Understanding Human Behavior in Health and Illness

THIRD EDITION

Understanding Human Behavior in Health and Illness

THIRD EDITION

Edited by

RICHARD C. SIMONS, M.D.

Professor of Psychiatry and
Coordinator of Human Behavior Course
School of Medicine
University of Colorado Health Sciences Center
Denver, Colorado

WILLIAMS & WILKINS
Baltimore • London • Los Angeles • Sydney

Editor: James L. Sangston
Associate Editor: Carol L. Eckhart
Copy Editor: Sally Lawther
Design: Bert Smith
Illustration Planning: Lorraine Wrzosek
Production: Anne G. Seitz

Made in the United States of America

First Edition, 1977
  Reprinted 1978, 1979, 1980
Second Edition, 1981
  Reprinted 1981, 1982, 1983, 1984

Library of Congress Cataloging in Publication Data

Main entry under title:

Understanding human behavior in health and illness.

  Includes index.
  1. Medicine and psychology. 2. Developmental psychology. 3. Psychology, Pathological. 4. Human behavior. I. Simons, Richard C. [DNLM: 1. Behavior. 2. Psychology, Applied. 3. Psychopathology. WM 100 U51] 726.5.U5 1985   155   84-13047
ISBN 0-683-07741-4

90 91 92 93 94
10 9

TO MY FAMILY

Preface to the Third Edition

These are very exciting times for psychiatry and indeed for all of the related behavioral sciences. The various contributors to this book, and I, hope that we have conveyed a sense of that excitement in this third edition. In just the past few years, there have been dramatic new advances in the diagnosis, classification, and epidemiology of the mental disorders; in infant, childhood, and adult developmental research; in the continuing discovery of the multiple biological factors that are involved in the etiology of mental illness; in the recognition of the importance of fetal and neonatal loss; in the study of the psychophysiology of stress and the interdependence that exists between physical health and mental health; in the development of consultation-liaison programs and other efforts aimed at the prevention of mental illness; in the care of geriatric and dying patients; and in the increasing breadth, specificity, and effectiveness of the various psychiatric therapies, to name only a few. Extensive revision of many chapters from the second edition and the addition of five new chapters in this third edition will hopefully reflect these advances in a way that will be meaningful for the beginning student of human behavior. But in our enthusiasm over this new knowledge and technology in the behavioral sciences (that parallel advances in all of the other medical specialties and medical sciences), we must never lose sight of the human being that exists in every patient who is to be the beneficiary of that knowledge and technology. In his book, *The Healing Heart*, Norman Cousins makes this point very eloquently:

There are qualities beyond pure medical competence that patients need and look for in their doctors. They want reassurance. They want to be looked after and not just looked over. They want to be listened to. They want to feel that it makes a difference to the physician, a very big difference, whether they live or die. They want to feel that they are in the doctor's thoughts. In short, patients are a vast collection of emotional needs. Yes, psychological counselors are very helpful in this connection—and so are the family and clergy. But the patient turns most of all and first of all to the physician. It is the physician who has most to offer in terms of those emotional needs. It is the person of the doctor and the presence of the doctor—just as much as, and frequently more than, what the doctor does—that create an environment for healing. The physician represents restoration. The physician holds the lifeline. The physician's words and not just his prescriptions are attached to that lifeline. This aspect of medicine has not changed in thousands of years. Not all the king's horses and all the king's men—not all the tomography and thallium scanners and 2D echograms and medicinal mood modifiers—can pre-empt the physician's primary role as the keeper of the keys to the body's own healing system.*

It is in that spirit that we offer this third edition.

Richard C. Simons, M.D.

_____

* *The Healing Heart. Antidotes to Panic and Helplessness* by Norman Cousins. Copyright © 1983 by Norman Cousins. Reprinted by permission of W.W. Norton and Company, Inc, New York, N.Y. Pp. 136–137.

Preface to the Second Edition

In the fall of 1977 a new course in human behavior was begun for the second year medical students at the University of Colorado Health Sciences Center in Denver, Colorado. Each week the coordinator of the course (R.C.S.) would visit a different one of the 18 discussion groups that meet following the two hour lecture presentations. During one of these visits to a particular group, the coordinator noted that one of the male medical students seemed rather distracted and had not said a single word. Before the end of the meeting the coordinator observed that the student had been very quiet, and asked for his thoughts, hoping to get some additional observations about the discussion in the group or about the lectures that morning. Instead, the young man said that he had not been paying attention at all, and in fact had not even gone to the lectures that day. He was preoccupied with an experience he had had the day before. He was a second year medical student who had been working on a clinical research project that involved collecting daily blood and urine specimens from seriously ill patients.

The patient on that particular day was a 60 year old woman suffering from small bowel syndrome, electrolyte imbalance, generalized osteoarthritis, and diabetes. The patient and our male medical student had had a good relationship during the preceding three months, but gradually over the preceding two weeks the patient had become more and more depressed and suspicious. There was a corresponding shift in her relationship with the medical student, whom she now saw as her persecutor (rather than as her friend and helper), and possibly even as the cause of her many chronic, debilitating symptoms. Finally, on the day before the discussion group meeting, as the student walked into her hospital room, the patient screamed at him and said, "Get out of here. I don't ever want to see you again. Why are you torturing me like this? I am through giving you my blood and my urine. You'll get no more from me. Leave me alone." The student was understandably overwhelmed,

and unable to deal with this angry outburst from a patient toward whom he had come to feel very close. He left the room devastated. He talked about feeling enormously guilty at asking a seriously ill woman for specimens of blood and urine, and even more guilty for having failed her in some inexplicable way. Tears began to come to his eyes.

Needless to say, the course coordinator, the two discussion group leaders, and the seven other medical students were profoundly moved by what was happening. It was already time for the discussion group meeting to end, but no one made a move to leave. There was a long pause. The student then spoke once more. "What upset me most about yesterday was that it reminded me too much of Peggy. Peggy was a 19 year old girl who died of leukemia last spring. She was beautiful and full of life. No one wanted to see her die. In fact, none of us could accept it. We fought against it. Every time she came into the hospital we fought to get a remission. We had to save her. But the last time she came into the hospital, she said very calmly, 'What are you doing all this for? Why are you putting in all these tubes? Can't you see that I don't want to go on any more? I just want to give up. Why can't you let me die in peace?'"

There was another long pause. The student's tears were quite evident by this time. Once again, he broke the silence. "I can't get Peggy out of my mind. I even dream about her—maybe because we were so close in age." Another pause. He then looked directly at the course director, and said, "What I want to know is—how is your course going to help me deal with these situations? I don't think a lot of strange theories are going to help me. But I do need something that will help."

It should not surprise our readers that the course coordinator was somewhat at a loss for words. This "silent" student—in fact this "absent" student who had missed the lectures that morning because of his depression—might well have been able to give those lectures himself. Or at least he would have been able to relate experiences that would have had a powerful impact on his entire class, just as they had had on his discussion group peers and teachers. Certainly no textbook nor prepared lectures could have given him what he had experienced firsthand in his elective research work. But perhaps a textbook or a course in human behavior might attempt to *start* with these experiences (and similar experiences of all physicians and other health care professionals), and then integrate those experiences within a broader conceptual framework. Might not such a broader framework begin with such immediately relevant concepts to physicians and other health care professionals as the continuity between past and present in all of human behavior, the range of adaptive and maladaptive reactions to illness and the regression that occurs in all physical illness, the ubiquity of defenses against anxiety and depression, the power of transference reactions for both good and ill in the responses of patients to their physicians and to the medical advice of those physicians, and the equally powerful reactions of physicians toward their patients?

Chapters in a textbook and lecture topics in a course can be changed and rearranged ad infinitum. Indeed, they should be, to keep abreast of current knowledge. But whatever the content of a human behavior course may be, the spirit that infuses such a course is what is critical. If the course attempts to involve the students emotionally and not just intellectually—if answers are provided where answers are known, but not simple answers for complex ambiguities, and not premature closure of further inquiry—if the students are seen as colleagues, and not as disciples to be recruited nor as patients to be treated, then the teachers of such a course will have to deal directly with the students' uncertainties, skepticism, and open disagreement. But hopefully at the end they will also have earned their students' trust and gratitude, and they will have learned from each other.

Readers of this second edition who are familiar with the first edition will notice that there have been a great many changes—in the organization and sequence of the material, in the content of retained chapters, in the deletion of other chapters, and finally in the addition of many new chapters. Nearly every one of these changes has come about because of our ongoing work with our students. We are grateful to them. They are very good teachers.

Richard C. Simons, M.D.
Herbert Pardes, M.D.

Preface to the First Edition

Of the many facets of life that are challenging and exciting to explore, perhaps none can surpass the area of human behavior. To say that this subject is complex needs little substantiation. To say that it evokes passion and controversy is self-evident. Indeed, it touches on issues close to each and every one of us as human beings. But, in addition, it is a subject that is vast and often quite mysterious. It has the fascination of seeming to be almost impossible to fully delimit or comprehend. Thus, it is a field that offers the promise of never being dull or repetitive.

Certainly to those of us in the health professions, this subject affects our lives and the lives of our patients in countless ways. The various biological, psychological, and sociocultural forces involved in human behavior will determine not only the health of our patients, but also the degree to which they can recover and cope with both physical and emotional illness. These same forces also have a critical impact on the healer, on the therapeutic team, and on the institution that renders health care. Thus, human behavior is a subject with which any student and any practitioner in the health professions should be familiar in more than just a "common sense" way. Only then can we render the best possible care, never losing sight of the common humanity that binds us to our patients.

There have been many different approaches to the study of human behavior. In some medical schools a group of behavioral scientists without immediate and ongoing clinical experience have attempted to teach human behavior to medical students. These attempts have, in general, not succeeded in involving the students, and the most typical complaint has been the remoteness of many of these areas of study to the immediate concerns of the medical student and the practic-

ing physician. This book is the outgrowth of a course that attempts a close integration between the many clinical aspects of human behavior and the behavioral sciences. First, a clinical issue or topic is presented to the students, either in the area of normal development and the life cycle, or in the area of the relationship between the mind and the body, or in the area of psychopathology. These are all areas which typically evoke questions and general curiosity, and this then permits the teaching of the behavioral sciences in a much more receptive climate. The student is now looking for the mechanisms and the theoretical concepts which organize and help to explain the widely varying and often mystifying clinical phenomena. This naturally evolving interest and curiosity turn the attention of the student to a sweeping range of work, from learning theory to sociology, from psychoanalysis to genetics, from ethology to neurochemistry. But these are now sciences to be investigated, not dogmas to be uncritically accepted.

In this book we will present the evolvement of this course in the teaching of human behavior. The various authors have all worked closely together in this effort to integrate the clinical aspects of human behavior and the behavioral sciences, and they have now focused on developing a readable, relevant, and informative text. Our goal has been to introduce the student in the health professions to the excitement and richness of human behavior, and to make available the data and concepts to which any health professional should be exposed and concerning which he should be knowledgeable. We welcome you to explore with us this vast and exciting subject.

Richard C. Simons, M.D.
Herbert Pardes, M.D.

Acknowledgments

The writing of a book such as this requires not only the dedication and commitment of a great many individuals, but the support of institutions as well. I would first like to thank my colleague and co-editor of the first two editions of this book, Dr. Herbert Pardes, for his unwavering support of medical student education programs in psychiatry throughout his entire professional career and for the personal encouragement that he has always given to me. Although I have now taken on the task of being the sole editor of this third edition, Dr. Pardes' continued involvement as a valued contributor and consultant means a great deal to me and to all of us associated with this book.

I also want to acknowledge the generous support of Dr. John W. Cowee, former Chancellor of the University of Colorado Health Sciences Center, who so steadfastly maintained a broad humanistic vision for the Department of Psychiatry at Colorado. In regard to the publishing company of Williams & Wilkins, Toni M. Tracy (Vice President and Editor-in-Chief) and the late James L. Sangston (Senior Editor) were the first to suggest and encourage a third edition; Norvell E. Miller, III (Director of Book Production) brought his long professional experience to bear in the overall production of the book; and Carol L. Eckhart (Associate Editor) and Anne G. Seitz (Production Sponsor) worked patiently and tirelessly with me on all of the daily details of the book's production. Among their colleagues at Williams & Wilkins to whom I also wish to express my appreciation are: Joseph Braden, Pamela Caras, Carolyn Donohue, Dan Donohue, Sara Finnegan, Timothy Grayson, Theda Harris, Wayne Hubbel, Sally Lawther, Terry Minton, Pat Nussman, Bert Smith, Bill Vinck, and Lorraine Wrzosek.

Mrs. Helene Ellinger (at the Downstate Medical Center in Brooklyn) devoted herself completely to every phase of the first edition of this book, as did Mrs. Marjorie McKee (at the University of Colorado Health Sciences Center in Denver) to the second edition and now to the third edition as well. I am deeply grateful and indebted to both of them for what they have given above and far beyond the ordinary call of duty over so many years. Other individuals at the University of Colorado Health Sciences Center who contributed in various ways to this third edition include: Aletha Arkie, Debra Becker, Jacqueline Brinkman, Maxine Conlon, Audrey County, Susan Domaschk, Bernice Douglas, Opal Every, Annette Ginnane, Joanne Haywood, Rosemary Heiser, Louise Kosenski, Naomi Miller, Maxine Peterson, Betty Preston, Dinah Rogers, Linda Greco-Sanders, Elaine Steffen, Imogene Tursick, Carolyn Zwibecker, and most especially Sheri Albrecht for her invaluable help to me and Mrs. McKee during the final stages of proofreading and indexing.

We hope that the illustrations in this book have a message of their own, equivalent to that of any words. Numerous individuals, museums, publishers, and film companies have given their permission for us to use these illustrations, and Mr. Mark Groth (also from the University of Colorado Health Sciences Center) photographed several of the illustrations.

Finally, I wish to thank my family (my wife Barbara and my children Lisa, Michael, and Kimberly) for sharing so much of me with this book, and for doing it so lovingly over so many years. Also, I wish to thank the following lecturers and discussion group leaders who have participated in the Human Behavior Course at the University of Colorado Health Sciences Center from 1981 through 1985. Their commitment to the teaching of medical students has made this book possible.

Richard C. Simons, M.D.

Stephen M. Allen, M.D.
Bernard Aoueille, M.D.
Elissa M. Ball, M.D.
Donald W. Bechtold, M.D.
Jon A. Bell, M.D.
Jon S. Berlin, M.D.
Henry H. Bible, Jr., M.D.
Thomas H. Budzynski, Ph.D.
Dorotha Graham-Cicchinelli,
  B.A.S.W.
Bettye Clement, Ph.D.
Erlyne Cooper, M.S.W.
Henry P. Coppolillo, M.D.
Deborah A. Coyle, M.D.
Thomas J. Crowley, M.D.
E. Earlene DalPozzo, M.D.
Donna M. DeSimone, M.D.
Steven L. Dubovsky, M.D.
Steven D. Dworetsky, M.D.
Robert N. Emde, M.D.
Gordon K. Farley, M.D.
Louis L. Fine, M.D.
Ronald D. Franks, M.D.
Robert Freedman, M.D.
Eugene V. Friedrich, M.D.
Ruth L. Fuller, M.D.
Warren J. Gadpaille, M.D.
G. Gail Gardner, Ph.D.

Michael H. Gendel, M.D.
William V. Good, M.D.
Margaret E. Grant, M.D.
Benjamin P. Green, M.D.
Robert J. Harmon, M.D.
Marita J. Keeling, M.D.
Darrell Kirch, M.D.
Joyce S. Kobayashi, M.D.
Carol L. Lassen, Ph.D.
Mark Leifeste, M.D.
Andrew S. Levitas, M.D.
W. Charles Lobitz, Ph.D.
John B. Lochridge, M.D.
John M. Macdonald, M.D.
Philip G. Madonna, M.S.W.
Harold Martin, M.D.
John H. McMurray, M.D.
Jeffrey L. Metzner, M.D.
Leslie J. Miller, Ph.D.
George L. Mizner, M.D.
Michael G. Moran, M.D.
Elizabeth Morrison, M.D.
Betty Ann Muller, M.D.
Emily Mumford, Ph.D.
Mary Jo Myers, M.D.
Calvern E. Narcisi, M.D.
Janice L. Petersen, M.D.

Francine J. Pokracki, M.D.
Robin D. Post, Ph.D.
David F. Raney, M.D.
Martin Reite, M.D.
Mark W. Rhine, M.D.
Joanne H. Ritvo, M.D.
Jonathan I. Ritvo, M.D.
Margaret Roath, M.S.W.
Jean E. Robinson, M.D.
Catherine J. Schieve, M.D.
Andrea Klein Schroder, M.S.W.
James H. Scully, M.D.
Andrew L. Selig, Ph.D.
Clifford H. Siegel, M.D.
Brandt F. Steele, M.D.
Jill Steinbruegge, M.D.
Mark Stone, M.D.
Johann Stoyva, Ph.D.
Carolyn S. Tank, M.D.
Marshall R. Thomas, M.D.
Hubert H. Thomason, M.D.
Troy L. Thompson II, M.D.
Wendy L. Thompson, M.D.
Carol E. Traut, M.D.
William H. Tullis, M.D.
Kenneth L. Weiner, M.D.
Michael P. Weissberg, M.D.
Sidney L. Werkman, M.D.

Contributors

William E. Bernstein, M.D.
Clinical Assistant Professor of Psychiatry
Faculty Member of Denver Institute for
  Psychoanalysis
School of Medicine
University of Colorado Health Sciences Center
Denver, Colorado

Michael Blumenfield, M.D.
Professor of Psychiatry
Associate Professor of Medicine and Surgery
Associate Director of Psychiatric Liaison
  Division
New York Medical College-Westchester
  County Medical Center
Valhalla, New York

Adolph E. Christ, M.D.
Associate Professor of Psychiatry
Director of Division of Child and Adolescent
  Psychiatry
State University of New York
Downstate Medical Center
Brooklyn, New York

Dorotha Graham-Cicchinelli, B.A.S.W.
Clinical Assistant Professor of Psychiatry
  (Social Service)
School of Medicine
University of Colorado Health Sciences Center
Denver, Colorado

William A. Console, M.D. (Deceased)
Formerly Clinical Professor of Psychiatry
Director of Division of Psychoanalytic
  Education
State University of New York
Downstate Medical Center
Brooklyn, New York

Henry P. Coppolillo, M.D.
Professor of Psychiatry
School of Medicine
University of Colorado Health Sciences Center
Denver, Colorado

Thomas J. Crowley, M.D.
Professor of Psychiatry
Executive Director of Addiction Research and

Treatment Service
School of Medicine
University of Colorado Health Sciences Center
Denver, Colorado

Robert Dickes, M.D.
Clinical Professor of Psychiatry
Training and Supervising Analyst
Faculty Member of The Psychoanalytic
  Institute
New York University Medical Center
New York, New York

Ferruccio di Cori, M.D.
Clinical Associate Professor of Psychiatry
Director of Research and Training in
  Psychodrama
State University of New York
Downstate Medical Center
Brooklyn, New York

Steven L. Dubovsky, M.D.
Associate Professor of Psychiatry and
  Medicine
Associate Dean for Faculty Affairs
School of Medicine
University of Colorado Health Sciences Center
Denver, Colorado

Robert N. Emde, M.D.
Professor of Psychiatry
Faculty Member of Denver Institute for
  Psychoanalysis
School of Medicine
University of Colorado Health Sciences Center
Denver, Colorado
Adjunct Professor of Psychology
University of Denver
Denver, Colorado

Gordon K. Farley, M.D.
Associate Professor of Psychiatry
Director of Day Care Center
Associate Director of Division of Child and
  Adolescent Psychiatry
School of Medicine
University of Colorado Health Sciences Center
Denver, Colorado; and

Adjunct Assistant Professor of Education
University of Colorado
Boulder, Colorado

Louis L. Fine, M.D.
Clinical Assistant Professor of Psychiatry
Clinical Associate Professor of Pediatrics
School of Medicine
University of Colorado Health Sciences Center
Denver, Colorado
Director of Psychiatric Consultation-Liaison
   Service
The Children's Hospital
Denver, Colorado

John L. Fleming, M.D.
Clinical Assistant Professor of Psychiatry
School of Medicine
University of Colorado Health Sciences Center
Denver, Colorado
Director of Clinical Affairs
Cedar Springs Psychiatric Hospital
Colorado Springs, Colorado

Ronald D. Franks, M.D.
Associate Professor of Psychiatry
Assistant Dean for Student Affairs
Associate Director of Psychiatric Inpatient
   Division
School of Medicine
University of Colorado Health Sciences Center
Denver, Colorado

Robert Freedman, M.D.
Associate Professor of Psychiatry and
   Pharmacology
School of Medicine
University of Colorado Health Sciences Center
Denver, Colorado
Staff Psychiatrist
Veterans Administration Medical Center
Denver, Colorado

Eugene V. Friedrich, M.D.
Assistant Professor of Psychiatry
Director of Psychiatry Internship Program
School of Medicine
University of Colorado Health Sciences Center
Denver, Colorado
Ward Chief in Psychiatry
Veterans Administration Medical Center
Denver, Colorado

Ruth L. Fuller, M.D.
Assistant Professor of Psychiatry
Director of Transitional Care

Director of Division of Community Psychiatry
School of Medicine
University of Colorado Health Sciences Center
Denver, Colorado

Warren J. Gadpaille, M.D.
Clinical Associate Professor of Psychiatry
School of Medicine
University of Colorado Health Sciences Center
Denver, Colorado

G. Gail Gardner, Ph.D. (Deceased)
Formerly Associate Professor of Psychiatry
   (Clinical Psychology) and Pediatrics
School of Medicine
University of Colorado Health Sciences Center
Denver, Colorado

Lewis Glickman, M.D.
Clinical Associate Professor of Psychiatry
State University of New York
Downstate Medical Center
Brooklyn, New York
Director of Psychiatric Consultation-Liaison
   Service
Kings County Hospital Center
Brooklyn, New York

William V. Good, M.D.
Assistant Professor of Psychiatry and
   Pediatrics
School of Medicine
University of Colorado Health Sciences Center
Denver, Colorado

Arthur Green, M.D.
Clinical Associate Professor of Psychiatry
Faculty Member of Columbia University
   Psychoanalytic Center
Columbia University College of Physicians and
   Surgeons
New York, New York
Director of Columbia-Presbyterian Family
   Center
New York, New York

Robert J. Harmon, M.D.
Associate Professor of Psychiatry
Director of Division of Child and Adolescent
   Psychiatry
School of Medicine
University of Colorado Health Sciences Center
Denver, Colorado
Adjunct Assistant Professor of Psychology
Smith College School for Social Work
Northampton, Massachusetts

Adjunct Assistant Professor of Psychology
University of Denver
Denver, Colorado

Joan Hittelman, Ph.D.
Clinical Assistant Professor of Psychiatry
Director of Infant and Child Behavior
  Laboratory
State University of New York
Downstate Medical Center
Brooklyn, New York

Carol L. Lassen, Ph.D.
Clinical Associate Professor of Psychiatry
  (Clinical Psychology)
School of Medicine
University of Colorado Health Sciences Center
Denver, Colorado

Norman B. Levy, M.D.
Professor of Psychiatry, Medicine, and Surgery
Director of Psychiatric Liaison Division
Coordinator of Psychiatric Liaison Services
New York Medical College-Westchester
  County Medical Center
Valhalla, New York

W. Charles Lobitz, Ph.D.
Clinical Associate Professor of Psychiatry
  (Clinical Psychology)
School of Medicine
University of Colorado Health Sciences Center
Denver, Colorado

John M. Macdonald, M.D.
Professor of Psychiatry
Director of Forensic Psychiatry
School of Medicine
University of Colorado Health Sciences Center
Denver, Colorado

George L. Mizner, M.D.
Clinical Associate Professor of Psychiatry
School of Medicine
University of Colorado Health Sciences Center
Denver, Colorado

Emily Mumford, Ph.D.
Professor of Clinical Sociomedical Sciences (in
  Psychiatry and Public Health)
Columbia University College of Physicians and
  Surgeons
New York, New York
Chief, Division of Health Services and Policy
  Research

New York State Psychiatric Institute
New York, New York

Herbert Pardes, M.D.
Professor and Chairman, Department of
  Psychiatry
Columbia University College of Physicians and
  Surgeons
New York, New York
Director of New York State Psychiatric
  Institute
New York, New York
Director of Columbia-Presbyterian Hospital
  Psychiatric Service
New York, New York

Janice L. Petersen, M.D.
Assistant Professor of Psychiatry
School of Medicine
University of Colorado Health Sciences Center
Denver, Colorado

Martin Reite, M.D.
Professor of Psychiatry
Director of Primate Laboratory
Director of Sleep Disorders Center
Director of Developmental Psychobiology
  Research Group
Director of Postdoctoral Research Training
  Program
School of Medicine
University of Colorado Health Sciences Center
Denver, Colorado

Mark W. Rhine, M.D.
Clinical Associate Professor of Psychiatry
Faculty Member of Denver Institute for
  Psychoanalysis
School of Medicine
University of Colorado Health Sciences Center
Denver, Colorado

Joanne H. Ritvo, M.D.
Clinical Assistant Professor of Psychiatry
School of Medicine
University of Colorado Health Sciences Center
Denver, Colorado

Jonathan I. Ritvo, M.D.
Assistant Professor of Psychiatry
School of Medicine
University of Colorado Health Sciences Center
Denver, Colorado
Director of Psychiatric Emergency and
  Consultation Services

Denver General Hospital
Denver, Colorado

Leonard Rosenblum, Ph.D.
Professor of Psychiatry
Director of Primate Behavior Laboratory
State University of New York
Downstate Medical Center
Brooklyn, New York

Mark Rubinstein, M.D.
Formerly Clinical Assistant Professor of
  Psychiatry and Attending Psychiatrist
New York Hospital-Cornell University Medical
  Center
New York, New York

Melvin A. Scharfman, M.D.
Clinical Professor of Psychiatry
Training and Supervising Analyst
Faculty Member of The Psychoanalytic
  Institute
New York University Medical Center
New York, New York

Andrea Klein Schroder, M.S.W.
Clinical Instructor of Psychiatry (Social
  Service)
School of Medicine
University of Colorado Health Sciences Center
Denver, Colorado; and
Psychiatric Social Worker
Division of Inpatient Psychiatry
Veterans Administration Medical Center
Denver, Colorado

Laurence Schweitzer, M.D.
Associate Professor of Psychiatry
Baylor College of Medicine
Houston, Texas
Deputy Director of Psychiatric Service
The Methodist Hospital
Houston, Texas

James H. Scully, M.D.
Associate Professor of Psychiatry
Director of Division of Psychiatric
  Undergraduate Education
Coordinator of Psychiatric Clerkship Program
School of Medicine
University of Colorado Health Sciences Center
Denver, Colorado
Director of Psychiatric Liaison Service
Veterans Administration Medical Center
Denver, Colorado

Richard C. Simons, M.D.
Professor of Psychiatry
Coordinator of Human Behavior Course
Training and Supervising Analyst
Faculty Member of Denver Institute for
  Psychoanalysis
School of Medicine
University of Colorado Health Sciences Center
Denver, Colorado

Brandt F. Steele, M.D.
Emeritus Professor of Psychiatry
Training and Supervising Analyst
Faculty Member of Denver Institute for
  Psychoanalysis
School of Medicine
University of Colorado Health Sciences Center
Denver, Colorado
Staff Psychiatrist of National Center for
  Prevention and Treatment of Child Abuse
  and Neglect
Denver, Colorado

Jorge Steinberg, M.D.
Clinical Associate Professor of Psychiatry
State University of New York
Downstate Medical Center
Brooklyn, New York

Johann Stoyva, Ph.D.
Associate Professor of Psychiatry (Clinical
  Psychology)
Director of Biofeedback Laboratory
School of Medicine
University of Colorado Health Sciences Center
Denver, Colorado

Dorothy Strauss, Ph.D.
Clinical Associate Professor of Psychiatry
State University of New York
Downstate Medical Center
Brooklyn, New York

Troy L. Thompson II, M.D.
Associate Professor of Psychiatry and
  Medicine
Acting Director of Psychiatric Liaison Divison
School of Medicine
University of Colorado Health Sciences Center
Denver, Colorado

Wendy L. Thompson, M.D.
Clinical Assistant Professor of Psychiatry
School of Medicine
University of Colorado Health Sciences Center
Denver, Colorado

Staff Psychiatrist
National Jewish Hospital and National
  Asthma Center
Denver, Colorado

Ursula Thunberg, M.D.
Clinical Assistant Professor of Psychiatry
State University of New York
Downstate Medical Center
Brooklyn, New York
Lecturer in Department of Social Work
New York University
New York, New York
Staff Psychiatrist
Stanley Lamm Institute
Long Island College Hospital
New York, New York

Kenneth L. Weiner, M.D.
Clinical Instructor of Psychiatry
School of Medicine

University of Colorado Health Sciences Center
Denver, Colorado

Michael P. Weissberg, M.D.
Associate Professor of Psychiatry
Director of Psychiatric Emergency Service
School of Medicine
University of Colorado Health Sciences Center
Denver, Colorado

Sidney L. Werkman, M.D.
Professor of Psychiatry
School of Medicine
University of Colorado Health Sciences Center
Denver, Colorado

Carl T. Wolff, M.D.
Formerly Coordinator of Human Behavior
  Course
State University of New York
Downstate Medical Center
Brooklyn, New York

Contents

Preface to the Third Edition .... **vii**
Preface to the Second Edition .... **ix**
Preface to the First Edition .... **xi**
Acknowledgments .... **xiii**
Contributors .... **xv**

PART I. HUMAN BEHAVIOR AND THE PHYSICIAN **1**

Section A/Why Learn About Human Behavior? **2**
    1. The Importance of Understanding Human Behavior to the Practicing
       Physician—Richard C. Simons, M.D. **2**
    2. The Role of Psychological Factors in the Development and Treatment of
       Medical Illness—Jorge Steinberg, M.D. and Richard C. Simons, M.D. **6**
Section B/The Doctor-Patient Relationship **14**
    3. The Participants in the Doctor-Patient Relationship—
       Ruth L. Fuller, M.D. **14**
    4. The Basic Models of the Doctor-Patient Relationship—
       Michael Blumenfield, M.D. **19**
    5. On Being a Physician—William A. Console, M.D. **27**
    6. On Being a Patient—Emily Mumford, Ph.D. **33**
    7. The Responses of Patients to Medical Advice—Emily Mumford, Ph.D. . **38**
Section C/The Mind-Body Relationship **48**
    8. The Psychological Reactions to Physical Illness—
       Michael Blumenfield, M.D. and Troy L. Thompson II, M.D. **48**
    9. The Psychological Aspects of Pain—Troy L. Thompson II, M.D. and
       Brandt F. Steele, M.D. **60**
    10. Conversion Disorder—Norman B. Levy, M.D. **68**
    11. Hypochondriasis—Mark W. Rhine, M.D. and
       Troy L. Thompson II, M.D. **73**
    12. The Psychophysiological Disorders: An Overview—
       Norman B. Levy, M.D. **79**
    13. The Psychophysiology of Health, Illness, and Stress—
       Steven L. Dubovsky, M.D. **90**
    14. The "Difficult" Patient **101**
      A. The Angry and Seductive Patient—Ronald D. Franks, M.D. **101**
      B. The "Difficult" Surgical Patient—James H. Scully, M.D.,
         Robert Dickes, M.D., and William E. Bernstein, M.D. **106**
      C. The "Difficult" Medical Patient, and the Importance of Consultation-
        Liaison Psychiatry—Troy L. Thompson II, M.D.,
        James H. Scully, M.D., and Wendy L. Thompson, M.D. **113**

PART II. CHILDHOOD AND ADOLESCENCE: THE YEARS OF GROWTH AND DEVELOPMENT **121**

Section D/The Beginnings of Life **122**
15. Pregnancy and the Expectant Couple—Joan Hittelman, Ph.D., Richard C. Simons, M.D., and Janice L. Petersen, M.D. **122**
16. Birth, Postpartum, and the Parent-Infant Interaction—Joan Hittelman, Ph.D., Robert N. Emde, M.D., and Richard C. Simons, M.D. **137**
17. Fetal and Neonatal Loss—Robert J. Harmon, M.D. and Dorotha Graham-Cicchinelli, B.A.S.W. **151**

Section E/The Early Years of Childhood **158**
18. An Overview of Child and Adolescent Development— Adolph E. Christ, M.D. **158**
19. The Infant—Melvin A. Scharfman, M.D. **165**
20. The Toddler—Melvin A. Scharfman, M.D. **182**
21. Ethology: Primate Research and the Evolutionary Origins of Human Behavior—Leonard Rosenblum, Ph.D. **197**

Section F/The Middle Years of Childhood **213**
22. The Pre-School Child—Melvin A. Scharfman, M.D. **213**
23. Sociology: Changes in Family Structure and Their Impact on Medical Practice—Emily Mumford, Ph.D **227**

Section G/The Later Years of Childhood **240**
24. The Grade School Child—Melvin A. Scharfman, M.D. **240**
25. Cognitive Development—Gordon K. Farley, M.D. **249**

Section H/Puberty and Adolescence **255**
26. Puberty and the Adolescent—Melvin A. Scharfman, M.D. **255**
27. Culture: Life Perspectives and the Social Meanings of Illness— Emily Mumford, Ph.D. **271**

Section I/Special Problems of Childhood and Adolescence **281**
28. Reactions of Children to Illness, Hospitalization, Surgery, and Physical Disabilities—Adolph E. Christ, M.D. **281**
29. Adoption, Foster Care, Day Care, and Other Living Arrangements— Ruth L. Fuller, M.D. **287**
30. Loss, Grief, and Mourning in Children—Henry P. Coppolillo, M.D. **293**
31. The Dying Child and Adolescent **299**
    A. Ethical Perspectives—G. Gail Gardner, Ph.D. **299**
    B. Clinical Perspectives—Ursula Thunberg, M.D. **303**

PART III. ADULTHOOD: THE YEARS OF MATURITY AND THE COMPLETION OF THE LIFE CYCLE **315**

Section J/Adult Sexuality **316**
32. Historical and Cultural Perspectives—Robert Dickes, M.D. **316**
33. The Physiology of the Sexual Response Cycle—Robert Dickes, M.D. . . . **324**
34. Sexual Myths and Misinformation—Robert Dickes, M.D. **338**
35. Sexuality in General Medical Practice—Robert Dickes, M.D. and John L. Fleming, M.D. **349**

36. The Psychosexual Dysfunctions and Their Treatment—Robert Dickes, M.D., Carol L. Lassen, Ph.D., and W. Charles Lobitz, Ph.D. **359**

37. The Paraphilias and Transsexualism—Robert Dickes, M.D. and Richard C. Simons, M.D. **376**

38. Homosexuality—Warren J. Gadpaille, M.D. **391**

Section K/Work **402**

39. Work and Creativity—Ferruccio di Cori, M.D. **402**

40. The Social Significance of Work, and Studies on the Stress of Life Events—Emily Mumford, Ph.D. **414**

41. The Choice of Medicine as a Career **423**
    A. Role Models and the Years of Training—Emily Mumford, Ph.D. **423**
    B. The Rewards and Hazards of Medicine as a Profession— Laurence Schweitzer, M.D. **432**

Section L/Early Adulthood, Marriage, and Parenthood **441**

42. Early Adulthood, Marriage, and Parenthood—Richard C. Simons, M.D. **441**

43. Marital Dysfunction, Separation, and Divorce—Richard C. Simons, M.D. and Dorothy Strauss, Ph.D. **452**

44. The Experience of Being a Single Parent— Andrea Klein Schroder, M.S.W. **464**

45. Parental Dysfunction and Child Abuse—Arthur Green, M.D. and Brandt F. Steele, M.D. **470**

Section M/The Middle and Later Years of Life **478**

46. Middle Age and the Climacterium—Dorothy Strauss, Ph.D. and George L. Mizner, M.D. **478**

47. Later Adulthood and Old Age—George L. Mizner, M.D., Dorothy Strauss, Ph.D., and Richard C. Simons, M.D. **486**

48. Loss, Grief, and Mourning in Adults—Carl T. Wolff, M.D. and Richard C. Simons, M.D. **498**

49. The Dying Adult **508**
    A. Historical and Religious Perspectives—Sidney L. Werkman, M.D. ... **508**
    B. Clinical Perspectives—Ursula Thunberg, M.D. **513**

PART IV. PSYCHOPATHOLOGY: THE CONTINUUM BETWEEN HEALTH AND ILLNESS **523**

Section N/Normality and Abnormality **524**

50. Normality Versus Abnormality, and the Concept of Mental Illness— Herbert Pardes, M.D. **524**

51. The Classification of the Mental Disorders—Richard C. Simons, M.D. and Herbert Pardes, M.D. **533**

Section O/The Multiple Etiologies of Mental Illness **541**

52. Biological Factors in Mental Illness **541**
    A. Genetic Factors in Mental Illness—Martin Reite, M.D. **541**
    B. Neurochemical, Neuroendocrine, and Psychopharmacological Factors in Mental Illness—Robert Freedman, M.D. **553**
    C. Biological Rhythms—Thomas J. Crowley, M.D. **564**
    D. Sleep and Sleep Disorders—Martin Reite, M.D. **569**

53. Psychodynamic Factors in Mental Illness, and the Concepts of Fixation, Regression, and the Unconscious—Herbert Pardes, M.D. **586**

54. Sociocultural Factors in Mental Illness, and the Epidemiology of the
    Mental Disorders—Emily Mumford, Ph.D. **597**
55. Learning Principles, Biofeedback, and Behavioral Medicine—
    Johann Stoyva, Ph.D. **607**

Section P/The Major Mental Disorders of Childhood and Adolescence **619**
56. The Syndrome of Mental Retardation—Herbert Pardes, M.D. **619**
57. The Pervasive Developmental Disorders of Childhood—
    Adolph E. Christ, M.D. and Gordon K. Farley, M.D. **628**
58. The Learning Disabilities of Childhood: Attention Deficit Disorder and
    Specific Developmental Disorders—Adolph E. Christ, M.D. **638**
59. Conduct Disorder, and the Problem of Juvenile Delinquency—
    Adolph E. Christ, M.D. **648**
60. The Eating Disorders, and the Psychophysiological Disorders of
    Childhood and Adolescence—Adolph E. Christ, M.D. **658**
61. The Symptom Disorders of Childhood—Gordon K. Farley, M.D.,
    Louis L. Fine, M.D., William V. Good, M.D., and
    Richard C. Simons, M.D. **671**

Section Q/The Major Mental Disorders of Adulthood **678**
62. The Schizophrenic Disorders—Mark Rubinstein, M.D.,
    Ronald D. Franks, M.D., and Richard C. Simons, M.D. **678**
63. The Affective Disorders **692**
    A. Mania and Bipolar Disorder—Mark W. Rhine, M.D.,
       Ronald D. Franks, M.D., and Richard C. Simons, M.D. **692**
    B. Depression and the Depressive Disorders—Richard C. Simons, M.D.,
       Mark Rubinstein, M.D., and Ronald D. Franks, M.D. **697**
64. The Phenomenon of Suicide—Lewis Glickman, M.D. **713**
65. Violence and the Physician—John M. Macdonald, M.D. **725**
66. The Substance Use Disorders—Thomas J. Crowley, M.D. and
    Mark W. Rhine, M.D. **730**
67. The Organic Brain Syndromes and the Organic Mental Disorders—
    Lewis Glickman, M.D. **747**
68. Psychiatric Emergencies in Medical Practice—
    Michael P. Weissberg, M.D. **759**
69. The Anxiety Disorders and the Dissociative Disorders—
    William A. Console, M.D. and Richard C. Simons, M.D. **764**
70. The Personality Disorders—Richard C. Simons, M.D. and
    John M. Macdonald, M.D. **772**
71. An Overview of the Psychiatric Therapies— Joanne H. Ritvo, M.D.,
    Eugene V. Friedrich, M.D., Jonathan I. Ritvo, M.D., and
    Kenneth L. Weiner, M.D. **780**

PART V. CONCLUSION **785**

Section R/Why Teach Human Behavior? **786**
72. Human Behavior and the Physician of the Future—
    Richard C. Simons, M.D. **786**

Name Index **789**
Subject Index **799**

PART I
Human Behavior and the Physician

Section A/Why Learn About Human Behavior?

CHAPTER **1** ## The Importance of Understanding Human Behavior to the Practicing Physician

Richard C. Simons, M.D.

"I know with certainty that a man's work is nothing but the long journey to recover, through the detours of art, the two or three simple and great images which first gained access to his heart."*

Albert Camus wrote that a number of years ago. I quote it at the beginning of this book because, as we approach this vast and complex subject of human behavior, it may be helpful to keep a few ideas clearly in mind. One, implicit in Camus' words, is that our past and our future, our art and our work, our birth and our death, are of a piece. They are all linked together by a continuous thread of memory and emotion, from the first experiences of our childhood to the last breath that we take.

Those of us who teach courses on human behavior may have to categorize the life cycle into various separate phases for teaching purposes, but it does not really happen that smoothly in life. One step only gradually leads to the next one, and oftentimes there have to be a few stumbles first, or at least some nostalgic glances backwards. The six year old boy may be pleased to find himself starting school, but he may also think how nice it would be to be two again, with mother always close by. The 11 year

old girl may look in the mirror and suddenly realize that she is becoming a young woman, but it may still be comforting to keep her childhood doll nearby (Figure 1.1).

Parents, seeing their children grow up, may wonder, "Where have all the years gone?" and wish that those years could be relived. The aged grandparent, blessed with a long life, may still feel that life at its longest is far too brief when the end finally comes. For others, burdened with sorrow and grief, a long life is too long, and they welcome death (Figure 1.2).

This cycle of life and death, this imperceptible yet sometimes all too sudden unfolding of the generations, is the great mystery of our existence. It is the privilege — and responsibility — of the physician to be able to participate in the significant events of this mystery from the beginning to the end. Our role was not always so central. In centuries past we were preceded first by the lawgiver, then by the priest, and most recently by the family of relatives and friends bound together by a common heritage and a commonality of interests. But in our age of mobility and modern science, it is the physician to whom we look increasingly to guide us through the awesome experiences of birth and parenthood, of growing up and aging, of separation and loss, and of illness and death.

Indeed, as our life cycle expands in longevity, so also do our statistics of mental illness. The

---

* From Albert Camus: an essay in appreciation, by Germaine Bree. The *New York Times* Book Review Section. January 24, 1960, p. 14.

Figure 1.1. *Girl at the Mirror* (1954) by Norman Rockwell. (Reprinted with permission from *The Saturday Evening Post* © 1954. The Curtis Publishing Company.)

psychiatric physician knows that 30% of all hospital beds in this country are occupied by the mentally ill and that one out of 10 individuals in this country will undergo a psychiatric hospitalization at some point in his or her life. A 1984 survey by the National Institute of Mental Health reported that the number of American adults suffering from a diagnosable mental disorder is approximately 20% of the population, and that only one in five of those afflicted seek help for their condition. For those who may understandably find it difficult to grasp the enormity of human suffering implied in these statistics, it has been estimated that mental illness represents an economic loss each year of over $25 billion. When this figure is added to the separately estimated cost of alcoholism ($25 billion a year) and drug abuse ($25 billion a

year) even the most hardened observer will have to be a little shaken.

But the nonpsychiatric physician knows that the problem of human frailty and emotional illness extends far beyond even these staggering statistics. Ask general practitioners, family physicians, or internists, and it is very likely that they will tell you that the single most common disease entity that they see in their practices is that of depression in all of its various emotional and somatic manifestations. Small wonder that suicide is rapidly approaching cancer and heart disease as the leading cause of death in our older age groups, that it is already a leading cause of death among adolescents and young adults, and that its incidence is rising dramatically even among children. These same nonpsychiatric physicians (depending on their practices and

Figure 1.2. *Self Portrait* by Käthe Kollwitz. (Courtesy of Roger and Ruth Loewi, Denver, Colorado. Photograph by Judith K. Thorpe.)

their particular specialties) will also tell you that anywhere from 20% to 30% of the physical symptoms of their patients are caused by psychological factors alone, without any organic etiology.

But there is another statistic far more important and impressive than any of these, of which every thoughtful physician and health care worker is well aware, and that is the statistic that involves 100% of patients. Every patient who becomes physically ill, for whatever reason, will have an emotional reaction to that illness. The causes of the illness may be psychological or organic or some combination of the two, but the reaction will always be an emotional one. Patients may feel anxiety, dread, or even terror. They may become sad and depressed, perhaps even to the point of experiencing despair. They may react in the opposite direction and feel a strange satisfaction in becoming ill, as though it were a punishment long awaited and well-deserved. They may even feel a sense of well-being so unwarranted as to constitute denial of a serious, life-threatening organic illness. Regardless of the type of reaction, *some* reaction will always be present.

Thus, with every illness, of whatever etiology, there will be a human being suffering from that illness. It is the task of the physician to be able to determine the cause or causes of the illness, then to treat the symptoms of that illness, and at the same time never to lose sight of the human being who is experiencing those symptoms.

To assist the physician in accomplishing this task is really the purpose of this book. We will go into considerable detail in subsequent chapters as we explore normal development and psychopathology, and the contributions that the various behavioral sciences can make to our understanding of human behavior in all its complexity. But as we focus on specific issues, it is important that we not lose sight of those "two or three simple and great images" which first gained access to our hearts, images which hopefully involved someone who cared and who understood. It is the privilege of physicians and their professional coworkers to be cast in the light of those same images, and thereby gain access to the innermost secrets of the human heart. No other profession is allowed to hear, to see, and to examine the most intimate aspects of people's lives, bodies, and emotions. But this will not happen unless we do care and strive to understand.

For of all the human needs that have been listed and categorized from time immemorial, perhaps the most fundamental of all is the need to be understood. It is as true for the youngest among us as for the oldest. An elderly lady died a few years ago in a geriatric ward of a hospital near Dundee, Scotland. No one knew very much about her, and at first it appeared as though she had left nothing of value. However, as a nurse was going through the old woman's possessions, she found something of immeasurable value, a bequest to all of us who aspire to help others, a bequest in the form of a poem:

What do you see nurses, what do you see?
Are you thinking when you are looking at me —
A crabby old woman, not very wise,
Uncertain of habit, with far-away eyes.
Who dribbles her food and makes no reply
When you say in a loud voice — "I do wish you'd try."
Who seems not to notice the things that you do,
And forever is losing a stocking or shoe.
Who unresisting or not, lets you do as you will,
With bathing and feeding the long day to fill.
Is that what you are thinking — is that what you see?
Then open your eyes, nurse, you're not looking at me.
I'll tell you who I am as I sit here so still;
As I do at your bidding, as I eat at your will,
I'm a small child of ten with a father and mother,
Brothers and sister, who love one another.
A young girl of sixteen with wings on her feet,
Dreaming that soon now a lover she'll meet;
A bride soon at twenty — my heart gives a leap,

Remembering the vows that I promised to keep;
At twenty-five now I have young of my own,
Who need me to build a secure, happy home;
A woman of thirty, my young now grow fast,
Bound to each other with ties that should last;
At forty, my young sons have grown and are gone,
But my man's beside me to see I don't mourn.
At fifty, once more babies play round my knee.
Again we know children, my loved one and me.
Dark days are upon me, my husband is dead,
I look at the future, I shudder with dread,
For my young are all rearing young of their own,
And I think of the years and the love that I've known.
I'm an old woman now and nature is cruel —
'Tis her jest to make old age look like a fool.
The body it crumbles, grace and vigour depart,
There is now a stone where I once had a heart;
But inside this old carcass a young girl still dwells,
And now and again my battered heart swells.
I remember the joys, I remember the pain,
And I'm loving and living life over again.
I think of the years all too few — gone too fast,
And accept the stark fact that nothing can last.
So open your eyes, nurses, open and see
Not a crabby old woman, look closer, see me!*

---

* Courtesy of the Peninsula Hospital Center, Far Rockaway, New York, and Greater New York Hospital Association.

CHAPTER **2** # The Role of Psychological Factors in the Development and Treatment of Medical Illness

Jorge Steinberg, M.D. and
Richard C. Simons, M.D.

In the preceding chapter our attention was called to the one person who makes it possible for all of us to be physicians, namely the patient. In referring to this person as a medical patient, or a surgical patient, or a psychiatric patient, we narrow our focus to one particular aspect and to one moment of his or her life. We are not going to attempt to define the concepts of health and illness in this chapter, but it is important for us to remember that both are always part of our lives, and that we function in a state which moves continually from one to the other.

Let us take a common clinical situation. A medical student is presenting a case. He mentions the woman's name, and proceeds immediately to describe the chief complaint. We ask him to stop, and indicate that we would like to know something more about the patient before he continues with his presentation. How old is she? What is her family background? Is she married or not? Does she have children? What is her appearance? How does she feel about herself as a person, and how does she feel about her illness? In other words, who is this person about whom we are talking? The student is somewhat amazed. He insists that the chief complaint is by far the most important piece of information, and all the rest is merely "psychosocial data." No one disagrees, of course, that the chief complaint is always crucial, but that is not the issue. The difficulty now becomes clearer. The student is presenting the signs and symptoms of illness, not a human being, and certainly not a human interaction of which he, the student, is an integral part.

Faced with illness, we all have the tendency to think in terms of a disease process, resulting from a causative organism or some metabolic physiological disequilibrium. We expect to arrive at a correct diagnosis, and then institute a treatment program so as to correct the disturbance. As we go through this chain of events, it soon becomes clear that we are regarding the illness as something foreign, something external which needs to be eliminated. We so often forget that it takes place in a human being. We think of signs and symptoms, of laboratory tests, of expected medical conclusions and recommendations. But who is this person who comes to us asking for help, and why at this particular time? Is the person young or old, male or female, poor or rich, alone and lonely, or with family and friends who are close and who care?

Confronted with illness, the patient not only wants us to know about his medical condition. He also wants and needs us to understand that he is now in pain and that he may be afraid. He may find himself in an unfamiliar place such as an office or hospital, surrounded by strangers who he hopes will help him. Illness forces him to relinquish a very important part of his autonomy, his sense of control over himself and his life. In such a setting, the individual by necessity reverts both physically and psychologically to a situation in which he has to be cared for by others. This dependence on other people enhances the sense of helplessness and vulnerability created by the disease process. It will reawaken the impact of previous life experiences and early childhood relationships. The patient's attitude towards his physicians and other caretakers will be colored by the way he was cared for when much younger, and very often this attitude will have a direct bearing on his response to medical advice and the ultimate outcome of the treatment program.

6

We now present a selection from a videotape interview of a 57 year old black man who was hospitalized because of a myocardial infarction. Dr. Moisy Shopper conducted this interview some years ago. Let us pay particular attention to what this man tells us about himself, about his illness, and about the setting in which it took place. Let us be sensitive to the powerful emotions within him as he tells us of his working in one place for 24 years. The place goes out of business, and after a few weeks he starts a new job. Let us see what then happens.

INTERVIEW WITH A PATIENT

Dr. S: You say you had never been sick in your life before this?

Patient: Never been sick. Three weeks ago tomorrow on the new job was the first time.

Dr. S: What kind of work did you do on this new job?

Patient: House wrecking. Never did it before. See, I worked on my job 24 years, and they went out of business this year, in June. I had not done anything from June up until three Fridays ago. Then I went on this new job and worked an hour and five minutes. It started hurting then — my chest. So I came home and got in the bed. Then I called the doctor to come, and I called the police and told them to send me an ambulance. So they sent one. Nobody home but me. My wife was working. They must have gotten me here to the hospital by 1:30 that Friday afternoon. But I never got into bed until about 7:00 that night.

Dr. S: That was a long wait.

Patient: Yes.

Dr. S: So you were hurting and hurting, and you had to wait a long time. It wasn't too pleasant. When did the doctor finally get to see you?

Patient: It must have been around 7:00 that night. He gave me a pill, and that pill did do it. It didn't hurt no more. But a few days later it started hurting all over again. You know, it hurt like before. But now it feels all right.

Dr. S: When you first got the pain in your chest, what did you think was wrong with you?

Patient: I don't know. I thought I had some indigestion, you know. Maybe I ate something bad. Felt like I wanted to vomit, only I couldn't vomit. You know, that's the way it felt. Like it might come up at any time. So I went into the restaurant, and I told the lady to give me a Alka Seltzer. I took that and it didn't do no good. Well, then she said she would give me a club soda or something. Whatever she gave me didn't do no good. So I went back on the job and lay down.

Dr. S: Was it lunch time or did you just take time off?

Patient: I just quit. It was five after nine, and I drank some warm water, and I spute up. And when I spute up, it kind of eased it a little bit. So I asked to drink some more warm water so I could spute up and ease it some more.

Dr. S: Did you have any idea that it might be something more serious than just indigestion?

Patient: Yes. I figured that out because the indigestion lasted so long. I told people at work that I must be having a heart attack. They said, "No, you don't have no heart attack." But I told them I knew something was wrong, because I never had anything like this before.

Dr. S: So you made your own diagnosis. You called the doctor yourself.

Patient: That's right, I never had pain like that before. So I called up.

Dr. S: Were you worried about the pain?

Patient: Seems like I wasn't worried too much about it. But seems like I couldn't rest no place, you know. First, I thought maybe I'm just tired, getting old and full of sweat, you know. But when I lay down, it was no good. When I sit up, it was no good. When I lean over, it was no good. Whatever I would do, it was no good.

Dr. S: What kind of work did you do before you took the wrecking job?

Patient: I was working in the coal yard 24 years. It was a nice place. I am real sorry they went out of business.

Dr. S: What kind of work did you do there?

Patient: Just loading the truck all day. They got a chute there. You have to hold the thing down for it to fall into the truck.

Dr. S: You pulled the lever that worked the machine?

Patient: That's right. That was nice. I felt like I could be a hundred years old and still handle that job. Maybe I wouldn't have gotten sick if I still had that job.

Dr. S: How did you feel when that place went out of business?

Patient: I felt so bad, to tell you the truth. I worked there 24 years.

Dr. S: Twenty-four years is a long time.

Patient: It sure is. Twenty-four years. They notify you a couple of weeks ahead telling that they're going to close up. Makes you feel bad. When you get to be an old man, where can you get a job? If I was a young fellow, I wouldn't worry about it. But when you reach a certain age, they don't want you no more. I went looking for a few jobs, you know, and they told me, "You're too old for this job."

Dr. S: That's what they would say to you?

Patient: That's what they told me. It wouldn't be hard work either, you know, but I was still too old.

Dr. S: What kind of jobs were you applying for?

Patient: All kinds of jobs. It didn't make no difference. But nobody wanted to hire me because I was too old. Everywhere I went — "Too old." They didn't want me.

Dr. S: How soon after this fellow closed up at the coal yard did you start looking for another job?

Patient: Well see, when he closed up, he gave me three weeks vacation. When the vacation was over, then I started looking for a job. And finally I got this hard job house wrecking. I am sorry the way it happened. If I hadn't went over there to that hard job, I wouldn't have gotten sick. Sorry I went over there. I didn't do myself no good. But you know how it is when you're used to working. You get tired laying around the house, you know.

Dr. S: You found it sort of like time was on your hands, and you didn't know what to do with it.?

Patient: That's right.

Dr. S: How will you try to spend your time now?

Patient: Well, to tell you the truth, I don't know. When I get out, I'll take it easy. I'll get up when I get ready. If I feel like walking out someplace, I'll walk out and take it nice and easy, that's all. I won't let nothing worry me no more.

Dr. S: You used to let things worry you and get you down?

Patient: Well, I couldn't get a job and that worried me. I just won't let things worry me no more, that's all. Worrying can kill you.

THE NEED FOR DENIAL

There are many issues which we could discuss as we review this man's clinical situation. He develops chest pain, and his first reaction is to offer himself a less serious diagnosis in order to relieve his own anxiety. He says that it must be indigestion. He needs to deny to himself the possibility that he might be having a heart attack. This is brought out by the interviewer's question, "Did you have any idea that it might be something more serious than just indigestion?" It is only then that he gives his own diagnosis of a heart attack. *Denial* is probably the most frequently observed defense mechanism on medical and surgical wards, a very important fact to be taken into consideration in obtaining medical histories. It is also interesting to note the way in which people close to patients may share this denial, and may even need it to a greater degree than the patients themselves. That was certainly the case with this man. When he told the people at work that he thought he was having a heart attack, they said, "No, you are not."

This sharing of denial may also include physicians, nurses, paraprofessionals, medical students, and all others involved in the care of patients. If we identify too closely with a patient in one way or another, we may find it extremely difficult to pay attention to the more serious implications of that patient's illness. That is the reason for the old adage, "He who treats himself has a fool for a patient." It is also the reason why it is usually best that we not treat close friends, relatives, or members of our family. A particularly striking example is the case of a physician quite experienced in the field of internal medicine who attributed his tarry stools to the ingestion of beets three days prior to the onset of his gastrointestinal hemorrhage.

The dangers of such denial become especially evident when we see colleagues as patients. Colleagues in the medical and nursing professions are going to come to us as patients. We have to remember that while medicine offers great emotional rewards and satisfactions, it also entails great physical and emotional stresses. That is why the incidence of suicide and drug abuse among physicians is so high. When a colleague comes to us with such a problem, very often we do not want to hear it, because it is too frightening and comes too close to home. We tend to minimize the problem, or we offer sympathy and friendly advice rather than establish an empathic relationship with the patient that will lead to the correct diagnosis.

EMPATHY

Empathy is something quite different from either sympathy or advice. Sympathy and advice usually give us a good feeling (even when the advice is not followed!), but empathy is often painful and demanding. Empathy requires that we be able to partially identify with the patient who comes into our office, and try to put ourselves in this person's place. We can then ask ourselves, "What is he or she experiencing? In what way are they in pain? What are they going through? What are they worried about? What would be happening to me if I were in a similar situation? How can I be of help?" Empathy allows us to be able to identify sufficiently with the patient so that we can have some understanding of his or her situation, but at the same time it allows us to maintain enough objectivity so that we can help the patient. Dr. Shopper's interview with our 57 year old patient is a good example of a warm and empathic approach that slowly and gently establishes a relationship of trust, in which the patient can begin to express his deepest feelings about the loss of his job and his subsequent heart attack.

THE LIFE SETTING

We turn now to the setting in which our 57 year old man became ill. He tells us of the great impact that the loss of his job had on him. His grief is obvious as he talks about his old job. In a very poignant and dramatic way, he establishes the connection in his own mind between his reaction to that important loss and his subsequent heart attack. He thus adds support to the conclusions of such workers as Thomas Holmes and Richard Rahe, who have documented the severe stress of many life changes, particularly those changes involving a loss of one kind or another. In this context we particularly want to mention the work of Arthur Schmale and George Engel who have formulated the concept of *the giving-up-given-up complex.* In a paper entitled "A Life Setting Conducive to Illness," George Engel points out that "illness is commonly preceded by a period of psychological disturbance,

during which the individual feels unable to cope." He also states that the giving-up-given-up complex is neither a necessary nor a sufficient condition for organic disease development, but is nevertheless often an important contributing factor.

As far as our patient is concerned, there is very little doubt that this man experienced a major life change and within weeks thereafter suffered a serious life-threatening illness. It is remarkable, but not surprising, that his myocardial infarction occurred on the morning he started a new job. The stress was not just in losing his old job; it was also finding himself in a situation which he may have never experienced before or at least not for a very long time. Lying around the house, feeling very much alone, he felt he was losing his sense of independence and his ability to provide for his family. Furthermore, he had a new task to accomplish as a result of the loss of his job. He had to find another one. But he is not 20 or 30 years old anymore. As far as society is concerned, he is an old man now, and he is constantly reminded of being too old. He feels unwanted and useless, and in this setting of loss, helplessness, and hopelessness, he has his heart attack (Figure 2.1).

THE FEAR OF DYING

Everyone sets ideals for himself. Getting older and becoming ill may require that people give up some of those ideals, or at least change the images that they have of themselves The individual's ability to do so may literally mean the difference between life and death, or an active and vigorous life throughout old age compared to a life of chronic invalidism. An understanding and supportive physician can be of enormous help in making this change. For example, our patient has to deal not only with his age and the loss of his job, but he also has to face a life-threatening illness. His preoccupation with death becomes clear when he expresses his determination to stop worrying about finding a new job. "Worrying can kill you," he says. The fear of dying, and the many different ways in which patients and their physicians may try to cope with this fear, will have enormous significance in the management of all seriously ill patients.

Some physicians may find it very difficult to

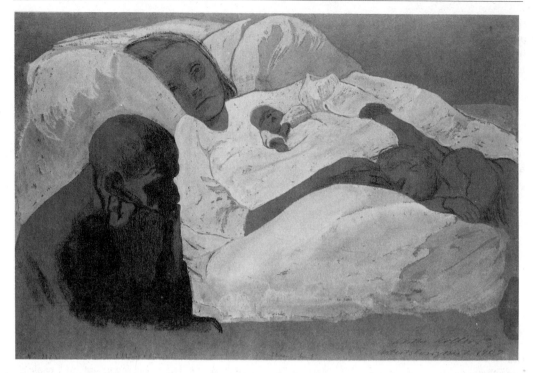

Figure 2.1. *Unemployment* (1909) by Käthe Kollwitz. (By permission of National Gallery of Art, Washington, D.C., Rosenwald Collection.)

talk with their patients about death. They may have a set approach to the subject, regardless of the needs of the individual patient. There will be much more material in later chapters about death and dying. Suffice it to say at this point that the overwhelming anxiety that patients may experience about the possibility of dying may have serious consequences in relation to their medical condition and their ability to follow medical advice. Conversely, dying patients may have far more awareness of their condition than their physician may realize, and they may be far more willing and ready to talk about their terminal illness than the anxious relatives, physicians, and others around them. It is also a well-known clinical phenomenon that when patients tell us that they are convinced that they are going to die soon, they often turn out to be right. This may reflect an accurate assessment on their part of the seriousness of their condition. It may also reflect a state of despair that may actually hasten death. In any event there are many surgeons who quite correctly will cancel elective surgery when they hear patients talking that way.

THE IMPACT OF HOSPITALIZATION

As physicians we are so used to being in hospitals practically every day of our lives that we may not recognize sufficiently what hospitalization may mean to people. An individual goes into the hospital as a patient, and he suddenly finds himself immersed in a strange and unfamiliar world. Doctors and nurses tell him what to do and what not to do. He is away from home and family, and the loneliness may become overwhelming. He has an illness about which he may feel bewildered and frightened, and thoughts of death may suddenly intrude themselves during the day and awaken him in terror at night. If he is placed in an intensive care unit (ICU), he is isolated even further, and surrounded by machines, continuous noise, and death. Small wonder that the incidence of "ICU psychosis" is so high.

How will these feelings affect the course of his illness and its management? Most of us develop a sense of belonging to a family, a home, a place of work. Suddenly all of that is taken away and we have to relate as patients to a new setting and to new people, including other patients. Some of these brief relationships may become very important and supportive, and another patient who goes home or who dies may entail still another major loss.

THE NEED FOR MASTERY

In the interview it is clear that our patient prides himself on being independent, on being able to take care of his own needs. It is essential to recognize how difficult it is for most patients to be in a dependent position. Some patients, in order to prove that they are not sick, may tend to do precisely what is not best for them medically. It may be very difficult for them to tolerate the helplessness and dependence of a serious illness. To need someone even for the most basic functions can be a major threat. To be washed, to be helped to go to the bathroom, or to have to use a bedpan may become quite unacceptable and intolerable.

Most patients need to feel that they are in control of their lives, that they have some mastery over their own destinies. It is usually quite helpful to engage the patient as an active participant in his treatment, rather than to permit him to be simply a passive recipient. This is extremely important in regard to diet, medication, and all other aspects of medical advice, as Dr. Mumford will describe later in the book. For example, eating may become a major issue with some patients. If they are used to eating particular types of food, trying to force them into a very restricted diet may prove to be a fruitless exercise. They may not tell the physician, but they will invariably go off the diet. It is much better to ally oneself with the patient and invite his or her active participation in the planning of the diet, the timing and the dosage of medication, and all other aspects of the treatment regimen.

A case comes to mind of a man with chronic renal disease. He had always been a strong, well built man. This image of himself was extremely important to him, and eating good food was part of it. As a result of his illness, he lost considerable weight and strength, and developed a severe depression with suicidal thoughts. The patient's wife was quite understanding of his needs, and realized the tremendous loss that his limited diet represented for him. She began to feed him more frequently and on smaller plates so that the portions of food seemed larger, and she also involved him more actively in the choice of those foods that were permissible. The man's physician learned a great deal from this wife's intuitive understanding of her husband's needs.

SEXUAL ACTIVITY

The life role of a man or woman may be drastically changed as a result of serious illness, and this may have a profound effect on the person's self-esteem. Difficulties in a previously stable marriage may be provoked, and the structure of a family may be seriously altered. The physician can play a crucial part in helping the patient find those activities that will most effectively restore his or her self-esteem and self-confidence. This is particularly true in regard to the advice given to patients regarding physical activity, especially sexual activity.

It is not uncommon for patients to be given vague and abstract instructions regarding their physical and sexual activity, and thereby be left to interpret their doctor's instructions according to their own needs or levels of anxiety. "Take it easy," seems innocent enough, and it is a piece of advice frequently given to patients. "Don't overdo it" or "Don't get too upset" are in the same category. We have to remind ourselves, however, that such comments may have a crippling effect on people who are very apprehensive about their health. Such a patient may take this casual advice as a warning and a prohibition, and inhibit himself or herself from going back to work, leading an active social life, or resuming sexual contacts. Many people believe that sexual excitement imposes too much strain, particularly on one's heart. They may abstain from sex even when the anatomical damage is minimal, unless their physician discusses with them frankly and realistically their capabilities and limitations. But this means that physicians have to be comfortable discussing sexual matters with their patients.

The sexual history is often ignored or given short shrift with the rationalization that it is too private, and that the patient will be too embarrassed to discuss it. Actually, it is often the physician who is too anxious and embarrassed to deal directly with this important aspect of everyone's life. Medical patients often have many questions in regard to sexuality, but they will not ask them if they sense that the physician would prefer to avoid this topic or is not interested in their personal problems. The patient may then say that everything is fine sexually, when actually it is not, and a conspiracy of silence will have begun.

THE LIFE CYCLE

The moving and eloquent poem quoted at the conclusion of the last chapter is a reminder to us of the importance of seeing our patients in the perspective of their life experiences. The past history, both medical and personal, thus becomes crucial in understanding our patients in their totality. This involves not only inquiring about childhood diseases. It means reviewing with our patients the progression of their lives through time, so that we can gain a sense of the continuity between their past, their present, and their future. And it will be to the nonpsychiatric physician that the great majority of patients will turn first, including those whose difficulties are emotional in origin.

A young woman is pregnant, and for a whole variety of reasons she begins to gain a great deal of weight. Eventually she starts to feel grotesque and ugly. She begins to worry whether her husband will still find her sexually desirable. It is very unlikely that she will first seek out a psychiatrist for help. She is going to want to talk to her obstetrician. This same woman may have a young son, who is becoming quite upset because of her pregnancy. He may have suddenly started to crawl again, or be asking to go back on the bottle, or be experiencing a return of earlier fears of being separated from his mother. He may even have started to wet the bed again. The mother is not going to first take her son to a child psychiatrist's office. She will take him to her pediatrician. She will ask, "What's happening here? I don't understand." Hopefully, the pediatrician will be able to help her understand, and will know that in the overwhelming majority of cases enuresis is caused by emotional conflicts, not by organic pathology in the urinary tract.

An older man is nearing retirement. He may be a man for whom work has been extremely important. His identity, his very existence if you will, has been defined by the kind of work that he does. Suddenly he is nearing age 65, and he finds that he is having some sexual difficulty. Perhaps, for the first time in his life, he is

impotent. He does not know that most erectile difficulties are caused by psychological problems rather than by organic problems, and therefore it is very unlikely that the first thing that will cross his mind is to see a psychiatrist. He is going to see his family physician, or his internist. Maybe he will seek out a urologist for a cystoscopic examination or a prostatic examination. These physicians will be the ones who will see that man first. Another man, such as our 57 year old patient, may actually have lost his job, and the loss will have such profound implications for him that it actually precipitates a serious medical illness.

We may see a woman in her late forties who is reaching menopause. Perhaps this is a woman whose children have always been very important for her. Her life may have been defined by her children, as the lives of other men and women are defined by their work. Perhaps she is a woman for whom physical attractiveness and youth are extremely important. Certainly we are still very much a youth-oriented, action-oriented, beauty-oriented culture. As that woman grows older, she faces many losses — the loss of her children, the loss of her childbearing capabilities and her physical youthfulness, possibly even the loss of her husband through death or divorce. She may begin to become depressed, and the depression may first be manifested by an aggravation of the normal menopausal symptoms that every woman experiences, and that most women handle without difficulty. She is not going to see a psychiatrist. She is going to see her gynecologist or her family doctor.

Other persons may turn to surgeons instead. They may give a history of having had one operation after another. One woman had many major operations by the time she was 40, beginning with an appendectomy at age 17 that produced a normal appendix. Her gall bladder, her stomach, portions of her bowels, her uterus — all had been removed. A brief interview with her revealed the fact that she was a twin, a fraternal twin. Her fraternal twin died when they were two, and frequently thereafter her mother would tell her that she was going to have to "suffer double" throughout her life — once for herself and once for her twin. She came to blame herself for the death of her twin, and so indeed her mother's prophecy came true. She "suffered double" many times over, and her repeated operations were motivated by her need to be punished, as well as by a fantasy of being reunited with her dead twin. She never saw a psychiatrist. But she certainly saw a surgeon, many surgeons, over and over again.

We shall spend the remainder of the book talking about how such reactions may come about in the lives of our patients. But as valuable as we hope such knowledge will be, the ultimate answers regarding each person's life must come from that person. Our patients will very quickly detect our interest, not only in their illness, but in them as human beings and in their unique life experiences. If we give them reason to trust us, they will in turn share with us their deepest feelings, their fears, and their hopes.

Suggested Readings

Engel GL: A life setting conducive to illness: the giving-up-given-up complex. *Ann Intern Med* 69:293, 1968.

Engel GL: The clinical application of the biopsychosocial model. *Am J Psychiatry* 137:535, 1980.

Leigh H, Reiser MF: *The Patient: Biological, Psychological, and Social Dimensions of Medical Practice.* New York, Plenum Press, 1980.

Peabody FW: The care of the patient. *JAMA* 88:877, 1927.

Waring EM: An interpersonal model for teaching psychiatry to medical students. *Psychosomatics* 21:998, 1980.

References

Console WA, Simons RC, Rubinstein M: *The First Encounter: The Beginnings in Psychotherapy.* New York, Jason Aronson, 1976.

Holmes TH, Rahe RH: The social readjustment rating scale. *J Psychosom Res* 11:213, 1967.

Vaillant GE, Sobowale NC, McArthur C: Some psychologic vulnerabilities of physicians. *N Engl J Med* 287:372, 1972.

Section B/The Doctor-Patient Relationship

CHAPTER **3** ### The Participants in the Doctor-Patient Relationship

Ruth L. Fuller, M.D.

In 1964 Norman Cousins was diagnosed as suffering from ankylosing spondylitis, an arthritic degeneration of collagen in the spine. Expert specialists gave him about a one in 500 chance for full recovery. With the help and encouragement of his physician, Dr. William Hitzig, Cousins decided to fight. He took himself off all analgesics, received Vitamin C in huge (25 grams a day) doses intravenously, and discovered the curative power of laughter in Marx Brothers films and clips from Candid Camera. To the amazement of the experts, he went on to a full recovery. In his book *Anatomy of an Illness* he draws some conclusions from his experience:

> I was incredibly fortunate to have as my doctor a man who knew that his biggest job was to encourage to the fullest the patient's will to live and to mobilize all the natural resources of body and mind to combat disease. Dr. Hitzig was willing to set aside the large and often hazardous armamentarium of powerful drugs available to the modern physician when he became convinced that his patient might have something better to offer. He was also wise enough to know that the art of healing is still a frontier profession. And, though I can't be sure of this point, I have a hunch he believed that my own total involvement was a major factor in my recovery.*

---

* *Anatomy of an Illness As Perceived by the Patient* by Norman Cousins. Copyright © 1979 by W.W. Norton & Company, Inc., New York, N.Y. Page 44.

Much has been written by others, before Norman Cousins, about this special human interaction between physician and patient. There have been romantic descriptions in literature, visual portrayals in art, and legal arguments in court as to the nature and limitations of this unique relationship. It would be highly presumptuous to assume that all of the nuances of such a complex, human exchange can be reduced to a description in a few pages, but what I propose to do is simply to introduce some of the basic issues about the participants in the doctor-patient relationship. In many ways, the rest of the book will be an elaboration of these basic issues.

THE PATIENT

Let me start with a picture of a patient. All of us have been patients long before we became doctors. A patient is a person with a name; of a certain age and sex; living in a particular household alone or with other people; from a heritage of importance to him or her; having hopes, wishes, dreams, fears, achievements, failures, and tasks of life yet to master; living in a particular neighborhood, society, and culture in a particular period of history; having a picture of his or her self-worth; and coming to a physician with a concern about his or her health. Whether a patient is seeing a doctor for the first time or after many times, there are certain expectations that this patient carries into the setting of the office, clinic, or hospital.

One expectation is that the doctor will be

knowledgeable about health and illness, and can tell the difference between the two. Although there are some patients who are committed to the maintenance of good health and the prevention of disease and illness, most patients see physicians because they feel badly or are aware that something is wrong. A second expectation is that the doctor will be helpful. To be helpful means to understand the presenting nature of the symptoms, to have a clear course of action for investigating the underlying problem, to have solutions for dealing with the problem once it is diagnosed, and to follow these solutions to the point of some resolution of the problem. A third expectation is that the doctor will allow the patient to participate in this process of diagnosis and treatment to the maximum degree possible. The nature of each of these expectations will differ uniquely for each patient, and will be influenced by a great many factors, including the patient's cultural background, physical and emotional state, personality style, childhood developmental experiences, earlier relationships with parents and siblings, and previous experiences with illness and with doctors.

THE DOCTOR

A doctor is also a person with a name; of a certain age and sex; living in a particular household alone or with other people; from a heritage of importance to him or her; having hopes, wishes, dreams, fears, achievements, failures, and tasks of life yet to master; living in a particular neighborhood, society, and culture in a particular period of history; having a picture of his or her self-worth; and coming to a patient with a body of information and skill in medical care. The physician also has a personality style, and has had earlier developmental experiences with parents, siblings, doctors, and illness. But in contrast to the patient, the doctor is asked to be aware of those personal reactions from the past that may be unrelated to the patient in the present and to be able to maintain some distance from these reactions. Thus, the physician is expected to be a respectful, knowledgeable professional who observes data, organizes the data, and then synthesizes the data in a meaningful way. The physician's resources for this task are the history, the physical examination, the laboratory, the experience of colleagues, the physician's own life experiences, and the mutual collaboration with the patient.

The History

The first resource is the obtaining of a history from the patient. The doctor-patient relationship begins as the two people involved start to talk with each other. In asking patients about their concerns and then listening carefully, the doctor establishes by that single act that what the patient has to say is important, and that the patient is the one person most uniquely experienced and acquainted with his or her illness. And, by listening with an attitude of total attention, physicians allow patients to tell their stories in their own ways. This process demands time and patience on the part of the physician. The time needed is always qualitative but not necessarily quantitative. For example, I observed a very experienced pediatrician who obtained a complete history from an anxious young mother concerning the perpetual crying of her firstborn infant in only 15 minutes. This young mother did not feel rushed, felt that she was well understood by the pediatrician, experienced a realistic resolution of her fears, and left the interview convinced that her infant had received good medical care — which indeed it had. At other times, many hours may be necessary to establish a clear picture of the diagnosis and the patient's psychological reactions to that diagnosis.

The Physical Examination (Figure 3.1)

The physical examination is the second resource that a doctor brings to the patient, and this experience can have a profound influence on the developing doctor-patient relationship. A patient expects a doctor to be thorough and confident in a physical examination. Patients may not necessarily expect certain humane preparations such as being told what part of the examination is coming next, its purpose, and whether or not it will be painful, but they will always be grateful for such respect and consideration on the part of the physician. Many patients remember only cold hands and cold instruments when asked about a physical examination. Others speak of their shame at having been examined thoroughly from head to toe. But there may also be some very positive memories. One 20 year old woman who was being examined by a prominent cardiologist on a hot summer's day remembered that she had been very thirsty, and that the doctor took the time to get her a drink of water. Cryptic groans, grunts, and grim-

Figure 3.1. Hippocrates sitting under his famous plane tree at Kos examining a patient. (By permission of Professor L. J. Bruce-Chwatt and the Wellcome Museum of Medical Science, London, England.)

aces by the physician usually inspire terror in patients who may be too frightened or shy to ask for a translation of such nonverbal responses, but who usually labor with an inaccurate picture of having an imminently fatal illness.

The Laboratory

The use of the laboratory is the third resource of the physician. Having established a relationship during which the history has been taken and the physical examination completed, here again that relationship can be enhanced by discussing with the patient the laboratory procedures to be pursued, their purposes, the risks (if any), and the discomfort (if any). It cannot be assumed that patients are familiar with these various procedures. For example, a 65 year old woman was being seen by a physician for a series of concerns including shortness of breath, joint pains, and muscle weakness. Before her appointment she had been suspicious of all doctors, but found this particular physician to be quite pleasant during the history taking and the physical. She was then told she would have to have some blood tests, an EKG, and X-rays. The EKG and

X-rays were acceptable to her, but she was quite disturbed about the blood sample because "he took a bottle of it." She felt that this "bloodletting" would worsen her condition, but said nothing to the doctor. She had looked distressed during the time the blood was being taken, but had not been told that the amount of blood taken was relatively small as compared to the total amount in her body. She never returned to this doctor. In talking about her experience later, it was clear that she felt that the bloodletting reflected how ill she was. She also thought that the taking of the blood was the beginning of the treatment rather than a diagnostic procedure. She did not want to see a doctor who still believed in bloodletting as a medical treatment. This is only one example of how a good working relationship can suffer an abrupt disruption if a patient feels that "all those tests" are not individualized but rather are followed automatically and without careful explanation by the physician. This particular physician was a very competent one, but his competence was of no benefit to this particular patient.

Some might argue that this elderly woman's reaction was due to her lack of education and medical sophistication. But look at a very similar reaction from a middle aged man who lacked neither education nor medical sophistication:

> There was the morbid fear of intrusive technology, fear of being metabolized by a data base, never to regain our faces again. There was resentment of strangers who came at us with needles and vials — some of which put supposedly magic substances in our veins, and others which took more of our blood than we thought we could afford to lose.*

Norman Cousins had even more to say about the technology of the modern laboratory following a heart attack that he suffered:

> The more exotic and sophisticated the technology, the greater the likelihood that patients will feel diminished or apprehensive. The physician who cannot afford the time to stay close to the patient during this experience had better find effective equivalents, for the ultimate impact of those tests can be harmful psychologically and there-

---

Anatomy of an Illness As Perceived by the Patient by Norman Cousins. Copyright © 1979 by W.W. Norton & Company, Inc., New York, N.Y. Pages 153–154.

fore physiologically. Patients cannot be blamed for retreating from encounters they find distasteful or upsetting. The argument that the procedures are necessary for the patient's own good misses the point, for the source of the patient's disquiet may not be the procedure itself so much as the climate or the context in which it occurs. The absence of human warmth during those experiences can figure more in the reactions of patients than the vaunted value of the tests.†

The Experience of Colleagues

The fourth resource that a doctor has is the use of colleagues with more information and experience as consultants. This process is true whether a medical student is drawing on the greater experience and knowledge of the cardiology resident to clarify the exact nature of a murmur in the chest of a long-distance runner, or whether the chief of medicine is consulting with a resident in gynecology about the cause of the right lower quadrant pain of a young, married woman. A relaxed and confident consultation with colleagues conveys to the patient a reasonable sense of humility and resourcefulness, not incompetence.

The Physician's Own Life Experiences

The most important resource of all to the physician is his or her own life experiences with parents, siblings, teachers, lovers, spouses, and friends. Human experiences of birth, death, loss, love, helplessness, and joy are universal. However, each of us lives these experiences in a unique way. We are of different sizes, shapes, colors, and personalities. We grow up in families and cultures that care about its members in their own special ways. We speak different languages, believe in different religions, and have different values, standards, convictions. Each of us works, loves, copes, and plays in a different way. It is the individual physician's ability to understand his or her own uniqueness that allows an appreciation of the patient's similar uniqueness. It is the further ability of the physician to juxtapose these differences against the commonality of all

human experience, and to use the resulting wisdom and empathy, that makes the doctor-patient relationship possible.

The Mutual Collaboration Between Doctor and Patient

The maintenance of the doctor-patient relationship continues with the physician explaining the results of the diagnostic procedures so that the patient understands the nature of the problem, the treatment prescribed, and the likely prognosis. If both doctor and patient collaborate together in this undertaking, with both recognizing that it is the patient's illness and not the doctor's, and that it is the patient's life and not the doctor's, many treatment "failures" can be avoided. I will conclude this introductory chapter with just a few words about some of these failures of patients to respond to medical advice.

I believe that the single most important reason for such failures resides in the inability of physicians to fully appreciate and continually keep in mind the complex needs and expectations of their patients. Dr. Blumenfield and Dr. Mumford will be speaking in more depth about some of these needs and expectations in the next chapters. Over the years, this neglect of the primary importance of mutuality in the doctor-patient relationship has evoked disappointment and anger in patients, nonmedical professionals, and concerned physicians. Several movements have developed in the past decade, such as the Holistic Medicine Movement, as well as self-help women's health care groups and ethnic minority health care groups. Each of these is concerned with a rethinking of the doctor-patient relationship so as to find new ways to practice medicine. One such organized effort in particular is the Humanistic Medicine Movement. Briefly, this movement addresses the dehumanization of medical care as characterized by "super specialization," "emphasis on technology," and "authoritarianism." Simply put, too many physicians are viewed as technicians with medical degrees who approach diseases or diagnoses, not patients, not whole people. What has been proposed by the Humanistic Medicine Movement is that three elements central to the doctor-patient relationship be emphasized: 1) The responsibility for health care should be mutually shared by both patient and doctor. 2) Illness should be redefined as a "creative oppor-

---

† *The Healing Heart. Antidotes to Panic and Helplessness* by Norman Cousins. Copyright © 1983 by Norman Cousins. Reprinted by permission of W.W. Norton & Company, Inc., New York, N.Y. Page 177.

tunity" for a patient to understand what gave rise to this particular illness at this particular time, and to modify his or her life accordingly. 3) It is the person rather than the illness that should be treated from the moment of the first appointment. To quote Norman Cousins once again:

> If I had to guess, I would say that the principal contribution made by my doctor to the taming, and possibly the conquest, of my illness was that he encouraged me to believe I was a respected partner with him in the total undertaking. He fully engaged my subjective energies. He may not have been able to define or diagnose the process through which self-confidence (wild hunches securely believed) was somehow picked up by the body's immunologic mechanisms and translated into antimorbid effects, but he was acting, I believe, in the best tradition of medicine in recognizing that he had to reach out in my case beyond the usual verifiable modalities. In so doing, he was faithful to the first dictum in his medical education: above all, do not harm.*

I would agree with Mr. Cousins that the heart of the issue still lies within the individual physician. The task of acting as a true synthesizer and collaborator rather than as some kind of omniscient and omnipotent authority may seem to be overwhelming at first, particularly when the young physician's resources have not yet become that familiar. However, with experience, the resources do become familiar, and so does functioning at the interface between the patient with the problem and the vast array of ever changing scientific information. This approach of mutual collaboration is ultimately far more rewarding than physicians trying to fit patients into a preconceived mold which suits the needs of the physician but not the needs of the patient. Plato said it very well a long time ago:

> Did you ever observe that there are two classes of patients in states, slaves and freemen; and the slave doctors run about and cure the slaves, or wait for them in dispensaries — practitioners of this sort never talk to their patients individually or let them talk about their own individual complaints. The slave doctor prescribes what mere experience suggests, as if he had exact knowledge, and when he has given his orders, like a tyrant, he rushes off with equal assurance

to some other servant who is ill. But the other doctor, who is a freeman, attends and practices on freemen; and he carries his inquiries far back, and goes into the nature of the disorder; he enters into discourse with the patient and with his friends, and is at once getting information from the sick man and also instructing him as far as he is able, and he will not prescribe until he has at first convinced him. If one of those empirical (slave) physicians, who practice medicine without science, were to come upon the gentleman physician talking to his gentleman patient and using the language almost of philosophy, beginning at the beginning of the disease and discoursing about the whole nature of the body, he would burst into a hearty laugh — he would say what most of those who are called doctors always have at their tongues' end: 'Foolish fellow,' he would say, 'You are not healing the sick man but educating him. It should not be your purpose to make another doctor out of him, only to cure him.' *

I would suggest — as does Plato — that the approach of the gentleman physician is perhaps not so "foolish" after all, and that it should be our purpose as physicians to help each of our patients become "another doctor" for themselves to the maximum degree possible. Dr. Albert Schweitzer would also agree. When Norman Cousins expressed his skepticism to Schweitzer about the effectiveness of the witch doctors who were working closely with Schweitzer, the latter replied half-smilingly:

> The witch doctor succeeds for the same reason all the rest of us succeed. Each patient carries his own doctor inside him. They come to us not knowing that truth. We are at our best when we give the doctor who resides within each patient a chance to go to work.†

Suggested Readings

Cousins N: *Anatomy of an Illness As Perceived by the Patient: Reflections on Healing and Regeneration.* New York, W.W. Norton and Co., 1979.
Cousins N: *The Healing Heart. Antidotes to Panic and Helplessness.* New York, W.W. Norton & Co., 1983.
Miller S, Miller S: First report of the Program in Humanistic Medicine, 1972–1973. The Program in Humanistic Medicine, San Francisco, California, 1974.
Reiser DE, Rosen DH: *Medicine as a Human Experience.* Baltimore, University Park Press, 1984.
Reiser DE, Schroder AK: *Patient Interviewing: The Human Dimension.* Baltimore, Williams & Wilkins, 1985.

---

* From *Dialogues of Plato.*

† *Anatomy of an Illness As Perceived by the Patient* by Norman Cousins. Copyright © 1979 by W.W. Norton & Company, Inc., New York, N.Y. Page 69.

---

* *Anatomy of an Illness As Perceived by the Patient* by Norman Cousins. Copyright © 1979 by W.W. Norton & Company, Inc., New York, N.Y. Page 48.

CHAPTER 4

The Basic Models of the Doctor-Patient Relationship

Michael Blumenfield, M.D.

"..Some patients, though conscious that their condition is perilous, recover their health simply through their contentment with the goodness of the physician."

Hippocrates (Figure 4.1)
Precepts, Chapter I

THE POWER OF THE DOCTOR-PATIENT RELATIONSHIP

There is no better illustration of the power of the doctor-patient relationship than when a medicine man cures a victim of a voodoo curse (Figure 4.2). Dr. Walter Cannon, the famous physiologist, vividly reviewed such a case originally described by Dr. Herbert Basedow in 1925:

'The man who discovers that he is being boned by any enemy is, indeed, a pitiable sight. He stands aghast, with his eyes staring at the treacherous pointer, and with his hands lifted as though to ward off the lethal medium, which he imagines is pouring into his body. His cheeks blanch and his eyes become glassy and the expression of his face becomes horribly distorted. . . . He attempts to shriek but usually the sound chokes in his throat, and all that one might see is froth at his mouth. His body begins to tremble and the muscles twist involuntarily. He sways backwards and falls to the ground, and after a short time appears to be in a swoon; but soon after he writhes as if in mortal agony, and, covering his face with his hands, begins to moan. After a while he becomes very composed and crawls to his wurley (hut). From this time onwards he sickens and frets, refusing to eat and keeping aloof from the daily affairs of the tribe.

Figure 4.1. Head of Hippocrates. (Courtesy of Dr. John Kelly, Denver, Colorado.)

Figure 4.2. Sculpture of priest with special divination bowl, board, and tapper, which are used to heal the sick in the Yoruba culture in Nigeria. (Articles from the collection of Dr. Jeffrey Hammer, New York, N.Y.)

Unless help is forthcoming in the shape of a countercharm administered by the hands of the Nangarri, or medicine-man, his death is only a matter of a comparatively short time. If the coming of the medicine-man is opportune he might be saved.' The Nangarri, when persuaded to exercise his powers, goes through an elaborate ceremony and finally steps toward the awestricken relatives, holding in his fingers a small article — a stick, a bone, a pebble, or a talon — which, he avows, he has taken from the 'boned' man and which was the cause of the affliction. And now, since it is removed, the victim has nothing to fear. The effect, Dr. Basedow declares, is astounding. The victim, until that moment far on the road to death, raises his head and gazes in wonderment at the object held by the medicine-man. He even lifts himself into a sitting position and calls for water to drink. The crisis is passed, and the recovery is speedy and complete. Without the Nangarri's intervention the boned fellow, according to Dr. Basedow, would certainly have fretted himself to death.

A more contemporary illustration involves a patient whom I saw in consultation. She was a 26 year old Mexican-American woman who was hospitalized on the dermatology ward for a rash of unknown origin. The consultation was requested because the patient was said to be very anxious. When I arrived to see the patient, the house staff no longer felt a psychiatric consultation was necessary since the patient's medical condition had taken a turn for the worse. She had had an unexplained fall in blood pressure with a very rapid pulse, and was going into

shock. I interviewed the patient immediately, and learned that she felt she was in the midst of a love triangle. The triangle consisted of the patient, her husband, and another woman who was competing for her husband's affection. The other woman had put a "curse" on the patient, who believed in the power of curses and hexes and was therefore convinced that she was going to die. It appeared that this belief on the patient's part was causing marked alterations in her autonomic nervous system which could potentially be fatal. All of the efforts of the medical staff were to no avail in alleviating her symptoms, and her condition had become quite serious. I explained the situation to the staff and advised that an anti-witch doctor in whom the patient believed might be helpful. It turned out that the patient's family had tried to bring in such a person to the ward but was refused permission by the staff. This anti-witch doctor or curandero was working at home for the patient using various herbs and potions. Once the patient was informed of this fact she made a rapid recovery.

These two cases not only illustrate the mind-body interaction but also demonstrate the powerful nature of the doctor-patient relationship.

BASIC CONSCIOUS MODELS OF THE DOCTOR-PATIENT RELATIONSHIP

The Model of Activity-Passivity

Thomas Szasz and Marc Hollender have described three basic models of the doctor-patient relationship, as outlined in Table 4.1. The first model, *activity-passivity*, is the oldest historically. It is not truly an interaction, but rather a relationship in which the active physician does something to the passive recipient, the patient.

Table 4.1
*Three Basic Models of the Physician-Patient Relationship**

Model	Physician's Role	Patient's Role	Clinical Application of Model	Prototype of Model
Activity-Passivity	Does something to patient	Passive recipient (unable to respond)	Anesthesia, acute trauma, coma	Parent-infant
Guidance-Cooperation	Tells patient what to do	Cooperator (obeys)	Acute infections	Parent-child or Parent-adolescent
Mutual Participation	Helps patient to help himself	Participant in "partnership" (uses expert help)	Most chronic illnesses, psychotherapy	Adult-adult

* Modified from earlier table by Thomas S. Szasz and Marc H. Hollender.

It is the model for many of the advances of modern medicine, such as surgery and anesthesia, and it is quite appropriate for the treatment of emergencies where the patient may be severely injured, bleeding heavily, delirious, or comatose. The prototype of this model is that of the parent-infant relationship.

The Model of Guidance-Cooperation

The second model, *guidance-cooperation*, is the one that underlies much of modern medical practice. This is an interaction in which the patient, troubled with symptoms such as those of an acute infection, actively seeks help from a physician, who tells the patient what to do and expects the patient to "obey" and cooperate with the recommended treatment. The patient is not expected to question, to disagree with, or to fail to follow the medical advice which he or she receives. In other words, this is a relationship between persons with unequal power, and the prototype of this model is that of the parent-child, or parent-adolescent relationship.

The Model of Mutual Participation

The third and final model, *mutual participation*, is one in which physician and patient have approximately equal power in a partnership or alliance, and in which both are working toward a mutually agreed upon goal. In this model the physician helps the patient help himself. This is the appropriate model for nearly all forms of psychotherapy, and it is also the necessary model in the treatment of most chronic illnesses, where the treatment program is carried out primarily by the patient. The model of mutual participation requires a more complex psychological development on the part of the two participants than either of the other two models, and therefore the prototype of this model is that of the adult-adult relationship.

PATIENT'S UNCONSCIOUS REACTION TO DOCTOR: TRANSFERENCE

The basic unconscious reaction of a patient towards the doctor originates from his or her experiences with important people in childhood. If patients as children had confidence and trust in their parents, they will more easily be able to put themselves in the hands of a doctor with this same trust and confidence. In a similar way, if patients had unreliable, neglectful parents, these experiences are going to interfere with their capacity to have confidence in even the most dedicated physician. In this latter case, such patients may remain aloof and suspicious, or may only be indifferent, but certainly not cooperative with the doctor. Patients who have unfulfilled needs for parental approval may try to gain the acceptance of a doctor by omitting or changing the facts. They will give an inaccurate history. They will tell the doctor things that they think the doctor wants to hear. The patient will have a greater need to please the doctor than to receive the proper treatment and get well.

The doctor-patient relationship ideally should be one of mutual participation between two adults with a common purpose. However, some patients are going to see the doctor as omniscient and omnipotent, much as the child sees the parents. Then, if something goes wrong in the treatment, such patients are going to be angry at the doctor. They will feel that the doctor, who should be able to take care of everything, has let them down. This phenomenon of having unconscious feelings towards the doctor based on previous relationships from the past can broadly be defined as *transference*. The development of transference is facilitated in cases of physical illness because of the psychological regression that invariably takes place. Patients return to earlier methods of psychological functioning, and this regression promotes and intensifies the development of transference feelings and reactions.

Characteristics of Transference

Transference is a ubiquitous phenomenon. It is characterized by intensity and inappropriateness. For example, instead of a patient being mildly annoyed at the doctor for something which calls for only minor annoyance, the patient will become furious at the physician. Another characteristic of transference is its persistence. If a patient reacts with an unrealistic or inappropriate annoyance to things that the physician does, this reaction is usually going to persist, and it may persist no matter what the physician does. It may recur irrespective of how the situation is handled. Sometimes a transference reaction will occur as soon as the patient meets the doctor. Other times it will occur even before the first meeting. Other types of transference will develop more slowly. However it begins, most patients will develop a transference that is not based on the conscious reality of what the physician does but rather on the persistence of unconscious infantile images.

"Positive" Transference

Patients may have some very strong positive feelings about their doctors. It is not uncommon for patients to feel that they have "the greatest doctor in the world" and that they have unshakeable confidence in him or her. As noted, they may form this opinion and develop this confidence even before they have met the doctor. Sometimes patients may even fall in love with their physicians. In such circumstances patients have overvalued and idealized the physician. This may lead to their working harder to get better, not necessarily because that is the realistic goal, but because they want to please the doctor, just as they may have wanted to please their parents earlier in their lives. In such cases they may very well want the doctor to reciprocate the admiration. They are going to want to be loved in return, and specifically they are going to want to be loved as they were loved or wanted to be loved when they were children. There is no stronger motivation than this for a patient wanting to get better, but there are inherent dangers as well. For example, such a "positive" transference can sometimes lead to overtly seductive or infantile behavior on the part of the patient towards the doctor. In such situations, the patient would be unaware that his or her sexual feelings towards the doctor are based on childhood relationships. These feelings can be quite intense despite the fact that the patient may only have limited professional contact with the physician. It is important that physicians understand the origins of these feelings and be cautious in establishing a personal relationship which may encourage unrealistic feelings derived from a "positive" transference. Otherwise the "positive" feelings can very rapidly shift to "negative" ones.

"Negative" Transference

Patients may develop an intense, resentful rage toward the physician, especially if their immediate hopes and expectations are not met.

This would be a "negative" transference. In one way or another, when the patient has such a "negative" transference, he or she will attempt to undermine the therapy. The patient will be opposing the physician just as the child may have opposed other members of the family. Of course, this is going to complicate the medical treatment. On a conscious level, the patient may want to do the things that are required, but unconsciously the patient may want to frustrate the doctor. Medicine may not be taken, or directions on the label may be misread. The number of ways the patient can find to undermine the therapy is truly unlimited. Such a patient, struggling with a "negative" transference, can be one of the most difficult problems with which the physician has to deal. This hostility can sometimes be very subtle, yet it can make the doctor feel very uncomfortable. This is especially true for young and inexperienced physicians. One such situation occurred with the following patient.

The patient was a 48 year old male who was reported to be a very difficult management problem for the house staff as well as for the medical students and nurses. The patient had a rare anemia. He would frequently argue with the nurses about the medication. He demanded to know his hematocrit and the results of all other laboratory tests. He seemed to have a way of putting down any new doctor or new medical student who came on the ward and did not know about his rare illness. An interview I had with the patient revealed that he had two brothers who were pharmacists, although he himself had never attended college. He had worked with his brothers in the pharmacy for many years and had actually dealt with doctors all of these years. There had been strong competitive feelings toward the brothers, who had achieved professional status while the patient had not. Now, during this hospitalization, he was aggressively competing with the doctors, and at one point in the interview he revealed in a slip of the tongue his unconscious thoughts when he said, "I am not a licensed physician . . . I mean a licensed pharmacist." He was struggling with an unconscious conflict from the past. The patient had a wish to outdo his brothers by becoming a physician, and he was now competing with the doctors on the ward as though they were his brothers. Some of this understanding of the patient was then utilized in the patient's management.

The patient was receiving some new medication, and his physicians were concerned about any possible side effects. The patient was enlisted as an active partner in making observations about the medication's side effects. He now felt that he was contributing in a meaningful way to the management of his treatment. He subsequently seemed to feel much less competitive towards the doctors and as a result became much less of a management problem.

Influence of the Doctor's Characteristics

Sometimes a single characteristic of the doctor can have a tremendous emotional significance to the patient and can greatly alter the type of transference that develops. For example, a black patient living in a ghetto may have a very distinct emotional reaction to a white physician based on previous experiences involving white authority figures. Such feelings could include fear, hopelessness, and anger, and they will hinder the medical treatment and the ability of the patient to cooperate with the physician. This point is illustrated in the following case history.

The patient was a black, teenage boy with sickle cell anemia. He was an extremely difficult management problem in that he did not follow instructions and usually was uncooperative with the medical staff. A new medical student, who happened to be black, rotated on the ward and was assigned to the patient. The student began to spend time with the patient. He showed the patient the microscopic slides of his blood cells and talked to him about these slides and about his illness of sickle cell anemia. The patient became a different person. He was no longer a management problem. In fact, at this point he developed a plan to become a physician. Obviously, the patient had begun to identify with the medical student. While it certainly is possible that such an identification could have occurred with any medical student who spent time with the patient, the fact that the student was black probably facilitated this identification.

The sex of the doctor may also be important in the type of transference that develops. We know that a doctor can take on the aspects of both mother and father, no matter what the sex of the patient or the doctor. A woman physician, however, might more easily evoke early memories of other women in the patient's life. The patient may view the female doctor as a mother with the patient functioning as a helpless child. The male patient may also view the female doctor as a threatening woman or as an attractive sexual object. While in such cases the patient may consciously and realistically accept the woman as the doctor who is there to help him, at the same time the patient would be responding unconsciously in different ways which are related to the transference. Obviously, the father type of transference may be more apparent where there is a male doctor. However, even here there is still a very strong element of a child being taken care of by the mother.

The age of the doctor can be a very deceptive factor in the transference. Young physicians and students frequently believe that they are going to be viewed as the children of their older patients. In some patients this may be the initial reaction, but the role of the doctor has too much emotional meaning to the usual patient for this to be the most significant factor of the transference. Also, since physically ill patients regress psychologically in certain ways, it is often the patients who will feel childlike and who will see parental qualities in their young physicians.

No two people's reaction to a particular doctor will be the same. To one individual it will be a certain characteristic of the doctor that will influence the transference. To someone else that characteristic may be relatively insignificant, whereas other characteristics may take on prime importance in the development of the transference. What is important to recognize with every patient is the power of the transference that will be a part of every doctor-patient relationship. It will be the unconscious part of the conscious, reality-oriented, mature alliance of the doctor-patient relationship.

DOCTOR'S UNCONSCIOUS REACTION TO PATIENT: COUNTERTRANSFERENCE

The doctor-patient relationship involves two people, and the other person is the doctor. Just as the patient develops what is called "transference," the doctor may develop something that, in the broadest definition, can be called *countertransference*. Counter does not mean against. In this case it means counterpart. It does not refer to the necessary empathy that a physician should feel for his patient, but rather it refers to conflictual feelings from the physician's own childhood. Just as patients may respond unrealistically and irrationally to their physicians, the same thing can happen in the response of the physician to the patient. The physician may find a certain pleasure in being considered a wonderful, outstanding, awesome person. Very often these feelings are derivatives of early childhood wishes to be omnipotent, magical, and omniscient. There is a stage of development in which every child engages in magical thinking. This type of thinking persists to some degree in the fantasies of adults, perhaps especially in the fantasies of physicians.

Although we know that the patient is often going to see the doctor as omnipotent, there is a great danger if the physician also sees himself or herself in the same way. In such a situation the patient is viewed as a helpless child, and the relationship is not one of two adult people working together towards a common goal but rather one of the doctor taking over and being the "good parent." Obviously, in some medical situations, such as the comatose or acutely ill patient, this type of relationship may be necessary. But in most situations, such as chronic illness or the recovery phases of acute illness, the patient will function and cooperate in an optimal manner when he or she can participate as an active and equal partner in the treatment with the physician.

Another example of countertransference can be seen in the very frequent tendency on the part of physicians to underdiagnose a colleague. When physicians begin to treat colleagues, they often tend to minimize their illnesses, and this is very dangerous. The reason this happens is that the treating physician is identifying with the patient-colleague. This type of identification, whether it happens in regard to a colleague or to any patient, is another form of countertransference.

Guilt feelings can emerge as a form of countertransference if the doctor, in the face of a realistic inability to help the patient, feels tremendously guilty about a particular medical situation. This most frequently occurs when a patient has died. The question, of course, is whether the doctor did all that could reasonably be expected to help the patient. Obviously, if the physician did not, then there would be some reason to feel guilty. Or, if the physician made a mistake, it would be appropriate to have guilt feelings. But if the guilt is felt about something over which the physician had no control, then the guilt is not realistic.

There will be some patients about whom the doctor will have intense feelings, not because they are patients but because they remind the physician of someone from the past. For example, perhaps an elderly woman patient could remind the doctor of his or her grandmother and this will evoke one kind of reaction. In another situation an older patient might remind the physician of one or both parents, and this might evoke a very different kind of reaction. One doctor might feel threatened or annoyed with an older patient, whereas another doctor might feel excessively affectionate and protective toward this same patient. Both sets of feelings can interfere with proper treatment. A surgeon may have the task of doing surgery on a man who brings back memories of his father or a particular teacher, and the surgeon may find himself unable to be completely objective. When this happens the doctor may want to refer the patient to a colleague, or may want to ask for a consultation with a colleague. Physicians who specialize in the field of psychiatry will learn to utilize these feelings of countertransference. They become a very important part of psychotherapy. However, no matter what field of medicine a physician may practice, it is very important to realize that doctors are going to react unconsciously to patients just as patients react unconsciously to doctors.

CLASSIC CASE HISTORY

The following case history has been well documented and has great historical significance. It illustrates some of the complications of transference and countertransference. The physician was Dr. Josef Breuer (Figure 4.3), a well-known internist in Vienna who was a student of Dr. Hering, the famous physiologist. He also was the physician who cared for Dr. Billroth, the world renowned surgeon, and many other prominent members of the medical community in Vienna at the turn of the century.

The patient was a 21 year old intelligent, attractive female who had a convergent squint, severe disturbances of vision, paralysis in the right upper and lower extremities, partial paralysis of the left lower extremity, weakness of the neck muscles, and periods of persisting sleep

Figure 4.3. Josef Breuer in 1897, at age 55. From *The Standard Edition of the Complete Psychological Works of Sigmund Freud, Volume II.* (By permission of Sigmund Freud Copyrights Ltd., London.)

walking, as well as many other symptoms including a cough. The symptoms of the patient had come on after the patient's father, of whom she was very fond, had become ill. The patient had devoted a great deal of time to nursing her ill father, and she deteriorated badly after he died. Dr. Breuer, her internist, noted that the patient seemed to have alternating states of consciousness which developed with regularity every day. During these periods of altered consciousness the patient would talk and tell stories. She would talk about her past and how it was when she was a little girl, as well as things that had happened in the not too distant past. She would wake up feeling quite calm and then would go back to her usual clinical state.

Dr. Breuer became very interested in this patient, and he began to see her on a daily basis. He began to hypnotize her, and during the hypnotic states he asked her to concentrate on each symptom. Eventually, she began to tell him about the circumstances that had occurred the first time that each of her symptoms had developed, and when she woke up that particular symptom was gone. For example, she told him that she began coughing for the first time while

sitting at her ill father's bedside and hearing the sound of dance music coming from a neighbor's house. She had felt a sudden wish to be there, and then became overwhelmed with self-reproaches and guilt feelings. Thereafter, whenever she heard rhythmic music she developed a cough. After this was brought out in the hypnotic state, the symptom of coughing disappeared.

In the same way her paralytic contractions, her anesthesias, her disorders of vision, the hearing problems, the neuralgias all disappeared. These symptoms were, so to speak, "talked away" by the patient with Dr. Breuer's help. At the time of this treatment the idea of a physician seeing a patient on an almost daily basis for a period of one and a half years was absolutely unheard of. The concepts of transference and countertransference were as yet undiscovered, and Dr. Breuer had no way of understanding or of dealing with the patient's transference and his own countertransference that were developing during the course of the treatment.

Dr. Breuer completed his treatment and he eventually wrote up the case. While it was not in his original description, eventually the facts surrounding the end of the treatment were documented. The patient had been cured of all her symptoms, and Dr. Breuer had decided to terminate the treatment. He told the patient he was terminating treatment and said goodbye to her. However, that evening he was called back to her house to find her in the throes of an hysterical childbirth. We now understand that this was related to the patient's transference which had been developing for some time. When Dr. Breuer entered the patient's room and asked what was wrong, the patient said, "Dr. B's baby is coming." Dr. Breuer was overwhelmed by the situation and had no way of understanding what was happening. He became profoundly shocked and took flight, abandoning the patient to a colleague.

In retrospect we can now see that Dr. Breuer had developed strong countertransference feelings for his beautiful patient. He had been spending a good deal of time away from his family, especially from his wife. He was very emotionally involved with this patient and interested in her case. Also, in Dr. Breuer's own background, his mother (who had the same first name as this patient) had died in childbirth

Figure 4.4. Sigmund Freud in 1891, at age 35. From *The Standard Edition of the Complete Psychological Works of Sigmund Freud, Volume II.* (By permission of Sigmund Freud Copyrights Ltd., London.)

when he was around age four. He had become, for his patient, the father whom she had lost, and she in turn had become, for Dr. Breuer, the beautiful mother he had lost as a young boy.

The reason this case history has such historic importance is because Dr. Josef Breuer subsequently collaborated with a young neurologist who encouraged him to publish this case history. The neurologist's name was Sigmund Freud (Figure 4.4), and this was the first case history in the *Studies on Hysteria* which Freud published with Breuer. Freud subsequently went on to make his discoveries of the unconscious as-

pects of the mind, of infantile sexuality, and of the universality of transference and countertransference reactions. But it was this case that marked the beginning of modern dynamic psychiatry. This case, in which transference and countertransference played such an important part, is Breuer's classic case of Anna O.

Suggested Readings

Balint M: *The Doctor, His Patient and the Illness.* New York, International Universities Press, 1964.

Bibring GL, Kahana RJ: Establishing the doctor-patient relationship. In *Lectures in Medical Psychology.* New York, International Universities Press, 1968, p 251.

Bowden CL, Burstein AG: *Psychosocial Basis of Health Care,* ed. 3. Baltimore, Williams & Wilkins, 1983.

Leigh H, Reiser MF: *The Patient: Biological, Psychological, and Social Dimensions of Medical Practice.* New York, Plenum Press, 1980.

Nemiah JC: The doctor and his patient. In *Foundations of Psychopathology.* New York, Oxford University Press, 1961, p 289.

Peabody FW: The care of the patient. *JAMA* 88:877, 1927.

Reiser DE, Rosen DH: *Medicine as a Human Experience.* Baltimore, University Park Press, 1984.

Szasz TS, Hollender MH: A contribution to the philosophy of medicine: the basic models of the doctor-patient relationship. In Millon T (ed): *Medical Behavioral Science.* Philadelphia, W.B. Saunders, 1975, p 432.

References

Basedow H: *The Australian Aboriginal.* London, 1927.

Breuer J, Freud S (1895): The case of Fraulein Anna O. Studies on hysteria. In *The Standard Edition of the Complete Psychological Works of Sigmund Freud.* London, Hogarth Press, 1955, vol 2, p 21.

Cannon WB: "Voodoo" death. *Amer Anthropol* 44:169, 1942.

Freud S (1912): The dynamics of transference. In *The Standard Edition of the Complete Psychological Works of Sigmund Freud.* London, Hogarth Press, 1958, vol 12, p 99.

Freud S (1915): Observations on transference love. In *The Standard Edition of the Complete Psychological Works of Sigmund Freud.* London, Hogarth Press, 1958, vol 12, p 159.

Pollock GH: The possible significance of childhood object loss in the Josef Breuer-Bertha Pappenheim (Anna O.)-Sigmund Freud relationship: I. Josef Breuer. *J Am Psychoanal Assoc* 16:711, 1968.

Pollock GH: Bertha Pappenheim's pathological mourning: possible effects of childhood sibling loss. *J Am Psychoanal Assoc* 20:476, 1972.

CHAPTER 5   On Being a Physician

William A. Console, M.D.

In this beginning part of the book, I would like to share with you some thoughts about being a physician and some of the basic principles that should operate in our work with all of our patients, regardless of our specialty.

Some time ago one of my psychotherapy patients, a 42 year old woman, came in for her regular appointment, took her seat, looked at me in a very anxious way and asked, "What is Osgood-Schlatter's disease?" As luck would have it, I knew the answer, and I said, "Who has the sore knee?" She said, "Louise," her 12 year old daughter. I told her in plain, common sense language that Osgood-Schlatter's disease is a relatively common affliction in young children. It is a disease in which something happens to the epiphysis of the tibial tuberosity that causes it to swell. It is rather painful, but by and large it is a self-limited affair, and it eventually straightens itself out, leaving no residual damage other than perhaps a little bump on the knee. I told her that it was of no long-term consequence that her child had this benign condition.

I was able, by giving my patient some factual information, to reassure her in a way that she had not been reassured by her family physician. He had merely told her that her child had Osgood-Schlatter's disease, and that he thought it wise to make a referral to an orthopedist. As we talked about it, it became clear that his diagnosis had made her feel very anxious, and as a result she had spent a rather sleepless night. She had thought of seeing another physician and had even thought that perhaps the first doctor was making up this disease. "What kind of nonsense is this ... Osgood Schlatter's disease?"

On another occasion, as I walked into my office at the medical school, one of the secretaries came out of her office with a book in her hand and tears in her eyes; she was obviously in distress. I greeted her, and she said, while trying to smile, "Doctor Console, I need some therapy."

I brought her into my office and asked her to sit down. She had with her a medical dictionary — the latest edition. "What is Scheuermann's disease?" she asked, at this point visibly shaken and crying. Scheuermann's disease is an osteochondritis of the vertebral body, much like Osgood-Schlatter's disease, which is an osteochondritis of the tibia. There is some rarefaction of the bone, but in general it is a self-limited condition that leaves absolutely nothing in the way of residual disability. What in the world had happened to cause this woman to feel so desperately upset?

Her 17 year old son had recently been accepted to college, and with the acceptance was the requirement that he go for a physical examination. He had gone for the examination with his father, and the physician had made a routine chest plate. When he looked at the film, he thought he saw some rarefaction in one of the thoracic vertebra, and he made the diagnosis — Scheuermann's disease. He asked the boy to wait outside in the waiting room, sat down with the father, and told him, "Your son has Scheuermann's disease. He should see an orthopedist. If you want me to make a referral I'd be happy to do so." The man was stunned. He went home and told his wife that their son had Scheuermann's disease. Now this is an athletic youngster, and her first thought was that his athletic activities were over and that he might be immobilized. It should be remembered that she is an intelligent woman who works in a hospital and has access to information about different diseases.

Well, together we looked up the dictionary's description of Scheuermann's disease, and we could both see from what the book said that it too was one of these self-limiting situations, just like Osgood-Schlatter's disease, and I reassured her to that effect. I reassured her on the basis of the facts that were available to both of us in

27

the dictionary. In addition, I told her that she should also speak to our medical consultant, who is a fine physician and who makes consultation rounds each day. I was sure that he would be glad to talk with her. When he arrived, she spoke with him, and he reassured her that this condition was of no consequence whatsoever. He even went beyond that. He obtained the X-ray film himself, looked it over, and even had his radiologist study it. Indeed, there was a serious question in both their minds as to whether there was anything pathological at all on the film.

Let me describe another situation. A man in middle age discovers that he is hypertensive. He is being treated by a member of the staff of a large teaching hospital who puts him on an antihypertensive drug. However, this doctor tells the patient that he will be leaving New York soon to accept a position at another medical school, and he suggests that the patient continue his treatment with a colleague, another man on the staff of the same hospital. The patient sees the new doctor, who examines him carefully. He raises the dose from three tablets to four each day and asks the patient to return for a check-up in about three weeks. He returns then, and the doctor takes his blood pressure and, explaining nothing, raises the dose to six tablets a day. He is asked to return in another three weeks, at which time the blood pressure is again taken and the dose is raised to eight tablets each day — two tablets, four times each day. The physician says nothing else and tells the patient to return again in three weeks. In three weeks he returns, whereupon the doctor takes the pressure, grunts his approval and says, "Very good. Stay on eight tablets."

This physician is completely unaware that he is dealing with a tense, anxious, and intelligent man who has access to some information about drugs. Such information is easy to come by. He has read that his drug is one of the newer ones for his condition, and that the manufacturer's recommendations are to start with three tablets each day and that the maintenance dose is four a day. He is now taking eight a day, which to him means that his hypertension is so bad, so completely out of control, that he is required to take twice the amount of drug recommended. He does the correct thing. He tells the doctor that he is sorry, but he does not think that they can work together. He goes to someone else who puts him on three tablets each day, and he stays

at that level thereafter — reasonably normotensive.

In this situation we are dealing not with a physician, but with a mechanic, who was apparently impressed only by numbers, who was unaware or uncaring that the numbers resided in a person. He was quite unaware that he may have *increased* his patient's anxiety and therefore his blood pressure by increasing the dosage of medication.

I could spend many pages in this anecdotal fashion, describing what occurs in the practice of medicine and what takes place in the name of treatment. There is absolutely no reason why any of these three people should have endured the kind of distress that I have described. There was no good reason for these people to have been made to feel so anxious. In each case, the doctor had been unaware that he was dealing with a person — not a machine and not merely a physiological conglomerate.

Let me cite another example. A good many years ago one of my first assignments was as a liaison psychiatrist to the Department of Medicine at the Long Island College Hospital in Brooklyn. I met weekly with a group of six senior medical students who were clinical clerks. On this particular occasion I went to the ward where a very intuitive and perceptive nurse was in charge, and she said to me, "Dr. Console, I've got a patient for you." She handed me a chart and told me the patient's bed number. I read the chart. I went and saw the patient for about 20 minutes, and then left him and went into one of the examining rooms where my six senior clerks awaited me. I looked at them and I said, "Who is taking care of Mr. Smith?" One jaw dropped. The other five looked at him and then looked back at me and announced that this was a medical case. So I said, "All right, I'm a medical doctor. Tell me about it."

The student gave a very nice description of this 43 year old unmarried gentleman, who 10 weeks before had been admitted to the hospital after he had been suddenly seized with severe chest pains that had radiated up his neck and down his left arm. He had been dyspneic. He had turned pale and was almost pulseless. His blood pressure dropped, and he presented a typical picture of a myocardial infarction. The man was admitted to the hospital where an EKG showed the characteristic changes of a cardiac thrombosis. His laboratory findings were commensurate with the diagnosis: blood count, sedimentation rate, and so on. The treatment in those days was pretty much rest in bed; we did not yet have intensive care units. Nonetheless, this man did quite well, and at the end of six weeks his EKG showed the changes one would expect when healing takes place. The sedimentation rate was normal. His blood count was normal. The chart said very clearly that this man had recovered. So they told him that he would be discharged. Plop! Back into bed. Reexamination. A whole series of new laboratory tests. More electrocardiographic studies. Two weeks later he was again told he would be discharged, and again he relapsed back into his bed.

So here it was, 10 weeks after the original admission, and they were about to tell him again that he would be discharged, and they were wondering what was going to happen. The student gave, as I say, a very adequate history and description of the onset and the course of the illness. He made it clear that, according to all the laboratory findings, the man was again well. I then said, "Fine. Then why is he still here? Tell me, what do you know of this man?" The student looked at me as though I was speaking in a foreign language and said, "I told you what I know about him." "No," I said, "What do you know about *him*? Who is this person? Where does he live?" So he grabbed the chart and said, "He lives at—" "No," I said. "I don't mean his address. I mean under what circumstances does he live? What is his life situation?"

The student did not know. He had not been taught to take this kind of history. But in the 20 minutes or so that I had talked with the patient, what had I found out? I had found out that this 43 year old man had been engaged to a woman for about 13 years, and she was understandably getting a little restless about her maiden state. The man lived with his widowed mother, and his mother was very reluctant to have him marry and leave her. And he was just as reluctant to leave her. Thus, he found himself caught between these two pressures: the girl urging him on to marry, and the mother quietly, but just as effectively, urging him to stay with her because she needed him. Why was he still in the hospital? It was not such a mystery any longer. It was not because of some strange exotic enzyme imbalance. It was because he was in conflict. He had two pulls in opposite directions. This is the fundamental nature of conflict. It is

a matter of being pulled here, being pulled there, and not knowing what to do. And what about this conflict? It had been pushed aside by his illness. To the girl who wanted him to marry, he could say, "I'm here. How can I get married?" To his mother who said, "Come home and look after me because I'm sick and I need you," he could say, "How can I? I'm here. I'm sick too." Perhaps, with some oversimplification, we can say that his conflict was at least temporarily resolved. It no longer existed. He was satisfied. There was no burden on him. Both his mother and his girl friend came to see him. They each sat at his bedside. They each said, "How awful. How terrible." And he was relieved of having to make a decision — until someone told him that he was ready to be discharged!

Let me give another example. A 40 year old woman went to see her doctor because of a very embarrassing and very distressing symptom. Suddenly, without any warning, she noticed that she had fecal incontinence. Some days before seeing the doctor she had noticed a brown fluid streaking down her stocking. It was feces. She had no idea how this happened. It persisted for a few days, and she went to see her family doctor. He did not know what it was all about either, so he referred the patient to one of his friends, a surgeon. The surgeon examined her and told her he would take her into the hospital and operate on her, and she would be cured. She went into the hospital and was scheduled for a surgical procedure that involved a cutting of the anal sphincter and a resuturing of it. Probably his idea was to take up the slack, tighten things up a bit, and in that way cure her rectal incontinence.

However, the original family doctor thought it would be wise to have a neurological consultation prior to surgery. At the time, I was the staff psychiatrist, and in those days being a psychiatrist meant that you were also a neurologist. So I saw this woman in consultation. I did a neurological examination on her and found nothing of any consequence. I saw nothing that questioned the integrity of the central nervous system. I completed my examination by putting on a rubber glove. I inserted my finger into her rectum, and she grabbed it like an old friend. With that reaction one would have to wonder about any failure of the integrity of the anal sphincter. It worked just fine. There was absolutely nothing wrong with it. I took off the glove, pulled the chair up next to her bed, and told her that I could find no neurological reason for her difficulty. She looked at me and said, "Doctor, could it be an emotional thing?" I said, "Perhaps it could be. Tell me."

And she told me. She told me how her husband had in the course of the prior five years or so developed a progressive muscular dystrophy. He had gone from a generalized weakness and difficulty in locomotion to being confined in a veterans' hospital on Staten Island. The woman lived in Brooklyn. She described how, every Sunday morning, she got up, made her breakfast, went to church, after church got a bus, took the ferry, took another bus to the hospital, and visited with her husband; then she came back, worked all week, and on Sunday morning went through all this again. She told me how her husband chided her for not visiting more often, despite the fact that she was making these regular visits on Sundays and was working during the week. Nevertheless, he was pressuring her about visiting more frequently, telling her how alone he felt, and she began to feel guilty. And it was on a Sunday morning after she had come home from church and was preparing for her weekly pilgrimage to the hospital that she developed her symptom. She noticed the fecal streak down her leg.

I did not have to do very much after that. In a way, she knew perfectly well what was going on. She was ready to submit to the surgery out of guilt. Because of her guilt she would accept this punishment. However, after only a few minutes of talking, she was dissuaded from this course. We postponed the surgery. When I saw her two days later she was walking around on the ward, and she said, "Dr. Console, look — I'm wearing stockings to show you how confident I am." Her symptom disappeared and never returned. She was discharged. I saw her in follow-up for about two years thereafter, and there was never any further difficulty.

One last case. I was asked to see a 23 year old Catholic girl who was in status asthmaticus. Status asthmaticus is a serious and potentially fatal asthma attack that does not subside. She was in an oxygen tent. She was in great distress. This was in May. I read her chart, and this admission in May was her fourth one to the same hospital for the same difficulty. She had first been admitted some five months before on the evening of December 25th. It appeared that

no one had reflected about why a 23 year old girl who had never before had any asthmatic difficulty, who was not known to be a person who had frequent winter or summer colds, who had no pulmonary infection whatsoever, who was a young, healthy, strapping girl — why such a girl, on December 25th, goes to the hospital with her first acute asthmatic attack and then is readmitted three more times within five months.

I went to this girl's bedside and asked the nurse to remove the oxygen tent so that I could talk to her. The nurse said, "She'll die if I take the tent off. She can't breathe." I said, "Take it off." Well, she did not die. We talked. I asked her to tell me what had happened on Christmas Day, the night she had her first attack. She described to me that she had been out on Christmas Eve with her boyfriend. She had been going with him for a year or so, and they were quite intimate sexually, but had never had intercourse. That evening he urged her to have intercourse, but she refused.

The next morning she had gone to church with her mother and father. After church they were preparing for their Christmas dinner when the boyfriend called. He appeared at the door. He was a little tipsy and was obviously amorously inclined. He and the patient went into the bedroom. The boyfriend again urged her to have intercourse, and against her wishes, in fact with great trepidation because her parents were in the next room, they had intercourse.

I asked her, "Were you afraid?" She said, "Yes. I was afraid. In fact he was breathing so hard that I put my hand over his mouth." I said, "And then what did you do?" She said, "Oh, my God!" It was a sudden insight. What had she done? She had held her breath. She had stifled her own loud breathing by holding her hand over her mouth as well. He left. The patient and her parents had dinner. She was very upset about what had happened. And after dinner, sitting in the living room with her mother and father, she experienced a difficulty in breathing, which soon became so severe that she had to be hospitalized that same evening.

What was she doing by having this symptom, a symptom which simulated the breathing that takes place in the excitement of intercourse? She had stifled her breathing while having intercourse, and now with her father and mother sitting there, she was confessing to them with her symptom. Her guilt was such that she had to make amends to her parents in some way. She had sinned in her parents' home on Christmas Day, and she was overwhelmed with her sin and with her guilt. And with this realization, there was an immediate and dramatic improvement in her asthmatic condition.

As I indicated earlier, I am addressing myself in this chapter to our treatment of our patients. What I have to say about treatment might not be what you are expecting to hear from a psychiatrist. I am not going to talk about formal psychotherapy because few readers of this book will go into psychiatry, and fewer still will be doing psychotherapy in the strict sense of that term. In a more general sense, however, you will be treating people, and you will be involved with them in what will hopefully be a therapeutic situation. Psychological pressures and factors come into play and have great meaning with virtually every patient whom we treat, and in that sense our dealings with people do involve a great deal of psychological treatment. Whatever treatment we do will be much better if we have an awareness of the manner in which people function psychologically, and a knowledge of the common anxieties and worries to which people are subject. Our treatment will be better if we use a minimum of trickery and obtain a minimum of narcissistic gratification. "Your son has Scheuermann's disease. See how smart I am."

Our first contact with the patient will involve obtaining a history. And in getting a proper history we are already starting the actual treatment of the patient, as can be seen very clearly in the three hospitalized patients I have just described. In taking a history, it is also possible to ask questions in a manner that suggests to the patient that he or she might be suffering from some serious illness, and this can be very frightening to the patient. In contrast, in taking a history we can say and do things which will create an atmosphere of confidence and of assurance. We can foster a feeling in the patient that we know and understand what is going on and that, therefore, the patient is in competent hands.

The next step in our relationship with the patient involves the physical examination, and here the same considerations hold, but to an even greater degree. For example, if we take someone's blood pressure and we have to go up and up to get the first sounds of pressure, we should not react to this by showing our concern. Even though the patient may not see the dial or the tube, he can see our faces, and he will be watching us very intently. The patient will watch for all of our reactions, and will read many things into them. If we are listening to someone's heart and we think we hear a murmur but are not sure if it is an early systolic or a late diastolic murmur, we should not show our doubt, or transmit our anxieties to the patient.

In the treatment of our patients, we should also avoid recommending or performing unnecessary manipulations and procedures. For example, if a woman brings her child to us with the complaint that he persistently wets his bed, we should not immediately recommend cystoscopy. We should have the courage to believe that in the overwhelming majority of cases involving childhood enuresis, the cause is a psychological one. Do not fix in the person's mind the idea of organicity or a physical disability with immediate physical manipulation. The same is true for the young man who comes to us and tells us that he is impotent. There is very little profit and potentially a great deal of harm to be done by examining him cystoscopically. Such maneuvers help fix in the young man's mind the idea of physical damage or dysfunction. In a sense, he may prefer to believe that this is the case. With unnecessary physical procedures we may reinforce this hope of his and thus preclude the psychological treatment that could really help.

Some might say that such an approach could end up in the physician's missing out on the detection of a physical problem. I am not suggesting the elimination of any necessary physical examination or laboratory test. Rather, what I am saying is that routine and unreflective instrumentation is really not at all helpful. By the same token, we would be doing this same patient a disservice if we immediately prescribed methyltestosterone for his impotence. To prescribe such a medication unthinkingly without a complete evaluation is to say to the patient, "I think that this is a hormonal deficiency." Again, I say that we must have the courage to state that the incidence of such a true hormonal deficiency is very small, and that if it were present, there would be other evidence of such a deficiency. Let me also say a few words about placebos. Such inert substances are often given to the patient with a big build-up. They must be taken at a certain time of the day, before meals, and so on. They are given with powerful suggestions to which many patients do respond, but more often than we may like to think, the patient soon discovers that he has been given something inert, and the physician then becomes a liar and a fraud.

Our treatment of patients will involve a relationship with them from the moment we meet them, from the taking of the history, to the physical examination, and then the more prolonged treatment itself, whether it be the administration of medication, or the performance of surgery, or whatever. Our treatment of our patients will involve a personal relationship over the course of many weeks, months, and even years, and will inevitably involve a great many psychological phenomena. Therefore, to the degree that we have some appreciation for and some understanding of human psychological functioning, we will be able to employ that understanding in the service of our patients. Only then will we be physicians in the truest sense of that word.

CHAPTER 6

On Being a Patient

Emily Mumford, Ph.D.

WHY PEOPLE SEE DOCTORS

In any month nearly 75% of the population suffers symptoms comparable to those presented to physicians every day. But only one-third of these potential patients will actually see or even phone a physician for help with the problem. Multimillion dollar sales of over-the-counter medications testify that many symptoms and illnesses are managed with home remedies and home treatment. Twenty thousand tons of aspirin, nearly 225 tablets per person, are purchased each year in the U.S. Even though people today seem readier than their parents were to seek medical attention, many still rely on self-treatment when they feel ill until perhaps some "last straw" spurs a call for professional help. Clearly, the presence of symptoms alone does not necessarily lead one to seek help. How then can we understand what leads people to define themselves as patients and to see a doctor?

Interaction Between Life Stress and Illness

To study these factors, mothers in 512 families that included 2,547 persons were asked by Roghmann and Haggerty to keep diaries for 28 consecutive days. Episodes of illness, stressful events, and calls or visits to physicians and pharmacies and pharmacists were recorded daily. Medical contacts — even when telephone calls were included — were significantly fewer than episodes of illness. One would expect that severity or potential danger implied by the symptoms would explain why medical attention was sought for a particular episode of illness, but severity only explained a part of the difference. *The occurrence of a stressful event* in the family at the time of the illness, or just before it, increased the probability about 50% that medical attention would be sought for symp-

toms. Even on days when there was *no* illness recorded, the occurrence of a stressful event in the mother's life increased by 80% the chances that there would be a medical contact, often for a child in the family, rather than for the mother herself. This particular interaction between life stress and illness implies that the visit for the child may be associated with the mother's needing help but neglecting her own health. When this is the case, the pediatrician may hold the key to the mother's health, either positively by guiding her toward help for herself, or on the other hand, negatively by reprimanding her for taking a doctor's time to see a well child.

The Need for a Diagnosis

It should not surprise us that the trigger for a visit to the doctor is often a distressing event in the family or some circumstance that generates vague feelings of discomfort. When they feel stressed, many people become particularly sensitive to sensations in their bodies, and they also have particular need for an explanation, a name, or a diagnosis for their distress. Interestingly, this paired phenomenon — sensitivity to bodily sensations when anxious or depressed, and the need to have a name to explain the vague distress — commonly affects medical students and student nurses. Medical and nursing education is often anxiety-provoking. Feeling vaguely anxious, many students fearfully entertain the possibility, and even come to believe for a time, that they have one of the dread diseases that they have studied. Therefore, we should expect that many lay people, when feeling some vague discomfort, will seek medical attention and a "diagnosis." In the encounter, patient and physician negotiate for a name for the problem, an answer for "What is wrong?" The diagnosis also establishes the sufferer's right to medical attention and help—it legitimates the sick role with all its rights, privileges, excuses, and obligations. Furthermore, in this society people come to understand that it is the doctor who is supposed to tell them what is wrong with them, and physicians have fought hard in legislatures and courts to retain the exclusive right to diagnose.

The Emphasis on the Physical

It is ironic then that in many, perhaps most, encounters between doctor and patient, information about nonphysical symptoms or events is implicitly declared "off limits." The result is that the name of the problem is likely to come up physical until dramatically proven otherwise. Reinforcing the tendency to cast problems in the somatic mold, many professors in medical schools insist that the student "prove" that the patient does *not* have any one of a series of physical diseases before even considering psychological and social problems, or referral for a social service, psychological, or psychiatric consultation. *Why the patient came or called this day* instead of a day or two earlier or later is rarely even inquired about in medical settings. Thus, the patient, reluctant to volunteer inner worries, is encouraged to ignore them and speak instead of physical sensations. The patient in such an exchange is, of course, being socialized by a role partner of high status. One effect of this unbalanced relationship is that the "language" of the person with higher status prevails, and patients are led to rephrase their complaints in physical terms, a factor which should be explored in the etiology of hypochondriasis. We need to know to what extent hypochondriasis is iatrogenically "caused" by prevailing medical attitudes, interests, and priorities.

WHY PEOPLE LEAVE DOCTORS

If the patient's actual problems do not happen to fit the physician's somatic interests, the patient either must learn to present approved symptoms or go elsewhere. Thus, the stage is set for many patients to leave feeling, if anything, more helpless or distressed than when they reluctantly asked for help in the first place. Physicians feel that their time has been wasted, and the gloomy prophecy of the skeptical patient is confirmed. When doctor and patient cannot even agree on the problem that they are trying to relieve, drop-out and failure to respond to medical advice are to be expected.

The Dissatisfied Physician

Disjunctions between the problems that trigger a search for help and the problems to which the doctor will listen thus contribute to mutually unsatisfying encounters and mutual criticism. Physicians complain of "crocks," "turkeys," "gomers," "doctor shoppers," "uncooperative patients," "hospital hobos," and the "worried well." These expressions refer to patients who seek medical attention frequently, but whose major problems do not seem resolvable by the physician. Trained to deal with diseased systems or organs, to look for physical signs and symptoms, to rely on X-ray and laboratory evidence of physical disease, many physicians are uncomfortable with the "softer" evidence of emotional difficulty. The widespread use of these slang pejoratives suggests that such patients are not uncommon, and that they are a continuing problem to the medical profession.

The Dissatisfied Patient

In fact, the effects of emotional and social distress on utilization of medical services appear to be most marked for those chronically ill patients who express the *most skepticism* about the benefits of medical care but who nevertheless seek medical help *most frequently*. This raises the possibility that a self-fulfilling prophecy may be at work to keep such persons wandering like an army of displaced persons through doctor's offices, clinics, and emergency rooms, from one doctor to another, with little benefit to health. Expecting little help but sufficiently distressed to seek it anyway, the highly skeptical or distrustful patient, when seeing a doctor, is likely to volunteer little about the social and emotional problems that may have compelled the visit on this day.

IMPACT OF EMOTIONAL AND SOCIAL STRESS ON MEDICAL PRACTICE

Emotional and Social Problems in Medical Practice

Given the importance of emotional and social stress in determining whether medical attention is sought, we should not be surprised to discover that medical practices are "crowded with vague complaints." An English general practitioner, Fry, described the most common diseases seen in his general practice as minor, benign, transient, self-limiting, and tending to remain undifferentiated and unlabeled from beginning to end of the episode. A succession of epidemiological surveys have rediscovered what clinicians have long known — that much of the time of most physicians in tertiary care settings, as well as in primary care settings, is spent with patients suffering from social and emotional problems.

Culpan and Davies screened 200 consecutive new patients who had been referred to the medical and surgical outpatient departments of a general hospital. On the medical services alone, 51 out of 100 consecutive newly referred cases suffered from psychiatric illness, and for 38 of these no relevant organic disease could be found. Letters from the doctors who had referred the patients to the hospital indicated that these patients had been diagnostic problems for extended periods of time.

An analysis by Harris of 500 consecutive cases admitted to the medical clinic of a Boston hospital found that 36% were suffering "emotional maladjustment." A report by Follman suggests that 50% of patients treated by general practitioners had emotional problems contributing to the visit. It is evident that the vast majority of the patients receiving medical treatment for explicitly psychiatric diagnoses receive it from general practitioners — not psychiatrists. D'Arcy reported that approximately 78% of emotionally distressed patients see only general practitioners. In Great Britain 30% of the general practice patients in one survey had been given prescriptions for tranquilizers, antidepressants, and other psychotropic medication. More than 68 million prescriptions each year are written in this country for so-called "minor tranquilizers" such as Valium and Librium, and most of these prescriptions are written by nonpsychiatric physicians.

Good physicians have always been aware that people turn to healers when they feel stressed psychologically or socially as well as physically. Ninety-six per cent of physicians surveyed by Smith, Anderson, and Masuda in Washington State indicated that a primary physician's role includes management of a patient's emotional problems. From 20% to 30% of their patients had significant emotional problems, and well over one-quarter of their time was devoted to dealing with such problems. These doctors also reported that most of the patients who required

psychiatric attention had initially presented with physical complaints.

Some people today feel strongly that the highly skilled surgeon, internist, pediatrician, gynecologist, or neurologist should not be expected also to be an expert in dealing with the emotional and social difficulties of their patients. They argue that it is enough to ask that these specialists be soundly based in their own fields and stay up-to-date with the latest technical advances. However, the consequences of selective inattention to a patient's emotional problems are likely to be: 1) unhappy or frustrating outcomes of doctor-patient encounters; 2) needless drain on physicians' time and the resources of the medical system through "doctor shopping"; 3) encouragement of patients to present all their troubles in physical terms; 4) the expensive following up of false clues and the ironic possibility that actual physical disease in these patients may be missed once they have been labeled as "crocks"; and 5) pressure on physicians to find a physical cause to the point where patients are exposed to excessive diagnostic work and, thus, are at greater risk for developing iatrogenic symptoms.

Mortality and Morbidity Rates in Psychiatric Populations

It unfortunately is true that any individual, like Job, may have more than one affliction at a time. Physical, social, and emotional problems tend to flock together. Mortality and morbidity rates in psychiatric populations suggest that psychiatric illness may be much more predictive of physical disease and even of death than is generally acknowledged. Death by suicide is, of course, high among psychiatric patients. But the excess mortality among psychiatric patients is not entirely accounted for by suicide. Babigian and Odoroff found that white female psychiatric patients were four times more likely to die from respiratory illness than their nonpsychiatric age counterparts. They also found that death from diseases of the circulatory system was three-and-one-half times more frequent in psychiatric populations than in the general population. In Scotland, the incidence of deaths among formerly hospitalized psychiatric patients was twice the expected rate, with the greatest excess occurring among younger patients. Amdur and Prizant reported that the prevalence of physical illness in psychiatric patient populations ranges from 33.5% to 61%.

In the 20 year follow-up survey of the Midtown Manhattan Study, psychiatric impairment rated from interview responses was one predictor of mortality. Among respondents rated emotionally "well" in 1954, only 17% had died during the ensuing 20 years, whereas 24% of those rated as suffering "mild to moderate" emotional impairment and 30% of those rated "severely impaired" had died in that same period. In addition, the respondent's subjective rating of his or her own health on a 4-point scale from "excellent" to "poor" in 1954 was statistically associated with survival over the next 20 years.

The "Worried Well" and the "Unworried Sick"

The term "worried well" is a misleading euphemism for persons who "bother" doctors when "there is nothing organically wrong." First, it wrongly implies that people with emotional problems probably are physically well. Second, it implies that if one is really sick, then one is not worried. Wrong again. There probably are no "unworried sick," just as there are probably no "worried well." Emotionally distressed people are more vulnerable physically, and physically ill people are often severely stressed emotionally. We have just presented evidence that patients with emotional problems have excess incidence of physical illness. There is also a good deal of evidence for the fact that physically ill people are also likely to experience emotional distress. Bergmann and Eastham studied 100 older patients hospitalized on medical services. Fifty-two per cent were found to be moderately to severely disturbed emotionally, and these patients had a mean stay of five and one-half days longer than patients who did not show evidence of emotional disturbance, though at admission the physical status of these two groups of patients matched.

If emotional distress compels many visits to physicians and if emotional distress is the usual companion of physical disease, it follows that the inclusion of outpatient psychotherapy in medical care systems may improve the quality and appropriateness of care, and might even sometimes lower costs of providing care. A series of studies to evaluate the effects of mental health intervention in medical and surgical settings provide evidence of the efficacy of such mental health intervention for medical and surgical patients.

Mumford, Schlesinger, and Glass have reviewed 34 studies of the effects of providing emotional support as an adjunct to medically required care for patients recovering from heart attacks or surgery. In some studies, experimental patients were informed about what to expect after surgery so they were not left needlessly bewildered or feeling they had no control over their situation. In other studies experimental patients were provided a chance to express some of their anxieties and to receive additional emotional support. In these 34 studies some 180 different outcome indicators were used including units of blood required, anesthesia time, and number of days in hospital post surgery. Many studies showed statistically significant benefits for the experimental patients who were provided psychologically informed care compared with the control patients treated "as usual." Thirteen studies compared the number of days of hospitalization for experimental and control patients. These studies reported an average hospital stay about two days shorter for the experimental patients.

Schlesinger, Mumford, and Glass have also studied the medical utilization patterns of patients suffering from chronic physical diseases, including diabetes, hypertension, ischemic heart disease, and chronic airway obstruction. In the third year following the diagnosis of any of these targeted chronic diseases, the charges for medical services of the group having at least seven mental health visits were on the average $371 lower than those of the comparison group that did not receive any mental health services. For people receiving relatively brief mental health treatment (under 21 visits) the savings in charges for medical care exceeded the total cost of the mental health treatment over the three years of the study. Such studies suggest that mental health treatments are needed by many patients who are not the "worried well," but rather the "worried sick."

DISCONTINUITIES BETWEEN MEDICAL TRAINING AND MEDICAL PRACTICE

Until recently in most medical schools comparatively little curriculum time and attention have been devoted to developing skills in perceiving and dealing effectively with the emotional difficulties of patients. Many physicians who were graduated one or more decades ago are inclined to believe that emotional disorders are "simply in the head" and none of their concern. It is said that most first year medical students are more interested in and alert to the emotional difficulties of patients than they are as graduates. In the faculty's zeal to provide students all that they will need to know for the highly demanding work of restoring or saving the hospitalized gravely ill patient, attention is repeatedly deflected from the emotional and social conditions of the ambulatory patients who will in fact account for most of the graduates' time. In our recent past, medical students seldom saw ambulatory patients, and rarely had an opportunity to learn to understand or deal with the emotional and social problems of these patients. Lacking the necessary skills to treat such problems, physicians would naturally not welcome them in their practices.

In view of the prevalence of symptoms associated with psychological disturbance in the offices of general physicians, it is sobering to read Eastwood's report that 19% of the male patients and 27.5% of the female patients had a psychiatric disturbance that was unknown to their own general practitioner. The much quoted North Carolina Study of Medical Practice found that only 17% of the physicians recognized and treated emotional problems with any competence. This leads to concern about the disjunction between the problems that many patients today bring to physicians and the ability of physicians to treat these problems. As Stafford-Clark put it, "The diagnosis of neurosis in patients complaining of physical symptoms is tantamount to the unmasking of an imposter — a process of scientific deduction which may bring credit and satisfaction to the doctor, but which is chiefly valuable in relieving him of any further responsibility towards the patient so skillfully discredited." The "discredited" patient is likely to leave the physician's office feeling diminished and more hopeless than when he or she arrived. If a return appointment is offered, it is not likely to be kept. And if anything goes wrong with diagnostic or therapeutic procedures, the "discredited" patient is more disposed than others to sue.

CONCLUSION

People see doctors because they feel they need help. The underlying causes of the visit may be emotional, social, or physical, and most often they are a combination of these. Vague feelings of physical distress, anxiety, and depression impel a search for an explanation or a name that permits a sense of mastery as well as direct help. Many of the symptoms that are most frequently presented to physicians generally are the very ones for which there is the strongest presumptive evidence that psychological factors play a significant role. *People leave doctors* or reject medical advice most often because they feel the doctor does not take the trouble to listen to them, and therefore does not understand them or the emotional and social stresses that may be prompting the search for help.

Suggested Readings

Fry J: Twenty-one years of general practice: changing patterns. *J R Coll Gen Pract* 22:521, 1972.

Mumford E, Schlesinger HJ, Glass GV: The effects of psychological intervention on recovery from surgery and heart attacks: an analysis of the literature. *Am J Pub Health* 72:141, 1982.

Mumford E, Schlesinger HJ, Glass GV, et al.: A new look at evidence about reduced cost of medical utilization following mental health treatment. *Am J Psychiatry* 141:1145, 1984.

References

Amdur MA, Prizant G: Health care issues in a psychiatric aftercare program. *Psychosomatics* 16:155, 1975.

Babigian HM, Odoroff CL: The mortality experience of a population with psychiatric illness. *Am J Psychiatry* 126:470, 1969.

Bergmann K, Eastham EJ: Psychogeriatric ascertainment and assessment for treatment in an acute medical ward setting. *Age Ageing* 3:174, 1974.

Culpan R, Davies B: Psychiatric illness at a medical and surgical outpatient clinic. *Compr Psychiatry* 1:228, 1960.

D'Arcy C: Patterns in the delivery of psychiatric care in Saskatchewan 1971–72: an overview of service sectors and patient volumes. *Can Psychiatr Assoc J* 21:91, 1976.

Eastwood MR: *The Relation Between Physical and Mental Illness.* Toronto, University of Toronto Press, 1975.

Follman JF: *Insurance Coverage for Mental Illness.* New York, American Management Association, 1970.

Harris HI: Efficient psychotherapy for the large outpatient clinic. *N Engl J Med* 221:1, 1939.

Roghmann KJ, Haggerty RJ: Family stress and the use of health services. *Int J Epidemiol* 1:279, 1972.

Schlesinger HJ, Mumford E, Glass GV: Mental health treatment and medical care utilization in a fee-for-service system: outpatient mental health treatment following the onset of a chronic disease. *Am J Pub Health* 73:422, 1983.

Singer E, et al: Mortality and mental health: evidence from the Midtown Manhattan restudy. *Soc Sci Med* 10:517, 1976.

Smith CK, Anderson JC, Masuda M: A survey of psychiatric care in family practice. *J Fam Pract* 1:39, 1974.

Stafford-Clark D: The contribution of psychiatry to modern medicine. *J R Soc Arts* November 1959, p 836.

CHAPTER 7   The Responses of Patients to Medical Advice

Emily Mumford, Ph.D.

When a superbly trained physician follows a careful history and an array of diagnostic tests with a cursory rundown of findings and recommendations during a brief talk with the patient, the result can be an exercise in futility. The patient's wife or husband who might otherwise support the medical advice is not enlisted on behalf of the physician's efforts. Family members may even be alienated by the inadequate attention given them. The patient may be too anxious to hear clearly, or even to know what questions to ask, and so leaves the physician unconvinced or confused, or both. The scene is set for rejection of the medical advice.

The physician's advice often has to compete not only with personal testimonials from well meaning friends and family but also with advertisements. Cartoons explain and reassure in terms the patient can understand, accept, and remember, and they are repeated daily. Ads with talking stomachs, gears and hammers causing pain, compelling portrayals of nasal passages with linings that shrink on contact with nasal mist—these and similar pretested products of skilled communications specialists are formidable competition for the doctor, particularly if he or she mistakenly assumes that the job is complete upon the writing of a prescription the patient cannot read.

Some patients never have these prescriptions filled. Some buy the prescribed drugs and take more, or less, than instructed. In one rooming house, occupants turned unused medication over to a motherly tenant who then dispensed from her drug cache whenever anyone became ill. Some patients decide to follow their aunt's advice because she listens to them and is, therefore, convincing about her favorite nostrum. Some patients feel that the doctor "doesn't understand my case," and so they set up their own regimens

without telling the doctor. Then again, the prescribed medicine may seem too costly, or it has not made the patient feel better, or there are unpleasant side effects, or so much relief there seems no need to finish the prescribed course of medication. Or the patient is so terrified by his perception of his illness that he has to deny it, and one way to deny a fearful reality is to ignore the advice directed to the management of that reality.

Many patients will not ask questions out of fear of annoying the doctor—or because they do not want to appear "dumb," or because the advice seems impossible to follow. ("He told me not to worry!") Such patients are very likely to leave the doctor's office frustrated and fearful. They have not been "helped" and may be resentful. The physician in such an exchange may also become frustrated, particularly when the patient then rejects the medical advice or fails to show at the next appointment.

Patients may be sincere in their wish to get better, and the doctor equally sincere in wanting a successful outcome. But failure to come to a working understanding can frustrate the achievement of their shared goal—improved health for the patient. Signing out against medical advice, missed appointments, failure to follow a regimen or to take medicine, all waste the physician's time, generate frustration among medical personnel, and lead to needless deterioration in patients' health.

EVIDENCE OF FAILURE TO COOPERATE WITH MEDICAL ADVICE

A number of factors tend to obscure the extent of rejection of medical advice. First of all, the culture of medical practice rests on assumptions of rational behavior, i.e., the patient has sought medical advice, sometimes at considerable expense, and therefore will follow this advice with reasonable compliance. Furthermore, modern medicine assumes a cultural belief in the efficacy of reasonable and scientifically informed actions on behalf of health. In this context it does not "make sense" that anyone but a disturbed person would seek medical advice and then ignore it. Such behavior does not "compute" in the language of logic and reason, and may therefore not be examined. In our culture it may even be threatening to the self-concept of the medical expert to consider seriously these cases of nonadherence, where the fruits of all that training and work are devalued by being ignored. One way to respond to any evidence of such disregard for good work is to reject the patient as deviant, hopelessly neurotic, beyond help, or "a crock."

A second factor that may obscure the dimensions of the problem of what people do with medical advice derives from the structure of much of modern medical practice. Characterized by brief encounters between the expert provider and the suffering person seeking help, the fact of defection from therapy and medical advice is often not visible to any one physician. Medical advice is associated with the emergence of large urban medical centers and clinics where the patient is seen by a range of highly trained specialists. These settings normally provide their physicians with less first hand data than the former general practitioner was given about the impact of his medical advice on the social and emotional lives of patients (Figures 7.1 and 7.2).

The increasing incidence of chronic illness is a third factor which tends to obscure the

Figure 7.1.   Painting by Ernest Hader of a physician treating the paw of a small dog. (By permission of The New York Academy of Medicine Library, New York, NY.)

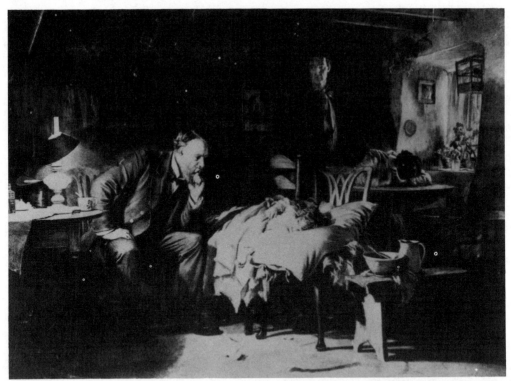

Figure 7.2. Painting by Sir Luke Fildes of a physician watching over a sick child. The worried father is standing in the background, and the mother is weeping with her head buried in her arm on the table. (By permission of The New York Academy of Medicine Library, New York, NY.)

patient's response to medical advice. Chronic illness by its nature places management of the daily medical regimen essentially in the hands of the patient and/or family and out of sight of the doctor. Relatively little of a physician's time is taken up with acute illness and hospitalized patients where problems of compliance are often less troublesome, and where, if the patient does not follow advice, the physician is more likely to know about it.

Therefore, the contemporary physician needs to be able to identify nonadherence potential during a brief encounter. He or she also needs tools for rapid calculation of the most effective strategies for assuring necessary patient cooperation for a wide range of patients, with their own individual orientations to health, to physicians, and to medical advice.

Milton Davis, author of a number of major studies of compliance, reviewed the literature and reported that the percentage of patients who fail to follow their doctor's advice ranges from 15% to 93%. Regardless of the variety of regi-

mens prescribed and the illness considered, at least a third of the patients in most studies had failed to comply with doctor's orders. Many of the studies indicate, either empirically or by implication, that doctors often do not give enough consideration to their role as interpreter and educator for patients, and the problem is compounded by the fact that many patients are reluctant to reveal their noncooperation to their physician. Why should they, when they want the doctor to like them?

In a study of tuberculosis patients, 95% said they were taking their prescribed medication faithfully. Physicians in the same clinic judged that only 80% of these patients were taking the medication as ordered. But para-aminosalicylic acid and isoniazid metabolite determinations done on urine samples brought in by these same patients indicated that only 70% of them had actually taken the drugs prescribed on the day of their clinic visit. How many had failed to take the medication on one or more days between visits is unknown. Physicians may sometimes wonder why medication is not working when, in fact, the patient is simply not taking it regularly. Haynes and coworkers reported that up to 50% of hypertensive patients fail to follow through with referral advice, over 50% of those who do begin treatment drop out of care within a year, and only two-thirds of the remainder consume enough of their prescribed medication to achieve adequate blood pressure reduction.

Hubert Caron and Carol Roth asked medical residents to estimate whether their hospitalized patients were adhering to an antacid regimen (ATR). Each resident's estimates were then compared with counts of antacid pills actually consumed by his or her patients in the hospital. The average patient had taken only 46% of the prescribed medicine, and the residents were unable to distinguish which patients adhered well and which ones had failed to take their medicine as prescribed. At least three different studies have found that physicians in office practices were not able to identify accurately which of their own patients were not taking medications as ordered.

PATIENT CHARACTERISTICS AND ADHERENCE

By the 1960's, because of a growing awareness of the importance of this problem, serious research attention began to be devoted to the subject of "noncompliance with medical orders." As the choice of the terms "compliance" and "orders" suggests, the search for explanations at first concentrated on the attributes of patients and particularly those attributes that are associated with inferior socioeconomic status.

Standard demographic variables were explored. Females seemed more disposed than males to default from medical advice—but there were contradictory findings. Lower socioeconomic status, particularly lower educational status, was found in some studies to relate to "noncompliance." However, here too the evidence was not conclusive. In fact, one study of patients who signed out of hospitals against medical advice found that the defectors had a greater ability to pay than the patients who stayed. One study of elderly patients suggested that the very old tended to be most often "noncompliant," and some of this failure to follow medical advice seemed to be the result of forgetfulness and of

inability to read the small print on labels of bottles. But other studies suggest that youth also appears to be associated with failure to follow medical advice.

Race or ethnicity or nationality has been shown in some studies to relate statistically to "compliance," a particular concern in view of the high incidence of chronic diseases in certain ethnic groups where noncompliance is also apparently high, and compliance with good medical advice might be crucial. Tuberculosis and hypertension are examples. Personality factors have been implicated in a number of studies of adherence to medical advice. For example, in a sample of alcoholic patients, dropout from outpatient therapy was associated with "field dependence" (a high score on a test devised by Herman Witkin to tap a subject's degree of reliance on background as an aid to perception). The import of "psychological readiness" is discussed in one study, and one team of investigators suggested that those patients who accepted treatment seemed to handle their anger more appropriately and appeared to be more willing to conform to social norms.

Gravity of the disease condition has also been considered as possibly predictive of compliance with medical advice. Logic suggests that where failure to follow advice might be most harmful, adherence would be better. However, the findings are distressing. Milton Davis found in his data that the patients with less severe medical illness were among the ones most likely to follow through with medical advice. Those with more severe illness were less likely to follow their physician's advice. Martha Hardy, in her follow-up on what happened with medical recommendations for pediatric patients, found that only half of the children received all the professional care advised—and these were usually the children with the fewest health problems. In a study of children with rheumatic heart disease it appeared that it was not the physician's diagnosis of rheumatic heart disease per se, so much as the degree to which the child's normal function appeared to the mother to be impaired, that determined the extent to which medication orders were followed. This presents a serious problem in management, since neither degree of discomfort nor even interference with daily activity is necessarily indicative of how potentially lethal an untreated illness may be.

Other social attributes of patients appear associated with how they behave toward medical advice. People who are "socially marginal" or those who live alone appear likely to defect from medical advice. Obviously, the patient in a hospital bed in an intensive care unit is constrained both by his social and physical setting to comply with medical orders. In the acute care context, relatively little is left up to the patient. However, even in that constraining context there appears to be much more noncompliance than is generally assumed. The convalescent in the hospital can, and sometimes does, accept the paper cup of pills from the medications nurse and then take all, some, or none of them. One seriously impaired cardiac patient devised his own exercise program in the hospital, vigorously working out behind his closed hospital door. He was assumed by staff to be an ideal patient because he never complained and always seemed cheerful and cooperative.

To summarize the literature reviewed thus far, a number of patient characteristics seem more or less associated with what at first was referred to as "compliance," and more recently has been called "adherence behavior" and eventually may be considered as the issue of "cooperation with medical advice." These variables are: age, sex, ethnicity, socioeconomic status, and the patient's attitudes toward health. But none of these attributes of patients explains enough of the differences between patients' responses to advice to provide much guidance for physicians.

The most conclusive evidence suggests that characteristics and social attributes of patients, in themselves, do not predict response to medical advice. A single patient may respond well to one bit of advice, and ignore the rest of it. One patient might be meticulous about medication, yet disregard orders about diet. Patients may vary in how they respond to a particular style of advice, to the content of the advice generally, and more specifically to various aspects of the advice. For example, one patient advised to follow a low cholesterol diet scrupulously avoided shell fish which he had never liked, and he always announced that he was not "allowed" by his doctor to eat clams. However, he often ate steak with potatoes fried in the meat fat, and chocolate mousse for dessert. Another patient carefully avoided lifting anything around his home, as advised by the doctor, but at the same time he did not give up skiing.

PHYSICIAN CHARACTERISTICS AND ADHERENCE

It is not surprising to find that physicians appear to vary in their ability to induce adherence behavior. Enthusiasm of physicians, permissiveness, length of experience, and "approach" have been reported to influence whether or not patients stay in therapy. But as with patient characteristics, there are contradictory findings. Even the length of time spent in one office visit does not predict compliance. Thus, a search for the answer by looking for attributes of physicians that predict whether or not patients will follow medical advice appears to be only a little more useful than looking for the answer among various characteristics of patients.

Logical next places to look for variables that can predict how patients will behave in response to medical advice are the source and context of the advice, the doctor-patient relationship itself, and the context where the advice is to be followed, i.e., the home. It is surprising that the question of "match," as it might predict productive encounters between doctor and patient, has only occasionally been the focus of study. The power of the doctor-patient relationship is evoked by physicians in political, educational, and philosophical discussions, explored in behavioral science courses, and suggested in studies of placebo results. It is idealized in press and prose as one of enduring, potentially therapeutic, and sometimes all-encompassing involvement. More recently, and directly to the point of our concern, at least five different sources of disjunction between patient and physician appear associated with failure to follow medical advice.

PATIENT-PHYSICIAN DISJUNCTION

I. The Problem of Different Medical Expectations

The degree of fit between expectations of patient and physician makes a difference in patients' adherence to medical advice. The doctor may expect that an essential part of a good physical work-up is to draw blood, yet some Puerto Rican patients may expect something different. One Puerto Rican patient complained: "He drew a half a cup of my blood and he didn't even pay me for it!" The physician may expect the patient to be ready, able, and willing to articulate a presenting complaint, but some Puerto Rican patients may expect the doctor to demonstrate his "powers" first. One patient reported to her friend, after visiting a physician: "How could he help me? He asked me, 'What is your problem?'" Many other patients, on the other hand, expect to be listened to and these patients are "put off" by a physician who allows no interruptions in a staccato barrage of questions that require only "yes" or "no" responses.

II. The Problem of Different Styles of Communication

A second source of disjunction between patient and physician is that the physician's style of offering advice and the patient's style of dealing with stressful situations and with new information may be incompatible. In various studies, neither a democratic nor an authoritarian teaching style has proved more productive for learning. The significant factor appears to be the "fit" or compatibility between teaching style and learning style. In medicine some patients respond best to a physician who discusses and advises. Other patients respond best to an authoritarian physician who questions decisively and then gives medical "orders" in the manner of a stern father. The authoritarian mode appears less acceptable to educated young adults than to older uneducated patients, and more feasible in the management of acute rather than chronic illness.

III. The Problem of Comprehension of Medical Advice

A third source of misunderstanding between patient and physician is that each may employ a vocabulary that is virtually incomprehensible to the other. The patient who says he is "taking it easy" may mean something quite different from what the physician assumes. The following sequence suggests a need for the doctor to determine what the patient really understands:
"Does it hurt here?"
"No"
"And here?"
"No"
"Are you constipated?"
"No"
"Do you know what constipated means?"
"No"

Evidence of a patient's failure to understand medical advice is not hard to find. In one clinic, diabetic children and their parents both answered a 15 item questionnaire. Thirty of the children knew fewer than half of the items which are important for them to know. Over one-half of the adult diabetic patients in one outpatient clinic made an error in dosage. Some thought they were supposed to take a dose different from that prescribed; others simply looked at the wrong calibration on the syringe. In one outpatient medical clinic no patient had a precise understanding of all of the words doctors commonly used in questioning them. Fewer than half had an exact knowledge of the terms "nausea," "lab exam," and "chronic." Thirteen showed a mistaken understanding of "diarrhea." Among patients on a low starch diet, 70% of those interviewed said they would not avoid prunes.

Some mothers in one clinic for handicapped children were proud of the fact that they "always" followed medical recommendations and had "confidence in the doctor." Yet, the purpose of various therapeutic measures and their expected results were frequently not at all clear—even to those mothers who took such pride in following recommendations. Therefore, while they adhered to the letter of the instructions, some were placing restrictions on their children which were outdated—or at best no help—and sometimes harmful. The meaning of "Don't let him be too active" may be one thing for the mother receiving the advice, and something else to the physician who gives it. Furthermore the physician may intend the advice to be followed during a brief recuperation period, while the mother takes it as a lifetime direction.

Not only is there much room for a patient's misunderstandings of medical advice, but physicians may even underestimate the real level of knowledge or the patient's ability to comprehend. If underestimation of a patient's knowledge were usually followed by more careful attention to explaining to patients, then underestimation might work on behalf of patients. However, in a study by Lois Pratt and her colleagues, the "physicians who seriously underestimated patients' knowledge were among those *least* likely to discuss illness at any length with the patient, compared with the physicians who did not seriously underestimate patients' knowledge." The problem is compounded when the patients who understand little are also the ones who are too frightened or too unknowing to ask for clarification. The need to give serious attention to the matter of the patient's comprehension emerges in surveys of patients' attitudes toward physicians both here and abroad. In Great Britain, a large percentage of people interviewed in Ann Cartwright's major survey were not only dissatisfied with the amount of information given them but were more dissatisfied on this issue than on any other of their medical experiences.

Patients do not routinely admit that they do not know a word or do not understand a question. When the physician asks, "Have you any questions?" and gets a "No questions" response, he may mistakenly assume that the patient understands. But absence of questions may also signify that people do not understand enough to know what questions to ask. Absence of questions may also indicate simple rejection of advice that seems unacceptable because it flies in the face of the patient's firm beliefs, or because it is only marginally comprehended, or simply seems overwhelming.

IV. The Problem of Different Perceptions

A fourth factor that contributes to incongruence in the doctor-patient exchange, and ultimately to defection from advice, is that doctor and patient may have very different perceptions of what actually happened in their meeting.

Barbara Korsch and Vida Negrete examined the exchanges between 800 mothers and pediatricians in a children's clinic. They found that most of the physicians believed they had been friendly and reassuring, but only half of the mothers shared this impression. When the exchanges were analyzed, it turned out that only a few of the doctors routinely used the mother's name when they spoke to her. At interviews immediately following their visit to the doctor, nearly 50% of the mothers were still wondering what had caused the baby's illness. Later in a home follow-up, the investigators found that only 42% of the mothers had actually carried out all the doctor's advice. Whether the mother was college educated or not, whether the pediatrician had spent a few minutes or nearly an hour with her, appeared to have little relationship either with the mother's satisfaction or with her compliance with the medical advice. But *the physician's expression of concern for her feelings* and *the fact of active exchange between them* did appear related to a successful outcome and to cooperation with the physician. In the Korsch and Negrete study, the children were more likely to receive the prescribed medicine if the *mother felt that the doctor had praised her as a mother and had established friendly and easy communication with her.* Similarly, Mary MacDonald and her colleagues found an association between a mother's estimate of how she was regarded by clinic personnel and her compliance with medical advice for her children.

Such findings are not surprising when we consider the state of the mother as she sees a physician about her sick child. Patients are exposed emotionally as well as physically in the physician's office. In this vulnerable position, people will be particularly sensitive to any perceived condescension or assault on their already jeopardized self-esteem. One way to respond to such a painful experience is to devalue the advice of the person who triggered the disquieting emotion. A hospitalized patient on a medical service told an interviewer, "The doctors here go their way and I go mine. They don't listen to me and I don't listen to them. Even here I just take the pills my doctor back in my home town gave me."

V. The Problem of Differences in Priorities and Beliefs

A fifth and apparently most significant aspect of the doctor-patient exchange is that a patient and a doctor can have very different basic assumptions about the probable benefits of following specific advice.

Persistence with a therapeutic regimen implies priorities and beliefs that doctors are likely to have—and many patients are likely not to have. First, there is a sense of order and routine in days and weeks that physicians take for granted. Also related to time, the physician may assume that everyone has a sense of the future as a reality that today's actions can and will influence. It is not surprising that a doctor—whose extended training is a testimonial to his or her commitment to the future—may tend to explain the long-run consequences of a therapeutic course in an effort to convince the patient of the need for following medical advice. It is also not surprising if some patients whose preoccupations are nearly all with today, and whose lives tend to bump from crisis to crisis, are not "sold" by arguments that promise benefits or lack of trouble at some distant date. One patient responded to the appointment clerk in one clinic when asked whether she would prefer to come in on Tuesday or Thursday: "How do I know how I will feel next week?" It can be misleading to assume that every person who seeks help from physicians fully shares the physician's assumptions of what can help. People who are convinced that their conditions are hopeless may see little reason to sacrifice daily pleasurable patterns because the doctor tells them to. This may stem from the patient's personal need to deny his illness, or from personal experiences with the illness, or from a lack of hope. Whatever the origin of lack of faith in the efficacy of medical advice, such disbelieving or despairing patients are likely to defect from treatment.

TYPES OF RESPONSE TO MEDICAL ADVICE

It should be clear by now that the simple idea of compliant or noncompliant patients is not very useful. Medical advice introduces a demand for some change in behavior in response to the physician's advice. In some cases the prescribed change may require major shifts in accustomed habits or significant sacrifice of daily pleasures.

A major force on behalf of the patient's efforts is the belief that medical advice really offers hope of improvement toward a cherished goal. However, it can be misleading to assume that all patients share the physician's goals. Promising that the patient can soon return to work if medical advice is followed may inspire someone whose self-esteem is tied to work, but be counterproductive to someone who hates his or her job. A busy executive who would "rather die with my boots on," may put work above health, but may also feel that nothing can really save him from a coronary anyway. "My father died of one and he never did a lick of work and he didn't smoke either!" Behavior is influenced not only by the relative value of an outcome to an individual, but also by the individual's expectation that a given course of action will result in that outcome. "It's God's will how long you will live."

The Retreatist Response

Two types of adaptation are associated with *the patient's lack of commitment or belief* in the

relative importance of benefits that can come through following the specific advice. The first, a *retreatist response* to medical advice, is likely with a patient who is unconvinced in the first place that the prescribed behavior can really benefit in the way he or she wants to be benefited, and in the second place does not really comprehend what he is supposed to do. Such patients are both uncommitted and left with inadequate means for pursuing the physician's advice. A character in the comic strip "Pogo" turned Voltaire around in a way that suggests the retreatist response to medical advice: "I don't understand what you say, but I'll defend to your death my right to deny it." While this response is maddening to many physicians, it is comprehensible. Feeling hopeless, and also bewildered by the advice, the patient is likely to flee from the site of fear and confusion—unless the physician can provide hope, or at least a clear understanding of what exactly is being recommended.

In attempting to overcome the frustrations of dealing with a potential retreatist response, some physicians try fear. Fear may work with some patients some of the time, but it is a most unpromising approach with the patient prone to the retreatist response. The doctor's threat of dire outcome may simply evoke more anxiety and activate further the patient's psychological defense of denial. Patients who already feel hopeless and unconvinced that a change in their own behavior can do much good, and who are also bewildered about exactly what is expected of them, are in a sense poised for flight. Fearful possibilities outlined in grim detail can simply trigger that flight from the physician who raised the spectre. The statistical relationship between actual morbidity or severity of illness and failure to follow advice is now more understandable. The more threatening the reality, the greater may be the urgency to deny any need to follow the doctor's advice.

The Ritualistic Response

The second type of response associated with absence of belief or commitment to the idea that one's own medically informed behavior may influence the course of illness is a *ritualistic response* to medical advice. It is seen among patients who have ample comprehension about what is expected and who want to please the doctor. The response may not be ideal, but it still can serve to improve health or reduce risk of illness. It is a kind of, "O.K. if you say so," response.

But ritualistic compliance can also be a problem. Patients may concentrate on the appearance of compliance rather than on full cooperation. Henry Dolger, author of *How To Live With Diabetes*, described a 10 year old patient whose urine charts were invariably excellent. One day when the doctor asked for her chart, she started to hand it over, then abruptly pulled it back. "Oh, no," she blurted, "that's next week's chart. Here's this week's. I'm sorry." Thus the physician can take little for granted with these patients. Particular care needs to be taken to assure that there is enough detail as well as understanding so that ritualistic order following has the desired effects. At the extreme of ritualism, the patient's response may be a nearly pathological compliance characterized by excessive acquiescence and gullibility. Rather than speak up to physicians, such patients may even jeopardize their health if being a good patient or having the doctor like them is an overriding desire.

In this adaptation, the patient's feeling about the physician is the major force for action on behalf of health. The emphasis is on being a good or bad patient, rather than on maintaining the best possible health. As Marc Hollender suggests, rather than being scolded by their doctor, such patients may conceal dietary indiscretions or get into balance a day or two before a regular appointment. Some even resort to bringing someone else's urine specimen, as did one woman who explained, "I want to keep my record good."

The Improvising Response

The second pair of adaptations depends on *the patient's sharing the physician's belief* about the efficacy of the particular medical advice. This believing patient's adaptation to the advice can be a *cooperative response* if the means for following the advice are available to him or her, or an *improvising response* if the means are not available.

Competing pressures from family or work situations, or lack of sufficient knowledge about the meaning or details of the doctor's advice, can leave the willing patient with inadequate means for following advice. The health-oriented patient may be convinced that his behavior can make a real difference, but still have too few details, or be left with orders that are virtually impossible to follow. Thus handicapped, the committed patient may adapt with an improvising response to medical advice. One patient, who because of his work was virtually unable to get to a clinic at the time it was open, improvised on behalf of adhering to the spirit of the orders his doctor had given. He had been going to the hypertension clinic for six weeks, but missed two appointments because of the exigencies of his tenuous work situation. He then came to the emergency room to get the medication which his clinic physician had suggested. In the clinic's statistics he would be counted simply as "noncompliant." Yet his failure to appear at the clinic had different origins from that of a retreatist response—and different implications for his health.

Since the conditions which give rise to the improvising response are different from those which seem to generate the ritualistic or retreatist responses, any attempts at reducing this type of nonadherence should call for its own strategies. For example, determining whether there are limiting factors that make following the advice an extreme hardship, and working out a compromise with the patient, leaves less up to chance and to the patient's guess about what is best to do when choices must be made.

Improvising behavior often stems from insufficient medical attention to instructing the patient. Patients may think they understand, but actually may not even know enough for appropriate questions. Such patients, though committed to cooperation with the physician, may strive mightily to follow advice with results that could range from beneficent to disastrous. A patient, discharged from the hospital following a myocardial infarction, had been told to "sit still." He did just that literally for days, terrified of moving. The improvising adaptation, like the ritualistic, is often not visible to the doctor since the patient thinks he is following the advice. With the good motivation implicit in this response, careful determination of the patient's level of understanding and the limitations of the situation, followed by discussion and educational efforts that take nothing for granted, would seem the most promising to change an improvising response to a cooperative response.

The Cooperative Response

Cooperative response to medical advice follows when the patient shares the physician's definition of benefits to be gained from the medical regimen, and where the patient and his family also have sufficient information and means to be able to cooperate with the intent as well as the letter of the advice.

Since the physician with a busy practice can never know how most patients are actually managing their illness vis-a-vis all of the medically relevant details, the fully cooperative patient must become the ideal. In this response, patient and physician are joined in a common effort, and the patient pursues the physician's advice with intelligence, asking for explanation when something is unclear and volunteering relevant information at office visits, in order to be able to cooperate fully.

CONCLUSION

It does not necessarily take extra time to notice what a patient believes about his illness, nor to determine what he understands about the advice he is given. It may only require that the physician *listen* for significant clues, and then *ask* patients to describe: 1) what they believe is wrong with them; 2) what they understand they are to do about it; and 3) what they expect by way of risks and benefits if they follow the advice. Written material and/or paramedical staff available to go over a diet or the dosage of medication or all other aspects of medical advice in careful detail, determining the patient's comprehension each step along the way and reinforcing what the physician has prescribed can be very helpful. When the issue of the patient's response to medical advice is attended to by the physician, time is gained, not wasted. In the final outcome there are few more tragically wasteful times spent than those times, however brief, when the physician offers carefully considered medical advice—and it is not followed.

Suggested Readings

Brody D: Physician recognition of behavioral, psychological, and social aspects of medical care. *Arch Int Med* 140:1286, 1980.

Korsch B, Negrete V: Doctor-patient communication. *Sci Am* 227:66, 1972.

References

Becker M, Drachman R, Kirscht J: Predicting mothers' compliance with pediatric medical regimens. *J Pediatr* 81:843, 1972.

Caron H, Roth C: Patient's cooperation with medical regimen: difficulties in identifying the non-cooperator. *JAMA* 203:120, 1968.

Cartwright, A: *Patients and Their Doctors: A Study of General Practice*. New York, Atherton Press, 1967.

Davis M: Variation in patients' compliance with doctor's orders: analysis of congruence between survey responses and results of empirical investigations. *J Med Educ* 41:1037, 1966.

Dolger H, Seeman B: *How to Live with Diabetes*. New York, Pyramid Books, 1958.

Elling R, Whittemore R, Green M: Patient participation in a pediatric program. *J Health Hum Behav* 1:183, 1960.

Freedman N, et al: Drop-out from outpatient psychiatric treatment. *Arch Neurol Psychiatry* 80:657, 1958.

Hardy M: Follow-up of medical recommendations. *JAMA* 136:20, 1948.

Haynes RB, et al: Management of patient compliance in the treatment of hypertension. *Hypertension* 4:415, 1982.

Hollender M: *The Psychology of Medical Practice*. Philadelphia, WB Saunders, 1958.

MacDonald M, Hagberg K, Grossman B: Social factors in relation to participation in follow-up care of rheumatic fever. *J Pediatr* 62:503, 1963.

Pratt L, Seligmann A, Reader G: Physicians' views on the level of medical information among patients. In Jaco EG (ed): *Patients, Physicians and Illness*. Gelencoe, Free Press, 1958, p 222.

Stunkard AJ: Adherence to medical treatment. *J Psychosom Res* 25:187, 1981.

Witkin H, Karp S, Goodenough D: Dependence in alcoholics. *Q J Stud Alcohol.* 20:493, 1959.

Section C/The Mind-Body Relationship

CHAPTER **8**   ## The Psychological Reactions to Physical Illness

Michael Blumenfield, M.D. and
Troy L. Thompson II, M.D.

"How sickness enlarges the dimensions of a man's self to himself."

Charles Lamb

There is a physiological and a psychological reaction to every disease process. Medical students routinely learn about the white cell response, the antibody response, and neuroendocrine responses. However, many patients report that their initial response to an incipient illness is a sense of psychological "dis-ease." This may simply be a vague apprehension or irritability which precedes overt physical symptoms. When actual physical symptoms develop, people begin to react emotionally in highly individualized ways. The appropriate question to consider at such times is not whether there is an emotional reaction, but rather what kind of psychological reaction is occurring and to what degree it may be affecting the patient.

The psychological responses exhibited by a patient depend on several factors. The first, of course, is the nature and severity of the physical illness itself. Obviously, a comatose or anesthetized patient will not exhibit his psychological reactions until regaining consciousness. A further factor is the special meaning that the particular illness and hospitalization may have for that patient. Another important element to con-sider is the characteristic personality style and coping patterns of that patient. The past experiences that the patient has had with illnesses, doctors, and hospitalization will also be important. Experiences of friends and family members with illness should also be considered. Finally, the doctors' and nurses' responses to the patient will help mold his psychological reactions to illness and to hospitalization.

Why should busy physicians worry about the psychological reactions of their patients? In addition to simply being humane, there are specific medical reasons why these psychological reactions should be diagnosed and treated. Patients with many organic disorders may have their physical conditions exacerbated if they become too anxious or depressed. For example, the overly anxious myocardial infarction patient will release catecholamines which can cause cardiac arrhythmias and lead to death. Or the overly depressed surgical patient may lose his will to live, and as a result of this "giving-up" may not survive the surgery.

COMMON REACTIONS TO ILLNESS AND HOSPITALIZATION

Rudolph Moos has described several major ways in which individuals react to the stress of illness. Initially, denying or minimizing the seriousness of the problem is common. Following

48

this initial reaction, often accompanied by regression, the patient will then begin to seek relevant information about the treatment and prognosis of his condition, thereby utilizing intellectual resources to help him cope. The patient will usually need reassurance and emotional support from family and friends. In some types of treatment the patient and/or family may need to learn specific illness-related procedures which are a part of the treatment, as indicated earlier by Dr. Mumford. The patient may mentally rehearse alternative outcomes of his illness and treatment to prepare himself for disappointments or bad news. Anxiety, depression, and anger are also common reactions to illness.

Denial

One of the most common initial reactions to any stress is the use of the psychological *defense mechanism* called *denial*. As defined by Dr. Simons in the glossary in Table 8.1, a defense mechanism is an unconscious mental process, protective in nature, used to relieve the anxiety and guilt arising from an individual's inner thoughts, feelings, wishes, and fears. The sequence involved in denial is that the patient perceives that a problem is developing, and this perception causes him or her to feel anxious. In response to this anxiety the patient rejects the upsetting perception, and thereby denies that the perception is accurate or significant. A physical analogy may be found in the pupillary response of the eye to light. To avoid overstimulation of the retina by too much light, the iris contracts. In the same way the defense mechanism of denial protects the person from too much psychological stimulation by a frightening perception of an external reality. All people use denial, and it may be quite useful to the patient as an initial reaction, as Dr. Dubovsky will discuss in a later chapter. However, it may be dangerous if it prevents the individual from making an important reality assessment. For example, if an individual denies the initial signs of cancer, it may prevent an accurate diagnosis and subsequent treatment from taking place. As Dr. Steinberg and Dr. Simons indicated in the second chapter, physicians themselves often use denial. This is one of the reasons why physicians should not treat themselves. There is a well-known story of the famous neurosurgeon who

denied his own symptoms of a brain tumor although they were painfully evident to the people around him. In such instances the consequences of denial can be tragic.

The following case history illustrates how a patient may use denial. A man in his sixties was admitted to the hospital with his second heart attack. He had always been a good athlete and was very proud of his physical strength. When he came to the hospital emergency room, he had a cardiac arrest and had to be resuscitated. He was told this a few days later, but he used a great deal of denial about its significance. The patient stated that he had been brought into the hospital with chest pain, that he had taken digitalis medication regularly prior to his admission, and that he had been under the treatment of one of the best cardiologists in town who checked over his electrocardiograms on a regular basis. He further stated that the doctors on the ward had told him that his cough might be related to "my heart—or something or other." But when asked, "So you have a heart condition?", he said, "Well no. I feel fine. I don't know that I have anything wrong. If I have any problem, let the doctors prove it to me."

This patient is using denial because he is quite anxious about what having heart disease would mean to him. He is not aware that he is using denial (as we said, a defense mechanism is an *unconscious* mental process), nor is it the task of the physician to try to "take away" the denial from such a patient as long as he is being cooperative with medically indicated treatment and as long as the denial is not hurting him in other ways. But it is important for the physician to recognize the strong needs of such a patient which prompt him to use this degree of denial. It is also important that the physician be aware if such a patient begins to use an excessive amount of denial. For example, such a patient may completely deny his heart attack and want to sign out of the hospital prematurely. Another patient may want to undertake some new endeavor which may not be advisable because of his illness. In these situations the physician may have to confront the denial, and then support the patient as the denial is given up.

Regression

All patients who are seriously ill, and especially those who are hospitalized, will demonstrate some degree of psychological *regression* (Table 8.1). This means that they will return to earlier ways of coping with psychological stresses. One patient may become quite assertive, demanding, and have "temper tantrums," while another patient may become silent and tearful. The developmental anxieties that will be mentioned shortly help to precipitate this regression to earlier childhood patterns of adaptation, as does the forced passivity and dependency that the patient develops toward his caretakers.

Control By Knowing

Another common reaction to illness, which is the opposite of denial, is seen when the patient wants to learn all he can about his illness and treatment. The patient is attempting to *control* the situation by *knowing* about it, and such patients may accumulate a tremendous amount of medical knowledge. Anxiety and fear are usually much greater when something is unknown. If the physician carefully tells the patient what will happen, the patient will later feel comforted when those occurrences actually take place. This will give the patient the sense that the physician knows what he or she is doing. However, sometimes too much information can be conveyed by the physician. There is usually no need for the physician to tell the patient the amount of blood loss that will occur during surgery or other upsetting details which serve no useful purpose. Some individuals have personality styles which prompt them to try to control every situation. They will find it particularly upsetting when they do not understand everything about their illness and treatment. It is important to recognize this need in some patients, to answer all of their questions as fully as is appropriate, and to allow them to participate as much as possible in their treatment. Other patients may not want to know anything except that the physician is doing his best. More will be discussed about these various personality types later in this chapter.

Anxiety

One of the nearly universal feelings that illness will evoke is *anxiety*. To the patient illness means the loss of function and the loss of

strength, physical as well as mental. Thus, illness is almost always perceived as a *danger situation*. The patient's previous life experiences, and the way in which he or she reacted to the danger situations of early childhood, are going to have an important influence on the current reaction to illness. These danger situations of childhood, first elucidated by Freud, will be discussed in more detail in later chapters by Dr. Scharfman. At this point it may be helpful to look at James Strain's summary of seven basic types of developmental fears and stresses associated with first the illness and then the treatment, including the hospital environment.

1) *Fear of the threat to basic integrity.* People want to believe they are self-sufficient, in control, the masters of their own destinies, and that their bodies are indestructible. Illness and hospitalization can abruptly challenge and reverse these universal, although irrational and narcissistic beliefs. 2) *Fear of strangers.* It is frightening to put one's life in the hands of total strangers in the hospital. The patient has no personal ties with these people, and is therefore uncertain as to whether they are competent to assure his survival and are sufficiently concerned with his full recovery. 3) *Fear of separation from loved ones.* Any illness that requires hospitalization is going to lead to a separation from people to whom the patient has been very close. If the physician can understand something of the patient's previous experiences with separations and what the reactions have been, it will be easier to understand and deal with the *separation anxiety* that will be evoked in response to illness and especially to hospitalization. Illness also brings out fears of death and dying. To most people death means the loss of those whom we love, and therefore anxiety about death is very often a derivative of separation anxiety. 4) *Fear of the loss of love and approval by loved ones.* Patients may fear the loss of their attractiveness or the loss of their ability to perform activities which are important to them as a result of their illness or surgery. 5) *Fear of the loss or injury of body parts.* Any illness can also evoke concerns regarding the loss of bodily integrity, and surgery on any part of the body will in particular evoke derivatives of *castration anxiety* in men and *mutilation anxiety* in women. This anxiety may well be intensified if the patient had surgery during the period in childhood

Table 8.1
Glossary of Defense Mechanisms

Defense Mechanism:	An unconscious mental process, protective in nature, used to relieve the anxiety and guilt arising from an individual's inner thoughts, feelings, wishes, and fears.
Compensation:	An unconscious defense mechanism by which a person tries to make up for an imagined or real deficiency, physical or psychological or both. It may also be a conscious process.
Conversion:	An unconscious defense mechanism by which the anxiety that stems from a psychological conflict is symbolically expressed in a motor or sensory somatic symptom. Seen in a variety of psychiatric disorders, it is particularly common in histrionic (hysterical) personalities.
Denial:	An unconscious defense mechanism in which an unpleasant aspect of external reality (including bodily perceptions) is rejected and disavowed, and at times is replaced by a more satisfying internal fantasy.
Displacement:	An unconscious defense mechanism by which an internal, unacceptable thought, feeling, wish, or fear is transferred to a more acceptable external person or situation, as seen in phobias.
Dissociation:	An unconscious defense mechanism by which a group of mental processes is split off from the rest of an individual's personality, resulting in an independent functioning of this group of processes, as seen in dissociative (fugue) states and multiple personalities.
Idealization:	An unconscious defense mechanism in which a person overestimates an attribute or the entire personality of another person.
Identification:	An unconscious defense mechanism in which a person takes into himself the attributes of another person and then patterns himself after this other person. It is to be distinguished from imitation, a conscious process, and introjection, an unconscious process.
Intellectualization:	An unconscious defense mechanism in which rational and logical reasoning is used to avoid facing an unpleasant and irrational thought, feeling, wish, or fear.
Introjection:	An unconscious defense mechanism in which a person takes into himself another person's (usually his parents') demands and value systems as if they were his own, so that he reacts to those demands and values whether or not the other person is actually present. However, the individual does not necessarily pattern himself after the other person as would be the case in identification.
Isolation:	An unconscious defense mechanism by which a thought or idea is separated and kept apart from its accompanying feeling or affect, as seen in obsessive-compulsive disorders.
Negation:	An unconscious defense mechanism in which an underlying wish is verbalized in the opposite terms of what is actually desired.
Projection:	An unconscious defense mechanism in which a person externalizes his conflicts and attributes to the outside world or to another person the thoughts, feelings, wishes, and fears that are part of himself but that are unacceptable to him, as seen in paranoid schizophrenia.
Rationalization:	An unconscious defense mechanism in which a person justifies an irrational thought, feeling, or behavior by making it appear reasonable and rational.
Reaction Formation:	An unconscious defense mechanism in which a person develops a socially acceptable attitude or interest that is the direct opposite of some thought, feeling, wish, or fear in the unconscious. It is a commonly observed mechanism in obsessive-compulsive disorders.
Regression:	An unconscious defense mechanism in which a person undergoes a partial or total return to earlier patterns of adaptation and behavior.
Repression:	An unconscious defense mechanism in which a person removes from consciousness those thoughts, feelings, wishes, and fears that are unacceptable to him. It is to be distinguished from suppression, a conscious process.

TABLE 8.1—*Continued*

Somatization:	An unconscious defense mechanism in which psychological conflicts are expressed in physical symptoms. The somatic expression may be a symbolic one without organic change (conversion), a more diffuse and generalized one without organic change (hypochondriasis), or one that involves actual organic change (psychophysiological disorders).
Sublimation:	An unconscious defense mechanism in which unacceptable wishes are diverted into personally and socially acceptable channels and thereby partially gratified. Sublimation may also be a conscious process.
Symbolization:	An unconscious defense mechanism whereby one idea or situation comes to stand for another because of some common aspect or quality in both. Symbolization is based on similarity and association. The symbols formed protect the person from the anxiety that may be attached to the original idea or situation.
Undoing:	An unconscious defense mechanism by which a person symbolically annuls something unacceptable that has already been done. Undoing is a form of magical ritual, commonly observed in obsessive-compulsive disorders.

* Table by Richard C. Simons.

when his or her *fears of bodily injury* were greatest, or had other anxiety-provoking medical experiences during this time in childhood. These fears may be based on real concerns (as in cases of surgical amputation of body parts), as well as what that body part may symbolize or mean to the patient's self-esteem and ability to enjoy his or her life. 6) *Fear of reactivation of feelings of guilt and shame*, which accompany fears of retaliation for previous transgressions. The patient may develop the idea that his or her illness is a punishment for some past sin of omission or commission. 7) *Fear of loss of control of developmentally achieved functions*. A patient's self-esteem can be severely affected by losing control of bowel, bladder, and other motor and sensory functions.

At times these various anxieties can become so overwhelming that the patient feels the need to either "fight or take flight." An anxious patient may try to pick a fight, or start an argument with the nurses or physicians, or threaten to sign out against medical advice. He or she may also refuse to sign a consent form for a needed procedure. At times some patients will be so psychologically overwhelmed that they may have a psychotic break with reality. For these reasons it is very important to continually assess a patient's psychological reactions and stability during any illness. Appropriate psychological treatment should begin immediately if the patient appears to be regressing precipitously. Certainly any surgical intervention may be perceived as an assault against a fragile patient's sense of bodily integrity and may precipitate an overt psychotic break.

Anger

A common way of dealing with fear is to become angry. Therefore, *anger* in patients is usually related to an underlying fear about their illness. Patients may deny that they are afraid and transform this unpleasant feeling into a feeling that they can more comfortably express—anger. Some patients will *displace* (Table 8.1) their concerns from one part of the body to another. Brian Bird describes a patient who was quite anxious following eye surgery. In the postoperative period, however, he became preoccupied and angry about developing urinary retention. He worried that he would never be able to use his bladder normally again. This patient had a much greater fear, namely that he would never be able to use his eyes again, but he displaced that fear and became upset about something else as a way of coping with his fear of blindness.

Depression

Any loss or threatened loss can lead to *depression*. As mentioned earlier, there are many potential losses associated with illness, surgery, and hospitalization, and this applies to a loss of a body part, as well as any loss of bodily function or bodily integrity. As will be discussed further in later chapters, depression may be manifested in countless ways, from overt weeping (Figure 8.1) to profound withdrawal (Figure 8.2).

SEXUAL FUNCTIONING

Since patients are frequently embarrassed to speak about sexual problems and doctors are

Figure 8.1. *Hopeless* (1963) by Roy Lichtenstein. (By permission of Kunstmuseum, Basel, Switzerland, Ludwig Collection.)

Figure 8.2. *No More Tears* (1947). Photograph by Vilem Kriz. (By permission of Vilem Kriz.)

sometimes reluctant to inquire about such matters, the effect that illness has on sexual functioning may go unnoticed. Patients are often afraid to resume sexual relations after becoming ill because they are concerned that such activity will aggravate their condition or may even be fatal. The fear of dying during sexual activity may be especially frequent with cardiac patients. For example, one patient developed premature ejaculation within 10 seconds of penetration after having his first heart attack. The patient explained that he was frightened that if he became too excited or exerted too much during intercourse he would have a fatal heart attack. When he and his wife were told these risks were minimal, their sexual relationship improved markedly. Sometimes patients may have had guilt feelings about their sexual activities prior to becoming sick, and they may actually feel that their illness is a punishment for these sexual activities. Such patients may withdraw from all sexual activities after becoming ill. Other patients may try to reassure themselves that they have not lost their sexual ability by engaging in an increased amount of activity.

PREVIOUS EXPERIENCES WITH ILLNESS

It is important to know about the patient's past experiences with illnesses. This inquiry should include not only the patient's previous illnesses but also those of family members with the same or different illnesses. For example, an intelligent young woman who wanted to have an abortion was quite frightened at the thought of going through with it. It turned out that her mother had died from an infection associated with an illegal abortion. The patient claimed that she was intellectually aware of the fact that there was a great deal of difference between the illegal abortion that her mother had and the procedure she would have in the hospital. Although she knew this intellectually, emotionally she continued to react as if the situations were the same. Another example can be seen in the *paradoxical depression* which may develop in patients recovering from an illness or surgery. The patient begins to become depressed just when he or she is starting to recuperate and doing well. This will appear "paradoxical" to the physicians, family, and often to the patient. However, if the patient's history is explored carefully, it is often found that a family member died of a similar illness before modern treatment was available, and the patient may be feeling guilty because he or she is going to survive. Both paradoxical depression and *survivor guilt* will be discussed in more detail in later chapters.

SPECIFIC PERSONALITY TYPES RELATED TO THE REACTIONS TO ILLNESS

Ralph Kahana and Grete Bibring have described seven basic personality types in terms of the psychological reactions to physical illness. These are of course generalizations, and many combinations and mixtures of these personality types may occur. However, for each of these personalities the essential psychological meaning of the illness and the response to it is different. Therefore, the doctor-patient relationship and certain management issues will also be different for each type. In general, these patients are not psychiatrically "ill" as such, but are individuals with rather fixed personality styles who react to the stress of illness in one of the following characteristic fashions. 1) The over-demanding *dependent personality*. These patients fear helplessness and have a great need for personal care. This is usually manifested during an illness by demands for endless attention, interest, and support by the family and the health care providers. 2) The orderly, controlled *compulsive personality*. Illness threatens these patients with the loss of control which is so important to them. In response they usually become even more psychologically rigid and overcontrolling. 3) The dramatic, captivating *histrionic* or *hysterical personality*. In these patients illness means they have developed a personal defect. They fear being unattractive or unappreciated, and they may react by becoming overly dramatic, emotionally labile, and sometimes seductively involved with their caretakers. 4) The long-suffering, self-sacrificing *masochistic personality*. Sometimes these patients unconsciously precipitate or perpetuate illnesses and other misfortunes in their lives in order to receive love and attention. They may also view the illness as a punishment or as an expiation for a deep sense of guilt. 5) The suspicious, querulous *paranoid personality*. These patients tend to blame others (especially physicians) for their illness or for their failures to improve by treatment. They tend to be very suspicious of anyone's attempts to help them and are oversensitive to any type of slight. 6) The superior, grandiose *narcissistic personality*. An illness

threatens the self-image of perfection and invulnerability of these patients. They want to be powerful and all-important, and are often grandiose, vain, and arrogant. Only the most eminent physician is good enough for them. 7) The shy, aloof *schizoid personality*. Their remoteness, unsociable nature, and lack of involvement with everyday events and other people are all protections from psychological stress. Illness threatens the tenuous psychological equilibrium of these patients, and they will often intensify their withdrawal in proportion to the degree of underlying anxiety. Few demands should be placed on these patients, but they should not be allowed to totally withdraw when they become ill. In a later chapter Drs. Simons and Macdonald will discuss each of these personality types in more detail.

FANTASIES ABOUT ILLNESS

Any time a patient becomes ill, he or she will immediately begin to develop fantasies about the cause and the nature of the illness. For example, a businessman who had just turned 50 was admitted to the hospital with severe epigastric pain radiating to his left chest. The physical exam, electrocardiogram, and blood cardiac enzymes were all normal. The patient was diagnosed as having a nonspecific gastrointestinal disturbance. When the patient was asked what he believed was the cause of his symptoms, he stated that he was certain he had cancer of the stomach, since his father had died of cancer of the stomach at the age of 50. After he had an opportunity to discuss these thoughts with his physician, he felt reassured and the symptoms disappeared.

No matter what the circumstances, every person will have some fantasy of why he or she has become ill, and these ideas may fit with the medical facts or be a complete distortion. They may be recognized as "foolish" by the patient, yet they can still be very important and meaningful to the patient. They can also determine if and when the patient will seek medical care. Another example is the case of a 38 year old male who had had a nine month history of sixth nerve palsy, headaches of unknown origin, nausea and vomiting, and weight loss. He told one of his physicians that he believed he had a rare disease related to the sexual intercourse he had while on a trip to Southeast Asia. He had felt very guilty about this and had only recently confessed it to his wife. He knew logically that his symptoms were not those of venereal disease but, nevertheless, this belief persisted and had delayed his seeking medical treatment.

Another example of the importance of fantasies about one's illness is seen in the following example. An intern had as a patient a 42 year old woman who was hospitalized with bronchial pneumonia. Although she was doing quite well, the intern asked her why she felt she had the illness. She was very relieved that he had asked her this question. She had recently undergone a hysterectomy and had become somewhat depressed after this surgery. She then developed the idea that there was an empty space in her body because of the hysterectomy. When she developed the pneumonia, she believed it was because this empty space had caused a draft in her bodily organs through her vagina. Although she was an intelligent woman, her life-long feelings of somehow being defective and inadequate were revived by the hysterectomy. Recognizing this, the intern was able to clarify the medical facts surrounding the hysterectomy and her pneumonia, and also to discuss some of her feelings that the hysterectomy had made her less of a woman.

The existence of some fantasy about one's illness is not limited to patients outside of the medical profession, as is illustrated in the next example. A medical colleague once expressed skepticism about the existence or importance of such fantasies in well informed patients. For example, he noted he had a toothache that day and doubted that he had any hidden thoughts about such a straightforward problem. When he was asked why he thought he had the problem, he said it was obviously because he had "poor gums." In the spirit of scientific inquiry he agreed to reflect on this explanation. His first thought was that he had inherited his gingival condition from his mother's side of the family. However, his sister did not have this condition. He then realized that he had always believed that his mother had given him all of the "bad things" but had given none to his sister. These reflections about his toothache revealed the remnants of his conflicts with both his mother and his sister. Like everyone else, he had constructed a fantasy about his illness which was in some way related to his own personal psychological makeup and his important past relationships.

REACTIONS TO ANESTHESIA AND SURGERY

Many patients are more concerned about the anesthesia than they are about the surgery. Anesthesia causes a complete loss of control and consciousness, which may be equated with death (Figure 8.3). Anesthesia also evokes fears of passivity and dependency, and fears of what the patient may do or say while anesthesized. Some of these fears may be partially understood by the fact that children are often told that a pet was "put to sleep" when it was killed by a veterinarian with an overdose of anesthetic. Also, many people explain death to children by saying that someone "went to sleep and did not wake up." Other patients are afraid that the anesthesia may not be effective, and that they may wake up during the surgery and experience overwhelming panic and pain.

The differentiation between a minor and major surgical procedure is usually one made by the surgical staff. A "minor" surgical procedure may

Figure 8.3. Illustration by Jan Vredeman de Vries (1605). (By permission of Perspectives, Dover Publications, Inc., New York, N.Y.)

be a major stress to the patient and his family. Also, elective surgery may be more psychologically stressful than a more major emergency surgical procedure because with an elective procedure the patient has more time to worry and consider the possible negative consequences. In addition to fears of passivity and dependency, and fears of pain, surgery also represents a threat to life in many cases and always involves a certain degree of threat to bodily integrity. Even if an organ or a part of the body is not removed during surgery, a scar will remain. Surgery will, therefore, always alter the body image to some degree.

Certain types of surgery often arouse more specific fears in addition to fears of death, mutilation, dependency, and pain. For example, surgery on the eyes or ears may arouse fears of blindness or deafness. Surgery near the genital areas is often anxiety-provoking. Male patients may become quite concerned about a hernia operation, a prostatectomy, or anal surgery. Women are often quite upset by a hysterectomy or mastectomy. And when it becomes necessary to perform such a procedure, no matter how much preoperative discussion takes place between surgeon and patient, the patient can never be truly prepared for the loss of such an important body part. When a woman awakens from anesthesia to discover that she has had a mastectomy, there is usually a profound emotional reaction. The symbolic equation of the breasts with femininity and desirability is usually quite important. This is true as well for the uterus, and in addition a hysterectomy may be linked to feelings related to motherliness and motherhood. The incidence of serious psychological reactions posthysterectomy is two and a half times greater than such reactions following gallbladder surgery, which usually involves a similar degree of physical trauma. Bernard Meyer reports the case of a young woman who, following a mastectomy, developed the delusion that her breast would grow back. Similar types of reactions may occur in men following penile surgery or orchiectomy.

Cardiovascular and brain surgery are often quite stressful due to the close association of those organs with life itself. Postoperative psychoses are not infrequent in these surgeries. Ileostomies and colostomies often are very upsetting. The patient may feel dirty and unattractive and be embarrassed by having to wear a colostomy bag. This may be reflected in diffi-culties with sexual functioning. Furthermore, following prostatic surgery or colostomy, up to 50% of males will be impotent due to the cutting of autonomic nerve plexuses.

Amputations forever alter the body image. It may be upsetting to realize that a former vital part of the body is now gone and "dead." Following the amputation of a diabetic foot, a patient said, "I have one foot already in the grave." Certain types of plastic surgery, such as rhinoplasty, may have either positive or negative psychological results. If the patient is psychologically stable, such a procedure may improve the body image and lead to greater emotional security. Psychological growth and improved interpersonal relationships may develop as a result. On the other hand, people who have such a procedure performed with the magical hope that it will solve all of their psychosocial problems are usually disappointed and are poor surgical candidates. A paradoxical reaction can also occur related to the surgical correction of a congenital or other chronic abnormality. If the person has incorporated such an anomaly into his body image, he may go through a period of mourning for the loss of the body part, even though it may have been abnormal or malfunctional.

For several days after major surgery patients are often apathetic and lethargic. This may be due to physiological stresses, but the patient may also be psychologically "dazed." The first sign that this lethargy is lifting is usually concern by the patient about his or her personal appearance. If lethargy persists for more than five to six days, psychiatric consultation may be needed. Anyone undergoing a surgical procedure may respond with some degree of anger. Any time injury is inflicted on a person, anger is evoked. The patient may wonder why this illness or accident happened to him. He may feel it is unfair and that he has been dealt a blow by fate. These feelings of anger will usually be increased if the surgery is not completely successful or if the pain or postoperative disability is greater than was expected. In our society, the expression of anger is generally considered to be undesirable. Therefore, many patients try to conceal this emotion from their physicians. Their anger may be indirectly expressed by complaints of pain, by making demands for narcotic medication, by continued disability and, sometimes, as a last resort to gain the attention of the physician, by litigation and malpractice suits.

REACTIONS TO THE INTENSIVE CARE UNIT

The intensive care unit can be a very psychologically stressful environment. Dr. Thomas Hackett studied patients with acute myocardial infarctions in the intensive care unit (ICU). These patients were attached to a number of monitoring devices, including electrocardiograms. Hackett found that most patients are reassured by the constant monitoring. However, others are distressed by the chronic, monotonous beeping of monitors and the lack of a normal sleep-wake cycle in some ICU's. Hackett found that the higher the patient's position in the socioeconomic strata, the less worried the patient was about irregularities on the electrocardiogram. Many white collar workers understood that any type of physical movement may cause some irregularity on the electrocardiogram, and were, therefore, less distressed by these EKG changes than blue collar workers who did not have this knowledge. Hackett also found that white and blue collar workers seem to have some knowledge about the myocardial damage that occurs in a heart attack, but the white collar workers had considerably more knowledge about the repair process that takes place. He found that the responses of these patients to their illness could be modified by education of the patients regarding the course of the treatment process. Later in the book Dr. Glickman will describe the serious disorganization (ICU psychosis) which can occur due to the combination of sensory deprivation, sensory overstimulation, and sleep deprivation in an intensive care unit, and some of the measures which can be taken to prevent and treat such severe psychological reactions.

REACTIONS TO HEMODIALYSIS

Franz Reichsman and Norman Levy have studied patients receiving chronic hemodialysis. They have found that these patients react in three psychological stages. The first stage is called the *honeymoon period*. This usually begins from one to three weeks after the first dialysis treatment and can last anywhere from six weeks to six months. In this stage, the patient seems to accept his or her intense dependency on the machine and on the dialysis process. There is still great stress and anxiety, but the patient is basically content, confident, and hopeful. The second stage has been termed *disenchantment and discouragement*. The confidence and hope have passed, and the patient begins to feel sad and helpless. This stage lasts anywhere from three to twelve months. This stage generally begins when the patients discover that they are not able to perform their usual activities, and they become depressed. They may also feel guilty over dietary indiscretions, and begin to feel ashamed about their illness. The third stage of these patients' reactions is their *long-term adaptation*. This begins when the patients are able to arrive at some degree of acceptance of their limitations. The patients may still have marked fluctuations in their sense of emotional and physical well-being, but there are longer periods of contentment alternating with the episodes of depression. As might be expected, the defense mechanism which is most commonly used during this period of long-term adjustment is that of denial.

REACTIONS TO TRANSPLANTATION

In recent years organ transplantation has created unique physiological and emotional situations. Kidney transplantations have been the most common procedure of this type. The situation is usually one in which a relatively young person has to suddenly deal with a life-threatening illness. In addition, the patient may have the task of asking a parent or a sibling to donate a kidney. Preexisting family conflicts can be heightened at this time, often with marked feelings of anger and guilt on the part of both donor and recipient. Dependency conflicts in the parent-child relationship can be especially heightened by the actual dependency that is imposed upon the patient by the illness. The fantasies and psychological reactions which occur in connection with organ transplantation are often intense. The transplant patient has the difficult psychological task of integrating an organ from someone else into his body image. The recipient of the kidney may even begin to develop some of the traits of the family member who was the donor through a process of identification. With a cadaver-donated kidney the patient may develop fantasies about the dead donor and react accordingly. In each transplant situation there is also the question of how an actual or fantasized cross-sex transplant will affect the recipient's feelings about his or her sexual identity. For example, a man on welfare fantasized that his transplanted kidney was from a wealthy woman, and he felt "less of a man" as a result. At times it may be best to diminish such reactions by telling the recipient some basic information about the donor. Steroid medication, which is frequently necessary in transplantation, can lead to changes in mood as well as changes in body image, secondary to the physical effects which often occur with steroid usage. It is possible that these various psychological factors may even influence the actual physical rejection of the new organ.

PATIENTS AT RISK FOR ADVERSE PSYCHOLOGICAL REACTIONS

In summary, we can say that there are several groups of patients who have greater risks of developing adverse psychological reactions in response to illness, hospitalization, and surgery. First, the patient with a prior history of psychotic decompensations or other psychiatric illnesses must be evaluated very carefully. Patients whose relationships with the medical staff or their families begin to deteriorate may be manifesting an underlying psychological problem. Patients who have unrealistic or magical expectations regarding a surgical procedure are at risk, as are depressed patients who express the fear or possibly even the conviction that they will not survive the surgery, as well as paranoid patients who are suspicious and unable to trust their physicians. Another group of patients seem to welcome illness and surgery. These are the masochistic personalities mentioned earlier who for various reasons need the pain associated with illness and surgery, and who may seek out multiple surgical procedures from different surgeons in the syndrome of *polysurgery*, which will be discussed further in a later chapter. Finally, patients who show too much or too little concern preoperatively are at risk. A mild to moderate degree of anxiety is realistic prior to most surgical procedures. The patient who denies feeling any type of anxiety is actually at greater risk for postoperative psychological problems than the patient who can admit to feeling some distress.

PSYCHOLOGICAL REACTIONS OF THE HEALTH CARE PROVIDERS

The physicians and nurses caring for a patient with a serious illness may also develop adverse psychological reactions. The health care providers must constantly monitor not only the patient's psychological reactions but also their own psychological reactions to the patient and his illness. This type of self-knowledge, sensitivity, and inquiry is essential to maintain effective doctor-patient relationships. A certain amount of emotional detachment is necessary for the physician. Surgeons especially need to have some emotional distance to allow them to do what they must do to the patient in an objective manner. This does not mean that the surgeon should be cold or detached. Such detachment may lead to problems in communication with the patient, family, and staff members if it is excessive. The patient who does not get better, or for whom treatment is ineffective, may threaten the physician's sense of competence and need to be in control. If the physician is not sufficiently secure and realistic about his own abilities and limitations, he may withdraw from the patient in response to these "failures." The patient who is dying may especially evoke feelings of failure, guilt, and shame in the careproviders even though they know realistically nothing more can be done. In addition, cancer and other potentially fatal illnesses can evoke fear and withdrawal reactions in many people, including some physicians. The physician also may develop negative attitudes toward the patient if the latter's illness is self-inflicted. This occurs with patients who have made suicide attempts or who have brought about their illness by their use of alcohol, cigarettes, and overeating, as only a few examples. Certain illnesses will have special meanings to the physician, just as they will have for each patient. As physicians and other health care providers, we must be willing to look within ourselves and face these wide ranging psychological reactions to the illnesses of our patients. Finally, it is important for health care providers to realize that illness and hospitalization do not always have negative results. The Chinese symbol for illness is a door which opens both ways. Some patients are able to utilize their experiences with a serious illness to reassess their lives, reorder their priorities, and redirect their futures in a more meaningful way.

Suggested Readings

Bird B: *Talking with Patients*, ed 2. Philadelphia, J.B. Lippincott, 1973.
Cassell EJ: Reactions to physical illness and hospitalization. In Usdin G, Lewis JM (eds): *Psychiatry in General Medical*

Practice. New York, McGraw-Hill, 1979, p 103.

Cirillo DP, Rubinstein M: *The Complete Book of Cosmetic Facial Surgery.* New York, Simon & Schuster, 1984.

Dubovsky SL, Weissberg MP: Reactions to illness. In *Clinical Psychiatry in Primary Care,* ed 2. Baltimore, Williams & Wilkins, 1982, p 149.

Glickman L: *Psychiatric Consultation in the General Hospital.* New York, Marcel Dekker, 1980.

Guerra F, Aldrete JA (eds): *Emotional and Psychological Responses to Anesthesia and Surgery.* New York, Grune & Stratton, 1980.

Hackett TP, Cassem NH (eds): *Massachusetts General Hospital Handbook of General Hospital Psychiatry.* St. Louis, C.V. Mosby Company, 1978.

Kempe CH: Nursing in a coronary care unit: a doctor-patient's view. *The Pharos.* Winter 1979, p 18.

Kimball CP: *The Biopsychosocial Approach to the Patient.* Baltimore, Williams & Wilkins, 1981.

Leigh H, Reiser MF: *The Patient: Biological, Psychological, and Social Dimensions of Medical Practice.* New York, Plenum, 1980.

Nemiah JC: Psychological complications of physical illness. In *Foundations of Psychopathology.* New York, Oxford University Press, 1961, p 256.

Reiser DE: Reactions to illness. In Reiser DE, Schroder AK: *Patient Interviewing: The Human Dimension.* Baltimore, Williams & Wilkins, 1985.

Strain JJ, Grossman S: *Psychological Care of the Medically Ill: A Primer in Liaison Psychiatry.* New York, Appleton-Century-Crofts, 1975, chapters 3 and 10.

References

Basch SH: The intrapsychic integration of a new organ: a clinical study of kidney transplantation. *Psychoanal Q* 42:364, 1973.

Blumenfield M: Patients' fantasies about physical illness. *Psychother Psychosom* 39:171, 1983.

Eisendrath R: The role of grief and fear in the death of kidney transplant patients. *Am J Psychiatry* 126:381, 1969.

Goldstein JH: Personal communication.

Hackett TP, Weisman AD: Psychiatric management of operative syndromes. *Psychosom Med* 22:356, 1960.

Hackett TP, Cassem NH: White vs. blue collar responses to having a heart attack. American Psychosomatic Society Meeting, Boston, 1972.

Kahana RJ, Bibring GL: Personality types in medical management. In Zinberg NE (ed): *Psychiatry and Medical Practice in a General Hospital.* New York, International Universities Press, 1964, p 108.

Meyer BC: Some psychiatric aspects of surgical practice. *Psychosom Med* 20:203, 1958.

Moos RH: Coping with the crisis of physical illness. In Freeman AM, III, Sack RL, Berger PA (eds): *Psychiatry for the Primary Care Physician.* Baltimore, Williams & Wilkins, 1979, p 25.

Reichsman F, Levy NB: Problems in adaptation to hemodialysis: a four-year study of 25 patients. *Arch Int Med* 130:859, 1972.

Strain JJ: *Psychological Interventions in Medical Practice.* New York, Appleton-Century-Crofts, 1978.

Thompson TL, II: Psychiatric aspects of open heart surgery. In Guerra F, Aldrete JA (eds): *Emotional and Psychological Responses to Anesthesia and Surgery.* New York, Grune & Stratton, 1980, p 51.

Viederman M: Psychogenic factors in kidney transplant rejection: a case study. *Am J Psychiatry* 132:957, 1975.

Winnie AP: Personal communication.

9 # The Psychological Aspects of Pain

Troy L. Thompson II, M.D. and
Brandt F. Steele, M.D.

THE IMPORTANCE OF PAIN IN MEDICAL PRACTICE

Pain symptoms are the most common complaint which patients bring to their physicians, and statistics illustrate the importance of understanding the differential diagnosis and appropriate treatments for various types of pain. Recent estimates indicate there were 18 million visits to physicians in the United States in one year for chronic low back pain, and 40% of the disability compensations paid in California in one year were for low back pain. Low back pain is now the most common cause of time lost from work in the United States, surpassing even the common cold. There are also about 12 million visits annually to physicians for chronic headache, and it has been estimated that 40% of Americans suffer some form of pain annually, with an economic cost of billions of dollars. The importance of this data is that the amount of medical care and the amount of disability related to pain symptomology far exceed that associated with any other single symptom.

TYPES OF PAIN

Pain serves the biological function of being a signal indicating the need for action to protect the person from further injury. While this is usually thought of as physical injury, the injury to be avoided may also be psychological in nature and outside the patient's conscious awareness. What we call "pain" is the interpretation in consciousness that certain stimuli reaching the cerebral cortex are signalling that some part of the body is injured. It is a *central* phenomenon profoundly affected by inputs from many nerve tracts and nuclei which contribute to the final mental concept of "pain." Although we commonly say "my toe hurts," we are really reporting the mental concept that stimuli impinging on nerve endings in the toe are unpleasant or damaging.

Neural phenomena which can be interpreted as pain may arise either from the peripheral nervous system, from the viscera, or even from psychological activities not directly related to external stimuli. Thus, we may recognize three general types of pain. In the first, the pain symptoms are directly related to physical injury and are proportional to it. In the second, the pain symptoms are totally psychogenic in nature; that is, they result from psychological conflicts which present in the form of physical symptoms. The third type, which is quite common and may create great difficulties in diagnosis and treatment, occurs when the initial physical injury is accompanied by psychological reactions which alter the character, severity, and duration of the pain, and thereby interfere with the understanding of the original injury and the recovery from it.

Thus, pain is not necessarily prima facie evidence of physical disease or proportional to actual anatomic injury. It cannot be seen, heard, palpated, or easily measured by objective laboratory tests. Even in cases of obvious organic illness it is very often necessary to evaluate the psychological factors which contribute to the patient's subjective interpretations of pain. Exploration of psychological factors is of particular importance in those persons who complain of chronic pain but who have little or no evidence of organic disease. The frequency of such situations is indicated by a report of Devine and

Merskey, who found that in 137 consecutive medical patients who had pain as their chief complaint, 75% had no organic disease focus which could be found.

PHANTOM PAIN

A clear example of the contribution of psychological factors to the sense of pain is that of *phantom pain* phenomena. Sharp pain, burning pain, pressure, or other unpleasant sensations are felt where some part of the body, which has been surgically removed, used to be. It is particularly common following amputated limbs, and as many as one-quarter to one-third of these amputees complain of such painful sensations. Although phantom pain may be explained initially on the basis of sensations generated at the ends of severed nerves, the pain persists long beyond the time when healing has occurred. An amputation causes a major change in the body image which is "painful" to accept, and the patient may be unable to grieve his loss. He psychologically denies it by feeling pain where the amputated part used to be. Such pain may be alleviated by discussing the loss with these patients and helping them deal with their feelings of grief and deformity. Some patients are helped by being told what was actually done in disposing of the amputated part of their bodies.

The following case history demonstrates one type of hidden concern which may underlie a phantom pain syndrome. A 48 year old woman had a surgically successful radical mastectomy for carcinoma of the breast. Afterwards she began to complain of severe pain as if it were in the nipple of the breast which had been removed. It persisted long after her wound had completely healed and was not relieved by several types of analgesic medication, nerve blocks, or surgical procedures to interrupt the pain pathways. Finally, during in-depth interviews, she was embarrassed to relate to her physician that the only time she felt relief was when she sat on her husband's lap and he gently stroked the area where her breast had been amputated. This woman's loss had caused her to feel less feminine and less appealing to her husband. She deeply feared she would not be sexually attractive to him and he would no longer love her. His caresses were reassuring and were the only "treatment" which really relieved the pain. After talking about these fears with her doctor and realizing that her husband did indeed continue to love her, she became less preoccupied with the loss of her breast. The pain soon diminished and eventually disappeared. She no longer "needed" it to maintain the fantasy that she still had her breast and was therefore still attractive.

PHYSIOLOGICAL VARIABLES RELATED TO PAIN TOLERANCE

Individuals vary greatly in their ability to tolerate pain. Both physiological and psychological factors contribute to this variation, but the pain threshold itself appears to be primarily related to several physiological variables. Ronald Melzack and Patrick Wall have postulated a *gate control theory* of pain perception in which there is a neurophysiological "gate" at the spinal cord level which may be opened or closed to incoming pain stimuli. This mechanism, which is still controversial, presumably facilitates or inhibits the intensity of pain stimuli reaching the cortex. According to Melzack and Wall, this "gate" may be affected by many factors associated with increased tolerance to pain, including the positive emotional state of the individual, analgesic drugs, acupuncture, biofeedback, meditation, relaxation exercises, physical activity, behavioral modification through positive reinforcement, hypnosis, guided imagery, and some neurophysiological treatments for pain such as transcutaneous electrical stimulators, brain electrodes, and dorsal column stimulators.

Endorphins and *enkephalins* are endogenously produced morphine-like substances in the central nervous system which may play an important physiological role in mediating the response to pain. Individual variations in the effectiveness of the endorphin system may partially explain the wide variations in pain tolerance among different people, or within the same person at different times and under different circumstances. An individual who is able to produce more (or better utilize) endorphins and enkephalins may be able to tolerate greater pain than the patient who has a relative deficiency in these endogenous morphines.

Some individuals have a *congenital absence of pain sensation*, which is seriously disadvantageous both physically and psychologically. Such individuals are prone to repeated traumatic injuries because they do not have the protective signal function of pain. They may also develop serious psychological problems stemming from the early developmental stage in which self-object differentiation takes place, since pain and discomfort help young children to determine their body boundaries and thereby to differentiate themselves from other people in their environment. Their need for others to interpret and protect them from "painful" reality may also lead to excessive lifelong dependence.

PSYCHOLOGICAL VARIABLES RELATED TO PAIN TOLERANCE

Acute Pain

There are three broad dimensions of pain: sensory, affective, and evaluative. Each is linked less to injury than to the overall body state. Pain must be sensed by the cortex in order to be described as pain. The person must be conscious and focusing attention on the perception to some extent for pain to exist. The immediate response to injury is directed toward protection and to destroying or escaping from the source of injury. Pain is seldom felt during this period. The affective dimension becomes more important in determining the response after the injurious events come under the person's control. Attention is then shifted to caring for the injury. Both *acute pain* and *anxiety* are felt during this stage. Although the pain threshold is largely physiologically determined, pain tolerance and endurance are greatly affected by psychological factors in the individual. Acute pain produces anxiety, and anxiety reduces pain tolerance and endurance; therefore, more pain is experienced by anxious patients. This may become a vicious cycle, but the opposite is also true, in that anxiety-lowering techniques such as meditation and behavior modification may help interrupt this cycle. For example, the Lamaze natural childbirth techniques lower anxiety and thereby increase the patient's pain tolerance. Other types of education about an illness and its treatment may do more to reduce the patient's anxiety level than a tranquilizer — and without the side-effects. The third, or evaluative, dimension relates to the meaning that the person attaches to the pain which is being sensed. As has been noted, the seriousness of the physical injury does not relate in a one-to-one fashion to the intensity of the pain that is subjectively experienced.

The role that the psychological meaning of the injury plays in affecting pain perception has been demonstrated by Henry Beecher. Beecher, a professor of anesthesiology serving in a field hospital during World War II, noticed that seriously wounded soldiers often complained very little of pain and refused pain medication. They were apparently so happy to be alive and to be removed from action that their pain was of little importance to them. Thus, the amount of pain experienced by these wounded soldiers was related to what the wound meant to them. Beecher compared these soldiers to civilians in the United States who experienced wounds with similar amounts of tissue damage. The civilians generally complained more about the pain and requested more analgesics. The civilians lacked the escape-from-danger meaning associated with the soldiers' injuries and usually had nothing to gain by their injury.

A further perspective on the role of psychological factors in the perception of pain is provided through the phenomenon of the elimination of pain sensations through hypnosis. In the previous section on phantom pain it was noted how certain emotional needs lead to the conscious perception of pain in the absence of any organic cause for it. In hypnosis it is possible through psychological mechanisms to create a state of anesthesia which prevents the conscious awareness of pain even though there is clear organic cause for it. Under the hypnotic suggestion that no pain will be felt, teeth can be extracted painlessly without the use of any other anesthetic. Other important practical applications of this phenomenon include the use of hypnosis in childbirth, and also in preventing pain during the frequent changes of dressings on severely burned children. Although the mechanisms involved in hypnotic anesthesia are not clearly understood, it seems obvious that there is an interruption centrally of nerve impulses which would otherwise be interpreted as "pain."

Chronic Pain

The chronic phase of reacting to pain usually involves inactivity of the painful part as a means of facilitating healing, but this inactivity may not always be helpful. In *chronic pain syndromes* or *idiopathic pain disorder* this phase is prolonged beyond the time which is necessary for biological recovery. The chronic pain may become an illness in itself rather than merely a symptom of another illness, and as such it may become a major psychological stress in its own right, causing regression, the emergence of some of the other psychological reactions which were discussed in the previous chapter such as anxiety, anger, and depression, as well as dependency on medication. The body can also change as a result of chronic pain, leading to altered cardiac, respiratory, endocrine, and gastrointestinal function. As only one example, a fear of aggravating the pain may result in limitation of movement, and this in turn can lead to hypoventilation and reduced circulation.

Chronic pain may significantly interrupt many aspects of a person's life. It may disrupt his position in his family and cause him to depend heavily on others. It may cause a decrease in his work abilities which may threaten his job. The hospital and doctor bills and the loss of income may result in significant financial problems. All of these consequences may lead to a great deal of anxiety, anger, and depression as noted above. The person may begin to frantically search for more treatments to relieve his suffering. As with acute pain and anxiety, *chronic pain* and *depression* interact to create a vicious cycle. A depressed person will focus more and more attention on his pain, and as a result become preoccupied with the pain and even more depressed. Treating the depression with appropriate medications and counseling may be necessary in order to break this cycle. Pain centers are beginning to develop around the country, utilizing the knowledge of many medical specialties (anesthesiology, internal medicine, psychiatry, neurology, and neurosurgery). The philosophy that guides all of these pain clinics is the realization that chronic pain is a complex syndrome in which biological, psychological, and sociocultural factors all play a part.

Pain in the Terminally Ill

Patients with advanced cancer or other terminal disorders may live their last months in severe pain. Although medications are available to relieve even the most severe forms of pain, some physicians are reluctant to prescribe them in adequate dosages or frequent enough intervals. Marks and Sachar have found that one of the reasons for this underutilization involves a fear of addicting the patient to a narcotic or other analgesic. Obviously, the fear of addicting someone who has only a few months to live does not make rational sense. However, many physicians are indoctrinated to feel that they are to be held personally responsible for drug addiction in any of their patients. Therefore, they may have great difficulty bringing themselves to prescribe large enough and frequent enough dosages of narcotics, even when they are medically indicated to prevent extreme pain. Terminal patients should be reassured that means are available to alleviate any degree of pain they may have. Patients should also be educated that it is wiser to let the doctor or nurse know when the pain begins or starts to worsen rather than trying to be stoic and long-suffering. Less total medication is often needed if it is given in lower dosages at regular intervals than if the pain is allowed to proceed to an excruciating level before treatment begins. It is also better to begin with a dosage that may be a little too high but will promptly break into the pain cycle, rather than starting too low and slowly titrating upward while the patient's anxiety steadily increases (along with the level of pain), and confidence that the physican can control the pain decreases. Gradually decreasing a slightly excessive dosage after the pain is under control is much easier and more humane.

Postoperative Pain

A similar exaggerated fear of creating addiction in surgical patients is often expressed by physicians and nurses who delay and withhold adequate pain relief in the early postoperative period. This delay only increases and prolongs pain. As a result the patient is likely to feel rejected, uncared for, more sensitive to pain, and not rarely, angry at the staff. Early and prompt relief of pain usually results in less anxiety, less sensitivity to pain, less total dosage of narcotics and earlier elimination of any need for them, as well as earlier postoperative activity. The only contraindications to full use of narcotics are adverse side effects or significant respiratory depression. It has been found that an empathic and thorough explanation of procedures and symptoms before and after surgery significantly reduces anxiety, thereby reducing the sensitivity to pain and the need for analgesics.

Pain and Punishment

The word "pain" is derived from the Greek word meaning punishment, and the two are closely linked from early childhood. Many children are punished through the infliction of some type of pain. In the Bible, Adam and Eve were punished by God for sinning by having pain introduced into their lives. This took the form of pain through childbirth for Eve and pain through hard work for Adam. Their "sins" involved the pleasure of taking a bite out of the forbidden apple from the Tree of Knowledge. Therefore, it is not surprising that many people feel guilty and fear some sort of painful punishment or retribution for becoming curious, for being aggressive, for enjoying pleasures of any kind, especially sexual pleasures, and for achieving success. A patient stated, "I get uncomfortable if things start going too well for me because I expect a disaster around the next corner to balance things out again." The frequency with which some people have accidents raises the possibility that they may be unconsciously bringing punishment on themselves, perhaps related to their fear of things going too well. Such *accident-prone* people may wish to punish themselves for some real or fantasized transgression, or for the psychological meaning that success has come to represent for them.

The Pain-Prone Patient

George Engel has described a group of *pain-prone patients* who repeatedly suffer from one or another type of painful disability without having a significant organic site of injury. They elaborate any pain beyond the degree of physical damage which is present and act as though the damage far exceeds that which is actually present. Engel found many of these patients to be masochistic personalities who unconsciously derive pleasure from pain. He also found that aggression, suffering, and pain were prominent features in the early family relationships of these patients. Harsh punitive attitudes, physical and verbal abuse, and constant threats of aggression as a means of control are common in such families. Painful physical illnesses also are common, and these patients may have learned the advantages of being sick by identifying with someone in their family who experienced illness and who used the illness to control others in the family.

The painful episodes in such pain-prone patients may be precipitated in several ways. Some may have a "success neurosis" in which they "need to punish themselves" if things begin to go too well. Others masochistically need to suffer continually, and feel better only when they are being punished in the long-suffering, martyr role. Some develop their painful symptoms when they experience a real, threatened, or fantasized loss. This may involve the loss of a person who is important to them, the loss of a goal, or the anniversary of an important earlier loss in their life. Pain may also appear if the person experiences excessive guilt, which is frequently associated with forbidden aggressive or sexual wishes. The pain may also represent an identification with an important figure from the past who suffered a similar symptom.

In taking a history from such patients several areas should be carefully evaluated. Did a sick sibling or parent receive inordinate attention because of their illness? Did the patient receive attention only when he or she was sick? Was crying or complaining of pain a way of communicating and obtaining love and affection in the family? Did a sick parent or other relative receive financial compensation by remaining ill? Although pain-prone patients may be found in all sectors of society, there are several factors in addition to those mentioned above which are associated with an increased incidence of this syndrome. These include greater age, lower socioeconomic status, and families of origin which included a greater number of siblings. The patient who has had painful illnesses or experienced painful medical procedures in childhood also tends to be more pain-prone in later life.

Secondary Gain

Many people who are sick experience some form of benefit from being ill. Such benefits are called *secondary gain.* If nothing else, the illness may serve to maintain gratifying relationships with medical health care providers. Some patients have few friends, and being able to see and talk with a physician provides a secondary gain in the form of a continuing social contact. Other patients find that, as long as they remain ill, their family and friends will give them more attention and respect than they do when they are well. In addition, government agencies in our society provide financial aid for those who remain disabled or ill. For those who are truly disabled, such assistance is very humane; however, such financial assistance may prevent some patients from taking the steps which could remedy their problem. The patient who has never enjoyed his or her work, may find that illness and disability payments provide a socially acceptable "out" from such responsibilities.

Some of the possible negative aspects of prolonging the "sick role" are demonstrated in the following case. A young man in his thirties who was a husband and a father had a great many financial and personal responsibilities. He pulled a muscle in his shoulder while doing some yard work and developed intense pain. He went to his physician who took a routine EKG. Unfortunately, the machine was malfunctioning, and he was initially told he had had a myocardial infarction. However, after that was disproved, the shoulder pain persisted and increased in severity. Eventually, he underwent several surgical procedures to interrupt his pain pathways. One of these operations accidentally resulted in a pneumothorax, which necessitated a lengthy hospitalization. He had to be out of work for six months and lost his job. Disability insurance was supporting his family. After discharge he hoped to gradually return to full-time work. However, he was told the insurance payments would stop the first day he went back to work. Since he did not feel ready to begin full-time work and was frightened of losing the insurance, he avoided taking even the simplest job. Realizing that they might have a life-long invalid on their hands unless they were more flexible, the insurance officials agreed to gradual decreases in payment after the patient had begun working. He was able to fully give up the payments and was working full time in about one year.

This man was psychologically susceptible to this "disability neurosis" for several reasons. He was raised in a family where everyone treated him as a frail, helpless child. He had developed a sense of impending disaster about his life and lacked the self-confidence that he could manage adult responsibilities. He had always felt like "an accident is waiting to happen." His self-image was that of a person who was too inadequate and ineffective to be a responsible worker, husband, and father. These fears had been amplified when he was a soldier in a combat area. He was constantly afraid of being injured or killed, and saw the sudden death of many of his buddies. Discussing these fears and gradually reducing the secondary gain he was receiving from his illness were both necessary aspects of his rehabilitation. Abruptly cutting off all of the

disability payments before he was ready to attempt independence would have probably resulted in his remaining a psychogenic invalid for the remainder of his life.

Psychogenic Pain

Psychogenic means "having its beginning in the mind." Therefore, *psychogenic pain* is pain caused by psychological stresses alone and represents an attempt to solve or avoid those stresses through pain. It is more socially acceptable to have a physical, rather than a psychological symptom, so many patients come to the physician with a physical symptom as a "ticket of admission." Some of these patients are aware of their underlying psychological distresses, will speak about them if asked, and can see a connection between those stresses and their pain. Others are completely unaware of any such connections and will deny any connection if one is suggested. The two most common causes of psychogenic pain are *conversion disorder* and *hypochondriasis*. In these two conditions no organic lesions or changes take place, in contrast to the *psychophysiological disorders* in which emotional stresses are associated with the development of actual organic changes in the target organ. All of these disorders will be discussed in the following chapters.

Munchausen's Syndrome (Factitious Disorder)

This syndrome is named for Baron von Munchausen, an 18th century legendary cavalry officer who went from tavern to tavern in Europe making up incredible tales about his supposed adventures. Patients with this syndrome do the same thing by mimicking the pains and other symptoms classically associated with a particular illness. They often go from hospital to hospital seeking elaborate medical procedures and surgery. They may be quite knowledgeable medically and very clever in fooling physicians into treating them for a multitude of disorders. For example, one patient would convince physicians he had hematuria by biting the inside of his cheek and spitting blood into the urinalysis container. Others mix sugar in their urine sample or blood in their stool specimen, carry falsified medical records or X-rays with them, and expertly develop all of the symptoms of an acute abdomen to precipitate a laparotomy. There are many different psychological reasons why patients behave in this sophisticated but ultimately self-destructive fashion. Some are psychotic and want the physician to "look inside" in the delusional hope that he will find and correct their "problem." Others may be quite masochistic and neurotic, and receive gratification of their intense dependency needs by placing their lives repeatedly in the hands of powerful physicians, whereas still others may be angry at doctors or authority figures in general. As one such patient admitted, "I enjoy fooling them and proving that they are stupid and that I am smarter than all of them." If such patients are discovered and confronted, and psychiatric treatment is suggested, they often are enraged and promptly leave the doctor's office or hospital, only to turn up elsewhere, sometimes in a different city. Several of these patients have been followed in the medical literature as they go from great to small medical centers around the world, changing their names and presenting with ever more fantastic symptoms.

The "Doorknob Comment"

The hidden reason behind a patient's pain complaints, the real reason he is coming to see the physician, is often revealed through an offhand comment made when entering or leaving the examining room. Such a "doorknob comment" may take many forms but is often prefaced with, "Oh, by the way, doctor." For example, "I really shouldn't be bothering you today, doctor, I'm sure I don't have heart disease or anything like that," will usually reflect an underlying fear of heart disease. Or as the patient leaves the office, he may say "So, you don't think I'm dying of cancer, right Doc?", even though he has mentioned nothing about a symptom he fears is caused by cancer during the examination. Other examples are, "Should I leave my disability form with your nurse on the way out?" or "So I guess having a little sex won't cause my ticker to break again?" The latter comment was made by a patient who was having difficulty returning to work and who developed marital and sexual problems following a myocardial infarction. He was afraid that returning to work and resuming an active sexual life would bring about another myocardial infarction and death. Too often, physicians ignore

"Let's schedule a follow-up for this wonderful patient —in seven or eight years."

Figure 9.1. Reproduced with permission from *More Cartoon Classics From Medical Economics.* Copyright © 1966 by Medical Economics Book Division, Inc., Oradell, New Jersey. All rights reserved.

such comments or brush them aside with a simple "Don't worry about that" or "Everyone has those problems at your age." Even though the patient is leaving the office and the busy physician is behind with the day's appointments, he or she should take another minute to explore these "doorknob comments." The patient may have been too anxious to reveal the real reason he made the appointment until he has one foot out the door. If a significant worry surfaces, it should be discussed then and there at least briefly, and then another appointment should be set up to do so at greater length, to insure that a hidden symptom is not being overlooked and that worried patients will have their questions answered and their anxieties allayed. The cartoon in Figure 9.1 may express the hostility that many physicians feel toward these patients, but it is not a very helpful way of dealing with them. Sensitivity in the physician to a patient's concerns is the cornerstone of establishing good doctor-patient relationships, and these are essential to managing the psychological reactions to pain and to physical illness.

Suggested Readings

Engel, G.L. "Psychogenic pain" and the pain-prone patient. *Am J Med* 26:899, 1959.
Hackett, TP: The pain patient: evaluation and treatment. In

Hackett TP, Cassem NH (eds): *Massachusetts General Hospital Handbook of General Hospital Psychiatry*. St. Louis, C. V. Mosby, 1978, p 41.

Luce JM, Thompson TL, Getto CJ, Byyny RL: New concepts of chronic pain and their implications. *Hospital Pract* April 1979, p 113.

Strain JJ, Grossman S: *Psychological Care of the Medically Ill: A Primer in Liaison Psychiatry*. New York, Appleton-Century-Crofts, 1975, chapters 7 and 8.

References

Beecher HK: Relationship of significance of wound to pain experience. *JAMA*, 161:1609, 1966.

Blumer D, Heilbronn M: The pain-prone disorder: a clinical and psychological profile. *Psychosomatics* 22:395, 1981.

Devine R, Merskey H: The description of the pain in psychiatric and general medical patients. *J Psychsom Res* 9:311, 1965.

Dubovsky SL, Groban SE: Congenital absence of sensation. *Psychoanal Study Child* 30:49, 1975.

Marks RM, Sachar EJ: Undertreatment of medical inpatients with narcotic analgesics. *Ann Int Med* 78:173, 1973.

Melzack R, Wall PD: Pain mechanics: a new theory. *Science* 150:971, 1965.

Meyer BC: Some psychiatric aspects of surgical practice. *Psychosom Med* 20:203, 1958.

Perry S: The undermedication for pain: a psychoanalytic perspective. *Bull Assoc Psychoanal Med* 22:77, 1983.

Spiro HR: Chronic factitious illness: Munchausen's syndrome. *Arch Gen Psychiatry* 18:569, 1968.

Wall PD: On the relation of injury to pain. The John J. Bonica Lecture. *Pain* 6:253, 1979.

10 Conversion Disorder

Norman B. Levy, M.D.

CONVERSION AND PERSONALITY

Conversion disorders are physical symptoms. Hence, they are also commonly seen by nonpsychiatric physicians, in particular family or general practitioners and also all other clinical specialists. Conversion disorders make up a considerable portion of the large number of patients who present at a physician's office with physical symptoms but without objective evidence of organic etiology. In contrast, the *histrionic* or *hysterical personality* describes a theatrical, seductive, emotionally labile personality. Historically the term "hysteria" is derived from the belief that these people suffered from a "wandering of the womb," and the condition was originally thought to be limited to women. However, many men also have hysterical personalities. The message, though masqueraded in terms of sexual seductiveness, often does not involve a true genital sexual desire, but rather a wish on the part of the hysterical person to be cared for. Therefore, the message is, "Come closer so that you can care for me," rather than, "so that we can have sexual intercourse." The hysterical personality tends to be more prone toward conversion symptoms, but conversion disorders are not limited to the hysterical personality. They occur among the whole range of personality types.

WHAT IS CONVERSION?

In conversion what is converted? It is a conflict between a wish and a prohibition. The wish can neither be consciously recognized nor carried through to action and is therefore converted into *symbolic body language*. This maintains *repression* of the wish, excluding it from consciousness and blocking it from action. Let me give an example of a conversion disorder.

A 29 year old white Italian-American construction worker was brought into the emergency room because of severe chest pain while engaging in sexual intercourse. The pain covered the left side of his chest, was knife-like in character, and intermittent, lasting one to three seconds and then stopping for one to three seconds. In the emergency room he was described as appearing calm, and was without physical findings. But because of a questionable electrocardiogram he was admitted to the medical ward for observation with a diagnosis of "rule out acute myocardial infarction."

On the ward a more detailed history was taken by the medical student and also by the liaison consultant. It revealed the following information. The patient did not actually develop the chest pain while having intercourse, but rather while he was with a woman who wanted to have sexual intercourse. They were in an advanced state of foreplay when he developed the pain. The couple then dressed and came to the emergency room. The patient had a past history of abdominal pains as a young child involving both lower quadrants, for which he received an appendectomy at the age of 16. Pathology lab findings were "normal appendix." A few months after the operation he developed upper quadrant abdominal pain. A diagnosis of gallbladder disease was tentatively made, and it was recommended that he receive gallbladder X-rays, but he did not. He also had a history of headaches which caused him to be away from work about one day each month.

One year prior to the onset of the current problem, his father had died, a man about whom the patient had many mixed feelings. His father died in the apartment of a young woman with whom he had been having an extramarital affair. The cause of death was attributed to a coronary. Family and friends jested that his father, a man with a reputation of being a Don Juan, had died of too much sex while in the act of making love. The patient had been most sensitive about this "joke," failing to see any humor in it and, indeed, finding any discussion of his father's death extremely anxiety provoking. Further history taking revealed the possibility that the patient may actually have been a virgin, or at least very limited in his sexual experiences.

In 19th century Vienna, Freud and Breuer were the first to describe the psychological aspects of this illness. It was the first psychological illness that Freud studied, understandably so for a neurologist. In late 19th century Vienna, the symptoms of conversion disorder tended to be rather dramatic. Gross tremors mimicking epilepsy were so common then that all conversions were divided into two groups, those with and those without epileptic-like seizures. Major paralyses of the voluntary muscles were also common presentations of conversion disorder, as well as sudden disruptions of the sense organs resulting in blindness, deafness, and global anesthesias. But that is no longer the case. Among most people today conversion disorders generally do not present in that way. They are more subtle and less dramatic. Nowadays the most common presentation of conversion disorder is in the form of *acute psychogenic pain*, as contrasted to chronic idiopathic pain, which is often due to a complex interaction between psychological and organic factors. I should add that the 3rd Edition of the *Diagnostic and Statistical Manual of Mental Disorders* (DSM-III) states that conversion disorder should not be diagnosed if the symptom is limited to pain. However, many workers in the field of consultation-liaison psychiatry do not agree with this restrictive definition. As was the case with the patient I just presented, acute psychogenic pain is a common form of conversion disorder in this country.

Let me recount a second case. A 21 year old soldier going into battle developed a paralysis of his right hand. Here, the wish is obvious, at least obvious to everyone but the soldier. The blocked wish is that he not go into battle. It may have something to do with his fear of his desire to kill, which has to be repressed and blocked from action. It may also have to do with his fear of being killed. The conflict presents itself in the body language of paralysis which can be understood symbolically if one knows the language. In the case of the 29 year old construction worker, the conflict is less apparent. His chest pain tells us that his symptom has something to

do with conflict over an identification with his father and conflict over sexual activity. The chest pain symbolically expresses his wish to be like his father, his fear of dying as his father did, and a prohibition against competing with his father.

OTHER CHARACTERISTICS OF CONVERSION

What are the other characteristics of conversion disorder? Remember that I said that conversion is a psychological illness, not an organic disease. Therefore, the pathway for the expression of conversion symptoms will *not* be pathophysiological, but rather will be determined by the mind's representation of that part of the body. For example, let us look back again at the case of the construction worker. Pathophysiologically, the innervations of the heart are such that myocardial ischemia presents itself not through precordial pain, but more characteristically through substernal pain, which is pressing or squeezing in quality rather than knifelike. The pain also tends to be persistent rather than intermittent, and tends to radiate to the left axilla and then to the medial portion of the left arm, left forearm, and left hand. This patient's presentation was not consistent with the pathophysiology of myocardial ischemia, which he did not know. The patient was involved in a psychological process and it was his psychological representation of what heart pain is that determined his symptoms.

I was once asked a question by a third year medical student having to do with just this point. The student had a patient with a midline anesthesia and had forgotten whether this was a characteristic of a conversion or of organic illness. It is unlikely that any symptom which is midline could involve pathophysiology because the innervations of the body are not linear. Such linearity would more likely have to do with the psychic representation of the body. The same is true for "glovelike" anesthesias of the hands and for "stocking" anesthesias of the legs.

I want to give an example of this point using a painting. Figure 10.1 is a painting entitled, *St. Francis in Ecstasy*. It is a beautiful and mystical 14th century painting in the Frick Museum in New York City. Look at St. Francis' hands. He has developed the stigmata of crucifixion in imitation of Christ. Here the lesion adheres to a

Figure 10.1. *Saint Francis in Ecstasy* by Giovanni Bellini. (Copyright The Frick Collection, New York, N.Y. Published by permission.)

mental concept of crucifixion rather than the anatomic reality, because, as we know from anatomy, a person's body weight could not be supported by nails through the palms. Crucifixion more likely took place with the victim having his wrists pierced by the nails.

A third characteristic of conversion is the choice of symptom, which often involves an *identification with an ambivalently held love object*. In the case of the 29 year old construction worker, the ambivalently held object was his father, and the patient's chest pain emulated the symptom which caused his father's death. Expressed another way, the son is trying to be like his father but is also unable to perform like him because of the conflicts surrounding their relationship.

A fourth characteristic often seen in conversions is *a history of a previous use of body language as a method of expression of conflict*. To return to our example of the construction worker, remember that he is a man who had an appendectomy for an anatomically normal appendix, after which he developed upper abdominal pain. He also had headaches a good deal of his life, causing absence from work one day a month. So, in all likelihood, he has used conversion symptoms in the past in the form of various bodily pains as a method of dealing with conflict. Usually by the time a patient presents himself to a physician with this illness, he has had a long past history of various conversion symptoms. It is rare that the physician sees conversion used for the first time.

A fifth characteristic of conversion disorder is a relative indifference shown by the patient to his symptoms, *la belle indifference*, beautiful indifference. In this same case, the patient in the emergency room was described as appearing calm. In conversion there tends to be a disparity between the severity of the "physical" symptoms and the intensity of the emotions shown by the patient. Usually a patient coming into an emergency room with a myocardial infarction is in great terror. This is a life-threatening disease with pain usually of great severity. In the patient having a heart attack there is usually some awareness, even among the most unsophisticated, that life is threatened. There is some body communication to the victim that he has an immediately life-threatening disease. Here, however, our patient presented himself relatively calmly. Why does this occur? In conversion disorder there is an unconscious awareness that the symptom involves a compromise, and therefore a temporary solution to a distressing conflict. This construction worker was being "relieved" by his chest pain of the challenge of having intercourse with a woman, thereby avoiding competition with his father and possibly dying as his father did. Therefore his presentation to the emergency room was not all "bad" for him, and his calm affect revealed his relief.

However, relative indifference is neither that unique a symptom nor so consistently present in conversion that it can in itself be diagnostic. There are many other reasons why people may present with indifference. For example, some people have certain defense mechanisms against anxiety which enable them to deny or isolate their feelings about a particular event or even a very serious organic illness.

Lastly, and very intentionally lastly, is the *absence of actual organic change* as a characteristic of conversion. There is no organic change because this is not a physical illness. It is a psychological illness expressed symbolically in physical terms. There are some exceptions to what I just said, such as stigmata and some other skin lesions. But in the vast majority of cases there are no actual organic changes. I have saved this characteristic of conversion for last quite intentionally, because usually these patients tend to be presented to liaison consultation services or on medical rounds as having a primarily psychological illness only after extensive work-up has shown no physical abnormal-

ity. In other words, the diagnosis has been made by exclusion and was not even considered among the initial differential diagnoses. This is a very frequent occurrence, and it is a most unfortunate one. It is best if a diagnosis of conversion is made before the patient is subjected to extensive physical examinations and laboratory testing, and the reason is more than just economic. It is also psychologic. The more extensive the work-up, the greater the impression the patient is given that he has a physical abnormality and the greater the tendency for the patient to be locked into his conversion disorder. This does not mean that I am suggesting that physical illness should not be ruled out, but too often the psychological aspects tend to be considered only when no physical abnormality is found. To the informed physician, characteristics other than the absence of physical signs enable the diagnosis of conversion to be made early or at least highly suspected.

THE TREATMENT OF CONVERSION

As I have just indicated, it is important that, wherever possible, the diagnosis be made early so that the patient can be reassured that his or her problem is not a physical one. Patients with conversion symptoms tend to be highly responsive to suggestion and reassurance. Conversion symptoms are often an *acute reaction* to some stress, and these patients may improve suddenly and dramatically with proper brief treatment and reassurance. However, their involvement in their physical symptoms is usually highly entrenched, and as a group they tend to be highly resistive to treatment by a psychiatrist. Of course, the motivated patient with conversion symptoms should be referred for psychiatric treatment. But, it is largely the nonpsychiatrist's task to treat these patients. At times patients with conversion symptoms need to be given a nonpsychiatric diagnosis, a benign one from which they know they will recover. In every case these patients need an understanding doctor who will respond empathically to their total life situation.

DIFFERENTIAL DIAGNOSIS

Conversion disorder should be distinguished from *hypochondriasis*, from *malingering*, and from the *psychophysiological disorders*. Dr.

Rhine and Dr. Thompson will discuss hypochondriasis in the next chapter. Conversion disorder and malingering often have the same dynamic roots, but the essential difference is that malingering is conscious and conversion disorder is unconscious. In regard to the psychophysiological disorders, conversion is a symptom in which a psychological conflict is expressed symbolically in physical symptoms without actual organic changes. Psychophysiological disorders, on the other hand, refer to a group of physical illnesses in which there are actual organic changes, and in which psychological factors play a major role in the onset and in exacerbations. I will discuss these psychophysiological disorders in Chapter 12, along with the important concept of "the giving-up-given-up complex."

Suggested Readings

Breuer J, Freud S (1895): Studies on hysteria. In *The Standard Edition of the Complete Psychological Works of Sigmund Freud*, vol 2, p 3. London, Hogarth Press, 1955.

Lazare A: Conversion symptoms. In Sederer LI (ed): *Inpatient Psychiatry: Diagnosis and Treatment.* Baltimore, Williams & Wilkins, 1983, p 157.

Rangell L: The nature of conversion. *J Am Psychoanal Assoc* 7:632, 1959.

Mark W. Rhine, M.D. and
Troy L. Thompson II, M.D.

HYPOCHONDRIA

Like many other psychological symptoms, most people have some degree of *hypochondria* (an overconcern with their health and bodily functioning) at certain times in their life. These concerns are often increased during periods of stress. For example, medical students often develop symptoms of the illnesses they are studying. This is especially a problem for them during times of stress, such as final examinations, but hopefully not because this is the first time they have studied the illness! A common stress-precipitated problem for many people is the *irritable colon syndrome*. This syndrome has been referred to by many names, including: functional bowel, spastic colon, mucous colitis, and nervous diarrhea. It is one of the most common and troublesome afflictions seen by physicians and is a leading cause of absenteeism from work. The symptoms usually include intermittent, diffuse, lower abdominal pain accompanied by either diarrhea or constipation. It is a diagnosis of exclusion and is often called "functional" because no demonstrable bowel disease or structural defects can be found.

Many people come to physicians with such symptoms fearing they have a serious illness. These patients are often derogatorily called the "worried well." A physician in general practice said he needed to know the diagnosis of patients on medically oriented television programs each week and the diagnosis of any patients discussed in Readers' Digest that month because many of his mildly hypochondriacal patients would come in fearful they had the same illness. These patients may also fear they have a disease which has been receiving widespread attention, due to a famous person having developed it or a national educational or solicitation campaign. These "worried and distressed" patients usually feel reassured and stop worrying about the illness if they are told they do not have it.

HYPOCHONDRIASIS

The illness of true *hypochondriasis* begins if the patient develops a chronically exaggerated concern over his physical health which interferes with his personal life or work. He may become obsessively concerned about some organ or illness, and feel he is incurably ill. The psychodynamic explanation of such symptoms is that anxiety is being displaced from some psychological conflict onto a bodily concern. The patient is unaware of the conflict existing in the unconscious portion of his mind. Often the organ which is selected for these concerns is one which is subject to the physiological expression of anxiety. Organ systems which are commonly associated with such anxiety include the gastrointestinal tract (*the irritable colon syndrome*), the heart and lungs (*the hyperventilation syndrome*), the skin and sweat glands (*hyperhidrosis*). In addition, muscles which are affected by muscular tension secondary to anxiety are also often involved, leading to a general feeling of weakness and fatigue, and the very common symptom of *tension headaches*.

TYPES OF HYPOCHONDRIASIS

Hostile Type

There are two broad diagnostic types of hypochondriacal patients. The first is the hostile type. They deny any dependency needs and must defend against feeling weak by being angry and "untreatable." They will dwell on their suffering and sacrifices, and often avoid physicians altogether. Dostoyevsky has given us the ultimate description of such a patient in *Notes From*

Underground:

I am a sick man ... I am a spiteful man. I am an unattractive man. I believe my liver is diseased. However, I know nothing at all about my disease, and do not know for certain what ails me. I don't consult a doctor for it, and never have, though I have a respect for medicine and doctors. Besides, I am extremely superstitious, sufficiently so to respect medicine, anyway (I am well educated enough not to be superstitious, but I am superstitious). No, I refuse to consult a doctor from spite. That you probably will not understand. Well, I understand it though. Of course, I can't explain who it is precisely that I am mortifying in this case by my spite: I am perfectly well aware that I cannot 'pay out' the doctors by not consulting them: I know better than anyone that by all this I am only injuring myself and no one else. But still, if I don't consult a doctor it is from spite. My liver is bad, well — let it get worse!

Dependent Type

The second may be called the dependent type. They unconsciously want a passive, childlike relationship with the physician, who is viewed as a strong authority figure. They will continue to complain and the physician will continue to try to help these "poor unfortunate people" with their suffering. Unfortunately, if the physician does not recognize the underlying hypochondriasis, the patient will not be helped, as the following letter to the head of a hospital surgical clinic documents:

Dear Dr.

I am writing to you again to see if you can be of any help. I wrote to you in April of this year. You advised me to see one of the gynecologists at your clinic. I did come out to see Dr. Smith. After we talked awhile, he thought I should see a psychiatrist, since I had had a lot of X-rays and tests and there didn't seem to be anything organically wrong. I didn't think and still don't feel that a psychiatrist would be of any help. I didn't even stay to let Dr. Smith examine me I was so disgusted, but he called my husband at work which I didn't exactly appreciate either, and told him that maybe a chiropractor would be of some help. Well, I went to one then and he said that it seemed to him that all my nerves and muscles were all

tied up in a knot, which is just what it feels like to me. He didn't want to work on me as he didn't feel that he could help me, but advised me to go to a neurosurgeon which I did. He told me that what I really needed was a real good general surgeon. I asked him to recommend one, but he said he couldn't. I am having trouble turning over and getting up and down. Now I have been like this ever since I had my first surgery in November of 1973. At that time I kept asking the doctor what was causing this and why I was having all the muscle spasms and he just kept saying he didn't know and wouldn't bother to find out either. Now I know there is something wrong somewhere and I am getting so tired of packing this load around I don't know what to do. In August of this year I went home and had some X-rays as I had been passing some horrible stuff in my stools and they just had a terrible odor to them. They put me on a fiber restricted diet and I kept on it even after I came home and kept passing gas and also I lost three pounds since August 9, and it doesn't seem to make any difference how little I eat I don't lose any more weight. Now I can feel something move in my lower abdomen. Sometimes so violently that it wakes me up at night. I have about come to the conclusion that they may have left something inside me or I have a fibroid tumor that they missed as he said I have these. Now I do know that it is possible that I could have had one on the outside of the uterus as this happened to a friend of mine, but her doctor had made her incision in the middle of her abdomen and found it but my doctor made his incision cross-wise and real low and it's possible that it could have been missed. Now another thing is that I have two places in my back that are just like small breaks, something is just pulling my back apart. I was trying to take some physical therapy treatments but they are just killing me. I am sure they would help my back if I had this thing out of my lower abdomen. I know this sounds like a weird story and you know if this wasn't happening to me and someone tried to tell me this, I would think they were a little rocky, but since it is happening to me, I just can't understand why, with the different doctors I have gone to, someone won't get to the bottom of things. You are just about my last hope as I don't believe I would trust any of these that I have gone to lately. I know I wouldn't let one of them operate on me. When I first saw some of them, they would say yes there was something wrong and then turn around and say there wasn't anything wrong.

Thank you,
Mrs.

This letter documents in exquisite detail the frustration of not only the patient but also of her physicians. Like so many of these patients, she has seen a good number of physicians, either because they refer her on out of their own desperation, or because she goes "doctor shopping" in the hope of finally finding somebody who can cure her. Yet, despite a wide variety of diagnostic tests and therapeutic regimens, her symptoms are no better. Not only have her physicians been unable to help her, but she relates that they seem to have lost interest in her. As so often happens, a psychiatric referral is finally suggested, but again as is so common, the patient rejects the idea, feeling that she has a physical problem and not an emotional one. Nevertheless, in spite of her disappointments with physicians, she continues in her search, and tells the head of the surgical clinic that he is her last hope. Should he become involved in the patient's care, we can predict that the story will go on unchanged, and that eventually he will prove to be as incompetent as her previous physicians (Figure 11.1). If such a patient will not accept referral for a psychiatric consultation, the physician should still speak with a psychiatrist to plan the best therapeutic approach.

THE FRUSTRATION OF THE PHYSICIAN

In the doctor's office, the hypochondriacal patient will present his or her complaints in the same monotonous detail as did this woman in her letter. As Lyon has pointed out, the doctor does not take a history from such a patient, but rather the patient gives a history, oblivious to any questions or comments the physician might want to make. The patient's bodily complaints are diffuse and generalized and involve various areas of the body, hence the sarcastic term "organ recital" often applied by weary physicians to these lengthy stories (Figure 11.2). Such patients seem to be aware of the most trivial physical sensations and describe the gravest consequences to minor aches, gas, or blemishes which most of us would ignore. At times, rather than complaining of symptoms, they will complain of a specific disease, generally a serious or even a fatal disorder. They talk at length of their illness, but rarely of anything else such as personal relationships or other interests.

The doctor's frustration stems from the fact that, although he can demonstrate no organic illness in spite of repeated diagnostic tests, the patient does not respond to reassurance and does not get well. Although there may be a brief

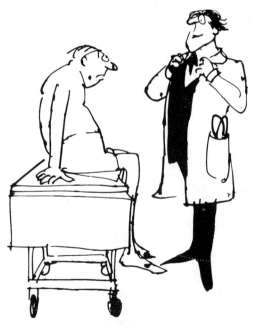

"Orthodox medicine has not found an answer to your complaint. However, luckily for you, I happen to be a quack."

Figure 11.1. Drawing by Richter. Copyright © 1969. The New Yorker Magazine, Inc.

"My eyes, ears, nose and throat hurt!"

Figure 11.2. Reproduced with permission from *Cartoon Classics From Medical Economics.* Copyright © 1963 by Medical Economics Book Division, Oradell, New Jersey. All rights reserved.

response to a change in treatment regimen, it is only temporary, and the patient returns to complain again of the fact that he or she is feeling no better. Since many people go into medicine to help others get over their illnesses, such patients who do not get better will eventually evoke a number of strong reactions in us. The physician begins to feel inadequate, helpless, guilty, irritated, even infuriated at this patient who is taking up his time when he might be treating somebody who is "really sick." It is this frustration that has inspired such labels as "crock," "turkey," "gomer" (an acronym for *get out of my emergency room* or *grand old man of the emergency room*), "wadao" (*weak and dying all over*), and "gok" (*God only knows*). At this point the phenomenon of "referred pain" may come into play — that is, referral to another clinic or colleague, often the newest doctor in town! Such feelings are human and are inevitable with such difficult patients, but nevertheless it is important, when we experience such feelings, that we ask ourselves what it is about the patient that disturbs us so. With hypochondriacal patients, we are often frustrated by our inability to help them get well.

UNDERSTANDING THE HYPOCHONDRIACAL PATIENT

How is it possible to resolve such a dilemma? It is important to understand that, since the patient continues to be sick in spite of all endeavors to help, the patient has a *need to be sick.* This may seem like a strange idea until we recall the instances when we ourselves may have used illness to get out of some undertaking which was unpleasant to us. Hypochondriacal patients tend to be individuals who have become overwhelmed by the tasks and stresses of life. Many of them have come from very deprived childhood backgrounds, frequently having to take on adult responsibilities at a very early age, often having to care for a sick parent or sibling. Later in life, when confronted with difficult tasks, they seem unconsciously to feel that it is now their turn to be taken care of and to be ill. Others may have discovered that the only time in their childhood when they received attention or affection from their parents was when they were ill, and they began to learn to use illness as a way of gaining the love and nurturance that otherwise was unavailable. Many of these dynamics are similar

to those described earlier for the pain-prone patient. Hypochondriacal patients have a very low self-esteem, and somehow seem to displace the sense that there is something wrong with themselves on to a worry that something is wrong with their body. Hypochondriacal concerns often increase during the involutional period of life (45 years of age and older) as certain physiological processes begin to fail, and as this loss in physical health and strength is accompanied by the loss of friends and loved ones through illness and death. In fact depression is frequently an important underlying factor in hypochondriasis.

We again want to emphasize that this process goes on at an unconscious level, out of the patient's awareness. It is as if these patients are unconsciously asking for the doctor to take care of them, as they were not taken care of as a child. Because such dependency wishes are not acceptable to the patient, they are denied and kept unconscious, and consciously the patient is aware only of a wish to get better. The physician, however, must understand that in spite of the conscious plea for help by the hypochondriacal patient, this patient has an unconscious need to remain sick. If the physician can understand and tolerate the patient's need to stay sick, and understand that all attempts at cure will be fruitless, the physician can then play a very useful role with such patients, and will also find his or her practice much more gratifying. It is useful to remember that there is nothing in the Hippocratic oath which requires physicians to cure all of their patients. But we are bound to *refrain from doing harm* to our patients. In the case of the hypochondriacal patient, it is harmful to initially confront the patient directly with the underlying psychological nature of his problem and his unconscious need to remain sick.

TREATING THE HYPOCHONDRIACAL PATIENT

If attempts to remove the patient's symptoms are not beneficial, what approach will work? First, we should not tell the patient, "It's all in your head," or imply that the symptoms are not real. Even though we may not be able to demonstrate organic pathology, the symptoms that the hypochondriacal patient experiences are indeed real, as real as any experienced by a patient with organic pathology. We should also not offer the empty reassurance, "There's nothing wrong with you." We should accept the patient as sick, and not attempt to take away his or her sick role. We should not promise a cure (which will be a relief to the patient who is experiencing a secondary gain from the illness), though we should indicate our interest in the patient's illness and our interest in following him to see if we can be of some assistance. It is important, however, to acknowledge to the patient (and even more importantly to ourselves) our limits in relieving his suffering. Perhaps the single most therapeutic action that we can take is to offer a return appointment. This appointment does not have to be a long one, and as time goes on such patients may be managed with very brief visits every two or three months.

The physician should not be afraid to charge for his time, which is a very valuable commodity to these patients. Diagnostic tests should be kept to a minimum and medications, when used, should be as innocuous as possible. It probably will not be possible to completely eliminate tests and medications, because they are an expected part of most medical treatment. Indeed, returning to the physician for medication may be the "symbol of sickness" that the patient can use to justify a continuing involvement with the doctor without having to acknowledge to himself that he really wants or needs a relationship with the doctor. Although one does not have to spend a long amount of time with such a patient, it is important during the time that is spent to listen carefully and respectfully to the patient's complaints. Initially all patients will spend the time reciting a long list of somatic complaints; as time goes on, however, some patients may begin to mention problems at home, at work, and so on, and it is then crucially important to respond to these psychosocial concerns. Occasionally it is possible to point out to the patient the connection of some external stress with an exacerbation of his physical symptoms, but great tact must be used here since most hypochondriacal patients are very resistant to seeing any emotional factors in their illness. Finally, one should be committed to following the patient on a long-term basis. If we find ourselves wanting to refer the patient, it is important to ask ourselves why. Psychiatric referrals are often refused by the hypochondriacal patient, and therefore the management of the hypochondriacal patient usually becomes the responsibility of the general practitioner or internist. The essence of treatment is the establishment of a supportive, sustaining relationship with one physician.

It is important to cut down on "doctor shopping" for another reason. If one physician follows the patient, he can be alert for changes in the patient's story which may indicate a true organic illness, necessitating further investigation. It is important to remember that hypochondriasis does not make one immune to physical illness. Despite the cartoon in Figure 11.3 hypochondriacal patients, like all the rest of us, do die of something. The above guidelines, based as all treatment should be upon an understanding of the patient's illness, can change the treatment of the hypochondriacal patient from a frustrating ordeal to a constructive aspect of one's medical practice.

DIFFERENTIAL DIAGNOSIS

Certain other conditions where there are somatic complaints without evidence of organic pathology may be confused with hypochondriasis. The malingerer can usually be identified because of the lack of a chronic medical history and because of some obvious immediate secondary gain from the illness, such as disability compensation or avoiding jail or a law suit. Certain normal individuals may be worried about their health, as the middle-age man who fears that he may have cardiac symptoms after several friends have had myocardial infarctions, or the preg-

"He didn't really die of anything. He was a hypochondriac."

Figure 11.3.   Drawing by Geo. Price. Copyright © 1970. The New Yorker Magazine, Inc.

Table 11.1*

Differential Diagnosis of Conversion Disorder and Hypochondriasis

	Conversion Disorder	Hypochondriasis
Definition	A *symbolic* expression of emotional conflicts in physical symptoms	A more *generalized* diffuse expression of emotional conflicts in physical symptoms
Personality type	Often seen in histrionic or hysterical personalities	Often seen in depressed and dependent personalities
Primary defense mechanism	Repression	Denial
Primary symptoms	Pain, or a single sensory (anesthesia) or motor (paralysis) difficulty	Pain, long history of multiple complaints, "organ recital," rarely a specific anesthesia or paralysis
Reaction to the illness	May show "la belle indifference"	Usually anxious and worried about the symptoms: wants tests, procedures, and medications; "doctor shopping"
Onset	Often an acute reaction to stress	Usually a chronic reaction to stress–a "way of life"
Response to treatment	May respond suddenly and dramatically to treatment	Rarely improves quickly–a chronic illness that usually requires long term supportive treatment

* Table by Richard C. Simons.

nant woman who fears that her mild abdominal pains may herald the onset of a miscarriage, but these individuals differ from the hypochondriacal patient in that they respond well to reassurance from the physician. The overtly depressed patient may show a preoccupation with somatic symptoms, but in addition will show other signs of depression such as sadness, guilt, insomnia, loss of appetite, and weight loss. The grieving patient may have a variety of somatic symptoms, but the history of a recent loss coupled with sadness and crying should alert the physician to an acute grief reaction. The somatic delusions of the schizophrenic patient have frequently such a bizarre quality that it is usually possible to differentiate them readily, along with the other symptoms of the schizophrenic illness. The patient with an organic mental disorder may focus on somatic complaints in order to avoid recognition of his failing mental capacities, but the latter can be demonstrated on a

mental status examination where disorientation, memory loss, impaired attention span, and other deficits will be evident. Finally, as Dr. Simons has summarized in Table 11.1, patients with conversion disorder differ from hypochondriacal patients in a number of rather distinct ways.

Suggested Readings

Barsky AJ, Klerman GL: Overview: hypochondriasis, bodily complaints, and somatic styles. *Am J Psychiatry* 140:273, 1983.

Dubovsky SL, Weissberg MP: Hypochondriasis. In *Clinical Psychiatry in Primary Care*, ed 2. Baltimore, Williams & Wilkins, 1982, p. 1.

Ford CV: *The Somatizing Disorders: Illness as a Way of Life.* New York, Elsevier Science, 1983.

Lipsitt DR: Medical and psychological characteristics of "crocks." *Psychiatry Med* 1:15, 1970.

Lipsitt DR: Psychodynamic considerations of hypochondriasis. *Psychother Psychosom* 23:132, 1974.

Luparello TJ: For some, illness pays. *Med Insight* 6:24, 1974.

Lyon JM: On the treatment of hypochondriasis. *Mount Airy Foundation Bulletin*, Denver, Colorado, Summer 1974.

CHAPTER **12** # The Psychophysiological Disorders: An Overview

Norman B. Levy, M.D.

Although the term "psychosomatic disease" is somewhat archaic and even misleading, it remains in common usage and is synonymous with *psychophysiological disorders*. The term refers to those illnesses in which the onset and exacerbation of organic disease are commonly seen in association with emotional distress. Examples of illnesses which have been termed "psychosomatic" include bronchial asthma, peptic ulcer, ulcerative colitis, essential hypertension, rheumatoid arthritis, neurodermatitis, and thyrotoxicosis. In recent years, the number of organic illnesses considered as "psychosomatic" has broadened beyond these original seven.

Every psychological illness has a physical component, and every physical disease has a psychological component. Anxiety is or may be associated with rapid heart beat, perspiration, dilation of pupils, and other somatic concomitants. Similarly, depression is also often associated with physical concomitants such as change of appetite, difficulty sleeping, and dryness of the mouth. There are also some psychophysiological reactions that are so common that everyone of us has experienced them. For example, anxiety may often be expressed somatically by episodes of diarrhea or urinary urgency, symptoms well-known to many medical students just before their examinations.

OVERVIEW OF PSYCHOSOMATIC CONCEPTS

Although the connection between mind and body was described by Hippocrates and other ancients, the term "psychosomatic" was not coined until 1818 and then not by a physician, but by the poet, Coleridge. Psychophysiological conditions were studied by Sandor Ferenczi, Felix Deutsch, and other early psychoanalysts who conceived of them in terms of unconsciously displaced expressions of conflict, akin to conversion symptoms. It was not until the 1930's and the work of Flanders Dunbar that the psychological components of these diseases were systematically described. Dunbar found both common personalities and common conflictual constellations among patients suffering from the same psychophysiological illnesses. She termed this the *personality profile*. In her view there are characteristics of personality style in each psychophysiological illness which distinguish it from other psychophysiological illnesses.

In the 1940's Franz Alexander (Figure 12.1) systematically separated the psychophysiological disorders from conversion disorder on the basis of involvement of the autonomic or sensory-motor nervous systems, respectively, and also on the basis of involvement of smooth muscle or skeletal muscle, respectively. Skeletal muscle and the sensory system were supposedly affected by conversion disorder, whereas smooth muscle was supposedly affected by the psychophysiological disorders via the vegetative or autonomic nervous system. He further divided the psychophysiological disorders themselves into the disorders of the parasympathetic autonomic nervous system and the sympathetic autonomic nervous system.

Alexander's concepts may be understood in terms of the fact that man is virtually the only animal which develops psychophysiological disorders under ordinary life situations. There are certain exceptions. A rat kept in a steel corset which restricts its activity will develop the gastric erosions of a peptic ulcer. Although some other animals do develop some other psychophysiological disorders these are usually under conditions of extraordinary stress produced by manmade experiments. By and large man is the only animal with the potential to develop such

Figure 12.1. Franz Alexander (By permission of Cedars-Sinai Medical Center and Curtis Studio, Los Angeles, CA.)

a wide variety of psychophysiological disorders. Civilized man is equipped with the same neuralhormonal physiology that his prehistoric ancestors needed in order to respond to physical emergencies. However, with civilization, threats to security occur predominantly in the mental and emotional spheres where such primitive defense arousal mechanisms can be inappropriate. Moreover, because threats associated with chronic anxiety are usually internal, undefined, and conflictual, they are not readily dispelled. They may persist indefinitely with the result that various organ systems remain chronically and inappropriately mobilized, thereby leading to psychophysiological illness.

Alexander formulated the hypothesis that issues involving dependency needs and wishes to be cared for are a function of the parasympathetic nervous system. If such wishes are blocked by conflict, hyperactivity and inadequate discharge of the parasympathetic nervous system may result and may lead to the development of specific psychophysiological illnesses, namely ulcerative colitis, bronchial asthma, or peptic ulcer. Similarly, the sympathetic nervous system, which controls the body's flight-fight patterns, may be blocked in its discharge because of conflicts around fear and anger. Such a blockage may result in hyperactivity of the sympathetic neuroendocrinological systems, leading to

such psychophysiological illnesses as hyperthyroidism, essential hypertension, and migraine headaches. Although this view is somewhat reductionistic and oversimplified, it served as an important model for psychophysiological illness for many years and still has considerable value.

In addition, Alexander expanded and refined Dunbar's work of describing the particular personality types and the specific conflictual situations seen in the various psychophysiological disorders. He helped popularize the concept of *psychosomatic specificity* in which specific personality types, specific life stresses, and specific psychological conflicts are seen as playing an etiological role in the genesis of each psychophysiological illness.

Following Alexander, Harold Wolff postulated that various bodily defenses are mobilized when the aspirations and needs of the individual are threatened. Depending upon the nature and the integrity of the physical structures participating in this protective reaction, these bodily defenses are either adaptive or maladaptive. If maladaptive, actual physical damage to organ systems can result. Later, Max Schur conceptualized the psychophysiological disorders as being the result of a regression to earlier, preverbal methods of handling life stresses and a *resomatization* of anxiety.

In recent years there have been at least two major theoretical advances in psychosomatic theory, the concept of the *somatopsychic-psychosomatic process* and the concept of *the giving-up-given-up complex*. I shall now discuss both of these concepts in much more detail.

THE SOMATOPSYCHIC-PSYCHOSOMATIC PROCESS

Concept of Organ Vulnerability

Using duodenal ulcer as a model, I. Arthur Mirsky hypothesized that certain diseases have their genesis either at birth or shortly thereafter as the result of some inborn, constitutional, *organ vulnerability*. Although there may be no signs or symptoms of any physical disease, this vulnerability of the organ may lead to psychological stresses surrounding the use of the affected organ system. These stresses may eventually result in the development of specific character traits and in the giving of special meaning to conflicts associated with the affected organ system. With the repetition of these same conflicts in later life, the psychological and physical stresses to the vulnerable organ may result in an actual organic lesion.

The somatopsychic-psychosomatic process is a theoretical concept which attempts to explain the genesis of the psychophysiological disorders. However, only in peptic ulcer has the somatopsychic-psychosomatic process been reasonably well proven. I will attempt to explain this concept of the somatopsychic-psychosomatic process by summarizing the investigatory data which led to its formulation, and then presenting a case of a patient with peptic ulcer which will be used to exemplify this theory.

Pepsinogen Secretion

The experimental evidence for this process which I shall cite is that reported by Mirsky, Weiner, Thaler, Reiser, and Weisman. To understand these data it is necessary to know that peptic ulcers are associated with a high degree of secretion of pepsinogen by the chief cells of the stomach, and that they may occur in the stomach, duodenum, or at the site of surgical anastomosis with the stomach. The duodenum is by far the most common site of peptic ulcer and the only location of the ulcers in the research I shall be describing.

There is considerable evidence showing that blood and urine pepsinogen levels measure the secretory function of the stomach. One such study of 203 people with well documented cases of duodenal ulcer showed that 94% of them had levels of pepsinogen one standard deviation above the normal adult population. The association between overall stomach size, chief cell mass in the stomach, and the secretory function of the stomach has been proven in a number of other studies. Thus, the secretory mass of the stomach seems to be dependent upon the number of chief cells, and both can be measured by blood and urine pepsinogen levels. Although the association between the secretory function of the stomach and duodenal ulcer has been proven, the exact nature of this relationship is not yet establlished. The fact that high serum levels of pepsinogen remain essentially unchanged after ulcers heal tends to confirm the idea that stomach secretory function is probably a predispositional factor and in all likelihood does not have a direct cause and effect relationship to peptic ulcer.

In a study of 200 neonates in which umbilical cord blood was used, it was shown that 12% of the infants had levels of pepsinogen at birth as high as that of adults with duodenal ulcer. This finding is particularly dramatic because children usually have much lower pepsinogen levels than adults and continue to have low pepsinogen levels until they are close to puberty. This study by I. Arthur Mirsky (Figure 12.2) established that stomach size and stomach secretory function vary greatly, even at birth. A longitudinal investigation of these neonates was planned and initiated in order to see which ones might develop peptic ulcer later in life, but unfortunately, it was not possible to continue the research to completion.

The Specificity Hypothesis in Peptic Ulcer

In his work, Alexander had hypothesized that conflicts surrounding dependency could produce a hyperactivity of the parasympathetic nervous system that might eventually lead to a group of diseases including peptic ulcer. By reviewing much clinical data, Alexander and his colleagues came to the conclusion that strong infantile wishes to be loved and cared for were present in people with ulcers, that these wishes tended to be repudiated in the form of a defensive pseudoindependence, and that at times of failure in coping with these needs, these people had an exacerbation of their ulcer symptoms. In Alexander's view, the frustrated desire to be cared for and to be nourished, leads to a continued

Figure 12.2. I. Arthur Mirsky

state of preparation for eating and helps produce the ulcer. This formulation is one example of the specificity hypothesis mentioned earlier.

The Investigatory Data

A study of 2,073 U.S. Army draftees was performed by Weiner and his colleagues utilizing both what was known factually concerning pepsinogen secretion, as well as Alexander's formulation of personality traits of patients with peptic ulcer. The subjects were young, basically asymptomatic, healthy young men who were all about to be exposed to the same stress, that of basic training. The draftees were given tests of their pepsinogen levels and were also psychologically tested. Two groups were separated out: 63 of the highest pepsinogen secretors and 57 of the lowest pepsinogen secretors. These two groups constituted the subjects for further study. Upper GI X-ray examination of these 120 draftees prior to starting basic training revealed that four had evidence of ulcers, one of which was active. All four with ulcers were among the group of 63 high secretors of pepsinogen. The X-ray studies were repeated between the eighth and sixteenth week of basic training, and an additional five were found to have developed an ulcer. Again, these five were among the group of high secretors.

Working with the hypothesis that people who are prone to or actually have peptic ulcer also have distinctive personality characteristics, Weiner and his colleagues studied these 120 subjects, attempting to differentiate high from low secretors without interviewing them, but using the findings from the psychological tests alone. Two psychiatrists and a psychologist working independently without any knowledge of the pepsinogen findings, looked for evidence on these psychological tests of major unresolved conflicts over oral dependency wishes. They successfully differentiated high from low secretors well within statistical significance (85% correlation). They also identified 10 subjects who they predicted would develop an ulcer based upon personality traits evident only on the psychological tests. Seven of these 10 did develop peptic ulcer, and all seven were high secretors. This classic study tends to confirm the validity of a specific personality type for peptic ulcer and the association between this personality type and high pepsinogen levels.

The Somatopsychic-Psychosomatic Process in Peptic Ulcer

In summary, these investigations established the following: 1) hypersecretion is a physiological process probably present at birth or in the earliest phase of life; 2) patients with duodenal ulcers are almost always hypersecretors and appear to have psychic conflicts related to frustrated oral dependency wishes; and 3) although healthy subjects who are hypersecretors may be identified either by their conflicts or by personality traits similar to patients with peptic ulcer, these hypersecretors may or may not actually develop an ulcer. Therefore, gastric secretion indicates that a subject may develop an ulcer but not necessarily that he or she will develop it. The development of an ulcer depends upon the presence of the predispositional factor of a large number of chief cells in the stomach, early childhood stress derived from this predispositional factor, and a repetition of this stress later in life.

Let us view this hypothesis in the following way. Just as abilities at mothering vary greatly, so also do the oral needs of children vary greatly and are dependent upon the rate of gastric secretion, which in turn probably affects sucking needs. The child who is born with a large, hypersecreting stomach is different from the child with a normal-sized, normally secreting stomach. A hypersecreting baby will be a baby who is constantly hungry and who will tend to relax less often, will tend to be satiated less frequently, and will be more trying and less gratifying to the feeding mother. If a child has a mother with poor mothering ability, i.e., poor ability to gratify oral needs, the chances of achieving oral satisfaction will tend to occur only if the child has a low oral drive, i.e., is a hyposecretor. The child with great oral needs, i.e., the hypersecretor, will be adequately gratified only if the child is matched with a mother with a great ability in mothering. Essentially, in this two person system of child and mother, the extent to which they are adequately matched will determine the degree of gratification of oral needs that that child experiences in early life.

The hypersecreting child who has inadequate mothering and, therefore, frustrated oral needs, will be left with a persistent desire to be cared for and will develop personality traits derived from this frustration. His dependency needs will tend to be denied as he enters adulthood and covered over by a pseudoindependent facade which may manifest itself in an ambitious drive to be a high achiever. Events later in life to which he will be particularly sensitive and vulnerable are those which interfere with his ability for receiving the support he needs under his veneer of independence.

Another associated set of factors is hereditary. Peptic ulcer tends to run in family lines and occurs in people with Type O blood to an extent well within statistical significance. Close relatives of gastric ulcer patients are three times as likely to have that disease as the rest of the population, and the same threefold increase in risk holds true for the close relatives of duodenal ulcer patients as well.

A Case History

Let us now turn to a case of a patient with a peptic ulcer which I shall use to exemplify some of the points I have just made. A 24 year old man with no family history of ulcer was admitted to the hospital with severe upper gastrointestinal bleeding. The history revealed that nine months prior to his birth his mother, then a 21 year old secretary in a large law firm, was robbed and raped in an elevator at knifepoint. The assailant fled and was never apprehended. Impregnated as a result of the rape, she had considerable conflict with her parents because of her wish to have the baby aborted and their wish for her to deliver the baby and then to put it up for adoption. Religious reasons were among the factors which resulted in her acquiescing to not having an abortion. But she then refused to give the baby up for adoption. She raised it herself.

The patient was breast fed for only one week and was told later in life that because of his mother's nipple tenderness and because he was biting his mother's breast, he was switched to the bottle. Shortly after his birth his mother started dating again, and fell in love with an older, divorced man whom she eventually married. The couple wanted children but repeated, spontaneous abortions prevented this. The patient recalled being told that he was a colicky baby. He was also enuretic at the time of his starting school at the age of five and at two other times when changed to new schools. He remembers his stepfather as a man who tried hard to be a good father. The patient said, "He would have been better if my mother and he had had

their own children. At times I felt that he resented me." When the patient finished high school, he became a cab driver and in a short time a cab fleet manager. Asked about college, he said, "I had the grades, but it was more important for me to work."

The symptom of heartburn was the first one referable to his gastrointestinal illness. It started immediately after graduation from high school and recurred when he became manager of the cab fleet. At the age of 21 he married a divorcee five years his senior. His marriage coincided with a period of relief from the heartburn. There was soon a dispute with his wife about their having children. He opposed it "on financial grounds," while she wanted children and thought they could afford them. A year and a half after their marriage they stopped the use of contraceptives. She became pregnant six months later. He soon had a return of his heartburn, and he was able to identify the onset of this symptom as occurring when he was first able to feel the baby's movements through his wife's abdomen. He remembered thinking, "Now that little bastard will take her away from me." A normal child was born after an uneventful delivery. Two weeks later the patient was admitted to the hospital because of massive gastrointestinal bleeding. The focus of bleeding was identified as occuring in the duodenum. A diagnosis of a bleeding peptic ulcer was made. He was treated conservatively, i.e., without surgery, and he had a good recovery.

Let us take this case and see to what extent it may fit the formulations given about peptic ulcer. We know nothing about this patient's pepsinogen level, since this was not measured. We were told that he does not have a family history of ulcer. However, this history only includes one half of this heritage. Our patient was a product of a rape, where there were major conflicts concerning his birth. He was forcibly conceived in a situation of terror. His conception led to a dispute between the mother-to-be and her parents, and resulted in a compromise in which his birth was something which his mother did not really accept, but rather was something to which she acquiesced after a struggle. We then learn that he could not be breast fed longer than a week and that he was colicky. After her marriage, his mother's repeated spontaneous abortions could not have helped matters. These abortions essentially meant that the desired babies did not come, and the couple was left with the product of a rape, a baby fathered by an unknown assailant.

Rejection certainly must have been a very important part of his childhood experience. Perhaps because of this rejection he had enuresis at times of important separations, particularly those associated with going to new schools. He had his first episode of heartburn after graduation from high school and then again when he took charge of running a fleet of cabs. It improved when he married an older, more socially and more sexually experienced woman. His gastrointestinal symptoms returned at the time when his wife was pregnant and after he was able to feel the life of the baby via its movements. His thought about the baby's competing with him for his wife's attention and care supports the speculation of his seeing the nurturing, mothering qualities of his wife as an extremely important part of her attractiveness to him. He presented with upper gastrointestinal bleeding two weeks after the birth of his child. The advent of the pregnancy and birth of the child was seen by him as having a special meaning. For most of us it would have been a happy occasion, but for him it represented a threatened loss of support encompassed in the thought, "Now that little bastard will take her away from me." In this setting a bleeding ulcer, or the bleeding of a preexisting ulcer, developed, requiring his hospitalization.

How does this case exemplify the somatopsychic-psychosomatic process? The early pathological process of duodenal ulcer is one of a larger-than-normal mass of stomach with a concomitantly large amount of gastric secretion. There are no manifestations of this in young children. However, the matrix for organ vulnerability of the upper gastrointestinal system has already been laid down. Concerning psychological development, our hypothesis states that a great deal depends upon the nature of the mothering system. If the child does not receive adequate nurture, he may be left with psychological traits associated with frustrated oral demands. Furthermore, he will tend to give special meaning to later events in his life which interfere with his dependent needs. Presented with sufficient stress, the vulnerable organ may develop an organic lesion, a peptic ulcer.

This child who later developed an ulcer received impaired mothering, and he developed a pseudoindependent personality style as a reaction against this. He refused college in order to support his parents and became a manager of a cab fleet. However, his going out into the business world was associated with the onset of his earliest ulcer symptoms. His going out on his own in business presented him with a conflict between his desire for further support from his parents and his wish to be independent and to support them. He experienced relief of these symptoms when he married an older, supportive woman. However, when the support of this woman was threatened by the arrival of a baby, his symptoms reappeared. His coping with his problems of dependency was further compromised when the baby was born and his wife's attentions to him diminished as he had feared. At that point he developed massive gastrointestinal bleeding.

The Somatopsychic-Psychosomatic Process in Other Psychophysiological Disorders

The somatopsychic-psychosomatic process may also be at work in other diseases, particularly those which have been associated with distinctive personality complexes, the so-called psychophysiological disorders. Of importance in understanding these illnesses is the fact that one cannot conclude that a particular personality type will lead to a specific psychophysiological disease. For example, presented with an individual who has conflicts surrounding orality and dependency, whose character structure is one of pseudoindependence, and who is threatened with the loss of a supporting system, one cannot conclude that this individual will develop a peptic ulcer. There are many people who have these same constellations of personality traits and conflictual situations who will never develop these diseases. A very central factor necessary for the development of a psychophysiological disease is that of organ vulnerability.

At the same time, although organ vulnerability is necessary in any given case, personality traits and conflictual situations in and of themselves can be predictive of the existence of a specific psychophysiological disorder. For example, presented with a group of patients all of whom had psychophysiological disorders, a team of coworkers of Franz Alexander at the Chicago Institute for Psychoanalysis were able to identify the specific psychophysiological disorders of patients within statistical significance. Their conclusions were based upon protocols describing the patients' histories but devoid of any specific information which would give a clue to the reader as to the particular illness that the patient had. Those diseases distinguished in the study were bronchial asthma, neurodermatitis, rheumatoid arthritis, essential hypertension, ulcerative colitis, peptic ulcer, and thyrotoxicosis.

Treatment of the Psychophysiological Disorders

Adequate treatment of the psychophysiological disorders requires focus upon the physical symptoms as well as the stress factors precipitating and otherwise contributing to the organic illness. Although in some instances a behaviorally trained specialist, such as a psychiatrist, psychologist, or psychiatric social worker may be involved in such a treatment, in the vast majority of cases the physician rendering the primary care is the only person treating the patient. In either event, an adequate knowledge of the personality types and characteristic stress situations seen in each of these disorders should be part of every physician's armamentarium. In addition, the physician must have an adequate history of what the life of each such patient has been, and the meaning to the patient of the life situations in which the disease originally appeared and has subsequently worsened. Thus, the physician's decisions on such issues as when to hospitalize, when to discharge, what to tell relatives, how to advise the patient on a wide variety of issues, and whether or not to refer the patient for psychiatric help can be made on the widest possible base of information.

Figure 12.3. Arthur H. Schmale

Figure 12.4. George L. Engel

THE GIVING-UP-GIVEN-UP COMPLEX

A more recent advance in psychosomatic theory is the concept of a life setting conducive to physical illness. This theory, which expands the scope of "psychosomatic" to include all organic illnesses and which attempts to unify medicine with psychiatry, was formulated initially by Arthur H. Schmale (Figure 12.3) and developed further by Dr. Schmale in collaboration with George L. Engel (Figure 12.4). This concept has been called *the giving-up-given-up complex*. It essentially answers the question, "Why do people become ill or die at the time that they do?" Folklore, poetry, and world literature reflect the interest of people throughout history in this question of why people fall ill at certain times. Nonphysicians generally take it for granted that a person's frame of mind has something to do with his or her propensity for illness or death. Discouragement, despair, humiliation, and grief are generally thought to be conducive to illness, whereas contentment, happiness, hope, confidence, and success are usually associated with good health. However, the physician, who in his or her everyday life may readily accept such a notion, rarely regards this concept of illness and death as a legitimate area for scientific interest and research.

Let me illustrate this concept of the giving-up-given-up complex by the following story told by Dr. Engel:

Charlie and Josephine had been inseparable companions for 13 years. In a senseless act of violence Charlie, in full view of Josephine, was shot and killed in a mêlée with the police. Josephine first stood motionless, then slowly approached his prostrate form, sunk to her knees, and silently rested her head on the dead and bloody body. Concerned persons attempted to help her away, but she refused to move. Hoping she would soon surmount her overwhelming grief, they let her be. But she never rose again; in 15 minutes she was dead. Now the remarkable part of the story is that Charlie and Josephine were llamas in the zoo! They had escaped from their pen during a snow storm and Charlie, a mean animal to begin with, was shot when he proved unmanageable. I was able to establish from the zoo keeper that to all intents and purposes Josephine had been normally frisky and healthy right up to the moment of the tragic event.

Let me give you another example. A famous novelist described the course of typhoid fever as follows:

When the fever is at its height, life calls to the patient: calls out to him as he wanders in his distant dream, and summons him in no uncertain voice. The harsh, imperious call reaches the spirit on that remote path that leads into the shadows, the coolness and peace. He hears the call of life, the clear, fresh, mocking summons to return to that distant scene which he had already left so far behind him, and already forgotten. And there may well up in him something like a feeling of shame for a neglected duty; a sense of renewed energy, courage, and hope; he may recognize a bond existing still between him and that stirring, colorful, callous existence which he thought he had left so far behind him. Then, however far he may have wandered on his distant path, he will turn back— and live. But if he shudders when he hears life's voice, if the memory of that vanished scene and the sound of that lusty summons make him shake his head, make him put out his hand to ward off as he flies forward in the way of escape that has opened to him— then it is clear that the patient will die.*

---

* From *Buddenbrooks* by Thomas Mann, copyright 1901. Translated by H. T. Lowe-Porter. (Reprinted by permission of Vintage Books, a division of Alfred A. Knopf, Inc., New York, N.Y.)

These are Thomas Mann's words in his book, *Buddenbrooks*, written in the year 1901. Mann was 26 years old at the time, writing about life as he saw it prior to antibiotics, prior to dynamic psychiatry, and prior to his acquaintance with Freud. What he has said in that memorable passage is that if the patient has a desire for life, he may live, but if he does not have the desire for life, then he will die.

In the February 13, 1975 edition of *The New York Times* the following article on inflation was featured on the first page:

When Mrs. Elsie DeFratus could no longer afford the cost of living, she died. She was nearly 80 years old and she had survived somehow for a long, long time on her meager widow's pension, frugally measuring it against the rising prices, scrimping and scraping and skipping meals, making do with less and less each day until finally, on a recent morning at an ancient hotel in the city, she crumpled quietly to the floor of her dark and tiny apartment. She weighed 76 pounds. An autopsy found no trace of food in her shrunken stomach. 'Malnutrition,' the coroner concluded. 'Surrender,' sighed an elderly friend, 'She just stopped believing tomorrow would be better.'

The concept of a life setting which is conducive to illness can be accepted by most people and may appear on page one of *The New York Times* and in many novels. When Thomas Mann wrote *Buddenbrooks*, there was no great uproar against him, because he was saying something that everybody already knew—that certain psychological states seem to be associated with good health and others with illness and death.

Characteristics of the Giving-up-Given-up Complex

Schmale and Engel have integrated this concept, which unifies folklore with lay and medical observations, into what they have called the "giving-up-given-up complex." This complex is not necessary for the formation of all physical illness. It does not, for example, set aside the germ theory of infectious disease. But it does explain one aspect of the relationship between physical illness and psychological state. The giving-up-given-up complex usually arises in response to a loss which may be real, fantasied, or threatened, and which results in depressive affects. Those specific depressive affects seen in association with this complex are 1) helplessness and 2) hopelessness. As defined by Schmale, helplessness refers to a feeling of impotence, failure, or frustration in getting the environment to help the individual, whereas hopelessness is a feeling that the individual himself can no longer cope with his or her problems. Other characteristics of the giving-up-given-up complex are 3) a self-image which is no longer one of competence or of being in control, 4) a loss of gratification from one's interpersonal relationships, and 5) a sense of disruption and discontinuity between past, present, and future. In this situation patients are reminded of other occasions in the past when they felt helpless and hopeless and which they could not resolve or master. This new situation now has a cumulative, "last-straw" effect, resulting in a feeling of giving up.

The giving-up-given-up complex, often transient and intermittent, occurs in everybody's life. It is usually short-lived, and in the ordinary course of life some solution eventually comes along and the symptom complex goes away. However, there are other times when prompt resolution is impossible. It is during these times that the individual is particularly prone to physical illness. In such instances the total biological economy is altered, and the ability to ward off and to deal with latent, potentially pathogenic or incipient physical problems is severely compromised. Examples of this are a latent diabetic becoming manifestly diabetic or a stable Ghon tubercle complex breaking down and becoming active. As mentioned, the giving-up-given-up complex is not essential for the development of an organic illness, but rather, it is a predecessor to the onset of many physical illnesses. It is a concept which organizes and explains something that has been known throughout history, but never understood scientifically.

This concept has been tested by a number of studies that will be cited later in this book. In a retrospective one done by C. Murray Parkes in England, widows and widowers were shown to develop organic disease within the first year after the loss of their spouses to a much greater extent than nonwidowed people of the same age. In a prospective study of a large number of naval personnel by Richard Rahe, based on earlier research done in collaboration with Thomas Holmes, physical illness was predicted solely upon changes in life events with an accuracy well within statistical significance.

Two Case Histories

Let me give you another example of this complex by presenting to you a patient whom I once interviewed. She was a 58 year old Syrian-born mother of four children who was admitted to the hospital for the treatment of acute rheumatoid arthritis. Thirty years previously, while she was hospitalized in Syria for a miscarriage, her husband secretly eloped to the Soviet Union with their two infant children. The patient grieved bitterly over the loss of her children, one of whom was not yet weaned from her breasts. The patient spoke of her sadness whenever she recalled the wetness of milk on her chest and remembered the lost baby. After a period of prolonged mourning, she began to think about the possibility of remarrying, and did so 10 years later. Her new husband and she left Syria for the United States.

Meanwhile, in Yerevan, the Armenian section of the Soviet Union, the older of the two children of the patient attempted to find her mother by showing a picture of herself and her mother to occasional Syrian visitors to their region. When relations between Syria and the Soviet Union improved, the number of Syrian tourists coming to this remote portion of the Soviet Union increased greatly. A Syrian tourist identified the picture, said that he knew the lady, and eventually obtained her address in the United States. The child of the patient wrote to her mother in America, and this letter produced an immediate and profound grief response in the patient. After unsuccessfully attempting all possible maneuvers to get permission for her children to emigrate to this country, the patient decided to visit them for a period of three months.

Upon her arrival in Yerevan, she met her children, and was immediately struck with the disparity between their economic status and her own. In her state of acute guilt over her relative affluence and her still unresolved mourning, she found herself unable to eat and curtailed her visit to only one month. When she disembarked from the plane taking her back to the U.S., she literally kissed the soil on the runway. She sadly explained the situation to her relatives the day after her return. The next day, she awoke in the morning with pains in her fingers, knees, and elbows, early symptoms of a disease which was to become a rather florid case of rheumatoid arthritis. It seemed a reasonable formulation that in her state of overwhelming guilt and inability to alter the circumstances of her daughters' lives, she experienced the emotions of helplessness and hopelessness, and developed the rheumatoid arthritis in response to her despair.

Let me present a second case. Several years ago Dr. Franz Reichsman and I conducted a four year study of the adaptation of patients maintained by hemodialysis. Historical data was obtained chiefly by tape-recorded and transcribed interviews of the patients themselves as well as their closest relatives. Of our 25 patients, 18 had a history of meaningful losses and separations preceding the onset of the uremic phase of their kidney illnesses. We wrote: "Of these 18 patients, nine reported feelings of helplessness in response to these life events. It is likely that stressful life events and the emergence of feelings of helplessness preceded the onset of uremic symptoms more often than elicted. While most patients spoke freely of their helplessness and sadness as responses to the uremic state, many seemed to deny or to withhold the occurrence of such feelings preceding their physical symptoms. These patients emphasized having been 'strong,' 'normal,' and 'not nervous' because they feared that acknowledging the existence of depressive affects prior to the onset of physical symptoms would stamp them as 'weak' persons and hence would jeopardize their acceptance into the program."

One of our patients was a 35 year old European-born housewife who was imprisoned with her father in a concentration camp during most of World War II. During these stressful and formative years she saw her father as a model and a fountain of strength not only for herself but also for the other prisoners. At the end of the war, their family emigrated to South America and then to the United States. Some years later her father developed a rapidly progressive case of acute leukemia which was refractory to treatment. He died six weeks after the onset of his illness. The patient said, "When he died my whole world collapsed. I felt let down and abandoned by everyone and I knew I could do nothing myself to change things." She raised both her hands with palms up and let them fall to her lap (a gesture of helplessness reported by Schmale and Engel) and said, "It was too much. I couldn't

take it anymore." Three weeks after he died, she experienced the nausea, vomiting, and headaches which were her earliest symptoms of the uremic phase of chronic glomerulonephritis. Hence, in the setting of her father's death, the patient experienced the affects of helplessness and hopelessness as part of the giving-up-given-up complex. She became highly symptomatic and entered an end-stage, uremic phase of an illness which must have been present but dormant for some time before this.

This is another example of the essential point that I want to reiterate in this chapter. The widest variety of physical illness may occur as a result of an alteration in the psychobiological economy caused by the giving-up-given-up complex. An awareness of the existence of such a phenomenon is of major importance in our understanding the enormous importance of life events and the stress of life changes, and the relationship of these life changes to the onset of physical illnesses.

Suggested Readings

Alexander, F: *Psychosomatic Medicine: Its Principles and Applications*. New York, W. W. Norton, 1950.

Engel GL. A life setting conducive to illness: the giving-up-given-up complex. *Ann Intern Med* 69:293, 1968.

Engel GL, Schmale AH: Psychoanalytic theory of somatic disorder: conversion, specificity, and the disease onset situation. *J Am Psychoanal Assoc* 15:344, 1967.

Mirsky IA: Physiologic, psychologic and social determinants in the etiology of duodenal ulcer. *Am J Dig Dis* 3:285, 1958.

Schmale AH: Giving up as a final common pathway to changes in health. In Lipowski ZJ (ed): *Advances in Psychosomatic Medicine. Vol 8: Psychosocial Aspects of Physical Illness.* Basel and New York, Karger, 1972, p 20.

Weiner H, Thaler M, Reiser MF, Mirsky IA: Etiology of duodenal ulcer I. Relation of specific psychological characteristics to rate of gastric secretion (serum pepsinogen). *Psychosom Med* 19:1, 1957.

References

Alexander F, French TM, Pollock GH: *Psychosomatic Specificity, Vol 1: Experimental Study and Results.* Chicago, University of Chicago Press, 1968.

Barchilon J: Analysis of a woman with incipient rheumatoid arthritis. *Int J Psychoanal* 44:163, 1963.

Cannon WB: *The Wisdom of the Body*, rev ed. New York, W. W. Norton, 1939.

Deutsch F: Psychoanalyse und Organkrankheiten. *Internat Z Psychoanal* 8:290, 1922.

Dunbar F: *Emotions and Bodily Changes.* New York, Columbia University Press, New York, 1935.

Engel GL, Reichsman F, Segal HL: A study of an infant with a gastric fistula. I. Behavior and the rate of total hydrochloric acid secretion. *Psychosom Med* 18:374, 1956.

Ferenczi S: *Further Contributions to the Theory and Technique of Psycho-analysis.* New York, Basic Books, 1952.

Holmes TH, Rahe RH: The social readjustment rating scale. *J Psychosom Res* 11:213,1967.

Levy NB (ed): *Psychonephrology I: Psychological Reactions to Hemodialysis and Transplantation.* New York, Plenum, 1981.

Levy NB (ed): *Psychonephrology II: Psychological Problems in Kidney Failure and Their Treatment.* New York, Plenum, 1983.

Mann T (1901): *Buddenbrooks.* New York, Vintage Books, 1952, p 591.

Moos RH, Solomon GF: Psychologic comparisons between women with rheumatoid arthritis and their nonarthritic sisters. *Psychosom Med* 27:135, 1965.

Parkes CM: The psychosomatic effects of bereavement. In Hill OW (ed): *Modern Trends in Psychosomatic Medicine,* ed 2. New York, Appleton-Century-Crofts, 1970, p 71.

Pollock GH: The psychosomatic specificity concept: its evolution and re-evaluation. In *The Annual of Psychoanalysis. Vol. 5.* New York, International Universities Press, 1977, p 141.

Rahe RH: Subjects' recent life changes and their near-future illness susceptibility. In Lipowski ZJ (ed): *Advances in Psychosomatic Medicine. Vol. 8: Psychosocial Aspects of Physical Illness.* Basel and New York, Karger, 1972, p 2.

Reichsman F, Levy NB: Problems in adaptation to hemodialysis: a four-year study of 25 patients. *Arch Intern Med* 130:859, 1972.

Schur M: Comments on the metapsychology of somatization. *Psychoanal Study Child* 10:119, 1955.

Weisman AD: A study of the psychodynamics of duodenal ulcer exacerbations: with special reference to treatment and the problem of "specificity." *Psychosom Med* 18:2, 1956.

West LJ: I. Arthur Mirsky and the evolution of behavioral medicine. In West LJ, Stein M (eds): *Critical Issues in Behavioral Medicine.* Philadelphia, J. B. Lippincott, 1982, p. xv.

Wolf SG, Wolff HG: *Human Gastric Function: An Experimental Study of a Man and His Stomach.* New York, Oxford University Press, 1943, 1947.

Wolff HG, Wolf SG, Jr, Hare S (eds): *Life Stress and Bodily Disease.* Baltimore, Williams & Wilkins, 1950.

CHAPTER **13** **The Psychophysiology of Health, Illness, and Stress**

Steven L. Dubovsky, M.D.

THE BIOPSYCHOSOCIAL MODEL

Psychiatry is sometimes accused of being an unscientific and impressionistic field, which is more concerned with unprovable theories about the nature of mankind than with the "hard data" of science. Medical practice, according to this notion, should only be concerned with observable data, such as physical findings and laboratory results, which quantify the disease process.

In an article in *Science* in 1977, Dr. George Engel (who is an internist as well as a psychoanalyst) pointed out that these assumptions are derived from a concept he termed the *biomedical model*. This refers to the concept that diseases are caused by one or a chain of biochemical or physiological changes that can ultimately be identified and measured (Figure 13.1). If one subscribes to this concept, one believes that all diseases have strictly biological causes, and conversely that entities for which no such biological cause can be discovered are not really diseases. Accordingly, biological changes must be found if psychiatric conditions are to be considered medical illnesses. In fact, evidence does exist that biochemical changes occur in certain psychotic illnesses (e.g., the schizophrenic and affective disorders), which some have maintained are the "real" causes of these so-called "functional" or "nonorganic" psychoses.

A related point of view holds that, since definite biological causes of all psychiatric illnesses have not been identified, they are not really diseases and should not be treated by a physician. Patients who do not suffer from any kind of known organic impairment, such as the neurotic patient, the hypochondriacal patient, many suicidal patients, patients suffering from personality disorders and sexual dysfunctions and addictions of various kinds, are not really "sick" but suffer instead from "problems of living." They do not have to be treated by a psychiatrist

or by any other physician, but could be equally well managed by a psychologist, social worker, minister, bartender, taxi driver, or even a guru. According to this view, such problems are "all in the head" (Figure 13.2).

According to Engel, when psychiatry or any other medical specialty adheres too closely to the biomedical model, the physician views illness only as a biological entity, separate from any psychological and social influences. Those who follow this model too closely might, for example, be very interested in a diabetic patient's blood sugar and insulin dosage, but would not be concerned with his emotional state or living conditions. As a result, they might not discover that because a patient has had a fight with his wife, or lost his job and is depressed, or needs to deny his diabetes, he is not taking his insulin as prescribed and not following his diet. As long as the physician's concern is only with the patient's laboratory values and clinical condition, without an awareness of the fact that the patient was simply not following the doctor's orders, control of the patient's diabetes would be impossible. Similarly, the doctor who attempts to achieve medical control of his patient's schizophrenia without taking into account the fact that the patient became psychotic when leaving home for college and attempting to achieve independence for the first time would not be very effective in treating the psychosis. Another example would be the large number of suicidal patients who visit a primary care physician before they kill themselves, complaining of some somatic symptom that is an expression of their depression. These patients have not heard of the biomedical model, and therefore they feel that it is their primary care doctor, not a psychiatrist or a minister or anyone else, who is the most logical person to diagnose and initiate treatment of their condition. If the physician does not do so, the results can be every bit as

Figure 13.1. From *Who's the Patient Here? Portraits of the Young Psychotherapist* by Stuart Copans and Thomas Singer. Copyright © 1978 by Oxford University Press, Inc. Reprinted by permission.

Figure 13.2. From *Who's the Patient Here? Portraits of the Young Psychotherapist* by Stuart Copans and Thomas Singer. Copyright © 1978 by Oxford University Press, Inc. Reprinted by permission.

fatal as missing a ruptured aneurysm. Thus, the question of whether or not a problem is an illness that requires medical attention is not only a matter of measurable biological phenomena, but also of the way in which the patient experiences the problem.

Engel concludes that the narrow definition of disease inherent in the biomedical model has created the same situation for all medical specialties, including psychiatry: the dichotomization of problems which confront the clinician into "diseases" and "problems of living," "organic" and "functional," "real" and "imaginary." This has resulted not only in an incomplete understanding of the multiple ways in which many biological, psychological, and social factors interact to produce states of both health and illness (*the biopsychosocial model*), but also incomplete management of both physical and emotional problems. Norman Cousins, in his book *Anatomy of an Illness* (already described in an earlier chapter by Dr. Fuller) makes the same point using the placebo as an example:

The placebo is proof that there is no real separation between mind and body. Illness is always an interaction between both. It can begin in the mind and affect the body, or it can begin in the body and affect the mind, both of which are served by the same bloodstream. Attempts to treat most mental diseases as though they were completely free of physical causes and attempts to treat most bodily diseases as though the mind were in no way involved must be considered archaic

in the light of new evidence about the way the human body functions.*

Psychosomatic medicine is that field which studies the interplay of psychological and physical variables in all conditions. Its adherents are often internists as well as psychiatrists who are dissatisfied with the dichotomization of the human condition into organic vs. nonorganic. They have produced a number of interesting findings in both animal and human experiments which have illuminated the ways in which people adapt in health, in illness, and in stress.

During the 1940's and 1950's psychosomatic research centered on the specificity theory described by Dr. Levy in the preceding chapter. This theory holds that any given psychophysiological illness is caused by specific emotional conflicts in a person who is psychologically vulnerable to suffer their effects when they are heightened by some specific stress, and who has an inborn predisposition or organ vulnerability to respond to stress in a specific organ system.

The specificity theory received great attention for many years. However, during the 1960's and 1970's, psychosomatic research focused more heavily on *nonspecific physiological factors* which

---

* *Anatomy of an Illness As perceived by the Patient* by Norman Cousins. W.W. Norton & Company, Inc., New York, N.Y. Copyright © 1979 by W.W. Norton & Company, Inc. Pages 56–57.

mediate between mind and body, in an attempt to delineate the ways in which a wide variety of *psychological stresses* may produce psychic or somatic decompensation. Recent psychosomatic research has also focused on the personality structures of people who insist that they are physically ill and present intractable somatic complaints for which no organic cause can be found, as well as on the emotional reactions of those whose illnesses seem primarily organic.

FLIGHT-FIGHT PATTERNS AS A REACTION TO STRESS

The natural reaction to a dangerous situation is to feel frightened or angry, or both (Figure 13.3), leading the individual either to run away and escape the danger (Figure 13.4) or to attack it and eliminate it (Figure 13.5). To prepare the body to take these actions, a number of physiological changes occur including 1) activation of the sympathetic nervous system, 2) suppression of the parasympathetic nervous system, 3) pituitary-adrenal-cortical activation leading to an increase in the secretion of catecholamines (epinephrine and norepinephrine) from the adrenal medulla, and 4) mobilization of the reticular activating system in the brain. The end result of these changes is to increase energy mobilization (through an increase in blood glucose and

Figure 13.4. From *The Savage Sword of Conan*, Marvel Comics Group, vol. 1. Copyright © 1977 by Conan Properties, Inc. Reprinted by permission.

Figure 13.5. From *The Savage Sword of Conan*, Marvel Comics Group, vol. 1. Copyright © 1977 by Conan Properties, Inc. Reprinted by permission.

Figure 13.3. From *The Savage Sword of Conan*, Marvel Comics Group, vol. 1. Copyright © 1977 by Conan Properties, Inc. Reprinted by permission.

free fatty acids), to increase heart rate and cardiac output (through an increase in circulating catecholamines), and to increase the capacity for physical activity (through an increase in blood flow to the skeletal musculature). This psychophysiological mobilization has been termed the *flight-fight reaction*. Unfortunately, modern man—trapped in a maddening traffic jam, or an unrewarding job, or some other continually stressful situation—is usually not as free as our prehistoric friend Conan was to either flee or fight!

The physiological components of the flight-fight mobilization can appear in reaction to external or internal threats, both real and imagined. The rapid heart beat, increased blood pressure, hyperventilation, and dry mouth of the soldier facing battle is no different from that of the student facing an examination or the phobic person facing the phobic situation. When the battle is won, the examination over, or the phobia cured, these changes abate and the flight-fight activation is terminated.

In the healthy person, the flight-fight activation has few consequences, except for the discomfort that it causes. However, the person who is vulnerable to its effects, or who is exposed to its chronic and unrelieved activation, may suffer adverse consequences. Imagine, for example, the patient who recently experienced a myocardial infarction and whose heart is vulnerable to the effects of circulating catecholamines. If he were frightened, could he not develop a dangerous cardiac arrhythmia due to the adverse effects on his heart of the excess catecholamine secretion which occurs during flight-fight activation?

In investigating this possibility, Thomas Hackett and Ned Cassem found that patients on the coronary care unit (CCU) during the immediate postmyocardial infarction period had three types of reactions to having had a heart attack. Some patients acknowledged the severity of their situation, and were quite anxious about their prospect for survival. A second group was less anxious; although they reported some frightening dreams, they were generally confident about their prospects for recovery. A third group seemed at times to be almost oblivous to the dangerous situation in which they found themselves. Not only did they express great confidence in their physician's ability to cure them, but they reported no nightmares and were even unaware of fatal cardiac arrests which had occurred in adjacent beds! When adjustments were made for physical variables that might affect survival, the patients who were the least anxious were most likely to survive, while those who seemed most "in touch with their feelings" were most likely to die.

Can our knowledge of the psychophysiology of flight-fight explain these phenomena? Bernard Lown and his coworkers immobilized dogs and then exposed them to a series of noxious electric shocks from which they could not escape. The dogs became visibly anxious, and their heart rates increased, accompanied by increased susceptibility to ventricular arrhythmia upon direct electrical stimulation of the heart during the vulnerable period of the T-wave. However, dangerous arrhythmias did not occur spontaneously. Next, the experimenters tied off a coronary artery in their experimental animals, creating an acute myocardial infarction. The animals were then put back in the slings and exposed to the frightening electric shocks. Once again, they demonstrated obvious flight-fight activation. But now in addition, without any electrical stimulation of their hearts, the dogs repeatedly developed ventricular tachycardia and ventricular fibrillation when they became frightened. This effect lasted for about three days, at the end of which time direct stimulation of the heart was again required to produce arrhythmia during flight-fight.

In a similar way, the hearts of anxious patients on the CCU may be most susceptible soon after infarction to the sympathetic activation that accompanies flight-fight, while patients who do not feel anxious are not as vulnerable. The observation that the *denial* of fear or anger abolishes the physiological changes of flight-fight suggests that the ability to ignore anxiety reduces the dangerous stress on the vulnerable heart. Clinical experience supports this notion, and many experienced cardiologists attempt to avoid emotional excitement in their patients in the immediate postmyocardial infarction period. As Norman Cousins says in his book *The Healing Heart*: "Free your heart-attack patients of panic. Panic is a killer." Reassurance, mild tranquilizers, hypnosis, and support from family members are useful adjuncts in this regard.

The ability to minimize or ignore frightening information may be of great help in promoting short-term survival in the heart attack patient; however, the results are quite different when denial occurs at other times. It is well known that 50% to 60% of deaths in victims of heart attack occur before the patient reaches the hospital. Some of these patients simply die without any warning; but others experience symptoms for hours before they seek medical attention. These patients' denial of their fear is a natural response when no immediate action exists which might terminate the flight-fight mobilization. However, when denial leads them to fool themselves that their symptoms are not severe enough for them to seek medical attention, a psychological defense mechanism which is useful once the patient reaches the coronary care unit becomes fatal. Another problem arises during the later period of convalescence. If the patient continues to minimize the seriousness of his situation, he may feel that he does not need to restrict his activities, watch his diet, or otherwise take care of himself, resulting in noncompliance with the therapeutic regimen. For example, a 42-year-old man I recently encountered with severe coronary artery disease was repeatedly warned by his physician to curtail his jogging and take up more sedentary activities commensurate with his degree of impairment. He died while on a three mile run.

It has also been postulated that at least some hypertensive patients whose cardiovascular systems are vulnerable in other ways to the effects of flight-fight might be chronically anxious or angry, and these emotional patterns lead to continuous activation of the sympathetic nervous system and ongoing stimulation of peripheral blood vessels. In fact, high pressured or anxious individuals are often referred to as "hypertensive." However, such an association, especially a causal one in which the flight-fight activation came first, rather than in reaction to the knowledge of having a serious medical problem, has not yet been convincingly demonstrated. To do so would require a prospective study of normotensive, anxious people with a vulnerability to high blood pressure (e.g., a strongly positive family history). Nevertheless, a number of new treatment approaches to hypertension are based on the speculation that chronic flight-fight activation at least exacerbates the condition, and are aimed at reducing sympathetic stimulation. Thus, hypnosis, biofeedback, meditation, and various relaxation exercises have all been demonstrated to be effective treatments for some forms of hypertension.

The long-term effects of chronic flight-fight activation on the heart have also been postulated in the "Type A personality." The anxious, pressured, impatient individual, who is intensely ambitious and competitive, who is unable to relax, who has a chronic sense of urgency, and who is quick to feel anger and hostility because of a low tolerance for frustration, is said to be more susceptible to coronary artery disease than his more relaxed peer (Type B). In a 1980 report Redford Williams and coworkers studied 424 patients who had undergone coronary arteriography for suspected coronary heart disease (CHD). They found a positive association between CHD and the global Type A behavior pattern, as well as one of its principal subcomponents—hostility. In 1983 Barefoot, Dahlstrom, and Williams reported on a 25-year follow-up study of 255 physicians who had taken a psychological test (the MMPI) in medical school. They found a positive prospective association between high levels of hostility on the MMPI, subsequent coronary heart disease, and total mortality from all causes. Further studies are needed to confirm these and similar findings. But clearly, all physicians should be informed about the characteristics of Type A behavior so as to be able to counsel their patients knowledgeably. Rehabilitation of Type A cardiac patients involves teaching them to react to the world with less anxiety and pressure, and to moderate somewhat their competitive, aggressive, success-oriented approach to life. It does not, however, require that they completely change their personality, and to suggest that they do so may make them even more anxious than before. If such patients can only follow a small portion of the advice of cardiologist Robert Eliot, they will be doing very well indeed: "Rule No. 1 is, don't sweat the small stuff. Rule No. 2 is, it's all small stuff. And if you can't fight and you can't flee, *flow*."

CONSERVATION-WITHDRAWAL PATTERNS AS A REACTION TO STRESS

While the psychophysiological changes of flight-fight prepare an individual to engage actively with his world, *conservation-withdrawal* is a psychophysiological state characterized by decreased interaction with the environment, decreased energy mobilization, and decreased activation of bodily systems. Thus, heart rate, blood pressure, and even body temperature decrease as does muscle tone and the general level of motor activity. This comes about through an activation of the parasympathetic nervous system and suppression of the sympathetic. George Engel and Franz Reichsman first conceptualized the conservation-withdrawal pattern in their classic paper on Monica, an infant with a gastric fistula, who would withdraw into depression and motor inactivity in the presence of a stranger and whose gastric secretion rates would correspondingly fall to their lowest levels at these same times.

An animal model for conservation-withdrawal can be demonstrated when an infant monkey is separated from its mother. Initially, it screams loudly and is very active in what appears to be a search for the mother. Soon, however, the infant stops this activity, curls up, and seems to withdraw from the environment. In contrast to its earlier state of flight-fight, its pulse and blood pressure are now low, and parasympathetic, rather than sympathetic, tone is greater (see Figure 21.17 in Chapter 21). It is easy to appreciate how the initial distress behavior might be useful in the wild, where it might be helpful in attracting the mother back; but if she did not come back, further such activity might attract a predator and it would be safer to withdraw and simply conserve energy until the mother returned on her own. Such a sequence also seems to be programmed into people, and human infants demonstrate the same sequence of events with prolonged separation from their mothers (e.g., hospitalization). Adults who are very sick also withdraw into themselves, and regress back to earlier, childlike behaviors.

In both animals and people, the state of conservation-withdrawal is activated when there is a stress the individual cannot control and terminated when it is no longer needed, for example, when the infant is reunited with its mother, or when the seriously ill patient improves. Sometimes, however, a state of diminished bodily activation seems to continue after conservation-withdrawal is no longer needed. In Figure 21.17 not only did the infant monkey continue to remain withdrawn, but his pulse progressively became slower and his body temperature remained subnormal. Eventually, his heart slowed to a standstill and he died of cardiac arrest, in the absence of any physiological or anatomical change that would explain his death. A similar sequence of events has been described by René Spitz in human infants separated from their mothers. Some of them remained withdrawn despite the availability of surrogate caretakers, and the death rate in this group was alarmingly high, especially if they received little emotional stimulation.

Heart rate is regulated in part by a balance between the activity of the sympathetic and parasympathetic nervous systems, and upsetting this balance in either direction can produce adverse effects. By shifting the balance in a direction opposite to that of flight-fight, can conservation-withdrawal also be dangerous to the vulnerable person? This possibility was investigated in animals by Curt Richter. Richter first attached heart rate monitors to wild rats and immersed them in a cylinder of water from which they could not escape. They developed a flight-fight reaction with increased pulse rate which persisted until they eventually drowned. Next, Richter clipped other rats' whiskers, which are important to the rat in helping it to adapt to everyday life. Again, the rats were immersed in water. This time, although their heart rates initially increased, they soon began to slow progressively until the rats developed cardiac standstill and died. Finally, Richter removed the rats with clipped whiskers briefly from the water a few times early in their immersion. Now they were able to swim for greatly extended lengths of time and once again developed a flight-fight reaction with increased heart rate, terminated only by drowning.

Richter wondered if the loss of a means of adaptation (i.e., the rats' whiskers) had somehow induced a state of extreme conservation-withdrawal which had adverse effects on the ability of the heart to meet the stress of being immersed in water. He hypothesized that something akin to a state of hopelessness was induced, and that this state could be reversed by removing the rats from the water, to give them "hope" of escape. This "hope" then allowed them to keep swimming until they drowned. He went on to speculate that a similar situation occurs in people who die of "voodoo death." Once they believe they are going to die, little can be done to save them, and many die of cardiac arrest. Only convincing them that their situation is not hopeless is likely to reverse these changes.

These hypotheses obviously go beyond the data from which they are derived. Nevertheless, clinical evidence exists that states of hopelessness are associated with increased mortality and morbidity from a variety of illnesses. For example, depressed patients who express a wish to die during open heart surgery are much more likely to die than patients with equivalent heart disease who do not feel hopeless, and some surgeons prefer to defer elective surgery on such patients until their emotional status can be improved. Similarly, the mortality from heart diseases in patients over the age of 55 is two to six times greater among people who have lost a spouse within the past six months than in age and sex matched controls. During the year following a flood in Bristol, England, the mortality rate was twice as great in those people whose homes had been flooded than in those whose homes had not. Studies in the 1950's by Blumberg, Le Shan and Worthington, and others suggested the possibility of a relationship between psychological factors and the development of neoplastic disease. Later studies by Greene and associates, Schmale and Iker, Horne and Picard, and others have shown that the course and even the onset of leukemia and lymphoma, uterine cancer, and lung cancer are associated with loss, hopelessness, and depression, while Bahnson and Bahnson, and others, have described strikingly similar defense mechanisms (i.e., denial, repression, and emotional inhibition) in many cancer patients. However, as Wellisch and Yager have pointed out, many more rigorously controlled studies will be necessary in order to convincingly demonstrate the existence of such a "cancer-prone personality." In 1946 Caroline Bedell Thomas began a fascinating three-decade prospective study on successive classes of medical students at Johns Hopkins to investigate whether physical and psychological profiles early in life would prove to be predictors of diseases suffered in later life. By the mid-1960's she had exhaustive data on 1,337 medical students. By 1977, 17 had committed suicide and 77 had developed cancer. To her surprise she found that the cancer victims were a good deal like the suicides in that both groups showed a remarkable alienation from their parents dating back to childhood. Such emotionally deprived and restricted individuals may be particularly vulnerable to the loss of social supports (spouse, friends, job) later in adult life.

These and similar observations have led Engel and Schmale to apply the term "the giving-up-given-up complex" (described by Dr. Levy in the preceding chapter) to those patients who express hopelessness, who feel helpless and powerless to influence their environment positively, who see their adaptive capacities as impaired, and who are unable to remember emotionally those times in which they were able to adapt successfully.

Such individuals are at risk for a whole range of physical and psychological illnesses. Conversely, those who feel hopeful, who enjoy a sense of being in control of their lives, and who have a social network (spouse, close friends and relatives, church membership, group associations) to call upon for emotional support appear to have a better chance for good physical health and longer life. A nine year follow-up study by Lisa Berkman and Leonard Syme of the 1965 Human Population Laboratory Survey of 6,928 adults in Alameda County found that people who lacked social and community ties had a death rate two to three times higher than those who had strong social support systems.

SUDDEN CARDIAC DEATH

Some researchers have speculated that sudden shifts from flight-fight to conservation-withdrawal may be particularly toxic to the vulnerable heart. According to Engel, this situation can occur in people who become emotionally excited in a situation from which they cannot escape and which they are helpless to control. Engel collected a file of 170 cases of sudden cardiac deaths occurring over a six year period. He classified the life settings in which the sudden deaths occurred into eight categories. Of these, six involved helplessness in one form or another: 1) the impact of the death of a close person; 2) during acute grief; 3) during the threat of loss of a close person; 4) during a period of mourning or on the anniversary of a death; 5) during loss of status or self-esteem; and 6) in a setting of personal danger or threat of injury, real or symbolic. The other two settings were: 7) after the danger was over, and 8) at times of triumph, success, or "happy ending." Common to all eight situations was an event impossible for the victims to ignore, and to which their response was overwhelming excitation or giving-up, or both. Engel speculated that these individuals had some underlying instability of the autonomic systems regulating heart rate and rhythm which broke down under the stress of rapid fluctuations between flight-fight (emotional arousal) and conservation-withdrawal (helplessness to control the situation).

Since sudden cardiac death is the cause of more than 400,000 deaths annually in this country (nearly a death a minute) and is the leading cause of death in the industrial world, greater knowledge of those at risk would have enormous preventive health implications.

THE EXPERIENCING OF PSYCHOLOGICAL STRESS AS A SOMATIC SYMPTOM

In recent years, psychiatrists have developed special units which aim to establish ongoing relationships with medical and surgical units in order to provide better service to patients with physical illnesses needing psychiatric care, and to their physicians. This branch of psychiatry is known as liaison psychiatry and may be considered the clinical arm of psychosomatic medicine. Clinical research by liaison psychiatrists has provided important insights into those patients who insist to their physician that they are suffering from a physical illness, even though little or no objective evidence of organic pathology can be found. The study of such patients has focused on the impairment early in life of their ability to tolerate emotional conflict, to differentiate emotions from physical sensations, to establish mature and independent relationships, and to obtain gratification of their normal needs for nurturance, closeness, and attention.

As will be described in more detail later in the book, the human infant initially experiences all types of discomfort (e.g., hunger, fatigue, pain, unhappiness) as generalized global distress. As the child grows, he begins to become aware of different types of experiences, and to differentiate them into physical and emotional. These categories may continue to be confused at times even into adult life (for example: "He stabbed me in the back" or "She broke my heart"). As the child continues to develop, he or she moves from what might be called a *somatic entity*, in which all stress is experienced in physical terms, to a partly psychic entity in which there is some differentiation of emotional feelings and bodily sensations, to a *psychosomatic entity* in which emotions and physical sensations can be differentiated from each other and in which emotional conflict can be tolerated without reverting to expressing it solely in physical terms. At the same time, the child learns that he can receive help in relieving both types of discomfort by communicating his needs directly.

Normal psychosomatic development can be interrupted by a number of adverse circumstances, some of which were described in earlier chapters on pain, conversion, and hypochondriasis. For example, an important caretaker may become ill and not be available to offer comfort during times of distress. The situation is worsened if the child must take care of the sick parent, resulting in his missing the prolonged dependency characteristic of early human development. The child may then learn that illness results in caretaking and attention from others, while the healthy must sacrifice in order to take care of the ill. This conclusion is compounded if his parents only paid attention to him when he was sick or had some physical complaint or injury, and ignored him when he was well. And because his parents were not available to help with psychosomatic development, he may never have learned to differentiate emotional from physical distress, and may actually think he is physically ill at times of emotional stress. This combination of experiences may result in conversion symptoms, hypochondriasis, and various "pain prone" states.

A PSYCHOPHYSIOLOGICAL MODEL FOR HEALTH, ILLNESS, AND STRESS

I will now attempt to demonstrate the complex interplay of psychological and physiological reactions to stress in the context of vulnerabilities and strengths which are determined in part by inborn biological tendencies and in part by environmental influences both early in life and later in development. These various factors are summarized and numbered (1–24) in Figure 13.6.

In contrast to the definition of "constitution" later in the book in Chapter 51 as the large number of more or less fixed factors (including genetic) with which the person enters the world, I will use "constitution" (1) to denote the total psychophysiological equipment, including both early environmental experiences (2) and genetic predisposition (3) that an individual brings to a stressful situation. People are born with and develop certain strengths, as well as certain vulnerabilities, in terms of their psychological makeup, their physical makeup, or both.

Whether or not an event is a stress (4) depends upon its meaning to the individual who experiences it (5). For example, the loss of a spouse might be extremely painful to a person who was very attached to the lost person, and possibly less painful if the couple were on the

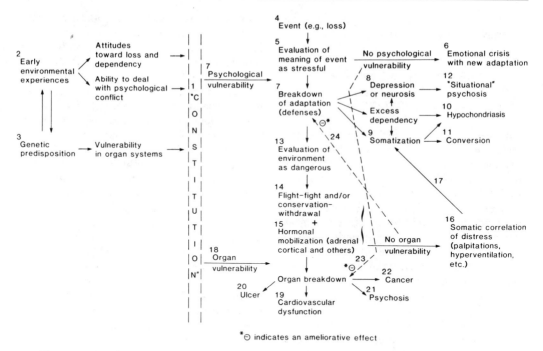

Figure 13.6. A psychophysiological model for health, illness, and stress. (By Steven L. Dubovsky.)

verge of a divorce. If the relationship had consisted of a complex mix of affection and anger (as do most relationships), the stress of the loss may be produced not only by the pain of losing someone to whom one was attached, but also by guilt and other feelings about the unresolved negative feelings toward the lost person.

Once an event is interpreted as stressful, various psychological coping mechanisms are brought into play to help the person adapt to the psychological pain he or she is experiencing. The healthy personality may come through a crisis with an even greater level of strength for having adapted to a difficult situation (6). People with emotional conflicts and psychological vulnerabilities which in some way coincide with the particular stress will probably experience a different outcome (7). For example, a patient who suffered the loss of an important caretaker early in life and who was exposed to significant deprivation because no one was available to take care of him, might be particularly sensitized to the effects of the loss of a significant person later in life, and might become depressed or develop other neurotic symptoms (8). Other patients, whose parents were physically present but emotionally absent due to physical illness or hypochondriasis, might express their emotional

distress through somatization (9), and develop either hypochondriasis (10) or conversion symptoms (11) in reaction to the loss of a supportive person later in life. Rather than feeling depressed, they might search for another caretaker in the form of a doctor. Another group of patients whose upbringing was characterized by intense, chaotic relationships with caretakers and inadequate development of their ability to regulate emotions and thoughts, might become so angry, anxious, or disorganized as to develop transient "situational" psychoses (12). When an individual is unable to respond effectively to a situation he interprets as stressful, either because of a psychological predisposition to the particular stress, or because of its overwhelming nature, his world begins to feel more dangerous (13). This results in the activation of flight-fight or conservation-withdrawal, or some combination of the two (14). The physiological effects of these may be ameliorated or exacerbated by the presence of such psychological variables as massive denial or extreme hopelessness. In addition, neuroendocrine and hormonal mechanisms may also be activated (15), leading to a breakdown of both organ systems and immune systems.

In the absence of inborn or acquired physiological vulnerabilities in any organ system, flight-fight activation will be accompanied by signs and symptoms of physiological arousal such as dry mouth, tachycardia, palpitations, perhaps mildly increased blood pressure, or the hyperventilation syndrome with shortness of breath, light-headedness, and numbness and tingling in the fingers and toes (16). People who are unaware of their inner psychological state may interpret these symptoms as signs of physical disease. If they are psychologically vulnerable by virtue of having been deprived of normal caretaking in childhood and thereby feel that their needs will only be met if they are sick, they may interpret these or other minor symptoms as indications of an illness which "forces" them to obtain caretaking from a physician and will be reluctant to relinquish their symptoms, even after the acute situation abates. This then becomes another pathway toward somatization (17). Patients with similar backgrounds who develop demonstrable organic disease may react excessively to the stress of their illnesses for the same reasons, while those who are threatened by dependency or incapacity may deny their symptoms and refuse to comply with the doctor.

In the presence of specific organ vulnerabilities (18), one or another organ system may break down when exposed to one or more of the nonspecific physiological changes caused by stress. Thus, the vulnerable myocardium may develop an arrhythmia under the stress of flight-fight and/or conservation-withdrawal (19) while the person whose congenitally high rate of pepsinogen secretion predisposes him to duodenal ulceration may develop peptic ulcer (20). The individual whose brain is predisposed to develop disturbances of neurotransmitter function may develop schizophrenia or severe depression under stress (21), disturbances which are more profound and severe than a transient situational psychosis. Is it possible that the immune surveillance system which monitors neoplastic cells may be vulnerable to disruption by the physiological effects of hopelessness in some individuals, resulting in the worsening or even the onset of some cancers? This is a new and intriguing area of interest in psychosomatic research (22).

In a recent prospective study of 15 spouses of women with advanced breast carcinoma, Marvin Stein and colleagues at Mt. Sinai Hospital in New York found lymphocyte stimulation responses to be significantly suppressed during the first two months following the death of the wife compared with prebereavement levels. And in another recent retrospective report, Alan Stoudemire movingly describes the onset of a malignant fibrous histiocytoma on his right tibia during a particularly stressful period of his life. These two very different studies are good examples of the richness and the many-sided aspects of this new field of *psychoneuroimmunology.*

Also of interest are the ameliorating effects of psychological strengths on physical disease and of physiological strengths on psychological illness. These possible interactions are shown in Figure 13.6 by dotted lines suggesting that the ability to handle psychosocial stress constructively may reduce the total amount of physiological activation to which vulnerable organs are subjected (23), perhaps favorably affecting the onset or course of physical disease, and that innate physiological strength may aid a person in coping with psychosocial stress (24), reducing the risk of psychological breakdown. Some evidence for these speculations is beginning to accumulate. A long-term follow-up study of college males by George Vaillant and his coworkers, initially begun over 40 years ago, has demonstrated a positive correlation between mental health and physical health. Vaillant also found that men who had stable childhoods and multiple social supports as adults were able to use their psychological defenses creatively, whereas men with unstable childhoods and few social supports as adults were more likely to use their defenses maladaptively and rigidly. Finally, the various studies cited by Dr. Mumford in Chapter 6 comparing medical and surgical patients who had psychiatric treatment and psychological support in connection with their physical illness, as compared with those patients who had not, found that the former were much freer of subsequent physical symptoms than the latter.

While the model which I have outlined in Figure 13.6 is a tentative one, open to change as new research develops, I believe it conveys the complex and ongoing interaction between psychological factors and physiological factors in all states of health, illness, and stress.

Suggested Readings

Cousins N: *The Healing Heart. Antidotes to Panic and Helplessness.* New York, W. W. Norton, 1983.
Eliot RS: *Stress and the Major Cardiovascular Disorders.* Mt. Kisco, NY, Futura, 1979.
Engel GL: The need for a new medical model: a challenge for biomedicine. *Science* 196:129, 1977.
Engel GL: The clinical application of the biopsychosocial model. *Am J Psychiatry* 137:535, 1980.

Engel GL: Sudden and rapid death during psychological stress: folklore or folk wisdom? *Ann Int Med* 74:771, 1971.

Hackett TP, Cassem NH (eds): *Massachusetts General Hospital Handbook of General Hospital Psychiatry.* St. Louis, C.V. Mosby Co., 1978.

References

Ader R (Ed): *Psychoneuroimmunology.* New York, Academic Press, 1981.

Bahnson CB: Stress and cancer: the state of the art. Part I. *Psychosomatics* 21: 975, 1980. Part II. *Psychosomatics* 22:207, 1981.

Bahnson CB, Bahnson MB: Role of the ego defenses: denial and repression in the etiology of malignant neoplasm. *Ann NY Acad of Sci* 125:827, 1966.

Barefoot JC, Dahlstrom WG, Williams RB: Hostility, CHD incidence, and total mortality: a 25-year follow-up study of 255 physicians. *Psychosom Med* 45:59, 1983.

Berkman LF, Syme SL: Social networks, host resistance, and mortality: a nine-year follow-up study of Alameda County residents. *Am J Epidemiology* 109:186, 1979.

Berkman LF, Breslow L: *Health and Ways of of Living: The Alameda County Study.* New York, Oxford University Press, 1983.

Blumberg EM, West PM, Ellis FW: A possible relationship between psychological factors and human cancer. *Psychosom Med* 16:277, 1954.

Bowlby J: *Attachment and Loss.* New York, Basic Books, 1969.

Cannon WB: Voodoo death. *Psychosom Med* 19:182, 1957.

Cassem NH, Hackett TP: Psychiatric consultation in a coronary care unit. *Ann Int Med* 75:9, 1971.

Cassem NH, Hackett TP (eds): The setting of intensive care. In *Massachusetts General Hospital Handbook of General Hospital Psychiatry.* St. Louis, C.V. Mosby, 1978, p 319.

Corbalan R, Verrier R, Lown B: Psychological stress and ventricular arrhythmias during myocardial infarction in the conscious dog. *Am J Cardiol* 34:692, 1974.

Cousins N: *Anatomy of an Illness.* New York, W.W. Norton, 1979.

Engel GL: A life setting conducive to illness: the giving-up-given-up complex. *Ann Int Med* 69:293, 1968.

Engel GL: Psychologic stress, vasodepressor (vasovagal) syncope, and sudden death. *Ann Int Med* 89:403, 1978.

Engel GL, Reichsman F: Spontaneous and experimentally induced depressions in an infant with a gastric fistula: a contribution to the problem of depression. *J Am Psychoanal Assoc* 4:428, 1956.

Friedman M, Rosenman RH: *Type A Behavior and Your Heart.* New York, Alfred A. Knopf, 1974.

Greene WA: The psychosocial setting of the development of leukemia and lymphoma. *Ann NY Acad of Sci* 125:794, 1966.

Greene WA, Miller G: Psychological factors and reticuloendothelial disease. *Psychosom Med* 20:124, 1958.

Horne RL, Picard RS: Psychosocial risk factors for lung cancer. *Psychosom Med* 41:503, 1979.

Karasu TB: Psychotherapy of the medically ill. *Am J Psychiatry* 136:1, 1979.

Kennedy JA, Bakst H: The influence of emotions on the outcome of cardiac surgery: a predictive study. *Bull Assn Psychoanal Med* 6:8, 1966.

LeShan L: Psychological states as factors in the development of malignant disease: a critical review. *J Natl Cancer Inst* 22:1, 1959.

LeShan L: An emotional life history pattern associated with neoplastic disease. *Ann NY Acad Sci* 125:780, 1966.

LeShan L, Worthington RE: Personality as a factor in the pathogenesis of cancer. *Br J Med Psychol* 29:49, 1956.

LeShan L, Worthington RE: Some recurrent life history patterns observed in patients with malignant disease. *J Nerv Mental Dis* 124:460, 1956.

Lown B, Verrier R, Corbalan R: Psychological stress and threshold for repetive ventricular response. *Science* 182:834, 1973.

Murphy GE: The physician's responsibility for suicide. *Ann Int Med* 82:301, 1975.

Parkes CM: *Bereavement: Studies of Grief in Adult Life.* New York, International Universities Press, 1972.

Richter CP: On the phenomenon of sudden death in animals and man. *Psychosom Med* 19:191, 1957.

Rogers MP, Dubey D, Reich P: The influence of the psyche and the brain on immunity and disease susceptibility: a critical review. *Psychosom Med* 41:147, 1979.

Schleifer SJ, Stein M, et al: Suppression of lymphocyte stimulation following bereavement. *JAMA* 250:374, 1983.

Schmale AH: Giving up as a final common pathway to changes in health. In Lipowski ZJ (ed): *Advances in Psychosomatic Medicine. Vol. 8: Psychosocial Aspects of Physical Illness.* Basel and New York, Karger, 1972, p 20.

Schmale AH, Iker HP: The affect of hopelessness and the development of cancer. Identification of uterine cervical cancer in women with atypical cytology. *Psychosom Med* 28:714, 1966.

Seligman ME: *Helplessness.* San Francisco, W.H. Freeman, 1975.

Shapiro AP: Physiological, psychological, and social determinants in hypertension. In West LJ, Stein M (eds): *Critical Issues in Behavioral Medicine.* Philadelphia, J.B. Lippincott Co., 1982, p 217.

Sklar LS, Anisman H: Stress and coping factors influence tumor growth. *Science* 205:513, 1979.

Spitz RA: Hospitalism: a follow-up report. *Psychoanal Study Child* 2:113, 1946.

Stein M, Schiavi RC, Camerino M: Influence of brain and behavior on the immune system. *Science* 191:435, 1976.

Stoudemire A: The onset and adaptation to cancer: psychodynamics of an ill physician. *Psychiatry* 46:377, 1983.

Thomas CB: Precursors of premature disease and death. The predictive potential of habits and family attitudes. *Ann Int Med* 85:653, 1976.

Thomas CB, Duszynski KR: Closeness to parents and the family constellation in a prospective study of five disease states: suicide, mental illness, malignant tumor, hypertension, and coronary heart disease. *Johns Hopkins Med J* 134:251, 1974.

Thomas CB, Duszynski KR, Schaffer JW: Family attitudes reported in youth as potential predictors of cancer. *Psychosom Med* 41:287, 1979.

Vaillant GE: *Adaptation to Life.* Boston, Little, Brown and Co., 1977.

Wellisch DK, Yager J: Is there a cancer-prone personality? *Cancer J for Physicians* 33:145, 1983.

Williams RB, et al: Type A behavior, hostility, and coronary atherosclerosis. *Psychosom Med* 42:539, 1980.

Wolf SG: New explorations in the psychobiology of sudden death. In West LJ, Stein M (eds): *Critical Issues in Behavioral Medicine.* Philadelphia, J.B. Lippincott Co. 1982, p 237.

14 The "Difficult" Patient

A. *The Angry and Seductive Patient*

Ronald D. Franks, M.D.

Of all the difficult cases with whom a doctor works, two of the most problematic are the angry and the seductive patient. The strong emotions evoked can strain even the most secure doctor-patient relationship. Such emotions are often intensified by unconscious transference reactions in the patient which in turn usually precipitate strong countertransference reactions in the doctor. The clinical situation can become so volatile that effective medical management may be severely compromised.

THE ANGRY PATIENT

Anger, whether expressed overtly or covertly, is not only uncomfortable for the doctor and the patient. It also interferes with effective treatment. The patient may openly and angrily challenge the doctor's competence, or conversely be more subtle and simply not comply with the doctor's treatment recommendations. The patient may caustically demand special considerations, procedures, and medications, or may appear very needy and dependent, yet reject any helpful suggestions. Inevitably, such patients generate angry counterreactions from their doctors. These responses may be either openly hostile or more subtle and disguised. The doctor may go so far as to have loud confrontations with such patients, even to the point of insulting or ridiculing them, often "justifiably" since they have not followed the treatment plan. Less obvious is the physician who expresses his or her anger by forgetting appointments, by not having time to return phone calls, or by losing interest in the patient. These angry transactions between doctor and patient are often examples of transference and countertransference. Anger felt by the patient, even if seemingly specific to some "error" by the doctor, is frequently exaggerated. The doctor comes to represent some important figure from the patient's past, and thus becomes the recipient of displaced or "transferred" anger. Countertransference reactions, on the other hand, are similar responses from the doctor in which the patient comes to represent some important figure from the doctor's past.

Causes of Angry Behavior

Before there can be any attempt to improve the doctor-patient relationship, the doctor must try to understand as much about the patient's anger as possible. First, is it *acute* or *chronic*? Obviously, those patients who are chronically angry are going to be less interested in talking openly about the reasons behind their anger and even less interested in changing their angry behavior. Those who are acutely angry, however, are usually more amenable to improving their relationship with their doctor. In either case, the causes for the patient's anger can usually be traced to two fairly common themes. Either patients have suffered some loss in relationships with others, or there has been some disturbance in how they view or value themselves. For example, a woman whose husband had recently died was quite irritable with her family physician. She snapped at him on several occasions, complaining that he probably would be unable to determine the cause of her abdominal pain. Although initially put off by her behavior, the doctor realized her anger was unusual, and so asked her about it. She talked about how hard it was to trust doctors since her husband's death. She then began to cry. Her grief was now obvious. The acute anger toward her doctor dissipated as she began to express her sadness. This patient illustrates the first of these themes, namely a loss in a personal relationship through the death of her husband. Her anger, in response to that loss, was displaced onto her doctor.

The second theme is demonstrated by a successful executive who had recently suffered a myocardial infarction. He was a demanding but congenial man prior to his illness, only to become "impossible" after being admitted to the coronary care unit. His doctor, being careful not to take the anger personally, asked the patient about this dramatic change in his behavior. The patient reluctantly described his fears of being a "cardiac cripple," and how threatened he felt. This significant change in self-image and the resultant fear of helplessness and worthlessness were disguised by the surface anger. As these underlying fears were more openly discussed, the anger gradually disappeared.

Treatment of the Angry Patient

As is evident from the above examples, working with these patients is very challenging. The doctor must contend with his own anger as well as that of the patient, not any easy task. It is essential for the physician to be as neutral and objective as possible. Otherwise, the anger could easily escalate to the point of disrupting an already tenuous doctor-patient relationship. To obtain this objectivity, it is very helpful for the doctor to ventilate his or her feelings prior to interacting with the patient. This direct expression of pent-up feelings about the patient can occur with friends or with other medical staff.

For example, a particularly difficult interaction with an angry patient left a surgeon feeling furious. As he entered the nursing station, he exploded, "Man, what a pain in the neck that guy is! I've had it! Someone else can take care of that 'turkey'!" After a few more strong comments, he began to get some relief and was able to ask himself, "Why does that man make me so mad?" He turned to the other staff to see if they felt the same way. Somewhat embarrassed, several nurses agreed. "Why?", he asked. The staff was not sure, but someone remembered the patient mentioning that his father had been treated at that same hospital 20 years ago. Now feeling more curious and less angry, the doctor returned to ask the patient why he was so upset. The patient glibly denied any difficulties, adding, "Just take care of my medical problems and mind your own business!" Again feeling rebuffed, the doctor commented, "I don't want to irritate you, but it's going to be hard for us to work together with you feeling this way. Maybe something is bothering you that might be useful

for us to talk about." "Like what?," the patient snapped. Acting on a hunch the doctor replied, "You told one of the nurses that your father was hospitalized here quite some time ago. Tell me what happened." The patient recounted how his father had been admitted for a rather routine evaluation, and due to some unexpected complications he had died, possibly as a result of mistreatment. "Are you afraid the same thing will happen to you?" "Yes", the patient replied, "Wouldn't you be?" The physician answered, "I guess I would be. How can we work together to reduce your fear?" This empathic comment helped the doctor and patient agree to talk in detail about every test planned and about all of the possible risks. The doctor even offered literature for the patient to read. And when the tests were completed, the patient was given straightforward information about the results. The remainder of the hospitalization was still difficult at times, but the foundation laid by the doctor helped him and the patient get through the worst periods without rupturing the doctor-patient relationship.

Those patients who are chronically angry are less likely to respond to the above approach. The defensive need for the anger is usually too strong to be easily relinquished (Figure 14.1). For these interactions the doctor does well to ventilate, as above, and then, when feeling more objective, try to determine how he or she might best *work around* this anger. The doctor may discover that for many of these patients the anger stems from the patient's fear of becoming either *too close to* or *too distant from* the doctor.

"You hate my guts, don't you?"

Figure 14.1. Reproduced with permission from *More Cartoon Classics From Medical Economics*. Copyright © 1966 by Medical Economics Book Division, Inc., Oradell, NJ. All rights reserved.

Those who fear closeness are afraid that they may become excessively dependent on their doctor. The anger serves as a convenient way of pushing the doctor away. Others, fearful of a too-distant relationship, become worried that the doctor does not care about them, and they get angry in anticipation of "inevitable" rejection. To work with the patient who is fearful of becoming too close, the doctor should put particular emphasis on forming an adult-adult, collegial type of relationship, being cautious not to infantalize the patient. Such patients are thus reassured that they will not be made to look weak during a time when they are in need of help. For those patients who are afraid of a too-distant relationship, a little more time, understanding, warmth, and reassurance will go a long way toward quieting the anger and lessening the fears of rejection. Admittedly, knowing which approach to use is not easy, and may require some experimentation with each individual patient.

For other chronically angry patients, the problems are rooted in the patient's low self-esteem and fears of inadequacy. The doctor may work with these concerns in several ways. First, he or she may try to give the patient control over as many nonessential aspects of the treatment as possible. This can include room location, timing of certain medications, change in visiting hours, and choice of diet, among others. The feeling of control and specialness will help lessen the patient's concerns about adequacy and acceptability. Finding an area of success in the patient's life, followed by appropriate compliments, will aid in combatting the patient's fears of worthlessness and lessen the transference fears that the physician is going to expose and humiliate the patient.

All these approaches to working around the chronic anger in this type of difficult doctor-patient relationship must not sacrifice good medical care. In a neutral, nonprovocative fashion, the doctor should clarify with the patient what behavior is tolerable and what behavior might threaten safe medical management. The approaches described previously can then be applied to hopefully improve the strained doctor-patient interaction. Obviously, the patient has a choice of changing doctors if he or she cannot abide by the limits established by the physician. But this is less likely if there is open and honest communication. In fact, such direct communication will more often than not lead to an improved therapeutic relationship, and a much less "difficult" patient.

THE SEDUCTIVE PATIENT

Patients, either men or women, who express intense sexual feelings toward their doctor are usually labeled "seductive." Some of these patients are very aware of their sexual feelings, while others have no appreciation of their seductiveness. They may touch their doctors, inquire about the intimate details of their doctors' lives, or display themselves flirtatiously during the physical exam. This behavior can progress to the point of the patient trying to seduce the physician through open expressions of love and wishes for intercourse. In most instances such behavior is the result of a transference reaction. As with the hate of the angry patient, such love is exaggerated and displaced onto the doctor because of whom the doctor represents to the patient. And like the angry patient, this seductive behavior usually elicits strong counterreactions and countertransference feelings from the physician. The doctor may become sexually aroused, but more likely may feel confused, anxious, or even angry. In fact, many physicians become so disturbed by seductive behavior that they will do anything to avoid these patients. Thus, they lose the opportunity to help these patients, who usually are trying to communicate something other than the wish to have a sexual encounter.

Causes of Seductive Behavior

For most of these patients, the seductive behavior stems from a few basic concerns. Probably the single most common one is the patient's *need for a close, giving relationship*. It often is the result of some acute disruption in one of the patient's personal relationships. For example, a female patient suddenly revealed that she found her doctor to be sexually attractive and openly propositioned him. Although initially flattered, the doctor soon discovered that the patient's seductive behavior was actually stimulated by her depression over the recent separation from her husband. Her grief and loneliness had become intolerable. The desire for an affair was an effort to escape from these depressed feelings. Wisely, the doctor focused on her feelings of despair, and this approach resulted in a gradual reduction in the sexual feelings. Nearly as frequent a cause for seductive behavior is the *low self-esteem* that is often precipitated by a disturbance in body image following a physical illness. This was seen, for instance, in a young man who had a colostomy due to chronic bowel disease. Afraid to face the possibility of no longer being attractive, he seductively turned to his female physician to reassure himself of his desirability.

In both of these patients the seductive behavior was a response to an *acute* stress. For some patients, however, sexually seductive behavior is not acute, but rather a *chronic*, characteristic way of relating to other people. This is especially true of certain *histrionic* or *hysterical personalities* to be described further in a later chapter. Only by repeated contacts is it possible to differentiate these chronic patients from the previous acute ones. Although the motivations for their seductive behavior may be the same, the behavior of the chronically seductive patient is usually deeply ingrained and more resistant to change. Again, although difficult to believe, these patients are *not* primarily interested in an actual sexual encounter. A third type of seductive patient is one who presents with *bizarre*, grossly inappropriate behavior, appearance, or both. This should alert the physician to the possibility of a psychosis. Such patients are usually trying to communicate that they are decompensating and desperately need help, not a sexual encounter.

Treatment of the Seductive Patient

Having recognized that there are different kinds of seductive behavior, and that these patients are usually trying to express much more than sexual feelings, the doctor can approach treatment in either of two ways. First, the doctor may choose to ignore the sexual advances of the patient and simply continue with the medical workup. This is the preferred approach for those patients who are chronically seductive. By not encouraging the behavior, most likely it will diminish and allow for a more constructive doctor-patient interaction. This approach, however, will only aggravate the seductiveness of a patient who is trying to deal with a more acute distress. For these patients, an empathic, inquiring response is indicated. This is particularly true if the seductive behavior is unusual for the patient. Direct questions about the patient's personal life such as changes in a love relationship, loss

of a job, concern over a physical illness, or a recent change in sexual functioning will usually lead to a marked lessening of the seductive behavior as the patient begins to describe the emotional stress in question. Occasionally, however, this questioning may lead to increased seductiveness. At this point, it is best to ask the patient directly if he or she is aware of having any sexual feelings toward you. This can be followed by, "Do you know why?", again hoping to enlist the patient's curiosity in discovering what factors are prompting the sexual feelings. The following case example will illustrate this approach.

A woman who was pregnant and in her last trimester began acting seductively toward her obstetrician. She would rub against him whenever possible, and constantly asked him questions about his personal life. Recognizing this behavior as unusual, the obstetrician decided to explore the possible underlying reasons for the change. He began by asking what prompted her and her husband to have a child at this time, and how each of them was feeling about becoming a parent. The patient quickly told how very difficult it was to think about becoming a mother, since she was afraid that her husband would no longer find her sexually attractive. Further discussion about her past history revealed that the patient's parents did not seem interested in each other as a husband and wife once they became parents. There was even a strong suspicion that after the birth of the patient's younger sister, the patient's father had had an affair. She now began to recognize that she was afraid that her husband would react in exactly the same way as her father did. In this transference reaction the patient was responding to her husband as though he were her father. After discussing the problem further, the obstetrician suggested to the patient that she share her concerns with her husband. As she did, the marital relationship improved considerably, and the patient's sexual interest in her obstetrician disappeared.

As might be anticipated, some of our patients, in contrast to the one just described, may become upset when we question them about their sexual feelings toward us. This may be due to having to face the psychological distress which is hidden behind the sexual behavior, or it may be due to the patient feeling rejected by our not responding physically to them. If we reassure them that we are concerned that something may be troubling them and that we can be most helpful by responding professionally rather than sexually, they will usually feel grateful rather than resentful.

An additional problem that female physicians are likely to encounter is the male patient who develops an erection during the course of a physical examination. For most men, this is an embarrassing response to the stimulation of the exam. Asking the patient if he would prefer waiting for a few minutes before continuing with the exam will usually alleviate the situation. In some cases, however, the erection will be due to a more overt sexual expression from the patient. In that case the guidelines described previously can be adopted. If these methods are not sufficient and the patient persists in his sexual behavior, then a more direct approach may be necessary.

The following case example demonstrates how a female physician worked with a man who developed strong sexual feelings for her. He was a lawyer who had been seen for approximately three years for management of his Hodgkins disease. During the course of the physical examination she observed that he had a partial erection. This was most unusual, as were his comments about how attractive he thought she looked. The doctor, feeling puzzled and also somewhat irritated, commented, "You have never mentioned my looks before. Any idea why you are talking about that today?" "Only that I've felt this way for some time," he replied. "How long?" she asked. "Maybe six months," he said. Her irritation disappeared as she realized that the patient was not trying to place her in a compromising situation, but rather was troubled with feelings that seemed irrational to both him and to her. This realization allowed her to begin exploring the origin of his feelings. She remembered that it was approximately six months before that he wondered aloud with her if he would ever get married, in view of his "fatal" disease. She had reassured him then that she believed his Hodgkins to be arrested and emphasized his good chances of survival. He had seemed relieved by her comments at the time, but now he revealed that when he had asked those questions, he was really trying to express how attracted he felt to her. She empathized with how difficult this must be for him, but stated that they needed to understand the source of these feelings rather than act on them. He understood what she was saying, and they agreed to meet

more frequently to talk over his concerns about his illness, including his fears of dying. They also decided to explore the realistic possibilities of his becoming involved with an available, more appropriate woman. Through the course of these discussions, the patient's sexual feelings toward the internist lessened and were replaced by feelings of warmth and respect.

His transference toward her can now be understood. He had hoped that she would accept him and be able to tolerate his disease which he feared other women could not. This fear stemmed from his childhood. His mother would become very frightened by any sign of illness in her children and would actually punish them for being sick. He was fearful that all women would respond to him in the same way that his mother had. A woman physician would be the best compromise, since she would be someone who was accustomed to disease, and hopefully would be less likely to be critical and rejecting. The internist, rather than labeling the patient as "difficult" and dismissing him, tolerated her feelings of confusion and irritation, recognizing them as a signal of underlying distress in the patient. She began to explore the meaning of the patient's behavior, believing that the source of his sexual feelings were not merely a physical attraction, but rather, much more complicated. This belief, and her willingness to work with the patient toward a mutual understanding of the problem, resulted in a successful treatment outcome for the patient.

Sexual Feelings Within the Physician

Thus far I have described a doctor-patient relationship involving sexual feelings coming primarily from the patient. Occasionally, however, it is the physician who feels strongly attracted to the patient, even if the patient is not acting seductively. For the most part, this is a normal and expected response. It usually requires nothing more than to recognize what is happening within oneself, and to consider it to be one of the benefits of human interaction. Obviously, such feelings should not be allowed to interfere with proper medical management or with a thorough psychological understanding of the patient. If, however, the physician feels close to acting on his or her sexual feelings, it is imperative to question whether or not this attraction is actually an avoidance of other, more serious problems. For example, a deterioration in one's own marriage or the stresses of other life crises may be prompting the physician to look to a patient for companionship and resolution of the personal problem. Or, as described earlier, it may be the patient who is avoiding other, more painful emotions by successfully getting the doctor to fall in love with him or her. If neither of these situations seem applicable and the desire for sexual involvement remains strong, it is then advisable for the physician to consult with a colleague. This could help to clarify unconscious motivations and conflicts of which the physician might be unaware.

Unfortunately, many physicians do become sexually involved with their patients. In a recent survey of 1,000 doctors, 460 of whom responded, 12.8% acknowledged some form of erotic behavior with their patients, with 7.2% admitting to intercourse. General practitioners appear to be at greatest risk in this survey, with 13% claiming to have had erotic contact with their patients and 9% acknowledging intercourse. Psychiatrists appear to be the least at risk in this survey: 10% admitted to some form of erotic involvement with their patients and 5% admitted having intercourse.

Clearly, all physicians may be tempted at one time or another to have sexual encounters with their patients. These encounters rarely fulfill the expectations of either the patient or the doctor, and are almost always damaging to the patient. Such damage has become increasingly recognized by civil courts and state licensing boards, which are now much more willing to find physicians guilty of malpractice. Such a judgment may result not only in economic loss and the loss of the license to practice for the physician, but also embarrassment, humiliation, and psychological turmoil for both the patient and the doctor. Thus, recognition that seductive behavior may be more complicated than it first appears can lead to more specific and empathic therapeutic interventions by the physician, resulting in help for a troubled patient rather than iatrogenic damage that then becomes truly "difficult" to undo.

Suggested Readings

Franks RD: The seductive patient. *Am Family Physician* 22: 111, 1980.

Franks RD: The angry patient. *Am Family Physician* 24: 123, 1981.

Groves JE: Taking care of the hateful patient. *N Engl J Med* 298: 883, 1978.

References

Burgess AW: Physician sexual misconduct and patients' response. *Am J Psychiatry* 138: 1335, 1981.

Kardener SH: Sex and the physician-patient relationship. *Am J Psychiatry* 131: 1134, 1974.

Kardener SH, Fuller M, Mensh IN: A survey of physicians' attitudes and practices regarding erotic and nonerotic contact with patients. *Am J Psychiatry* 130: 1077, 1973.

Kardener SH, Fuller M, Mensh IN: Characteristics of "erotic" practitioners. *Am J Psychiatry* 133: 1324, 1976.

B. The "Difficult" Surgical Patient

James H. Scully, M.D., Robert Dickes, M.D., and William E. Bernstein, M.D.

In the chapter on "The Psychological Reactions to Physical Illness," Dr. Blumenfield and Dr. Thompson discussed many of the most common reactions to surgery and to anesthesia. In this chapter we are going to focus in more detail on the "difficult" surgical patient.

A surgeon once told another specialist that in medicine there are surgeons and then there are all other physicians who are consultants to surgeons. His tongue-in-cheek remark has a grain of truth in it. There is a sense of drama in treating patients who are seriously ill, and surgical illness often takes center stage (Figure 14.2). The surgical patient experiences, in reality, a confirmation of what most patients wonder about whenever they go to a doctor, even if it is for a routine examination when they are feeling well. All of us frequently imagine that our doc-

Figure 14.2. *The Dawn of Abdominal Surgery* by Dean Cornwell. Dr. Ephraim McDowell, about to perform the first successful ovariotomy on Jane Todd Crawford, Danville, Kentucky, 1809. (Courtesy of Wyeth Laboratories, Philadelphia PA.)

tors will tell us that there is something wrong with us. This fantasy has become a reality for the patient who requires surgery.

When surgery is the prescribed treatment for illness, patients will react in different ways and will assign multiple meanings to that recommendation. These meanings will be highly influenced by the regard that the patient has for the surgeon. If the patient has trust and confidence in the surgeon's diagnostic and surgical skills, the patient will agree with the recommendation and hope for a beneficial outcome from the surgery. But there are also many other spoken and unspoken concerns, with unconscious as well as conscious meanings. Apprehension about pain, loss of bodily form and function, dependency, and death are prominent. The total surrender of control to another during the time of anesthesia and surgery can be a harrowing experience. No one is ever quite the same after surgery as one was before. Both the illness and the treatment for it have associated risks, as well as benefits. The risks combine to make the patient feel highly vulnerable. Confidence and dread hang in a delicate balance. The extent of organic pathology, the skills of the surgeon, and the characteristic ways in which the patient has reacted to critical events during his or her life are key factors that tip the balance towards a favorable or an unfavorable surgical course and outcome. Each of these three factors is crucial, and each can evoke feelings of anxiety, shame, guilt, and anger. The multiple ways that these painful affects are expressed and withheld bear upon the topic of this chapter. When a patient's expressions of and protections against experiencing these painful feelings deviate from the expectable, that patient likely will be regarded as "difficult."

The great advances of modern surgery have tended to turn some surgeons' attentions away from these emotional reactions of their patients. In fact, to some surgeons, the ideal patient is anesthetized. Thus, it often surprises a surgeon that in spite of an excellent surgical result, the patient suffers an emotional breakdown. Only when this happens does the surgeon then ask for a psychiatric consultation. If the psychological difficulties develop slowly, it may be a long time after the surgery before the psychiatric consultation is requested, and the referring physician may not even realize that the surgery was associated with the patient's emotional difficulties. Plastic surgeons are an exception, because they are usually well aware of the psychological consequences of altering a person's body image, especially when the demands for facial or other changes are based upon minor variations of little realistic consequence.

More psychiatric consultations should be requested in advance of surgery, especially in mutilating operations which affect the patient's body image. Any operation that threatens a person's basic self-esteem and psychological balance may require psychiatric help. Sexual functioning is often adversely affected in such operations. In this chapter we shall discuss preoperative difficulties, postoperative difficulties, and the effect of certain surgical procedures on male and female sexual functioning.

PREOPERATIVE DIFFICULTIES

Patients Who Refuse Surgery

The fears of death, mutilation, dependency, and pain can become so overwhelming that the patient decides to leave the hospital, thus delaying what might be life-saving surgery. Any patient obviously has a right to refuse surgery, and to operate on someone without his or her permission is considered an assault by the law. Nevertheless, the reason why the patient is refusing surgery must be evaluated. The patient may be using massive denial to cope with the anxiety caused by the reality of the illness and the possibility of surgery. The patient may also be out of touch with reality because of delusions due to psychosis or confusion due to an organic brain syndrome. Psychosis and organic brain syndromes are not absolute contraindications to surgery, but a psychiatric consultation should always be obtained. There is an increased risk of suicide postoperatively in these patients. Furthermore, the medications used to treat the psychosis may have various cardiorespiratory side effects, such as hypotension, and should be monitored carefully. In patients with an organic brain syndrome, there is an additional risk be-

sides the potential refusal to undergo surgery. There is a strong correlation between an organic brain syndrome preoperatively and a postoperative delirium. When a physician is faced with such a patient who refuses necessary surgery, the risks involved must be evaluated. In an emergency situation where the patient will die or be seriously impaired if the surgery is delayed, the surgeon must do what is needed and obtain the necessary legal protection for the surgery. If it is not an emergency, help from a psychiatric consultant can be obtained. The psychiatrist can then try to enlist the patient's cooperation by aiding the person to recognize and deal with the anxieties that are prompting the refusal for surgery. It does not usually help to confront the patient's denial directly as this only causes the patient to become even more frightened.

The Depressed Patient

A 58 year old executive was admitted to the hospital for coronary bypass surgery following a myocardial infarction. During the admission examination the surgeon noted that the patient looked sad, and asked him about his feelings regarding the surgery. "I don't care what happens to me anymore" replied the patient. "Do whatever you want." The surgeon cancelled the bypass surgery, and quite appropriately so. Patients who are seriously depressed for whatever reason are at a much greater risk to develop complications following surgery, and usually the more severe the depression, the more severe the complications will be. Other patients fully expect to die from the surgery and are resigned to their fate. This belief may be the result of some cultural or religious meaning of the surgery to the patient. For instance, the patient may believe that he has been cursed and will die from the surgery as a result of the curse. There is a high mortality rate from surgery in patients who believe they are going to die. In these cases, the surgery should be delayed if at all possible until the patient's beliefs can be explored and hopefully modified.

The Paranoid Patient

Another group of patients who are potentially difficult in the preoperative as well as in the postoperative period are the paranoid patients. These patients tend to project their hostile and anxiety provoking ideas and feelings onto others. They then blame these other people for their problems. These patients tend to be overly concerned with the physical exam, and become preoccupied with the details of the ward. They want to know what is going on because they do not trust anyone. It is useful to recognize this suspiciousness as a coping mechanism and not take it personally. The doctor regularly should explain as much as possible about what is going to happen and share information with all patients, but especially with the above types of patients. Great care should be taken, since they may resort to litigation if they feel neglected or mistreated by the physician. It may be particularly hazardous to perform plastic surgery on such patients, especially any plastic procedures involving the face.

The Polysurgery Patient

Another group of very difficult patients are those who are able to get doctors to operate on them over and over again. Often there is no organic pathology at first. In some instances, however, organic pathology is present and leads to the initial operation. This then triggers the syndrome. After several operations, postsurgical complications can develop, such as adhesions and obstructions, which may or may not need further surgery. Usually these patients present their symptoms in such a way that surgery seems the only solution, a solution which they urge. Dr. Karl Menninger has described some of the possible meanings of surgery for these patients. It may be an avoidance of some event more feared than the surgery itself. It may be a search for love through submission. It may represent a trial that is necessary in order to feel worthy and accepted. It may be a punishment for a pervasive feeling of guilt, the cause of which is usually unconscious. The 40 year old woman described at the end of Chapter 2, who had multiple operations beginning with the removal of a normal appendix at age 17, would be an example of a polysurgery patient motivated by a particular form of guilt. In her case she felt guilty for having survived her fraternal twin sister who died at the age of two.

POSTOPERATIVE DIFFICULTIES

Postoperative Delirium

Dr. Blumenfield and Dr. Thompson have already discussed some of the common reactions after major surgery. One of the less common but quite serious reactions is that of postoperative delirium (acute organic brain syndrome). In a later chapter Dr. Glickman will describe the symptoms of both the acute and chronic organic brain syndrome. Suffice it for now to say that the patient may develop cognitive defects, decreased level of consciousness, and motor deficits, as well as delusions, hallucinations, and assaultiveness. These symptoms may become life threatening. There are several conditions in which postoperative delirium is more likely, for example following open heart surgery. Besides the anxiety associated with this high risk surgery, there are major physiological changes such as decreased cerebral blood flow, decreased oxygenation, dehydration, and electrolyte imbalance, all of which may result in an acute organic brain syndrome and delirium. In addition, the thoracotomy involved in open heart surgery causes considerable postoperative pain, and these patients usually require large doses of analgesics which also reduce cardiopulmonary function. Postoperative delirium may also be the result of a withdrawal syndrome in a patient who is addicted to alcohol or some other drug and then is unable to take the addicting substance because of the surgery. The withdrawal symptoms begin during the postoperative period. Withdrawal from alcohol and barbiturates can cause an agitated delirium which is life threatening, and must be diagnosed and treated promptly. The signs and symptoms of these withdrawal states will also be discussed later in the book by Dr. Glickman.

Postoperative Depression

Postoperative depressions are common. They can be understood as a reaction to a loss — a loss of a body part, a loss of a bodily function, a loss of a cherished self-image, a loss of emotional supports. Surgery may result in other losses as well. For example, the patient may have expected too much from the surgery. Following the operation the patient must deal with the fact that the fantasied expectations of a cure have not been realized. For instance, the patient may have had the fantasy that a back operation would remove all his pain, but must now face the reality of some continued pain. The depressed patient who lies in bed without moving is more susceptible to complications such as pulmonary emboli and pneumonia. The patient who is depressed also tends to be more demanding of physicians and nursing staff and thus provokes their anger. The patient's lack of progress may also serve as an added provocation to the staff. It is important for health care professionals to be aware of both the patient's and their own feelings, and recognize them as understandable, so that they will not react negatively and punitively to the patient.

MALE SEXUAL FUNCTIONING

The Urinary Apparatus

Any portion of the male urinary apparatus (kidneys, ureters, and bladder) may require an operation. These organs are not directly involved in sexual performance and, therefore, any interference with sexual functioning is usually secondary to the general response to the surgery. The normal patient, following convalescence, should have no problem resuming sexual activity. Operations on the urethra, however, can cause considerable pain and organic interference, thus affecting both urination and ejaculation, and patients should be prepared for such temporary results.

The Testes

The effects of surgical removal of the testes depend in part on the age of the patient. Testicular removal before puberty usually results in impotence in the adult male. This is not necessarily due to the loss of the testes, but to the fact that the child has not developed a mature sexual pattern. In the stable adult male, bilateral orchiectomy need not produce impotence. The physiological facts of erection must be explained to a patient facing the removal of the testes so that the dangers of psychic impotence are lessened. More surgeons should adequately inform their patients about the physiology of erection and take the time to reassure them about their specific fears. If this is not done, then the man is left to deal with his multiple anxieties alone, thus making adjustment much more difficult. The loss of the testes due to carcinoma or to an accident, and the subsequent emotional shock, require that each man receive the education and specific help necessary for the best recovery possible. Sexual activity can continue. The inability to father children can be a serious blow to masculinity and self-esteem. In addition, the fear of losing his wife's love adds to the depression. The surgeon must be alert to the fact that testicular loss can cause a depression even in the normal male and must be prepared to make a psychiatric referral when necessary.

The Vas Deferens

Changing sexual societal roles, plus the increasing emphasis on limiting family size, has made vasectomy a relatively common operation. Previously, the woman bore the burden of contraception by the use of the "pill," the intrauterine device, the rhythm method, or surgical interruption of the uterine tubes. Many now consider vasectomy as the operation of choice since fallopian tube interruption is more complex and carries greater risk. Careful psychiatric evaluation should be done to make certain the individual is stable, understands the nature of the operation, and realizes that the sterility is usually permanent. There are more frequent adverse psychological reactions to vasectomy than is generally recognized.

The Prostate

A man's sexual performance can also be affected by operations on the prostate gland. Prostatectomy typically causes retrograde ejaculation. The patient who is aware of this result and has had a stable sexual relationship usually adjusts without major difficulty. The commonest cause for surgical removal of the prostate gland is hypertrophy, especially in the elderly. Many of these men expect to be impotent following surgery. This expectation can be a self-fulfilling prophecy. The disappearance of the ejaculate is at times used as proof of sexual incompetency. Skillfull reassurance and instruction in the anatomy and physiology of the sexual act is crucial.

Carcinoma of the prostate often requires extensive pelvic dissection. The resultant impotence and, possible urinary incompetence, are usually organic in origin. These men should be told before the operation about the resulting loss of potency and the other complications, including sterility, since a vasectomy is now often performed at the same time as a prostatectomy. Erectile ability cannot be recovered by psychotherapy when dissection has destroyed the significant innervations. The spouses and patients, however, can be taught that much sexual activity and pleasure remain even without penile insertion.

Neurosurgery

Many types of neurosurgical operations can affect sexual function. This is particularly true for neurosurgical operations which result in neuronal destruction in the central nervous system as well as vertebral fusions which may result in severing of local nerves. Thus, certain operations can create erectile or ejaculatory dysfunction of a permanent nature. Depression is frequent following such postoperative results. Attempts at helping these patients to function sexually must first take account of the depression. The spouse must be involved in the sex therapy for these individuals, although people may come for therapy only when the male is involved, since vaginal containment for the woman remains possible even after she has had major surgery. So much emphasis is placed upon penile performance as a measure of masculinity that the emotional situation for the male who cannot have an erection or ejaculation is much more serious. In the treatment, the importance of the penis must be deemphasized for such couples. The pleasures available from oral contacts, fondling, bodily embraces, and genital manipulation are significant, and need to be stressed. New surgical procedures are also being developed for organic impotence due to defects in the blood supply to the penile corpora. The value of these approaches remains uncertain.

FEMALE SEXUAL FUNCTIONING

The Breasts

For many women the importance of childbearing and physical attractiveness are often of paramount importance, and any operative procedure involving the breasts or the reproductive organs requires special attention. Carcinoma is the most frequent cause for breast amputation. Commonly the immediate response to mastectomy is the fear of loss of attractiveness and of love. Our culture emphasizes a woman's value in terms of her physical attractiveness with a special role assigned to breast development. Thus, the loss of a breast often makes the woman feel ugly and, therefore, unwanted. These feelings may lead her to provoke a rejection in advance. She may also refuse to discuss her appearance and scar with anyone close. This contributes to a growing alienation, creating a vicious cycle of rejection and counterrejection. The man, confused by these events, may seek sex elsewhere. The ensuing marital difficulty can even lead to divorce. This occurs just when the woman is most in need of support, understanding, and love.

The physician's role in the above noted situations is to restore communication between the partners, and to help them to verbalize and discuss their fears. Encouraging the pair to resume lovemaking is important. The absence of the breast and the presence of the scar should be dealt with via looking and touching. Loving partners usually manage the difficulties quite well.

The emotional trauma of mastectomy to the single woman without a partner is apt to produce an even more severe reaction. The absence of the support of a companion lessens her security and confidence in her attractiveness. All physicians should be aware of these facts and, if possible, arrange preoperatively to have family or friends involved in helping these women deal with their fears. Actively seeking out a sex life is important. The prospective partner should know about the mastectomy prior to lovemaking. Many men will not lose their interest.

Reconstructive surgery for the amputated breast is to be recommended, since it helps many women regain their psychological equilibrium. In fact, one reason why the radical (Halsted) mastectomy is being performed less and less is that it does not leave sufficient tissue for reconstruction. The woman should be helped to develop a realistic concept of what the reconstructed breast will be like. Unrealistic expectations should be carefully explored and corrected so that a serious disappointment in the reconstruction does not occur.

The Uterus

A woman's psychological response to the loss of the uterus is quite varied and depends on many factors, including the reason for the operation, the woman's acceptance of its necessity, her age, her psychological maturity, and the stability of her sense of her femininity. Her response is influenced by her own as well as her culture's attitude toward childbearing. Her husband's attitude is also extremely important. Some men reject the woman as no longer truly feminine because of their own unconscious fears as well as their desires for children. Carcinoma of the uterus with its serious prognoses imposes a much greater psychological burden than does removal for fibromyomata. As a rule younger women react more unfavorably especially those wanting children.

Even under the best of circumstances, complete psychological recovery following a hysterectomy may take many months. This is because much psychological response is based upon unconscious thinking which does not have a logical basis. For example, any operation may be viewed, unconsciously, as a punishment. This is especially true of operations on the sexual apparatus. The person views the organic pathology as the punishment for sexual behavior. Great guilt is still attached to sexual thoughts and sexual activity by many people. Physicians must be aware of this, and should take steps to prevent a depressed patient's sexual behavior from being severely inhibited.

It is also important to recognize the contention of many concerned people that at least some hysterectomies may be performed for less than compelling medical reasons. Hysterectomy is the nation's second most frequently performed operation, after tonsillectomy, and the rates vary considerably from group to group and from country to country. Twice as many hysterectomies are performed for insured persons as for the uninsured. In prepaid health plans where peer review discourages unnecessary surgery, rates of hysterectomies are as much as 25% lower than in fee-for-service health plans. Hysterectomies are performed two and a half times as frequently in the United States as in England and Wales, and four times as frequently as in Sweden. While there are many factors that may explain such findings, all physicians need to reflect on any economic motives that might prompt certain procedures, as well as the attitude among some male professionals that a woman's uterus is not really that important. It is unlikely that they would feel the same way about an operation on their own genitals or reproductive organs.

The Ovaries

What is applicable to the breast and the uterus also applies to the ovaries, especially to bilateral removal. Unilateral oophorectomy, in a properly informed woman, rarely precipitates a psychiatric crisis. However, bilateral oophorectomy has been known to have an even more profound psychological effect upon a woman than hysterectomy. This is due to the belief that the true seat of femininity is in the ovaries and not

elsewhere. Hysterectomy alone does not induce such women to develop a major psychiatric crisis, whereas hysterectomy plus bilateral oophorectomy is much more likely to create a major emotional upset. The physician, therefore, must be aware of the implications involved in this triple loss. It is also important to remember that the ovary produces hormones necessary to the female reproductive cycle, and that estrogens as well as androgens influence a woman's general behavior as well as her sexual activity. The surgeon should aid the patient to consult with her internist or endocrinologist to insure the appropriate hormonal replacement, or other supportive measures if hormonal replacement is not possible because of malignancy.

CONCLUSION

All physicians, including surgeons, have become increasingly attentive to their patients' psychological responses to illness, and an ongoing collaboration between psychiatrists and other specialists in medicine can only benefit both the patients and the physicians. As Dr. Dubovsky has already indicated in Chapter 13, George Engel has offered an expansion of the traditional biomedical model to a *biopsychosocial* model that would encourage the appreciation of the complex interaction between biological, psychological, and social factors in all states of health and illness. By taking such a biopsychosocial model into consideration, physicians have an expanded base of information which they can utilize in the assessment of their patients' diagnoses and treatment, and in predicting the outcome from illness, hospitalization, and surgery. Through such an expanded understanding, we might well be able to bring about a considerable decrease in the incidence of "difficult" surgical patients.

Suggested Readings

Dickes R: Medicine, surgery, and sexual dysfunction. In Grinspoon L (ed): *Psychiatry 1982: Annual Review.* Washington, American Psychiatric Press, 1982, p 35.

Engel GL: The need for a new medical model: a challenge for biomedicine. *Science* 196:129, 1977.

Notman MT, Nadelson CC (eds): *The Woman Patient. Volume 1: Sexual and Reproductive Aspects of Women's Health Care.* New York, Plenum Press, 1978.

Surman OS: The surgical patient. In Hackett TP, Cassem NH (eds): *Massachusetts General Hospital Handbook of General Hospital Psychiatry.* St. Louis, C.V. Mosby Co., 1978, p 64.

References

Barchilon J: *Malpractice and You.* New York, Ace, 1975.

Barnes AB, Tinkham CB: Surgical gynecology. In Notman

MT, Nadelson CC (eds): *The Woman Patient. Volume 1.* New York, Plenum Press, 1978, p 203.

Belt BG: Some organic causes of impotence. *Med Asp Hum Sex* 7:152, 1973.

Blachy PH, Starr A: Post-cardiotomy delirium. *Am J Psychiatry* 121:371, 1964.

Castelnuovo-Tedesco P: Organ transplant, body image, psychosis. *Psychoanal Q* 42:349, 1973.

Console WA, Simons RC, Rubinstein M: The polysurgery woman. In *The First Encounter: The Beginnings in Psychotherapy.* New York, Jason Aronson, 1976, p 115.

Deutsch H: Some psychoanalytic observations in surgery. *Psychosom Med* 4:105, 1942.

Dlin BM, Perlman A: Sex after ileostomy and colostomy. *Med Asp Hum Sex* 6:32, 1972.

Engel GL, Romano J: Delirium: a syndrome of cerebral insufficiency. *J Chronic Dis* 9:260, 1959.

Goldwyn RM: The woman and esthetic surgery. In Notman MT, Nadelson CC (eds): *The Woman Patient. Volume 1.* New York, Plenum Press, 1978, p 271.

Hollander MA: Hysterectomy and feelings of femininity. *Med Asp Hum Sex* 3:6, 1969.

Huffman JW: The effect of gynecological surgery on sex relations. *Am J Obstet Gynecol* 59:915, 1970.

Kahan EB, Gaskill EB: The "difficult" patient: observations on the staff-patient interaction. In Notman MT, Nadelson CC (eds): *The Woman Patient. Volume 1.* New York, Plenum Press, 1978, p 257.

Kennedy JA, Bakst H: The influence of emotion on the outcome of cardiac surgery: a predictive study. *Bull NY Acad Med* 42:811, 1966.

Kimball CP: A predictive study of adjustment to cardiac surgery. *J Thorac Cardiovasc Surg* 58:891, 1969.

Kimball CP: Psychological responses to the experience of open-heart surgery. I. *Am J Psychiatry* 126:348, 1969.

Kimball CP: The experience of open-heart surgery. III. Toward a definition and understanding of post cardiotomy delirium. *Arch Gen Psychiatry* 27:57, 1972.

Lipowski ZJ: Delirium, clouding of consciousness and confusion. *J Nerv Ment Dis* 145:227, 1967.

Menninger KA: Polysurgery and polysurgical addiction. *Psychoanal Q* 3:173, 1934.

Notman MT: A psychological consideration of mastectomy. In Notman MT, Nadelson CC (eds): *The Woman Patient. Volume 1.* New York, Plenum Press, 1978, p 247.

Pasnau RO, Gitlin MJ: Psychological reactions to sterilization. *Psychosomatics* 21:10, 1980.

Pollock GH, Muslin HL: Dreams during surgical procedures. *Psychoanal Q* 31:175, 1962.

Richards DH: *Depressive Illness after Hysterectomy.* Rockville, MD, Physicians International Press, 1973.

Rodgers DA, Ziegler FJ, Levy N: Prevailing cultural attitudes about vasectomy: a possible explanation of postoperative psychological response. *Psychosom Med* 29:367, 1967.

Roeske NCA: Hysterectomy and other gynecological surgeries: a psychological view. In Notman MT, Nadelson CC (eds): *The Woman Patient. Volume 1.* New York, Plenum Press, 1978, p 217.

Rosen JS, Nanninga JB, O'Connor VJ: External sphincterotomy: effect on penile erection. *Arch Phys Med Rehabil* 57:511, 1976.

Titchener JL, et al: Psychosis in surgical patients. *Surg Gynecol Obstet* 102:54, 1956.

Wabrek AJ, Wabrek CJ: Mastectomy: sexual complications. *Primary Care* 4:803, 1976.

Weisman AD, Hackett TP: Predilection to death: death and dying as a psychiatric problem. *Psychosom Med* 23:232, 1961.

Zohar J, et al: Factors influencing sexual activity after prostatectomy: a prospective study. *J Urol* 116:332, 1976.

C. The "Difficult" Medical Patient, and the Importance of Consultation-Liaison Psychiatry

Troy L. Thompson II, M.D.,
James H. Scully, M.D., and
Wendy L. Thompson, M.D.

PSYCHIATRIC DISORDERS IN GENERAL MEDICAL PRACTICE

As Dr. Mumford has already indicated in Chapter 6, most patients turn first to their primary care physician rather than to a psychiatrist or other mental health professional when they are in physical or emotional distress. In spite of this well known fact, many physicians are still not aware of the importance of psychiatric disorders in their practice of medicine. Some of the reasons given for avoiding the psychiatric aspects of patient care are that the physician's job is to care for medical and not psychiatric disorders, that it is too time consuming to take a thorough psychiatric history, that psychiatric treatment is beyond the capability of the physician, and that it would be upsetting to the patient to talk about emotional conflicts. Actually, patients who have emotional stresses are usually relieved when the physician recognizes these stresses; however, uncovering emotional conflicts may be upsetting to the physician. Furthermore, while sophisticated psychiatric treatment is beyond the capability of most primary care physicians, this is not an acceptable excuse to avoid diagnosis of psychiatric disorders. Heart surgery is also beyond the training of most primary care physicians but few would view this as justification for not listening to the heart or not doing other basic screening tests to determine if consultation with or referral to a cardiac surgeon is indicated.

It also must be noted that under our current method of financing medical care in this country, the rewards are far less for taking a careful psychiatric history, engaging in patient education, and utilizing nontechnological approaches in diagnosis and treatment. Time spent in the operating room or performing technical procedures is reimbursed by insurance companies and other third party payers at five to ten times what is paid for the same amount of time in educational, counseling, or history-taking activities. In the long run these current policies may be much more expensive, since many patients who do not have their questions answered or who are not counseled and educated in management of their conditions may ultimately require longer hospitalizations and more expensive medical care. Furthermore, over-reliance on technical and laboratory procedures rather than utilizing skills at history taking and physical examination tends to put more emotional distance between the physician and patient. This is sometimes called practicing "defensive" medicine because of fears of malpractice suits. Paradoxically, those physicians who know their patients best and have a personal relationship with them are much less likely to be sued than those who interpose excessive technology between themselves and their patients. A malpractice attorney who defends doctors once said he viewed it as a bad sign if the physician did not remember the patient and had to request the medical records to determine who the patient was after learning of a potential malpractice lawsuit. Over-reliance on "objective" measures may actually lead to misdiagnosis. Case example: A 34 year old successful business executive came to his family physician complaining of severe substernal chest pain of one day's duration. He appeared frightened and anxious, and was worried that he might be having a heart attack. Vital signs were normal, and the cursory physical examination revealed no abnormalities. Electrocardiogram was within normal limits. The patient was admitted to the coronary care unit of a hospital,

and only after coronary angiography was also reported as normal did anyone sit down with the patient and discuss his concerns in more detail. The patient's pain had begun on the tenth anniversary of his father's death from a myocardial infarction. The patient had had a stormy relationship with his father and had been unable to attend the funeral. He had felt guilty about this as well as many other aspects of his relationship with his father, and had never talked about his guilt with anyone. A psychiatric consultation was obtained, and the patient was discharged from the hospital to work on his unresolved grief about the death of his father in psychotherapy. The patient's stay in the hospital cost over $10,000 as well as many days of unrelieved anxiety for the patient and his family.

Another impediment to helping patients deal with the emotional aspects of their illnesses is a dualistic, "either-or" type of thinking. This kind of thinking leads to "mind" versus "body", "organic" versus "functional", "real" versus "not real" illnesses, and other terms such as "gomer", "crock", or "turkey." These terms often reflect the physician's discomfort with emotionally disturbed and needy patients, and the physician's difficulty in seeing such patients in a comprehensive, biopsychosocial perspective. Reductionistic thinking may then emerge at these times. This kind of thinking is characterized by attempting to explain all behaviors through the smallest possible unit or system. For instance, assuming that a patient's violent behavior may be explained entirely by his personality style rather than appreciating that there may be a disorder of brain function would be reductionistic, as would assuming that a patient's postoperative depression is entirely due to disordered physiology without considering the meaning of the surgery for that particular patient. This kind of reductionistic thinking is a very powerful factor in expanding scientific knowledge but may be counterproductive when dealing with an individual human being. Obviously molecules, atoms, and neurotransmitters ultimately make up the human brain, but that does not mean that the laws that govern brain neurochemistry can ultimately be used to explain all of the problems that may arise at higher levels of psychological and social functioning. Nor can psychosocial conflicts ever be divorced from their biological and neurological roots. We hope to demonstrate the importance of a systems-oriented, biopsychosocial approach to all patients as we discuss several different variations of the "difficult" medical patient.

THE "DIFFICULT" MEDICAL PATIENT

Psychiatric Illness in Medical Patients

Glass and colleagues found that 83% of new patients seeking care at a university hospital outpatient medical clinic had a psychiatric diagnosis. Thompson and colleagues found that about two-thirds of patients in a similar setting had at least one major psychosocial distress and about a third of those patients had two or more types of significant psychosocial distress. It should also be noted that in the latter study the internal medicine physicians did not recognize significant psychosocial distress in 14 of 17 areas of functioning in their patients. This was largely due to inadequate screening efforts and not taking careful psychosocial histories that would have elicited psychiatric symptoms.

Medical Illness in Psychiatric Patients

As Dr. Mumford has also indicated in Chapter 6, psychiatric patients are not immune from medical illness, and indeed may be at higher risk for medical illness than the general population. One study by Koranyi found that 43% of psychiatric outpatients had one or more medical illnesses, and half of these disorders had not been diagnosed by the primary care physicians who referred the patient to the psychiatric clinic. Patients who were self-referred or referred by social agencies and who had a medical illness were almost always undiagnosed.

Medical Illnesses Presenting as Psychiatric Disorders

Almost all patients who develop a medical or surgical illness have some form of psychological reaction, as was discussed in Chapter 8. A mild degree of anxiety, depression, or insomnia is normal in response to physical illness and should lead to a discussion of the patient's concerns about the illness rather than to immediate prescription of a tranquilizer, antidepressant, or sedative. However, a number of medical illnesses may initially present with psychiatric symptoms, and all physicians should be alert to this

fact (Table 14.1). Proper treatment in such cases can only result from correct diagnosis of the underlying medical illness. Failure to recognize the underlying physical disorder and attempts to treat the psychiatric symptoms via the usual psychiatric treatments will obviously be inadequate and may lead to a dangerous progression of the medical illness. Patients who have a psychiatric history are particularly at risk for such oversights. Clearly a psychiatric disorder does not make one immune to medical illness. For example, patients with hypochondriasis all die of something other than their primary psychiatric disorder.

In one particular study, Hall and colleagues found that almost 10% of patients being treated in a psychiatric outpatient clinic had medical disorders that were producing their psychiatric symptoms. Cardiovascular or endocrine disorders were most frequent, but disorders of almost every organ system were identified. Nearly 30% of these patients were psychotic. Many had delusions and hallucinations, and these symptoms were particularly confusing to physicians who did not recognize that they were of organic origin. Psychosis is not always due to schizophrenia, mania, or depression. It can also develop secondary to disorders of the central nervous system, metabolic disturbances, toxins, infections, tumors, or trauma. Even commonly prescribed medications alone or in combination may cause psychiatric symptomatology (Table 14.2).

Medical Evaluation of Psychiatric Patients

General observation of the patient may reveal a great deal about his or her physical health. Is the gait normal in walking from the waiting room? Is the patient well groomed and the clothing appropriate to the season and weather? Observe the posture and look for involuntary movements. Does the patient look robust and healthy, or pale with loose fitting clothing, suggestive of weight loss? Do the skin, hair, and eyes look healthy? Is the patient alert and attentive? Is the speech of a normal tone and rate? Because of the increased prevalence of medical illness in psychiatric patients, a medical evaluation should be considered for all patients who present with psychiatric symptoms. The index of suspicion that a medical illness is present should be especially high when: 1) the patient has devel-

Table 14.1*
Medical and Neurological Illnesses Which Commonly Cause Psychiatric Symptoms

Illness	Onset and sex	Medical symptoms	Psychiatric symptoms
Addison's disease (adrenal cortical insufficiency)	adulthood, M = F	hypotension, skin pigmentation, weight loss, weakness	depression, apathy, may lead to toxic psychosis
Cushing's disease (hyperadrenalism)	adulthood, M = F	"moon" facies, buffalo hump, striae, truncal obesity, fatigability	memory loss, depression, anxiety, euphoria, may progress to thought disorder
Hypoglycemia	adulthood, M = F	sweating, hunger, dizziness, weakness	anxiety, depression, confusion
Hypoparathyroidism	late adulthood, more females	muscle spasms, tetany, hyperreflexia	anxiety, depression, may lead to toxic psychosis
Hyperparathyroidism	late adulthood, females 3:1	weakness, peptic ulcers, renal calculi, myalgias, fractures	anxiety, depression, may lead to toxic psychosis
Hypothyroidism	early to middle adulthood, females 5:1	dry and puffy skin, cold intolerance, thinning hair, weight gain	anxiety, depression, "myxedema madness" may resemble schizophrenia
Hyperthyroidism	early to middle adulthood, females 3:1	tremor, weight loss, sweating, heat intolerance	rapid onset mimics anxiety attacks; slower onset mimics depression
Pheochromocytoma	adulthood, M = F	intermittently elevated blood pressures, headaches	anxiety, fear, panic
Intracranial tumors	adulthood, M = F	depends on location—headaches, vomiting, papilledema, seizures	personality changes, depression, anxiety, delusions, symptoms of organic brain syndrome (OBS)
Malignant, solid tumors	any age, M = F	related to site of carcinoma	"distant" effect of carcinoma, depression common
Pancreatic carcinoma	late adulthood, males 3:1	abdominal pain, weight loss, jaundice	depression, sense of impending doom
Alzheimer's disease	middle to late adulthood, perhaps more females	extrapyramidal symptoms	symptoms of OBS, depression, anxiety
Chronic subdural hematoma	all ages, more late adulthood	headache, papilledema, gait disturbance, seizures, progressive focal neurological deficits	memory loss, depression, agitation, personality changes
Multiple sclerosis	early adulthood, more females	impaired vision, nystagmus, ataxia, scanning speech, other motor or sensory losses	euphoria, personality changes, mood swings
Myasthenia gravis	all ages, more early adulthood, females 2:1	muscle weakness, increasing fatigue with activity, diplopia	irritability, depression
Normal presssure hydrocephalus	middle to late adulthood, M = F	increased reflexes, gait disturbance, urinary incontinence	confusion, memory loss, depression
Acute intermittent porphyria	young adulthood, more females	abdominal pain, paresthesias, weakness	severe anxiety or withdrawal, emotional lability

Table 14.1—*Continued*

Mitral valve prolapse	young adulthood, more females	often asymptomatic	acute and chronic anxiety, agoraphobia, panic attacks
Pernicious anemia	mid to late adulthood, more females	glossitis, peripheral neuritis, weakness	depression, if prolonged may lead to OBS
Systemic lupus erythematosis	young adulthood, females 8:1	butterfly rash, multiple symptoms depending on organ systems involved	cerebral vasculitis may cause varied and variable symptoms, anxiety, depression, thought disorder resembling schizophrenia
Wilson's disease (hepatolenticular degeneration)	adolescence to young adulthood, males 2:1	Kayser-Fleischer rings, liver and extrapyramidal symptoms	anger, depression, sudden outburst, may resemble schizophrenia

* Table by Troy L. Thompson II, M.D. Modified from earlier tables by Martin (1979) and Hall (1980).

Table 14.2*

Psychiatric Symptoms Caused by Commonly Used Drugs

Drugs	Type of drug	Psychiatric symptoms
Benzodiazapines	minor tranquilizers, sedative-hypnotics	depression, euphoria, anxiety, apathy, fatigue
Cimetidine	ulcer treatment	confusion, headache, psychosis
Clonidine	antihypertensive	vivid dreams, insomnia, nervousness, fatigue, depression
Corticosteroids	antiinflammatory, immunosuppressive	euphoria, insomnia, mood swings, depression, psychosis
Digitalis	cardiac glycoside	bad dreams, restlessness, headaches, weakness, apathy
Ephedrine, terbutaline	decongestant, antiasthmatic	anxiety, restlessness, insomnia, weakness, palpitations
Estrogens	female hormone, birth control pills	exacerbation of latent migraine, depression
Furosemide	diuretic	headache, restlessness
Insulin	treatment of diabetes	anxiety, restlessness, nightmares
Isoniazid	antituberculous	depression, nightmares, toxic psychosis
Levodopa	antiParkinsonian	depression, dementia, psychotic episodes, insomnia, euphoria
Lidocaine	IV for cardiac arrhythmias	euphoria, apprehension, vivid hallucinations, OBS, agitation or drowsiness
Methyldopa	antihypertensive	nightmares, depression, mild psychoses, fatigue
Methylxanthines	bronchodilators	anxiety, insomnia, palpitations
Phenobarbital	anticonvulsant	agitation, anxiety, nightmares, insomnia, hallucinations, thought disorder
Propranolol	antihypertensive, antianginal	depression, insomnia, occasional symptoms or OBS, vivid dreams
Reserpine	antihypertensive	depression, possibly psychotic
Thyroxine	thyroid hormone replacement	anxiety, tremulousness, insomnia

* Table by Troy L. Thompson II, M.D. and Wendy L. Thompson, M.D.

Table 14.3*

Several Problems for Which Psychiatric Consultation Should Be Sought

Immediately
1. The patient is suicidal or homicidal or has a recent history of severe psychiatric illness.
2. The patient is psychotic or has very disturbed behaviors.
3. The patient is becoming overwhelmed by some psychogical reaction.
4. The doctor-patient relationship is severely disrupted.
5. The patient is threatening to leave against medical advice (AMA).

Within a day or so:
1. The patient is becoming more anxious or depressed, or is developing persistent insomnia.
2. The patient's behaviors are beginning to interfere with optimal medical management.
3. The relationships with the doctors, nurses, family, or others are beginning to deteriorate or show signs of significant distress.
4. The patient has a history of significant psychiatric illness, even though he or she appears to be well compensated at present.
5. The patient is taking psychiatric medications, especially if side effects are present or they are at risk of developing.
6. Some psychotherapy or advanced type of counseling is needed to prepare the patient for surgery or a specialized procedured (e.g., CT scan, hemodialysis).
7. The patient may need some type of psychiatric disposition following discharge (e.g., psychotherapy, mental health clinic, rehabilitation program).

* Table by Troy L. Thompson II, M.D. Modified from Dubovsky and Weissberg (1982).

oped psychiatric symptoms for the first time over the age of 40, or the current psychiatric symptoms differ from prior symptoms; 2) the onset of the symptoms is slow or insidious; 3) there is no clear psychosocial precipitant in the patient's life; 4) there is no family history of psychiatric illness similar to the patient's symptoms; or 5) apparently competent psychiatric treatment has been ineffective.

Psychiatrists should refer their patients who need a complete physical examination to an internist unless the psychiatrist has maintained physical examination skills and general medical knowledge. Likewise, other physicians should refer their patients with questionable psychiatric symptoms to a psychiatrist for consultation, since these physicians are rarely as skilled or up-to-date in general psychiatric knowledge. Psychiatrists should do careful medical histories and be keen observers, maintaining a high degree of suspicion of physical illness in their patients. Furthermore, the psychiatrist should not assume that a patient who has been referred to him by another physician, even an internist, has been thoroughly screened for medical illness that may be producing the psychiatric symptoms. The referring physician may not have done a complete mental status examination or considered all of the medical possibilities. It should also be remembered that psychiatric symptoms may be the earliest indication of a medical illness even before laboratory tests are positive. A progression of medical symptoms should lead to immediate consultation with the primary physician for further evaluation.

Patients With Both Medical and Psychiatric Illness

As is clear from all of the above, some patients have both medical and psychiatric illnesses. In such cases it is very important for the primary care physician and the psychiatrist to collaborate in order to formulate a unified treatment plan. Any changes in diagnosis, treatment, or prescription of medication should be discussed to avoid adverse drug interactions or contradictory treatment approaches. Both the primary care physician and the psychiatrist need to be able and willing to use a broad biopsychosocial approach to their diagnostic thinking and their treatment planning.

IMPORTANCE OF CONSULTATION-LIAISON PSYCHIATRY

Reasons For a Psychiatric Consultation

When a physician requests a psychiatric consultation, it is important to clarify what the physician wants the psychiatrist to do (Table 14.3). The physician may simply desire confirmation of his or her psychological understanding of the patient, or may want the psychiatrist to take over completely the psychosocial management of the case. Obviously, the psychiatrist and attending physician must communicate and discuss their expectations of each other, otherwise a great deal of misunderstanding, disappointment, blame, and counterblame may result. These expectations may be completely different from one patient to the next, even when the medical conditions are the same.

Often patients are admitted to medical wards for an extensive workup of somatic symptoms. In the course of the evaluation the physician may become aware that the patient has a psychiatric disorder that may be underlying the somatic complaints. Some physicians wait before consulting a psychiatrist until they have exhausted all of the technological and laboratory procedures in an attempt to rule out biomedical illnesses; by then the physician, the patient, the family, and nursing staff are feeling frustrated, confused, and helpless. The magical wish for the psychiatrist to then enter the picture and quickly explain all the symptoms on psychological grounds is almost always unrealistic. It is wiser to consult a psychiatrist earlier when the medical issues may still be unclear if the patient or family are beginning to become very upset. "An ounce of prevention is worth a pound of cure" is just as true for psychiatric disorders as it is for medical or surgical disorders. A psychiatric evaluation can be carried out simultaneously with laboratory or other diagnostic efforts in sorting out the confusing symptomatology.

If the psychiatric disturbance is severe enough, the patient is usually transferred to the psychiatric ward of a general hospital or to a separate psychiatric hospital once the medical or surgical illness is under control. In some cases the patient's psychiatric condition can be managed on the medical or surgical ward or as a psychiatric outpatient after discharge. Ongoing outpatient psychiatric follow-up is usually recommended where there is a long-standing or recurrent psychiatric condition.

The consulting psychiatrist may also attempt to assure that the patient understands his or her illness and is appropriately involved in the decision-making regarding the recommended treatment. Some physicians have the attitude that they know what is best for their patients and that their patients should accept their physician's wisdom without question. Unfortunately, such an approach may meet with resistance from many patients, especially those who have very independent or oppositional personality traits. On the other hand, some patients may prefer to "know nothing" about their illness or treatment and may passively want the physician to make all the decisions. Psychiatrists can help the physician assume the most appropriate role with different patients or even with the same patient at different times during the course of the illness. In Chapter 7 Dr. Mumford discussed the many different factors involved in the failure of patients to cooperate with medical advice. For example, a large percentage of patients do not take medications as prescribed or for as long as needed. In part this may be because the physician did not take the time to answer the patients' questions about the medication, explain the need for dosage and duration of treatment (as with a course of antibiotics), and discuss possible side effects. Other patients may not trust or have confidence in the physician's diagnostic skills and therapeutic recommendations. Still other patients' lack of compliance may be due to memory difficulties or psychiatric disturbance. Many physicians respond initially to the noncompliant patient by becoming frustrated and angry. Some think and a few say: "If the patient doesn't follow my good advice, then he deserves to stay ill." Such reactions seldom do anything to improve the compliance, and may well make the lack of cooperation even worse. A better approach is to attempt to understand the reasons why the patient has been uncooperative and to try to correct these causes. Consultation-liaison psychiatrists may play a helpful role in such cases by consulting with physicians as well as with patients. They conduct teaching conferences for other physicians to discuss the common psychiatric disorders, techniques of interviewing, issues of patient education, basic counseling approaches, and negative attitudes towards patients with emotional conflicts that impair their ability to cooperate with medical advice. They may also help nursing staff to better deal with difficult medical patients.

Patients' Reactions to Psychiatric Consultation

Most patients are aware when they are having significant psychiatric symptoms, such as anxiety and depression, and are usually relieved to have a specialist in that area to talk with and from whom they can receive recommendations. However, it is critical that the physician prepare the patient for a psychiatric consultation. Patients who are not told that a psychiatrist is coming by to talk with them almost always become angry and distrustful. Some patients who are not properly prepared feel they have been "bad" and that the psychiatrist has been sent as a punishment. The explanation for recommending a psychiatric consultation should be straightforward and brief, the same as it would be for a cardiologist or other specialist who has been asked to consult. The physician might say, "I have noticed that you are fairly anxious or depressed, and I would like a specialist in this area, a psychiatrist, to come by and talk with you. This should help me to provide you the best care with this problem. Do you have any questions about that?" If the physician does not think the patient has a serious mental condition it can be comforting to convey that by saying something such as, "Many people are frightened to talk to a psychiatrist because they think it means they have a severe mental problem or that they are crazy. I do not think that is true in your case, but even moderate anxiety or depression may delay your recovery, or make it more uncomfortable than it might be otherwise." It is also wise as well as courteous to tell the patient when the psychiatrist will visit or, if the exact time is not known, to say, "I imagine the psychiatrist will come by this evening or some time tomorrow. After the visit I will talk with the psychiatrist and discuss our thoughts with you on my rounds tomorrow."

When properly prepared Schwab found that the great majority of patients were positive and accepting of psychiatric consultation. Those who were well prepared for the consultation and were able to have their questions answered benefited more from the psychiatric consultation than those who were not well prepared. Levitan and Kornfeld, as well as others, have found that effective psychiatric consultation may significantly reduce the length of hospitalization and health care costs. Patients who have had psychiatric intervention may also be able to return home rather than go to a nursing home or other institution. The overall goal of consultation-liaison psychiatry is to assure that the patient's unique biological, psychological, and sociocultural situation is included in the treatment planning, in the belief that such an approach will lead to many fewer "difficult" medical patients.

Suggested Readings

Hall RCW (ed): *Psychiatric Presentations of Medical Illness: Somatopsychic Disorders.* Jamaica, NY, Spectrum, 1980.
Martin MJ: Physical disease manifesting as psychiatric disorders. In Usdin G, Lewis JM (eds): *Psychiatry in General Medical Practice.* New York, McGraw-Hill, 1979, p 337.

References

Boston Collaborative Drug Surveillance Program, Boston Univ. Med. Ctr. Psychiatric side effects of nonpsychiatric drugs. *Semin Psychiatry* 3:398, 1971.
Dubovsky SL, Weissberg MP: *Clinical Psychiatry in Primary Care,* ed 2. Baltimore, Williams & Wilkins, 1982.
Glass RM, et al: Psychiatric screening in a medical clinic: an evaluation of a self-report inventory. *Arch Gen Psychiatry* 35:1189, 1978.
Hale ML, Abram HS: Patient's attitudes toward psychiatric consultations in the general hospital. *Va Med Mon* 94:342, 1967.
Hall RCW, et al: Physical illness presenting as psychiatric disease. *Arch Gen Psychiatry* 35:1315, 1978.
Kimball CP: The challenge of liaison medicine. In Pasnau RO (ed): *Consultation-Liaison Psychiatry.* New York, Grune & Stratton, 1975, p 269.
Koranyi EK: Morbidity and rate of undiagnosed physical illnesses in a psychiatric clinic population. *Arch Gen Psychiatry* 36:414, 1979.
Levitan SJ, Kornfeld DS: Clinical and cost benefits of liaison psychiatry. *Am J Psychiatry* 138:790, 1981.
Lipowski ZJ: Consultation-liaison psychiatry: past, present, and future. In Pasnau RO (ed): *Consultation-Liaison Psychiatry.* New York, Grune & Stratton, 1975, p 1.
Martin MJ: A brief review of organic diseases masquerading as functional illness. *Hosp & Comm Psychiatry* 34:328, 1983.
McKegney PF: Consultation-liaison teaching of psychosomatic medicine: opportunities and obstacles. *J Nerv Ment Dis* 154:198, 1972.
Schwab JJ, et al: Medical patients' reaction to referring physicians after psychiatric consultation. *JAMA* 195:1120, 1966.
Strain JJ, Grossman S: *Psychological Care of the Medically Ill: A Primer in Liaison Psychiatry.* New York, Appleton-Century-Crofts, 1975.
Thompson TL II, Thompson WL: Treating postoperative delirium. *Drug Ther* 8:30, 1983.
Thompson TL II, Stoudemire A, Mitchell WD, Grant RL: Underrecognition of patients' psychosocial distress in a university hospital medical clinic. *Am J Psychiatry* 140:158, 1983.
Thompson TL II, Moran MG, Nies AS: Psychotropic drug use in the elderly. *N Engl J Med* 308:134 (Part I) and 194 (Part II), 1983.

PART II
Childhood and Adolescence: The Years of Growth and Development

Section D/The Beginnings of Life

CHAPTER 15 **Pregnancy and the Expectant Couple**

Joan Hittelman, Ph.D.,
Richard C. Simons, M.D., and
Janice L. Petersen, M.D.

The reader may well ask why we have chosen to begin our study of the life cycle with pregnancy. There are several reasons. First of all, each developmental stage of the life cycle offers the opportunity for growth, for change, for the mastering of old conflicts and the finding of new solutions, and each stage also entails the risk and the danger of failure and regression. This is true of every stage, from childhood and adolescence, through adulthood, to aging and death. We do not like to think about death very much, but it is the final stage of life, and very often the way in which we meet our own deaths is an indication of how we have lived our lives. Right up to the end, each stage of life offers the opportunity for psychological growth and the danger of regression. We believe that this opportunity and this danger can be seen with particular clarity in pregnancy.

Pregnancy (and parenthood) is also the one stage of life that inevitably involves and affects many other human beings. Pregnancy is an important developmental experience not only for the woman, but also for the man, the fetus, the other children, and the extended family. No other experience in a person's life so dramatically affects the lives of so many others. The introduction of a new member into any existing group changes the nature of that group, and the change is particularly profound when a new member is added to a dyad. Indeed, the most dramatic effects of pregnancy occur in first pregnancies. While less dramatic, subsequent pregnancies bring with them new problems along with new joys and require, once again, a reorientation and role change for each member of the family. Thus, the birth of an infant is not an isolated biological event. It requires the creation of a new social system for the baby's very survival, not to mention his or her physical, emotional, and intellectual development. The psychological transformation of a woman into a mother and a man into a father is absolutely essential for the health of the infant, and for the stability of the newly expanded family.

A final reason for our beginning with pregnancy is that it is a condition in which the mind-body relationship is vividly demonstrated. In no other developmental stage do we see quite so clearly the powerful effect that the body has on the mind, and that the mind in turn has on the body. In pregnancy there are both profound physiological changes and profound psychological changes, and there is a continual and intimate interaction between the two.

PREGNANCY AS A NATURAL PROCESS

Pregnancy and birth are natural processes, and like all natural phenomena, they possess their own homeostatic balance which can be threatened by untimely intervention. Any intervention, medical or otherwise, into a balanced homeostatic system must be carefully evaluated, taking into consideration the potential advantages as well as the possible disruptions.

The extent to which the medical profession views pregnancy as "natural" rather than as an "illness" varies from country to country. In some Western European countries, such as Holland, France, and England, trust in the natural process of pregnancy and delivery seems to result in a greater reliance on midwives and nonhospital births, and a decreased use of drugs, Caesarian sections, and episiotomies. Rather than proving harmful, such medical practices seem to correlate with more symptom-free pregnancies, a higher rate of spontaneous births, and a lower rate of infant mortality.

A greater awareness of the natural course of pregnancy and birth is gaining strength in this country, as witnessed by increased restraint in medical intervention, decreased use of drugs, the "natural" childbirth movement, father-coached deliveries, renewed interest in home deliveries and rooming-in, and the development of many midwifery programs.

While men and women may intellectually recognize that pregnancy and birth are natural processes, they do not easily have faith in the ability of the body to deliver safely a healthy baby. Unlike other animals, our conscious minds are easily alienated from our bodies, and thus we do not seem to know instinctively how best to assist in birth. We rely instead on society's understanding of such processes. Indeed, society, and in particular the health professions, can enhance the experience of pregnancy, increase the chances of a healthy birth, and foster the development of a caring family. On the other hand, society and medicine can also further alienate women from the natural processes of their bodies, increase the chances of an impaired birth, and disrupt family unity. The more we in the health professions understand both the biological and the psychological processes of pregnancy and birth, the better will we be able to evaluate the impact of any particular intervention, and the better will we be able to design health care programs that truly serve the expectant couple.

PREGNANCY AS A PERIOD OF CHANGE AND CRISIS

Pregnancy is an intense period of rapid and uncontrollable changes — in terms of physical development, fluctuating emotional states, the formation of new identities and roles for husband and wife, and the shifting of marital relationships. Because of these changes, Grete Bibring wrote that "every pregnancy includes intrinsically an element of crisis as an indispensable factor of the process." By crisis, she did not mean pathology but rather a "turning point with the unsettling and dislodging of habitual solutions."

Each couple will respond to this crisis of pregnancy differently, depending on each partner's individual past history and characteristic response to earlier crises, the couple's present marital adjustment, and the support systems currently available to them. During this period, the expectant mother may experience more mood swings than usual. At times she may appear very euphoric, whereas at other times she may become very quiet and reflective, even to the point of being withdrawn. Her sexual interests may also shift suddenly during the course of pregnancy. She may be easily aroused sexually on one occasion, and a short time later she may lose interest in sexual pleasures altogether.

Perhaps it is the state of pregnancy itself that allows her to assert her fluctuating needs and feelings with a persistency and intensity not otherwise characteristic of her. As the woman-with-child, she may view herself and her needs with new-found importance and thus allow herself (often with the expressed permission of her husband) gratification of needs previously denied. Considering the changes in his wife, it is no wonder that this is a time of strain for the husband. In addition to dealing with all of his own anxiety set off by her physical, emotional, and sexual changes, as well as his own impending fatherhood, he is expected to provide continued emotional support for his wife. Under these circumstances, he may become overly sensitive to the changes in his wife and may perceive her emotional and sexual withdrawal as a personal rejection of him. His response can vary anywhere from an oversolicitous attempt to gratify all her wishes to a complete withdrawal from the overwhelming demands of the situation. For some, this may involve a retreat into work, sports, or even sexual affairs.

While each couple will react to each pregnancy differently, all couples must cope with certain basic issues. Together they must face real changes in their lives. They must prepare for and adapt to their new roles as parents, and this invariably brings up unresolved conflicts from their own childhood and fears about their ability to parent. They will have to adapt to a shift in their relationship, usually involving the wife's increased emotional and financial dependence on her husband for an extended period of time. Together they must prepare themselves to face a potentially painful and perhaps life-threatening experience in which they hope for the fulfillment of a dream — a perfectly healthy baby — but realistically they know that they may be tragically disappointed. Some babies do die during pregnancy and in childbirth, and some are born damaged. It is no surprise then that both parents may experience moments of doubt and resentment, even to the point of wishing they were not going to have the baby.

With so many issues and concerns, it is unfortunate that our society all too often demands that the expectant couple appear blissfully happy, thereby placing unnecessary pressure on them to hide their real feelings from others and sometimes even from themselves. By not allowing their real feelings to emerge, they are unable to accept these feelings as normal. Instead, such ambivalent feelings about the pregnancy become an additional source of stress and guilt. While the couple may have to pretend with their friends and relatives, hopefully in the presence of their doctor or midwife they can let down their masks and breathe a sigh of relief, knowing that someone recognizes that pregnancy is not an uncomplicated, blissful experience. The more a couple can deal openly and honestly with their fears and resentments, the more they can experience the joys and wonders of pregnancy.

The doctor can help minimize unrealistic fears by explaining to the couple all of the medical procedures involved in pregnancy and birth in the simplest, clearest language possible. For example, many women are delighted to hear the normal heartbeat of their infant in utero. This experience can help turn a worried fantasy into a reassuring reality. And why shouldn't the father hear too? His fears and worries are just as real. Why ignore him? Encouraging the father to become involved with the baby as early as possible in the pregnancy will help assure the attachment of both parents to the infant at birth.

PREGNANCY AS A BIOPSYCHOLOGICAL STATE

Pregnancy is a biopsychological state in which both biological and psychological factors mutually interact, that is, physical processes have psychological effects and vice versa. Physical

and hormonal changes in the pregnant woman affect her internal feeling state, her sensitivity to external stimuli, her sense of herself and her body image, and her sexuality. All of these emotional changes in turn have a profound impact on her physical well-being. During pregnancy, psychological stress can increase her physical discomfort; physical symptoms can disturb her psychological equilibrium; and both can interact to induce a wide variety of disturbances.

The first and most obvious physiological change is the enlargement of the uterus and the breasts, and there is a normal weight gain in every pregnancy. However, there are times when the enlargement and the weight gain become so great that the woman feels grotesque. When this phenomenon of fluid retention is carried to its extreme, with elevated blood pressure, edema, and albumen in the urine, we have the condition known as *preeclampsia.* If convulsions occur, we then have the serious medical emergency known as *eclampsia* or *toxemia of pregnancy.* This is not an uncommon condition. It occurs mostly in first pregnancies, and can be practically eliminated through good prenatal care. Interestingly, toxemia is unique to humans. It is not seen in any other species. What occurs physiologically is an abnormal retention of sodium and water with vasospasm and with reversible renal lesions. No one has yet discovered a specific organic cause for toxemia, and psychological factors have been implicated in this condition, possibly in combination with some as yet unknown organic factor.

Nausea, or morning sickness, is another very common physical reaction during the early weeks of pregnancy. Again, the exact causes of this nausea are as yet undetermined. However, this normal physiological feature of pregnancy may progress to vomiting, and this may in turn lead to the potentially fatal condition of continued and unremitting vomiting known as *hyperemesis gravidarum.* At this point, psychological factors may be involved, particularly intense ambivalence over being pregnant and becoming a mature woman and mother. Unless psychiatric treatment can be instituted quickly and effectively, the pregnancy may have to be terminated in order to save the life of the mother. Obstetricians and psychiatrists who have had the opportunity to see women with this condition have described a very striking fantasy. Many of these women express a terror of seeing the fetus or pieces of the fetus in the vomitus, even though intellectually they know that the baby is in the uterus, not the stomach. This fantasy vividly expresses their conflict — their fear of being pregnant, and at the same time their fear of losing the baby.

The conflict over becoming a more mature woman, and eventually a mother, is also an important etiological factor in *anorexia nervosa*, a disturbance with similar symptoms of vomiting and weight loss, but which occurs earlier in a woman's life. It is seen primarily in young girls and women, with onset most often either at the time of puberty, or at critical times of separation from the family, such as graduation from high school and college. The girl is frightened of becoming a mature woman and, on a deeper level, especially terrified of becoming pregnant and thereby no longer able to be a child herself. These young girls develop a common pattern of symptoms. On the surface it appears as though they are refusing to eat, and are progressively losing weight. Actually, in secret they gorge themselves with all kinds of different foods, then become upset at the "bulge" in their stomachs and the possibility of "gaining weight" (namely, becoming pregnant). At this point they go into a panic and induce vomiting, often by putting their fingers down their throats. The weight loss is progressive, and at times the patient's weight falls to as low as 60 or 70 pounds. The appearance of these emaciated young women is truly bizarre. As their breasts flatten, their body contours disappear, and their menstrual periods cease, their outward appearance reflects their inner wish. They no longer look like attractive young women of 14 or 18 or 22. Rather, they look like thin, scrawny prepubertal boys of nine or ten. As in the case of hyperemesis gravidarum, this condition is a medical and psychiatric emergency, since many of these young women will die unless effective treatment is instituted.

Conflicts around being pregnant and becoming more mature may also be involved in some cases of *habitual spontaneous abortion* where there is no organic pathology involved. It has been found that the most common organic cause of habitual spontaneous abortion is cervical incompetence. This causes a relaxation of the cervical opening around the third or fourth month of the pregnancy, resulting in dilation of the cervix and the loss of the fetus. Other organic causes include "blighted ovum," hormonal deficiency, anatomical problems of the uterus such as bicornuate uterus, and incompatible blood type. But, in some other cases of habitual abor-

tion, psychological factors and external stress appear to be involved in the loss of the fetus. In a nine-year study conducted by Edward C. Mann at the New York Hospital-Cornell Medical Center on over 400 women who had a history of three consecutive miscarriages, emotional factors were involved in many of the cases where no detectable organic pathology was found.

There is another phenomenon of pregnancy that demonstrates even more vividly and convincingly the power of the mind in regard to the body, and that is the condition known as *pseudocyesis* or false pregnancy. In pseudocyesis the wish for a fantasied baby may be so strong (for a wide range of different psychological reasons) that the woman develops all of the signs and symptoms of pregnancy. Her uterus enlarges. Her breasts swell. Her periods stop. She develops morning sickness. She proceeds this way through the nine months of pregnancy, only to discover at the end that she is not pregnant. There is no fetus. Pseudocyesis is as dramatic a demonstration of the mind's influence on the body as exists in medicine.

The mind can also work in a diametrically opposite way to pseudocyesis that can be just as startling, namely *denial of pregnancy*. There are interns and residents who have had the experience of being in an emergency room and having a women come in with severe abdominal pain. The intern immediately thinks of an acute abdomen, possibly due to appendicitis or a ruptured ovarian follicle. He examines the woman and is amazed to find that she is pregnant and is in labor, and that she did not know that she had been pregnant for the previous nine months. This is truly a remarkable example of the defense mechanism of denial that was mentioned earlier in the book. Not only would such a woman have to have a great capacity for denial, but she would have to have a history of menstrual irregularity and a certain kind of body frame to permit such denial to operate. But such cases do occur, and invariably they will involve intense fears over being pregnant and becoming a mother.

THE STAGES OF PREGNANCY

The First Trimester

Pregnancy is not a unidimensional experience but a progressive sequence of stages which for convenience is usually divided into three trimesters. The first trimester is dated from the moment of conception to the end of the third month of pregnancy, but experientially it begins somewhere in the second month when the pregnancy is confirmed. The beginning months of the pregnancy are merged into the prepregnant period when the couple, dispensing with birth control, tries to conceive. If this period does not take too long, it can be a very joyful and sexually arousing experience. However, if conception takes longer than expected, anxiety, fear of infertility, guilt, and mutual blame can turn sexual relations into a chore and threaten the marital adjustment. For couples harmonious in their wish to conceive, enormous relief and fulfillment come with the news of a definite pregnancy. For others who were not expecting the pregnancy, it can be tragic news, requiring the immediate decision of whether or not to have an abortion. The acceptance of the pregnancy is the main issue confronting both husband and wife, and the resolution of their feelings will affect the entire course of the pregnancy.

During the first trimester, the first physical changes become noticeable. The expectant mother's breasts swell. The nipples and areola area darken and become tender. She may feel the urge to urinate more frequently, and her bowel movements may become irregular. Chronic fatigue, sleepiness, heightened olfactory sensitivity, nausea, and even vomiting are common early symptoms. For some, these symptoms represent a disruption in their daily lives that can evoke much anxiety. Extreme discomfort may be a sign that the expectant mother is under too much stress either from her own unresolved conflicts or from external pressures. Both husband and wife may need time to discuss the problems that may be exacerbating the condition.

Women in the first trimester of their first pregnancy often experience decreased sexual desire. However, some women, freed from the pressure either to conceive or to avoid pregnancy, experience an increased interest in sexuality at this time. For such women the first trimester can be a very romantic period. In a study done by Masters and Johnson, a majority of women in the early months of their first pregnancy restricted their sexual activity for fear of damaging the fetus. A wife's sudden and unexplained decrease in interest in sexual intercourse can be very threatening to her husband if he mistakenly equates it with a rejection of himself as partner and lover. Other women may not have been able

to experience an orgasm prior to becoming pregnant, but once they become pregnant and master whatever anxiety they may have had about becoming a mother, they may then be able to experience an orgasm.

During the early months of pregnancy the expectant mother often finds her attention directed inward. She may become more reflective, finding herself daydreaming about her pregnancy and her baby. She may become more preoccupied with her own body, and may develop various concerns about the state of her health and the health of the fetus as well. This is normal and expected, and a very common concern among pregnant women is the fear that the child may be deformed. When there are serious conflicts in regard to the pregnancy, these may be reflected in persistent and exaggerated fears about the health of the baby.

The pregnant woman may also spend time thinking about her relationship with her own mother, and may begin to make a reassessment of that relationship. Old conflicts with the mother may resurface. Not infrequently, by the end of the pregnancy many women have resolved many of these conflicts with their mothers, and a new equality of shared motherhood exists between them.

The demands of the small nuclear family may place additional strains on the couple at this time in the pregnancy. Accustomed to the woman's emotional support, her family may feel hurt, neglected, and angry by her need to rest and her emotional withdrawal. She, in turn, may feel guilty and compensate by overextending herself. A couple who recognizes that fatigue and withdrawal are common aspects of pregnancy and is not threatened by it, can find practical ways of providing the extra attention that is needed for the care of young children and the home. It is also important to involve the other children in the pregnancy from the very beginning (Figure 15.1).

Since a pregnant woman's attention is naturally drawn toward herself, she is very receptive to learning about her own and her unborn baby's health and nutritional needs. Early mothering begins when a woman changes her diet and "eats for two," takes prenatal vitamins, cuts back on smoking, abstains from unnecessary medication and alcohol, and has regular prenatal medical checkups. Doctors and nurses interested in her and her baby's development can be very helpful at this early stage by answering the woman's

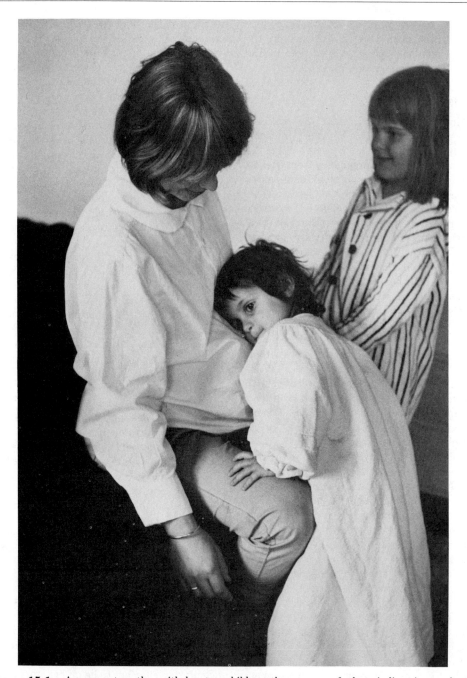

Figure 15.1. A pregnant mother with her two children, the younger of whom is listening to the fetal heartbeat. Photography by E. Niggemeyer. From *Children and Their Mothers*, Hill and Wang, New York, 1964. (Published with permission of Reich Verlag, Lucerne, Switzerland.)

many questions, providing accurate information, and recommending up-to-date reading materials.

By the end of the first trimester the young husband often feels burdened with the worries and responsibilities of becoming a father. He may spend time assessing the family's finances, taking on an extra job, or working overtime. He, too, may spend time thinking about his relationship to his own father, and worry about whether or not he can live up to his own image of parenthood. How much easier it is to criticize the ways in which one's parents failed than to find the resources within oneself to do better.

The Second Trimester

During the second trimester the woman's body changes noticeably. Her waist thickens, her belly begins to show, her breasts enlarge. No longer can she hide her pregnancy from friends, relatives, or even the casual observer. Looking at herself in the mirror, she will see a mature woman's body where months before there was a slimmer, more youthful figure. Depending on her feelings toward her femininity and her own mother, she may find this new look attractive or ugly. Some men find the pregnant woman's ripening, fertile body very sexually arousing, whereas others are repulsed by their perception of a "distorted, fat" body. Both men and women may find these drastic physical changes quite frightening, partly because they are a reminder that the pregnancy is progressing out of their control.

Some men react to their wives' fertility with envy and jealousy, feeling that their own lives are empty and sterile in comparison. Others, identifying with their wives' creative energy, develop new creative interests for themselves. Some so closely identify with their wives that they show a weight gain comparable to their wives' and experience nausea, stomach distress, abdominal bloating, and even "sympathy pains." Such an identification is the basis for a condition known as the *couvade syndrome* in which expectant fathers develop symptoms similar to those of their wives during pregnancy and labor. It is named after the couvade ritual, a magical practice known for centuries throughout practically every country in the world, in which an expectant husband goes through a pretended childbirth at the same time that his wife goes into labor.

During this period of the second trimester sexual activity may decrease for some women, whereas other women experience heightened sexual tension and an increased desire for sexual intercourse. Men respond differently to their partners' changed bodies and changing sexual demands. Some find these changes very gratifying. Others may be frightened by the changes. Toward the end of the second trimester, the male superior position becomes uncomfortable for the woman. Couples who are at ease with one another sexually can try other positions which keep the man's weight off the woman's abdomen. The female superior position, the side-to-side position, or the rear-entry position will be more satisfying.

Despite an occasional leg cramp or indigestion or some swelling of her wrists and ankles, most of the early symptoms usually disappear, leaving the pregnant woman more comfortable and energetic. Many seem to possess a glow of good health and well-being. Feeling well, she often has the creative energy to develop new interests. Many women become interested, perhaps for the first time, in such basics as gardening, sewing, knitting, and baking.

Around the fourth or fifth month, the expectant mother experiences for the first time the baby's movement. This is usually a very exhilarating moment for her. No longer is the baby just an idea or a dream, but now is reassuringly alive and real. As the movements become stronger, the father can share her joy, and for the first time, reach out and make contact with his offspring, touching a limb as it travels across the mother's belly. This experience confronts the couple with the reality of the infant's impending birth. Feelings which before were only vaguely conscious now become very real. Plans will begin to take shape for the infant's layette, room, and name. Increasingly, couples are wrestling with the issues of hospital vs. home births, natural vs. anesthetized deliveries, rooming-in vs. nursery care, breast vs. bottle feeding. Here again, physicians and nurses can be extremely helpful by responding to questions and providing the most objective information available.

The Third Trimester

During the last trimester, the pregnant woman's body is at its fullest. To balance her extra weight, she will develop the characteristic posture of pregnancy — leaning backward with legs spread slightly apart. It becomes increasingly uncomfortable for her to lie on her stomach. By now the baby's kicking may prevent her from getting a full night's sleep. As she approaches term, she may be very tired and uncomfortable.

The last month may seem to drag on interminably as the couple anxiously waits for the signs of labor. With so much attention directed toward the coming birth, they will find themselves actively preparing for the baby. A great deal of energy is spent cleaning and readying the home, decorating a room, or buying a crib and layette. The intensity of these preparations is such that some have compared it to the nesting instinct in other animals. While it is not terribly important what the couple does in terms of specific preparation for the baby, what does matter is that they are beginning to parent, in that they are already spending their time, energy, and money on the baby and making room for him or her in their home.

Couples in their second pregnancy often worry that they will be unable to love this new baby with the intensity of feeling they have for their first child. These untested feelings of love are in no way different from those felt in the first pregnancy, except that then there were no vivid parental feelings with which to compare. Many parents worry that they will not be able to make the transition from cherishing a fantasy baby to loving the real one. While only the presence of the living baby can calm this fear, the understanding of those around them can at least assure them that this is a common experience in the development of parental feelings.

As all of her energy becomes more and more channeled into the birth process, the woman's thoughts may increasingly dwell on her fears of being hurt or injured during the delivery. By the end of the last trimester she has probably quit her job or taken a maternity leave. She will find herself becoming more physically, emotionally, and financially dependent on her husband. Because of the intensity of her own concerns, she may overlook her husband's anxiety. The couple is usually very grateful for any help that will reduce their mutual anxiety. More and more people are attending childbirth classes and visiting the labor and delivery rooms before the birth. There are many classes, books, and films about labor and delivery which provide detailed information on what both husband and wife can expect, and give specific instructions as to how the father can be helpful during labor and delivery. The closer the couple feels toward each other, the more support they can offer to each other and thereby further enhance their marital bond. If they have become alienated from each other, these last months can be a terrible strain on their marriage with each feeling more abandoned and alone.

Increasing sexual tension poses an additional strain on the expectant couple. Despite intense orgasms, the wife may feel continued unrelieved sexual tension due to vasocongestion. Most couples decrease the frequency of sexual intercourse as they approach term, nonetheless, because they often fear injury to their baby. In addition, most doctors prescribe abstinence for the last four to six weeks of term. Some people are able to adjust to this interference in their love making by increasing manual and oral contact; others may refrain altogether. It is during this trying period that a sizeable proportion of husbands seek out extramarital affairs to relieve sexual frustration and to deal with their anxieties over their impending fatherhood. Masters and Johnson found that in a sample of 79 husbands, over 15% had an extramarital affair during this period. Most couples, however, are able to face the strains of pregnancy together, and in so doing actually enrich their lives and strengthen their marital relationship.

THE ROLE OF HEALTH CARE PROFESSIONALS

What can the midwife, doctor, and/or nurse do to help during this critical stage in the lives of the expectant couple? The formation of a trusting relationship is very important for the pregnant woman. Since she is experiencing a dramatic physical and emotional change in her life, attention and concern need to be given to both these aspects of her pregnancy. Feeling particularly vulnerable, she is in need of support from those around her. The more the doctor can encourage the expectant father to participate in the early stages of parenting, the less burdened and alone the pregnant woman will feel. This can take the form of encouraging the father to attend the monthly checkups and to participate in parents' childbirth classes (Figure 15.2).

The more detailed information they can learn about what to expect from pregnancy and delivery, the less anxious they will feel. It is easier to fear something real, than to worry about unknown dangers. While there is nothing the doctor can do to keep the expectant couple from worrying, he can assure them that the incidence of serious problems is rare and that worrying about injury to the woman and to the fetus is normal. Books, films, and parents' classes are particularly helpful in this regard, especially if parental discussion is encouraged.

Since the parents' experience of pregnancy and delivery will affect the early and tentative parenting behavior, they should be encouraged

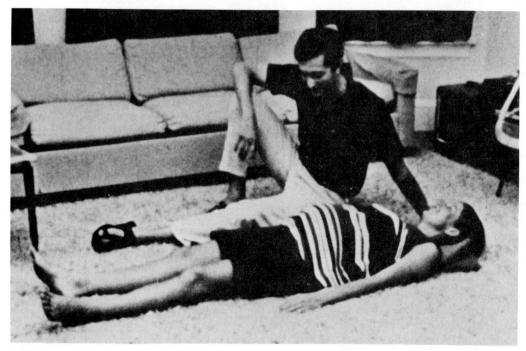

Figure 15.2. A husband and pregnant wife practicing childbirth exercises in a Lamaze class. From the film *Not Me Alone.* (By permission of Polymorph Films Inc., 331 Newbury St., Boston, Mass. 02115.)

to take responsibility wherever medically possible for the decisions affecting the pregnancy, labor, and delivery. If a doctor is unable to accept their choice, for example, home delivery or natural childbirth, he should advise the parents of his reasons, and if they want to pursue their preference, he should make an appropriate referral.

Stress has been shown to interfere with the course of pregnancy, and thus the doctor, nurse, or midwife should be alert to stress and anxiety in his or her patients. Allowing the expectant parents to express their feelings can help reassure them that they are not alone and that someone else cares. If the problem seems to require more specialized skills, the couple can then be referred for counseling. But even in these instances, in fact especially in these instances, the physician, nurse, or midwife should maintain continued contact with the expectant couple, rather than develop the attitude that the couple is now in the hands of "experts" and no longer has need of him or her. In point of fact, their need for a stable, reassuring person capable of helping them through the pregnancy and delivery will be greater than ever as they examine their anxieties in counseling or psychotherapy.

ADOLESCENT PREGNANCY

Out-of-Wedlock Pregnancies

Although we have focused on pregnancy in the married or committed couple, we cannot ignore the increasing number of women who conceive without having a permanent relationship to the baby's father. In 1980, 666,000 out-of-wedlock babies were born in this country, accounting for nearly one of every five births. This represented more than a 50% increase since 1970, when 400,000 out-of-wedlock babies were born. And nearly half of those unmarried mothers in 1980 were teenagers.

The majority of today's adolescents are sexually active. Yet despite this rise in sexual activity, teenagers tend to be rather erratic in their use of contraceptives, if they use them at all. As a result, fertility rates are quite high among adolescents. A 1981 study by the Alan Guttmacher Institute (a research affiliate of the Planned Parenthood Federation of America) reviewed some 100 existing studies on adolescent sexuality and pregnancy, and reported the following: 1) by age 19, four of five males and two of three females have had sexual intercourse, with 16 being the average age for the first experience; 2) the number of sexually active teenagers increased by two-thirds during the 1970's; 3) nearly two-thirds of the sexually active adolescent females never used contraception or did so only erratically, and nearly half said they did not think they could get pregnant; 4) over one million teenage pregnancies occur each year in the United States, and unless current trends are reversed four of every ten girls now age 14 will become pregnant at least once during their teenage years; 5) of these teenage pregnancies, half proceed to birth (22% are out-of-wedlock, 10% are made legitimate by marriage, 17% are postmarital conceptions) and half end in either miscarriage (13%) or abortion (38%).

Why are adolescents less likely to marry the baby's father prior to delivery than are women over 20 years of age? Some teenagers feel either that they are too young to marry, or that the baby's youthful father is unable to provide them with continued emotional or financial support. Since many of those teenagers are from lower socioeconomic backgrounds, the unwed mother's concern about the father's future is unfortunately realistic. Many of these adolescent mothers also fear that such marriages are all too likely to end up in divorce. Indeed, in the long run these youthful marriages are more likely to end in divorce than later marriages. And the younger the couple, the greater the chances of the first marriage failing.

Despite their reluctance to marry, most unwed mothers maintain contact with the baby's father throughout the pregnancy, according to a study by Gabbard and Wolff. Approximately one third of unwed fathers offered some financial support to the mother during pregnancy and the early postpartum years, but those who do not marry tend not to continue the relationship or the financial support. Within three to five years after the birth of the baby, only 8% of the unmarried fathers offered any financial support and only 16% remained in weekly contact with their baby's mother. And since the young unwed mother is neither emotionally nor financially independent, she often lives at home with her family of origin and needs their support as well as public assistance. In 1975 approximately half of the $9.4 billion spent in the federal Aid to Families with Dependent Children program went to families in which the mother gave birth while in her teens.

Causes of Adolescent Pregnancy

Why do so many adolescents find themselves pregnant? As we have mentioned, teenagers engage in sexual activity without making effective use of contraceptives. There is often no reliable source of contraceptive information available to them. Many teenagers have heard about the dangers of the pill and the IUD, and have generalized their suspicions to all forms of contraception. The diaphragm is often seen as "messy" and requires the teenager to accept full responsibility for her sexual intentions prior to intercourse. Relying on the condom means that the teenager must insist that her partner use it effectively, a somewhat "unromantic" position for her to take. Teenagers of both sexes are often not yet ready to accept responsibility for adult sexuality. They may find it easier to allow themselves to be overwhelmed by passion than to recognize that they are likely to engage in sexual intercourse and to take the necessary precautions to avoid pregnancy. Instead, many teenagers deny the connection between sexual intercourse and pregnancy, and delude themselves into believing that they will not get pregnant.

In some communities, teenage pregnancy is commonplace. The teenager who is pregnant remains in her community, attending school, continuing to date and engage in her usual activities. Like many of her friends, she too is pregnant. It no longer has the stigma of a shameful event. As a result of her pregnancy, she may actually receive preferential treatment and heightened social status among her peers. In such communities, teenagers do not feel the same pressure to avoid pregnancy. Given the change in sexual mores, the unavailability of meaningful employment for large segments of the adolescent population, and the relatively easy access to public assistance, unwed motherhood becomes for many adolescents a viable option to choose. For those teenagers whose future prospects appear otherwise bleak, having a baby can provide a focus and meaning to their lives.

For other teenagers, becoming pregnant may be a desperate attempt to cope with disturbing emotional conflicts. They may be trying to resolve an adolescent identity crisis by reinforcing their feminine identity. Pregnancy may be a compensation for depression; the baby becomes a gift to themselves to ease their loneliness and isolation. For others it may serve as a way of extricating themselves from an unhappy, conflict-ridden family life. By having a baby they can turn to public assistance to help free themselves from what may be an unbearable family situation. For some it may be part of an adolescent rebellion, a way of getting revenge against parents and society.

Complications of Adolescent Pregnancy

In general, the consequences of early pregnancy can be quite severe. In addition to the increased risk of divorce in adolescent marriages, the teenager faces the increased probability of impoverishment and emotional crisis. Pregnancy during the teen years means that the young girl faces a double crisis: that of adolescence and that of pregnancy. Her own development is not yet complete, and already she must make room in her life for her baby. At first she may be pleased, even excited by the prospect of her pregnancy, but over time she may begin to feel quite derailed from her future hopes and plans. She may limit or stop her education, and curtail the development of her work skills. As a result, she is more likely to experience job dissatisfaction and unemployment, with markedly reduced income levels, compared to those women who delayed child bearing past the age of 20.

While some teenagers will have uneventful pregnancies and deliver normal healthy babies, pregnant teenagers also have an increased risk of medical complications. They generally seek prenatal care late, increasing the risk to mother and baby. In a study of 884 pregnant teenagers delivering at Kings County Hospital Center in Brooklyn, teenagers were found to have a higher incidence of uterine dysfunction, contracted pelvis, anemia, preeclampsia, toxemia, and partial separation of the placenta at birth. While some of these problems are attributable to immature physical development, others are probably related to social and emotional factors. According to a report by the Committee on Adolescence of the American Academy of Pediatrics, there are two major health complications directly related to the young age of the mother: preeclampsia (leading to an increased risk of infant death), and an excessive number of low-birth-weight babies. The babies of teenagers are also at risk for later developmental problems, including

neurological, psychological, and intellectual difficulties.

After reviewing the research literature, the Committee on Adolescence concluded that delaying the first pregnancy until the late teenage years or early 20's substantially diminished complications of pregnancy, low-birth-weight infants, and subsequent abnormal child development. They suggest that the problems can be resolved "only through open discussion, adequate training of health care personnel, and more effective delivery of health care and health education and, finally, more research."

The Role of Health Care Professionals

What can be done about these complications of adolescent pregnancy? As with any problem in medicine, the first step is prevention. Health care professionals can take an active role in educating adolescents and their parents about the extent of teenage sexuality and about the need for effective contraception. In order to maximize the likelihood that adolescents, who are often hesitant and uncomfortable in talking about their sexuality, will utilize counseling and contraception, such services need to be easily accessible, individualized, and confidential. Health care professionals can be advocates for the provision of such services in their community. Once the pregnancy has occurred, the teenager will benefit from counseling to help her determine how she wants to deal with the pregnancy. She will appreciate a nonjudgmental, informative, clarifying approach. If she decides to continue the pregnancy, she should be encouraged to obtain regular prenatal care, perhaps at a special clinic for pregnant adolescents if one is available. Nutritional education should be a routine part of all prenatal care, since proper nutrition is essential for normal fetal development. The expectant mother should be encouraged to work out a plan for completing her education. Special educational programs that provide child care as well as classes on child development and parenting skills are becoming more common. Involvement of the adolescent mother's family should be actively encouraged. Such support has a strongly favorable effect on the well-being of both the mother and the child. For those young mothers and their families who have limited financial resources, a social service evaluation may be necessary to arrange financial assistance. When pregnancy is a result of inadequate knowledge about reproduction and contraception, further education after the delivery is warranted. Such interventions by health care professionals can help to minimize the disruptive effects of teenage pregnancy and maximize the developmental potential of both mother and child.

UNWANTED PREGNANCY

For many women, pregnancy and childbirth are highly desired. But for others, pregnancy is unplanned, unwanted, and disruptive. Unwanted pregnancy is not only an issue for adolescents; it is a problem for women of any age. An unmarried woman faces caring for herself and the child without the support of a husband. A married woman may be coping with financial hardship or marital discord that is further exacerbated by the unwanted pregnancy. The resources of some families are already strained by multiple children; another child can be a significant burden. Older women who have already completed their families may be looking forward to increased freedom as their children grow up; they may reject the role of mothering another infant again. Whatever the situation, an unwanted pregnancy evokes strong conflicts. To her surprise, the woman may experience pleasure at her ability to get pregnant and create a new life. On the other hand she may feel depressed, angry, anxious, or guilty about the pregnancy, and may react with passivity or impulsivity. Counseling is an invaluable service for helping the woman come to terms with her feelings about an unwanted pregnancy.

Principles of Counseling

Counseling the woman with an unwanted pregnancy requires that the health care professional set aside his or her own values about pregnancy in order to allow the woman to arrive at a clearer understanding of her wishes and choices. Avoid being moralistic. Try to understand the patient's life situation and the reasons for her ambivalence about the pregnancy. Explore all of her alternatives, which may include marrying to legitimize the pregnancy, bearing the child within a preexisting marriage, bearing the child out-of-wedlock, relinquishing the child for adoption, or terminating the pregnancy by an induced abortion. Discuss the patient's reactions to these alternatives and discuss also the

potential for support from family, friends, the father of the child, and social services. Whatever her choice, allow her to explore her feelings and come to some acceptance of her decision. Inquire about any contraceptive difficulties that may have contributed to the pregnancy and then provide the necessary information. With counseling, the crisis of an unwanted pregnancy can become an opportunity for enhanced maturity and an increased sense of responsibility for one's actions.

Induced Abortion

This topic brings up many legal and moral issues, but the fact is that in 1980 there were over one and a half million induced (or "therapeutic") abortions in the United States, double the number in 1973. This choice is most common for the unmarried woman and the overburdened multiparous woman. A minority of women apparently show little concern about this procedure; they appear to use it as a means of birth control and may have multiple abortions. However, most women find the choice more difficult. They come to the decision more reluctantly as the best resolution for a situation where they feel emotionally unprepared for the child. Adolescents (and older women) who make this choice tend to come from intact families with a higher socioeconomic status, and tend to have better academic records and higher educational and vocational aspirations than their peers who carry the pregnancy to term. Once the decision has been made and the procedure carried out, the patient usually experiences a feeling of relief. Various studies have shown minimal psychiatric morbidity after induced abortion, especially compared to bearing an unwanted child, and especially if the abortion occurs in the first trimester before fetal movement is perceived. There is no question that induced abortions conducted under the proper surgical conditions can save both the emotional and the physical life of the woman with an unwanted pregnancy. Ford and his associates studied a group of 500 women who requested therapeutic abortion from 1968 to 1970. They identified one group of women in particular who benefited greatly from the abortion, namely the "tired mothers" who had come to look upon themselves as "baby factories." Senay and Nadelson have reviewed a number of other studies which have shown the vast majority of women with an unwanted pregnancy are improved following the abortion. However, it is also important to keep in mind that for certain women, abortions are not without psychological risk. Even when there is every medical and psychiatric indication for the abortion, there may still be long-range emotional consequences. The most common sequelae is regret over the loss of the pregnancy and guilt over having induced the loss. Such women may need to grieve the lost child, and may even experience an anniversary reaction that occurs each year at the time of the abortion or at the time when the baby would have been born.

Relinquishment of the Baby

Some women who are not prepared to care for a child find that abortion is not a suitable choice. For these women, continuing the pregnancy, bearing the child, and then giving it up for adoption become important options. Relinquishment is the legal process of giving custody of the child to the adoptive parents. This occurs less frequently now than it did in the past. In the early 1960's, 90% of out-of-wedlock babies were relinquished, as compared to less than 5% in the early 1980's. A study by Leynes suggests that adolescents who give up their infants for adoption are more mature and function better intellectually than those who keep the unwanted child. After the birth, these mothers must then grieve the loss of the baby that has been part of their bodies for nine months. The sadness and regret are often mitigated by a sense of having done "the best thing for the baby" or "helping someone else (the adoptive parents) have a baby they can love."

Keeping the Unwanted Child

Many women decide to keep the unwanted child. Some can adapt to their circumstances, resolve their mixed feelings about the pregnancy, and effectively care for the infant. Such an adjustment is facilitated if the woman has adequate income, as well as support from the father of the child or her own family. However, for those women who are financially impoverished, socially isolated, and emotionally strained, the unwanted child can be a considerable burden. How can a woman show sustained responsiveness to the needs of an infant when she is unable to have her own needs met? Where there is unresolved hostility toward the pregnancy, there can be impaired attachment at birth, and an increased incidence of subsequent child neglect and abuse. A Swedish study by Forssman and Thuwe showed an increased incidence of antisocial behavior, school problems, and mental illness in children born to women who had been denied abortions. Health care professionals can assist such mothers in many ways. A social service evaluation may be requested to arrange financial assistance. Child care services can be arranged to provide the overburdened mother with needed relief. Any supportive relationships with family, friends, or the father of the child should be encouraged. Mental health services should be recommended if needed. If child neglect or abuse is suspected, the health care professional is required to notify child abuse agencies for further evaluation and intervention.

THE PROBLEM OF INFERTILITY

Incidence of Infertility

How different from the unwanted baby is the problem of infertility. *Infertility* is defined as the failure to conceive a pregnancy following one year or more of regular sexual intercourse without contraception, or the inability to carry pregnancies to a live birth. Infertility is primary when there has been no previous pregnancy, and secondary when it occurs after one or more successful pregnancies. It has been estimated that 15% of our population in the childbearing years are infertile at any given time (about one in every five to six couples of childbearing age), and the incidence appears to be increasing. One reason may be the increased prevalence of venereal disease that causes scarring and blockage of the reproductive organs in both sexes. Another may be the increasing tendency of many women to delay marriage and childbearing until later in life, past the supposed period of peak fertility in the mid and late twenties. Finally, certain contraceptive methods (i.e., IUD and induced abortion) may lead to infertility as a result of scarring, infection, and cervical incompetence, while other contraceptive methods (i.e., the Pill) may cause prolonged cessation of ovulation in some women.

Causes of Infertility

Menning has stated that an organic or physical basis for the infertility can be found in approximately 90% of couples who have been thoroughly evaluated. In about 40% of these cases the difficulty lies with the man, in 40% with the woman, and with both in the remaining cases. In the female the problem may involve: 1) a mechanical barrier to fertilization due to scarring and adhesions of the uterus, ovaries, or Fallopian tubes secondary to venereal disease, pelvic inflammatory disease (PID), or endometriosis; 2) endocrine disorders of the thyroid, adrenals, or the hypothalamic-pituitary-ovarian axis that cause dysfunction of the normal menstrual cycle; and 3) structural disorders of the uterus (congenital absence, malformation, retroversion, fibroid tumors) and the cervix (cervical incompetence, cervical stenosis, abnormal cervical mucus).

In the male the problem may involve: 1) inadequate sperm production (due to mumps with orchitis, undescended testicle, variococoele, prolonged elevation of the scrotal temperature, exposure to chemical toxins and certain drugs); 2) inadequate sperm motility (due to endocrine disorders or prostatic disease); and 3) blockage of the vas deferens (due to venereal disease, injury, vasectomy). Some of the causes of combined infertility include: 1) an immunologic reaction (of some women to sperm, and of some men to their own sperm); 2) problems of coital technique, such as the use of positions in intercourse that do not facilitate the movement of sperm to the cervix, or the use of spermicidal lubricants; and 3) psychological conflicts that may lead to psychosexual dysfunctions and avoidance of intercourse.

New Treatment Approaches to Infertility

Just within the past few years there have been dramatic developments in the treatment of infertility that have helped approximately half of infertile couples become pregnant. These include synthetic hormones that can stimulate various phases of the menstrual cycle; microsurgery for unblocking Fallopian tubes, removing variococoeles, and reversing vasectomies through reconnection of the vas deferens; laser laparoscopy for removing adhesions and endometriosis; improved techniques of artificial insemination of a fertile wife by a donor; the use of "surrogate mothers" who become pregnant using the sperm from the husband of an infertile wife; and perhaps the most dramatic develop-

ments of all, in vitro fertilization and the "test tube" baby, and embryo transfer.

Psychological Problems of Infertility

There still remain many infertile couples who to date cannot be helped with this major life crisis, and the psychological conflicts that they face may be considerable. Following the initial period of surprise and denial, many older couples may realistically fear that time is running out on them. For others, profound doubts may emerge about their masculinity or femininity, their sexual desirability, and even their worth and self-esteem as human beings. Jealousy and resentment of couples with children may become unbearable. The grief and mourning for the lost parenthood and the loss of control over their lives may progress to chronic depression and a profound feeling of being alone, isolated, and defective. An inaccurate or premature diagnosis of psychogenic infertility (and the accompanying admonition to "relax") may add further to the anger, shame, guilt, and sense of failure. The necessity for intercourse to occur at specified and scheduled times during the woman's ovulation may seriously detract from the spontaneous pleasure of sex, and may even lead to psychosexual dysfunction in one or both partners. And the continuing cycle of hope and anxiety, ending in despair as the menses begins, may become so emotionally exhausting for some couples that they eventually just give up. If they then decide to adopt, it is important for them to know that the pregnancy rate following adoption appears to be the same as for those couples who do not adopt, despite many myths to the contrary.

Health care professionals can assist these couples greatly through empathic support and individual counseling, and also through referral to Resolve, a self-help organization for infertile couples which was founded in Boston in 1973 by Barbara Eck Menning, who was herself infertile. Resolve now has chapters in over 35 states, and provides information on infertility, makes referrals to infertility specialists, and sponsors peer-support groups. Individual counseling by health care professionals and self-help group support may allow infertile couples to appreciate those inner sources of worth that are unrelated to reproductive capacity. Counseling may also help such couples to rediscover the pleasures of sex for its own sake, to consider the alternatives of either adoption or childfree living, and perhaps most important of all, to face their grief. As we shall see in Chapter 17, with couples who have experienced fetal or neonatal loss, such grief never entirely disappears. But hopefully it can become less intense, as one infertile woman has described:

> My infertility resides in my heart as an old friend. I do not hear from it for weeks at a time, and then, a moment, a thought, a baby announcement or some such thing, and I will feel the tug—maybe even be sad or shed a few tears. And I think, "There's my old friend." It will always be part of me.*

Suggested Readings

Bibring GL: Some considerations of the psychological processes in pregnancy. *Psychoanal Study Child* 14:113, 1959.

Howells JG (ed): *Modern Perspectives in Psycho-Obstetrics.* New York, Brunner/Mazel, 1972.

Menning BE: *Infertility: A Guide for the Childless Couple.* Englewood Cliffs, NJ, Prentice Hall, 1977.

Notman MT, Nadelson CC (eds): *The Woman Patient. Volume 1: Sexual and Reproductive Aspects of Women's Health Care.* New York, Plenum Press, 1978.

Reiterman C (ed): *Abortion and the Unwanted Child.* New York, Springer, 1971.

Teenage Pregnancy: The Problem That Hasn't Gone Away. New York, Alan Guttmacher Institute, 1981.

References

Barglow P, Brown E: Pseudocyesis. To be and not to be pregnant: a psychosomatic question. In Howells JG (ed): *Modern Perspectives in Psycho-Obstetrics.* New York, Brunner/Mazel, 1972, p 53.

Benedek T: The psychobiology of pregnancy. In Anthony EJ, Benedek T (eds): *Parenthood: Its Psychology and Psychopathology.* Boston, Little, Brown, and Co., 1970, p 137.

Bohman M, Sigvardsson S: A prospective, longitudinal study of children registered for adoption. *Acta Psychiatrica Scandinavica* 61:339, 1980.

Boston Women's Health Book Collective: Childbearing. In *Our Bodies Ourselves.* New York, Simon & Schuster, 1973, p 157.

Chertok L: The psychopathology of vomiting of pregnancy. In Howells JG (ed): *Modern Perspectives in Psycho-Obstetrics.* New York, Brunner/Mazel, 1972, p 269.

Coleman AD, Coleman L: *Pregnancy: The Psychological Experience.* New York, Herder and Herder, 1972.

Collins JA, et al: Treatment-independent pregnancy among infertile couples. *New Engl J Med* 309:1201, 1983.

Committee on Adolescence, American Academy of Pediatrics. Statement on teenage pregnancy. *Pediatrics* 63:795, 1979.

Ford CV, Castelnuovo-Tedesco P, Long KD: Abortion: is it a therapeutic procedure in psychiatry? *JAMA* 218:1173, 1971.

Forssman H, Thuwe I: One hundred and twenty children born after application for therapeutic abortion refused. *Acta Psychiatrica Scandinavica* 42:71, 1966.

Gabbard G, Wolff J: The unwed pregnant teenager and her male relationship. *J Reprod Med* 19:137, 1977.

Greenglass ER: Therapeutic abortion and psychiatric disturbance in Canadian women. *Canad Psych Assoc J* 21:453, 1976.

Howells JG: Childbirth is a family experience. In Howells JG (ed): *Modern Perspectives in Psycho-Obstetrics.* New York, Brunner/Mazel, 1972, p 127.

Jessner L, Weigert E, Foy JL: The development of parental attitudes during pregnancy. In Anthony EJ, Benedek T (eds): *Parenthood: Its Psychology and Psychopathology.* Boston, Little, Brown, and Co., 1970, p 209.

Lamb E, Leurgans S: Does adoption affect subsequent fertility? *Am J Ob Gyn* 134:138, 1979.

Leynes C: Keep or adopt: a study of factors influencing pregnant adolescents' plans for their babies. *Child Psychiatry* 11:105, 1980.

Mai FM: Conception after adoption: an open question. *Psychosom Med* 33:509, 1971.

Mann EC: Spontaneous abortions and miscarriage. In Howells JG (ed): *Modern Perspectives in Psycho-Obstetrics.* New York, Brunner/Mazel, 1972, p 233.

Masters WH, Johnson VE: *Human Sexual Response.* Boston, Little, Brown, and Co., 1966.

Mazor MD: The problem of infertility. In Notman MT, Nadelson CC (eds): *The Woman Patient. Volume 1.* New York, Plenum Press, 1978, p 23.

McCarthy J, Menken J: Marriage, remarriage, marital disruption, and age at first birth. *Family Plan Perspect* 11:21, 1979.

Nadelson CC: "Normal" and "special" aspects of pregnancy: a psychological approach. In Notman MT, Nadelson CC (eds): *The Woman Patient. Volume 1.* New York, Plenum Press, 1978, p 73.

Nadelson CC: The emotional impact of abortion. In Notman MT, Nadelson CC (eds): *The Woman Patient. Volume 1.* New York, Plenum Press, 1978, p 173.

Nadelson CC, Notman MT, Gillon J: Adolescent sexuality and pregnancy. In Notman MT, Nadelson CC (eds): *The Woman Patient, Volume 1.* New York, Plenum Press, 1978, p 123.

Phipps-Yonas S: Teenage pregnancy and motherhood: a review of the literature. *Am J Orthopsychiatry* 50:403, 1980.

Ringrose CAD: Psychopathology of toxaemia of pregnancy. In Howells JG (ed): *Modern Perspectives in Psycho-Obstetrics.* New York, Brunner/Mazel, 1972, p 283.

Senay EC: The psychology of abortion. In Arieti S (ed): *American Handbook of Psychiatry,* ed 2, vol 1. New York, Basic Books, 1974, p 535.

Shore EG: Prenatal influences on child health and development. In Notman MT, Nadelson CC (ed): *The Woman Patient, Volume 1.* New York, Plenum Press, 1978, p 21.

Solberg D, Butler J, Wagner N: Sexual behavior in pregnancy. *N Engl J Med* 288:1098, 1973.

Tietze C: Teenage pregnancies: looking ahead to 1984. *Family Planning Perspec* 10:205, 1978.

Trethowan WH: The couvade syndrome. In Howells JG (ed): *Modern Perspectives in Psycho-Obstetrics.* New York, Brunner/Mazel, 1972, p 68.

Weir WC, Weir DR: Adoption and subsequent conceptions. *Fert Ster* 17:283, 1966.

Zelnik M, Kantner JF: Reasons for nonuse of contraception by sexually active women aged 15–19. *Family Plan Perspect* 11:289, 1979.

---

* *Infertility: A Guide for the Childless Couple* by Barbara Eck Menning. Copyright © 1977 by Prentice Hall, Englewood Cliffs, N.J. Page 117.

CHAPTER **16 Birth, Postpartum, and the Parent-Infant Interaction**

Joan Hittelman, Ph.D.,
Robert N. Emde, M.D., and
Richard C. Simons, M.D.

Childbirth is the moment the expectant couple has been anticipating for the past nine months. They have been coping with a changing physical and psychological reality and attempting to grow into the new parenting role. The extent to which they were able to support each other's confidence and emotional growth during pregnancy will play a crucial factor in the way in which they respond to the crisis of childbirth.

An important factor in the experience of childbirth is the degree to which the expectant mother can surrender herself to her basic bodily urges during labor and delivery. Any factors that might inhibit a birthing woman can complicate her labor. If she tends to be embarrassed or humiliated by the birth process, she may fight against the experience by becoming tense. This could in turn increase her pain and slow down her labor. In the hospital setting, she may feel as though she is on public display as unfamiliar faces come and go, examining her most private and intimate parts. An unfriendly or critical attitude by the staff can further inhibit a woman from relaxing. On the other hand, the intimacy of a familiar setting with trusted birth attendants, especially her husband, can allow her to let go of her inhibitions and involve herself fully in the unique bodily experience of childbirth.

OPTIONS FOR THE COUPLE

Physicians must be aware of the potential dehumanizing effect of the hospital on expectant mothers, especially those who deliver in a city hospital for lower socioeconomic class patients. Such hospitals may separate the woman from her family, remove her personal effects and clothes, give her little personal attention, and

expect her to fit into the hospital routine. Despite these obvious discomforts, most couples deliver in a hospital rather than at home. What is the expectant couple seeking in the hospital delivery? With the advances of modern medicine for assessing and treating pregnancy and birth complications, childbirth no longer poses the same threat it did a century ago. These advances include: amniocentesis, ultrasound, electronic fetal monitoring, increasing safety of Caesarean sections (due to improved anesthesia, antibiotics, and blood banks for transfusions), the development of a vaccine against Rh disease, and intensive care units for premature babies. As a result, the infant death rate has dropped from 20 infant deaths per 1,000 live births in 1970 to 11.2 per 1,000 in 1982.

Thus, these advances, more available in the hospital setting than in home births, can prevent serious injury or death to the mother or baby. But in a normal, healthy, uncomplicated delivery, they may be unnecessary. During this past decade, when most of these advances were first introduced into American obstetrical practice, the Caesarean section has tripled—from about 5% in 1968 to about 15% in 1978 nationally, and to rates as high as 20% to 25% in some hospitals by 1982. Studies have shown that analgesia and anesthesia, administered to the mother during labor, delivery, or Caesarean section, rapidly enter the fetal bloodstream and can affect the newborn's state of alertness at birth. Since the newborn does not eliminate medication as effectively as does an adult, drugs given to the mother during labor and delivery can remain in the newborn, depressing the capacity to process auditory and visual stimuli. Unmedicated babies are more alert and nurse better for the first month of life compared to those whose mothers received medication during labor and/or delivery.

Birthing centers and birthing rooms are now offering both a safe delivery and a homelike atmosphere in the hospital. The mother can labor and experience delivery in the same room accompanied by her spouse and other family members. The birthing room is often decorated in a homelike atmosphere with comfortable chairs and tables, perhaps a T.V., and often a specially designed bed which can be used for both labor and delivery. The mother can choose the position she finds most comfortable in which to deliver. No longer does she have to be rushed from labor room to delivery room, holding back the delivery by restraining from pushing. Instead she can labor and deliver in a natural and comfortable setting with the knowledge that in an emergency, staff expertise and life-saving equipment are just down the hall.

More and more, the task of today's physician is to sift through our advanced technologies in order to know which technologies give the best options to patients and their families. This strategy takes account of the fact that families are taking an increasingly active role in choosing their birthing environment. Pregnancy and childbirth are not illnesses; they are now recognized as developmental crises containing opportunities for individuals and families to grow. As a result, today's physician must be trained and sensitive to a variety of psychological aspects of family-centered perinatal care. It is perhaps not coincidental that obstetrics, which used to be a male dominated surgical profession, is now attracting significant numbers of women as well as men.

PREPARED CHILDBIRTH

Many hospitals have attempted to modify their procedures to give more attention to the special needs of the pregnant woman and the developing family unit by incorporating classes for prepared childbirth and by encouraging the father's participation in labor and delivery. Most prepared childbirth classes in the United States are a consolidation of two major schools: Dick-Read's "natural childbirth" and Lamaze's "psychoprophylactic." Generally their goal is to help a mother reduce excessive pain during childbirth, to give her and her partner the tools to cope with an unmedicated labor, and to teach

her how to work with her body so as to ease and shorten delivery. Since fear is related to tension and pain, these approaches attempt to reduce fear by education. Childbirth films are shown and the couple is taken on a tour of the labor and delivery rooms.

Each stage of labor and delivery (effacement, dilation, transition, expulsion) is described. For each stage, specific breathing techniques are suggested that help the woman work with her body. In addition, the couple is taught how to help the woman relax her muscles, both to conserve her energy and to prevent the buildup of tension. During the early stages of labor she is encouraged to relax and concentrate her attention on coordinating her breathing with the wave-like contractions. By taking each contraction one at a time, she usually develops confidence in her ability to maintain control and to distract herself from much of the pain and discomfort.

The couple needs to be forewarned about the transition stage (7 to 10 centimeters dilated), for this is usually the most difficult stage of labor with which to cope. It is not uncommon for the mother to shiver uncontrollably, to vomit, and to feel intensely vulnerable. Some cry; others may ask for medication. Emotional support by staff and husband at this point is important for helping the mother so that she can remain awake and alert for the expulsion of the baby. Using specific breathing techniques, the birthing mother can avoid premature pushing, and when it is time, she can expedite the baby's passage through the birth canal. Studies have reported that prepared mothers have better childbirth experiences and better immediate relations with their babies compared to unprepared women. Prepared women had shorter labors, fewer medical complications, and needed less obstetrical medication. Prepared women also felt that they had played an active role in their baby's birth. And a study by Sosa and coworkers found that when birthing women were provided a supportive companion, they had shorter deliveries, fewer perinatal problems (including Caesarian section and meconium staining), and better mother-infant relationships than those who delivered alone.

Indeed, the father has come to play an active role in prepared childbirths. Having been encouraged to attend the classes with his wife, he comes prepared with an armament of techniques to handle discomforts (backaches, cramps, thirst) and to remind her of the breathing and relaxation exercises they practiced together. Since some hospital environments and staff may still be hostile to the couple attempting a prepared birth, the husband's role is also to protect his wife, in her vulnerable condition, from anyone who might try to interfere with their goals. He is urged to stay by her side (especially during the transition stage) for fear that in his absence, she might be given unwanted medication. Even when the hospital environment is supportive of prepared childbirth, his presence is needed to offer her his love, compassion, and support.

Many couples find this a very moving experience which brings them closer together as parents, enriching their love for each other and the newborn. One mother wrote to her childbirth teacher, Sheila Kitzinger: "To see this helpless little baby . . . emerge into the world must surely enrich and strengthen any marriage. For us, it was a tremendously moving and rewarding experience, never to be forgotten" (Figure 16.1).

Most husbands and wives look forward to sharing this experience together, but some husbands may cope with their fear of childbirth by avoiding the childbirth experience. The crucial issue is that alternatives and options and choices be provided for each individual and each couple. It is no more helpful to require all fathers to attend deliveries or to require all mothers to be with their babies immediately after delivery, than it was in the past to exclude fathers from the delivery and to immediately separate mother and baby. If couples can face their own anxieties and wishes, and mutually come to terms with them, then they can be the best judge of the method of childbirth that suits them best. For the physician to protect them from the burdens of early parenting by deciding for them the form that childbirth should take is to infantilize them. Expectant parents need all the honest information they can get to help them discover for themselves the way in which they want to greet their newborn child.

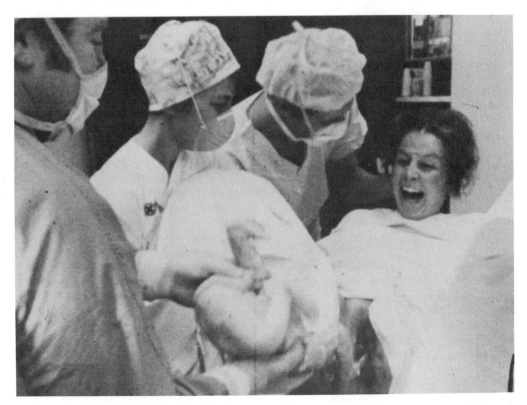

Figure 16.1. Exquisite and unsurpassed joy on the face of the mother as she sees her newborn baby at the moment of birth. Her husband is present, supporting her head. Obstetrician is holding the baby. From the film *Not Me Alone.* (By permission of Polymorph Films, Boston.)

EARLY PARENTAL DISAPPOINTMENT

Since most couples' worst fears about a damaged baby do not materialize, there is often an initial feeling of relief and accomplishment. For some parents, seeing their baby for the first time may be an exquisitely poignant experience. In Tanzer and Block's book on natural childbirth, a father described his joy at seeing his baby: "It was all so powerful I felt as though my head might come off, that I might simply explode with joy and a sense of profound participation in a profound mystery" (Figure 16.2).

Others, though, are disappointed with the baby. The infant conceived in their minds and cherished for many months may not be the infant who is now their son or daughter. Their fantasy baby may have looked more like the magazine pictures of a fat-cheeked four month old rather than their molded-headed, wrinkled-

Figure 16.2. *Father and Child* (1930) by Gustav Vigeland. Bronze. Placed in the Vigeland Sculpture Park, Oslo, Norway. (By permission of Vigeland Museum, Oslo, Norway.)

skinned newborn. The baby may be one sex and the parents are delighted. Or the baby may be another sex, and the parents are deeply disappointed. Or the husband and wife may have completely different reactions to the baby's sex and personality. Hoping for a baby of a particular sex, one mother described her disappointment in Tanzer and Block's book: "And I remember Paul waking me, Paul and the nurse, and telling me I had a little girl, and I was so disappointed. And I said, 'I'm sorry,' because I knew he was disappointed."

Parents who believe that there are certain attitudes they should have to be "good" parents, and other attitudes they should not have or else they will be "bad" or "inadequate" parents, may begin to hide their feelings from themselves. Hiding one's disappointment does not relieve it, but rather only makes it more inaccessible to understanding and modification. An accepting attitude in those around the new parents can help them begin to accept their real feelings and begin to deal with them.

When a baby is born with a defect, Solnit and Stark observed that the mother and the father go through a period of mourning for the loss of the perfect baby they were expecting. If this grief is prolonged, the ensuing depression and parental unavailability may have deleterious consequences on the infant's development. The physician may be able to play an important role in being available to facilitate this parental grieving. Infants born with physical handicaps (absence of limbs, facial malformations, bony malformations) are less appealing from the outset. From a therapeutic and preventive standpoint, it is helpful for the physician to acknowledge deficits, so that the parents can begin to appreciate other rewarding aspects of their handicapped infant.

Strategies for helping parents "tune in" to other rewarding features of their infants is beautifully illustrated in the work of Selma Fraiberg with congenitally blind babies. Not only is the blind infant's appearance different, but the rewarding communication system of eye-to-eye contact is absent in the congenitally blind. When Fraiberg began her work, a large proportion of these infants became socially withdrawn, developed stereotypic behaviors, showed retarded language development, and were often regarded as "autistic." Fraiberg noticed an interference in the mother-infant relationship from the earliest postnatal months. There was a diminution of affective interchange, and often an avoidance of pleasure and play by the mothers. Fraiberg developed an intervention program in which she helped these parents understand the cognitive development of their children, their nonvisual communicative patterns, and the ability of these infants to be pleasing in a variety of ways. As a result, the affective interchange was restored, and the mothers enjoyed their blind babies much more. The so-called "autism" syndrome in these infants was eliminated.

EARLY PARENT-INFANT CONTACT

Initially parents need to spend time getting to know their baby. Observing mothers and their newborns, Klaus, Kennell, and their coworkers recorded on video tape an orderly and predictable pattern of behavior on the part of mothers when presented with their nude newborn shortly after birth. Starting with fingertips touching the infant's extremities, they proceeded to massage and encompass the infant's trunk. An intense interest in waking their infant in an effort to establish eye contact was also noted. Emde and his coworkers observed that during the first two postpartum hours, the unmedicated infant is not only "wide awake" but is capable of visual pursuit and has an inviting, wide-eyed appearance often interpreted by parents as a display of "wonderment."

In further studying the development of attachment in mothers toward their babies, Klaus and Kennell found that early contact between the mother and infant positively affected the development of attachment toward the infant for as long as at least one year after delivery. However, unlike some species which require early contact for acceptance of their young, humans are more complicated and flexible in their attachment process. As other studies have shown, early contact is not a prerequisite for warm, maternal feelings, but it may enhance this process. Loving and parenting are not "fixed" by critical events such as postbirth contact, but rather represent lifelong developmental processes.

The above not withstanding, long separations from neonates have been shown to have serious consequences for later attachment. Mothers separated from their sick or premature infants for weeks or months in hospital nurseries may have difficulty in the adequate development of attachment. For example, studies have shown that premature babies suffer a much higher incidence of child abuse and neglect.

Therefore, health care professionals should be conservative about any intervention that separates mother and baby in the period after birth. To assure the proximity between mother and infant and thereby encourage the development of parental attachment, newer hospitals have designed rooming-in units which allow mothers easy physical access to their babies and continued visual contact, while at the same time providing nursing care to both mother and baby so as not to overstrain the mother in the immediate postpartum period. Similarly, in an effort to allow fathers more proximity to their babies, many hospitals have instituted fathers' hours during which the father can get acquainted with his baby by touching, holding, and/or feeding his son or daughter. One father described his feelings of getting to know his baby in a *New York Times* article on fathers' hours: "I really didn't have that proud father feeling. . . . But as I hold the baby, I'm getting prouder and prouder, stroking his face a lot, feeling his skin, smelling him—it's a kind of enjoyment that I can have now while we're alone" (Figure 16.3).

In addition to physical contact, the mother's emotional state is particularly important. If she

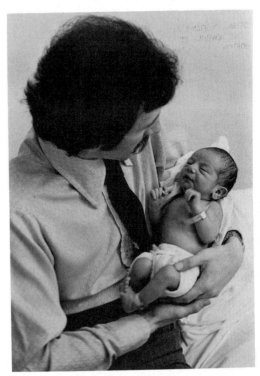

Figure 16.3. Father holding his newborn baby. From the film *Adapting to Parenthood.* (By permission of Polymorph Films, Boston.)

has been sedated or has prolonged physical discomfort, she may find it difficult to turn her attention to her newborn. The anesthetized mother, not having seen her baby at birth, must rely on the staff's word that the infant is indeed hers.

THE POSTPARTUM COUPLE

Couples who expect their lives to return to normal after the delivery, that is to their prepregnant state, will be rudely awakened by the stressful reality of the postpartum period. While some couples may receive preparation for pregnancy and childbirth, few will be adequately prepared to cope with the biological and psychological changes following childbirth. Mothers and babies are now leaving the hospital within days of delivery, but little provision is made by the hospital or the birth attendants for the mother's continued recuperation or for the infant's care. Myths and misconceptions on the nature of maternal love and conflicting schools of childbearing can further complicate the process of loving and caring for an infant. All too often couples approach the task of parenting hoping for an all-knowing maternal love to spontaneously emerge, instead of seeking out information and skills that will allow the couple to face the difficult task of caring for a newborn. Ignorance of postpartum stress and lack of social supports make this a period of high risk for emotional disturbances and marital problems.

If the husband or wife expects the wife's body to function at its prepregnant level immediately after the delivery, they may be disappointed, even frightened, by the postpartum physical and sexual discomforts. This period can place an unexpected strain on the marital bond of an unsuspecting couple who may be hoping to finally return to life as usual. As the mother's body begins the process of recovery, she may have painful uterine contractions, itchy and irritating episiotomy stitches, a draining fatigue, hot flashes and nighttime perspirations, and sensitive and perhaps engorged breasts. She may find the blood-stained vaginal discharge disturbing and her overweight postpartum figure disappointing.

If a couple is expecting to return to their prepregnant sexual pattern after the sixth week checkup, both husband and wife may be alarmed to discover the wife's lack of sexual interest. In a study by Masters and Johnson, almost 50% of the women interviewed at three months postpartum had low or negligible levels of sexual desire. They refrained from intercourse because they experienced excessive fatigue, weakness, and pain on coitus. Also, they were afraid of permanent physical harm from too early coital activity. Direct observation of the postpartum vagina indicated that women two months after delivery were slower to arouse, lubricated in reduced quantities, and climaxed with reduced intensity. If the husband and wife are unprepared for this, they may mistakenly view these normal physical changes as a sign of the wife's "frigidity." They may fear that she has substituted maternal love for sexual pleasure. The sexual strain of the postpartum period is sometimes expressed by the husband's seeking sex outside of his marriage. From the last months of pregnancy through the sixth week of continence, over 20% of the husbands interviewed by Masters and Johnson had engaged in extramarital sexual activity, many for the first time.

The more information a couple has to deal with the sexual difficulties of the postpartum period, the less strain they will experience. A simple suggestion such as the use of sterile jelly or contraception cream for a sexually interested but nonlubricating wife can help ease a tense sexual situation. Couples need to be encouraged to experiment with different sexual positions that may enhance both partners' sexual pleasure.

Most new mothers will face a period of transitory emotional disequilibrium in the months following childbirth. Many will experience a lack of energy and chronic fatigue. Mood swings with episodes of crying, anxieties and fears, and confused and distracted thought processes may be seen. If the couple expects the new mother to bask in the well-being of maternal bliss, they may be disappointed by the postpartum mother's general deterioration in mood. Instead of feeling all-giving, she often feels very needy herself. The demands of other children at home can be overwhelming to the new mother. Trying to maintain her family, social, and professional obligations at her prepregnant level of efficiency without additional help will be an exhausting, often impossible goal that may leave her feeling guilty and depressed. Furthermore, the difficulty of handling a sick or colicky infant or multiple births can result in an intense period of strain.

In the book *Our Bodies, Ourselves* one mother described how she responded when her triplets were quite young:

"Over a period of time I noticed that my mind suffered. I dropped out on everything that had been going on before the babies were born. My recall of facts and images, especially those predating the birth, was sharply impaired. It was like becoming senile. All of my psychic energy was going into sustaining the babies and the family."

Some even less fortunate mothers will face a psychiatric disturbance severe enough to warrant hospitalization, and some of them may be permanently incapacitated. They may suffer a *postpartum psychosis* with hallucinations, severe depression, and possibly even suicidal and/or infanticidal impulses. Postpartum disorders are really a very common phenomenon. It has been estimated that as many as one of every two to three women may develop "maternity blues," a self-limited adjustment disorder with depressed mood. About 5% to 10% of women will suffer a diagnosable postpartum major depression during the first three months following delivery, and a small number of these (about one to two of every 1,000 births in this country) will go on to develop a postpartum psychosis.

While some researchers have emphasized the importance of hormonal imbalance and deficiency in the etiology of postpartum disorders, others have focused on the role of psychological and social factors in the etiology and prevention of postpartum disorders. Using questionnaires, Gordon, Kapostins, and Gordon were able to identify women as high risk for postpartum distress on the basis of their own and their husbands' personal and social histories. Relatively brief postpartum difficulties were associated with more personal stress, such as an illness or death in the family, whereas postpartum reactions of longer duration tended to be associated with problems in the current social environment, such as lack of experience in childcare, lack of practical help from others, and lack of support from husbands and relatives.

Using this information, the authors devised a postpartum program for pregnant women and their husbands. The expectant mothers who took these special prenatal classes had less postpartum distress than did the control group. Considering the importance of the social factors in perpetuating postpartum difficulties, it is not surprising that when husbands accompanied their wives to these classes, half as many of these women developed postpartum adjustment problems as did those women whose husbands did not attend. Obstetricians and public health nurses who incorporated these principles into the management of maternity patients were also successful in reducing postpartum distress.

PARENT-INFANT INTERACTION

Myths that have romanticized maternal love have placed an unnecessary burden on parents as they take their first tentative steps in the early relationship with their baby. The notion that maternal love is automatically delivered along with the baby or that it resides solely within the personality of the mother unfortunately leaves the parents and the health profession with an unrealistic and oversimplified understanding of the complex and dynamic interaction between parent and child.

There are several such myths or misconceptions that have made the process of parenting much more difficult. One is the myth that all newborns are basically the same, a "tabula rasa" which is shaped entirely by the environment and especially the mother, and which does not really contribute very much to the parent-infant interaction. As will be discussed in more detail in Chapter 19, nothing could be further from the truth. Newborns are not all the same. They differ on many behavioral measures, and the various ways in which they differ have a direct effect on their parents.

For example, individual differences have been observed in the neonate's intensity of response to various auditory, visual, and tactile stimuli, and these differences show significant day-to-day consistency. This is true even in the way in which they suck milk from a nipple. Each newborn has his or her own characteristic reflex sucking pattern. Other behavioral measures that are relevant to social relatedness have been observed to differ widely among newborns, including the degree to which infants orient to animate and inanimate objects, their muscle tone, their tension states, their temperament and irritability, their cuddliness, and their activity patterns. These measures along with others are included in Brazelton's Neonatal Behavioral Assessment Scale.

Thus, each newborn enters life with his or her own unique individuality, and this in turn will profoundly affect his or her parents. Studying the mother-infant interaction, Osofsky and Danzger observed that there was a high degree of correspondence between the responsiveness of the mother and that of the baby. The mother's auditory stimulation was related to the auditory responsiveness of the infant, her visual stimulation to the infant's auditory and tactile responsiveness, and her tactile stimulation to the infant's visual, auditory, and tactile responsiveness. Since the baby's behavior was consistent when interacting with the experimenter as compared to the mother, the authors concluded that the infant's responsiveness was probably affecting the mother's behavior, and in so doing, contributing to the interaction.

The reader may wonder: How can a helpless infant affect anyone? The answer is that there has been a growing respect for the extent of the young infant's behavioral competence and biological endowment. Neonates can hear, see, taste, and smell. They are capable of maintaining visual fixation and pursuit, and of making visual discrimination. They are capable of making or breaking eye contact, a measure that has a very powerful effect on their mothers. When they experience displeasure, they can express it by crying, or they can avert their eyes, powerful aversive stimuli to most parents. Thus, the young infant is no longer considered a passive, neutral creature absorbing his or her personality from the environment, but rather as already a unique individual with a capacity, however limited, to affect its caretakers.

In order to understand the impact of the infant on its parents, one has to understand the emotional state of the parents. They have conceived the baby for their own personal reasons. One common need of parents is to be in a mutually gratifying relationship with their baby. As a result of this desire on the part of the parents to gratify and be gratified by the baby, very small responses or gestures by the baby can have a profound impact on the parents, encouraging them to repeat the parental behavior that elicited the desired response, whether it was stimulating a baby to smile or quieting a crying child.

Although learning theorists have traditionally described how mothers "shaped" their baby's behavior, we are now beginning to appreciate how much babies "shape" the behavior of mothers and other adults in their social environment. Indeed, if we look at interactions between a parent and infant, it is the parent who accommodates most to the young baby's activities. The baby has a much more limited capacity to accommodate to the parents' activity. Then, as the baby develops, the situation begins to change. By the end of the first year interactions between the baby and the parent are more nearly symmetrical with initiations and accommodations more equally distributed between them. Perhaps one definition of parenting the very young infant could be a willingness and capacity to accommodate to the infant's needs and unique individuality.

We have come to appreciate the reciprocal interacting nature of the parent-child relationship. Each partner influences and is influenced by the other, even during the neonatal period. As Sameroff has pointed out, there are inherent rewards in this reciprocal functioning, intrinsic pleasures in experiencing the back and forth rhythms of this unique social interaction (Figure 16.4).

While individual differences in early infancy can be identified as temperamental patterns that persist in later infancy and early childhood, the effect they will have on a particular child and its social environment is very much dependent on how the infant's temperament is perceived and reacted to by the parents. Thomas, Chess, and Birch, studying parental perception of infant temperament in 85 families and 133 children over a period of six years, identified nine relatively stable temperamental qualities in infancy and early childhood. Children under two years of age who were described as "difficult" characteristically were irregular in biologic functions (sleeping, eating) and were slow to adjust to changes in the environment, often reacting intensely with loud crying and temper tantrums. Pleasure was also expressed loudly, but these children were unhappy more often than happy. As many as 70% of these children developed behavioral disturbances later in childhood. The other 30% were able to adapt, although slowly, to the parental and environmental demands made on them. Thus, the "difficult" child was obviously not an easy one to raise, and most parents of such a child were unable to help their child adapt. Many of these parents developed feelings of self-doubt, anxiety, and helplessness in their efforts at nurturing these children. It is important to point out that not all "difficult"

Figure 16.4. *Mother and Child* (1928) by Gustav Vigeland. Bronze. Placed in the Vigeland Sculpture Park, Oslo, Norway. (By permission of Vigeland Museum, Oslo, Norway.)

children become problem children. The authors believe that the parents' ability or lack of ability to help the child adapt to social demands played a crucial factor in the development of pathology in these children. In contrast to the "difficult" child, the "easy" ones were predominantly positive in mood, highly regular in their biological rhythms, and rapidly adaptable, with positive reactions in new situations. Most of these children did not develop behavior problems later, and their parents tended to perceive themselves as effective, skillful, and confident. Thus, the misconception that all infants are the same encourages parents to ignore each child's unique individuality, burdens them with unwarranted guilt, beclouds their perception of their child, and interferes with their ability to help their children cope with their social environment.

After a 25-year follow-up of these same 133 children, Thomas and Chess (*American Journal of Psychiatry*, vol 141, p 8, 1984) concluded: "In tracing individual developmental sequences we have found the concept of *goodness of fit* ... to be very useful. Goodness of fit results when the properties of the environment and its expectations and demands are in accord with the organism's own capacities, motivations, and style of behaving. When this *consonance* between individual and environment is present, optimal development is possible. Conversely, poorness of fit involves *dissonance* between individual and environment, so that distorted development and maladaptive functioning occur." For Thomas and Chess the essential goal of parent guidance is to identify the poorness of fit between child and environment that is responsible for the behavior disorder, and then to work out a strategy with the parents that can change the poorness of fit to a goodness of fit.

The second misconception is a corollary to the first one, and that is that everything that happens in the development of the child is going to be completely dependent on the mother or mothering figure. This notion can make parents overly anxious about their performance, and leads to such stereotypes as the "good" mother or the "bad" mother, the "overprotective" mother or the "rejecting" mother. It also implies that one mothering person is necessary for normal development and that multiple caretaking would be detrimental. It completely ignores the influential role played by the father or grandparents or parent substitutes in the child's development. The research on the kibbutz in Israel, as well as similar research in the United States, indicates that children raised in extended families, or where parents share caretaking with others, will thrive as long as the other caretakers provide loving relationships. The important factor is not the number of caretakers but the quality of care they provide.

In actuality, just as each newborn is unique, so is each parent-infant interaction. Rather than thinking in global terms such as "good mother"—"bad mother," it is more helpful to think in terms of a mutual harmony of the mother's and father's needs and the infant's needs, or a mutual disharmony of the parents' and the infant's needs, and this is going to vary over time. Let us take the baby's sucking reflex as one example. One baby may be an active, vigorous sucker. A mother who is a fairly active woman, who likes to give a lot and who likes to receive a lot, is probably going to be pleased with that particular infant. She is going to feel good about her mothering. There is going to be a mutual harmony of needs. But another baby may be a much more sluggish, less active sucker, with irregular sleep-hunger cycles which make it difficult for the mother to know when the baby needs to nurse again. It is easy to see how this same mother with this second baby might come to feel that she is not a "good" mother. If a pediatrician can sit down with her and explain to her that every infant is different, every woman is different, and therefore every interaction is different, then perhaps she can be helped to see that she need not blame herself for being "inadequate," but rather can begin to accept both the baby and herself.

To take another example, certain mothers and fathers and families are going to be very comfortable with an infant or a newborn, a completely dependent child, but when that child begins to separate, begins to individuate, begins to express his or her own needs, then at that point, there may be a disharmony. Or the difficulty may come later, in the rebellion of adolescence. All through the life cycle, it is a question of the degree of mutual harmony, or disharmony, between the parents and the children. Parents and children both must somehow deal with the task of individuation and separation throughout the life cycle.

This brings us to a third misconception, one that is really at the opposite end of the spectrum from the idea that the mother is all-important. It is the idea that some parenting figure or figures are not really crucial for development. If the child is raised in a clean, hygienic environment and its physical needs are met, then that is all that is required for development to proceed normally. This is not true. Someone—whether it be the biological mother, or an adoptive mother, or the father, or the grandparent—must give that infant the attention and the love that is necessary for the establishment of a trusting relationship with other people, and the development of a healthy capacity for human relationships. That is not going to come about simply by a proper formula in a bottle in a germ-free environment. Stimulation (auditory, visual, tactile, and kinesthetic) in response to the infant's needs and emotional involvement by the caregivers are essential for normal development (Figure 16.5).

Children raised in impoverished environments, particularly in large institutions where they are given minimal individual attention, rarely held or cuddled, and given few objects with which to play, often become unresponsive and retarded in language, cognitive, and motor development. In a classic study of *hospitalism*, René Spitz compared infants raised in three environments: those raised at home; those raised by their mothers in a nursery of a prison; and those raised in a hygienic but emotionally sterile foundling home. He found that the infants in the first two groups developed adequately. However, the children in the foundling home showed, from the third month on, extreme susceptibility to infection, illness, and death. By age two and a half years, only two of the 26 children in the foundling home could speak a few words or walk.

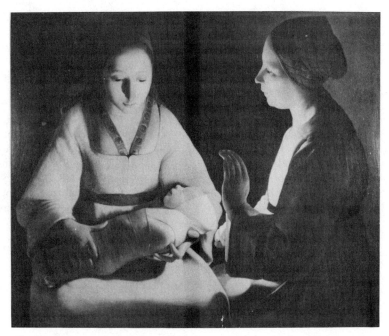

Figure 16.5. *The Newborn* (1630) by Georges de La Tour. (By permission of Museum of Fine Arts, Rennes, France.)

Various kinds of stimulation in infancy have been shown to have positive developmental effects. For example, handling of neonates has improved their visual interest. Kinesthetic stimulation of prematures has improved their feeding patterns with additional weight gain on comparable amounts of formula. In later infancy the human voice has been found to be the most effective conditioner of infant vocalization.

Human contact is also necessary for social-emotional development. Just as parents become emotionally attached to their babies when they spend time in close contact with them, babies also become attached to the stable caretakers in their environment. Human contact appears to have emotionally toned significance from the earliest days of life. Neonates differentially respond to animate and inanimate events. When mothers were asked to remain completely unresponsive to their infants, that is to look at them with a still face for three minutes, infants as young as two weeks typically responded by withdrawing and turning to self-quieting behaviors after attempting to reengage the mother.

Similarly, neonates also "tune in" to certain biological rhythms of their caretakers as shown in the studies of Sander and his coworkers. Babies housed with single caretakers established day-night sleep cycles sooner than did babies in routine hospital nurseries. Switching caretakers at 10 days of age can cause disruption of infant rhythms and increased fussiness. There are studies by Macfarlane to suggest that within the first week of life the neonate is already beginning to differentiate his or her mother from others by the characteristic odor of her breast milk.

Furthermore, infants raised in inadequate institutions with changing caretakers do not become emotionally attached to these caretakers. They may become withdrawn and develop disturbed patterns of relating. While we know that extreme forms of deprivation are detrimental to infant development, we know less about the effects of specific kinds of parenting patterns or practices. Much seems to depend on the specific individual needs of the infant and the capacity of his or her parents or other caretakers to meet these needs.

THE NEW PARENTS

The days and weeks after the birth are a time of reorientation, for both the mother and father. Instead of being a time of intuitively knowing the infant's needs and blissfully meeting them, this is often a time of stress as the parents adjust to the baby's physical presence and learn to cope with the baby's needs. The physical separation at delivery between the mother and baby places an emotional strain on the mother, who has grown used to being united with her baby throughout the pregnancy. Many women feel anxious when the newborn is away from them for any length of time. As the mother comes to terms with her feelings over the loss of her infant-in-utero, she can begin to recognize her baby as separate from herself with his or her own needs. The father who has probably per-

ceived his wife and baby as one throughout the pregnancy must also adapt to the reality of his baby as separate and differentiated from his wife.

Caring for a separate baby outside the mother's body requires new adaptations. No longer can the parents rely on biological forces within the mother's body to protect and nurture the baby. Now specific infant needs must be paired with specific gratifications. To calm a distressed infant requires skills in baby care for which many couples with their first baby are totally unprepared. Little in the mother's or the father's long years of formal education has prepared

Figure 16.6. *Mother With Child in Arms* (1916) by Käthe Kollwitz. (By permission of Philadelphia Museum of Art: Given by Carl Zigrosser.)

them for the day they bring a baby home from the hospital. They must learn the fundamentals, the tricks of the parenting trade, at the same time that they are discovering the unique aspects of their baby. Parents of firstborns are often shocked by the extent to which their life styles must change to accommodate the physical and emotional needs of the newborn. Because many couples in our society live far from their families, the burden of coping with the baby often falls entirely on the parents and frequently just with the mother.

Even for experienced parents who know the fundamentals of baby care, frequent feedings are exhausting and often tedious. Persistent crying can be worrisome and annoying. For first-time parents who may not have already established social relationships with other parents, the early months can be lonely as they face the realization that a profound, not altogether welcomed, disruption in their lives has occurred. Many parents hide their disappointment and annoyance because they mistakenly confuse their resentment of an emotionally and physically draining situation with their feelings toward their baby. As parents learn that resenting the internal state of discomfort created by the newborn is not the same as rejecting the baby, they can be freer in their expression and acceptance of both their resentment and their love. Beyond this, they can enjoy the special rewards of coming to know their baby as a unique human being who responds to them.

CONCLUSION

In this chapter we have tried to present the parent-infant relationship as a mutually dynamic interaction in which each member is affected by and affects the other members. While there may be uncommon cases in which parents and child are so alienated from one another that they may be inaccessible, the members of most families are to some degree attached to one another and thus are influenced by the needs and reactions of one another. It is not beneficial for the parent to try to live up to an idealized image of a "good" mother or father, or to try to create an idealized "normal" child. Rather, as parents begin to accept their own and their infant's unique individuality and different needs, they can better help the baby and themselves cope with the varying and unpredictable demands and stresses of life (Figure 16.6).

Suggested Readings

Anthony EJ, Benedek T (eds): *Parenthood: Its Psychology and Psychopathology.* Boston, Little, Brown, and Co., 1970.

Brazelton TB: *On Becoming a Family: The Growth of Attachment.* New York, Delacorte Press, 1981.

Brazelton TB: *Infants and Mothers: Differences in Development.* New York, Delacorte Press, 1983.

Call JD, Galenson E, Tyson RL (eds): *Frontiers of Infant Psychiatry.* New York, Basic Books, vol. I, 1983; vol. II, 1985.

Cath SH, Gurwitt AR, Ross JM (eds): *Father and Child: Developmental and Clinical Perspectives.* Boston, Little, Brown, & Co., 1982.

Karmel M: *Thank You, Dr. Lamaze.* Philadelphia, J.B. Lippincott, 1959, and Garden City, NY, Dolphin Books, 1965.

Kitzinger S: *The Experience of Childbirth.* New York, Taplinger, 1972.

Klaus MH, Kennell JH: *Parent-Infant Bonding.* St. Louis, C.V. Mosby, 1982.

Kliman GW, Rosenfeld A: *Responsible Parenthood.* New York, Holt, Rinehart, & Winston, 1980.

Osofsky HJ, Osofsky JD: *Answers for New Parents.* New York, Walker & Co., 1980.

Stern D: *The First Relationship: Mother and Infant.* Cambridge, MA, Harvard University Press, 1977.

References

Arms S: *Immaculate Deception: A New Look at Women and Childbirth in America.* Boston, Houghton Mifflin, 1975.

Bell RQ, Harper LV. *Child Effects on Adults.* New York, Halsted Press, 1977.

Birns B: Individual differences in human neonates' responses to stimulation. *Child Dev.* 36:249, 1965.

Boston Women's Health Book Collective. Childbearing. In *Our Bodies, Ourselves.* New York, Simon & Schuster, 1973.

Bowes WA, et al: The effects of obstetrical medication on fetus and infant. Monographs of the Society for Research in Child Development, vol 35, 1970.

Bradley RA: *Husband-Coached Childbirth,* rev ed. New York, Harper & Row, 1974.

Brazelton TB: *Neonatal Behavioral Assessment Scale.* Philadelphia, J.B. Lippincott, 1973.

Brazelton TB: The origins of reciprocity: the early mother-infant interaction. In Lewis M, Rosenblum L (eds): *The Effect of the Infant on its Caregiver.* New York, Wiley, 1974, p 49.

Brazelton TB, et al: Early mother-infant reciprocity. In *Ciba Foundation Symposium 33: Parent-Infant Interaction.* New York, Associated Scientific Publishers, 1975, p 137.

Brody S: *Patterns of Mothering.* New York, International Universities Press, 1956.

Butterfield PM, Emde RN, Platt BB: Effects of silver nitrate on initial visual behavior. *Am J Diseases of Children* 132:426, 1978.

Chertok L: *Motherhood and Personality: Psychosomatic Aspects of Motherhood.* Philadelphia, J.B. Lippincott, 1969.

Coleman RW, Kris E, Provence S: The study of variations of early parental attitudes. *Psychoanal Study Child* 8:20, 1953.

Dalton K: *Depression After Childbirth.* New York, Oxford University Press, 1980.

Dick-Read G: *Childbirth Without Fear.* New York, Harper & Brothers, 1954.

Dodson F: *How to Parent.* Los Angeles, Nash Publishing, 1970.

Doering SG, Entwisle DR: Preparation during pregnancy and ability to cope with labor and delivery. *Orthopsychiatry* 45:825, 1975.

Emde RN, Swedberg J, Suzuki B: Human wakefulness and biological rhythms after birth. *Arch Gen Psychiatry* 32:780, 1975.

Emde RN, Gaensbauer TJ: Modeling emotion in human infancy. In Immelman K, et al (eds): *Behavioral Development: The Bielefeld Interdisciplinary Project.* New York,

Cambridge University Press, 1980.

Emde RN: Emotional availability: a reciprocal reward system for infants and parents with implications for prevention of psychosocial disorders. In Taylor P (ed): *Parent-Infant Relationships.* New York, Grune & Stratton, 1980.

Etzel BC, Gewirtz JL: Experimental modification of caretaker-maintained high-rate operant crying in a 6- and a 20-week old infant (Infans tyranno-tearus): extinction of crying with reinforcement of eye contact and smiling. *J Exp Child Psychol* 5:303, 1967.

Fraiberg SH: *Insights From the Blind: Developmental Studies of Blind Children.* New York, Basic Books, 1977.

Gewirtz JL: The course of infant smiling in four childbearing environments in Israel. In Foss BM (ed): *Determinants of Infant Behavior,* vol 3. Boston, Methuen, 1965, p 205.

Gordon RE, Kapostins E, Gordon KK: Factors in postpartum emotional adjustment. *Obstet Gynecol* 25:158, 1965.

Hazell LD: *Commonsense Childbirth.* New York, Tower Publications, 1972.

Hittelman J, et al: Mother-infant assessment of the LeBoyer "non-violent" method of childbirth. Paper presented at the meetings of the American Psychological Association, September 1980.

Kaij L, Nilsson A: Emotional and psychotic illness following childbirth. In Howells JG (ed): *Modern Perspectives in Psycho-Obstetrics.* New York, Brunner/Mazel, 1972, p 364.

Kennell JH, et al: Maternal behavior one year after early and extended postpartum contact. *Dev Med Child Neurol* 16:172, 1974.

Kitzinger S: *Giving Birth.* New York, Taplinger, 1971.

Klaus MH, Kennell JH: Mothers separated from their newborn infants. *Pediatr Clin North Am* 17:1015, 1970.

Klaus MH, et al: Human maternal behavior at the first contact with her young. *Pediatrics* 46:187, 1970.

Kron RE, Ipsen J, Goddard KE: Consistent individual differences in the nutritive sucking behavior of the human newborn. *Psychosom Med* 30:151, 1968.

Leboyer F: *Birth Without Violence.* New York, Alfred A. Knopf, 1975.

Maccoby EE, Feldman SS: Mother-attachment and stranger-reactions in the third year of life. Monographs of the Society for Research in Child Development, Vol 37, 1972.

Macfarlane JA: Olfaction in the development of social preferences in the human neonate. In *Ciba Foundation Symposium 33: Parent-Infant Interaction.* New York, Associated Scientific Publishers, 1975, p 103.

Masters WH, Johnson VE: *Human Sexual Response.* Boston, Little, Brown, and Co., 1966.

Osofsky JD, Danzger B: Relationships between neonatal characteristics and mother-infant interaction. *Dev Psychol* 10:124, 1974.

Paykel ES, et al: Life events and social support in puerperal depression. *Brit J Psychiatry* 136:339, 1980.

Provence S, Lipton RC: *Infants in Institutions.* New York, International Universities Press, 1962.

Rutter M: Parent-child separation: psychological effects on the children. *J Child Psychol Psychiatry* 12:233, 1971.

Sameroff A: Motivational origins of early cognitive and social behavior. In Immelman K, et al (eds): *Behavioral Development: The Bielefeld Interdisciplinary Project.* New York, Cambridge University Press, 1980.

Sander LW, Julia HL, Stechler G, Burns P: Continuous 24-hour interactional monitoring in infants reared in two caretaking environments. *Psychosom Med* 34:270, 1972.

Seiden AM: The sense of mastery in the childbirth experience. In Notman MT, Nadelson CC (eds): *The Woman Patient. Volume 1: Sexual and Reproductive Aspects of Women's Health Care.* New York, Plenum Press, 1978, p 87.

Shaw NS: *Forced Labor: Maternity Care in the United States.* New York, Pergamon Press, 1974.

Solnit AJ, Stark MH: Mourning and the birth of a defective child. *Psychoanal Study Child* 16:523, 1961.

Sosa R, et al: The effect of a supportive companion on perinatal problems, length of labor, and mother-infant interaction. *N Eng J Med* 303:597, 1980.

Spitz RA: Hospitalism: an inquiry into the genesis of psychiatric conditions in early childhood. *Psychoanal Study Child* 1:53, 1945.

Spitz RA: Hospitalism: a follow-up report. *Psychoanal Study Child* 2:113, 1946.

Spitz RA, Wolf KM: Anaclitic depression: an inquiry into the genesis of psychiatric conditions in early childhood. *Psychoanal Study Child* 2:313, 1946.

Stern DN: Mother and infant at play: the dyadic interaction involving facial, vocal, and gaze behaviors. In Lewis M, Rosenblum L (eds): *The Effect of the Infant on its Caregiver.* New York, Wiley, 1974, p 187.

Svejda MJ, Campos JJ, Emde RN: Mother-infant "bonding": failure to generalize. *Child Development* 51:1980.

Tanzer D, Block JL: *Why Natural Childbirth.* New York, Doubleday, 1972.

Thomas A, Chess S, Birch HG: *Temperament and Behavior Disorders in Children.* New York, New York University Press, 1968.

Thomas A, Chess S: *Temperament and Development.* New York, Brunner/Mazel, 1977.

Thomas A, Chess S: Genesis and evolution of behavior disorders: from infancy to early adult life. *Am J Psychiatry* 141:1, 1984.

Vietze PM, et al: Contingent interaction between mothers and their developmentally delayed infants. In Sackett GP (ed): *Observing Behavior.* Baltimore, University Park Press, 1978.

17 Fetal and Neonatal Loss

Robert J. Harmon, M.D. and
Dorotha Graham-Cicchinelli, B.A.S.W.

A marriage just as I wished. A pregnancy just as I hoped ... And I feel good ... The apartment is bathed in sunlight, and in my head the baby is, too ... Everything is perfect. I see him, this baby. He is there a little more at each dawn ... I touch him, I feel him, I breathe him ... I wait for the first awakening more and more feverishly, the first smile, the first tooth ... And then, one night, hemorrhage. Panic ... Here's the taxi, the hospital ... 'Madame, you must not think any more about the child.' Not think any more about the baby? About 'my' baby? About the one I waited more than eight months for? ... I think I'm going to die of pain. My husband is there, close ... He kisses me ... I want to cry. Or to sleep. All I want is to sleep. Sleep so I won't have to think anymore, sleep so I won't see my husband cry anymore ... I want to bury my dreams and my sorrow. When I wake up, sympathetic faces walk past me, but ... they will never understand what I feel. It was a girl, they say. She would have lived, but ... she is dead. It's an 'accident.' No ... For me, it's failure. And jealousy ... Why all the others and not me? When I returned to the house, there was no more sun, no toys, no colors. The silence of the hours to come. An empty room. What is it, a mommy without a baby?*

The physical and psychological effects of the loss of a parent, a spouse, a child, or some other loved one on the bereaved are now well accepted, and the stages of grief and mourning in response to such losses will be described in detail in Chapter 48. However, only in recent years have we begun to understand that perinatal death— whether miscarriage, fetal loss, or neonatal loss—is equally, if not more devastating than

---

* From "C'est quoi, une madam sans bébe?" by M. A. *F Magazine*, No. 26, April 1980. Copyright © 1980. Reprinted by permission.

the death of those we have known and loved over a longer period of time. As many couples have described, the loss of a parent is the loss of one's past, while the loss of their baby is the loss of their future.

PERINATAL LOSS

Advances in medicine have significantly decreased the infant mortality rate over the last 50 years, yet the fact remains that some pregnancies fail and some babies die. Perhaps it is the unlikelihood of this event today that makes its impact so tragic and often lasting. Family members, friends, and even some professionals question how a couple can feel so devastated by the death of a child they did not even know or love. The answer is really quite simple. The expectant parents have been doing just that— coming to know and love their unborn child and getting ready to welcome its birth.

Until recently, the degree to which the expectant couple develops an attachment to its unborn child has not been fully appreciated. But it is now well recognized that attachment to the unborn child often begins prior to conception and certainly with most couples occurs at some point during their pregnancy. With the advent of better birth control techniques, many couples are delaying pregnancy until their careers are established and their finances are somewhat more stable. Because a great deal of discussion about pregnancy now takes place during courtship and early marriage, often the child has been prepared for and dreamed about for many years. Then, when conception does occur, the new medical techniques of ultrasound and amniocentesis provide the parents with pictures of, and in many cases knowledge of the sex of, their unborn child. This information confirms a sense that this is a real developing person, one who is known, experienced, and loved. The mother's bodily changes, the baby's heartbeat, and the onset of fetal movements all further confirm to the parents that their child is a reality. Concurrent with the creation of this new human being is the creation of a new life for the parents. Changes begin to occur, including altered career plans, a move to a bigger apartment or house, and preparation of the infant's room.

When the pregnancy ends in tragedy and dreams collapse, such hopes and plans for the future are lost. Sadness and guilt replace joy and anticipation. The couple fears that they will never be able to have a child and that they can no longer rely on their bodies. They have failed to fulfill their own parents' dreams of grandparenthood and their friends' expectations of good news. They have lost their new-found identity, and their whole future may seem meaningless. One mother stated: "Now what? I've quit my job. I'm supposed to be home nursing my baby, yet I'm home alone. My breasts make milk for no one; I feel useless, without purpose. I've lost my future." Another mother said: "I felt like I walked around for months with a shadow of sadness totally covering me, and nothing I could do would make it go away. I would imagine myself a tree whose branches were covered with snow wondering when I was going to break." Irrational guilt over what they fear they may have done or not done to make the baby die may be the most troubling symptom of all. One mother admitted with embarrassment: "I know this probably isn't true, but I can't help but think if I'd eaten better or exercised less maybe my baby would have lived." These feelings are even stronger if there are no known reasons for the baby's death. Parents whose child has died with birth abnormalities feel the guilt of carrying defective genes. But good genetic counseling does seem to allay some of these fears. Parents who have the most difficult time with irrational guilt are those that remain in a free floating atmosphere of unanswerable questions. Guilt over whether they should have taken that trip, had intercourse so close to delivery, painted a room, moved that box, are only a few examples of such self-torturing. Often these thoughts may not be shared with the spouse. Many months following one couple's loss, the wife admitted to her husband that she knew he blamed her for the death of their child. She was surprised to learn that the husband actually blamed himself for not helping her enough with the household chores. Such irrational feelings are very common and must be addressed by the physician. Otherwise these couples may harbor a terrible burden of guilt all of their lives.

MISCARRIAGE

In *miscarriage* or *spontaneous abortion* (loss occuring from conception to 20 weeks gestation), there is often the fear that there will be difficulties with future pregnancies and doubts about ever having any children. The physician must be aware of the sense of loss and acknowledge the couple's fears of future problems. Statistically, miscarriage is the most common failed pregnancy. This is why physicians and health care providers often view it as a medical problem and treat it in a mechanical manner. They are confident that most couples will eventually complete a successful pregnancy. Many physicians do not consider these patients as obstetrical high risks until after three miscarriages. But by this time fear of the unknown has played emotional havoc with the couple's life. The mother in particular becomes preoccupied with issues of physical dysfunction, genetic abnormality, and management of the next pregnancy. Without appropriate physician counseling she may severely and inappropriately restrict her sexual, physical, and work activities.

The physician may be confident that the couple will soon complete a successful pregnancy; the couple, however, is not that confident, and their fears should be explored and discussed. The couple must be allowed to mourn the loss of the child that was to be. Talking about the experience makes it become more real. The pregnancy can end so abruptly, often simply with bleeding and a curettage, that it is hard for the couple to believe that this has happened to them. Thus, it is important that when possible the couple be allowed to see what is expelled from the uterus, so they know with certainty that the pregnancy is over. Often the mother herself will ask—was I really pregnant or was this just a dream? Many couples are reluctant to discuss a miscarriage. They are afraid people will not understand the emotional significance they have attached to this pregnancy. And for couples dealing with longstanding fertility problems, a miscarriage becomes paramount over all other concerns in their lives.

FETAL LOSS

Fetal loss is death occurring from 20 weeks gestation to a full term, nonliving infant. With improved diagnostic tools, physicians often are able to diagnose fetal death before delivery. Although diagnosis before delivery does not take the grief away, it does allow for some anticipatory grieving by the parents to begin. From the moment an ultrasound is performed or a fetal scope discovers no heartbeat, a couple's worst fears become reality. It is very important for the physician at this point, even though he or she is as surprised and saddened as the parents, to be clear and precise with the couple about what has occurred and how they can manage this unexpected outcome together. The physician's time and understanding, plus discussions and reading material offered to parents, can help them prepare for the difficult decisions they will have to make at the time of delivery. In some situations it may be advisable for the mother to carry the pregnancy until labor occurs on its own. Many ambivalent feelings arise while carrying a dead baby to term, and thus the physician needs to help the mother deal with these feelings and to be very clear as to the advantages of vaginal delivery over Caesarian section. At the time of the diagnosis fathers seem more resigned to the infant's death than the mothers, who do not fully believe their baby is dead until delivery has occurred. Concerns of injury to the mother seem foremost in the fathers' thoughts.

Death, even if anticipated, is still a shock when it actually arrives. Instead of a baby's cry filling the delivery room, there is only lifeless silence. Unexpected death diagnosed at the time of delivery carries the most shock, not only for the parents but for physicians and medical staff as well. Often futile resuscitation measures are performed in an attempt to avoid the inevitable task of confirming the infant's death. "I can't believe my baby is dead" is a common response. Shock helps insulate the tragedy by delaying the impact. Feelings of numbness are common during the first minutes, hours, or days after a stillbirth. One woman recalled: "I felt paralyzed and was amazed at how calm I must have appeared right after the delivery. I wondered if the nurses thought I was being callous. I was totally numb." Another mother quoted by Borg and Lasker said: "When I saw the fetus, the fantasy became a person and it was more than the death of a fantasy; it was a real baby I lost."

Stillbirth, as with any other perinatal death, is plagued by a flood of questions and emotions. "Why us? Why my baby? What did I do wrong?" Many couples will start by blaming God, the doctor, the hospital, and finally themselves, particularly if there is no apparent reason for the baby's death. Inability to have eye contact with their baby produces an anguished void for parents, making it difficult for them to attach an identity to their child. Later in their mourning process, this void can be devastating for the couple, making it much harder for them to effectively grieve their loss without the benefit of loving memories.

NEONATAL LOSS

The death of a newborn up to the first 28 days of life characterizes *neonatal loss*. Premature birth, congenital abnormalities, or brain damage due to lack of oxygen are a few of the conditions responsible for early infant death. The parents' attachment process is somewhat different than in the other losses previously described, even though the stages of grief remain the same. At birth the parents are able to see their infant born living, and often have eye contact with the child, thereby creating an attachment outside the womb that signifies to the parents that this pregnancy was real, that this child is indeed theirs. Even though the outcome of this new life results in early infant death, the attachment the couple has experienced permits a more effective grief response. In our experience, it seems that parents who have been able to attach to their live newborn go about initial grieving with more intensity, but may arrive at a resolution phase sooner than their counterparts who experienced fetal loss or stillbirth.

STUDIES ON PERINATAL DEATH

The literature on perinatal death has primarily focused on two issues. The first has concerned maternal grieving and psychopathology following neonatal loss. In one study by Cullberg, it was reported that 33% of women studied one to two years after neonatal loss showed serious mental difficulties, including psychosis, phobias, anxiety attacks, and depression. In another study by Rowe and colleagues, 23% of women were described as showing a prolonged grief reaction. In a later, more systematic, study by Harmon and colleagues in 1984 of 38 mothers who had experienced a neonatal death, mothers were interviewed at three and nine months following the death of their infant and given supportive treatment in the context of the study. All women in the study were married at the time of their infant's death, and their infant had lived at least three days and no longer than 14 days. Most mothers described the death of their infant as having had a major impact on their functioning, although by nine months things seemed to be going better. For example, at three months only 23% of mothers felt that they had adjusted reasonably well, but by nine months 68% felt this was true. The fact that 75% of the mothers emphasized that the period from two to four months was extremely difficult seemed to be due to the fact that family and friends had become less emotionally available to them and expected them to be "back to normal" by this time. And although things seem to be going well in general by nine months following neonatal loss, it should be noted that 74% of the mothers interviewed then were still describing feelings of depression related to their baby's death. At nine months, 42% continued to have episodes of crying about their baby, and 53% described themselves as irritable because of their infant's death. It is also important to note that in this particular study some positive effects were described by nine months following the loss. It had been a widespread clinical impression that there is often an increase in marital difficulties following pregnancy loss. However, in this study, only 10% of the mothers described themselves as having marital difficulties while 50% described their relationship with their husband as having become closer as a result of dealing with the loss together. This particular finding illustrates the adaptive functioning that many couples can show following a loss if given appropriate support from family, friends, clergy, or health care professionals. However, without such support, severe marital difficulties may ensue, leading to an increased evidence of separation and divorce among such unsupported couples.

Although several authors (Peppers and Knapp; Borg and Lasker) have provided clinical descriptions of the effects of miscarriage, to our knowledge there have been no systematic studies of early pregnancy loss with the exception of a 1983 dissertation by Swanson-Kauffman. Twenty women who miscarried *prior to fetal movement* were interviewed on two occasions shortly following their loss. In all instances, the women emphasized that they had experienced the loss of a real child. Although the initial grieving was quite intense, as in the research on neonatal loss described above, within four to six weeks most of these women had dealt with their loss and were ready to think about another pregnancy. The findings from this study suggest that couples who have experienced a miscarriage are able to psychologically think about another pregnancy within a few months following their loss. Thus, though it is usually suggested that couples experiencing fetal or neonatal death wait six months to a year before beginning another pregnancy to allow them to adequately grieve the loss of the dead child, couples experiencing first trimester miscarriages may not require such an extensive grieving period.

The second group of studies on perinatal death has focused on relationships between parental grieving and the behavior of health care professionals. In one study by Benfield and colleagues, it was demonstrated that the attitude of hospital personnel, family, and friends, often had a negative effect on parental grieving. It was the observation of these authors that health care professionals frequently find it difficult to cope with neonatal death themselves and thus are not able to help families deal with their loss. In the previously cited study by Harmon and colleagues, it was demonstrated that through appropriate staff education and the development of a neonatal loss program, health care professionals can learn to be more emotionally available to parents. The grieving process can thereby be facilitated, and more appropriate and adequate follow-up care and support for such families can be provided.

HELPING PARENTS DEAL WITH PERINATAL LOSS

It may seem hard to believe, but not so many years ago some hospitals, at the request of the doctors or family, destroyed the records of stillborn babies. This procedure denied the pregnancy's occurrence as if it was a nonevent, one that was shameful and needed to be hidden. Some hospitals still feel that the less said about the death the better. However, many hospitals have come a long way in helping the couple deal with their tragic loss.

The physician and the hospital staff must

work as a team to help couples deal with the immediate event of death and also be available to empathize and educate parents about the grief they will encounter following their loss. One mother looking back on her loss of a few years ago said: "No one said anything to me; in the recovery room the nurse told me to take these pills to dry up my milk and asked what we wanted to do with the baby's body. Then they sent me to the GYN floor where no one even knew what had happened. There were times I'd wake up and wonder if I'd really had a baby. God knows I wanted to deny my baby was dead, and it seemed instead of the hospital helping me to realize it, they fed into my denial. I was so scared. I wanted someone to teach me how to grieve."

Many hospitals assume that when a mother has delivered a dead infant, she does not want to be on the obstetrical ward with echoes of crying babies and mothers in happier circumstances. However, it has been found that most mothers want a choice of being allowed to remain on the obstetrical ward or being transferred to another medical floor. One mother put it this way: "I'd been planning for months to deliver my baby and enjoy my stay in the hospital with all the other mothers and babies. When my baby died I felt I'd been cheated out of my baby and also out of the obstetrical experience—as if I was an outcast. I wanted to hear the babies cry; it signaled hope for me." Another way in which mothers who have suffered a perinatal loss may feel like an outcast is that they are seen as harbingers of bad luck. One mother cried when she recalled, "I could feel my friend tense and bristle when I picked up her newborn baby—as if I were a baby killer."

Based on the premise, emphasized by Lindemann and others who have studied mourning, that full expression of emotional reactions in a grieving person is necessary for a healthful resolution of grief, the physician and medical staff can help to facilitate grief in a number of ways. To enable parents to experience the reality of their dead child, it is important that the staff feel comfortable in allowing parents the opportunity of seeing, touching, and holding their infant. Being able to experience their baby by touch and caress helps confirm the reality of its existence and its death. It is found beneficial for parents to be gently encouraged to hold their infant immediately after delivery or in the recovery area. If at first parents decline or are

emotionally unable, the parents should be informed how long they have to make their decision and the baby should be offered to them two or three more times during that interval. Allowing parents private time alone with their baby is important. Parents can examine the body, bathe the baby, and say goodbye to their child.

In perinatal deaths where the fetus is poorly developed, macerated, or has congenital anomalies and malformations, it is important that the physicians and staff be comfortable in presenting these babies to parents and be capable of pointing out positive features of the baby as well as the problems. Preparing parents by describing the baby's condition is essential, thus making them feel less uncomfortable and reducing the shock of seeing their malformed infant. More often than not what may appear grotesque to the staff can be seen as beautiful by parents. Parents will nearly always find one positive body aspect upon which to focus.

Another important aid to parents is a picture of their baby. In the Harmon, et al. study, 86% of parents either received pictures of their babies, or wanted them. This finding supports the premise that parents want and need to have memories of their child. Photographs are one positive and concrete way of facilitating the grief process as a reminder that the baby was a real person, not a fantasy. Being able to name their child is another way parents can acknowledge the child's reality. Often couples will not use the name they have chosen had the baby lived, but they still feel more comfortable and respectful of their baby if they can give him or her an identity. In stillbirth, since birth certificates are not issued, many couples make certain their baby's name is registered with the bureau of vital statistics, again ensuring for posterity that this child will not be forgotten. Remembrances such as identification bands, the infant's measurements, footprints, or a lock of hair become important mementos to most couples.

All couples express a feeling of being overwhelmed at the awesome task of expecting to know how to handle burial plans for their infant. Most fathers are left alone to "call around" for bits and pieces of information regarding the arrangements. Yet, those that have agreed to "let the hospital handle it" have subsequently worried about what the hospital actually did with their baby. Having hospitals provide a list of area funeral homes or having the hospital chaplain counsel the parents on options will give parents some tangible information. Explaining the procedure of how the hospital manages the remains of the baby will dispel the worst imagined fears. A funeral, a small private service following a cremation, or a memorial service in honor of the dead infant helps in facilitating grief. It signifies to the couple and their family that this event and their baby are worthy of time and attention. With support of family and friends who share in this ritual and the couple's sadness, a funeral can help begin the mourning process and gives a specific place for parents to visit where they can be with and grieve for their baby. Many couples and families will plant a tree or even a garden in honor of their baby as a way of never forgetting this loved infant. If physician and staff educate parents to the options and choices open to them, it will help prevent any regrets the parents might later feel as to the decisions they have made. Even if the parents subsequently regret the choices they have made, they will not forget that the choices were there, and they will be grateful to those that gave them information and comfort.

Couples have expressed being greatly helped by the physicians and nurses who expressed sadness and empathy, and took the time to listen to them and educate them about the feelings they were experiencing. On the other hand, hospital personnel who made comments like "You're young, you can have another baby," to the mother, or "Chin up, you must be strong for your wife," to the father, or were overly cheerful, or abrupt in dealing with the loss were later viewed with great anger by the couple. Many doctors and nurses interpret this anger as direct blame from the parents, as if they are accusing the staff for the baby's death. On the contrary, the parents look to physicians and nurses for support, care, and understanding in a frightening and tragic course of events, and this anger is an expression of their disappointment over these failed expectations. To expect the physician to meet all the needs of the grieving couple is unrealistic. But physicians can take the initiative in educating the hospital staff, in providing reading material and lists of funeral homes, in encouraging counseling time with the hospital chaplain or social worker, and in developing fetal and neonatal loss support groups. These are excellent ways of ensuring that the couple is not forgotten in their grief. Many doctors are now beginning to schedule specific follow-up interviews with the parents following their loss. These meetings not only assure the couple that the doctor really does care what happens to them, but they also give the physician an opportunity to assess the couple's ability to cope with the loss and to note the progress of the normal grief process. In this way doctors can become alerted to possible pathological grief reactions and then refer the mother, the father, or the siblings for appropriate counseling and also to support groups.

PARENT SUPPORT GROUPS

Recently, parent support groups are being formed nationwide to meet the needs of grieving couples who have suffered a perinatal loss. In these groups, many attend as couples; however some, mothers mostly, attend alone. Father involvement greatly enhances the group discussion. Many women who have come alone often find the other fathers helping them understand why their husbands are having difficulty being as supportive as they would wish. Sharing positive as well as negative memories of the pregnancy and delivery, plus some of the frightening feelings accompanying grief, helps each couple feel less isolated and more normal in their reactions to their baby's death. Many parents, mothers in particular, will comment: "Everyone in this room has described exactly what I feel. Thank God, I thought I was going crazy." Ways of managing tactless remarks from family and friends, returning to work, coping with siblings and grandparents, and dealing with the symptoms of grief—these are just a few topics parents discuss. Thus parents suffering a similar loss form a common bond that allows them to feel understanding and empathy with each other. Leaders provide education and explanations of grief reactions while helping to dispel, if possible, any misinformation that might have been acquired regarding the pregnancy, delivery, or loss. Photos, mementos, poems written by parents, are often shared during and after meetings. A policy of open-ended meetings provides participants the opportunity of coming to meetings sporadically, rather than regularly if they so wish. Many couples do return after long absences from the group, especially during holidays, or "due date" anniversaries.

RESOLUTION OF GRIEF

As will be described further in Chapter 48, the final stage of grief is one of *reorganization.* Thoughts begin to turn toward the future, former acquaintances are renewed, and interest returns in previously enjoyed activities. Now is the time the couple may think about investing in another pregnancy or pursuing other options open to them for completing their family. The loss of the baby is still a remembered event; however, time helps soften the initial pain of grief, and brings relief and resolution. When the couple begins discussing another pregnancy, friends and professionals tend to view this reinvestment as the final cure-all for the couple's loss. Although for most couples, having a healthy subsequent child goes a long way in resolving their grief, may couples are surprised when they find themselves suddenly becoming sad, remembering vignettes of the former tragedy. This final phase of reorganization never arrives all at once, and unfortunately for some parents never completely arrives at all. Peppers and Knapp, in their book *Motherhood and Mourning,* describe this experience as "shadow grief," one that is present as a dull ache, the marks of an experience not shared or known by many, one that leaves an indelible scar. The couple can laugh and enjoy life, yet there is always this constant pain that sometimes surfaces, often prompted by the baby's birthday, death day, hearing the child's name, or seeing other children that are the same age as their child would be. One mother has described this feeling very poignantly: "Right after it happens you must go through all the phases of loss immediately in order to function. Then the grief comes in waves and you deal with that. But even after you think you have resolved the loss, the pain may be diminished but not the memory. After six years and two children, I'm in an o.k. place. But the memory of my lost baby can never completely go away."

Suggested Readings

Berezin N: *After a Loss in Pregnancy.* New York, Simon & Schuster, 1982.

Berg B: *Nothing to Cry About.* New York, Sea View Books, 1981.

Borg S, Lasker J: *When Pregnancy Fails.* Boston, Beacon Press, 1981.

Friedman R, Gradstein B: *Surviving Pregnancy Loss.* Boston, Little, Brown, and Co., 1982.

Pizer H, Palenski CO: *Coping With a Miscarriage.* New York, The Dial Press, 1980.

Peppers LG, Knapp RJ: *Motherhood and Mourning.* New York, Prager Scientific, 1980.

Schiff HS: *The Bereaved Parent.* New York, Crown Publishers, 1977.

References

Benfield DG, Leibs SA, Vollman JH: Grief response of parents to neonatal death and parent participation in deciding care. *Pediatrics* 62:171, 1978.

Chez RA, et al: Helping patients and doctors cope with perinatal death. *Contemporary OB/GYN* 20:98, 1983.

Cullberg J: Psychosomatic medicine in obstetrics and gynecology. In *Proceedings of the Third International Congress, London, 1971.* London, S. Karger AG, 1972, p 326.

Friedman R, Cohen KA: Emotional reactions to miscarriage. In Notman MT, Nadelson CC (eds): *The Woman Patient. Vol 3.* New York, Plenum Press, 1982, p 173.

Harmon RJ, Glicken AD, Siegel RE: Neonatal loss in the intensive care nursery: effects on maternal grieving and a program for intervention. *Journal of the American Academy of Child Psychiatry* 23:68, 1984.

Kennell JH, Trause M: Helping parents cope with perinatal death. *Contemporary OB/GYN* 12:83, 1978.

Klaus MH, Kennell JH: *Parent-Infant Bonding,* St. Louis, C.V. Mosby, 1982.

Kubler-Ross E: *On Death and Dying.* New York, McMillan, 1969.

Lindemann E: Symptomatology and management of acute grief. *Am J Psychiatry* 101:141, 1944.

Rowe J, et al: Follow-up of families who experience a perinatal death. *Pediatrics* 62:166, 1978.

Schwiebert P, Kirk P: *When Hello Means Good-Bye.* Portland, OR, University of Oregon Health Sciences Center Press, 1981.

Stewart M: Perinatal death review. Presented at District VIII Perinatal Section Conference, 1982.

Stewart M, Harmon RJ, et al: Perinatal death: an interdisciplinary approach to follow-up. Unpublished manuscript, 1983.

Swanson-Kauffman K: The unborn one: a profile of the human experience of miscarriage. Doctoral dissertation, University of Colorado School of Nursing, 1983.

Whitfield JM, et al: The application of hospice concepts to neonatal care. *Am J Diseases of Children* 136:421, 1982.

Section E/The Early Years of Childhood

CHAPTER **18** ## An Overview of Child and Adolescent Development

Adolph E. Christ, M.D.

One of the fascinations that child and adolescent development holds for many of us is its complexity. There are a number of *systems* or perspectives that need to be interwoven in order to understand any given child and adolescent. By synthesizing all of these various systems, the physician can better understand the child and then convey this understanding to the child, to the family, and to the school. For the sake of clarity, let us look at a number of these systems, one at a time, in order to gain an overview, before we focus in more specific detail on the years of childhood and adolescence.

THE PSYCHOLOGICAL PERSPECTIVE

Intellectual Development

It was not so long ago that the homunculus theory was fairly universally accepted. That is the theory that states that inside the male sperm is a tiny but fully developed person, only requiring nurturing in the maternal womb in order to grow. Well into the 19th century this idea that a child is but a miniature adult was still quite widely accepted. It has only been fairly recently that we have come to realize that not only are children different from adults, but children are different from one another. For example, one of the basic ideologies of the French Revolution was that all men are created equal. A concomitant noble thought was that all children should

receive an equal education in order to take advantage of this equality. It was therefore most dismaying to find that, given equal opportunity, some children learned and others did not learn. The French government then asked a French psychologist, Alfred Binet, to study the problem. Taking questions and problems that first and second graders could on the average answer, Binet began to find that there were major differences in various children's ability to learn and to be taught. It then became possible to set up a standardized equation of Mental Age over Chronological Age and get a fraction that became known as the I.Q. (Intelligence Quotient). Thus, a 10 year old who knew what the average seven year old knows, but not what the eight year old knows, would earn an I.Q. of 70.

Psychosexual and Emotional Development

Whereas Binet looked at these differences, Sigmund Freud was more interested in understanding *why* certain emotionally disturbed adults thought as they did. The importance of the unconscious mind — a part of oneself that is totally out of awareness — was illuminated by Freud at the turn of the 20th century. A major contribution of Freud's was that in the gradual and painstaking reconstruction of the onset of an emotional illness in an adult, he identified certain stages of psychosexual development in childhood as indicated by Dr. Simons in Table 18.1. Further, he found that emotional conflicts and danger situations (Table 18.1) during these early developmental stages played a major role in later emotional disturbances in adulthood.

Ego Development and Object Relationships

Freud also described the stages of ego development and object relationships (Table 18.1), specifically the oedipal stage, the latency stage, and adolescence. Margaret Mahler and her coworkers later delineated the preoedipal stages into the autistic stage, the symbiotic stage, and the stage of separation-individuation.

Cognitive Development

Another major contributor to our understanding of development is Jean Piaget. Unlike I.Q. or other achievement tests which can tell us a great deal about what an individual has learned, Piaget's descriptions of the sequential changes in cognitive ability tell us much more about *how* an individual thinks and learns. Fascinated by the so-called "errors" that children made (for example, if a four year old is asked why the river flows as it does, he might answer, "Because the men are rowing the water"), Piaget described the sequences in levels of thinking through which children progress, and demonstrated the ways in which the thinking process is significantly different in each of the stages of cognitive development (Table 18.1). Piaget's work is invaluable not only for the educator, but for all those who work with disturbed thinking from whatever cause.

THE BIOLOGICAL PERSPECTIVE

Physical Development

The pediatrician Arnold Gesell was one of the great contributors to our knowledge in the area of physical development, and it is not necessary to belabor the point that individual differences in genetic endowment and in physical development can have important emotional consequences. For example, junior high school is an excellent place to study these differences. The boy with a delayed adolescent growth spurt has a hard time — not one hair has yet developed on his chin or face. His genitals are still tiny in

comparison to his classmates'. His voice is an unwavering soprano. His feelings of insecurity are enormous. In contrast, the 11 year old girl who is fully developed may be pleased that she is the envy of her classmates, but she is often traumatized by sexual overtures that her precocious physical development stimulates in older boys or young men.

Neurological Development

Unfortunately, the least known and understood part of development, the question of *where* a child thinks, has remained virtually unanswered. The clinical material is there, but the orienting framework is almost totally absent. An illustrative case is that of a 12 year old boy with a history of a severe temporal lobe injury at age eight, who developed severe memory problems. He could retrieve what he had learned, but had virtually no automatic memory — that is, he could not remember how he came to the clinic, whether by car or by bus, whether with his mother or his father. He did very well with skills learned before age eight, such as playing checkers, but showed no evidence of having learned new skills since the injury, and his thinking style was that of a well practiced eight year old. Thus, cognitive changes may be closely associated with concomitant changes in the brain cortex.

But before one can plot these cortical changes in time, we need a clarification of where in the cortex certain functions take place. Much interesting, but very preliminary, work is going on in this science of neuropsychology, and one of the most imaginative pioneers is the Russian neuropsychologist, A. R. Luria. Luria has organized the cerebral cortex into three functional units: 1) areas of the cortex having to do with wakefulness, sleep, and the general state of alertness of the brain itself; 2) areas of the cortex that take in sensory experiences and combine them into functional patterns; and 3) areas of the cortex that analyze and synthesize this information so that abstract thinking, symbolic processes, and other higher cognitive activities can take place.

An injury to this third part of the brain will not stop an individual from seeing, hearing, tasting, and feeling, but will greatly hamper intelligent thought. Birch and Goldfarb, working with severely emotionally disturbed, psychotic children, describe the inability of these children

Table 18.1
*Stages of Development**

Chronological Stage of Life	Psychosocial Stage (Erikson)	Stage of Ego Development and Object Relationships (Freud-Mahler)	Stage of Psychosexual Development and Primary Area of Pleasure (Freud)	Primary Danger Situation (Freud)	Stage of Cognitive Development (Piaget)
The infant (birth to 18 months)	Basic trust vs. mistrust	Autistic Symbiotic Beginnings of separation-individuation	Oral (mouth and skin)	Fear of loss of the object	Sensory motor (birth to 24 months)
The toddler (18 months to 3 years)	Autonomy vs. shame and doubt	Completion of separation-individuation	Anal (anus and urethra) (body musculature)	Fear of loss of the love of the object	Preoperational (2 years to 7 years)
The pre-school child (3 years to 6 years)	Initiative vs. guilt	Oedipal	"Phallic" (genitals)	Fear of bodily injury Castration anxiety in boys Fear of genital penetration and mutilation in girls	Preoperational (2 years to 7 years)
The grade school child (6 years to puberty)	Industry vs. inferiority	"Latency"	"Latency" (intellect)	Fear of the conscience-guilt	Concrete operational (7 years to 11 years)
The adolescent (puberty to late teens or early twenties)	Identity vs. role diffusion	Adolescence	"Genital" (sexual intercourse with orgasm)		Formal operational (from 11 years on)

(Separation Anxiety brackets the Primary Danger Situations of the infant and toddler rows.)

* Table by Richard C. Simons.

to put together information coming from different sensory experiences. Luria's third functional unit has this task. Thus, even though an organic cause for the childhood psychoses is in no way proven, we have in Luria's work a possible localization for those functions that are specifically impaired in this group of children. Much more work is needed before we can truly understand psychotic children as well as children with minimal brain dysfunction, and can begin to sort out the multiple etiologies of these disorders.

THE SOCIOCULTURAL PERSPECTIVE

The Family Setting

Homo sapiens is totally dependent for survival on a parenting figure. This is true not only for such functions as eating, but for emotional development as well. The tragic consequences of emotional isolation of young infants from their mothers were vividly described by René Spitz in his papers on hospitalism and anaclitic depression. These children, raised in hygienic isolation, failed to thrive, failed to grow, became retarded, and had a very high mortality rate.

Thus, not only is physical survival dependent on good parenting, but so also is emotional survival, and the parental impact on children is continuing and crucial. A few examples may suffice. Psychiatric consultation on three eight year old boys, all students in a special school, disclosed that all three had I.Q.'s of around 70. All three had moderate learning disabilities, and prenatal and birth histories consistent with possible but minimal central nervous system damage. The first was a delightful child, liked by all, a slow but eager student. The mother was a bit slow herself, but warm and realistic about her son. She genuinely enjoyed his growth, however slow. She had faced and accepted the fact that he would need special schooling. The second boy was more troublesome, provoked fights, lied, and cheated. He was born out of wedlock. The mother was promiscuous, and the father had trouble with the law and did not support the child. Thus, the personality disturbance in both parents was similarly present in the child. The third boy was described as bizarre and totally unpredictable at times. He needed much more support and structure than the others. The mother's appearance was most unusual — her hair was disheveled and her clothes did not match. Her view of her son, despite numerous

sessions with the teachers and social workers, was that he would "snap out of it" and go on to college. Her approach to raising him was: "The world is unpredictable. He just has to learn that. If I tell him I'll be home at five, I make sure it's four or six, but never five. Only that way will he learn how the world really is." This mother had been told numerous times by various professionals that a retarded, possibly brain damaged child needs predictability and structure for him to begin to organize his inner and outer world, but she could not change her way of relating to him.

In summary, all three boys had possible mild brain damage with secondary retardation. The form of the parental interaction added an important ingredient in each boy's ability to cope.

The School Setting

With nursery school, kindergarten, and more recently, day care centers for children of working mothers, the importance of school even for the very young child is enormous. Now the interweaving of factors becomes important in a very real and practical sense.

School and Development. The earliest school experiences are in great part socialization experiences. The four or five year old who first goes to school is flooded by contacts with new people—teachers, peers, and older children in the play yard who can be kind, disinterested, or often nasty and frightening. Above all, the initial impact of school is the separation from home, from mother. An initial fear reaction of crying and clinging to mother is not at all uncommon, and may even develop into a "school phobia." But the fear involved in this "phobia" is the fear of separation from the mother.

Around the third grade, printing is changed to script writing, reading now requires answers that are no longer verbatim in the text, and social studies and history are being introduced. The addition and subtraction that have been memorized up to now are changed as word problems are introduced. The child now needs to move to a new kind of thinking, which has been described by Piaget, as concrete operational thinking.

Junior high school is felt by many to be one of the most difficult stages. The boys range, even in the same grade, from soprano-voiced, four feet tall, hairless, latency age children to bass-voiced, bearded, six feet tall young men. The girls similarly are concerned about onset of menses and breast development. Socially, parties take on a different meaning. One male teacher may suddenly be the focus of a mass crush by the girls, and various flirtations are endlessly discussed. The school, therefore, much more than the home, is now the area where many of these developmental issues are experienced. Parents start to complain: "We are just a hotel — a source of money — and an occasional snarl or fight seems to be our only reward."

The separation and individuation of adolescence become still more of an issue for the juniors and seniors in high school who are facing college and careers. For some, even marriage becomes an issue at this age. Again, much of this is lived out in the school, with peers, and with the teachers. One 17 year old girl, who had been a model student, began skipping classes. As she discussed it with me, it became clear she was "trying out" leaving the school prior to being forced to leave at graduation. During the last two weeks of the senior year in most high schools, such absenteeism takes on epidemic proportions. For some adolescents this time of separation and individuation can be very anxiety-provoking, and the independence and relative lack of external limits and controls that suddenly face them in college can precipitate a reaction as severe as an acute schizophrenic breakdown.

School and Family. It is normal for parents to identify with their children, and to wish better things for them. "My son will not have the problems I've had. He will get a good education and go on to Harvard — not drop out of high school and end up with a manual job the way I did." This quotation can be altered a thousand-fold, each time giving the same message. Such expectations can also reflect the parent's unconscious use of the child as a status symbol. "My son is having a hard time deciding among Harvard, Columbia, and the University of California. He has been accepted at all three with full scholarships." "He's a chip off the old block. This is the third year he is top in his class." "My daughter has been asked for dates by every boy in her class." These are just a few of the fantasies that parents have and discuss with each other as they are changing the diaper of their four month old child. The hard reality of the impartial school can start to undermine these fantasies, and intense resentment of school, teacher, or child can result.

Another complicated interaction is that between parent and teacher or principal. It is usually impossible for a teacher to perceive the child, or convey to the parents that the child is as unique and special as the parents feel the teacher should. Another situation is one in which the parent, having been a student, will continue to react to the teacher as he or she did to his or her teachers. Uncritical acceptance of the teacher's word as law, excessive praise of the teacher, or hostility toward the teacher as a harsh disciplinarian are just a few of the many variations on this theme.

School and Psychopathology. It is not unusual for the more disturbed child to flunk out after three weeks of kindergarten. For some parents this may be the first time that they are actually confronted with the degree of their child's abnormality. Mild retardation may not be picked up or suspected until the second or third grade. Developmental unevenness, particularly with boys, can make reading a nightmare. This is also the time that the learning disabilities become more pronounced. The hyperactive, distractible child with a short attention span, who has difficulty with reading and with mathematics, and who cannot organize the material in some logical sequence, will by the second, third, or fourth grade be in serious trouble. It is not unusual for such a child to have a deep sense of failure by this time.

The shy, withdrawn, quiet, depressed child will often be overlooked because in early grammar school the other problems mentioned above clamor for the teacher's attention. Early adolescence may be the first time that these more neurotic children are noticed. It is not unusual for surprised teachers and parents to witness severe breakdowns of such a child in high school, or see other major personality changes under the impact of the adolescent process. The top A student may suddenly take a nose dive in grades. More ominous is the onset of school phobia at this late age. A somewhat borderline child who has marginally adjusted may suddenly become severely phobic of school and adamantly refuse to go to high school. Unlike the kindergartner or the first grader with such a school phobia, these adolescents are often suffering from a much more profound disturbance, not infrequently a schizophrenic disorder.

The Environmental Setting

It is hard to know where to start with the impact of the environment on children and adolescents. The biblical curse, "And the sins of the father shall be visited on to the fourth generation," may have more validity than we have heretofore suspected. Benjamin Pasamanick drew our attention to the impact of the prenatal environment on the future child. Describing the concept of *developmental casualty*, he argued that any factor that caused a substantial incidence of central nervous system fetal or infant mortality must result in an even larger number who survive with some residual central nervous system damage. Subsequent research at large medical centers which provide services for many ghetto population families has confirmed his original hypothesis. The incidence of miscarriage, of prematurity, and of natal and postnatal mortality is much higher as: 1) the income goes down, 2) the mother is under 17, 3) the mother is unmarried, 4) the diet of the mother is deficient, 5) the incidence of welfare goes up, 6) the mother is of a minority race, and 7) the prenatal care is poor or absent. And where the above factors are present, one also sees a statistically significant increase in: 1) retardation, 2) antisocial behavior in the older child, 3) learning disabilities, and 4) truancy and school drop out.

The ghetto environment, where there are the greatest stresses and strains just for survival, brings with it much more frequent and severe home disruptions. The young child who by age five or six has lived in such a situation for several years is forced to develop a keen sense of survival, because the present is so chaotic and so totally unpredictable. Such youngsters may have learned which drunk can and which one cannot safely be rolled. They may be able to ride the subways and survive on the streets for several days, but may be totally lost and begin to evidence seriously disruptive behavior in a "confining" school.

While doing a home visit on a youngster living in such a ghetto, I could sense the pervasive fear and suspicion that many people felt toward each other. A small-time drug pusher lived next door, and several apartment houses had been burned out across the street and were being used as "crash pads" by heroin addicts. Older children demanded protection money on a regular basis, or else they would badly beat up and injure the younger children. A gang offers a sense of belonging, but the price is high. One very bright 10 year old told me that in order to join his street gang, he had to steal a T.V. set. Another 11 year old described stealing a bicycle from an

acquaintance. When I asked him if he felt guilty, he scornfully said, "He deserved it. He should never have left it out like that." The incidence of drug and alcohol usage is enormous — as a way of belonging to the group, and as a way of dealing with chronic resentment and frustration. Whatever the combination of factors, it is hard for these children not to participate in drug use.

Similarly, the environmental pressures for sexual involvement on the preteen and teenage girl in the ghetto are enormous. As one mother told me: "I told all my daughters to go straight. But I know human nature. So I also told them that if they get pregnant, they can bring the child home. But they better not bring the father home. Husbands are nothing but trouble."

However, it is important to remember that environmental pressures are by no means limited to the ghetto. As one 13 year old girl told me: "We are middle class. My parents are both professionals. But I'm one of the poorest in the private school I go to." She felt deprived and ashamed. She was on the fringe of the popular group, but felt bitter rage that her parents could not give her the money and clothes she needed to keep up with the others. Her solution? "A few times I've stolen money so I could invite them out. You just can't always be invited out and not pay back."

The Psychosocial Setting

In his book, *Childhood and Society,* Erik Erikson attempted to integrate the stages of ego development and the stages of psychosexual development within the larger family, environmental, social, and cultural settings. These psychosocial stages (Table 18.1) will be described in much more detail in subsequent chapters, as will the stages of ego development, psychosexual development, and cognitive development.

AN OVERVIEW

In summary, then, we have looked at some of the various systems that affect each child and adolescent and their families. No single factor can be looked at in isolation, but each, like building blocks, contributes to the final edifice. I have found it very helpful to think of the child as a magnet, surrounded by a number of other magnets, each of which is more or less powerful, and each of which contributes to the point in space where the central magnet is suspended. The genetic endowment of the child, the normal developmental stages and stresses, the family relationships, the interactions in school with teachers and peers, and the larger sociocultural environment, are all important factors that interact with each other.

The stage is now set. Each of the systems we have described is like a spotlight, each able to highlight a different complementary perspective on the child. The psychosexual developmental system answers the question *why* the child thinks the way he does; the cognitive developmental system shows *how* the child thinks; the neuropsychological system may some day help us understand *where* certain thinking is localized in the cortex; the interpersonal and social system of family, peers, and school places the child in a *total* environmental context. Unlike a stage, you can never shut off one spotlight completely. Rather, as you will see in the chapters later in the book describing the clinical syndromes of psychopathology, different parts of the total system are involved to different degrees in one syndrome as compared to another. Even when the etiology is clear, as in Down's syndrome, all systems are still affected, and the physician must be able to understand the child and the family from each of the perspectives described, in order to be able to intervene intelligently and helpfully.

References

Birch H (ed.): *Brain Damage in Children.* Baltimore, Williams & Wilkins, 1964.

Erikson EH *Childhood and Society.* New York, W.W. Norton, 1950.

Goldfarb W: An investigation of childhood schizophrenia: a retrospective view. *Arch Gen Psychiatry* 11:620, 1964.

Luria AR *The Mind of a Mnemonist.* New York, Basic Books, 1968.

Luria AR: *The Working Brain.* New York, Basic Books, 1973.

Miller JG: *Living Systems.* New York, McGraw-Hill, 1978.

Pasamanick B, Knobloch H: Brain damage and reproductive casualty. *Am J Orthopsychiatry* 30:298, 1960.

19 The Infant

Melvin A. Scharfman, M.D.

In this second part of the book I am going to be discussing normal development, from birth through adolescence. I will devote some of the later chapters to periods of development which span a number of years, such as latency and adolescence. Thus, it may seem strange that I am devoting this entire chapter to the first year and a half of life when, to the casual observer, little may seem to be happening at first. But a great deal is happening from the very beginning. This is a period of life when we can see clearly the relative balance between biological endowment and environment or, to put it another way, between *nature and nurture*. Both exist; both are important; and both interact from the moment of conception onward. It is impossible to talk about the process of development if either one or the other is left out.

THE DATA OF PSYCHIATRY

Before we proceed further, we should talk about the kinds of data with which we deal in this field. Dynamic psychiatry is less than 100 years old and, in the beginning, many of the theories that were formulated about human development were based upon observations made by people who were treating pathological conditions. That is one source of our data, a valuable but limited source, based on retrospective studies. We assume that certain things went wrong in the development of patients who later display certain specific difficulties.

A second source of data, one which has become prominent during the last 30 years, is that of direct observational studies. Investigators have spent years in newborn nurseries or on home visits, making long-range observations and descriptive studies of pregnancy, of infancy, and of the behavior of children of all ages, thus adding to the previous observations of patients

the perspectives of normal behavior. During the past 10 to 15 years in particular, there has been an enormous number of these direct observational studies on newborns, and all that we can attempt to do in this chapter is to give a very brief overview of some of the main findings of these studies.

The third source of data is what may be broadly referred to as research. Research on people is obviously limited, since we do not want to cause harm to human beings. We have to rely for our experimental controls on accidents of nature, situations which have come about without our intervention and allow us to study the effects they have on development. Some examples would be the studies of children in orphanages made by René Spitz, or Anna Freud's observations of the children who were sent out of London for reasons of safety during the blitz of World War II. These are studies which were not planned as experiments, but were recognized by investigators as fulfilling experimental conditions. Another form of research is the limited control experiment which would not be expected to damage the child: for example, dropping a book so as to make a loud noise and observing the strength of the infant's startle response. This is obviously not going to do any damage to the infant, yet it can provide a good source of data.

There is a fourth source of data consisting of inferences made from observations and experiments done on other species. A good example would be the famous experiments made on newborn monkeys by Harry Harlow and his coworkers. In this sort of investigation, of course, one must always question the validity of any correlations made between human and nonhuman data. In any event, it is important to remember that the information I will be describing in regard to normal development comes from data of varying sources.

PRENATAL PERIOD

In child development we always have to deal both with the biological endowment and with the environment, and that is true even before birth. The infant in the uterus is already the bearer of a very complicated evolutionary pattern, a pattern which makes him or her uniquely human, with the potentialities for developing certain traits that no other species possesses to the same degree. The nature of his intelligence, for example, and his ability to communicate are different from those of any other species. At the time of conception, of course, there is a specific genetic endowment which is unique for each individual. This is more than a determinant for certain characteristics such as blue eyes or long fingers. Part of what is transmitted is also a potential, a genetically predetermined blueprint for a sequential unfolding in the process of development. It is not accidental that most children will learn to crawl before they learn to walk, or that most children will learn to walk before they can be toilet trained.

The child in the uterus also enjoys a relatively selective and very protective environment where there is a very low level of stimulation, even though that child is already able to respond to stimuli with certain basic reflex patterns such as kicking or sucking motions. Fetal monitoring devices, such as fetoscopy and ultrasound scanners, have demonstrated that four senses (vision, hearing, taste, and touch) function prior to birth. Furthermore, the prenatal infant can be conditioned to respond to certain specific stimuli, and, therefore, it would be accurate to say that conditioned learning actually begins in utero.

We know that an infant in utero can be affected by a number of different things. For example, if the mother, in the course of her first three months of pregnancy, happens to develop a viral illness, such as German measles, it may cause specific kinds of damage to the heart, brain, or other organs in that infant. If the mother is a diabetic, that will influence the nature and development of the child in other ways. This is equally and disastrously true if the mother is a drug addict. This is an area about which we do not know a great deal, and one in which there is a great deal of investigation going on at this time, but we do suspect that even more factors can affect the fetus than we may presently realize. After all, the mother's blood is transmitted to the child through the placenta and the umbilical cord. This means that anything that affects the contents of the mother's circulatory system may also affect the child. Some people believe that, for example, if the mother is very anxious, it will increase the amount of adrenocortical hormones in her bloodstream, and that these hormonal effects will be transmitted to the infant. This is a matter which is still under investigation, but we can at least say that something about the mother's emotional state during her pregnancy may be transmitted to the fetus while it is developing.

BIRTH

There are also theories, less convincing, about the effects of the experience of birth on the newborn. This is a question about which there has been a great deal of controversy, and several elaborate and unproven theories have evolved about the nature of the "birth trauma." What we do know now is that the nature of an infant's ability to perceive is such that he or she can have little conscious awareness of what occurred in the process of birth.

The nature of the birth experience can, of course, have an effect on development when it goes beyond what we consider to be a normal birth. As we have become a more technologically advanced society, we have made birth a more technological process. We may use anesthesia, which, improperly given, can affect the child by inducing a degree of relative reduction of oxygen and thereby affect potential cerebral functioning. (Other effects of anesthesia, even properly given, have been described by Drs. Hittelman, Emde, and Simons in Chapter 16.) The use of forceps improperly applied can cause organic damage to the brain. These would be two examples of pathological events during birth.

What we know about normal birth is that it is an experience that leads to a tremendous change in the stimulus level to which infants are exposed, a change during which they go from a relatively stable environment with a regulated temperature, an absence of light, and a blunted tactile stimulation, rather abruptly into the external world, where they are exposed to multiple stimuli. Most children, if they have not been anesthetized through the mother's bloodstream, will react shortly after birth by crying, one of the ways that the newborn has of reacting to these new stimuli.

Children at birth, then, have had nine months of complicated interaction with their intrauterine environment. But it certainly does not look that way when we first see them, because newborn babies are uniquely dependent creatures, less able than the young of most other species to take care of themselves. They are born as relatively immature organisms, and it will take a long time for their basic biological endowment to be completed.

REFLEXES AND TENSION STATES

There are, however, certain attributes which the newborn does have, a repertoire of characteristics which will help him or her to survive. These are *reflexes* and *biological tension states*. If you stroke a baby's cheek, he will turn towards the touch, the so-called *rooting reflex*; if you put something into his mouth, he will suck it, the *sucking reflex*. They are both reflexes which aid in feeding.

There are a number of other reflexes, more or less adaptive, with which the child enters the world. The *Moro*, or *startle reflex*, is a gross discharge with flexion of the extremities in response to sudden stimulation. The child is also born with the potential to withdraw a limb from a painful stimulus, and with pupillary reflexes, so that if a light stimulus is too intense, the child will close his eyes. The baby also has less adaptive reflexes. He has a *palmar grasp reflex*: if you put your finger into his palm, he will contract his hand and cling to it. This is sometimes called the "Daddy's reflex," since its only function in the human being is to make fathers feel happy because they believe that the baby is recognizing them! It is, however, a very important reflex in primates, who cling to the mother's body and hair by using the palmar grasp.

Even less adaptive is the *Babinski reflex*. That simply means that, if you stroke the sole of the baby's foot in a particular way, the toes will hyperextend and spread apart, as opposed to the normal adult response, which is to close down. In an adult the Babinski reflex is one sign of certain kinds of neurological damage. But it is normal in newborn infants. The newborn infant has a positive Babinski, which disappears after a few months.

Besides these reflexes, the infant is born with certain kinds of biological tension states; he has certain *needs*. If these needs are not met, they lead to an increase in tension, and in the young infant, the tension is discharged through crying. The tension state which immediately comes to mind, of course, is hunger, but here we are using words in an imprecise way. We say that the newborn is hungry, that he wants to eat, but if we think about it for a moment, we realize that the infant does not know that he wants to eat. When his blood sugar gets low enough, he enters a tension state and begins to cry, but he has no idea, in the way that you or I do, of why he is crying. I will talk a little later about how the child begins to learn how to alleviate these states of tension.

DIFFERENCES IN NEWBORNS

All newborns are endowed with the same basic biological needs and reflexes, but there are also readily observable differences between infants, as was discussed in Chapter 16. For example, there is an enormous difference in the level of the threshold of stimulation. One child will be easily awakened by noise and light and touch, while another will sleep on, all but impervious to these stimuli. The same child may also have very different responses to each one of these stimuli. Children are also born with differences in their autonomic sensitivity. If you present a given stimulus to a child and subsequently monitor him for heart rate, skin temperature, respiration and so forth, you will see that various children will respond differently to the same stimulus. Some appear to be much more labile in their autonomic nervous system response, while others are more stable.

Children differ, too, in their degree of what has been called the level of alertness. Most of us think of infants as spending their time either sleeping or eating; but much work has been done in recent years which indicates that there is also a well defined waking state. During these periods, even in the earliest months, children lie awake, beginning to explore their environment. This is the time when the newborn utilizes his capacity to respond to visual stimuli, and the amount of time that different children spend in this state varies considerably. There are many other differences in newborns that have been studied by a variety of investigators, such as differences in their level of motor activity, their sucking behavior and other reflexes, their tension states, their discharge patterns (such as crying), their moods and temperament, and their emotional expression.

MYTHS ABOUT NEWBORNS

In the past we have tended to think of the newborn as a relatively passive, undifferentiated organism who behaves primarily to reduce tension and stimulation. If we look at all of the new data emerging from the laboratories of neonatal investigators, a very different view emerges. There is now abundant evidence to indicate that the nervous system of the neonate is built for action prior to reaction. The newborn has definite stimulus needs for both soothing and arousal, and these needs prompt active engagement with the environment from the very beginning of life. Furthermore, rather than being undifferentiated, the newborn has actually undergone a considerable amount of differentiation during fetal life, and arrives with a rather complex behavioral repertoire to aid both in survival and in active involvement with the environment. Finally, the newborn's wakefulness and visual interest in the world are not simply directed toward reducing biological tension states such as hunger, since a newborn will interrupt a feeding to look at a new and novel stimulus. Wakefulness itself can be prolonged by such a stimulus, and an endogenous sleep-wakefulness rhythm exists in the newborn whether fed or not. To quote Robert Emde and Jean Robinson in an excellent review paper: "It is no exaggeration to state that the newborn is active, stimulus-seeking, and creative in the ways he begins to construct his world."

PARENTING

Children are born with different strengths of needs. But these same children, with their unpredictable variations in tension states and sensitivities, are also born into an environment which has variable ways of meeting these needs. Sometimes we call this the "average expectable environment," and what we have come to realize is that, given a certain attention to basic needs, there is a great deal of latitude in the manner in which they can be met. The newborn must be provided for or he will die, but there is an enormous range of ways in which these needs can be met.

The person who will determine how those needs are met is going to be the caretaking person, usually the mother, but that will vary greatly in different social, cultural, and economic settings. We would like to assume that this caretaking person will be aware intuitively of many of the child's needs. But that, too, is a relative matter. In our society, we have moved further and further away from certain basic biological experiences. It is possible that some readers of this book, especially if they are medical students, have seen a child being born. But if you go outside of the medical schools, you will find that a great many people, unless they have had a child themselves, will never have seen the birth of a baby. Unless you yourselves are parents, many of you may never have seen a child fed or diapered or, for that matter, perhaps have never even had a chance to hold an infant. At another time in history that would have been highly unlikely. There was a time when most births took place in the home, when everybody would have seen a birth, observed the care of a newborn, and helped to care for the young infant. We have moved far away from those earlier times, and that also means that we have mothers or mothers-to-be who have had no experience in caring for a newborn infant. Nor do we have the extended family available to the same degree any longer, the grandmother or older sister or mother living in the same house or around the corner who can help the new mother to deal with some of the things that she does not know intuitively.

Mothering does not appear to be an innately acquired pattern or response in human beings. As a matter of fact, there have been animal studies which indicate that mothers of other species such as monkeys also have to learn by observing other members of their species. We can assume that most mothers will learn if they are given a little time. A mother will probably be quite different in the handling of her first child as compared to subsequent children; and of course she will bring to the entire task of parenting her own personality, as will the father.

As was discussed in Chapter 16, the whole question of the fit between parent and infant is a fascinating one. A young woman brings certain expectations to motherhood. She anticipates having a certain kind of baby, and how that actual baby fits in with her expectations will play a large part in determining how they adapt to one another and how the baby develops. The same is true for the father. One mother may want a baby who is very active, who is awake a lot so that she can play with him. What if that mother gets a sleepy child? She might be distressed; she would probably try to stimulate the child, encouraging more reactivity. That is what we mean by the interaction that occurs from birth onward between the child and his or her environment. The less responsive child would probably become more responsive because the mother was stimulating it. Or the reverse can be true, so that a mother who wants a quiet baby and instead gets an alert child who is awake most of the day, might be convinced that the baby was hungry all the time. She would want him to go back to sleep and so she would feed him whenever she saw him lying awake. This is bound to affect his developing personality in some way.

THE BEGINNING OF MEMORY

Assuming that we have an average expectable environment and a reasonably responsive mother or mothering figure, we can return again to the baby. We have found that infants do not develop well if they are constantly exposed to excessive stimulation or deprived of stimulation. If we get too much stimulation, there is distress; but if we do not get enough stimulation, that also creates problems. There also has to be some kind of balance in an infant's life between gratification and frustration. The best way to demonstrate this is through the model of feeding.

The child has a biological tension state resembling hunger, and he has a rooting and a sucking reflex. Since he has no motor coordination, he needs something else; he needs the parents. At the beginning, the child does not know that it is hungry. It does not know what it wants, but only that something, in some vague biological sense, is not right. So along comes the mother, and each time the infant communicates by crying that he is hungry, the mother will, presumably, feed him. As she does so, we have to assume that the child lays down some vague memory traces of the experience that alleviated his tension.

As a matter of fact, in the first feedings of newborn babies, they may be crying so much that they do not even get around to sucking. Their tension state is so great and their discharge of that tension in the crying is so intense that they are unable to recognize the thing that is put into their mouths. After a couple of feedings, though, something will have changed: they will have learned something. What they will have learned is that the thing that got into their mouths alleviated their tension. At some point babies will begin to anticipate that relief when they enter the hunger-tension state. And that means that some kind of memory trace has been laid down. From what we know about newborn infants, their sensory apparatuses are rather rudimentary, and their perceptions are not very acute. They may not clearly see the mother or the bottle. But although their perceptions are unsophisticated, they do have the capacity to lay down a *memory trace*. When an experience has been recorded and reinforced a number of times, then the next time that they experience that particular tension, they will begin to revive the memory of what relieved it before. They will know that something is coming that is going to make them feel better.

This all sounds rather imprecise, but those of you who have had contact with infants will have observed just this process. A newborn infant, when he is hungry and crying, will not quiet down when the mother walks into the room. He will continue to cry when she turns on the light, when she picks him up, when she runs the water to warm the bottle. The baby will continue to cry all the time until the bottle is actually in his mouth and he is sucking, because he is subject to a tension state which he has no way of regulating. We say that he has no way of delaying his need for gratification. But after awhile, within only a few weeks, you will see something quite different. Now, when the mother comes into the room, the baby will quiet down when she turns on the light or picks him up. He will stop crying because he will be anticipating something which is going to happen.

A child at that age does not have much capacity to anticipate, but we see that he does have some. Something about the experience which alleviated his tension in the past is now enough to curb his tension for a short period of time. And that "thing" is any component of the experience which relieved the hunger in the first place. There is a whole range of sensory and kinesthetic experiences that become part of the feeding experience, and eventually parts of the environment are also incorporated into it, so that any part can begin to represent for the child the fact that the whole thing is going to happen soon. Because the mother always turns on the light, or makes noise rattling the pots, the child soon begins to know that this one stimulus will bring on the whole activity, and he will be able to expect that he is going to be fed soon. In this way, the feeding experience becomes one of the first learning experiences of the baby's life.

In this pattern of feeding, the development of the neonate is dependent on both his genetic endowment and his environment, on his biological needs and reflexes interacting with the care he receives from the mothering figure. But babies develop in other ways during this period, and each area of development will have as a requirement an adequate caretaking person. We have learned from pathological development what happens when the mothering needs of infants are not met. We know that if you raise an infant, feed him adequately, change his diapers, and do all of the rest of the things he needs, but do not provide the additional stimuli in the way of the body contact, verbalization, and love that we call "mothering," then you will have a child who does not develop normally. This has been demonstrated vividly with primates. In the experiments done by Dr. Harlow, infant monkeys were bottle-fed and provided with surrogate mothers constructed out of wire and cloth. Although the infants' biological needs were met, they did not grow up to be normal; they could not relate to other monkeys, and they could not reproduce spontaneously. Human beings are not very different, and the human parents' essential role in the first few months of life is to meet both the physical and emotional needs of the infant.

Someone once described the mother of the neonate rather ingloriously as the "tension regulator." It is not an easy job, whatever we call it, not only because a new mother often has to do without much sleep, but also because she does not get any feedback from the infant. He does not recognize her, nor give her any reactions she can take as an indication that she is doing a good job. Most mothers survive this period in part because they endow the child with all kinds of qualities that are not really there. What the new mother actually loves is a projection of what she wants. Luckily, this is usually enough to keep her from resenting too greatly the constant demands made on her by the infant. And the balance between biology and environment will soon provide her with some response from the baby: a smile.

THE SMILING RESPONSE

Human beings are born with a kind of innate reflex pattern called "endogenous smiling" which is not, at first, intentional. In normal development, assuming that a child has had an adequate mothering experience for the first couple of months, he or she will begin to smile at the mother, and also at a human face or anything approximating a human face, "exogenous smiling" stimulated from the outside. Children's early perceptions are not very specific, so that you can elicit the smiling response in children by anything that vaguely resembles a human face, such as two circles in a triangle. But the smile is something to which the parents respond very strongly, because it is the first sign of emotional feedback from the baby. The parents for the first time have an indication that they are now dealing with something which is more than just a mass of biological needs.

By the time he or she is around two to three months old, the infant will begin to smile selectively, recognizing the mother. We call this a *social smile*, from which the parents get a very special pleasure that makes the rest of parenting much easier (Figures 19.1 and 19.2). A smile may seem like a frivolous thing, but it is one of the landmarks of infant development; René Spitz terms it *the first organizer of the psyche*. If an infant does not begin to smile by a certain time, then we feel there may be something seriously wrong with that child's development.

If you consider it, you will see that the smile is important in that it indicates that the child is beginning to respond selectively and specifically to an externally perceived object. For the most part, the first two or three months of life are a time during which the child does not have a clear discrimination between himself and the external world. He is in what Margaret Mahler terms the *autistic stage of development*. "Autistic" is also used in a pathological sense to describe a group of children who show a specific severe disturbance (infantile autism) in which they cannot discriminate between themselves and external objects. However, the normal child is not in a parallel situation to an autistic child. The normal infant is involved in an active, stimulus-seeking interaction with its environment, and therefore is in a phase of beginning differentiation from the very moment of birth. Early differentiation proceeds as an active, unfolding developmental process in the normal child, and it is this process of early differentiation that is disrupted in the autistic child.

In addition to the social smile, there are other changes taking place at around two months of age which suggest a major developmental change — a "biobehavioral shift" as Robert Emde calls

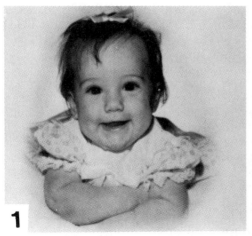 

Figure 19.1. A three and one half month old baby girl smiling.
Figure 19.2. A three and one half month old baby boy smiling.

it. These changes include: an increase in the ability to sustain long periods of sleep; a shift to a diurnal pattern of nighttime sleep and daytime wakefulness; increased attentiveness, eye-to-eye contact, and visual scanning of the mother's face; a decline in "fussiness"; an increase in cooing and babbling; and a new capacity for maintaining the effects of learning through habituation and conditioning.

THE BODY IMAGE

The newborn's view of his own body is incomplete. He cannot say, "This is me and this is my mother." As a matter of fact, if you look at a newborn you will see that he will follow his own hand passing in front of his eyes in the same way as he would follow a pencil. He does not know the difference between sucking on a pacifier and sucking on his own finger when it happens to find its way into his mouth. He does not have a well defined sense of his own body.

Development of the *body image* is one of the other important events which begins in the first few months of life. It is a very important concept. When you deal with adult patients you will see that their psychological stability depends to a considerable degree on a stability in their views of their bodies, and any time anything happens to change the view of the body, the whole psychic functioning is affected. Surgeons know that when a patient undergoes a surgical procedure in which something about his or her body is changed, the patient's whole view of himself or

herself will change. The same thing happens if there is a chronic illness. If you have ever lost a lot of weight, or gained a lot of weight, or even if you have had a radically different hairstyle, then you might have had a very peculiar feeling when you looked at yourself in the mirror. Who is that? Is it really me? We call this the body image. It takes a long time to develop and it is slow to change. But the newborn baby has no body image. He begins to develop it by virtue of a number of biological factors.

The first is something called "two-point touch"; that means that when he touches his own body, he feels it in two places. The thumb in the mouth is experienced in two places, while the pacifier is felt in only one. A child explores his body even in the early months, although not volitionally because of his poor motor control. But his own palm falling against his cheek is felt twice, on the face and the hand, while the sheet against his cheek is felt only on his face. In that way, he begins to develop an awareness of the boundaries of his own body. However, during the first three months this is not well defined.

REALITY TESTING

Another discrimination laid down in the early months of life is the distinction between reality and not-reality. This is a more complicated matter. The newborn will not be able to distinguish between himself and his mother. He does not know how the nipple got into his mouth, or who brought it to him, or whether it is going to come back again. We think that when the infant experiences hunger tension, he revives the memory of what happened to him previously to alleviate that tension, and in the beginning, he will not know the difference between that mental picture and the object outside himself in the real world. In other words, he will be doing something which, in an adult, we call hallucinating. When he is imagining the "thing" which alleviated his tension in the past, for a brief period of time he will not know that "thing" is not really there.

This is a complicated concept, but it can be demonstrated quite convincingly. If a child is hungry, and not just wanting to suck, and if he accidentally gets his thumb into his mouth, then he will start to suck on it. We believe that at those times he is picturing other times when he was fed and the tension went away. He is having a mental picture that he is sucking on a bottle, and that seems to be sufficient to alleviate the hunger temporarily. But obviously, the hunger does not go away, and this heralds a very important step in development. He begins to know that there is a difference between the mental picture that he has of something and the thing itself, outside of himself in the real world. He is developing the beginnings of what we will later refer to as *reality testing*, the capacity to differentiate between the mental image of something and the thing in reality. If you think about it for a minute, you will see that this is another way of defining the barriers between me and not-me. It is an important function, and one which is related to a good deal of later psychopathology.

BASIC TRUST VS. MISTRUST

It requires experience for reality testing to evolve, but fortunately, certain experiences are universal. Everyone, no matter how coddled, has to wait sometimes; everybody has moments when his needs are not met immediately. Frustration seems to be necessary in some degree for differentiation, to allow the human being to develop out of this early "autistic" phase. What is important in the first months of life is that there be a balance between gratification and minimal kinds of frustration. It is not necessary to set up the frustrations; they take place naturally and inevitably in an endless variety of ways between parent and child. What is most important about this balance is that the child begins to develop some feelings of confidence or, to use

the term originated by Erik Erikson, some *basic trust*. The child has to begin to feel that when he needs something, there will be someone around to provide it. Infants who do not have adequate mothering never develop a feeling of basic trust, never have the confidence that somebody is there to help them, to make them feel better. Obviously, this is not a trait which is completed in the first few months of life, but it is in this period that it has its beginnings.

THE FURTHER DEVELOPMENT OF ATTACHMENT

Investigators in the field of child development call the next months of the first year of life the *symbiotic stage of development*, a term also designated by Margaret Mahler. They use the word with the same meaning with which we are all familiar in biology, but not quite so literally: in general, the symbiotic phase refers to an interdependent relationship, a stage of mutuality between the mother and the infant. Not only is the infant responding to the mother; the mother, especially with the advent of that first smile, has begun to interact with the infant in an increasing number of ways which go far beyond feeding or diapering. She will play with the infant, talk to him or her, try to elicit more smiles, and use a wide range of physical contacts. These stimuli all act on the infant, causing him to become more and more attached to her in a specific kind of way.

One of the tasks which lies ahead for the infant is to learn to separate himself somewhat from his mother, but before this separation can be accomplished, he must first become attached to her. The nature of that *attachment* in human beings is a subject about which there are a number of ideas. In the lower order of animals, we know that the attachment to the mothering figure can be effected in different ways. You may know about the work of Konrad Lorenz with bird species. Lorenz has noted a phenomenon which he called *imprinting*, a process by which whoever is introduced into a baby bird's life at a specific biological point will be accepted by the bird as its mother (Figure 19.3). A dog, passing in front of a duckling at the proper moment, will be, forever after, its mother. This is one of those instances in which it is dangerous to take the analogy to animal behavior too literally. There is no evidence of imprinting as such in human beings. Rather, we believe that

Figure 19.3. In a famous experiment, Konrad Lorenz demonstrated that goslings would respond to him as if he were the natural mother, through the phenomenon of imprinting. (Reprinted by permission from Hess, E.H. Imprinting: an effect of early experience. Science *130:*133, 1959.)

the infant's attachment to its mother is a response to a series of repeated interchanges with her in which the infant's tensions are reduced and in which a variety of stimuli is presented to the infant.

The attachment to the mothering person is variable in its intensity, since there are socially as well as psychologically different styles of mothering. We are most accustomed to the style in which a single person, usually the biological mother, is the one who provides almost all of the early interaction with the infant, but there are many other styles which still allow the infant's needs to be met and development to proceed. There are social organizations in which mothering is shared by a number of women: for example, a kibbutz or a large farm family. There are other social organizations in which infants

are removed for periods of time from their biological mothers and raised by someone else, i.e., a nanny, as used to be the practice in many upper class European families. Today, many young couples, especially among the most highly educated, try to share the child-rearing between them. There are other families where the parenting has to be shared by siblings and grandparents. Because various people are used to one system, they may have certain prejudices in its favor, but we all accept the fact that, regardless of the way in which the infant is raised, he or she will develop some specific form of attachment to the person or persons who are involved in the parenting. The kind of attachment the infant develops towards the mothering person or persons will ultimately prove to have a profound effect on the kinds of relationships developed later on in life.

I have already mentioned the important balance between gratification and frustration. It is obvious that if we do not gratify certain needs, the human infant will not be able to survive. On the other hand, there are inevitably, in the course of development, varying degrees of frustration which the infant will encounter. The fact that the newborn infant had to wait between the first pangs of hunger-tension and the time when he was given the bottle helped the infant develop a mental representation of the outer world. In the very first months of life the infant has no inner capacity to tolerate frustration and cannot wait for satisfaction. As months go by, however, we begin to see some capacity to delay gratification, and this has many critical implications for the kind of child he or she will become.

Remember that the balance between gratification and frustration is something that most mothers reach intuitively. "Intuitively" is a rather imprecise way of saying that a mother gets some sense of how long her infant can wait, how long he can be allowed to cry, how long he will be satisfied by her presence, or her voice, or by being held. There is some variation even in the earliest days in the degree of intensity with which any infant expresses his demands, but mothers vary even more in how they handle the demands. There are some mothers who have a great deal of difficulty in letting their infants wait at all. They seek to anticipate the child's needs and satisfy these needs almost before they are manifested. These are the mothers who are present as soon as the infant awakens and begins to make some small noises in the crib, and who try to feed him or her even though the infant has not yet communicated any wish to be fed. Such a mother is concerned about her child's waiting too long, and does not like to hear any crying. She anticipates the infant's needs to such an extent that she does not allow the capacity to delay gratification to be developed fully.

There are, of course, other mothers at the very opposite end of the spectrum. These are the mothers who never seem to be able to meet the infant's needs quite adequately, who let him wait too long in a variety of different situations, so that he is never fed until he has become frantic or even until his hunger cries have subsided with exhaustion. As might be expected, one of the most common manifestations of either an excessively indulgent or an excessively frustrating approach in these early months is the development of *feeding difficulties* of one kind or another.

As children grow older, they begin to show specific behavior patterns which we think are related to this early interaction with their mothers. There are some very young children — and, as a matter of fact, some older children and even some adults — who cannot wait at all. They have never really developed a capacity to control whatever tensions they are experiencing, but always seek to obtain an immediate reduction in that tension. These are the people who, when they are adults, have great difficulty in controlling their own impulses. But there are others, at the opposite extreme, who seem to expect nothing of life. They appear to have no sense that life can provide anything pleasurable, and these are the people who, we think, may have been frustrated in too many instances, and who never had their needs adequately met as infants. We see this attitude of pessimism in sad young children and also in depressed adults. Somewhere in between there lies the great majority of people who have a healthy wish for gratification but who are also able to tolerate delay and who have a "basic trust" that that gratification can eventually be achieved.

STRANGER ANXIETY OR DISTRESS

While the infant is achieving this basic trust, he or she is of course becoming more and more attached to the mother. The infant evolves an increasingly sophisticated repertoire of memories of her, and begins to have certain expectations of her, recording each of his experiences

with her in his memory. As this happens, the infant will begin to reach outward, comparing the other people in the world to the mother and also to the father. If you watch young infants who are handed to a stranger, you will see them begin to explore the other person. They "check out" what the other person is like, touching his face, his glasses, patting his hair and staring at him; sometimes they will even seem to taste him. This is what Dr. Margaret Mahler, one of the people who have worked extensively with this age group, has called the "customs inspection." We believe that what the infant is doing in this inspection is comparing the stranger with the mental images he has of his mother; if the stranger passes the inspection, if there are enough similarities, then there will be no reaction of anxiety.

At a certain point in development between seven to nine months, the child may begin to show a different reaction to the presence of a stranger. He or she begins to become anxious whenever a stranger is present. Of course, we do not really know whether this is anxiety in the adult sense. But even when the stranger is someone who has been relatively familiar, the child will now begin to manifest some kind of discomfort or distress, perhaps just a momentary look of confusion or maybe a long spell of crying. Acquaintances and even relatives who were accepted with no difficulty in the first months of life will go over to the infant, and the child may start to scream hysterically until he is handed back to his mother. Obviously he is reacting to the presence of the other person — we call this phenomenon *stranger anxiety* or *stranger distress* — but he is also reacting to the absence of his mother. In fact, he has made an increasingly sophisticated mental image of his mother, and he compares other people to that image. When they do not match, he may react with confusion and tears. This is a time of differentiation, differentiating self from mother and mother from other people, and it represents another major biobehavioral shift in development.

One way that we know that it is the absence of the mother as well as the presence of a stranger which is discomforting, is that many children at this same age, that is at around eight months, will also begin to develop *sleeping problems*. As soon as mother takes a step towards the door, the baby will begin to scream, even though he seemed to be half asleep. He does not want her to leave, so he cries, and she returns.

She gives him a bottle or pats him and, when he has quieted down, she then makes another attempt to leave the room, only to be met with renewed screams. If the mother complains to her pediatrician, it is likely that he will suggest that the baby is teething and, in fact, this sleep difficulty does take place during the period when the teeth are erupting. But we believe that what is at issue is that something has happened to the child's mental image of the mother. He now recognizes her as different from himself and different from others, but he cannot hold that image of her in his mind when she is not physically present. Piaget describes this as *recognition memory*. The capacity to evoke the image of the absent mother is not present until 18 months of age or later, an achievement called *evocative memory*. Thus, when the mother is physically absent for any period of time, the infant may manifest anxiety over this separation.

THE BEGINNINGS OF SEPARATION AND INDIVIDUATION

The psychological task of the next few years is to learn to hold this image in mind as a step towards dealing with separation. Before the infant can begin to master separation, he first has to become attached to the mother. Having made the attachment, the infant then has the problem of learning to let go, of being able to know that someone still exists even when that person is not physically present. When we look at young children we can see a variety of behaviors which have to do, at least partially, with their attempts to master this problem of *separation anxiety*.

For example, if you take an infant at six or seven months and present him with something that he wants, such as a bottle or a brightly colored toy, and you put the object right in front of the baby but cover it so that he cannot see it, the infant will not initiate any move to get to it. It does not exist anymore; "out of sight, out of mind." By the time the child is a year old, however, he will react very differently in this situation. He will move immediately towards the hidden object and try to remove the thing which is hiding it. It seems that the younger child was unable to find the bottle, because once it had disappeared from his visual field its image did not stay in his mind, while the older child had developed the capacity to maintain the image, or *mental representation*.

Children in the second half of the first year of life do a variety of things to help them deal with their anxiety over the fact that objects disappear. At heart, of course, it is the mother they would like to be able to keep with them all the time. But since this is impossible, children have a variety of ways of playing out the loss and regaining of objects. For example, babies universally play peek-a-boo, the game in which the player practices making something disappear and then come back. He is controlling the very existence of other people whenever he closes his eyes and then reopens them.

There is another, more annoying game which is played by infants. Somewhere toward the end of the first year, because of a growing physical maturity, infants in a highchair will take a spoon or a cup and fling it to the floor. When the mother picks it up, the child will giggle and throw it down again. Wearily, the mother hands it back, and once again the child giggles and tosses it down, even as the mother gets more and more upset. Perhaps she would not be so annoyed if she realized that this game is not just a provocation. The child is playing at making something go away and come back. Infants will do the same thing in their cribs when they take whatever cuddly toy they have and drop it out of reach. The parent hands it back. After all, this may be the one animal the child absolutely needs to have in order to sleep. But he is still playing, and he flings it back. We regard this behavior as an attempt at mastery, at trying to deal with the fact that life does not remain constant. Things that the child wants can disappear, and he or she is trying to learn how to bring back an object that has been lost.

Maturational factors are also an influence. Somewhere around six months of age, there is a shift in human infants from palmar grasping to the beginning of the uniquely human response of thumb-forefinger approximation. When an infant can bring his fingers together in this way, he is much more effective in picking up something and, after a period of practice, getting it into his mouth. Children begin to practice this hand-eye-mouth coordination. They will reach for everything that is presented to them, bring it into their visual field, and then put it into their mouths.

This skill has a number of implications. The child will now begin to explore his environment. He will be able to control some of the kinds of stimuli to which he has been exposed, so that he is no longer just a passive recipient, but can try to initiate and repeat pleasurable experiences. Soon he will try to feed himself. When the bottle is put in front of him, he will begin to reach out, grasp it, and pull it toward him. Although he is scarcely a model of self-sufficiency, he is now a little bit less in need of his mother. As his maturation proceeds, there will be a number of areas in which the child begins to practice doing things for himself, and as he succeeds, he will feel less and less vulnerable to his mother's absence.

Another maturational skill which comes into play at this time and which will help the child deal with separation from his mother, is locomotion. Somewhere around the sixth to eighth month, the baby will begin to crawl (Figure 19.4). At first he will stay very close to his mother's feet. Then he will crawl a short distance away, but will scuttle right back and grab her, touching her ankles or doing something else to get back into physical contact. Gradually he begins to be able to move further and further away and to stay away for longer and longer periods of time; but still he will rush back to

reassure himself by touching the mother. She represents a special kind of safety for him. There are films of monkeys showing how the mother extends her hand as the infant moves in a wider and wider circle around her. But should anything startle the baby monkey, he will jump directly back into physical contact with this mother.

As children begin to crawl further away, they gradually come to rely less on direct physical contact. Soon they are satisfied if they can simply turn around and check to see that the mother is still there. Some more adventurous youngsters will even crawl out of the room where the mother is. Eventually, most children will not even need the visual contact; they will be able to remain at a distance but within hearing of the mother's voice, so that the physical contact has been replaced by a visual or auditory contact.

TRANSITIONAL OBJECTS

We have been talking about a gradual process, one which extends over many months, and which includes first the attachment to the mother and then the ability to move away from her successfully. As you may imagine, it is a process which is often accompanied by a certain amount of anxiety, and children have different ways of dealing with this separation anxiety. Towards the end of the first year of life, for example, many infants become attached to a specific object, which we call a *transitional object*. You are probably familiar with Linus, in the comic strip "Peanuts," who walks around with a blanket all the time. Other children cling to a teddy bear or a bottle or a doll (Figure 19.5). In the mind of the child, these objects are a link to the mother. Because of the child's way of thinking, the fact that the blanket has some of the qualities that remind him of his mother makes it usable as a substitute for her. It is warm or soft or cuddly; it acquires a specific odor. It is important to the child that this object stay just the same. Any attempts by mother to wash it or to replace it with a nice new animal are met with tears and anger. The clean blanket or the new teddy bear just do not work; they are no longer effective as a link to the mother.

The need for a link to the mother is most intense, of course, at times of separation, and the most frequent of these separations is sleep. Most children use some kind of transitional link to the mother before they go to sleep. This may

Figure 19.4.   A one year old boy crawling.

be the bottle or blanket or stuffed animal, or it may be an even more direct link. Some mothers sing to their babies at bedtime. When the children get a little bit older, the mothers will talk to them or tell them bedtime stories. Older children are also reluctant to be alone as they go to sleep, so they may have a glass of milk and listen to the radio for awhile. Even we adults retain some derivatives of this emotion, and so we, too, look for links to the external world before we go to sleep and lose our contact with other human beings. Some people have a snack every night; some watch the late movie on television; others say that they cannot drop off to sleep until they have read for awhile. This is a derivative of our early feelings about losing touch with others; human beings do not like to be alone, and although they learn to tolerate it, they still remain vulnerable (Figure 19.6).

For example, you may have had the experience of arriving in a new school or a new city. You will probably remember feeling a momentary sense of estrangement, perhaps even of panic. In order to overcome this feeling, you probably looked around for something familiar, something that reminded you of your earlier experiences. Maybe you called home. Many people, when they have to go away from the people to whom they are attached, carry something from home with them as a link: a picture of the family or a particular desk lamp. When children go to camp, it is a good practice to give them something from home to take with them. This is especially important to remember when children are sent to the hospital. This is a time when they are not only away from home, but in a frightening situation. Instead of buying a new bathrobe and slippers for a little girl who is going to have her tonsils removed, the parents are best advised to make sure that she takes her oldest and most familiar things with her.

I am not suggesting for a moment that most people, once they are grown, react to separation in the way that infants do. People mature, they have the ability to remember the people they care about when they are away from them, and they are able to deal with the experience of separation. But the anxiety which older children

Figure 19.5. A two year ten month old girl cuddling and kissing her doll.

Figure 19.6. A four year old girl asleep with her dolls, later versions of earlier transitional objects.

and adults feel when they go away on their own is an echo of the fact that, at some point early in development, the child fears losing what is familiar. It will take a long time to learn that someone can be out of his sight but still exist.

DISTURBANCES OF DEVELOPMENT

There are many things that can go wrong during this period of learning. For example, there are mother-child pairs who cannot seem to arrive at the proper balance between gratification and frustration when it comes to separation. The mother is the basis of the young child's security, and of course she — or at least the mothering person — should be with the child a great deal of the time. But in order for the child to learn to cope with becoming a separate person, he will have to learn how to deal with her absence. In other words, an infant has to have the experience of being left alone for some period of time; mother or father cannot always be there. Some young parents, those who perhaps have troubles of their own about separation, will try never to leave their babies, and we see one sort of difficulty in the development of these children. There are other mothers who leave the child alone too much of the time, with the result that those children have other kinds of difficulties. Indeed, if these children are left alone for extended periods of time, or if they are raised in orphanages or foundling homes where there is inadequate stimulation and emotional contact, they will *fail to thrive*, with resulting intellectual and social impairment.

There are also disturbances which occur when the child who has formed a strong and healthy attachment to his mother is suddenly deprived of her presence. Sometimes children are unavoidably placed in hospitals during the second half of the first year of life. Under the best circumstances, they are in daily contact with the parents, who are encouraged to take over part of their care: visiting them, feeding them, and playing with them. But occasionally it happens that a child is suddenly deprived of all physical contact with the parents through a serious illness. What then may happen is that the child becomes withdrawn and unresponsive. We call this an *anaclitic depression*, meaning a reaction to the loss of the person on whom we were leaning. It is a term which can also be used, for example, to describe the depression which occurs in adults who have lost their husbands or wives. It may not be the best term for these children, but it does describe the reason for their terrible condition. There are several films, such as those made by Dr. René Spitz, which show very dramatically the marked emotional and physical impairment of infants which may result in such situations of *hospitalism* if they persist over a long time (Figure 19.7).

Children suffering from *infantile autism* are unable to form any attachment to the parents from the very beginning of life. There are other children who negotiate the initial period of attachment well, but who are then unable to separate from their mothers. They become arrested in the symbiotic stage in what has been called *symbiotic psychosis*. They never develop any reliable sense that they are separate individuals, or that the mother can leave them and still come back. Such children seem to be all right when the mother is present, but will become quite disorganized and confused and unable to function when she is away. Later in life we are familiar with other, less extreme examples of people who have trouble with separation. Some will develop manifest anxiety at every real or threatened separation throughout their lives. Many adult neurotic reactions involve such separation anxiety. For others, their whole character structure may center around fantasied fears of loss and magical ways to avoid those dangers.

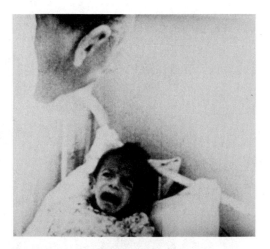

Figure 19.7.   A one year three month old emotionally deprived child, suffering from "hospitalism" and a "failure to thrive." Child's size is only that of a three month old infant. From the film *Somatic Consequences of Emotional Starvation in Infants.* (By permission of René Spitz Film Library, Department of Psychiatry, University of Colorado Medical Center, Denver.)

Such persons may feel that whatever they have will be taken away or "lost" — their loved ones, their money, their possessions, their job. They may need to acquire more and more as a protection, but it never suffices. Their entire lives may be lived under the cloud of such fears, including fears of death, which is the ultimate separation. They are so afraid of dying that they cannot enjoy living. There are other children who show other developmental disturbances related to the first year of life. These manifest themselves as unevenness in the development of the ego, where one or more of the ego functions to be described below fails to develop appropriately. More will be said about such problems when the syndromes of childhood and adult psychopathology are discussed later in the book.

THE FUNCTIONS OF THE EGO

You will have seen that by the time the child reaches the end of the first year of life, he is quite different from what he was at birth. He has gone through a period of increasing psychic differentiation. In order to organize and follow this process we will be using certain concepts to explain what happens in development and behavior. These concepts of *ego psychology* are working formulations around which theories of human development are organized. They are not presented as absolutes. They are not "real" in an anatomical sense, although sometimes when they are used they may sound that way. They have been modified many times with the appearance of new data, and we can be sure they will be modified again in the future. Their purpose is to help us understand our observations.

The psychic apparatus appears limited at birth. We have observed that experiences are necessary to leave a psychic representation, a mental picture. Thus, we talked about tension states resulting from biological needs. They have, however, no form, no mental representation. The child does not know he is hungry, or what will satisfy that hunger. Only actual experiences of satisfaction lay down memory traces. When subsequently the same tension is experienced, the mental picture of that satisfying experience will reappear, however vague or ill defined.

The wishes to find in reality what appears as a mental picture of the earlier satisfaction, the search for gratification, operate to motivate behavior. These have also been called *drives* or

impulses. The first year of life has been called the *oral stage of psychosexual development*, because the oral zone is the primary area of pleasure and the area where gratification is sought during this first year. This is much more than hunger in the usual sense, since oral pleasures will include many different elements – the sucking, the sensation in the lips and palate, the taste, the visual aspects of the experience, the warmth of mother's body, and her smell. It is all of these pleasures for which the infant searches again and again, and the mother is the magic source of satisfying these wishes. That part of the psychic organization that mediates between the child's wishes and reality is called the *ego*. It is really a concept of a group of functions that will become more cohesive and integrated as development proceeds.

One of these functions of the ego is based upon the sense of self, upon the sense of one's own body. During the early, undifferentiated phase in human development, when the child could not differentiate himself from the mothering person, the child had at most a very primitive ego. He had no sense of the boundaries of his own body. As he developed a more discrete sense of himself, of his own body and its limits, he then made a step in the direction of having a body sense or *body image*, which is part of what we call the ego.

Another one of the ego's functions is the regulation of the interchange with other people, in other words *object relationships*. If we look backward, we see that the child moved from a phase in which he could not differentiate himself from the mothering person to one in which there was a mutuality of interchange which we called symbiotic. But after that, as the child perceived his mother as a separate person, he also evolved an increasingly complex set of wishes and interactions with her. The regulation of these wishes and the need for other objects are part of what we postulate is mediated by the ego.

Another function of the ego is the *control of drives*, so as to tolerate frustration and delay the discharge of tension. We talked about the fact that at the beginning the infant had no capacity to delay or to wait for anything. By the end of the first year of life, we see that infants can wait — not very long, but they can wait. Not only can they wait but they can accept substitute gratifications rather than to have to immediately get what they want.

As mentioned earlier, another function of the

ego is *reality testing*, the capacity to discriminate between internal perceptions and the presence of objects in the external world. As a neonate, the child could not do that; he could not distinguish between his wish for the bottle and the actual presence of the bottle. By one year of age, however, the child has some degree of reality testing, although it is still very fluid. He is still in a stage where certain inner conditions are easily attributable to the outside world, and where certain external things are being internalized.

The ego has another group of functions about which I have not yet talked, the *defensive functions*. I have not talked about them yet because at the beginning of life the infant has very little in the way of any defensive function. He has very limited means of dealing with an increase in tension and keeping it from becoming intolerable. He is entirely dependent for this upon the intervention of outside forces. But as he develops, he will acquire a repertoire of ways of handling certain tensions. By the end of the first year of life we begin to see some of them. For example, if he is afraid of his mother's not being there he can *displace* his wish to cling to something else — onto a teddy bear or onto his bottle. During this first year there are very primitive and very rudimentary precursors of what we will talk about later as *the mechanisms of defense*.

We should mention, in order to complete the picture of this multifaceted theoretical construct, that the ego has another group of functions which we call *autonomous*. These are the structures that do not derive from any kind of conflict and which are not dependent upon conflict for their development. These are functions such as *perception, memory, thinking, emotions* or *affects, motor capacity,* and *speech*. These are innate givens. They are affected by the environment but not as much as the other functions that we have been discussing. During all of the periods of development which I will describe, the ego is going to be evolving in an increasingly complex way, and these various functions of the ego will have a very specific impact on how the child will relate and adapt to the reality of the outside world.

The thought processes of the infant and young child were called *primary processes* by Freud, really meaning the first way of thinking. We will talk about this much later when we discuss pathology. What primary process means is that the thinking is in pictures. In the first year of

life there is no use of symbols, no verbal representations. Thinking is animistic, which means that it does not differentiate an inanimate object from a live one. The infant will therefore continue to talk to an inanimate object, or strike out at a table if he happens to bump into it because he attributes to it qualities of being alive. Furthermore, "No" does not exist in the infant's mind. "No" is an abstract concept. Negatives do not exist at this point in life. All of these characteristics are part of what we call a primary process way of thinking. It is enough at the moment to say that this is very different from the way in which we as adults think most of the time, and we will see how this kind of thinking changes in the course of development. Jean Piaget referred to this early period of thinking as the *sensory motor stage of cognitive development*, as Dr. Farley will discuss in his chapter on cognitive development.

From the point of view of motor control, which is another of the autonomous ego functions, we have seen how the child has gone from functioning solely on a reflex basis through a whole series of maturational steps. He has begun to crawl, he can stand, and he may be able to take his first steps at this point. He has also become increasingly sophisticated in terms of hand-eye-mouth coordination, and has now gone beyond a palmar grasp to the capacity to pick up an object. His speech apparatus also matures, so that one begins to see toward the end of the first year of life, either the first few words or at least the babbling kind of speech which is the first vocalization of a young child. We will be talking more about this development of speech in the next chapter.

Suggested Readings

Brazelton TB: *Infants and Mothers: Differences in Development.* New York, Delacorte Press, 1983.

Call JD, Galenson E, Tyson RL (eds): *Frontiers of Infant Psychiatry.* New York, Basic Books, vol I, 1983; vol II, 1985.

Cath SH, Gurwitt AR, Ross JM (eds): *Father and Child: Developmental and Clinical Perspectives.* Boston, Little, Brown & Co, 1982.

Erikson EH: Trust vs basic mistrust. In *Childhood and Society.* New York, W.W. Norton, 1950, p 219.

Fraiberg SH: *Every Child's Birthright: In Defense of Mothering.* New York, Basic Books, 1977.

Lidz T: Infancy. In *The Person.* New York, Basic Books, 1976, p 123.

Mussen PH, Conger JJ, Kagan J, Huston AC: The prenatal period. In *Essentials of Child Development and Personality.* New York, Harper and Row, 1984.

Mussen PH, Conger JJ, Kagan J, Huston AC: The first two

years. In *Essentials of Child Development and Personality.* New York, Harper and Row, 1984.

Prugh DG: *The Psychosocial Aspects of Pediatrics.* Philadelphia, Lea & Febiger, 1983.

References

Emde RN, Gaensbauer TJ, Harmon RJ: Emotional expression in infancy: a biobehavioral study. Psychol. Issues 10, monograph No. 37. New York, International Universities Press, 1976.

Emde RN, Robinson J: The first two months: recent research in developmental psychobiology and the changing view of the newborn. In Noshpitz JD, Call JD (eds): *Basic Handbook of Child Psychiatry*, vol 1. New York, Basic Books, 1979, p 72.

Escalona SK: *The Roots of Individuality. Normal Patterns of Development in Infancy.* Chicago, Aldine, 1968.

Freud A, Burlingham DT: *War and Children.* New York, International Universities Press, 1943.

Freud A, Burlingham DT: *Infants Without Families.* New York, International Universities Press, 1944.

Harlow HF: *Learning to Love.* New York, Jason Aronson, 1974.

Korner A: Individual differences at birth: implications for early experience and later development. *Am J Orthopsychiatry* 41:608, 1971.

Lewis M, Rosenblum L (eds): *The Effect of the Infant on its Caregiver.* New York, Wiley, 1974.

Mahler MS: On the concepts of symbiosis and separation-individuation. In Mahler MS, Furer M (eds): *On Human Symbiosis and the Vicissitudes of Individuation.* New York, International Universities Press, 1968, p 7.

Mahler MS, Pine F, Bergman A: *The Psychological Birth of the Human Infant.* New York, Basic Books, 1975.

Spitz RA: Hospitalism: an inquiry into the genesis of psychiatric conditions in early childhood. *Psychoanal Study Child* 1:53, 1945.

Spitz RA: Hospitalism: a follow-up report. *Psychoanal Study Child* 2:113, 1946.

Spitz RA, Wolf KM: Anaclitic depression: an inquiry into the genesis of psychiatric conditions in early childhood. *Psychoanal Study Child* 2:313, 1946.

Spitz RA: *The First Year of Life.* New York, International Universities Press, 1965.

Spock B: *Baby and Child Care.* New York, Simon & Schuster, 1975.

Wolff PH: The causes, controls, and organization of behavior in the neonate. Psychol. Issues 5, monograph No 17. New York, International Universities Press, 1966.

CHAPTER 20

The Toddler

Melvin A. Scharfman, M.D.

THE SECOND YEAR OF LIFE

The continuing process of *separation and individuation* is the dominant theme of the second year of life. This theme is played out over and over again in each area of development throughout the life cycle. For much of the initial part of this second year of life, the child will continue to practice the mastering of separation from the mother or mothering figure. With the added impetus provided by the achievement of free upright locomotion and the development of speech, the child will have a more active role in determining closeness and distance to the mother, and will be able to explore a much wider segment of the world around him or her. This time of life, called the "practicing period" by Mahler, is one in which the toddler has been described as having a "love affair with the world." By about 18 months, the child is truly a more separate person. The toddler is aware of this separateness, and with that realization there comes a movement back toward mother. The child leaves to enter the wider world but then comes back for "refueling," to reestablish close bodily contact and safety. The world he or she sets out to explore contains many dangers, and mother's help and reassurance are needed before further development can be achieved. This time of moving away and then returning to mother is called "rapprochement." Let us now turn to the more specific developments of this second year of life.

THE DEVELOPMENT OF SPEECH

Because speech is such a uniquely human achievement, I will discuss it first. Actually, most children do not speak well until they are around two, but the beginnings of speech occur at the end of the first year. Somewhere around that time, children begin to say what we regard as their first words, although they have been babbling for awhile before this. The babbling of infants takes a fairly regular form in any culture; it consists of a repeated consonant and vowel sound. An infant will be saying "la la la" or "da da da" or "ma ma ma" whether he lives in Grand Rapids or in China. In order to understand what happens to these sounds we must refer to *learning theory*. We assume that some prehistoric mother, hearing random combinations and wanting to believe that the child was recognizing her, began to reinforce the sounds. That is, she heard the noise "ma ma ma" and, every time it was said, she responded to it with a smile. She had decided that "ma ma ma" was the word that was going to be used for the most important person in the child's life, namely herself. This kind of reinforcement goes on with every child, because babbling inevitably predates intentional speech. In every society, the words used to designate the parents are derived from those early combinations of sounds that are really the infant's babbling. There is "da da da," daddy; "pa pa pa," papa; and "na na na," nana, a word for grandmother. We reinforce a sound which occurs in the evolving development of the child, repeating and responding to the child's saying, "ma ma," until he begins to learn to identify that sound with the presence of the mother.

The early acquisition of language by children is limited to just such a naming of objects. There is no continuity, no abstraction, simply the beginning of the ability to identify a visual representation with a particular sound which is then reinforced by the mother. If the child who can repeat the word "cookie" is handed a cookie, it is not long before he is able to make the connection between the object and the sound. But that reinforcement of response is essential. It is largely through the medium of the mother or the mothering figure that the child's language is expanded in the course of the next few years into a much more sophisticated kind of verbal communication. This is especially true in the early stages of the child's acquisition of language. You may have had the experience of being with a very young child who says something or other which is understood by nobody but his mother. For example, somewhere in the course of his second year, some little boy might say, "Bobby lunch." Only Bobby's mother will know whether the child is saying that Bobby wants lunch, that Bobby is eating his lunch, or that Bobby is playing with his lunch. She will expand his vocabulary by supplying the intermediary words, and the child will gradually learn to expand his own vocabulary in order to be able to communicate with someone besides his mother. The acquisition of the capacity to communicate first with the mother, then with the family, and finally with the rest of the world is another step towards the child's independence and separation from his mother and from his family.

THE DEVELOPMENT OF LOCOMOTION

The second major accomplishment of the second year is locomotion. The age at which the ability to stand erect is achieved is somewhat variable, but it occurs somewhere around the end of the first year of life. It is a function of the completion of the myelinization of the spinal cord, a process which proceeds at different rates among different children. Myelinization and neurological development in general occur somewhat earlier in girls than in boys. On an average, therefore, most girls will stand earlier than boys. Girls will also generally learn to walk earlier than boys, and they will learn to use language earlier than boys.

Whatever the age at which it happens, the child enters into a whole new world when he begins to walk. He now has greater control over what happens to him. He has the capacity to explore his environment actively. He can leave his mother rather than wait to be left by her. As he begins to explore the world around him, which he does very hesitantly at first, but with expanding confidence, he will also be calling on his mother to play a very different role in his life. For much of the first year of life, the mother has served to meet the child's basic needs. During the second year she begins to act as his protector, a protector from all of the trouble that he will inevitably encounter as he begins to walk.

AUTONOMY VS. SHAME AND DOUBT

The walking of children is at first very unsteady, not at all what it will be within a few months. They walk by alternating their feet with a kind of three point stand, leaning their bodies forward to balance the weight. When they begin to walk up steps, they do it one step at a time, pulling the second foot up to the same level as the first. They practice constantly. There seems to be a great pleasure for children in mastering the experience of locomotion, and if you have ever taken care of a child who is between 18 months and two years of age, then you know that they practice this pleasurable experience all the time. The child likes nothing better than to keep moving about, running, climbing, falling, getting up, and falling again. If he tries to climb into a chair, he may fall off, but then he will get right up and try it again and again until the task has been accomplished. There is clearly a great pleasure derived from mastering motor functioning, one which makes the child practice all the time. The child is practicing all kinds of newly acquired skills. However, as he practices these skills, he faces the possibility of getting into difficulty.

If a child of this age is walking along and comes to the top of a flight of stairs, he has no way of knowing that he should stop or else he will fall down and hurt himself. If he is climbing, he does not know that he is climbing out onto a windowsill and can fall out of the window. And if he is running, he does not know that he should stop at the curb. Mother has to intervene to protect him all the time. In the same way, he will be exploring textures, colors, and new objects which he finds in his wanderings. If he crawls under a sink and sees a brightly colored bottle labeled, "Lye," he will not know what it is and will make some attempt to taste it. And if he sees an expensive glass ashtray on a coffee table, the child will probably want to pull it down and examine it. In fact, the baby who has now become a toddler can get into a lot of trouble. He can hurt himself, and he can damage the things around him. All of which means that his mother is going to have to begin to say "No" to him in one way or another. How a mother sets limits in a wide variety of areas is one major determinant of the later development of the child. One kind of mother may be overzealous in her setting of limits, and thereby overprotective from this early point in the child's life. She begins to curb his initiative, his willingness to explore and to try out new things. Another mother may be constantly critical, saying "No" and blaming the child for everything, whereas still another mother may be unable to set limits of any kind. One of the better known observers in the field of child development, Erik Erikson, feels that the nature of such experiences during this second year of life will make the difference between whether a child develops a *sense of autonomy* with a capacity for later initiative and pleasure, or is burdened with a sense of *shame and doubt*.

THE CONCEPT OF "NO"

"No" can come to mean (to the child) a variety of different things, depending upon how the mother presents this concept. She may not actually use the word "No," but she will be doing a lot of what is called, in learning theory, "negative reinforcement." This ranges all the way from removing the temptation or diverting the child's attention, to speaking sharply and to slapping the child. Whatever way the "No" is presented, the mother is now in the position of having to act as a protector of the child, as what can be called his "auxiliary ego." Remember what we said earlier about the ego; it is a concept we use to indicate the child's sense of himself and his capacity to mediate between his inner wishes and the environment. His ego is still very immature at this point, and the mother has to serve as an auxiliary. It is she who has to protect him from external dangers. The child is not at all eager to have this protection. He does not know about all the potential dangers; all he wants is to be able to move around and explore. At the same time, he is also trying to achieve a greater degree of separation from the mother, by constantly moving away from her and then returning for reassurance. From the child's point of view, mother's restrictions on him are incomprehensible and often intolerable.

Until this time, the child — boy or girl — has been identifying primarily with the mother; that is, the child takes on some of her characteristics by imitating her. Children now begin to identify with the mother who is saying "No." By the end of the second year of life, children are pretty much saying "No" automatically. They can be, at this time, negativistic, difficult to handle, and in constant opposition to the mother. Oddly enough, this is in actuality an extension of the child's identification with the mother, but it is understandably difficult for most mothers to appreciate this. The child wants to be more independent. But mother is saying "No" and the child says "No" right back to her. The child does this both to maintain independence from her and also as an imitation of her. This is the developmental phase that is called the "terrible twos" in so many popular articles (Figure 20.1).

We said earlier that the child's vocabulary at this age was for the most part limited to nouns, to the names of concrete things. "No," on the other hand, is an abstraction. Dr. René Spitz, one of the people who have concerned themselves deeply with this period of life, believed that the use of the word "No" introduces a whole new level of communication for the child; it is the beginning of the communication of abstract concepts. Incidentally, children learn to say "No" before they say "Yes," just as they learn

Figure 20.1. *Angry Boy* (1930) by Gustav Vigeland. Bronze. Placed in the Vigeland Sculpture Park, Oslo, Norway. (By permission of Vigeland Museum, Oslo, Norway.)

to shake their heads from side to side before they learn to nod "yes." It is likely that this is biologically determined.

THE INTERNALIZATION OF LIMITS

Such *negativistic behavior* probably feels like the last straw for the mother, coming as it does at a time when the child is wearing the mother out in her need to limit and protect the child. Fortunately, the child is also learning. This learning takes place on several levels. One particular phenomenon of central importance results from the child's imitation and identification with the parents in their role of setting limits and of indicating the "do's and don'ts." The child begins to internalize these rules. He begins to develop what we will later talk about as a *superego*, a *conscience*. This development begins in a very rudimentary way. You can sometimes observe how children internalize, or identify with what the mother is doing or has done to them. If the child has just walked into the bedroom and pulled open 15 drawers and dumped out the contents, mother may then come in and say, "No, you mustn't do that." Maybe she slaps his hand, and then puts the drawers back in order. Twenty minutes later the child goes back to the same set of drawers and is curious about what is in there. You will see some children who go through a series of steps. First they look around. "Is mother around?" If she is not around, then they may reach for the drawer and you will literally see some children who then say, "No," and slap their own hands.

What are they doing? They are taking the mother's command and setting up some kind of psychic organization within themselves that will begin to effect a controlling and modifying influence on their behavior. They are beginning to *internalize a control system*. Some people never adequately internalize a control system. There are some people who go all through their lives really very much like the child who is looking over his shoulder to see who is watching. They do not have any stable internal set of values or controls. They operate on the idea, "Am I going to get caught? Am I going to get punished?" We all know people like this. If the cop is watching, they do not cross the street against the red light. But if he isn't, they go right ahead even if it is a crowded traffic situation. Or they might steal something, or cheat in business. No one has a perfect conscience. There is no such thing. But

there are people who do not really adequately internalize a conscience. At the other extreme there are those who internalize an excessively harsh group of prohibitions, which are too punitive. Some people become so strict within themselves that they cannot allow themselves to do anything that would bring them pleasure. They retain the kind of rigid rules with which the child is presented in "do" or "don't," with nothing in between — no flexibility.

We expect that these beginning internalizations will change and be modified many times as development proceeds. We are discussing just the very beginnings of this process. Both what is desired and what is disapproved by the parents in the child's behavior will begin to be internalized. This will not be static. Behaviors which are not acceptable at this age may be quite all right just a short time later. For a toddler, walking to the head of a flight of stairs may be forbidden. He learns that, and a few months later, has to unlearn it so that he can walk down the stairs. In many areas such changes will take place and are necessary. The value system that is beginning to be internalized must retain flexibility for the most effective functioning in the reality of life.

SEXUAL DIFFERENCES

Among the other things which the child internalizes by imitation and identification are those related to differences between boys and girls. The whole area of whether or not there are basic constitutional differences other than those of sexual anatomy has been the focus of much recent interest and research. One of the areas where such differences seem to be significant is in the area of aggressivity as seen in motor activity. In all studies done, in humans and other species, males seem to be more muscularly active and more prone to physical aggression. Categories, of course, overlap, and some girls may be more active than some boys, but there is a clustering of boys on the side of greater physical aggression and girls on the opposite side, even in young infants.

It is not, however, just a question of biological endowment. The nature of our expectations of a child begins to play a role here. By and large society operates with certain stereotypes about what is masculine and what is feminine. Parents are much more likely to act in a positive, reinforcing way to physical aggressiveness and physical activity in a boy than in a girl. They may shake their heads in despair, but they will probably be smiling at the same time. They will reinforce behavior in a girl which is more subdued and gentle. They will smile at a boy when he climbs to the top of the jungle gym, but they will run to grab his sister off the lowest bars. Similarly, although boys and girls are different in their degrees of muscular activity, that difference is reinforced and encouraged by the way in which we play with each of them. In picking up a boy, we tend to swing him up, to toss him high, while we are more gentle and protective picking up a girl. Other studies indicate that the mother's tone of voice is different when she is talking to a boy than when she is talking to a girl.

These observations are supported by animal studies, which show that mother monkeys behave differently with their male infants than they do with their females. Once more we see an interaction between the biological endowment and reinforcement from the environment. For example, since boys are, in general, more active during this second year of life and more apt to get into mischief, their mothers have to be intervening more frequently in limiting physical aggression and motor activity, and in trying to control behavior. The girl's development, on the other hand, is likely to be somewhat less restricted by the mother at this point. She will not have the same needs for limits to be placed on her activity, and she will therefore have less conflict with the mother during this time than her brother does. Both the boy and girl will be internalizing the parents' response to them. They will be acquiring some sense of how they are expected to behave as a boy or as a girl.

We know that children of this age already identify themselves as boys or girls (Figure 20.2). They do not necessarily have any specific interest in genital differences or in sexual functioning, but they are developing a sense of what is masculine and what is feminine, which we call *core gender identity*. Two year old children will be able to discriminate between playmates and say, "This is a boy" or "This is a girl." They are not doing any anatomical inspection, but they have a sense of their own gender. They are beginning to define a picture of what is masculine and what is feminine through experiences with their parents and their parents' expectations. Although this is much simpler than what their later perception of sexual identity will be, it is an essential beginning. What is important

Figure 20.2. A 21 month old girl, dressed up in her best Sunday clothes. Even at this early age, she is very much a "young woman."

is that the child sees the mother in one role and the father in another.

While we are discussing sexual differences, we ought to say something about the father. We have not mentioned the father very much as yet, and for a very good reason. In our society he is not around much of the time. Maybe he should be, but he is not. The father is absent for a variety of reasons and as we move towards a more and more technological society, many fathers will probably be further and further removed from any real participation in the upbringing of their children. As families move to the suburbs and traveling time is added to the father's hours at work, he becomes less and less a part of the child's early experiences. It is mostly the mother who is left to deal with the early period of development.

We have, therefore, the problem of the father who comes home from work and plays with his wonderful children for half an hour before they go to sleep. The mother then begins to complain about the awful day that she had with the baby — how defiant he was, how negative, how destructive. The father thinks she must be out of her mind, since the baby, when father was with him, was just wonderful. Why does this happen? It happens because the father is, at this point, in an ambivalence-free role. That is, he is not the one who is saying "No" to the child. He is not the one who is cleaning up the messes or stopping the child from falling downstairs or breaking something; the mother is doing all of that. The mother is put into a role in which she is going to be viewed ambivalently, while to most children the father is just a big, strong, wonderful person who comes home and plays with them and never says "No." It is something that really has a very important effect upon the child, because sex roles are among the many things that the child is learning at this time.

Thus, the sense of masculinity or femininity will be experienced by children in terms of how they see their parents. Changing cultural patterns of parenting roles can be expected to affect these attitudes. The effects of a father being the primary caretaker while the mother works is something about which we know very little as yet, but it is a pattern which is occurring with increasing frequency. Other patterns such as communal parenting, which have not been common in our society, may also help us learn more about the development of our perception of what is masculine and what is feminine.

TOILET TRAINING

Another major area involving parental values is toilet training. At the same time that the child is going through a struggle to become separate from the mother and is practicing saying "No" to her, he or she is also at the age when, in our society, we think that toilet training should be underway. Not every society begins toilet training at the same time or in the same way, but there does seem to be a biological timetable which tells us when such training can first be initiated.

We know that children can be trained before they are a year old, because they are equipped with a reflex pattern, a gastrocolic reflex. This operates from very early in childhood. If the mother wishes, she can train a child through conditioning at a very early age. We hear about children who are trained before they have voluntary control of their sphincters. This can be done most easily with children whose gastrocolic reflex is quite strong. The mother regularly puts them on the potty right after they have eaten, and soon they respond to the feel of the toilet seat by producing a bowel movement. However, that is not a popular or a widely accepted practice in our society. We think it is far better if children can participate in the experience voluntarily.

There are a few things that we can say that should be prerequisites in terms of beginning to toilet train a child. First of all, the child should have complete innervation of its sphincter. In other words, the child should be able to control voluntarily its sphincter, otherwise the parent is going to have a very difficult problem. One can gauge that indirectly by the sophistication of walking. When a child is just toddling around, he or she does not yet have adequate sphincter control. When a child can run in a given direction and turn or stop, this is a good indication that myelinization has been completed, and that the child has the capacity for sphincter control.

Secondly, it helps for children to be able to communicate verbally, so that they can tell their mother when they have to go to the toilet. That becomes absolutely necessary in our culture because of the way toilets are designed. Children cannot really utilize them on their own. Put yourself into the child's world for a moment. For a child to sit on a toilet can be a very scary thing. First of all, their feet are off the ground and children do not like that feeling very much. They would rather have their feet down on the ground. Furthermore, that hole looks awfully big and the child can literally fall into it. Thus, we have a potty seat (a device that is put on a toilet, a modification of the old kind of potty chairs) to keep the child from falling into the bowl. It is a little easier for children to first learn how to go to the toilet using a potty chair that is on the ground, because they can walk over to it themselves, can look at it, and can actively participate in what is happening (Figure 20.3). However, for the most part, American parents do not do that. We put them on the toilet. Some children become very frightened of such experiences and may develop certain fears and early phobias.

Keep in mind that the young child does not have a very well defined sense of his body. He does not really know where he begins and where he ends. He will know best those parts of his body that he sees and touches most often. He will not know very much about his rectal area. He does not touch it that much. Children ini-

Figure 20.3. A mother toilet training her young son. The interaction is a joyful one, rather than a struggle. Photograph by Thomas Höpker. From *Children and Their Mothers*, Hill and Wang, New York, 1964. (By permission of Woodfin Camp, New York, New York.)

tially do not know that feces are not an integral part of the body, or that bowel movements will occur regularly and predictably. They view feces as something that they are losing, as a part of their body that can be permanently lost. When the mother begins to urge a child to make a "B.M.," or whatever euphemism she uses for it, and then applauds when the child finally performs, the next thing she does is flush the toilet and away it goes. Imagine yourself to be a two year old child for a minute, or a year and a half old, and try to figure out what is happening: "If what I did was so great, why did she throw it away?"

Feces are viewed by the child as something that he loses. In order to surrender something of his own (and it is a surrender for a child), he has to have something positive to balance this loss. The something positive is the love for the mother. He will give up something because it is less painful to give it up than it is to run the risk of losing his mother's love, or facing her disapproval. That is the reason why children will allow themselves to be toilet trained. Children are really much more effectively trained by using their need of love than they are out of fear

of punishment. Children can be trained either way. They can be trained by threats or they can be trained by the positive encouragement to be more grown-up and thereby more acceptable to mother and father. In fact, during this second year of life the primary area of pleasure appears to shift from the mouth and skin to the general body musculature, and more specifically to the increasing pleasure in control that the child experiences over the elimination of urine through the urethra, and the elimination of feces through the anus. That is why Freud designated this period of life as the *anal stage of psychosexual development*.

Thus, it is possible to teach children to use the toilet without a tremendous amount of conflict, but it is not so easy in our society, where toilet training is a source of great conflict. Why is this so? In our toilet training of the child we reflect a whole set of the unspoken values of our society. We exert a lot of pressure on children to be trained because we live in a society which calls for a repudiation of anal interests. Just how far we have gone in this direction, in the repudiation of anything connected with dirt, feces, or urine, will become clear through the number of television commercials for soaps, perfumes, and deodorants. Over and over again we see admonitions to have the cleanest laundry on the block and to be the best smelling person in the neighborhood. We place a great emphasis on renouncing bad smells. This unspoken complex of values is transmitted to the child through the mother, who may begin to react to the child as dirty and smelly and think that it is time to start toilet training. If the mother herself has acquired strong needs to conform in this area, she may be unduly forceful or negative in training the child, or start before the child is able to voluntarily cooperate. Some mothers are even competitive about how early their child is trained, as if it were a mark of distinction for them.

The more flexible mother will recognize that training takes time, that it is not something that takes place the day she decides she is tired of washing diapers or thinks the child is old enough. He may or he may not be old enough but, even if he has the capacity, training will have to be something that extends over a period of time, a gradual process. Under such conditions, training need not present any great problems. If training greatly interferes with the child's need to be independent, then it is better to wait awhile until the child feels a little more confident in himself or herself. Otherwise, training can become a struggle for independence by the child. The mother may become impatient or angry. She may misinterpret the child's lack of interest as defiance. Or the child, dealing with a mother who is constantly restricting him, limiting his behavior, and trying to make him conform, learns that this is the one area which his mother cannot control. He says to her, "You can't make me do this." Some children will then engage in a struggle that really is about independence, control, and individuation, but the struggle will be joined over the issue of bowel training. The child refuses to have his bowel movements in the toilet. As he does so, the mother becomes more and more insistent. The more insistent she is, the more defiant he becomes and they get into a not uncommon conflict, one which is the prototype for certain kinds of characterological patterns in later life. Remember that this issue becomes a matter of conflict for the most part between mothers and children who are having other kinds of problems. It is not really the toilet training, but rather the whole context of the relationship surrounding the struggle for separation and independence.

We talked earlier about the differences in development between boys and girls. Myelinization is completed earlier in girls than in boys, making them more mature physically. They are also likely to be less active than boys, and therefore they evoke less controlling behavior in their mothers. Both of these factors are involved in making the girl easier to train. The girl is able to control her sphincter, to walk to the potty, to make her needs known, and even to manage the small muscle movements needed to pull down her pants before the boy is able to perform these acts for himself. But there is also the fact that mothers and daughters are in less conflict over control at this period in the child's development. If mother has not been snatching the child away from the street all day long, then there is not such a ready environment for resentment and defiance. By and large, girls during this period are not in as much difficulty with their mothers. It does make the negotiating of toilet training a much easier matter for them.

There is one more area of conflict in toilet training which adds to the difficulties which boys have, and it is such a simple one to remedy that it seems surprising that it causes so much trouble. When a mother trains a girl, she will teach her to sit down, whether she is going to urinate or defecate. When she trains a boy, she may very well start out in the same way. She tries to train the boy for both functions in the same manner as she would train the girl, but that does not fit either with the way in which the boy sees his father behave or with his own anatomy. It is much easier to train a boy for bladder control if he is taught to stand at the toilet to urinate from the beginning, but this is not a thought which comes naturally to many mothers. Fathers, of course, can be of considerable help in this very area if they will take the time to be available to their sons.

EARLY DANGER SITUATIONS

At the age we are discussing, conflict exists most often when the child's wishes or demands are limited or prohibited by the mother. The child learns gradually that continued expression of a given behavior will not be accepted by the mother. For the child there is then a potential danger: *the fear of loss of mother's love and approval.* This danger largely supersedes the major danger of the first year, *the fear of loss of the mother.* These two dangers together constitute *separation anxiety.* The child will attempt a variety of solutions so as to prevent these potential danger situations. These attempts at coping are early models for what will be mechanisms of defense — ways the ego tries to deal with wishes which, if fulfilled, would lead to a potential danger.

Let us go back to the situation of toilet training. Some children know by now, since mommy has told them a number of times, that they ought to have their B.M.'s in the toilet. However, they just had a B.M. in the kitchen. What they may do is walk over to the toilet with the B.M. in their pants and sit on the toilet. It is as if to say, "What I did in the kitchen doesn't count, because now I'm doing what you wanted me to do." It is a way of trying to *undo* something they recognized would bring them into the danger situation of losing mother's love. You can see very young children separating themselves in another way from the unpleasant consequences that they may anticipate. Mother may have walked into the kitchen and said, "What smells?" The child looks around, under the table, at the dog, and says, "Not me." This unpleasant business is all outside. It has nothing to do with the child. He tries to *isolate* himself from whatever is unpleasant or would bring him into a situation of potential danger. Other children react by a kind of scrupulous adherence. That is, mother tells them that they have to be clean and they become very clean. They give up entirely the child's normal wish to be messy. They become very meticulous. You may see little children like this. They are hardly walking and yet, if they get a dirty spot on their dress or their shirt, they become very upset. They want to be clean all the time. They go through massive repudiation of what would be a normal interest in dirt and messiness at this time. This is another defense mechanism, one which, when we talk about it later, we will call *reaction formation*.

All of these forms of behavior are normal in a child. The child initially saw no reason to control his bowel movements. He had no aversion to feces, no disgust at the odor, no discomfort at the feeling, and no reason to prefer the use of the toilet. He learns that this is objectionable to his mother and that he must change his behavior. Normally such acceptance is gradual, extending over many months. Even more gradually some of the patterns of behavior evolved in dealing with this conflict will begin to function autonomously. They will continue but now free

of conflict. For example, in later childhood and adulthood, people will be clean for their own sake, not because they must be clean in order to please the mother.

In some children and adults, not a small number in our society, problems may arise in handling this conflict and lead to distortions in later personality development. I indicated earlier that the larger issue is one of separation and individuation. The child opposes too much external control. When it threatens him with submission, which means a loss of self-esteem and independence, he may become obstinate and defiant. Certain character traits may then develop and persist throughout life. For example, we think adults in our culture should have a certain quality of tenacity — that is, given a job to do, they should be able to remain with it until it is finished. There are people who cannot do this. Instead of being able to complete a task, they become obstinate and stubborn. They are very much like the child who says "No" to everything. They develop a characteristic personality which is based on resisting whatever they are asked to do. This is obviously not very adaptive. Another characteristic trait of people who have had difficulties at this phase of development is that they are indecisive. They are like the little child who cannot decide whether he should produce or not produce. Some people persist in this pattern. They are indecisive in every aspect of their lives. They can never come to a decision, very much like the child who becomes constipated because he does not want to let go. He cannot decide whether or not to let go, and he is stuck at that point. There are many adults who are "stuck" in the same way.

When neuroses and personality disorders are discussed later in the book, some that are specifically related to this phase of development, namely the *obsessive-compulsive disorders*, will be described in more detail. Prevention of some of these patterns can be achieved by an understanding of the child. It requires time for the child to feel enough confidence in himself or herself to accept imposed limitations. Many children are not able to participate in toilet training at this age. They are not yet secure enough in their own autonomy and independence. It is much better under such circumstances to postpone training until a little later when the child can accept it more readily and can participate in it without being caught up so much in the struggle over separation and individuation. An increasing sense of autonomy will more likely be the result, rather than the beginnings of shame and doubt.

THE THIRD YEAR OF LIFE

During the third year of life children achieve further consolidation in ego organization and an increasing sense of their own individuality. Verbal communication increases rapidly and there is an increasing use of more abstract words and concepts. Play serves the purpose of defining and experimenting with roles, as well as of expressing a rapidly expanding fantasy life. There are increasing capacities to tolerate frustration and to remain separate from mother and father for longer periods of time. The world of the child widens and other family members as well as playmates become more important. By the end of this third year children have a more stable image of themselves and a more stable inner representation of the mother and father that they can retain in their absence. Continuing identifications with the parents as well as other people occur, and there is increasing internalization of societal attitudes with the beginning of superego formation. Bowel and bladder control are achieved. In the latter half of the third year the child shows an increasing interest in sexual differences, and reactions to these differences appear. Let us consider these events in more detail.

VERBAL, CONCEPTUAL, AND MOTOR DEVELOPMENT

Children's verbal abilities expand rapidly during this year. They are very interested in learning the names of all the new objects and experiences they encounter, and "What is it?" or "What's its name?" are frequent questions. They use more complete sentences with a subject, object, and verb. Numbers are abstract concepts which the child can now begin to understand. (They know what two of something or three of something means.) Time also begins to mean something, and "later," "tomorrow," and "soon" can now be understood. This is related to the growing capacity to delay as well as to cognitive maturation. Equally interesting is the increasing use of pronouns, something that has not been possible earlier. It is only by age three that the child begins to speak about I, you, he, and she, and in that way to differentiate not only self from object, but also different objects from one another.

It is very important for a three year old to be able to divide people into different groups. At this age children begin to become very concerned about their own identifications. They become very possessive of whatever labels are attached to them — Mary or girl or blue-eyes — particularly because their sense of individuality is still somewhat tenuous. It is easy to tease three year olds; they will become very upset if you play around with their names. You sometimes see adults play this game with little children: "You're not Sam; I'm Sam." The child will become anxious and insistent. This is so upsetting because the labels that the child is using are an integral part of his sense of himself or herself, and if they are switched, anxiety appears. It is quite an experience to see somebody tell a little girl, "No, you're not a girl. You're a boy," or vice versa, and see the child's violent reaction to such teasing. Their identity is very important to them. They feel very threatened. Gender identity is now an increasingly important part of the self.

Three year olds are also very concerned with size, and they compare everything in these terms. They are typically very interested in knowing who is taller and shorter, and they like to have their mothers make a mark on the wall to show them how much they are growing. This is another form of categorization, so that we have: boy-girl, brown hair-blonde hair, bigger-smaller. There has been some very interesting research in this area by Piaget which has taught us about the child's cognitive abilities. Piaget calls the thinking of the child at this age *preoperational*, and Dr. Farley will be discussing this stage of cognitive development more fully in Chapter 25. Basically, children of this age are impressed with what is visible and tangible, and they are relatively unsophisticated in making judgments about relationships. Some of Piaget's experiments have shown us that children of this age have a very limited idea of what is more or less. If you give them a container which is tall and very skinny and another which is shorter but of greater volume, and ask them which holds more, they will invariably choose the taller object. They do not yet have the ability to conceptualize beyond the one dimensional idea that taller means more.

Motor control has become much more sophisticated by age three. When they were two, children could not run and change direction at the same time; if they tried, they were likely to run headlong into something. By three they are able to change direction with great agility. They no longer just climb up stairs; they go flying up and down with no difficulty at all. Their fine motor coordination is also much more sophisticated. If you had given the two and a half year old an outline to fill in with a colored crayon, he would have gone far outside the boundaries. He is unable to keep the color inside a defined area. By the time he is three, he will be able to accomplish this with some precision. The same improvement in fine motor coordination is true in the use of the small muscles of the eye. Three year olds are able to discriminate small differences between objects very clearly.

The most noticeable fact about their motor control, however, is their tremendous exuberance. All of the new body movements have to be practiced and perfected. They run and jump and dance and swing, and can continue such activity all day long with obvious pleasure in the repetition and mastery.

PLAY, SOCIALIZATION, AND FANTASY

The play of the three year old is enlivened not only by a rich fantasy life, but also by a newly complicated social awareness. This is a process which extends over many years; in a sense, it began when the baby first identified his mother as a being other than himself. At three, with his increasingly active sense of himself, the child is ready to accept the existence and cooperation of others. When we see two year olds at play, they are likely to be wrapped up in their own concerns. They like to play; they enjoy handling toys; they tolerate the presence of other children to varying degrees and for varying periods of time; but there is not much in the way of joint play. The term for what they do, among nursery school people, is "parallel play." That means that several two year olds will sit side by side, each finger painting or pushing a truck, but none of them interacting with the others (Figure 20.4). Somewhere around three years of age we begin to see the development of "joint play," in which two or three children will cooperate in a game or a project. At first this does not include too many children, nor does it last for very long, but there will be some degree of cooperation in throwing a ball or playing school or building a sand castle.

Figure 20.4. A young girl hand painting. From the film *A Long Time to Grow — Part I.* (By permission of Department of Psychology, Vassar College, Poughkeepsie, New York.)

Along with this social behavior comes an increasingly rich fantasy life. As language develops and the ability to abstract and conceptualize becomes more advanced, the child enjoys exercising these mental processes. He fantasizes, he makes things up, and he does in fantasy what he cannot do in reality. This makes his mental apparatus much more interesting, but it also can create some difficulties. For example, the three year old crosses the line between fantasy and reality with great fluidity. That means that if he happens to be playing that he is Superman and pretending that he can fly, he may just decide to try it. If he is lucky, he will make this attempt by jumping off a table; but children have been known to jump off much higher things because they were carried away by their fantasies and not able to fully appreciate reality limitations.

The second complication of the developing fantasy life is one with which parents find it extremely difficult to deal, and that is that children at two and one half and three seem to be awful liars. They are always making up stories, stories about where they went or what they saw or who, precisely, spilled the cocoa. Why is he or she such a liar? Most of the stories that small children make up are very transparent, and it is all too easy to tell when they are lying. The problem is that a child of this age believes that his parents are omniscient. He believes that his parents know everything that he is thinking, but he is not absolutely sure, and so he wants to test this and see if it is true. He makes up some ridiculous story and tells it to his mother just to see if she will know that he made it up. If the parents do not recognize that what the child is doing is exercising a potentially healthy aspect of his personality, which is the capacity to fantasize and be creative, then they will see it simply as lying. Such parents may react with righteous indignation to this behavior. Parents need to be reassured that children do this all the time and that it is not a matter of major concern. They do not have to pretend to accept his fabrications, but they can joke with him about his imagination. A large number of parents, however, become extremely anxious about this behavior, fearing that the child will not know the difference between reality and fantasy or that he will turn into a chronic liar and never tell the truth.

With some children, the increase in imaginative play takes on a specific form. A child who is especially sensitive about being criticized or abandoned by a parent will make up an imaginary companion who does all the bad things in his house. When a lamp is knocked off the table or the cat is let out, then it is always George who did it. George is someone who exists only in the child's thoughts, a figure onto whom all of the child's unacceptable actions and feelings are projected.

SELF AND OBJECT CONSTANCY

During much of the third year the child is struggling with ideas of "good" and "bad." Those feelings and behaviors that are approved by mother are easily introduced as part of the *self-representation* — a "good" self. The "bad" initially is disowned by putting it outside the self, as onto the imaginary George. It takes time to get these two views integrated into a stable and constant view of oneself as an individual.

In a parallel way each child has a "good" and a "bad" mother. The "good" mother is the one who takes care of you, stays with you, satisfies your needs. The "bad" mother is the one who stops you from doing things, is angry or critical, or especially is the one who leaves you. During the third year the child also has to integrate these different views of mother into a single *object representation*. From the latter part of the second year on, as mother has to introduce some limits on the child's behavior, she is more likely to be perceived as "bad." When mother is physically present the child can accept his anger with his "bad" mother because his "good" mother is with him. He may *project* his "bad" feelings outside. The child with the imaginary compan-

ion will say, "George's mommy is mean. He hates her." Other children will be angry with a pet or with a doll. When the mother is absent, the "bad" mother feelings are reinforced because the child is angry that she is gone. He may be unable to retain the image of his "good" mother. When she returns, she is refound as the "good" mother. The child cannot retain the full object representation of mother in her absence — he "loses" her when he is angry at her for leaving. Many parents have returned home from a short trip looking forward to greeting their loved and missed child and expecting a warm welcome. When they walk through the door, instead of a hug and a kiss, they may be ignored for awhile. The child is angry and has "forgotten" that he loves and misses them. Of course, he will usually soon "remember" and welcome them back. It is also a way of saying, "You left me. Now I'll leave you."

It takes time for the child's mind to retain the image of mother in her absence. We know from Piaget that a child can remember a toy when it is hidden and look for it long before this, but there are not such strong and mixed feelings about the toy. It will only be somewhere between age two and three that the child will be able to retain a stable image of the parents when they are absent and tolerate their absence well. In Piaget's terms it is only then that the child has a reliable evocative memory. We call this *object constancy*, and it is a major achievement in development. It indicates a fusion of the "good" and "bad" object representations and is a requirement for the development of appropriate object relationships. Object constancy is dependent on repeated experiences of tolerable degrees of frustration, prohibition, and absence combined with sufficient physical presence, gratification, and pleasure.

GENDER IDENTITY

The growth in his fantasy life leads the three year old to enjoy playing with miniature versions of grown-up objects such as dollhouses, baby dolls, trucks, and guns. Through this kind of play, the child has a comfortable, although magical, feeling that he or she has control over the bigger, real objects in the world. The little boy may envy his father's ability to drive the family car, and so he shoots his own toy car across the room, telling everyone that he can drive faster and faster. It has been traditional for boys to play with trucks and guns and tools, while girls play with dolls and brooms and high-heeled shoes. Such sex-bound traditions regarding what interests boys and girls are being increasingly questioned at this time. Many people believe that society should not stereotype such activities because this may limit the child's interests and pressure the child into overly confining future sexual roles.

What we can say is that a child increasingly chooses to play the role of the parent of the same sex, and that this choice is connected with the child's wish at this point to consolidate his or her gender identity. This process begins very early (Figure 20.5), and continues throughout childhood (Figures 20.6 and 20.7). If mother is a doctor, then the little girl will play at being a doctor. It does not matter whether this identity is boy-truck, girl-doll, but it does matter that the child be able to identify with the rest of the people in the world who are of the same sex. Self-definition and identity are the tasks to which these concerns are related. At three, the child feels his or her identity and category much more markedly than before. Although children in their fantasy lives may be varying mixtures between male and female, on another level they will be very protective of their gender identity, as we indicated earlier.

We said that gender identity has very little to do with anatomical knowledge. A few years ago, if you had asked a three year old how he told the difference between boys and girls, he might have said that boys had short hair and girls had

Figure 20.6. A two and one half year old boy trying on his father's hat.

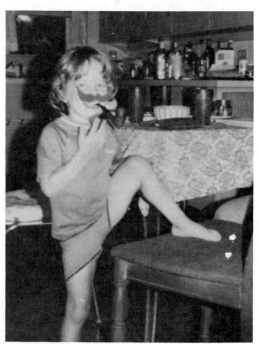

Figure 20.7. A four year old boy who is very happy being a "grown-up man" with a moustache and a pipe.

Figure 20.5. A young boy (age 14 months) with his father's pipe.

long hair; that boys wore pants and girls wore dresses. Those criteria are no longer valid, but then, they never did constitute the real difference between the sexes. Children certainly know boys from girls. But they do not like to tell adults just how much they know. Some of their knowledge in this area is connected with anxiety, as we will discuss shortly. Of course, there are also adults who do not like to think that children know anything in this area.

Avoidance of this issue only confuses the child. We adults already confuse children enough because of our own conflicts over sexuality. For example, no one would think of telling a child that his eye was a "see-thing" or that his nose was a "smeller"; but when it comes to identifying sexual organs, you will find that most people use some sort of avoidance. Proper words for the organs are not used. Instead many parents use terms such as "pee-pee," or "sissy," or some other word which describes the function rather than the proper name of the organ. Many people feel uncomfortable about having these things spelled out too clearly, and they are self-conscious about having children use the proper terminology. There is no reason for this; the child is perfectly capable of learning and using the appropriate words for everything.

The young physician may be surprised to discover that many of his adult patients do not know the proper names for their sexual organs. In fact, many patients have an enormous amount of confusion about their own anatomy. In this area there is something of a difference between the sexes, in that women are more likely to be confused and vague about their genitals than men because their genitals are much more difficult to visualize. For example, some women will characteristically have difficulty in localizing sensations in the pelvic area or in the genitals. You ask such a woman what hurts her, and she will say, "It's down there," indicating an area roughly between her navel and her knees. She is not specific in telling the doctor because the sensations themselves are probably not specific and localized. Confusion about anatomy becomes apparent in the use of language. Women will talk about having a stomach ache when they really have menstrual cramps, or about a baby being in the stomach rather than the uterus. They have an early confusion about their own anatomy. It is interesting to note that, for other reasons entirely, men have a similar confusion about the female genitalia.

Let us return to toilet training to understand some of the factors involved in this confusion. Toilet training draws the child's attention to the anal-genital-urethral area. Partially through the mother's actions in cleaning the child, she pro-

duces pleasurable sensations. The child begins to explore both visually and tactilely this area of the body as attention is drawn to it. In this pursuit, the boy has a different and easier task. His genitals are external and more easily accessible visually and tactilely. He is more easily able to distinguish between the functions of urination and defecation, as well as to obtain pleasurable sensations from touching his genitals.

Young girls, on the other hand, have a different experience. Girls have more difficulty visualizing the genital area and are much less likely than boys to explore their genitals, especially the inner aspects of their anatomy. The fact that the same position is used in urinating and defecating probably adds to the girl's confusion. It is not uncommon to find that a girl has the fantasy that there is only one common opening through which urethral, anal, and genital functions are performed, analogous to the cloacas of certain animal forms. Here, too, the names used by parents can contribute to the confusion. Little girls may be told they have a vagina, but the term is often used in a global way to designate the external genital area, the labia, and the clitoris, including the urethral and vaginal openings. This lack of specificity in naming the various parts of the girl's genitals contributes in later life not only to varying degrees of vagueness about anatomy, but sometimes to feelings of dirtiness or smelliness, which were connected in childhood with urethral and anal functions, now carried over and transferred to the genital area. While this sometimes occurs with boys as well, it is much more common in girls.

These anatomical and biological aspects are, of course, just one factor in sexual differentiation. In recent years there has been a great deal of controversy over this issue. It can be looked at from the point of view expressed by Freud that "anatomy is destiny," or from the opposite view that gender identity is entirely determined by society. There seems to be something to be said for each position, with neither being completely correct. We do know that gender identity and behavior begin with genetic transmission, with whether a person has an X or Y chromosome. We also have some evidence from laboratory studies on other species that the fetal sex hormones secreted by both sexes affect sexual behavior in later life. At the same time, we also know that environmental factors are of enormous influence. Investigations done by John Money and Robert Stoller indicate that such factors can override biology at times – that children experience themselves and function in the sexual role in which they have been reared, even if it is contradicted by the genetic, chromosomal determination of their sex. Dr. Dickes and Dr. Simons will be discussing these issues in greater detail in their chapter on transsexualism.

We noted earlier that parents in general tend to treat girls and boys differently. In these actions there begins to be transmitted an organized set of values that reflects the attitudes of both the culture and the individual family, and it is this set of values which will determine for each child what it means to be a boy or a girl in that particular sociocultural setting. It is here that we see introduced many matters that have very little to do with true masculinity or femininity. We begin to say things such as, "Boys don't do that; it is sissyish." If a boy wants to pretend in play that he is the mommy and he happens to have parents who are apprehensive about how such behavior will affect his masculinity, they will discourage the behavior. Or if a girl tries to play football, her father may withdraw from her some of the approval which she seeks from him. This behavior is typical of our society, but its roots go far back in history, long before our modern society and psychiatry. Interestingly enough, there has generally been far less acceptance of "feminine" behavior in boys than of "masculine" behavior in girls. We are not as distressed if a little girl is a tomboy. If she insists on climbing trees or playing football when she is five or six, this behavior is often thought of as "cute"; but if a boy of that age wears beads, plays with dolls, and acts effeminate, then not only his parents but all of society will react harshly to him. There must be some explanation of this fact, since it is a phenomenon which is by no means limited to our culture.

Further, in virtually every culture throughout recorded history there has been a tendency to give masculinity a more preferred status, to elevate what is male and devalue what is female. We can ask ourselves where this biologically unfounded bias had its beginnings and why it should have persisted. What leads men to repudiate so strongly femininity in themselves and to devalue women? Why have women for so long, even when aware of it and resenting it, often accepted an inferior status? The answers to such questions are undoubtedly complex and much is still unknown. In Chapter 22 we will consider some factors present in children of this age that may help us to answer some of these questions.

Suggested Readings

Brazelton TB: *Toddlers and Parents: A Declaration of Independence.* New York, Delacorte Press, 1974.

Call JD, Galenson E, Tyson RL (eds): *Frontiers of Infant Psychiatry.* New York, Basic Books, vol I 1983, vol II 1985.

Erikson EH: Autonomy vs. shame and doubt. In *Childhood and Society.* New York, W. W. Norton, 1950, p 222.

Fraiberg SH: The first 18 months, and 18 months to three years. In *The Magic Years.* New York, Charles Scribner's Sons, 1959, pp 62–103 and 107–176.

Lidz T: The toddler. In *The Person.* New York, Basic Books, 1976, p 165.

McDevitt JB: The toddler: from sixteen to thirty-six months. In Wiedeman GH (ed): *Personality Development and Deviation.* New York, International Universities Press, 1975, p. 63.

Mussen PH, Conger JJ, Kagan J, Huston AC: Development during the second year. In *Essentials of Child Development and Personality.* New York, Harper & Row, 1984.

Prugh DG: *The Psychosocial Aspects of Pediatrics.* Philadelphia, Lea & Febiger, 1983.

References

Mahler MS: On the concepts of symbiosis and separation-individuation. In Mahler S (ed): *On Human Symbiosis and the Vicissitudes of Individuation.* New York, International Universities Press, 1968, p 7.

Mahler MS, Pine F, Bergman A: *The Psychological Birth of the Human Infant.* New York, Basic Books, 1975.

Spitz RA: *No and Yes. On the Genesis of Human Communication.* New York, International Universities Press, 1957.

21 Ethology: Primate Research and the Evolutionary Origins of Human Behavior

Leonard Rosenblum, Ph.D.

A very reasonable question that a reader might have would be: "What is the relevance of a chapter on ethology and primate research in a volume having to do with human behavior?" I do not want to bore you with a long introduction to the chapter itself, but I think it does help to have at least some historical perspective.

SIGNIFICANCE OF COMPARATIVE BEHAVIORAL RESEARCH

As early as Aristotle, there was an interest in variations in animal behavior as well as in animal physiology and morphology. That interest continued for a time but then was lost for many centuries, and did not reappear until the period following Darwin's pioneering work on evolution. The thrust of this renewed interest was that if in fact we could trace the evolutionary origins of the morphological features of man—his nose, his arms, whatever features happened to be of interest—perhaps then one could, with diligence and care, also trace the evolutionary beginnings of similar behavioral developments in early mammals and even submammalian forms.

At the end of the 19th century, an interest in psychology, psychiatry, and behavior began to develop out of the prevailing materialistic view of science. There was always the implication that all behavior was ultimately dependent upon physical, neurological structures in some manner or means, however complex and difficult to determine. Certainly Freud always believed this. Despite our frequent failures to ascertain the physical basis of behaviors, we nonetheless still maintain our confidence that the kinds of psychological phenomena in which we are inter-

ested must have their ultimate basis in various physical structures of the organism. If this is so, then one can presumably trace the evolutionary origins of man's behavior in lower animals, just as one can look for the evolutionary origins of man's morphological structure in lower animals.

Thus, in the wake of Darwin's work towards the end of the 19th century, there was a flurry of activity attempting to pull together all kinds of anecdotal information about the origins of man's most noble and least noble properties—ranging from his altruism to his aggression, from his asceticism to his sexual behavior. Books were published that compiled all kinds of bits and pieces of information of the kind with which we are all familiar—the dog that loved his master; the bird that flew halfway around the world to find his family again; the porpoises that helped their mates; the whole panorama of human frailty and human nobility that various animal lovers around the world thought could be seen originating in the instinctual behavior of more primitive animals, or at least "primitive" from some points of view. There have always been others who have felt that we are the more primitive and degenerate of all the species, but I will not get into that debate in this chapter.

These searchings for the origins of man's higher, more complex mental characteristics, which were so actively pursued in the 1880's and 1890's and at the turn of the 20th century, began to run into a number of difficulties. It is common, for example, to read the description of some missionary working his way through Africa, who has studied the behavior of various animals by shooting them down ("Let's open their stomachs to see what they eat"). There are others who have studied the complex behavior of animals by keeping them in the backyards of their houses and taking notes over a period of years. These approaches are obviously fraught with a number of difficulties that can be summarized very simply—they do not meet the standards of reproducibility, of objectivity, and of precision, that we demand of our sciences. Furthermore, as is true with science in general, when such problems become apparent there often tends to be a reaction, a sort of, "That's all garbage; forget about that. We can't make any sense of that. It's not science." Science requires a great deal of detail, of quantification, of control, and hence all of this early, nominally anecdotal, nominally nonscientific material on animal behavior was essentially rejected and buried in the first couple of decades of this century.

At this point, what is loosely called behaviorism came to the fore and people like John Watson and others began to talk only about the kinds of readily quantifiable, motoric elements of animal behavior that could be studied in great detail and were physiologically manipulable. You could cut things up and snip things off, and thereby manipulate various aspects of behavior in what was then purported to be a scientific rather than an anecdotal fashion. There is considerable question now about how "scientific" all of these activities were, but nonetheless that was the thrust of the early work in animal behavior in the first decades of this century. However, as we began to look at animal behavior within this kind of learning theory-reinforcement framework, it became obvious that there were a great many things about animals that did not readily fit into the learning-reinforcement model. As scientists, we seemed to be left with many aspects of animal and human behavior that we could not easily explain, and that were not particularly dependent upon the offering of food or heat or light or whatever other reinforcements we may have had in mind.

So we turned once again to what we may loosely refer to as "instinct theory," the notion that, "Well, if we can't see how the animal learns this kind of behavior after it's born, then it must have been born with the behavior." For lack of anything better, we returned to various kinds of instinct constructs and then, as before, the pendulum swung back in the earlier direction and we went overboard with instinct theories. There were people like McDougall in the early years of this century who had lists of the instincts of man—gregarious instincts, fighting instincts, maternal instincts, filial instincts, food-getting

instincts—any kind of behavior in any fragmentary form whose origins we could not readily explain was essentially written off as an instinct. Stated rather simplistically, "Why do salmon swim upstream?" "Because they have an instinct to swim upstream." "Why, at the end of their spawning, do they swim downstream?" "Because they have an instinct to swim downstream." And as is often the case in various domains of science, at least in their early stages of development, we think that by labeling something with a given name we have somehow explained it. In point of fact we have only provided a name to label our ignorance.

Around about the middle of the 1930's and early 1940's there arose, primarily in continental Europe and subsequently England, a new science of behavior, *ethology,* which attempted quantitatively to determine, and then assess these presumptively instinctual and acquired behavior patterns in various animal species. *Predator-prey relations* were a primary focus of some of the earlier work. Why did an animal attack some particular kind of opponent? What features of the opponent actually elicited the attack? By using artificial models of competitors, one could attempt to determine what aspects of the competitor actually elicited the kind of attack behavior in which we might be interested, and in this way we could get some more precise understanding of those elements of the stimulus array that actually control the behavior in question. Out of the ethological movement, led off in the 1930's by Konrad Lorenz and followed by people like Tinbergen and Hinde and Thorpe and others, many concepts have been developed, such as "imprinting" and "action-specific-energy." We are not going to be able to devote time to concepts like "action-specific-energy," which bears a certain resemblance to concepts like "libido" in psychoanalytic theory—a kind of hydraulic model of instinctual energy that goes rushing through the organism nestling here and bursting out there. There is obviously a certain amount of predictive efficacy to concepts like action-specific-energy, just as there is to libido, but many of the essential features of these concepts escape our experimental grasp and I want to deal in this chapter with more concrete and observable data.

In any event, the question that ultimately must be asked of the modern studies of animal behavior is, "What does the study of animal behavior offer us in terms of our interests as scientists, as physicians, as students of human behavior?" Clearly nothing in the study of animal behavior can allow us to draw direct conclusions about the behavior of man or the origins of his behavior. Indeed, what I will in part be trying to emphasize in this chapter is that we often cannot even generalize our conclusions from one primate species to another closely related primate species. Single fragments of behavior of the white rat, of a given monkey, or of any species, cannot, in and of themselves, be generalized. We cannot draw conclusions by leaping gaily from one branch to another in the phylogenetic tree. What we can attempt to do, is to define the variables in such a way that we can more meaningfully test hypotheses at various nonhuman levels in the phylogenetic order, so as then to improve our hypothesis testing at the human level.

There is, after all, an unending series of possible questions (and approaches to the answers to those questions) that become relevant in terms of the study of human behavior. By a careful series of comparative studies at the nonhuman level, where we can manipulate environments and quantitatively follow the behavior of our animals through a large period of their life span, we can attempt to derive principles which will hopefully be worthy of assessment at the human level. That is the contribution of comparative psychology and ethology to the study of man's behavior, the degree to which these sciences assist us in the testing of hypotheses at the human level, and subsequently in the ordering of priorities for the investment of our resources as a society. There are limitations, to be sure. We cannot shift our techniques easily from one species to the other, but perhaps we can make some meaningful movements in the appropriate direction.

SOCIAL ISOLATION REARING

I would now like to discuss with you some of the work that has been done in recent years with primates, focusing especially on the critical relationship of primate infants to the social milieu within which they develop and, in particular, on the infant's relationship with its primary caregiver. In most cases, primate infants are born in a state of considerable helplessness which takes a rather long period of time to overcome, and thus, as in man, the nonhuman primates are dependent upon other figures in their immediate surroundings in order to insure their survival. What happens when that kind of normal, nurturing relationship (nurturing not simply in a physical, food, heat, protective sense, but in the general care-giving sense of social stimulation as well) is disrupted?

Figure 21.1 shows the normal mother-infant

Figure 21.1. A normal Pigtail macaque mother grooming her young infant while it clings to her ventral surface.

monkey attachment relationship. This of course is only one particular species, one about which I will be speaking more later, the Pigtail macaque. Under normal circumstances, the Pigtail infant, at birth, climbs onto the mother's ventral surface where it is held and protected, and where it spends much of the day with the nipple in its mouth, nursing from the mother or just simply maintaining oral contact with the mother's nipple. This is a strongly pacifying, quieting kind of behavior that Pigtail infants do for long periods of time—around 70% or 80% of the time that infants in these species are on the mother they maintain nipple contact—and this is true even when they are as much as a year or so of age. At that age they are spending less time on the mother, but when they are on her they still maintain a good deal of nipple contact. Thus, this behavior does appear to be something in the way of support for the idea of some kind of oral drive. Clearly the oral stimulation is very effective in placating, soothing, and comforting the young primate.

Figure 21.2 shows what normally happens in most monkeys that are gregarious, group-living animals. These are from another species, the Bonnet macaque. Many mothers and infants may be found within small, relatively cohesive groups. After a few weeks of age both Bonnet and Pigtail infants begin to engage in various forms of social play with one another, although such play behavior emerges more rapidly in the more gregarious Bonnets.

As their dexterity and locomotive capacity and coordination increase, chasing and running after one another are mixed with the bouts of physical play. This is the common pattern of behavior that is seen in infants after about four to six weeks of age and that continues for the first couple of years of life. It gradually wanes as puberty approaches, which in these animals occurs at around three or four years of age.

But what happens when one raises such infants not with their mothers, not in a social group but in fact in *social isolation*—social isolation even more severe and overwhelming than that which has been described by René Spitz in his papers on hospitalism and anaclitic depression? After all, the children Spitz described were handled somewhat, they had some degree of

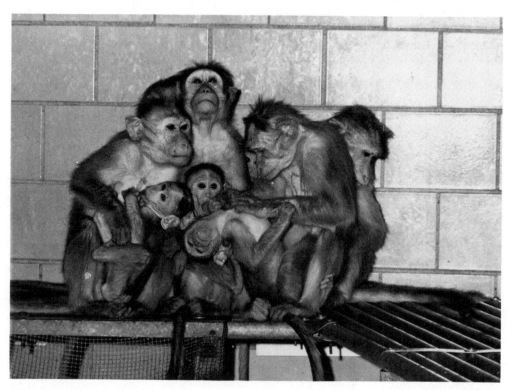

Figure 21.2. A group of Bonnet macaque mothers and their infants huddled close together in characteristic fashion.

visual stimulation, they had all of their physical needs cared for, but they were in large measure deprived of social and psychological stimulation. With monkeys one can manipulate such social isolation to the extreme. One can, within six hours or so after the time that the infant is born, place that infant monkey into complete social isolation. One can feed it by bottle and keep it warm artificially, and then allow it to emerge, three, six, nine, or twelve months later and attempt to assess the degree of devastation that such isolation rearing may have had on the subsequent course of its social development.

The infant in Figure 21.3 is a close relative, a member of the same genus as the monkeys in the previous figures. This infant is the more common Rhesus macaque. This figure illustrates the kind of behavior that one sees in young and older isolate-reared Rhesus infants. These infants at a year of age will barely move, will fail to interact with other animals, will not approach or explore even simple, inanimate objects when they are presented with them. Such isolate animals display a large array of what, at the human level, are referred to as autistic behaviors—self-clasping, rocking behavior, self-orality, and often rather destructive, self-directed aggression. This can be seen in the adult animal depicted in

Figure 21.4. An older Rhesus monkey raised in isolation during infancy, shown biting and clutching his hand with contortion of the lower limbs during a period of heightened arousal. (Courtesy of Dr. H.F. Harlow.)

Figure 21.4 who was reared in social isolation for the first year and a half of life and then spent the next three to five years living in a cage in the regular monkey colony, but continued to show very extreme degrees of self-biting and self-mutilation. There is documentation of animals severely injuring themselves by biting, pulling hair, distending of the nipples in females by constant sucking, and a variety of other aberrant behaviors. Massive disturbance of the animal's normal behavioral development is the common result.

In quantitative terms, if one compares in Figure 21.5, six month isolates and twelve month isolates (that is, animals reared in social isolation for either six months or twelve), with animals raised in a normal laboratory environment with varying degrees of social stimulation, and also tested at twelve months of age, it is clear that social play in the twelve month isolates is completely absent. Play appears to some extent

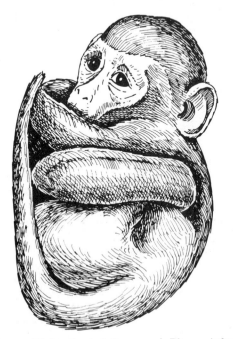

Figure 21.3. An isolation-reared Rhesus infant rolled up in a tight ball, clutching itself in the corner of its cage. (Courtesy of Dr. H.F. Harlow.)

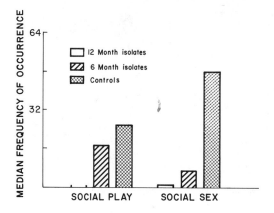

Figure 21.5. Comparison of social play and sexual behavior in 12 month and 6 month isolates, and normally-reared control subjects. (Courtesy of Dr. H.F. Harlow.)

in the six month isolates but is significantly less frequent than one sees in normal controls even though these isolates spent only the first six months of life in isolation and then had six months of normal stimulation. If one examines sexual behavior (the early elements of sexual behavior in these animals involve mounting on the part of males and sexual presentation on the part of females), this behavior is virtually totally absent in the twelve month isolates and also the six month isolates, but is quite prominent in the animals reared under normal conditions of social stimulation. Thus, we see marked deficiencies in social play, and in the initial elements of sexual behavior development in the six and twelve month isolates. If you look at the aggressivity of these animals, i.e., the degree to which they act aggressively towards various kinds of partners, Figure 21.6 shows that the isolates are appreciably more aggressive towards all kinds of partners with whom they are presented—adults, age-mates, juveniles, males, females, whatever. It is clear then that we observe a decrease in the kind of positive, affiliative elements of social behavior (play and sexual behavior) and a very marked increase in destructive, aggressive behavior when animals are raised in social isolation.

SEX DIFFERENCES AMONG ISOLATES

These classic early studies, carried out by Harry F. Harlow and his students on Rhesus macaques, have now been modified in very important ways. One cannot any longer make sim-

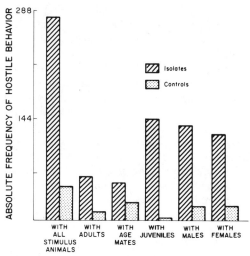

Figure 21.6. Comparison of aggressive behavior towards social partners of various types in isolate-reared and normally-reared Rhesus infants. (Courtesy of Dr. H.F. Harlow.)

ple statements about the impact of early stimulation or the lack of such stimulation upon infant monkeys. One must now qualify that statement in terms of the species and gender of those infant monkeys. A variety of recent data now suggests that early isolate rearing, deprivation of any kind, has a much more severe and continuing effect in some species than others. And in the Rhesus monkey the male infants raised in isolation show more profound disturbance than is the case with the female infants raised in isolation. That is not to say that female Rhesus infants are not disturbed by, nor that their social development is not disrupted by, severe deprivation in early infancy, but rather the range and the extent of that disturbance is less than is the case with male infants raised under comparable conditions. One sees this particularly in terms of sexual behavior. Male Rhesus isolates are almost completely inadequate as adults when it comes to sexual behavior. They will virtually never mount females. The distortion of their sexual behavior is such that even when sexually aroused by a receptive female who may sexually present to them, such isolate-reared males in response to this sexual stimulus may begin to masturbate or manually manipulate their own genitals or may even begin to thrust towards the wall. On the other hand, females raised in social isolation, when presented with a sexually active and patient male, may indeed not only be induced to perform in relatively appropriate sexual fashion, but indeed, conceptions take place and such females then bear young. Their behavior as mothers, however, is quite distorted.

"MOTHERLESS-MOTHERS"

When these females, who had been raised with varying degrees of early deprivation, the so-called *motherless-mothers*, now have their first-born young, one sees very dramatic evidence of the impact of early deprivation on these animals. In marked contrast to the type of females illustrated in Figure 21.1, such "motherless-mothers" are severely destructive of their young infants. The infants of these aberrant mothers, instead of being allowed to cling to their mothers' ventral surface, are continuously rejected, are pulled away from the nipple and not allowed to nurse, and are even physically abused, sat upon, bitten, and struck. Survival itself is at stake in some cases and when the infant does survive, it is only as a result of the intervention of the experimenters who continue to bottle feed such infants on careful schedules and periodically remove the infant from the abusing mother. In general, after a couple of months, the mothers settle down in varying degrees. Compare the normal Rhesus mother (Figure 21.7), clutching the baby to her breast, threatening, not her own infant, but rather those who would

Figure 21.7. A protective threat response by a normal Rhesus mother whose infant nurses at her breast. (Courtesey of Dr. H.F. Harlow.)

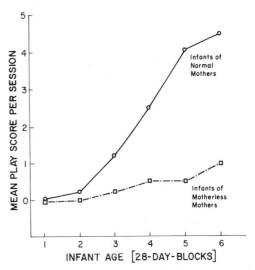

Figure 21.8. Comparison of the development of one form of social play in the infants of "motherless-mothers" and normal mothers during the first six months of life. (Courtesy of Dr. H.F. Harlow.)

approach her and possibly offer some degree of danger to her and her infant.

Under natural conditions the age at onset of weaning occurs in relationship to the fact that females in the wild normally have a baby every year and since gestation lasts about five and a half months, the mother is becoming pregnant with next year's infant when this year's infant is about a half year of age. At this point the mother's estrogen titers are starting to rise, and lactation is decreasing, so that around four to six months of age, weaning behavior begins to increase rather rapidly in the normal mother with regard to her normally reared infant. But the motherless-mother reared infant receives that kind of high level of rejection much too soon, much too dramatically, much before it is capable of coping with it in the sense of being able to interact with others, and move from the mother freely in the environment. There is one further concomitant of this form of aberrant maternal behavior, as indicated in Figure 21.8. Whereas the infants of normal mothers show a very marked and dramatic development of social play, the infants of motherless-mothers fail to show normal peer interaction development.

For reasons that we do not understand at present, these motherless-mothers, when induced to have a second pregnancy, appear to lose, in large measure, this pattern of severe rejection and act with their second infant for all intents and purposes as a normal mother does. The available data on this phenomena are still not complete, but it does appear that something about the experience of raising the first infant, however inadequately and inappropriately, markedly alters the subsequent maternal behavior of the motherless-mother. One additional point is worth noting, however. Infants that receive appreciably higher levels of maternal aggression and punitiveness, at adulthood are significantly more aggressive themselves. The subsequent social behavior of motherless-mother infants is thus distorted, and the kind of aggressive behavior typical of isolates to a certain degree appears in similar fashion in the rejected motherless-mother infant.

EXCESSIVE PEER ATTACHMENT: "TOGETHER-TOGETHER" ANIMALS

Before I move on to some studies of more normal mother-infant relations, let us first consider the question of what might happen if you raise an infant monkey not with a normal mother and not in complete social isolation but simply with another peer. In Figure 21.9 are two Rhesus infants, raised from the first days of life with one another. These infants are referred to in the literature as *together-together* animals, a term coined by Harlow. When we did this work on the development of the together-together animals, some important findings regarding their social behavior development emerged. They did not show the pattern of autism that one sees in the complete social isolates. There was no self-mutilating behavior. These animals did not rock. They did not "self-clasp," but as can be seen from Figure 21.9 they do a great deal of clasping of their partner.

Figure 21.9. A pair of "together-together" infants clinging tightly to one another's ventrum.

There is a characteristic waning of ventral contact along with increasing interaction with the social and physical environment that normally progresses at a fairly rapid rate when infants are raised by a mother to whom they cling. This maturation fails to emerge in the together-together animals. At three to seven months of age, when normal mother-reared infants are actively playing with their peers at every possible opportunity, these together-together animals continue to cling to one another, and to show a marked degree of orality with regard to one another, sucking on one another's fur, ears, and skin. In short, they show a kind of regressive pattern of development, manifesting at a half year or nine months of life, behavior that in the normal infant essentially passes from the repertoire by two or three or four months of life. Being reared with peers, then, is not as devastating as being reared in the absence of any social stimulation at all, but the inappropriateness and singularity of this kind of rearing is in and of itself debilitating in terms of the normal pattern of social behavior. These infants are not at six or nine months or a year of age able to interact appropriately with peer groups of normally reared monkeys.

VARIATIONS IN NORMAL MOTHERING AND SOCIAL MILIEU

Let us now look at studies done in the laboratories of the Downstate Medical Center on the more general factors that influence the pattern of mother-infant relations when an infant and a normal mother are raised under more normal, albeit laboratory conditions. In Figure 21.10, we see one of the species groups that we have utilized in our laboratory, the Pigtail macaque. Notice the spacing of these animals within the available laboratory area. This is the kind of basic breeding and observational group that we use. Each contains a male and four or five breeding females. Compare the Pigtail type of adult spacing pattern with that seen in Figure 21.11, in a second member of the same genus, the Bonnet macaque, where the animals are grouped in a dramatically different way. These patterns of social interaction among wildborn adults, brought into the laboratory for breeding purposes as adults, are very reliable phenomena that occur under a variety of living conditions. But what is most important for our consideration here, is that these patterns are not disrupted

Figure 21.10. A breeding group of Pigtail macaques containing a male, four adult females, a mother and her baby, and an adolescent male.

Figure 21.11. A group of five Bonnet females, including three mothers and their infants, sitting together in close contact with one another.

by the birth of infants within the group. The species-characteristic adult structure and pattern of interaction continue when infants appear.

The infant normally, of course, appears at the mother's ventrum and clings to her in both species. She protects the infant in both species and will allow no harm to come to it. So this is not the difference between the two species. It is not that one type of mother does not care and the other does, but rather the difference lies in the nature of the kind of social stimulation that the normal mother in each of the two species allows and offers her young infant. The Pigtail mother not only remains spatially separate from her peers but when those other animals attempt to approach, to explore, to examine her young infant, as seen in Figure 21.12, they are actively rejected by the Pigtail mother. If she is not sufficiently dominant to attack, she will flee with her young infant and thereby see to it that the infant does not have any opportunities in early life to interact with other members of the social group. As Figure 21.13 clearly shows, the Bonnet, on the other hand, even before the placenta is eaten (which it usually is), allows her

peers to come in close contact with her and to begin to explore her new infant. Thus, infant interaction with other members of the group, for the Bonnet, begins in the first hours of life.

The Pigtail mothers continue to remain aloof of their peers. Their infants grow up, at least in the first weeks of life, in this kind of separated, socially less interactive environment, whereas the Bonnet infant grows up from the first days of life in a melange of social stimulation from other mothers, other babies, and males. What are the consequences of these different patterns of social relations within these two types of genetically close, but socially quite disparate monkeys? One difference that we see, which is rather dramatic, is the response of the infants in these two species to the birth of a sibling.

When the mother of a one year old Pigtail infant gives birth to a second baby, we often see a rather marked disruption in the ongoing behavioral development of the older sibling. The loss of the mother's ventral surface serves as a relative rejection of the older infant, and this results in the kind of pattern seen in Figure 21.14: a marked decrease in activity, a marked drop in play, a change in body posture to a

Figure 21.12.   A Pigtail threatening away another adult female of the group who has attempted to explore her young infant.

Figure 21.13. Two Bonnet mothers seated in contact. The smaller infant is only a few hours old with the placenta still attached, yet the mother has already reestablished contact with a female group member.

Figure 21.14. An older Pigtail offspring showing signs of depressed behavior following the birth of its younger sibling, who now clings to its mother's ventrum.

sustained hunching-over, as well as an increase in self-orality (thumb-sucking). Notice the eye closure in the infant of this figure. There is, we believe, a degree of somewhat transient, but nonetheless clear, depressive behavior manifested by Pigtail infants when their mothers give birth to the next offspring. We never see this kind of depressive disruption in Bonnet infants whose mothers have given birth to subsequent infants. Bonnet infants just continue along their way.

What happens to the relationship of the older infant with its mother? The bond is by no means broken regardless of the older infant's frustration, rejection, or even depression, following the birth of the second infant. In Pigtails, the older infant continues to orbit about and to direct much of its behavior towards its mother; and, indeed, if one comes into the laboratory, for example in the late evening, one sees the older infant sleeping now not at the mother's ventrum as it has done in the past, but at her back, while her younger infant now has the place at the ventrum. When second, third, and fourth infants appear in Pigtails they all continue to

manifest this kind of orienting behavior directed towards the mother, and as a consequence, very cohesive, highly interactive, consanguinal family groups emerge in Pigtails. We never see that kind of pattern emerge in Bonnets.

If one has the opportunity to study a Pigtail and a Bonnet group over a period of many years during which each mother has a number of offspring, we continue to see striking differences in their social patterns. Figure 21.15 illustrates the kind of pattern we see in Pigtails. We see depicted the mother, her newborn black infant, her three year old, her four year old and her six year old offspring. Even when grandchildren are born, the Pigtail familial unit remains highly cohesive. (The breeding male is not a part of this group at all. Males, although they may express some paternal behavior, do not have an investment, in these species at least, in any particular offspring; indeed in wild groups, where several males may be present, no male is the certain father of any given infant.) We do not see this same kind of family cohesion in Bonnets. The Bonnet attachment pattern, compared to that of Pigtails, is less intense initially

Figure 21.15.   A Pigtail family containing the mother (second from the right), with her newborn dark infant clinging to her, and three of her prior offspring, including her adult son seated at the far left of the picture.

Figure 21.16. The two adopted infants of a Bonnet female, who still holds her own biological offspring at her ventrum, while her two foster infants cling to her and attempt to nurse.

and wanes more rapidly, and thus tends to be relatively less selective and is dispersed among the entire social group.

DISRUPTION OF NORMAL MOTHERING

Finally, there is one further dramatic indication of the difference in the intensity of infant attachment seen in Pigtail and Bonnet infants as an outgrowth of the kind of social structure of the two species and as a consequence of the correlated differences in maternal behavior of the two species. This difference has its most compelling effect when the mother is lost. One sees a very marked and dramatic difference in the response of infants of these two species when one experimentally removes the mother.

In Bonnets, the general reaction when the biological mother is removed is for the infant initially to be disturbed. One has to physically pull the infant from the mother's body to effect separation. There may be a degree of agitation, some running back and forth, and vocalizing. But very quickly the Bonnet infant separated from its mother at four to six months of age,

when a good deal of dependence upon her is still maintained, turns and redirects its affiliative, filial patterns to other members of the group. This may be to the group at large, even the adult breeding male of the group, but most generally to some other female in the group who ultimately adopts the separated Bonnet infant (see Figure 21.16). If the foster mother herself has a young infant or is lactating for other reasons, she may nurse the young infant and allow the young infant Bonnet to cling to her. Bonnet infants generally pass through a separation period maintaining this close relationship withtheir foster mothers, so that there is very little destruction of ongoing social behavior and development. The infant continues to play, to locomote, to explore. Its affective behavior is not particularly disrupted. So strong is the bond that often develops between the foster mother and the separated Bonnet infant, that when the biological mother returns, the infant may not return to her, or will only gradually shift from the foster mother back to the biological mother after a week or two of transition. Such is the response to separation in Bonnet infants.

Figure 21.17. A depressed Pigtail infant several days after separation from its mother.

The Bonnet response stands in marked contrast to that which we see in Pigtail. In the Pigtail infant, as with Bonnets, when the mother is removed there is a very marked period of initial agitation. The infant races back and forth, cooing the "localization call" of young monkeys—a very plaintive, high-pitched, easily locatable call. However, within twenty-four to thirty-six hours, that period of initial agitation disappears, and most such separated Pigtail infants pass then into a period of very marked, very severe depression.

As shown in Figure 21.17, the infant closes its eyes and rolls up into a ball, spontaneous locomotion virtually ceases, and exploration of the environment disappears. Of greatest significance, however, is the fact that social play is not only no longer initiated by such a separated infant, but that even the initiatives of others will not elicit a response. Behaviorally and in terms of physical appearance, this is a severely depressed infant. If it is a male, penis-sucking is a frequent occurrence. In fact, self-orality in general is very markedly increased. Such a depression lasts for a week to ten days. During much of that time, it is as if the infant simply

were not there. And perhaps that is the essential nature of this depressive behavior—avoiding all encounters and dangers, conserving energy, "keeping a low profile." The depressive reaction does not occur in all infants—those showing less clinging before separation are less depressed during separation—but in some infants the depression can be quite severe. Indeed, in some cases the infants will fail to drink and must be given fluids, otherwise the animal will dehydrate rapidly and die. In most cases, however, they manage to continue to eat and drink adequately though doing little if anything else.

After a week or ten days, the depression begins to lift gradually. The infant begins to sit up more. Its eyes are open more. It begins initially to explore the environment in its immediate surroundings. Within the next week or so it begins to respond to play initiations of its peers and gradually by the end of a month of separation, such an infant looks quite normal to the casual observer. In quantitative terms, in terms of our detailed observations, we know the separated infant is still showing less than normal levels of exploration and locomotion, still somewhat high levels of self-orality and affective disturbance. But it is in general quite markedly recovered from the earlier separation reaction. When the mother is returned at the end of the month of separation, the Pigtail infant almost immediately reasserts with tremendous intensity the earlier bond to the mother and spends the next two or three months in very intensive close clinging to the returned mother. Thus, the previously separated six or seven month old clings to the mother and hesitates to venture independently into the environment much in the fashion of a three or four month old. One can, therefore, detect a very marked regression in the mother-infant relationship in such previously separated infants.

There are some questions that may be raised with regard to the nature of this depressive reaction that I have described. How do we know that we are not simply dealing with an infant whose milk supply has been cut off and who is feeling terrible for a week, or an infant who no longer can sleep at its mother's ventrum and hence is an infant whose sleeping patterns have been disturbed? As a means of assessing that kind of question consider first the following. When human children are separated by being transferred to the hospital with some serious illness, they pass through a kind of agitated state, then a weepy withdrawal, and finally apathy and then placidity. This is a fairly common sequence in hospitalized children. What happens when such children are exposed to their mothers or some other primary caregiver during the course of the hospitalization? One often gets a kind of reversion of the earlier, more severely depressed symptomatology.

Bearing that whole complex in mind, we carried out a study on separation with this special feature. Pigtail infants separated from their mothers were observed every day in the normal fashion with their mothers gone, but then several times each week their mothers were presented to them in a small restraining chamber at the front of the pen in order to determine their reactions to the separated mother.

As has often been noted in the responses of children to brief encounters with their mothers during a prolonged separation, our separated monkey infants' responses to the lost maternal figure were generally quite dramatic. Although individual responses varied, for at least several weeks each of the separated, previously depressed infants, whose spontaneous behavior during the observation periods when the mother

was absent appeared relatively normal, responded to the brief reappearance of their mothers by the rapid reemergence of the full depression pattern. Generally these young infants, playing or moving freely about the pen when the mother was absent, would upon her reintroduction stop playing and locomoting virtually immediately, withdraw to some other bar or corner of the pen, begin the plaintive cooing of the separated infant, change their posture into the characteristic rolled-up one described earlier, and show the closed or drooping eyelids so characteristic of the depression pattern. In general, during the time their mothers were present these young infants remained withdrawn and motionless, quite in contrast to their behavior in her absence, only periodically looking at the mother, perhaps cooing briefly, then dropping their heads and closing their eyes once again.

It is important to note that this repeated depression pattern appeared only as a response to the infant's own mother, and did not reflect some generalized response to the placement of a new animal in the group. The presentation of mothers of the other separated infants failed to evoke anything remotely resembling the repetitive depression pattern that I have just described. It is perhaps also of interest to note that the reelicited depression pattern was restricted in time to the period of the mother's presence and disappeared virtually immediately upon her removal from the pen. This potential for repetitive reappearance of the depression pattern argues strongly against any simplistic hypotheses of the type we described earlier that might suggest that the depression pattern is merely the result of metabolic disturbances in the young separated infant. Although this material cannot be interpreted to suggest that no physiological disorders play a role in this depression pattern, it is my view that these data leave little doubt that the essential nature of the depression pattern lies in *the infant's psychological response to the loss of the mother.*

One final point. These infant monkey responses to separation parallel another pattern seen in human children. Although in this study the physical restraint of the mother complicates matters somewhat, it was nonetheless the case that separated infants generally failed during the repeated brief returns of the mother to move towards the returned mother, and instead either avoided contact with her or lapsed into the repetitive depression pattern. This intriguing failure of such infants to overtly approach the mother directly suggests the possibility of some form of parallel with the avoidance behavior shown by some separated children during initial reunions with their separated primary attachment figures.

In summary then, it is our view that these experimental studies of the behavioral development of nonhuman primates provide an appropriate setting within which key elements of development may be manipulated and studied in ways that are ethically and often physically impossible to implement at the human level, and may provide us with the methods to test hypotheses about the dynamic interrelationships which mediate the development and expression of human behavior.

Suggested Readings

Harlow HF: *Learning to Love*. New York, Jason Aronson, 1974.

References

Harlow HF, Dodsworth RO, Harlow MK: Total social isolation in monkeys. *Proc Natl Acad Sci USA* 54:90, 1965.

Kaufman IC: Biologic considerations of parenthood. In Anthony EJ, Benedek T (eds): *Parenthood: Its Psychology and Psychopathology*. Boston, Little, Brown, and Co., 1970, p. 3.

Kaufman IC, Rosenblum LA: Depression in infant monkeys separated from their mothers. *Science* 155:1030, 1967.

Kaufman IC, Rosenblum LA: Effects of separation from mother on the emotional behavior of infant monkeys. *Ann N Y Acad Sci* 159:681, 1969.

Mason WA: Early social deprivation in the nonhuman primates: implications for human behavior. In Glass DC (ed): *Environmental Influences*. New York, Rockefeller University and Russel Sage Foundation, 1968, p 70.

Rasmussen KLR, Reite M: Loss-induced depression in an adult macaque monkey. *Am J Psychiatry* 139:679, 1982.

Reite M: Maternal separation in monkey infants: a model of depression. In Hanin I, Usdin E (eds): *Animal Models in Psychiatry and Neurology*. New York, Pergamon Press, 1977, p 127.

Rosenblum LA, Kaufman IC: Variations in infant development and response to maternal loss in monkeys. *Am J Orthopsychiatry* 38:418, 1968.

Rosenblum LA: Infant attachment in monkeys. In Schaffer HR (ed): *The Origins of Human Social Relations*. New York, Academic Press, 1971, p 85.

Section F/The Middle Years of Childhood

CHAPTER **22** The Pre-School Child

Melvin A. Scharfman, M.D.

AGES THREE TO SIX

The years between ages three and six bring about major changes in the child's life. They constitute the time during which there is a shift from a world largely centered around the child's relationship to the mother to one involving both parents. In that context, specific constellations evolve in the relationship with each of the parents and there is a restructuring of those relationships by the end of this period. The child will shift from a more egocentric view of the world to one in which there is a sharper recognition and acceptance of reality. Some magical thinking is still present, and at times the line between fantasy and reality is still not sharply drawn. However, there is a shift in the direction of more logical thinking and an increasing use of thinking to replace trial action — the ability to anticipate the consequences of a given action without actually doing it. In general, there will be a degree of "taming" of affects with more moderate expressions of feelings. The child by six is calmer and more reasonable. Increasingly during this time there will be a more internalized regulation of behavior through the consolidation of the conscience, with feelings of guilt and self-approval more prominent as determinants of behavior. The child will be laying the foundation for movement into the larger social world of school by being able to relate to adults as something more than parental substitutes. Interests in and curiosity about the world increase as the intensity of involvement within the family con-

stellation subsides. Let us consider how some of these changes come about.

THE "PHALLIC PHASE"

Just as the first year of life was called the *oral stage* and the second year of life the *anal stage*, the stage of psychosexual development which we are now discussing was called the *phallic phase* by Freud. It is an interesting misnomer since "phallus" would be, by definition, a male term. Freud was, of course, aware of this and its use reflected the way he thought children experienced themselves at this time — namely, as concerned with whether or not they had a penis, and as classifying people in this manner. Certainly the use of the term reflected the culture in which Freud lived in Central Europe, which was male-dominated. Ancient Greece and Ancient China also stressed male superiority, and Christianity, Judaism, and the Moslem religions all contain prejudicial views of women. Freud knew this, and it is one of the things to which he tried to address himself. Paradoxically, some of his hypotheses have been used to support the idea of male superiority, while at the same time he searched for clues as to why this idea has persisted for so many centuries.

The term "phallic phase" is, as we said, a misnomer, but does indicate that there appears to be an increased interest at this age in the genitals by children of both sexes. We do not know why this happens, but it has been confirmed repeatedly by observations of young chil-

213

dren. There have been studies which indicate that there is a rise in the secretion of sexual hormones around age three. This higher level is maintained until age six, at which time the level decreases, not to rise again until prepuberty. These studies are suggestive but not totally reliable, since they are limited in number. Whether or not it is due to hormonal activity, we do see a rise in genital interest around the age of three. Children shift from a more general interest in their entire bodies to a specific interest in their genitals.

Infants in the first months of life explore their genitals in the course of their random discovery of the whole body. Although there are erections in infants this age, the boy does not seem to have any specific interest in the erection should he encounter it with his hand. It is an incidental phenomenon. Girls also explore their genitals as they do any other part of their bodies. But by age three children become much more specifically interested in their genitals and, so far as we can guess from observation, the genitals begin to be a much more specific source of pleasure than previously. Children at this age are masturbating more often, stimulating themselves rhythmically, and obviously finding pleasure in this activity.

With this new interest in their bodies, we begin to see another kind of concern. We notice children becoming very interested in the loss and restitution of body parts. If a little boy finds a worm, he will be absolutely fascinated with the idea that if it is cut in half, the halves will grow back. Starfish become a matter of great interest now. Children ask if it is really true that starfish can grow lost legs, and does that mean that if they lost an arm or a leg, that it would grow back? A *fear of bodily injury* or damage or mutilation is the concern they are expressing in these varied ways.

Contact with children of this age makes one aware of the fact that they are the chief consumers of Band-Aids in the United States. They are always running to mother with cuts, bruises, mosquito bites, and imagined injuries, and mother has to examine each blemish carefully. Something is required for this dreaded injury. Mother will probably kiss it and then put on a Band-Aid. The child walks away, satisfied with the fact that he or she is all healed. We may find this behavior funny or annoying, but it is important that we recognize that it springs from

BAND-AIDS

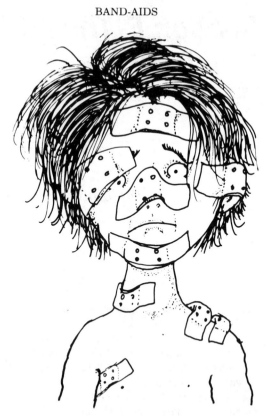

I have a Band-Aid on my finger,
One on my knee, and one on my nose,
One on my heel, and two on my shoulder,
Three on my elbow, and nine on my toes.
Two on my wrist, and one on my ankle,
One on my chin, and one on my thigh,
Four on my belly, and five on my bottom,
One on my forehead, and one on my eye.
One on my neck, and in case I might need 'em
I have a box full of thirty-five more.
But oh! I do think it's sort of a pity
I don't have a cut or a sore!

Figure 22.1. "Band-Aids." From *Where The Sidewalk Ends*. The Poems and Drawings of Shel Silverstein. Copyright © 1974 by Shel Silverstein. By permission of Harper & Row Publishers, Inc., New York.

an intense concern about something being wrong with the body (Figure 22.1).

Boys and girls go through this same stage, but they go through it differently. All children initially assume that everyone in the world is built just like themselves. When they discover that this is not true, they react in quite different ways according to their sex. We do not know why this happens, and we do not even know whether it is a universal phenomenon, but we can be fairly sure about what has been observed in the study of many, many children in this society. Let us consider the boy's reactions first.

CASTRATION ANXIETY IN THE BOY

The boy at age three is very involved, as we said, in the pleasure he gets from touching his penis and exploring that part of his body. At the same time he begins to view his penis as something to show off, and many a little boy has embarrassed his parents by walking into a living room filled with company with his pants off. He just wants to share his pride with them. Or he will be standing to urinate and boast proudly to his father, "Daddy, watch this. I'm big." He attributes to his penis qualities of size, importance, and power. Some of this undoubtedly has to do with his view of his father, because the father is generally viewed as being so big and strong. In his growing identification with the males of the world, the boy begins to want to be bigger and stronger himself, and that includes wanting to show off his genitals. It is not so much that he wants to do anything special with his penis; he just expects to impress everybody. Boys this age are very interested in impressing the world, in telling other children that their fathers, their brothers, their cars are the biggest and strongest. At this point in development boys are concerned with size and with "showing off."

From this time on, we have an intensely proud and competitive little boy, tremendously interested in his genitals. Somewhere along the line his initial assumption that the rest of the world is built just the same as he is will be shattered. He will find out that it just is not true. It may happen when a baby sister is born or when he catches sight of an older girl in the house, or when he is bathed with another child. Most children will have had opportunities to observe one another long before they turn three. However, by age three, when a boy looks at a little girl's genitals, he comes to a special conclusion. Given his concrete and preoperational mode of thinking, when he notices that she looks different from him, he concludes that something bad happened to her, and that whatever happened to her might also happen to him. He becomes worried about his genitals and develops what we call *castration anxiety*. At this time of life cas-

tration anxiety becomes the next major danger situation for the boy. It is a concern based on the observation of the differences between males and females.

Earlier we discussed separation anxiety and the fear of loss of love. The fear of damage to the genitals in both sexes is now added to the hierarchy of danger situations. In the boy this fear takes on the specificity of castration anxiety, whereas in the girl it is experienced as a *fear of genital penetration and mutilation*. As with the other situations of danger, the child will have various ways of coping with this danger. For the three year old boy, castration seems a real danger. It is so real and so frightening, that some boys will deny what they see and insist that the girl is actually just like them, only she has male genitals hidden inside her. This is the reason for the many rag dolls which have been pulled apart, so that young surgeons might explore their inner anatomy. Children of this age have a limited concept of the contents of the body. To them it is like a big circle, with things going in at one end of the body and coming out the other. Not a great deal is known about what goes on in between. So the boy can conclude that everybody is really the same. Girls have a penis inside the body and, therefore, he has nothing to worry about. This is one of the ways of dealing with castration anxiety.

Alternatively, he can conclude that the girl's penis got lost but that it will come back. It will reappear, he is sure; and so we see the interest in regeneration which I mentioned earlier. Children play games that indicate their fantasies about things that are lost coming back. Many little boys play a game in which they hide their penis between their legs and then let it pop out. They scream with delight when it pops out because that proves their hypothesis that what you cannot see is really not gone at all, but was only an illusion of absence.

The boy has another option. He can become frightened by what he has seen of the female genitalia, and that fear can extend to where the girl herself becomes frightening, someone to avoid, someone to scorn, and someone whose activities have to be severely regulated. This behavior is motivated by the anxiety of little boys. It was Freud's idea that most societies which have tended to deprecate women have done this in response to the males' castration anxiety. For example, there is a long history of man's avoidance of a menstruating woman, based on the assumption that the woman is sick, diseased, and dangerous. Where would such an attitude originate? The roots of this attitude may be based on the fact that the thought of blood on the genital area made men nervous because it tended to confirm their fears of castration. They then institutionalized their avoidance of it, just as they tried to institutionalize the separation and deprecation of women in other ways.

Long before he is an adult and able to determine the rules of society, the little boy will for these same reasons want to avoid girls. He will tease them and make fun of them and call them names. This is one response to the anxiety that arises from the perception of the difference between male and female genitals. That same fear may be displaced onto other areas of the body with the boy then terribly worried about any cuts and scrapes. Boys who have had no trouble getting their hair cut can suddenly start to put up a terrible battle when someone wants to take them to the barber. Three year olds' conversations are full of threats like, "I'm going to cut your head off. I'm going to cut off your legs and chop you up into little, little pieces." In this way they are dealing with their own fears of being injured by threatening to injure other people. They can also reassure themselves, and do, by exhibitionistic behavior and by constantly touching themselves. If you watch boys of this age, you will see that they spend half of every day holding onto their genitals. They do this not only for the pleasurable sensations but also because they feel worried and need this reassurance.

All of these reactions of the little boy are normal at this age. Remember that in these reactions the woman is the source of danger. Up to this time the boy has identified with his mother. This feminine identification is now itself a danger, and any activity seen as feminine may be viewed as dangerous to the boy's growing masculinity. Of course, some of these reactions may persist into adulthood. Some men must avoid any activity they identify as feminine and they become caricatures of masculinity. If tenderness and affection are seen as feminine, they will be unable to express those feelings. They may be unable to wash a dish, or prepare a meal under such conditions. Some will even be unable to ever love a woman.

More specific forms of psychopathology provide vivid examples of these childhood fantasies

persisting into adulthood. For example, *transvestites* literally act out the fantasy of the woman with a penis. They are dressed as a woman, but they still have a hidden penis. *Exhibitionists* are also struggling with a childhood fantasy as a central part of their illness. It is very important for an exhibitionist to display his genitals in a public place; but it is also important that he get a specific response from the woman who sees him. He has to scare her. Only when he sees the reaction of fear from the woman does he feel that he has accomplished his task. He is actually saying, "When I looked at you as a young boy, I was frightened. Now I want to turn the tables and frighten you." At the same time, through the frightened response of the woman, he reassures himself that his penis is still intact, much like the three year old who ran about displaying his penis.

The confusion in the child's concept of the female genitals can also be seen in adults who are *voyeurs*. Characteristic of Peeping Toms is the fact that although they look, they never really see. They look only under circumstances where they cannot see the woman's genitals clearly. We think that this has something to do with their own confusion, and with the wish to keep on believing that the woman is not really different after all. They are trying to look at her genitals, but they are not at all sure that they want to see them. This is not so uncommon; normal men may also remain terribly confused about the specific details of female anatomy.

Even beyond the area of anatomy many men seem to experience confusion about women in general. There are social and poetic conventions about the "mystery and illogic" of women. It is said that men can never understand women or know what they want, because women are so puzzling and mysterious. There is no logical basis for this idea. There is no reason why it should be harder for men to understand women than for women to understand men. Yet throughout history we find references to the idea that women are very difficult to comprehend. It may be that what is difficult for men to comprehend is their anxiety about women.

FEAR OF GENITAL PENETRATION AND MUTILATION IN GIRLS

Freud was among those who found women a puzzle, but at least he acknowledged his bewilderment. Certainly some of his formulations about the psychology of women appear to most contemporary observers to be biased and reflective of the societal view of women of his time. In some areas his ideas appear to be generalizations that have not been confirmed by direct observations of children. Subsequent work by a number of female analysts has added much to our knowledge of the development of girls at the age we are discussing, as well as to our knowledge in many other areas. In fact, for a field which has been said to hold a somewhat biased view of women, psychiatry is a specialty in which women have been more active contributors than in almost any other branch of medicine, and one where their contributions have found acceptance and their status has been unquestioned from the very beginning. Perhaps if we look at some of Freud's ideas about the girl's development, we may be able to place his thinking in better perspective.

Early understanding of psychological development was derived from the clinical study of adult patients experiencing conflicts of different types leading to interferences in their functioning. As is not unusual in medicine, pathology led to insights about normal function. Only much later was normal development studied by direct observation of infants and children, including the use of longitudinal studies. Many early formulations were found to be correct, others were slightly modified, and still others were found to be incorrect and extensively modified. That is the method by which theory-building should proceed, as an open-ended process, always changing.

The clinical study of adult female patients pointed to the importance of early childhood experiences in shaping development, just as did that of male patients. The nature of the experience of a girl's reaction to the awareness of sexual differences was one important experience, and we will see similarities as well as differences from the boy's range of reactions. Let us now consider the girl's response when she makes the discovery that she does not have the visible organ which boys have. One reaction similar to that of the boy is a concern over genital injuries. She may feel she has already been damaged or injured, that she has lost something. Or she may feel that in any kind of sexual involvement, especially with the large penis she may have seen on her father or older boys, she will be injured and her genitals torn apart and mutilated.

Freud's ideas stressed *penis envy*, the reaction that the girl would want what she saw but did not have. This is certainly not foreign to the child's way of thinking since the boy envies the mother's capacity to have a baby. His envious wishes, however, are discouraged by most parents in our society as I indicated earlier. He is not allowed to want to be a girl. But what about the girl who wants a penis or wishes to be a boy? In our society, this has been viewed quite differently. There are some little girls who fantasize that they have a penis and that it is hidden inside, just as the boy fantasized. Other little girls hang a gun where a penis would be and play cowboy, or place a stick there and ride a horse. Many parents, especially those who value a boy more, react to this behavior as "cute," or at least do not react as negatively as they would do to a boy who is expressing wishes to be a girl and to have breasts and babies. Such parents may thus encourage in the girl the persistence of the fantasy of a hidden penis, which might otherwise be given up more readily and easily.

Penis envy exists in many little girls this age and is quite normal, just as *breast envy* and *womb envy* exist in many little boys. The persistence of these fantasies into later life is quite another matter. A multitude of factors contributes to the eventual outcome. We mentioned parental expression of preference for a boy. Such parents would already have influenced a little girl to feel less than pleased with herself. She would be identifying with a mother who probably saw herself as devalued. Her father may have been less affectionate with her. If such a girl has brothers who are clearly favored over her, her feelings of jealousy and envy may be intensified. On the other hand, a warm and affectionate relationship with the father can help the girl to overcome envy or jealousy of a younger brother, or to correct an identification with a mother who has a negative image of herself as a woman. The major point is that for many girls the reaction at this age will be transitory if it is not reinforced by the family environment, by society, or by conflicts or trauma in the later course of their lives. That, of course, is still all too often the case even with our changing views of women. Hopefully this will change as more equal opportunities for women become a reality.

What are some of the other ways the little girl may react to the differences between the sexes? Some little girls will become resentful and deprecatory, taking a "sour grapes" attitude: "I don't have it, but who wants it anyway?" Other girls deny what they have seen and then react with shock to the sight of the penis many years later. Many girls react as if the fantasy that they were damaged or injured was a reality. They feel inferior and inadequate, and accept this as reality. They may go through life with such an image of themselves and will be unable to ever feel complete. Any of these reactions can appear in the course of normal development without necessarily becoming important factors in later life. On the other hand, they may continue to operate throughout life and leave a lasting mark on the personality.

The impairing nature of such childhood fantasies prevents many women from achieving a full acceptance and enjoyment of themselves as women, and a full utilization of their talents and abilities. Freud may not have been right about the universal and persistent nature of penis envy, but he did point to an interference in development that is quite common. Freud also felt that the girl's wish to have a baby was a wish arising out of the wish to have a penis. We now know that girls show such wishes much earlier as part of an identification with their mothers, just as boys do. We discussed earlier that the normal girl already has a good sense of herself as a girl long before this phase, and therefore does not simply see herself as a boy without a penis. That does not mean that she may not have some fantasies of herself as a boy, just as a normal boy may have fantasies of being a girl. All children have such wishes, which they act out in the various roles they take on in their play. Such fantasies are normal, natural experiences, and, in fact, the increasing role of fantasy and the changing nature of these fantasies are central to the oedipal stage of development, as we shall now see.

THE OEDIPAL STAGE

This period in the child's development was designated as the *oedipal stage of development* as a consequence of Freud's description of the *Oedipus complex*. The name was chosen from Sophocles' tragic play *Oedipus Rex*, a play about a man who unknowingly murdered his father and eventually married his mother. He then blinded himself when he discovered what he had done. It seems a long way from such a story to what is now considered a normal phase of the child's development. What then does this "Oedipus complex" have to do with normal development?

For most of the first three years of life the child's world has centered on its relationship with the mother. Father has certainly had a role during that time, but one which, in the usual family, has not been as central as that of the mother. Why the child's focus now shifts to a *triangular relationship* is not certain. Various theories have been formulated , some describing a phylogenetically determined pattern of response, others a specific biological timetable, and still others a culturally determined change. We may not know for certain why this shift occurs, but it is not too difficult to observe if one looks at children between ages three and six. We will follow the development of the girl and the boy separately as they go through this experience. We will attempt to indicate the range of solutions possible and some of the ways these solutions will color the child's subsequent development.

In its simplest form, the oedipal stage means the time when the child develops a possessive attitude toward the parent of the opposite sex. Because of these wishes to have exclusive possession of that parent, the child is brought into a position of rivalry or conflict with the parent of the same sex. These rivalrous feelings are certainly complicated by the fact that there are always affectionate feelings toward the parent of the same sex and not just competitive rivalry and resentment. It is the balance between these feelings, based also on the real relationship with each of the parents, that determines the individual's unique experience during this phase of development and the nature of the resolution which is achieved.

In addition, we need to consider the child's mode of thinking. The child may express the wish to marry the parent of the opposite sex or the wish to have a baby with this parent. Marrying someone does not mean to a four year old what it means to an adult, nor does having a baby. The child's earlier experiences determine what such wishes mean, influenced by both the child's knowledge of the real world and the nature of the child's fantasies. Also, the child's thinking is still magical and preoperational. If a child is angry and wishes a parent to disappear, he or she may feel it will happen. Wishes and fantasies are not yet sharply discriminated from reality. They will become more so during these years. Let us turn to a consideration of this process.

THE GIRL'S OEDIPAL STAGE

The little girl of three has gone through some of the reactions we have just described in discovering that she is different from boys. She may have passed through this stage relatively uneventfully. Such a girl will continue to identify with her mother, and her dominant motivation in becoming more interested in father would be part of the wish to be like her mother and have what her mother has. Other girls may have had other experiences, as we indicated, and may still have feelings of having been deprived anatomically. Such girls frequently conclude that their fantasied deficit is mother's fault because it is the mother who produces the babies.

Children of this age really do not know exactly how babies are made, but they do have a pretty good idea that the mother has a lot to do with it. Frequently, in the child's thinking the father is left out of the process altogether. As a result, it is the mother who is blamed for the fact that the girl feels that she has been born in an incomplete form. This will be especially true if there are brothers in the family. After all, if mother was able to make them one way, why has she made the girl differently? Accompanying this common misconception, there is a turning away from the mother.

Such a girl may turn more strongly toward her father with a wish that he compensate for her feeling deprived. In any event, most girls will begin to turn toward their fathers with increasing interest. Some will still have very positive feelings toward the mother at this time, whereas others will be more disappointed or angry with her. All these will be factors in the intensity of the oedipal wishes and conflicts, and in the nature of their resolution. But if the girl is to take a step toward being able to have relationships with men in later life, it will begin with this turning toward the father. The nature of the father's reaction to his little girl's interest is of great importance. Fathers, for the most part, find it easier to demonstrate affection towards little girls than towards little boys, and many girls can be quite effective in eliciting this kind of response. During this phase the girl wants to have her father all to herself. She becomes very possessive of his attention, and will often be unwittingly humorous in her callous elimination of the mother from the family's plans. One little girl, for example, asked her mother at dinner, "How old are you, mommy?" When the mother asked why she wanted to know, the girl announced that she had just been wondering when the mother was going to die so that then she could marry daddy and keep house for him. Depending on where she was in this phase of development, she might decide that this would not really be such a good idea after all, because then she would not be able to go to school or play with her friends, but she first expresses her wish to take her mother's place. If you listen to children, it is not very difficult to hear them expressing wishes of this kind.

What does she want with her father? That is one of the areas where people get into difficulty, imagining that the child's thought processes are as sophisticated as those of the adult. The little girl wants her father for a great many things that one cannot express except in the most general terms. It is simple to say that she wants to marry him, but what does that mean to a little girl? It means that she wants the loving attention that her mother has. She already knows that there are two parents in the family, that they have some special private life together, and that she wants to be part of that life and have her father all to herself. She may want daddy to talk nicely to her, to cuddle and kiss her. She may want him for any of her many fantasies about what her parents do in private. It is very common for a girl of this age to say that she wants to have a baby with her father, but we cannot assume from this statement that she has any understanding of the specific prerequisites for producing a baby. Rather, she will want something in accordance with her fantasies, depending very much on her experiences, and the information that has been given to her. At any rate, however she perceives it, the little girl does want the exclusive possession of her father, and this wish will put her into conflict with her mother.

She will be torn by this conflict because for all children the wish for exclusive possession is an ambivalent feeling. For the entire three or four years of her life the little girl has been very much attached to her mother, and she will continue this attachment. As a matter of fact, just as she wishes to have exclusive possession of her father, so will she at other times want to have an exclusive relationship with her mother. At those times she may feel that her father is an intruder. The dominant picture at this time, however, will be a turning from the mother towards the father, a movement that will create conflict with her need and affection for her mother. The end result will enhance the girl's already established identification with her mother. Both girls and boys identify with their mothers in their earliest years. In the resolution of the oedipal stage, the girl's growing cognitive ability allows her to recognize that it is highly unlikely that she will ever achieve exclusive possession of her father, and that through that wish she runs the risk of alienating and angering her mother. She concludes that the best thing for her to do is to become as much as possible like the person who does have the father, so that one day she can marry someone like him (Figure 22.2).

When we discuss the boy's resolution of the oedipal phase, we will see that it is accompanied by a great amount of anxiety. There is no such similiar degree of anxiety involved in the girl's oedipal attachment to her father, nor is it brought to as abrupt an end as in the case with the boy. The only thing opposing it, outside of

Figure 22.2.   A four and one half year old girl with her mother's hat and her "own" telephone.

the recognition of the reality factor, is the child's mixed feelings towards her mother. She will not want to risk the loss of mother's love. But she will continue to have a close, intense, and romanticized relationship with her father through much of her childhood, a relationship which will certainly last until adolescence. It will be quite acceptable for the girl to want to flirt with her father, to sit on his lap, to want him to pay attention to her and to think that she is special. The girl's attachment to her father does not stop at the age of six, and it will still be acceptable for her to retain it as she moves into adolescence and even into adulthood. Not so long ago there was a tradition at women's colleges of having a "Fathers' Weekend," a time when the fathers came to visit their daughters and acted as their dates, the weekend culminating with a dance at which the fathers acted as their daughters' escorts. One cannot imagine such a weekend at a boys' school. Assuming that there are still some boys' schools left it is difficult to conceive of a "Mothers' Weekend" being held there.

For that matter, if a woman in our society chooses to marry a man who is 10 or even 15 years older than she, nobody seems particularly concerned. This is even more common in other cultures. In many societies it is expected that a man will marry a woman 15, 20, or more years younger than himself. Yet, if the reverse occurs, if a man chooses to marry a woman 10 or 15 years older than himself, people might be wondering what is wrong with him, perhaps joking that he is marrying his mother. Logically, there is no difference at all in the two situations, only in the attitude formed by the nature of the resolution of the Oedipus complex. While the girl is able to retain her ties to her father, the boy is forced to put aside his attachment to his mother.

One of the most important things that happens with even a partial resolution of the Oedipus complex is that there is an intensification of identification with the parent of the same sex and, along with this, an internalization of certain values and prohibitions. It has been said that the resolution of the Oedipus complex is what gives the superego a unique character. By superego, we mean, in a general way, the value system or conscience of an individual. At the time of the resolution of the Oedipus complex, this value system will have a childish quality. The little girl will have a set of ideas in her mind of what things she can do to please her parents and what things will displease them. There will be prohibitions — "Mommy does not like you to use certain words" — which are part of the superego, and a positive model — "Daddy likes you to be soft-spoken like Mommy" — which forms the *ego ideal*. But at age six, these ideas are still a very undeveloped guide for later behavior. They will be modified as development proceeds.

Freud believed that, because girls did not have as decisive and intense an ending to the oedipal stage of development as boys, they did not develop as strong or independent a superego. He felt that women did not have as powerful a value system as men, and that girls were not able to channel their conflicts into higher attainments as successfully as boys. These ideas are simply not true, stemming as they did from a misunderstanding of many aspects of female development. We know now that there are both earlier and later identifications which structure, modify, and contribute to the final superego organization in both men and women, and that both sexes are equally capable of developing strong, flexible, and independent consciences.

We have given you a very simplified picture of the normal process of the oedipal phase in the little girl. Of course, there are many variations in the way that resolution may occur. For example, the girl at this time decides that she will marry and have a baby just as her mother did. This is one group of experiences open to women, but in fact not every woman will choose to marry, or to stay home with little children. Whether or not the woman who chooses to live a different kind of life will be comfortable with these decisions will depend partly on the experiences and attitudes that were part of her environment as she proceeded in her development. She will have an early identification with her mother, and then later in life, a part of her own personality may come into conflict with this picture of what a woman should be. There may be things that change in her later development, such as societal attitudes that allow for other pathways and possibilities in life. She will have the opportunity as she goes on in her life to restructure some of these early identifications. The intensity of the identifications and the kinds of changes which occur in her life will determine whether or not she can resolve this successfully.

At this point in our society there is considerable questioning of the simple model of marriage-and-babies which most girls accepted as part of their ego ideal when they were very young. How will this affect current and future generations of women? How many will choose not to marry or not to have children? We do not know. That will depend upon many things. It should be clear, however, that there are innumerable variations possible for the girl going through the oedipal phase which can lead to a good integration of her personality structure. There are many different channels of development and ways in which one can fulfill one's potential which should not be labeled as pathological.

Some girls have trouble successfully going through the oedipal phase because of events which happened in their earlier development or in their family structures. Suppose, for example, that the father dies or abandons the family when the child is two. That little girl may be so disappointed in her experience of being female that she may feel like a failure as a woman. Another girl may be well into the oedipal phase when a little brother is born. She may feel envious of the boy, and this may revive earlier feelings that she had of feeling deprived as a girl. At the same time she may experience disappointment in her father because he gave a baby to her mother, and not to her. This girl might go backwards in her development, abandoning her attachment to her father and feeling that she could only capture her father's attention if she were a boy. This, of course, would depend upon the family constellation, on how men and women were viewed by the family, and on what kind of relationship she had observed between her mother and father.

There are also some women who never leave the oedipal stage. Such a girl goes on into adulthood feeling very much that she is still a little girl who wants her daddy all to herself. The problem is that she wants men just as the little girl wants her daddy. What this means is that what she wants from a man is to be held, to be comforted, and to be given all sorts of affection, but she stops short of a sexual relationship. Such women are often frightened of sex, perceiving the sexual relationship as they must have when they were children — as an activity in which they could be hurt, injured, and torn apart. They view men as big and frightening, people with whom they could not possibly anticipate having any kind of pleasurable sexual experience. Women like this are seen not infrequently. They are very good at getting men to want to be with them. They seem quite seductive, but they are totally unable to imagine anything in the way of an adult sexual relationship. They are really like little girls, arrested at the point in psychological development where they have turned toward a man, but never having gone beyond their original attachment to their fathers.

There are other common variants of sexual choice springing from the resolution of the oedipal stage. There are some women who will choose men who are very much like their fathers in looks or occupation or behavior. Other women, who have been severely disappointed by their fathers, will grow up expecting nothing from men, having the need to deprecate them or to compete with them unendingly, and hoping for little in the nature of a positive relationship.

We ought to emphasize the fact that the course which we have described for the girl is, as it will be for the boy, an oversimplification. For one thing, it presupposes an intact family with the father in the house, with the parents serving as caretakers, and without any special influence from siblings. There are countless other variations in the family structure which can still produce a child whose sexual behavior is within the normal range. For example, there are many households in which there has been a divorce, so that the father is less of an influence on the little girl's life than would otherwise be the case. What will happen to that child is variable, depending in part on whether a grandfather, uncle, or older brother is around to show her affection, in part on whether the mother remarries immediately, and in great part on the father's continued interest and the mother's ability to set aside her resentment of the father. We cannot go into all of the possible variations, but it is important to realize that it is not at all so simple a course as I have described. Our picture has been one-dimensional and schematic, like a laboratory drawing. But life is rarely that simple.

THE OEDIPAL STAGE IN THE BOY

Let us turn now to the parallel course of development in the boy, again presenting a somewhat schematic and oversimplified pattern. We saw that the girl had to switch her attachment from her mother to her father. The boy's initial attachment is to the mother, and this remains true through the oedipal phase. He does not have to make such a shift in his love object as does the girl. Instead he has to shift his identification from the mother to the father, and he also has to shift his role in relation to the woman, to move from a position in which he derives pleasure from a predominantly passive role to one in which he will have pleasure in an active relationship to the woman. In his early life, his pleasures came from things being done to him, from being bathed and fed and powdered and kissed. He has to move into a position where the roles are more evenly balanced, and he will also have to give up his mother as the object of his wishes and turn his interest to other women.

During the oedipal phase the boy moves into a possessive relationship with his mother and into a competitive relationship with his father. Just as with the girl, it is easy to recognize this when we listen to the talk of little children. While the boy likes and admires his father, he is also expressing sentiments of a very different nature when he delightedly waves goodbye to his father every morning and looks forward to remaining at home alone with his mother. When the father returns, he may be greeted in a somewhat ambivalent fashion, sometimes with a sharp blow to the stomach or a kick in the shins as he is presumably being embraced and welcomed home. The point is that there is ambivalence in the relationship and that the boy becomes aware that, in his wish to have exclusive possession of his mother, his father is his rival— not only a rival, but one with whom the boy cannot hope to compete successfully. He will want to be bigger than daddy, to be stronger than daddy, to have everything that daddy has, but he will soon gain the awareness that this is not realistic.

It is not as easy for the boy to deal with this as it is for the girl. She can go on loving her father while she is strengthening her identification with her mother. The little boy goes through a more frightening period. Children, you remember, believe that their parents know everything that they are thinking. When the little boy, therefore, is wishing that his father would just go away so that he could be alone with his mother, he is also convinced that his father knows what he is thinking. And he is afraid that, should the father know what he wants to do to him, then father will retaliate.

He may have different levels of fear of his father, but we know that among these fears, he will probably develop the idea that his father will castrate him. This does not make much sense to an adult. After all, fathers do not do such things to their children. They do not even threaten castration. Why, then, should the boy have such a fear? It is based partly upon his recent awareness and observation of the difference between himself and a girl. For the little boy, the observation of the girl's genitals is demonstrable proof that such a thing as castration can happen. We said earlier that children all believe that everyone is originally made as they are, and that when boys notice that girls do not have a penis, then they fear that theirs could be taken away from them. Their penis is now also a source of pleasurable sensations, including fantasies of being as strong and as powerful as father. These fantasies are the source of great anxiety, the fear being that the father will know about these thoughts and punish the boy for having them. It is the body part which offends that will be punished in the boy's thoughts. It is this castration anxiety which makes the boy's passage through the oedipal phase much more tumultuous than the girl's. This fear puts him under much more pressure to modify the nature of his oedipal wishes and to give them up compared to the girl. The worst thing that the girl can imagine happening to her as a result of her oedipal wishes is that her mother will not love her any more. This is a bad enough prospect, but one which does not have the intensity of the boy's fear of physical punishment and castration. It is for this reason that the boy's oedipal phase comes to a more abrupt end than the girl's.

As we saw a little earlier, most boys will show the effects of this conflictual period for some years afterwards. They will, typically, be frightened of girls, avoiding contact with them whenever it is possible. If you have ever worked with a group of children of around six years of age, you know that it is very difficult to get them to join hands and form a circle. The boys do not even want to touch the hands of the girls. They act as though there is something especially frightening about girls, something which is a reminder of the danger that they imagine they have passed through so recently. This is the age when little boys are interested in supermasculine role models. The boy wants to be a policeman or an astronaut or a soldier, an almost caricatured masculine role which protects him from the dangers of anything which threatens his masculinity. This is the period when the boy,

realizing that he cannot defeat his father, decides that he might as well join him, and moves into a phase of wanting to be like his dad. He not only internalizes the idea of masculinity, but even exaggerates it somewhat. He also internalizes certain models of behavior which he acquires from his father.

There is a series of prohibitions which will form his superego, but these prohibitions have a particularly childlike quality to them, as is the case with the girl. For example, one of the things that the little boy believes at this time is that he should not get too much pleasure or excitement from contact with his mother. If he is to grow up able to have the capacity to enjoy a relationship with a woman, he will have to modify this childhood stance in later years. Therefore, there is not a fixed structuralization of the supergo at this point. It is rather that certain basic tendencies get organized now, and a particular imprint on the personality is determined.

A boy can go through as many different variations in his oedipal development as the girl does. There are men who never outgrow their fear of women, who remain all their lives like the six or seven year old who deprecates girls and runs around trying to scare them. We see other men who seek to reassure themselves constantly throughout their lives about their masculinity, largely because of residual anxiety from the oedipal stage. They will restrict their learning experiences to what are considered masculine pursuits, denying any interest in music or poetry. When they are fathers they may be outraged at the notion that they might occasionally give the child a bottle or wheel the baby carriage, fearing that this might make them less masculine.

There are other disturbances of greater and lesser magnitude which come from different resolutions of the oedipal stage. Suppose, for example, that there is a father who is altogether too overwhelming for his little boy, who constantly puts him down, teases him, and belittles him. The child may feel at a total loss. He can never compete or win against such a father, and he may give up the idea that he might ever hope to be like his father or get someone like his mother. This boy may regress or retreat in his development, deciding that the safest thing for him to do is to submit and to please his father, since the danger of competing with him is too great. He may grow up to be a rather passive and submissive person. Possibly he may become someone who is latently or overtly homosexual, a man who finds it safer to be in the company of men than in the company of women. Of course, this is not the only determinant of *homosexual behavior*. Countless factors contribute to such an outcome, an outcome sometimes fixed even before the oedipal stage. An impaired sense of early gender identity, an overly intense attachment to one's own body, and various body traumas are just a few factors contributing to later homosexuality. Nor does the father have to be domineering and threatening. An absent or weak father can fail to provide enough of a model of masculinity and this can lead to a similar result. We call these patterns negative resolutions of the oedipal conflict, which cause boys to abandon any competitive feelings toward men and, instead, seek the love and approval of men by submitting to them. At the same time they are usually unable to love a woman.

There are also men who display unresolved positive attachments to a parent. We all know men who are bachelors 40 or 50 years old who live at home with their mothers. The father may be dead or merely unimportant in the family structure, while the mother remains for these men their primary love object. Other men, because of their ambivalent attachments to their mothers, divide women into two categories. These men have one category of nice girls, girls who resemble their mothers and sisters in some aspect, but with whom they cannot have a sexual relationship. Then there is another category of girls who by their education, ethnic background, socioeconomic level, or appearance are different from the women in their families. These women are safer, which in this case means nonincestuous, and with them a sexual relationship is possible. It may not, however, be accompanied by any feelings of tenderness or affection. This is a phenomenon which is not unusual among adolescents and often occurs transiently in the course of growing up. Most people are able to go beyond this and to develop relationships in which sexuality and tenderness are combined toward the same woman. Some men never achieve that. They can feel love or affection for their wives or girl friends, but can only enjoy sex with someone else.

Sexual dysfunctions in both women and men are also at least partially based on unresolved conflicts from this stage of development. We need not go on with the whole range of sexual malfunctions; it is enough to say that most of the problems which physicians encounter in this area are at least partially related to difficulties in the resolution of oedipal conflicts. This is one of the reasons psychiatrists are interested in this stage of development. Another is that what we call *neurotic symptoms* make their first appearance at this time and may have significant influences on later functioning. The most prominent of these symptoms are nightmares and phobias. Neurotic symptoms in adults willl be discussed later in the book, but perhaps a few words about the *symptom disorders of childhood* are in order here.

CONFLICT AND SYMPTOMS — NIGHTMARES AND PHOBIAS

If we return to the average expectable reactions of children around the oedipal stage of life, then we notice that it is normal for children to develop certain symptoms at this time. For example, there will be a great many disturbances in sleep patterns. Children have trouble going to sleep and, once asleep, they will be awakened by *nightmares.* Why are they afraid to go to sleep (Figure 22.3)? Because Frankenstein is hiding in the closet or because Dracula might

AFRAID OF THE DARK

I'm Reginald Clark, I'm afraid of the dark
So I always insist on the light on,
And my teddy to hug,
And my blanket to rub,
And my thumby to suck or to bite on.
And three bedtime stories,
Two trips to the toilet,
Two prayers, and five hugs from my mommy,
I'm Reginald Clark, I'm afraid of the dark
So please do not close this book on me.

Figure 22.3. "Afraid of the Dark." From *Where The Sidewalk Ends.* The Poems and Drawings of Shel Silverstein. Copyright © 1974 by Shel Silverstein. By permission of Harper & Row Publishers, Inc., New York.

come in the window. These fears, fantastic as they seem to the adult, are perfectly expectable at this age, in part due to the still immature state of the ego. It is a time when children begin to develop transient *phobias*. They are afraid of dogs, robbers, tigers, or monsters. These fears are extremely common, and they usually resolve themselves in a few years.

Let us return to the little boy who is in a very ambivalent relationship with his father. He wishes that his father would go away, or even that his father would die. He also is afraid that his father knows just what he is thinking. At the same time, he also loves his father, enjoys being with him, and wants to be just like him. This is a dreadful predicament for the child. How can he go on having such intense conflicting feelings? One way in which children of this age handle such feelings is by the formation of a phobia, a fear which has an adaptive value for them. They take the conflict that they are experiencing in relationship to their parents, and they displace it onto some outside object so that they do not have to experience both love and fear for the same person. The child may suddenly develop the fear that a dog is going to bite him, even though he has never had a bad experience with a dog. Or he may be unable to go to sleep at night because a tiger might come into his room, no matter how many times you assure him that there are no tigers in the neighborhood. The point is that the fear has been displaced from the father onto an object which is easier to avoid. The boy who is having hostile wishes toward his father and is afraid that his father will retaliate against him for those wishes will displace the whole conflict onto gorillas. It would be intolerable for him to have to live in the same house with someone of whom he is so afraid, and it is much easier to avoid the zoo than to avoid his father. In this way, he is handling his conflict by the formation of certain symptoms.

In most children, these symptoms are time-limited. They disappear as the child moves on in development and becomes more comfortable with his own feelings. In other people, such fears persist throughout life, but even in these people they may not seriously interfere with functioning. Many phobias can be present without an interference in adaptation. If a man or a woman has a fear of heights, that need not interfere with their life at all. They can just avoid skyscrapers, airplanes, and driving in the mountains and can function quite successfully. Some of these fears, when they persist into adult life, may become personality traits which have lost their connection with the conflicts which originally caused them, and may lead to a *phobic* or *avoidant personality structure* — people who are constricted by unrealistic fears throughout life and use avoidance to deal with these fears.

Phobias in children can be most troubling to parents and, therefore, are often brought to the attention of physicians. Sooner or later you may very well be asked about a child who has developed a sudden intense fear, and the parents will want to know if something should be done about it. The answer, most of the time, is no. Only if it interferes grossly with the child's functioning should there be any consideration of initiating treatment to help the child. Consider, for example, the child who is afraid of dogs. His family might simply decide not to buy a dog until he is over this problem. But if that fear is not limited, but rather begins to spread, i.e., if the child begins to avoid going outside the house or to school or to other children's houses because he might see a dog there, then his present functioning and his future development could be affected. If this freedom to function is constricted by the symptom, then we would think that something should be done to help the child to understand and overcome the fear. But by and large, nightmares and transient phobias occur as the result of the child's attempts to deal with his or her oedipal conflicts and they do not ordinarily require intervention.

INITIATIVE VS. GUILT

Most children will emerge from this conflictual time of life very much changed. Perhaps the most important change has to do with the structuralization of the superego and the ego ideal. What this means is that there is a shift from conflicts in which the child's wishes come into opposition with the outside world to one in which there is now mainly *intrapsychic conflict*. The child's unacceptable wishes will be opposed by an internalized agency, the superego, and guilt arising from disapproval by the superego becomes the last danger situation. In Erik Erikson's terms, the child will either develop an increasing *initiative* and sense of mastery as a result of this regulatory agency, or else be burdened by an exaggerated feeling of *guilt* over inner drives and wishes.

What happens to these childhood conflicts?

Surely most people do not remember very much from that time of their lives. It is because of a defense mechanism called *repression* which keeps certain memories of feelings and events from consciousness — they remain unconscious. In later life we will see the effects of these experiences or derivatives of them. Only in children can we observe them directly. Much of the first five or six years is not available to us as conscious memories. For most people, remembrances of childhood start with the grade school years except for an isolated memory or two. This is one reason why much of what I have been saying will seem so strange and foreign to most people unless they observe it in their children or in patients whom they treat. Others, of course, learn about it if they themselves undergo psychotherapy or psychoanalysis. There is much that is strange and mysterious in the mind of the child and in the unconscious, but we need to learn about it if we wish to understand some of the disturbed patterns of functioning to which we as physicians will be exposed, as well as to understand more about the normal functioning of children.

Suggested Readings

Bibring GL, Kahana RJ: Sexual differentiation; the oedipus complex and its resolution. In *Lectures in Medical Psychology*. New York, International Universities Press, 1968, p 84.

English OS, Pearson GHJ: Irrational fears and phobias. In Harrison SI, McDermott JF (eds): *Childhood Psychopathology*. New York, International Universities Press, 1972, p 375.

Erikson EH: Initiative vs. guilt. In *Childhood and Society*. New York, W.W. Norton, 1950, p 224.

Fraiberg SH: Three years to six. In *The Magic Years*. New York, Charles Scribner's Sons, 1959, pp 179–282.

Lidz T: The preschool child. In *The Person*. New York, Basic Books, 1976, p 195.

Lidz T: Childhood integration. In *The Person*. New York, Basic Books, 1976, p 246.

Mussen PH, Conger JJ, Kagan J, Huston AC: The preschool years. In *Essentials of Child Development and Personality*. New York, Harper & Row, 1984.

Prugh DG: *The Psychosocial Aspects of Pediatrics*. Philadelphia, Lea & Febiger, 1983.

References

Blum H (ed): Supplement on Female Psychology. *J Am Psychoanal Assoc* 24: 1976.

Jacobson E: Development of the wish for a child in boys. *Psychoanal Study Child* 5:139, 1950.

Maccoby EE, Jacklin CN: *The Psychology of Sex Differences*. Stanford, Stanford University Press, 1974.

Money J, Ehrhardt AA: *Man and Woman, Boy and Girl*. Baltimore, The Johns Hopkins University Press, 1972.

Nelson JB: Anlage of productiveness in boys: womb envy. In Harrison SI, McDermott JF (eds): *Childhood Psychopathology*. New York, International Universities Press, 1972, p 360.

Ross JM: The development of paternal identity: a critical review of the literature of nurturance and generativity in boys and men. *J Am Psychoanal Assoc* 23:783, 1975.

Schafer R: Problems in Freud's psychology of women. *J Am Psychoanal Assoc* 22:459, 1974.

Stoller RJ: The sense of maleness. In *Sex and Gender*. New York, Science House, 1968, p 39.

Stoller RJ: The sense of femaleness. In *Sex and Gender*. New York, Science House, 1968, p 50.

CHAPTER 23 Sociology: Changes in Family Structure and Their Impact on Medical Practice

Emily Mumford, Ph.D.

The family in any society, as many marriage rituals specify, is supposed to manage its members "in sickness and in health," and everywhere the family and the patterns of response to illness are intricately intertwined. However, we have a family system that provides limited resources for coping with infirmity, and this becomes a special problem since we also have such great expectations about what should be done in response to illness.

OUR FAMILY SYSTEM

Four characteristics of our family are remarkable, and each of these characteristics has implications for medicine. First, the units of this system tend to be *small*. Second, they are *geographically mobile*. Third, the units are packed with affect and *very breakable*, though paradoxically the larger system made up of them appears quite durable. Fourth, many of the functions, which have been managed primarily by the family in other cultures, have been *redistributed* away from the family, and into other institutions. It should be clear that not all families in this country follow this same pattern, which is a product of the middle class members of industrialized societies and urban environments. However, elements of both the positive and negative aspects of this system appear so frequently and with such impact on health statistics that close attention should be paid to them. Each of these characteristics of our family system implies increasing demands on modern medicine and its practitioners, and these same characteristics are also related to the preeminence of medical experts in our society, the competition to gain admission to the medical profession, and the emergence of the giant medical centers.

VARIATIONS IN FAMILY SYSTEMS

Before turning to the contemporary family we should briefly establish where it fits in the range of family forms across different cultures. First, our family system is *monogamous*. The legal and social expectation is one wife to one husband—at least at any one time. One might more accurately say we have a form of "serial monogamy." A second structural variation in family systems is the pattern of descent, i.e., *patrilineal* following the father's line, or *matrilineal* following the mother's line, or *bilineal* where both the male and female parents are considered of equal importance in regard to descent.

The place where the newly married couple is supposed to live tends to follow the pattern of descent, though there are exceptions. The term *patrilocal* refers to the pattern in which the new couple moves into the residence of the groom's father. The *matrilocal* family lives in the home of the bride. Our pattern is *neolocal*, that is the young family is expected to set up its own new home. *Patriarchal* and *matriarchal* designate where the power or authority is supposed to rest. Here, as with other aspects of family systems, the terms designate what is either expected or socially preferred or legally sanctioned. But in any system not every family conforms to a dominant pattern, and this is probably especially true in the matter of power, where personality factors have large play. For example, an American male temporarily in Saudi Arabia inquired wistfully of an English-speaking Mohammedan business man, "Why do you only have one wife, when your wealth, religion, and the law all would allow four?" The Mohammedan marriage is referred to as patriarchal, and yet the Arabian husband's response was, "My wife won't let me!" American marriages are often referred to as *companionate*, suggesting a partnership of equals, but here also the reality often varies from the norm. However, in spite of exceptions, the dominant family structure of society does influence what the social expectations are, what is likely to happen, and how large numbers of people will probably behave.

UNIVERSAL FUNCTIONS OF THE FAMILY

Except in philosophy, fiction, or utopian experiments, the family everywhere serves several essential functions for its society. These universals are reproduction, protection, socialization, status placement of the child, social control, channeling of affect (or designating whom one can and should love), and physical maintenance and care for its members. Societies vary remarkably in the extent to which the family is left as the primary institution to fulfill these functions, and societies also vary in the way these functions are structured.

Plato among others envisioned a society without families in which reproduction would be seasonal, and defective children and those born out of season in the Republic would simply be eliminated. All other children were to be separated from the biological mother, and the social control of children, as well as the care and maintenance of them, would be out of the hands of the family. Consequently, the child's position in the society would be beyond family influence.

Since the *Republic*, other philosophers as well as social reformers and religious leaders have also proposed reallocation of family functions. Some say the wish to eliminate the family expressed by certain philosophers has its origins in the personal problems that each one of them had experienced with his own family. Others insist that these reformers and philosophers were facing an inevitable fact—that redistribution of family functions is the only way to achieve true equality of opportunity for children. Among the 19th century American social experiments, Oneida and the early Mormon colonies each sought to create a perfect society by restructuring the family to conform to ideals set forth by their religious leaders. The early Soviet kolhoz and the Israeli kibbutz were developed to give trained experts, instead of parents, primary responsibilities for socialization, maintenance, and social control. Such a system obviously tends to equalize opportunities for children by removing the variables of the family's position and its social, intellectual, and material resources as influences on the child's opportunities.

To date, none of these experiments has succeeded in spreading far enough into society to eliminate families. Most of the experimental colonies that have survived eventually developed accommodations to allow small nuclear families to exist within and around them. Thus, it seems that in theory the family can be eliminated, but in history it has demonstrated durability as the basic mediating agency that links individuals to society with all the good and bad that this implies.

Harry Stack Sullivan once wrote that people everywhere are more alike than different. This is as true of families as it is of individuals. But in both cases, the differences that do exist can have important consequences. The mother-infant unit, biologically determined, is at the core of every family system, but from there on a wide range of social inventions determines what is expected—and what usually follows. In addition to the mother and her infants, each family system includes in its units some male, either the biological father, the putative father, or someone with socially designated responsibilities to the unit. This unit, the *nuclear family* of a female and her children and an adult male, is apparently universal.

The earliest mother-infant interaction is also probably more alike than different from one culture to another. But the length of time allowed for this close relationship, the exclusiveness of it, and the social approval of its continuation as a basic bond vary widely from one society to another. We tend to assume that everywhere husbands and wives love each other and that parents love their children. But what is sometimes called our *affectionate family* may be a relatively rare form. The apparently cold acceptance of ubiquitous infant death in Europe between 1500 and 1700 is hard for us to fathom, and so is the fact that in mid-19th century England several attempts had to be made before a law was passed to prohibit hiring children under 10 for arduous factory work (Figure 23.1). Evidence of increasing personal concern by husbands and fathers from the early 18th century on, particulary among affluent families, is offered by steadily increasing expenditures on

Figure 23.1. Lower class children at work in a factory in 18th century England. From the film *Invention of the Adolescent*. (By permission of Perennial Education Inc., 1825 Willow Road, Northfield, Illinois 60093.)

wives and children—clothes, books, pets, jewelry, and toys,

Incest taboos appear universal, though how many different relatives are considered "off limits" also varies. In addition everywhere the family appears to fulfill the essential functions for its society, but the extent to which the family carries the sole or primary reponsibility for managing these functions varies. All of these functions except for reproduction and affection are shared by other agencies in our society.

SMALL NUCLEAR FAMILIES AND SOME CONSEQUENCES

Our family units seldom have more than two generations in one household, as witnessed by the emergence of nursing homes and retirement villages as a major industry. This system of small nuclear families in contrast to the larger *extended family* has also been found in some primitive societies. For example, the Indians of Interior Canada had a form similar to ours. It is also a form which appears adapted for the social change and geographic mobility necessary in industrialized areas. Its units can move rather easily in response to the opportunities and demands of the work market. Ours is a family system compatible with, and dependent on, highly developed institutions that take over a

large share of family functions including physical care and maintenance.

Modern medical practice and the institution of medicine (as it has been elaborated in this society) and our family system are highly interdependent. The medical sector needs families to produce many able, highly motivated aspirants willing to compete for admission to medical school, and willing to postpone today's pleasure in favor of future occupational positions. The medical system also needs a large public ready to turn to the medical expert for help with a wide range of problems and disposed to cooperate with technically competent advice. The family in turn needs medical experts to fulfill many functions that extended families have managed in other places and other times.

Absence of extended kin leaves the couple somewhat free and beyond the control of their parents, but they are also without the help of those kin who, living together, could provide aid, especially when sickness occurs or when a new member is born to the little unit. Moreover, the couple in the nuclear unit who presumably married for "love," are somewhat adrift in a society where most transactions are with strangers or acquaintances. This, of course, intensifies the role of feelings between the marital partners. In other systems, kinsmen engaged in cooperative tasks are available to dissipate intense emotion between the marital partners or at least to provide other possible alliances within the family group of adults. In contrast, the small family where affect is concentrated appears resistant to intrusion on its personal as well as its physical boundaries. Its members are expected to lavish attention on each other, almost exclusively. It is too small to accommodate an extra adult comfortably, and its members tend to be jealous over affection as well as over punishment.

A student from Nigeria once told me that one of the first things that struck him in New York City occurred as he walked by a play yard. There were children playing and one little boy was teasing a little girl to the point of tears. Several female adults appeared to ignore the exchange until at last the little boy's mother noticed. This, the student said, would have been inconceivable in the village where he grew up. Any child misbehaving in this way would be spanked by any female in a village where everyone was related. By the same token, the student from Nigeria said that in his village any child who cried would be picked up by any woman because most of the women were related in one way or another, and practically anybody could feed the child and did. In contrast to this we do not even like strangers or other people to feed our pets, let alone punish our children.

There is a growing concern about the battered child in this society. The extent to which abuse of children has become more visible as more people appear at emergency rooms instead of in the offices of local physicians and the extent to which it actually has increased in incidence is at this moment not known. There is some indication that it might actually be on the increase. However, in the long perspective of history, what is new is that we now find it so shocking that a parent might either mistreat or neglect a child. The stresses and strains imposed by the rather isolated small family, the confined living space in cities, and the great expectations we have for how much parents should do for children, all impose tremendous strain on parents of young children, and it is to the medical and educational sector that they turn with the hope that "somebody will do something."

GEOGRAPHIC MOBILITY

We are a remarkably mobile population. Little family units on wheels go off on vacation. The first home of a bride and groom is often too small as children arrive and grow, so the family moves. After children grow up and leave home, the couple may again search about for a new home for retirement, perhaps in Florida or California.

Frank Lloyd Wright once said that he thought the United States was tilted to the West so that everything loose lands in Southern California. Californians think that everybody is moving in on them and one year 33,000 arrived to settle there from Nebraska alone. But the same year, about 10,000 went the other way, leaving California for Nebraska. In one recent year one million people left the farm to live in cities. But that same year one half a million people moved from city to farm. For every two people moving from city to suburb, between one and two persons move from suburb to city. Moving is big business. In some suburbs within a five year period, half the people had moved from one house to another or from one suburb to another or to a city, or a small town.

Geographic mobility, except in nomadic tribes, implies that young people separate from their parents. It is difficult to move all your cousins and your aunts and your grandparents unless you travel by camel and live in a tent. Urbanization and specialization are other factors that have contributed to change in the kind of family system we have. Social mobility through occupational efforts also impels moves from one home to another. The son who aspires to a better life style than his father's is approved of in our society, but this has not always been so.

BREAKABLE FAMILIES

In many societies, affection between husband and wife is not a necessary requirement for stability, nor for choice of a partner. However, family units such as ours which tend to be created out of emotion, can also be torn apart by emotion. If there is great expectation for the amount of emotional satisfaction expected in marriage, then the potential for great disappointment is also high, and if the reason for marriage is "love," then it follows that not being "in love" might become a reason for separation. Since it is assumed that "love and marriage" go together, when love disappears dissolution and a search for new partners often follow.

One in three marriages now ends in divorce, and the ratio appears to be moving rapidly toward one in every two marriages. The paradox is that with such instability of individual units, the system is still viable. We are among the most avid creators of family units. This little, fragile, isolated unit, full of affect, is still most important statistically and also socially. Between the ages of 35 and 45 some 86% of the males in this society are married—as are a little over 85% of the females. An additional 6% are formerly married and perhaps looking to do it again. The remarriage rate is very high.

Most societies have not had such a high proportion of the people in this age range married. There were other places people could go or stay instead of forming a new family unit. There was religion, for example, and there was physical as well as psychological and social support available within the extended family for unmarried aunts or uncles who could live out their lives going to the same family gatherings and being an integral part of the fabric of their society without having to form their own family through marriage. The persistent findings that the formerly married are at risk physically as well as psychologically are consistent with the idea that for many people marriage provides a required emotional attachment, a mooring in a sea of strangers.

Other factors contribute to the breakdown of family units, as Dr. Simons and Dr. Strauss will indicate in a later chapter on separation and divorce. In a rapidly changing society one partner can develop or progress upward at a faster pace than the other, leaving someone who was once a close companion, now embittered and out of place in a new social context. Also, increasing numbers of women work. Being able to earn enough so that they can support themselves, wives as well as husbands are more free than previously to decide that this romantic love was not "the real thing."

Our system does put a terrible burden on the young to pick their own mate rather than having elders select one on possibly more rational grounds. While this "do it yourself" mate selection is somewhat rare in the history of family forms, it works in a way, and our divorce statistics do not necessarily mean that we have more or less happiness in marriage than former societies, where most partners, once they were married, had practically no options for change.

VARIATIONS IN DISTRIBUTION OF FAMILY FUNCTIONS

In many societies it is the family that provides the ultimate physical *protection* for its members. Shakespeare's plays about the War of the Roses, where family fought against family, are examples. At that time the family that fought together was able to stay together. Today, institutions, such as the military and the police, take over this function. The state is empowered to intercede if a child's parents do not protect it, or if they are abusive. In many other societies the parental rights over children have been complete, even to the extent of infanticide. *Care and maintenance* of children, while still provided by the family, are sometimes shared by state or voluntary agencies. Care and maintenance of aged family members increasingly take place outside the family, and so does care for the sick child or adult.

The responsibility for *socialization* of children at increasingly younger ages is now shared between the family and the educational system. Nursery school, kindergarten, and elementary school all place children outside the family and in narrowly restricted age groups under the charge of someone unrelated but trained, the teacher. In such conditions, the chance for identification with peers rather than with the family is enhanced. The commitment to separateness of education from the family is exemplified when a child, whose mother is a teacher, is carefully assigned to someone else. Even for the very young child still entirely within the family, outside guidance via "experts" is almost regularly pursued. This sharing of responsibility for the socialization of children has its advantages, especially in view of what I have described thus far about the fragility of the small, isolated nuclear family.

Through the educational system much of *social control* also moves from family and teacher to peer groups, which have the power to create fads and fancies in clothing, music, and manners, and to generate norms that have a powerful hold over their members. At early ages the child begins to become more dependent on approval of peers. Ultimately *status placement* moves out of the hands of family and even peers and into the arena where careers are forged—the higher educational system. Often the family has limited access even to know what goes on in that arena.

In contrast to the situation of guilds or family farms or family businesses, young members of our society must go out to learn an occupation. Even when a son plans to enter the same field as his father, if the career is in a profession, the father is empowered to handle neither his son's education nor his licensing. Sons and daughters are thus separated geographically, physically, and intellectually from their parents. Consistent with this, the value climate in our society holds *achieved status* as far more important than *ascribed status*, i.e., that given by birth.

In the extreme cases, such as societies built on a caste system, birth determines which people shall be untouchable. In feudal societies, one's family determines who shall be king and who shall be a serf, and the occupations that people in between can follow. At the other end of the continuum, where other institutions including religious, occupational, and economic systems are fully developed and relatively independent of the family, the child's life chances are not so fully determined by birth. However, even in these situations the early socialization that parents provide out of their own life experience influences where their child is likely to go and the options he or she is likely to perceive.

As the developing individual spends decreasing amounts of time with the family, its potential for social control is compromised. True, by virtue of tastes and values developed partly in the family, the range of mates likely to be considered is strongly influenced by the family. However, the search for a mate to form a new family takes place largely within the peer group and away from the family. College students away from home seek and find their own mates, and parents may be informed or introduced only after the couple has come to its own decision, and parents unwilling to risk alienating their offspring may try to learn to live with the choice. Moreover, since the expected basis for mate selection appears to be romantic love—something which to date has been much eulogized and defamed but never objectified—rational or other arguments by parents are unlikely to carry much weight, and the parents in our society seldom have powerful social or economic sanctions available to them to lend force to their arguments.

Channeling of affect or emotional ties is the one function that is probably left more to the family in our system than has usually been the case in other societies. By virtue of the way family members respond to him daily, and which ones he sees most often, by virtue of the people with whom he is allowed to be, and also those he is supposed to avoid, the child gains an impression of where his primary ties are supposed to be, whom he is expected to love, and even which categories of people are outsiders or enemies. The tragedy of *Romeo and Juliet* suggests the personal consequences when expected affiliations and enmities are not honored by offspring in a family system different from ours. Similar tragic endings to romantic out-of-bounds attachments appear in the literature of Ancient China, of Japan, and of India. In each of these societies the extended family was the primary source for socialization, maintenance, social control, and for defining social status, and mate selection was very definitely the business of the parents. It would follow that affective ties strong enough to impel a couple to marry — when they are generated outside the expected or approved lines — would elicit powerful sanctions.

Where partners are selected by the extended family and held together by them rather than by the husband-wife bond, introduction of a second or a fourth or even a fortieth wife does not necessarily challenge the family unit. The two forms of *polygamous* marriage — *polyandry* (multiple husbands) and *polygyny* (multiple wives) — do not depend primarily on affect or on what we would term romantic love between man and wife to hold the family together. In the first place, the status difference between male and female in most polygamous systems militates against the couple's forming the kind of ties that in themselves would be strong enough to assure stability. In the second place, the marrying couple may have seen each other only briefly, if at all, before the marriage ceremony. In marriage they are held together by the potentially powerful sanctions of extended families.

Among the polyandrous Toda, a buffalo herding group high in the hills of South India, one female marries one male, but at the same time becomes the wife to all his brothers. Marital privileges rotate among the brothers, generally by the month. With pregnancy there is no need, fortunately, to determine the biological father. Brothers decide as a group who shall "give the bow" in a ceremony prior to birth and the term "father" among the Todas includes all males of the father's clan and generation. Primary loyalty and bonds are expected to rest between brothers and between sons and father, rather than any male and a wife.

The contrast between our contemporary family and that of the Irish farmers of County Clare illustrates the significance of differences between two systems which at first appear similar. The Irish countryman family is monogamous as is ours, and *patronymic*, i.e., the bride takes the groom's name. However, the Irish family, unlike ours, is patrilocal and also its marriage units appear more durable and apparently provide more continuity between generations than does our system.

As described by Conrad Arensberg, when the "old man" or the head of an Irish family of County Clare decided that it was time for him to step down and turn over his land to one son of his choosing, he let it be known that he was "casting about" for a proper bride for his son to start a new family. A first choice selected, the father would then send a neighbor "matchmaker" to find out whether the girl's father would like to "join families." If the answer was positive, then a long series of negotiations was set in motion between the two families and the matchmaker. The father of the girl might "walk the land" with the son's father to determine the worth of the property to which his daughter would move, "whether there be good water and the condition of the buildings," and therefore the amount of dowry that should go with her. In a sequence of bargaining sessions, laced with whiskey, toasts, and sometimes "blarney" and humor, the two "old men," the matchmaker, and the chosen son negotiated terms for a marriage contract that would set in motion an extensive shift of roles in both families.

Marriage contracts were elaborate documents that usually specified the rights of the "old man" and the "old lady" in the house as well as the terms of the dowry the bride would bring. The use of a cow and the best room of their house might be reserved for the groom's parents. The contract drawn and the marriage performed, the old couple moved into their room and the bride arrived. Children followed and pretty soon the circle was completed. The dowry that the bride brought provided a dowry for a daughter on the groom's side so she could then be married and move to a new home. Any additional money provided some funds for sons who were not to inherit the land. It was at this time that other children of the family might be impelled to "travel," i.e., go out to find work away from the land, a pattern that contributed as much as the potato famines did to emigration from Ireland to America.

Such a system that delayed marriage until the "old man" decided it was time for him to step down in favor of one son, not surprisingly, was one where marriages occurred late, and where unmarried males living with the parents were referred to as "boys" even though they might be in their 40's, a pattern that probably imposed considerable strain on young men so dependent on their father and his decisions. In 1930, in County Clare, only 12% of the males aged 30 to 35 were married. Contrast this with the comparable statistics in the United States at the same time when 76% of all the males aged 30 to 35 were married.

It is obvious that in this situation the "boys" in the family were under a combination of economic, occupational, social, and other pressures to stand by the marriage contract once it was signed. The potential for social control of young adults was enhanced by several aspects of this system. On the small farms and also in small shops, families worked together in interrelated tasks that made for a high degree of visibility of each member's performance. Any behavior that might threaten the family's solidarity or standing in the community could be sanctioned quickly and effectively before it became a habit. Both males and females who wanted to stay on the land were obliged to learn their adult roles from their parents rather than from an "expert" in the educational system. In such a setting, "the way my father did it" could more legitimately be invoked as justification for any action than it could ever be in occupational settings characterized by learning outside the family, by rapid change, and by obsolescence.

Moreover, the young adults were dependent on parents for decisions about when and whom to marry. The "girl" needed a dowry and the "boy" needed his father's decision to turn over his land. After marriage, since the new couple lived in the home of the groom's parents, it would be surprising if many of them could ever become very independent of those parents. Since both sets of in-laws had created the marriage they often were motivated to see that it lasted. Their families were joined in a society that referred to extended kin as the "friends," or the people on whom one can depend to help out in times of need. In this system, as late as the 1930's, birth, sickness, and death were primarily managed within the family setting.

CONSEQUENCES OF REDISTRIBUTION OF FAMILY FUNCTIONS

In contrast to the Irish farm family of County Clare, where religious, family, and economic commitments on behalf of marital stability could be reinforced by the social structure, our families have rather limited means of social control over their young adult members. Social control rests more with peers, first in school and later in occupations. There is less continuity between generations. There is less stability of the marital relationship, and individuals in this family system are much more dependent on external agencies to serve a wide range of functions.

Scientific advance makes its own contribution to disjunction between generations and contributes a force for reliance on experts rather than tradition. In science the father cannot really educate his son in the most up-to-date methods or the latest findings. The young man who has just completed his Ph.D. degree in a highly specialized area is far ahead of his father in terms of the latest information, and sometimes even ahead of the methods of the professor who taught him. This tends to break down the expectation that tradition, or the older generation's reply that "it has always been done this way," is the best basis for action.

Technological advance also has the same kind of consequence. With the advent of the computer, the old accountant, no matter how good he was when young, is out of date in his methods and information unless he has made consistent efforts to keep abreast of the rapid advances and changes in his field.

Rapid change and small families impel people to seek help from experts for an increasing array of problems. Specialized competence through education and license rather than kinship determines whose advice is considered best. The most interesting aspect of redistribution of family functions is the *caring function*. In the past, the family has been largely responsible for whatever care its family members might receive "in sickness and in health."

In medieval Europe and into the 18th century, birth and also most care of the nonindigent sick and, therefore death, was intimately woven into the fabric of family life. The adult individual was assumed to be the best judge of whether he was dying, and he was supposed to decide when to call for the sacrament of extreme unction. He knew the ritual. He had seen it often before and at first hand in a society characterized by high birth and death rates, and big extended families living and working in close proximity. The dying person was therefore expected to preside over the ritual of his own dying. Should he forget his role, priest or family members kept the routine moving. They all knew it well, and they all had in common an abiding faith in immortality and in the continuity of their system.

Dying was also a neighborhood event. As late as early 19th century in parts of Europe, passersby who met a priest bearing a last sacrament formed a little procession and followed him into the sick room to pay their respects, and to gain any last wisdom, or gifts, that the dying person might want to bestow. Relatives, friends, and neighbors might be present during the dying process. Children were brought in and not only for a few minutes. They were part of the group waiting for death (Figure 23.2). The possibly mistaken notion that children should be protected from life's realities apparently occurred to few parents. Paintings of death scenes were not unusual—and they often show a roomful of people of all generations. At death, even into the 19th century in the United States, the family washed the body, laid it out, draped it in a winding sheet, and ordered a plain coffin from the local carpenter who had also helped them build their houses.

But by the second half of the 19th century, family members were beginning to hide from the patient the gravity of his condition—and to keep children as far as possible from the experience. By the 1930's to 1950's, the modern hospital complexes were beginning to emerge and were becoming associated in the public mind with miracle breakthroughs and reprieve from death. Medical advances allowed growing numbers of people who previously would have been destined to die at early ages to enter the hospital, stay relatively briefly, and then return home to live for years. Care of the sick as well as cure and even birth moved to the hospital, the domain of experts. Then dying, once so familiar in the flow of family and community life, became increas-

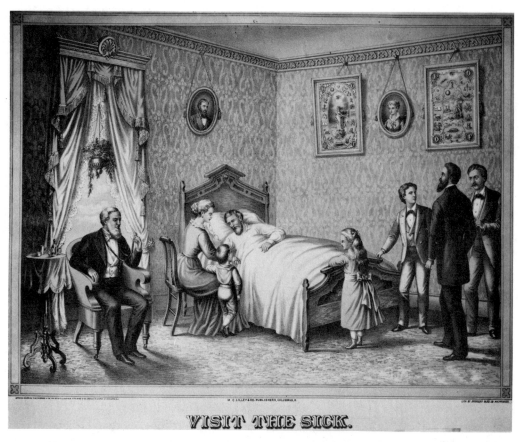

VISIT THE SICK.

Figure 23.2. *The Sick Room* (1877) by M.C. Lilley. (By permission of The Bettmann Archive, New York City.)

ingly hidden, alien, and separated from ordinary life. In 1935, 34% of all deaths occurred in hospitals, while by 1961 some 61% took place in hospitals, and another expanding number in nursing homes, the new extension of the hospital (Figure 23.3).

Fantastic developments such as Forest Lawn proudly claim to minister "not to the dead, but to the living." Bodies there are "housed" and "laid to rest in their plots," not buried in graves. One of our major industries has as its central interest the creation of greater life-like qualities in the dead. People "pass on" or "depart." They do not die, and every effort is made to see that the cadaver can look "better than life." Family mobility is reflected here too. One in 10 of all the dead are shipped from one place to another for burial. (Train fare for a corpse is double the cost of a single first class ticket for a live passenger.) The preoccupation over what to do with,

and where to put the body, is also rather new. During early medieval days, the dead were put near where the living were—under the floor of a church, or nearby. If space got crowded, bones of the nonillustrious deceased were dug up and reburied in a heap to make way for newcomers.

It is suggested that we make so much of funerals because death has become so strange and isolated an event. Now that we can talk about sex, "death" may have become our new taboo topic. Ashamed that we did not or could not do much for the dying, many people dissipate a large share of any insurance benefits on the funeral. The new site for dying, the hospital, leaves the next of kin in alien territory, alone, and feeling like unwelcome outsiders. The physician, not the priest, must certify when death occurred, and its cause, and now we hear debates in medicine about what exactly can be taken as the determinants of when death has occurred.

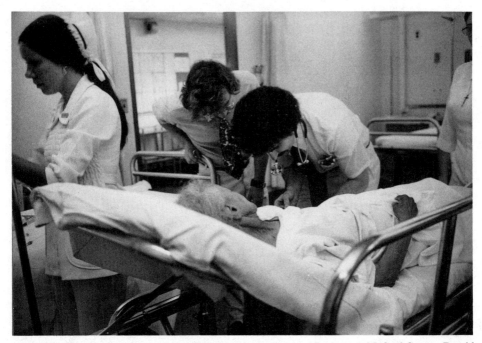

Figure 23.3. Elderly man dying in the hospital. (By permission of Downstate Medical Center, Brooklyn.)

The physician, not the patient, is assumed to be the best judge about whether the patient is dying.

Advance in the science and technologies of medical diagnosis places the physician in the uncomfortable new position of foretelling probabilities of imminent death. For example, the diagnosis of cancer of the esophagus in a patient who may be relatively symptom-free implies a set of dire predictions as well as painful medical treatment. Thus, the relatively new issue the doctor must handle is whether and when to tell a patient and his family that the patient is mortally ill.

We also demand alternately that the physician both prolong life and relieve suffering. With the expansion of life-sustaining possibilities, allowing the patient to die sometimes becomes an act of will in the hands of physicians—and a highly visible act, such as in the Karen Quinlan case, or where headlines read, "Who pulled the plug on Mary Jane?" Again, medicine is called upon to fulfill an essential function formerly managed in the course of family life.

The burden placed on the physician is doubly stressful because the medical practitioner and his environment, the hospital, are dedicated to the saving of life, and the people in medicine are motivated to conquering disease and superbly

trained for that. We can assume that people who work in hospitals have all the fear and prejudices of their fellow citizens against any acceptance of death as a routine of life to be handled with the help of ritual. But, in addition to that, their medical devotion to restoring and saving life may even make the men and women of medicine particularly susceptible to distress in the face of death. They may too readily see it as a sign of failure. And, until recently, their medical education and training have provided little in the way of systematic help for them in handling this family task that has now largely been turned over to the medical profession without anyone's ever having planned it that way.

In hospitals, where death usually occurs, it goes against the grain—hence, sudden screens, an attendant and cart from the underground morgue, and presto, the patient never was in that bed. In their effort to manage their own stress, people of medicine may tend to avoid the humanity of the dying person at the same time that they administer heroically to his failing body, and they may also tend to avoid the bewildered family members who expect more than medicine can deliver.

Recently, articles in medical journals as well as the lay press have dealt with what physicians and nurses can do to make the patient's dying days more comfortable, more amenable to self-respect; others discuss when and how and whether to tell the patient about imminent death. Seminars and courses on death and dying have proliferated, often in response to demands from medical students. Elisabeth Kübler-Ross in Chicago and Cicely Saunders in London have toured both continents urging that more attention be paid to the comfort and dignity of a dying patient. In the future perhaps more attention will also be paid to the issue of where the patient's relatives fit into this setting.

It is a cruel twist for the physicians—who legitimately devote their energies to saving life and delaying death—to be asked to attend to the humanity of the dying also. They, too, for the most part, have grown up in families where there was no intimate, first-hand experience in watching death occur. They come to this experience as little trained for coping with death as the patient and the family who expect the doctor to help them, but it is the physician who is now most often the one who must convey the sad news to the survivors. The wife or the husband or the sons and daughters of the deceased are often "told" in the waiting room or in the corridor in an embarrassed flurry, asked permission for an autopsy, and left to go home alone. This is a vastly different situation compared with the time when death occurred at home. Members then grieved together, supported one another, and were themselves the first to know when death occurred.

Moreover, the aftermath of death, or for that matter the break-up of a family for any reason, often results in the survivor's search for further help from the doctor. The mortality figures for widows and widowers during the six months of bereavement are much higher than they are for an equivalent population of married people or equivalent populations of never-married people. Numbers of visits to clinics, to emergency rooms, and to doctors' offices increase markedly during the six months following the death of a spouse. As Colin Parkes and others have demonstrated, a range of disorders from severe depression to respiratory and coronary disease relate statistically to the break-up of a family unit. Since the physician is the first point of contact with bereaved family members, if he or she does not intercede before the stress of loss expresses itself in physical deterioration of the remaining members, no one else is likely to do so.

The other most obvious event, aside from the care of the ill, that has moved to the hospital and out of the family, is birth. Having a baby was, in the past (Figure 23.4) and in many countries today still is, a matter handled in the family setting. (For example, today in Holland 70% of all births take place in the home.) Where birth is a family-centered event, youngsters grow up seeing babies born, and the adolescent girl in many societies has been around long enough to have made at least some kind of ritual contributions to the birth. But, in our society the woman in labor is rushed to the hospital, where an array of trained strangers is responsible for guiding her through the experiences of birth and initial care of her newborn (Figure 23.5).

Hence, another primary function that had

Figure 23.4. Spanish birth scene from the 17th century. (By permission of The New York Academy of Medicine.)

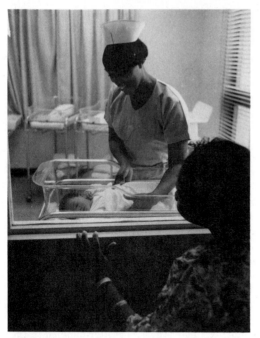

Figure 23.5. Newborn in nursery with mother looking on from the outside. (By permission of Downstate Medical Center, Brooklyn.)

been performed in families is now assigned to a large institution, the hospital, and it means that when the primiparous female arrives at the hospital, she has had practically no experience to guide her. She may have read about it or she may have attended a course given by a professional, but these are still removed from personal experience. One woman said that if she had been able to have a "dress rehearsal," her first delivery would have gone better. In other family systems most females have the equivalent of a dress rehearsal before they give birth by virtue of being around when female relatives gave birth.

When the contemporary mother of a nuclear family arrives home with her baby she has no large number of relatives to help her out, or to fill in when she does not feel well, or to support her through the process of learning how she is supposed to raise a youngster. Thus, once again the modern woman turns to experts, to a book, to the medical profession. Pediatricians are called about all manner of things that in another society a female relative would answer. Dr. Spock was said to have raised two generations of children—and he was sometimes blamed for all their problems.

THE CONTEMPORARY FAMILY AND MEDICINE

It is suggested that because of its small size and high charged affect, with no extra adults in the home to help out, the nuclear family of today can no longer by itself cope adequately with illness. When any member gets sick, it is necessary to send him to the hospital in order to give him the benefits of technological and scientific advance. But it also may be necessary for another reason—to get the sick person out of a home whose resources are too limited to manage the extra burden of an infirm member. Moreover, sending the sick person out to the hospital may be good for the family in an unanticipated way. A child used to getting attention from his parents, then observing that in illness his brother or sister gets much more, and is also excused from school, may learn the benefits of increased attention in illness. Talcott Parsons suggests that where much attention is given to the sick and there are no extra adults to help out, someone is likely to feel relatively deprived and notice that illness can offer desirable attention. Illness in this sense may be socially communicable if it is not removed to the hospital.

In the situation of acute and short-term illness where the patient goes to the hospital temporarily, the family system works fairly well with the medical system in a neat and distinct division of labor. The patient moves to the *doctor's domain*, the hospital, where the family may only visit. Then, when nearly recovered, the patient is turned back to the family, who presumably can carry on as before. However, with chronic illness it is another matter. In chronic illness the family and the way it functions become necessarily relevant in determining how the patient cooperates with medical advice, because the patient is in the *family's domain*. If the family is only tolerated by physicians as visitors or as intruders while the patient is in the hospital, then those family members are unlikely to be able to continue the therapeutic regimen knowledgeably.

Partly because of the family system that we have elaborated, the expectations for what the medical sector can do and will do are tremendous. The patient may not realize fully that he is coming back to the physician again and again after he has lost his wife because he wants something else besides medicine, but indeed the expectations are there, and with great expectations, there is also the possibility of great disappointment. The public, both patients and relatives of patients, very much want all kinds of help but they hate the wanting of it, and often they do not know how to articulate "where it hurts." Thus, the members of our small family units turn ever more to medicine as well as to other special institutions for functions once managed by extended families. This contributes to the prestige and the power of the medical enterprise today, but at the same time it demands a new resolution of age-old problems and new forms of articulation between the medical and the family systems.

Suggested Readings

Bloch DA: Family systems perspectives on the management of the individual patient. In Grinspoon L (ed): *Psychiatry 1983: Annual Review II*. Washington, American Psychiatric Press, 1983, p 203.

Lidz T: The family. In *The Person*. New York, Basic Books, 1976, p 45.

Reiss D: Family studies: reframing the illness, the patient, and the doctor. In Grinspoon L (ed): *Psychiatry 1983: Annual Review II*. Washington, American Psychiatric Press, 1983, p 172.

Vincent CE: The family in health and illness: some neglected areas. In Millon T (ed): *Medical Behavioral Science*. Philadelphia, W.B. Saunders, 1975, p 522.

References

Aries P: *Western Attitudes toward Death from the Middle Ages to the Present*. Baltimore, Johns Hopkins University Press, 1974.

Arensberg CM: Arranging the marriage in rural Ireland. In Goode W (ed): *Readings on the Family and Society*. Englewood Cliffs, NJ, Prentice-Hall, 1964, p 68.

Geiger K: Changing political attitudes in totalitarian society: a case study of the role of the family. In Bell NW, Vogel EF (eds): *The Family*. Glencoe, NY, Free Press, 1960, p 173.

Glaser BG, Strauss AL: *Awareness of Dying*. Chicago, Aldine Publishing Co, 1965.

Goode WJ: *After Divorce*. Glencoe, NY, Free Press, 1956.

Goode WJ: *World Revolution and Family Patterns*. Glencoe, NY, Free Press, 1963.

Heinzelmann F, Bagley RW: Response to physical activity programs and their effects on health behavior. *Public Health Reports* 85:905, 1970.

Mitford J: *The American Way of Death*. New York, Simon and Schuster, 1963.

Moroney RM: *Families, Social Services and Social Policy: The Issue of Shared Responsibility*. Washington, DC, DHHS Publication No. (ADM) 80–846, 1980.

Parkes CM: *The First Year of Bereavement*. New York, John Wiley & Sons, Inc, 1974.

Parsons T: Definitions of health and illness in the light of American values and social structure. In *Social Structure and Personality*. Glencoe, NY, Free Press, 1965, p 257.

Queen SA, Habenstein RW, Adams JB: *The Family in Various Cultures*. Philadelphia, J.B. Lippincott, 1961.

Section G/The Later Years of Childhood

CHAPTER **24** ## The Grade School Child

Melvin A. Scharfman, M.D.

When I was One,
I had just begun.

When I was Two,
I was nearly new.

When I was Three,
I was hardly Me.

When I was Four,
I was not much more.

When I was Five,
I was just alive.

But now I am Six, I'm as clever as clever.
So I think I'll be six now for ever and ever.*

THE "LATENCY" PERIOD

In this chapter we will consider some six or seven years in the development of a child – the grade school years, from the first grade on until approximately the start of junior high school. I indicated previously that with the resolution of the oedipal conflicts, there was a general taming and modulation of the drives, and a consolidation of ego growth and superego functioning. When this phase in life was first given a name by Freud, he called it *the latency period.* Latency may seem like another misnomer because if you look at children of this age they are anything but "latent." They are tremendously active physically, interested in learning, and involved

---

*From *Now We Are Six* by A. A. Milne. Copyright © 1927, by E. P. Dutton & Co., Inc. Copyright renewal, 1955, by A. A. Milne. (Reprinted by permission of E.P. Dutton.)

in all kinds of social interaction. What Freud was referring to specifically was the child's psychosexual development. Having arrived at a certain point in terms of the oedipal wishes, there then is a period of time when no new sexual aims are emerging.

However, we also know that the term "latency" is a term that is relative to the particular society in which the child is growing up, and very much influenced by the way in which a society structures itself. In some societies children are accepted much more quickly into areas which, in our society, we view as the exclusive domain of adults. There was a time in our own society when most latency age children were working and earning money, and indeed there are still areas in our society today where children this age are working and helping to contribute to the income of the family. Usually these children are from lower socioeconomic groups of the population. They also tend to be much more directly exposed than most other children in our society to experiences involving sexuality, birth, and death.

At an earlier time in history all of these experiences were fairly accessible to children. Then society began to change, and we began to communicate to children that they should not know about such matters. Children responded by avoiding these areas in their overt behavior. In particular, children in our society have been viewed as if they should know nothing about sexuality. When they ask questions, the answers are frequently not forthcoming or are evasive. If they show their curiosity more directly, this frequently leads to criticism. We do know that in other societies children are treated quite differently and therefore react quite differently. Such children appear to have a different kind of latency, but it is still the time during which they are prepared for their adult roles in that particular society. They learn the limits imposed upon the expression of aggressive and sexual behavior. Societies differ in how much such feelings are allowed direct expression and the form of such expression, but there are always limits. Children's energies are forced to find other channels of expression, those appropriate to a given society.

This curbing of excessively threatening sexual and aggressive impulses contributes greatly toward the enhancement of learning. Learning is also aided by maturational changes in cognitive development. Children achieve what Piaget calls the *stage of concrete operations*, which will be discussed by Dr. Farley in the next chapter. They think much more logically and coherently. There is much less magical thinking. Thoughts are checked more closely against observations in reality, and causal relationships can be un-

derstood. Learning is no longer tied as strongly to imitation and identification, but is pursued more for its own sake as latency proceeds.

Latency is also a time of learning the rules of society and the ways that one can function as part of a group in that society. This much seems common to all societies, and there seems to be a universal quality to these years that transcends the shifts of history. Look at the painting by Bruegel which is several hundred years old (Figure 24.1). If you look closely at this painting you will see many of the games that all of us played when we were children — jacks, Johnny-on-the-pony, London Bridge. These games have been transmitted unchanged from generation to generation over the centuries. Furthermore, the children in this painting are all in groups. Thus, learning along social lines also proceeds: the learning of social roles for the boy and girl, the learning of what is allowed with adults and with peers, what is allowed in school and at home, what is work as opposed to play. The child is learning his or her place in society with all its

Figure 24.1. *Kinderspiele* by Pieter Bruegel. (By permission of Kunsthistorisches Museum, Vienna.)

privileges and its limitations during this time. Let us look at how some of this takes place.

THE LATENCY AGE BOY

As we saw earlier, the four or five year old boy wants to be big and powerful, but he is also quite capable of being very destructive, and we can observe how boys of that age will threaten each other: "I'll cut your head off! I'll chop your arms off!" By the time they move into the latency period of life they still have a wish to be big, to be strong, to be powerful, to be a hero, but something is different about latency age heroes — whether the hero is Batman or Superman or the cowboys in the movies or the space explorers. They all have one thing in common — they do good and fight evil. All of their superpowers and strengths are directed into socially acceptable channels. They all have magical powers — Superman can fly and has X-ray vision, and Batman has all his special equipment — but it is always in the service of good. They do only good things and they do not do bad things. This is the result of the internalization of a control system that we talked about earlier, a value system, the superego.

One can see other residues of the recent past in these children, again through their heroes, because there is another thing that latency age heroes have in common. The latency age hero is one who avoids contact with women. Batman does not have a girl friend, he has only Robin. Superman has a girl friend but everyone knows they are never going to marry. The cowboy has his horse and that is all! These heroes all avoid heterosexuality, and if we look at the behavior of young boys this age, we see the same thing. They act as if girls are something to be avoided at all costs, and their modes of relating to girls are fairly characteristic. They tease them, they put them down and call them names, they chase them home from school, and try in various ways to attack the girls, but they would never acknowledge that they enjoy the company of a girl. As a matter of fact, a little boy this age who plays with a girl is very likely to be considered a "sissy."

There are several reasons why this is so. One is that the boy of six or eight or nine is still trying to separate himself from his attachment to his mother, and so he moves away from anything even remotely related to his identification with his mother. He is trying to consoli-

date his masculinity by becoming to a certain extent a caricature of what he thinks is masculine. He exaggerates all of the masculine qualities which he wants to possess. The second reason is that any kind of physical contact with a girl has become something that is connected with considerable anxiety. She reminds him of the danger of castration, and he will avoid her. There are, of course, some men who never overcome this anxiety in the course of their lives, as I noted earlier. Furthermore, since most of our grade schools are still matriarchies, the boys are also jealous of the girls, who they feel are better understood and favored by the predominantly female teachers.

The boys are going through a rather stormy time in general because of another interesting phenomenon that has to do with biological maturation. If we remember back to the sixth grade and junior high school, the girls were always taller. If we look at the school pictures from that time in our lives, it may be a shock to see that the girls were three or four or maybe even six inches taller than the boys who stood next to them in line! Going to a party of 12 and 13 year olds can provide a similar experience. All of the girls are several inches taller than those little boys who are walking around with them! This adds to the boy's feelings of insecurity and fears of being overwhelmed by girls, and fosters the defenses of deprecation and avoidance.

THE LATENCY AGE GIRL

I indicated in an earlier chapter that girls do not resolve their oedipal attachment in the same way as boys, and if we look at latency age girls we will see this manifested in a very obvious way. In contrast to most boys at this age, the average girl is not afraid to talk about her fantasy that she wants to marry when she grows up. It is quite open, on the surface, and acceptable. The girl's romantic fantasies are reflected through her daydreams and the stories that she reads. She is like Sleeping Beauty, waiting for her Prince Charming to come along and wake her up. She tends to admire boys and may even try to emulate them in different ways. There are a fair number of girls at this age who are tomboys. This is one area where we can see some of the competitiveness the girl is feeling, because there is nothing that a tomboy likes better than to beat the boys at their own games. The girl on the block who can hit the baseball farther than the boys represents the ultimate humiliation for the boys. Nothing could be worse than that.

The girls this age are doing much better than the boys in practically every area. They are certainly doing much better in school. They are, for the most part, reading before the boys are able to read. They behave better in class. They do not seem to have the same kind of need to be constantly roaming around and getting into mischief as the boys do. Their learning is less involved with conflict. Girls at this age are also much better coordinated than the boys, and they can do certain things that the boys cannot do. They may not do quite as well when it comes to gross strength, but as far as their coordination is concerned, they are far ahead of the boys.

THE PEER GROUP AND THE "RULES OF THE GAME"

There is something, however, that both girls and boys at this age have in common, and that is the need to organize themselves into groups, groups that tend to exclude adults to a considerable degree and that operate much more as an organization of peers. Within this peer group there is a tremendous emphasis upon learning, upon mastering new functions, upon trying out different kinds of roles, and upon secrecy. Think back to this time in your life. In these groups you invented secret languages, and then you went home and you talked in this secret language that nobody else was supposed to be able to understand, certainly no grown-ups. These groups or clubs also reflected the internalization taking place at this age, the need for controls and structure, because the most important things about these clubs were the rules. You and five other children got together and you had a meeting. You were going to form a club and you spent two hours drawing up all the rules of how to become a member of the club, and what the dues and initiation rites were, and where the club would meet, and how often. Of course, the club did not do anything. But that was because the only purpose of the club was the organization!

One sees at this age a tremendous need on the part of the children to organize and categorize, to do things by the rules, and to try to do them correctly. As part of this need to categorize, children this age become interested in hobbies and they start to collect things — rocks, leaves, model airplanes, baseball cards, stamps, coins.

They collect anything they can get their hands on. Everybody collects something, organizes it, and puts it in order, and it is also very important to be able to know certain things. You have to have your facts right and you certainly have to know how to play the game. Go down to a schoolyard and watch a group of eight year old kids trying to play basketball. They may not really manage to get the ball up to the hoop, but they know all about how you commit a foul and they are yelling at each other, "You double dribbled." They can barely even dribble, but they are learning the rules and so they know all about double dribbling and the three second rule.

There are also the kinds of magical thinking that we all remember, such as, "Step on a crack, break your mother's back," or touching every third lamppost on the way to school. These are rituals that are organized to control impulses that might break through, directed against both aggressive impulses and also any kind of manifestations of sexual interest. In fact, latency age children look to a certain extent like one group of adult patients. They look very much like obsessional neurotics, because obsessional neurotics also organize and order things. They collect everything and they are overly concerned with rules because, like these children, they show an overdominance of superego controls. They have a need to be "right," with all of the oversimplified notions of right and wrong that children this age have. "You must do the right things." And sometimes children in these middle years are so relentless in their pursuit of doing "right," that if somebody else breaks the rules they beat him up. Those are the "rules of the game."

SOCIALIZATION

This then is a time of social movement, of moving a great deal from beyond the primary family of origin into the larger social organization. There are a number of factors that are of great importance to children in terms of how they make this transition toward socialization in a widening world. One is the nature of their experiences in school. Another has to do with the peer group available to them. A third involves the larger outside influences. This becomes important in terms of a phenomenon such as television which takes children beyond their immediate friends and beyond their day-to-day experiences in school. Let us first consider some of the aspects of school.

School is a place where one is supposed to perform and where it is very important to be accepted. Whether or not it is constructive, in our society one learns a certain amount of competitiveness in school, and a need for achievement is communicated. Obviously, in many segments of our society this need for achievement is overemphasized. But to be able to achieve is one basis for being accepted. Whether the achievement has to do with who can hit a baseball the farthest or who gets the highest marks in school, you have to be able to achieve. School is an area where large groups of children experience difficulty because they are not able to achieve, not because of any lack of innate ability but because of some of their earlier experiences.

If children grew up in a relatively deprived environment where they did not have the stimulation that we normally associate with a middle class or upper middle class family, then they have not had the same exposure to words, to vocabulary, to trying out new ideas, to reading, or even to a television set. When they enter school, they are disadvantaged and are unable to keep up with the other children. When this happens they may experience a tremendous blow to their self-esteem and just give up or drop out. This is very characteristic of many latency age children. If they feel they cannot make it, they give up. And if there is no one around to encourage them in what they are trying to do, then they quit for good. They may be labeled "a dope" or "stupid," and their ability to learn may be compromised for many years regardless of their innate intellectual endowment.

All of us have probably had this experience while playing a particular sport. Some people do well and stay with it. Others try and fail, and unless they happen to have someone around who is willing to spend some time assisting them, they just quit. You can see this in the boy who does not know how to throw a baseball, and then decides that baseball is not for him. He may then avoid not only baseball, but all other sports as well. The same thing is true for many children in terms of school. If they meet with initial failure, or if expectations are made of their ability to perform without taking into account the fact that they have had a different earlier experience, then school becomes a turn-off for them and they can no longer relate to school. Obviously, some of the experimental educational efforts that have been made in recent years, such as the various Head Start programs, are partly an attempt to compensate for the deprivation in the early experiences of these children and the lack of the stimulation necessary for the normal maturation of the intellectual processes.

School will be very important in another way, a way that has many ramifications in our society. How many of us had a male teacher before we entered the sixth grade? As I said earlier, in our society at least, nearly all the elementary school teachers are women. Why is that? For one thing, it indicates something about our society's attitudes toward intellectuality and toward being a teacher. In fact, we even connect too much education with not being very manly. The boy who does well in school but cannot throw a football is not our national hero. We do not really respect learning and education, and so we do not encourage our male children to have that as their life's goal.

The result of this attitude is that most of our grade school teachers are women. Many of them are very talented and responsive and understanding, but some of them have a great deal of difficulty dealing with the boys in their class. They may not understand the much greater degree of conflict and tension that boys at this age experience, or their need to deal with this tension by activity. Thus, they tend to be much more critical of the most active boys while rewarding passivity.

Social cruelty as well may be first encountered in school. Children begin to be cruel to a peer by excluding him or her from their group because he is "different," because he looks "funny," because he is good in school and bad in sports, whatever the reason. Children begin to decide who is "good," and who is "no good," based upon what they have perceived of the values of the larger society. This is the age when all of the derogatory ethnic expressions that you hear on television, on programs such as "All in the Family," are transmitted to children. They learn all of the terms to exclude somebody. These values may be reinforced or may conflict with what takes place within their families or their schools. Thus, the child may grow up perfectly comfortable within his primary family and think his parents are nice, warm people. They are good to him. They are reasonable. He loves them. He wants to be like them. Then he moves out into the world of school, and the world of the peer group, and he learns that his parents are not part of the social in-group. They may be the wrong color. They may be the wrong religion. Perhaps they are immigrants and do not speak English very well. As a result, the child is exposed to a devaluation, not only a devaluation of his parents, but a devaluation of himself because he does not meet whatever has been introduced as the new standard. The child will be comparing the values of his parents with the new values of the outside world, and the discrepancy between these value systems may cause the child a great deal of distress.

Let us talk further about the peer group. The peer group develops a group morality and the children in the group then operate according to that particular value system. A great deal depends upon the nature of the group morality. Children who have not had the opportunity for adequate internalization of values within their homes and families may adopt different attitudes about what is right and what is wrong when they get together in a group. They may very well abrogate the ordinary rules of society, organize around antisocial behavior, and become a gang. That is why it is so important to introduce these children to adults or older teenagers to whom they can relate and who are not directly connected with either the school or the family — group leaders who can help these children achieve control, mastery, and self-respect. Children this age need heroes, they need adults whom they can use as models and who are acceptable within their subgroups. So you have one generation of children that wants to grow up to be Babe Ruth or Amelia Earhart, and another generation that wants to be Muhammad Ali or Olivia Newton-John. They may choose heroes and heroines from sports or politics or the movies or the world of rock music. If, on the other hand, you introduce these children to the antihero, the one who disavows the need for any kind of restraint, limits, or controls, then you are going to see children who are overtly aggressive and destructive. They may terrorize other children or even adults, destroy property, become truant, steal, or otherwise defy the rules of society.

The latency age child is trying on different social roles all the time. One day he is pretending to be a great basketball player. The next day he may practice at being an astronaut. That same afternoon he could be a Boy Scout, the next day he will be something else. He tries on different roles to see how he fits in with the range of roles offered by society, and the more he or she feels excluded from some of those roles, then the more narrow the path from which to choose. The roles that society offers to children of both sexes at this particular age are of tremendous importance in terms of their future life choices.

INDUSTRY VS. INFERIORITY

Despite all of this fluctuation in roles that has been described, this is still a period of life when by and large children seem least troubled. This is not an age of maximum problems. It is a relatively happy and delightful time of life. As a matter of fact any of us who may have worked in camps as a counselor or as a teacher's assistant, know that children in the third, fourth, and fifth grades are the easiest to teach and to manage. They get along well. They enjoy things. They are willing to learn. They are curious (Figure 24.2). They can function constructively as a group. This is a time of consolidation, of intellectual and physical growth, of increasing mastery. It is the stage of life in Erik Erikson's psychosocial framework in which the child de-

Figure 24.2.   *Boy Seated in a Tree* (1913) by Gustav Vigeland. Bronze. Placed in the Vigeland Sculpture Park, Oslo, Norway. (By permission of Vigeland Museum, Oslo, Norway.)

velops *industry*. Of course, nothing in human development goes along a straight line — there are always ups and downs, periods of progression and regression — but this is still one of the longest periods in the child's life of relatively calm consolidation. And if this consolidation does not take place, if instead the child develops a pervasive sense of *inferiority*, then there is going to be a great deal of difficulty a few years later in junior high school when the biological pot begins to boil again with the onset of puberty.

THE PHYSICIAN AND THE LATENCY AGE CHILD

I want to conclude with a few words about some of the difficulties children this age do have, and some of the reasons why they might come to the attention of a physician. Since so much of the child's life is organized around school, the most common difficulty that one encounters is the child who presents as a problem in school. There are various kinds of such problems.

One such is the child who has a *learning disability*, and there will be an entire chapter devoted to this problem later in the book. This is a very complicated area, and there are many factors involved in an activity such as learning how to read. First there is the biological apparatus, and in this context it is important to remember that children mature at different rates, and that girls tend to mature somewhat earlier than boys. There are biological givens that one needs in order to be able to learn how to read. The eyes have to be coordinated to follow the written word, and there has to be an integration of perceptual and fine motor skills.

There are indeed children who present with a reading difficulty who do have perceptual motor difficulties as a result of some kind of minimum brain damage. This can be demonstrated with various neurological and psychological tests. However, it is my impression that we have indiscriminately applied this diagnosis of *minimal brain dysfunction* (MBD) to many children who do not have actual brain damage but are really suffering from slower maturation rates, social deprivation, emotional illness, and many other factors that cause them to learn and to read more slowly. Not only are they misdiagnosed, but since amphetamines do appear to be of help for some children with MBD, these same drugs are being given to many other children inappro-

priately without an adequate diagnostic evaluation. This is maltreatment, yet the number of American children who are taking amphetamines during their elementary school years is staggering. Careful evaluation can correct this error.

The second most common problem that presents itself is the *conduct disorder*, but once again this is a very subjective diagnosis that is often overapplied and misapplied. For example, a boy may be having a rather stormy time and he may start to get disruptive in class, and so the teacher says, "This kid is impossible. He's a behavior problem. Send him to the school pediatrician or to the school psychologist." *Hyperactive child* or *hyperkinetic syndrome* is probably the most frequently incorrect pediatric diagnosis of this particular generation, for which there is again a very wide misuse of drugs, especially the amphetamines and the barbiturates. Many of these children are simply normally active, trying to cope with all kinds of emotional conflicts that have nothing to do with any sort of psychiatric syndrome. Most of them simply cannot sit in a classroom for hours on end without effective and stimulating teaching, frequent breaks in the schedule, and opportunities for athletics and other physical activities. They are often approached in the wrong way. The answer to these complex social and cultural problems is not to drug these children at an early age to get them to "behave" or to correct their "learning disability." It may be cheaper and easier but it does not work. Nevertheless, it is widely done, and it is one of the most glaring examples of the widespread misuse of drugs in our society.

Another school-related problem is that of the *school phobia*. Compulsory school attendance brings any child who does not attend to the attention of the school authorities. Some children may be *truanting* and not be phobic at all. The phobic child is unable to leave his house, usually more specifically his mother, in order to attend school. Such a child experiences great anxiety upon the enforced separation, and wants to stay home. The truant does not have this anxiety, nor is such a child likely to be home with the parent. A child who has a school phobia is not malingering or pretending. Rather the phobia is a sign of some psychological problem which should be properly evaluated and treated. There are many different etiological factors that can lie behind such a symptom, and different therapeutic approaches that can be used, de-

SICK

"I cannot go to school today,"
Said little Peggy Ann McKay.
"I have the measles and the mumps,
A gash, a rash and purple bumps.
My mouth is wet, my throat is dry,
I'm going blind in my right eye.
My tonsils are as big as rocks,
I've counted sixteen chicken pox
And there's one more — that's seventeen,
And don't you think my face looks green?
My leg is cut, my eyes are blue —
It might be instamatic flu.
I cough and sneeze and gasp and choke,
I'm sure that my left leg is broke —
My hip hurts when I move my chin,

My belly button's caving in,
My back is wrenched, my ankle's sprained,
My 'pendix pains each time it rains.
My nose is cold, my toes are numb,
I have a sliver in my thumb.
My neck is stiff, my spine is weak,
I hardly whisper when I speak.
My tongue is filling up my mouth,
I think my hair is falling out.
My elbow's bent, my spine ain't straight,
My temperature is one-o-eight.
My brain is shrunk, I cannot hear,
There is a hole inside my ear.
I have a hangnail, and my heart is — what?
What's that? What's that you say?
You say today is . . . Saturday?
G'bye, I'm going out to play!"

Figure 24.3. "Sick." From *Where The Sidewalk Ends*. The Poems and Drawings of Shel Silverstein. Copyright © 1974 by Shel Silverstein. By permission of Harper & Row Publishers, Inc., New York.

pending upon the evaluation. One common denominator in all treatment approaches is prompt intervention to return the child to school as soon as possible, since once the phobia is established as a persistent pattern, it is much more resistant to treatment. In his poem and drawing, "Sick," Shel Silverstein humorously conveys the way in which physical symptoms may be an expression of school phobia (Figure 24.3).

Enuresis is a problem often presented to the physician by children in this age category. The average child will have achieved both bowel and bladder control by age three and a half or so. Many parents, however, are reluctant to see persistent wetting as a problem. They may be embarrassed by it and feel they have to hide it. It is a symptom in which there is frequently collusion among family members to keep it a secret from the outside world. Often it is only when the child cannot stay at a friend's home overnight or is embarrassed by going to an overnight camp that help is sought. Children who have such a problem are frequently made the object of jokes and name calling by other children, and some children develop personality problems such as inhibition and constriction secondary to such experiences. Obviously, this is another problem requiring a proper evaluation. Enuresis is two to three times as frequent in males as in females, and it is a very common problem. It has been estimated that approximately seven per cent of the population will still be enuretic after the age of seven. Organic factors are the cause in only about 5% of these cases, but they must first be ruled out. If present, they must be treated appropriately. Psychogenic and developmental factors are by far the most frequent cause, and again a full evaluation is required to determine the appropriate intervention. Various treatments such as conditioning apparatuses or drugs are often used without such an evaluation. While they may be useful, they are best used only when it is clear what kind of disturbance the child may have. Psychotherapy may be indicated as the primary treatment or in conjunction with other methods. Very often the parents also need guidance and counseling in order to be able to help the child overcome the wetting. Again, the earlier the appropriate intervention can be made, the better the results. *Encopresis* (fecal soiling) is usually a much more serious problem that requires an extensive medical and psychiatric evaluation.

Another common problem that one may encounter in pediatrics or general practice or psychiatry, is that of *social maladjustment*. These are the children who are the loners, who do not fit in, who are not accepted for one reason or another by their school group, and in whom we immediately decide that there must be some kind of problem. There may be or may not be a problem. Some very creative and gifted people in our world have grown up as "loners" who have not simply accepted the organization of their peers or "adjusted" to the world as they found it. A common example would be a boy who is interested in poetry and literature. He may be excluded by his friends. He may well be a loner. We can either make a value judgment that he is "queer" or a "sissy" or a "faggot," or we can try to appreciate his interests and direct them in a positive way, and not immediately come to the conclusion that just because he does not fit in with the group, there must be something wrong with him.

A final major difficulty that begins to manifest itself in children this age is what we call *delinquency*. People often wonder what it would be like to grow up in a socioeconomically deprived, or broken home. Well, it is a very different world and one has to understand the behavior that follows as a consequence of that different world. The child who grows up with inadequate housing, poor food, a disrupted family structure, is also regularly exposed much more to violence and to sexuality. The whole environment is different, as Dr. Christ will discuss in his chapter on juvenile deliquency. These children are continually overstimulated in terms of violence and sexuality, and understimulated in terms of the other kinds of activities and interests that could provide outlets for their sexual and aggressive impulses. Furthermore, they often do not have

the kind of models available that could lead to any degree of redirection of those energies. So what one sees in this environment is a group, but a different kind of group. It is not a group that is going out in the schoolyard to play stickball. It is a gang that is going out to beat up somebody or rob or rape or whatever. This is the result of this peculiar combination of deprivation on a material level and overstimulation in the other areas, the very areas where it is so important for children this age not to be too stimulated. Children need balance and they need limits. Since we are now flooding our middle class and upper middle class children with violence and sexuality in a different form, through the movies and magazines and television, it will be an interesting "experiment in nature" to see what effect this is going to have. We may be quite disturbed by the end results. It may be that the chapter on "latency" in future books on human behavior will not exist, because there will no longer be any time for children to consolidate a sense of ego mastery without being overwhelmed by sexual and aggressive stimuli. Only time will tell what kind of an adult emerges from such a childhood.

Suggested Readings

Bibring GL, Kahana RJ: Early school years: the latency period. In *Lectures in Medical Psychology*. New York, International Universities Press, 1968, p 121.

Erikson EH: Industry vs. inferiority. In *Childhood and Society*. New York, W.W. Norton, 1950, p 226.

Farley GK, Eckhardt LO, Hebert FB: School phobia. In *Handbook of Child and Adolescent Psychiatric Emergencies*. New York, Medical Examination Publishing Co., 1979, p 102.

Gerard MW: Enuresis: a study in etiology. In Harrison SI, McDermott JF (eds): *Childhood Psychopathology*. New York, International Universities Press, 1972, p 418.

Johnson AM, Falstein EI, Szurek S.A., and Svendsen M. School phobia. In Harrison SI, McDermott JF (eds): *Childhood Psychopathology*. New York, International Universities Press, 1972, p 410.

Lidz T: The juvenile. In *The Person*. New York, Basic Books, 1976, p 273.

Mussen PH, Conger JJ, Kagan J, Huston AC: Middle childhood. In *Essentials of Child Development and Personality*. New York, Harper & Row, 1984.

Pierce CM: Enuresis and encopresis. In Kaplan HI, Freedman AM, Sadock BJ (eds): *Comprehensive Textbook of Psychiatry*. ed 3, vol 3, Baltimore, Williams & Wilkins, 1980, pp 2780 and 2788.

Prugh DG: *The Psychosocial Aspects of Pediatrics*. Philadelphia, Lea & Febiger, 1983.

Sarnoff CA: *Latency*. New York, Jason Aronson, 1976.

CHAPTER 25 Cognitive Development

Gordon K. Farley, M.D.

THE IMPORTANCE OF COGNITIVE DEVELOPMENT

In order to understand children, one needs to understand more than psychosexual development and more than psychosocial development. Children do not spend all of their time thinking about sex and aggression. Much of their time is spent in problem solving, interacting with, discovering, changing, and learning about their world. In fact, some people have postulated a third drive in addition to sex and aggression, and that drive has been called the *drive for mastery*, the drive for competence, the effectance drive. This drive for mastery is very much related to cognitive development. In order to understand how to talk to children and also adults, one should have some general understanding of their stage of cognitive development. It is the stage of cognitive development that will determine how a child or adult views his or her body and understands his or her bodily functioning. This understanding has a very important role when one wishes to get children and adults to comply with medical treatment or to submit to all the mysterious, threatening, and often painful things that we as physicians do to them.

The one person who has been most prominent in the study of cognitive development is the Swiss psychologist, Jean Piaget (Figure 25.1), who was very interested in what he called "genetic epistemology." Genetic epistemology is the study of how humans gain knowledge. Piaget's interest in intellectual development in children began at the time that he was working to standardize an I.Q. test of Cyril Burt's with some children in Paris. He became more interested in the wrong answers that children gave to questions than in the right answers. He thought that perhaps these wrong answers could tell us something about how children think and how they view the world. He then spent much of the rest of his life studying these "wrong answers."

What I would like to do in this chapter is to briefly review the characteristics of the four stages of cognitive development and relate these characteristics to general medical practice.

THE STAGES OF COGNITIVE DEVELOPMENT

Sensory Motor Stage (Birth to Two Years)

The first stage that Piaget has defined is what he calls the *sensory motor stage* or the stage of sensory motor intelligence. During this stage the infant begins with a comparatively dim awareness of his or her surroundings in the world and his or her relations to the people in these sur-

Figure 25.1. Jean Piaget. (By permission of The Jean Piaget Society, Temple University, Philadelphia.)

roundings. There are two main tasks of this stage. One task is for the child to establish some kind of primitive notion of causality or *causal thinking*. We can see this happening in the crib. When the infant moves in the crib and the mobile that is hanging over the crib or attached to the crib moves, the child is likely to move again, trying to get the mobile to move again. This is what Piaget has called "making interesting sights last." An important point here is that Piaget, as have others after him, views the infant not as a passive, receptive organism soaking up knowledge like a sponge, but rather as an active and interactive organism that operates on his or her environment, seeks new experiences, seeks stimulation, and learns that his or her actions have causal effects on the environment.

There is another important task in this stage, namely, "the conquest of the object." During this period of time the child establishes what is called *object permanence* or *object constancy*. That is, the child reaches a stage of cognitive development where there can be an *internal mental representation* of the objects in the external world, including both things and people. For an infant of less than one year of age, "out of sight" is literally "out of mind." If one takes the favorite rattle of a six month old child and hides it somewhere, the child no longer searches for it. The child merely looks puzzled and goes on to another activity. For that infant, the rattle has ceased to exist. Similarly, when the child's mother is out of sight, the child's mother is for the most part out of mind as well. This has many important implications regarding the hospitalization of children. If one can remember that a child of this age may have either no mental representation of the mother or a very hazy one, then there may be many ways in which a physician who has to hospitalize a child can keep the image of mother alive in the child's mind, the image of the mother as a comforting person. The physician can use pictures of the mother and other family members, can talk to the child about the mother, can bring familiar objects from home, and can use familiar routines from home around toileting and feeding in the hospital. Frequent telephone contact even with a two year old can be beneficial. Best of all, the physician can demand that the hospital allow the parents to be with the child as much as possible.

Through primitive causal thinking and the development of object permanence, the infant gradually builds up and develops internal mental representations of the objects of the external world, as well as an internal mental representation of his or her own body.

Preoperational Stage (Two to Seven Years)

The next stage is the *preoperational stage*, and this is one of the more interesting stages of cognitive development. The move from the sensory motor stage to the preoperational stage marks the transition from the *plane of action and sensation* to the *plane of thought*. The characteristic that makes this stage so interesting is that, although the child's understanding of the world is far from logical and is in many ways mysterious, the child has the verbal ability to communicate these beliefs to adults.

Piaget's way of questioning children is relevant. Piaget was the original open ended questioner and was very good at eliciting unusual beliefs from children by asking them such questions as, "Where do dreams come from? Where did the sun come from? What makes the wind blow?" Preoperational thought in children marks the appearance of what is called the *symbolic function*, and it is during this time that a child learns that a name stands for an object and is a symbol for an object, and also that two sticks put together at an angle can symbolically represent an airplane, or a pencil can represent a rocket, or a doll can represent a baby. This is really the time of flowering of both language and imaginative play in children, and that is one reason why it is so delightful a time of life.

There are some interesting beliefs that children display at this time. One of the beliefs is that the name of the object is actually a part of the object, that the name resides in the object. The name "truck" is not just an arbitrary name that is chosen, but it is actually a part of the truck. The other belief that many children have is that any name *they* assign to an object is *the* name for the object. For example, a child that names his doll a "muzzy" may not be able to understand why nonfamily members do not know what he is talking about when he mentions his "muzzy." I know of a two year old who called his toy steam shovel his "dig dugger" and was very irate with those who named it anything else.

Egocentrism is another interesting feature of preoperational thinking in children. What is meant by this is that the preoperational child is literally unable to put himself in another's place. Piaget had an interesting and well-known experiment in which he set up a scene of mountains on a table with a small mountain in front and two large mountains behind, each mountain with distinctive features. He would seat the child on one side of this scene and ask that child to describe what is looked like. The child could do it very accurately, saying that there is a small mountain in front and there is a larger one in back on the right and another larger one in back on the left. Then Piaget would ask the child, "What would it look like from the other side of the table?" The child would very carefully describe what he had just seen from his side of the table, and would literally be unable to put himself in another's place behind the table. One of the implications of this finding is that we cannot ask a child of this age to keep quiet because his mother has a headache. The child is unable to put himself in his mother's place, to feel what it is like to have a headache, and to have a child demanding something. Many adults regard egocentrism as "moral perversity" in children when actually it is none other than their inability to function at a higher cognitive level. It is often helpful for physicians to explain this to parents.

Another characteristic of this stage is called *animism*. Children of this age believe that everything that moves is alive and has feelings and thoughts. Bushes, automobiles, planes have feelings. Children at this age also believe that their feces are alive, since they are moving around inside them, and that the feces have thoughts, intentions, and feelings. As a result, the child may believe that the feces only come out when they want to, and will not come out when they do not want to do so. This belief has many implications for toilet training, because, if a child feels that his feces are a living part of him, he may not want to give them up so easily. Adults often regress to animistic thinking. One morning I had a hard time starting my car, and began cursing at it, then coaxing it, and finally pleading with it as though it were alive. On another day I saw a medical student swearing at the dollar changer in the cafeteria saying, "Come on you son of a bitch, give me that last five cents." We were both attributing animate characteristics to inanimate objects. There was an article a few years ago in the newspapers about a woman in Philadelphia whose car failed to start for the fourth time, and she beat it to death

with a sledge hammer! We all do such things at times, and there is nothing so terribly strange about it.

Another characteristic of this stage is that of children being unable to distinguish between physical and psychological causality. I remember clearly an incident with my son who threw a ball and knocked down the light fixture in his room. I asked him why he did it. He said, "I didn't do it. It already wanted to come down by itself." He was four years old at the time. This characteristic has important implications for medical practice, since children who are unable to distinguish between psychological and physical causality may think they get sick as a punishment for wrong doing or bad thoughts. They may feel guilty when somebody in their life is injured or dies or leaves because they had some angry thoughts about that person, and in their mind they may feel that they have caused the person's injury or death or departure.

Another quality of the preoperational stage is *artificialism*. By this it is meant that children of this age believe that all things are made by humans and for humans, and that everything has a use. At this age one gets the unanswerable questions from children such as "What is snow for?" or "Why do we have dirt?" Children at this age are also unable to reason using verbal propositions. They can sometimes reason using concrete examples in front of them, but when using only verbal propositions they are unable to reason. For example, one gives a child of this age the following problem: If Mary is taller than Sue, and Sue is taller than Judy, who is the tallest, who is the shortest, and who is in between? The child of this age cannot solve the problem using verbal reasoning. Another one of my sons at age six put up his third, fourth and fifth fingers, naming them each in turn and saying, "Mary is taller than Sue, and Sue is taller than Judy, the tallest one is Mary, that's easy." Thus, if children are given a concrete picture, they can do certain kinds of reasoning, but without a visual representation, they cannot.

This brings up an important point for medical practice. It is that, generally, we as physicians tend to talk to children rather than show them. Most operations, procedures, and medical treatment plans are explained to children in verbal terms. The doctor comes in and he says, "Your appendix is a little thing that dangles on the end of your cecum. Well, it's diseased, it's all swollen up, and if we don't cut it out, it's going to hurt you." The preoperational child is not likely to understand any of this, and in fact is very likely to misunderstand just what that "little thing that dangles on the end of your cecum" really is! One of the things we can do to help children understand medical procedures is to draw them, play them out with dolls or figures, model with clay, and use other visual representations. One very useful technique is to use play objects to explain surgical procedures and equipment, and thereby help children reduce their anxiety over the situation and increase their sense of mastery. Another technique that has been useful to me when working with physically ill children is to ask them to draw what they think is wrong with them on a piece of paper or model it with the use of clay. What they draw or model can be exceedingly revealing of their fantasies about the nature and the cause of their illness, and this knowledge can often be extremely valuable in the physician's treatment of the child.

Another well-known characteristic of preoperational children is the inability to conserve. What this means is that when something changes in appearance, the child does not realize that the thing which has changed still retains and "conserves" some of its characteristics. A classical experiment performed by Piaget is one in which he takes some clay, rolls it up into a ball, and asks the preoperational child to look at it. Then he puts it on a table, smashes it down into a flat pancake, and says to the child, "Is it more now?" The child says, "Yes." Piaget rolls it back up into the ball and says, "Is it less now?", and the child says, "Yes." Piaget straightens it out into a long shape like a weiner and says, "Is it more now?" and the child says, "Yes." What the child does not realize is that although the object changes in shape, it still "conserves" its original mass or volume. Another way to understand this inability to conserve is that the preoperational child is able to attend to only one property or dimension at a time. While there are many determinants to "penis envy" or "breast envy," surely the preoperational child's concept that what is bigger is better, and conversely that what is smaller or possibly not immediately visible at all is of less value, is an important factor.

There are many other examples of illogical preoperational thinking, and we should realize that in times of stress, we may all regress to such thinking. This was brought home to me

vividly when, as an intern, I dropped a unit of blood on the floor. It contained only 500 cc, but no one could convince me that there was not at least two gallons there—that is a failure of conservation! We see this in the operating room when novice surgeons consistently tend to over estimate blood losses. Spread out on all the sponges and drapes, the blood loss looks like it is much more than it really is. The principle here is that any visual display can sometimes be overwhelming for adults as well as for children. There are several different kinds of *conservation* including length, volume, area, number, and continuous quantity. For example, if one were to pour a given amount of liquid from a short fat beaker into a tall thin beaker, adding or subtracting nothing, a preoperational child would say that there is more liquid in the tall, thin beaker. The usual progression is that children are first able to conserve continuous quantity, later number, length, and area, and still later volume.

Another characteristic of preoperational thought is that the preoperational child feels that all questions have answers and that adults know what these answers are. Children usually get over this by the time of adolescence, and then they feel that adults know nothing. This latter phenomenon has been termed by some "the stage of cognitive conceit." Adolescents feel that if an adult does not know the answer to one thing, then the adult does not know the answer to anything. In the preoperational stage, however, it is very characteristic that all answers are believed to be known. I can remember talking with my son after a great snowfall in Denver. He was four or five years old at the time, and there were three feet of snow on the ground. He said, "Dad when will the snow melt?" I tried to explain to him that it depends upon the temperature, the saturation of the ground, the sunlight, the humidity, and so on. He could not really understand that I did not know the exact instant that the snow would melt, and his disappointment was apparent.

The last characteristic to be noted of the preoperational stage is that these children think things can occupy only one class at a time. They do not understand that it is possible to be two things at the same time. David Elkind gives the example of asking a preoperational child, "Can you be both an American and a Protestant?" The child answered, "Only if you move." I remember asking my younger son, David, if he had a brother and he said, "Yes." I said, "What is your brother's name?", and he said, "Steven." Correct so far. I said, "Does Steven have a brother?", and David said, "No." His view here was that Steven cannot both be a brother to him and be a person who has a brother himself at the same time, from whence may come the saying, "My brother was an only child." This is also part of egocentrism, the difficulty that children at this age have of seeing what something looks like from another person's viewpoint. David could not see what he looked like from Steven's viewpoint. Another consequence of not being able to conceive of something occupying more than one classification at the same time is the difficulty that children have in understanding that a person can have mixed feelings toward another human or toward an event. It is hard for young children (and indeed for many adults) to believe that one can love and hate another person at the same time. And yet such *ambivalence* is inevitable in all human relationships.

Concrete Operational Stage (Seven to Eleven Years)

The next stage of *concrete operations* is a delight to see. At this time children can begin to do amazing things mentally. It is no accident that such concentrated teaching and learning in schools go on at this time, from the ages of approximately seven to eleven. Concrete operational children are able to reason using factual verbal propositions. They can solve "who is taller" problems, they can conserve volume, length and area, and are able to maintain the idea of constancy over apparent change. A child of this stage, when given the problem of pouring a liquid from a short, fat container into a tall, thin container, can understand that the amount of the liquid is unchanged, that nothing has been added or taken away. The same child can also attend to both dimensions, height and thickness, simultaneously, and can understand that they compensate for each other in a reciprocal way.

A key to these new found abilities is the ability to reverse processes mentally. Children of the preoperational stage cannot reverse processes mentally. The concrete operational child knows that if something can be done, it can also be undone. If you can flatten the clay ball out, you can also round it up again; if you can lengthen it, you can also shorten it. This capacity for

reversibility has medical implications. Children below the stage of concrete operations have a hard time understanding that if a bone is broken, the bone can also heal. They think that if a bone breaks, it is forever weakened. I think physicians often encounter the belief on the part of children and adults that once they get sick in a part of their body, then that part of their body is damaged forever. For example, if they get pneumonia they may believe that their lungs will be "weak" for the rest of their lives. This is a problem of reversibility. It is the ability to reverse mental processes that gives concrete operational children the *ability* to *conserve*.

Children at this age are also able to put themselves in another's place. They can describe what the mountain scene of Piaget looks like from the other side of the mountain. They can also use multiple classifications and see that things can occupy two or more classifications simultaneously. One medical implication of this capacity is that preoperational children have difficulty in understanding that there are varying degrees of illness. For example, one can have a minor illness like a cold or one can have a serious illness like leukemia. At the age of seven and older, children are able to understand that there are classifications of illness. There are serious illnesses, moderately severe illnesses, and minor illnesses. The physician should remember, however, that there are wide variations among children as to when they are able to distinguish minor from severe illnesses, and when they are able to understand the finality of death.

Formal Operational Stage (Eleven Years and Older)

The stage of *formal operations* is supposed to start around the age of eleven. Approximately 70% of adults do not achieve formal operations as defined by certain Piagetian tests, but may achieve formal operational thinking in other areas. There are a number of characteristics of formal operations. One characteristic is that the adolescent can think about and can reflect on his or her own thinking. John Conger reports hearing an adolescent say, "I began to think about my future, then I began to think about why I was thinking about my future, and then I began to wonder why I was thinking about thinking about my future." That is not only thinking about thinking, but thinking about thinking about thinking! Children in concrete operations are unable to do this.

Another characteristic of formal operations is that adolescents can reason about and use *contrary to fact propositions*. For example, an adolescent who has reached formal operations can solve the following problem: If you lived in a land where snow was black, what color would coal be? Young children below eleven cannot solve this problem and are really unable to conceive contrary to fact situations. In some ways thinking about the future is really a contrary to fact proposition because we are not yet in the future.

Another characteristic of this stage is the emergence of what is called "scientific thinking," or "propositional thinking" or "hypothetico-deductive reasoning." Formal operational adolescents can consider several variables simultaneously. They can consider the possibility of *multiple causality* rather than linear causality (only one thing causing one other thing). They can hold variables constant, manipulate a single variable, and think probablistically rather than with certainty. They can think about what are likely or possible or hypothetical outcomes rather than what is the only certain outcome. To these thinkers, the actual or the real outcome is only one of a number of possible outcomes. It is for this reason that adolescents tend to be preoccupied with abstract thought, verbal metaphors, ideal solutions, and utopian schemes. The failure of both male and female adolescents to use contraception when having intercourse despite a wish to avoid pregnancy may be thought of as a failure to develop formal operations. They do not consider the possible outcome (pregnancy), but only consider the past actual outcomes (nonpregnancy) and do not believe that a pregnancy can result from intercourse since it had not in the past.

One last characteristic of formal operations is egocentrism, but of a different type from what was described earlier. It is fair to say that children of all ages are egocentric. However, the type of egocentrism changes. In infancy, it is something like this: "Only I exist; the world and I are one and inseparable." In early childhood the thought is: "What I think is right is right, my view is the only view." By adolescence, egocentrism takes a new form. At this time the adolescent has a strong belief that he or she is

the center of others' attentions and interests, and is under constant observation. The thought here is: "Others care about me, are watching me, are interested in me and how I look. My tastes and my peers' likes and dislikes are the only important tastes, the only worthwhile tastes that have ever existed." An example of this is the following: A few years ago I asked my teenage son if people his age were still interested in disco music. His reply was, "Aw Dad, gimme a break, you've got to be kidding. Get outa here, I mean it. Disco sucks. None of us at our high school have been able to stand disco for over six months."

I would like to conclude with one last thought. The question of whether cognitive development in children can be speeded up was often asked of Piaget. He has come to refer to this question as "the American question." Can we do it faster, can we do it earlier, can we do it cheaper? To this he gives what others have called "the Swiss answer." He says, "Kittens at the age of four weeks have achieved object permanence but that is as far as they get." His answer is just as applicable to all other aspects of development as well. Man's far more complex cognitive, sexual, and social functioning is achieved only through complex cognitive, psychosexual, and psychosocial developmental progressions that cannot be speeded up, however difficult that may be for a society dedicated to personal initiative and free enterprise to accept.

Suggested Readings

Piaget J: The stages of the intellectual development of the child. *Bull Menninger Cl* 26:120, 1962.

Piaget J: The relation of affectivity to intelligence in the mental development of the child. *Bull Menninger Cl* 26:129, 1962.

Additional Readings in Piaget

Brearley M, Hitchfield E: *A Guide to Reading Piaget.* New York, Schocken Books, 1959.

Flavell JH: *The Developmental Psychology of Jean Piaget.* Princeton, NJ, Van Nostrand Co, 1963.

Ginsburg H, Opper S: *Piaget's Theory of Intellectual Development,* ed 2. Englewood Cliffs, NJ, Prentice Hall, 1978.

Inhelder B, Piaget J: *The Growth of Logical Thinking from Childhood to Adolescence.* Basic Books, New York, 1958.

Phillips JL: *Piaget's Theory: A Primer.* San Francisco, W. H. Freeman & Co, 1981.

Piaget J: *Science of Education and the Psychology of the Child.* New York, Orion Press, 1970.

Piaget J: *The Origins of Intelligence in Children.* New York, International Universities Press, 1952.

Piaget J: *Play, Dreams and Imitation in Childhood.* New York, W. W. Norton, 1951.

Section H/Puberty and Adolescence

CHAPTER **26** **Puberty and the Adolescent**

Melvin A. Scharfman, M.D.

The grade school period, particularly the latter part, was described as a time of relative stability of psychic functioning, with increasing mastery in the areas of socialization and cognition. As a result, most latency age children seem able to channel discharge of impulses into appropriate pathways, a mechanism known as *sublimation*. However, biological changes are beginning to take place which will lead to considerable disequilibrium over the next several years. I am referring to the increasing activity of the sexual hormones. This activity occurs during a period of life that is called prepuberty or preadolescence. *Puberty* itself refers to the specific physical effects of the hormonal activity, namely the development of secondary sexual characteristics, the onset of menarche in the female, and the onset of seminal emissions in the male. *Preadolescence* is a term used to describe the initial psychological process of adapting to the increased tensions resulting from these bodily changes.

PREADOLESCENT TENSION

The preadolescent youngster is characterized by a tremendous increase of tension, a tension which is experienced at first as being without any specific direction or aim. Many 11 or 12 year old children seem literally to be unable to sit still. Their feet are always moving, they tug at their ear lobes, they twist their hair, they wiggle around in their seats. Their increasing inner tension is also manifested in many vague

physical complaints. The preadolescent youngster may frequently say, "I don't feel like going to school today. I don't feel well. I have a stomach ache or a headache." This does not mean that these youngsters are malingering. Something is happening inside their bodies, and they do not know exactly what it is. There is a head of steam building up with no place to go as yet. Although we believe that the tension which is felt has to do with changes in the sexual hormones, the tensions themselves are not experienced as specifically sexual or as necessarily connected to sexual thoughts. Rather they are felt as diffuse bodily tension.

There are already considerable changes in the body, both external and internal. The year or two before the specific phenomena of puberty is a time of marked increase in growth. This growth is most marked in the arms, legs, and neck, and contributes to the gawky look of youngsters this age. In boys the shoulders begin to broaden, in girls the hips. The girls also begin to develop more subcutaneous fat and start to look rounder and softer. Some breast enlargement occurs. One of the early external changes is the appearance of pubic hair. Only later in puberty does axillary hair appear and some facial hair in boys. There are also changes due to growth of the external genitalia, which are more noticeable in the boy. The testes become larger and more pendulous, and the penis enlarges. The sebaceous glands are more active, leading to oily skin and often acne, a source of great concern. The youngsters sweat more and the perspiration has a stronger odor, another source of concern. Change of voice also begins to occur, most noticeably in the boys.

All of these bodily changes focus the attention of these youngsters on their bodies. They become self-conscious and preoccupied with their bodies. The mirror becomes an important part of life and will remain so for some years. In fact some preadolescents and adolescents cannot live without a mirror. Are they beginning to develop any hair in the pubic area or under their arms? For the girls, are her hips getting a little bit wider? Is there any kind of budding development of breasts? For the boy, is his penis getting any bigger? Preadolescents anxiously check daily for new evidences of maturity, for signs that they are growing. They compare their progress with that of their friends. Those who are slower to mature as well as those who mature early may develop feelings of discomfort about being different. Factual knowledge about the different rates of maturation may help youngsters deal with some of these concerns.

PUBERTY

I said earlier that the most specific phenomena of puberty were the occurrence of menarche in the girl and seminal emissions in the boy. One point to stress is the extent to which boys and girls differ in the age of onset of puberty, and therefore the chronological differences that constitute the periods called preadolescence and adolescence in the two sexes. The average age of puberty seems to be occurring somewhat earlier with succeeding generations for reasons that are not entirely clear. At the present time the average age of menarche appears to be about 12½, with a range between age 10½ and 15. Sperm production in the boy occurs at about age 14½, with a range from 12½ to 16½. Thus, it can be seen that the bodily phenomena we have been discussing occur about two years earlier in the girl than in the boy. As a result, girls between the ages of 11 and 14 are usually quite a bit taller than boys their own age, often towering over them. This is only one of the differences which will contribute to the different experiences of boys and girls during this prepubertal period. Let us now turn to some of the psychological differences during preadolescence, keeping in mind that we are discussing girls between approximately age 10 and 12½, and boys between 12 and 14½.

THE PREADOLESCENT BOY

Boys this age are very much concerned with their bodily changes as indicated earlier, especially as they begin to approach puberty. Some boys will have had the peak of their growth spurt starting just before puberty, but many will not. Another change which will be occurring during this time is the increase in the size of genitalia. Along with this genital change, in response to the increased hormone production, comes the occurrence of more frequent erections. These may occur in conjunction with some sexual thoughts, but frequently they do not. A preadolescent boy may find himself with an erection while sitting in a classroom or playing a game without knowing how it came about. This reflects a response to the hormonal activity that does not yet fully relate to the psychological experience of object oriented sexual wishes. Only later in the course of adolescence will this occur. Even when preadolescent boys begin to masturbate more frequently, as they often do, it is more a response to nonspecific tension than to conscious sexual thoughts. They masturbate for relief of tension which their generally active physical behavior has not fully discharged.

Socially, they are especially involved with groups of other boys in various sports activities. There frequently is a great interest in bathroom jokes and "dirty" language, and concomitant disinterest in cleanliness. Most boys will continue to behave in an anxious and hostile manner toward girls, belittling them and trying to avoid them. When there are girls around, the boys will tend to brag, boast, and tease. This difficulty in relating to women is seen most clearly in the pubertal boy's relationship with his mother. While in many ways he is quite dependent upon his mother, the pubertal age boy has a strong need to deny this dependency and appear independent. Unsure of their manliness, they are very threatened by any controlling or dominating behavior on the part of the mother. They may become involved in arguments over the simplest request made by the mother, such as to straighten up their rooms. They prefer to fight rather than to feel they are submitting. Many mothers feel rejected and hurt by this behavior, and are unable to understand that the boy is rejecting being mothered rather than rejecting the mother personally.

Boys this age are also short tempered and can easily lose control. They shout instead of talk, and slam the doors to shut out adults. They live more in a world of other boys. They compare themselves with other boys in terms of how strong or tall they are, how they can run or hit a ball, even how far they can urinate or spit. Support from the group of peers is very important as the pubertal boy begins to try to separate from his parents.

THE PREADOLESCENT GIRL

The preadolescent girl is also very concerned with her body and her appearance. She may feel that she is too fat, too thin, too tall, too short— too anything. In addition to these self-criticisms, she also complains about her mother. Prior to this time she has not really turned away from her mother in the way that the boy has, but now she does try to do so. For many girls this separation from the mother leads them to turn more toward boys. When this occurs with boys nearer to their age, they become the active pursuers of the boys. However, since boys of their own age are maturing more slowly and are still uncomfortable with girls, girls this age tend to seek out somewhat older boys. One special form of this behavior is the "crush" experienced by preadolescent girls. They may romantically idealize a male teacher, a movie or television star, or a rock music performer. Preadolescent girls formed the largest part of those involved in the adulation accorded to the Beatles some years ago, or to Frank Sinatra even earlier, and more recently to the Rolling Stones and The Who. We can see still other ways of dealing with the dependency on the mother from which the girl is trying to separate herself. Preadolescent girls tend to have very close relationships with one other girl, sharing all their secrets with her rather than with the mother. Such girl friends talk to each other endlessly, and can tie up a telephone for hours on end. Other girls turn to a diary as their confidant, "sharing" the thoughts there which they no longer communicate to their mothers. Girls this age are much less likely to form groups in the way in which boys do. Even when they do, it quickly leads to more one-to-one relationships.

THE BEGINNING OF ADOLESCENCE

The period of time we have been discussing, preadolescence, is arbitrarily concluded by the occurrence of puberty, which then marks the beginning of *early adolescence*. Preadolescence is a time when we see the psychic restructuring that will take place more extensively during adolescence. Just as preadolescence represents a stage of gradual transition from latency to adolescence, so also is adolescence a time of gradual transition from childhood to adulthood. Adolescence is in some ways a culturally specified period, most evident in technological societies. Prior to the Industrial Revolution (and the resulting specialization of work), young children became "adults" very early, and adolescence as a separate developmental phase as we now know it, did not really exist (Figures 26.1– 26.3). In some primitive cultures there is still no such stage as adolescence. Instead of prolonged education, there are rituals, sometimes called *puberty rites* or *rites of passage*, which mark the transition from childhood to adulthood. These rituals may range from brief ceremonies to a vigorous testing of skills that extends over several weeks, but they cannot compare to a developmental period which in our society extends over seven or eight years or even longer before the time that one enters adulthood with all its prerogatives and privileges. We sometimes tend to discuss adolescence as if it were an innate developmental phase that occurs inevitably because of the immaturity of the human organism, rather than seeing it as a stage that is also at least partially instituted by society. Young people growing up in different societies and cultures have very different experiences during this time of life. With this in mind, I will now for the most part discuss adolescence as it is experienced in our society. A good starting point is to consider the developmental tasks of adolescence that lead to the next phase of the life cycle, young adulthood.

THE DEVELOPMENTAL TASKS OF ADOLESCENCE

One of the major tasks that must be accomplished by young people during adolescence is that of *independence from the childhood parental ties*, and freedom from the childhood conflicts that involved the parents as the most important objects of aggressive or sexual feelings. It is this developmental task that has led Peter Blos (in his book *On Adolescence*) and others to designate adolescence as a second period of separa-

Figure 26.1. A 17th century painting of the "men of the family," ranging in age from about 10 years (on the left) to about 40 years (on the right). The clothes and demeanor are strikingly similar, the only difference being the beards of the two older men. The children are clearly "little adults," and there is little distinction between them and the older men of the family. From the film *Invention of the Adolescent*. (By permission of Perennial Education, Northfield, Illinois.)

Figure 26.2. Another painting from the film *Invention of the Adolescent*, again showing a young child appearing in both dress and demeanor as an adult. (By permission of Perennial Education, Northfield, Illinois.)

Figure 26.3. A strikingly different view of childhood following the Industrial Revolution, The "innocent" and "idyllic" nature of childhood as distinct from adulthood is now emphasized. From the film *Invention of the Adolescent.* (By permission of Perennial Education, Northfield, Illinois.)

tion and individuation. The difficulties of attempting to achieve this goal affect the adolescent's feelings and behavior in many ways, and are an important contribution to making the adolescent appear so incomprehensible to most adults. Since these attempts are especially prominent in early adolescence, I will be discussing them in greater detail shortly.

The second major developmental task of adolescence is the *achievement of a capability for heterosexual relationships outside the family boundaries.* This includes the ability to function on a genital sexual level, and the ability to integrate sexual feelings with tender, affectionate, loving feelings so that mature sexual love becomes possible. This process takes considerable time and extends well into middle and late adolescence and beyond. It is this task which Freud had in mind when he designated adoles-

cence as the *genital stage of psychosexual development.*

Finally the *consolidation of a firm sense of identity* should occur during adolescence. Erik Erikson views this as a central task of the adolescent period, a failure of which leads to *role diffusion.* The concept of identity is a complicated one that includes a sense of one's individual identity, a continuity of one's personal history, and an inner sense of one's belonging to a group. It means finding one's place within one's self and within society. The adolescent period allows for many experiments with different roles before they are synthesized into a sense of who one really is. The questions of, "Who am I?" and "Where do I fit into the scheme of things?" are the central ones for these years.

These three tasks form the background for that period we call adolescence. Their completion will mark the individual's entrance into young adulthood. For some, one or another of these tasks may extend well beyond any chronological definition of adolescence as the "teen years," especially in our society, where protracted adolescence is so very common. Let us, however, first turn to the events of early adolescence, especially the task of separation from the parents.

EARLY ADOLESCENCE—A TIME OF TURMOIL

The early adolescent seems to be in a state that is difficult for most adults to understand. Parents, in particular, are often at a loss to be able to deal with someone they thought they knew but who now seems changed. Changeability and contradiction are characteristic for youngsters at this time. They want to be independent and reject parental control, appearing at times extremely rebellious. At the same time they conform almost sheepishly to their peers' standards of dress, music, and behavior. They seem to be completely self-centered and materialistic one moment, then suddenly shift to an altruistic giving of themselves in the service of some social cause or political ideal. They can be extremely inconsiderate and tactless one day, remarkably sensitive the next. Their moods can change within minutes from being on top of the world to feeling that everything is hopeless. Consistency is totally missing, and these rapid shifts and contradictions seem hard to comprehend.

In many ways these contradictions are inevitable, because they represent a disruption of psychic organization that is necessary for reintegration at a new level. The stable structure of childhood is no longer suitable and it must change. Whether it slowly crumbles or is more dramatically smashed, it must adjust to meet a new series of challenges. For some youngsters much of the agitation is experienced only internally, in others their overt behavior and functioning are disrupted. But either way some degree of turmoil is a prerequisite for growing up. Even the process of wanting to be grown up and to be more independent is caught up in these contradictions. Let me give an example from an interview with a 15 year old boy. One day he began, "Well, this is it. I've had it. I can't take it any more. This is the end with my mother. I

have to leave. I'm moving out on my own. I'll get an apartment of my own or live with a friend. I don't care what I do, but I can't live here. She is impossible. I can't take it." After awhile I asked how all this had started and just what it was that had caused him to be so angry. He shifted in his chair and said, "Well, you know how it is. When I get home from school I like to have a snack. A glass of milk and cookies or something. Today I went to the refrigerator and there was nothing there. Nothing!" The adolescent wishes to feel grown up, yet in many ways still feels like a child. The young adolescent struggles with this conflict much of the time. Demands are made to be given new freedoms and to be treated as an adult, while at the same time there are still strong wishes to be taken care of as a child. Nowhere is this clearer than in the relationship to the parents.

INDEPENDENCE FROM THE PARENTS

One can see derivatives of the wish to gain a greater degree of freedom and separation from the parents in the adolescents' attempts to take over a greater degree of control of their own bodies. They insist on wearing only the clothes they wish to wear, in wearing their hair in a style that pleases them, on bathing only when they wish, or eating only when they wish, or sleeping only when they wish. In each of these areas they may become involved in a struggle with the parents, especially if the parents have a need to impose their own standards. Adolescents also attempt to control and integrate as their own their increasing sexual feelings. Particularly for the young adolescent boy, masturbation becomes a way of trying to master these feelings and bring them under some degree of self-regulation.

Earlier in the book we discussed the separation and individuation of young children from their parents, and the differentiation of their own bodies from their mother's body. While this process leads to the capacity to discriminate the self from other objects, the child for many years continues to feel that the parents are really responsible for taking care of his or her body. It is only during early adolescence that youngsters attempt to more fully claim their bodies as their own. Like many aspects of adolescence this can lead to an overreaction. Adolescents may announce that they will be responsible for their own body functions, but then may neglect them or abuse them. We can see derivatives of this feeling that their parents are still responsible for their bodies in the behavior of youngsters who get into difficulty through sexual activity or drug abuse. It is not uncommon to hear such young people say, "Boy, it would kill my parents if they knew what I was doing." They act as if it is really the parents who will suffer the consequences of their behavior, rather than having a clear awareness of their bodies as their own. Here again parental attitudes can contribute greatly to such a conflict.

In many other areas the adolescent is also trying to become more independent. The early adolescent plagues the parents for permission to stay out late, to have an unchaperoned party, or to have more money available. In many of these demands the youngsters seek far more than they expect to get. They attempt to make the parents feel unfair about any limits that may be imposed, yet at the same time they make it clear that they need limits to be set. Many young people are not only unable to impose limits adequately on themselves, but also feel that the absence of any limits is an expression of parental indifference or neglect. In the course of treating a number of young people, it is a rather common experience to find that after an initial period of praising their parents for being "open-minded and liberal," youngsters may later indicate that such permissiveness is really seen as an emotional abandonment by the parents. One young girl, who had extolled her parents for their granting of various freedoms, returned from a weekend stating, "Look at my mother. I went away for the whole weekend and she didn't ask who I was with. I don't think she even cared if it was my girl friend or if it was a boy friend. All she asked was whether I had a nice time. She really couldn't care less about what happens to me." Of course, if this mother had asked, the girl might have become angry, or lied in order to cover up having done something of which her mother might not approve. But she would not have felt that her mother was indifferent.

It is very difficult for many parents to know how to achieve some balance between granting increasing freedom and responsibility while still imposing appropriate limits in keeping with the youngster's level of functioning. Many parents are overly concerned that their children will be angry with them or criticize them as being "old-

fashioned" or exceedingly harsh. It is important to remember that this kind of criticism appears to be necessary to the young adolescent. He or she needs to feel that there is some opposition, something against which to rebel. Parents who are more secure within themselves and in their relationship with their children can tolerate their youngsters' anger and criticism, knowing that the time will come when this too will pass. This is a time of stress for many parents, and often their own internal pressures contribute to the conflict and the turmoil of adolescence.

The adolescent process can create a variety of pressures for parents. While young adolescents are trying to gain a greater sense of themselves as separate individuals, many parents experience this attempt as an indication that they are beginning to lose their child. Particularly where the adolescent is the last child or an only child, the parents may feel the pressure to reevaluate their own lives and goals, which for many years may have been stabilized by the presence of their children. In addition, simply having children of adolescent age means that parents are confronted with the fact that they themselves are getting older. This is something which in our society seems particularly difficult to accept. We are very strongly youth oriented, and most people seek to look and to feel younger. The pleasure of maturity, a time of life that in other cultures brings increasing respect and admiration, are less in our own society. We do not look kindly upon aging, and one sees many parents trying to compete with their youngsters.

It is not at all uncommon to see the fortyish mother wearing the same hair style as her teenage daughter, dressing in jeans, dancing to the latest music, or using the teenager's language. Sometimes such a mother enters into an overt competition with her daughter, and if the young girl has questions about her own attractiveness or desirability, she may develop marked feelings of inferiority. She may feel that it is impossible ever to compete sexually with her mother, and she may then accept a devalued view of herself. Similar phenomena may sometimes be seen in a father's relationship to his teenage son. As the youngster is attempting to succeed in sports, schoolwork, or in dating girls, the father may be in active competition. He may need to prove that he can defeat his son in athletic events, that he is smarter in all areas, and that he certainly knows more about girls. Here, too, some boys accept a sense of defeat and inferiority, feeling as though they can never compete adequately with their fathers.

If the parents are overly concerned with the feelings that they are concluding ther own lives while their youngsters are beginning theirs, then the youngsters do indeed become rivals. The mother may be envying her daughter's physical attractiveness or the attention she gets from young men. The father may be envying his son's emerging physical prowess or be jealous of the young girls he sees his son dating. Particularly for parents who are not secure within themselves or for those who have had a tenuous marriage, this can be a time of great stress. It is partially to such experiences that the idea of a "conflict of generations" is attributed. Many other parents, of course, are able to maintain a reasonable relationship with their children during this process, granting increasing freedom to their youngsters in an appropriate way and looking forward to the time when they can enjoy their own lives without so much focus on their children.

DEFENSIVE FUNCTIONS IN ADOLESCENCE

The struggle of the adolescent to remove himself or herself from the attachment to the parents is a very intensive one. It extends over a considerable period of time and is fraught with many changes and conflicts. Why is this so? I have already discussed the tremendous increase in drive intensity in prepuberty and early adolescence. It is the parents who are the initial objects of these drives. This is another way of saying that there is a revival, usually unconscious, of oedipal conflicts in early adolescence. However, there is a considerable difference between this revival in adolescence and the earlier oedipal conflicts. The five year old child who is angry with his daddy may wish to be able to hit him or beat him up, but he knows that physically this would be impossible. However, a 15 year old has the physical capacity to put such aggressive wishes into action. Even more frightening are the adolescent's sexual feelings. At age five one could not do very much about one's sexual wishes and fantasies, but a 15 year old can. What this means is that these conflicts are experienced in different ways which are much more threatening. It is this intensity that leads to the equally intense attempts to free oneself from

one's attachment to the parents. Let us consider some of the ways in which the adolescent attempts to do this.

One mechanism of defense used in this process is what Anna Freud called *reversal of affect*. What this means is that the adolescent defends himself or herself from the threatening feelings of attachment to the parent by reversing them into the opposite. Such an adolescent states, "I can't stand my mother or my father. I can't be in the same room with them. I hate them." This defense is not entirely a successful one, although commonly used. Its operation indicates only a partial step toward separation, inasmuch as the parent remains the focus of an intense emotional attachment. By reversing the affect, the adolescent has moved to a somewhat more comfortable distance, but the intensity of the attachment is still present. In later adolescence we will see that such extreme reversals are no longer necessary, and the adolescent who is less intensely involved will not need this kind of defense.

Another defense utilized both in early adolescence and throughout the course of adolescence by some youngsters is that of *displacement*. The intense attachment to the parent is shifted onto someone else. This is related to the phenomenon of the "crush" that we discussed earlier. Usually the object of displacement is someone who is older than the adolescent, not uncommonly a teacher or a friend's parent. In relation to this person, the adolescent experiences a degree of the idealization and intense attachment that is a reflection of what had gone on much earlier in relationship to the parents. As intense as these attachments may be, they are also quite transitory. An adolescent can enter into this kind of "crush" for a brief period of time, and then shift the feelings onto someone else, sometimes overnight. Yet such attachments may have many positive consequences for later development in the sense that they may contribute to partial identifications, something we will consider later. Youngsters involved in these kinds of displaced love relationships are sometimes quite vulnerable. This occurs when they encounter an older person who takes advantage of the youngster's love and turns it into a more specific sexual relationship. Such relationships have been portrayed from time to time in a variety of novels and movies, such as *The Graduate*. Certainly it is a common clinical finding that the object of the early adolescent's sexual feelings is someone who is a thinly disguised substitute for the parents.

Equally common in adolescence is for the intense emotional involvement, when it is withdrawn from the parent, to be shifted not to someone else but onto the self. It is this phenomenon that accounts for the narcissistic involvement so characteristic of adolescents, the intense concern with the body, with appearance, with the feeling that the whole world is centered around them. Later on when we discuss some of the disturbances in adolescent development, we will see that there are some youngsters who seem to be fixed at this point. Having withdrawn from their involvement with their parents, they invest themselves with all of their available emotions, and have a great deal of difficulty in experiencing subsequent emotional relationships with other people.

Normal adolescents may wish to withdraw from the world for very brief periods of time. Many go through phases in which they feel that their privacy is absolutely not to be invaded. They put "Do Not Disturb" signs on the door or lock their rooms, and become furious if anyone attempts to intrude into their private sanctuaries. However, the normal adolescent may move quickly from such a period into another in which he is intensely involved with everything going on around him. To become arrested in this otherwise transitory involvement with the self is an indication of something seriously wrong with the process of development.

Before we look at adolescents as they move on to involvement with people their own age, I would like to mention two other defenses, both described by Anna Freud in her classic book, *The Ego and the Mechanisms of Defense,* namely *intellectualization* and *asceticism.* If one looks at the adolescent in our society in recent years, one would think that these defenses are less common now than they might once have been. Yet, we do see youngsters who manifest in significant ways such patterns of reaction. Asceticism refers to the adolescent who attempts to massively repudiate drive gratification in all forms, and who goes through periods of self-denial by not allowing himself or herself any pleasure in eating, sleeping, expressions of anger, or sexuality. Perhaps in recent years the closest to this phenomenon that we have seen are those youngsters who have become engaged in a preoccupation with eastern religions, part of whose doctrine

centers around asceticism. These youngsters go through varying periods in which they deny themselves all the pleasures of the flesh. It does seem that in our present society one is more likely to see excesses of indulgence rather than asceticism, but we do see patterns in which brief periods of deprivation alternate with extreme self-indulgence. The utilization of this kind of massive defense was described by Anna Freud as related to the nature of the threat that the adolescents feel from the intensity of drives. Afraid that they will be overwhelmed by impulses, they may resort to this global attempt at self-control and self-discipline.

As for intellectualization, it is certainly quite evident in many adolescents. It is related to the fact that there is a significant development in the level of cognitive functioning and abstract thinking during adolescence, as Dr. Farley has noted in his discussion of Piaget's *stage of formal operations.* What is relevant here is that this otherwise normal development process can be utilized for defensive purposes. Some adolescents engage in highly abstract intellectual discussions which essentially are related to unconscious problems involving family ties and family organizations, which they are attempting to resolve. Thus, one sees adolescents who discuss endlessly the varying forms of possible organization of a society: democratic, socialistic, and dictatorial. Such youngsters, aside from whatever else in the way of real interest they have in such discussions, are also dealing with how they feel their own families should be organized. It is indeed difficult to draw a line and say when certain intellectual interests of adolescents should be considered a defensive function, and when they essentially represent highly successful adaptations and a movement to better levels of integration.

THE CAPACITY TO LOVE

Let us now follow the adolescent on the path toward a love relationship. One thing that happens in the normal adolescent developmental process is that at some point there is a shifting of love interest onto someone of the opposite sex who is closer in age. This shift may be gradual or it may come about rather abruptly. It is not unusual for young boys or girls to suddenly decide that someone who had been sitting next to them in school for two years and toward whom they had been indifferent, now becomes the object of their love. The adolescent "crushes" that I discussed may resemble some of these early attachments, but they are essentially different. This early love relationship may take varying forms. One form seems to be just a step removed from the kind of narcissistic preoccupation that some adolescents have gone through. That is, they make an early choice of a love object on a narcissistic basis. This means that when the young adolescent boy chooses his first girl friend, she is liable to be valued by him not in terms of what she is or even what he feels about her, but rather in terms of what the other boys think about her. This phenomenon is what leads to the choice of the most popular girl, the prettiest girl, the one who enhances his own esteem in the eyes of his friends. The same phenomenon may occur when the girl chooses the handsomest boy, the best athlete, or the smartest boy. Such choices are relatively narcissistic and not what we hope will evolve later in development as a more lasting object relationship. Such a phase is of course not a necessary phenomenon in normal development, but it is nevertheless a frequent one.

Whether or not they have gone through this specific phase, the next step of finding someone to love is one that is very characteristic of adolescence and may go on for quite a long time. The early feelings of love are quite romantic and are sometimes called "puppy love," but they are really the beginning of tender feelings for some-

one of the opposite sex (Figure 26.4). Such feelings are usually quite idealized and highly romantic. They are called romantic because they have some of the characteristics of romantic love as described in literature. It is a love relationship in which there is a split between the feelings of love, affection, and tenderness on the one hand, and sexuality on the other. It is not easy for adolescents to integrate feelings of love and sexual feelings, and this integration is usually a gradual process. Of course, one can look at many current early adolescent love relationships and can see that they are quite explicitly sexual. This, however, does not mean that an integration between love and sexuality has necessarily taken place, and we will consider some of the effects of the trend toward earlier explicitly sexual relationships shortly.

In the more usual and perhaps in some ways more appropriate developmental process of adolescence, there is a gradual integration of sexual feelings and experiences into a relationship with someone toward whom one also has feelings of love and tenderness. The adolescent tends to experiment, and gradually to integrate and master one step at a time on the path toward genital sexuality, rather than covering the distance in one great leap.

There is a related pattern of development in which the adolescent, most frequently the boy, literally splits sexuality apart from a love relationship. In this situation the boy may have two girls, one of whom he idealizes and feels that he loves, but with whom he has very little explicit

Figure 26.4.   An adolescent boy and girl. From the film *Adolescence: The Winds of Change* by John Janeway Conger, in consultation with Jerome Kagan. (By permission of Harper & Row, 10 East 53rd St., New York, N. Y. 10022.)

sexual involvement. He may simultaneously have another girl toward whom he does not have such feelings of love, but with whom he does have a sexual relationship. This particular pattern as it appears in adolescence is somewhat more common among boys, just as it may be more common in adult males. It is possible that this difference is accounted for by the different oedipal resolution in the boy and the girl. As I discussed in earlier chapters, the boy will feel a greater prohibition against any persistent sexual feelings connected with his mother or sister. It is this phenomenon which accounts for the splitting off of sexuality from love, and which requires time for working through in adolescence. It means that the successful ability to integrate these feelings is dependent upon a modification in the superego which originally forbade such feelings in connection with a childhood love object. The superego of childhood must, of course, be modified in many ways to allow normal adult functioning, but this is one of the important modifications that is necessary.

As was indicated, girls do not have the same kind of experience. They are more likely to have retained some connection between love feelings and the expression of some degree of sexual interest. This is one reason why the adolescent girl in many ways finds it much easier than the adolescent boy of equivalent age to accept the sexual relationship as part of the love relationship. It may also be a factor in leading adolescent girls to seek someone a few years older than themselves, someone who would have been able to move further along on this path than a boy their own age.

Let us turn for a moment to some of the possible effects of the so-called sexual revolution on adolescent behavior. There seems to be no question that changes in society's attitudes toward sexuality, the widespread availability of sexual information, and the availability of contraception have had profound effects. These appear not only in the extent to which adolescents talk more openly about their sexuality, but also in the greater frequency of sexual experiences during the adolescent process. It is also clear that many of these young people are not emotionally equipped to deal with these experiences in a constructive way. Often they engage in initial sexual experiences because of peer pressure. They are simply viewed as not grown up enough by their peers if they choose not to have intercourse at this time. There are, of course,

many other pressures operative. The sexual impulses of adolescence are intense and demand some outlet. Adolescents are physically mature and yet, in the structure of our society, they are certainly not psychologically mature. They are not able to support themselves. They cannot marry if that would be their wish. As a matter of fact, for most adolescents "being grown up" seems a hundred years away. The prolongation of the period before they are viewed as socially able to function on an adult level increases the pressure felt by many adolescents. For some, sex becomes a temporary palliative. It serves to make them feel more grown up. For many others, sex remains an isolated function in which they are technically proficient but without the accompanying sense of emotional involvement. Others find it difficult, in spite of the recent modification of some of society's attitudes, to function without a sense of guilt. This is a real problem facing many adolescents because the sense of pressure and the need for some discharge is quite real.

What outlets do adolescents use when they choose not to engage in sexual intercourse? Many adolescent jokes indicate that one of their outlets is through involvement in motor activities, particularly competitive sports. Adolescents joke with each other, suggesting that one of them run around the block a few times and take a cold shower if he feels sexually tense. In fact, their involvement with sports does partially serve to discharge some of their sexual tensions. This may take the form of playing football, basketball, tennis, swimming, or extend to drag races with their cars. In one way or another they seek to involve themselves in activities that provide excitement, emotional involvement, and some form of physical discharge. Work, of course, also becomes an outlet for some of these adolescent pressures, whether it be school work, a job after school, or a hobby. More frequently, however, none of these outlets really adequately resolves the tension.

Many adolescents continue to masturbate as their primary form of sexual discharge. Such masturbation remains a source of guilt in spite of the available information that it is not in any way physically damaging. These adolescents who experience guilt over this activity are generally guilty about the nature of the fantasies that accompany their masturbation. These fantasies are frequently grandiose, exploitative, or sado-masochistic, revealing the same difficulties in integrating sexuality with love and affection that are manifested in their day-to-day relationships. Masturbation, particularly for boys, is very common during adolescence, so common that we would be concerned about a boy who had never masturbated. This is not quite the same for girls, although masturbation by girls is by no means infrequent. Masturbation is one means the adolescent uses in an attempt to master his or her impulses, and will usually become less frequent as some real relationship begins to develop. The essential problem of the adolescent in this area is one of an appropriate timetable for sexuality. There are adolescents, particularly toward the latter part of adolescence, who can have meaningful and satisfying real relationships including sexual relationships, but this remains a most difficult area for many adolescents.

All of this is preparatory to the fact that somewhere in the course of adolescence the capacity for a full relationship with someone of the opposite sex should develop. This is the achievement of *genitality*. Genitality means more than just the fact that sexual tensions are discharged by the genital route. It implies the capacity for the integration of such sexuality with love, affection, and tenderness. Achievement of this level of functioning during the latter phases of adolescence is of essential importance. One of the reasons that adolescence in our society is such a disturbed time may be the fact that many obstacles are placed in the path of such achievement by an institutionalized prolongation of childhood and adolescence. We live in a society in which the period of time before one really becomes capable of having available the prerogatives of the adult world has been extended further and further. This prolongation of adolescence has many implications for the completion of the third developmental task, namely the consolidation of a sense of identity.

IDENTITY CONSOLIDATION

One of the central concerns of adolescents is to define their sense of who they are and what they wish to do. Up to the time of early adolescence the most significant identifications have almost always been with the parents, more specifically with the parent of the same sex. With the attempt to achieve emotional distance from the parents, this identity begins to change, and

there is a corresponding search for new models. These models may at times be the objects of intense admiration and idealization. A school teacher, particularly one with whom there is some extended personal contact, may be chosen. The parent of a friend, someone's older brother or sister, an athletic or creative hero or heroine are other possibilities. Sometimes the adolescent's identification with this new model is quite striking, with the assumption of that person's manner of dress, hair style, or speech. Whatever their nature, such identifications occur and contribute to some modification in the identity of the adolescents and in their sense of themselves. Such relationships also introduce changes in the superego and the ego ideal. Previously accepted values are examined and challenged, and new values considered. There are changes in what one hopes to be, as well as modification in what is felt to be acceptable.

To all of these identifications other factors affecting identity are added in middle and late adolescence. The choice of vocation becomes a major concern. Few such decisions are seriously made before this time except perhaps for certain youngsters with special talents in music, art, and dance. Such youngsters may already know what they wish to be and will stay with that choice. Most adolescents try out many different possibilities either in their fantasies or in brief experimentations before they have any sense of what they wish to do. Some go to college just because they do not know what they want to do. Middle class youngsters in particular may graduate from high school and be well into college before they have any defined sense of vocation. Working class youngsters are more likely to decide upon an occupation earlier. They have, of course, fewer choices. It is becoming increasingly common in our society that such decisions occur later and later. The actual entry into the vocation is, of course, even later than that decision.

In fields such as medicine, law, engineering, and a host of others which require extensive postgraduate training, it is not unusual to see students in their mid-twenties or even later who have not yet engaged in their chosen occupation. They are, of course, for the most part not financially independent during this prolonged period. For many, such as the medical students who might be reading this book, the time when they will finish their training and be able to earn a living seems light years away. This situation affects not only their sense of themselves but also affects decisions such as marriage and the raising of a family. While in these fields the examples are relatively dramatic, they are reflective of a trend in our contemporary society. The social changes brought about by our advancing technology and by a broadening democratic structure with its erosion of class barriers have brought many benefits, but they have also created problems. Advancing technology means that there is a need for a considerably smaller labor force but one which is much more highly educated and skilled. Some sociologists feel that, in addition to humanitarian and other altruistic motivations, compulsory education is in part an outgrowth of the need to limit the entrance of young people into the job market. They are kept for longer and longer periods in schools which are not always oriented to providing the kind of education which will equip them for productive occupations. At the same time unskilled, semiskilled, and even skilled labor positions are relatively devalued in our society. This places a greater emphasis upon so-called white collar occupations, with concomitant pressure upon everyone to achieve a college education. One finds many young people who graduate from college, not only uncertain of what occupation they wish to pursue, but unprepared to pursue it, or if they are prepared, unable to find employment in that occupation. Obviously, there are no easy solutions to these problems, but it does seem that this prolongation of adolescence contributes significantly to the confusion of many young people about who they are, where they belong, and where they are going. In a sense they hang suspended between the world of childhood and the world of adulthood for a long time.

The changing social structure also has its effects. In less complex cultures, the choices open to young people are much fewer. At one time, even in our society, a boy stayed within the class boundaries in which he was born and not infrequently entered whatever occupation the father had. For the girl the choices were even narrower. Few occupations, other than to become a wife and mother, were open to women. Now, there is, at least theoretically, no limitation on choice of occupation or on the achievement of economic or social status. That, of course, is not always true in fact, but it is clear that there is a much wider range of choices available to young people. While very few would wish to go back to that social system which

narrowed occupational choice and social mobility, the widened range of choices and movement creates additional problems for many young people. Identity consolidation and the sense of self are probably easier to achieve in a less complicated world. Certainly we do seem to be presented with increasing numbers of people in their early twenties and even in their late twenties and early thirties who are essentially experiencing some of the uncertainties in regard to identity that we would usually associate with adolescence.

EMOTIONAL PROBLEMS DURING ADOLESCENCE

It is not possible to cover in any detail the wide range of emotional disturbances that can occur during the phase of life designated as adolescence. Many of the disturbances will be covered in greater detail in later chapters of the book. This section will be limited to indicating some of the patterns of disturbance most closely associated with the adolescent period.

First, of course, one could mention what has been discussed more extensively above, namely *protracted adolescence*. In its own way, protracted adolescence contributes to several other conditions encountered by the clinician dealing with adolescents. Considering what has been described above in terms of the disruptions of psychic structures and their subsequent reorganization, one can be tempted to think of much of adolescence as in some sense pathological. This, of course, is not so. Erikson used the term "normative crisis" in discussing adolescence, and this seems a useful way in which to view many of the events which occur. Erikson also viewed this time as one during which there was a "psychosocial moratorium," meaning that this was a period during which there was societal approval and institutionalization of a transitional period for experimentation and growth. But the prolonged extension of this period brings with it certain problems. Erikson has designated one such problem as *role diffusion* (also known as *identity disorder*), referring to a phenomenon in which there is essentially a fragmentation of the sense of identity with a failure to incorporate and synthesize new identifications occurring during adolescence. These youngsters appear to have cast off an earlier sense of themselves but fail to find some new and more integrated sense of themselves. They appear as confused, aimless, and uncertain in regard to their life goals with impairment in both their social and occupational functioning, and as a result they have failed in one of the essential developmental tasks of adolescence.

Other aspects of adolescent behavior also seem related to the extended time period with its prolonged delays in assuming the functions of a young adult. Some of the psychosocial phenomena of recent years may be reflections of this. We have gone through a period of adolescent social protests and political involvement. As this activity subsided, there was a marked increase in the use of drugs by the adolescent population. Thus, there was a change from an active quest for greater involvement in determining social or political direction to a position of apathy and escape when the quest appeared futile. This now appears to be subsiding to some extent and is being replaced by a return to conformity, with an emphasis of working hard in school to achieve practical ends, despite the fact that jobs are scarce. The essential problem, however, remains the same. We have not as yet found the optimal way for adolescents to participate constructively in our society, with appropriate outlets for their enthusiasm and energy. It would go well beyond the scope of this chapter to consider those changes in society that might facilitate such a development. It does seem, however, that as a society we cannot ignore what looms as an ever increasing adolescent population. A large percentage of our population is under age 25, and a great many of these individuals are still involved in protracted education and training, and thus feel less than full members of society.

Another form of emotional disturbance during adolescence appears in the youngster who remains unable to participate in that restructuring and resynthesis that is required for growth. Some of the young people who appear to be completely free of any of the disruptions associated with adolescence are in this category. They may be free of disruptions in terms of their external behavior, but they remain constricted and rigid in their intrapsychic functioning. Since we think that adolescence should be a time of change in growth in the ego and the ego ideal and a time of modifications in the superego, youngsters who do not allow for such growth because of their rigidity fail to develop emotionally. On the other hand, there are some adolescents who appear to move through adolescence

relatively smoothly and progressively, and still manage to achieve the necessary internal changes. They are usually favored in their environmental circumstances, have good peer relationships, and have parents who encourage their independence. The Offers have described such adolescents as the "continuous growth group," in contrast to the "surgent growth group" (characterized by cycles of progression and regression) and the "tumultuous growth group" (characterized by recurrent self-doubts, conflicts with parents, and less stable family backgrounds).

Another common problem during adolescence which is frequently overlooked is that of *depression*. All adolescents may at times experience feelings of depression and may even have limited suicidal fantasies in which they wonder what the world would be like without them and if anyone would miss them. That is all part of the emotional changes within the boundaries of normal adolescent behavior. However, the relatively high number of adolescent suicides is proof enough that major depressions also occur during adolescence. Although the country's overall suicide rate has not varied much in the past 50 years, the rate for adolescent suicides has more than tripled between 1965 and 1985. For a long period of time such suicides were concealed as accidents, and therefore they were thought to be less frequent than was actually the case. Such adolescent depressions are also sometimes masked by other behaviors such as drug use or sexual promiscuity. A serious assessment must be made of possible depression when we see adolescents who are having difficulty in functioning.

For all the years since Kraepelin first designated *schizophrenia* as dementia praecox, it has been common to associate the onset of schizophrenia with adolescence. There is certainly some truth in this in that early signs of a schizophrenic disorganization may first become manifest during adolescence. Not all clinicians agree as to the continuum between early adolescent schizophrenic-like disturbances and the usual clinical syndromes that evolve into chronic schizophrenia in adulthood. Some feel that these acute disturbances occurring during adolescence may represent, at least in some cases, a rather different process, one which is less related to genetic and biochemical disturbances than some other patterns seen in adult schizophrenia. Whatever the truth may be, we do see adolescents in whom disorganization and disintegration become quite prominent in conjunction with a withdrawal from involvement with family, friends, school, and work. Where such a pattern continues for any period of time, a careful evaluation by a clinician familiar with adolescents is indicated.

There are, of course, many other disturbances that can occur during adolescence in addition to the usual psychopathological syndromes. *Delinquency* has been very much associated with adolescence, and *antisocial personality* patterns first appear during adolescence in many cases. Other youngsters may be involved in similar behavior which does not have the same meaning or consequences. The instability for short periods of time of superego functioning in adolescence may lead to brief involvement in symptomatic delinquent behavior for youngsters who are subsequently able to function quite normally. Isolated experiences of breaking laws are not infrequent in normal adolescents, or at least in adolescents who do not subsequently evolve into antisocial personalities. Again, a careful evaluation is indicated.

Finally, *anorexia nervosa* is a syndrome whose onset is most frequent during early adolescence. It is far more frequent in girls, usually pubertal or early adolescent. A sudden loss of all interest in eating, with marked weight loss that becomes not easily reversible, is the characteristic symptomatology. It is a syndrome which may have a variety of underlying conflicts. The fact that this frequently occurs in youngsters who are in many other areas functioning extremely well and are high achievers may lead the unfamiliar observer to underestimate the seriousness of this illness. It is again a disturbance which requires a careful evaluation by someone familiar with adolescents.

TOWARD ADULTHOOD

What can we say about the indications that an adolescent has moved toward young adulthood? It was said that adolescence was a stage of development that could be defined in developmental terms as related to the achievement of certain tasks. It has no sharp endpoint as such but must be looked at in terms of relative developmental achievements. Very few adolescents complete all of these developmental goals by the end of their teenage years. What may be central is rather that the goals begin to seem reachable,

that there is a defined sense of direction. There should be a considerable degree of freedom from the emotional intensity and dependency of earlier relationships to the parents. This does not mean that there should be no relationship with the parents. Rather, there should be more mutuality in that relationship and some sense of affectionate, respectful feelings between adults rather than between parent and child. They need not agree all of the time, but they can still respect each other's positions. The adolescent's sense of self-respect develops most in an atmosphere of respect by the parents and by society, something all too often not present. The adolescent takes himself or herself seriously and needs to be viewed that way.

There should have developed the capacity for a meaningful continued relationship with the opposite sex, whether or not there has been a full and satisfactory sexual relationship. At least there needs to have evolved the capability for such a relationship. The achievement of a stable and full degree of what Erikson calls the "capacity for intimacy" may not occur until later. Certainly, permanent marital or even other long-lasting relationships may not yet have taken place. In fact, marriages taking place between adolescents have not had a very good prognosis. The current trend to later marriages may in part be a reflection of the phenomenon of the prolongation of adolescence discussed earlier.

The sense of identity should be more stable with a greater degree of certainty about who one is and where one is going, even if one may not yet be there. There should be the capacity to anticipate future goals and to delay immediate gratifications in order to attain these goals. Time is seen in better perspective, with past, present, and future all equally meaningful, rather than an emphasis only on the here and now.

If these tasks are reasonably close to achievement we can expect that something of a satisfactory adulthood has a good change of developing. Where there are serious failures in any of these areas, the kind of adulthood that develops will be compromised to a greater or lesser degree.

Suggested Readings

Adelson JB: The mystique of adolescence. In Harrision SI, McDermott JF (eds): *Childhood Psychopathology.* New York, International Universities Press, 1972, p 214.

Bibring GL, Kahana RJ: Puberty and adolescence. In *Lectures in Medical Psychology.* New York, International Universities Press, 1968, p 131.

Blos P: *On Adolescence.* Glencoe, NY, Free Press, 1962.

Dulit EP: Adolescence. In Wiedeman GH (ed): *Personality Development and Deviation*. New York, International Universities Press, 1975, p 189.

Erikson EH: Identity vs. role diffusion. In *Childhood and Society*. New York, W. W. Norton, 1950, p 227.

Esman AH (ed): *The Psychology of Adolescence: Essential Readings*. New York, International Universities Press, 1975.

Finch S: *Adolescent Suicide*. Springfield, IL, Charles C Thomas, 1971.

Fine LI: *"After All We've Done For Them": Understanding Adolescent Behavior*. Englewood Cliffs, NJ, Prentice-Hall, 1977.

Freud A (1936): *The Ego and the Mechanisms of Defense*. New York, International Universities Press, 1946.

Freud A: Adolescence. *Psychoanal Study Child* 13:255, 1958.

Group for the Advancement of Psychiatry. *Normal Adolescence*. Report No 68. New York, Group for the Advancement of Psychiatry, 1968.

Lidz T: Adolescence. In *The Person*. New York, Basic Books, 1976, p 306.

Mack JE, Hickler H: *Vivienne: The Life and Suicide of an Adolescent Girl*. Boston, Little, Brown, and Co, 1981.

Mussen PH, Conger JJ, Kagan J, Huston AC: Adolescence. In *Essentials of Child Development and Personality*. New York, Harper & Row, 1984.

Offer D, Offer JB: *From Teenage to Young Manhood*. New York, Basic Books, 1975.

Prugh DG: *The Psychosocial Aspects of Pediatrics*. Philadelphia, Lea & Febiger, 1983.

Sorenson RC: *Adolescent Sexuality in Contemporary America*. New York, World Publishing, 1973.

References

Anthony EJ: Two contrasting types of adolescent depression and their treatment. In Anthony EJ, Benedek T (eds): *Depression and Human Existence*. Boston, Little, Brown, and Co, 1975, p 445.

Conger JJ, Petersen AC: *Adolescence and Youth*. New York, Harper & Row, 1984.

Erikson EH: *Identity: Youth and Crisis*. New York, W. W. Norton, 1968.

Feinstein SC: Adolescent depression. In Anthony EJ, Benedek T (eds): *Depression and Human Existence*. Boston, Little, Brown, and Co, 1975, p 317.

Hendin H: Growing up dead: student suicide. *Am J Psychotherapy* 29:327, 1975.

Josselyn IM: *The Adolescent and His World*. New York, Family Service Association of America, 1952.

Keniston K: *The Uncommitted: Alienated Youth in American Society*. New York, Harcourt, Brace & World, 1965.

Weller RA, Weller EB, Herjanic B: Adult psychiatric disorders in psychiatrically ill young adolescents. *Am J Psychiatry* 140:1585, 1983.

27 **Culture: Life Perspectives and the Social Meanings of Illness**

Emily Mumford, Ph.D.

"Medicine is an exquisitely sensitive indicator of the dominant cultural characteristics of any era, for man's behavior before the threats and realities of illness is necessarily rooted in the conception he has of himself and his universe."* Each society's culture provides its members with a system of vital ideas that gives some coherence to the crucial events of birth, illness, and death, and a measure of predictability in social life. Beliefs, customs, values, preferences, and perspectives, while products of social interaction, in turn shape behavior and the meanings that people assign to the events of the life cycle.

THE NATURE OF CULTURE

While most cultures include some physical conditions under a concept somewhat akin to our notion of illness, there are marked variations in four interrelated aspects. These are: the beliefs about causation, the conditions that qualify as "sickness," the expectations about what the afflicted person should do, and the expected actions of others in response to that person's condition.

These culturally generated definitions around health and illness can become self-fulfilling. The concept of the *self-fulfilling prophecy* simply means that when people act on the basis of their beliefs and shared definitions, the actions make the beliefs come true. Regardless of the original objective reality, if most depositors in a bank believe that its financial integrity is threatened—and if many of them act on the basis of that belief to cause a "run on the bank"—their prophecy is likely to be fulfilled.

"Bone-pointing" or black magic among the

---

* E. Pellegrino. "Medicine, history, and the idea of man." *Ann Am Acad Polit Soc Sci* 346:9, 1963.

isolated natives in the northern territory of Australia offers an extreme example of self-fulfilling prophecy. The unhappy victim believes in the power of magic and so do the people around him. Once cursed by the "magical rite," he appears stricken by terror. He may refuse water and food and suffer dehydration. His kinsmen abandon him. According to reports, deaths have resulted from the actions set in motion by the malevolent prophecy.

Populations, acting on their definitions and beliefs, for example a conviction of illness as "fate" or "God's will," can profoundly influence morbidity and mortality statistics. Our value commitment to activism, to active intervention in nature, has led us to massive investments in sanitation, health research, education, and health services, with consequent reduction in infant mortality and infectious disease.

Beliefs about the reasons for illness are often held tenaciously. As Stanley King points out, the beliefs of a Navajo from a remote reservation cannot be dismissed as "mere superstition"; to the Navajo they are real and sensible. In Mexico among the Tepoztecans, there are "hot" and "cold" diseases, just as there are "hot" and "cold" foods. A mother who is convinced that her child is suffering from a "hot" disease brought on by the adultery of her husband, knows that the child needs a "cold" medicine. If she goes to a *curandero* (Fig. 27.1), she tells him or her that the child is suffering from a "hot" disease, but if she goes to a doctor, she says nothing. If the doctor's medicine does not work, the mother attributes it to the fact that the doctor did not understand the nature of the illness and gave the child a hot medicine instead of cold. On the other hand, if the curandero does not effect a cure, her explanation is of a different kind. She now believes that the heat of the disease was so great that there was no medicine cold enough to

Figure 27.1. A *curandero* in Taos, New Mexico. Photograph by Richard Spas. (By permission of Richard Spas, Stables Gallery, Taos, New Mexico.)

counteract it; her faith in the curandero and her distrust of doctors continue.

Three common misconceptions of the nature of culture can stand between well intentioned medical efforts and desired outcome. The first is an assumption that deeply held beliefs and values can be changed by reason and argument or if that fails, by fear. This concept of culture was satirized in the comedy *The Teahouse of the August Moon*, when the beleaguered colonel railed, "I'll teach these natives Democracy if I have to kill everyone to do it." Habits and some aspects of culture such as clothing style appear relatively amenable to rapid change. However, values and preferences that are acquired early and unconsciously are much more intransigent.

Elaine and John Cumming, in reporting the untimely demise of one mental health program, commented, "It was evident that we had been trying to change ideas that were very deeply and firmly held and that the more we tried to dislodge them, the more tightly people held on to them and the angrier they became at us for trying to take them away."

A second misconception of the nature of culture is that only other people are under the influence of culture—"What *I* do is based on reason and objectively verifiable fact. What *they* do is culturally conditioned." Part of the conceit of many Americans is that they believe they are entirely rational and not influenced by culture.

Yet much of the action in and around hospitals would be inconceivable without our seldom questioned faith in the value of life, and our obligation to help the infirm. We are least aware of the influence of culture when it is our *own*.

A third mistaken notion about culture is that its impact is limited to trivial matters of taste and preferences. In each culture, shared expectations and preferences are invested with a range of feeling from trivial choices that are easily changed to emotionally charged beliefs or values for which an individual would die.

DEFINITIONS OF ILLNESS

Certain diseases—frequently those accompanied by severe or violent onset and those most often shortly followed by death—seem included in the concept of illness in most societies. The plague and smallpox are examples. Many other conditions which we presently define as illness have been in other times and places considered simply a part of normal living. The skin disease pinto (dyschromic spirochetosis) has been so common among many South American tribes that the few men who were free of the disease's discoloration were regarded as pathological—and unmarriageable. When malaria was very common along the Mississippi Valley in the mid-1800's the backwoodsmen said, "He is not sick, he's only got the ague."

Always included in the concept "illness" is some notion of the extent and limits of social responsibility for the person who is socially defined as "ill." Among the Kubu of Sumatra the person who became ill with a fever was considered dead to the society even before his physical death. Thus, the Kubu assumed little or no responsibility for aiding anyone whose illness was accompanied by fever. In Ancient Greece, where balance and beauty of mind and body were ideals, every cultured layman was supposed to know the basic principles of medicine. City-states hired physicians to help keep the population healthy. But the Greek community physician was not encouraged to waste his time by continued efforts on behalf of anyone who was grotesquely impaired, nor was the physician expected to prolong the life of the infirm person who appeared to be mortally ill.

The heroes of the old Arab epics were epileptics. Seizures were taken as a sign of leadership and thus the man "suffering" from such attacks was more likely to be followed then pitied, or treated, or ostracized. In Biblical Mesopotamia, leprosy was viewed as deserved punishment for sin. Thus, added to the leper's physical distress were contempt, blame, and the very real tribulations of ostracism and occasional attack. In contrast the early Christians saw the infirm as "blessed," and the meek sufferers could provide their benefactors with "grace." One consequence of this view was the opening of religious hospices or havens for care—though not necessarily for treatment nor for cure of the sick.

Many cultures have included the belief that certain conditions were caused by sorcery or spirit intrusion and, therefore, the afflicted person should have help to exorcise the spirit which had entered. The ancient Egyptians, acquainted with the human body through their religiously inspired custom of embalming important people who died, held a belief that many illnesses were caused by putrefaction in the intestines. An obvious remedy for such disorders was catharsis. Flushing out the body as though it were a series of canals is still a practice followed by some people today. To the Chinese, illness was due to imbalance, a concept consistent with a belief system that emphasized harmony in nature. Akin to the practices based on the balance between hot and cold, which many Puerto Ricans hold today, cure for the Chinese depended on restoration of the balance of elements. To the Jehovah's Witness, there will be no death for a faithful believer. Therefore, worldly medical interference might indicate a lack of faith and would be of little value anyway for the believer who expects to be made perfect within the next few years when the world is scheduled to end.

THE CULTURAL SUPPORTS OF MODERN MEDICINE

Of course, people in every society generally would like good health. But not every culture gives the deliberate striving toward health and physical comfort the high priority and backing that we afford it. Not too many years ago when people listed the necessities of life, they said, "Food, clothing, and shelter." Most people today would give a list of at least six: food, clothing, shelter, education, employment, and health care. We thereby have doubled within a lifetime the list of those things we consider the basic necessities of life. We have come to believe that the sick person has a right to expect help from strangers—the professionals—and the right to

be excused from normal obligations during the time the professionals declare him ill. This expresses itself in some union contracts that entitle the individual to a certain number of "sick days."

Active intervention on behalf of health is consistent with our tendency to intervene toward improvements generally. Tocqueville's 1835 observation on his visit to America seems to hold today: "There reigns in America a popular faith in the progress of the human mind. They are always expecting that improvements will be discovered in everything, and in fact they are often right."

We are a nation of busy bodies dissatisfied with what is—seeking for youth, for cosmetic improvements, for health, for relief from restlessness or sleeplessness, for stimulants against tiredness or sleepiness, for expert advice about how to enjoy sex, or a stylist's advice about how we should want our homes and ourselves to look (Figure 27.2). We are afraid of obsolescence and old age. We buy hair pieces to cover baldness, depilatories to remove hair, and have plastic surgery to change a profile or smooth marks of age. We are encouraged to believe in magic, only our magic is science, often medical science. The layman wants very much to believe that money,

Figure 27.2. Cover from *Vogue Magazine.* (By permission of Condé Nast Publications, Inc.)

public and private, will buy health. A Massachusetts Mental Health program included a slogan in all its brochures: "Mental Health can be purchased." The professional may want to believe it too and may have his own need to see himself as the marvelous, nearly miraculous healer portrayed in fiction and on television.

Community hospitals get front-page coverage for adding shining new pieces of equipment to "do the latest thing" in surgery. Television cameras are invited into hospitals to get on-the-spot coverage of dramatic breakthroughs and Christiaan Barnard became a public celebrity for doing heart transplants. Magazines and newspapers can increase readership with articles on "new medical breakthroughs," often in advance of adequate proof or research into untoward side effects. Mass media responds to and also stimulates curiosity about hospitals and the people in them, and it often tells the public what it very much wants to believe—that medical science is wonderful and that doctors can answer nearly all the needs of the person in trouble.

For millions of television viewers, Dr. Welby—or his current counterpart—acts as religious confessor, psychiatrist, moral preceptor, father, and friend. Superb clinical skills and dedication are assumed. They have young colleagues who may be gruff, sometimes unruly, but even they serve as benign big brothers for patients. If the young colleague challenges the system of practice, he is likely to be "put down" by some dramatic reality and then helped to manage it with the gentle and wise guidance of "the real doctor." Like Pony Express riders, these doctors see to it that neither social nor financial obstacles, family difficulties, emotional stress, personal danger, nor threat to their professional standing can get in the way of treatment. Against that fiction, the ordinary doctor whom most patients see can be as disappointing as today's heavy-footed postman compared with a Pony Express rider from days gone by.

The promises of scientific breakthroughs and the promises implicit in popular fiction about interns and family doctors and surgeons all feed the imagination and whet the appetites of Americans for still more and better health care. This is "good news and bad news." Physicians are at the top of the social ladder. But in stimulating the public to expect so much, the profession raises the probability of much disappointment, of anger—and of malpractice action.

This press for "more and better" is true not only in medicine. As John Kenneth Galbraith has suggested, much of our industry depends on the whetted appetites of the population for new models of everything. Advertising daily suggests new ways to be wasteful of vital resources. People are stimulated to feel they need air conditioning for summer and central heating for winter, a television, or an extra phone, or two cars. Such definitions of needs are costly. It is cheaper to perspire than to air condition. It is more economical to keep warm by putting on an extra sweater than to heat the whole house. But hotels have even begun to heat the outside as well as the inside by installing infra-red lights to warm the sidewalks of their entrance ways.

Much has been written on the desire of the American people to appear successful, and more has been said about our almost childish commitment to progress and change. There is also a kind of striving to belong. And the way to belong, if you have just arrived and do not know anybody, is to seem to fit, and to seem to be trying to get ahead. Many Americans work all day, rush home to refinish furniture, or to tutor a little son so that he will compete well at school, or they join a volunteer citizen's group to circulate a petition against the smog they helped create by driving home. Four out of five households in the country have at least one car, and cars tie up cities, pollute air, kill thousands annually, beguile young men, impress young women, and consume increasingly precious fuel.

All this implies dissatisfaction with what is, and most often a conviction that some place else will be better. There is pretty good evidence that this belief in progress and possibility actually does land people in situations where they can sometimes do better. If you are convinced that life can be better, then you can at least consider the possibility of making moves that will improve things. But such restlessness can also be destructive.

For example, surveys indicate that everyone in America would like more money. As a matter of fact, in one study, regardless of income, rich and poor respondents said they would be satisfied if they could only earn about 20% more. Observers have remarked about the importance of appearing successful. There may be something to that, for today there are many businesses that survive by renting people things they could not afford to own. In New York now you can rent a limousine with a uniformed chauffeur. You can rent silverware, table linens, a butler, a maid, an oil painting, mink coat, some chairs. While in some places it may be more a situation of, "You either have it or you don't," in our large urban centers, it is often more, "Now you have it and now you don't."

The individual can live meagerly in most places and splurge occasionally, so he looks wealthy then. The typist in an office can spend a week at a luxury hotel in a kind of "let's pretend." Accelerated credit buying and expense accounts aid this strange living on several different status levels at one time. The young man in an advertising agency may make less than a secretary, but he is allowed to take clients to lunch at the city's most expensive restaurants, and his company pays. He thus eats like a very wealthy man at lunch but has frankfurters and beans for dinner. His wife does the family laundry, and his expensive suits may come from a resale shop.

These probabilities for a kind of momentary affluence or the appearance of it further stimulate aspirations and desires. It means that many people live beyond their present incomes, and it also contributes a spur to their efforts to move up. Individuals and groups tend to become what they think they are, and a taste for riches, conveniences, and the good things of life is said to be easy to acquire with only a little practice.

Part of all this striving expresses itself in the American urge for education. The desire to have one's children eventually go to college is often related more to upward mobility than to any commitment to learning for its own sake. The median number of school years completed is steadily going up. Then there are the special schools—and the whole adult education industry. Adult education offers everything from "abrasives" through "zoology," and is a gold mine of information on the variety of pursuits of our strange, restless people, and, incidentally, one of the major pursuits of the adult unmarried male and female is to find a spouse. These courses serve the useful secondary function of allowing people to meet informally without being as obvious as attending a singles bar.

Adult education and a wide assortment of therapeutic groups also testify to the American people's commitment to the concept that experts should be consulted for a wide range of problems. Having gained both time and money to devote to the improvement of ourselves, we then expect an expert to do it for us. Other societies have relied more on tradition, religious prescrip-

tions, family solidarity, or feelings of personal loyalty as the preferred guides for deciding important matters. Not so with us. "The way it used to be done," or "What the family thinks," often carry strong negative connotations in our society. "What the experts say," in contrast, has the ring of approval. While some cultures will accept science only when it is cloaked in ritual, ours tends to accept magic and ritual only when it is cloaked in the scientific method. Computerized astrological charts may be an example. We now turn to the scientific expert rather than to family members, or the church. Some say that the architecture of many of our giant medical centers is reminiscent of the cathedrals in France, and that this is only fitting, since faith in science occupies such an analogous central position in our belief systems and social structure.

Americans also appear to feel strongly about the value of the individual. Individual life is given the primacy that the family or religion has been given in other societies. This commitment to individual human worth, along with our striving for the new and improved, and our insistence on comfort at any cost, have added to our faith in science, and have contributed in large measure to very real scientific and technological medical achievements. Convinced that each human life is precious and that scientific advance is in itself a most worthy and attainable goal, we encourage large numbers of our most able people to devote their energies and attention to science and particularly to medical science. More conditions are included in the concept of illness than has apparently been true in any other society, and more people are able to live longer with chronic illness. In this society illness tends to be viewed as a mishap, which should be amenable to correction with the help of experts. We seem to believe that health, or in its absence extension of life, is an end in itself worth pursuing, rather than a means to allow us to move on to other goals.

CULTURE AND THE ROLES OF PATIENT AND PHYSICIAN

Built on our faith, and reinforcing it, is a set of expectations for what doctors and nurses should do, how they should behave, and what we have a right to expect from them. Complementary to this is a cluster of expectations and ideas about the person who is sick. Sociologists call this the *sick role* or the *patient's role.* The medical professions in America are built on the middle class culture and its perspectives, relationships, and beliefs. Patients from this middle class background can often function in ways that fit nicely with the expectations of doctor and nurse. The patient who best conforms to the expectations of the patient role allows the professional to function most easily in the *professional role.*

People in the patient role are supposed to detail relevant physical symptoms to strangers in a hospital, and, unlike many social expectations, this is not reciprocal in kind. I am expected to tell the doctor about my bowel movements, but in exchange the doctor does not have to tell me about similar personal details. The patient is expected to believe that a specialist he may never before have seen can help even more than a layman who loves him and has known him for years. Patients are expected to try not to show too much emotion when they talk with the doctor for that would interfere with their telling all the details the doctor needs to know. Patients are expected to follow medical advice and not to decide that a friend who once had a similar symptom has a better remedy. Patients are supposed to want to and expect to get well and to demonstrate this by cooperating actively with the doctor and nurse.

It should be clear that the role as described here is an "ideal" that parallels the ideal image of the physician as it is portrayed in the mass media, and as it has evolved over time in the treatment of acute illness. As such, this role of the patient is probably more accepted in the white native-born middle class than in some other ethnic and socioeconomic groups, and it is everywhere more an ideal than a reality. Moreover, this ideal role may reflect the treatment of acute illness in a hospital much better than it does the treatment of chronic illness in an ambulatory setting. The acutely ill patient is by virtue of his or her condition more dependent and more constrained toward compliance than is the ambulatory patient with chronic disease. The outpatient with chronic illness cannot expect to recover fully, and is less obviously dependent on the physician and nurses. Therefore, the advice of family and friends about daily management often outweighs the advice that a physician gave in a consultation some months

back, as I discussed earlier in the chapter on responses to medical advice.

THE MODERN MEDICAL CENTER AND THE HOSPITAL CULTURE

Cultural predilection for change and for problem solving through research and consultation with experts gives rise to new definitions and expectations, and also to new facilities. The emergence of the modern hospital complex exemplifies this interaction. As late as the turn of the century, the large public hospital was still viewed as a place for the poor and the abandoned to go to die. Not a few municipal hospitals were combination prison and alms houses. People at that time were likely to feel a sense of surprise and gratitude if they survived a hospital stay. Many did not. Approximately 10,000 of the 13,000 amputations performed by Army surgeons in the Franco Prussian War proved fatal. Since social perceptions tend to outlast the reality that gave rise to them, it is not surprising that older people a few decades ago were excessively fearful of approaching the hospital for help. Today rich and poor people alike come to the hospital, and these new patients expect more different kinds of help when they arrive.

In 1935, in the United States, there were fewer than nine hospital admissions per 1,000 population; in 1964, the figure had climbed to 149 admissions per 1,000. By 1974, the ratio was 169 to 1,000 and now seems to have leveled off. In addition, outpatients visits have doubled in a 10 year period. Emergency room visits have spiraled. Thousands of ambulatory patients flow in and out of the hospital daily, demanding and receiving a wide range of services.

As often happens, progress whets appetites for more progress. So, at the time when hospitals are able to treat more patients effectively and in shorter periods of time, demands for still more effective treatment will increase, not diminish. A paradox of all societies is that improved situations do not necessarily increase satisfaction. Quite the opposite. As things get better, more people will have a taste for improvement and be impatient with what is.

The large hospital today could not function without two basic perspectives about time. The first is a belief that time is valuable and is to be employed, scheduled, and saved, and not wasted, "killed," or lost. The second is commitment to an orderly sequence in which events in a future time can be influenced through the way we spend our minutes today. Such conceptions of time have very real consequences. Time and money are invested in research, increasing the probabilities of scientific advance.

The search for natural causes through the scientific method is valued inside the hospital even more highly than on the outside. The model of the open mind that is willing to admit uncertainty is highly valued in the teaching hospital and often reinforced by approval. "That is a good question"; "We are not certain"; "I agree, we should run another test first"; and "We'll do research on it" are reactions that are rewarded on many teaching rounds. Physicians are the product of childhoods where wanting to know "why" brought parental interest and encouragement, in contrast to many cultures where children may be punished for demanding a reason. However, what is reassuring acknowledgment of the present limits of knowledge between colleagues, may be extremely disquieting to a patient or to family members who desperately need to believe that the doctor knows everything and has final and certain ways to cure.

Our medical culture is also imbued with the conviction that a wide range of discomforts, disabilities, and complaints is appropriately brought to a trained expert because the expert is willing to search for a cause and a cure. But it would be a mistake to assume that people of different ethnic groups all have the same conceptions about what legitimately is to be brought to the physician for help, and what should be done in response.

ETHNIC DIFFERENCES IN PRESENTING COMPLAINTS

Even within our own society, the patient contributes more to the doctor-patient exchange than simply describing physical symptoms and expressing the hope that the doctor will help. Depending on the ethnic heritage, the patient also brings special values, beliefs, priorities, and attitudes developed over the years. Before arriving to see a physician, the cultural meaning of symptoms, and the social implications of particular disorders, have already influenced the decision to seek medical help.

Irving Zola studied the selective differences in the symptoms which patients bring to the doctor by comparing diagnostically matched patients from different ethnic groups. All patients were new admissions to the Eye, Ear, Nose, and Throat Clinics of Massachusetts General Hospital. He found distinct cultural patterns of response to symptoms and to definitions of illness. Even when Italian patients had a diagnosed eye or ear disorder, they did not locate their chief complaints there, nor was that the primary focus of their concern. Related to this, Italian patients presented a significantly wider assortment of bodily dysfunctions than did the Irish patients. Irish patients tended to deny pain as a feature of their disorder. For example, two women with diagnosed presbyopia and hyperopia were each asked, "What seems to be the trouble?" The Irish patient said, "I can't seem to thread a needle or read a paper." But the Italian woman with the same diagnosis reported, "I have a constant headache and my eyes seem to get all red and burny." When the interviewer asked, "Anything else?" the Irish patient said, "No, I can't recall anyting." The Italian patient said, "No, just that it lasts all day long and I even wake up with it sometimes." The Italians tended to seek medical aid after their symptoms interfered with social or personal relations or when they were experiencing a situational or interpersonal crisis. But Irish patients tended to see a physician only after they had received the approval of others who urged their visit and in a sense legitimated the search for help. In contrast, the Anglo-Saxon patients came for help only after their disorders caused interference with some of their specific vocational or physical activities. Among people committed to a work ethic, inability to perform appears to trigger a search for help.

The Navajo Indians have very few words for pain in contrast to our large assortment of terms, e.g., "sharp," "throbbing," "dull," "gripping," "piercing," "aching." The Navajo is supposed to bear pain in silence, and Navajo women tend not to cry out in childbirth. This led one physician mistakenly to assume that Navajo women were not experiencing pain and therefore needed little medication for it. Within a year after this physician's arrival at a Navajo reservation hospital, the Navajo women were no longer going to the hospital to give birth. One woman had told another that birth in the hospital was no less painful than it was in their own homes.

In his study of patients in one veterans' hospital, Mark Zborowski described differences in response to pain between males from three ethnic groups: Jews, "Old Americans," and Italians. The Italians cried out when in pain, but as soon as they got relief, they seemed to bounce back with good humor. The "Old Americans" tended to be stoical and quiet when in pain, and almost clinical in their attempts to tell the doctor the exact position, timing, and nature of the pain. Jews expressed themselves openly about pain as did the Italians. However, where the Italian seemed relieved and relatively untroubled once the pain subsided, Jewish patients continued to worry and question the meaning of the pain, the probable and possible consequences of it, and they also worried about possible later effects from the medication to relieve the pain. The Jewish patients more often asked whether another doctor should be consulted.

Marvin Opler studied a sample of 30 Irish patients and 30 Italian patients in the same psychiatric service. Nearly all of the Irish psychiatric patients tormented themselves with guilt about sex and three-fourths of them had elaborate and fixed delusions. In contrast, the Italian psychiatric patients in the same hospital demonstrated no evidence of such Puritanism and less than one-third gave any evidence of delusions. But the Italians had histories of repeated outbursts of behavior—temper tantrums, assaults, destruction of property, and suicide attempts. In the hospital they tended to be overtalkative, excitable, disposed to hysterical outbursts, and somewhat difficult to manage. Only four of the 30 Irish patients showed any history of behavioral aberrations, and in the hospital they tended to be passive and withdrawn. On the basis of the Italians' less inhibited interest in bodily functions, Opler had expected that Italian patients would be more prone than the Irish to hypochondria, and this appeared to be the case.

People from different ethnic groups also hold different expectations about what physicians are supposed to do—and not do—when the patient does seek help. To the Puerto Rican who believes he has only a fixed amount of blood to last a lifetime, drawing blood in a diagnostic workup "diminishes" him. In Mexican folk medicine blood holds a dominant place. If it is too thin, or too much of it is lost, a man's sexual vigor is jeopardized. Difficulties getting blood donors from Chicano populations may relate to this concept. Folklore about blood in the United States includes the idea that it is supposed to thicken in winter and thin out in summer. Too much salt can cause blood to thin. One respondent said, "I always take my special compound every fall. It thickens my blood and makes me ready for cold weather." Alongside of scientific medicine in the United States goes a brisk business in patent medicine. "I give my children a dose of cathartic once a week and they don't have near the sickness other children do." Or, "My husband takes aspirin all winter. He hasn't had a cold in years. It just shows what a little doctoring at home will do for you."

GOOD FOOD AND BAD

The relative importance that people place on food, as well as the foods which "taste good," varies from one culture to another, and everywhere food is associated with early childhood memories, especially with important holidays and celebrations. Like so many other aspects of culture, food preferences are little influenced by argument. That early commentator on America, Alexis de Tocqueville, wrote this comment home to his mother in France: "The absence of wine at our meals at first struck us as very disagreeable, and we still can't understand the multitude of things that they succeed in introducing into their stomachs here. . . ."

Edwin Weinstein systematically recorded the content of delusions and hallucinations of neurological patients from three ethic groups: Puerto Ricans, those from St. Croix, and the French speaking natives of St. Thomas. He found patterned differences in the content of delusions that reflected essentially different priorities of the three cultures. Unlike the Crucians and those from St. Thomas, food was a focus of the delusions of many Puerto Rican patients, reflecting the fact that food is an extremely important element in social relationships among them. To the dismay of the medical staff in the hospital, Puerto Ricans tended to cling to their diet of beans and white rice, and they often would not eat except when their relatives brought in food.

There are many examples of our own ethnocentrism which cause us to fail when we try to change food preferences and practices. Walt

Disney made entertaining, creative films for health education. One film made for Arabian countries showed a farmer whose plate of food was covered with a swarm of very large animated flies. The intent of the film was to encourage a change in the Arab's way of handling food by showing how flies carried germs and caused illness. However, the Arab audiences commented afterwards that now they understood why Americans got sick. The reason was that Americans have such large flies, but Arabs did not, therefore Arabs do not get sick from flies. Thousands of dollars of educational efforts had been expended and the films were enthusiastically received in Arabian countries. Yet the educational effort mistakenly assumed that everywhere people accept the concept that germs cause illness. No decrease in the target diseases of diarrhea and dysentery was noted, even though the films themselves were quite popular. Some examples of failure in our own campaigns, e.g., to wipe out smoking, should be reexamined in this context.

There have, of course, been many successes in reducing or nearly eradicating target diseases. One World Health team was able to change the food habits of the Zulus enough to eliminate kwashiorkor and pellagra—but only after 12 years of effort to find ways to change food habits without challenging deeply held beliefs.

A golden brown substance of library-paste consistency that adheres to the roof of the mouth when eaten, is considered revolting by the people of many cultures. Americans consumed close to seven hundred million pounds of it in a recent year. But in spite of our efforts to encourage other people to enjoy peanut butter as a nutritious supplement to inadequate diets, so far we remain somewhat unique in our special liking for this food.

Food not infrequently becomes an issue with patients in hospitals, especially since loss of appetite is a frequent companion of illness. A prescribed bland diet offers familiar tastes and textures to the person who grew up loving vanilla custard, ice cream, and mashed potatoes. The same diet may be a much bigger problem for the man who grew up accustomed to the explosive taste of hot peppers and the assertive crunch of fried things. Stanley King describes an Italian patient who steadfastly refused the diet offered him after major surgery in spite of the efforts of nurses and dieticians. Finally one social worker heard him say that the gruel that he was supposed to eat "is the kind of food we

fed pigs on the farm." How could he trust the hospital to take care of him if they fed him food that he would give to pigs?

But middle class American patients do not escape from culturally bound problems with the food tray. They may get their cultural shock from the tray that brings cool, gelatinous pot roast and gravy, ice cream awash in its melting, and tepid coffee. Having grown up to the strains of, "Eat your food while it is hot" and "Hurry, the dinner will get cold" and the parents' insistence on "hot lunch for school children," these patients may feel particularly abandoned when presented with chilly foods. The fact that the hospital tray is usually faced alone, after a lifetime of eating in the reassuring presence of relatives and friends, does not help.

As with food preferences, each culture has what Edward Hall refers to as its own definition of "body space," or the distance felt appropriate before privacy is invaded. Hall describes a kind of "conversational waltz" when people from different cultures talk. One moves closer in conformity with his culturally based comfortable conversational distance, while the other moves back to establish his comfortable distance. A room to oneself and no visitors may be treasured in the middle class culture, but not to a Puerto Rican who grew up on streets with noisy children and blaring radios. One Puerto Rican woman said, "Moving here to the housing project was really the social worker's idea. You never see any movement on the street, not one little domino or card game or anything. This place is dead. People act as if they're angry or in mourning. Either they don't know how to live or they are afraid to. It's true what the proverb says: 'May God deliver me from quiet places; I can defend myself in the wild ones.'"

The culture that has given rise to the modern hospital benefits many. However, it may sometimes be productive for the people who are an integral part of the modern hospital to take note of how much of the daily life in hospital routines rests upon its own culture. It may be as Nietzsche suggested, "Invisible threads are the strongest ties." If you hope to understand a man, find out what he takes for granted.

Suggested Readings

Graham S: Sociological aspects of health and illness. In Millon TB (ed): *Medical Behavioral Science.* Philadelphia, W. B. Saunders, 1975, p 531.

Mumford E: *Medical Sociology: Patients, Providers, and Policies.* New York, Random House, 1983.

Opler MK: Schizophrenics and culture. *Scientific American,* August 1957, p 117.

White KL: Life and death and medicine. In Millon TB (ed): *Medical Behavioral Science.* Philadelphia, W. B. Saunders, 1975, p 499.

Zborowski M: *People in Pain.* San Francisco, Jossey Boss, 1969.

Zola IK: Culture and symptoms—an analysis of patients' presenting complaints. *Am Sociol Rev* 31:615, 1966.

References

Cumming E, Cumming J: *Closed Ranks: An Experiment in Mental Health Education.* Cambridge, Harvard University Press, 1957.

Hall E: *The Silent Language.* Greenwich, CT, Premier Books, 1965.

King S: *Perceptions of Illness and Medical Practice.* New York, Russell Sage Foundation, 1962.

Koos E: *The Health of Regionville.* New York, Columbia University Press, 1954.

Malinowski B: Culture. *Encyclopedia of the Social Sciences* 3: 621, 1967.

Mumford E: Puerto Rican perspectives on mental illness. *Mt Sinai J Med* 40:768, 1973.

Nichter M: Idioms of distress: alternatives in the expression of psychological distress. *Culture Med and Society* 5:379, 1981.

Pellegrino E: Medicine, history, and the idea of man. *Ann Am Acad Polit Soc Sci,* 346:9, 1963.

Pierson G: *Tocqueville in America.* Garden City, NY, Anchor Books, Doubleday, 1959.

Weinstein E: *Cultural Aspects of Delusion.* Glencoe, NY, Free Press, 1962.

Section I/Special Problems of Childhood and Adolescence

CHAPTER **28** Reactions of Children to Illness, Hospitalization, Surgery, and Physical Disabilities

Adolph E. Christ, M.D.

In order to understand the frequent and enormously important problems of illness, hospitalization, surgery, and physical disabilities among children, we must orient our thinking along four dimensions, each of which contributes to the child's unique and individual reaction, and each of which helps to clarify the way in which the physician and nursing staff should handle the total situation. These four dimensions include the developmental stage of the child, the child's ability to cope, the type of stress, and the family's and hospital staff's reaction to the stress.

DEVELOPMENTAL STAGE

It would be helpful for us to review in our minds the chapters on development at this time. An awareness of the developmental stage of a given child enhances our understanding and appreciation of the concerns that illness, hospitalization, and physical disabilities will evoke in that child. For example, a seven month old infant does not have the cognitive capacity that would make explanations of present and future events, such as a hospitalization, meaningful. Rather, this child reacts to people as friend (familiar) or foe (stranger). In addition, our seven month old has by now experienced vaccinations and other injections, and will set up a healthy wail at the sight of a white coat. One might say that a child's only friend at this age is the mother. Obviously, every effort should be made to work out a live-in arrangement for the mother if a young infant requires hospitalization.

For a somewhat older child, the problem is quite different. A 19 month old who was hospitalized with a fever of unknown etiology was described as very whining and irritable. She screamed when staff approached her, then screamed again when they left, had started soiling although recently toilet trained, and would ingest nothing but milk. This child had clutched at the mother at the beginning, so that the mother had to pry her arms off in order to leave. The child would scream for two hours after each visit. The mother finally decided not to visit the girl, because "Visits just make her upset and harder to manage." Immediately after the mother stopped visiting, the girl developed the above-mentioned symptoms of irritability, soiling, and refusal to eat. Such a child, in transition between the various subphases of the individuation-separation stage of development, will usually respond much more to the psychological stress of separation, and unless there is a great deal of pain or other physical distress, be nearly oblivious to the physical aspects of the illness. Reinstituting frequent visits by the parents, bringing a few favorite toys for her, reassuring the mother that the crying behavior of the girl after visits was to be expected, and educating the nursing staff resolved this difficult management problem. A similar situation is vividly depicted in James Robertson's film, *A Two Year Old Goes to the Hospital* (Figures 28.1 and 28.2).

Figures 28.1 and 28.2. Laura, a two year old girl, has been hospitalized for the repair of an umbilical hernia. She is frightened (Figure 28.1) and depressed (Figure 28.2), and she clings to her teddy bear. From the 1952 film *A Two Year Old Goes to the Hospital.* (By permission of James Robertson, Robertson Centre, London, England. Distributed by New York University Film Library, 26 Washington Place, New York 10003.)

A four or five year old sees the world very differently compared to the two younger children described above. His thinking is preoperational, i.e., magical and unidimensional. Psychosexually he is in the phallic-oedipal phase. Hospitalization for a tonsillectomy for this young child generates anxiety related both to separation and castration fears. For example, a five year old boy, hospitalized for appendicitis, was acutely agitated and very disruptive on the ward. During the psychiatric consultation, he explained to me that he was going to be put to sleep and then cut open. He told me a dream that he had had the night before in which his finger had fallen off. In playing with a doll, he busily cut the doll with a tongue depressor (his pretend knife). His "knife" kept slipping and cutting the doll's thigh, and sometimes even the

doll's "tushy." A girl the same age will also be experiencing fears of being mutilated in a hospital, and will need the support of parents and hospital staff in dealing with these fears (Figures 28.3 and 28.4).

Adolescents, on the other hand, are (mostly) beyond all such "childish" concerns. Their thinking is concrete or formal operational, and they can make excellent use of explanations, the more detailed and technical the better. They can think about the future, and will react very differently to such catastrophies as amputation and cancer. They have more defenses available, such as rationalization, but under severe stress they

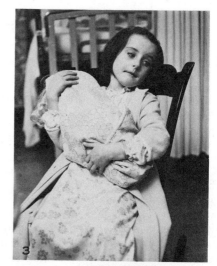

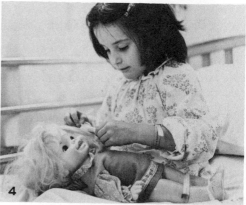

Figures 28.3 and 28.4. The film *When a Child Enters the Hospital* follows a somewhat older girl and her mother through the child's hospitalization and surgery. The girl clings to her doll now instead of a teddy bear (Figure 28.3), and attentively dresses her doll (Figure 28.4). (By permission of Polymorph Films, Boston.)

too will regress and become infantile, dependent, demanding, and depressed. Such regression can tax the ability of doctors and nurses to be empathic, and this rejection will produce even further stress on the adolescent patient.

These different reactions in children of different ages emphasize the need to be fully aware of the developmental stage of the given child, and the major concerns and anxieties at each stage.

COPING ABILITY

A normal, well adjusted youngster is indeed a wonder to behold in most severely stressful situations. The mobilization of inner resources and the excellent use of the environment are indications of such coping abilities. This child will make friends with other children on the ward as well as all the nurses. He will busy himself by helping prepare charts, play "Doctor", give roommates shots, and operate on dolls. On the other hand, the less effective the preexisting adjustment, the fewer the coping mechanisms that will be available to the child. In addition, the added stress of illness will usually aggravate any preexisting emotional disturbances, which in turn will often make the child more demanding and therefore less appealing. The passive-dependent child becomes, "What a baby. You change his dressings!"; the passive-aggressive child, "You know what that little monster did? He tried to trip me."; the schizophrenic child, "He is weird—a real kook." The new situation severely compounds the anxiety that is already present. The relatively few coping mechanisms of such a child are decreased under the impact of the acute stress, and busy nurses and doctors stay away from these "less appealing" children.

SPECIFIC STRESS

Aside from the importance of the developmental level and the coping ability, the nature of the specific stress is also critical to an understanding of a given child's reaction to physical illness. A new acne pustule on the cheek of an adolescent girl that erupts just before an important date, a broken arm or leg, an amputation following a car accident, and a diagnosis of acute fulminating leukemia—these are all acute stresses, the first two being reversible, whereas the last two involve irreversible consequences. On the other hand, there are chronic illnesses such as ulcer-

ative colitis or asthma that may have acute exacerbations and may or may not be reversible with proper treatment. Finally, there are certain forms of brain damage that may be relatively irreversible. It is important to ascertain whether the specific stress on the child or adolescent is acute or chronic, and whether the effects are reversible or irreversible.

An example of a chronic illness and the reactions it evoked can be demonstrated in a 14 year old girl who was diagnosed as diabetic at age six. During her early years she had trouble with the insulin injections, and would at times sneak candy and go off her diet. A week after her 13th birthday, whatever stability she had acquired with diet and insulin evaporated, and she went into a diabetic coma. When I first saw her in psychiatric consultation, she looked like a prostitute—with heavy makeup and a skin-tight mini dress. Her pretty face was a mask of scorn and contempt. It was not until after many sessions together that she was able to talk about what it was like for her to be diabetic. She began to express venomous rage at her parents, teachers, and doctors, and was quite surprised to find that I did not become angry at her and retaliate. "Teachers are all stupid and boring. Doctors never tell you anything; they are just interested in money. And parents are the worst." Occasional suicidal ruminations were another manifestation of her depressive moods. Only after many more sessions was she able to identify the origin of her rage—"Why did I have to be the one to have diabetes?" As so often happens, the rage over her condition was turned against herself (depression, suicidal ruminations, diabetic comas), and also unleashed on the significant adults in her life (parents, doctors, and teachers). Viewing the illness as a punishment is a very frequent unconscious reaction. Gradually, it also became clear that she blamed the diabetes for all of her problems—why she wasn't popular, why she had lost the election for class secretary, why she had not been invited to her rival's slumber party. This girl exemplified how a chronic illness can complicate normal developmental tasks, and in turn can be used as an excuse (and rationalization) for all of the difficulties associated with those tasks.

There are, of course, many chronic conditions that may interfere with important developmental accomplishments, particularly the child's acquirement of a realistic body image and an adequate sense of self-esteem. Birth defects, chronic disabilities and illnesses, unusual features such as a very tall or a very short stature—anything that sets the child apart from other children—may play havoc with the child's self-esteem.

A young child under the age of four or five will make little differentiation between an acute or chronic illness. Later on the child will understand a good deal about the nature and severity of his or her illness, but may need to deny what he knows, and in this denial the child may be aided and abetted by the parents. A nine year old boy was brought to the child guidance clinic by his mother, who was concerned that he was not keeping up in school and might have to repeat the third grade. Only after about 30 minutes in the interview did she state that he had leukemia and was being treated with medication. The mother's becoming preoccupied with a relatively minor problem is an example of a defense mechanism called *displacement* ("I am not concerned about the leukemia which will kill my child, but about his failing in school.") In addition, her "forgetting" about the leukemia is an example of her *denial.* These defense mechanisms are used frequently by the parents of children having incurable illnesses, and also by the children themselves. Defense mechanisms operate automatically, and without conscious awareness. The physician who is unaware of these defenses so often used by children who have such chronic and irreversible problems, and by their parents, can be very puzzled by what seems to be a lack of concern. He may facilitate the use of such defenses by thinking: "Who in his right mind wants to talk to a nine year old and his mother about the fact that the boy is dying?"

This boy willingly came to see me, but talked mostly about school and how he disliked the medicine that he had to take. He needed to remain on a very superficial level until he felt he could trust me. Only then did he begin to use some of the play therapy toys to plan out elaborate games of war. He was particularly preoccupied with the details of the killing of the soldiers, Indians, and cowboys. In the course of this play he talked about his great uncles, great aunts, and his grandparents, what illnesses they had had, and how they had died and been buried. These deaths spanned a 20 year period, and the boy's preoccupation with the deaths of his ancestors really reflected his anxiety over his own impending death. This very gradual, indi-

rect approach to his feelings about leukemia was essential in helping him to begin to deal more directly with his fear, panic, and rage. This child and his mother may intellectually have known about his severe illness, yet not have emotionally accepted their reactions to it. The process of facilitating that acceptance must be approached most sensitively. Acceptance of the illness can bring to the family a degree of comfort, and a focus on what can still be accomplished despite the tragic nature of the situation.

FAMILY AND HOSPITAL STAFF REACTION TO THE STRESS

Family

The interaction of the "normal" parent and the "normal" child in an acute stress situation sometimes flows so naturally as to be nearly invisible, much as a smoothly flowing river can appear immobile. The regression of the child does not throw the family into disequilibrium because well integrated parents will be able to gratify and support the child. Child and parents are sufficiently open about their feelings and reactions, and they can tell each other what they need. The father is automatically more supportive of his wife, and rather than reacting with jealousy at her increased involvement with the child, he will feel pleasure and pride in her competence as a mother. It must be understood and expected, however, that the majority of "normal" parents will at some point react with anxiety to their child's acute illness or hospitalization, and they will regress, and be more irritable, demanding, dependent, frightened, and depressed. In short, the parents will be different from the way they usually are.

A different dimension is presented with the chronically ill child. Asthma, diabetes, epilepsy, the spastic or retarded child, all alter the dependence-independence axis of interaction between parent and child. Indeed, the "overprotective" parent was once thought to be a specific etiological factor in the causation of many of the psychosomatic disorders of childhood. A comparison of such parents with the parents of children with other chronic illnesses such as poliomyelitis raised serious questions about whether this interaction is a cause or an effect. The current view is that overprotectiveness is a normal reaction of a parent to a chronically ill or disabled child, and guidance of the parents by the physician can be extremely helpful in curbing excessive and harmful overprotectiveness.

A quite different situation occurs when one or both of the parents of the ill child have a psychiatric illness. The reaction of such a parent to the child's illness may then be quite unpredictable. This parent may react to the child's illness as though it were a personal narcissistic injury and become severely depressed by the situation, or become unreasonably enraged at the child or physician. Careful therapeutic work with such parents often clarifies that the child is not only a child to these parents, but may unconsciously represent for them someone from their past, such as their own parent, or a hated sibling.

For example, a mother, whose own parents had died when she was quite young, had been in a number of foster homes. Without being aware of it, she looked for mothering in all her relationships, including the one with her adolescent daughter. The mother often became furious at her daughter. As the mother once said, "She always wants me to take care of her. She has to learn that the world isn't like that. I have to work, so the least she can do is clean the house and do the cooking. I can't do everything." The girl, on the other hand, said, "I have to do everything—cook, clean the house, take care of my little sister. It doesn't seem fair. Sometimes I actually feel like I'm the mother!" In another instance an adolescent described how she handled the fights between her parents: "Mother just doesn't seem to understand that dad wants her to take care of him most of the time. It's like I have to explain that to her, and then she is a little better for awhile." In either of these situations, the parent will react to an illness on the part of her child with helplessness, rage, and feelings of, "Who is going to take care of me?"

An equally difficult problem presents itself where the child's illness itself becomes the catalyst for precipitating a parental neurotic reaction. A 25 year old mother of a five year old girl reacted in a very disturbed way when her daughter was hospitalized following a febrile convulsion. In consultation with me the mother began to describe her severely retarded brother who was epileptic, to whose care she had devoted an excessive part of her adolescence and young adulthood, and who had died in status epilepticus. She was not consciously aware of her relief and subsequent guilt at his death, but with the hospitalization of her daughter, she experienced an uncanny dread and a feeling of being punished, which she could not understand. Indeed, she feared she was losing her mind, and had terrible nightmares of her daughter dying and of dying herself. She clung so to the nurses and doctors that they began to avoid her because of her excessive repetitive questions and her constant need for reassurance regarding her daughter's condition.

Nursing Staff and Physicians

As professionals, we are in no way immune to feelings and emotional reactions. Indeed, recognizing and using our feelings can mean the difference between a cold technician and a warm human being who can earn the patient's trust. For the sake of clarity we might separate these reactions into three types: *selective emotional reactions, empathy,* and *countertransference.* As human beings, we all have propensities to respond to some situations selectively. Those of us who enjoy teaching and parenting may respond more easily to the child or parent who is more dependent, who needs the reassurance of having a professional who is definite and certain and who explains things carefully. Others of us may prefer the more independent patient or parent, who wants a minimum of contact and who wants to be left alone to figure things out for himself. Again, there are some of us who like a fighter, who feel most comfortable with a patient or parent who argues, questions, challenges. Others will feel very uncomfortable with such a patient. Recognizing the *emotional "fit"* is important, for as professionals we need to learn to respond to the needs of our patients rather than forcing them to adjust to us.

There are specific situations and illnesses that arouse strong emotional reactions in all of us. The provocative delinquent who sabotages every treatment effort, or the adolescent girl suffering from anorexia nervosa who refuses to eat, may well evoke feelings of frustration and anger in all of us. Quite different is the situation of the pretty two year old who has a brain tumor, or the five year old who has leukemia. The physician and nurse readily accept the role of healer, but are much less comfortable with the role of caring for the dying child. The emotional reactions we experience to such tragedies are complex and painful—guilt that we cannot cure the child, resentment at not being "competent," perhaps even relief that, "It is not me or mine." These are not unusual reactions. The emotional involvement from us that may be needed by the child or parent can too easily be forgotten, and our busy schedules can easily serve as an excuse for avoiding our dying patients.

A very important part of being able to establish an emotional "fit" with another human being involves the process of *empathy*, namely the ability to understand how someone else feels, the ability to put ourselves in someone else's place. Empathy can be developed with practice and effort, so that we can gradually increase the number and types of people with whom we can empathize. The other side of this same coin is a phenomenon that has been called *countertransference*. As Dr. Blumenfeld has already stated, countertransference is an unconscious, irrational reaction on the part of a professional to a patient, not because of who that patient is in reality, but rather because that patient comes to represent someone from the professional's own past. For example, a parent was very controlling and bossy with an 11 year old. The professional who observed this felt very angry—more so than the situation actually warranted. The professional's mother had herself been a very bossy and controlling person. Those of us in psychiatry who specialize in working with such feelings and reactions find that psychotherapy for ourselves is essential in order to become aware of these unconscious reactions in ourselves. The greater the awareness of one's own past, and of one's reaction to one's past, the greater the possibility that we can understand the influence of the past in our reactions to current situations.

In conclusion, let me say that there are certain guidelines for all of us in medicine who work with patients and their families. The first is that all children and parents who experience a catastrophic illness or a hospitalization are helped by sensing interest, warmth, and competence in the professional. Second, keeping in mind the developmental stage of the child, his or her coping capacity, the type of illness, and the specific parental reaction to it can lead us to many ways of being helpful. For example, a good defense against anxiety is *intellectualization*:

getting information and explanations. Realistically, a parent's understanding in some detail of what a spinal tap is will not improve the illness or its treatment, but it will decrease fear and anxiety, and provide a feeling of some control. A surgeon was treating an eight year old boy with second and third degree burns of the chest and stomach. The postage stamp skin grafts had collected serum, and the serum needed to be squeezed out so that the graft would not die from lack of circulation. This is an extremely painful procedure, one that sometimes has to be repeated a number of times. The surgeon helped the child "control" the pain. He said, "I'll roll the pencil and squeeze the water out. It will hurt. But it has to be done. You hold your breath while I do it, and as soon as you let your breath out, I'll stop. I'll start again when you take a deep breath." Recognizing that this boy would be more comfortable having some control over what happened to him, and then giving him that control—i.e., the ability to stop the pain when it became intolerable—resulted in a decrease in the total amount of time that the procedure usually took, and gave the child a feeling of pride and mastery. This was in striking contrast to another severely burned child whose arms and legs had to be held by four strong nurses and orderlies while he screamed helplessly as the serum was removed from the grafts. Taking the time to listen and to learn about the patient and the family will always pay rich rewards. With enough information one can gradually come to see the situation as the patient or family does, and then be in a position to be truly empathic and helpful.

Suggested Readings

Bowlby J, Robertson J, Rosenbluth D: A two-year-old goes to the hospital. *Psychoanal Study Child* 7:82, 1952.

Farley GK, Eckhardt LO, Hebert FB: Reactions to illness, hospitalization and surgery. In *Handbook of Child and Adolescent Psychiatric Emergencies.* New York, Medical Examination Publishing Co, 1979, p 88.

Jessner L, Blom GE, Waldfogel S: Emotional implications of tonsillectomy and adenoidectomy on children. *Psychoanal Study Child* 7:126, 1952.

Prugh DG: *The Psychosocial Aspects of Pediatrics.* Philadelphia, Lea and Febiger, 1983.

CHAPTER **29** **Adoption, Foster Care, Day Care, and Other Living Arrangements**

Ruth L. Fuller, M.D.

Children in a family usually come by way of biological birth to two individuals married to each other. Although it is accurate to say that this experience is the most common, parenthood is achieved in a number of other ways by many adults. In this chapter, we will look at various routes to parenthood, and a number of different child-caring and child-rearing arrangements.

ADOPTION

Motives for Adoption

Adoption is the assumption of parenthood on the part of one or two people by way of the law rather than by way of biology. When couples adopt, the usual reason for pursuing this route to parenthood is infertility. Another reason for adoption may be a conscious decision not to add to the world's population explosion.

The single parent presents another reason for adopting a child. The single parent, male or female, is ready to assume the responsibilities of parenthood but for a variety of reasons has also chosen to remain single. Single parents vary in age but are generally closer to 30 to 40 years of age, established in their careers, and relatively set in their life styles. Single and couple adopters may want to expand their families and go on to another aspect of the life cycle, namely that of providing for the next generation. The wish to have legitimate heirs to carry on the family name in future generations may also be a motivating factor. However, this is probably not as strong a motive as it was in earlier decades, or as it may still be in other cultures. For example, traditionally, boys have been the ones to carry on the family name, and for that reason might seem to be the more desirable of the two sexes for adoption. But in our country girls are in much greater demand. The reasons for this phenomenon are not clear, but may be related to the fact that girls are generally considered to be easier to raise, and tend to remain closer to their families for longer periods of time than boys.

The Family Romance

Although adoptive parents still form a minority among all parents, their numbers are growing. It is therefore necessary for the future physician to understand some of the issues that arise in the process of adoption. One very important aspect of the psychodynamics of adoption has to do with the impact of this fact on the child who is the adoptee. The adoptee has two sets of parents, biological and adoptive. The significance of this situation is made clearer if I briefly review one aspect of the normal course of human development. At the age of approximately four to five years, the child begins to move away emotionally from his or her parents. Some children may actually pack their bags and leave home, which in most cases means going as far as the end of the block! Because of the aggression inherent in the oedipal conflict, as well as the inevitable frustrations and disappointments of growing up, the parents with whom the child lives are often seen as mean, cruel, or bad. The oedipal child develops the fantasy that he or she cannot possibly belong to such discredited parents but rather must have been stolen or adopted from a good, beautiful, possibly even royal family. This phenomenon is called the *family romance*, first described by Freud in 1909. The family romance ends when the child becomes able to accept the fact that the parents who care for him in the daily routine of life, whether loving or angry, "good" or "bad," are the same people. The adopted child has a much more difficult task of resolving the family romance since this child does indeed have another set of parents in reality. It follows then that the issue of when and how to tell adopted children of the fact of their adoption is extremely important.

It had once been universally recommended by adoption agencies that the child be told as early as possible, for example, around two years of age, and this is still the policy that is most frequently followed. The rationale has been that the child's ability to understand this difficult concept would evolve over the years in a manner similar to the child's gradual assimilation of other information about life. Secrecy and dishonesty were to be avoided, and the child was to be given whatever information he or she could integrate and tolerate. Recent investigators, including Marshall Schechter and Herbert Wieder, have emphasized instead the importance of taking into account the developmental stage of each particular child and the family setting in which disclosure takes place. Certainly, the precipitous disclosure of the actual existence of a "real" set of biological parents different from the adoptive parents can be devastating for an oedipal child's emotional development. For example, if a four or five year old adopted child is furious with his adoptive parents and has mobilized the family romance fantasy of a set of "real, noble parents," disclosure of the adoption at that point in development could cause the family romance fantasy to persist. The actual or psychological search for the biological parents may then continue for the rest of the child's life with an idealization of the biological parents and an aggressive disavowal and disparagement of the adoptive parents. Such a failure of resolution at this stage of development may well influence all future development. Supporters of the earliest possible disclosure argue that such an inopportune disclosure during the oedipal period is less likely to occur if the concept of adoption has been introduced to the child in the earliest years as speech and language are beginning to develop.

An example of such an inopportune disclosure was seen with Matthew, age six years. He was taken to the principal of his school by a very concerned teacher. For weeks he had done no work. He fought constantly with his fellow students, and on that particular day, he had hit his teacher. Matthew had been a good student academically, and his behavior had been excellent up to that point. When the principal asked Matthew, "What's wrong?", he began to scowl

and finally scream out his story. His sixth birthday had taken place three months before. After opening his presents at a family dinner, his mother suddenly told him that she had something else for him. At that point, he was abruptly informed that he had been adopted. He reacted to this news quietly at home, but his distress was vividly seen in school. Matthew's questions were the basic questions of all adopted children: "If this mother that I have known up to now is not my real mother, then who is my mother?" "Who is my father?" "Who am I?"

There is surprisingly little documentation as to the effects of disclosure of adoption at particular times in children's lives. There are some workers in this area who strongly believe that later disclosure, for example during the latency school-age years when a difficult concept such as adoption can be better understood, may be much more realistic than disclosure during the earliest years, which may be extremely traumatic and disruptive to the young child's developing personality. There appears to be universal agreement that disclosure during the oedipal years may be quite hazardous.

Another decades-old tradition of having "sealed records" concerning biological parents is also being reevaluated. There is a growing movement by organizations of adoptees, such as the Adoptee's Liberty Movement Association, to have the law of sealed records changed to a law requiring that the entire case history of the biological parents be made available to adoptees when they come of age or even earlier. We know that the adolescent has a number of issues to settle in order to reach psychological adulthood, and one of the most critical is that of identity formation. This process has been described by Erik Erikson as the formation of a concept of oneself that is internally consistent as well as being consistent with one's environment. The questions of "Who am I?" "Where did I come from?" "What are my biological origins?" "What is my heritage?" are pursued and answered during adolescence. For some adoptees, these questions may have no answers. The adoptee may be a true foundling who was deposited on the doorstep of a hospital. However, in those studies that have been done (especially by Sorosky, Baran, and Pannor) about the effects on adoptees whose biological parents are known and who receive information about their biological parents, it appears that most adoptees are better able to resolve their fantasies about their biological parents after learning about them and after meeting them. Thus, it would seem that knowledge of one's genealogical background is better than ignorance. Most adoptees have usually been disappointed by reality, but have felt considerable relief in finally having some answers to the mystery of their "family romance." The important thing for the physician and all those working with adoptive families to recognize is that the desire of the adoptee to search for the biological parents is rooted in certain fundamental needs regarding identity, and should not be dismissed as either ungrateful or pathological behavior.

Other Problems of Adopted Children

At this point, one may ask the question of whether or not there are other special problems for the adoptee besides the issues of identity formation and the resolution of the family romance that will come to the attention of a physician. There are indeed several such special problems. The adoptee invariably struggles with the doubt as to whether he or she is really loved or wanted. The adoptee may quietly attempt to be the most perfect child that the parents could ever have had or, as is more often the case, noisily and provocatively force the adoptive parents to continually reaffirm their love. The latter mode of behavior has been misunderstood by many adoptive parents as evidence of the child's lack of affection for the parents. The truth of the matter is that this more aggressive behavior in adopted children usually is motivated by their greater need for affirmation and affection. Adoptees often feel painfully worthless, and see themselves as so undesirable that no mother or father could want them. Similarly, the child's fantasies concerning the reason for its abandonment may lead to the conclusion that, "There is something so wrong with me that my real parents had no choice but to give me away." Adoptees also develop symptoms involving action, for example, overt sexual and aggressive behavior, or running away. It is important for physicians to recognize the turmoil and the doubt that most adopted children experience, so that they can be of help to the children, the other siblings in the family, and the parents.

Adoptive Parents

Special problems are also seen with adoptive parents. If the original reason for adoption was the infertility of one or both parents, a dilemma arises. The adopters may continue to emphasize the differences between the special adopted child and the ordinary natural child, or follow the opposite approach by denying any differences between these two modes of creating a family. The parents' pursuit of either route leads to a distorted view of the child and, therefore, to distorted parenting. For example, when the child presents some unacceptable aggressive or sexual behavior, natural parents may blame each other or their own parents. Adoptive parents tend to blame the unknown biological parents and the fantasied "faulty" genetic makeup of the child. Under these circumstances it is easier for the adoptive parents to deny any contribution that they may have made to the less desirable aspects of their child's behavior. Adoptive parents may feel highly competitive with the biological parents for the ultimate love of the adoptee. The biological parents are perceived as a constant threat. This competition is reflected in the adoptive parents' concern that the adoptee will turn against them when the "truth" about the adoption is known. Thus, adoptive parents often struggle with their own version of the family romance. Just as the child in the family romance feels that the everyday parents are not the better parents, so also may the adoptive parents think the same thing. These concerns can lead to excessively indulgent behavior on the part of the adoptive parents.

Adoptive parents often feel this stress especially acutely at the time of the adoptee's adolescence. As the adoptee pursues the question of his or her biological background, the adoptive parents may view this pursuit as evidence that their youngster is being lost to the biological parents. The adoptive parents may then discourage the adolescent in these strivings, and may even attempt to forbid any search for the biological parents. If the adoptive parents do have some information that the youngster seeks, they may withhold or distort it, usually to the detriment of their relationship with their child. They thus may bring about the very distrust and rejection which they so fear. Adoptive parents may also err in trying to resolve their fears by encouraging their adopted children to seek out their biological parents when the adoptee may have no desire to do so, or by joining in the search at a time of great turmoil, such as in early adolescence, when it might clearly be much wiser to wait a few years until some of the normal integration of later adolescence has taken place.

Interracial Adoption

All of these potential problems in adoption are usually compounded even more by *interracial adoption*. By interracial adoption, I mean not only children of different ethnic but also of different religious and cultural backgrounds from their adoptive parents. This issue has aroused a storm of controversy in our society. At times the battle grounds have been firmly and passionately drawn, those totally for and those totally against interracial adoption. How ever, physicians must take a broader and more scientific view.

Let us look back in history. Up until recent years, social agencies had tried to match adoptees and adopters by color (and coloring), religion, country of origin, and culture. The result of this procedure was that many potential adopters went childless, while many children of Black, Hispanic, Oriental, Native American, and especially mixed backgrounds, remained in child-caring institutions. In most recent years, perhaps greatly influenced by the fewer number of children available for adoption, perhaps influenced by the growing demands of single parents and certain minority group parents for adoption, the thinking has changed. Minority group children are now being adopted by couples and single parents with increasing frequency. The argument against such adoptions had been that the child would not be brought up in the manner that his or her heritage had prescribed. For example, a Catholic Black child in a White Protestant home would be deprived of the natural heritage of the biological parents. The argument for such an adoption is that having a loving parent of any color or creed is far more desirable than having no parent.

Racial prejudice is a vast topic that is beyond the scope of this chapter. However, in considering the issues in interracial adoption, it would be a significant omission not to address this question at all. In any comprehensive discussion of the roots of racial prejudice, one must consider historical, cultural, economic, political, social, and psychological factors. Prejudice is based on one or several false beliefs about a group of people, or about an individual because he or she is a member of that group. The children of such a group are always the most defenseless

targets for such prejudice, and the children of interracial marriages and interracial adoption are even more potentially vulnerable targets. Furthermore, in the usual situation, the adoptive parents may or may not choose to tell the child that he or she is adopted, and the child in turn may or may not choose to disclose the fact of the adoption to others. In interracial adoption, however, the child who is of a different racial background from the adoptive parents has no choice in the matter, and must negotiate with the outside world the obvious physical fact of his or her adoption.

The issues of identity and biological heritage become even more complicated and important in interracial adoption. Not infrequently, interracial adoptees may come to feel they are betraying their cultural and biological heritage if they become devoted to the adoptive parents. However, it is most important to remember that many successful interracial adoptions do occur and are occurring with increasing frequency. Unfortunately, while many more children of mixed or minority backgrounds are being adopted than ever before, the majority of such orphaned or abandoned children are still cared for by another means, that of foster care.

FOSTER CARE

Foster care is a system in which parenting is assumed on a temporary basis by one or more foster parents or by an institutional staff. Foster care can be given up to age 18 or even longer. Within the definition of foster care, we can see a built-in problem. The relationship between the foster parent and the foster child is a temporary one, as compared to the adopted child who belongs to the adopters, for better or worse, for life. The foster child does not know how long he or she will remain in the foster home. Arrangements have been as brief as a matter of days to as long as 18 or 20 years, or even until the completion of advanced educational pursuits. If we look back to the early years of child development, there is a great need for consistent, uninterrupted parenting. The foster child lives with the threat of a possible interruption of parenting at any time. The interruption may be a return to the biological parents, a move to another foster home, a move to a group home, or a move to a large, impersonal child-care institution. If foster care has fulfilled its purpose in providing a temporary shelter for a child or children during a family crisis or tragedy, leaving the foster home poses less difficulty. But if placement in foster care results in a prolonged, fruitless wait for the time the child will belong to someone, somewhere, then the effect is almost always detrimental to the child. An extreme but not uncommon form of waiting is seen in the "ping-pong" phenomenon. The child is moved from biological parent to foster parent, then back to biological parent, then perhaps to an institution. It is nearly impossible to convince children they are loved, valued, and wanted when their experience tells them that such is not the case.

This was brought home to me vividly in the case of a 13 year old girl who had been in 13 foster homes. She said she could mark every birthday by her 13 placements. At this point she was going back for her usual visit with her biological parents. They made a point of always picking her up from the foster home just prior to the expiration date of the statute of limitations defining abandonment. They would keep her about two months and then bring her back to the foster care agency as "impossible." This girl told me the home she liked best was the eighth placement in which she was the youngest of four children, the other three being boys. She was treated as the only sister in that family. She was taught how to roller skate, bicycle, and swim. She felt saddest about leaving that home because with them she felt for the first time that somebody really loved her. Prior to that time she was convinced that no one would ever want her for more than six months because she was so bad. When I talked to her about what she expected after this approaching visit with her biological parents, who were perfectly within their legal rights to come and get her and then take her back, she said, "The next time I think I would rather not go to a foster family because it's getting harder to leave. I think I'd rather go to a residential school. I'd rather go there because that way at least the building is always there." She was moving in the direction of wanting to relate to a building rather than to people, and understandably so.

I recall another case — a seven year old boy who was placed in foster care by his biological mother when he was five days old. Approximately every two years (at age two, four, and six), she demanded his return, kept him for a few months, and then gave him up again. Now she was demanding him back again, but this time the foster mother was refusing because she said that the boy returned from weekend visits with the biological mother hungry, dirty, and with many suspicious bruises all over his body. Then, after one of those weekend visits, the child did not return. The foster mother went to court and was told the boy was with the biological mother and would remain with her, since that was her legal right. The boy had absolutely no preparation for what was to happen. He had just left for what was supposed to be a usual weekend with his biological mother, and did not return to the foster mother for whom he had come to care a great deal. This was a tragic situation. With the more recent developments in children's rights, there has been a redefinition of what constitutes abandonment by the biological parents, and a greater willingness by the courts to terminate the parental rights of biological parents who are clearly unable to parent. With these changes, along with a reemphasis on the temporary nature of foster care, it may be possible to prevent such tragic occurrences in the future.

From the point of view of the foster parent, he or she must have the capacity to receive new children with enthusiasm and yet not know for how long these youngsters will remain. The turmoil of giving up a child or children must be experienced over and over again by foster parents. The foster parents are constantly reminded that they are temporary parents, and thus must deal with their own wishes for a permanent parent-child relationship. It is not unusual for foster parents to apply for adoption of one or more of their foster children. Here, we encounter another dilemma. If the desired child has not been released for adoption, the child may then be removed from the very foster parents requesting adoption. The reasoning had been that the foster parents had become too "involved" with the child and, therefore, placement in another foster home would be made. The thinking in child-care agencies is now shifting to the rights of the child in this situation, and there is much debate about the subject. The question is as follows: if the child has known only one parent (or set of parents), is not the child entitled to remain with these psychological parents rather than be forced to return to the biological parents whenever the biological parents may wish to have the child returned? How are the wishes and abilities of the parents to be assessed? How are the wishes and needs of the child to be weighed? How are the best interests of the child to be determined? These are important questions that are going to be addressed with increasing frequency to the physicians of the future.

DAY CARE

Day care is a method of shared parenting that is rapidly becoming a way of life in the United States. We are well into an era in which more than 50% of mothers work outside of the home and a minority of women are full-time parents. With this increase in working mothers, day care has become a critical necessity for many families. However, we still know very little about the long-term benefits and the long-term liabilities of day care. Parents will turn to physicians for guidance in this area, but our answers to their questions about the effect of day care on the intellectual and emotional development of their children cannot be as definite as we would wish. Nevertheless, the physician should at least be able to support parents in their quest for quality day care. Parents should locate the day care parent or the day care center whose approach to children is compatible with their own, and whose resources and staffing patterns will provide sufficient attention to each individual child. A physician who makes the effort to become acquainted with the highest quality day care facilities in his or her community will provide an invaluable service to working parents.

OTHER LIVING ARRANGEMENTS

Briefly, I would like to mention that there are other ways in which families are formed and maintained. With the increasing divorce rate millions of children are being raised by single divorced parents, and then by stepparents when the single parents remarry. It may be that with this increase in single parenting and stepparenting due to divorce, more attention is being paid to other living arrangements involving members of the extended family. These variations have often had a long history in many, often minority, cultural groups. For example, informal adoption of, or foster care for younger siblings, is often provided by older siblings in many cultural groups. Grandparents and great-grandparents will often assume the parenting responsibilities for grandchildren and great-grandchildren. Teachers have sometimes become informal foster parents to students and protegees. Similarly, it is not unusual for an adolescent to live with an uncle, godparent, cousin, or family friend when the turmoil of that period cannot be negotiated in the original home. Older adolescents will sometimes share living space and parent each other. Adults have become formal and informal adoptive parents of other adults. Group parenting may be formal, as in a commune, or informal, as in a shared house. Homosexual couples are increasingly asking to adopt children, or to raise the children of one of the homosexual partners. These and other variations in child care and child-rearing will be presented to the physician, and questions will be asked about the benefits and liabilities of such arrangements. There are no preset answers to any of these questions, and each situation must be assessed individually on its own merits.

Suggested Readings

Freud S (1909): Family romances. In *Standard Edition of the Complete Psychological Works of Sigmund Freud*, vol 9. London, Hogarth Press, 1959, p 235.
Krementz J: *How It Feels To Be Adopted*. New York, Alfred Knopf, 1982.
Kuzma K (ed): *Working Mothers*. Los Angeles, Stratford Press, 1981.
Notman MT, Nadelson CC: Maternal work and children. In Nadelson CC, Notman MT (eds): *The Woman Patient*, vol 2. New York, Plenum Press, 1982, p 121.
Schechter MD: Observations on adopted children. *Arch Gen Psychiatry* 3:21, 1960.
Schechter MD, et al: Emotional problems in the adoptee. *Arch Gen Psychiatry* 10:109, 1964.
Schechter MD: About adoptive parents. In Anthony EJ, Benedek T (eds): *Parenthood: Its Psychology and Psychopathology*. Boston, Little, Brown, and Co, 1970, p 353.
Siegal-Gorelick B: *The Working Parents' Guide to Child Care: How To Find the Best Care for Your Child*. Boston, Little, Brown, and Co, 1982.
Sorosky AD, Baran A, Pannor R: Identity conflicts in adoptees. *Am J Orthopsychiatry* 45:18, 1975.
Wieder H: On when and whether to disclose about adoption. *J Am Psychoanal Assoc* 26:793, 1978.

References

Allport GW: *The Nature of Prejudice*. Cambridge, MA, Addison-Wesley, 1954.
Comer JP: *Beyond Black and White*. New York, Quadrangle Books, 1972.
Erikson EH: *Identity: Youth and Crisis*. New York, W.W. Norton, 1968.
Friedman RM, et al: Length of time in foster care: a measure in need of analysis. *J Nat Assoc Soc Workers* 27:499, 1982.
Goldstein J, Freud A, Solnit AJ: *Beyond the Best Interest of the Child*. New York, Free Press, 1973.
Hampson RB, Tavormina JB: Feedback from the experts: a study of foster mothers. *J Nat Assoc Soc Workers* 25:108, 1980.
Stuart I, Abt L (eds): *Interracial Marriage*. New York, Grossman Publishers, 1973.

30 Loss, Grief, and Mourning in Children

Henry P. Coppolillo, M.D.

Grief is ubiquitous in the human condition, and children are not spared. If we recognize that grief occurs not only when there has been a death in the family or the loss of a loved one through physical separation, but also when a cherished and familiar pattern of interacting with the world is discontinued or when a treasured aspiration must be surrendered, we can see how early in life our children become introduced to this affect. While in this section we will explore the phenomenon of grief and mourning using a death in the family as an example, we will return to the broader issue of grief in the daily life of children as an important concern of the physician.

THE DEATH OF A GRANDPARENT

Tommy was a happy young boy of seven. His family consisted of a father who was 40, a civil engineer, a mother 38 years of age, and a sister who was 13. Three years earlier, Tommy's paternal grandfather had died, and his widowed grandmother came to live with Tommy's family. Six months after the grandmother came into the home, Tommy's mother returned to her teaching career as grandmother provided some help with the general household chores as well as care for Tommy. Tommy and his grandmother developed a tender and loving relationship as she became an integral part of the home and family.

One morning in May, Tommy awakened at his usual hour and arose from bed to go running downstairs to watch his favorite television shows while his grandmother or mother made breakfast and gently fussed at him to wash and dress lest he be late for school. Yet today, even as he was hopping down the stairs on one foot at a time (getting his legs in condition for next year's

skiing), he noticed there was something different in the home. The hum and rattle that usually came from the kitchen was stilled. The smell of food was absent. Dad's car was still in the driveway, and the whole house felt to him like church felt some Sunday mornings — hushed and solemn.

When Tommy reached the kitchen, he *knew* that something was indeed wrong. He saw the kitchen was empty before he heard the call from the living room. When he reached the living room, his mother and father looked strange. A vague memory of another time in the past when he had seen them this way began slowly to form but was interrupted by his mother saying, "Tommy, we have to tell you something." Tommy was startled by the low and gentle tone of her voice that was at the same time painful and compelling. In an instant his mind flashed to the possibility that they had been informed of some misbehavior of his at school or that they had changed their mind about the bicycle that they had promised him for this spring. But it was neither of these because mother, taking him gently by the shoulders, went on to say "Grandmother didn't wake up this morning. She went to sleep last night and didn't wake up." For a moment Tommy thought he would never learn to understand grown-ups. They made such big deals about such trivial issues. Patiently, therefore, he offered the obvious solution by saying, "Let's go wake her up." Again, he felt perplexed by the look of pain on his parents' faces. Finally Mother said, "No, Tommy. She'll never wake up again." Tommy knew what that meant. The memory that had just started to form when he walked into the living room returned. He remembered when they had told him that Grandpa had gone to sleep. He knew that he had never seen him again. He remembered putting this together with what the teacher had told them about the class's pet guinea pig that had disappeared from the cage last year and had never come back. Died! That was the word, and Tommy wasn't going to have it! "You mean she died," he said. This time Father answered, and he was crying. "Yes, Tommy, she died." "No!", Tommy yelled and ran to his bedroom. He didn't want it to be true, and he wasn't going to listen to his parents trying to convince him that it was true. He didn't want Grandma to be dead. He threw himself on his bed and buried his head in his pillow, actively telling himself that his parents were mistaken and that all they needed to do was to try harder to awaken her.

After a few minutes, his father came into his room and sat on the side of the bed. He tried to talk to Tommy, but Tommy wanted none of it. He just wanted Dad to go get Grandma up. He rolled off of the bed away from Dad and went over to the toy chest where the football that Grandma had given him rested. He picked it up and held it to him while his mind raced and searched for possible explanations for all the confusing thoughts and feelings he had. His father, detecting the turmoil in Tommy, touched his son on the shoulder and said that he seemed to want to be alone for now. He added that he would be downstairs with Tommy's mother and hoped Tommy could come down to join them when he felt like it.

Indeed, later that morning Tommy felt hungry and while preparing breakfast for him, his mother was able to explain to Tommy how grieved she and Tommy's father and sister were about the loss of Grandma. Tommy felt better in knowing that Mom understood how he felt and that he and Mom and Dad could talk about Grandma.

Tommy did not go to school for the next couple of days. He and his sister had a relative stay with them during the time that Mom and Dad were at the wake and funeral. Several times over the next couple of days, Tommy was able to play or enjoy the company of others without the sad, anguished feelings he had when he thought of his grandmother. During one play period he picked up the football that his grandmother had given him. After holding it a few moments and looking into space, he burst into tears and ran into his room.

The next evening, the family was sitting down to have dinner, and the mother noticed that she had inadvertently set a place for the grandmother. She began to cry at this, and Tommy immediately joined her in tears while father struggled to remain in control as he tried to answer his daughter's questions about the crying. Somewhat later in the evening, the family settled down and resumed their activities.

Tommy began once more to settle into his comfortable and happy life. A couple of days later following dinner, in response to a playmate's invitation to join him outside, Tommy responded that he wanted to stay home and watch television with Grandma. He then remembered that Grandma was no more, and his grief and sadness returned and stayed with him for a relatively shorter period of time. In the next week or two this remembering of his grandmother with a flood of grief occurred several times, but each bout was relatively shorter and the intervals between them became longer. At the same time he began to remember his grandmother with a tender warmth and in a somewhat idealized fashion. She bought him the best toys, and she was the one who baked the best cookies ever made. Occasionally his parents would see him do things alone which he had formerly done with his grandmother, such as watch a television show that had been a favorite of hers or tend some flowers that they had planted together. In addition to these observations, they noted that Tommy gradually began to be more friendly and accepting of the attentions of an elderly woman neighbor who had been an acquaintance of his grandmother.

THE STAGES OF MOURNING IN CHILDREN

Why are the issues of grief and mourning of interest to healers of the mind and body? The behavior of animals lower on the phylogenetic tree tends to consist of more fixed automatic patterns of adaptation. As we look at higher animals, we see that the fixed patterns of behavior that serve adaptation tend to drop out, and in their place we see processes that require thought, choices, and creative problem-solving activities on the part of the individuals. In a word, instincts are replaced by a dynamic psychological process that integrates the individual's biological capacity with his psychological and social experience to achieve an adaptation to both the demands of the outside world as well as the demands of his inner world of wishes and needs.

The ability to grieve and to mourn a loss is one of the psychological acquisitions of higher animals, including humans, that serves this process of adaptation. In human beings when this process is not successful following any significant loss, we can see a number of breakdowns in the ability to adapt physiologically as well as psychologically and socially. Grief is a frequent component of any illness that causes a person to experience himself as handicapped, diminished, or restricted in his state or in his abilities. The process of mourning necessary to alleviate this affect of grief is a part of the healing process upon which the outcome of illness and the reacquisition of health may be heavily predicated. With these observations in mind, the process of grief in children may be examined.

Immediately after a child comes to understand that a loss has occurred and to realize the significance of that loss to him or her, there is a period of shocked disbelief and outrage. Often this stage may be accompanied by exclamations of denial. When Tommy shouted "No!" to the heavens and all who could hear him, that single word was expressing his outrage and his denial. This reaction is really not very different from that which occurs in adults, as Dr. Wolff and Dr. Simons will indicate later in the book. In adults, however, the expression of those reactions that appear illogical or irrational, like the denial or the anger, are often inhibited or muted. In children they tend to be expressed very directly. In some cultures in which affective expression is more direct than in our culture, it is not unusual to hear the dead gently and tenderly reprimanded for having abandoned the bereaved. Shakespeare gives us an example in Act V. of *Romeo and Juliet*. When Juliet awakens and finds that Romeo has committed suicide with poison, she cries, "Oh churl! drunk all, and left no friendly drop to help me after?"

This stage of shock, outrage, anger, and denial may last from hours to days in the normal child. Gradually from this state the child will pass into another pattern of mourning. In this second stage, which may last from days to months, one can see cycles of intense grief, sometimes mixed with guilt or regret, succeeded by periods of the child's usual behavior or by mild sadness or even cheerfulness. The episodes of grief can be occasioned by a reaction to a stimulus or a spontaneous memory. At these moments a number of qualities or traits, or perhaps the special significance, of the lost person are recalled, and with each cycle of grief we can see that a specific trait or a specific meaning the person had for the child is remembered, reviewed, and then surren-

dered. When Tommy held his football, he recalled his grandmother's generosity as one of her most cherished qualities. But during these same periods of grief, Tommy may have recalled that he had sometimes disobeyed or discomfited his grandmother, and then the sadness and anguish would be accompanied by regret and perhaps even guilt and self-accusation. Each of these periods of acute sadness tends to be shorter than the preceding one, and the intervening period of normal functions tends to be longer. In Tommy's case, the periods he could play without internal disruption were longer after his momentary lapse around the television show episode than they had been during the day or two immediately after his grandmother's death.

Another quality of this second stage of grief that is exemplified by Tommy's thought that he would watch television with his grandmother is the child's search for the lost one. This seeking process may appear as a misperception. A person passing on the street, a voice on the telephone, the sound of movement from the bedroom, may evoke the image or momentarily induce the conviction that the departed is there. The intensity of these misperceptions may range from a momentary and quickly dispelled illusion to a deeply moving and sometimes frightening hallucination. It must not be thought, however, that an hallucination in this instance is a symptom of severe psychopathology. Here it is only a sign of healing.

A final note regarding this stage of the process of mourning has to do with the nature of human relationships. Often during this phase of the process the bereaved will reject any substitute for the lost person and tends to withdraw from attempts of others to comfort him. When his father came into Tommy's room and attempted to comfort him, Tommy withdrew. Any early attempt of the elderly neighbor lady to provide Tommy with the generosity or warmth that Grandma had given when alive would have been turned down by the boy. Grief must run a certain course before a substitute object can be accepted.

In the last stage, the episodes of acute grief grow further apart and are accompanied by a number of other phenomena that promote healing. As the anger, chagrin, and longing for the lost object become more manageable, the mourner begins to assume some of the qualities of the lost person. This most often occurs outside of the child's awareness, and in this way the mourner unconsciously keeps part of the lost person alive within. Examples of this process can be seen in Tommy's turning to tend the flowers of which his grandmother was so fond. As these identifications are being processed psychologically, sad, lonely, and angry feelings surrounding the death and the dead person are gradually replaced by memories that are imbued with tenderness and fondness. The memory of an interchange with a lost loved one may even serve as a comforting thought during moments of distress. Bolstering these positive memories is the tendency to idealize the departed person. Both children and adults alike embellish the positive traits of the dead, and forget or minimize painful or negative memories. In some cultures this tendency is ritualized to the point that no dead person is referred to only by name, but rather as "your *sainted* Grandmother" or "the blessed George" or "the good soul."

Finally, the irreplaceability of the loss fades, and the bereaved child invests in new interests. Tommy could, after a time, begin to accept the cookies of the elderly neighbor lady and with them her interest and fondness for him. As the objects of the past become cherished, the objects of the present become important. The film *The Day Grandpa Died* (Figure 30.1) beautifully depicts all of these stages of mourning in a young boy following the death of his grandfather. In the next chapter on "Death and the Dying Child," Dr. Thunberg will present other clinical examples of losses in childhood — the loss of a body part, the loss of a sibling, the loss of a parent, and the loss of a peer. While all of these losses in childhood are dramatic and momentous, there is another aspect of childhood loss which I would now like to emphasize.

ACHIEVEMENT AND ABANDONMENT OF DEVELOPMENTAL MILESTONES

In a subtle and almost imperceptible way, small bouts of grief comingle with joy and satisfaction to comprise the affects that accompany each stage of development in the life cycle. In a first grade class that has just been informed that all the children will be promoted to the second grade, one would not have much trouble perceiving the expressions of joy and satisfaction. But look a bit closer! There is Johnny with just a tinge of sadness breaking through about having to leave Mrs. Jones, the first grade teacher. If Johnny feels comfortable enough, he will reveal his conviction that there will never be another teacher like her or that a particular, pleasurable activity of the first grade will never be available again.

Probably most of the parents who have watched their child toddle away from them as the child acquired the ability to walk experienced the happiness of witnessing a new phase of their youngster's development even as they distantly and dimly felt the sadness of the disappearance of their fat, cuddly infant. Judging from the number of times the toddler expresses anger and frustration, we might speculate that the child may also be experiencing some sadness at losing the days of unconditional love and approbation as he or she becomes introduced to the concept that love must now be earned by using the newly achieved capacity to move responsibly ("Don't walk in the flower bed. Don't go near the street.").

At each stage of development, even as we exult in acquisitions of the new stage, something lost from the old must be sadly relinquished. We can enjoy sipping vintage wines only when we have given up the investment in college freshman beer busts. It may well be that these episodes of minor brushes with the grief process are necessary to prepare human beings for the collisions with grief that inevitably appear in the course of every human being's life, including the realization of our own impermanence.

Figure 30.1. A young boy with his grandfather. From the film *The Day Grandpa Died*. (By permission of BFA Educational Media, 2211 Michigan Avenue, Santa Monica, California 90406.)

PATHOLOGICAL MOURNING IN CHILDREN

In those instances in which grieving for a lost person has been suppressed, either by external influences or the child's own inabilities to grieve, one possible pathological outcome is a child who withdraws from human contacts in significant ways. The picture is often one of an apathetic, isolated child who shows very little interest in making human investments. When the child has, by training, been taught to be polite or gracious, it may seem that he is relating well until the relationship is subjected to closer scrutiny. Then the observer will see that while the motions of relating are being carried out, little that is personal or significant is ever communicated, and no sense of liking or loving another person is ever conveyed by the child. Special attachments to teachers and playmates are not observed, and separations from significant members of the child's environment do not seem to cause the child distress.

In the case of inadequate mourning of a lost function or body part, two signs are present. The first is that there is no history of the anger and sadness related to the loss that are evidence of normal grief work. Secondly, the child shows little or no investment in developing compensatory capacities, whether these are in the form of learning to use a prosthesis or in the area of using another sensory or motor modality to compensate for the lost one. While in adults this may appear as medical noncompliance, in the child it appears as "laziness" or simple passive resistance.

In certain instances the child may go through a period of pseudogrieving. In these cases the child may speak of the loss but does so without any real, internally generated feelings. Sometimes this occurs in instances where health care professionals are zealous but not very well prepared technically to manage the situation. They may do all of the talking and tell the child what he or she is supposed to feel without the child having initiated the interaction in any way. Often the child will comply by nodding or indicating agreement to almost anything the worker says without any real changes having occurred. In some other instances the youngster receives subtle but definite clues from the parents or other adults in the environment that they cannot or wish not to tolerate his grief (Figure 30.2). This situation is closely related to those instances in which children are so concerned about their parents' grief that they literally must neglect or repress their own feelings. Again, these

Figure 30.2. *Starvation* (1924) by Käthe Kollwitz. (Courtesy of Roger and Ruth Loewi, Denver, Colorado. Photograph by Judith K. Thorpe.)

are often compliant children who may have a rather marked capacity to express things dramatically and well. The only trouble is that what they are expressing is imitative rather than internally generated.

Finally, I would like to address a consequence of pathological grief whose impact has probably been, as yet, only partially appreciated. This is the topic of *childhood depression.* Children can and do become depressed, and one way in which the depression can come about is through deviance in the process of mourning. At times the depression can manifest itself in clamorous and open rebelliousness and hostility at home or in school, at other times in somatic symptoms, and at still other times in a quiet, despairing sadness. In any form, the depression can be diagnosed by a physician who looks carefully at the child's interpersonal relationships, his preferences and avoidances, and his responses to empathic questioning.

The prognosis of childhood depression, when not alleviated, is not good. At best the child's satisfaction and joy in the accomplishments of growth and development are blunted and submerged in self-doubt and self-denigration. At worst, children can suicide. In some cases, though they are infrequent, a child's self-destructive behavior is clearly labeled "suicide" by the family. More frequently we see situations in which ingestion of poisons, falls, and other actions that are fatal to children are labeled "accidents." But they are not always accidents. One study estimated that the number of self-poisonings among children ages five to 14 may be five times the number of cases of meningitis that occur in that age group. And as I just indicated, suicide in children may be even more underreported than suicide in adults. Bakwin has estimated that the ratio of actual childhood suicide attempts to reported attempts may be as high as 50 to one. Shaw reports that the suicide rate is three times higher among children whose families have recently moved, and it is also higher among male children. Finally, Pfeffer and her colleagues found that among approximately 100 children referred for psychiatric hospitalization at a New York hospital, 33% had threatened or attempted suicide.

These are indeed sobering statistics. But in concluding this chapter, it would be well to recall that grief should not be viewed in a lugubrious or mystical context. It is, in fact, part of the necessary preparation for each new step in the life cycle. As one last example, we can recall when it became time for us and an admired and respected teacher to part. If the meeting had any meaning at all, both teacher and student were gratified by the exchanges of the encounter, and both were a bit saddened by the necessity for its termination. Yet each carried away something from the other that went beyond the substantive knowledge that was shared. The teacher faced his new group of students with a bit more empathy, sensitivity, and youthful enthusiasm, left with him by the student who had just departed. The student left with an identification with a certain number of the teacher's traits, attitudes, and values that becomes a support system with which to face a taxing and demanding world. Hopefully every encounter between a physician and a patient will provide the same mutual enrichment.

Suggested Readings

Anthony EJ: Childhood depression. In Anthony EJ, Benedek T (eds): *Depression and Human Existence.* Boston, Little, Brown, and Co, 1975, p 231.

Bemporad JR: Childhood depression from a developmental perspective. In Grinspoon L (ed): *Psychiatry 1982: Annual Review.* Washington, American Psychiatric Press, 1982, p 272.

Bowlby J: Grief and mourning in infancy and early childhood. *Psychoanal Study Child* 15:9, 1960.

Freud A: The role of bodily illness in the mental life of children. *Psychoanal Study Child* 7:69, 1952.

Kashani JH: Epidemiology of childhood depression. In Grinspoon L (ed): *Psychiatry 1982: Annual Review.* Washington, American Psychiatric Press, 1982, p 281.

Poznanski EO: The clinical characteristics of childhood depression. In Grinspoon L (ed): *Psychiatry 1982: Annual Review.* Washington, American Psychiatric Press, 1982, p 296.

Watson E, Johnson A: The emotional significance of acquired physical disfigurement in children. *Am J Orthopsychiatry* 28:85, 1958.

References

Bakwin H: Suicide in children and adults. *J Am Med Wom Assoc* 19:489, 1964.

Cobb S, Lindemann E: Neuropsychiatric observations after the Cocoanut Grove Fire. *Ann Surg* 117:814, 1943.

Gould R: Suicidal problems in children and adolescents. *Am J Psychotherapy* 19:228, 1965.

Kashani JH, et al: Current perspectives on childhood depression: an overview. *Am J Psychiatry* 138:143, 1981.

Kohut H: Forms and transformations of narcissism. *J Am Psychoanal Assoc* 14:243, 1966.

Pfeffer CR: Suicidal behavior of children. *Am J Psychiatry* 138:154, 1981.

Pfeffer CR, et al: Suicidal and assaultive behavior in children. *Am J Psychiatry* 140:154, 1983.

Shaw C, Schelkun R: Suicidal behavior in children. *Psychiatry* 28:157, 1965.

Toolan JM: Suicide and suicide attempts in children and adolescents. *Am J Psychiatry* 118:719, 1962.

31 The Dying Child and Adolescent

A. *Ethical Perspectives*

G. Gail Gardner, Ph.D.

"The hour of departure has arrived and we go our ways—I to die and you to live. Which is better God only knows."

Plato

TO DIE OR TO LIVE

Is it better to die than to live? This question and others related to it are rarely asked in discussions dealing with terminally ill children. Instead, in this age of high technology, we presume too often to know all the answers: "More is better. If we can prolong life, we must. If any adults—especially physicians—do not believe in these efforts, they must pretend that they do. Death is bad. Children are too young to understand any of this. At all costs, children should be protected from death and from any knowledge of death."

When adults are terminally ill, they can usually exercise rights of self-determination that allow them to experience dying as a final process of life that needs to be mastered. Having the right to informed consent, they can insist on complete information about their medical condition and make decisions accordingly. They can choose further treatment or they can refuse it. They can select their doctors. They can seek support and guidance from family, friends, clergy, and other health care professionals.

Legally, dying children have no such rights. At issue, however, is whether they have such rights based on moral and ethical grounds. I believe they do. I will devote this chapter to defining those rights and to attempting to understand why physicians tend to neglect or disregard them.

THE RIGHT TO KNOW

One often hears that children should be spared the knowledge that they are dying, as if such knowledge imposes unnecessary suffering on them. On the contrary, when a physician informs a child that his or her illness is terminal, it is often the physician who suffers most. Those of us who work frequently with dying children and adolescents know that they usually accept the idea of death much more easily than adults. When we try to delude a dying child—for example, by defining leukemia in relapse as "anemia"—we pay a large price for our own comfort. First, we convey some of our own anxiety about death to the child and therefore create the very problem we want to avoid. Second, we destroy any possibility of trust, for the child probably already knows that death is inevitable or at least very likely. Children with cancer, for example, figure out that the sign "Oncology Clinic" refers to cancer and not just to anemia. They read the mail from the Cancer Society. They watch television programs about cancer and note the similarity to their own symptoms. They hear people talk.

Is there an age below which children do not conceptualize death as final? If so, we could perhaps maintain our own comfort by not talking about death to patients below this age. Unfortunately, child development research is not as helpful here as one might hope. In the next part of the chapter, Dr. Thunberg will review several studies of healthy children who have little reason to be concerned with death, and she will quote several authors who have concluded that the age of a reality-based awareness of death is as high as seven or eight years. However, in the case of younger children who are actually dying, understanding the nature of death becomes immediately relevant and may therefore occur much sooner. I know a four year old boy who said: "I have leukemia. That is a bad disease and you could die from it. When you die, they put you in the ground and you just can't do anything anymore." I know a six year old leukemic boy who said: "Why are they going to bury me in my good clothes when I die? I'm just going to rot. They should bury me in my old jeans and give my good clothes to orphans or to poor children."

I do not mean to suggest that all dying four year olds know they are dying or that physicians should talk candidly about death with all dying children of any age. Some children may be truly ignorant about death, and others may have a strong need for denial that should be respected. What is crucial is that physicians listen to verbal and nonverbal communications from dying children, and base their communications about death not on their own needs or anxieties but on the needs and anxieties of the child. And in any given case, if the physician cannot do this, then he or she should turn to some other health care professional who will be able to talk appropriately with the child.

Parents sometimes state that they absolutely do not want death discussed with their child. In such cases, I try to learn the reasons for their position. If a parent claims that the child is "too young to know," then I share my general knowledge about the issue, and ask the parent simply to listen for two weeks to the child's spontaneous comments. The result is often very surprising to the parent. One mother of a six year old leukemic child insisted that he could not possibly be concerned about death "because he is such a happy child." She agreed to two weeks of listening with an open mind. During that time, the child asked several questions about a nearby cemetary: "Are your parents with you when they bury you there? If they bury you *down* there, how do you get *up* to Heaven?" The boy also reported a dream that he called "The Dream of the Firewitch." He said: "I dreamed there were many ghosts going around in circles holding fire. I felt scared. I was afraid they might catch me and fire me. And I guess I would die. I hid under a desk." (Figure 31.1). Following these events, the mother changed her mind and asked me to discuss death with her son and to help her to do the same.

Sometimes I agree that a dying child really has no idea that he or she is dying. Then I encourage the parents to continue their listening attitude, and I suggest that we may want to discuss death with the child at a later time. Occasionally, despite evidence to the contrary, parents adamantly insist that a child does not need or want to talk about the possibility of

Figure 31.1. Drawing of "The Dream of the Firewitch."

death. They do not want the child to hear about death at all. In such cases, I express my disagreement but respect their wishes. If I did otherwise, I would only alienate the parents and then be unable to help them or the child.

THE RIGHT TO SHARE

Having talked once about death with a dying child, physicians have a tendency to consider the job done, without any need to discuss the subject again. Many parents then follow the example of the "experts." We rationalize that we will help the child most by exuding constant optimism and hope. Again, we pay a price. We create a conspiracy of silence with the result that the child bears the burden of dying utterly alone and takes on the added responsibility of shielding all of us from our own pain.

The job is not done after the initial discussion. The dying process continues, and the child who is cut off from further communication may develop fantasies about death that are far worse than reality. I have seen children, initially comforted by faith in eternal life, begin to doubt such faith after seeing family members who cry but refuse to talk. These children wonder why people cry if heaven is really such a wonderful place. Becoming aware of their parents' grief and also their worries about medical costs, dying children may add irrational guilt and shame to their confusion. They may conclude that they are dying because they are bad children.

If we take the time to learn about the concerns of dying children throughout the dying process, we can do much to lighten their burden. Again, if we carefully observe verbal and nonverbal cues, we will usually know when they need to talk. We should also inform parents about the child's continuing need to share, and encourage them to facilitate a climate of sensitive honesty and openness. For those parents who cannot bring themselves to talk with their children about death, we can remind them that sharing is not limited to verbal communication. One can share by touching or holding a child. One can share by crying together or by enjoying something together or by doing anything special together.

THE RIGHT TO LIVE

The dying child is also a living child. As much as possible, dying children have a right to all of the experiences of healthy children: a wholesome family environment, peer relationships, school, sports, special activities, holidays, and so on. The sensitive physician can allow dying children to know and to share the reality of death and still enjoy a relatively normal life with as few constraints as possible. In addition to counseling parents about home activities, physicians need to monitor any of their own behavior that may compromise the child's right to live a normal life. For example, if a child's illness requires that he or she be in the hospital on a weekend that would otherwise include participation in sports or church attendance, so be it. But we need to think twice about keeping the child in the hospital over the weekend if we know that little or nothing will be done until Monday. All too often, we claim to determine the course of medical care based on the patient's needs when we really consider the convenience of our own schedules first. The result is unnecessary hospitalization.

Given that many medical procedures create anxiety and/or depression in children and adolescents, we need to think more carefully about

ordering any procedures of questionable value. I am not talking only about so-called "heroic" efforts such as the use of respirators for children who are obviously dying; fortunately we see less of these efforts now than in the past. Rather, I am questioning the use of "routine" procedures. I have seen physicians insist on "routine blood tests" when everyone knew a child would be dead within a week. When I protested, I was told that it was "just a finger-stick" and that the information would be "useful." "Useful to whom?," I wondered, as the child turned to his parents and wept. To give another example, when a child is obviously dying, I have seen physicians insist on continuing supplemental tube feeding in order to achieve weight gain. In one case, the feedings were stopped only when the parents pleaded for a more normal end to their child's life. Why do physicians engage in this kind of mindless behavior? I believe they often do it in order to stave off their own feelings of helplessness in the face of death. If they would spend the same amount of time and effort talking and playing and comforting the dying child, they would become aware of doing a far greater service.

Physicians can facilitate the experience of a normal life even when a hospitalized child is only a few days from death. I know a physician who arranged for a dying child to shoot his new but unused BB gun on the hospital roof. The event turned into a party for the child, the family, and the entire medical team. The atmosphere was one of victory, not defeat.

THE RIGHT TO DIE

In the case of many dying children and adolescents, there comes a time when one can reasonably continue treatment or one can reasonably stop. Physicians can then take one of three positions. First, they can limit the decision-making process to the medical team. Second, they can include the parents. Third, they can also include the child.

It seems to me that, if physicians give dying children and adolescents the right to know, the right to share, and the right to live, then it is only logical to give them the right to participate in the decision to terminate treatment and to die. This last right does not pertain when there is a good possibility of survival following treatment or when the child's judgment is obviously limited or impaired. But the rational child or adolescent who is obviously dying can be asked straightforwardly whether he or she wants everything possible done to prolong life.

I have known children who answered with a categorical "Yes." I have known others who asked to be kept alive, but only under certain conditions such as "until my father gets here." Still others have answered with a categorical "No" and have gone on to request that they die either in the hospital or at home. In the last category, the youngest child I have known was 10 years old. He said he was ready to die. His parents agreed. When his wish was granted, no one felt helpless. We had done our best for him. We had understood his needs and met them. When he died, we felt satisfied and even enriched.

I am aware of cases in which decisions to limit or terminate treatment for dying children are delegated to the courts, even when the child, the family, and the medical staff all agree that death is inevitable. When there is complete agreement among the persons involved, it seems unreasonable that a stranger should be expected to make the best decision. The problem is usually that physicians—for either personal or legal reasons—feel compelled to override their own good medical judgment. This legalistic approach does minimize the physician's anxiety and the risk of lawsuits. But it also violates both medical integrity and the rights of dying children. Medicine is not only the science of healing bodies. It is also an art in which physicians can use their personal skills to enhance the lives of people, including dying children and adolescents.

OTHER MEMBERS OF THE FAMILY

In working with terminally ill patients, physicians also have a significant impact on other members of the family. This impact is most likely to be positive when the dying patient's rights have been respected. Some parents share their own positive feelings associated with the death of a child; the sensitive physician can use this information to help dispel his or her feelings of anxiety and helplessness in relation to dying

patients. For example, one mother, whose 12 year old son David had died of leukemia, wrote the following letter to one of her son's caretakers:

Dear Dr.__

Why does one cry for the dead? The answer depends on who dies, and how, and why, and whether one feels negligent or responsible for the death, or whether one feels unfinished about the relationship—"I should have made amends, etc." In David's case, a young person dying, one cries that it seems unnecessary—I rebelled at that all fall. But now the deed is done, and that which has been fought against with all of man's skill has come to pass. How, then, to make meaning out of it? I am as bewildered by how one copes with accidental death, or violent death, as anyone, but this is not ours to cope with, by the mercy of God. We have only the strong memories that David died in calm, surrounded by the best care and love anyone could have. So no feelings of negligence, or broken relationship to mend. I could cry for his unfinished life, if three score years and ten is most important, but if I believe that God is personal, and cares more for me and my loved ones than even I know how to, then how should I grieve that he is with God. And how could I doubt this personal God, after my experiences of the past month? And do I grieve for my loss of a son? Yes, if he were truly out of touch— but Dave is so real to me—not externally but internally—bound up in all that I cherish and wonder at and reflect on, that his reality is very present, very real, very full of meaning. And so I rejoice, mainly, that God should so bless me as to make meaning out of chaos.

Suggested Readings

Gardner GG: Childhood, death, and human dignity: hypnotherapy for David. *Int J Clin Exp Hypnosis* 24:122, 1976.
Kellerman J (ed): *Psychological Aspects of Childhood Cancer.* Springfield, IL, Charles C Thomas, 1980.
Kubler-Ross E: *On Children and Death.* New York, MacMillan, 1983.
Stinson R, Stinson P: *The Long Dying of Baby Andrew.* Boston, Little, Brown, and Co, 1983.
Veatch RM: *A Theory of Medical Ethics.* New York, Basic Books, 1981.
Warner R: *Morality in Medicine: An Introduction to Medical Ethics.* Sherman Oaks, CA, Alfred Publishing Co, 1980.

B. Clinical Perspectives

Ursula Thunberg, M.D.

THE DEATH OF A CHILD

In our own society, the fact that children die seems quite strange to us. Yet, if we lived in some other country, the death of children might be an accepted reality. For instance, the World Health Organization was trying to introduce contraception to some of the more economically impoverished countries and encountered serious difficulties. This was so because the infant mortality was high, and the parents felt that the more children they had the better it would be for them, since then there would be somebody to take care of them when they grew old. Indeed, until antibiotics and vaccinations were discovered, even in this country the death of children was an accepted fact.

For Americans, who place a high priority on prenatal care, well baby clinics, and ongoing pediatric care, the death of a child is a very shocking experience. It is something to which we cannot get accustomed. A child is supposed to grow up, become independent, and fulfill his or her life goals. To deal with the death of a child is extraordinarily difficult for medical personnel and for the parents of the child. They often feel responsible and guilty for what is happening. Where a healthy child will gain mastery, a dying child will start failing. Where the healthy child will grow, the dying child will start wasting.

THE CHILD'S AWARENESS OF DEATH

Generally around three or four years of age, through the death of a pet or the death of a family member, the child becomes aware of death. In play-therapy sessions, Gregory Rochlin interviewed children from the ages of three to five about their ideas regarding death. A three and a half year old felt that dying was going out of the house without boots, being exposed to the weather, and disobeying the parents. In contrast, a five and a half year old associated dying with being gone. One could see a growing awareness of the true meaning of death with advancing mental development.

In the 40's in Budapest, Hungary, Maria Nagy studied 378 school children from ages six to 10 years. She had them make drawings on the theme of death, and then talked with them about death. In her data, children under five did not recognize death as final. They saw it as sleep or departure, and they felt that life and death were not mutually exclusive. According to their ideas, people remained alive in the grave. They were growing. They knew what was going on. However, from five onward, the child was able to imagine death as final, inevitable, and universal. For six and seven year olds there was a more personalized awareness of death. They were able to see that their parents and they themselves might die. In addition, many children explained that life ended in death but that there was a soul that lived on. In considering the answers of these children, we have to recognize the cultural and religious background of this population. They were either Protestant, Catholic, or Greek Orthodox — Christian faiths predominantly. The children were growing up in a cultural setting where there were many books with pictures from the Middle Ages, with much imagery of death as a person or skeleton (Figure 31.2). Thus, when she analyzed her data, Nagy found that many of the older children imagined death as a frightening person or some other frightening figure.

A similar study was done by Sylvia Anthony in England. After age eight, the children in her study understood the biological essentials of death. School children often thought about it. They played out their fantasies in games at home and at school, and generally associated death with separation and fears of retaliation. When they were asked what dying meant, they often associated it with lying helplessly on their backs or going to the hospital.

More recent studies have indicated that adolescents comprise the group of the population that thinks least about death. In one study, 90% of the adolescents said that they rarely thought about death in any personal way, which also tells us something about the attitude of the young medical student coming to the hospital.

Figure 31.2. *Death Swoops Into a Group of Children* (1934) by Käthe Kollwitz. (By permission of National Gallery of Art, Washington, D.C., Rosenwald Collection.)

Very often medical students are still struggling with many adolescent conflicts. If the young medical student is suddenly exposed to death over and over again in the hospital, it can be quite a shocking experience. No wonder that doctors then tend to avoid the dying patient. The need for proper emotional preparation of the medical student during the preclinical years is very, very important.

HOW THE CHILD FACES DEATH

How a child actually faces death will very much depend upon its stage of development. A young child, around six to eight months, becomes aware when the mother leaves and responds with crying. To make some definite statement about how a young, nonverbal child will respond to dying is very difficult if not impossible, because we can observe that this response might be very much influenced by the attitudes of the people around the child. An anxious mother will make a child very anxious. A mother who avoids the child will also make the child anxious. On the other hand, a very supportive mother may be able to make the child

feel quite comfortable and relatively at ease. I will now describe some of the cases that I have followed over the years to enable us to see how different children and different parents have responded to the tragedy of a dying child.

Joe

Joe was a three and a half year old boy who had multiple metastases to the brain as a result of an eye tumor. The metastases were actually starting to bulge out of his head, and he looked very ugly. He was also very emaciated. From the time he was seen initially until the time he died, which was about a year and a half, he never spoke. Either he was severely deprived or he was actually brain damaged. When I started working with the mother, I learned that she would become very angry and frustrated and would hit Joe. When speaking to her, I learned that she felt that he was bad and evil, because he did not do the things he was supposed to do for his age. I had to work with her very patiently, explaining to her how his illness affected him. I would also work with the mother and child together, and would make comments to the mother in his presence. For instance, when she said, "Joe is evil. He's bad. He's naughty," I would say to her, "No, he's not bad. He's not evil. He's upset. He's angry." Eventually, she was able to become more understanding and supportive of her son. In fact, she was one of the few mothers who took her child home to die. When he had totally wasted, when no more transfusions could be given, when nothing more could be done, she decided that he would be happier if he were at home. Since there were several older teenage siblings who could help her to take care of him, she took him out of the hospital and brought him home, where he died. I spoke with her afterwards, and she indicated it had been a very comfortable experience for him. He drifted into sleep in his own home setting.

Joan

In another case, Joan's mother dropped out of the picture the last two months before the girl died and simply did not show up anymore. She had generally been a very ungiving mother, and in spite of my working with her as well as with the grandmother, the family gave no emotional support to this six year old girl. She had a brain tumor and became increasingly paralyzed from the waist downward. She became nonverbal after several convulsions. I would see her twice a week, and our whole relationship consisted of my pushing her wheelchair, giving her a lollypop, and talking to her. All she could do was look at me. She could not talk. When the girl became terminal, the mother did not respond to a telegram. She did not have a telephone. She did not come and visit. Joan finally died on the ward with a nurse present.

Casey

Casey was a four year old girl who had been operated upon at the age of nine months for a blastoma of the liver. She had been considered cured but returned at the age of three years with multiple metastases to the lung causing severe destruction of lung tissue and increasing respiratory distress. She was a beautiful and ingratiating child. She did not like to talk very much, but she loved to draw. She would take markers of all different colors and then make circles. She called it doing her "homework." Figures 31.3 through 31.5 illustrate the progressive diminution of lines and circles in the drawings as Casey became weaker and weaker.

During her last weeks in the hospital she could breathe only by sitting up in the bed with many pillows behind her. Both parents were very supportive to the child. They learned that when she was sitting in the rocking chair on the ward she was more relaxed than when she was in bed, and

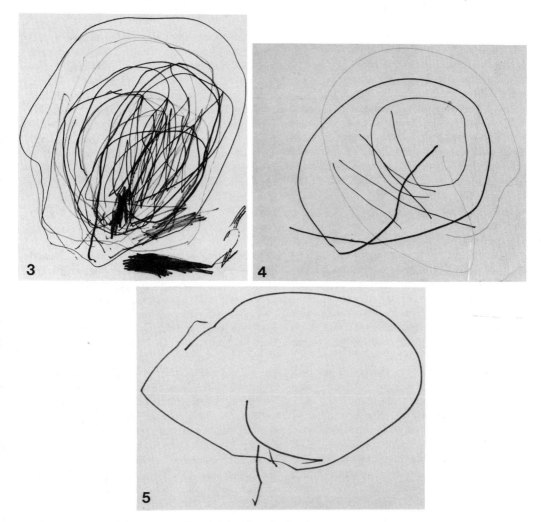

Figure 31.3. Drawing by Casey in October.
Figure 31.4. Drawing by Casey in November
Figure 31.5. Drawing by Casey in December shortly before her death

so one or the other of the parents would always sit with her on their lap, and rock her in the rocking chair. This seemed to ease her respiratory distress. One evening the mother said, "We want to take Casey home. We know she's going to die, and we want her home." Casey was taken home the next day. She died there, again in relative comfort, supported by her parents and family. The parents of Joe and Casey had made their decisions because they had observed that their children always appeared happier at home, more relaxed and more at ease. It is also interesting from a cultural point of view that both of these families were black. Black families are often extremely supportive of any member who is ill, and this was certainly true in these two cases.

Sandra

Over the years several children have told me that they knew that they were about to die, and that the end was near. This material is rarely reported in the professional literature, but I am convinced that this phenomenon is not a rare one. The rarity of such reported cases is probably related to the fact that the physician does not generally stay with the child when it actually reaches the final phase of life. The general tendency is to avoid the child and to leave it in the company of the parents or the nursing staff, because the experience is too painful.

Sandra was an only child, dying of leukemia. I had followed her for about three years before she went into her last final relapse at age six. At least once a day during her last hospitalization, I would go up to the ward, mornings or evenings, whenever I had the time, and see her. I got a call one day at noontime that I should come quickly. It was from her mother who was up on the ward and who said, "Sandra requests that you come over immediately." I did so and saw that Sandra was lying very quietly in her bed, not looking well but in no apparent pain. I said to her, "How do you feel?" She said, "Not good." I said, "You'll get better." She said, "No, I won't." She did not say anything else, so I spoke at her bedside with the mother and found that at the same time that she had asked for me, she also had requested the mother to fetch the father from work. She wanted to see him. Nobody knew why she was so insistent on seeing all the people she loved. That evening around five o'clock, she went into a coma and died six days later, never recovering consciousness.

Robert

Robert was a four year old boy who had had an abdominal operation for the exploration of a tumor. I saw him the day after the operation. He had no fever but he complained about a severe bellyache, which was quite natural. I then said to him, "Well, you'll soon be better," thinking that he would receive radiation treatment, that there was nothing terminal about the situation, and that he would get better, at least temporarily. Bellyache and all, he threw himself around in the bed, looked angry, and said, "No, I won't." He refused to talk to me from then on. I came back the next morning. He had died during the night of cardiac arrest.

Matthew

Matthew was another child who had a premonition of impending death. This was an eight year old youngster who was hospitalized during the first crisis of an acute myeloblastic leukemia. When I first saw him, he was anxious, in fact panicky. I had no way of knowing if this was his typical way of reacting to stress or if this reaction was specifically triggered by the hospitalization and the illness. The mother told me that he was always very clingy, but that he was not usually so whiny and tearful. All he ever said to me was, "I want to go home. When can I go home? I'm afraid to be here." He had good reason to be afraid, because he was very, very ill.

Twenty-four hours before he died, he showed a change of affect. He became quiet and composed. He responded to me positively and said that he felt good. There was no more questioning about, "When do I go home?" No more turmoil. I left the ward, and the next day received a call that he had died that same evening at eight o'clock. I spoke with the mother at home. "You know," she said, "after you left he was so sensible and quiet. Then he asked that his younger brother be called because he wanted to talk alone with him." This mother was a very unusual person. She did as Matthew asked, and she let the children talk alone for an hour. She does not know what happened during that hour. When she came into the room to get the younger brother, Matthew told her that he was going to leave her soon. She asked him what he meant, and he said that he was going to die. At that point the mother became very upset, and he reassured her and told her that she need not get so upset. A few hours later he began to hallucinate that Martin Luther King was standing in the corner of the room beckoning to him. Then he drifted into a coma and died.

THE LOSS OF A BODY PART

There are many losses that are an integral part of normal development. Many of these have already been discussed by Dr. Scharfman, and they will be discussed in more detail in a later chapter on loss, grief, and mourning in adults. Besides these normal developmental losses, there are other losses that are not generally shared by all children.

I was once asked to consult preoperatively and postoperatively on a 10 year old boy who, because of a malignancy of the thigh, had to have his leg amputated. This boy was a very bright, alert, well-developed youngster. When I saw him, he had already been told by the physician about the planned operation. His mother also had spoken with him about it. As in all such cases, one must first try to establish a relationship with the child, and then explore how much the child really understands of the issues involved. When I asked him about the operation, he said that he had a bad leg, and that he needed to have his sick leg taken off because otherwise the illness would spread to his whole body, and he would die. I agreed with him that that was the reason the leg was being amputated. When a child responds with as direct and clear a statement as this, however much the directness may shock the therapist or the medical staff, it is important to respond with equal directness and honesty. The child will respect the honesty of the therapist, physician, or nurse. If the child then gets better, nothing has been lost by honesty. If the disease progresses, at least the supporting adult has not proven himself or herself to be a liar, and can therefore be trusted again when needed.

When I asked this boy what he thought would happen after the operation, he verbalized his fantasy of getting a powerful artificial leg like the "Six Million Dollar Man," the hero of a TV show who has exceptional power and strength because of "bionic" artificial limbs which he received following an airplane crash. He asked me if he would get a leg like that. Here was a very agile 10 year old boy who in two days was going to be without a leg. I had to gently explain to him that his artificial leg was not going to be

quite like that, that his new leg would not have special batteries and powers, that he would be without any leg for several weeks until the wound from the operation had healed, and that he would first have to use crutches in order to be able to walk. He then asked if the new leg would keep growing like the other leg, and I had to explain that it would not, and that from time to time he would need to get a new, larger artificial leg.

He then told me that he had already warned his friends that when he came home, if they dared to laugh at him or tease him because he only had one leg, he was going to beat them up. So this boy had already thought about the reactions he might get from his friends, and he was preparing for them. He had even thought about what he was going to do in the summer time, when he would be swimming. People were going to see his artificial leg. Again, I agreed with him. He would probably have to take it off at the beach, but that would not prevent him from swimming. He looked very thoughtful and a little disgusted. He had not quite anticipated this kind of reality. I then asked him if he had any questions about the operation itself or about any of the surgical procedures. He asked if he would be awake during the operation and if he would feel any pain. I explained the process of sedation and anesthesia to him, and assured him that he would not feel any pain during the operation. However, he might be nauseous afterwards for awhile, and I reassured him that he would receive medication for any pain that he might have during the first few days after the operation.

He then said, "You know, I am really very much afraid, but I try not to show it." I told him that he did not have to try too hard to show any special courage, because it was very natural to be afraid of losing one's leg. He smiled, and then told me that we could not talk any longer, because it was time for his favorite TV show, *The Six Million Dollar Man!*

I saw him again two days after the operation. When I came into his room, he was in quite a different mood. He was sitting in bed, TV off, looking depressed. He told me that he did not feel like talking. I said that I thought he looked awfully unhappy, and he responded by saying that he felt very sad because his leg was taken away. He did not want to talk further with me.

Two days later, four days postoperative, he was sitting in his bed and drawing pictures, at the same time that he was watching some program on TV. He smiled and looked cheerful and said that he felt much better. Eight days later when I visited, he was sitting in his wheelchair, skillfully racing around on the ward much to the consternation of the nursing staff. I brought him a boat model to work on, and he at once volunteered the information that in the morning he had walked around on his crutches and was already getting used to them. He said that he had the funny feeling that his leg was still there, though he knew that it had been cut off. The phenomenon of *phantom limb* was explained to him, and he felt reassured that this strange feeling would disappear eventually.

Two days later this boy went home. I saw him several more times after that in the outpatient clinic. He was always very alert and outgoing, moving freely around on his crutches and later without difficulties on his prosthetic leg. Thus, in a period of just a few days this boy passed through a stage of preoperative anxiety to a stage of postoperative depression and finally returned to his normal presurgical behavior.

THE LOSS OF A SIBLING

Loss of a sibling can be a terribly difficult emotional experience for children. Siblings have both loving and competitive relationships. When a sibling dies, the surviving children will pass through a whole range of ambivalent feelings before the mourning has been resolved, as can be seen in the following case.

A seven year old boy had had a very close relationship with his sister, a nine year old girl who died after a five year illness with leukemia. She had been the dominant sibling. Any game that they played was initiated by her. She gave the directions as to how the games were to be played. She liked to boss him around, tell him what to do, how to behave. They were very fond of each other and he admired her. They were the only children in the family. After the last relapse of her illness, she was transferred to a specialized cancer hospital for a trial with experimental drugs. Her brother was not able to visit her during these last three weeks of her life. He could only see her stand at her hospital window on the third floor and wave down to him. He reacted with great sadness and anxiety to the separation, and to the concomitant frequent absences of the mother from the home. This sister made some remarkable drawings during the course of her illness which reflect her fantasies about death and dying (Figures 31.6–31.8).

After the sister died, the family brought him to the funeral parlor. This decision had been discussed with me, since I had known both children in the pediatric oncology clinic over a period of five years. He saw his sister in the coffin and showed only curiosity. He did not become upset. The same was true at the funeral, which the boy attended. Over the next few days I spoke several times on the phone with the mother, who reported that the boy was constantly talking about his sister. He was reminiscing about the things they did together. The mother allowed the boy to talk about the sister even though this was emotionally very hard on her. The mother then decided that she wanted to have me see him for awhile in order to help with his reactions to the death of the sister.

He came to see me in the play room of the clinic that he had always attended with his sister during her visits to the same clinic. He initiated the session with the statement that he and his sister used to come to the clinic together, and he smiled sadly when he said this. His behavior, which usually was that of an active, vivacious boy, was quite different on this occasion. He moved slowly and looked around the room. He then began to play with several small dolls, with which both he and his sister had played in the past. They came in both a white and a black doll set. This time, in contrast to the past occasions when he had played with his sister, he chose to play only with the black set of dolls. He put one of them on a car, and when asked what was happening he said that there was a funeral. He then continued with the funeral game, finally moving one of the dolls back and forth in the air. I asked him what was going on. He said that the doll was an angel who was flying. I then asked him if he was perhaps thinking of his sister. He said that he was and he stated, "She is an angel now. Mommy told me so. I miss her a lot." He then stopped talking and quietly went on playing with the dolls. When he was leaving he said that he was going to be back soon. Though he came back a few more times, this was the only time that he played out a subject directly related to the death of his sister.

A year later a new baby sister was born, and he was deeply disappointed because she was constantly screaming and was not able to play with him. Over the months, though, he became

Figure 31.6. "A girl was bad and ran away from home because her mother was angry and tried to hit her *and she got black all over.*"

Figure 31.7. "The girl came out from the house without permission, and then she laughed, because her hat fell off. Her mother saw her and got very mad, but she was still laughing. Then her father came out and she stopped laughing, because he hit her so hard she started crying. *Then the house got all black and fell in and all the people in her house died.*"

Figure 31.8. "The sun and the snowman are happy, *but the girl is sad. Some of the snow is black, and the snowman is melting.* The girl is wearing a green dress, and pink shoes and a pink hat, *but it all comes out black. A flower is growing inside her.*"

fond of her. His tendency to compare his infant sister with his dead, older sister gradually disappeared, and he eventually became quite attached to this younger sister. This case is only one example of how the death of a sibling can affect the emotional development of another child in the family. What form the reaction takes is very much dependent on the relationship between the dead child and the surviving children, their ages at the time of the loss, and the overall support available within the family.

THE LOSS OF A PARENT

An 11 year old girl reacted to the death of her mother by stealing large sums of money from both relatives and strangers. She bought candy with the stolen money, which she then gave away to her friends and classmates. She also began to have increasing problems in school. Eventually she was referred to me for treatment. She was the older of two sisters. As I explored the past history, I learned that she had been the child who had always had problems relating to the mother, and who had been designated by the parents as being the more difficult of the two children to handle. The younger sister was a sweet, ingratiating little girl who never presented any problems to the mother, and who had clearly been the mother's favorite. On the death of the mother, the older girl showed no apparent emotional reaction, in contrast to the younger girl who became quite upset and wept desperately.

During a period of three months of therapy the older girl did not once speak about her dead mother. Although nothing was said about the mother, she spent a great deal of time talking about other families in the neighborhood. Many of the mothers in those families were described by her as not being very nice to their children, often scolding them, and beating them, and not showing very much understanding for them. Clearly she was speaking about her own mother. I allowed her to verbalize her anger toward her mother in this disguised fashion, and gradually her stealing subsided and her school work began to improve.

As this case shows, reactions to parental loss in children can take many different forms. Again depending on the quality of the family relationships, loss can be followed by normal grief and mourning (the younger sister) or by various disturbed reactions (the older sister). In this case the older sister expressed her anger by taking money, and her need to be loved by handing out the candy to friends. The famous etching by the Norwegian artist, Edvard Munch, entitled *The Dead Mother* (Figure 31.9) depicts the terror and devastation experienced at the loss of a parent. These were feelings that Munch himself experienced at the death of his mother from hemorrhagic tuberculosis when he was five. Munch never recovered from this tragic loss, and later in his life he suffered a psychotic breakdown.

A more normal grief reaction, albeit none the less poignant and moving, can be seen in the following poem written by nine year old Scott Sanchez and read at the funeral of his father, Charles Sanchez, a fireman who died in a supermarket blaze in Brooklyn, in January, 1976:

> To my dear father I will never forget.
> Life is the sun that gives us light.
> Life is the stars that shine at night.
> Life is the soil that makes plants grow.
> But the answer to life, no one knows.
> Our Life is the sun that lights the sky.
> Life is the moon that's floating by.
> Life, dear life, that is on what we rely.
> Life is the answer to when and why.
> Life is the sun that gives us light.
> Life is the stars that shine at night.
> Life is also each and every breath.
> Life is not only life, it is also death.

THE LOSS OF A PEER

Children in a tumor clinic will perceive (even if they only rarely talk about it) one another's state of health or another child's absence because of death. One six year old girl, who had just been discharged from the ward after she was in remission, spontaneously talked about her friend, Martha, being very sick. When I asked her how sick Martha really was, she said, "She is so sick that she might die." This girl was able to accurately perceive the seriously impaired state of health of her friend.

One 12 year old boy, who never spoke about

Figure 31.9. *The Dead Mother* (1901) by Edvard Munch. (By permission of Munch Museum, Oslo, Norway.)

the children who had left the clinic during the time that he attended, began to reminisce once about all the children who never came back because they had died. He said that sometimes he and some other children talked about it. But he did not like to do so, because, "It makes me feel creepy." When I asked him to explain what he meant by "feeling creepy," he said that it made him sad, and it reminded him that it may also happen to him some day. He spoke in detail about a teenage friend from the clinic who had died only two weeks before, and described his feeling of disbelief on hearing that his friend had died. He also described the reaction of the other boys in the neighborhood who had been friends with the youngster who had died. "They behaved funny. They could not believe it. They all stayed home and did not talk to one another. Nobody felt like talking."

Grief and mourning can thus take various forms in children, depending on their ages, family settings, and sociocultural backgrounds. Grief reactions will be strongly influenced by religious and cultural beliefs, and if we are to gain a proper understanding of the child's response to loss, these various factors must be taken into consideration.

THE DEATH OF AN ADOLESCENT

Adolescence is a transitional period in an individual's life. Rapid changes take place with the development of secondary sexual characteristics, growth spurts, and beginning sexual functioning. During this time the adolescent is very much aware of these ongoing changes in the body image, as well as changes in psychological development and interpersonal relationships. The adolescent is in the process of exploring his own values and norms for living and acting, sometimes accepting those of his parents, at other times challenging them. Gradually the bonds to the parents are loosened, and a new stage of separation and individuation takes place. Peer relationships become extremely important, and are filled with competition. There is competition in the physical area in regard to looks and strength, in the sexual area in regard to prowess with partners of the opposite sex, and in the intellectual area in regard to academic achievement. Also, the majority of adolescents generally live very much in the present, and have little concern for either the past or the future.

When we begin to consider the tragedy of a teenager with a malignant disease, we have to consider all of these developmental factors in order to be able to explain the various reactions of the dying adolescent. Many of the drugs used in the treatment of malignant diseases emotionally affect the adolescent more than children of a younger age because of the teenager's preoccupation with physical appearance. Hormones, for example, can drastically change the looks of a youngster by increasing weight gain and causing a puffiness of the face. Others of the anticancer drugs affect the growth of normal cells and lead to diminished height and muscle development. Radiation therapies may cause loss of hair. Slowly progressing malignant diseases lead to loss of weight and strength, and progressive emaciation.

John

John, a 16 year old boy with malignant lymph node disease, was the oldest of four boys. He was walking in the street with his second youngest brother, a very well developed 13 year old boy, when they met a friend of the brother. This boy asked the younger brother if John was his younger brother. John told me about this incident the following week. When I asked him what he felt at that time, he said that he walked away. "If I had not walked away, I would have hit him, I was so mad." He then tearfully talked about the fact that all the other fellows in the class had begun to date girls, but that no girl was interested in him because he looked so thin. Another 12 year old boy with a malignancy, who had a twin sister, became quite resentful because his twin sister was growing taller and faster than he was.

Barbara

The emotionally healthy teenager with a malignant disease, although aware of and reacting to the progress of the disease, will often learn to compensate for the increasing physical incapacitation in other ways. For example, a 14 year old teenage girl with a chronic hereditary kidney disease came from a family where the father died of the same disease after a transplant. A younger sister had also received a transplant, and Barbara herself had received a transplant. Barbara developed bone complications, which necessitated her walking on two tall crutches. She became increasingly angry, because she was not able to participate in any of the social activities in which her classmates were involved. She complained bitterly that they went out dancing with boys, and met among themselves to listen to records, while she was awkwardly moving around with her crutches or else staying at home. Finally, because of increasing bone destruction, an operation to replace the diseased hips with artificial ones was suggested, and she agreed immediately. She managed the operation remarkably well, both medically and emotionally. She did not display any preoperative fear, nor did she show any of her characteristic angry tantrums postoperatively. She was determined to be able to move around normally and to do what the other teenage girls of her class were doing. Her medical course was without complications. She recovered rapidly and after several weeks went dancing with the other girls.

During a long course of illness this girl had to be absent from school many times, at first for dialysis several times a week for six to eight hours at a time, later for medical follow-ups, operations, and hospitalizations. In spite of this she was able to remain a grade A student in her class and progress with her classmates. She was proud of her achievements, especially since her illness caused her frequently to feel irritated or physically exhausted for several days at a time. It required an enormous effort on her part to be able to achieve so much.

Karl

Teenagers generally are quite aware of the seriousness of their illnesses. Even if for some reason the parents are not willing to discuss the illness with them, they often utilize clues from the physician and the nursing staff. Sometimes, while the ward staff is busy, they may look at their own charts, and then go to libraries and read about their diseases, acquiring quite sophisticated and anxiety-provoking knowledge. If their parents indicate that talking about the disease is too upsetting for them, the adolescent boy or girl might then approach some member of the medical staff for clarification or information. In some cases the loyalty to the parents and the parents' attitude about the disease is so strong that the youngster will not talk about it either. His fear and anxiety might then be indirectly expressed by acting out behavior, especially in his therapeutic relationships. This becomes one among many reasons why the treatment of the dying adolescent may be an extremely trying experience for the medical and therapeutic staff.

Karl is an example of such an adolescent. Karl was a 14 year old boy with leukemia who needed several hospitalizations for prolonged courses of medication. His parents had told the medical staff that under no condition did they want him to know about his illness, and they believed that he had no knowledge about it. Even after he had clearly indicated in many different ways that he knew everything about his illness, the parents denied that such was the case. They refused to allow Karl to be seen by a psychiatrist on an outpatient basis, and did not approve of my seeing him when he was hospitalized. This boy rarely talked about his illness, but instead would criticize everything he could about me — my accent, my clothes, my lamentably poor ability to play cards. When I would tell him that he was criticizing me because he was upset about something else, he would smile. At one point in the final phase of his disease, after an especially prolonged barrage of verbal attacks against me, he said that I must be getting very tired of him. When I reminded him that I always came back to see him, no matter how angry he got at me, he grinned and went on to beat me mercilessly in the chess game we were playing.

It is usually because of their own anxieties that the parents of a teenager refuse to discuss a fatal illness. However, as in all other interruptions of communication between people who are emotionally close, the end result of such a breakdown is isolation and anger on both sides. Karl's parents never even shared the knowledge of the seriousness of their oldest boy's disease with the younger children. As a result, the other children could not understand why Karl sometimes did not have to go to school, or why the parents took so much time from work and home to take him to the clinic, or why they spent so much time at the hospital. This led to resentment and attention-seeking behavior by the other children, causing the parents in turn to feel angry and frustrated with the other siblings and to blame Karl for all these difficulties.

When Karl finally died, the parents and I were in the hospital room together. The mother was still denying that her oldest son was dying, even though he was in a terminal stupor. The father, who was able to realize what was happening, finally began to talk about the many happy times that he had shared with his oldest boy. He spontaneously brought up his decision not to talk about the illness with his son, and said that he felt that it had been a good decision. This was not the time to discuss all that had happened. It was the time simply to be supportive, and to allow these parents to talk about the past and the many happy and loving moments that they had shared with their son. As I listened, I finally understood more clearly why they had never been able to discuss Karl's illness with Karl or with anyone else. It was because the pain of losing him was simply too great to bear.

Billy

The dying teenager represents a special problem for the medical staff. As the medical team most directly concerned with the care of a dying child or adolescent consists of interns and residents and in some cases medical students, and also young nurses and social workers, they very frequently identify strongly with the adolescent who is so close in age to them. This identification often leads to very personalized reactions by the staff. This problem is compounded by the fact that teenagers possess an adult's capacity to reason and to provoke. If a dying adolescent is too upset to talk about his or her illness, the anxieties may be expressed in other ways. One of the most common defenses is to see the staff as the enemy. It is often very difficult for inexperienced staff to deal with such provocative behavior.

Billy was a 17 year old boy, with a long history of illness, who was hospitalized shortly before he died. He had arrived very ill with a high fever, and was not responding to medication. I came over one evening with a medical student, and Billy was very upset. He was talking about blowing up the hospital. Everyone had better watch out. I just listened to him as he was screaming and yelling. Everything came out in a tremendous pressure of speech, in great turmoil. I looked at him and said, "You know, you sound awfully upset," and he suddenly became quiet and smiled at me. Then he did what he had always done over the years with me. He started to attack me in a teasing manner. I often wear an old army jacket for a coat, and this time he said, "God damn it, Thunberg, you are such a big shot around here. Can't you afford a fur coat? Do you always have to run around with these sloppy jackets?" When I initially entered the room, I thought he might be having a psychotic break. When I left, it was apparent that what I had encountered was a tremendously upset teenager who knew that he was very ill and was afraid that something terrible might happen to him.

I came back the next day. He had visibly improved on medication. I asked him if I could get him something. "Yes," he said, "you can get me a ham sandwich and a beer." Well, sandwiches and beer are against the ward rules, but every now and then other things are more important than the rules. So I got him the ham sandwich and beer. When I returned, he was dressed. I sat down and said to him, "Well, when are you leaving?" He said, "Not yet. Something has come up." I am so used to seeing all kinds of people in the hospital that it did not register on me that there was a pretty teenage girl sitting in the room also. Billy was grinning at me. He repeated the double entendre, "Something has just come *up*." He was enjoying himself immensely. I knew that he was teasing me about something, but it still had not registered yet. He said, "There she is." What had "come up" was an attractive girl on the volunteer staff, as well as something else. They had met during an earlier hospitalization and had started a relationship, and Billy was certainly not interested in talking to me at that moment. So I said to him, "Well, I see you have better company. I'll leave and I'll see you next time." I left. He went home and about two months later he died.

Shirley

The realization that a teenager can die brings death very close to home for all of us. This is why working with the dying adolescent is so difficult. But this is also why therapy with the dying teenager can be a very enriching and gratifying experience. Many adolescents will show great strength in dealing with their life realities, and can even be quite supportive to the needs of their parents during this time of crisis.

Shirley was a 14 year old girl who at the age of 10 had been diagnosed as having lymphoblastic leukemia. She was an extremely attractive girl who was the center of attention in her large family. At the time of her last relapse, she sought me out, complained about her fatigue, and began to weep. She said that she could not talk with her mother about it, because the mother was worried about the grandmother who had just been hospitalized with a serious case of diabetes. Shirley did not want to upset her mother further.

When she became worse physically, she also became more depressed about her condition. She shared her depression with me, but kept it from her mother so as not to upset her. Thus, the mother was helped to deny the fact that Shirley's illness was now terminal. On the last day of her life, Shirley told her mother about another girl who had the same disease that she had. Shirley told her mother that this girl had just died. Actually this girl was doing well at the time, was at home, and was attending school. Clearly Shirley was talking about herself. After Shirley died, the mother asked me about this last communication from her daughter. She said that she could not understand why Shirley had done this. She accepted my interpretation that her daughter wanted to communicate to her how very ill she was, without at the same time upsetting her too much. This is only one example of the extraordinary sensitivity and empathy of which some dying adolescents are capable.

Suggested Readings

Farley GK, Eckhardt LO, and Hebert FB: The dying child. In *Handbook of Child and Adolescent Psychiatric Emergencies.* New York, Medical Examination Publishing Co, 1979, p 66.

Nagy M: The child's theories concerning death. *J Genet Psychol* 73:3, 1948.

Prugh DG: Psychosocial aspects of management of fatal illness. In *The Psychosocial Aspects of Pediatrics.* Philadelphia, Lea & Febiger, 1983, p 483.

Solnit AJ, Green M: Psychologic considerations in the management of deaths on pediatric hospital services. Part I: The doctor and the child's family. *Pediatrics* 24:106, 1959.

Solnit AJ, Green M: The pediatric management of the dying child. Part II: The child's reaction to the fear of dying. In Solnit AJ, Provence S (eds): *Modern Perspectives in Child Development.* New York, International Universities Press, 1963, p 217.

References

Anthony S: *The Child's Discovery of Death.* New York, Harcourt Brace, 1940.

Evans AE: If a child must die. *N. Engl. J. Med.* 278:138, 1968.

Fleming J: The problem of diagnosis in parent-loss cases. *Contemp. Psychoanal.* 10:439, 1974.

Furman E: *A Child's Parent Dies: Studies in Childhood Bereavement.* New Haven, Yale University Press, 1974.

Furman RA: Death and the young child. *Psychoanal. Study Child* 19:321, 1964.

Kastenbaum R: Time and death in adolescence. In Feifel H (ed): *The Meaning of Death,* New York, McGraw-Hill, 1959, p 99.

Natterson JM, Knudson AG: Observations concerning fear of death in fatally ill children and their mothers. *Psychosom. Med.* 22:456, 1960.

Pollock GH: Childhood parent and sibling loss in adult patients: a comparative study. *Arch. Gen. Psychiatry* 7:295, 1962.

Rochlin G: How younger children view death and themselves. In Grollman EA (ed): *Explaining Death to Children.* Boston, Beacon Press, 1969, p 51.

Steinberg S, Weiss J: The art of Edvard Munch and its function in his mental life. *Psychoanal. Q.* 23:409, 1954.

PART III

Adulthood: The Years of Maturity and the Completion of the Life Cycle

Section J/Adult Sexuality

CHAPTER **32** **Historical and Cultural Perspectives**

Robert Dickes, M.D.

SEXUALITY AND THE PHYSICIAN

Many people are eager to learn about sexual behavior, but for varied reasons. Some are curious about other people's performance and are titillated by their discoveries. Some wish, competitively, to compare other people's performance with their own, and some wish to discover ways to improve their own techniques. Physicians and other therapists, however, must study sexual behavior as part of their training as healers of the sick, and, above all, they must learn to do no harm. This may strike the reader as self-evident, but it is unfortunately the case that many doctors know little about sex and are embarrassed to discuss the subject with their patients. Because of their own emotional difficulties, some physicians cannot learn about this fundamental aspect of all human behavior and, as a result, behave punitively toward those who come for help. These doctors often cause much suffering. It is our hope that all young physicians will at the very least learn enough to avoid behavior which can lead to great unhappiness and even human destruction.

I wish to illustrate this point with the story of a young woman of 16 who was very much in love with a young man. She indulged in "heavy petting" with him in spite of her conviction that it was morally wrong. She did resist all his endeavors to force her to have intercourse. Eventually, her boyfriend threatened to leave her if she did not give in and at least relieve him of "sexual tension" by practicing fellatio. He convinced her that this was necessary for his health. For this reason and out of fear of losing him, this young woman agreed to engage in oral-genital sexual contact. Later she was totally overwhelmed, thought she had made the wrong decision, and was convinced she had become a "pervert." Full of despair, she felt forever damned, and suicide seemed the only way out. In her desperation, she decided to see her family doctor, a man she had known all her life. She poured out her heart to this physician, told of her self-loathing and of her belief in her perversion and damnation, and asked for help. The doctor's only response to this girl was to agree that she was indeed a pervert and that he had no help to offer to such a person. The young woman, feeling utterly hopeless, went home and killed herself. Thus, a life was tragically ended.

One might think that anyone, particularly a physician, should have been more sensitive and that what I have just described is unusual. Let me then add the sequel to the lecture in which I told this tragic story to a group of medical students. I told the story as a prelude to the point that doctors above all should avoid doing harm to anyone, and that this doctor's function was to help the young woman understand that she had not done anything perverse. The doctor should have known this but he did not. Not only was he ignorant of the facts, but his hostile attitude was the final humiliation which pushed his patient into suicide. I thought I had succeeded in making my point until I was met by an angry delegation from the class on the following day. They took me to task for my immoral attitude and defended the doctor for his "honesty." They claimed that, "All he did was tell the truth. He was morally obligated to do this."

This group did not accept the fact that the vast majority of normal people do engage in oral-genital contact from time to time, and they were not impressed with all of the evidence verifying the universality of this behavior throughout recorded history (Figures 32.1–32.4). They believed that only their own code was correct and any other type of behavior was abominable. They further believed that all sexual behavior was biologically based, therefore relatively fixed. Those who deviated from *their* standards simply had done something radically wrong. I pointed out to them that, in spite of his or her personal beliefs, a physician has a more primary moral obligation to do no harm and that the doctor could have sent his young patient to a minister or a priest or a psychiatrist to either save her soul or her mind, or both. I reminded them that the physician's duty is to help and not condemn. Only then did some of these students begin to realize that other approaches existed, although others in the group still believed that something must be morally wrong with any person who would engage in what they considerd to be aberrant sexual behavior.

GREECE

The concept that sexual behavior is fixed and immutable on a religious or biological basis is not borne out by a study of past cultures. It is true that sexual drives are founded upon a biological basis, but methods of obtaining gratification have varied enormously from one histor-ical period to another, and from one culture to another. Even what may seem to be similar practices may have acquired, over the span of centuries, quite different meanings. Many of us have read or heard that the Greeks were bisexual and regularly practiced homosexuality. There is indeed evidence that the Greeks engaged in

Figure 32.2. Mochican pot depicting fellatio. (Reprinted from the book *Studies in Erotic Art*, published by Basic Books, New York, 1970, by permission.)

Figure 32.1. Greek cup depicting fellatio. (By permission of The Louvre, Paris.)

Figures 32.3 and 32.4.   Love play—cunnilingus (top) and copulation (bottom). Two scenes from Koshiba-gaki Sōshi, a Japanese handscroll attributed to Fujiwara Nobuzane (1176–1268). (Reprinted by permission from the book *Studies in Erotic Art*, published by Basic Books, New York, 1970.)

homosexual activities. When we talk about Greek homosexuality, however, we often translate it in terms applicable to the present day. We assume the behavior to be entirely erotic in character, performed for pleasure, and often obligatory in the sense that the individual is impotent with the other sex.

Actually, the Greeks had a very different idea about homosexuality. I can do no better to illustrate this than to quote from a tablet from the seventh century B.C. which was found at a small temple on one of the Greek islands. The inscription stated: "Invoking the Delphic Apollo, I, Crimon, here copulated with a boy, son of Bathycles." Such a temple inscription written today in a religious place would be considered obscene and sacrilegious. Yet, in many ways, the ancient tablet explains the Greek outlook on male homosexuality, because in ancient Greece pederasty was a central factor in the upbringing of boys and youths. This applied only to noble youths and involved a teacher-pupil relationship, one in which the older male was considered the mentor of the younger one and was responsible for all his acts. This was one of the major ideas in Greek upbringing and had deep religious significance. These relationships were under the control of the state and the authorities had a very considerable hand in their management. The Greeks believed that this kind of sexual relationship enabled the young recipient or passive partner to "take in" the manly qualities of the elder teacher. It should be noted that both the soliciting man and the boy had to be from good families and that this mentor-pupil relationship was not available to the lower classes.

The relationship was considered so important that its establishment was highly formalized. A ritual existed by means of which a boy would be chosen. The man who wished to be the mentor and lover of the young boy would first discuss the matter with the boy's parents, primarily the boy's father, since wives had little say in ancient Greece. If the parents consented, a formal announcement of the intent would be made. Following this announcement, a mock capture was enacted, after which the boy went to live with the man who now became his mentor and stood "in loco parentis" to the youngster. The mentor at this point became responsible for the boy's entire conduct, which included his becoming a brave warrior. In fact, when the Greeks went into battle, battalions were often made up of paired lovers who would defend one another to the death and would rather die than shame their partners. The Spartans were especially noted for this and were merciless in their behavior toward a boy who misbehaved. His mentor would also be severely punished if improper battle behavior occurred.

Although pederasty played such an important role in a youth's upbringing, he was expected at a later age to marry and to have children. The boy's homosexual relationship terminated when he began to grow a beard and develop other secondary sexual characteristics. From this time on he was not expected to be the passive partner in a homosexual relationship but was expected to have full heterosexual relationships with women.

Of course, the Greek relationships with women were peculiar by our standards and these deserve far more extensive discussion than is now possible. Women for hire were divided into three categories, the pornae or common prostitutes, the auletrides or flute players who entertained with dance and music (as well as spending the night), and finally the highest level, the hetaerae, who served as companions and intimate female friends. These women often held a higher status than did a wife. A wife's place was one of confinement to the home and to her domestic duties. Her task was to raise the children and take proper care of her husband who was absolute master. History does not record what the wives thought of this system.

ROME

Sexual behavior took a different turn during the long course of Rome's history. The moral approach to sexuality and to women in early Rome is perhaps best exemplified by the story of the rape of Lucretia by Tarquinius. Lucretia, "defiled," killed herself, knowing that this would ease the stain upon her husband's honor and that he would prefer this to her living as a symbol of dishonor. Legend has it that retribution then overtook the Tarquin clan and led to their overthrow and to the establishment of the Roman republic. However, this retribution was not so much to avenge Lucretia as to avenge her husband. The attitude toward rape in those days thus in some ways parallels our own. Suicide, it should be noted, was not yet a mortal sin but rather was a virtue in a woman who at the time was required to be spotless regardless of the circumstances.

Custom had changed very considerably by the time of Catullus, the poet, who lived in the first century B.C. By this time, the emancipated wives of Roman patricians went about freely, escorted by male admirers and lovers, who even entered the ladies' homes. Indeed, any Roman gentleman could pursue a Roman wife, not his own, of course, quite openly. Neither would be subject to reproach as long as good manners were observed. Catullus made no secret of his love affair with Clodia, the wife of the governor of the province in which Catullus was born. The Romans by now believed that loving someone else's wife was quite the thing to do. Licentiousness increased in Imperial Rome and involved many sexual excesses. The conduct of many of the emperors and empresses is too well-known to be repeated here.

What about male sexual behavior? The men were often bisexual and potent with both sexes. All of us know about Julius Caesar, the great general and political leader who seemed the epitome of all that is austere and masculine. Our history books, however, have altered the truth.

How many readers know that Caesar, in his youth, was a perfumed dandy, kept his body devoid of hair, and engaged in homosexual activity? We do not like to know about such things, but Caesar was long known as the Queen of Bithynia because of his affair with the King of Bithynia. He was mocked for this relationship not because of the homosexuality per se but for the fact that he was the passive partner in the relationship. By this time, passivity was equated with submission and weakness. Caesar was also known as "the husband of every woman and the wife of every man." His sexual activity did not detract from his stature as a general. But his foppishness was another matter. The following remark is attributed to Cicero: "When I see his hair so carefully arranged and observe him adjusting it with one finger, I cannot imagine that it should enter into such a man's thoughts to subvert the Roman State." Please note that Cicero was not concerned with either Caesar's lechery or his homosexuality, only his effeminacy.

Hadrian may also be used to illustrate the fact that the Romans did not view pederasty as an abnormality. *Pederasty*, it should be remembered, is most commonly defined as coitus per anum with boys and should not be confused with sodomy. *Sodomy* is defined as carnal copulation between humans and beasts. It has also come to mean anal copulation between two humans, including anal penetration of a female. Hadrian lost his beloved Antinous, who was drowned at the age of 20. Hadrian's love of this young man was quite open, and the grieving emperor had Antinous buried at the Porta Maggiore of Rome. Poets wrote words of consolation and none belittled Hadrian's grief. Hadrian was no fop. He was a fine general, shared his soldiers' hardships, and was thoroughly respected. As we will see, the Judeo-Christian tradition is about to break sharply with that of the Graeco-Roman world.

THE RISE OF CHRISTIANITY

Profound changes in people's attitudes toward sexuality coincided with the rise of Christianity and its emphasis on the value of sexual abstinence and the denial of the needs of the flesh. As St. Paul said, "It is good for a man not to touch a woman." This concept of abstinence, even in marriage, took hold and the celibate union of Ammon and his unnamed bride set an example for centuries. So famous did this third century couple become that many gathered about them to practice asceticism. Ammon and his wife lived in total continence, moved from their luxurious home into the desert, and lived in a rude hut. Even this arrangement was too intimate, and they moved into separate huts and practiced self-mortification. Thus, the ideal marriage was the one never consummated. There are many stories telling of the success of such marriages, and also stories of how such marriages failed because they were consummated.

Certain variants of the continent marriage also developed and flourished during the second to sixth centuries. These were spiritual marriages in which virgins known as agapetae became spiritual wives of the clergy without, of course, marrying. These people's relationships were supposed to be entirely devoid of sexual contact, and any failure was more profoundly sinful since the contact would have taken place outside the matrimonial bond. Needless to say, these failures did occur and the church eventually condemned all of these types of relationships. Many other varieties of sexual activities could be described, such as courtly love, and the sources of the early asceticism of the church might also be discussed. My purpose, however, remains that of emphasizing the variability of human sexual behavior so that as physicians and therapists we remain tolerant and become knowledgeable enough to aid our patients.

A corollary to the fight against sexual pleasure on the part of so many monks was the fact that the status of woman was constantly in question. Her role as a temptress superseded her role as mother and child rearer. Woman was described as the gate of Hell, the unsealer of the secrets of the forbidden tree, and the first deserter of the divine law. In 585 A.D., the Council of Macon even debated the proposition that a woman did not have an immortal soul. The Council decided in favor of woman possessing a soul but resolved their problem of her sexuality by declaring that she would become sexless at the Resurrection! These attitudes toward women necessarily struck at the very foundations of marriage. It was considered godly for a man to fail to marry or to leave his wife to become celibate for the glory of God. The Council of Trent in 1563 actually condemned the doctrine that marriage was as good as celibacy. The church's attack on sexuality continued unabated, and women were urged to renounce marriage and remain virginal.

Fortunately for the race, only a few succeeded in following these dictates, and most continued to marry and produce children. The effects of the fulminations against sexuality in all its forms, however, are still with us today.

The church's attitude toward marriage was gradually resolved as old Roman customs were discarded and marriage gradually came under the domination of the clerics. In time, marriage became a sacrament, not dissoluble, and thus, under the protection of divine law. But this should not be taken to mean that sexual pleasure became acceptable. As St. Jerome said, "He who too ardently loves his own wife is an adulterer." St. Augustine also must be accorded a prominent place in the fashioning of attitudes of guilt, not only toward sexual behavior but even sexual thoughts and urges. These became sinful as well. It was Augustine who maintained that "marital lust," meaning sexual desire, was justified only when it had the sole and immediate aim of producing children. Of course, if sexual desire is present, the aim of pleasure already interferes with procreation as the sole aim of sexual union. Thus, love between the sexes which would combine both the spiritual and the physical was considered evil. A latter day outcome of this attitude is represented by the concept of the "pure," therefore nonsexual, wife. Even today, these ideas are regularly promulgated. The following is extracted from a series of admonitory teachings offered to high school girls taking a course in sex education. These notes state the following: "For some girls, the sexual act holds no particular attraction beyond motherhood." Concerning a girl's interest in boys it states: "You may even let him kiss you and yet feel no stimulation. Sexual desire in a girl may not come until after her marriage. In some women it never comes." That is what is presented as the ideal. After according the male the right to sexual feelings, this document points out that it is the girl's responsibility to control him. Finally, the teaching concerning intercourse states: "As a purely sensual practice for pleasure and amusement alone—*it is meaningless and degrading.*" (Italics in the syllabus.) We can see in these attitudes the continuation of ideas dating back to the earliest beginnings of Christianity.

THE REFORMATION

The Reformation brought a marked change in the sexual mores and behavior of both church men and the lay public. The Protestants now stated that marital sex was wholesome and no longer proclaimed the virtues of celibacy. Luther broke the ban against marriage for the clergy and believed that celibacy was really an invention of the Devil. He no longer considered marriage a sacrament but declared it a civil matter. He fathered six children and in many ways bore himself as any other husband, at times considering his wife a great treasure and at other times grumbling bitterly about his lot. On the whole, he considered sexual love as natural and necessary.

The Reformation was not, however, monolithic, and John Calvin pursued a different path. He extolled asceticism, preached about mankind's sexual depravity, and disapproved of all frivolity. It was punishable, even by imprisonment, to dance at weddings, sing, curse, or wear extravagant clothes. Sexual transgressions received the severest punishment. Adultery was punishable by death, and fornication by exile. Thus, mixed messages were delivered about so basic a human drive as the sexual urge. Ambivalence concerning sexual conduct plagues our generations even unto this day.

THE VICTORIAN PERIOD

This ambivalence was clearly evident in the 19th century. The old attitudes toward sexual activity, now modified into permissiveness toward marital sexuality, became a social taboo against the open mention of anything even remotely related to sex. It was better to commit adultery than to mention it in polite society. Manners now demanded an amazing artificiality. It was considered ungentlemanly to offer a woman a leg of a chicken rather than one of the upper parts. Some librarians even went so far as to separate books by male authors from those written by women. As for the genitals—that became unrecognized territory, at least publicly. The taboos against the mention of sex spread to include a taboo against mention of the excretory functions. The reason for this is obviously based upon the anatomical fact that the sexual organs and the excretory functions are so closely linked. The public prudery of the Victorians also extended to courtship procedures which prevented engaged couples from spending any time alone together. Chaperones were provided who not only prevented sexual embraces but also made it enormously difficult for the "lovers" to even get to know one another as human beings.

THE SCIENTIFIC REVOLUTION

All this has changed, of course, and our century has witnessed a tremendous revolution. Most people think that this revolution consists of the present frankness and openness regarding our sexual involvements with one another. They may also cite the stress on equality for women and the recognition of her sexual rights. I do not think that this is the real revolution. After all, during the long and varied history of human sexual interaction, there have been many periods during which both men and women were openly sexual. The basic revolution, I believe, is the scientific revolution which involves the use of the scientific method and its application to the study of ourselves as well as to the study of the heavens and all other natural phenomena. However, we must not make the mistake of believing that studies in physiology and biochemistry inevitably led to the study of sex. The study of the circulatory system or the lungs is not so emotionally charged, and such work proceeded in an atmosphere of respect and admiration for the participating scientists. This was not the case in regard to investigations which touched upon sexual matters.

The first great discoverer in this field was Sigmund Freud, who began his career as a highly regarded neurologist. He made important scientific discoveries about the brain, and prior to the time that he became committed to research into the human psyche, he was liked and welcomed by his colleagues. However, the publication of the first of his psychological findings which have so profoundly altered our lives led to ostracism by his colleagues and condemnation from all sides. People even crossed the street when they saw him approaching and considered him a dirty, vile man. It is suitably ironic that in his personal life Freud was rather straitlaced and an extremely moral man.

One of the most important things to understand about Freud's works is the fact that he introduced the first rational approach to the observation of what had previously been the totally mysterious productions of the mind. Freud made sense out of what had been considered basically beyond understanding, and in the process he discovered the unconscious mind. His method of observation, termed free association,

led his patients to unravel the meaning of their symptoms. In the course of this work, Freud was astonished by the repetitive role sexual repressions played in his patient's illnesses, and in the earliest part of his career he believed that most neurotic difficulties related to sexual traumas. He later extensively elaborated on his first hypothesis and assigned great importance to aggression and to other factors. In terms of the current revolution of sexual enlightenment, he wrote about masturbation, removed the myths about its dangers, and almost single-handedly broke the bonds of Victorian repression and thereby opened the way for further careful study of human sexual development.

Freud's work was almost entirely related to the study of psychological factors. It remained for Masters and Johnson to carry further the objective and scientific approach to sexuality begun by Freud into the study of male and female physiological responsiveness during actual sexual activity. They discovered that physiological sexual responsiveness showed relatively little variation from one person to another. Thus, the body's response is as fixed as the psychic response is varied. We will devote the next chapter to a discussion of the physiological responses to sexual stimulation. We must always keep in mind, however, that psychological factors can greatly influence this responsiveness.

FURTHER CONSIDERATIONS ON HOMOSEXUALITY

It has been pointed out that the Greeks and Romans accepted homosexuality as part of normal living. The first fulminations against homosexuality appear in the Old Testament and have been part of the Judeo-Christian tradition ever since. The Middle East, however, developed its own cultural approach to homosexuality. Rape of a man by a man has been accepted in this culture right into the 20th century. One incident may be used to illustrate this.

In the 15th century, the Sultan Mehmet was concerned about the loyalty, and therefore the degree of submission, of one of his most famous generals, the Megadux Notarus. To test the general, the Sultan asked for the use of the general's eldest son for pederastic purposes (anal sexual penetration). Notarus refused. The Sultan then demanded, in order of age, the use of each one of his other sons. Each request was refused. The

Sultan then indicated that he would kill all the children and Notarus as well, if Notarus refused to give him one child. Notarus had only one request in reply, namely that the Sultan kill his sons in his presence and before he himself was killed, because he was afraid that they might weaken and he knew that he would not. The request was granted and all were killed. The general was greatly honored by the people because he refused to submit. Had he submitted he would have been ridiculed for the rest of his life, and the would-be penetrator, in this instance the Sultan, would have been honored for his strength. Apparently, no blame was attached to the Sultan for what we would perceive as senseless cruelty and "perverse" sexual behavior. The intent of these acts, however, in the very different cultural setting of the Middle East, was primarily aggressive and not sexual. The issue was one of power, not erotic pleasure.

The approach of the ancient Norsemen toward homosexuality was somewhat like that of the Turks. Overt and conscious aggression played an important role, and the issue of primary importance was one of dominance and submission, not sexual pleasure. There was no shame attached to being the dominant, therefore the conquering, male. The shame was attached only to submitting and to being what the Norse called "argr," a term of crude abuse. It was considered disgraceful in ancient Scandinavia to submit to and be used sexually by another man to whom one should be equal.

Homosexuality in the United States has had a very different meaning and history than in these cultures just mentioned. There has never been any honor attached to the penetrator, and the act itself has been considered criminal even between consenting adults. Only lately has this punitive legal approach begun to be modified by law in some states. However, little emotional change has taken place as yet in the average person's loathing for these acts, which are considered "unnatural." Homosexuals themselves have not given any special distinction or honor or power to the person who fulfills the male role of penetration, nor have they considered the person who is penetrated as dishonored. Frequently, partners will even reverse roles. Con-

sciously, therefore, the role of aggression has receded into the background, and the erotic element has assumed a much more overt significance. Further, many obligate homosexuals consider their sexual behavior normal even though they are quite incapable of performing the sexual act with women. This attitude differs widely from that of the Greeks, the Romans, and others who have been described as practicing homosexuality. In these cultures, total and obligatory homosexuality was not considered desirable or acceptable, although homosexual contacts between young boys and older men under very strict and time-limited circumstances were socially acceptable.

In contrast, our own culture has considered any form of homosexuality as undesirable and pathological. This viewpoint has been challenged more and more openly by organized groups of homosexuals. They state that these conceptions of homosexuality are degrading and incorrect, and they have fought against both the medical model of homosexuality as an illness and the developmental model of homosexuality as a developmental disturbance. They have gained considerable influence and have been supported by many psychiatrists in their efforts to have the term homosexuality deleted from the diagnostic and statistical manual published by the American Psychiatric Association. The deletion of the term, however, will not enlighten us about the causes of homosexual behavior. Our approach to the study of homosexuality, as well as toward all other forms of behavior, must remain scientific rather than political. Data gathering and hypothesis testing still are the best ways to approach the problems of human behavior. Eventually, as knowledge accumulates, our formulations will more and more closely approximate the truth.

Suggested Readings

Freud S (1905): Three essays on the theory of sexuality. In *The Standard Edition of the Complete Psychological Works of Sigmund Freud*, vol. 7. London, Hogarth Press, 1953, p 125.

Hunt MM: *The Natural History of Love.* New York, A. A. Knopf, 1959.

Licht H: *Sexual Life in Ancient Greece*, ed. 10. London, The Abby Library, 1971.

Vanggaard T: *Phallos.* New York, International Universities Press, 1972.

CHAPTER 33 The Physiology of the Sexual Response Cycle

Robert Dickes, M.D.

THE RESEARCH OF MASTERS AND JOHNSON

We owe almost all of our information about the physiological responses to sexual stimulation to the work of William Masters and Virginia Johnson. At first, their reports were received with great skepticism. The criticisms ranged widely, from slurs upon their scientific reputations for studying such a subject as sexual responsiveness to innuendoes about their personal characters. These slurs were in many ways similar to those hurled at Freud for daring to be the first to study sex scientifically. Thus, the attitudes of the 19th century toward Freud and his coworkers have continued. We should thus not forget that the second half of the 20th century is by no means free of prejudice, and that the right to learn and to teach is not guaranteed by the Constitution.

Many communities object not only to the teaching of sexuality in the schools but to any scientific study of sexuality as well. These communities do not even want known facts communicated to the public. They base their objections on moral and religious grounds and claim that correct sexual knowledge is dangerous to their children and inherently evil. We need not be concerned with this type of criticism in this volume, but we do need to deal with a different type of critique, namely that which masquerades as scientific. One of these criticisms is that the patient population used in the Masters and Johnson research was improperly chosen. This criticism would seem to negate the importance and correctness of the most complete and objective studies of sexual responsiveness ever done. Let us therefore examine the patient population and the experimental approach of Masters and Johnson rather carefully.

During the first 29 months of their project, Masters and Johnson worked with 118 women and 27 men, all of whom were prostitutes. Out of this group, eight women and three men were finally selected for further anatomical and physiological study. In addition to the prostitutes, a second group of subjects was also studied. These came from the academic community of a large university hospital complex. Remarkably enough, the published text which contains the reported results does not include material from the prostitute population, but rather contains information derived primarily from the higher socioeconomic and intellectual group from the university complex. Thus, the sample was distorted. A skewing of this type, however, does not necessarily lead to false results, and this sample population was quite large; 382 women whose ages ranged from 18 to 72, and 312 males with an age range from 21 to 89 years were observed. Over 10,000 complete sexual cycles were studied.

The sexual cycles were studied under markedly artificial conditions. The women used the knee chest position. This position provided an opportunity to observe and record with special instrumentation the intravaginal physiological responses to sexual stimuli, which were provided by means of plastic penises having the same optics as plate glass. This allowed observation of the vaginal interior by using cold light illumination. Many types of observations and recordings were made, and the equipment was adjustable for physical variations in size, weight, and vaginal development. In the experiments, the rate and depth of the "penile" thrust was initiated and controlled by the responding woman. A period of orientation and practice was necessary before the subjects could be studied properly.

Obviously enough, many critical remarks may

be made concerning the experiments, and I exclude remarks related to prudery or other nonscientific attitudes. Masters and Johnson have questioned their results themselves. They pointed out the artificial nature of the experimental situation as compared with the natural situation of intercourse in privacy. They were also aware that the instrumentation itself could possibly vary the results. Thus, legitimate objections can be raised concerning the experiments. However, these objections may be answered satisfactorily. Many types of scientific observation modify the phenomena under study. If the size of the disturbance is small, however, the final measures will be sufficiently accurate to give a reasonably faithful report of the events. This has turned out to be the case for the observations on the subjects in question. The distortions, if any, are not large enough to significantly alter the findings. Furthermore, there is no way of studying intravaginal responsiveness other than by instrumentation. By now, many camera recordings have verified the essential accuracy of the work of these two pioneers in the field. Masters and Johnson also verified their own work by showing that the experimental intravaginal studies gave results that corresponded in every way with those obtained from self-manipulation.

One of the first points to be noted is that the human sexual response is generalized and is not confined to the breasts and genitals. The skin becomes flushed, muscle groups may show increased tension, the blood pressure and heart rate go up, and it may be said that the entire body, in one way or another, joins in the symphony of sexual responsiveness. Thus, it is no accident that people say, "Let us make beautiful music together." Response builds upon response as each person interacts with his or her partner. The better the communication and feeling between the two participants, the better and more complete will be the pleasure. Even rectal contractions have been noted during orgasmic response, and these responses are significant in the consideration of some paraphilias.

Masters and Johnson divided the sexual response cycle into four major sequential stages: the *excitement, plateau, orgasmic,* and *resolution* phases. Since the external genitalia (Figures 33.1–33.3) and the woman's breasts show the most changes, I will confine most of this chapter to describing the changes in these organs. I will describe each organ separately and ask the reader to integrate the multiple organ sequences which occur simultaneously (Tables 33.1 and 33.2).

THE FEMALE SEXUAL RESPONSE

The Breasts

The first signal of a woman's rising sexual excitement given by her breasts is nipple erection (Figures 33.4 and 33.5). This frequently occurs first in one nipple and then in the other. The erection is due to contraction of muscle fibers and not because of increased blood flow, which is responsible for so many of the other changes noted in the body. Occasionally, some women raise questions concerning the amount of their nipple erection. Large nipples usually show less increase in size than do those of average size. Very small nipples may show little change and inverted nipples may not evert at all. The relative anatomical change in size is, however, not significant. The ultimate pleasurable response to stimulation is primarily a psychological matter and not an anatomical one. Those women who raise questions concerning nipple erection are anxious and the questions should, therefore, be answered seriously and re assuringly.

During the excitement phase, the increased blood flow to the breast creates a venous engorgement which may show as a pattern on the skin. The engorgement also increases the size of the breast, which is more noticeable when the woman is lying down. The patterning of the skin is more noticeable when the woman is standing. Marked variability in all these physiological responses is to be expected not only in different women but in any given woman. Variable responses are not necessarily due to pathological factors, and any questions should alert us to the person's reasons for asking. Once again, the answers should be directed toward alleviating anxiety, provided organic pathology has been ruled out. Careful examination and attention to a patient's psychic state as well as physical needs are the hallmarks of a good physician.

The first stage of arousal shades imperceptibly into the next phase, termed the plateau phase. In this phase, the areola, the pigmented area surrounding the nipple, becomes engorged with blood (Figure 33.6). This so elevates the

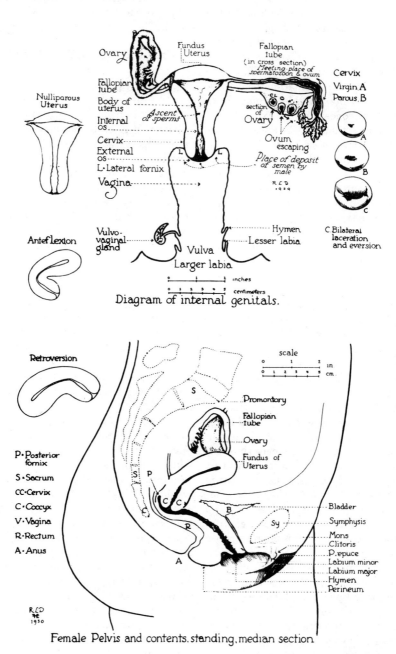

Diagram of internal genitals.

Female Pelvis and contents, standing, median section

Figure 33.1.   Female pelvis and contents, frontal and median (standing) sections. (Reproduced by permission from Dickinson, R.L. *Atlas of Human Sex Anatomy*, ed. 2. Williams & Wilkins, Baltimore, 1949.)

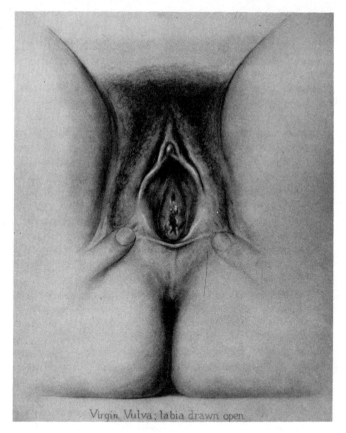

Figure 33.2. Female external genitalia, labia drawn open. (Reproduced by permission from Dickinson, R.L. *Atlas of Human Sex Anatomy*, ed. 2. Williams & Wilkins, Baltimore, 1949).

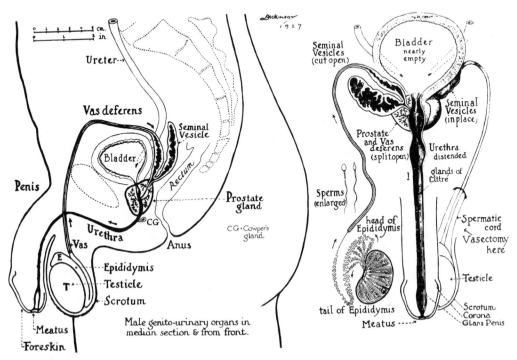

Figure 33.3. Male genitourinary organs, median and frontal (standing) sections. (Reproduced by permission from Dickinson, R.L. *Atlas of Human Sex Anatomy*, ed. 2. Williams & Wilkins, Baltimore, 1949.)

327

Table 33.1

*The Female Sexual Response Cycle**

	I. Excitement Phase (several minutes to hours)	II. Plateau Phase (30 sec. to 3 min.)	III. Orgasmic Phase (3–15 sec.)	IV. Resolution Phase (10–15 min. if no orgasm, ½–1 day)
Skin	No change	Sexual flush: inconstant; may appear on abdomen, breasts, neck, face, thighs. May resemble measles rash	No change	Flush disappears in reverse order
Breasts	1. Nipple erection 2. Venous congestion 3. Areolar enlargement	Venous pattern prominent. Size may increase one-fourth over resting state. Areolae enlarge: impinge on nipples so they seem to disappear	No change	Return to normal
Clitoris	Glans: glans diameter increased Shaft: variable increase in diameter. Elongation occurs in only 10% of subjects	Retraction: shaft withdraws deep into swollen prepuce	No change (Shaft movements continue throughout if thrusting maintained)	Shaft returns to normal position in 5–10 sec. Full detumescence in 5–10 min.
Labia majora	Nullipara: thin down, flatten against perineum Multipara: rapid congestion and edema. Increase to 2–3 times normal size	Nullipara: may swell if phase II unduly prolonged Multipara: become enlarged and edematous	No change	Nullipara: *increase* to normal size in 1–2 min. or less Multipara: *decrease* to normal size in 10–15 min.
Labia minora	Color change: bright pink in nullipara and red in multipara. Size: increase 2–3 times over normal	Color change: bright red in nullipara, burgundy red in multipara. Size: enlarged labia form a funnel into vaginal orifice	Proximal areas contract with contractions of lower third	Return to resting state in 5 min.
Vagina	Vagina: transudate appears 10–30 sec. after onset of arousal. Drops of clear fluid coalesce to form a well lubricated vaginal barrel. (Aids in buffering acidity of vagina to neutral pH required by sperm.)	Copious transudate can continue to form. Quantity of transudate generally increased by prolonging preorgasm stimulation	No change	Some transudate collects on floor of the upper two-thirds formed by its posterior wall (in supine position)
Upper two-thirds	Balloons: dilates as uterus moves up pulling anterior vaginal wall with it. Fornices lengthen; rugae flatten	Further ballooning occurs, then wall relaxes in a slow tensionless manner	No change; fully ballooned out and motionless	Cervix descends to seminal pool in 3–4 min.
Lower third	Dilation of vaginal lumen occurs. Congestion of walls proceeds gradually	Maximum distension reached rapidly; contracts lumen of lower third. Contraction around penis aids thrusting traction on clitoral shaft via labia and prepuce	3–15 contractions of lower third and proximal labia minora at ¾ sec. intervals	Congestion disappears in seconds. (If no orgasm, congestion persists for 20–30 min.)
Uterus	Ascends into false pelvis in phase I	Contractions: strong sustained contractions begin late in phase II	Contractions strong throughout orgasm. Strongest with pregnancy and masturbation	Slowly returns to normal position
Rectum			Inconstant rhythmical contractions	All reactions cease within a few seconds

* After table from *The Nature and Evolution of Female Sexuality* by Mary Jane Sherfey.

Table 33.2
The Male Sexual Response Cycle*

	I. Excitement Phase (several minutes to hours)	II. Plateau Phase (30 sec. to 3 min.)	III. Orgasmic Phase (3–15 sec.)	IV. Resolution Phase (10–15 min.; ½–1 day if no orgasm)
Skin	No change	Sexual flush; inconsistently appears on abdomen and spreads to the chest, face, and neck. Can include shoulders and forearms. May resemble measles	Widely spread flush if present persists	Flush disappears in reverse order of appearance
Penis	Erection within 10–30 sec.	Increase in size of glans and diameter of penile shaft. Deepened coronal and glans coloration	Ejaculation: marked by 3–4 major contractions at 0.8 sec. intervals followed by minor contractions	Partial involution of the erection in 5–10 sec. with variable refractory period. Complete detumescence in 5–30 min.
Scrotum and testes	Elevation of testes toward perineum and tightening and lifting of scrotal sac	Marked increase in size of testes over unstimulated state due to vasocongestion	No change	Return to normal size due to loss of vasocongestion. Testicular and scrotal descent within 5–30 min.
Other	Inconsistent nipple erection	A preejaculate of a few drops of mucoid fluid which may contain viable sperm. This is not the ejaculate. Pulse: may reach 175 per min. Blood Pressure: rise in systolic 20–80 mm, diastolic 10–40 mm. Respiration: increased	Partial loss of voluntary muscular control along with ejaculation. Rhythmical contractions of the rectal sphincter may be noted. The heart rate, blood pressure and respirations may increase further. Respirations up to 40 per min.	Return to quiescent state in 5–10 min.

* After table prepared by Virginia A. Sadock, M.D., from Masters and Johnson data.

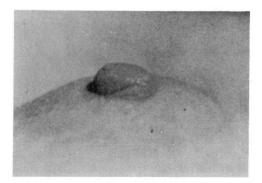

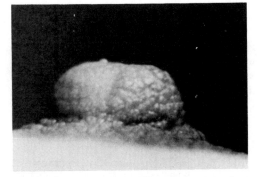

Figure 33.4. Nipple erection in early excitement phase. From the film *Physiological Responses of the Sexually Stimulated Female in the Laboratory* by Gorm Wagner, M.D., of the Institute of Medical Physiology, University of Copenhagen. (By permission of Focus International, New York City.)

Figure 33.5. Close-up of nipple erection (side view) in later excitement phase. From the film *Physiological Responses of the Sexually Stimulated Female in the Laboratory* by Gorm Wagner, M.D. (By permission of Focus International, New York City.)

Figure 33.6. Following genital stimulation both the nipple and the areola are erected. A milk drop is seen exuding from the top of the nipple. From the film *Physiological Responses of the Sexually Stimulated Female in the Laboratory* by Gorm Wagner, M.D. (By permission of Focus International, New York City.)

areola that an illusion may be created that the nipple is losing its erection. This is not the case. The nipple retains its erection into the resolution phase. As the areolae enlarge, the breast increases in size. This process began in the excitement phase but now becomes much more visible. Just prior to the orgasm and at the height of breast enlargement, the total increase in breast size may be as much as 20% to 25% over the size of the woman's breast when she is unaroused. After a woman has nursed a child, however, such increases in size are not usual, since nursing increases the venous drainage system and thus decreases the effects of the vasocongestion of sexual excitement.

The skin of the breasts may show a pinkish mottling which usually first appears over the upper abdomen and then spreads to the breasts. This pinkish mottling, which may cover a wide area of the body, is termed the *sex flush* and is part of the generalized response to sexual excitement which mounts until orgasm is reached. The breast shows no special response during orgasm itself.

Following orgasm, the skin or sex flush disappears and the areolae quickly return to their quiescent state. The nipples tend to stay erect and return to their prearousal state more slowly. This difference in timing may create the illusion that the nipple is becoming erect again. The fact is that the engorgement in the surrounding tissue subsides quickly and the nipple subsides more slowly. The disappearance of the engorgement of the breasts which caused the size increase proceeds at an even slower rate, and it

may be 5 or 10 minutes before the breast returns to its resting contour. The speed of the return is related to the size of the venous drainage system. The larger the drainage system, the sooner will the breast decrease in size.

One may, at this point, raise the question as to why it is important to know such details of normal physiology. Clinical situations in which such knowledge is important do occur and not infrequently. Physicians who are knowledgeable and comfortable about sexual matters will hear about these matters and thus be able to be helpful. This is not true of those who are ignorant or uncomfortable when faced with sexual questions. This is illustrated by the story of a young woman who came to her physician complaining that her breasts became tense and tight when she felt sexually excited. She was so concerned about this that she thought she ought to avoid sex lest she develop cancer. The physician looked grave, examined her carefully, and told her that he found nothing wrong. He asked her to return in three months for a reexamination and possible further study if the condition did not subside. The results of such an approach are easy to predict but much harder to correct. The woman began to worry even more after this encounter with her physician and became quite inhibited sexually with her husband. She finally sought help for this latter disorder. The effect on her life and her marriage would have been quite different had her original doctor known enough to tell her that the tenseness she felt was due to a normal breast enlargement during sexual excitement. He could have helped her overcome her anxiety, and she would soon have lost her fear of the tenseness in her breasts. She might even have enjoyed it!

Let us now turn our attention to the female genitals and how they respond to sexual arousal. I am assuming that the reader is familiar with the anatomy of these organs. The physiological responses of the female genitals are directly influenced by psychic factors as well as physical factors. I will, in this chapter, concentrate on the physical responses.

The Clitoris

The clitoris, although enclosed by the vulva and not visible until the labia are parted, will be considered first because of its uniqueness in function (Figure 33.7). It is the only organ which functions solely for sexual pleasure; the penis, its anatomical counterpart, serves as an excretory organ as well as being the major organ of sexual pleasure for the male.

During the excitement phase the clitoris increases in size although the increase may be minute. The rate of enlargement is quicker with mons stimulation close to the clitoris (Figures 33.8–33.10). Slower and less extensive engorgement is noted in the response to fantasy, breast stimulation, or intercourse. In this phase more than half of the subjects showed no obvious enlargement of the head (or glans) of the clitoris. Enlargement of the glans clitoris should not be compared with the erection of the penis, which is dependent upon venous filling of the cavernous sinuses in the shaft or body of the penis. Total clitoral body erection is not observed normally.

Masters and Johnson report that during the plateau phase, the clitoris universally retracts and becomes less accessible to view or touch. They also report at least a 50% reduction in the total length of the clitoral body. This has not been confirmed by all other investigators. However, the importance of the retraction should not be overlooked. Many couples, unaware of the normality of retraction, stop active stimulation of the mons and hunt for the clitoris. This interferes with their spontaneity and responsiveness, since they believe that direct contact is essential for increasing pleasure. Actually, most women prefer the stroking to be close to the glans and not directly upon it.

No direct information concerning the clitoris

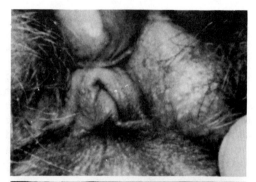
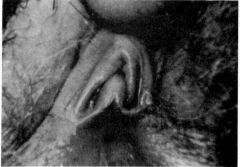
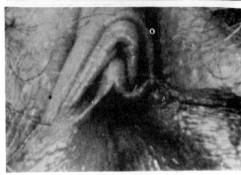

Figures 33.8–33.10. Close-up views of the progressive enlargement of the clitoris and surrounding tissues with stimulation. From the film *Physiological Responses of the Sexually Stimulated Female in the Laboratory* by Gorm Wagner, M.D. (By permission of Focus International, New York City.)

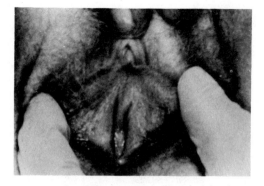

Figure 33.7. Soft, unstimulated head of the clitoris visible under the prepuce upon spreading of the labia. From the film *Physiological Responses of the Sexually Stimulated Female in the Laboratory* by Gorm Wagner, M.D. (By permission of Focus International, New York City.)

is available for the orgasmic phase due to the retraction of the clitoris, which makes it inaccessible to observation.

The clitoris, in the end or resolution phase, returns to its resting position in 5 to 10 seconds after the last orgasmic contraction. One should be aware, clinically, that the cycle of responsiveness of the clitoris is the same regardless of the method used to reach orgasm. Positioning, self-manipulation, or intercourse do not influence this sequence.

Many questions emerge at this point, such as: 1) Are there any differences between the clitoral and vaginal orgasm? 2) If there are differences, what do these signify? Freud believed that there was an important psychic difference between the two types of orgasm. These matters cannot be discussed in this chapter, which is devoted to physiological response patterns, but they will be discussed in the chapter on sexual myths and misinformation. The external female genitalia and the vagina will be discussed next.

The Vulva: The Labia Majora

Since the woman's obstetrical history affects the sexual physiological response of the labia majora, the nulliparous woman (a woman who has not borne children) will be described first. During the excitement phase, the labia flatten and then turn outward. They also become elevated upward and outward away from the vaginal outlet. This anatomic displacement away from the midline may be a secondary effect due to the protrusion caused by the rapid engorgement of the labia minora and the early vasocongestion of the external third of the vagina, which take place simultaneously with the changes in the external labia. No further changes occur in the labia majora in the plateau phase or during orgasm. The labia rapidly return to the normal midline position during resolution. Prolonged sexual stimulation without orgasm leads to a marked engorgement and possible edema. This engorgement may then take several hours to abate. The multiparous woman's (a woman who has borne children) labia majora respond differently to sexual stimulation. The labia, instead of thinning, become markedly distended due to vasocongestion. The movement away from the midline is present but less than in the nullipara.

The Vulva: The Labia Minora

The labia minora may increase as much as threefold in diameter by the time the full plateau phase is reached. Then they may actually protrude through the major labia, having lengthened by about one centimeter and adding to the length of what is termed the vaginal sexual barrel. It should be noted that in many women, the labia normally protrude even in the resting state. The engorged labia also develop vivid colors during the plateau phase. These colors range from bright pink to red to a deep wine color. Masters and Johnson have used the term *sex skin* for the labia minora. They state that the more brilliant and definite the color changes, the greater is the sexual excitement. Women do not obtain orgasmic pleasure without first developing these specific color changes. The color loss is rapid after orgasm.

The Vagina

The vaginal response to sexual stimulation follows a basic pattern regardless of whether the stimuli are primarily somatogenic or psychogenic in origin.

A lubricating transudate appears on the vaginal walls within 10 to 30 seconds after effective sexual stimulation begins, therefore in the stage of initial excitement (Figure 33.11). Individual droplets appear scattered throughout and then coalesce to form a smooth slippery surface over the entire vaginal barrel. This substance, a transudate, results from the marked dilation of the venous plexus which surrounds the vaginal barrel. This whole process of lubrication is so rapid that in less than one minute a woman may be physiologically ready for entry. The psychological "set" is another matter, and very often, women and men prefer an appropriate period of foreplay. Thus, physiological and psychic events need not coincide.

As the excitement phase continues, the inner two-thirds of the vagina expands and relaxes. The vaginal inner arches also expand, and the

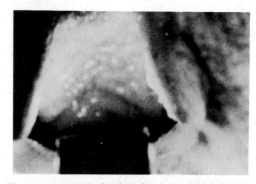

Figure 33.11. Individual droplets, of a lubricating transudate appearing on the vaginal walls in the early excitement stage. From the film *Physiological Responses of the Sexually Stimulated Female in the Laboratory* by Gorm Wagner, M.D. (By permission of Focus International, New York City.)

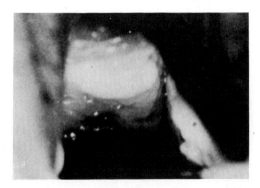

Figure 33.12. Tenting effect in the excitement phase, producing considerable expansion of the inner portion of the vagina. From the film *Physiological Responses of the Sexually Stimulated Female in the Laboratory* by Gorm Wagner, M.D. (By permission of Focus International, New York City.)

cervix and body of the uterus are pulled out of the true pelvis and up into the false pelvis, creating a *tenting effect* (Figure 33.12). Thus, the inner portion of the vagina expands considerably. Total vaginal length may increase by as much as three centimeters in length and four centimeters in its interior width. The outer third of the vagina, however, shows little dilation. The normal vaginal color darkens to a deeper red.

The vasocongestion noted in the excitement phase continues to develop in the plateau phase until it is so marked that the lumen of the outer third of the vagina is reduced in size by as much as one-third from the distention noted in the first phase. When this degree of vasocongestion occurs, the peak of the plateau level has been reached. The vasocongestion now encompasses the entire outer third of the vagina and the engorged labia minora. This is the anatomic foundation for the area which is termed the *orgasmic platform.* The rate of vaginal lubrication which was so rapid in the excitement phase can slow during the plateau phase, especially if the level of sexual tension is extended for a long time.

It is important to note that when orgasm occurs, the vaginal response is confined to the outer third of the vagina or to its orgasmic platform. This area responds regularly and strongly at approximately 0.8 second intervals with a number of contractions, which range from three to five contractions up to 10 or 15 with each orgasm (Figure 33.13). There are no other physiological responses of the vagina during the orgasmic phase. I have mentioned the ballooning

of the inner two thirds of the vagina noted in the earlier phases of excitement. This area is inactive during orgasm. The possibility of becoming pregnant is enhanced by this quiescence.

During resolution, the localized vasocongestion dissipates and the lumen of the outer third of the vagina increases. The expanded inner portion of the vagina returns to its unstimulated state. The cervix also returns from its elevated position in the pelvis. These events may take three to four minutes. The mucosa resumes its basic coloration more slowly.

The Uterus

As noted earlier, the entire uterus is elevated into the false pelvis and the cervix shifts from its usual position. This elevation is coupled with the changes in the inner portion of the vagina, creating a tenting effect. The elevation of the uterus is not complete until the plateau phase. Contractions of the body of the uterus occur during orgasm. These begin in the fundus, proceed to the midzone, and end in the lower uterine segment. The contractions, regular at first, become irregular but recurrent, and the extent of the contraction roughly parallels the intensity of the orgasm that the woman experiences. The excursion of the contractions decreases as the orgasm diminishes in its intensity. Pelvic vasocongestion, which may be extensive, is relieved with the occurrence of orgasm. Within five minutes, 50% of the pelvic vasocongestion disappears, and the remainder in 10 minutes. The

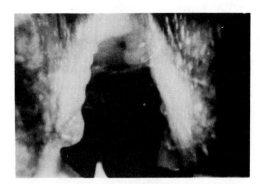

Figure 33.13. Vagina during orgasm. Considerable increase in volume is seen. A large droplet of lubrication can be seen in the lower left corner of the vaginal outlet. From the film *Physiological Responses of the Sexually Stimulated Female in the Laboratory* by Gorm Wagner, M.D. (By permission of Focus International, New York City.)

vasocongestion may persist for hours in the absence of orgasmic relief if the sexual activity has been prolonged.

THE MALE SEXUAL RESPONSE

The male sexual response is also conditioned by psychic factors which may enhance both the performance and the pleasure or hinder it sufficiently to prevent the man from functioning at all. Such failures, when they occur, cause considerable anguish but they may not signify any serious psychological difficulty. Repeated failures, however, indicate the need for expert help. Repeated failure in a woman also indicates a need for help but again does not necessarily indicate serious psychopathology. Physicians should know that brief treatment for sexual difficulties has already helped an enormous number of people, and they should be prepared to make the appropriate referral. Discussion of such treatment methods will be taken up in a later chapter.

The Penis

The male response to sexual tension, noted in the earliest part of the excitement phase, is penile erection (Figures 33.14 and 33.15). This may occur when there is only a minimum of sexual excitement. The excitement phase may be brief or prolonged, and the erection may be partially lost and regained many times during prolonged foreplay.

Erection is, of course, the most obvious sign of sexual arousal and a few generalizations con-

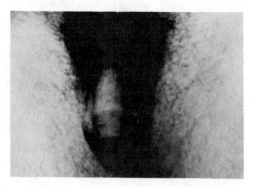

Figure 33.14. Soft, unstimulated (flaccid) penis. From the film *Physiological Responses of the Sexually Stimulated Male in the Laboratory* by Gorm Wagner, M.D. (By permission of Focus International, New York City.)

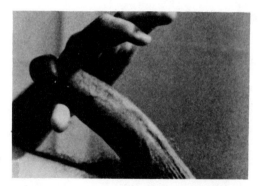

Figure 33.15. Erect penis following stimulation. From the film *Physiological Responses of the Sexually Stimulated Male in the Laboratory* by Gorm Wagner, M.D. (By permission of Focus International, New York City.)

cerning this are in order. Erections are under the control of higher and lower nervous system centers. The higher centers control the psychic aspects of sexual response and therefore also influence the erection. This should not be taken to mean that erection is under voluntary control. It is not, and efforts to "will" an erection do not work. Treatment based on such an assumption is only harmful. The conspicuous nature of the erection tends to cause people to overlook other more generalized responses. Just as in the woman, the pulse rate increases, and the blood pressure goes up. Nipple erection may occur along with the skin sex flush. It should also be noted that erections can and do develop in infants and in the very old. Stated another way, the capacity to develop an erection is, in the healthy male, lifelong.

During the plateau phase, the penis, which is already fully erect, develops an additional minor vasocongestive increase which is confined primarily to the coronal area of the glans. This additional increase in diameter occurs as the orgasmic phase approaches. The penis itself may develop a deep mottled reddish color which is related to the venous stasis. Approximately 20% of the subjects showed this color change.

In addition, a preejaculatory secretory emission occurs during the plateau phase (Figure 33.16), and these droplets of fluid may contain sperm.

The sensations of orgasm and ejaculation coincide. The ejaculation (Figure 33.17) develops when regular and recurrent contractions of several muscles occur in relation to one another.

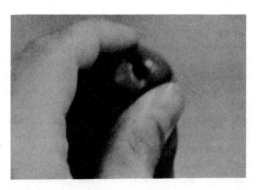

Figure 33.16. Preejaculatory droplet in the urethra during the late plateau phase. From the film *Physiological Responses of the Sexually Stimulated Male in the Laboratory* by Gorm Wagner, M.D. (By permission of Focus International, New York City.)

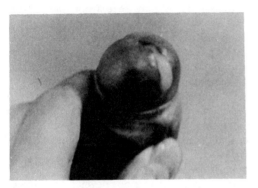

Figure 33.17. Ejaculation of semen during orgasm. From the film *Physiological Responses of the Sexually Stimulated Male in the Laboratory* by Gorm Wagner, M.D. (By permission of Focus International, New York City.)

well past the end of the refractory period of resolution. When erection has been maintained for many minutes intravaginally, the penile vasocongestion, and therefore the erection, may continue for some time after ejaculation. Penile involution is therefore variable and dependent upon the extent and intensity of the stimulation. The process is slower when sexual stimulation persists and is faster when asexual stimuli are intruded. If the penis is removed from the vagina, involution proceeds more rapidly.

The Scrotum

As excitement rises, there is a noticeable tensing and thickening of the scrotal skin. This is due to a localized vasocongestion and contraction of smooth muscle fibers. This causes a constriction which produces a marked decrease in the internal diameter of the scrotal sac. There are no other specific scrotal sac changes in either the plateau or orgasmic levels of sexual excitement. During resolution, there is a rapid loss of the congested, tense appearance of the scrotum. A minority of about 25% exhibit a slow resolution with a delay in the loss of the tension induced by the congestion and muscle fiber contraction.

The Testes

Both testes elevate in the excitement phase (Figure 33.19). The elevation is due to the shortening of the spermatic cords brought about by the contraction of the cremasteric muscula-

Contractions involve the entire length of the penile urethra. This forces the seminal fluid from the prostate and membranous portions of the urethra through the urethra, to the meatus, and then to the outside. The explosive force and frequency of the contractions decrease rapidly after the first three or four expulsions.

Detumescence (loss of erection) during resolution occurs sequentially in two phases. The first phase is present during the early part of the refractory period of resolution, a period during which reerection and orgasm do not occur. The initial involution of the erection reduces penile size about 50% and is quite rapidly accomplished (Figure 33.18). The second phase of penile involution returns the penis to its flaccid state. This may occur slowly enough to extend

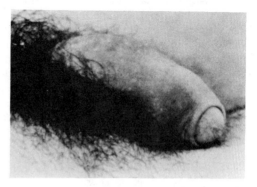

Figure 33.18. Partial loss of penile erection immediately following ejaculation. From the film *Physiological Responses of the Sexually Stimulated Male in the Laboratory* by Gorm Wagner, M.D. (By permission of Focus International, New York City.)

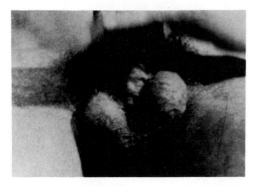

Figure 33.19. Elevation of the testes during the excitement phase. From the film *Physiological Responses of the Sexually Stimulated Male in the Laboratory* by Gorm Wagner, M.D. (By permission of Focus International, New York City.)

ture. As the testes elevate, they undergo a shift in their axes of suspension. The superior pole turns anteriorly and when the testes are completely elevated, the posterior pole comes into direct contact with the perineum. If the excitement phase is maintained for more than 5 to 10 minutes and no progression in sexual tension follows, the cremasteric musculature relaxes. The testes and the scrotal sac return to their unstimulated position. If sexual tension continues to mount, the testes maintain a tight apposition to the perineum. This is the preejaculatory position and is of extreme physiological importance.

Full elevation of the testes is required for a full ejaculatory sequence. Partial elevation results in a marked reduction in the ejaculatory pressure. When the testes reach full apposition to the perineum, plateau has been reached and orgasm is certain if stimulation is continued. The testes in plateau increase in size by as much as 50% due to vasocongestion. The longer the plateau, the more severe is the testicular vasocongestion and the greater the amount of enlargement. The nature of the testicular reaction during orgasm is unknown. During resolution, the return of the testes to their unstimulated state may be rapid or slow.

THE SEXUAL RESPONSE IN OLDER WOMEN AND MEN

Older Women

Diminution in the sex flush is noted. There is also a marked reduction in the vasocongestive

reaction of the breast after age 50 and therefore breast enlargement is either decreased or absent. Orgasm remains essentially the same but resolution occurs more quickly since there is less vascular engorgement. The labia majora do not show the usual flattening and elevation. The labia minora show a reduced vasocongestion with a loss of what was earlier described as the labial sex skin reaction.

The major changes in sexual response concern the vagina itself. It undergoes specific involutionary changes. The walls of the vaginal barrel become tissue-paper thin, and there is a shortening of both the length and width of the vaginal barrel. Some loss of expansive ability is also noted. In younger women, the vaginal lubrication takes place within 10 to 20 seconds. Once the individual woman is beyond the mid-fifties and past 60, it may take from one to three minutes before any definite production of vaginal lubrication can be observed. The inner two-thirds of the vaginal barrel expands more slowly and the local vasocongestion in the outer third of the vagina is significantly reduced after senile involution of the vaginal walls and constriction of the barrel. Thus, the orgasmic platform develops less fully, but when it is developed, the central lumen of the senile vagina, although constricted, is still proportional to that of a younger woman.

In orgasm, contractions develop with the exception that the contractile phase is reduced in duration. In resolution, there is a rapid involution of the entire vaginal barrel. The uterus also shows changes and, in the average woman 5 to 10 years past the cessation of menstrual flow, the uterus and cervix are essentially equal in length. There is some evidence that the uterine contractility noted in orgasm may cause a cramping pain. Due to this factor, many women who have never had sexual discomfort previously may note distress after menopause.

These specific changes which occur after menopause can be corrected with intravaginal endocrine replacement therapy, and those individuals who develop difficulty can return to effective sexual performance. The use of these endocrine preparations restores the vaginal mucosa to its earlier state and thus the painfulness of intercourse ceases. The pain of uterine contractions can also be relieved by combinations of estrogen and progesterone. However, there are considerable risks to oral estrogen therapy, and these will be discussed in some detail in the chapter on the climacterium.

Older Men

As in women, the sexual response in the older man is basically related to the slowing and lessening of vasocongestion in the sexual organs and the accessory sexual organs. Nipple erection is reduced and the sexual flush does not develop. In general, the older the male the longer it takes to achieve full erection regardless of the techniques used to induce the erection. Once achieved, the erection may be maintained for extended periods of time without ejaculation. Regardless of the variety of the sexually stimulating activity, the ability to maintain erections over long periods of time without an ejaculatory sequence is associated with the aging process. Once the erection has been attained and then lost without an ejaculatory opportunity, older males have difficulty in returning to excitement phase responsiveness regardless of continuation of previously effective stimulating techniques. The full erection is not obtained until just before the ejaculatory experience. The aging male experiences not only an increase in glans circumference but also increases in length and diameter of the entire penile shaft just prior to ejaculation.

In general, the ejaculatory process shows the same slower reactive qualities inherent in other aging processes. The man over 50 exhibits marked reduction in ejaculatory distance, 6 to 12 inches being the average distance, as compared to double this distance for the younger man. The older male will also have fewer expulsive contractions as well as less force in expelling the seminal fluid. The refractory period lasts for a much more extended time, especially after the age of 60. Penile detumescence is so rapid that the first and second stages so characteristic for younger men cannot be delineated. Scrotal responsiveness and testicular elevation is reduced. Older males have been observed to ejaculate with the testes elevated only one-third to one-half the way to the perineum. Prostatic contractions notable in young men are not present in the older man.

This type of information needs emphasis because any change in functioning of the sexual apparatus is very apt to be disturbing to many people, and unless they can be reassured as to the normalcy of the change, fears develop that may induce a marked inhibition of the person's sexual performance in general. Reassurance is of great value to the anxious person, and this is especially true in regard to sexual functioning in older people.

Suggested Readings

Masters WH, Johnson VE: *Human Sexual Response*. Boston, Little, Brown, and Co, 1966.
Sadock VA: Sexual anatomy and physiology. In Grimspoon L (ed): *Psychiatry 1982: Annual Review*. Washington, American Psychiatric Press, 1982, p 9.

CHAPTER 34 Sexual Myths and Misinformation

Robert Dickes, M.D.

A number of sexual myths which concern both women and men will be considered in this chapter, and these myths will be discussed primarily in terms of physiological responsiveness. However, although I will be confining the discussion in this chapter to the sexual response cycle, I must add that love, mutual respect, and object constancy contribute a great deal to lasting sexual pleasure. But before pursuing these issues, let us first proceed on the principle that knowledge in and of itself is rewarding and can help to lead a person away from fear. There has certainly been far too much ignorance and fear attached to sexuality throughout human history.

CLITORAL SIZE AND STIMULATION

Many people think that the size and shape of the clitoris are directly related to the effectiveness of a woman's performance in intercourse. This idea has no foundation in fact. During active intercourse with the woman in the supine position, the body of the clitoris rarely contacts the penis. The shift in the location of the clitoris during the plateau phase makes the possibility of contact even less likely, and therefore the clitoral anatomy is of no significance in the development of sexual pleasure. The increasing pleasure derived from the clitoris during intercourse in the supine position is not dependent upon clitoral contact from the penis but is derived secondarily from the penile thrust. This thrust deep into the vagina places pressure upon the sexual platform which includes the labia minora. This creates a bilateral downward pull upon the hood of the clitoris by traction. The withdrawal of the penis releases the pull, and the glans and body of the clitoris return toward their usual position. Thus, the rhythmic motion of the couple creates its own mechanism for clitoral stimulation, and this is sufficient in most instances to bring the woman to climax. Attempts to produce direct penile-clitoral contact

are not only unnecessary, but they lead to an awkward positioning that is uncomfortable for both partners.

The assumption of the lateral or female superior position does permit direct stimulation of the clitoris by the penis, provided the participants place their pubic symphyses in apposition, one against the other. Thus, direct stimulation is possible, in addition to the secondary stimulation just described for the supine position. The clitoral pleasure response may, therefore, develop more intensely in these positions. Some women report that they achieve their greatest intensity of response when they assume the female superior position. Many sex therapists make use of this knowledge for women who have difficulty in reaching climax. In addition to the extra stimulation, the woman has better control of movement and therefore can intensify her pleasure.

Masters and Johnson take issue with this approach and do not seem to be impressed with these various attempts to increase clitoral stimulation, since every position provides indirect stimulus to the clitoris. It is true that many women can do very well without direct stimulation, but in certain cases, more stimulation, including manual manipulation, is necessary. There are women who benefit from the extra stimulation and learn to become orgasmic as a result. They then can usually become capable of full responsiveness in any position once they gain experience in achieving orgasm.

MASTURBATION IN WOMEN

No two women are alike in personality or in anatomy, nor do they masturbate in similar fashions. Some rub their thighs together with pressure on the clitoris. Others stimulate the mons pubis. Most concentrate on the areas adjacent to the clitoris itself. The majority of women avoid direct manipulation of the glans, but many women will manipulate the shaft of the clitoris. Right handed women will rub the right side and left handed the left side. Some prefer light touch and some require rather heavy pressure. These preferences may well be influenced by the neuroanatomy of the clitoris. Variations in the quality and number of different nerve endings in the clitoral body and glans have been noted. These nerve endings could then be responsible for the different preferences women display. The importance of the mons pubis is often overlooked but it is an area of considerable sensual value. Masturbation by stimulation of the mons pubis remains effective even after clitoridectomy (surgical removal of the clitoris). The labia minora and the entire perineum also possess great sensual potential.

THE DISTENSIBILITY OF THE VAGINA

There are a large number of people who have many fears concerning vaginal penetration. One of the beliefs they harbor is that the vagina is easily damaged. Other beliefs include the idea that it is the penis that is easily damaged, or that the vagina is unclean. These are sexual myths that interfere with a person's ability to enjoy intercourse and it may become the physician's task to dispel these erroneous notions.

Viewed biologically, the vagina is indeed an ideal penile container and is an organ that can provide great pleasure both for the man and the woman, provided that both can be free of anxiety and are uninhibited in their sexual expression. A woman worrying about the fragility of her vagina or its ability to distend and contain the penis without damage is not going to experience the full pleasure normally available to her. She should know that the vagina is a very strong organ capable of withstanding severe pressure on its walls and that it is, for all practical purposes, infinitely distensible. The process of childbirth can be used to explain these points to any couple. A child's head and body pass through the vaginal canal without damaging the vaginal organ. If there is damage during delivery, it is primarily perineal damage usually due to uncontrolled expulsion. This danger does not exist in intercourse. The vagina can, therefore, contain even a very large penis.

Too rapid entry, however, can be experienced as painful. If mounting occurs too early in the excitement phase before a woman is psychologically ready, as well as before vaginal expansion and lubrication have occurred, the woman may experience some difficulty in accommodating the penis. Presuming, however, that the distress is not too great, involuntary vaginal expansion usually takes place rapidly and the difficulty disappears. There is no resultant damage to the vagina. Of course, no man should attempt entry before his partner indicates her readiness and desire for entry. By the same token, a woman should deny entry until ready. She should be free to tell her partner how she feels. Open communication between the two participants is essential in generating sexual pleasure and fulfillment.

VAGINAL SIZE

Not only can a small vagina encompass a large penis, but a large vagina can encompass a very small penis and provide sufficient sensation for both to experience perfectly normal sexual pleasure. The vaginal walls are normally in close apposition to one another and the vaginal space, which is essentially variable, is only a potential space. The introduction of one or two fingers into the quiescent vagina will quickly demonstrate that the walls of the vagina surround and touch the fingers. The smallest penis is hardly smaller than a finger and, therefore, it can extend the vagina and supply sufficient stimulation to the woman and in turn receive sufficient stimulation.

The vagina, when a woman is stimulated, undergoes many changes, among which are changes in the labia minora and the outer third of the vagina. These engorge and enlarge, thereby encroaching on the lumen of the vagina. This narrows the vaginal opening and forms a cuff which supplies a gentle yielding pressure on the penis. Another factor which aids in minimizing the importance of penile size is that, regardless of the position chosen for intercourse, much of the clitoral and labial stimulation is derived from the mutual pelvic motion which supplies pressure and friction to the necessary parts. Thus, much of the clitoral stimulation is secondary, and it is only in the lateral and female superior positions that direct clitoral-penile contact can be achieved. So once again, penile and vaginal size is of little importance.

THE CLEANLINESS OF THE VAGINA

The myth that the vagina is unclean is almost ubiquitous and is as widely accepted by women as by men. Both sexes are wrong in this belief. The healthy vagina is essentially bacteria free and is incapable of inducing any disease in any man. The mouth, an organ far more acceptable in our (men's and women's) body schema, harbors many types of bacteria. Many diseases are transmitted by the apparently healthy mouth. Yet mouth-to-mouth contact is rarely feared in our culture. The reasons for this fear and dislike of the vagina are based on ideas concerned with unconscious fantasies and are not related to reality.

These ideas cannot be discussed in any detail in this context. Suffice it to say that the underlying fears are related to ideas of penetration and wounding with subsequent bleeding, and also to ideas of a single cloacal opening, rather than to any real knowledge of anatomy and physiology. Scientific knowledge of the menstrual cycle and its full meaning is an extremely recent discovery in terms of the length of the time span of the human species. Our unconscious ideas were formulated long before scientific discovery became part of our history. In any case, the point to be made is that the vagina is neither unclean in a biological sense nor dirty in the psychological sense. In itself it can do no harm to a man. This is a necessary piece of information and must be imparted to people by physicians. It is especially reassuring to women who have believed in this sexual myth to know the truth.

FANTASIED PENILE DAMAGE BY THE VAGINA

There are many myths about the damage that women can do to men during intercourse. One of these concerns the vagina and the female superior position, and it contains a kernel of truth which contributes to the reluctance of both men and women to use this position. The myth states that damage can occur when the woman assumes the superior position and lowers herself abruptly as the penis enters the vagina. The damage is thought to occur when the penis strikes the vaginal walls. It must be remembered that the vagina is quite distensible and spacious enough to prevent damage. In addition, the walls of the vagina are lubricated and thus aid in easy entry. Therefore, even if the woman's descent is rapid, no real danger is present.

There is a way, however, in which a woman can injure the erect penis when she is in the superior position. She could strike the erect penis a rapid and forceful blow with her body with the sadistic intent of doing harm. Such an injury would not involve the vagina, however, since no entry is effected and the penis is struck by the thigh or some other body part. This is the kernel of truth in the myth of penile injury by the vagina. However, I have never heard of even a violently psychotic woman behaving in such a fashion. Further, a woman does not seek too-rapid entry. The danger for all practical purposes does not exist. Most of the remaining types of damage which are blamed on a woman's vagina belong completely to the realm of myth and fantasy (Figure 34.1). The vagina is, of course, subject to disease as is any organ of the body and may, therefore, harbor some specific infection which requires treatment. My remarks apply to the healthy vagina.

VAGINISMUS

A very common fantasy occurs early in children who have observed two dogs stuck together after the act of intercourse. These children, and many adults as well, are unaware of the anatomical differences between the male dog and the human male. The dog penis contains a bony structure and the bulbus glandis, an extension of the corpus cavernosum urethra. The constrictor vestibuli muscles of the female dog contract around the engorged bulbus of the male dog, causing the locked together position which may last 10 minutes.

The situation for the human is very different. No such penile bone exists and *vaginismus*, when it does occur, prevents *entry* of the penis, not removal. Orgasm and muscular contractions of the vagina not only do no harm to the penis but rather increase the pleasure for both. Vaginismus is one of the sexual dysfunctions treatable by therapy and even though fantasy suggests that the clamped-down vagina will damage the penis, the facts refute the fantasy. The vagina is not a weapon, and even though it is a strong muscular organ, it is incapable of cutting through the penis or of cutting off its essential blood supply.

Figure 34.1. *The Purgatory of Fiery Vulvas.* Japanese print. (Reprinted by permission from the book *Studies in Erotic Art*, published by Basic Books, New York, 1970.)

THE FEMALE ORGASM

There has been much discussion as to what constitutes a normal female orgasm. Freud was insistent upon the idea that a "clitoral orgasm" was a sign of immaturity and that only "vaginal orgasms" could be termed healthy. Unfortunately, the distinctions between these two types of response were never fully clarified in the early analytic literature. Freud's ideas concerning female responsiveness, based upon subjective and psychological data from his patients, dominated psychological thought for a great many years. Only recently has any challenge to these ideas gained credence.

The apparent challenge came from Masters and Johnson and was based primarily upon their physiological discoveries. The results of their work indicated that although the orgasmic experience varies greatly in duration and intensity among different women and even at different times in the same woman, the clitoris and vagina always react in "consistent physiological patterns." Masters and Johnson demonstrated that the fundamental physiological orgasmic response was the same regardless of the site of stimulation or the way in which the orgasm was achieved. They concluded that the clitoral and vaginal orgasms "are not separate biological entities," but rather that both the clitoris and the vagina participate physiologically in every orgasm. They, therefore, seem to contradict Freud and his comments about the existence of clitoral and vaginal orgasms. Yet, Masters and Johnson do report subjective responses which differ in terms of what is felt locally by the woman and how extensive the feeling is anatomically. Women have reported orgasms experienced primarily in the clitoral area as well as orgasms experienced primarily in the vaginal and deep pelvic areas. Of course, orgasm may also be experienced over a much more widely distributed area with a merging of both clitoral and vaginal sensations. This latter type of orgasm is more complete and satisfying.

The contradictions between Freud on the one hand, and Masters and Johnson on the other, are more apparent than real. Masters and Johnson were discussing the *physiological* response when they stated that there is no such thing as a "clitoral" versus a "vaginal" orgasm. Their work includes the discovery that *all* orgasms include clitoral responsiveness and vaginal contractions regardless of the person's subjective experience. Freud and other analysts such as Helene Deutsch and Phyllis Greenacre were referring to a woman's subjective *psychological* experiences when they described "clitoral" versus "vaginal" responses. It is possible, if the inhibition is sufficient, for a woman to have vaginal contractions as Masters and Johnson have described and yet not experience *any* of the usual pleasure that accompanies these contractions. The physiological machinery may work, therefore, but the woman may not be able to experience the totality of pleasure that would normally be available to her because of certain psychological conflicts. Viewed in this light, Freud's original remarks concerning female orgasm may now be more understandable. His remarks concerning clitoral orgasm refer to an inhibition of normal vaginal pleasure as compared to the more widespread orgasmic response experienced by the uninhibited woman. Thus, there is a very wide range of orgasmic response, and a given woman may experience orgasms that range from a minimal to a maximal response. The amount of response is, of course, dependent upon many circumstances. The sexually normal woman, however, has the complete range available.

A woman is capable of producing a number of successive orgasms provided she is stimulated again before her sexual tension has fallen below the plateau phase level. She is also capable of staying in an orgasmic state for a fairly long time. *Status orgasmus* has also been described by Masters and Johnson. This state consists of a series of rapid recurrent orgasms between which no plateau phase response can be noted. Status orgasmus may last from 10 to more than 60 seconds.

MULTIPLE ORGASMS

Women, when masturbating, may frequently enjoy repeated orgasms before they feel satisfied.

They stay at plateau levels between the repeated orgasms and stop only when tired. Mary Jane Sherfey has carried this concept further and considers three to six orgasms as a necessity. She goes on to state that, "... no matter how many fully satisfying orgasms (a woman) may have she will not feel completely satiated until she is completely exhausted." This represents the beginnings of a new myth that women cannot be satisfied unless they have multiple orgasms continued to exhaustion. Sherfey's comments are contradicted by much clinical evidence that most women do not require multiple orgasms for complete satisfaction. This in no way contradicts the fact that repeated orgasms are harmless and enjoyable, just as masturbation is also harmless and enjoyable.

SIMULTANEOUS ORGASMS

Many people believe that simultaneous orgasms are the necessary goal of all sexual intercourse. A large number of people also believe that simultaneous orgasms will produce a pregnancy. Some even believe this is necessary for pregnancy. In actuality, fertilization does not depend upon female orgasm at all. A woman may become pregnant without orgasm and even without penetration. The deposition of sperm at the vaginal orifice has been known to produce pregnancy. Attempts at contraception, therefore, should not rely on avoiding entry and allowing the male to ejaculate upon the vulva. I have observed several cases in which young girls became pregnant following practices based upon such misconceptions.

Orgasm for both women and men need not be simultaneous for a satisfactory sexual relationship although such simultaneity is highly pleasurable. What is most significant for pleasure is that each of the partners have the opportunity for climax with the help of the other. Usually, a man will climax more quickly than will a woman. Under average circumstances, however, most women can climax shortly thereafter. Remember that penile detumescence takes place in two stages. The first stage can reduce the penile erection by about 50%. The remaining degree of erection is often sufficient for a woman to climax satisfactorily. If the woman requires additional stimulation, manual or otherwise, this should not be considered as abnormal or as a sign of failure on the part of either the man or the woman. Such ideas of failure have caused many people much discomfort and even great anxiety and interference in their interpersonal intimacy. In some couples, failure to have simultaneous orgasms becomes a source of contention and unhappiness. Simultaneity is not necessary for a fulfilled sexual relationship, and couples should not place such demands on one another.

THE ARTIFICIAL VAGINA

Myths exist concerning the functioning of the artificial vagina, and many students are curious about the effectiveness of the constructed organ and its ability to respond. The five patients with artificial vaginas reported upon by Masters and Johnson all lubricated in the excitement phase and demonstrated the normal lengthening and dilation of the inner portion of the vagina. The degree of elasticity of the barrel was, however, diminished. The vasocongestive phenomena of the plateau phase are quite marked in the artificial vagina and may be of such proportion as to diminish the central vaginal lumen by as much as 50%. Orgasmic responses are similar to those present in women possessing normal vaginas except for a vivid change in mucosal color from rather gray or purplish red to a very striking bright red. Resolution is accomplished in a manner that is basically similar to that of the normal woman. In brief, the surgically constituted vaginal barrel can be quite adequate for all sexual needs. It cannot, however, function in terms of reproductive needs unless it is normally rather than surgically attached to the uterus. Moreover, not all the surgically constructed vaginas function this well. Some tend to close off, bleed, or manifest other difficulties.

SPILLAGE FROM THE VAGINA

A few significant points concerning this function should be mentioned. The anatomic angulation of the vagina is of great importance when the organ is considered as a seminal receptacle. When a woman is in the supine position, there is a natural gravitational tendency for a seminal pool to develop on the posterior wall of the inner half of the vaginal barrel. The phenomenon of cervical elevation produces a bulbous or tenting expansion of the midvaginal plane. This increases the circumferential diameter of the entire inner two thirds of the vaginal barrel. The creation of the orgasmic platform in the outer third of the vagina creates a 50% constriction. Thus, the orgasmic platform produces a stopper-like effect in the outer third of the vagina and delays the loss of the seminal pool.

In resolution, the anterior vaginal walls and the cervix of the anteriorly placed uterus return to their previous positioning more rapidly than the posterior or lateral walls of the vaginal barrel. In this manner, the cervix is quickly immersed in the constrained seminal pool. This portion of the ejaculate that is not lost is usually contained within the depths of the vagina for a matter of hours unless the woman assumes special positions to rid herself of the semen. Semen raises the pH (acid-base balance) of the vagina, a fact which is significant for the viability of the sperm. That portion of the ejaculate which is lost coats the entire vaginal mucosa and is an aid, therefore, in changing the normally acid state within the vagina to an alkaline one. The pH fact is mentioned here because some women have an unfavorable reaction to the spilling out of semen. The spillage is an aid in conceiving. Knowledge of this biological usefulness may help these women toward a more favorable view concerning the spillage. This change in attitude, if effected, can increase their coital pleasure.

PENILE SIZE

The penis is almost always the focus of all clinical considerations concerning male sexual performance. This is rightly so, since effective erection is necessary for intercourse to take place at all. Erection and performance are therefore required of the man. The woman need not be aroused in order to have intercourse. Thus, different psychological factors related to biology enter into sexual performance for the man and for the woman. Both types of factors must always be considered and weighed accordingly.

Several myths exist concerning the penis. Just as many people believe that the size and shape of the clitoris is related to its effectiveness in intercourse, so do many believe that the size of the penis is important for effectiveness in performance. It has been presumed in many cultures that the larger the penis, the greater the sexual prowess of the individual and the more pleasure he can supply to his partner (Figures 34.2 and 34.3). This latter matter has already been discussed earlier in this chapter. People have presumed that there is great variation in the size of the normally erect penis. Masters and Johnson, once again, are among the few who have actually measured a number of penises in both quiescent as well as in the erect state. They

Figure 34.2. Mochican drinking cup with huge penis. The ancients had a sense of humor, because the cup has a perforated rim which forces the drinker to use the phallic spout. (Reprinted by permission from the book *Studies in Erotic Art*, published by Basic Books, New York, 1970.)

Figure 34.3. Scenes from Yōbutsu-Kurabe (The Phallic Contest). A 19th century copy of a 12th or 13th century original Japanese print (Reprinted by permission from the book *Studies in Erotic Art*, published by Basic Books, New York, 1970.)

reported that the average size of the penis in the flaccid state in one group measured from 7.5 to 9 centimeters in length. These men were then compared to a similar number of men (40) whose penile length measured 10 to 11.5 centimeters. The smaller penises increased in length by an average of 7.5 to 8.0 centimeters at full erection. In contrast, the men whose organs were significantly larger in the flaccid state demonstrated an increase in length of 7.0 to 7.5 centimeters.

Thus, the evidence does not support the concept that the larger penis increases more in size than does the smaller organ. In fact, the results demonstrate that the opposite is true. The greatest single increase in size, in their study, occurred in the smallest flaccid penis and the smallest increase in size occurred in one of the largest organs. Erection, therefore, tends to equalize the size of the organ. I wish to stress again, though, that the actual size of the penis has no effect on the pleasure of both participants. Size has no relevance to performance, which includes the capacity to love, the skill to arouse one's partner at a suitable pace, and the ability to be orgasmic and also permit one's partner to reach a climax as well. Nor does the size of the penis bear any relationship to frequency of performance. The latter is much more dependent on other matters.

Sexual activity is related to appropriate hormone supply in the brain and genitals and to some other, as yet unidentified, factors. Of course, general physical health is of the utmost importance in a consideration of either the ability to obtain an erection or the degree of desire manifested by any individual. Several diseases are related to a failure of both the sexual appetite and the person's ability to respond to stimulation. These include certain diseases of the nervous system, diabetes, chronic illness such as those which affect the liver and kidneys, and other types of disease as well. Alcohol is a notorious offender and deserves special notation since some people believe alcohol helps one to be sexually effective. Shakespeare was right when he said that whiskey or wine may whet the appetite but that they dull the performance. The same is true of most other drugs. Anyone treating sexual dysfunctions must be alert for organic factors at all times, but psychic factors are, of course, by far the most common causes of sexual dysfunction. Depression is a prime example of this. Anxiety and fear are also heavy contributors to sexual malfunction.

THE PENIS AS A DANGER

The penis has also been the subject of alarming myths and misconceptions along with the vagina. One myth emphasizes the value of an overly large penis, but another emphasizes the damage that can be done by an average size penis. This myth emphasizes the role of the penis as a weapon that can cause great harm. Thus, the penis is variously viewed as a snake or sword; a knife or lance that can poison, pierce, or tear; or as a gun that can not only pierce and tear but also shoot (Figures 34.4 and 34.5). Each of these weapons is made of cold steel and this alludes to the hardness of the penis as if it too were made of cold steel. I remember a woman who was fearful all during intercourse until she reassured herself that the penis was not an unyielding piece of metal. She had to learn by feel that the head of the penis is flexible and much softer than she had imagined. Both sexes, therefore, have their fears of each other's organs. In most cases, these fears are but dim images in the mind and of no consequence, but occasionally they acquire great force, and it is necessary for the skilled physician to help the patient dispel these fears.

CIRCUMCISION

Some ideas about circumcision must be included under the rubric of sexual myths. It has generally been accepted as fact by a number of people that circumcision is a good cure for premature ejaculation. They believe that removal of the prepuce or foreskin exposes the glans penis to more stimulation. This, they think, desensitizes the head of the penis and allows the individual to "withstand" more stimulation during sexual interaction. The dulling of the response mechanisms in the skin is supposed to allow the person to have a much slower and less sensitive reaction to stimulation, and therefore able to withhold ejaculation for a much longer time. An equally common but contradictory myth is that a circumcised penis is more sensitive, and therefore *more* vulnerable to premature ejaculation. These are both misconceptions. There is no evidence that the circumcised penis is either more or less sensitive to sexual stimuli than is the uncircumcised penis. There is also no evidence that circumcised males demonstrate either more or less premature ejaculation than

Figure 34.4.   Wooden male sculpture with penis as a snake. Broddenbjerg, North Jutland, 4th century B.C. (Reprinted from the book *Primitive Erotic Art*, published by G.P. Putnam's Sons, New York. By permission of National Museum, Copenhagen, Denmark. Photo courtesy of Weidenfeld and Nicolson Limited, London.)

Figure 34.5. Image of the god of war made from pine wood, with penis as a corkscrew dagger. Zuni Pueblo, Arizona, 19th century. (Reprinted from the book *Primitive Erotic Art*, published by G.P. Putnam's Sons, New York. By permission of National Museum of Natural History, Paris, France. Photo courtesy of Weidenfeld and Nicolson Limited, London.)

do uncircumcised males. No clinical distinctions can be noted in the two groups.

THE MALE ORGASM

The physiology of the male orgasm was briefly described in the preceding chapter. We should repeat at this point that a preorgastic secretory emission occurs in the male. It is mucoid in character and usually totals no more than two or three drops which escape involuntarily from the urethral opening. Occasionally, a rather considerable amount is secreted and has been mistaken for an ejaculation by the involved partners and the physician they consult. I know of one case in which the amount equaled that of the ejaculate which followed. The distinction could be made by the fact that no resolution phase took place after the outpouring of the fluid. The penis maintained its plateau phase size and the man had no subjective orgastic response. It is important to know about the possibility of a preejaculatory fluid, since this substance may contain motile sperm. This is one of the reasons why the coitus interruptus technique for contraception should not be recommended.

A few seconds before ejaculation, the man experiences a sense of *ejaculatory inevitability.* This feeling develops as the seminal fluid collects in the prostatic urethra. Ejaculation cannot be delayed once this feeling of inevitability is passed. This is an important point in terms of treating an individual for premature ejaculation. Another myth is that men who ejaculate prematurely are usually "passionate." Actually, they are quite anxious and not in control of their ejaculation. A man suffering from this symptom must learn to recognize the point of ejaculatory inevitability and stop before it has been passed. He may then start again. This technique is the basis for most brief treatment approaches for premature ejaculation. The contractile phase of orgasm sets in immediately after the premonitory response. Rhythmic recurrent contractions are noted in the urethral sphincter and in the group of superficial and deep perineal muscles. These contractions are accompanied by powerful subjective feelings of pleasure which may vary in intensity throughout the expulsive phase. They also vary in intensity from time to time. Pleasure is also related to the volume of the ejaculate. A larger volume is experienced as more pleasurable than is a lower volume. Second and third orgasms with ejaculation are experienced as less satisfying than is the first response. This may be related to the decrease in the volume of the ejaculate.

MASTURBATION IN MEN

Masturbation has been viewed as an evil ever since the biblical injunction against its practice was set down in the Old Testament. Volumes have been written about its deleterious effects and the practice has been viewed as causing impotence, insanity, and many other ills, both mental and physical. None of this is true. Genital manipulation of the sexual organs begins in earliest infancy and is continued by both sexes throughout their early years or until satisfactory relationships are established with the opposite sex. Masturbatory patterns are established after the onset of puberty. Present day estimates indicate that over 90% of males masturbate at some time or another, and the actual incidence may be even higher. In fact, a history in a young man of complete avoidance of masturbation may well reflect some serious underlying emotional disturbance.

It is worth noting that men as well as women develop individual techniques for masturbating. This is so despite the fact that a much higher percentage of boys than girls indulge in group masturbation and they can, in this way, observe the techniques others use. Group masturbation was uncommon for girls in the past. It seems more common now. Thus, the less frequent masturbation previously noted among women may be cultural rather than biological. Some males use very light touch on the ventral surface of the penis. Some prefer strong grasping and stroking movements, a practice which others find objectionable. Other men stimulate the glans alone. There are also men who will not use their hands but prefer to rub their penis against a convenient object. These preferences bear no relationship to whether or not a man is circumcised. Many men report that the glans becomes quite sensitive to any pressure or confinement immediately following ejaculation. It should be noted that women also report similar sensitivity of the clitoral head.

In the main, most males center their fears about masturbation on the ejaculatory phase and not on manipulation. Many men fear that too frequent ejaculation leads to a loss of physical strength. Athletic coaches and trainers, for example, forbid intercourse to athletes and prevent wives from being at training camps. According to this myth, women deplete men of their strength. Presumably it is the loss of semen that is responsible for this depletion. There is no evidence to support this idea. In fact, the absence of women may place the athlete on edge and make him more irritable rather than more relaxed. Perhaps being irritable may be useful

in a prizefighter. Normally, however, it is contentment that we seek, and contentment and calm are conducive to good physical and mental health. Frequent intercourse is in no way injurious, and neither is frequent masturbation.

GERIATRIC SEXUALITY

The timelessness of the sexual drive has been demonstrated again and again in old people of both sexes. There is, however, a cultural bias against the expression of sexual desires in older people. This prejudice has been so powerful that many who are over 60 are overwhelmed with shame and guilt about their sexual wishes and activities. There are even people in their fifties who feel that they should have passed beyond sexual desire. This attitude toward sex is no more than a continuation of the earlier attitudes so prominent in the church in previous centuries. Yet, the striking fact that has emerged from all studies of sex in old age is that the sexual behavior of people in their advanced years correlates strongly with their earlier sexual behavior. Those who were active and successful in their youth continue their activity into their seventies and some into their eighties and nineties. Good health is, of course, an important factor but not necessarily so, since an active sex life has been conducted by people with advanced chronic illnesses. Older people should be encouraged toward active sexual expression. It is healthy and rewarding.

Suggested Readings

American Medical Association Committee on Human Sexuality. *Human Sexuality*, Chicago, American Medical Association, 1972.
Lief HI (ed): *Medical Aspects of Human Sexuality*. Baltimore, Williams & Wilkins, 1975.

References

Glenn J, Kaplan EH: Types of orgasm in women: a critical review and redefinition. *J Am Psychoanal Assoc* 16:549, 1968.
Masters WH, Johnson VE: *Human Sexual Response*. Boston, Little, Brown and Co, 1966.
Masters WH, Johnson VE: *Human Sexual Inadequacy*. Boston, Little, Brown and Co, 1970.
McCary JL: *Sexual Myths and Fallacies*. New York, Van Nostrand Reinhold, 1971.
Sherfey MJ: The evolution and nature of female sexuality in relation to psychoanalytic theory. *J Am Psychoanal Assoc* 14:28, 1966.

CHAPTER 35 Sexuality in General Medical Practice

Robert Dickes, M.D. and
John L. Fleming, M.D.

Human sexuality is affected by a large number of factors and concerns, all of which are the province of the physician. The previous chapter has focused on the important education which the physician can provide in regard to the sexual myths and misinformation of patients. The following chapter will focus on the role which physicians can play in the treatment of their patients' sexual dysfunctions. The purpose of this chapter is to review other issues of adult sexuality which concern patients and which will not be covered elsewhere in this book. In this chapter, the term "sexuality" refers to more than the mechanics of the sexual act. It includes the tender and affectionate feelings between the couple, as well as other aspects of their relationship which may be affected by their sexuality.

THE ATTITUDES OF PHYSICIANS TOWARD SEXUALITY

Almost any medical or surgical problem brought to a physician can unfavorably affect sexual behavior. Furthermore, many sexual problems may masquerade as medical problems. Headaches, backaches, fatigue, or other physical symptoms may consciously or unconsciously represent ways to avoid sex. Most patients will not talk to a doctor about sexual problems if the doctor does not seem interested or gives the clear message that he is or she is uncomfortable talking about sex. Most often these messages are unintended and are outside the physician's awareness. Physicians will often take exhaustively detailed histories of each body system and its functions and yet not ask any questions about sexual function. If a sexual problem is brought up, some physicians may become embarrassed and change the subject. Some physicians even avoid examining the genitalia during the regular "physical" and may therefore miss serious pathology. The physician who communicates a critical, judgmental attitude toward sex that closes off all further discussion may also damage his or her patient psychologically. Burnap and Golden interviewed a group of physicians about the sexual problems of their patients and how these problems were handled. They reported that physicians who asked routinely and naturally about sexuality found definite sexual problems in approximately 14% of their patients. (This percentage would be higher in patients with selected illnesses.) Physicians who took a sexual history only when it seemed indicated found sexual problems in about 8% of their patients. Those physicians who felt uncomfortable asking about sexual matters found sexual problems in only 2% to 3% of their patients.

There are many reasons why a physician may fail to inquire about a sexual problem. First, the physician may need to deny the existence of a sexual problem of his or her own. Second, the physician may not feel that a sexual problem can be treated once identified. Third, physicians may be concerned that their patients might consider a sexual history as immoral or unethical. Fourth, as already discussed earlier in the book by Dr. Franks, physicians may be afraid of the sexual feelings which patients may develop toward them; and fifth, they may be afraid of the sexual feelings which they themselves may in turn develop toward their patients. None of these concerns can realistically justify the avoidance of the sexual history.

The reluctance to deal with sexual problems is also exemplified by the failure, until very recently, of most medical schools to provide adequate education about human sexuality. It was not until 1969 that the American Medical Association finally endorsed formal teaching of human sexuality as part of a core curriculum, and stated that it should be continuous throughout the entire four years of medical school. Despite these pronouncements, resistance to sexual education remains, and medical school curriculum committees are often reluctant to assign required hours of instruction in sexual matters in contrast to elective hours. By 1973, all but five of the medical schools contacted by Lief and Karlen had programs on human sexuality. But these programs and the faculty involved in them varied greatly in terms of quality. Only 68% of the schools listed a course on human sexual behavior as a required course. The median number of hours offered throughout the four years in all medical schools was only 21, surely an insufficient amount of time for the creation of the group of knowledgeable physicians the public needs.

It is important that all physicians not only learn about human sexuality and the available methods of treatment for the sexual dysfunctions, but also are comfortable and tolerant of other people's sexual attitudes and behavior. Patients have a right to expect their physicians to know about sexuality and to be able to counsel them wisely. Not only are sexual problems far more common than is generally recognized, but as we noted, sexual conflicts and fears can manifest themselves in a multitude of physical symptoms, and medical illness can in turn evoke a great many sexual concerns and difficulties. Sexuality is important and must not be overlooked.

TAKING A SEXUAL HISTORY

There are a variety of strategies that can be helpful in taking a sexual history. Many physicians find that they and their patients are most comfortable if the physician sets the stage, and while questioning the patient about the various systems for clues to illness, lets the patient know that there will also be an inquiry about sexual matters. This must be done with both tact and firmness. One can start with a statement such as: "Many people have some concerns or questions about their bodies and their sexual functioning which they have not had a chance to ask a doctor about. What questions have you had along these lines?" If there are problems, follow-up questions then proceed naturally from this initial introductory approach. If the patient fails

to respond, it is the doctor's responsibility to gently question the patient. This kind of introduction goes a long way towards reassuring patients that it is appropriate to raise whatever questions they may have. Even if there are no questions, the patient is unlikely to feel intruded upon and will recall in the future the interest of the physician if sexual problems do arise.

Some physicians prefer to ask questions about current functioning first and then proceed to more remote times. "Are you currently satisfied with your sexual life?" Such a question can be followed by questions about interest, function, frequency, number and types of partners, and recent changes. Other physicians prefer to ask questions along developmental lines. They start the inquiry with questions about childhood sexual interests and sexual play, sex education experiences at home and in school, age of menarche or first ejaculation, reactions to these events and other bodily changes of puberty, same-sex behavior and experimentation in childhood and adolescence, and masturbation. With this as background, they then ask about current sexual functioning and satisfaction. No matter what method is followed, it is often helpful for the physician to indicate the universal nature of many sexual experiences such as masturbation. It is also important for the physician to close by asking if the patient has any other sexual concerns which may not have been discussed. This leaves the way open for the patient to bring up further questions or problems at any time in the future. Though this summary has been brief, more detailed discussions of questions to ask and possible phrasings of them in taking a sexual history are available in the suggested readings at the end of the chapter.

SEXUALITY AND MEDICAL ILLNESS

Acute Illness

Any acute illness accompanied by fever, pain, toxicity, or debility can cause a diminution in sexual interest and performance. Most patients understand the situation, and when the acute episode is transient, they cope well. They have much more difficulty with longer-term illness. Acute cardiovascular episodes are much greater psychological hazards because of their life-threatening potential. Many people still believe that exercise is dangerous and especially sexual exercise. Present-day knowledge indicates that the reverse is true.

Cardiovascular Disease

The heart and the blood vessels are assumed in the mind of the public to be among the great offenders which interfere with sexual functioning. Many people believe that myocardial infarction will prevent normal sexual functioning following convalescence. This is related to the myth that intercourse per se is taxing and dangerous to the heart. The risk, however, is in no way different than that of exercise such as climbing one flight of stairs. The physician must reassure the patient who is capable of such exercise that he or she is also capable of intercourse. Just as proper exercise is beneficial to the heart, so is sexual activity and intercourse.

Convalescence at home and before returning to work places the patient and spouse in much more contact. This proximity can activate sexual wishes and cause anxiety since such patients often believe in the danger of sexual activity to the heart. These patients usually have little understanding of anatomy and physiology. The physician must, therefore, carefully explain what has happened and describe the healed state of the heart. The spouse must also be instructed and encouraged, because the spouse will usually be just as convinced as the patient, if not more so, of the dangers of both exercise and intercourse. In many ways the spouse is the key figure in postinfarction recovery. Several studies have shown that two-thirds of both male and female postmyocardial infarction patients report marked dissatisfaction with their sexual lives, including decreased coital frequency. Most of these changes appear to be based on faulty assumptions by the patients that sexual activities are unsafe, and therefore to be avoided.

The psychological treatment of sexual problems caused by other cardiovascular difficulties such as emboli, peripheral vascular problems, and cerebral hemorrhage or occlusion is based on the same principles. These patients need corrective information and reassurance, and they need physicians who understand the causes of their anxiety and know how to address their patients' concerns in clear and specific ways. Almost all victims of cardiovascular injuries recover sufficiently to engage in a full range of sexual activity. This must be pointed out to the patient, and full activity should be encouraged as soon as practical. Otherwise there may be a disruption of a previously well-functioning marriage.

Endocrine and Metabolic Disorders

Many glandular disorders impair sexual function. Those affecting erectile functioning include acromegaly, hypopituitarism, hypogonadism, pituitary basophilism (Cushing's syndrome), and hyperprolactinemia. Addison's disease in its later stages and hormonal deficiencies based on various chromosomal abnormalities also adversely affect sexual function in both men and women. Spark and colleagues have reported a study in which serum testosterone levels were obtained on 105 consecutive patients with erectile dysfunction. Thirty-seven of these patients (35%) were found to have previously unsuspected disorders of the hypothalamic-pituitary-gonadal axis. Because of these many medical illnesses which may cause sexual difficulties, it should be a rule that any patient who reports a change in previously successful sexual functioning must have a thorough investigation for organic disease prior to instituting any psychological treatment.

Diabetes mellitus is an example of a chronic metabolic illness involving cardiovascular and neurological lesions which affect potency in males. The inability to obtain an erection is, rarely, the first complaint the patient notes. But about 50% of all male diabetics and nearly 90% of male diabetics with any diabetic peripheral neuropathy report erectile dysfunction eventually.

Women suffering from diabetes are less vulnerable to loss of function. Some report eventual loss of orgasmic pleasure and, related to this, show less interest in sexual activity. However, women can still help a partner reach climax during normal genital union. Partners who care for one another can find this very rewarding. Furthermore, in one study by Ellenberg, approximately 80% of diabetic women report no change whatsoever in their sexual functioning even when diabetic neuropathy was present. This is another example of the fact that the sexual function of men is generally more vulnerable to disruption than that of women.

Chronic Illness

Many chronic progressive illnesses produce progressive sexual dysfunction. These include multiple sclerosis, emphysema, uremia as the end result of renal damage, Hodgkins disease, Parkinsonism, sickle cell anemia, atherosclerosis of the small penile vessels, and many other debilitating conditions. Crippling diseases such as rheumatoid arthritis are associated with sexual dysfunction, as are lesions of the central nervous system and spinal cord, such as the various paraplegias. All produce their own particular types of difficulty, as do the various surgical procedures previously discussed in the chapter on the "difficult" surgical patient. Peyronnie's disease may cause erectile dysfunction in men, and vaginismus and dyspareunia in women may be caused by vaginal infections, pelvic inflammatory disease, endometriosis, or episiotomy scars. It is necessary in each case to assess the degree of organic contribution to the sexual problem. Consultations with experienced experts may well be indicated. The needs of both partners must also be assessed. Only following such a careful approach can appropriate therapeutic interventions be instituted. The human ability to adapt is, in these instances, of great advantage. The importance of penile entry and genital union needs to be addressed in those instances in which erections are unobtainable, so as to allow the couple to enjoy sexual pleasure, however achieved. A good relationship will facilitate the necessary modifications of their usual sexual conduct and allow a couple much enjoyment. However, the shift in focus in the marriage induced by the illness and sexual dysfunction is at times so great as to create major difficulties in a previously satisfactory marriage.

Iatrogenic Illness

The physician may not only enhance an existing sexual dysfunction but may even induce one. A doctor's prudery and disapproval concerning any sexual practice can adversely influence the patient. The so-called "missionary" position in intercourse is the only morally permissible one in the minds of some physicians. Other doctors condemn any type of masturbatory activity. They also object to oral sex and other behaviors. These physicians are unable to help their patients. In many instances, their attitudes add to people's sexual tensions and difficulties. Such physicians, hopefully, will be aware of their attitudes and refer patients in a nonjudgmental way to qualified experts.

SEXUALITY AND DRUGS

The search for suitable aphrodisiacs has been apparent for generations but, to date, no such drug has been found. Among the drugs which have been praised as aphrodisiacs are alcohol, marijuana and its active principle tetrahydrocannabinol (THC), as well as the hallucinogenic LSD. Amphetamines and others have also been mentioned. However, Shakespeare's comment on alcohol, that it provokes the desire but takes away the performance, remains correct. Acute intoxication as well as chronic alcoholism are known to produce sexual dysfunction in both men and women. Morphine, heroin, methaqualone, barbiturates, and amphetamines are all known to adversely affect sexual behavior.

Special mention must be made of THC (tetrahydrocannabinol, which is the active ingredient in marijuana), LSD, and Cantharides. These substances have often been touted as aphrodisiacs. LSD is a much stronger hallucinogen than marijuana and is known to produce profound alterations in both the state of consciousness and the perceptual experience. The LSD user reports that his or her visual imagery is enhanced, sometimes strongly, and that there is a "crowding in" of numerous thoughts which are unrelated to one another or to the ongoing sexual process. Therefore, the actual sexual pleasure response may not be increased even though the user reports it as "unusual and exciting." The LSD user also reports that at times he or she notes a very marked detachment from the sexual experience and from the sexual partner. This is hardly conducive to the close interpersonal relationship sexual union is supposed to achieve. Most people believe that the purely sexual response is enhanced by emotional closeness and the satisfactions engendered by loving. Furthermore, the response to LSD is extremely varied and the individual user cannot foretell the effect of the next dose. "Bad trips" are well known. People with severe emotional disorders are much more prone to respond unfavorably to such drugs, and they are often the very people who feel they need LSD in order to function better sexually. Therefore, LSD leaves much to be desired as an aphrodisiac. The same comments would also apply to cocaine, when the "high" is often followed by a "low" that involves depression, apathy, and loss of sexual desire.

Marijuana is also widely used. The controversy concerning the long-term effects of this drug continues. There are those who believe that sexual responsiveness is enhanced by the drug and that orgasm is improved. This may be related to reports that the drug has the effect of enhancing muscle contraction and that an increased awareness of muscle contraction accompanies the muscle response. These reports require verification. As yet, many of the reported subjective responses are anecdotal. The truth awaits scientific verification. The normal individual is likely to do very well sexually without the use of special drugs.

Cantharides or Spanish fly has long been accepted as an aphrodisiac. It is actually a toxic drug which causes irritation of the urethra and bladder, and this irritation is thought to increase sexual drive. The *priapism* (a more or less persistent erection) which can result is due to the toxic irritation and is not related to sexual drive. It is a very dangerous drug and has been known to cause permanent damage to the penis and even death.

Most medications have little or no effect upon sexual desire or function. A few, however, may cause either erectile or ejaculatory failure, or both. These medications include the tricyclics and MAO inhibitors used in the treatment of depression, thioridazine (Mellaril) and haloperidol (Haldol) used in the treatment of schizophrenia, and virtually any of the antihypertensive drugs. Cimetidine, digoxin, propranolol, narcotics, and anti-neoplastic drugs also impact on erectile capacity and sexual desire. If the physician does not inquire about the possible effects of these drugs on erection and ejaculation, still another "iatrogenic illness" may be produced.

There are few reports concerning the woman's sexual response to these drugs. Women generally seem less vulnerable to these pharmacological agents. Their response pattern, contrary to the male's, is less obvious and therefore researchers may have overlooked their vulnerability. There also may be reluctance on the part of women to discuss their difficulties or on the part of physicians to ask women about their difficulties. Much research remains to be done so as to increase our knowledge of the female sexual response pattern to various pharmacological agents.

BIRTH CONTROL

For many physicians, their knowledge about birth control methods has been limited to the purely mechanical and pharmacological aspects of the various methods. This factual knowledge base is essential but is not in itself complete (Table 35.1). Choice about which contraceptives to use are affected by factors related to how the birth control method may affect a couple's sexuality. Intercourse-dependent methods such as foam and condom usually require a pause in the lovemaking to insert or apply the device, a pause which can in some people interfere with the increasing sexual excitement and be emotionally distancing. This interruption in the lovemaking tends for some people to establish a biphasic lovemaking—a fun time and then a serious time. Once the device is in place effort is to be concentrated on performance, meaning entry and orgasm. Only "serious" actions may be permitted following the use of the contraceptive device. It is these aspects of the intercourse-dependent devices which may trouble the couple. Partner cooperation can sometimes heal the breach—the woman can put the condom on the man as part of stimulation, or the man can help to insert the foam. A diaphragm may be inserted in advance of intercourse, although many women fail to do this.

The intercourse-independent methods such as the pill, IUD, vasectomy, and tubal ligation do not interrupt the act of lovemaking and would seem to avoid many of the above emotional pitfalls. However, other potential problems are encountered. The use of the surgical methods requires a permanent shift in a person's self-image, which normally includes an awareness of sexuality and the ability to be fertile. This ability to be fertile is lost in the operative procedures. Some individuals cannot tolerate this even though they may consciously seek the operation. Careful presurgical evaluation of the patient is needed.

Much of our society tends to view sex for procreation as permissible, whereas sexual expression for recreation is much less acceptable. Besides this dilemma, there are other worries. These intercourse-independent methods create an ongoing permanent or semipermanent change in one's body—either in its hormonal or physical state. There are realistic concerns about taking these kinds of steps. The long-term effects of the pill, for example, are as yet unknown. In spite of such concerns, most patients are able to use the method of their choice effectively, especially if they can be encouraged to discuss these concerns with their physicians.

SPECIAL SITUATIONS

Rape

The crime of rape has profound effects on a woman's social, psychological, and physical adjustment. Most physicians are not aware of its

Table 35.1

Comparisons of Birth Control Methods

Control Method	Male	Female	Coitus-dependent	Coitus-independent	Temporary	Permanent	Behavioral	Nonbehavioral	Mechanical	Chemical	Vaginal	Nonvaginal	Effectiveness Index (Composite of Pearl Index and Life Table data)
Abstinence	X	X	X		X		X						0
Condom	X		X		X			X	X		X		2–5
Diaphragm		X	X		X			X	X		X		5–12
Foam, jelly, film		X	X		X			X		X	X		3–10
Suppository		X	X		X			X		X	X		2–5
Breast feeding		X		X	X		X					X	Avg. of 6 mos. amenorrhea
Tubal ligation		X		X		X		X	X		↖	X	.01–.5
Vasectomy	X			X		X		X	X			X	.01–.5
Hysterectomy		X		X		X		X	X			X	0
Pill		X		X	X			X		X		X	0–4
Withdrawal	X		X		X		X						No data (>20?)
Douching		X	X		X		X				X		30–40
Rhythm		X		X	X		X					X	20–40
Injectables and implants	X	X		X	X			X		X		X	.01–1
Sexual behavior technique	X	X	X		X		X					X	No data (<5?)
Intrauterine device		X		X	X			X	X			X	1–5
No birth control													65–80

Results depend on the particular method and proper use. The majority of failures are due to the user, not the method. Figures cited are estimates derived from various studies. They are of greater use for relative rather than for absolute comparisons.

* From Diamond, M. in *Human Sexuality: A Health Practitioner's Text*, edited by R. Green, ed. 2, p. 70. Williams & Wilkins, Baltimore, 1979, by permission.

devastating impact on women's health or its increasingly frequent occurrence. To cite statistics from only one large urban center, New Orleans, the current number of rapes is such that one woman in 20 is at risk of being raped *each year* in that city. This is a health problem of grave magnitude and warrants discussion.

How do rape victims react? Ann Burgess and Lynda Holmstrom have worked extensively with patients at the rape crisis unit of Boston City Hospital. Together they have identified the *rape trauma syndrome* which consists of both an acute phase and a longer-term phase of reorganization following a forcible rape or its attempt. The syndrome can be understood as a *post-traumatic stress disorder*, and consists of behavioral, psychological, and somatic reactions. In the acute phase, physical symptoms predominate. These include symptoms from actual physical trauma, such as bruises, as well as symptoms from skeletal muscle tension, e.g., tension headaches, gastrointestinal complaints, and genitourinary tract symptoms. Emotional reactions

are also present in this acute phase, including fears of death and of being harmed, humiliation, anger, a wish for revenge, shame, guilt, and often irrational self-blame. Roughly half of the victims express these feelings openly, but the other half, whom the authors have labeled "controlled," do not outwardly show these feelings though they internally struggle with them.

After several weeks, the woman enters a reorganization phase during which the initial disorganization is restructured. This is an active phase which is not merely a forgetting. Nightmares, especially ones of being trapped or helpless, emerge as do other sleep disturbances. Phobias are common, especially fears of being alone, or being out of doors (if the rape occurred there) or indoors (if that was the setting for the rape). Fears of crowds, strangers, and people behind them also are commonly seen. Physical moves, such as changing living situations, occur in half the patients. Six out of 10 victims experience major disruptions in preexisting romantic relationships, with many of these relationships ending. Over 80% of the victims experience adverse reactions in their sexual lives; nearly 40% become totally sexually abstinent for some months. These alarming consequences are mild compared to those experienced by the one in five victims who suffer overtly maladaptive adjustments to their rape—as defined by the emergence of severe alcohol or drug abuse or overt suicide attempts. Four to six year follow-up studies show slightly over one in four women victims still do not feel "back to normal," and of those who do feel back to normal, half required years, and not months, to achieve this result.

Many women and women authors have pointed out that the recovery from rape is not helped by the victim's experience at the hospital, assuming she even reaches it. Some understanding of the seriousness of what the victim has been through is necessary. Rape is not a sexual crime, but a crime of violence. Perhaps a clearer statement is that rape is not primarily an expression of intense erotic feelings but rather is an act of hatred that involves a sexual activity. Fundamentally, most rapists are lashing out violently in an attempt to shore up their own self-esteem, to feel powerful by humiliating someone else, the victim. The effect on the victim is devastating. Too often, her experience at the hospital is only a further assault against her own shaken sense of self-control. She is a coerced "patient." She is only at the hospital because of the rape, and thus hospital care, too, is forced on her by the rapist. Unless she chooses to ignore the risk of physical damage, pregnancy, and venereal disease, she must go to the hospital. The routine there involves further violations of her body: venipunctures, IV lines, pelvic exams, intramuscular penicillin, commands to produce urine, long delays for the examining resident to appear, perhaps exposure half nude in the lithotomy position, and little privacy as police and others stand about outside the flimsy cloth screens. These further violations of the victim's human dignity cannot and should not be tolerated. They are a second rape.

How do health care providers react to rape victims? Most are outwardly polite and professional but rarely address the enormity of the patient's emotional needs. There are several reasons for this. First, they are busy with the problems of repairing the victim's lacerations, collecting medico-legal evidence, attending to prevention of pregnancy and venereal disease, and assigning follow-up care appointments. Second, the physician may unconsciously blame the victim for the assault and, as we have seen, self-blame is one of the features of the acute reaction of many victims. This tendency to blame the victim is, in most cases, a form of denial. It serves to minimize the overwhelming sense of helplessness and powerlessness that the victim has experienced. It is easier for all concerned to rationalize this away by assigning blame somewhere, even to the victim, than to become truly aware of how helpless we all potentially are to crimes of violence. A third reason for avoiding contact with the patient can be the fear of becoming too entangled in the patient's problems—legal, as well as emotional.

For all of these reasons, rape crisis teams are proving to be the most effective method of dealing with the rape victim's complex needs. These teams, usually composed of women staff and volunteers, are on call 24 hours a day to be with victims throughout their wait in the hospital emergency room, the exams, the police interviews, and the follow-up appointments. Team home phone numbers are given to victims with assurance of complete availability. The difference in patient care, from both an emotional and physical standpoint, can be dramatic. In one Albuquerque hospital, only 8% of rape victims returned for follow-up appointments for repeat venereal disease and pregnancy checks when the standard emergency room routine was followed. Eighty-six per cent of patients returned when a rape crisis unit began operation, and of those returning, nearly 90% did in fact have complications requiring further treatment—problems which apparently went unrecognized before. The major role of the rape crisis team is to provide crisis-oriented psychotherapy to begin the emotional healing process. Some patients may well require referral for further psychotherapy on a longer-term basis. With this special effort and, in many cases, special programs, rape victims can be helped to resume in time a full participation in their sexual, social, and psychological lives.

Sexuality in the Hospital

Many people think that hospitalization, as distinct from the illness leading to the hospitalization, is enough to repress a patient's thoughts and feelings about sex. In some cases, patients are too ill to be interested in sexual activity per se, yet important aspects of their self-esteem may still be dependent upon their feeling sexually attractive. The postmyocardial infarction patient worried about his sexual capability, the surgical patient with facial or breast modification, the patient with a new colostomy or ileostomy or ureterostomy, all are examples in point. These patients often develop an emotional crisis about their self-worth, which will include sexual worth as well. The reactions of spouses, family, friends, ward staff, and other patients are quite important. For such a patient, the opportunity for masturbation in private may be essential for reestablishing an internal sense of self-worth. For others, the opportunity for a private conjugal visit may be necessary for both the patient's and the spouse's self-esteem. Most hospital settings are not physically geared for patients' sexual needs. It is also true that ward staff, including physicians and nurses, are not emotionally geared for such patient needs and often either ignore or condemn them. There are exceptions. On one renal transplant ward where long convalescent stays are common, a change in nursing policy permitted spouses to spend the night with patients who were healthy enough to tolerate sexual activity. These patients and spouses became noticeably less depressed. Sexual intercourse may not have occurred in all instances, but a marital and human interchange did.

Occasionally, staff members will discover patients involved in sexual activity. The reaction of the observer is rarely based upon a true assessment of the act as related to the patient's actual physical situation and psychological needs. In fact, the usual reaction is condemnatory and hostile. For example, a nurse disturbed a young man masturbating behind the closed door of his private bathroom. She had entered without knocking. She became extremely hostile and demanded his immediate dismissal. She said she was not being paid to take care of such obnoxious young men. The patient, who had been hospitalized for 4 months, was totally dependent on the hospital life support systems for pulmonary function. He was only attending to necessary needs. The nurse should have knocked before entering. But having done what she did, she should have apologized and withdrawn gracefully. We all understand patients' needs to eat, sleep, and excrete. It is time we recognized that patients also have sexual needs.

The recognition of these sexual needs does occur in some hospitals. At one large institution, patients were noticed walking to the visitors' parking lot where camping vehicles could be parked and an opportunity for private sexual expression was thus available. On one occasion, a patient in hospital gown, IV intact, emerged from the door of a recently bouncing camper and strode back into the hospital, more secure with himself and his relationship with his wife. There was much discussion about what to do among staff members. It was finally recognized that such compelling needs are better off gratified than frustrated. No physical harm came to these patients, and much psychological and physical relief was obtained. Among the worries patients often have concerning a long hospitalization is that a sexually frustrated spouse will seek gratification elsewhere. Relief of such worries can only be beneficial. This is not to state that patients who are in an extremely precarious physical condition should be encouraged to engage in sexual activity. In fact, most such patients are not interested. Staff attitudes ought to be based on a clear and accurate assessment of the genuine physical risks involved, if any, and not on a misguided or hostile moral stand which denies needs which are universally important. We need to reassess many of our attitudes toward hospitalized patients.

For example, in her book, *Heart Sounds*, Martha Lear pointed out that it was only when her physician-husband was a patient that he became appalled, not only at how house staff treated patients, but how he himself had behaved as a physician. He never knew how badly staff treated patients, since the patients rarely complained about how they were infantilized or patronized. Patients were given orders, and they and their caretakers expected them to obey. "It was as though, by the simple act of signing in, patients forfeited the right to be treated with respect," says Lear. She described one incident in which two men burst into Dr. Lear's room, one yelling at him and demanding why he had done something or other and accusing him of being a troublemaker. Dr Lear, not knowing who the man was, asked him to identify himself. The man turned out to be the medical resident, and it soon became apparent that this resident was in the wrong room. He and his partner left, evidently without apologizing. We will not include other incidents from the book. However, we wish to note Martha Lear's observation that the only other place where people may break into rooms without permission is in a prison. This incident did not involve sexual activity, but it does reveal the insensitivity which many hospital staff continuously show in regard to patients' needs for privacy, respect, and consideration. How much more true this is for sexual needs!

CONCLUSION

The physician in a general medical practice is frequently confronted with the sexual concerns of his or her patients, even when their presenting problems are not primarily sexual in nature. An awareness that human sexuality is the final common pathway of a multitude of biopsychosocial forces can alert the physician to potential problems. With a healthy curiosity, a genuine concern, an adequate history taking procedure, and a knowledge of some common sources of difficulty, the physician can effectively learn to deal with and treat a very common source of human discomfort, so that it can be restored to a universal source of human pleasure (Figure 35.1).

"I love the idea of there being two sexes, don't you".

Figure 35.1. Copyright © 1940 James Thurber. Copyright © 1971 Helen W. Thurber and Rosemary T. Sauers. From *Men, Women and Dogs,* published by Harcourt Brace Jovanovich. Originally printed in *The New Yorker.*

Suggested Readings

Dickes R: Medicine, surgery, and sexual dysfunction. Grinspoon L (ed): In *Psychiatry 1982: Annual Review.* Washington, American Psychiatric Press, 1982, p 35.

Green R (ed): *Human Sexuality: A Health Practitioner's Text,* ed 2. Baltimore, Williams & Wilkins, 1979.

Group for the Advancement of Psychiatry. *Assessment of Sexual Function: A Guide to Interviewing.* Report No. 88. New York, Group for the Advancement of Psychiatry, 1973.

Hilberman E: *The Rape Victim.* New York, Basic Books, 1976.

Holmstrom LL, Burgess AW: *The Victim of Rape: Institutional Reactions.* New York, John Wiley & Sons, 1978.

Kaplan HS: The effects of illness on sexuality. In *The New Sex Therapy.* New York, Brunner/Mazel, 1974, p 75.

Kaplan HS: The effects of drugs on sexuality. In *The New Sex Therapy.* New York, Brunner/Mazel, 1974, p 86.

Lear MW: *Heart Sounds.* New York, Simon & Schuster, 1980.

Lief HI (ed): *Sexual Problems in Medical Practice.* Monroe, WI, American Medical Association, 1981.

Lief HI, Karlen A: *Sex Education in Medicine.* New York, Spectrum Publications, Division of John Wiley & Sons, 1976.

References

Abramov LA: Sexual life and sexual frigidity among women developing acute myocardial infarction. *Psychosom Med* 38:418, 1976.

Brownmiller S: *Against Our Will: Men, Women and Rape.* New York, Simon & Schuster, 1975.

Buffum J, et al: Drugs and sexual function. In Lief HI (ed): *Sexual Problems in Medical Practice.* Monroe, WI, American Medical Association, 1981, p 211.

Burgess AW, Holmstrom LL: Rape trauma syndrome. *Am J Psychiatry* 131:981, 1974.

Burgess AW, Holmstrom LL: Adaptive strategies and recovery from rape. *Am J Psychiatry* 136:1278, 1979.

Burnap DW, Golden JS: Sexual problems in medical practice. *J Med Educ* 42:673, 1967.

Cole TM: Sexuality and physical disabilities. *Arch Sex Behav* 4:389, 1975.

Cole TM: Sexuality and the spinal cord injured. In Green R (ed): *Human Sexuality: A Health Practitioner's Text,* ed. 2. Baltimore, Williams & Wilkins, 1979, p 242.

Comarr AE: Sex among patients with spinal cord and/or cauda equina injuries. *Med Asp Hum Sex* 7:222, 1973.

Currey HLF: Osteoarthrosis of the hip joint and sexual activity. *Ann Rheum Dis* 29:488, 1970.

Diamond M: Sex and reproduction: conception and contraception. In Green R (ed): *Human Sexuality: A Health Practitioner's Text,* ed. 2. Baltimore, Williams & Wilkins, 1979, p. 58.

Dickes R: The new sexuality: impact on psychiatric education. In Karasu TB, Socarides CW (eds): *On Sexuality: Psychoanalytic Observations.* New York, International Universities Press, 1979, p 243.

Ellenberg M: Impotence in diabetes: the neurologic factor. *Ann Int Med* 75:213, 1971.

Ellenberg M: Sexual aspects of the female diabetic. *Mount Sinai J Med* 44:495, 1977.

Felice M, et al: Follow-up observations of adolescent rape victims. *Clin Pediatr* 17:311, 1978.

Green AW: Sexual activity and the postmyocardial infarction patient. *Am Heart J* 89:246, 1975.

Green R: Taking a sexual history. In Green R (ed): *Human Sexuality: A Health Practitioner's Text,* ed. 2. Baltimore, Williams & Wilkins, 1979, p 22.

Hilberman E: The impact of rape. In Notman MT, Nadelson CC (eds): *The Woman Patient. Vol. 1: Sexual and Reproductive Aspects of Women's Health Care.* New York, Plenum Press, 1978, p 303.

Jackson RW: Sexual rehabilitation after cord injury. *Paraplegia* 10:50, 1972.

Johnson WE: The handicapped: recreational sex and procreational responsibility. In Money J, Musaph H (eds): *Handbook of Sexology.* Amsterdam, Elsevier/North Holland Biomedical Press, 1977, p 933.

Karacan I, et al: Nocturnal penile tumescence and diagnoses in diabetic impotence. *Am J Psychiatry* 135:191, 1978.

Kaufman A, et al: Follow-up of rape victims in a family practice setting. *South Med J* 69:1569, 1976.

Lief HI: Sex education of the physician. In Fink PJ, Van Beuren O, Hammett FA (eds): *Human Sexual Function and Dysfunction.* Philadelphia, Davis, 1969.

Martin LM: Impotence in diabetes: an overview. *Psychosomatics* 22:318, 1981.

Pauly IB, Goldstein SG: Physicians' perception of their education in human sexuality. *J Med Educ* 45:745, 1970.

Rada RT: Commonly asked questions about the rapist. *Med Asp Hum Sex* 11:47, 1977.

Reich P: A historical understanding of contraception. In Notman MT, Nadelson CC (eds): *The Woman Patient. Vol. 1.* New York, Plenum Press, 1978, p 161.

Schiavi RC: Sexuality and medical illness: specific reference to diabetes mellitus. In Green R (ed): *Human Sexuality: A Health Practitioner's Text,* ed 2. Baltimore, Williams & Wilkins, 1979, p 202.

Segraves RT: Pharmacological agents causing sexual dysfunction. *J Sex Marital Ther* 3:157, 1977.

Soloff LA: Sexual activity in the heart patient. *Psychosomatics* 18:23, 1977.

Spark RF, White RA, Connolly PB: Impotence is not always psychogenic: newer insights into hypothalamic-pituitary-gonadal dysfunction. *JAMA* 243:750, 1980.

Wagner NW, Sivarajan ES: Sexual activity and the cardiac patient. In Green R (ed): *Human Sexuality: A Health Practitioner's Text,* ed 2. Baltimore, Williams & Wilkins, 1979, p 192.

CHAPTER **36 The Psychosexual Dysfunctions and Their Treatment**

Robert Dickes, M.D., Carol L. Lassen, Ph.D., and W. Charles Lobitz, Ph.D.

This chapter will focus on some of the more common types of psychosexual dysfunction which do not involve severe gender identity disturbances or unusual sexual choices. These dysfunctions are often found in people who are able to love, form good relationships, and marry. Their sexual adequacy in terms of pleasure, however, is far from satisfactory. They suffer greatly from their inability to perform well, lose a good deal of self-esteem, and in the past often felt quite hopeless as far as help was concerned. The dysfunctions most commonly encountered are orgasmic difficulties in women and ejaculatory and erectile difficulties in men. Until recently, the methods of treatment were lengthy, time consuming, and expensive, since the disorders in question were thought to be invariably due to serious and deep-seated psychopathology.

The discoveries of Semans, and Masters and Johnson, have introduced new knowledge and new methods of treatment for people suffering from the common disorders mentioned above. They have taught us that sexual dysfunctions need not originate in major psychic illness and can be related to simple failures and fears. People, for example, worry about the demands their lovers make. They also have fears of being rejected and humiliated which can interfere with their performance. Men are particularly worried about fears of performance and many women fear rejection.

The increasing awareness that sexual failure is not necessarily related to deep-seated pathology has been verified by the many successes accomplished by brief treatment directed at overcoming these obstacles to performance. The essential feature of the treatment introduced by Masters and Johnson is the use of special sexual tasks assigned to the couple as a sort of home-work to be done between sessions. Masters and Johnson see their patients for two weeks in daily sessions and report excellent results. So do other workers who have introduced modifications of this original approach. They may see patients once weekly, since many people cannot afford the necessary time off from work for daily sessions. The results of this variation are also reported as excellent. It should be noted, however, that this type of treatment is directed primarily to the specific sexual difficulty of the couple and cannot be used as a substitute for those individuals with other types of symptoms or character difficulties related to more deep-seated psychic pathology. Such brief treatment is also of little use to those couples who essentially are ill suited to one another.

THE CAUSES OF SEXUAL DYSFUNCTION

Before proceeding to a discussion of specific syndromes, it might be helpful to discuss first some of the causes of sexual dysfunction and to consider the basic principles of brief sex therapy. These are discussed in considerable detail and in a most useful fashion by Helen Singer Kaplan in her two books, *The New Sex Therapy* and *The Evaluation of Sexual Disorders.* The etiology of most psychic difficulties may be divided into the earlier causes, therefore deeper and more remote, and the more immediate causes. Deep and immediate causes or failure often unite to produce the overt dysfunction. Thus, a neurosis beginning in childhood can join with present day inhibitions related to anger at a spouse to produce a psychic stress powerful enough to cause a sexual dysfunction. The strategy of brief sex treatment is to focus upon the immediate causes of the failure and to attempt to remove those factors which are producing the "overload." Removal of the immediate causes of the psychic stress often sufficiently lightens the burden on the individual to permit pleasurable and satisfactory responsiveness. The deeper causes of difficulty may be left untouched. These deeper factors should be brought into focus in the treatment only when they interfere with the success of the brief therapy.

The stress that is placed upon the immediate causes of sexual dysfunction should not blind us to the power and importance of the so-called deep or remote causes of sexual failure. These deeper causes are often in themselves of sufficient power to prevent a person from achieving sexual satisfaction. When this is the case, brief therapy will probably be inadequate. Longer-term psychotherapy or psychoanalysis are then among the treatments of choice.

Organic Conditions

Although the majority of sexual dysfunctions are primarily psychological in origin, a sufficiently high percentage of them are caused by organic factors to warrant a complete medical evaluation in every case. For some years it was estimated that approximately 10% to 20% of people seeking help for sexual dysfunctions had some organic pathology which contributed to the disorder. Recently, however, the incidence has been estimated to be much higher. For example, in a recent major study by Wagner and Green, and another by Spark and colleagues, as many as 35% of the patients seeking treatment for erectile dysfunction were found to have demonstrable organic abnormalities, particularly hypothalamic-pituitary-gonadal disorders. The various organic conditions that can lead to sexual dysfunction have been described in the preceding chapter and will not be repeated here. However we do want to emphasize certain principles in the treatment of these patients. When the organic problem can be treated medically or surgically, the sexual dysfunction often can be ameliorated. Yet there is always the danger that the quest for a medical or surgical treatment will prevent the clinician from investigating the possible psychological factors involved, and may result in inappropriate interventions. A common example is the frequent prescription of testosterone injections for a man's erectile problems even though his testosterone levels are within normal limits. Very often the placebo effect does not occur or is not maintained and the patient becomes discouraged, with an exacerbation of the psychological conflicts that caused the disorder in the first place. Furthermore, when an organic factor is contributing to a sexual dysfunction, the problem is often exacerbated by psychological factors. The most common example of this is in early stages of diabetes when the erectile failure due to neuropathy is aggravated by *performance anxiety*. Proper treatment in these situations requires attention being given to *both* the organic and the psychological factors contributing to the dysfunction. Finally, as noted in the preceding chapter, many patients with irreversible organic conditions, such as a spinal cord injury, can be helped by sex therapy to adjust to their dysfunction and develop alternative sexual behaviors.

Immediate Factors

One of the most common immediate causes of sexual failure is the phenomenon known as *spectatoring*, a name applied by Masters and Johnson to the act of watching one's own performance while engaged in sexual activity. This spectatoring is usually highly self-critical and consists of such anxious questions as: "Am I going to have an erection? Will I be able to come? What if I don't? Will he or she like me?" Such a critical watching of one's self is highly detrimental to successful sexual achievement. This type of behavior has long been understood as a *splitting* of the person into the doer and the watcher. Such splitting always interferes with any type of performance, and it is often a manifestation of an obsessional disorder which has its roots in childhood. However, the contribution of Masters and Johnson was the discovery that such splitting is not necessarily due to a long-standing, serious, obsessional disturbance, but rather in many cases is related to a fear of repeating previous sexual failures in adulthood. They found that such spectatoring can be successfully overcome by appropriate interventions in brief treatment.

Other immediate causes for sexual dysfunction arise from what Helen Kaplan terms the "antierotic environment created by the couple which is destructive to the sexuality of one or both." One such cause for a couple's failure to enjoy sex would be the couple's inability to do the things that they each find exciting. Fear of failure also plays an important role in producing an inhibitory anxiety. This is often coupled with an exaggerated sense of pressure to perform. Another factor is the fear of rejection which causes an overconcern with the need to please one's partner. Such overconcern can prevent one from spontaneously enjoying the sexual interchange and pleasure. Open communication about what one wishes and enjoys is a great aid to better sex, and it is a pity that so few people are able to confide in one another. Failure to talk to one another openly leads to lessened pleasure and is therefore a very important factor in producing sexual dysfunction.

It seems strange that some adults know so little about sexual techniques. Yet people cannot know without being taught. It is even stranger that there are people who object to this teaching. These very objectors are themselves often ignorant about sexual matters, and are opposed to the sexual freedom which they themselves could enjoy. Ignorance has caused much misery throughout human history, and much tragedy could be avoided if sexual knowledge were to be given at the proper time. For example, people often do not know how to touch one another or how to tell their partners what gives them pleasure. The partner then remains ignorant and both suffer as a result.

Such ignorance is often manifested in simple lack of knowledge about one's own sexual responsiveness. Many individuals, particularly women, but men as well, are not aware of their own requirements for attaining sexual pleasure and sexual arousal. Sexual response is "natural," i.e., it is a capacity that is given at birth, but it is also a learned skill. The further up the phylogenetic ladder a species stands, the greater the role that learning plays in adult sexual union. Our culture does not encourage sexual curiosity, exploration, and mutual learning; in fact it tends to discourage it. People can attain adulthood in our society having learned very little about their own bodies and erotic responses. With so little self-knowledge, it is difficult indeed to share one's sexual desires and preferences with a partner.

Certain myths also interfere with pleasure. For many years, people have been told that if they cannot achieve mutual orgasm they are failures. Nothing could be further from the truth. So long as both can achieve a satisfying orgasm and they are happy with the result, then the sexual union has been a success. Mutual orgasms are indeed a great pleasure, but they are not the ultimate measure of a fulfilling sexual relationship.

Ignorance of anatomy can also contribute to tragedy, and knowledge can help avoid it. Some years ago, a young man presented for treatment. His life was, as he put it, ". . . falling to pieces." He had been at the point of asking a young woman whom he loved very much to marry him. She was beautiful as well as intellectual. They shared mutual interests and both were pursuing similar graduate studies. He had long needed an operation for a hernia, and it was finally performed successfully. During his hospital stay the young woman visited regularly. Shortly after his leaving the hospital, when they were being somewhat intimate, he felt a pain in his groin and lost his erection. The next time they were together he was very self-conscious and had a similar unfortunate experience but without the pain. He then decided that the "operation on his sexual apparatus" had damaged him and he was "through." He became withdrawn from the young woman and she, in hurt, retreated from him. Matters were going from bad to worse when he was referred for treatment.

He was a thoroughly unhappy young man who believed that permanent damage had been done to his genital apparatus. He had no knowledge of his own body and thought that a hernia operation was ". . . doing something to the internal sexual organs." The operative procedures were clarified and he was reassured that no damage had been done to any organ, let alone any of his sexual organs. The patient was much relieved and needed only a second visit to learn about spectatoring and its bad effects on performance. This reassurance and education relieved him of his anxiety. He called the young woman, and soon thereafter they were married. Reports about them indicate that both are apparently successful in work and in love.

Deeper Factors

There are other causes of sexual difficulty based upon deeper intrapsychic factors. Many of these have already been discussed in the earlier chapters in the book on childhood development. Essentially our society has been hostile to human sexual expression. The present-day modifications and increased sexual freedom have not penetrated very deeply as yet. In general, the search for sexual pleasure is frowned upon, and children especially are taught that sexuality is bad. Young boys are threatened if they touch their penises, and little girls are severely censured if they display sexual interest. It should be no surprise that after such early indoctrination many people feel conflicted and guilty about sexual expression. We need only examine religious pronouncements to realize the extent of the restrictive forces and their effects on the young. These same youngsters, when grown, are expected, via the rite of marriage, to cast all doubts away and function freely and well. Sometimes it does work this way but often it does not. The strength of the sex drive and the innate endowment of the individual may overcome all obstacles to good functioning. This is more a tribute to the human ability to transcend unfavorable beginnings than a tribute to our present method of handling sexual development.

It is also an ironic twist of fate that the characteristics that people most value about themselves may sometimes become contributing factors in disrupting their sexual lives. The man who prides himself on being strong, logical, independent, and "tough" also may have a hard time being sufficiently tender to meet his wife's needs, or to permit his own needs for affection and caring to be met. The woman who values her role as a good wife and mother but sees that role as incompatible with being a sexually passionate woman will inhibit her response to sexual stimulation in order to maintain her valued image of herself as a "good woman." Hard driving successful "workaholics" may apply the same standards of goal attainment and determined "success" to their own genital responses, only to discover that "trying harder" does not work in the arena of sexual activity, but the very activities they have not had time for, relaxation and pleasure, do.

Interactional Factors

There are other causes of sexual difficulty that relate to the interactions between the couple. These are important because the sexual difficulties often are only a reflection of the more pervasive difficulties in the marital relationship. Sometimes it is easy to determine the fact that the two do not care for each other, or that one is disinterested without the other knowing it. At other times, the involved people may not be aware of their own disinterest in and rejection of each other. Such couples should not be accepted for brief treatment since one or the other or both will sabotage every attempt to help.

There are, of course, many reasons for marital discord other than true incompatibility or real disinterest. People who live together must make compromises and be prepared for frustrations and disappointments in their interactions with each other. These frustrations may lead to anger and rebellion which may be expressed primarily in acts of sexual revenge. A woman who is full of rage toward her husband is not apt to be a pleasant bed mate. A man who is contemptuous of his wife's values is no better. When rage and fear of rejection exist in either partner or in both, it is no surprise to find that they are "no good" with each other in an act which requires trust and mutual abandonment to pleasure. Often the patients are unaware of the interfering, deep-seated hostility. Part of the therapeutic task may require relief of this anger through ventilation, and help in the resolution of the underlying difficulties.

Lack of communication is another important factor. A couple came complaining that when one was interested in sex, the other was not. Neither could fathom the reasons and they insisted that they cared for each other. They wished to save their marriage, which they believed was in jeopardy because of the sexual incompatibility. A careful history revealed the following. Everything had gone well in their marriage until they bought a house that was more expensive than they had anticipated. The man was rather frightened by the added burden but nevertheless he went ahead and bought the house for his wife. He was unaware of his resentment over what he felt was an unwarranted purchase. His wife was equally unaware of how he really felt. Pressured by the purchase of the house and the mortgage payments, he worked unconscionably long hours and was often exhausted and disinterested in sex. This made his wife feel unwanted, and she grew increasingly frightened and resentful. The few times he wanted sex turned out to be the times when she was disinterested. It is important to understand that both of these people were unaware of their own feelings of anger and of their partner's feelings. They had been assigned the usual tasks in sex therapy, but somehow could never seem to get together to do them. Tactful confrontations led them to learn of their resentments toward each other. When the wife learned about her husband's feelings about the house, she broke down and wept, saying that she did not care about the house but only about him. The results of the treatment were good, and the two people were able to resolve their difficulties and return to their earlier sexual compatibility, thus demonstrating the importance of adequate communication.

Another factor that often leads to marital and sexual difficulty is a struggle for power. The need to control the people in one's environment is usually unconscious and is often related to a fear of losing control and of intense underlying rage. If each spouse fights for domination, a destructive struggle occurs, and is usually carried into the bedroom where any compliance with the wishes of the other is viewed unconsciously as a defeat. The treatment of such people may be more difficult than those previously described since the "controllers" may not be able to give up their need for power. For example, treatment with one particular couple went smoothly until the rather passive husband began to demand that the wife do the "exercises" recommended by the sex therapists. She, however, could only be involved in something if she initiated it. She had already described her alienation of many men by "coming on too strong," and had never been able to permit any man to pursue her. The woman was then gently confronted with her need to control. Sex therapy frequently consists of much more than the simple assignment of sexual tasks. A certain amount of psychotherapy is usually an essential ingredient in such treatment. Sex therapy has the limited goal of improving or curing sexual difficulties. When a bad marital situation exists, a broader goal is required. Sometimes one or both partners require extensive individual psychotherapy. At other times, marital therapy is indicated.

Not all sexual disharmony is due to hostility. The couple mentioned earlier who bought the house are essentially loving. A man may avoid sex because he fears he may fail. A woman may avoid sex because of fears of penetration, or she may permit the man to try but then fail him at the last moment. One such story deserves to be told to emphasize how a single unconscious movement can seriously damage a relationship. A young man and woman who had been married

for more than a year came for help because the marriage could not be consummated. Every time he tried to penetrate, he failed. Surgical removal of the hymen was of no avail and vaginismus was not present. At that point, both patients felt it was the man's problem, since the wife desired penetration, or so she said. However, discussion revealed that the man's erections were good. What could be wrong? Both were instructed to note carefully what actually happened. The young man finally discovered the trouble. Each time he tried to enter his wife's vagina, her hand got in the way. She deflected the penis to the side and thus prevented entry. This had been entirely unnoticed by both of them, since both were excited and it takes only a slight touch and a momentary deflection to defeat entry. That such acts can happen and be unknown to both parties is very hard to believe, yet psychiatrists are continuously confronted with the power with which the unconscious mind can deceive people about their own motivations and acts. This is only another illustration of the facts of everyday medical and psychiatric practice.

Depression

Loss of sexual interest and inability to perform sexually are very frequent concomitants of a severe depression, and the depression usually requires special treatment before undertaking sex therapy. Mild cases of depression may be more difficult to diagnose since in these patients sexual functioning may be relatively intact. However, their sexual arousal may be reduced as well as their pleasure and frequency of sexual contact. Depression is an important diagnosis for the physician to consider whenever a sexual complaint is the presenting problem. Furthermore, the physician must make a distinction between sexual dysfunction or disinterest which is secondary to depression, and depression which is secondary to sexual dysfunction. When the depression is primary, sexual dysfunction is only one symptom among all the other symptoms of depression: anhedonia or the inability to experience pleasure, sleep and appetite disturbances, physical symptoms, and interpersonal withdrawal. In those instances where the sexual dysfunction is primary, it is not unusual for such patients to be depressed and disheartened, to feel that they are failures as men or women, and to consider themselves as inadequate sexual partners. In both situations (where the depression is primary and where the sexual dysfunction is primary) suicide is an ever-present danger that must be continually assessed.

BASIC PRINCIPLES OF BRIEF SEX THERAPY

The Diagnostic Approach

The basic principles of brief sex therapy, a form of psychotherapy, will now be discussed. Two major distinctions separate brief sex therapy from the usual forms of psychotherapy. The first is the assignment of specific graduated sexual "exercises" to be performed between visits. These exercises carried out away from the therapeutic hour are as much a mainstay of the therapeutic process as are the actual sessions held with the therapists. The concentration on the specific sexual problem rather than on any underlying psychological difficulties constitutes the second difference from the usual psychotherapeutic approach. There are a number of varied formats for conducting sex therapy. One such format that is fairly standard is as follows. The couple is seen together by a male and female team of cotherapists for about one hour. A careful sexual and general psychiatric examination is performed. If the history indicates that sex therapy may be helpful, further visits are arranged. Before the second visit, an internist and a gynecologist complete a thorough diagnostic evaluation. These reports can be of great value in reassuring patients regarding the absence of organic causes.

The second visit consists of individual interviews by the therapist of the same sex. This allows the patient a greater freedom to speak out in private and separate from the spouse. At times, much information is revealed in this session which was not made available at the first meeting. The third session is also an individual session but with the therapist of the opposite sex. The fourth session is termed the "round table" at which time the problems are discussed in the light of the information gathered. If the couple is not suitable for brief sex therapy, recommendations as to the best treatment method are offered and discussed, and referrals are made if requested. If the couple is suitable for sex therapy, this is recommended and discussed. The final decision is the patients'. Treatment

from this point on is tailored to the needs of the couple.

Sensate Focus Exercises

Originally, Masters and Johnson followed a standard routine with their patients regardless of the deep-seated problems, the diagnoses, or the presenting complaint. All couples are advised to abstain from coitus and follow the same routine of *sensate focus exercises*. Only after the couple has developed a suitable increase in sexual pleasure do these workers introduce the specific techniques applicable to the individual complaints. Helen Kaplan presented a more flexible approach. At times she omitted some sensate focus exercises and turned directly to tasks specific to the problems presented. It is also the practice of many other sexual dysfunction clinics to follow a flexible approach and to pay particular attention to the dynamic factors which interfere with therapeutic progress.

Sensate focus exercises are a key factor in most brief sex therapies. (Figures 36.1–36.3). These are nondemanding, mutually pleasurable explorations of one another's bodies. Both vaginal entry and orgasm are prohibited at first. Each partner explores the other's body and helps find ways of heightening the erotic experience. Genital touching is excluded during the first few sessions and attention is focused on giving and receiving pleasure without demands for performance. Only later is genital stimulation advised and introduced into the pleasuring routine. The goal, at first, is to increase the couple's awareness and sensitivity to nonorgasmic sexual or sensuous pleasure. It is only after this goal is achieved that specific sexual activities are recommended that address the individual problems of the couple. These exercises and goals vary depending on the patients' needs. The length of the treatment, though short, also varies and depends on the couple's rate of progress. Although 15 sessions are usually enough to complete the treatment, the number of sessions should be left open-ended, since a specific time limit introduces enormous psychological pressure on both the patients and the therapists.

The Role of Masturbation in Development and in Sex Therapy

Many clinics and sex therapists now recommend self-stimulation as an auxiliary treatment

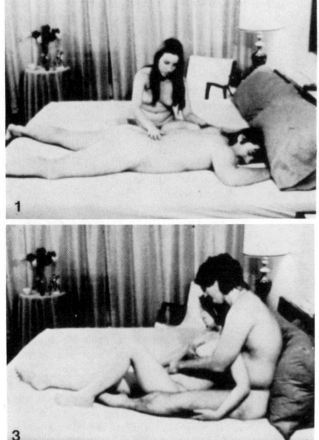
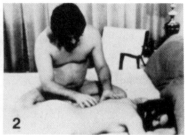

Figures 36.1–36.3. A couple explores each other's body. From the film *An Experiment in the Teaching Methodology of Sensate Focus.* (By permission of EDCOA Productions, Englewood, N.J.)

technique for a variety of sexual dysfunctions, with documented positive results. Since masturbation was for so long in such bad repute, both with the general public and in the professions, the rationale for this procedure is presented here.

The strongest statement that can be made about the value of self-stimulation concerns not only its normality, but also its highly significant role in sexual development. It is virtually universal among men of all cultures and widely practiced among women. It is common among the married as well as among the single. The practice of self-stimulation in women is highly correlated with the development of a gratifying sexual relationship with a mate. Masturbation is also commonly observed in species other than the human being.

Once roundly condemned as the cause of a myriad of emotional and physical disabilities, to be controlled if necessary by medical and surgical therapies, the professional attitude toward self-stimulation has shifted dramatically in the past 50 years. Credit for this change goes to those scientists who were willing to violate cultural taboos to report their studies and observations.

Developmentally, tactile exploration of the genitals evolves into an early form of masturbation at about eight months. René Spitz demonstrated that the occurrence of infantile self-stimulation is strongly positively correlated with overall physical and intellectual development and with the quality of nurturing care. Boys typically continue to fondle and stimulate their genitals throughout childhood and later adulthood. Girls, however, begin to adopt more covert methods like rocking or squeezing their thighs together as early as the second year of life.

At this point it is worth noting the remarkable sequential interaction that occurs among the various components of childhood and adult sexual development. Maternal fondling and nurturing of the infant, and the child's own genital play, provide the foundation for comfort with physical touch, nurturance, and sexual excitement in adult sexual exchange. Early touching of one's genitals and body is also one of the many developmental manifestations of childhood learning and curiosity. Such learning lays the groundwork for enjoyment in peer play, including exploration of the bodies of playmates. In its turn, experience and comfort with peer play are major contributing factors to the achievement of adult sexuality. Masturbation also helps permit the child to come to know and to trust the reality and sensations of his or her own body, so as to gain the confidence to explore and to trust other realities outside of the body.

Masturbation in later years, particularly during adolescence, takes on the additional developmental task of sexual "practice." This form of rehearsal has several dimensions, including appreciation of one's own physical sensations, the learning of one's sexual preferences and desires, the acceptance of oneself as a sexual being, and the "trying on" of various partners in fantasy. Thus, one sees throughout childhood and adolescence the interweaving of masturbation with touch, nurturance, curiosity, learning, peer play, reality testing, adolescent "practice," sexual comfort, and sexual fantasy in a complex pattern that results in the formation of mature adult sexual functioning.

Self-stimulation programs are currently utilized in the treatment of orgasmic dysfunction, premature ejaculation, erectile failure, and sexual disinterest. In the treatment of these syndromes, masturbation exercises have a specific value in increasing sensory awareness. This is especially true for women suffering from orgasmic dysfunction, since such women are more likely to have missed the experience and the developmental learning that take place with self-stimulation. In this instance, women are instructed to begin with visual appreciation and tactile exploration of their total bodies (Figure 36.4), to give themselves permission and approval, and with increasing comfort to progress

to observation, exploration, and stimulation of the genitals. For these women, body exploration and self-stimulation are prescribed as a parallel process to sensate focus exercises.

This "relearning" approach offers a variety of therapeutic advantages. First, a woman begins self-exploration without the additional distracting concern about what her partner is thinking (spectatoring). Second, as she learns about herself, she has much more information about her own sexual preferences to share with her partner. Third, she goes strictly according to her own pace and can focus fully on her own psychological and erotic "blocking points." These are then discussed in therapy. Fourth, if she has a fear of losing control in orgasm, she may be able to begin to permit that letting-go more easily in privacy. Fifth, self-stimulation can be a very successful mechanism for undoing the "Sleeping Beauty" myth. The Sleeping Beauty myth maintains that no woman is really sexual until the "right man" comes along. Until then she is psychologically prepubescent, naive, and virginal in her desires. Only this Mr. Right can awaken her passion, and without him (or with a man who does not awaken her with the "right" approach), she remains or returns to a passionless state. This can be a very damaging myth in mature sexual relationships. A woman affected by this myth cannot allow herself to know her own desires and finds it doubly difficult to communicate them. Her partner inevitably feels inadequate because he has to take the responsibility for having to arouse her to prove he is her chosen lover. Self-stimulation can help to demolish this myth and replace it with a sense of sexual maturity and responsibility. When a woman acknowledges to herself that she is both a giver and receiver of sexual pleasure, she can no longer deny that she is a sexual being. It is not conferred upon her by a man. *She* must take part in making a good sexual experience happen.

In the treatment of male sexual dysfunctions, masturbation exercises can be used to learn the stop-start technique for premature ejaculation, and to learn confidence in the ability to gain, lose, and regain an erection without panic. Furthermore, the reestablishment of sexual confidence in an individual without a partner may be essential before he has the courage to pursue an intimate relationship with a woman. Thus, at this point it is accurate to state that, along with sensate focus exercises, self-stimulation exer-

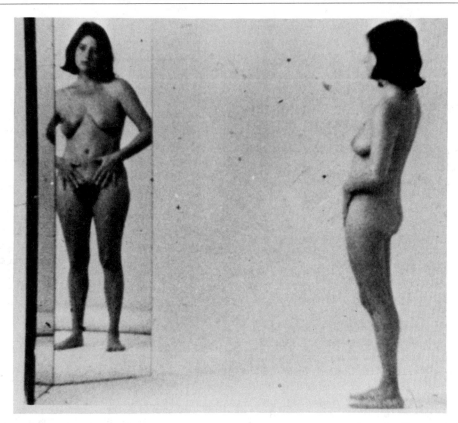

Figure 36.4. From the film *Reaching Orgasm*. Produced by Cort Media Productions. (By permission of Human Sexuality Program, University of California at San Francisco.)

cises have become a second major and accepted technique in sex therapy in the promotion of sexual learning and change.

Ethics and Training in Sex Therapy

Before leaving the topic of basic principles and accepted therapeutic techniques, it should be noted that some therapists adopt approaches that differ widely from these generally accepted models. Some of these "therapy" variations reach a level of questionable practice. Some therapists wish to observe their patients' sexual activity; some may recommend group sex. It is wise to keep in mind that individuals with sexual difficulties have already been traumatized by their inhibiting values and by their failure experiences. Self-esteem is sometimes at such a significant low that one or both members of the couple may comply with therapeutic demands that are not in their own best interests. Thera-

pists who encourage or prescribe such questionable practices in our view run the risk of further damaging their patients' sense of competence, sexual pleasure, and self-esteem.

There are also groups of "clinicians" who have had no training in the theories of human psychology, the dynamics of psychopathology, or the techniques of psychotherapy. These "clinicians" use the standard methods advocated by Masters and Johnson but they use them in a mechanical fashion without any understanding of their patients' resistances and responses. These untrained workers use sex education and strong reassurance, and deal only with obvious and superficial factors related to their patients' problems. They do help a certain number of people but their capacity to help is severely limited. It is our belief that sex therapy is a form of psychotherapy and that well trained therapists are prepared to deal with more than just the sexual difficulties. The difference between success and failure may well rest on the tact and skill with which the deeper resistances to improvement are understood and managed.

SYNDROMES OF SEXUAL DYSFUNCTION AND DISORDERS OF SEXUAL DESIRE

Masters and Johnson first differentiated and elaborated the various categories of *sexual dysfunction* and presented scientifically validated treatment methodologies to relieve those dysfunctions. In addition, there is another category of sexual difficulty which is not a dysfunction but a disorder, and which has come increasingly to the attention of sex therapists. Helen Kaplan; Kolodny, Masters, and Johnson; and Robert Stoller have all independently described the phenomena and treatment of *disorders of sexual desire*.

Thus, it is now diagnostically useful to consider a triphasic conceptualization of sexual sequence and sexual difficulties, as proposed by Helen Kaplan. The first phase, prior to the actual onset of sexual arousal and response, encompasses sexual interest, initiation, and receptivity. *Sexual desire disorders* include inhibited sexual desire and aversions (phobias).

The second and third phases involve the now classic *sexual response cycle*, and are defined by characteristic physiological changes of the body. Problems that occur in these two phases are of a *dysfunctional* nature, such that expectable physiological responses of the response cycle do not occur or occur prematurely. With increasing knowledge, it is now apparent that the three diagnostic phases have implications for the focus and depth of sex therapy.

The sexual dysfunction syndromes are better known and better understood, and will be described at length. Treatment of the sexual desire disorders is more complex and will be discussed briefly at the conclusion of the chapter.

The Second and Third Phases (The Sexual Dysfunctions)

Helen Kaplan divides the cycle of sexual response into a *phase of genital vasocongestion* (or the phase of mounting sexual excitement), and a *phase of reflex clonic contractions* which is primarily muscular and which constitutes the

orgasm. This approach does not contradict the findings of other researchers whose work essentially described the process of mounting sexual excitement culminating in orgasm as though it were a unitary process. It is true that each phase follows the next, but the mechanisms underlying vasocongestion differ from those related to orgasm. Thus, the sexual response cycle actually is composed of two differing and somewhat independent components. The vasocongestive phenomena are related to vaginal lubrication and swelling in the female and to penile erection in the male. The two common sexual dysfunctions related to vasocongestive phenomena are *general sexual dysfunction* ("frigidity") in the woman and *erectile dysfunction* ("impotence") in the man. Orgasm in both sexes is related to the regular reflex clonic muscular contractions. The dysfunctions related to this phase are *orgasmic dysfunction* (inability to achieve orgasm) in women and *premature or retarded ejaculation* in men.

The separation of the two processes is further verified by the facts that each component involves different anatomical structures, namely the blood vessels for the congestive excitatory phase, and later the musculature for the orgasm. Two different areas of the nervous system innervate the components of the biphasic cycle as well. The parasympathetic section of the autonomic nervous system mediates the vasocongestive phenomena of the excitement phase, whereas the sympathetic section of the autonomic nervous system is the essential mediator of the orgasm. Of course, higher brain centers also contribute to the end result and may inhibit either phase of the cycle.

Kaplan's approach serves some very useful clinical purposes. It is known that both excitability (vasocongestion) and orgasm show differing vulnerabilities to physical trauma, drugs, and age. Since the controls for both aspects of the response cycle are located in different areas of the nervous system, it is entirely possible for one phase of the cycle to be impaired while the other is not. The treatment for dysfunctions of the two phases will also differ. The treatment, for example, for a man who suffers from premature ejaculation differs from the treatment of a man with erectile dysfunction. By the same token, the treatment of a woman who can lubricate and respond with excitement but is nonorgasmic differs from that offered to a woman who does not respond to sexual stimulation. Let us now consider these individual syndromes in somewhat more detail.

General Sexual Dysfunction

This designation refers to the syndrome which many have termed "frigidity" in the past. Such women experience little or no erotic pleasure upon stimulation. Coupled with this is a lack of physiological response, and vasocongestion is absent, as is lubrication. The lack of response is not always so extreme and sometimes a little lubrication may be noted after penile entry. Women who cannot respond often find sexual activity unpleasant and try to avoid it. Lesser degrees of this type of dysfunction are noted in women who enjoy cuddling and closeness as long as it does not lead to more overt sexual action and coitus. Many of these women are also non-orgasmic, but this constitutes a separate difficulty. General sexual dysfunction may be primary or secondary. Primary refers to women who have never experienced sexual pleasure. The secondary type refers to those women who previously experienced arousal but seem no longer able to enjoy sexual experiences, especially those that lead to coitus. Some women seem not to mind their inability to respond, while others are quite disturbed about their lack of responsiveness.

The sexual response is under the control of the autonomic nervous system. The same is true for breathing, eating, and many other functions. A person under emotional tension can have any of these processes disrupted. If a woman is angry or fearful, proper vasocongestion cannot occur and the stages of sexual excitement fail to develop. As we have seen, the causes of the anxiety or other interfering emotions may be deepseated and remote, but often enough the causes are more immediate. They include spectatoring, inability to communicate, and the other factors previously mentioned. The aim of treatment is to free the woman from these interfering forces. The therapist tries to help the couple develop a relaxed and nondemanding atmosphere during lovemaking, and with this goal in mind sensual exercises are prescribed.

The first task utilizes sensate focus exercises. The couple is advised to avoid coitus and orgasm until an appropriate stage of responsiveness is reached. The couple is also told to limit their actions to caressing each other. The wife, in this case the apparent patient, is told to caress and pleasure her husband first in order to alleviate her guilt over receiving pleasure. The husband, who also will eventually gain in pleasure, must be willing to defer orgasm and gratification. If he is not willing, this must be dealt with in such a way as to make him a willing collaborator. The success of treatment always depends on both parties.

After the patient develops erotic responses to the sensate focus exercises, light genital play is introduced. The body is caressed as are the nipples, vaginal entrance, and clitoral area, with the man paying particular attention to the woman's wishes and feelings. The touching must not be demanding upon the man's part and the sexual play must be gentle and tender. If the woman is dry, a suitable lubricant may be used.

When genital caressing has become a positive experience, with considerable erotic response, intercourse may then be permitted. It is to be initiated by the woman when she is ready. Thrusting must be at her desired pace. Therapists usually advise that the thrusting be slow and tentative and that the woman focus all her attention on her own vaginal sensations. Most women report that pleasurable vaginal responses are increased when the thrusting is under her control. Masters and Johnson, who initiated this treatment method, advise the couple to use the female superior position but other positions may be used. The man is advised to withdraw if his urge to ejaculate begins to get too intense, and to continue caressing his wife to maintain her arousal. After a time, if the woman is experiencing high levels of arousal and is on the verge of orgasm, she is encouraged to do whatever will intensify the erotic experience and *permit* orgasm. "Making an orgasm happen" is rarely successful. Focusing on and maximizing the erotic pleasure creates the phenomenon of orgasm. If the woman cannot reach orgasm on this occasion, thrusting is continued to provide the man with orgasmic release.

The effectiveness of the exercises depends upon the fact that they are geared to the woman's needs. Her desires dictate what is done. It is extremely important for the woman to focus her attention entirely on her own sensual pleasure even when she is stroking her husband. Usually some difficulties in carrying out the exercises emerge in the course of treatment. The woman may report that caressing tickles rather than excites, or that she begins to think of other things just when she starts to feel sensuous pleasure. Other defenses to avoid sexual excitement may also be reported. Thus, these erotic exercises are extremely useful in highlighting the patient's psychodynamic problems. A good therapist takes advantage of this and tactfully aids the patient in overcoming the obstacles. This is another example of the fact that good training is needed to be able to conduct sex therapy. Most women respond to the treatment outlined above, especially if the dysfunction is related to more recent and immediate difficulties. Those women who suffer from more generalized, deep-seated difficulties are more suited to longer-term therapy.

Orgasmic Dysfunction

The woman's inability to reach orgasm via intercourse is probably the most common sexual complaint of both women and men, although they complain for different reasons. Men feel their "pride" is at stake and that they have failed if the woman does not reach orgasm. They also feel they have left the woman unsatisfied. Women, too, feel that they have failed and they also may feel unrelieved of their sexual tension, although this is not always the case. Some women reach orgasm some of the time and some not at all. About 10% of women never achieve orgasm. It is well known that many a woman's orgasmic difficulty is related to the fact that her lover may not continue the foreplay and the penile thrusting for the length of time needed for her to climax. Lest men be too alarmed, it should be remembered that in most instances, women can climax within less than 10 minutes of intercourse, provided there has been adequate foreplay. In addition, many women can achieve orgasmic release very quickly by automanipulation. This fact may be used in treatment.

It should be kept in mind that although 90% of women are orgasmic by some means, perhaps 40% of those do not attain orgasm with intravaginal penile thrusting alone. This is a high enough proportion to be considered a normal variation. Such women may be orgasmic, and gratified, by genital stimulation before or after coitus or concurrently *during* coitus. Just the information that such a sexual pattern is not at all unusual may be all the reassurance a woman or her partner needs.

If the decision is made to treat the absence of orgasmic response *in intercourse*, the aim of treatment depends upon an understanding of the contributing factors. The problem may be as simple as inadequate stimulation prior to coitus, or as complicated as fear of loss of control in the context of close physical intimacy. In the instance of overcontrol, the patient must be taught to pay strict attention to her own premonitory sensations, especially those erotic feelings which occur just before orgasm. The sexual premonitory sensations must not be shut off and the patient must allow herself to continue on to orgasm.

The woman who has never had an orgasm requires a different treatment program from the woman who develops a secondary orgasmic dysfunction. The following discussion will apply to secondary dysfunction which is the most common. It is important that the therapist identify the existing difficulties between the two partners and also the patient's intrapsychic problems which contribute to the inhibition of orgasm. Treatment must always take account of the inner psychology of the couple. When necessary, the problems must be interpreted. In addition, erotic tasks are assigned with the purpose of so increasing the woman's sexual arousal that she is almost orgasmic by the time entry into the vagina is made. This is combined with teaching the woman to become aware of her own responsiveness and to enjoy it. The use of clitoral stimulation is very helpful in accomplishing the above goals. The exercises follow what Kaplan has called the *stop-start* teasing approach. Foreplay is started in a teasing manner, interrupted at times, and always nondemanding in type. Coitus is not to be attempted until the woman is thoroughly aroused. The vagina is then entered. Thrusting is slow and nondemanding, and at a suitable time, the couple separates. During the withdrawal period, clitoral and other stimulation is continued. The cycle of entry and withdrawal is repeated several times. The female superior position is useful since the woman can press her clitoris against her husband's pubic bone. This provides added stimulation and may help lead to orgasm. In addition, the woman can control her movements. Manual clitoral stimulation by the man may be added and the thrusting is continued until the woman feels close to orgasm. Manual stimulation is then stopped and the woman thrusts actively until orgasm is achieved. Another method involves the woman using self-stimulation. She stops the self-stimulation as she approaches orgasm and completes the act by active thrusting.

During all the above series of exercises, the patients discuss their successes and failures with the therapists who help them with the emerging problems. The importance of this accompanying psychotherapy cannot be stressed too strongly. Most women do very well on this treatment plan.

Premature Ejaculation

This difficulty is considered by many to be the most prevalent male sexual disorder. It occurs widely in men who appear to have no major psychiatric disorder, as well as in those who have identified psychopathology. In fact, the original Kinsey reports considered the extremely rapid ejaculation which occurs within a minute as normal! Others give different time limits, and there has been much discussion as to what constitutes adequate time delay. Helen Kaplan's approach is probably more useful. She redefined the problem in a way that eliminates the question of time and considers premature ejaculation as the inability to have voluntary control of ejaculation. Kaplan thus avoids the time question and considers the much more crucial problem to be that of establishing voluntary control over the ejaculatory reflex. Prematurity is then said to exist when the man cannot exert voluntary control once a high level of sexual arousal has been reached. We would consider 10 to 15 minutes as a reasonable time to be able to delay orgasm. Kaplan considers the failure of control as due to an absence or diminution of the perception of erotic sensation once intense arousal is reached. This apparent failure in perception also applies to the premonitory sensations in the penis.

Many men who have difficulty in gaining ejaculatory control have attempted to delay their ejaculation by trying to think nonsexual things. They may also try fist clenching and other devices that do not work, since once the sexual excitement climbs high enough they ejaculate. These people use condoms, anesthetic ointments, and other devices to decrease their sexual responsiveness. These methods also fail and defeat the objective of sexual pleasure. Treatment is best directed toward aiding the man to reach intense levels of sexual excitement and still maintain control over his ejaculation. Those

methods which focus on the male genital sensations which precede orgasm are extremely effective in helping the patient achieve the voluntary control he seeks.

The wife must be a willing participant in the treatment process, and she must understand that the treatment must first focus on the man's premature ejaculation. Unless this is done, she herself is deprived of pleasure. Once the man has succeeded in controlling his ejaculation, attention may be directed toward any sexual problem present in the wife. Her problems are often not apparent until the man's problem has been solved. She may be nonorgasmic, for example, and this might not even be discovered until her husband's prematurity has been cured. The wife may also be resistant to treatment because she may fear loss of her husband if his sexual performance improves, and there may be other reasons for her to fear a good result. The therapists must be alert to all factors that may impede treatment and deal with them as indicated.

Two main methods of treatment exist, the Semans technique of *stop-start* and the Masters and Johnson *squeeze technique* (Figures 36.5–36.11) which is really a modification of the stop-start method. In the stop-start approach, the couple is told to use only enough foreplay to induce an erection. The man then lies on his back while his wife stimulates his penis (Figure 36.5). He is to pay attention to his own sensations only. As soon as he feels the premonitory urge to ejaculate, he signals his wife to stop the stimulation. The premonitory sensation then disappears, usually before erection is lost. Stimulation is begun again. If the erection is lost, the couple should realize that this is of little consequence since it can be regained. Once erect, the stimulation sequence is repeated and again stopped. Ejaculation is permitted on the fourth sequence. The use of a lubricant is helpful and is advised. It is important to explain to the patient that the control attempted is over only the external stimulation, and he should avoid any attempt at conscious control of the ejaculation. Stopping the stimulation at the proper time is enough.

When the patient has acquired a sufficient degree of control, intercourse is begun with the female in the superior position (Figures 36.6–36.8). The man controls the movements and signals the stop of thrusting when he is preorgasmic. This is repeated and orgasm is again

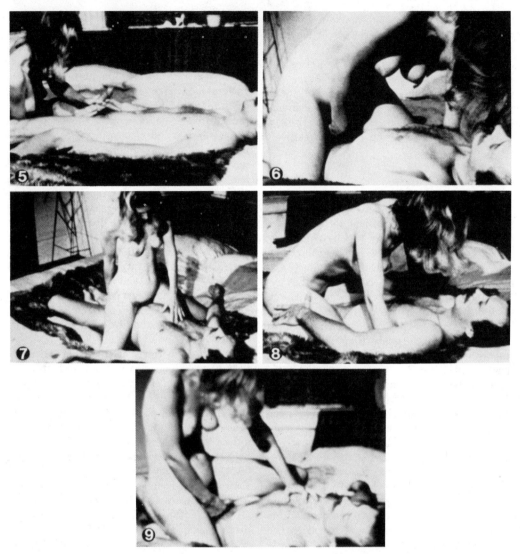

Figures 36.5–36.9. From the film *Squeeze Technique*. Produced by the National Sex Forum. (By permission of Multi Media Resource Center, San Francisco, Calif.)

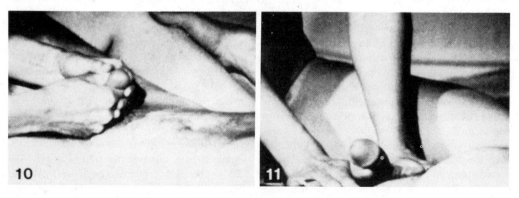

Figures 36.10 and 36.11. From the film *Squeeze Technique*. Produced by the National Sex Forum. (By permission of Multi Media Resource Center, San Francisco, Calif.)

permitted on the fourth time. The male superior position is the last one tried since it is the most stimulating to the man. The results of this treatment method are excellent, as are those of the Masters and Johnson squeeze technique which requires the woman to place pressure on the coronal area of the penis (the area just back of the head of the penis) just before the man reaches orgasm (Figures 36.9 and 36.10). The erection is lost (Figure 36.11), and stimulation is then begun again, just as in the stop-start method.

Erectile Dysfunction

Men who suffer from primary erectile dysfunction have never been able to have sexual intercourse. Some may even have been married for years without consummation of the relationship. Secondary erectile dysfunction is much more common, and occurs in a man who has previously maintained sufficient erectile capacity to achieve intercourse. No accurate figures exist, but a majority of males have had some transient episodes of erectile failure at one time or another. This is of no significance and usually disappears. It is the frequent occurrence of failure that signals the need for help. This should be sought as soon as possible since the longer the problem exists, the more difficult it is to remedy the situation. Special care should be taken to rule out organic disease before beginning treatment, since secondary erectile dysfunction may be the first indication of an underlying organic problem. Previously, it had been believed that erectile problems were either the manifestation of organic processes or of severe psychological problems. It may, however, be due to more immediate factors such as those previously described and can occur even if no major psychopathology exists.

The treatment of erectile dysfunction is quite complex and depends on the special factors noted in the patient. The treatment should be brief and should avoid developing into long-term therapy, which requires a different approach. The first instructions to the couple are to engage in nondemanding caressing, each partner taking turns at caressing the other. As is usual in brief sex therapy, coitus and ejaculation are temporarily prohibited. Genital touching may or may not be advised depending on the special circumstances in which the couple are involved. Great emphasis is placed upon the development of nondemand sexual pleasure for its own sake. The couple is also specifically advised not to

strive for erection and not to be worried about an erection if it does occur and then disappears. A stop-start technique can be used to teach the couple that the erection may be regained. The husband is also taught to suppress distracting thoughts and not to worry about his wife's pleasure. He is to concern himself only with his own pleasure. Intercourse is recommended when the couple is ready. They are to separate without orgasm in order to prevent vaginal containment from becoming a command signal for orgasm for the woman. The man is advised to use erotic fantasies or any other means to obtain an erection. These function as transitional methods until he gains confidence.

Drugs have been used as an aid in some cases, and although the use of testosterone had fallen into disrepute, it has recently again been thought to be of some advantage. Helen Kaplan mentions the use of Afrodex (a combination of johimbine, testosterone, and nux vomica) as helpful. In due course, however, all drugs should be discarded. Most important in the treatment of erectile dysfunction is the skill with which the therapist handles the patient's emotional problems. These vary from person to person and can greatly tax the therapist. The outcome for the patient is dependent upon the length of time he has had erectile dysfunction, the cooperation of his partner, and the state of his psychic health. Most reasonably healthy men respond well to skillful treatment.

As knowledge increases concerning the various organic causes of erectile dysfunction, attempts are being made to surgically deal with the particular condition in question. In the case of vascular disease, surgeons are instituting bypass anastomoses to correct the circulatory obstruction. In other cases, artificial inserts known as penile implants are placed in the penile sinuses. At present, all of these surgical procedures are still in the experimental stage, and caution must be maintained concerning their long-term effectiveness and eventual widespread use.

Group Treatment of Sexual Dysfunctions

One of the latest developments in the treatment of sexual dysfunctions has been the extension of the basic principles of sex therapy to a group treatment approach. Typically, the diagnostic workup is done with each couple separately. Then the treatment instructions are done with several couples in a group led by one or two therapists. As with the treatment of sexual dysfunctions in an individual or couple format, "homework" exercises are prescribed, and no sexual activity takes place within the therapy group itself. The advantages of the group format are: 1) the treatment is more cost-effective in terms of professional time; 2) the couples are able to benefit from each other's experiences and progress; and 3) the couples discover that they are not alone in their problems. This commonality is usually enhanced by limiting the group composition to couples who have the same sexual dysfunctions. For example, groups will be composed of couples who have a problem with orgasmic dysfunction or with premature ejaculation. The research literature supports the efficacy of this type of treatment; the outcome results for couples treated in groups appear to be as favorable as for those couples treated in the more traditional way. An additional use of the group treatment format involves those individuals with sexual dysfunctions who do not have regular partners.

Some of the greatest successes with group treatment have occurred for women who have never had an orgasm by any means. They are usually seen in all-women groups led by female cotherapists. This setting provides a comfortable forum for exploring issues around female sexual development and for discussing the importance of masturbation in the treatment of this problem. In addition, men who do not have regular partners and who experience erectile dysfunction have also been treated successfully in therapy groups. For these men, the group setting offers a valuable forum for discussing our culture's myths and expectations surrounding male sexual performance. Such groups may also incorporate social skill training for these men so that they are able to learn how to deal with their sexual anxieties when they are in the presence of a new sexual partner, and thereby feel more relaxed and comfortable in the interaction. Although these groups are typically led by male therapists, it has been found useful in the latter stages of the therapy process to involve female cotherapists when the patients are learning and practicing social skills.

The First Phase (Disorders of Sexual Desire)

Kolodny, Masters, and Johnson describe two diagnostic categories that are characterized by inhibited sexual initiation or inhibited sexual receptivity. *Sexual aversion* is identified by a pervasive negative reaction to sexual activity which is of phobic proportions. *Inhibited sexual desire* is marked by loss of interest in sex. Inhibited sexual desire is a more frequent phenomenon than sexual aversion. In both instances, the sexual response cycle may be intact, with erection or lubrication, ejaculation or orgasm occurring without difficulty when a sexual encounter does take place. The contributing factors involved in the etiology of the desire phase disorders are similar to those involved in the dysfunctions, with this difference: According to Kaplan, the causal factors in the desire disorders relate more frequently to the "deeper" factors and to the more severe relationship factors. In addition, these complex factors tend to be less conscious. She also reports that desire disorders are far more resistant to successful treatment. By contrast, Kolodny, Masters, and Johnson report very low failure rates, at least for treatment of sexual aversion, but they also appear to be very stringent in assessing motivation for treatment before accepting a couple. Our clinical experience would tend to confirm the greater difficulty in resolving inhibitions of sexual desire, and the frequent necessity for longer-term sex therapy or psychotherapy.

Conclusion

In concluding this chapter, it is well to reiterate that no matter what the dysfunction or disorder, male or female, the active participation and enthusiastic cooperation of the partner is a crucial factor in the reversal of the sexual difficulty. Next to the motivation of the patient there is nothing so curative as a concerned lover. Sexual intimacy indeed involves two people. The dysfunction affects *both* partners, and it takes *both* partners to resolve it in a mutually satisfying intimate exchange. It should also be emphasized that this has been an abbreviated presentation of the origin and treatment of sexual problems. The bibliography is an important resource for those who wish to learn more. Physicians should keep in mind that patients with minor difficulties related to misinformation or inadequate technique may well respond to simple suggestions and reassurance, but more difficult cases should be referred for appropriate therapeutic treatment.

Suggested Readings

Kaplan HS: *The New Sex Therapy.* New York, Brunner/Mazel, 1974.

Kaplan HS: *The Evaluation of Sexual Disorders: Psychological and Medical Aspects.* New York, Brunner/Mazel, 1983.

Masters WH, Johnson VE: *Human Sexual Inadequacy.* Boston, Little, Brown, and Co, 1970.

Meyer JK: *Clinical Management of Sexual Disorders.* Baltimore, Williams & Wilkins, 1976.

References

Belliveau F, Richter L: *Understanding Human Sexual Inadequacy.* New York, Bantam Books, 1970.

Kaplan HS: *Disorders of Sexual Desire.* New York, Brunner/Mazel, 1979.

Kinsey AC, Pomeroy WB, Martin CE: *Sexual Behavior in the Human Male.* Philadelphia, W.B. Saunders, 1948.

Kinsey AC, et al: *Sexual Behavior in the Human Female.* Philadelphia, W.B. Saunders, 1953.

Kolodny R, Masters WH, Johnson VE: *A Textbook of Medical Sexuality.* Boston, Little, Brown, and Co, 1979.

Lassen CL: Issues and dilemmas in sexual treatment. *J Sex Marital Ther* 2:32, 1976.

Lobitz WC, Baker EL: Group treatment of single males with erectile dysfunction. *Arch Sex Behav* 8:127, 1979.

Mills KH, Kilmann PR: Group treatment of sexual dysfunctions: a methodological review of the outcome literature. *J Sex Marital Ther* 8:259, 1982.

Semans JH: Premature ejaculation: a new approach. *South Med J* 49:353, 1956.

Spark RF, White RA, Connolly PB: Impotence is not always psychogenic: newer insights into hypothalamic-pituitary-gonadal dysfunction. *JAMA* 243:750, 1980.

Stoller RJ: *Sexual Excitement: Dynamics of Erotic Life.* New York, Pantheon Books, 1979.

Wagner G, Green R: *Impotence: Physiological, Psychological, Surgical Diagnosis and Treatment.* New York, Plenum Press, 1981.

37 The Paraphilias and Transsexualism

Robert Dickes, M.D. and
Richard C. Simons, M.D.

In the third edition of the American Psychiatric Association's Diagnostic and Statistical Manual of Mental Disorders (DSM-III), those conditions that had previously been termed sexual deviations or sexual perversions are now termed *paraphilias*, emphasizing that the deviation or perversion (para) exists in that to which the individual is attracted (philia). There was no adequate DSM-II category for the syndrome of *transsexualism*, which is characterized by an individual experiencing intense discomfort and dislike for his or her anatomical sex and by persistent behavior patterns in that individual usually associated with the opposite sex. In DSM-III, transsexualism is now listed as a *gender identity disorder*. In this chapter we shall discuss both the paraphilias and the syndrome of transsexualism.

THE PARAPHILIAS

Impairment in the Development of Sexual Orientation and Object Choice

As we discuss the individual paraphilias, we shall also try to briefly review the process of psychosexual development, since an understanding of the paraphilias requires some knowledge of earlier developmental states. At birth, the infant is incapable of distinguishing between itself and the outer environment. This has been called the "undifferentiated" or autistic stage. There is, therefore, no relationship to another person as we know it later in life. Adult relationships are only attained via a long developmental sequence, which begins with this undifferentiated state. This earliest period merges imperceptibly into the next or symbiotic stage when the mother-child pair functions as a unit. In this

period, the child is able to recognize distinctions between itself and mother but only intermittently and imperfectly. This symbiotic stage is slowly superseded by the stage of separation-individuation. The child emerges gradually from the symbiosis with the mother and begins to develop its first representation of self.

This phase of separation-individuation is a crucial period of life, during which time disturbances in the parent-child relationship may well set the stage for later difficulties in the establishment of mature, adult object relationships and sexual orientation. One group of the paraphilias is characterized by an *impairment in the development of sexual orientation and object choice*, leading either to the choice of a nonhuman object for sexual arousal, or to the choice of inappropriate human partners. In *fetishism*, an inanimate object is substituted for a person, usually an article of a woman's clothing. *Transvestism* is an extension of fetishism in which a man becomes sexually aroused wearing women's clothes. In *zoophilia*, an animal is the source of sexual arousal, and in *urophilia* and *coprophilia* the products of excretion. In regard to inappropriate human partners, in *pedophilia* a child is the source of sexual arousal, and in *necrophilia* a dead person.

There is still a great deal of controversy as to whether *preferential* or *obligatory* (*exclusive*) *homosexuality* (a person of the same sex is exclusively the source of sexual arousal, and heterosexual relationships do not bring about sexual arousal) should be considered as one of the paraphilias. In 1975, the term homosexuality was deleted from DSM-II, and the declaration was made that homosexuality is not a psychiatric disorder unless the person experiences discomfort about his or her sexual orientation. Dr. Gadpaille will discuss this controversy more fully in the next chapter, but we agree with his position that preferential or obligatory homosexuality is a developmental disturbance and therefore an impairment in sexual orientation *within the context* of what appears to be a powerful biological pressure towards heterosexual arousal and what certainly is a powerful psychological and social pressure towards continuation of the human species. However, this is *not* to imply that homosexual men and women necessarily suffer from more conflicts than heterosexual men and women, *nor* that homosexual men and women are less creative, productive, or socially responsible than heterosexual men and women, *nor* that there is any justification for the homophobic discrimination that exists throughout the world against homosexuals. As concerned citizens we all must work toward the elimination of discriminatory laws against homosexual men and women. We must also always keep in mind that a disturbance in one line of development (the sexual) does not necessarily imply disturbances in other areas of development, such as the capacity to work, to love, and to be creative. Homosexual men and women, including homosexual physicians, have made and will continue to make outstanding contributions in all areas of life. Nevertheless, as scientists, it is still our obligation to expand our knowledge of the origins, not only of homosexual behavior, but of all other behavior as well, and to work to improve our treatment techniques for all of those who request our help.

Impairment in the Development of the Aggressive Drive

The development of relatedness to other people is paralleled by development in the realm of the drives. Freud originated the concept of the dual drives of sex and aggression, both of which contribute to sexual behavior. Neither drive can be observed in pure form, and the two are regularly fused, but in varying proportions. There is, for example, no sexual act or act of love that does not contain some aggression, even if it is only enough to overcome obstacles and sustain the necessary activity for successful performance. It is important to know that the manifestations of the aggressive drive are essential to life. They need not be destructive, and are not necessarily "aggressive" or "hostile" in the usual sense. There is still much to be learned about the maturation and development of the aggres-

sive drive and how it fuses with the sexual drive. But we do know that *aggressive impulses* play an important and pathological role in many of the paraphilias, as Robert Stoller has described in his book, *Perversion: The Erotic Form of Hatred*. Furthermore, there is a group of the paraphilias in which the aggressive impulses have become almost completely dominant over the sexual impulses and obliterate any sense of shared intimacy, equality, and tenderness. In true *sexual masochism* the individual needs to receive punishment, pain, and humiliation on a conscious level as a condition and requirement for conscious sexual arousal and gratification. (This is in sharp distinction to the *masochistic personality*, in which both the punishment and the resulting sexual gratification from the punishment exist on an unconscious level, not a conscious one.) In true *sexual sadism*, the individual needs to inflict punishment, pain, and humiliation on another person as a condition and requirement for conscious sexual arousal and gratification. *Rape* and *sexual murder* are properly viewed as extensions of sexual sadism, in which sexuality merely becomes the vehicle for violent hatred and murderous rage.

Impairment in the Development of the Sexual Drive

In its earliest phases, the manifestations of the sexual drive are infantile in nature and do not show the characteristic behavior of the adult, in whom the *partial drives*, as they are called, have come under the domination of the genital needs. The pleasurable experiences of childhood include looking, exhibiting, kissing, touching, and other forms of behavior which later are considered as normal, important, and universal aspects of adult sexuality. However, in a third and final group of the paraphilias, one of these early partial drives of childhood sexuality becomes preferred to the exclusion of genital union, and becomes the primary mode of sexual arousal and gratification. In *voyeurism*, looking becomes the primary mode of sexual excitement, in *exhibitionism*, being looked at becomes primary, and in *frotteurism*, rubbing is the preferred mode of sexual pleasure.

Definition

Perhaps we are now ready to offer a definition of the paraphilias. They are conditions in which there is an avoidance of adult, human, hetero-sexual, genital relations, with an *habitual* and *required* use of other outlets or objects or persons for sexual gratification, or else an involvement in heterosexual relations only under certain *habitual* and *required* conditions. They may involve an impairment in the development of sexual orientation and object choice, an impairment in the development of the aggressive drive, or an impairment in the development of the sexual drive. They are the end result of many different interacting factors—biological, psychological, and social. And they are usually associated with a great deal of anxiety, shame, and guilt, and very little freedom, flexibility, shared pleasure, and conscious choice. They serve an important, unconscious, defensive function, and protect the individual from the overwhelming panic that is generated whenever an opportunity for normal intercourse without compulsive exclusions or obligatory conditions is presented. Whatever the paraphilia, it bears the hallmarks of infantile sexuality carried on into adult life, and is evidence of a failure to establish mature, heterosexual relationships. Finally, with the exception of preferential or obligatory homosexuality and sexual masochism, the paraphilias are almost exclusively male, for reasons which Dr. Simons will discuss in more detail in Chapter 42.

FETISHISM

It is not possible to discuss all of the paraphilias described above, but we shall try to discuss one in sufficient detail so as to hopefully make them more understandable. The general model may then be applied to other paraphilias. *Fetishists* demonstrate an erotic fixation on objects or body parts which are quite inappropriate for intercourse but are a condition for sexual satisfaction. Objects used by fetishists include shoes, underwear, or other inanimate objects which have become invested with sexual interest. Body parts may also be used, such as hair or the foot. Some degree of "fetishism" is quite commonplace and well within normal limits, so long as the person is capable of normal intercourse and does not require "props" in order to perform successfully. We are referring here to the normal overestimation of the beloved (an old-fashioned term!) that often extends to his or her possessions. It may also be noted that a transitional stage on the road to full fetishism may be ob-

served in people whose partners must fulfill special criteria such as a particular body configuration, or a special hair distribution or color. A spectrum may be said to exist ranging from the normal, or near normal, to the severely pathological behavior of the full-fledged obligatory fetishist. Such spectrums exist for all paraphilias as well as all other illnesses, which range from the mildest to the most severe. We will discuss the development of full-fledged fetishism since it so clearly illustrates the factors involved in the development of these aberrations.

An understanding of any of the paraphilias requires a knowledge of the person's early development. Fetishism is no exception. It is necessary to know about the individual's childhood, about the objects associated with this period, and about the parental behavior. Peculiar to fetishism are the objects. Many infants very quickly learn that thumb or hand sucking is pleasurable. At times, a bit of a blanket or a bit of cloth gets into the mouth or may be held in the hand. These objects are soothing to the child, and may then acquire special importance as a defense against anxiety, especially at bedtime when the child is left alone in a darkened room. Later, the object may acquire a value equal to that of the mother and may then be termed a *transitional object*. Transitional objects are quite commonplace, and many children possess them. They aid children in dealing with their fears of separation from the parents and form a bridge to the external world.

The parents soon learn that the treasured object gives the child comfort and that it can be used as a pacifier. This provides the parents with a means of avoiding direct conflict with the child's demands. They may notice the child's increasing anxiety over separation from them as the child's cries increase in volume and intensity. The parents, unable to stand their own increasing tension, give the child its special comforter in order to quiet it and avoid a confrontation. This increases the value of the object to the child. Such parents, especially those beset by many problems, may continue to encourage the child to use inanimate objects in order to lessen the demands made upon them. They train the children to turn to these objects for gratification and support instead of to themselves, a rather damaging procedure. Later, the child may transfer its investment in the original object to new objects such as a toy, a doll, or teddy. The importance of these new objects becomes enhanced when they serve as an aid in diminishing tension and relieving the anxiety of deprivation and separation. This too may be detrimental since a child should be learning to tolerate these normal frustrations without the obligatory need for inanimate objects.

We have mentioned the use of transitional objects to reduce bedtime anxiety. The next tension producing period is that of weaning. Once again, the child is separated from a loved object. In this case it is the breast or the bottle. Tension is again countered by the child's use of an inanimate object which it can continue to suck and fondle. The use of such an object prolongs the bedtime thumb or blanket sucking, and the mouth continues to play an important role at a time when its importance should diminish. Another tension producing period develops when the child must surrender to the parent's demands to produce a stool at the proper time and place. Thus, the child loses control of another precious object, its stool. Adults consider the stool as ill smelling and disgusting, and are aware of the need to control the process of defecation. The child, however, has a very different point of view. The child considers its stool as part of itself and does not like to give up control of any body part. Young children do not object to their own feces, and will lie in it and even smear it over themselves with pleasure. It is only after the child adopts the parental attitudes that the stool becomes devalued. The fetishist often reveals the infantile character of his paraphilia by requiring his fetish to smell bad and to be dirty. These smells often resemble those of unwashed bodies and remind one of fecal odors.

The struggle between the parent and fetishistic child for bowel control may rage with great severity far in excess of what one observes normally. One fetishistic patient, an adult, recalled this period very vividly. His mother was an extremely aggressive and controlling woman whose determination to win out was matched by her son's stubborn refusal to submit. His mother regularly inspected his stool, commented unfavorably on it, and humiliated the boy. The child then refused to defecate. He was kept on the pot for hours but he never gave in. Finally, when taken off the pot, he would defecate on the floor. Another tactic was to defecate before being put on the pot. His enraged mother would then beat him unmercifully. In spite of this, she never won. Finally, in desperation, she allowed him to take his special toy with him into the bathroom. The child, sensing the "victory," capitulated and defecated promptly as required.

It would seem that peace had been established and that success had been achieved. The solution, however, was a failure for both mother and child. The inanimate object gained what the mother had lost. This inadequate mother, hostile, demanding, and unable to love, was an unsuitable person for childrearing. She neither loved her child nor permitted him to interact with her in ways suitable for his proper growth. She forced him to work out his problems with inanimate objects rather than with herself. A good mother would not have begun bowel training so early, nor would she have made a war out of it. Is it any surprise that his fetish was a dirty, ill-smelling, brown, teddy bear?

Thus, as time passes, the comforter or transitional object comes to represent many things—first the parents who are lost at bedtime, then the lost breast or bottle, then the lost stool. As the child begins to develop, new meanings are added to the old ones. The beloved toy becomes the focus for the child's own feelings and develops a new use, a disadvantage that is really a further step from normality. Since the child has transferred his feelings to the toy, he may say, "Wah Wah" (or whatever name is used) "is angry." This allows the child to deny that it is he or she who is angry when frustrated. The stage is thus set for the child to continue to deny the state of his or her own feelings. The situation is further complicated when the object also symbolizes the parent. The child may then be angry at the toy instead of the parent. This prevents the child from appropriate interactions with living people and handicaps the child in developing relationships with peers, including those of the opposite sex. The stage is also set, therefore, for future sexual difficulties.

A very large group of children make use of these special objects to relieve anxiety and depression caused by separations from the mother and other frustrations. Such children, and they constitute the large majority, are never so reliant on their comforters that these equal the mother in importance, or that normal developmental processes suffer. The interests of the normal child extend as the child grows, and the special object is no longer needed to overcome anxiety or other difficulties. The object thus loses its special value and is appropriately discarded. A small number of children whose parenting has been poor, and who have been aided and abetted in the enhancing of the importance of the inanimate object, grow to value the toy more than the mother. These children are unable to discard these transitional objects.

The great discovery of the anatomical differences between the sexes occurs at about the age of three. Up to this time, when interest shifts to the genitals, the child believes that both sexes have similar organs. This belief persists in spite of observations to the contrary. The infantile mind can deny reality even more easily than adults, so the idea that children only accept the anatomical differences at so "late" an age should not be too strange. Boys especially try to deny the absence of male genitals in their mother, to whom they regularly attribute these organs. The truth is accepted with the greatest of reluctance, and some people grow to maturity never having really given up the original idea that everyone possesses male genitals. Of course, this idea is repressed (unconscious) and is not easily accessible. The life of a transvestite, however, is living testimony to this idea. He is, after all, a man masquerading as a woman. The "secret" his strange behavior emphasizes is that underneath the woman's dress is a being who is male. If this is true for him, it is also true for other "women." In this way he confirms his fantasy that all women have penises. "If you cannot see it, it is there hidden in the pubic hair. If small, it will grow." These remarks are those of an actual patient who was a transvestite.

At the time the child makes the discovery of sexual differences, erotic interest centers on the genitals. Boys in particular are observed manipulating their genitals, much to the distress of many a parent. Prohibitions against this masturbatory activity are often coupled with threats about the loss of the penis or possible damage to it, so that the child comes to believe in the possibility of castration. The belief is strengthened by his observations of the genitals of girls. They must have already suffered these consequences, so he thinks. Another factor in his acceptance of the idea that he can lose his penis is the actual experience of losing his teeth. Solidly attached organs, even as strong and hard as teeth, can become detached and lost. The normally brought up boy weathers all the vicissitudes of these growth periods, nursing and weaning with its loss of the nipple, bowel training with its loss of the stool, and now his penile erotic interest and his accompanying fears of castration.

It is at this time of life that the transitional object becomes invested with genital sexual interest, and some children have been observed engaging in masturbation with these toys, which now may be called *childhood fetishes*. Such a child has truly transferred its love from mother to the comforter. This state of affairs only develops when the mother regularly deflects the child's interests in her to an interest in the inanimate object. She has taught the child to love something other than a living person.

Object relationships to people normally are undergoing a maturational process at the same time as all the above events transpire. The child reaches school age and now is required to give up his attachment to mother, deal with the loss of his intimacy with her, and make new attachments in the outside world, as well as deal with his fears of organ loss. The normal child makes the adjustment fairly well, the girl more easily than the boy. It is entirely different for the budding fetishist. The young fetishist, the child who by now is using his special or transitional object in a sexual way, has already suffered damage to his ego. This is due to the unfortunate interactions of the earlier developmental periods which have helped center his interests and dependence on inanimate objects. He is, in fact, already dependent on an inanimate object for sexual gratification. Such a child is not able to make a satisfactory transition to teachers and other children, or from home to the world at large.

Development continues during the school years, and the ego grows in strength. The conscience is also consolidated, and the power of the sexual drive decreases during this prepubertal period. The urge to use the childhood fetish for sexual purposes correspondingly decreases, and the fetish no longer serves sexual goals in an obvious way. Some future adult fetishists continue to use these objects for solace and support during latency. They carry their toys with them wherever they go and turn to them to support their efforts toward making various adjustments in the world. Those who are less damaged may even appear perfectly normal during this quiescent time. If upbringing improves and the child has a strong enough ego, the difficulties may actually be overcome. But this is not always the case.

The onset of puberty, with its great upsurge of sexuality, changes the whole picture. It is at this time that the earlier difficulties resurface, although in an altered form. The demand for interaction with one's peers and especially with the opposite sex are difficult enough for the essentially normal person. It is intolerable for the boy or girl who has in early life been taught to substitute an inanimate object for the mother. The fetishist has failed regularly in the major tasks of development and now, in adolescence, he is once again unable to master his anxieties and succeed in his new tasks. He retreats, therefore, to old methods and seeks out some inanimate object which represents the original, long-forgotten, childhood treasure. The path he follows is the one already prepared by his childhood interactions, and he deals with his anxieties by the use of a fetish that is now much more complex in meaning than the original childhood fetish. These complexities derive from new additions to the earlier meanings of the fetish. The use of the object is once again overtly sexual, as it was in childhood, but the physical responses are those of the adult, and orgasm and ejaculation are achieved. Unfortunately, the fetishist has come of age.

Each fetishist has his own particular choice of object. These are as varied as are the individual fetishists and are related to the unique experiences of their childhoods. The basic principles for the emergence of the fetishism, however, remain the same. *The fetish represents a means of overcoming anxiety related to the loss of precious objects which ultimately represent body parts.* Primary in the fetishist's concerns is the fear of loss of his most precious possession, his penis. He needs to deny the possibility of this loss, a possibility nurtured by his loss of the nipple, feces, teeth, and the mother herself. Not the least of these losses was what for him was a shocking discovery, namely that his mother did not have what he firmly believed she once possessed, a penis. His discovery of the anatomical differences between the sexes thus has a profound and lasting effect upon him. Women from then on are disparaged, and he tries to reassure himself against the loss of any of his body parts through the use of his fetish. The fetishist's infantile theories of intercourse also include the fear that he can lose his penis during intercourse and become like a woman. Thus, sexual intercourse becomes invested with terror for him, and he either turns to his fetish for sole sexual gratification, or else engages in intercourse but only with the use of his fetish as a precondition. We are very well aware of how strange all of this must seem. Let us remember, however, that fetishism itself is even stranger. Think for a

moment! A man makes love to a rubber garment, a shoe, a bottle, or to some other dirty "disgusting" object. He cannot bear the sight of an undressed woman or a close view of her genitals. Must not the reason for such events also seem strange and unusual to us? It is the patients themselves who have taught us about their "unknown" childhoods. They deserve full credit for the tremendous efforts they have made to undo the harm that was done to them and for the difficulties they endured in their work toward normality. It is not easy to recall the distress of one's childhood. Yet those who are successful teach us what we know and what we are now presenting to you.

TRANSVESTISM

We shall now discuss one other condition which is less common than is fetishism, with its spectrum from the near normal to the most bizarre and severe, but which is an extension of fetishism. In *transvestism*, a man is compelled to fetishistically cross-dress in women's clothes as a means for maintaining heterosexual functioning, since most transvestites are heterosexual and not homosexual. It is very important to distinguish transvestism from obligatory male homosexuality. All three of these conditions—fetishism, transvestism, and obligatory male homosexuality—are interrelated in that each contains within it an attempt to avoid acknowledging and accepting the genital differences between men and women, and the castration anxiety attendant upon such acceptance. The absence of a penis in a woman is basically unacceptable to these men. But the transvestite and the obligatory male homosexual handle their conflicts very differently. While both types of men have reported an intense fear and dislike of a woman's genitals, a fear and dislike based on infantile theories similar to those of the fetishist, the transvestite is usually heterosexual (often married and with children), and wears women's clothes to maintain the fantasy of a woman with a penis (the "hidden trick"). In contrast, the obligatory male homosexual does not fetishistically cross-dress, and even a very effeminate male homosexual may only occasionally cross-dress but without fetishistic sexual excitement. Furthermore, the obligatory male homosexual avoids the female genital at all costs, and is compelled to choose other men who also have a penis as sexual partners. Finally, both the transvestite and the obligatory male

Table 37.1*

Differentiation of Transvestism, Homosexuality, and Transsexualism

	Fetishistic Cross-Dressing	Gender Identity	Sexual Role Behavior	Sexual Orientation	Erotic Pleasure in Genitalia
Male transvestite	Yes	Masculine	Masculine	Heterosexual women	Yes
Male homosexual (obligatory)	No	Masculine	Variable	Homosexual men	Yes
Male transsexual	No	Feminine	Feminine	Heterosexual men	No
Female transsexual	No	Masculine	Masculine	Heterosexual women	No
Female homosexual (obligatory)	No	Feminine	Variable	Homosexual women	Yes

* Table by Richard C. Simons.

homosexual experience intense erotic pleasure in their penises, and their gender identity is masculine (Table 37.1). This now leads us to a discussion of sexual identity, gender identity, and the syndrome of transsexualism.

SEXUAL IDENTITY

Any given individual's *sexual identity* has four components: 1) the *anatomical sex*, either male or female; 2) the *gender identity*, either masculine or feminine; 3) the *sexual role behavior*; and 4) the *sexual orientation*. Let us examine each separately.

Anatomical Sex

The anatomical sex is determined by three factors: 1) *genetic* (the genotype or chromosomal configuration); 2) *gonadal* (the presence of testes or ovaries); and 3) *hormonal* (the effects of various hormones acting in an appropriate sequence which ensures the differentiation of the external genitalia and the development of the appropriate sexual cycles or rhythms). We can observe anomalies and disturbances relating to all three of these factors.

Genetic anomalies include *Klinefelter's syndrome*, where an extra X chromosome (XXY) produces phenotypic males with small testes who are sterile and suffer from testosterone deficiency and *Turner's syndrome*, where an absent second sex chromosome (XO) produces phenotypic females who are small in stature and do not develop secondary sex characteristics at puberty.

If gonadal abnormalities occur, these result in types of *true hermaphrodism*, in which both ovarian and testicular tissue is present, and

where the external genitalia may be male, female, or ambiguous.

Hormonal abnormalities, on the other hand, lead to *pseudohermaphrodism*, in which there is a discrepancy between the internal gonads and the external genitalia. For example a *female pseudohermaphrodite*, a female baby with ovaries, but with a masculinization of the external genitalia, may result from the *adrenogenital syndrome*. This is a congenital adrenal hyperplasia in the fetus in which the adrenal glands become hyperactive and produce too many androgens— i.e., testosterone and other male hormones. Female pseudohermaphrodism may also result from an androgen-producing tumor in the mother during pregnancy, or from androgens given to a pregnant woman to prevent abortion. A *male pseudohermaphrodite*, a male baby with testes, but with feminine-appearing external genitalia, may result from the *feminizing syndrome* in which there is a genital end organ insensitivity to androgen stimulation, or from inherited metabolic errors. These include the deficiency of *17-beta-hydroxysteroid-dehydrogenase* (one of the enzymes necessary to produce testosterone from cholesterol) and the deficiency of the enzyme *5-alpha-reductase* which causes decreased in utero production of dihydrotestosterone and feminization of the external genitalia.

All of these abnormalities of anatomical sex, especially where the external genitalia are ambiguous, make the child vulnerable to an error in sex assignment. In the great majority of these cases, as John Money and others have shown, the sex of assignment and rearing will prevail if the correct diagnosis is not made before 18 months of age and certainly no later than three years of age. Therefore, early diagnosis is crucial. For example, female pseudohermaphrodites can be raised as females with hormonal therapy and surgical correction, but male pseudohermaphrodites with the feminizing syndrome must be raised as females because androgen therapy will not produce male genitalia nor male secondary sex characteristics. However, a 1979 report by Imperato-McGinley and colleagues would seem to indicate that male pseudohermaphrodites suffering from a deficiency of 5-alpha-reductase have been "induced" sufficiently in utero by testosterone (which is not 5-alpha-reductase dependent) so that they may be able to be "activated" at puberty by normal plasma levels of testosterone. Even though raised as girls in the 23 interrelated families in three rural villages in the Dominican Republic, these males responded to testosterone at puberty with masculinization of the external genitalia, and development of male secondary sex characteristics such as deepening of the voice and muscular changes. Of the 18 subjects studied, 16 successfully assumed a male gender identity and a male sexual role, over a period of several years. Imperato-McGinley and her colleagues claim that this study shows that gender identity is not unalterably fixed in early childhood, but is continually evolving and becomes fixed only with the biological events of puberty. Yet, the almost complete absence of extensive psychological, sociocultural, and anthropological data in the Imperato-McGinley study cautions against any final conclusions at this time.

Prenatal Hormones

Many animal experiments, and some other human "experiments in nature," have established the critical role played by the sex hormones during prenatal life. Not only are these hormones crucial for the subsequent differentiation of the male and female sexual organs, but they also appear to "program" the brain during fetal development for later masculine or feminine behavior as well. More specifically, genetic material contained in the sex chromosomes causes either testes or ovaries to develop from the embryonal gonad. If testes develop, they secrete testosterone, which causes the other reproductive structures to develop as male. In the absence of testosterone, the reproductive structures will develop as female.

In a series of brilliant experiments begun in the late 1940's, the French physiologist, Alfred Jost, was able to demonstrate that the basic

anatomical state of all fetuses is female, and that the addition of androgens (testosterone) during a "critical period" is necessary for the differentiation of male genitalia. The male rabbit fetuses castrated in utero by Jost were born with female external genitalia, whereas the ovariectomized female rabbit fetuses were also born with normal female genitalia, thereby demonstrating that it is prenatal testosterone and not prenatal estrogen that determines sexual differentiation.

Similar experiments with rats produced the same results. Male rats were chemically castrated in utero during the "critical period" of the 16th to 20th day of pregnancy through the use of cyproterone acetate, a drug which blocks the effects of circulating androgens. These male rats were born with mammillary glands, a vaginal pouch, and a miniaturized penis indistinguishable from a clitoris. In contrast, female rats given testosterone during the critical period in utero developed masculinized genitalia, even including prostate glands and scrotal sacs.

Researchers then began to wonder whether prenatal hormones could also affect subsequent masculine and feminine behavior in addition to the differentiation of the external genitalia. William C. Young, Arnold Gerall, and their colleagues demonstrated that female guinea pigs that had been given testosterone prenatally responded to testosterone at puberty with a high level of male instead of female copulatory behavior, including mounting of other females and pelvic thrusting. Robert Goy of the University of Wisconsin found similar results with female rhesus monkeys that had been given testosterone prenatally.

In another group of experiments by Ingeborg Ward at Villanova, pregnant rats were subjected to a high degree of environmental stress, and their offspring were followed into adulthood. The male rats that were stressed prenatally showed far less male copulatory behavior with females in heat than did those male rats stressed after birth and other male rats not stressed at all. All three groups of rats were then castrated and given estrogens. The males stressed prenatally assumed the female lordotic position of arching the back and presenting the raised genitals to other males, whereas those male rats stressed postnatally and those not stressed at all did not show this female behavior. It was then discovered that the prenatally stressed rats had suffered a decrease in testosterone production. While one must be very cautious about generalizing from animal experiments to humans, it may nevertheless turn out to be that the old wives' tales of stress during pregnancy are far more significant than we had ever realized! Maternal stress may influence prenatal hormonal production, which in turn affects prenatal development, which may in turn lead to abnormal behavior in the adult. If we did not know about the prenatal stress and its hormonal effects, we would be unable to explain the later homosexual-like behavior of these male rats.

In fact, on the basis of a series of similar rat and hamster experiments, Dörner has postulated that an absolute or relative androgen deficiency in the human male fetus at a critical period of differentiation (between the fourth and seventh months) may lead to a "neuroendocrine predisposition for homosexuality" in the adult male resulting in obligatory homosexuality (group 6, exclusively homosexual, in the Kinsey classification), despite subsequent normal testosterone production and normal secondary sex characteristics. However, it is important to remember that this hypothesis has yet to be proven in humans, and also that it does not exclude the coexistence of environmental factors in the etiology of human homosexuality.

Many subsequent experiments have established the presence, at least in lower animals, of a sexually dimorphic nucleus located in the hypothalamus, an important structure at the base of the brain. These hypothalamic cells appear to be involved in the development of neurohormonal mechanisms which function as a sort of built-in clock for determining the body's sexual rhythms. If androgens are present in sufficient quantity prenatally, the hypothalamic cells become organized into a "male" pattern—i.e., the steady, noncyclic release of pituitary hormones at puberty, and "masculine" sexual behavior. If androgens are absent prenatally, the hypothalamic cells become organized into a "female" pattern—i.e., the cyclical release of pituitary hormones at puberty (leading to estrus in animals and the menstrual cycle in women), and "feminine" sexual behavior. Of course, the ultimate sexual identity is the result of many different forces and factors, especially environmental experiences, as we shall now see in our discussion of gender identity. But what we want to emphasize here is that we are only at the beginnings of our knowledge about the prenatal and postnatal hormonal influences on sexual behavior and sexual identity.

Gender Identity

Gender identity can be defined as the sense of masculinity or femininity as understood within a particular culture or society, and subject to all of the prejudices and stereotypes of that culture or society. The development of gender identity is determined by sex assignment and parental rearing, and thus is essentially psychological and social, in contrast to anatomical sex which is biological. Anatomical sex and gender identity are usually congruent, but they can develop in conflicting and even opposite ways as we shall see in our discussion of transsexualism.

The development of gender identity begins at birth and is essentially established sometime between 18 months and three years of age. The individual's anatomical sex, of course, enters into the development of an appropriate gender identity. However, attitudes displayed by the parents to the child have a profound effect upon the ultimate outcome. In contrast to animals, humans are much more plastic and flexible, and much more responsive to psychic stimuli. This is especially related to the human's unique capacity for symbol formation. The human responds to purely internal conceptual constructs which are beyond an animal's capacity. These constructs can markedly influence a person's physiological and biochemical responses, and lead to variations in behavior that may overcome many an inherent biological difficulty. By the same token, culture and environment, because of their powerful influence upon human emotional development, can alter behavior regardless of the presence of a normal or a pathological biological endowment. This can be illustrated clinically.

Young girls suffering from the adrenogenital syndrome have adrenal glands which secrete excessive amounts of male hormones. These infants appear highly masculinized, including their external genitalia, but their internal organs remain female. Psychologically, these children behave very much like boys. They show no interest in dolls and behave like aggressive "tomboys." They also prefer boys' toys, playthings, and clothes. One would think that such women might grow up to become transsexual. Nearly all, however, go on to full heterosexuality and motherhood. They are no more likely to become transsexual than more feminine girls who do not show "tomboy" behavior, although there does appear to be a somewhat higher incidence of homosexuality in these girls on long-term follow-up. But in most instances the handicaps of the original adrenal malfunctions are overcome through experience and learning, and these psychological factors outweigh the original biochemical insult. This should be expected. Multiple influences are at work to produce the end results of human behavior, and these are not simply the byproducts of various chemical effects.

The following case from *Man and Woman, Boy and Girl* by John Money and Anke A. Ehrhardt illustrates this even more clearly. One of two male identical twins was castrated at the age of seven months. During what was supposed to be a simple circumcision by electrocauterization, the boy's penis was accidentally amputated, thus effectively terminating the twin's ability to function as a male. When the child was 17 months old, the parents finally accepted medical advice to reassign the child's gender and raise him as a girl. At a later date, reconstructive surgery and hormonal therapy successfully created an artificial vagina. The parents were able to change their attitudes appropriately, and the child grew up behaving quite happily and accepting of herself as a girl. The identical twin brother grew up just as accepting of himself as a boy. In this case, the role of culture and environment was clearly apparent through the ability of the parents to determine the outcome of the child's gender identity. It also demonstrates the enormous flexibility which humans possess.

Sexual Role Behavior

By sexual role behavior, we mean a person's preference for the sexual, social, physical, or other qualities that are associated with either the masculine or feminine role in a particular society. And there can be a preference for certain qualities associated with the opposite sex without there being an impairment in either gender identity or sexual orientation. For example, there are many men who possess so-called "feminine" qualities who nevertheless have a well consolidated masculine gender identity and who are heterosexual, and there are many women who possess "masculine" qualities who have a well consolidated feminine gender identity and who are heterosexual.

There are also many homosexual men and women who clearly prefer some aspects of the sexual role of the opposite sex, but who do not suffer from the gender identity disturbance of transsexualism. However, the words "active" and "passive" are rarely helpful in categorizing the complete behavior of these homosexual men and women. For example, one homosexual, whose anatomical sex was male and whose gender identity was masculine, "actively" sought out and pursued other homosexual men, but then wanted to be "passively" penetrated by these men in his anus and thereby function sexually in the role of the woman. Another homosexual, whose anatomical sex was female and whose gender identity was feminine, "passively" wanted to be pursued by other women. But once wooed and won, in the sexual relationship with the other woman she played two roles—that of the man who "actively" penetrated the other woman with her finger or tongue, and that of the mother who "actively" nurtured the other woman.

Finally, in transsexualism, which we will discuss shortly, the individual belongs anatomically to one sex but has an intense dislike for the genitalia and the gender of that sex, and wants to function socially and sexually as a member of the opposite sex. Thus, both the gender identity and the sexual role behavior are of the type usually associated with the opposite anatomical sex in transsexualism.

Sexual Orientation

By sexual orientation we mean a person's preferential or obligatory sexual arousal by either heterosexual, homosexual, or inanimate objects.

TRANSSEXUALISM

The newborn infant does not know whether it is male or female, let alone masculine or feminine, and only develops the sense of maleness or femaleness as it matures. Cues to behavior are supplied to the infant in the earliest months of life primarily by the mother. Neonatal research has shown that most mothers treat boys and girls differently from the first hours of life. Each sex is handled or fondled in accordance with its assigned gender, and this applies to dressing, feeding, and all other matters of behavior and contact. The child is so young that these learning experiences are nontraumatic and not conflictual. They are, so to speak, the "built-in" earliest experiences that are accepted without question, and they form the basis of the child's earliest *core gender identity*, the first and most fundamental sense that one truly belongs to one's anatomical sex.

As the child grows older, more and more attitudes related to what is considered masculine or feminine behavior are communicated to enhance the behavior expected for each sex. This indoctrination is continuous and exerts great force on the growing child. Parents teach each child the behavior appropriate for its sex and also reflect to the child the expectations of the individual culture. Most parents provide the average expected attitudes to their children, and therefore few children experience problems in gaining their correct gender identity. There are parents, however, who fail to provide the child with the appropriate cues and instead treat the child in a fashion that is thoroughly inappropriate for the child's anatomical sex. These inappropriate signals function as mandates to the growing child and confuse the child concerning its proper gender identity. Sometimes the confusion may be so great as to lead the child to develop the syndrome of *transsexualism*, the most extreme form of gender disturbance. These individuals believe themselves to be of the sex opposite to that of their actual body. An anatomically normal male, for example, believes himself to be a woman trapped in a man's body. He seeks surgical remodeling and hormone treatments so as to become as much of a woman as is anatomically possible. Although physically a male and able to recognize his maleness without delusional distortion, he has nevertheless developed a feminine gender identity. The reverse would be true in the case of the many fewer female transsexuals who are anatomically normal women who have developed a masculine gender identity.

Differential Diagnosis

The cross-dressing of the male transsexual must not be confused with that of the transvestite. The male transsexual does not experience fetishistic sexual excitement with cross-dressing as does the transvestite. Furthermore, the gender identity of the male transsexual is feminine, and his sexual role behavior is truly and totally feminine in walk, talk, and gesture. It does not show the angry and fearful identification with women that the "effeminate" male homosexual reveals in his mocking caricature and exhibi-

tionistic mimicry of femininity. The male transsexual does not experience erotic pleasure in his penis, wishes to have it surgically removed, and desires a vagina so as to be able to have heterosexual intercourse with a heterosexual man and not a homosexual. The male transsexual does not consider himself a homosexual, but rather a female who wants to be loved as a woman by a normal man. In fact, he feels ashamed of his penis and male appearance, which he considers as repulsive because of his total feminine identification. In sharp contrast, fetishists, transvestites, and obligatory male homosexuals all take intense pleasure in their penises, and cannot tolerate the idea that women do not possess a penis. They may occasionally fantasize themselves as women, but they never really imagine themselves as being without a penis. Such individuals may become psychotic or feel overwhelmed with guilt about their sexuality, and seek surgical removal of the penis. Physicians must be very careful to make the correct distinctions between all of these conditions and transsexualism, and be aware that surgery is absolutely contraindicated for the transvestite, as well as for the fetishist and the obligatory male homosexual (Table 37.1).

The same diagnostic features are true for the female transsexual, whose gender identity is masculine, and whose sexual role behavior is truly masculine and does not show the angry and fearful identification with men that the "butch" homosexual woman reveals in her mockery and mimicry of masculinity. The female transsexual does not experience erotic pleasure in her vagina, wants it transformed surgically into a penis, and desires a penis so as to be able to have heterosexual intercourse with a heterosexual and not a homosexual woman. The female transsexual does not consider herself a homosexual, but rather a male who wants to be loved as a man by a normal woman (Table 37.1).

Etiology of Male Transsexualism

There is still much to be learned about the etiology of transsexualism. While some investigators have postulated an hormonal or possibly even a genetic disturbance prior to birth, these have not yet been demonstrated. What has been documented, by Robert Stoller in his two volumes, *Sex and Gender Volume I: On the Development of Masculinity and Femininity*, and *Sex and Gender Volume II: The Transsexual Experiment*, is the parental behavior of the parents of transsexual patients. Since there are many more male transsexuals than female transsexuals and since Stoller has been able to study many more parents of male than female transsexuals, we shall begin with his observations of these parents.

Stoller has studied the special relationship that exists between male transsexuals and their mothers. He has reported that these women, although appearing feminine, were quite aware of feeling neuter rather than womanly. Some of these women were also chronically depressed. None of them enjoyed sexual relations, which they permitted only infrequently. As children, these women had been tomboys, dressed as boys, and played only with boys. They failed to establish any close relationships with girls. The onset of puberty, however, led them to reject their more masculine behavior, at least on the surface. Subsequently, each of the mothers of the male transsexuals studied selected one of their male children, usually a "beautiful" male child, to whom they devoted a rather peculiar and special attention. They indulged themselves in close, usually skin to skin contact, with this chosen one of their children and attempted to maintain a blissful union with the boy in question. The boy was treated as an extension of the mother, and an extreme symbiosis was created between the child and the mother. Such a symbiosis is decidedly detrimental and results in an overwhelming and very early identification of the boy with his mother. This prevents him from establishing a true separation and individuation from the mother, and from developing a masculine gender identity, masculine role behavior, and a heterosexual orientation toward women. Thus, the femininity of the male transsexual is shaped from the first day of life and is related to his mother's wish for him to be a graceful and beautiful part of her own body. She does not find the child's anatomical sex any hindrance to her behaving toward her son as if he were a continuation of herself. In fact, she welcomes it, because this son represents the maleness and the overvalued penis for which she herself had yearned as a little girl. By unconsciously turning her son into a little girl she not only keeps him and his penis close to her forever, but also takes her revenge against all males.

Furthermore, the fathers of these boys provided no help to their sons. They were mostly absent from the home, and even when physically present they were so emotionally passive and remote as to be psychologically absent. They therefore offered no suitable masculine image with which these boys could identify so as to overcome the abnormal feminine identification with the mother. These fathers neither objected to the mother's dressing the boys as girls nor to their treating the boys as girls, and therefore did not protect their sons from the mother's behavior. The impact of the behavior of such parents is overwhelming and the child, unable to resist the blissful symbiosis with the mother, which is interrupted by neither the mother nor the father, becomes incapable of developing a normal masculine gender identity.

We often deal with parenthood and especially motherhood as if it were something sacred and as though all mothers and fathers do well by their children. Judges have taken children away from the finest of foster parents and returned them to obviously unsuitable parents as though the blood tie transcended every observed type of misbehavior on the part of the natural parents. Unfortunately, many parents do not really wish their children well, and use them for unsuitable purposes related to their own psychic pathology. This is certainly the case with the parents of male transsexuals. The mother shapes the boy's developing gender identity so that he never takes pleasure in his penis and instead develops a feminine gender identity which cannot be shaken. The histories of such individuals indicate that by the age of three they are already dressing as females and are insistent upon this. They will improvise girls' clothing for themselves out of any type of cloth if suitable female garments are not available. These boys even insist on sitting to urinate! The parents of such boys never seriously discourage this behavior. In fact, they consider it "cute," even when these boys begin to speak of themselves as girls and express the belief that they will grow up as women rather than as men. As a result, the adult male transsexual gives a history dating back to his earliest memories that indicates that he had always considered himself as feminine in spite of possessing male sexual organs.

The transvestite presents a very different childhood history. During the earliest months of his life and in the nonconflictual period before he is able to know about maleness or femaleness, he is cued differently than is the transsexual. The transsexual is unequivocally cued as a female regardless of his anatomical appearance, while the transvestite is essentially treated as masculine but in an ambiguous and sometimes hostile way, so that his developing masculinity is flawed but nonetheless fixed. In early childhood he may have been encouraged to wear girl's clothes by a sister or his mother or some other female in an effort to humiliate him and to undermine and attack his masculinity, but he still forms a masculine gender identity, albeit one that is certainly conflicted. Fetishism and transvestism are closely linked, as we have noted. The transvestite-to-be may, as a prepubertal child, put on female garments, often with the knowledge of his mother. If she enjoys his excitement, she will not discourage his use of her garments. These episodes may not occur frequently, and the child is considered normal. After puberty, however, the wearing of women's clothing is accompanied by increasing sexual excitement, with erection and masturbation. Those transvestites who wear only one or two female garments are closest to fetishistic men in their behavior. However, many transvestites dress completely in women's attire and like to pass for women, thus appearing on the surface like a transsexual. However, the transvestite, in contradistinction to the transsexual, is always sexually excited by his masquerading as a woman. He is fully aware of being a male when dressed as a woman, and he regularly becomes sexually aroused. Further, he cannot maintain the fiction of being a woman for very long, and sooner or later gives himself away by actions that reveal his masculine identity. When normally garbed as a man, he is quite masculine rather than feminine in appearance and mannerisms, and he is attracted to women. He cross-dresses only intermittently when in the grip of his compulsion.

Etiology of Female Transsexualism

In their many years of work with this syndrome, Stoller and his colleagues have not been able to identify the same etiological cluster in the parents of female transsexuals, namely a mother with a particular personality pattern and a father with a particular personality pattern. Many of the mothers of female transsexuals appear to have been withdrawn and depressed early in their daughter's life, and the fathers neither supported their wives nor encouraged their daughter's femininity. Rather they encouraged the little girl to take over some of their own tasks as husbands and fathers. The little girl then begins to feel very protective toward her mother, has conscious thoughts of taking care of her as a husband, and begins to develop increasing masculine behavior which is not discouraged by either the mother or the father. Whether these initial findings will be substantiated or invalidated by further study remains to be seen.

Treatment of Transsexualism

We have already commented on the crucial importance of making a proper diagnosis, and the need to distinguish transsexualism from transvestism and homosexuality. This is sometimes very difficult, if not impossible, because of confusing histories, distortions and misrepresentations of the history by patients seeking sex change surgery for a whole variety of different reasons, and also situations in which there is an actual mixture of several of these syndromes. Clearly, surgery should only be considered in the most extremely feminine men and the most extremely masculine women, without mixed pictures, where there is reasonable certainty of the diagnosis of transsexualism. But even in these cases, continuous hormonal treatment, supportive psychotherapy, and living and working in the role of the opposite sex are all necessary before *any* surgical procedures are begun.

Furthermore, it is important to remember that not all surgical interventions are equally successful. Modern surgical techniques and improved estrogen treatment have aided greatly in breast development and in the surgical creation of an artificial vagina for male transsexuals. However, as Stoller and others have reported, not all artificial vaginas function successfully or without difficulties. As a rule, they are very short and have a tendency to shrink or even close up on themselves without constant use. Frequent dilations are therefore necessary, and the artificial organ often bleeds or becomes infected afterwards. Scar tissue overgrowth has also been reported and may be a hazard, as well as rectovaginal fistulas, cystitis, and urethritis. In regard to female transsexuals, androgen therapy can produce secondary male sexual characteristics and an enlarged clitoris, and bilateral mastectomies and a hysterectomy can then be performed. But to date, attempts at the surgical reconstruction of penises for these females have not been very successful, and these patients need to be prepared for this sober reality.

Stoller, Green, Money, and others, have commented on the inadequacy of follow-up studies both in terms of quality and quantity on all those patients who have had sex change operations since 1953. We still know relatively little about those patients who truly benefit from sex reassignment procedures, since the most successful cases establish new lives in new locations, become integrated into their communities, do not wish to be reminded of their past or to be identified as a transsexual, and therefore are lost to follow-up. We also know relatively little about the frequency of postoperative surgical complications and long-term psychiatric complications in these patients.

In 1979, Meyer and Reter reported on their follow-up findings on 100 patients of the Johns Hopkins Gender Identity Clinic, 34 of whom had received surgery and 66 of whom had not been operated upon at the time the follow-up was begun in 1971. Follow-up data was eventually published on only 15 of the operated group (an average of 5.2 years after surgery) and on 35 of the unoperated (14 of whom subsequently received surgery but were evaluated separately from the operated group). Although the subjects who had had surgery did not regret the surgery and showed a trend toward social and sexual improvement following the surgery, Meyer and Reter concluded that the postsurgical improvement was not significantly different from that which occurred in the subjects who did not have surgery. The marked improvement which the surgical patients experienced with hormonal therapy and living in the role of the opposite sex prior to the surgery was not taken into account in the study. Shortly after the publication of the Meyer-Reter study, the Chief of the Department of Surgery at Johns Hopkins announced that sex reassignment surgery would no longer be performed at that institution.

It is important to note that the findings and the conclusions of the Meyer-Reter study are highly questionable and controversial, and have been sharply criticized on several methodological grounds by Money, Green, Pauly, Satterfield, Hunt and Hampson, and others. Nevertheless, even if it can be conclusively shown that the sex change operation is socially and sexually beneficial for properly selected patients, we still need to be aware, as John Money says, that "the reassignment procedure itself, finalized with surgery, does not solve all of the life problems that may be attendant upon the gender identity confusion." In the few patients that Robert Stoller has been able to follow in depth over many years, the true tragedy of this condition becomes apparent. Even if the surgery is successful, and the patients experience great psychological relief at finally being able to function as a man or a woman as the case may be, they still must live their new lives in the constant fear of being discovered. To whom can they then turn for the affection so desired? Can they ever tell their heterosexual partners the truth and still maintain the relationship? If not, how do they live with the despairing feeling of being dishonest with someone they love? Since these patients are not delusional and cannot simply deny the past, can they ever completely forget that life began in the opposite sex and that "in the depths of their identity" they know that they are still members of the anatomical sex into which they were born? As one of Stoller's patients said, a female transsexual who committed suicide after many years of successfully living and working as a man: "I'm all dressed up and no where to go." There is still so much more that we need to learn about this most extreme and tragic of all the sexual disorders.

Suggested Readings

Money J, Ehrhardt AA: *Man and Woman, Boy and Girl*. Baltimore, Johns Hopkins University Press, 1972.

Stoller RJ: *Sex and Gender Vol. I: On the Development of Masculinity and Femininity*. New York, Science House, 1968.

Stoller RJ: *Sex and Gender Vol. II: The Transsexual Experiment*. New York, Jason Aronson, 1975.

Stoller RJ: *Perversion: The Erotic Form of Hatred*. New York, Pantheon Press, 1975.

References

Bak RC: The phallic woman: the ubiquitous fantasy in perversions. *Psychoanal Study Child* 23:15, 1968.

Benjamin H: *The Transsexual Phenomenon*. New York, Julian Press, 1966.

Dickes R: Fetishistic behavior: a contribution to its complex development and significance. *J Am Psychoanal Assoc* 11:303, 1963.

Dickes R: Psychodynamics of fetishism. *Med Aspects Human Sexuality* 4:39, 1970.

Dickes R: Parents, transitional objects, and childhood fetishes. In Grolnick S, Barkin L, Muensterberger W (eds): *Between Reality and Fantasy: Transitional Objects and Phenomena*. New York, Jason Aronson, 1978, p 305.

Dörner G, et al: A neuroendocrine predisposition for homosexuality in men. *Arch Sexual Behav* 4:1, 1975.

Dörner G: *Hormones and Brain Differentiation*. New York, Elsevier Scientific, 1976.

Gadpaille WJ: *The Cycles of Sex*. New York, Charles Scribner's Sons, 1975.

Gadpaille WJ: Biological factors in the development of human sexual identity. *Psychiatr Clin N Am* 3:3, 1980.

Goy RW, Wolf JE, Eisele SG: Experimental female hermaphroditism in rhesus monkeys: anatomical and psychological characteristics. In Husaph H, Money J (eds): *Handbook of Sexology.* Amsterdam, Excerpta Medica, 1976, p 136.

Green R: *Sexual Identity Conflict in Children and Adults.* New York, Basic Books, 1974.

Green R: Children called "sissy" and "tomboy," adolescents who cross-dress, and adults who want to change sex. In Green R (ed): *Human Sexuality: A Health Practitioner's Text,* ed. 2. Baltimore, Williams & Wilkins, 1979, p 150.

Green R, Money J (eds): *Transsexualism and Sex Reassignment.* Baltimore, Johns Hopkins Press, 1969.

Greenacre P: Perversions: general considerations regarding their genetic and dynamic background. *Psychoanal Study Child* 23:47, 1968.

Greenson RR: Dis-identifying from mother. *Int J Psychoanal* 49:370, 1968.

Herschkowitz S, Dickes R: Suicide attempts in a female-to-male transsexual. *Am J Psychiatry* 135:368, 1978.

Hunt DD, Hampson JL: Follow-up of 17 biologic male transsexuals after sex-reassignment surgery. *Am J Psychiatry* 137:432, 1980.

Imperato-McGinley J, et al: Androgens and the evolution of male-gender identity among male pseudohermaphrodites with 5-alpha-reductase deficiency. *N Engl J Med* 300:1233, 1979.

Jost A: Problems of fetal endocrinology: the gonadal and hypophyseal hormones. In Pincus G (ed): *Recent Progress in Hormone Research.* New York, Academic Press, 1953, p 379.

Lothstein LM: Sex reassignment surgery: historical, bioethical, and theoretical issues. *Am J Psychiatry* 139:417, 1982.

Marmor J (ed): *Homosexual Behavior: A Modern Reappraisal.* New York, Basic Books, 1980.

Meyer JK, Reter DJ: See reassignment: follow-up. *Arch Gen Psychiatry* 36:1010, 1979.

Money J: (quoted in): *Medical World News,* April 30, 1979, p 11.

Money J: Sex assignment in anatomically intersexed infants. In Green R (ed): *Human Sexuality: A Health Practitioners' Text,* ed. 2. Baltimore, Williams & Wilkins, 1979, p 136.

Money J, Hampson JG, Hampson JL: Imprinting and the establishment of gender role. *Arch Neurol Psychiatry* 77:333, 1957.

Newman LE, Stoller RJ: Nontranssexual men who seek sex reassignment. *Am J Psychiatry* 131:437, 1974.

Pauly IB: (quoted in): *Psychiatric News,* June 19, 1981.

Person E, Ovesey L: The transsexual syndrome in males. I. Primary transsexualism. *Am J Psychotherapy* 28:4, 1974.

Person E, Oversey L: The transsexual syndrome in males. II. Secondary transsexualism. *Am J Psychotherapy* 28:174, 1974.

Phoenix CH, et al: Organizing action of prenatally administered testosterone propionate on the tissues mediating mating behavior in the female guinea pig. *Endocrinology* 65:369, 1959.

Saez JM, et al: Familial male pseudohermaphroditism and gynecomastia due to a testicular 17-ketosteroid reductase defect. I. Studies *in vivo. J Clin Endocrinol Metab* 32:604, 1971.

Satterfield S: (quoted in): *Psychiatric News,* July 16, 1982.

Stoller RJ: The term "transvestism." *Arch Gen Psychiatry* 24:230, 1971.

Stoller RJ: Boyhood gender aberrations: treatment issues. *J Am Psychoanal Assoc* 26:541, 1978.

Stoller RJ: Fathers of transsexual children. *J Am Psychoanal Assoc* 27:837, 1979.

Ward I: Prenatal stress feminizes and demasculinizes the behavior of males. *Science* 175:82, 1972.

Young WC, Goy RW, Phoenix CH: Hormones and sexual behavior. *Science* 143:212, 1964.

CHAPTER 38 Homosexuality

Warren J. Gadpaille, M.D.

ATTITUDES TOWARD HOMOSEXUALITY

The fact that a person is homosexual does not define him or her any more than does the fact that another person is heterosexual. Sexual orientation is only one facet of a person's life. But for many historical and psychological reasons, homosexuality often arouses very strong emotions in all of us, including physicians. This chapter's goals are to provide a background for physicians treating homosexuals, as all physicians do, and to counteract some of the preconceptions and overgeneralizations about homosexual activity. Whether a physician realizes it or not, 1% to 3% of adult female and 3% to 6% of adult male patients are predominantly or exclusively homosexual, and up to half of all people have engaged in various kinds of homosexual activities sometime during their lives. There are relatively few generalizations that can be scientifically validated about even exclusive homosexuals, much less about half of all patients.

As will be discussed below, the great majority of homosexual experiences occur in those who are, or will become, predominantly heterosexual. But this chapter will give particular attention to adult preferential or exclusive homosexuality because that is the category about which there is so much confusion, misunderstanding, and prejudice. The term "preferential," in this context, does not imply that this kind of homosexuality results from conscious choice, any more than heterosexuality does; the awareness of one's sexual preference is conscious, but not the source of that preference. Here, "preferential" applies to those who may be able to function heterosexually, but are more readily and pleasurably aroused by those of the same sex even when opposite sex partners are available and willing.

Homosexual activity occurs in all mammalian species studied for its incidence, and in most if not all human cultures; however, adult preferential or exclusive homosexuality does not occur naturally in any species other than humans. (For a more detailed discussion of the cross-species and cross-cultural data, and references to the original research, see Gadpaille, 1972 and 1980a.)

There is a wide variety of human cultural attitudes toward homosexuality. The majority of cultures in which the attitudes are known are accepting of some expressions of both male and female homosexuality. Acceptance is quite different from approval, however. Karlen's careful study of historical anthropological data indicates that genuine approval applies chiefly to juvenile and adolescent homosexuality and to nonpreferential or nonexclusive adult homosexual behavior. Preferential or exclusive adult homosexuality is virtually universally regarded as deviant. There is no known human culture in which adult preferential homosexuality is (or was) the behavioral norm.

In all mammals, including humans, the hypothalamus and perhaps other portions of the brain are organized during fetal or early neonatal development by the presence or absence of fetal androgens, for both physiology and behavior that is sex-specific. As Dr. Dickes and Dr. Simons discussed in the preceding chapter, fetal androgens during the critical periods organize the hypothalamus for later acyclic gonadotropin production, male reproductive behavior, and masculine social behavior. The absence of fetal androgens results in later cyclic gonadotropin production, female reproductive behavior, and feminine social behavior. Both the physiology and the behavior can be reversed by reversing the critical-period androgen exposure, regardless of chromosomal or gonadal sex. A major consequence of this fetal central nervous system

(CNS) organization is an innate heterosexual bias. Under normal biological conditions, it is easier to elicit a sexual response to an opposite sex member of the same species than to a same-sex one.

Males are biologically more vulnerable to disruption of sexual function than are females. One reason just noted is that male and masculine development requires that something be added to the basic CNS predisposition toward femaleness, and whenever a development is more complex, it is also more susceptible to disruption. In lower species, males are more distractable from mating than are females, and decortication destroys the sexual responses and function of males but not of females. Among primates, as Dr. Rosenblum has discussed earlier, privation conditions that interfere with the social learning necessary for adult sexuality disrupt the sexual function of males more totally and permanently than that of females. This kind of evidence demonstrates that male sexual function is more dependent upon learning—and therefore more susceptible to mislearning—than is female sexual function.

As one ascends the phylogenetic scale, the role of postnatal learning increases and the immutability of biological predisposition lessens. In humans, the importance of postnatal experiences is at its maximum, almost obscuring the innate biological factors. Innate characteristics are quite fragile, and idiosyncratic rearing experiences can distort or destroy them. But the data from fetal endocrinopathies, sexual anomalies, and the few available experiments are unanimous in demonstrating that humans retain the fetal CNS "programming" of sexuality common to all mammals. This evolutionary continuity reveals itself also in greater human male psychosexual vulnerability. Even in the area of postnatal learning, the more difficult task falls to boys, who must disidentify with their first love objects (the mother, or some mothering female) before they can achieve a male and masculine gender identity—as Dr. Simons will discuss further in his chapter on early adulthood.

Nevertheless, our species' evolution has continued to load the gene pool for those sex-linked traits, including that of adult heterosexual bias, conducive to species survival. The biologically normal human newborn is not a sexual *tabula rasa*, however vulnerable its innate tendencies may be to the overriding influence of postnatal experiences.

Against this background, adult preferential or exclusive homosexuality is viewed as *an adaptive response to some disruption of or interference with the natural process of psychosexual development*. Some specific and unnatural, although perhaps quite subtle influences are necessary to disrupt heterosexual orientation permanently in the absence of any biological abnormality. However, this view implies little else that is generally applicable to adult preferential homosexuals, and nothing at all about the vast majority of people with other kinds of homosexual experiences. Equally as important, since there are so many unfortunate misconceptions about homosexuality, one must be very clear about what *cannot* be assumed simply by knowing that a person is primarily aroused by, or is sexually active with, others of the same sex.

Unless one takes a careful history, the fact that homosexual activity has occurred is not clinically useful. One must know which of the many varieties of homosexual activity is involved because some may have implications for therapeutic intervention and others may not.

In the Christian religion and in some other religions, there are injunctions against homosexuality, so that for those who accept these religious tenets any homosexual activity is sinful and unacceptable. But in humanitarian terms, homosexual activity between consenting peer partners does not label someone evil or bad. Unless homosexuality itself is arbitrarily defined as a crime, there is no evidence of a higher incidence of criminality or antisocial behavior among homosexuals than among heterosexuals.

Homosexual people do not by definition function less well than heterosexuals, or even have a more impoverished sex life. Masters and Johnson studied committed and highly functional homosexual and heterosexual couples, and found that the homosexuals were the more sensitive to the partner's needs and responses, took more time in whole body sensuality and foreplay, communicated more freely about their emotions and sensations during sexual interaction, and were the more egalitarian than were heterosexuals. Of course, their findings may not apply to the general population of either group. But a recent large study of lesbian and heterosexual women found that the lesbians reported themselves to be more sexually active and orgasmically responsive, and more satisfied in their sexual relationships, than did their heterosexual counterparts. And there are more homosexuals who feel satisfied and are productive in their lives than there are those who cannot function effectively because of emotional conflict over their sexual orientation.

Most importantly, one cannot automatically assume that homosexual activity is, or is symptomatic of, an illness according to the medical model: a condition with a known (or knowable) cause, typical onset and course, pathognomonic symptoms, and implications for prevention and therapy. Clearly it sometimes can be, just as some expressions of heterosexuality are grossly pathological. Even in instances where it is indicative of disorder, what to do about it is the sole right and choice of the individual except in specific instances of its misuse against others. A wide variety of homosexual behaviors and persons, perhaps a majority, probably fall outside the above medical model and reflect a broad range of motives, origins, and individual and cultural meanings.

VARIETIES OF HOMOSEXUAL EXPRESSION

Preferential or exclusive homosexuality deserves the fullest discussion and will be covered in a separate section.

Developmental homoerotic activity may occur at any or all immature developmental stages in both boys and girls. It is found in most or all cultures, is a part of normal sexual curiosity and experimentation, and is usually not prognostic of adult homosexuality. Kinsey and his coworkers found that 33% of females and over 50% of males reported homoerotic play by age 15.

Pseudohomosexuality is homosexuality by default. It has been described chiefly in males, but complementary motivation may occur in females. Contrary to the primarily erotic motivation of preferential homosexuals, pseudohomosexuals' primary conflicts concern dependency and power, which they associate respectively with femininity and masculinity. If men see themselves as inadequate or weak compared to other men, they may unconsciously make the equation, "I am nonmasculine = I am feminine = I am homosexual." This may then be acted out in homosexual behavior. In childhood these men often were passive and isolated from their peers, but few remember wishing to be girls or feeling erotic attraction to other males. Masturbatory fantasies and dreams may have homosexual content, but the emotional components concern power and submission more than eroticism.

People of either sex whose natural tendencies or developmental conflicts give them an inadequate sense of masculinity or femininity are at risk for pseudohomosexuality, a condition that characteristically arises from deep conflict and is accompanied by severe emotional distress. Sometimes the fear of being homosexual or of being homosexually attacked can accelerate into an acute panic state and require emergency psychiatric intervention.

Situational homosexuality occurs among preferential heterosexuals in enforced same-sex environments such as some armed forces assignments. Usually these people revert to their heterosexual preferences when they return to normal social settings, and little psychopathology develops unless the experience precipitates a pseudohomosexual panic or a more lasting pseudohomosexual maladaptation. In some same-sex environments such as boarding schools or prisons, additional characterological qualities (forceful coercion and fearful submission) often color the homosexual experience.

Exploitative homosexuality is that form which those with the social and physical power, as in inmate subcultures, use to coerce the weaker and more fearful to be sexual objects, usually in anal intercourse but sometimes also through fellatio. There may be unconscious sexual identity conflicts in some exploiters, but usually these are acts of violence and rage in which the penis is used as a weapon and symbol of dominance, as in heterosexual rape. Sexual exploitation in the service of power, dominance, and underlying rage also occurs in all-female environments. Male exploiters characteristically do not think of themselves as homosexual and rarely seek therapy for sexual conflicts.

Enforced homosexuality complements exploitative homosexuality. The violence to one's masculine or feminine self-image is severe, and therapy is urgently indicated, but the facilities and circumstances usually make it difficult or impossible. There is a general professional consensus that a preexisting sexual orientation conflict is necessary before a primarily erotic homosexual preference can develop, but there is one report by Sagarin of preferential homosexuals who claim never to have been aware of homosexual tendencies before their experience as coerced sexual partners in prison.

The above two kinds of homosexual experiences raise an important issue. For most middle class American homosexual males, the masculine or feminine identity implications of the insertor or insertee roles carry little conscious importance, although the unconscious implications may be quite significant. The roles are often alternated, and relatively few express a strong preference one way or the other. But this is not true everywhere and in all groups. Even in Western culture, there are some Latin American cultures and some United States ethnic groups in which the roles are sharply dichotomized with respect to masculine and feminine meaning. Only the insertee regards himself, and is regarded, as homosexual and feminine and is so stigmatized. The insertor does not consider himself homosexual; he usually does not hide his activity, his masculinity is not compromised within his group, and he suffers no social stigmatization. This can be true whether the insertor acts with intimidation and violence as in prisons, or with mutual consent, as in some Latin American groups; this dichotomy is also reported in some male adolescent groups.

Bisexuality is a large category that is poorly understood. Bisexuals report themselves to be sexually functional with either sex. However, except for the small group of ambisexuals, it cannot be assumed that they do not have a preference for one sex or the other. In a society that stigmatizes homosexuality, bisexuality is usually found in those whose erotic preference is homosexual; otherwise, the social consequences would not be worth risking.

Ambisexuality is a subgroup of bisexuality that is theoretically distinguished by the fully equal capacity to function in and enjoy sexual activity with both sexes. In the quite small group thus categorized by Masters and Johnson in 1979, no differences in sexual performance, observed or reported erotic pleasure, or physiological sexual response were detectable, regardless of the partner's sex.

Variational homosexuality is the consciously voluntary expression of the desire for sexual variety, and probably has many different roots. One may be freedom from social bias, but others may include conflict over heterosexuality, unconscious homosexual preference, or difficulties with emotional commitment to one partner with the long-term implications and responsibilities of that commitment.

Ideological or *political homosexuality* is a recently more visible type, found most often among women in the feminist movement. It is frequently an aggressive denial of any sexual need for or dependence upon men, or is used as

a negation of any innate psychological sex-linked differences. Sexual identity conflicts may certainly find expression in this behavior, but by definition, psychopathology is denied by the proponents. Nonetheless, doubts, conflicts, and psychotherapeutic needs are emerging in people who have found that such ideological homosexuality does not solve their sexual problems nor is it compatible with their basic sexual identity.

PREFERENTIAL OR EXCLUSIVE HOMOSEXUALITY

The term "homosexual" generally refers to this group of people. This spontaneous, popular distinction from others who are homosexually active may have some basis; cross-species and cross-cultural data suggest that this form of homosexual behavior is not only quantitatively but also qualitatively different from other expressions of homosexual behavior. In preferential homosexuals, their response to same-sex persons is primarily erotic, genital, and affectional; this is in contrast to that of all the other varieties except possibly ambisexuality.

The true numbers of any stigmatized or illegal group cannot be determined. Estimates have ranged as high as 10% of males and 6% of females in the United States, but these figures usually derive from nonrepresentative samples. More representative populations yield estimates of 1% to 3% of females and 3% to 6% of males, with no significant differences among the various ethnic groups. That means that about six to eight million people in the United States today are homosexual. Biological factors, such as those mentioned earlier, may account for the higher frequency worldwide among men.

Contrary to popular misconceptions, perhaps a majority of those who are preferentially or exclusively homosexual at any given time have experienced heterosexual intercourse (from 33% to over 66% of males and from 60% to 85% of females, depending upon the study), and a large minority continue to have some degree of heterosexual activity. Many have been married and, of those, one-half to three-quarters have had children.

The label "homosexual" implies a unity that does not exist because, aside from a shared sexual orientation, this group of people is made up of as diverse human types and personalities as are heterosexuals. Bell and Weinberg proposed one possible typology into which approximately 70% of their study population (about 1000) of nonpatient homosexuals could be fit. There were those who were *coupled*, living in a quasi-marriage with one partner (the length of the partnership varied widely). Of the 686 males, the "close-coupled" (9.8%) desire considerable fidelity and closeness. The "open-coupled" (17.5%) consider a regular partner important for sex and affection but, despite considerable jealousy, agree to additional sexual partners. The *functional* group (14.9%) have a high level of sexual activity and more sexual partners than the other groups, little regret over their homosexuality, and relatively few sexual problems. The *dysfunctionals* (12.5%) have more regret over their homosexuality and more sexual problems than the others. The *asexuals* (16.0%) have little sexual interest, little activity and few partners, and also have many sexual problems. Seventy per cent of the female homosexuals were similarly classifiable, but there were about three times as many close-coupled, and far fewer functionals, dysfunctionals, and asexuals.

Obviously, one could construct many different typologies of either homosexuals or heterosexuals; this one does serve the purpose of indicating some of the sexual variety within a group that is usually designated by a single label. However, it is impossible to know whether the sample population of Bell and Weinberg is representative of all preferential homosexuals, and a serious flaw exists in their inability to classify about 30% of their sample into the categories they themselves devised. This unclassified percentage is nearly twice as large as that in any of their specific categories. Furthermore, since Bell and Weinberg compare their classified homosexuals with the control group of heterosexuals in many dimensions, the omission of such comparisons with this unclassified 30% group renders the conclusions of this study difficult to evaluate.

There are differences as well as similarities between male and female preferential homosexuals. As shown in the data cited earlier, more females than males have had and continue to have heterosexual intercourse. About two-thirds of each sex reports "tomboyism" or "sissiness" in childhood. But in a comparison group of heterosexuals, 16% of females were also "tomboys" whereas only 3% of males were "sissies." Thus, cross-gender behavior is more prognostic of adult homosexuality in boys than in girls.

And cross-gender behavior in either sex does not necessarily continue into adulthood, so that the majority of homosexuals are not recognizable by opposite sex mannerisms or social behavior.

The major behavioral differences are in the number of partners and frequency of partner change. In Schäfer's 1977 study, homosexual males averaged 15 times as many partners as did homosexual females, and 11 times as many males as females had more than 50 sexual partners. In the Bell and Weinberg study, one-third of the black and nearly one-half of the white males had had over 500 different sexual partners; another one-quarter and one-third, respectively, reported between 100 and 500 partners. Fifty-one per cent of the blacks and 79% of the whites reported that more than half of their partners were strangers, and 38% and 70%, respectively, had sex only once with over half of their partners. In contrast, only 12% of black and 7% of white lesbians had 50 or more different partners, and only 6% reported that over half their partners had been strangers. The 1977 Schäfer study reported that homosexuals of both sexes shift partners more often than heterosexuals do, and that the difference is much greater between homosexual and heterosexual men. Comparison of number and frequency of change of partners with the heterosexual control group is omitted from the Bell and Weinberg study. Both studies show a greater incidence and longer duration of close, quasi-marital pairing among women, and more importance placed upon sexual fidelity in female than in male homosexual couples.

PSYCHODYNAMICS AND THE ISSUE OF "ILLNESS"

The discussion here is limited to what is known of the etiology of adult preferential homosexuality in those relatively few who have been in psychoanalysis or in other kinds of intensive psychotherapy, or who have otherwise made themselves available for study—a small proportion of all homosexuals. The speculative possibility of a biological etiology must be mentioned, though it is by definition not a psychodynamic factor. It is conceivable that atypical or aberrant fetal hormonal (or other) influences that organize the embryonic CNS for ultimate heterosexual arousal and responsivity could reverse that heterosexual bias, or diminish or neutralize its strength. There is no direct evidence for this basis of homosexuality in humans, but it cannot as yet be ruled out. Primate and other mammalian experimental evidence, and clinical evidence from various human endocrinopathies and genetic disorders suggest that some such altered biology during fetal development may play an as yet undefinable role in some instances.

The nature and relevance of postnatal rearing and psychological experiences for the development of homosexuality remains controversial. One source of homosexuality that is clear to those who have worked intensively with homosexual males in psychoanalytic therapy lies in unconscious conflict that develops from a child's emotional response to various postnatal experiences and parental influences that render heterosexuality unappealing or unattainable. The range of influences that could have that effect is endless, but some seem to be found more commonly than others. The most extensive research is reported by Bieber and his colleagues, in which the majority of male homosexual patients were found to have grown up with a close-binding, overly intimate mother and a detached or hostile father. Such mothers infantilize the son, undermine his development of masculinity through overprotection, interfere with his moving out into the rough-and-tumble world of little boy peers, and make him inappropriately into her companion and confidante. The father is emotionally unavailable as an object of identification either because he is detached and indifferent, or hostile and punitive. The mother is usually openly disrespectful and derogatory toward the father and makes the son an ally against him—behaviors which further remove the father as a person deserving of respect and identification, and devalue the boy's masculinity by devaluing his father. The psychological consequences for the boy (mostly unconscious) are that he identifies with his mother rather than his father and is afraid to be a scorned masculine person for fear of losing her love. In addition, his father's distance or hostility deprives him of the opportunity to learn to see his father realistically rather than as the all powerful oedipal rival. Both his overcloseness with his mother and his exaggerated perceptions of his father conspire to make him fearfully avoid masculine competition with other men for women in the future.

This brief summary is not a caricature, nor even a particularly extreme description. Many case histories of male homosexual patients reveal such dynamics over and over again. But even though it is the most typical constellation of early childhood influences in the histories of male homosexual patients, it is only one. And obviously, the dynamics would have to be different for females. One constellation among female homosexuals found by Kaye and his colleagues is essentially complementary: the mothers were hostile toward the little girl and not encouraging of her femininity, and the fathers were puritanically overprotective, emotionally distant, and jealously attacking of any budding interest in boys. In another pattern the mother is unloving and overtly prefers any male siblings, while the father is withdrawn and, by not being demonstratively affectionate and thus showing that he cherishes her as a little girl, fails to protect his daughter from the mother's destructive influence.

In trying to understand the intrapsychic dynamics of homosexual patients, there are two important principles to keep in mind. One is that there is no one etiological background for any state of being, whether homosexuality, heterosexuality, or anything else. Any number of experiences, operating in concert with the particular cognitive capacities and developmental levels and vulnerabilities of different children, can combine to interfere with the ability of a child to identify with parental adults of the same sex in his or her sexual orientation. The second principle is that these influences and emotions need not be in immediately accessible conscious memory. Most of these experiences had their decisive impact by the time the child was five or six years old; while some were dramatic, often they were subtle but pervasive. These facts, plus the inevitability of repression of many early painful and conflictual childhood memories and emotions, mean that most people do not recall the origins of their sexual object choice; they even unwittingly "rewrite" their own biographies by remembering their childhoods quite differently from what they actually were. This does not mean that psychiatrists have simply inferred such backgrounds without data; such histories were spontaneously recounted under circumstances that facilitated the recovery of repressed memories, and were often independently corroborated. It does mean that one cannot depend upon unstudied conscious memory to reveal early unconscious psychodynamics.

The recent research by Bell, Weinberg, and Hammersmith questions the validity of most psychodynamic explanations of homosexual development. In their interviews with hundreds of homosexual men and women, the histories given by most of those respondents did not seem to corroborate the family constellations and emotional conflicts found in analytic patients. There seemed to be little correlation between early parental relationships and later sexual orientation, and their data were interpreted as supporting a biological explanation. These data are important and useful in understanding the conscious self-concepts of homosexuals, but they cannot scientifically be seen as negating psychoanalytically derived historical and etiological data. The two kinds of information arise from different levels of awareness, and one need not contradict the validity of the other.

There are also social learning theories that add to the understanding of adult preferential homosexuality. Intrapsychic conflict alone would not fully explain why two children with at least apparently similar backgrounds could develop different sexual orientations; such an explanation requires an understanding of how the continuing parental influences and expectations differed for the two children. Differing cultural expectations also affect what one learns from specific experiences. For example, there is an Oceanic culture in which all males spend their adolescence isolated from females, and are in exclusive homosexual relationships with the preferentially heterosexual adult males of the tribe (who had had the same adolescent experience themselves). Since their early childhood experiences did not impair their capacity for heterosexuality, and since the culture expects them to be preferentially heterosexual when they reach marriagable age, they do not learn to regard themselves as (nor do they become) homosexual. Social learning theory also explains many developmental phase manifestations of homosexuality in this culture. But sometimes such theories minimize or deny the role of unconscious conflicts and of the biological substrate that can set the stage for unconscious conflicts. As general explanatory theories, they are insufficient to explain adult preferential homosexuality because of the one-sided position they take in the nature/nurture interaction, neither extreme of which is scientifically tenable.

A major, and essentially unanswerable, question is whether any such psychodynamics as described above can be extrapolated to the millions of adult homosexuals about whom no such information is available. There are studies of nonpatient homosexuals in which family constellations and evidence of emotional conflicts typical of the patient groups were also found. But again it cannot be known whether or not those study groups were representative of adult preferential homosexuals in general. There is no disagreement that any of these psychodynamics or family constellations can be found in some heterosexuals. What makes the difference is unclear. If (or where) atypical fetal biology plays a role, some children may have less resilience against relatively minor developmentally disruptive influences that might also be found in the backgrounds of many heterosexuals.

The much more important question of whether or not preferential homosexuals are psychiatrically disturbed is highly controversial, and the issue has become more political than scientific. In 1974, the American Psychiatric Association voted to remove homosexuality from its classification of mental illnesses. In 1977, another survey of 2500 psychiatrists found that 69% regarded homosexuality as a pathological adaptation. However, psychological test surveys of nonpatient homosexuals fail to reveal significant pathology in the majority of those tested. Comparisons with heterosexuals vary from finding more to less psychopathology in the homosexual groups. In the Bell and Weinberg study, homosexuals showed more social and psychological problems than did heterosexuals in the majority of a variety of measures, including job stability, psychosomatic symptoms, tension, depression, and suicidal ideation and attempts; female homosexuals showed fewer and smaller differences from their heterosexual counterparts than did male homosexuals with theirs. But when the homosexual/heterosexual comparisons were broken down according to the typology described earlier, the "dysfunctionals" and the "asexuals" provided the bulk of the pathology. There were no significant differences between the heterosexual controls and the "close-coupled," "open-coupled," and "functional" homosexuals in the problems reported.

The belief is widely held among sociologists, and many psychiatrists as well, that the greater incidence of social and psychological problems among homosexuals is caused by social stigmatization and discrimination and its consequent psychological stress. This explanation is reasonable and attractive because such conditions do cause stress that results in morbidity among the victims. Yet the one study, by Weinberg and Williams, of such problems in homosexuals in both discriminatory and nondiscriminatory social environments failed to find that those in the nondiscriminatory environments had fewer psychosocial problems than those in the discriminatory environments.

The practice of having sex with very large numbers of partners, most of whom are and remain strangers, is generally considered evidence of psychopathology. There are no exactly comparable data for heterosexuals, but what data exist indicate that heterosexual partner numbers and frequency of change is typically only a small fraction of those found in many (chiefly male) homosexuals. To what extent this assessment of pathology is a culture-bound moral prejudice rather than a valid psychiatric judgment is not clear. There are some cultures in which premarital heterosexual contacts among nonincest-tabooed partners are entirely free, and the number of partners is limited only by local population and accessibility; one cannot make automatic assumptions in all cultural milieux about either the causes or the consequences of many casual sex partners. Perhaps homosexual males are freed from the constraints imposed upon heterosexuals by women, who can and often want to bear children, and who thus have an understandable vested interest in commitment, marriage, and family.

Clinical experience, however, is that whenever anyone, whether heterosexual or homosexual, develops a life style into adulthood characterized by casual sex with numerous partners who are and remain strangers, such behavior typically indicates significant psychopathology. It is evidence of shallow, narcissistic, impersonal, often compulsively driven, genital-oriented rather than person-oriented sex, and of conflicts in the capacity for intimacy and commitment. This is an orientation-blind clinical judgment; it applies regardless of the partner preference of the individual. And it clearly does not apply to those homosexuals who are able to establish close, committed partnerships.

A developmental statement that is valid for every adult preferential homosexual is that he or she did not make a firm and lasting identification with the heterosexual orientation of the parent of the same sex. In clinical populations this is typically reflected in conscious or uncon-

scious hostility toward people of the same sex, which is defended against by the desire to love and be loved by these people of the same sex. Hendin has found this hostility in a nonclinical population also. To whatever extent this dynamic is a valid generalization, such ambivalence could provide one explanation for the frequent impersonality of homosexual encounters, the repetitive turning from one partner to another, and the great difficulty most homosexuals have in achieving and maintaining a committed, enduring relationship that is both sexual and affectionate. This speculation, even if sound, is bound to be incomplete, however, because it does not explain why the same failure of identification seems to affect female homosexuals less than males.

It is obviously inappropriate to stereotype all adult preferential homosexuals as emotionally disturbed and socially dysfunctional. The disruptions in psychosexual development that predispose to homosexuality do seem to contribute to difficulty in fusing one's needs for sex and intimacy in a workable and gratifying relationship with another person, but many people can surmount these difficulties. There is little reason to presume that this adaptation disrupts overall function or mental health any more than other kinds of pathogenic developmental influences cause various degrees of emotional conflict and dysfunction in perhaps the majority of heterosexuals. The only difference is that the developmental traumata in heterosexuals disturbed or constricted different aspects of their lives than their sexual orientation. The majority of homosexuals appear to be both socially and psychiatrically satisfied and functional, though perhaps homosexual males often suffer from an impoverishment of interpersonal commitment and intimacy with their sexual partners.

CLINICAL IMPLICATIONS

The fact that a patient is homosexually active has practical medical significance. Just as it is important to know if a woman is or may be heterosexually active because of the relevant medical and contraceptive issues, it is clinically important to know of homosexuality. Failure to do so can lead to missing atypical manifestations or loci of some illnesses or lesions. For instance, in the Bell and Weinberg study, two-thirds of the male homosexuals had had some venereal disease at least once. The physician who did not know of a patient's homosexual activity could overlook examining for a rectal lesion, or fail to culture or do appropriate microscopic examination of rectal or pharyngeal specimens even in the presence of suspicious symptomatology.

There are other medical conditions that have an unusual incidence or epidemiology in male homosexuals, related to their more frequent practice of anal intercourse than is true of heterosexuals. Because the anus is less elastic than the vagina for accommodation of the erect penis, anal and rectal fissures, fistulas, and infected fissures and hemorrhoids are more common. Nonspecific urethritis due to fecal pathogens can occur. Infectious hepatitis is transmitted primarily via the fecal-oral route and homosexual males are at particular risk. Various intestinal parasitic diseases, such as amebiasis and giardiasis, can be contracted through anal intercourse; the diagnosis can easily be missed in a patient who has not been exposed through any of the usual epidemiological routes, if the physician fails to inquire about homosexual practices. And the recently emerging acquired immune deficiency syndrome (AIDS) is a usually fatal condition of still unknown etiology that affects homosexual males in much greater proportion than other population groups.

Relatively few homosexuals spontaneously identify themselves as such to a physician, and very few doctors routinely ask such questions. It is important to remember, however, that any patient may be homosexually active, even someone who is married and has children, and whom the doctor has known for a long time. Many doctors believe that they would offend their patients by asking questions about homosexuality and that patients would deny it anyway. Both offense and denial may happen under even the best of circumstances, but neither possibility justifies taking an inadequate history, and both can be greatly minimized by a matter-of-fact, nonjudgmental attitude. Often a patient with homosexual activity is eager to discuss it with an understanding physician because it is related to the reason for seeking medical help, even though he or she would not have mentioned it unless asked.

The majority of homosexuals profess no desire to become heterosexual. For adult patients, it is a mistake to express one's own preference and try to persuade them to change; that will usually be taken offensively, destroy rapport, and perhaps drive them away from necessary medical care. It is appropriate, however, after some sense of trust is established, to inquire nonjudgmentally, "Have you ever felt unhappy over being homosexual, and wished you could be different?" There are those who do want to change and perhaps could, but are afraid to express it because they are convinced it is impossible.

With children and adolescents, the physician is in a somewhat different ethical position. First, it is necessary to determine whether the homosexual behavior is simply a nonprognostic developmental experience or is prognostic of adult preferential homosexuality. The distinction is not always easy, but there are some helpful signs. (More is known about the childhood of male homosexuals than of female homosexuals.) Boys who are likely to become homosexual are more often effeminate and loners, are over-protected and afraid of physical harm, avoid rough boys and rough-and-tumble games and sports, and often prefer to play with girls and prefer girls' games and toys. The comparable manifestations of tomboyism in girls are not as often prognostic, but in both sexes, when masturbation with erotic fantasies begins, those fantasies are more often homosexual than heterosexual. Also, the feeling of being in love with a same-sex person (not just a nonerotic "crush"), or the voluntary involvement in sexual activity with a same-sex adult, are often indicative of future homosexuality, as is, obviously, the conscious awareness of homosexual erotic preference.

Children and adolescents cannot be expected to comprehend fully the consequences of their actions or of specific lifestyles. While neither "bad" nor "wrong," homosexuality carries with it more disadvantage than advantage in most societies. With young people it is ethically appropriate to inform them about the possibilities of change, to urge change, and where permissible to involve parents in providing psychotherapy for the child and themselves as well.

Whenever therapy to effect a shift to heterosexuality is indicated for a child or voluntarily sought by an adolescent or adult, there is the additional problem of finding competent therapy. This always requires a psychiatrist or other specially trained mental health professional, but many psychiatrists are no better informed about homosexuality nor better trained to help effect such a shift than are primary care physicians. It is necessary for the referring physician to inquire directly about a psychiatrist's specific interest and experience in working with such patients. Therapy with children, especially if their parents are concurrently involved, can be very successful; therapy with adolescents is often less successful. With adults, psychoanalysis has generally had the best results. Approximately one third of such patients become exclusively heterosexual, one third become preferentially heterosexual, and one third are unchanged. Recently, Masters and Johnson have reported an unusually high success rate (79%) of shift to heterosexuality by homosexuals dissatisfied with their homosexuality using intensive behavior modification techniques, but these results await further confirmation.

For those patients whose homosexual activity is not preferential or exclusive, it is useful to determine what category of homosexual behavior is involved. Persons subjected to enforced homosexuality, even when it was long past, may have serious emotional problems. Developmental homoerotic play may severely frighten an adolescent boy or girl, and undermine the sense of masculinity or femininity. And a knowledge of the patient's cultural values is important; it would insult a male insertor from some cultures to refer to his behavior as homosexual. Preferential homosexuals who have no interest in changing may still need psychotherapy. An inability to form attachments may benefit from professional help regardless of orientation. Homosexuals can suffer from sexual dysfunctions just as heterosexuals can, and the dysfunctions can be successfully treated.

Basic to all good patient care with homosexuals is an accepting and nonjudgmental attitude. This is sometimes difficult or even impossible for some physicians to achieve, because physicians are only people with a particular kind of professional training, subject to the same stereotypic thinking, prejudices, inhibitions, conflicts, and ignorance as other people. When personal attitudes interfere with an optimal doctor-patient relationship and good patient care, the ethical course is to explain one's dilemma openly and refer the patient to a colleague known to be comfortable with such patients. A sick homosexual patient is nothing more than a sick person, entitled to be treated with dignity and respect, and with whatever medical or psychiatric care he or she may require.

Suggested Readings

Bieber I, et al: *Homosexuality: A Psychoanalytic Study of Male Homosexuals.* New York, Basic Books, 1962.

Gadpaille WJ: Cross-species and cross-cultural contributions to understanding homosexual activity. *Arch Gen Psychiatry* 37:349, 1980.
Hendin H: Homosexuality: the psychosocial dimension. *J Am Acad Psychoanal* 6:479, 1978.
Karlen A: *Sexuality and Homosexuality.* New York, W.W. Norton, 1971.
Marmor J (ed): *Homosexual Behavior: A Modern Reappraisal.* New York, Basic Books, 1980.

References

Bartollas C, Miller SJ, Dinitz S: The "booty bandit:" a social role in a juvenile institution. *J Homosexuality* 1:203, 1974.
Bell AP, Weinberg MS: *Homosexualities.* New York, Simon and Schuster, 1978.
Bell AP, Weinberg MS, Hammersmith SK: *Sexual Preference.* Bloomington, Indiana University Press, 1981.
Carrier JM: "Sex-role preference" as an explanatory variable in homosexual behavior. *Arch Sexual Behav* 6:53, 1977.
Churchill W: *Homosexual Behavior Among Males.* New York, Hawthorn, 1967.
Coleman EM, Hoon PW, Hoon EF: Arousability and sexual satisfaction in lesbian and heterosexual women. *J Sex Research* 19:58, 1983.
Davenport W: Sexual patterns and their regulation in a society of the Southwest Pacific. In Beach FA (ed): *Sex and Behavior.* New York, John Wiley & Sons, 1965, p 164.
DeFries Z: Pseudohomosexuality in feminist students. *Am J Psychiatry* 133:400, 1976.
DeFries Z: Political lesbianism and sexual politics. *J Am Acad Psychoanal* 6:71, 1978.
Evans RB: Childhood parental relationships of homosexual men. *J Consult Clin Psychol* 33:129, 1969.
Ford CS, Beach FA: *Patterns of Sexual Behavior.* New York, Harper & Row, 1951.
Gadpaille WJ: Research into the physiology of maleness and femaleness. *Arch Gen Psychiatry* 26:193, 1972.
Gadpaille WJ: Homosexuality in adolescent males. *J Am Acad Psychoanal* 3:361, 1975.
Gadpaille WJ: Biological factors in the development of human sexual identity. *Psychiatr Clin N Am* 3:3, 1980.
Gagnon JH, Simon W: *Sexual Conduct.* Chicago, Aldine, 1973.
Green R: *Sexual Identity Conflict in Children and Adults.* New York, Basic Books, 1974.
Grundlach RH: Childhood parental relationships and the establishment of gender roles. *J Consult Clin Psychol* 33:136, 1969.
Hooker E: The adjustment of the male overt homosexual. *J Proj Tech* 21:18, 1957.
Hooker E: Parental relationships and male homosexuality in patient and non-patient samples. *J Consult Clin Psychology* 33:140, 1969.
Kaye HE, et al: Homosexuality in women. *Arch Gen Psychiatry* 17:626, 1967.
Kinsey AC, Pomeroy WB, Martin CE: *Sexual Behavior in the Human Male.* Philadelphia, W.B. Saunders, 1948.
Kinsey AC, et al: *Sexual Behavior in the Human Female.* Philadelphia, W.B. Saunders, 1953.
Masters WH, Johnson VE: *Homosexuality in Perspective.* Boston, Little, Brown, and Co, 1979.
Medical Aspects of Human Sexuality: Sexual survey #4: Current thinking on homosexuality. 11:110, 1977.
Ovesey L: *Homosexuality and Pseudohomosexuality.* New York, Science House, 1969.
Reiss AJ, Jr: The social integration of queers and peers. *Social Prob* 9:102, 1961.
Sagarin E: Prison homosexuality and its effect on post-prison sexual behavior. *Psychiatry* 39:245, 1976.
Saghir MT, Robins E: *Male and Female Homosexuality.* Baltimore, Williams & Wilkins, 1973.
Schäfer S: Sexual and social problems of lesbians. *J Sex Res* 12:50, 1976.
Schäfer S: Sociosexual behavior in male and female homosexuals: a study of sex differences. *Arch Sex Behav* 6:355, 1977.

Schwartz MF, Masters WH: The Masters and Johnson treatment program for dissatisfied homosexual men. *Am J Psychiatry* 141:173, 1984.

Snortum JR, et al: Family dynamics and homosexuality. *Psychol Rep* 24:763, 1969.

Weinberg MS, Williams CJ: *Male Homosexuals.* New York, Oxford University Press, 1974.

Weinberg TS: On "doing" and "being" gay: sexual behavior and homosexual male self-identity. *J Homosexuality* 4:143, 1978.

Section K/Work

CHAPTER **39** **Work and Creativity**

Ferruccio di Cori, M.D.

The dual capacity to love and to work, so Freud said, is the expression of normality. Work takes a wide variety of forms, however, some of which fall at the farthest boundaries of normality, if not a bit beyond.

WORK AND CREATIVITY

Is drudgery an expression of normality—work which is one more monotonous element in a dreary, compulsive life? Is extremely dangerous work—stunt driving, for example—an expression of normality? Depending on your viewpoint and tolerance for the unusual, we might equally well question the normality of political agitation as a line of work, or pornographic performing, or corporate spying, or mercenary soldiering. But regardless of the form it takes, work represents structure. It organizes time, it provides an outlet for drives, it satisfies both financial needs and familial obligations.

Because different individuals are dominated by different impulses, we often see one able and sensitive man or woman locked into the most routine work while his peer in ability and sensitivity is producing at a highly creative and rewarding level. Among the factors that differentiate the two is the relative strength of the need for self-expression. When that need is at its most intense, the foundation for creativity is laid. Assuming the raw potential is there upon which to build, we then have the makings of an actor, an artist, a playwright—in short, a creator.

THE SCOPE OF CREATIVITY

Of course, the gratifications of creativity are not confined exclusively to the highly gifted. The delights of a more modest level of creativity

were brought home to me some years ago when I attended a band concert in Staten Island. Tchaikovsky's *1812 Overture* was being performed, and performed most stirringly, up to the point at which the boom of cannon is written into the score, whereupon several unidentifiable bangs rang out instead. I was the guest that evening of the conductor, and so made my way backstage at the end of the concert. There I found a uniformed policeman who had, on cue, been firing his pistol into a garbage can. I complimented him on his performance, and he grinned with pride. "Would you believe?" he said. "I didn't even have a rehearsal!"

Another time in other circumstances, I was strolling in Greenwich Village, New York's traditional artist's section. An outdoor art show was in progress, and among the exhibitors was a little woman sitting hunched and unassuming on a camp stool alongside the fence on which her work was displayed. Prominent among her wares was nothing less than the *Mona Lisa*. And in the lower left hand corner of the canvas was a small, discreet label: COPY.

From this we may gather that a certain amount of self-deception enhances the pleasures of amateur creativity. And why not? For the most part, Sunday painters are not entirely blind to the fact that, no matter how many Sundays they devote to their art, they will not emerge as tomorrow's Picasso. And "Chopsticks" playing pianists, however much they enjoy their productions, are nevertheless aware that they are performing with two fingers rather than the 10 that Rubinstein preferred.

THE NEED TO CREATE

Work and ego gratification tend to be intimately related. Consider, for example, the chess master who, on the rare occasions when he lost a game, would invariably exclaim, "How can one lose to such idiots!" He thus rebuked himself for his failure to win, but at the same time he denigrated his opponent as even less apt than himself. He refused even to acknowledge the individuality of his opponent, who became merely a part of an undifferentiated pack of idiots. So in one fell swoop the chess master punished himself, thereby assuaging his feelings of guilt, and belittled his opponent, thereby protecting his own ego.

Romantic notions to the contrary notwithstanding, the creative process is subject to dissection. Creative activity begins in the unconscious. For illustrative purposes, let us say it is the unconscious of a poet, William Blake. Blake has decided to write a long narrative poem on the French Revolution. His unconscious is aswirl with a welter of incoherent impressions, tales of war, nightmares of war, fantasies, and facts. All this material must be culled and filtered before it can be transformed into poetry, and that is the task of the preconscious. The preconscious serves as the dragoman, the official interpreter of the unconscious for the conscious. It selects what is usable and conducts the material forward into consciousness. At the same time it represses the impressions which will not serve. Having done so, the preconscious yields to the conscious, and white-hot creative inspiration strikes. Out of a mass of verbal, visual, auditory, perhaps olfactory impressions, Blake has, by a process of which he is unaware, selected what he needs. He begins: "The dead brood over Europe, the cloud and vision descends over *chearful* France," and so on. Incidentally, Blake himself would no doubt have scoffed at this brief examination of the anatomy of creativity. "I will not reason and compare," he wrote. "My business is to create." Blake, as you may know, is a haunting figure who stands alone in 18th century English literature. He developed into a mystic and a visionary whose poetry has special meanings all of its own.

According to George Bernard Shaw, "The true artist will let his wife starve, his children go barefoot, his mother drudge for her living at 70, sooner than work at anything but his art." It is something of a cliché, the artist's unswerving devotion to his work, regardless of poverty and discomfort, his own and others'. Like most clichés, it is quite true. Actors do indeed pound the pavements, month in, month out, in relentless quest of a role, supported by the labors of a spouse or the munificence of parents. Painters in fact do survive on welfare payments in factory-district lofts, which is the present-day equivalent of starving in a garret. Dancers and singers, those supposedly free and unconventional spirits, lead lives of the most arduous discipline. Poets apply endlessly for foundation grants, tutor, ghostwrite executive speeches—do anything that will keep a roof over their heads and still allow them time to create. One would be hard put to imagine an accountant or a shopkeeper or an electrician pursuing his chosen line of work with such monomaniacal ardor. Why only the artist?

The artist is highly narcissistic. A paycheck as sole reward for a job well done is flat and flavorless to him. He feeds on applause. And for applause he needs an audience. A living, breathing cheering audience for the musician, the actor, and the dancer—performers take their applause direct. Whereas the writer, the painter, and the composer are fed by collective anonymous applause, one step removed. No matter, their audience is real enough to them. The narcissism of the nonperforming artist, who does his creating in solitude, is simply displaced onto his creations—poems, sculptures, whatever they may be. His art becomes his beloved child, and he is content to devote his life to improving and perfecting it. "Blessed is he who has found his work; let him ask no other blessedness," Carlyle wrote. But then, Carlyle was speaking for himself. He was an artist.

A life devoted to creativity is necessarily the province of the dedicated artists among us. But creative minds also abound in spheres of activity as diverse as politics and advertising. Moreover, the great figures of history, the ones who left the world a different place than they found it, were also creators in the highest sense of the word. Plato was a creator. So was Galileo. So was Christ. Each of them stood upon what had gone before and jumped into the unknown, overleaping a hundred intermediate steps to arrive at a new, unsuspected, dazzlingly self-evident truth, which is to say, each of them moved along a path illuminated by pure creative inspiration.

It is a well-known fact that creativity as high as this is often ignored, ridiculed, or violently rejected in its own time, only to be revived and venerated later on. There is probably little truth in the notion that the creator's contemporaries are so riddled with envy of his brilliant achievement that they conspire to destroy him in revenge. More likely they are simply bewildered. Unable to follow the creator in his inspired leap from known to unknown, his contemporaries reject his achievement with sincere and total incomprehension. Years pass during which the more pedestrian minds in the field bridge the gap, taking intermediate step after plodding step, until they reach the pinnacle to which the creator had long before jumped. At this point the work of an unrecognized and forgotten genius is resurrected and acclaimed. Van Gogh comes to mind as a prominent example of this phenomenon. He is also an artist who suffered periodically from profound depressions and eventually committed suicide. Countless others whose gifts were eventually recognized were initially discouraged by their well meaning but tradition-bound elders. Verdi, for example, applied in his youth for admittance to the Conservatory of Milan and was firmly rejected. The professors at the conservatory felt that he lacked musical aptitude. The poet and Nobel laureate Quasimodo was expelled from school. His work was not up to par. Papers were scored on a scale of zero to 10, and Quasimodo's invariably got a zero. His professor, genuinely baffled by the strange work of the student, showed one of Quasimodo's papers to a fellow instructor who, as it happened, had a sharper eye for unorthodox but brilliant writing. The big zero was already in place on Quasimodo's paper. The instructor read it and returned it to his colleague. "I'd suggest," he offered, "that you put a one in front of the zero."

THE SOURCES OF CREATIVITY

Thus far we have been treating the artist as a flower born in full bloom. We have considered the source of the need to create without questioning the source of the talent that permits satisfactory expression of the creative urge. Rare talent is often referred to as a "gift," presumably a gift from God. And if we regard genetic makeup as a gift, then the reference is, to an extent, correct. Actually the source of artistic talent is threefold.

The first element, the seed from which talent grows, is the genetic component. It is pure potential. It is the perfect pitch with which a Bach or a Mozart is born. It is Michelangelo's capacity to envision accurately the human form, even in the most distorted postures, without reference to a living model. It is Giotto's ability to draw a perfect circle freehand.

The second element of the compound called talent is early childhood stimulation and the influence of the parents, both direct and indirect, in modifying the direction the child's life will take.

The third element is environment, which can destroy potential genius as easily as nuture it. Thus, we may safely assume that a Raphael born in 15th century New Guinea rather than 15th century Italy would have produced no memorable artwork in his life. A Beethoven who lived a few hundred years earlier, when the church still discouraged the playing of musical instruments on the theory that it might distract worshippers from holy thoughts, would have composed no symphonies. Conversely, the dazzling quantity and quality of literary output in Elizabethan England or of painting and sculpture in Renaissance Italy are in no small part attributable to an environment that encouraged, prized, and rewarded such production.

We can only speculate about the legions of potentially immortal geniuses who, throughout the centuries, must have lived and died having produced nothing: illiterate Shakespeares who spent their lives in the coal mines; potential Bernhardts who cooked and cleaned and tended their children from morning to night, and made a scene once in awhile just for the sheer dramatic pleasure of it. The first, the genetic element of artistic genius, was theirs. The other two—stimulation and environment—were lacking.

THE PERSONAL VISION OF THE ARTIST

The artist reinterprets reality, making his personal vision universal. Consider the pointillists of 19th century France, who laid unmixed color down on their canvases in tiny side-by-side patches, leaving it to the eye of the viewer to perform the blending task. Study their paintings, and whenever you see water or grass shimmering under intense sunlight thereafter, you will see them through the eyes of the pointillists.

Sunlight was the pointillists' inspiration. Their exploration of its nuances was without end. But inspiration may be found anywhere. For Fasanella, the New York primitive painter, inspiration is billboards, ball games, shop windows, subway kiosks, milling but never anonymous crowds. For Robert Frost, inspiration is the silence of snow, the austere and gentle landscapes of rural New England. For Proust, the famous madeleine—a teacake just like the one his aunt had given the narrator when he was a child—evoked the whole unforgotten world of *Remembrance of Things Past.*

This is not to suggest, of course, that artists wait, pen poised, for inspiration to strike. To the contrary, artists who practice their art with any degree of continuity learn to seek out inspiration. With time they become more and more skilled in promoting the requisite flow between conscious, preconscious, and unconscious. They learn to use exterior stimuli for purposes of evoking interior stimuli. The painter who floods his studio with the sound of a particular kind of music would be an example. The cork-lined room of Proust is an example in reverse. Only in the total absence of outside stimuli was he able to plunge into the real and imagined past and reemerge with the *Remembrance.*

The artist's vision is an intensely personal vision. But no matter how original his conceptions may be, in the long run he cannot elude the influence on his work of the emotional experiences common to us all. This is why the same highly personal and nonderivative mode of creative expression is so often arrived at independently by different artists of different times and different cultures.

Some two thousand years ago, a small bronze statue was molded (Figure 39.1). It depicts the elongated form of an adolescent boy smiling ambiguously. It is called *The Evening Shadow*—a superb example of Etruscan art and a supreme demonstration of the way an artist, working only with the most limited materials, can transmit a mood across milennia: the poetic, mystical, and mysterious aura that pervades the dusk of the day when shadows lengthen and linger. It is the Etruscan expression of a style of sculpture whose present modernistic exponent is the sculptor Giacometti but whose origin antedates recorded time. *Nihil novum sub sole*—nothing is new under the sun. But because the little bronze continues to move us, its nameless creator has achieved immortality. The immensity and depth of the creative unconscious, in its primitive as well as its most sophisticated expressions, are a puzzle which is not subject to easy solution. If

Figure 39.1. Bronze statue, *The Evening Shadow.* (Courtesy of Dr. Ferruccio di Cori, New York, N.Y.)

we ask ourselves, "Are the stars beautiful?" the answer is, "Yes." If we ask, "Why?" the answer is more complicated.

THE PERSONAL EXPERIENCES OF THE ARTIST

Obviously, the artist does not create in a vacuum. Like everyone else, he has a family life and a social life, money worries, problems of health, and so on. And the events of his life, both momentous and mundane, affect the nature of his creative output. Tchaikovsky was in the process of composing his Fourth Symphony at the time he married. But his marriage represented an effort on his part to control his strong homosexual trends, and the sorrowful mood of the symphony accurately reflects the pain of a man under the strain of intolerable conflicts. Predictably, his depression became so severe that he was unable to complete his opus. At this point, Tchaikovsky's brother removed him from the marital abode and took him to a sanitarium in Switzerland for a rest cure. There the composer improved dramatically, so much so that he was able to go back to the uncompleted work. He finished it with an unmistakable climactic upsurge of sweeping grandeur, and the last movement is a poetical and creative testament to the recovery and replenishment of the ego.

Caruso, so the story goes, placed an immensely painful personal experience at the service of his art. He was justifiably famous for his unique rendition of *Pagliacci*, the finale of which he sang in the most heart-rending fashion. The unfailing passion he invested in the line, "Ridi, Pagliaccio" (laugh, clown, laugh) was explained by the great tenor himself. At each performance he relived on stage his discovery of his wife betraying him with her chauffeur. Assuming there is some truth to the tale, it demonstrates the remarkable resilience of the man who, instead of succumbing to despair, was able to dilute and channel the impact of the incident by utilizing it as the fulcrum of a highly creative act—a clinical classic of sublimation.

But emotionally charged experiences are not the only ones that affect an artist's productions. Chagall, who chooses to live in close contact with nature, never grows jaded by its beauties. He paints myths, not field flowers. And yet he is wont to exclaim in near anguish over his longing to capture on canvas the miraculous colors he sees in his surroundings. He is inspired by the most ordinary, everyday experience, such as a brief stroll in the country. And in this, he is not alone. Trees, sky, water, clouds are a fount of creative stimulation for many artists. It is almost as if they had a womb that could be fertilized by the seed of what they see.

Creative expression can be sparked by the most casual experiences. A woman, who is not a poet but who is endowed with a highly creative potential, came home one day from the supermarket. "What's in the shopping bag?" she was asked. "Food," she replied, picked up a pencil, and proceeded spontaneously to write, directly on the bag:

> Food
> essence
> of lost wombs
> parenthesis of love
> given
> when the mouth demands
> fulfillment
> and gasps . . .

Another example: an immigrant to this country, teaching in Brooklyn for many years, is driving through one of the older and poorer sections of the borough. Someone in the car with him says, "Everyone in Brooklyn is either old or black." In that moment, a poem takes shape in his mind, a poem that captures the hope that Brooklyn and New York have held out to so many citizens from other lands. He calls it, *The Green Light:*

> Everyone is either
> old or black
> in Brooklyn,
> vestiges of an era
> when walls
> kept houses
> divided
> and yet 'twined
> by shrills
> of children
> who grew up
> as Americans,
> old flags whirring
> their flutters
> on the battlement
> of their hearts
> and oatmeal
> pouring
> out of Jewish bowls
> into the arteries
> of people
> who kept
> Brooklyn
> a museum
> beyond
>   and above
> the bridges
> of faith
> while waiting
> for a green light.

Another aspect of creativity that lends itself to speculation is the artist who produces in his life one outstanding work and one only. Pietro Mascagni composed his brilliant opera *Cavalleria Rusticana* at the age of 19. He continued composing for the rest of his life. But this particular work, this lyrical and passionate story of an unresolved mother-son relationship that sprang from his unconscious when the composer was 19, is the only music that ever won him glory. This phenomenon is even more common in the literary arts. A number of playwrights have written a single splendid play only to fall into obscurity afterwards. The terrors of the second novel—the one an author must write after he has produced one highly acclaimed book—are legendary among writers. Fear of success is a too obvious, too facile catch-all explanation for this phenomenon. It is as if a volcano were to explode once, then become forever dormant, as if the need to create at the highest level available to the artist could, in some cases, be permanently assuaged by one magnificant, creative burst. The ego is satisfied, and the creative unconscious seems to have appeased its hunger forever.

THE COMMUNICATIONS OF THE ARTIST

Fully realized creativity—the output of genius—speaks to all people for all time: its message is universal. It is almost inconceivable that a time might come when viewers will not stand in humble awe before Michelangelo's men and women, too perfect to be anything but gods; when the elegant, wistful melodies of Chopin will fail to evoke in listeners an answering catch of the heart. But every work of art, masterpiece or not, offers us, the audience, multiple mes-

sages. There are surface messages, such as the plot of a play or the subject of a painting. There are intellectual messages of style and technique, and emotional messages whose impact is easier to experience than to analyze. And there are hidden messages, sometimes unknown even to the artist himself.

Consider Andrew Wyeth's well known painting, *Christina's World* (Figure 39.2). The juxtaposition of the three stimuli—the figure in the foreground and the two houses on the horizon at top—is in itself intriguing. If we move one layer below the surface, we see the poignancy of the faceless girl's strained posture and the bleakness of the empty field. Penetrate to the next underlying stratum, and we become aware of the reason for the juxtaposition of the central elements: Christina is physically handicapped. Her arms are too thin and sinewy, her hands are too bony and tense. Her twisted torso and disheveled hair speak of a powerful forward impetus, but her legs and feet are immobile. The painting tells us that she longs for security, represented by the houses far away. We can see that the artist sympathizes with her strivings. But he has painted a featureless, near limitless field for her somehow to cross, and he does not want us to

Figure 39.2. *Christina's World* (1948) by Andrew Wyeth. Tempera on gesso panel, 32¼ × 47¾" (Collection, The Museum of Modern Art, New York, N. Y., by permission.)

Figure 39.3. Painting of a woman emerging from a forest. (Courtesy of Dr. Ferruccio di Cori.)

know whether or not she will reach the houses. Will she attain her goal or yearn forever in that wistful élan? We must bow to the artist, challenged by the mystery he has presented to us.

Another painting of a woman alone in the silence of an oppressively monotonous landscape (Figure 39.3) tells a very different story. Here is a forest the thickness and immensity of which blot out the sky, and a women, very small by contrast, stepping out of the trees. She has emerged from a situation that is destructive and overpowering; she has no face, no arms, she is nothing but a breeze-touched gown. But she stands in a clearing lit by the sun, and now she can be reborn. The limelight of the clearing is the only message, the only communication.

The poet finds himself making a direct appeal to the emotions of his reader, bypassing the intellect. Yet he must use the intellect to do so since his medium is words. Thus, the reader finds that poetry is in fact a rebellion against language, and that some of the greatest poets write very much as if they were recreating language as they go along.

Robert Frost's *The Road Not Taken* is a stylistically conservative poem. It has meter and rhyme, and it is in no sense obscure. It begins thus:

Two roads diverged in a yellow wood,
And sorry I could not travel both
And be one traveler, long I stood
And looked down one as far as I could
To where it bent in the undergrowth;

Clearly, the aging Frost is speaking of life choices, ruminating, in the second half of his life when the major battles have all been fought, on the direction taken and the compromises made. (Frost is another artist who suffered profound depressions, especially during his early creative years.) In two more five-line stanzas, with carefully controlled nostalgia, the poet further develops his theme. Then he concludes.

I shall be telling this with a sigh
Somewhere ages and ages hence:
Two roads diverged in a wood, and I—
I took the one less traveled by,
And that has made all the difference.*

The poem intentionally leaves us hanging. Frost will not say whether or not, in retrospect, he is

---

* From *The Poetry of Robert Frost*, edited by Edward Connery Lathem. Copyright © 1916, 1923, 1969 by Holt, Rinehart and Winston. Copyright © 1944, 1951 by Robert Frost. (Reprinted by permission of Holt, Rinehart and Winston.)

pleased with the choice he made long ago. But look again at the third and fourth lines of the last stanza for the answer. "I" followed by a forced and lengthy pause—so much like a pause in music the length of which sustains the emphasis of the passage, or a pregnant silence on stage that stresses the significance of what has just occurred or is just about to occur—and then a second "I." Those two "I's" tell us that the poet reached an ego decision about which he has no regrets. They tell it with superb economy of means and elegant sophistication of style.

But Frost does have regrets about growing older, as he expresses so poignantly in another poem, *To Earthward.*

Love at the lips was touch
As sweet as I could bear;
And once that seemed too much;
I lived on air

That crossed me from sweet things,
The flow of—was it musk
From hidden grapevine springs
Downhill at dusk?

I had the swirl and ache
From sprays of honeysuckle
That when they're gathered shake
Dew on the knuckle.

I craved strong sweets, but those
Seemed strong when I was young;
The petal of the rose
It was that stung.

Now no joy but lacks salt,
That is not dashed with pain
And weariness and fault;
I crave the stain

Of tears, the aftermark
Of almost too much love,
The sweet of bitter bark
And burning clove.

When still and sore and scarred
I take away my hand
From leaning on it hard
In grass and sand,

The hurt is not enough.
I long for weight and strength
To feel the earth as rough
To all my length.*

CREATIVITY AND EMOTIONAL ILLNESS

Clues to the infirmity of the artist are concealed in a small watercolor presented to me by one of my patients (Figure 39.4). Purportedly, it is the young man's attempt to reproduce in an impressionistic fashion the environment of my office—and in fact, in its superficial aspects, it is fairly accurate. But this patient is deaf. His psychotherapy is conducted by means of writing and lip reading, and much spontaneity is thereby lost. In his painting the patient expresses his frustration and dissatisfaction with his therapeutic progress—quite unconsciously—by producing for his psychiatrist a symbolic representation of his own inner ear and the environment of a psychotherapeutic relationship that he fears may be hostile.

Another of my patients is a shy and withdrawn woman in her thirties who has never been able to free herself of her narrow and restrictive upbringing. One day she presented me with a drawing of a delicate, rather dreamy face of indeterminate sex (Figure 39.5). It was, she said, the patient whose session followed her own the

*From *The Poetry of Robert Frost*, edited by Edward Connery Lathem. Copyright © 1916, 1923, 1969 by Holt, Rinehart and Winston. Copyright © 1944, 1951 by Robert Frost. (Reprinted by permission of Holt, Rinehart and Winston.)

Figure 39.4. Painting of Dr. di Cori's office. (Courtesy of Dr. Ferruccio di Cori.)

Figure 39.5. Drawing of a young man. (Courtesy of Dr. Ferruccio de Cori.)

Figure 39.6 and 39.7. Paintings of cupolas. (Courtesy of Dr. Ferruccio di Cori.)

previous week, and whom she had briefly seen. She had found it inconceivable that so beautiful a young man should require psychiatric attention. Accordingly, he had captured her imagination; hence the drawing. But in reality, what this insecure woman finds inconceivable is that this man or any man could desire her. Nor can she herself consciously desire a man; her rigid upbringing has forbidden it. But a young man she sees in her psychiatrist's waiting room is acceptable to her unconscious because he is under the aegis of a protective and approving father figure. And to that figure, the psychiatrist, she brings the image of the one she desires, symbolically disguised.

There is a story behind the paintings shown in Figures 39.6 and 39.7. The artist, a dynamic and restless Florentine, was by profession the American correspondent of an Italian newspaper. He married a young English girl when he was in his fifties, and shortly thereafter he was recalled by his employer to Italy. It was the first time in 20 years that he had seen the Renaissance splendors of his native land, and he was ravished by the beauty that surrounded him. He was a demanding, rather childish husband; and when his young wife told him she was pregnant, he was overwhelmed by conflicting emotions.

He had been haunted all his life by an obsessive oedipal dream in which his mother caressed him while his father stood by, approving and at times even supervising. Now a prospective baby was suddenly threatening him with annihilation by replacement. He withdrew into a search for the original maternal figure. And in a fury of activity, he began to paint. He painted night and day, and all he painted was churches—the cupolas and bell towers of churches. He produced hundreds of canvases. Almost by chance, his work came to the attention of the criticis. It was acclaimed, and he found himself a successful artist. Knowing his story, it becomes possible to look at his paintings and see, not just cupolas, but also the breast of his childhood yearnings.

A creative expression may release submerged and repressed material in concealed form. It was true for the woman who drew her fellow patient, the deaf boy who painted my office to look like an inner ear, the father-to-be who painted cupolas. It follows, then, that illness can sometimes be treated by eliciting, tapping, and nurturing the sources of a patient's creativity. Assuming the patient has a creative potential he can be brought to explore, his outpourings can have significant cathartic value. The following poem was written by a man who, in a crisis of despair, was able to express his gloom in a sudden creative outburst. From then on, through poetry, he retraced his life's steps in his treatment.

Bereft I look askance
over the stairway
in the dimlighted air
of the new dawn.
   I peer into the stile
and its design
intrigued step by step
by its ascent.
   I stoop
slowly descending
   by the rail
and thinking of the years
   that moved uphill
or plunged down
   or soared high
and I wonder at my balance
   and my skill.
Cloudy is the horizon
host to a downpour.
Too bare is the field
   no longer green.
My wings are clipped
and if I dare to fly
I'll be plummeting fast
   in a tailspin.
Unsteady and faltering
is my climbing
   now.
Unlikely is the summit
   to be seen.

The sport is game
but the hazard is
   shrouded
   and the eye is too
   fogged
to be keen.

The poem externalizes and exemplifies the entire concept of depression. Its symbolism is by no means inaccessible. The stairway of the second line is the man's past. The ascent he describes is his earlier success. But now he foresees only disaster (the clouds on the horizon). He lacks confidence in his ego resources (clipped wings). Sorrowfully, he accepts his limitations (the unreachable summit). And the "eye" which is too fogged to be keen is also the "I" or ego. The production of this poem marked a turning point for this man. Stimulated to continue with this medium of approach, he recovered successfully from his deep depression.

CREATIVITY AND THE PHYSICIAN

Unquestionably works of art contain hidden messages, decipherable by those with a grasp of the codes that the unconscious employs. It is the physician's role to be aware of the sources of creativity and to be sensitive to the innate assets an individual may harbor within himself. Distorted or mangled though they may be by trauma and stress, they are capable of being revived when acceptance and encouragement are offered. It may thus fall to the physician not only to identify the roots of creativity but to nourish them and help them grow as well.

A housewife, momentarily under the spell of her role as provider of food for her family, writes a poem about food on a shopping bag. A journalist, delighted and horrified by the pregnancy of his young wife, finds relief from tension in painting church cupolas. These are examples from everyday life. For the giants of creativity, the germinative burst which briefly inspires a housewife-poet becomes instead a self-fueled torch, bright enough to burn for centuries. Thus Galileo, who proclaimed an unexpected truth for which the world was not yet ready, paid for his provocative understanding of the correct relationship between earth and sun with his freedom. His creative thinking was denied and his work reviled. It was a punishment imposed upon him by a society that was too limited and too

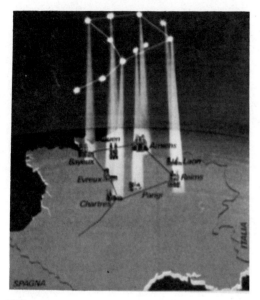

Figure 39.8. France's eight Gothic cathedrals, projected into the sky to form the constellation Virgo.

frightened to appreciate the breathtaking flights to which a creative mind can aspire.

The complexity of human nature is such, however, that understanding may permanently escape us; and some messages, by their nature, must remain forever concealed from the expert in codes of the unconscious as well as from the interested observer. In 1118, nine knights left France for Jerusalem. Before the King of Jerusalem, Baldwin II, they pledged their vows of poverty, chastity, and submission. They were known as the Knights Templars. Their mission was a secret one. Among the ruins of the Temple of Solomon they were to search for the tables given by Moses to King Solomon and preserved in the crypt of the Temple. These were special tables written by rulers of wisdom, who merged knowledge with love and understanding of humanity. It is unknown if the tables were found. But 10 years later the knights returned to France, having surrendered their wealth, rank, and worldly possessions; and before the Council of Troyes they requested permission to form a secret religious order, which was thereupon instituted. Two years later, construction was begun on France's first great Gothic cathedral. Almost simultaneously, about the year 1130, in an unprecedented frenzy of architectural activity, seven more cathedrals began to rise: Chartres, Paris, Reims, Lyons, Amiens, Rouen,

Bayeux, Evreux—and each of the eight cathedrals was dedicated to Notre Dame, the Holy Virgin. It was long afterwards that a strange thing was noticed. If one were to draw a projection into the sky from the eight cathedral cities, the result would reproduce in miniature the constellation Virgo—the familiar zodiac representation of the Virgin Mary (Figure 39.8). On the very land where the Celts, the Gauls, and other pagans had observed the rituals of Mother and Child (the Black Virgin was discovered under Chartres), a later people with a desire to raise a testament to their faith lifted their voices in a song of creativity, soaring upward, as if a message could be transcribed and read for centuries in the sky above them. The deep enigma of the projection remains unsolved. What was it that led innumerable individuals to create, in independent and farflung representations, an overwhelming symbolic affirmation of their Supreme God?

At the end of his *Divine Comedy*, the great poet Dante had to describe the Supreme Being. At that point he surrendered the strength of his creativity. His cosmic instinct warned him to desist, and he ended his immortal poem with the famous verse, *All' alta fantasia qui mancò possa*—"To the high fantasy here power failed."

At this clearing, we scientists, physicians, and, first of all, humanists must pause from time to time to assess the immensity of human creativity and possibility. We know that a positive attitude on the part of the physician toward a patient's personality and creative assets can actually modify the prognosis of an illness and even lengthen that individual's life span. The privilege given us to assist a suffering humanity, however, does not place us in a superior station of life, nor does it provide us with limitless powers. We should be simply more attuned than others to the mysteries concealed within the unopened books of those lives entrusted to us. Not by hubris hazed but with a deep sense of commitment we must remain receptive toward what the human mind and body signal to us. It is in answer to these messages, whispered by the individual torn in distress, that we can lift a hand to offer the vessel of our knowledge, limited though it may be by our human nature. And more we may not be able to do. If myths have meaning, then the image of Icarus—arrogantly defying the prohibition against flying too close to the God-Sun, and then plunging into the sea with his melted wings—still carries a powerful warning.

Suggested Readings

Arieti S: The rise of creativity. In *The Intrapsychic Self.* New York, Basic Books, 1967, p 325.

Edel L: The madness of art. *Am J Psychiatry* 132:1005, 1975.

Gedo JE: *Portraits of the Artist.* New York, The Guilford Press, 1983.

Niederland WG: Psychiatry and the creative process. In Freedman AM, Kaplan HI, Sadock BJ (eds): *Comprehensive Textbook of Psychiatry,* ed. 2, vol. 2. Baltimore, Williams & Wilkins, 1975, p 2462.

CHAPTER **40** # The Social Significance of Work, and Studies on the Stress of Life Events

Emily Mumford, Ph.D.

THE IMPORTANCE OF WORK

Four hundred employed men were asked, "If by some chance you inherited enough money to live comfortably without working, do you think you would work anyway?" Eighty per cent answered "yes." They would definitely continue to work even if they did not need the money. The "no" responses were concentrated among unskilled laborers, generally the people whose work affords the least social esteem and the least autonomy in the way their work is done. Ninety-three per cent of the men who said they would work regardless of economic necessity volunteered as their reason, "To keep interested or occupied." Other reasons that were echoed by many were: "Work keeps a man healthy," "It is good for a person to work," and "It gives a feeling of self-respect."

Studs Terkel's popular book, *Working*, is crammed with quotations from interviews with workers in over 100 occupations and these convey four aspects of work today. First, occupation influences the conception an individual holds of himself and the world around him. Second, occupation is used as a social locator. Third, among people who do not like their work, there is a sense of frustration, a feeling of being "just a machine," or of being treated like one, and anger over the lack of autonomy and social esteem. "A monkey could do my job." Fourth, there is a remarkable tendency to cast work in terms that elevate it, that make it special and important, either as contributing to humanity or as providing a source of power and autonomy.

A grave digger:
> Not anybody can be a grave digger ... you have to make a neat job. . . . A human body

is goin' into this grave. That's why you need skill when you're gonna dig a grave.

A stock broker:
> When you're dealing with a person's money and investments, you deal with his hopes and ambitions and dreams.

A fireman:
> I worked in a bank. You know, it's just paper. It's not real. Nine to five and it's shit. You're lookin' at numbers, but now I can look back and say, 'I helped put out a fire. I saved somebody.' It shows something I did on this earth.

A hooker:
> In the outside society, if I tried to be me, I wasn't in control of anything. As a bright, assertive woman, I had no power. As a cold manipulative hustler, I had a lot. . . . All I did was act out the reality of American Womanhood.*

Through work in this society, many people manage to feel needed or at least in control of some aspect of their lives. Freud, in *Civilization and its Discontents*, wrote that no other aspect of life ties an individual so securely to reality and to society as does work.

George and Caroline Vaillant have reported on a study of 456 inner city men prospectively followed from age 14 until age 47. They found

---

* From *Working: People Talk About What They Do All Day and How They Feel About What They Do*, by Studs Terkel. Copyright © 1974 by Pantheon Books, a division of Random House, Inc., New York, N.Y. (Published by permission.)

that *capacity to work in childhood* predicted the success of these underprivileged men at their work as adults, and also surpassed all other childhood variables (including socioeconomic class) in predicting later mental health and capacity for interpersonal relationships. Furthermore, many people—though seriously distressed by mental disorders and though seriously handicapped in their family relationships—still manage to function well, sometimes even brilliantly, in their work.

DIFFERENT CONCEPTS OF THE MEANING OF WORK

Some claim that the ancient Greek concept of work as punishment and degradation is diametrically opposed to the work ethic as we know it. That society, in which all physical labor was relegated to slaves, provided the superior Greek man with the necessary leisure for thought, enjoyment, and perfection of mind and body. However, as early as 800 B.C., Hesiod wrote that work is "no disgrace," a claim which must at the time have seemed a bit outlandish. Even as late as the first century A.D., Seneca, the Roman, proclaimed, "Work is not a good. Then what is a good? The scorning of work."

With the Reformation and its emphasis on individualism, and with the emergence of guilds and crafts which had their own status, including identifying costumes, occupations began to be an important alternate route, outside of family, for social position. Shakespeare noted the personal meaning of occupation in the lament about Othello's retirement from a brilliant military career: "Farewell. . . . Othello's occupation's gone!" sounded an ominous forecast of the eventual destruction of a proud man.

The work ethic of the Protestant sects continued to enhance the social and personal significance of work to a point where it came to be for many people an end in itself. At first, work was thought to be "good" for everyone. Today's attitude toward work, and particularly work identified as a profession, is a conception far from that of the 18th century "gentleman of leisure" who stood near the top of a social pyramid.

However, even today some people question whether working more to get more makes sense. A tourist in Mexico wanted to buy a dozen baskets from a craftsman. "No, senora. If I sold you so many I wouldn't have any left to sell." In this country, the "Flower Children" of the

1960's, and many others, challenged the older generation's commitment to working, to getting, and to spending. The point is that some tension over whether work is good in itself or just a necessary evil probably exists everywhere. But there are differences between cultures in the relative significance attached to occupation.

THE PRIMACY OF ACHIEVED STATUS IN TODAY'S SOCIETY

In the absence of extended family, caste, clan, or religion as a means of social placement, our society relies most heavily on occupation as the means of identifying where people "belong" in the social structure. In this context, it is not surprising that the struggle of minority groups takes place primarily over the right of access to better jobs and the right to equal chances for the education required to get better jobs. The feminist movement also sees the way to improvement of women's lot, generally, to depend on improvement of their chances to move up the occupational ladder as well as to command equal pay for equal work.

The emergence of second and even third careers after mandatory retirement in this society testifies to the vital significance of work for many men and women. Able to retire on a pension, they cast about for something else to do, something which will give them a "place," something to keep them from dropping into the residual category, "old people," or the people who used to be foremen, brokers, merchants, or police. The aged are seen as "useless" when they are no longer a part of the work and achievement arena, like work horses put out to pasture.

For many adults an immediate response to the question "Who am I?" is to name an occupation or an educational sequence leading to an occupation, particularly if they are in a profession or moving toward one. "I am a medical student." "When you grow up, what are you going to be?" appears to be a favorite way for some adults to try to relate to a child in our occupation-oriented culture, where career decisions imply a wide array of predictions about the years to follow. Thus, people in our society tend to locate each other by means of occupation. Another evidence of the importance we attach to work as a social locator is our resourcefulness in upgrading what we do for a living by the use of euphemisms. A "vice president," "sales representative," "sanitary engineer," and "maintenance man" may be a copy editor, door-to-door salesman, garbage collector, and the fellow who cleans the incinerators, respectively.

With occupational achievement as the primary source of identity for the self as well as the locator for social position, the individual can venture free of his family; he can forge his own place and "prove himself." Not a few parents are ambitious for their children to move above them on the occupational ladder, and boast of the work their sons and daughters do. This is satirized in the story of a mother at the seashore who sees her son swimming far out and in obvious difficulty: "Help, help, my son, *the doctor*, is drowning!" Such occupational preoccupation has many benefits to individuals and to the society. However, the emphasis on achievement in work also means that the individual must justify himself by his or her own efforts daily. It is not so much what you did, but what you are doing that counts. The author of a best seller is asked, "And what are you working on now?" Upward mobility through work becomes an end in itself for some, rather than a means to other goals. The restless striving of many middle-aged managers, proprietors, and professionals suggests that in this ethic the individual becomes his or her own harsh taskmaster.

Three indicators of socioeconomic status are commonly used in today's surveys: income, education, and occupation. Of these, occupation stands alone as the most powerful predictor of attitudes, of lifestyle, and also of health behavior. To many people, the agony of unemployment — particularly loss of occupational status that had lent some prestige — derives from a corrosive sense of worthlessness as well as from economic hardship, and these psychological stresses can be devastating. Sociologist M. Harvey Brenner has estimated that during the period 1940–1973, each 1% increase in the national unemployment rate in this country was associated with a number of increases in social stress indicators: deaths from cirrhosis of the liver (1.9% increase); deaths from cardiovascular–renal disease (1.9% increase); homicide (5.7% increase); suicide (4.1% increase); and state mental hospital admissions (3.4% increase). A more personal reaction was reported in The New York Times: "Dr. John R. Coleman, president of Haverford College, took an unusual sabbatical in 1973 working at menial jobs. In one instance he was fired as a porter-dishwasher. 'I'd never been unemployed. For three days I walked the streets. Though I had a bank account, though my children's tuition was paid, though I had a salary and a job waiting for me back in Haverford, I was demoralized. I had an inkling of how professionals my age feel when they lose their job and their confidence begins to sink.'"

THE PROFESSIONS

The centrality of work in determining style of life, associations, and friends is most remarkable in the professions. And in all discussions of professions, medicine is cited as the prototype. A close look at the issues that generate heated controversy over proposed changes in delivery of health care reveals at once the remarkable solidarity of the medical profession and its characteristic insistence upon the exclusive right of its members to provide special services without nonprofessional supervision. "Paraprofessional," "semiprofessional," and such terms suggest the struggle of other groups to be included in the valued designation. A consequence is that the category "professional" accounts for an increasingly large portion of the labor force in census statistics.

Professionals more often express satisfaction with their work than do nonprofessionals, and among professionals there is more blurring of work and nonwork in hours, friends, and leisure activities. In view of the relationship between a person's core identity and occupation, and the significance of work to social esteem, it is no surprise that a doctor's advice to "cut down on work" or change occupations or stop work is for some people the least likely medical advice to be followed. For some, and particularly for professionals, the advice is tantamount to saying, "Stop being what you are. Find another identity."

OCCUPATIONS AND HEALTH

Since work — keeping busy for pay — takes so much of man's and now woman's life, and since it has replaced the family as a primary source of status placement, it follows that occupation is significant for a sense of well-being and for health. Occupational identification is traditional in medical case presentations, e.g., "This is a 43 year old white male stock broker who first began having abdominal pains.... " Considerable information is condensed by occupational designation. For the physician, the patient's occupation provides clues to the types of physical as well as social and psychological stress which may be crucial in understanding certain symptoms. Occupation predicts something about a patient's education, lifestyle, his eating, drinking, and sleeping patterns, his leisure activities, his priorities, and his circle of friends.

The earliest attention to the impact of occupation on health was directed to the most obviously occupationally induced diseases, e.g., cancer of the scrotum among chimney sweepers and "black lung" among miners. In this tradition, the etiology of a wide range of specific diseases (such as asbestosis) was identified and it is now estimated that as many as 20% of all cancers may be job-related in some way.

Another series of studies began to be directed to the possibility of other less obvious, less palpably noxious factors of occupation that might relate to illness. For example, Robert Karasek has found that people who have little control over their jobs (e.g., assembly-line workers) have higher rates of heart disease than people who can control the pace of their work. The same is true for those whose work makes high demands on them but allows little independent decision-making (e.g., secretaries and telephone operators). Clearly the effect of chronic dissatisfaction with work on health needs much more attention. In one study for an insurance company, disaffection with work predicted mortality in a five year period better than any other social indicator. Eventually it followed that change in or loss of occupation in itself began to be considered as potentially deleterious to health.

STUDIES IN LIFE STRESS AND ILLNESS

In laboratory studies, Hans Selye traced the physiological patterns in the flight-fight response. Since neither response is at times possible, particularly for a laboratory animal, this physiological preparation can be maladaptive. Selye's concept of the *stress response* starts with a *stressor* or agent, for example, an electric shock to a laboratory animal who can neither run nor fight. Selye and others found that, depending on the mediating factors which might increase or decrease the impact of the stressor, an *adaptation syndrome*, accompanied by specific chemical changes, take place.

This concept of stress, originally conceived in purely physiological terms, was followed by investigations of stress in humans. Lennart Levi and his colleagues in the Laboratory for Clinical Stress Research in Stockholm demonstrated experimentally that catecholamine output increases in situations which are perceived by the individual as threatening. Out of the same group of investigators, Tores Theorell and others studied a panel of 21 rehabilitated survivors of myocardial infarction who participated in repeated weekly observations over several months. Among the most commonly reported events entered in their diaries were: "conflicts at work," "change in work hours and conditions," and "been home from work because of disease." Comparison between weekly diary entries and analysis of urine collected each week led the investigators to report that observation weeks without reported life changes had catecholamine levels significantly below the average of the individual subject. Observation weeks with reported life changes had elevated urine epinephrine and norepinephrine levels.

Meyer Friedman and Ray Rosenman did bi-weekly blood tests on 18 tax accountants between January and June. The average serum cholesterol of the group was 206% to 217% in the slack season, rose sharply in March and peaked at 232% by mid-April. Blood-clotting time dropped to five minutes by April 15, then went back to 8.8 by June, the relatively calm work days after the tax rush. They concluded that responses to stressful situations are associated with alterations in blood-clotting time (Figure 40.1).

Thomas Holmes and Richard Rahe, working as clinicians, developed a list of 43 life events which they believed might trigger stress because, whether desired or not, change and adjustment would be demanded. People were asked to rate each event on a scale to indicate the degree of readjustment each might demand, i.e., "If marriage had an adjustment score of 500, how much adjustment — and what score would you assign to a change of jobs?" The results of their studies and later replications suggest that "fired at work" and "retirement" were viewed by many of their respondents as among the top 10 of the potentially most stressful events (Table 40.1). Scaling the items in descending order of the magnitude of change and adjustment, "death of a spouse" received the highest score.

It should be clear that this "Life-Event Scale" is not a real scale of stress. It is simply a scale

Figure 40.1. Former President Nixon in a wheelchair with his left leg raised because of phlebitis shortly after his resignation from the Presidency. (By permission of United Press International.)

based on how stressful a sample of respondents thought different events would be. The individual filling out the scale might not be experiencing excessive stress even though his or her score of Life Change Units (LCU) is very high. The meaning of the event, the presence or absence of social supports, and the flexibility or coping style of the individual are only a few of the intervening variables contributing to how stressful to the individual a very high score may be. Nevertheless, high scores do show a statistical association with visits to physicians.

The point of discussing the life event research here is that while major family events are increasingly being associated with stress in the minds of physicians, the potential major impact of work changes may still tend to be overlooked. Any set of circumstances which demands or signifies a change in the individual's life pattern can reasonably be considered as a possible precipitator of stress. Stressors seem to have the properties of being both additive and nonspecific in their outcomes, and they are implicated in a wide range of illness conditions studied to date. Perhaps most important, stressful events are closely related to visits to physicians.

Since the development of the Holmes and

Rahe Social Readjustment Rating Scale, a large body of literature reports correlations between high score on the scale and visits to a physician for a wide range of physical, as well as psychological problems. Rahe, Mahan, Arthur, and Gunderson followed 2,463 Navy-enlisted men, 125 Navy officers, and 96 Marine-enlisted personnel aboard three cruisers. In addition to all sick bay calls, the investigators collected three research questionnaires from each member of their "captive" sample: a personal history, a health opinion survey, and a military version of the Holmes and Rahe schedule of recent experiences. This uniquely controlled study allowed the researchers to chart the percentage of total sick calls for each week of each of three cruises. Each ship's operation schedule was plotted against sick bay episodes. Illness reporting was highest during periods of change in the ship's operations. In addition, when men were categorized as high or low risk on the basis of their scores on the initial questionnaire about recent life events, the "high-life-change" individuals made 50% more visits to the dispensary than did the individuals who had low scores on the life-change scale.

There are at least three explanations for the

Table 40.1

The Holmes-Rahe Social Readjustment Rating Scale

Life Event	Mean Value
1. Death of spouse	100
2. Divorce	73
3. Marital separation	65
4. Jail term	63
5. Death of close family member	63
6. Personal injury or illness	53
7. Marriage	50
8. Fired at work	47
9. Marital reconciliation	45
10. Retirement	45
11. Change in health of family member	44
12. Pregnancy	40
13. Sexual difficulties	39
14. Gain of new family member	39
15. Business readjustment	39
16. Change in financial state	38
17. Death of close friend	37
18. Change to different line of work	36
19. Change in number of arguments with spouse	35
20. Mortgage over $10,000	31
21. Foreclosure of mortgage or loan	30
22. Change in responsibilities at work	29
23. Son or daughter leaving home	29
24. Trouble with in-laws	29
25. Outstanding personal achievement	28
26. Wife begins or stops work	26
27. Begin or end school	26
28. Change in living conditions	25
29. Revision of personal habits	24
30 Trouble with boss	23
31. Change in work hours or conditions	20
32. Change in residence	20
33. Change in schools	20
34. Change in recreation	19
35. Change in church activities	19
36. Change in social activities	18
37. Mortgage or loan less than $10,000	17
38. Change in sleeping habits	16
39. Change in number of family get-togethers	15
40. Change in eating habits	13
41. Vacation	13
42. Christmas	12
43. Minor violations of the law	11

remarkable consistency of these findings that suggest that recent life changes are associated with episodes of illness. First, the investigations just cited of Theorell, Levi, Rahe, and Holmes,

provide evidence that argues for a causal chain from event, to perception of threat, to physiological stress response in a vulnerable person, to additive effect, and to illness.

Second, other investigators, for example, Bruce and Barbara Dohrenwend, suggest that some part of the relationship between event and illness that has been reported in surveys may be contributed by the appearance of transient symptoms in response to stress. The sleeplessness and appetite loss, often associated with recent bereavement, are examples. Changed sleeping patterns following retirement is another example. Thus, the change may not trigger actual physical disease, but may simply produce passing symptoms in response to the event itself.

Third, taking still another approach, David Mechanic and Irving Zola are among the investigators who add that correlations between life event and illness onset could be the result of events triggering a search for help from physicians. An existing illness or symptom may have been there all along but not brought to the attention of medicine until some "last straw" propelled the patient to feel anxious or in need of help. The fact that many of the diseases associated with high stress scores seem to be chronic ones — for example, high blood pressure and diseases of the heart and kidneys — argues for the importance of stress as a trigger in the search for help with an existing but previously untreated medical problem. In this line of reasoning, the subsequent contact with a physician means that the illness may then be first diagnosed; thus, the correlation between event and illness. For some patients, the event may have caused neither the illness, nor the symptom, but simply made the condition seem less tolerable and ultimately more likely to be caught up in statistics.

Whatever the causal relationship, the correlations between life events and visits to physicians are reported in many contexts. But it should also be noted that there appears to be wide variation in individual susceptibility to symptoms, to illness, and to the need to visit a physician, even in the presence of an accumulation of what would seem to be a stunning burden of stressful events. The apparent vulnerability of people who are isolated with no supporting kin suggests that social situations may be powerful mediating factors on health status. There is also the possibility that stress, coped with well, strengthens one to cope with the next stress. The impact or threat of any given change may vary greatly. Perhaps people exposed to sufficient — but not too much — change and stress that was successfully handled early in life respond differently to major change than those either previously underexposed to change, or overexposed and unable to surmount early crises successfully. At the present state of knowledge, we can only hope that more research attention will be paid to the many people who though faced with potentially noxious demands for change remain alive, well, and buoyant.

LIFE EVENTS AND THE CHANGING FACE OF EMERGENCY ROOMS

The burgeoning literature that implicates life events in stress, including changes in occupational status as well as changes in family and financial status, has a number of implications for the delivery of health services today. It also has implications for the clinical practice of medicine as well as for medical research. In all three areas, ignorance of the recent life events of patients becomes increasingly consequential.

The increase in emergency room utilization and other walk-in services may best exemplify the implications of life events for future delivery of health services. As expectations for the benefits that medicine can provide expand and as families become less able to handle crises, it might be predicted that more people will bring in more different kinds of problems for help — to the places that are always open (Figure 40.2). The shortage of physicians available to see patients at night is often cited as "the cause" of increasing emergency room use. But there are many factors that appear to contribute — and the increased utilization is by no means concentrated at night and on weekends.

In 1971 there were some 60 million visits to emergency rooms in this country. Ten years later the number of visits had exceeded 80 million. The increase cannot be explained on the basis of an upsurge of traumatic accidents. Instead, it appears to reflect a shift in the nature of problems that are brought to the emergency room. Today the victims of social trauma are more numerous than are victims of physical trauma in many large emergency rooms.

It is no longer news to "discover" that many people who visit emergency rooms or doctors' offices suffer from psychological and/or social problems along with physical ones. It is also not

Figure 40.2. A busy waiting room in a clinic. From the film *Hospital*, produced and directed by Frederick Wiseman. (By permission of Zipporah Films, Boston, Mass.)

surprising to find that people suffering from psychiatric or social trauma may also be at risk physically. However, as I noted in Chapter 6, in practice these facts may often be forgotten as each specialist concentrates on the problems of particular interest in his or her specialty.

Some tension between patients and staff of emergency rooms may be generated if the institution allocates space and personnel on the basis of norms that arose in the 1940's when the emergency room served a different function. In those days, problems tended to be viewed as either physical or other, and the emergency room was a place for acute physical distress often consequent to an accident and requiring an ambulance and hospitalization. Today the patient brings to the emergency services as well as to outpatient clinics and private offices a wide range of social as well as physical problems, and not the least of these relates to trouble in work or to the lack of work. To label this trend "misuse" of the emergency room may be to miss the point. It has become, without anyone planning for it, the first place of recourse for large populations, and the likelihood of success in efforts to "educate" the public to behave differently is unpromising. Emergency room utilization today presents modern medicine with an accomplished social fact which can be seized as an opportunity for effective intervention on behalf of health before problems spiral into irreversible chronic illness. It also can be the most propitious site for preventive measures.

We found striking evidence of the relationship between recent life events and visits to the emergency room of Kings County Hospital,* a large municipal hospital serving several ghetto populations in Brooklyn. Patients interviewed in our study were asked whether they had experienced within the past six months any one of a brief list of events selected from the Social Readjustment Rating Scale developed by Thomas Holmes and Richard Rahe, and later revised by Eugene Paykel and others. We added a few questions to determine whether patients recently had been robbed or mugged, or had their homes broken into. For each of the life events where we could establish reasonably reliable community baselines, more of the population of emergency room visitors had suffered the experiences than would be expected, unless such

experiences were in some way associated with a search for help in the emergency room.

Fifteen per cent of the emergency room respondents said there had been a change in their work hours, and 22% had experienced a change of job or the nature of their work. The emergency room sample for the same time period also included a rate of robberies nearly six times what should be expected unless these social traumas were in some way associated with a subsequent search for help or reassurance in the emergency room. A 1975 *New York Times* article reported that retired persons who were victims of crimes suffered "horrendous" after-effects. Many became depressed and isolated even to the point of malnutrition and serious deterioration of their physical health. Without occupation and already tenuously tied to social life, the assault of any crime against them appeared to have an accumulated impact, to be the "final straw."

The responsiveness to our interviewers by patients who had suffered a recent loss suggests an urgency in their need to talk, and supports the notion that social problems are related to some emergency room visits. "Thank you for interviewing me." "Good luck with your study." "Will you visit me if I have to be hospitalized?"

Each generation apparently has been more ready than the previous one to use hospital services, at first for acute illness and inpatient treatment, eventually for specialized outpatient services, and now for much more, including a request for help following some stressful life event. For people whose work is their primary tie with society, we can expect that something about work or the lack of it has impelled many a patient to seek help at a particular time. The problem to be solved now is what to do with the new pattern. All too often, neither patient nor physician acknowledges, and neither may consciously know, why the patient with a chronic illness came to the emergency room or the office or clinic on this particular day, and what it is that the patient really wants or really needs from his visit. Yet such knowledge may at times be crucial for determination of the optimal treatment to be recommended, and the future responses of the patient to this medical advice.

Suggested Readings

Barrett JE, Rose RM, Klerman GL (eds): *Stress and Mental Disorder.* New York, Raven Press, 1979.
Dohrenwend B, Dohrenwend B (eds). *Stressful Life Events and Their Contexts.* New York, Prodist, 1981.
Mumford E: Professions: issues and organizations. In *Medical*

---

* Emily Mumford, Laurence Lusk, Reuben Margolis, Herbert Pardes, Ted Plimpton.

Sociology: Patients, Providers, and Policies. New York, Random House, 1983, p 247.

Terkel S: *Working.* New York, Pantheon Books, 1974.

Vaillant GE, Vaillant CO: Natural history of male psychological health: work as a predictor of positive mental health. *Am J Psychiatry* 138:1433, 1981.

References

Arthur RJ: Life stress and disease: an appraisal of the concept. In West LJ, Stein M (eds): *Critical Issues in Behavioral Medicine.* Philadelphia, J.B. Lippincott, 1982, p 3.

Brenner MH: Impact of unemployment and economic loss on mental and physical health. In Barrett JE, Rose RM, Klerman GL (eds): *Stress and Mental Disorder* New York, Raven Press, 1979, p 161.

Friedman M, Rosenman RH, Carroll V: Changes in the serum cholesterol and blood clotting time in men subjected to cyclic variation of occupational stress. *Circulation* 17:852, 1958.

Freud S (1930): Civilization and its discontents. In *The Standard Edition of the Complete Psychological Works of Sigmund Freud,* vol 21. London, Hogarth Press, 1961, p 64.

Holmes TH, Rahe RH: The social readjustment rating scale. *J Psychosom Res* 11:213, 1967.

Karasek R, et al: Job decision latitude, job demands, and cardiovascular disease. *Am J Public Health* 71:694, 1981.

Levi L: Occupational stress: a psychophysiological view. *Occup Ment Health* 2:6, 1972.

Mechanic D: *Medical Sociology: A Selective View.* New York, Free Press, 1968.

Paykel ES, Prusoff BA, Uhlenhuth EH: Scaling of life events *Arch Gen Psychiatry* 25:340, 1971.

Petrich J, Holmes TH: Life change and onset of illness. *Med Cl No Amer* 61:825, 1977.

Rahe RH, et al: The epidemiology of illness in naval environments. Illness types, distribution, severities and relationship to life change. *Milit Med* 135:443, 1970.

Rahe RH: Subjects' recent life changes and their near-future illness susceptibility. In Lipowski ZJ (ed): *Advances in Psychosomatic Medicine. Vol. 8: Psychosocial Aspects of Physical Illness.* Basel and New York, Karger, 1972, p 2.

Selye H: *The Stress of Life.* New York, McGraw-Hill, 1956.

Theorell TT, et al: A longitudinal study of 21 subjects with coronary heart disease: life changes, catecholamine excretion and related biochemical reactions. *Psychosom Med* 34:505, 1972.

Zola I: Pathways to the doctor: from person to patient. *Soc Sci Med* 7:677, 1973.

CHAPTER 41

The Choice of Medicine as a Career

A. *Role Models and the Years of Training*

Emily Mumford, Ph.D.

THE FLEXNER REPORT

"Welsh, we are lucky to get in as professors, for I am sure that neither you nor I could ever get in as students." William Osler is said to have made this statement as a comment on the "unusual" admission requirements to Johns Hopkins Medical School circa 1890. The requirements included an A.B. degree or its equivalent! At the time, only six of the many licensing bodies in the country specified any premedical education, and five of these required less than high school graduation.

Diploma mills and proprietary schools were described in 1910 in distressing detail by the apparently tireless Abraham Flexner, who had undertaken a major study of medical education, funded by the Carnegie Foundation. The National Medical University in Chicago offered, as an inducement to medical students, a free trip to Vienna, provided the student paid his fees regularly in cash for three years! The "teaching hospital" of this school had two patients. It was a day when some medical schools went after paying students with the apparent commercial greed of today's schools of driving, dancing, and karate.

Only three of the country's 155 medical schools received a clean bill of health in the Flexner report. Those pre-Flexner days were clearly ones when the term "physician" covered a wide range of educational background and proficiency. A few sons and fewer daughters from families with means went to the best schools here, then traveled abroad to work in one of the fine English or Scottish teaching hospitals of the day. A few went for advanced studies at the great French or German universities. Those others less well-to-do took whatever courses they could, in schools that were either the cheapest, or demanded the least qualifications for admission. Some received diplomas through mail order or night school. With such diversity caught up in the title "doctor," it is not surprising that the social standing of physicians varied widely and depended largely on individual background or "breeding," as it was then called. There are stories from these early days of some physicians who were consigned to eat with the servants after the expected house call on a wealthy patient.

The Flexner report of 1910 led to major changes in American medical education. All medical schools began to be "created equal." They also became equally costly in terms of time and money, and difficult to attend for anyone but wealthy or middle-class students. Night schools, correspondence schools, impoverished schools, and schools for black students were among the 92 schools that closed or merged during the big clean-up of American medical education. The authority of the American Association of Medical Colleges and committees empowered to accredit schools was assured. The standards set for all schools enhanced the public's chances of getting a well trained physician and contributed significantly to the exclusivity, prestige, and career attractiveness of the profession of medicine in America. At the same time, they had a conservative effect on educational innovations, and recruitment of the poor.

The new obligatory combination of university and hospital in American medical education combined the best aspects of English hospital training and German university study of the day. Johns Hopkins was the prototype. The new form

423

created fertile soil for specialization and advances in medical research, and soon competition between college graduates became an essential fact of recruitment, selection, and training in American medicine.

GETTING INTO MEDICAL SCHOOL

In 1983, some 520 qualified students applied to one state medical school; 480 of those with the highest grade point averages and other qualifications were interviewed for the 132 positions available. Across the nation more qualified applicants were rejected than were admitted to American medical schools.

In their efforts to gain admission, students today apply to many different medical schools (five had been the average number of schools to which an applicant applied in 1968 and eight in 1978). Some students who are refused admission by all schools spend the next year working in hospitals or related settings, or taking extra courses, hoping to improve their chances when they reapply the following year. According to a study of unaccepted applicants to medical school, two and a half years following nonacceptance, approximately 27% of the respondents had finally enrolled either in United States or in foreign medical schools—in Mexico, Belgium, Italy, England, France, or a Caribbean island. An additional 40% were still intending to reapply yet another time.

In 1968, I mailed a questionnaire to all applicants for the opening year of the Mt. Sinai Medical School and received nearly 1,000 usable questionnaires back. This response was excellent, but since the questionnaires were clearly for research and not for admission purposes—and so stated—none of us had anticipated what was to happen. We were deluged with phone calls from applicants, and from their parents and friends as well, who hoped we might intercede with the admissions committee on their behalf. We also received many calls from applicants asking for an interview or pleading for a change in the whole process of selection. The urgency of this wish to be admitted was also communicated by respondents' comments written in the margins of the questionnaires. Many students held positive views of the admission process: "It is a challenge worth meeting if medicine is what you want." "I came out of the situation a more mature individual." "I learned a great deal about myself in the process." Comments also conveyed some disaffection over the process of trying to be admitted—even among successful candidates: "I fit in, so I got in. My general impression is that the procedure is biased and unfair." "I did not enjoy routinely selling myself nor did I enjoy the apprehension resulting from competition with other students."

This phenomenon of a large pool of highly qualified applicants, willing to compete for admission, presents an embarrassment of riches. It attests to the continued desirability of medicine as a career. Medical schools today have their choice among the country's top students. One consequence of the increased competition over admission and the need for acceptable, objective criteria for selection has been the inflation of grade point average among applicants. Another has been the almost yearly increases in average MCAT (Medical College Admission Test) scores. However, MCAT scores and GPA's (Grade Point Averages)—above the high level required for admission—fail to predict much more than ability to score well on similar exams in medical school. For example, clinical performance as evaluated by professors in the final two years of medical school does not correlate significantly with MCAT nor with undergraduate GPA scores.

Moreover, many educators, and students, worry about the implications of accelerating competition over exam performance in the premedical years and believe it to be potentially counterproductive. Concentration on exam performance reduces the chances that students will do anything which might contribute to their own personal development at the risk of lowering a grade point average or of not knowing enough "to score" on the MCAT. The aspirant's wish to pursue additional activities, such as taking non-required courses, reading independently, or helping fellow students, can be overwhelmed by the zeal for admission. Moreover, selection committees, swamped with applications, cannot know all applicants well enough to feel comfortable relying fully on "subjective" impressions. Members of admissions committees may have to justify their choices in legal proceedings, and MCAT scores are "objective"; and since medical education is both expensive and relatively slow to change its form, there is an institutional reluctance to "take a chance," or to select applicants on new criteria. The result in part may be that too many capable people have sacrificed, to an unfortunate extent, the richness of undergraduate learning, and have been forced to learn competition as a way of life.

SPECIAL QUALITIES OF THE MEDICAL SCHOOL YEARS

Diversity

The composition of medical school classes has changed in ways that portend significant future developments in the medical profession. In the 1920's, practically no medical student was married. It was not considered appropriate to bring a wife to "join a fraternity," or to "enter the priesthood." But by the 1960's, 60% of the senior medical students were married. This shift means that the newer recruits to medicine are less exclusively under the influence of medical peers and professors. Classes in medical schools today, as compared with those of the 1940's and 1950's, represent more diversity of backgrounds, of premedical majors, of career aspirations, of race, and of ethnicity. There are also significantly more females in today's medical school classes than at any time since the turn of the century, around 40% compared with about 7% in the 1930's. This is partly a result of government funding and affirmative action policies, and partly a product of change in social attitudes.

Personal Characteristics

This trend toward diversity makes it increasingly misleading to speak of medical students as though they were all alike. However, there are still some dominant personal characteristics. For example, by the very fact that they have arrived, medical students demonstrate extraordinary energy, determination, and ability to put off immediate gratification on behalf of future goals. Karl Menninger's 1959 description of basic attributes shared by many medical students seems accurate even today. He suggested that people who go into medicine tend to react to stress with efforts to change something, that they incline toward intellectualization of problems, and that they appear to have strong needs to feel independent and be in control.

Insulation

Once admitted to a school, the medical student's experience is remarkably different from all other graduate education. The small amount of attrition between admission and graduation, and the degree of standardization of course sequence, is in marked contrast to Ph.D. programs where relatively few matriculated students eventually receive the degree. Particularly in the social sciences and humanities there is wide variation in the number of years between admission and degree, and wide variety in the educational and independent experiences leading to the degree. The fact that the medical educational sequence is standardized and prolonged, with considerable sacrifice demanded and with sharing of intense experiences throughout, increases the probabilities that medical graduates will identify strongly with their profession. Many medical students have trouble explaining to an outsider "what it's like," and they soon find that only someone in the same boat with them really understands the medical school experience. "Gallows humor" shared by fellow medical students at once expresses and relieves the intensity of some of these experiences, and also serves to draw together groups of people who are learning ways of coping with all of the facts to be absorbed, and all of the demands, anxieties, and charged new experiences to be managed. But at the same time such humor, based on subjects and sights which laymen actively avoid, may be incomprehensible or even shocking to an outsider, if overheard. Thus, by their work, hours, humor, problems, and aspirations, medical students are drawn together and separated from outsiders. They tend to limit their social contacts to other medical students and physicians—the only people who can fully understand what it means to say, "We had a cardiac arrest today and. . . ." Out of this background of sharing, the reluctance to voice criticism of a colleague to an outsider is both predictable and understandable.

The Fate of Idealism

Several studies have followed students over the four years of medical school. "The Fate of Idealism in Medical School" encapsulates one set of findings that suggests that incoming first year medical students express enthusiastic convictions about what a physician should and could be; but by their fourth year, they express very different perceptions. The implications of such change, reported in more than one study, have been debated by medical students and faculty members, as well as by social scientists. It is important to distinguish between naiveté and idealism in such discussions. A part of maturity as a professional involves an accurate perception of the limits of one individual's ability to change social patterns or organizations or professions. It is possible to retain an ideal, and at the same time to become more realistic about one's limits. On the other hand there may be an attrition in idealism due to continuous exposure to human suffering. One defense against anxiety is to become somewhat desensitized to the stimulus or the source of it. At some phase of their education, students come to realize that they can face with equanimity situations of human suffering which might have sent them into near panic at an earlier time. The range of response to this realization varies widely. Some take pride and congratulate themselves over having come to a new, more effective self. Others express serious concern and self-doubt: "Am I becoming dehumanized by this experience?" Some students say that faculty members do not treat students with enough respect as individuals; and since the senior physicians are role models, their manner toward students may be emulated when the student relates to patients. Additionally, the intense pace of medical student life, the excessive demands for memorization, and the tendency to reward exam skill rather than knowledge about and consideration for the patient, may all darken the lustre of the profession and tarnish the original ideal image.

Competitiveness

The fact that many students arrive at medical school with great expectations and have exerted great efforts to be admitted also raises the likelihood of considerable disaffection when they experience "more of the same grind and no patients, anywhere!" Also, having been at the top of their class in college, many students find themselves in the middle or near the bottom of the medical school class, at least in terms of study habits and ability to absorb facts. Having been the pride of family and friends for gaining admission, they are, on arrival, just one among many medical students. Such a situation can generate considerable anxiety. "Will I be able to make it?" "How well am I doing?" "Will I know enough?" In view of the very low attrition rate in medical school, extremes of competitiveness are not logical, but they are understandable.

Classes made up of top students, all of whom have been successful competitors for admission, are asked to master larger amounts of material and are further stressed by faculty comments about impending board examinations, and how much more there is to learn in each subspecialty. The self-doubts raised in the process not surprisingly focus anxiety on whatever means of evaluation a school uses. Heated debates over the best means for evaluating how well students are doing take place continually across the nation.

Evidence to date suggests that neither pass/fail nor any variant of letter grades is a panacea. Ideally, examinations and feedback from them should be purely an educational experience that allows students to monitor themselves. Most people agree that the real issue should be, "Do I know enough of this subject to provide a sound basis for my next phase of training and my eventual responsibility for clinical and/or research decisions?"

Serious research, and experiments with various systems of evaluation measured against long-range as well as short-range educational objectives, should be a part of any ongoing educational enterprise. It seems paradoxical that in the medical centers, where scientific research and rapid advance flourish, the curricula, evaluation procedures, and teaching methods are determined more by tradition, faith, and opinion, rather than by the results of careful evaluation.

In view of the internal and external pressures to "measure up" and the massive amount of material that needs to be mastered, it is understandable that some students may look for indications of how well they are doing compared with other students—even to the point of becoming preoccupied with grades and competition against fellow students. It is not that competition in itself is bad, but rather it is competition over the wrong goal—grades—which appears to be destructive. Doing away with grades is one obvious way to structure student relationships toward more mutual help and learning, the ideal of education as well as of professional deportment. But even in the absence of grades, some students cast about for other symbols to reassure themselves about how well they were doing vis-a-vis other students. Though the ideal of the profession is that of colleagueship of peers, the external society relies largely on competitive attainments for evaluating its members.

The ranking of students may be closer to patterns of the larger society than to the professional ideal.

Specialization

Many students move away from their original intentions to enter general practice and opt for a specialty at some point during their training. While this move appears more frequent in some schools than in others, it seems to be a general trend that has persisted for many years. In the 1950's, 60% of the first year class of one school said they were going into general practice; by the fourth year the proportion was down to 16%. The fact that professors and other potential role models are recognized specialists and are "board certified" contributes to specialization. In surveys of medical students in some medical schools, the specialists gained in prestige, and "general practice" showed a decline when freshmen and senior responses were compared. In addition, as a student becomes aware of how much there is to know, one way to be able to gain a sense of mastery, of "knowing enough" to function and to keep up in a rapidly advancing science, is to become highly specialized. The opening of family practice departments in medical schools is a counterforce to the precipitous decline in the ranks of physicians prepared to provide comprehensive primary care to large numbers of patients.

The press toward specialization that is fostered in the educational experience has increased the significance of a second half of medical education that expanded with relatively little planning or coordination since World War II—extended house staff training in the specialties.

THE HOUSE STAFF EXPLOSION

From 1910 to 1930, house staff training beyond the internship was an option taken by relatively few medical school graduates. Compared with the standardization of the four years of medical school, the lengthening years of specialty training even today represents a wide range of educational experience, from superb to quite bad. The fact is that every graduate of an American medical school is virtually assured entry into some residency program, though not necessarily the one of his or her first choice.

Compared with the enormous number of applicants to medical school positions, there are still unfilled spaces in some house staff programs, and graduates of foreign medical schools (FMG) have filled many of these residency positions. By 1982 there were 18,020 first year positions (PGY-1), and 4,380 of these were still being filled by an FMG (half of whom were U.S. citizens). The demand for the services provided by house staff physicians has contributed to this situation, and so has the attractiveness of American training and practice.

Several facts should be noted about this postgraduate phase of the medical career. First, in contrast to the relative stability in the structure of medical schools since the post-Flexner reforms, house staff programs have undergone dramatic changes, and will probably continue to change. Second, the physicians who are interns, residents, and teaching or reseach fellows, who have stayed on for still more years of training, represent more than 15% of all physicians in practice today. Since more of the older physicians are nonspecialists, house staff representation within specialties, and particularly within subspecialties, is much greater. Between 1931–32 and 1973–74, the number of physicians in hospital training programs rose from a little over 7,000 to more than 60,000, and by 1982 there were more than 69,000 residents on duty. The impact of the services provided by house staff members compared with all physicians in the country is most obvious in hospital-based care. Residents provide almost all of the service in the expanding emergency rooms, where increasing numbers of patients present for most of their medical care each year. They also predominate in hospital-based clinics.

The house staff phase of training is dramatic, stressful, and extremely influential in the individual development of the physician. In sum, the experiences and difficulties of house staff physicians today highlight and possibly forecast both the personal problems of the medical career and the possible future improvements in the quality of life in that career.

JULY ONE THROUGHOUT THE LAND

The day that most interns and residents start their year is, throughout the nation of hospitals, a day of speeches, packets of information, assignments, uniforms, introductions, and much expectancy (Figure 41.1). Many new arrivals

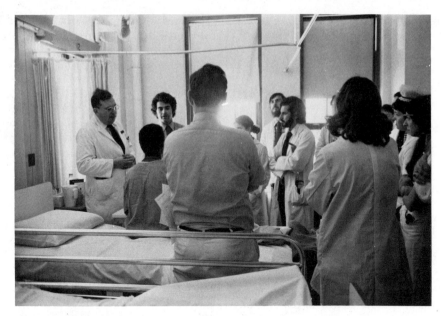

Figure 41.1. Attending and house staff on bedside rounds (Courtesy of Downstate Medical Center, Brooklyn.)

have, by that day, accumulated enough stress points to rank them high in the risk factors that predict illness on the Holmes and Rahe scale, discussed in the preceding chapter. Recent marriage, a move, a new job, change of work hours, graduation, promotion, debts—all these characterize the recent events in the lives of new house staff.

Incoming house staff members each year must be among the nation's hardiest specimens in order to function as well as they do. Most arrive with highly charged expectations. On one July first, as I was observing a group of interns (PGY-1's) being introduced to their resident, one turned to me and said, "This is *it*!" Another was asked by a chief resident to "draw blood on Mrs. J." The intern rushed off with the necessary equipment; but in a few minutes, he returned to ask sheepishly, "But where is Mrs. J?" One grabbed my arm as I started to follow a group on their first rounds in the hospital: "I've been here three hours and I don't know where the toilet is! Can you tell me?" Added to the stress from many people, places, and protocols they do not yet know is the unfortunately common sleep deprivation encountered during the early "shake down days" when each patient "work up" takes longer than it will a few months hence (Figure 41.2).

Not a few male residents report that during

their first year they suffered erectile difficulties for the first time in their lives. They had not admitted it to anyone and assumed their own problem was atypical. But in Great Britain, 55% of the male and female house staff officers in one survey reported that during their first six months, they had suffered some sexual dysfunction. The situation of the female house staff physician has received too little attention, as Malkah Notman and Carol Nadelson, among others, have suggested.

There is evidence of other stresses and strains in the marital relations of house staff physicians. Robert Coombs describes a study of wives of male medical students, interns, and residents. Loneliness, doubts about whether they were still attractive enough to interest their husbands sexually, and reports that their spouses expected a kind of deference that was "intolerable" were common complaints. Coombs suggests that some of the husbands appeared to assume the same role with their wives that they took with nurses and patients, i.e., an "authoritarian" manner intolerant of both disagreement and criticism. Wives of MD's have higher rates of suicide, of alcoholism, and of drug addiction than the rest of the population of married females.

One resident said, "Do you know how you become a doctor? By sticking your neck out, and

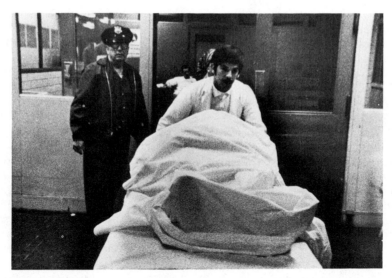

Figure 41.2.   House staff physician rushing patient to the emergency ward. From the film *Hospital*, produced and directed by Frederick Wiseman. (By permission of Zipporah Films, Boston, Mass.)

every step of the way you are scared." Most interns and most residents get through the experience with only occasional crises which are successfully managed and which even contribute to their development. However, some are casualties of their unwillingness to admit a need for help. In his July first welcoming speech to the new medical interns, the chief on one service explained, "Don't be ashamed to ask for help, or to admit you don't know something." This is a theme of introductions in all hospitals, but is supported by action in only some. Since July first is shortly followed by a traditional exodus of vacationing senior staff, the "call on us any time," followed by an almost immediate departure, does convey two conflicting messages. Moreover, the invitation for a call for help—either in the minds of the arriving resident, or the faculty member—may only include "help" with a patient's complex and "interesting" medical problem. The understandable emotional difficulties of the person under the fresh white coat and black plastic name tag are sometimes assumed not to exist, or considered inappropriate for attention.

We know that the medical profession in general suffers from high rates of marital problems, alcoholism, drug addiction, and suicide. Estimates of the rates of addiction for physicians run from 30 times to 100 times the rates for males in the larger population. Such statistical uncertainty suggests that we do not have very reliable means of determining the exact numbers, and it also suggests the extent to which the problem is kept underground.

The common tendency for self-medication by doctors appears to begin in medical school and may be particularly marked in the house staff years. Clinical studies of addicted and alcoholic physicians report that many began early in their careers to assume that their own special knowledge of drug action and problems of addiction somehow made them less vulnerable to addiction than lay people. In a study which compared physicians' beliefs and practices concerning patients with what the physicians themselves did when ill, 9 out of 10 doctors said that by all means a person should have a personal physician; but only 3 out of 10 could specify any physician they themselves had consulted about their own health. Most doctors feel very strongly that a patient should not medicate himself ("He who has himself as a patient has a fool as a doctor") and believe that doctors should not medicate themselves. Yet, even so, most physicians confess to self-medication without having sought expert advice. Thus, in addition to the occupational hazards of fatigue and stress, and the major life changes that require adjustment, there is a built-in hazard in physicians' reluctance to admit a need for personal help. The feeling that the physician should somehow be able to "go it alone" may be a prime destructive factor during the house staff years.

Objectively, conditions of the house staff training experience have improved in many ways. Any professor over 50 will be happy to tell you how little he was paid as an intern and how many hours he worked each week. Stipends today provide much more than subsistence, and the hours of work demanded today are less punishing on most services. Some of these improvements, both in the educational experience and in the conditions of work, have been brought about by the impact of house staff members acting in concert. Thus, one ray of promise through the somewhat chaotic picture of house staff training is the emergence of groups of articulate and vocal house staff who are addressing themselves to the problems of becoming a physician.

As such groups of young physicians have more time, energy, and sense of control, they may be encouraged to consider more fully the quality of their own lives as physicians. For example, several national conferences called by house staff members have attracted participants from all over the country. Among the subjects that have been discussed are: delivery of health care in the nation, the quality of training provided in a range of hospitals, the physician and his or her family, the quality of life of the physician, sexuality, the dying patient, and the need for omnipotence. A continuing theme at these conferences is that the physician must set priorities and recognize limits, and must learn when it is necessary to say "no" to demands from the public, from patients, from the profession, and from oneself. With such open sharing of the problems and the limits in their work, as well as the pride in that work, physicians can move toward significant future improvements in the quality of their lives.

THE LATER YEARS OF PRACTICE

Overwork

Two patterns observed in many house staff programs can set the stage for later disaffection in medical practice. The first of these is a tendency to idealize overwork as though it is an end in itself, and the second is a preoccupation with rare diseases that present a diagnostic challenge or that call for heroic medical intervention. The rhetoric of overwork expresses itself in comparisons about how little sleep house officers managed in the past week, or tales told by attendings of how long their hours on duty used to be.

Overwork has been used to justify an error, rudeness to a patient, neglect of family, or drug abuse beginning in the house staff years. When it becomes an end in itself and a source of pride, overwork can lay the groundwork for chronic fatigue, persistent irritability, and eventual dissatisfaction with medical practice.

In Vaillant's study of a group of healthy Harvard students that began over 20 years ago, physical health, capacity for work, and capacity for love and altruism appear to be closely associated. The happiest people were also the healthiest and the most productive. The difference between the many whose lives fulfilled the rich promise of their youth and the few whose lives did not are instructive. No life was lived without adversity, without problems. The significant differences were not in the magnitude of good or bad events since graduation, not in the isolated traumas of childhood, but rather in the pattern of human interaction. It was the daily relatedness with people, the active engagement in life, and the positive adaptive coping patterns that evolved in response to adversity that separated productive and generative lives from the bored and frustrated ones.

Physicians especially must learn to recognize and to manage adversity and disappointments constructively. It is not constructive to lash out at others or to become absorbed in self-criticism. It is not constructive to work past exhaustion when that is done in a frantic attempt to ward off inner feelings, or to achieve some kind of illusory perfection, or to avoid any kind of external criticism. Overwork, sleep deprivation, and isolation from human interaction may lead to feelings of hopelessness and helplessness in medical schools and hospitals just as in prisoner of war camps. As a result medical students and house officers and ultimately practicing physicians may be disenfranchised of their right to self-determination and robbed of much of the enjoyment available in their work. When people believe they are not doing an adequate job unless they are in a state of exhaustion, they are not likely to muster the individual or group resources necessary to make realistic or wise decisions about the priorities in their lives.

Heroics

A preference for problems that require heroic medical interventions expresses itself in the use of terms like "interesting patient," referring to medical, not personal attributes. Those patients who do not require such virtuosity become "crocks," "turkeys," "gomers," "worried well," "hospital hobos," "uninteresting" or "nuisances" who "misuse medical services." A preoccupation with heroics and rare diseases and its corollary, a quest for omnipotence, may lead to neglect of interpersonal skills and to an underestimation of the importance of the small daily actions of relief and comfort in medical care. If only saving a life or making a dramatic intervention is taken as important, then indeed "nothing can be done" for most patients.

However, in most doctor-patient relationships it may not be the big events that determine satisfaction as much as it is the ongoing patterns that are made up of smaller events. William Osler advised his medical students: "Nothing will sustain you more potently than the power to recognize in your humdrum routine, as perhaps it may be thought, the true poetry of life— the poetry of the commonplace, of the ordinary man, of the toil-worn woman, with their joys, their sorrows, and their griefs." That advice is confirmed in studies of contemporary physicians and career satisfactions.

Ann Cartwright and her colleagues interviewed physicians and their patients to determine areas of consensus and sources of satisfaction on both sides of the doctor-patient relationship. Some 46% of the doctors said that their personal contacts with patients were the source of their greatest enjoyment. Most (71%) of the physicians who "enjoyed practice very much" estimated that only about 10% of their consultations were about "trivial problems." In contrast, among the physicians who were unhappy with their work, 18% reported that one-half to three-fourths of their patients presented "trivial complaints." These unhappy and cynical physicians who thought that a higher proportion of their consultations were for trivial, unnecessary, or inappropriate reasons had more patients who thought that the prestige of physicians had diminished within the last 10 years. Impressions of physicians that patients "demand their rights" too much was also strongly associated with the largest estimates of "trivial complaints."

Trivializing patients' complaints demeans patients and the practice of medicine. It is bad for doctors in that it contributes to unhappiness in the medical career and robs physicians of a major potential source of emotional rewards, i.e., the knowledge that most patients can be helped significantly in one way or another and will be grateful for that help. Sometimes that help may consist of a gentle hand, a respectful remark, a considerate glance, or even a moment of silent but attentive listening to a patient who needs to tell a story, who desperately needs to know that he or she matters to someone, and is understood. Trivializing patients' complaints is also bad for patients who must leave such an encounter feeling more frustrated and helpless, and with their self-esteem more diminished, than when they arrived for help in the first place. Finally, trivializing patient complaints also leads to flawed doctor-patient relationships. A study by the California Medical Association reports that physicians who have been sued for malpractice are often characterized by a need for their patients to be overly dependent on and grateful to them, but also by a tendency to fear and dislike these very same patients and to demean their complaints.

Thus, attention to the fears, concerns, and complaints of patients is not only humane, it is also "good medicine" for both the patient and the doctor. The more powerful our techniques, the more invasive our heroic interventions, the more urgently will patients need to have their humanity attended along with their organ systems. "High tech" may also accentuate needs for "high touch". And, the "touch" that may mean the most will often be the small but caring actions that comfort people when they are most vulnerable (Figure 41.3).

Figure 41.3. Elderly man talks to a young house staff physician about placement in an old age home. From the film *Hospital*, produced and directed by Frederick Wiseman. (By permission of Zipporah Films, Boston, Mass.)

Suggested Readings

Coombs RH, Boyle BP: The transition to medical school: expectations versus realities. In Coombs RH, Vincent CE (eds): *Psychosocial Aspects of Medical Training.* Springfield, Ill, Charles C Thomas, 1971, p 91.

Coombs RH: The medical marriage. In Coombs RH, Vincent CE (eds): *Psychosocial Aspects of Medical Training.* Coombs RH, Vincent CE (eds): Springfield, Ill, Charles C Thomas, 1971, p 133.

Keniston K: The medical student. *Yale J Biol Med* 39:346, 1967.

Menninger KA: Psychological factors in the choice of medicine as a profession. In Hall BH (ed): *A Psychiatrist's World.* New York, Viking Press, 1959, p 477.

Mumford E: *Interns: From Students to Physicians.* Cambridge, MA, Harvard University Press, 1970.

Notman MT, Nadelson CC: Medicine: a career conflict for women. *Am J. Psychiatry* 130:1123, 1973.

Raskin M: Psychiatric crises of medical students and the implications for subsequent adjustment. *J Med Educ* 47:210, 1972.

Stein LI: The doctor-nurse game. *Arch Gen Psychiatry* 16:699, 1967.

References

Association of American Medical Colleges. Graduate of foreign medical schools in the United States: a challenge to medical education. *J Med Educ* 49:813, 1974.

Becker HS, Geer B: The fate of idealism in medical school. *Am Sociol Rev* 23:50, 1958.

Boyle BP, Coombs RH: Personality profiles related to emotional stress in the initial year of medical training. *J Med Educ* 46:882, 1971.

Cartwright A: *Patients and Their Doctors.* London, Routledge and Kegan Paul, 1967.

Funkenstein DH: Current medical school admissions: the problems and a proposal. *J Med Educ* 45:497, 1970.

Levine DM, Weisman CS, Seidel HM: Career decisions of unaccepted applicants to medical school. *JAMA* 232:1141, 1975.

Lewis CE: Illness behavior and academic performance among medical students. *Arch Environ Health* 12:776, 1966.

Peterson O: An analytical study of North Carolina general practice. *J Med Educ* 31:2, 1956.

Reiser DE, Schroder AK: Becoming a doctor. In *Patient Interviewing: The Human Dimension.* Baltimore, Williams & Wilkins, 1985.

Vaillant GE: *Adaptation to Life.* Boston, Little, Brown, & Co, 1977.

B. The Rewards and Hazards of Medicine as a Profession

Laurence Schweitzer, M.D.

Medicine as a rewarding profession? That idea will surely come as no surprise to any of us. It embodies the tradition and folklore of centuries. But medicine as a hazardous profession? To whom? We hope not to the patients. If not, can the work be hazardous to the physician? That certainly is a startling proposition, yet it appears more true now than ever before in the history of medical practice. In this chapter I will attempt to discuss both the rewards and the hazards of the medical profession. Much of what I say will also be applicable to all the health-related professions.

THE DEMANDS OF MEDICAL PRACTICE

For the most part, the public understands very little of what it is really like to practice medicine. Our relationship to a physician has usually been that of a patient, and in this context we have directed our attention to our own bodies, sensations, experiences, and needs. Stop for a moment and consider what it is like for the other person, that is for the doctor who is continually subjected to the demands of this very one-sided, and if you will, rather self-centered contact. Perhaps viewing things from this perspective allows us to appreciate the impact of the profession on the social and psychological life of the physician.

To begin this other look at medicine, we should first have a clear description of what a physician's day-to-day life is like. We can then go on to consider the possible psychological meanings of this life style, and draw some inferences about the origins of the satisfactions as well as the hazards of this work.

A Typical Week

A rather fine description of a doctor's work week can be found in the Milbank Memorial Fund Study of Doctors' Work. The following excerpt has been quoted from this study.

> The week began for Dr. Stanley at 2:17 A.M. Monday with the phone ringing.

Mrs. Jones was ready to deliver. One hour later he was on his way home from the hospital. Aftercare for Mrs. Jones had been left in the capable hands of the hospital staff.

The alarm clock next woke Dr. Stanley at 7 A.M. Fifty minutes later he was scrubbing, and 8 o'clock sharp he was getting into his gown and gloves to help Dr. Stevens, a surgeon, remove a gallbladder from one of Dr. Stanley's patients. Right after that, he acted as Dr. Steven's assistant while one of Steven's patients had a bowel tumor removed. It was now 11 A.M. Fifteen minutes for coffee and some talk with the others in the doctor's lounge. Then back to the operating room, to give an anesthetic while one of his colleagues removed the tonsils and adenoids of a six year old girl. Then they switched ends of the table, and Stanley removed a pair of tonsils from one of his young patients. Together they went for another quick coffee, and a coffee room debate over whether the family doctors were going to have to stop giving anesthetics now that there were anesthesiologists on the staff of the West Urbanville Hospital.

It was now 12:30 P.M. and Dr. Stanley was off and running to visit five other patients who were in the hospital under his care. This took 30 minutes. Seventeen minutes with the patients' charts and the nurses on the wards, and walking from ward to ward; 13 minutes with the patients. Extra tests were ordered for Mr. Raimey with jaundice. The nurse was asked to speed up getting the results of the stomach X-rays on Mrs. Peters, which had been ordered to make sure there was no trouble there, before the arrangements were completed for her gallstones to be removed. Mrs. Jones, whom he had delivered during the night, was fine, and he peeked through the glass at her baby, who looked pink and contented. He'd go over the baby in more detail before the little guy went home. Finally, he spent five minutes with Bell, who was dying of cancer.

It was 1 P.M. Dr. Stanley stopped in the records room and telephoned his office. He took three messages and asked his secretary to pick up a sandwich for him. He signed off three charts on patients who had been discharged from the hospital the previous week, made two of the phone calls relating to the messages and decided the third could wait. On the way to the office he dropped in for 10 minutes at a nursing home to visit three elderly patients.

2:20 P.M. Finally at the office. Mondays were always hell. Ten minutes to gulp the sandwich and review the afternoon's work.

2:30 P.M. Twenty patients were to be seen before 6:30 P.M. Five an hour, one every 12 minutes. Two new patients, 18 return patients. Six with new conditions, 14 with chronic conditions, or returning for review where there was not apparent disease. These four hours were interrupted by 27 minutes of telephone calls concerning patients—some from patients themselves, others from specialists and other doctors concerning patients,.

6:30 P.M. Four more phone calls to make, including the one waiting since morning. As a result, two house calls had to be made. These took one hour.

At 7:45 P.M., home and dinner. Two calls waiting after dinner. One required telephone instructions. The other about a patient's cut leg, required a 40-minute visit to the emergency department at the hospital. The intern could have done it himself.

Home again just before 10 P.M. That was it; no more leaving the house until the following morning. It had not been an unusual day.

* * *

During this one day we have followed Dr. Stanley and have found him to be a busy, conscientious doctor. His main contacts with specialists were in the operating room or in hurried telephone calls from his office. He knew he was relatively inaccessible to his patients for many hours during the week and that his records were unavailable to those who saw his patients during his absence. He would have liked to have spent time more with his patients' psychosocial problems, but this would have crippled each morning's work in the Urbanville Hospital. During the remainder of the week, Dr. Stanley had not a single direct contact with any social workers or with the community's health-related welfare agencies.

He earned about $1,200 during the week; his office overhead left him with about $750. During the week he managed his own practice at the business-administrative end. He kept track of the work he did as he did it, and he supervised the feebilling system maintained by his combined secretary-receptionist-billing clerk-girl Friday. He decided how many telephones to have, how to run his miniature laboratory, and so on. In the hospital he was just another G.P. or family doctor, in his office he made all the decisions—he was independent, yet he often felt he was on a treadmill.

Dr. Stanley emerges from this vignette as a dedicated and conscientious physician who by any reasonable standard is available to his patients and is familiar with their particular problems. Dr. Stanley is well informed and competent in areas of surgery, obstetrics, general practice, and applied psychology. His life is very much taken up with his practice and his patients, and he spends the greatest part of his time listening to the problems of other people. From what we see, it is rare for him to spend any substantial time engaged socially with friends or colleagues. During this week there was little time for any nonprofessional conversations, and no one to whom he could unburden himself during his long working day. In fact, one of the most dramatic aspects of Dr. Stanley's life is its essential loneliness (Figure 41.4). He has a great deal of contact with people, but these contacts are dominated by the needs of his patients and offer little opportunity for the gratification of his own psychosocial needs. In short, his work demanded continuous involvement with others while denying him reciprocal opportunities. Would we prescribe such a life for any of our own patients?

Dr. Stanley should not be taken to represent an unusual physician. Moreover, I will add my personal impression that the pressures of time, social isolation, and the demands of the doctor-patient relationship are captured with great clarity by this vignette.

The Nuclear Family

Other equally important factors impinge on doctors that are not examined or appreciated by any study limited to a description of time and activity. For example, what do you imagine has been the effect on the doctor-patient relationship as the extended family has become frag-

Figure 41.4. *Weary Country Doctor.* Coffee and a smoke in the hospital kitchen at 2 A.M. ends one day for Dr. Ernest Guy Ceriani. In a few hours, another would begin in his endless job as the only physician for Kremmling, Colorado. Photograph by W. Eugene Smith. (By permission of W. Eugene Smith.)

mented and its source of internal support dissipated? To whom have these isolated nuclear families turned for advice, counseling, and support? Increasingly, it has been the family practitioner and more recently, the specialist. This reliance on the physician becomes even more intense when medical science extends the life of the fatally ill patient, and thereby often extends the suffering of the patient, the family, and the physician.

In the past, a network of extended family ties provided a large measure of comfort and support to its members, especially at the time of death. Contemporary life, with its emphasis on social and geographic mobility and its disruption of the extended family, has placed many additional burdens on the physician. These new demands are as often spiritual and psychological as they are physical, and require us to regularly deal with our own most sensitive concerns. For example, how does the physician feel as he supports the life of a dying patient, all the while knowing that he is causing great anguish to the patient's family? Moreover, how does the doctor simultaneously provide emotional support to both? How does a physician deal with illnesses that were formerly fatal and now are only crippling, leaving the survivor bitter and resentful toward the physician who preserved life but not its quality? How does the physician, who is often isolated and alone in his work, regard the patient who asks for his help, but who he knows will turn with a vengeance on him when disillusioned with the results of the physician's best efforts.

The Physician's Own Family

Finally, what is the effect of all this stress and commitment on the doctor's family? We know from a variety of studies that doctors' marriages are less durable than those of other professional groups. Moreover, the long hours and continuous deprivation of the physician-father or physician-mother are also very punishing on the doctor's children. It is an often repeated joke that if you ask a doctor's child what he wishes to be when he grows up, he will reply, "A patient." I would add that this is not merely apocryphal. A woman, whose father is a physician and had an office in the home, has told me that as a child she did truly wish to be a patient, and always chose to be the patient in any doctor games that were played.

The preceding austere observations on the physician's lot may darken what each of us has privately romanticized and idealized as the physician's experience. I do not want to draw the conclusion that all is sacrifice and renunciation without recognizing that the rewards of medical practice are very substantial and meaningful. If we examine just a few medical specialities, perhaps we can have a clearer picture of the special tasks and the particular gratifications of each.

EXAMPLES OF PARTICULAR MEDICAL SPECIALITIES

Pediatrics

The pediatrician's work affords him the opportunity to do more than treat childhood illnesses. Although he participates in the development of each child that he treats, an important part of his time is spent providing education and reassurance to anxious parents. This regular contact provides him with an additional patient about whom we generally pay too little attention, the family unit. The pediatrician has the

opportunity to promote not only the healthy growth of the child but the family as well.

Pediatricians who listen carefully to parents' concerns will often hear elements of irrational fantasies about bodily functions that cause much anxiety. A common example is when parents complain about "...eating problems." Common sense and experience suggest that anybody, large or small, eats when hungry and food is available. (We are assuming that there is no primary eating disturbance in the child.) Yet parents are often driven to desperation because a child who is well nourished and well developed, and who has a past history of eating regularly, does not finish everything that he or she is given. The pediatrician is often sought out by the parents who hope for an ally in their struggle about how much is enough. In such cases, the "patient" is the family unit, and the "illness" is an irrational pattern of behavior on the part of the parents based on certain misconceptions. The simple act of listening to the parents' concerns generally elicits these ideas. Such a discussion between a pediatrician and a parent can be extremely helpful in resolving these attitudes, and is an example of primary prevention of the very best sort. The result is often an immediate and dramatic improvement in the parent-child relationship.

The reader may well ask what is helpful in all of this. Is it merely catharsis and if so, why should a pediatrician spend his time this way? Catharsis alone is not the best explanation for the therapeutic effect that talking to an interested and informed physician has. Rather, the therapeutic effect seems to derive from two other sources. The first is the fact that the use of the spoken word enables people to judge their own ideas more clearly. Ideas that remain as unspoken thoughts can be quite fanciful and are often influenced primarily by our feelings, just as daydreams are likely to be. Putting ideas into words actuates a critical and evaluating function of our mind that is not always present in silent thought. Second, when the speaking occurs in the presence of an acknowledged expert, these critical and evaluative functions can be strengthened by identification with the pediatrician's careful, thoughtful, and objective approach. The net effect of this experience is often a reorganization of the parents' concepts of their child's behavior, and the replacement of misconceptions with the physician's realistic and empathic understanding.

These comments apply generally to all areas of medicine. We work most effectively with all patients, but in particular with those who demonstrate irrational behavior, when we listen first to find out what the patient's ideas actually are. Our remarks and educational interventions will then be more judicious, pertinent to the patient's anxieties and misconceptions, and more easily assimilated by the patient.

Surgery

Few of us attack disease as directly or as efficiently as the surgeon. His work brings him into daily and repetitive contact with patients who are seriously ill and often near death. On his daily rounds he confronts a regular complement of acutely ill patients who may have appeared relatively healthy only a day before he operated on them. Moreover, their acute physical distress and postoperative pain often breed a disillusionment and bitterness to which the busy surgeon can only give nodding recognition. He is absorbed by still other stresses. These are dying patients whom most of us gladly avoid. They, more than any group of patients, represent a blow to our professional narcissism and self-esteem, and confront us with a keen personal sense of our own mortality. The stress of surgical practice is particularly intense since many surgical patients may die as a direct result of the surgical intervention.

It is no small wonder then that surgeons have been described as "cold and unfeeling." Who could absorb such punishment on a daily basis and not defend themselves? Indeed, it is a sad and undeserved misjudgment to say that the surgeon is unfeeling or, worse yet, that he is merely sublimating his sadistic wishes. The truth of the matter is that the surgeon often feels too much, and these feelings may be dealt with in a defensive fashion through attention to the technology of a surgical procedure, rather than its emotional significance for the patients.

Although the price of a surgical practice is great, the rewards are equally so. Where else can one intervene so directly and efficiently so as to literally take the disease in one's hands and cast it out? What bond is deeper between patient and physician than that between the surgeon and a recovered patient? Yet, the rewards of a surgical practice extend far beyond the surgeon's relationship to physical illness. As with the pediatrician, these rewards find their clearest expression in our opportunity to realize our essential humanity through our relationship to our patients. The surgical treatment should be understood as one vehicle that promotes this end. The other is the surgeon's ability to listen to his patients, tolerate their anxiety and pain, and provide an empathic understanding of human frailty. The physician's ability to exercise his expertise and bring empathic understanding to the patient is the physician's greatest gift and reward. We have seen how this may occur in a pediatric situation. Now let us consider how a surgeon can do very much the same. To do this I will have to digress briefly to review one aspect of psychological development—that of "the body image."

We have long been aware of the fact that people's earliest concepts of themselves begin with the establishment of certain mental representations of their bodies as separate from the rest of the world. Dr. Scharfman has already discussed this development sequence in some detail. The resulting set of early concepts relating to our bodies is our first "self" and is referred to as "the body image." It is never completely factual or accurate, since it is first developed by the child between the ages of one and three. As a result, this set of ideas about the body contains inconsistencies and fantasies that children commonly use in order to account for their own observations and experiences. As an example, many children theorize that the fluids that enter their mouths and leave via their urethra flow through a direct connection of tubes or an equivalent plumbing system. Other children think that fluids—and later feelings—travel through their bodies by way of elaborate systems that have a diffuse type of interconnection. Another common idea that children have is that babies are conceived by swallowing something, and that they are then born through a large cloacal opening that is indistinct from the rectum.

Many of these early ideas and body concepts are not completely corrected by later experience or factual information. They remain in our unconscious up to and throughout our adult life. We can hear the derivatives of these childhood theories in our daily conversations with patients. It is common for us to hear a patient indicate that his "system" is not working right, or that something got into his system and has "traveled" from one part of his body to another, causing him distress. Still another example is a commonly expressed explanation of uncomfortable feelings being the result of "my nerves."

Keeping the preceding comments in mind, we can begin to appreciate the meaning of surgeon and the surgery to the patient. It is the surgeon whose tools, indeed whose very hands, enter into a person's body to make or disrupt connections as well as to remove its parts. As a result, the surgeon becomes indispensable to the patient who must now make a new and modified body image. The postoperative patient desperately needs the surgeon to help him repair the damage done to his psyche as well as to his body. The changes caused by surgery disturb concepts that are often fundamental underpinings of our sense of self-esteem. These changes can cause patients to become apprehensive, anxious, depressed, and confused.

It is the surgeon's unique ability to understand these concerns while dealing effectively with the patient's physical illness that allows the greatest reward of the surgical practice. Quiet discussions in which patients can ventilate their anxieties about their bodies often relieve them of unrealistic and unwarranted anger at the surgeon. The sense that someone understands is one of the most reassuring and comforting of all human experiences. The lack of this rapport may leave physically recovered patients quite emotionally distressed, and perhaps even furious in the mistaken feeling that their bodies were wantonly invaded and injured. Such irrational feelings uncorrected by the realistic explanations of an empathic surgeon not infrequently lead to malpractice suits. It is my impression that such suits are often the expression of a patient's frustration at having been unable to establish a meaningful dialogue with his or her physician, and this is especially true in cases where surgical procedures have been performed.

Obstetrics

The obstetrician is generally the first to know and to announce the happy news that a couple will soon become parents. As such he is doubly fortunate in being able to observe the unfolding of this transformation of a couple into a family, to participate personally in this rich and human experience. The obstetrician's counsel and wisdom can often make the difference between a harmonious rather than a chaotic and disruptive introduction of a child into the husband and wife dyad. In order to appreciate the obstetri-

cians' role, it is helpful again to review some of the psychology involved in this part of our life cycle.

In general, the wish to be unique in the eyes of those whom we love is a normal and ubiquitous human emotion. In certain cases where parents feel competitive with their own children for love and affection, this wish proves to be a major barrier to establishing a mature, parenting relationship. Often a husband becomes jealous, even petulant, at his pregnant wife's growing interest in the unborn child and her affection for the child after its birth. It is the obstetrician who can be alerted to these problems and who can then discuss this matter openly with the couple as a form of primary prevention. Very often, such interventions may actually preserve the new family and help it begin in a healthy way. There are other ways in which the obstetrician becomes involved with the family unit. These include genetic counseling, as well as family planning. From this perspective we can see that the role of the obstetrician should not be limited to the mother nor to the delivery process. The obstetrician has an important relationship to the entire family.

The problems of an obstetrical practice for the physician often originate in precisely those same areas that we have identified as providing the greatest potential sources of gratification. That is to say, once one becomes involved with families, it requires wisdom, strength, and patience to handle such problems effectively, and to withstand the family's wish to have the physician champion each member's point of view. These pressures may often serve to confuse the physician's self-concept and undermine his or her relationship to the new family.

THE VULNERABILITIES OF PHYSICIANS

There are many factors other than the physical or emotional pressures of a physician's work that may lead to special vulnerabilities. Dr. George Vaillant and his coworkers have compared a group of 47 physicians to 79 socioeconomically matched controls during 30 years of adult life to determine if physicians suffer higher rates of dysfunction. Their findings indicated that physicians as a group showed greater marital instablity, a higher incidence of alcohol and drug abuse, and a greater need for psychiatric treatment. When physicians with a history of a traumatic childhood were compared to a matched group of nonphysicians, the physician group was twice as likely to experience difficulties in one or more of the three areas studied. The authors also found that poor childhood experiences doubled the expectation of later life difficulties regardless of occupational choice.

These data point to childhood experiences as a contributing factor in later life disturbances. However, when the effect of childhood experiences is taken into account and controlled for, emotional problems are still significantly more frequent among physicians. Clearly other factors must be operative, and this fact provides additional justification for viewing our work itself as predisposing to life difficulties.

Dr. Vaillant has noted that the character traits of most physicians tend to promote a need to care for other people and a corresponding difficulty in allowing themselves to be cared for. As Vaillant says: "Doctors need permission to cherish themselves and admit that they, too, have needs." The adage, "Physician, heal thyself," is followed all too often in the form of drug and alcohol abuse by the overworked, underloved physician who has given his all to his patients in the hope that he shall also find solace and support in the process.

The altruistic character structure that Dr. Vaillant describes is one that often places a tremendous burden upon physicians and prevents them from attending to their own legitimate needs. We have all known physicians who feel guilty about expressing and gratifying their needs for rest, companionship, and the support of their loved ones. The physicians of physicians must be alert to this problem, especially since patients often want their physicians to be completely selfless and without needs of their own. The result of this largely unconscious union of the physician's altruism and the patient's wishes can sometimes be the literal destrucion of the physician's life. The suicide rate among male physicians is about 15% higher than the expected rate among the general male population, and the suicide rate among female physicians is three to four times as high as the expected rate.

It becomes clearer now that something in the nature of our patients' problems and in our relationship to patients can threaten our own emotional well-being. Furthermore, if we acknowledge the potentially synergistic role of our own personalities in this matter, we can better understand the rewards and hazards of the physician's life.

One of the most serious consequences of such stresses can be the development of an emotional illness in the physician himself. I think that such cases are more common than we would like to recognize. A frequent form of such an illness is a disturbed pattern of work or social adjustment. Who does not know a physician whose family rarely sees him, but whose patients have access to him at every hour of the day and night, every weekend and holiday? Examples in the opposite direction are also common. We all know physicians who regularly fail to return phone calls, or who keep patients waiting for excessively long periods of time. In such situations, the physician has fallen victim to his own conflicts. Indeed, we ourselves may be the greatest and most frequent hazard we face.

The question of how to deal with such reactions is complex. When such feelings lead to behavior that is inappropriate and uncontrolled, the physician would be well served to seek psychiatric consultation and help. In other cases, it is often sufficient to identify the presence of these feelings and to trace them back to their source in a relationship with a particular patient. The physician is then alerted to the operation of a specific unconscious reaction to that particular patient, described earlier in the book by Dr. Blumenfeld as a "countertransference" reaction, and can then attempt to institute a more helpful and appropriate form of behavior.

PERSONAL RECOLLECTIONS

The physician's professional experience is qualitatively different from that of other care givers. He is not only required to deal regularly with life and death matters, but he alone has the final responsibility to intervene to sustain life in the face of certain death. The demands for empathy that these situations make are often profoundly disturbing for the physician.

As a third year medical student, I served a clerkship on an orthopedic service in which a teenage girl was slowly dying of cancer. She had developed a sarcoma of her tibia, and had had successive amputations at her knee, midthigh, and finally at her hip joint in an heroic effort to eradicate this malignancy. It was all to no avail, and she now had a large fungating tumor growing out of the stump where her thigh had formerly been attached to her body. She was dying, and she was acutely aware of this fact as well as of our anxiety and distress. She had been placed at the furthest point from the nursing station and was the most isolated patient on the unit. The effect of this isolation did much to unnerve her, but I think it was our anxiety and reluctance to be involved with her that was most painful. I know that as a young medical student I was deeply shocked at the inevitability of her death and felt guilty over my contrasting good fortune. I recall trying to pass by her doorway quickly so as not to be seen or to see her. It was only when she repeatedly cried for help that any of us went to her. At these times she would scream at the top of her lungs that she did not want to die, that she wanted to live!

As time passed, her condition worsened and these episodes became more and more frequent. We wondered what more we could do for her. Gradually we came to recognize our own anxiety and our avoidance of this patient. We began to think not so much about her impending death but rather for the first time began to ask how we could help her live with her illness. There was of course something of an unwelcome mortification in accepting the fact that cancer would ultimately take her. It was our preoccupation over preserving our feelings of omnipotence that had prevented us from seeing our proper role in this girl's terminal illness. As her physicians and nurses, we came to see our responsibility to help this young woman live the remainder of her life as best she could. This rather simple yet profound realization further enabled us to talk to her, whereupon we discovered some remarkable things. We learned she had a life goal that was very important to her, although she was aware that she would die shortly. She wanted to graduate from high school with her classmates. This goal was not beyond hope since she had continued to study while in the hospital, and unknown to us had passed all of her courses! She was now painfully depressed at the prospect of not being able to be at her graduation. After learning this, we made special efforts to get her to her graduation ceremony and to have her receive her diploma with her classmates. On her return to the hospital she was a new person. She was happy, and grateful to the medical staff for being able to understand her wishes for the first time. She died two days later.

This experience moved me most deeply, and I shall never forget this patient. She taught all of us who treated her how important it is for physicians and nurses to confront their own anxieties and to deal with them honestly, so that they do not interfere with our humane treatment and understanding of our patients.

Conversely, physicians sometimes develop too much empathy. This problem generally occurs when we treat a medical colleague. We very often identify with the other physician and experience a host of painful feelings that have more to do with ourselves than with our colleague-patient. This reaction can lead to a denial of real illness and to the frequent errors in diagnosis and treatment that physicians and the families of physicians regularly experience. Another personal example can serve to highlight this problem.

I had suffered from recurrent respiratory infections over a period of a year, and on the advice of my physician I entered the hospital for a bronchogram. The procedure required that a small needle be passed through my trachea in order to inject the radiopaque material into the respiratory tree. The procedure was accomplished uneventfully, and since I felt so well following the X-rays, I suggested to the intern that I be allowed to return home that same evening. Routine hospital practice required that I should remain overnight for observation. The intern, perhaps somewhat intimidated by my age and faculty position, eventually agreed that I could leave. Shortly after my return home I began coughing up a good deal of the dye and quickly developed a dissecting subcutaneous emphysema. The air spread upwards from my trachea to my face, and in no time at all I took on the appearance of a boiled potato.

My reason for wanting to leave the hospital was to ensure that I would see my own patients on the following day, which happened to be the day before my summer vacation. I had been concerned that I might not see my patients if there was any delay in my discharge, and rather than leave my fate to those most competent to oversee it, I took matters into my own hands. "Physician, heal thyself!" The result was that my patients saw a physician whose face and neck were grotesquely swollen by air and who looked nothing like the doctor they had known before. I certainly did not help to relieve their separation anxieties, nor were they reassured that nothing bad was likely to happen to me during the vacation.

CONCLUSION

We have seen how the unique and dramatic nature of our contact with patients and the impact of life and death matters can profoundly affect us. I have also talked about the problem of avoiding empathy and the opposite problem of developing too much empathy. I have also noted how the demands of our profession and our own altruistic and perfectionistic character traits may drive us into work patterns that impose enormous stress on ourselves and on our families, and make it impossible for us to truly enjoy all of the rewards and gratifications of medical practice. We and our families then become vulnerable to emotional illness.

In conclusion, it is my belief that those of us in the medical profession, and indeed in all of the health-related professions, can best fulfill our obligations to our patients if we are aware of our own needs, anxieties, and vulnerabilities. It is time to change the adage "Physician, heal thyself" to "Physician, understand thyself and be tolerant of thine own needs."

Suggested Readings

Coombs RH: The medical marriage. In Coombs RH, Vincent CE (eds): *Psychosocial Aspects of Medical Training.* Springfield, Ill, Charles C Thomas, 1971, p 133.

Menninger KA: Psychological factors in the choice of medicine as a profession. In Hall BH (ed): *A Psychiatrist's World.* New York, Viking Press, 1959, p 477.

Scheiber SC, Doyle BB (eds): *The Impaired Physician.* New York, Plenum, 1983.

Stoudemire A, Rhoads JM: When the doctor needs a doctor: special considerations for the physician-patient. *Ann Int Med* 98:654, 1983.

Talbott GD, Benson EB: Impaired physicians: the dilemma of identification. *Postgrad Med* 68:56, 1980.

Vaillant GE, Brighton JR, McArthur C: Physician's use of mood-altering drugs. *N Engl J Med* 282:365, 1970.

Vaillant GE, Sobowale NC, McArthur C: Some psychologic vulnerabilities of physicians. *N Engl J Med* 287:372, 1972.

Wolfe S, Badgley R: The family doctor. *Millbank Memorial Fund Quarterly* 50:4, Part II, April 1972.

References

Bissell L, Jones RW: The alcoholic physician: a survey. *Am J Psychiatry* 133:1142, 1976.

Carlson GA, Miller DC: Suicide, affective disorder, and women physicians. *Am J Psychiatry* 138:1330, 1981.

Johnson RP, Connelly JC: Addicted physicians: a closer look. *JAMA* 245:253, 1981.

McCue JD: The effects of stress on physicians and their medical practice. *N Engl J Med* 306:458, 1982.

Pearson MM: Psychiatric treatment of 250 physicians. *Psychiatr Ann* 12:194, 1982.

Rose KD, Rosow I: Physicians who kill themselves. *Arch Gen Psychiatry* 29:800, 1973.

Waring EM: Psychiatric illness in physicians: a review. *Comp Psychiatry* 15:519, 1974.

Section L/Early Adulthood, Marriage, and Parenthood

CHAPTER **42 Early Adulthood, Marriage, and Parenthood**

Richard C. Simons, M.D.

THE TASKS OF ADULTHOOD

When does early adulthood begin? In our age of prolonged adolescence, lengthened education, increasing work specialization, and decreasing job opportunities for even the most highly skilled and well trained, that is becoming an ever more difficult question to answer. But it is becoming just as difficult to know when the developmental phase of early adulthood comes to an end, and gradually gives way to middle age. This is not only because of our lengthened life span. Many other factors are operating as well to alter our traditional concepts of the life cycle, and to cause a shift in the age-specific tasks of early and later adulthood.

For example, puberty is occurring at an earlier and earlier age, as are sexual experimentation and close sexual involvements among young adolescents. Furthermore, many young adults are marrying at a much earlier age than ever before and having children at a much younger age. The average young woman marries in her early twenties, gives birth to her first child within the first year or so after marriage, has borne all of her children within the next five to six years, and is entering her last-born child in grade school by the time she is in her early thirties.

Thus, active parenthood is becoming much shorter in duration than in previous generations, the children are leaving home and marrying when their parents are still relatively young, and grandparenthood is coming at an earlier age than ever before for many people. It is no longer uncommon to see grandparents in their forties, and consequently dramatic changes are taking place in the relationships between these younger grandparents, their children who are now young parents themselves, and their grandchildren.

At the same time that the traditional tasks of marriage, parenthood, and grandparenthood are occurring at younger and younger ages, other young people in increasing numbers are experiencing doubts as to whether the rewards of marriage and especially of parenthood are worth the sacrifices. As a result, many of these young people are living together for long periods of time before marrying, and sometimes without ever marrying. If they do marry, they may have no children, or at most only one or perhaps two, in contrast to the much larger families of previous generations.

Thus, we have these three divergent trends. First, a delay in the true independence and autonomy of adulthood because of prolonged education, protracted financial dependence on parents, and decreased work opportunities. Second, an earlier and earlier onset of genital sexuality, marriage, parenthood, and grandparenthood. Third, a revolutionary shifting of values among increasing numbers of young people, with greater emphasis upon a commitment to oneself and to another person in a relationship that may not include either marriage or parenthood.

It would be foolhardy to attempt to predict what the future will bring in the face of trends such as these. Are there then any anchors around which we can attempt to conceptualize the increasing complexity of young adulthood? Despite the divergence and sometimes the turbulence of these various currents of modern life, it would seem that Freud's prescription for a rewarding life is just as apt now as when he offered it, perhaps even more so: "To love and to work." For a man who wrote and discovered so much, Freud could be very succinct at times. Notice that he did *not* say, "To marry" or "To have children" or "To make money" or "To be famous" or "To be happy" or "To have mutual and multiple orgasms" or "To become one with the mystical universe." What he said was much simpler, and yet much more profound, and indeed much more difficult to achieve, than any of these stereotypes of "normality." "To love and to work" are truly the essential tasks that face the young adult in every culture and in every generation. These are the tasks for which the growth, development, and maturation of childhood and adolescence have prepared each individual, and these are the tasks that will require a lifetime to complete. Let us look at each one, even if only briefly.

TO LOVE

The Uniqueness of Human Sexuality

A good many chapters of this book have dealt with the developmental phases of childhood sexuality, and the many different aspects of adult sexuality. But perhaps we should pause for a moment, and reflect about the uniqueness of human sexuality. What are the features that set human sexuality apart from the sexual functioning of all other animals? There are several. Human sexuality is first of all independent of reproduction, and this is not true in other mammalian species where the sexual act is intimately tied to reproduction during the estrous cycle. Furthermore, with the advent of modern contraceptive measures, the separation between human sexuality and reproduction is more complete than ever before. Human sexuality is also both a physiological and a psychological phenomenon, and the relationship between these two parameters is complex and ever present. Again, in contrast to all other animal species, there is tremendous variation from culture to culture, and within any given culture from one historical period to another, in terms of the prevailing attitudes, values, and mores as to what is normal and what is abnormal, what is acceptable and what is unacceptable as far as sexual behavior is concerned.

Along with this enormous cultural and historical variability, there is a biological unfolding, a sequential maturation of the sexual drives that is relatively independent of culture, environment, and experience. For example, the biological phenomenon of puberty is going to take place no matter what a particular society, culture, family, or religion thinks about sexuality. The sexual drive is one of the fundamental urges of human existence. It can be denied, suppressed, even outlawed. But it will never disappear. However, while this biological unfolding and instinctual urgency are undeniable facts, it is also a fact that in humans, again in contrast to all other species, culture, experience, and learning all play a tremendous role in shaping each person's ultimate sexual behavior. As a result, there are remarkably different patterns of sexual gratification in different individuals, despite the similar, sequential maturation of the sexual drives.

The Differences Between the Sexes

Thank heavens for the differences, to paraphrase many old jokes and songs. But the differences contribute to the difficulties between the sexes, as well as to the love and the sexual pleasure. To begin with it is far more difficult for many women to achieve full orgasmic capacity than it is for most men. Kinsey in 1953, Hunt in 1975, and Hite in 1976 all arrived at strikingly similar figures: approximately 10% of American women never experience orgasm, and well over half of sexually active women do not regularly experience orgasm during intercourse. There are a number of reasons for these findings. First, the woman has two primary erogenous zones, the clitoris and the vagina, whereas the man only has one, the penis. And while the clitoris and the vagina participate physiologically in every orgasm, the complete integration of these two structures 1) into the woman's mental representation of her genitalia, 2) into her psychological response to sexual stimulation, and 3) into her experiential perception of sexual pleasure and orgasm, is difficult to achieve. Another very important reason is the fact that the girl's genitals are, for the most part, internal and hidden, in contrast to the boy's, and therefore there is much more confusion and vagueness among girls and women as to the precise anatomy of their genitalia.

In addition, the little girl has to change her primary love object from the mother to the father if she is eventually to establish a heterosexual rather than a homosexual object choice. The little boy does not have that task, although he does have the even more difficult task of changing his primary figure of identification from the mother to the father. It is also important to remember that a woman's sexuality is much more closely tied to reproduction than a man's. Historically, over the centuries women have had to deal with many realistic fears in regard to pregnancy and childbirth. It has only been rather recently in the long history of human civilization that death during pregnancy and childbirth was not relatively common, and women still die in childbirth today even with the most modern of obstetrical procedures.

Finally, throughout all of recorded history, there has been much more sociocultural repression and restriction of sexuality in women, and a much greater readiness to allow sexual freedom to men. Nor has this discrimination ended at the sexual level, but rather has extended to every level of human functioning. All known societies have discriminated in one form or another against women. Some communist countries, despite their widespread curtailment of human freedom and their flagrant racial and religious discrimination, have made determined efforts to end discrimination against women, and in our country the Civil Rights Movement and Women's Liberation Movement have made enormous progress in opening up greater opportunities for women and for minority groups. However, according to a 1984 report by the Bureau of Labor Statistics: 1) the percentage of women in the medical, legal, and engineering professions is still considerably lower in the United States than in Russia and in most Western European countries; 2) women are markedly underrepresented in many other professions and occupations for which they are qualified; 3) women are still paid less than men for the same work, and generally receive less prestigious positions and promotions; 4) women are the first to be fired when there is a shrinking job market; and 5) there is still a "double standard" against women in regard to receiving credit and borrowing money.

Thus, for all of these biological, psychological, and sociocultural reasons, many women have a more difficult time achieving full orgasmic capacity than do most men. However, the paradox is that this does not necessarily mean that women have a more difficult time coming to terms with life or achieving a stable gender identity. In fact, the opposite appears to be the case. Boys seem to have much more difficulty adjusting to reality than do girls, and this appears to continue to hold true later in life as well. In nearly every emotional disturbance of childhood and adolescence, there is a higher ratio of boys than girls — mental retardation, childhood psychosis, behavior disorders, learning disabilities, delinquency, enuresis. The one exception is anorexia nervosa. Later in life the rate of murder, suicide, alcoholism, drug addiction, gambling, criminality, assaultive behavior, homosexuality, paraphilias, transsexualism — all are much higher in men than in women. So a woman may have more difficulty experiencing orgasm, especially if her lover is not patient and knowledgeable. But men appear to have more difficulties in every other area of human functioning, including establishing a stable masculine identity. As one woman with a sense of humor once said, "I wouldn't mind having a penis for a month or so, just to find out what it feels like. But I often wonder if it really is worth all that trouble."

Intimacy vs. Isolation

Erik Erikson has described young adulthood as the time when one must achieve *intimacy*, or risk the failure of *isolation*. Here, too, we see differences between the sexes, in part because of sociocultural attitudes, in part because of more intrinsic biological and psychological factors. Our American society still allows women more emotional expression, and thereby a greater ease and comfort with intimacy, than it does to men. This is certainly one factor in the greater capacity of many women to integrate love and sexuality. Our society is much more tolerant of "tomboy" behavior in girls and "masculine" behavior in women, than it is of "girlish" behavior in boys and "feminine" behavior in men. Another aspect of our society that needs to be emphasized in this regard is the structure of our grade schools. They are still primarily matriarchies, despite the recruitment of more and more male teachers in recent years. As a result, just as the young boy is struggling to separate himself from his mother and identify with his father, he finds himself starting school, surrounded by female teachers as the primary authority figures and the primary models for identification. This is surely a major reason for the much higher incidence of learning difficulties and behavior problems in boys during these early school years. Such school settings make it even more difficult for the boy to shift his primary figure of identification from the mother to the father. This "dis-identification" is a task that many young men never fully and successfully accomplish.

But these social and cultural factors are not the only ones operating to undermine a boy's development of a solid masculine identity. Both biological and psychological factors are also at work. We know from the work of Jost and others that the basic anatomical state is female, and that an additional endocrinological development in the form of a surge of androgenic hormones is required for the formation of a masculinized fetus, whereas no additional sex hormones are required for femaleness. As Richard Green concludes: "Thus, a developmental system (anatomical maleness and behavioral masculinity) requiring the addition of specific amounts of specific substances at critical times is much more vulnerable to natural error," leading to incompletely masculinized males who are behaviorally feminine to various degrees.

Furthermore, as was discussed earlier in the book, the resolution of the oedipal conflict is quite different in the two sexes. The girl enters the oedipal conflict with an intense attachment to her mother, and only gradually relinquishes that in favor of a shift to her father. The eventual attachment to the father may then be maintained for many years, and this is culturally accepted. It is a very different situation for the boy. His overt attachment to his mother is dramatically relinquished under the impact of castration anxiety, and there are strong cultural sanctions against a boy's prolonged involvement with his mother, which continue for the rest of his life. For example, it is socially acceptable for an older man to marry a much younger woman, but it is not socially acceptable, even in our supposedly more enlightened age, for a younger man to marry a much older woman. There is no logic to this social taboo, especially since women tend to outlive men by seven to eight years, and it would therefore make much more social sense for wives to be several years older than their husbands. But there are profound, unconscious reasons for these social attitudes, and they can be changed only very slowly.

Thus, both the external culture and inner psychological forces combine to make the mother a much more forbidden figure for the boy, than the father is for the girl. Hence, the

way has been prepared for a much greater split between sexuality and love in men as compared to women. It is usually difficult for most women to completely give themselves sexually unless they care for the man. It is much easier for many men to function well sexually without necessarily feeling love or affection for the woman. Indeed, for some men it is impossible to put the two together. If they love, they cannot desire. And if they desire, they cannot love. And so the women in their lives are split into two types — the "good" women whom they idealize and love but with whom they avoid sex, and the "bad" women whom they desire sexually but toward whom they feel disgust and contempt.

As has always been the case, the poets knew all of this before the scientists. William Butler Yeats, considered by many to be the greatest poet in the English language after Shakespeare, was passionately in love with a remarkable Irish nationalist, Maud Gonne, and for 13 years he courted her devotedly but hopelessly. She realized that Yeats' love for her was based on an idealized vision that gave creative urgency to his poetry, but did not really include a sustained sexual desire for her as a woman. She eventually married someone else, and Yeats continued writing his exquisitely lyrical poems. He expressed his celibate idealization of Maud Gonne in many poems, but perhaps most poignantly in the beautiful *When You Are Old*.

> When you are old and grey and full of sleep,
> And nodding by the fire, take down this
>   book,
> And slowly read, and dream of the soft look
> Your eyes had once, and of their shadows
>   deep;
>
> How many loved your moments of glad
>   grace,
> And loved your beauty with love false or
>   true,
> But one man loved the pilgrim soul in you,
> And loved the sorrows of your changing
>   face;
>
> And bending down beside the glowing bars,
> Murmur, a little sadly, how Love fled
> And paced upon the mountains overhead
> And hid his face amid a crowd of stars.*

---

*From *The Collected Poems of William Butler Yeats.* Copyright © 1906 by Macmillan Publishing Co., Inc. Renewed 1934 by William Butler Yeats. (Reprinted by permission of Macmillan Publishing Co.)

Shakespeare is a greater poet than Yeats if only because the range of his art was broader and deeper. There was no human experience that Shakespeare did not describe, whether derived from love or hate. Certainly the hatred in love, or more accurately, the contempt and hatred of sexuality devoid of love, have never been expressed more powerfully than in Shakespeare's Sonnet 129:

> The expense of spirit in a waste of shame
> Is lust in action; and till action, lust
> Is perjur'd, murderous, bloody, full of blame,
> Savage, extreme, rude, cruel, not to trust;
> Enjoy'd no sooner but despised straight;
> Past reason hunted; and no sooner had,
> Past reason hated, as a swallow'd bait,
> On purpose laid to make the taker mad:
> Mad in pursuit, and in possession so;
> Had, having, and in quest to have, extreme;
> A bliss of proof, and prov'd, a very woe;
> Before, a joy propos'd; behind, a dream.
> All this the world well knows; yet none knows well
> To shun the heaven that leads men to this hell.

The capacity for true intimacy requires an integration of both love and sexual desire. It is free from excessive idealization as well as contemptuous hatred of the other person. And it rests on a secure sense of one's own self and one's own boundaries. Sexual desire, orgasmic fulfillment, and commitment to another do not pose any threat of personal dissolution. Two people can give themselves completely to each other, and at the same time be enriched by the giving, not depleted. The identity of each becomes even further consolidated and expanded through their intimacy, not fragmented nor diminished (Figures 42.1–42.4).

In contrast, the art of the great Norwegian painter, Edvard Munch, reflects the terror of

Figure 42.1. *The Kiss* by Auguste Rodin. (By permission of Alinari/Editorial Photocolor Archives.)

Figure 42.2. *Man and Woman.* Wood sculpture by Richard De Walt. Private collection. (Photograph by Judith K. Thorpe.)

Figure 42.3. *Man and Woman* (1930) by Gustav Vigeland. Bronze. Placed in the Vigeland Sculpture Park, Oslo, Norway. (By permission of Vigeland Museum, Oslo, Norway.)

Figure 42.4. Two lovers. From the film *Human Sexuality: Heterosexual Intercourse* by Paul R. Miller, M.D. (Copyright 1974, Paul R. Miller, M.D., Reno, Nev. Published by Williams & Wilkins, Baltimore, Md.)

sexual love and intimacy. He suffered many severe deprivations during his childhood, the most overwhelming being the death of his mother from tuberculosis when Munch was five years of age. He witnessed her death following a massive pulmonary hemorrhage. Seven years later, when he was 12, he witnessed the death of his younger sister, Sophie, who also succumbed to tuberculosis.

As an adult, Munch had many stormy affairs with women, but he never married. He viewed women as vampires who would rob him of his masculinity and destroy him. Stanley Steinberg and Joseph Weiss have described the pervasive isolation of Munch's life: "Munch was an unusually lonely man. Closeness, whether it involved friendship with a man, sexual intimacy with a woman, or even looking at a person, was frightening to him. He suspected his men friends of plotting against him. A sustained sexual relationship was impossible for him since he felt it would sap his strength. His concept of closeness between two individuals as revealed in his art was of a destructive incorporation of one by the other."

This theme of intimacy as dangerous and destructive is expressed in a great many of Munch's works, especially in those painted prior to his psychotic break in 1908 when he was 46 years old. In *Attraction* (Figure 42.5) the mood is one of despair and imminent doom, rather than one of joy and pleasure. In two different versions of *The Kiss* (Figures 42.6 and 42.7), the lovers are progressively incorporated by one an-

Figure 42.5. *Attraction* (1896) by Edvard Munch. (By permission of Munch Museum, Oslo, Norway.)

other, with a corresponding blurring and loss of their personal identities. The natural conclusion of this theme is depicted in *Death and the Maiden* (Figure 42.8), where sexual intimacy is equated with complete annihilation.

Marital Choice and Parenthood

In view of all that we have said thus far, is it any wonder that marriage and parenthood entail

Figure 42.6. *The Kiss* (1895, dry point) by Edvard Munch. (By permission of Munch Museum, Oslo, Norway.)

so many conflicts, along with so many rewards? Not infrequently, physicians are the first to be presented with marital and parental difficulties, even though the "patient" may initially be the child rather than the parents. While it may not be possible to obtain all of the answers, at least we should have some questions in our minds whenever we see such a troubled couple or family.

Why did these two people marry? What were they looking for in each other? What were they hoping to receive from each other? What were the experiences in the individual life history of each that led them to make the choice that they did? Is the spouse unconsciously viewed as a parent, or a sibling, or possibly even a child, rather than as a peer? Or is the spouse perceived as someone defective and inferior who needs to be "helped," or as someone incestuously overvalued who needs to be "rescued," rather than as an equal to be loved? What were the unrealistic expectations that were brought to the marriage that have now led to bitterness and disappointment?

If the couple has chosen to have children, why? What were their conscious and their unconscious motivations? There are many healthy reasons for having a child, not the least of which

is the inner developmental need to complete one's own life cycle and to give life and sustenance to a new generation (Figure 42.9). This is what Erik Erikson refers to as *generativity*. But there are other external pressures toward parenthood — religious, social, and family — that may hinder one's capacity to give freely and generously to one's children. There are also other internal motives that place unrealistic expectations on the child and lead to disappointment, just as with a spouse. It is a universal wish of all parents to live on through their children, to perpetuate themselves through their offspring. But if the child is meant to replace someone from the past who has been lost, the chance of parental disappointment in the child is much greater. The same is true if the child is a gift of love to one's parents rather than to one's spouse, or conversely if the child represents an act of competition with or rebellion against one's parents. There is more inevitable disappointment if the motives lie even deeper in the past — if the child represents an attempt to consolidate and confirm an unstable identity as a man or a woman; or if the child represents solely an attempt to relive our own childhoods, either to give to the child what we ourselves

Figure 42.7. *The Kiss* (1902, woodcut) by Edvard Munch. (By permission of Munch Museum, Oslo, Norway.)

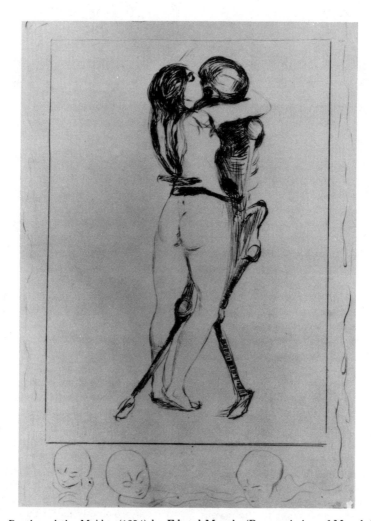

Figure 42.8. *Death and the Maiden* (1894) by Edvard Munch. (By permission of Munch Museum, Oslo, Norway.)

never had, or else to become young again through a child that is only an extension of ourselves and not truly a separate person.

Finally, are the parents experiencing some specific conflicts connected with the particular developmental stage of their child? Some parents may love an infant, but not a rebellious toddler or a sexually curious five year old. And

Figure 42.9. *Family Group* (1948–49) by Henry Moore. Bronze (cast 1950), 59¼ × 46½ inches, at base: 45 × 29⅞ inches. (Collection, The Museum of Modern Art, New York. A. Conger Goodyear Fund.)

since adolescence is such a painful time for all of us, very few parents can survive the turmoil of their adolescent children with equanimity.

TO WORK

This is a vast topic that literally encompasses all of life, since loving also requires work and effort. Many of the questions that were just raised in regard to marital choice could also be slightly rephrased to apply to occupational choice. Why do people choose a particular occupation or profession? Are they receiving sufficient rewards and gratifications? Are they capable of making a commitment to their work, similar to the commitment that is necessary for love and intimacy? Does their work allow some sense of participation and creativity? Are they able to love and to play as well as to work? Do they receive inner satisfactions from their work that are independent of external success? Are they able to allow themselves to achieve to the fullest of their abilities, or are there unconscious limits that they have set for themselves that cannot be surpassed? Does the person only identify himself or herself on the basis of work, or is there a deeper identity independent of work?

These and many other questions could be asked in regard to both loving and working, these two essential tasks of life that must at least begin to be addressed in young adulthood. Count Leo Tolstoy said it all several decades before Freud: "One can live magnificently in this world, if one knows how to work and how to love, to work for the person one loves, and to love one's work." Time, history, and culture have brought many changes in the various forms that love and work can take, and there will be many more changes to come in the years ahead. But the element of commitment is necessary in every age and in every society in order for one to begin to love and begin to work. Without that commitment, we simply have that cold enemy of us all — indifference. Phyllis McGinley needed only a few words in her poem, *A Choice of Weapons* to make the point:

> Sticks and stones are hard on bones.
> Aimed with angry art,
> Words can sting like anything.
> But silence breaks the heart.*

---

* From *Times Three* by Phyllis McGinley. Copyright © 1954 by Phillis McGinley. Originally appeared in *The New Yorker*. (Reprinted by permission of The Viking Press.)

Suggested Readings

Anthony EJ, Benedek T (eds): *Parenthood: Its Psychology and Psychopathology.* Boston, Little, Brown and Co, 1970.

Colarusso CA, Nemiroff RA: *Adult Development.* New York, Plenum Press, 1981.

Erikson EH: Intimacy vs. isolation. In *Childhood and Society.* New York, W. W. Norton, 1950, p 229.

Freud S (1910, 1912, 1918): Contributions to the psychology of love. In *The Standard Edition of the Complete Psychological Works of Sigmund Freud,* vol. 11. London, Hogarth Press, 1957.

Kimmel DC: Young adulthood: identity and intimacy. In *Adulthood and Aging: An Interdisciplinary, Developmental View.* New York, John Wiley & Sons, 1974, p 77.

Lidz T: Marital choice. In *The Person.* New York, Basic Books, 1976, p 410.

Menninger KA: Work as a sublimation. In Sze WC (ed): *Human Life Cycle.* New York, Jason Aronson, 1975, p 413.

Nadelson CC Notman MT: To marry or not to marry. In Nadelson CC, Notman MT (eds): *The Woman Patient. Vol 2.* New York, Plenum Press, 1982, p 111.

References

Green R (ed): *Human Sexuality: A Health Practitioner's Text,* ed 2. Baltimore, Williams & Wilkins, 1979, p 158.

Greenson RR: Dis-identifying from mother: its special importance for the boy. *Int J Psychoanal* 49:370, 1968.

Hite S: *The Hite Report: A Nationwide Study on Female Sexuality.* New York, Macmillan, 1976.

Hunt M: *Sexual Behavior in the 1970's.* New York, Dell, 1975.

Kinsey AC, Pomeroy WB, Martin CE, Gebhard PH: *Sexual Behavior in the Human Female.* Philadelphia, W.B. Saunders, 1953.

Steinberg S, Weiss J: The art of Edvard Munch and its function in his mental life. Psychoanal. Q. 23:409, 1954.

Troyat H: *Tolstoy.* New York, Doubleday, 1967, p 158.

43 Marital Dysfunction, Separation, and Divorce

Richard C. Simons, M.D. and
Dorothy Strauss, Ph.D.

The stresses which may be imposed upon a marital relationship are many and varied. Whether a given marriage is to survive and flourish (and many do—the doomsayers not withstanding) depends not only upon the nature of these stresses, but also upon how one or both partners will measure individual, personal needs vis-a-vis the requirements for mutuality of the marriage. Present-day social and cultural conditions may, indeed, play a role in the increase in reported marital discord. However, the predominant factor may be an unwillingness to forego personal independence and self-indulgence rather than the emergence of new or more numerous social factors. It would be both naive and inaccurate to deny the existence of a substantial number of troubled marriages in earlier times and other places. We need only the evidence of countless novels and plays to inform us that there have been tormented marriages as long as there has been marriage. Let us look at just a few examples.

IBSEN AND STRINDBERG

Henrik Ibsen

The great Norwegian dramatist, Henrik Ibsen, has an undeserved reputation in the public's mind as the author of "social" dramas which have lost their relevance—*A Doll's House, Ghosts, An Enemy of the People.* On the surface, these plays dealt with such contemporary issues of the time as "emancipation of women," venereal disease, and the conflict between public and private morality. But Ibsen's genius as a dramatist went far beyond that of a mere propagandist or polemicist. He was a true rebel and a radical individualist, able to penetrate into the deepest truths of the human spirit. In *Hedda Gabler* (Figure 43.1), he gave us the consummate portrait of a woman consumed by pride and revenge, controlling her husband, Tesman, as though he were a puppet. Just as *A Doll's House* portrays a mockery of marriage, so also does *Hedda Gabler*, except that now the husband, Tesman, is the "doll," rather than the wife, Nora. Hedda continues to destroy everyone and everything around her, until finally her murderous hatred is turned against herself in suicide.

In another masterpiece, *Rosmersholm*, Ibsen goes even further in his exploration of unconscious forces. Rebekka West, a fiery, intelligent, and "freethinking" young woman, joins the household of Johannes Rosmer, and in her uncontrollable yearning for the forbidden Rosmer, drives Rosmer's childless wife, Beata, to suicide. For awhile, she and Rosmer are happy together. But then she begins to learn, bit by bit, that the man who raised her and adopted her as a young girl, and whose mistress she subsequently became, was actually her biological father. Overwhelmed with guilt at this realization, and aware that she has reenacted the very same oedipal drama with Rosmer and his wife, she persuades the malleable Rosmer, himself guilt-ridden, to enter into a joint suicide pact. The play ends with their jumping off the very bridge from which the wife had earlier killed herself.

Finally, in one of his last plays, *The Master Builder*, Ibsen presents a marriage that has been dead for years. It is a play with strong autobiographical overtones. Master Builder Halvard Solness launched his architectural career by building a successful project on the ashes of his wife's ancestral home. In the fire that burned down his home, Solness's children perished, and his wife, Aline, never recovered from her grief and mourning. She remains a tragic and pathetic

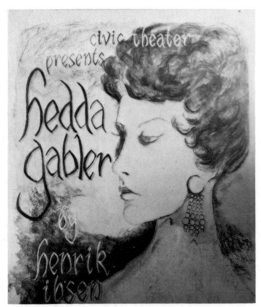

Figure 43.1. *Hedda Gabler* by Henrik Ibsen. (Poster by Alice Logan. Photograph by Mark Groth.)

figure hovering in the background, as the beautiful, young Hilde Wangel comes to express her admiration for the aging Solness and to claim him for herself. Hilde remembers him from her childhood as the greatest of all men, and she goads him to again "dare to do the impossible." Yearning to regain his lost youth through her, haunted by the fear that he will be overtaken by younger rivals, guilty over the career that grew from the corpses of his children, he builds a tower and climbs to the top to place a wreath there. As Hilde waves excitedly from below urging him on, Solness becomes dizzy and confused, and plunges to his death. As Robert Brustein commented in his book, *The Theatre of Revolt*, "It is a great cathedral of a play, with dark, mystical strains which boom like the chords of an organ."

August Strindberg

Even more autobiographical than Ibsen's *The Master Builder* is the astonishing early play by the great Swedish dramatist, August Strindberg (Figure 43.2). The play is *The Father*, autobiographical because it mirrors the paranoid sufferings of its author. No other play is more explicit in its violent hatred of women and of everything feminine. The story can be summarized very briefly. The Captain is a freethinking atheist who is both a cavalry officer and a scientist. His marriage to his religious wife, Laura, has been emotionally barren for years, and a quiet equilibrium of mutual contempt and distance has been maintained. However, when the Captain attempts to educate his daughter, Bertha, as a freethinker like himself, open warfare breaks out between the couple. Laura proceeds to plant seeds of doubt in the Captain's mind about the true paternity of their daughter, driving him deeper and deeper into a jealous rage and paranoid suspiciousness, until finally he becomes violent and is taken off in a straitjacket to be committed as insane.

As the Captain lies helpless at the end of the play, Laura asks him if he believes that she is his enemy. He answers:

> Yes, I do. I believe all you women are my enemies. My mother did not want me to come into the world because my birth would give her pain. She was my enemy. She robbed my embryo of nourishment, so I was born incomplete. My sister was my enemy when she made me knuckle under to her. The first woman I took in my arms was my enemy. She gave me ten years of sickness in return for the love I gave her. When my daughter had to choose between you and me, she became my enemy. And you, you, my wife, have been my mortal enemy, for you have not let go your hold until there is no life left in me.

But before this last harrowing climax, there

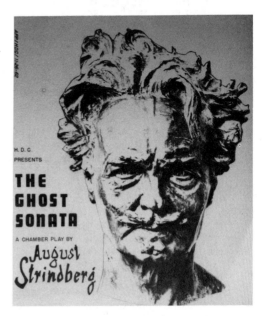

Figure 43.2. August Strindberg.

is an earlier scene in which the poignant humanity of each is revealed, and the mutual longing that first brought them together. He yearned as a son for a mother, and she in turn yearned for a child to nurture. As long as he was the child, and she was the parent, they were happy together. It was only when they were forced to recognize their mutual fear and revulsion over sexuality that they began to hate each other.

Laura: (laying her hand on his forehead.) What? You, a man, in tears?

Captain: Yes, a man in tears. Has not a man eyes? Has not a man hands, limbs, senses, opinions, passions? Is he not nourished by the same food as a woman, wounded by the same weapons, warmed and chilled by the same winter and summer? If you prick us, do we not bleed? If you tickle us, do we not laugh? If you poison us, do we not die? Why should a man suffer in silence or a soldier hide his tears? Because it's not manly? Why isn't it manly?

Laura: Weep, then, my child, and you shall have your mother again. Remember, it was as your second mother that I came into your life. You were big and strong, yet not fully a man. You were a giant child who had come into the world too soon, or perhaps an unwanted child.

Captain: That's true. My father and mother had me against their will, and therefore I was born without a will. That is why, when you and I became one, I felt I was completing myself—and that is why you dominated. I—in the army the one to command—became at home the one to obey. I grew up at your side, looked up to you as a superior being and listened to you as if I were your foolish little boy.

Laura: Yes, that's how it was, and I loved you as if you were my little boy. But didn't you see how, when your feelings changed and you came to me as a lover, I was ashamed? The joy I felt in your embraces was followed by such a sense of guilt my very blood seemed tainted. The mother became the mistress—horrible!

Captain: I saw, but I didn't understand. I thought you despised my lack of virility, so I tried to win you as a woman by proving myself as a man.

Laura: That was your mistake. The mother was your friend, you see, but the woman was your enemy. Sexual love is conflict. And don't imagine I gave myself. I didn't give. I only took what I meant to take. Yet you did dominate me. . . . I felt it and wanted you to feel it.

Captain: You always dominated me. You could hypnotise me when I was wide awake, so that I neither saw nor heard, but simply obeyed. You could give me a raw potato and make me think it was a peach; you could make me take your ridiculous ideas for flashes of genius. You could corrupt me—yes, make me do the shabbiest things. You never had any real intelligence, yet, instead of being guided by me, you would take the reins into your own hands. And when at last I woke to the realisation that I had lost my integrity, I wanted to blot out my humiliation by some heroic action—some feat, some discovery—even by committing *hara-kiri*. I wanted to go to war, but I couldn't. It was then that I gave all my energies to science. And now—now when I should be stretching out my hand to gather the fruit, you chop off my arm. I'm robbed of my laurels; I'm finished. A man cannot live without repute.

Laura: Can a woman?

Captain: Yes—she has her children, but he has not . . . Yet you and I and everyone else went on living, unconscious as children, full of fancies and ideals and illusions, until we woke up. Right—but we woke topsy-turvy, and what's more, we'd been woken by someone who was talking in his own sleep. When women are old and stop being women, they grow beards on their chins. What do men grow, I wonder, when they are old and stop being men? In this false dawn, the birds that crowed weren't cocks, they were capons, and the hens that answered their call were sexless, too. So when the sun should have risen for us, we found ourselves back among the ruins in the full moonlight, just as in the good old times. Our light morning sleep had only been troubled by fantastic dreams—there had been no awakening.

Laura: You should have been a writer, you know.

Captain: Perhaps.

Laura: But I'm sleepy now, so if you have any more fantasies, keep them till tomorrow.

Captain: Just one more—a fact. Do you hate me?

Laura: Sometimes—as a man.*

---

* From *The Father* by August Strindberg, translated by Elizabeth Sprigge. Published in *Six Plays of Strindberg* by Doubleday and Company. Reprinted by permission of Collins-Knowlton-Wing. Copyright © 1955 by Elizabeth Sprigge.

THE CAUSES OF MARITAL DYSFUNCTION

Intrapsychic Factors

One might compile a long and elaborate list of causes of marital dysfunction, such as "poor communication," inadequate sexual gratification, parental interference, the burdens of children, conflicts in roles, and differing expectations. Yet these are no more than symptoms of the core problems which underlie any failure to establish a committed and intimate relationship. The tendency of embattled partners is toward projection and self-justification, rather than toward mutual understanding and introspection. Thus, the root of the difficulties is often obscured. The marital setting is often utilized for the playing out of individual conflicts that existed long before the marriage. The marriage can then become a continuing vehicle for the displacement of the intrapsychic conflicts of one or both partners. Or the promised intimacy of the relationship, while greatly desired, may also be too threatening, and can only become bearable when it can be disguised and diluted through constant fighting.

Turning first to some of the developmental influences which interfere with the establishment of a peer relationship between adult partners, we have to consider the enormous importance of the early relationships with siblings and parents. The love and hatred of parents and siblings are powerful forces in human development, and have also been documented in novels and plays throughout history. Early conflicts with parents are indeed important causes of difficulties in later adult relationships, especially in marriage. But also of considerable importance, in our experience, are the relationships with siblings, and in fact sibling conflicts may be the more immediate and more accessible to the patient in treatment. Not infrequently, only if these are addressed first will the underlying conflicts with the parents come to the surface. A man may indeed be reacting to his wife as though she were his mother, but he may also be reacting to her as though she were a loved or hated sister.

Children who have no brothers or sisters are not spared difficulties because of the absence of sibling rivals and competitors for the parental affections. In fact, some studies have suggested that only children may have even more difficul-ties in marriage than individuals raised with siblings. "His Majesty, the Highness," can no longer be the center of attention, and the unbridled narcissism that is sometimes the fate of only children comes to a rude awakening in the marital relationship.

Later, as the child becomes an adolescent, he or she recapitulates the illusion of "romantic love," which so typified the literature of the Middle Ages, and yet which historically had nothing to do with marriage. The medieval celebration of romantic attachments, told in song and story, usually described the passions of lovers not available to each other. Hence, a romantic union was rarely consummated, or if it was consummated, it was not obliged to stand the test of daily living. We are all familiar with the galaxy of star-crossed adolescents, knights in shining armor, and immaculate and undefiled beloveds of literature. The difficult task of reflecting about oneself and one's prospective mate can thus be avoided through the romanticism of the courtship. Both partners cling to the fantasy that the marriage will remain a continuous courtship, and that "love," not work, will conquer all.

In our time, not only is it assumed that romantic love will very often lead to marriage, but indeed that it should be a prerequisite for marriage. What was that popular song a few years ago?

> Love and marriage
> Love and marriage
> Go together like a
> Horse and carriage
> Let me tell you, brother
> You can't have one without the other.

Such a romantic view of love has little to do with the stress and strain of everyday reality. It revives infantile wishes to be nurtured and taken care of, thereby generating an illusion of security. The beloved is not loved as a person, but only as the source of satisfaction for all needs. Disappointment and bitter resentment are the inevitable consequences of such unrealistic expectations. Even if it were possible for someone to fulfil all these needs, the demanding partner, angered at his or her own dependence, would inevitably project hostility onto the spouse.

What may appear on the surface to be a reasonable assumption, that marital failures caused by unrealistic romantic illusions might diminish or even disappear with the greater frequency of premarital sex, has not been adequately supported by either cultural or anthropological studies. Kirkendall, Burgess, and others have found little effect upon romantic idealization as the result of premarital sexual activity with the partner who later becomes the mate. This type of coupling seems to be motivated by a variety of factors ranging from desire for a steady sex partner to fear of loneliness. Although the single lifestyle has become more prevalent and openly acceptable, the "singles scene" appears to hold only short-lived appeal for many who are dependent upon it for finding companions. Thus, the need to dream and hope for the idealized love object remains and may even be intensified by the current trend of moving in and out of sexual relationships with a greater degree of freedom.

In conclusion, despite the fact that romantic love often impairs critical judgment and fosters the wish that the partner can magically return one to the state of infantile security and pleasure, it seems to be an integral part of our culture to approve mate selection on the basis of romantic love as an assurance of the "pursuit of happiness." Thus, even though peers may marry, the ability of each to establish a peer relationship of true equality will be limited to the degree that each expects total gratification from the other.

In addition to these intrapsychic factors based on childhood and adolescent conflicts, there are also certain developmental stages and tasks of adulthood which may contribute to and possibly even create marital difficulties. The process of "growing-up" is uneven at best for every individual, and to expect that it will be an exact parallel process for any two individuals is simply unrealistic.

Daniel Levinson and Roger Gould, expanding upon the earlier writings of Erik Erikson, have worked out detailed descriptions of various developmental stages of adulthood which suggest that critical points occur throughout the life span. Erikson referred to early adulthood as the time of intimacy vs. isolation. Elaborating on this concept, Levinson labeled the early and mid-twenties, when most first marriages occur, as "provisional adulthood." This is seen as the period of doing what one has been "programmed to do." The reflection and life experience necessary for achieving a sense of proceeding in a self-selected direction, according to Levinson, takes place with the passage from the twenties to the thirties. Berman, Sacks, and Lief see this

as a time of major threat to many marriages, especially two-profession marriages. The wife makes a developmental shift from a dependent and insecure person to that of an independent, competent, and attractive woman, and this may result in a marked discrepancy in the growth rate of the partners and a new set of priorities in the marriage. The husband is likely to be more inclined to settle into the traditional tasks of rearing a family and consolidating gains, while the wife becomes conflicted by the choices newly available to her.

In one-professional marriages, it is still the husband who is for the most part involved in some stage of professional training, although this may change as more women enter the career world. Robert Coombs, among others, has written about the great strains on the medical marriage, not the least of which may be the growing disparity in education, if not always in personal maturity, between the medical student about to graduate or the resident in specialty training, compared to the wife married while in college. As one young wife of a medical student lamented to Coombs, "Our marriage is mainly affected because he will soon have his medical degree and I have absolutely nothing; I feel inferior to him." There may be other strains as well, as the cartoon in Figure 43.3 so poignantly conveys.

While this type of developmental threat to marital stability undoubtedly is more dramatic in the two-profession and one-profession marriage, its occurrence appears to be on the increase in general in those marriages where the original common interests and objectives become too restrictive or unsuited to various changing views of the self. Marital dysfunction, at this time, may assume a variety of forms. There may be a burst of extramarital sexual activity, usually to compensate for some kind of emotional deprivation that the dissatisfied partner believes is now built into the marital relationship, or to "make up" for previously denied sexual experimentation. Increased withdrawal, both emotional and physical, may occur, and power struggles and bitter quarrels replace the earlier affectionate and sexual bonds. The two partners, once allied in mutual hope and expectation, become sworn enemies, and the bedroom is turned into an armed camp.

Interpersonal Factors

Marriage can also be viewed as a transactional system wherein reciprocity is central and lack

"Sure, honey. . . . I'll take you down to the office Saturday and give you a few tests."

Figure 43.3.   Reproduced with permission from *Cartoon Classics From Medical Economics.* Copyright © 1963 by Medical Economics Book Division, Oradell, N.J. All rights reserved.

of reciprocity leads directly to dysfunction. The system itself sets up needs by which it is maintained, and a change in any single component, regardless of how apparently trivial, produces change in all aspects. This broader view, which extends the examination of marital dysfunction beyond the individual personality problems of each of the involved members, is expressed by Berman and Lief when they observe that "marital therapy must be related not only to a person's intrapsychic conflicts but, more importantly, to current environmental, family, and spouse-related phenomena."

These authors conceptualize marital dynamics as existing along the three critical dimensions of power, intimacy, and inclusion-exclusion. Each partner is seen as having the task of resolving conflicts between 1) the wish to please, and any personal need for dominance; 2) the need for closeness, and the need for separateness and distance; and 3) the priorities of the marriage, and the priorities attached to activities and persons external to the marriage. According to Berman and Lief, the more rigid and fixed the solutions of the couple, the more dysfunctional the marriage.

Sager and Kaplan take a somewhat different view of the marital interaction. They concep-

tualize it in terms of "contractual dynamics." They postulate that marital discord begins when the needs of one of the partners are not met. The disappointed partner experiences this failure as a conscious, deliberate, and hostile effort by the other partner not to meet the terms of the "marriage contract," even though the defaulting spouse may be totally unaware of what these terms are supposed to be, or may be totally incapable of fulfilling them. Each partner then becomes furious at the other, and the marital dysfunction is expressed in a continuing battle to exact revenge and establish a quid pro quo balance. These are usually the marriages that contain broad areas of conscious deception from the very beginning, because of each spouse's fear and anxieties about being acceptable and desirable as a marriage partner.

Both of these transactional approaches to marital dysfunction, namely maintenance or impairment of equilibrium within the marital milieu (Berman and Lief) and satisfaction or disappointment with the covert, or unexpressed contractual conditions (Sager and Kaplan), recognize the importance of the type of relationship that exists within the marriage. But each approach assumes that disequilibrium and disappointment lead to marital dysfunction. Actually, many marriages are based on a complementary match of needs, and many of these needs may be quite neurotic and unrealistic. And yet, an equilibrium is very definitely established, and each partner may express relative satisfaction with the marriage "contract." It is only when one of the partners changes and wants a more equal or symmetrical relationship that the marriage becomes "dysfunctional" in a clinical sense.

For example, sadomasochistic marriages are notoriously difficult to change or to end. But there are more subtle variations on this theme that are equally resistant to outside intervention. As long as one partner needs to be a father or a mother and has an available child in the spouse, or the rescuer has a partner who needs to be rescued, or the "master" has his or her "slave," then the marriage may stay in balance for many years and never arrive at the point of dissolution. Although we often tend to think of the "masters" as men, this may be quite naive and culturally biased, because just as many women can fit this model too. We see this especially in wives of the chronically alcoholic or unemployed, or the wives of inept "dreamers" for whom nothing in the real world seems adequate enough for their unique talents, or self-doubting women who deliberately choose severely handicapped husbands.

While sexual dissatisfaction is often given as the cause of marital breakdown, this complaint, as we have noted, is very often simply the symptom of an underlying conflict which utilizes the bed for the battleground. Sex readily lends itself to abuse in the conflicted marriage. It may be used to exploit, to punish, to reward, or to meet personal neurotic needs. The partner may be rendered sexually incompetent because of intrapsychic conflicts or interpersonal difficulties in the marriage, and then sex becomes the job to be worked on or the thing to be "gotten over with." Sex can acquire the symbolic quality of a language for transmitting messages between partners, and in the dysfunctional marriage the messages are frequently all negative. Sexual dysfunction may, indeed, exist as a primary problem in marriages. But, if the potentials for a mutually beneficial relationship exist, the marriage can be expected to improve along many dimensions as the sexual difficulty responds to treatment.

Too often, therapists and patients are misled into thinking that improvement in the sexual difficulty will inevitably lead to improvement in the marital relationship. If the marriage is basically a good one, then sex therapy can be of enormous benefit. But if the marriage is basically unsound, then therapy limited only to the sexual difficulties may actually make matters worse. It is important to keep in mind that there are many unhappy, basically uncommunicative marriages in which the mechanics of sex are satisfactory, and there are also marriages of trust, love, and mutual respect that can and do survive even the most profound of sexual disturbances, such as a paraplegic injury.

Children

The event with possibly the greatest potential for disrupting the stability of the marital dyadic relationship is the introduction of children. Most marriages are entered into with the expectation that children will be born in due course, but the intention to raise a family is rarely the motivation for getting married. In fact, in recent years, young couples are deciding increasingly against having any children at all.

The motivations behind a wish for children are most complex and may involve a response to external pressure, or inner needs which may be only vaguely realized or entirely beyond awareness. In any event, the new arrival changes the system and requires that the parents restructure their relationship. This restructuring may lead to an even more rewarding, more committed, more enduring relationship. But it may also lead to disruption.

So, regardless of whether we view marriage in terms of intrapsychic needs, or interpersonal transactional dynamics, or both, this often fragile alliance or system is now at risk by the addition of a new set of demands. The shift of attention to the child creates an opportunity for a muting and a softening of the marital conflict, but it also creates the opportunity for a new conflict over power and authority, and for the building of exclusionary alliances. Popular assumptions to the contrary, studies of family interaction repeatedly demonstrate that, in conflict-prone marriages, children do not improve the relationship between the parents. Rather, they become pawns to be utilized by one spouse against the other.

Social and Cultural Factors

Up to this point, the emphasis of our discussion of marital dysfunction has been upon intrapsychic factors and interpersonal processes, and it is therefore appropriate to turn now to the influence of cultural norms and social institutions. While the intimate nature of the marital relationship makes it distinctly personal and unique to each couple involved, it is both shaped by and responsive to the explicit and implicit expectations and mores of the society in which it exists. J.R. Udry, in *The Social Context of Marriage*, proposes that four basic belief systems affect marriage in America: the Judeo-Christian tradition, democratic egalitarianism, individualism, and secularism. The dramatic shifts which have taken place within these belief systems have not only altered the expectations and demands with which partners enter marriage but they also tend to disturb the equilibrium of long standing marriages. It is particularly the concept of secularism (the substitution of social change for religious values) that appears to exert the major impact upon marital adjustment. Marriages viewed as sacred obligations, hence maintained by inviolate traditions, have grown noticeably fewer in this country in recent decades as a result of increasing secularism.

Sociologist Jessie Bernard, who has written extensively on the subject of marital adjustment, maintains that there are two types of marriage: his and hers. Hence, there are two distinctly different perspectives upon dysfunctional relationships. It is Bernard's contention that because we operate with a double standard of mental health which approves, in women, the equation of conformity with satisfactory adaptation, tolerance of marital dysfunction is a commonplace experience for many women. Bernard's conclusion is that most women accept marital tension as long as companionship and sociability are provided even in limited amounts by their husbands. Thus, for Bernard, any reduction of marital dysfunction would have to involve an upgrading of the wife's role in the marriage. However, this suggested upgrading may *increase* dysfunction from the point of view of the husband, inasmuch as men, too, have internalized social norms. If the husband's model of a desirable wife is still that of a spouse educated and socialized to discharge her marital obligations with enthusiasm as well as competence, her failure to perform at a peak level of nurturance becomes a serious disappointment.

As a social force, the feminist movement, sometimes called the women's movement, inevitably influences marriage. Marriage, in common with all social institutions that have long histories, tends to hold on to worn-out stereotypes, in particular sex-role sterotypes, in the interest of preserving those traditions which are perceived as essential foundation stones. It is these sex-role stereotypes that the women's movement opposes, not marriage itself. Not all women are comfortable with "liberalization" from these stereotypes; nor are all men threatened by what they interpret as shifts in equilibrium between the sexes. But within this range of ambiguity and ambivalence, many women want to legitimize their nonfamily oriented aspirations. Thus, any examination of the reasons for marital stability or disintegration now requires that a set of new social questions also be considered. Perhaps the decision not to marry, now made far more often than in the past, and also the decision not to have children, reflect an increased sense of independence not only for many women, but for many men as well.

Thus, traditional marital patterns are changing, and rightly so. Ideally, modern marriage should be an alliance and a partnership of equals, not a struggle for power and domination, nor a replay of a parent-child model. But individual and marital therapists who unwisely attempt to transmit recent changes in cultural norms too rapidly to as yet unprepared patients and marital couples may be doing far more harm than good. Injunctions to passive women—and passive men—to "liberate" themselves from marriages viewed as "dysfunctional" by the therapist but not necessarily by the participants, may be much more destructive and disruptive than helpful.

SEPARATION AND DIVORCE

As has already been stated, by no means do all dysfunctional marriages terminate in either separation or divorce; and some marriages which may appear dysfunctional to outsiders remain functional to the very end. We will not consider desertion or abandonment in this chapter because they do not constitute a third alternative in the same sense. When desertion occurs, there is no opportunity for negotiation and decision making between the spouses, and even states with restrictive divorce laws permit a fixed period of desertion as grounds for legal divorce.

Separation may serve various purposes. It provides time for trial and exploration to the undecided. To those who cannot face a return to the single status, it offers a sense of quasi-security. For particularly impulsive or needy people, it protects them against a new marital entanglement during a time of uncertainty and readjustment. Separation may also be the only form of relief available or acceptable in particular instances where religious or cultural or extended family pressures against divorce are quite strong.

Whether a troubled couple chooses separation or divorce or remaining together cannot be taken as a measure of the unhappiness or even the pain characterizing the relationship. Tolerance levels vary greatly, as do the degrees of investment that each partner has in the marriage. In this country, at the present time, the major obstacles to divorce are economic and religious. Children, once the major reason given for persisting in a difficult marriage, are becoming less and less of a deterrent. Easing of the divorce process, including no-fault provisions in 48 of the 50 states, has increased public acceptance of divorce. Greater employment opportunities for women, practically universal availability of contraception, and an increasingly censure-free attitude toward casual sex have removed many of the traditional blocks to marital dissolution.

Published data indicate a very marked rise in the number of divorces granted annually in the United States during the past several decades. While divorce to marriage ratios provide us with projections which are rather tentative, current trends seem to indicate that 33% of first marriages, 40% of second marriages, and nearly 50% of all remarriages will end in divorce. The divorce rate doubled during the decade 1960–1970, and doubled again during the decade 1970–1980. The number of children involved in divorce has tripled in the last 35 years. Currently, more than one million children each year suffer the breakup of their families. The divorce rate is also rapidly increasing among older couples after the children are raised. Among couples married from 15 to 19 years, divorce rates have increased 100% since 1960, and among couples married over 20 years, divorce rates have increased 50% since 1960.

The divorce rate is higher in the United States than elsewhere, but this does not necessarily mean that there is greater marital dysfunction here, because divorce laws and social customs vary greatly. In some countries, especially in South America, divorce is very difficult to obtain unless one is rich. Italy only recently passed a conservative divorce law after years of heated and passionate debate. Even in countries where

a divorce is easy to obtain, it may bring social stigma and loss of face—for example, India and Japan.

In regard to some other statistics, the divorce rate is now higher than formerly among couples from a lower socioeconomic background, so that divorce, in this country at least, is no longer a luxury for only the wealthy. Divorce appears to be more frequent among couples in whom the parents of one or both of the spouses have been divorced or separated. The rate is also higher in couples who marry in their teens, between the ages of 15 and 19.

However, both statistical evidence and clinical observation indicate that most individuals who divorce enter second and even third marriages. Despite the many problems that step-families face, five out of six divorced men and three out of four divorced women remarry within three years. We may well then ask, how are we to interpret the rising divorce rate, what motives inspire this uncoupling followed by renewed coupling, and what does all this portend with respect to marriage as a social institution? There seems to be little reason to doubt that myths and illusions may be attached to divorce just as they are to marriage. If we exclude from consideration the teenage marriages which terminate following a brief trial and error period, we find that divorces are sought by partners in all age groups.

Whereas, in some cases, the divorce is the product of a painful, nonremediable situation, it is equally true that, in others, it represents an illusory pursuit of "self-expansion," "catching-up," "being really appreciated," "excitement," and "youth." If this be the case, and these neurotic conflicts are still operative, then in all likelihood they will interfere with the establishment of a good relationship in the second marriage just as they did in the first. However, some of these neurotic needs may change with time and maturity, and as Freud observed many years ago in his three essays on *Contributions to the Psychology of Love*, once the resentments and grievances from the past have been spent against the first spouse, a second marriage may turn out much better.

There are, to be sure, instances when divorce is a constructive, growth-producing step. To persist in a hopelessly destructive relationship is more an indication of pathology than of mental health. But even here a word of caution is in order, because the divorced person must still face the anxiety of independence, the loss of the network of married friends, the depression and possibly even the despair of loneliness, the intense ambivalence toward the ex-spouse, the sense of failure and shame, and the guilt associated with inflicting pain upon children.

THE CHILDREN OF DIVORCE

Our clinical impression is that, although marriages are no longer held together "for the sake of the children," considerable denial operates in parents of both sexes with respect to what marital disruption means to children. At the very least, it means partial separation from one of the two most important people in the child's world. For other children, depending on which parent is given custody and the arrangements worked out for visitation, it may mean, quite literally, the end of that world altogether. Several recent studies have shown that children may indeed respond to divorce with mild to severe depression, physical illness, accidents, and other symptoms.

In 1971 a social worker, Judith Wallerstein, and a psychologist, Joan Berlin Kelly, began a five year study of 131 children from 60 divorced families in a northern California suburb. (Eighty-eight per cent of the families were white, 9% interracial, and 3% black.) Wallerstein and Kelly found that very few of these children had felt pleased or relieved by the divorce, even in those cases where there had been evident conflict between the parents. Preschool children (three to five and one-half years old) frequently assumed that they were in some way personally responsible for the divorce. They were frightened, bewildered, sad, and irritable. They tended to deny the separation, at the same time regressing in their behavior. The younger school-age children (six to eight year olds) showed the most pervasive sadness of all. These children in particular expressed intense yearning for more contact with their fathers, and their grief was matched in turn by the grief of many of the fathers. Children in this age group also experienced much greater conflicts in loyalties than did the preschool children. Older school-age children (nine to 12 year olds) were able to cope more effectively and tended to hide their depression better, but still felt rejected, betrayed, abandoned, and lonely. What distinguished this group from all of the younger children was a fully conscious, intense anger that often led to an alignment with one parent against the other.

Adolescents (13 to 18 year olds) were generally able to deal with the divorce the most realistically of all the age groups, but many still felt deprived of the normal time and parental supports that should have been available to them for growing up and achieving independence. Finally, in all four groups, there was a continuing desire to see the parents reunited and a fantasy that this reconciliation would eventually take place. In their five year follow-up of these 60 families, Wallerstein and Kelly were surprised at the severity and duration of the disturbances. They found that 31% of the fathers and 42% of the mothers had not yet achieved psychological or social stability, and that 37% of the children and adolescents were still moderately to severely depressed. Wallerstein and Kelly conclude their study with a strong recommendation for widespread counseling services for divorcing parents and their children over an extended period of time following the divorce.

We still have much to learn about the effect upon children of living in a single-parent family as compared with living in an intact but conflicted setting. More research in this area is greatly needed, because one out of every five children under 18 today (about 12 million of the country's 60 million children under 18) is living in a family with only one parent, usually the mother. A 1982 Census Bureau Report showed that in 1970, 11% of all families with children at home were maintained by one parent, but by 1981 this proportion had increased to 21%. It is estimated that 45% of all children born in any given year will live with only one of their parents at some time before they are 18.

In this regard, it is important to note that fathers are increasingly being awarded custody of the children, at their request and sometimes at the request of the mothers. In fact, the number of children living with divorced fathers has increased considerably over the last several years. Both spouses are also increasingly requesting regular and prolonged visiting time with the father when the wife retains custody, largely out of the conviction that children benefit from extended contact with both parents. Finally, to avoid the terrible pain of custody battles in court and the child feeling torn between the mother and the father, parents are increasingly turning to joint custody and equal responsibility in caring for the children. As of 1983, 27 states had embraced the concept of joint custody. Such an arrangement obviously works best when both parents live in the same town and are on friendly terms with each other. But the children may still be caught in the middle when the court imposes joint custody on parents who live in different towns or who will not even speak to each other.

These cases of joint custody stand in sharp contrast to other divorces in which *neither* parent wants custody of the child or children. In more and more cases, the woman is abandoning her family without even waiting for a formal separation, and increasing numbers of married women are being reported as simply "missing." In previous times, this usually happened only with fathers. If there is no extended family to care for these children, they become wards of the state, abandoned to orphanages or foster homes. These human tragedies, resulting from an abdication of all parental responsibility, are occurring more and more frequently. Rabbi Earl Grollman may be right when he says that divorce can be even more traumatic than death. "Death has closure, it's over. With divorce, it's never over."*

FAMILY DISORGANIZATION

Urie Bronfenbrenner, professor of family studies at Cornell University, believes that the progressive disorganization that has taken place in the American family over the past several decades is a major factor in the degree of "alienation" and "estrangement" between young people and adults in our society today. Divorce is unquestionably a factor in this family disorganization, as is urbanization, mobility, the separation of residential and business areas requiring long hours of commuting, the shrinking of the extended family, and the rapid rise in the proportion of working mothers. The percentage of today's mothers who work outside the home far exceeds the proportion that existed in 1950; and, as Bronfenbrenner has pointed out, the greatest increase has occurred for mothers of preschool children. In 1980, 43% of married mothers with children under six were working outside the home. Of the seven million small children affected, there were day-care openings for only 1.6 million. It should also be noted that the inflationary economy which began to domi-

nate the later years of the seventies decade has been a major cause of "the two-paycheck marriage." It has forced many family-oriented women out of the home, and sweeping changes in our society have resulted. In 1980, 51% of married American women were working outside the home, and so, for the first time in our history, working wives outnumbered housewives.

The related mental health statistics for children and adolescents are alarming. The rate of suicide among children age 10 to 14 is twice as high as it was 20 years ago, and the rate of suicide among adolescents age 15 to 19 is more than three times as high as it was 20 years ago. Violent crimes by children are on a rapid rise, and the rate of armed robbery, rape, and murder among adolescents has doubled within the past 10 years and tripled over the past 20 years. There have been concomitant increases in school dropouts, drug and alcohol offenses on school property, burglaries of school buildings, and assaults on teachers.

If present trends continue, it is estimated that one out of every nine youngsters will appear in juvenile court before the age of 18! In a later chapter, a related phenomenon will be described—a dramatic rise in the reported number of cases of child abuse and child neglect during the past decade. As Bronfenbrenner again points out: "The most severe (child abuse) injuries occurred in single-parent homes and were inflicted by the mother herself, a fact that reflects the desperation of the situation faced by some young mothers today." Clearly, parenthood and especially motherhood are no longer held in the same high esteem in our rapidly changing society as they once were.

WHAT DOES THE FUTURE HOLD?

In view of the extent and severity of marital dysfunction, the surprising finding is not the rising divorce rate but the persistent and repetitive choice of marriage as still the optimum arrangement for the great majority of adults. Marital distress may originate in a broad spectrum of causes which include both intrapsychic and interpersonal factors. In addition, social and cultural pressures have intensified the way in which marriage is experienced during the critical phases of adult development. Thus, marriage becomes caught up in the current contagious

---

* From "Children of Divorce." *Newsweek*, February 11, 1980, p. 63.

"search for the self" which encourages self-indulgence and impulsive behavior, instead of the growth that can occur when partners stay together and work out painful but appropriate solutions.

We have not been concerned in this chapter with alternative life styles and fashions ("swinging," "swapping," open contracts, homosexual marriages, group marriage) because the subject under examination has been the present state of marriage, and because there is no indication of its demise in the foreseeable future. What does seem possible is an increase in what might be termed "serial monogamy," a series of several marriages during a lifetime. It is a prospect not inconsistent with the vicissitudes of a greatly prolonged life span for many more persons. All of these issues will require more time and study in order to be better understood. Perhaps the most salutary outcome will be twofold: a more realistic appraisal of what the marital relationship can be expected to provide, and a broader acceptance of the belief that a truly equal relationship can actually enrich the individual growth and development of both its partners.

Suggested Readings

Francke LB: *Growing Up Divorced.* New York, Simon & Schuster, 1983.

Goldstein S, Solnit AJ: *Divorce and Your Child: Practical Suggestions for Parents.* New Haven, Yale University Press, 1984.

Levinger G, Moles OC (eds): *Divorce and Separation: Context, Causes and Consequences.* New York, Basic Books, 1979.

Wallerstein JS, Kelly JB: *Surviving the Breakup: How Children and Parents Cope with Divorce.* New York, Basic Books, 1980.

Weiss RS: *Marital Separation.* New York, Basic Books, 1975.

References

Berman EM, Sacks S, Lief HI: The two professional marriage: a new conflict syndrome. *J Sex Marital Ther* 1:242, 1975.

Berman EM, Lief HI: Marital therapy from a psychiatric perspective: an overview. *Am J Psychiatry* 132:583, 1975.

Bernard, J: *The Future of Marriage.* New York, World, 1972.

Bronfenbrenner U: The origins of alienation. *Sci Am* 231:53, 1974.

Bronfenbrenner U: The split-level American Family. In Sze WC (ed): *Human Life Cycle.* New York, Jason Aronson, 1975, p 179.

Brustein R: *The Theatre of Revolt.* Boston, Little, Brown, and Co, 1962.

Burgess EW, Wallin P: *Engagement and Marriage.* Philadelphia, J.B. Lippincott, 1953.

Coombs RH: The medical marriage. In Coombs RH, Vincent CE (eds): *Psychosocial Aspects of Medical Training.* Springfield, Ill, Charles C Thomas, 1971, 133.

Eisenstein VW (ed): *Neurotic Interaction in Marriage.* New York, Basic Books, 1956.

Freud S (1910, 1912, 1918): Contributions to the psychology of love. In *The Standard Edition of the Complete Psychological Works of Sigmund Freud,* vol 11. London, Hogarth Press, 1957, p 163.

Goode W: *After Divorce.* Glencoe, IL, Free Press, 1956.

Gould R: *Transformations.* New York, Simon & Schuster, 1978.

Hartmann H: *Essays on Ego Psychology.* New York, International Universities Press, 1964.

Hetherington EM, Cox M, Cox R: The aftermath of divorce. In Stevens JH, Jr, Matthews M (eds): *Mother-Child, Father-Child Relations.* Washington, DC, NAEYC, 1977.

Kirkendall LA: *Premarital Intercourse and Interpersonal Relationships.* New York, Julian Press, 1961.

Levinson DJ, et al: *The Seasons of a Man's Life.* New York, Alfred A. Knopf, 1978.

McDermott JF: Divorce and its psychiatric sequelae in children. *Arch Gen Psychiatry* 23:421, 1970.

Nadelson CC, Notman MT: To marry or not to marry. In Nadelson CC, Notman MT (eds): *The Woman Patient. Vol 2.* New York, Plenum Press, 1982, p 111.

Persky H: Personal communication.

Sager CJ, et al: The marriage contract. In Sager CJ, Kaplan HS (eds): *Progress in Group and Family Therapy.* New York, Brunner/Mazel, 1972, p 483.

Sander FM: *Individual and Family Therapy: Toward an Integration.* New York, Jason Aronson, 1979.

Udry JR: *The Social Context of Marriage,* ed 2. Philadelphia, J.B. Lippincott, 1971.

CHAPTER 44 The Experience of Being a Single Parent

Andrea Klein Schroder, M.S.W.

THE SINGLE-PARENT FAMILY

Most of us tend to think of the phenomenon of the single-parent family as a quite recent variation of American family life. It is therefore surprising to learn that in the decade of 1900 to 1910 more children experienced some form of marital disruption in their families than did children in the decade from 1950 to 1960. The prevalent cause of marital disruption in the first decade of this century was the death of a parent. Children born in the 30's were likely to find themselves in a single-parent family as the depression forced fathers to move around looking for work, frequently leaving the family behind. Later in the 40's, fathers went abroad to fight during the Second World War. Now parents leave increasingly because of marital separation and divorce.

The perspective that the single-parent family is an old phenomenon is not to belittle the significance of the statistics pertaining to single-parent families today. Currently, approximately 20% of all children under age 18 are living with one parent only, and nearly half of these children have experienced a parental divorce. It is only within perhaps the last 10 to 15 years that much has been formally studied and written about the experiences of the single parent. Much of the literature pertains to women, since the great majority (90%) of single-parent homes are still headed by the mother. In the past, the courts almost unanimously awarded custody to the mother. More recently, fathers are beginning to gain custody of their children in increasing numbers; in fact the number of single-parent families headed by the father doubled from 1970 to 1981 and will probably continue to accelerate as more states enact joint custody laws. This phenomenon suggests that society is changing its rigid view that only the mother is the capable nurturer.

Most studies that have examined the experiences of single parents are grim reminders that being a single parent is stressful at many different levels. Schlesinger and Ilgenfritz, in their studies involving single mothers, found the following problems: difficulties rearing the children, sexual concerns, hostility toward men, fears of being alone, hesitancy in reestablishing social relationships, financial difficulties, and loss of self-esteem associated with a sense of shame and failure. The costs of litigation and maintaining two households can reduce the family income enormously. The majority of women experience a substantial drop in income at the time of divorce. And a recent Census Bureau Report found that less than 25% of divorced, separated, or single mothers receive any child support. Hetherington, Cox, and Cox found the households of divorced families to be more disorganized than two-parent families. They described divorced parents as feeling more anxious, depressed, angry, rejected, and incompetent. Hetherington, in another study of 48 nursery school age boys and girls, found more difficulty parenting (especially mothers with sons), poor communication with children, less affection with the children, parental inconsistency in disciplining, and lack of parental control over the children.

The literature on single parents does contain some positive notes. In a chapter titled, "Divorced Mothers: The Costs and Benefits of Female Family Control" (in Levinger and Moles' excellent book *Divorce and Separation: Context, Causes and Consequences*), Janet Kohen and her colleagues observe that most of the 30 divorced mothers in the study felt that they were doing a good job raising and disciplining their children. They described feelings of mastery, control, and emotional growth since becoming single parents. As one of the women said, "Nothing is easier, but it feels easier." The chapter, "Fathers By

Choice: Divorced Men Who Receive Custody of Their Children" by Kelin Gersick (also in the Levinger and Moles book) leaves one with a positive impression about the capabilities and motivations of fathers as single parents. These men who chose to raise their children were older, well educated, longer married, and themselves a product of a healthy two-parent family. Their identification with two competent parents was suggested as one of the factors motivating them to get custody of their children.

EFFECTS OF DIVORCE ON CHILDREN

The current literature dealing with the effects of divorce on children appears to be changing in focus from attempts to prove simple cause and effect relationships between behavior and parental absence to a broader, and seemingly more balanced perspective. In fact, several recent studies have shown that divorce does not have any one single impact on children. Rather than attempting to prove certain predetermined notions about either the positive or the negative effects of divorce on children, research in this area should instead look for *all* of the possible effects and what it is about divorce that specifically troubles children at different age levels.

THE TASK OF REESTABLISHING THE FAMILY

Paul Bohannan has accurately described what he calls the overlapping stresses of the emotional divorce, the legal divorce, the economic divorce, the coparental divorce around the custody of the children, the divorce from a shared community of family and friends, and the psychic divorce. It is no wonder that everyone, researcher and layman alike, concludes that the first year following the separation is the most difficult for all members of the family.

Let us look at what is involved in the process as parent and child adjust to a new family pattern. Robert Weiss in his chapter entitled, "The Emotional Impact of Marital Separation," again in the Levinger and Moles book, describes some of the major themes. One is the persistence of the marital bond. We need only recall the traditional words of the marriage ceremony, "For better or for worse, for richer or for poorer, in sickness and in health, until death do us part," to appreciate that the formation of such a strong, all-encompassing bond is the expecta-

tion of marriage. Regardless of the quality of the marriage, the fact that two people share many of the same daily experiences and settle into daily habits and patterns determined largely by the mutual influences of each other, strengthens the injunction from the marriage vows. This bond of habits, patterns, and experiences is not automatically erased when the suitcases are packed or the divorce proceedings begin. This persistence of the bond is described as a feeling of being pulled back even to what is perceived as bad. It is not necessarily related to liking, admiring, or respecting the other partner. We see evidence of the tenacity of the marital bond by looking at the behaviors of both partners following the actual separation. Rarely are the interactions between the two partners objective or matter-of-fact—the angry phone calls to argue about a trivial point, the difficulty in attending to some of the factual business of the divorce and separation, and, in disturbed individuals, the suicide attempts and threats of disaster.

These attempts to "hang on" to the departed person become understandable when we realize the terrible fear of being alone that most people experience when they first separate. I remember shortly after my husband left, lying in bed one night trying to go to sleep. All of a sudden I was overwhelmed with anxiety. I thought, "My heart is going to stop beating right now. I know I will die right now." As I usually did not feel this way, I began trying to understand where this panic was coming from. Was I that angry at my husband? Did I want him back? Was I worried about a job? Was I worried about the responsibility of the children?—all these questions ran through my head. After some time I looked at the clock. Fifteen minutes had elapsed, and I remember thinking, "Here it is, 15 minutes gone by, and I haven't died yet. Maybe I'll be all right." From then on, each time this feeling of raw panic set in, I was able to recall surviving those first 15 minutes, and the anxiety subsided.

As the reality of the separation starts edging its way into awareness, both parents and children begin the very painful process of grieving for the person who has left. These grief responses include: 1) the tendency to organize one's thinking around the image of the lost person—rehashing the last days together, the conflicts, the discussions, what went wrong, how that person looked; 2) the urge to make contact—the toilet is stopped up and he probably knows the name of the plumber, or perhaps I'll just drive by to see her for a moment; 3) anger toward the person, and for children, the double issue of anger also toward the parent who remains; 4) guilt for having caused the loss—maybe it is wrong of me to feel this way, perhaps I should have been more willing to give in on this or that point; 5) presence of the "alarm reaction," i.e., hypersensitivity to the return of the lost person—when will he come? Will he be on time? When the phone rings, is it she who is calling?; and 6) the maintenance of intense fantasies—maybe we'll get back together again some day, or conversely, he or she won't ever be responsible and can't be depended on for anything. Children particularly maintain intense fantasies that the parents will reunite, and also fantasies about what they (the children) may have done to cause the separation.

When the intense distress around the separation subsides, and frequently this takes up to two years, a wistful state of loneliness appears. This loneliness is almost like awakening from a deep sleep, recognizing again the people around you, your friends, your children, but feeling only superficially connected to them and being most aware that there is no one primary bond to another person. I remember one beautiful fall Saturday morning attending a soccer game with my son. I was watching the mothers and fathers of the other children sitting on blankets in the grass sipping their morning coffee and exchanging familiar comments and nods with each other. I remember thinking that the soccer coach was very handsome, wondering if he was married or single, trying to decide if and how and when I wanted to get to know him. As my children and I walked home, I remember breathing in the crystal clear air of that fall morning, feeling that it was such a beautiful and romantic day, but that there was no man in the world with whom I could share it.

The waning of the anger, the emergence of tender feelings and happy memories, the settling back into a routine of mealtimes and bedtimes and weekly trips to the grocery store, cause ambivalence about what has happened. Often the ambivalence finds its expression in the little bittersweet memories that seem to emerge from nowhere—reflections about a happy moment together before the divorce, fond memories about some personal quality of the spouse that in former days excited one or made one happy. Once life settles down again, one may start entertaining fantasies about a quiet weekend

away with the former spouse. Not infrequently, a luncheon engagement is arranged. Another expression of the ambivalence is the preoccupation with the dating habits of the former spouse, and some sadness or anger if he or she has begun a new relationship. Many times, the ambivalence is experienced more directly through legal proceedings and property settlements that drag on bitterly and without resolution.

Children also struggle with their ambivalence once life begins to settle down again—aware on the one hand that life has probably become more stable and comfortable, yet concerned that some tie be kept in some form to the parent who is no longer in the family. A divorced friend told the following story. Her children saw their father infrequently despite the fact that the father lived in the surrounding neighborhood. The children seemed to tolerate the infrequent visits and this new relationship to their father. A larger house about a mile away went on sale, and my friend went to look at it with the thought of moving there. In discussing the potential move with her children, they were excited about the possibility of living in a bigger house and said, "Even if we move, we'll still be close to Daddy." I was surprised that for as long as five years after my divorce, periodically my children came to me asking for the story once again about how and why the divorce happened. They were still trying to work through their ambivalence about the divorce.

SOME SPECIAL ISSUES FOR SINGLE PARENTS AND CHILDREN

Discipline

Disciplining children is hard work whether there are one or two parents. It is no secret that in a two-parent household the disciplining of the children not infrequently stirs up conflicts and arguments between the parents, and there have been times when I have not minded being the only one to lay down the law with the children. However, the energy required to be the single disciplinarian is tremendous and constant. It is not possible to say when tired, "Go talk to your father (or your mother) about that." And for the single parent, there is no reinforcement when the limits are set. The firm backup by another adult is missing. Nor is there a buffer for either the parent or child in the heat of the disciplining anger. In the single-parent family, the child is not permitted even the luxury of the comforting fantasy that "Daddy loves me anyway" when mother is being the tyrant or vice versa. The lack of a buffer to the disciplining parent is perhaps a more troublesome issue if we acknowledge that as parents we get trapped from time to time in our own past developmental conflicts and play these out in a very subjective way in disciplining our children. The tendencies to be overly permissive or overly punitive are difficult to control when there is not another adult close at hand to monitor us.

The issue of single-parent discipline is additionally complicated for the parent who does not live with the children, but who sees them usually away from the home in new surroundings and for a limited period of time. For such parents, it is difficult to know where and when to intervene, to appreciate the full context of the child's behavior, and to be consistent with the limits and structures that are set down at home. And who wants to be an ogre when the period of time with the child may be brief? Nevertheless, such inconsistency can undermine the efforts of the parent at home in setting limits and in structuring the child's world.

Assuming Roles Culturally Ascribed to Someone Else

I remember crying after a particularly tough day of disciplining my children. The thoughts and feelings that spilled out were: "I wasn't cut out to have to be so harsh and forceful with the children. I always imagined that being a mother meant providing a home that smelled of cookies baking as the children happily walked in after school, playing peek-a-boo with a laughing and happy baby, reading bedtime stories, and getting the children snuggled in cozy for a good night's sleep. I hate having to be the iron hand that keeps the troops in line." Children, I think, are as confused and at odds with the multiplicity of roles as are the parents. One evening during a particularly rowdy bath time, I was booming orders at the children. My oldest son looked up at me and said, "Mom, you sound just like a father." My reply was, "Yes, I feel like a father sometimes and I don't like it because I'm a woman." Especially for young children, the boundaries for role modeling can easily become

blurred in the single-parent family despite the fact that we live in an age where fortunately both men and women are more flexible in interchanging tasks and roles. In the single-parent family, there is only one person for the child to observe.

Reinforcing the Child's and the Parents' Identity

One evening I was standing in front of the mirror putting on makeup in preparation for going out on a date. My five year old son stood at the bathroom door watching the process. After a while he said, "Mom, when I'm six, will I be a girl?" I replied, "No, you'll always be a boy." Suspecting that there was more to this question than just idle curiosity, I said, "I wonder why you'd think that?" In a rather awkward way he replied, "I don't know." I said, "I think it's hard not having a daddy around. You boys never get a chance to see how men get ready to go out—all the things that they do like shaving, combing their hair, and straightening their tie." He replied, "I know, but you were a girl when you were six." I said, "That's right, and you will be a boy when you are six and you will grow up to be a man."

It is not unusual for children around the age of five to experience some fantasies about what it would be like to be a member of the opposite sex. Sorting out the confusion about which parent with whom to identify is a task of normal development at this stage. The child in a single-parent family does not have the benefit of a daily demonstration of behaviors that can be associated with one sex or the other. In many cases, the issues of identification are much more specific than that women do this and men do that. Children need the personal reference, that is, my mother does, enjoys, dislikes these kinds of things, and my father does, enjoys, dislikes those kinds of things. When my oldest son was 10 years old, he told me on a Sunday morning that Beethoven was his favorite composer, and that he thought for sure he would play football when he grew up. The stimulus for this came from the night before when a male friend of mine had been over for dinner and had talked about his love of both Beethoven and football. Having tangible traits to emulate is difficult when the parent of the same sex as the child does not reside in the home.

Should single parents attempt to be supermen or superwomen? Should single mothers take lessons in football and volunteer to be the team coach? Should single fathers take sewing lessons and start making curtains for the kitchen? I suspect every single parent goes through a period of feeling bad and perhaps guilty that certain activities are not going to become part of the family as they had before. It is probably less confusing and in the end less overwhelming for children if single parents can appreciate and communicate their own limits. "I don't like to play football but let's see if we can find someone to play with you." Or, "I just don't think I'm going to be able to bake cookies, so let's go out and buy some." Such comments convey a sense of personal identity and integrity to the child, and a realistic sense of one's own limitations.

Use of Social Support Systems

Recently I had a conversation about single parents with my children's pediatrician. He has a warm and easy way of dealing with his patients and their parents. He always seems to be as interested in the "extracurricular" activities of his patients and their families as he is about the medical symptoms at hand. I was curious to know if he looked at single parents as a group, and if so, what it was about them that he tried to evaluate. He replied that he paid particular attention to single parents and that he was most interested in assessing two areas: support systems and financial resources. I asked him what he did if he found a single parent who was lacking in either. His reply was that he suggested appropriate community resources to patients and in some instances made the referral phone calls himself.

The roots to establishing new social support systems are invariably there in the fond traditions of family life before the divorce. Perhaps the tradition was sweet rolls on Sunday morning. Maybe it was Friday night at the movies, or Wednesday afternoon picnics. But the reluctance to take the initiative in entertaining old friends is common following a divorce and also following the death of a spouse. And, not infrequently, the first attempts at entertaining leave one feeling even more lonely when everyone has gone home—it's just not like it used to be. Looking to new people, groups, and experiences requires the ability to move beyond the definitions of the past. In this instance, single parents

usually have some advantage over divorced individuals with no children, because frequently it is the children who pull the parents along if the parents will let them. It is quite unusual today to be the only single parent at McDonald's in the evening. There is a nice comradery and at times almost a humorous acknowledgment when single parents meet each other in public with their children. Many pleasant adult friendships have developed through encounters of this sort. Children usually are not as shy as their parents in this situation. Some wonderful stories have been told about children making matches between single parents.

Dating and Sexual Relationships

"God, Mom, it's about time," said the 11 year old son of a friend following the evening when mother's boyfriend had slept overnight at the house for the first time. The issue of dating and resuming sexual relationships following divorce is and should be one that calls for considerable thought and sensitivity when conducted in the presence of children. A divorced friend said to me one time in anger, "You surely don't expect me to never sleep with another man until Sally is through the oedipal period, do you?" Dating and falling in love, when that happens, is rarely as simple as boy meets girl and they live happily ever after. When dating is conducted in the presence of the watchful eyes and ears of the children, the issues are even more complex.

My first date, approximately a year and a half after the divorce, was with a delightful but somewhat shy middle-aged bachelor. Within two minutes after my friend arrived and was introduced to the children, my then six year old son took my friend's hand, led him around the house for a tour, and then sat him down in the living room with the comment, "You sure are handsome." And then with escalated enthusiasm he said, "Do you think you'll marry my Mom?" There have been many other awkward moments subsequently which I shall not document.

Balancing the needs of the children with the parent's needs for adult companionship and sexual relationships is difficult. At best, it requires maturity and a sense of humor. The single parent's first dating attempts are frequently not very smooth, and perhaps largely experimental as the parent struggles to reshape and reestablish feelings of self-esteem as a man or women. Many of the first dating experiences are more adolescent than adult in their tone. It is difficult to run a family and a household when you are preoccupied with a crush, and particularly difficult to deal with the needs of children. If the children are adolescents themselves, the situation may be practically impossible.

The intimate workings of the adult male and female relationship are demonstrated to the children on a daily basis in a two-parent family. In most single-parent families, this powerful daily demonstration does not occur, or it occurs in a somewhat distorted fashion as the cast of characters changes from time to time, depending on the frequency of the dating. When a new person walks into a family to date the parent, the children will have no say about what manner of stranger this might be. Such a situation will obviously trigger a multitude of reactions in the children. Whether or not the questions are ever asked explicitly, the child will wonder: Is this new person going to stay around for a while? Should I make the effort to get to know him, or her? Will he or she make the effort to get to know me? Will he or she monopolize my mother's or father's time and affection? What will he or she do if I am naughty or affectionate? How will my life be changed? If I like this person and then they stop seeing my parent, will I ever see them again? What will happen to my other parent if this parent marries again?

Following my first dates, my children would usually ask, "Mom do you think you'll marry him?" During this time, my two boys were especially fond of the service station attendant where we regularly bought gas. Several times they said they thought I should marry him. These instances provided a very nice opportunity to talk with my boys about the nature of male and female relationships, specifically that they are mutual, that they take time to develop, and that they are not a matter of short-term fantasy. A friend of mine, who was raising adolescent children and dating, told of many lovely discussions with his 19-year old son in which there was a mutuality of giving and sharing advice and perspectives about male and female relationships. The parents' ability to mature in their own handling of intimate relationships will in the end be the most positive model of all for their children. And the ability to mature in intimate relationships is as much an issue for married as for single parents, and equally important for their children.

Suggested Reading

Levinger G, Moles OC (eds): *Divorce and Separation: Context, Causes and Consequences.* New York, Basic Books, 1979.

Wallerstein JS, Kelly JB: *Surviving the Breakup: How Children and Parents Cope with Divorce.* New York, Basic Books, 1980.

Weiss RS: *Going It Alone: The Family Life and the Social Situation of the Single Parent.* New York, Basic Books, 1979.

References

Bloom BL, Asher SJ, White SW: Marital disruption as a stressor: a review and analysis. *Psychol Bull* 85:867, 1978.

Bohannan P (ed): *Divorce and After.* Garden City, NY, Doubleday and Co., 1970.

Gersick KE: Fathers by choice: divorced men who receive custody of their children. In Levinger G, Moles OC (eds): *Divorce and Separation: Context, Causes and Consequences.* New York, Basic Books, 1979, p 307.

Hetherington EM, Cox M, Cox R: The aftermath of divorce. In Stevens JH, Jr, Matthews M (eds): *Mother-Child, Father-Child Relations.* Washington, DC, NAEYC, 1977.

Ilgenfritz MP: Mothers on their own—widows and divorcees. *Marriage and Family Living* 23:38, 1961.

Kohen JA, Brown CA, Feldberg R: Divorced mothers: the costs and benefits of female family control. In Levinger G, Moles OC (eds): *Divorce and Separation: Context, Causes and Consequences.* New York, Basic Books, 1979, p 228.

Longfellow C: Divorce in context: its impact on children. In Levinger G, Moles OC (eds): *Divorce and Separation: Context, Causes and Consequences.* New York, Basic Books, 1979, p 287.

Schlesinger B (ed): *The One-Parent Family.* Toronto, University of Toronto Press, 1969.

Weiss RS: The emotional impact of marital separation. In Levinger G, Moles OC (eds): *Divorce and Separation: Context, Causes and Consequences.* New York, Basic Books, 1979, p 201.

CHAPTER **45 Parental Dysfunction and Child Abuse**

Arthur Green, M.D. and
Brandt F. Steele, M.D.

HISTORY OF CHILD ABUSE

Maltreatment of children has been recognized since the dawn of history in various forms: *physical abuse, neglect, emotional abuse, sexual abuse,* and *infanticide.* Infanticide has been practiced for many reasons since antiquity, and laws against it have existed since the time of Hammurabi nearly 3,000 years ago. Other forms of abuse have been condoned or largely disregarded by society until the 19th century when the overt abuse of small children in the labor force during the Industrial Revolution led to the passage of child labor laws in England. Societies for the prevention of cruelty to children developed in America and England following the great publicity given the case of Mary Ellen in New York in 1874. She was an illegitimate child who was cruelly maltreated by her adoptive mother and stepfather, and was finally taken into protective custody through the legal action of the American Society for Prevention of Cruelty to Animals on the grounds that a child, too, was a member of the animal kingdom.

Both before and after this, public and private social agencies did much work to rescue abused children, but it was not until the 1950's that the medical profession took any significant interest in the problem of child abuse. At that time, radiologists discovered the curious coincidence of fractured skulls, subdural hematomas, and multiple fractures of long bones on the X-rays of children with alleged accidental injuries, and decided these were nonaccidental injuries inflicted by the caretakers of the unfortunate victims. Dr. C. Henry Kempe and his colleagues at the University of Colorado Medical Center became concerned not only with these children who had suffered fractures, but also with chil-

dren suffering from multiple bruises and lacerations (Figure 45.1), and in 1962 they published an article on "The Battered Child Syndrome." This article aroused the interest of the medical profession and led to increasing effort being directed toward the diagnosis and treatment of these children and their families.

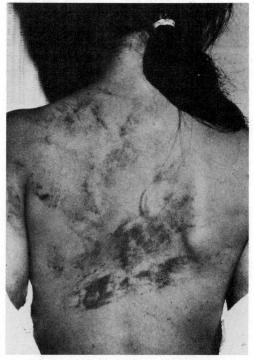

Figure 45.1. A seven year old girl with strap marks on her back. Example of child abuse. (Courtesy of Drs. Henry Kempe and Barton Schmitt, Department of Pediatrics, and Dr. Brandt Steele, Department of Psychiatry, University of Colorado Medical Center, Denver.)

INCIDENCE OF CHILD ABUSE

The actual incidence of child abuse is unknown and is probably next to impossible to determine accurately. Laws requiring the reporting of child abuse have been passed only since the mid-1960's and have led to a constantly increasing number of cases reported to authorities. Such statistics may still be misleading, since many states report only physical abuse of a serious nature and do not report cases of neglect (Figures 45.2–45.5). Workers in the field of child maltreatment estimate that a minimum of nearly one million children are abused and neglected in the United States each year, and close to a corresponding number of children are sexually abused. In fact, reported cases of sexual abuse are increasing even more rapidly than other cases of maltreatment. All of these statistics represent simply an increased reporting of maltreatment, and there is no solid evidence that child abuse itself is on the increase. Mortality statistics are even more difficult to obtain and to validate, but it is estimated that some two to three thousand children die each year in the United States as a result of repeated abuse or prolonged neglect. Maltreatment of children is thus a problem of major proportions with a morbidity and mortality much greater than that due to other more widely recognized causes of death in children such as infectious diseases, leukemia, and accidents. Although maltreatment of children is reported more commonly among lower socioeconomic groups, particularly in core poverty areas of large cities, it occurs in all socioeconomic levels, in families of all gradations of educational achievement, in upper class suburbs, in small towns and agricultural areas, among devout members of various religious denominations and among those of no religious affiliation whatsoever, and among members of all racial and ethnic groups.

THE REPETITIVE CYCLE OF CHILD ABUSE

The most common denominator in all the varieties of maltreatment, ranging from burns

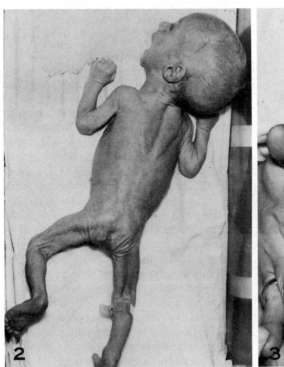 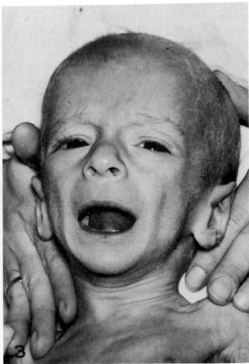

Figures 45.2 and 45.3. Three month old baby boy suffering from a "failure to thrive," secondary to caloric deprivation. Weight is only one ounce over birth weight. (Courtesy of Drs. Henry Kempe and Barton Schmitt, Department of Pediatrics, and Dr. Brandt Steele, Department of Psychiatry, University of Colorado Medical Center, Denver.)

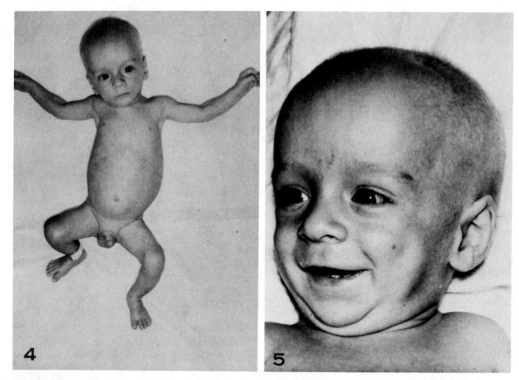

Figures 45.4 and 45.5. The same infant three weeks later after hospitalization. (Courtesy of Drs. Henry Kempe and Barton Schmitt, Department of Pediatrics, and Dr. Brandt Steele, Department of Psychiatry, University of Colorado Medical Center, Denver.)

and bruises on through severe lacerations, multiple fractures, visceral injuries, starvation and failure to thrive, brain injuries, and death, is that all of these conditions are the result of acts of commission or omission by the caretakers of the child. Standards have been developed to enable pediatricians and other physicians to separate these nonaccidental traumas from similar-appearing metabolic or infectious diseases or accidental injuries. Much more difficult than the technical diagnosis of maltreatment is the problem of the physician's own personal responses to this situation in which those who are supposed to love and care for the child have been the very ones who have damaged the child. In the face of such a situation, the physician's own dismay and anxiety may be very distressing. He or she may manage it as society has always handled child abuse, by denying it and looking for organic causes for the injuries, or accepting the lame, unconvincing stories of accidents. On the other hand, the physician may feel a strong identification with the helpless, mistreated child

and may respond with a surge of righteous anger toward the abusing parent or caretaker. Neither of these responses is very useful in dealing with the problem. Much more helpful is the realization that the physician is seeing the reenactment of an old drama. Almost without exception, abusing parents were significantly neglected or physically abused in their own earliest years. They are merely repeating with their own children the way they themselves were treated by their own parents.

Thus, it is obvious that the damage to the child's emotional and personality development is probably of greater import than any physical damage to his or her body, that these effects are long-lasting, and that such early childhood experience leads to later dysfunction as a parent. This repetitive cycle of parental dysfunction leading to child abuse, and the abused child later becoming a parent who repeats the child abuse with his or her own children is a fascinating and tragic problem. We shall now look more closely at the participants in this cycle.

THE ABUSED CHILD

One of us (Arthur Green) conducted a study at the Downstate Medical Center in Brooklyn from 1970 to 1972 which corroborated and enlarged on the findings of the other author of this chapter (Brandt Steele) in regard to the psychological and psychodynamic factors involved in child abuse. In this study, 60 abused children and their mothers served as subjects of the investigation. The children ranged in age from five through 12. Thirty nonabused neglected children and 30 nonabused normal children and their mothers served as controls. All of the children received psychiatric and neurological examinations and psychological testing. The results revealed that the abused children exhibited marked impairment on most of the psychiatric, psychological, and neurological measures compared to the normal controls.

Twenty-five per cent of the abused children were retarded with an IQ of less than 70. They also manifested difficulties in object relationships and impulse control. They suffered from a poor self-concept and distorted body imagery. They were more anxious and depressed than their normal counterparts. Almost all of the abused children demonstrated serious academic or behavioral problems in school. They were overly aggressive, impulsive, and inattentive in the classroom, and had obvious learning difficulties. Approximately one-quarter of the abused children engaged in self-destructive behavior, in the form of suicide attempts, suicidal gestures, and various forms of self-mutilation. This symptom seemed to represent a primitive, learned behavior pattern originating in the earliest painful encounters with their hostile parents.

In addition, about one-third of the abused children were found to be neurologically impaired. Since abused children with severe head trauma (skull fractures, subdural hematomas, cerebral hemorrhages) were excluded from the sample, this central nervous system impairment might be considered antecedent to and a *cause* of the abuse rather than its result. This hypothesis was supported by case studies which revealed that some of these abused children had been deviant since birth, and that their physical or behavioral abnormality proved so burdensome to the parents that it provoked parental abuse. In numerous other cases, the neurological

and psychological trauma was clearly the *result* of the abuse and contributed to the child's deviant behavior, leading to a vicious cycle in which the resulting behavioral aberrations stimulated even further abuse.

THE ABUSING PARENTS

Mothers of these abused children generally described poor relationships with the important people in their lives. They were often detached from their own parents, whom they regarded as critical and ungiving. As children, they frequently experienced physical abuse, neglect, and exploitation by their parents. They also manifested a high incidence of conflict with their spouses or boyfriends. They complained about the failure of their men to provide adequate physical and emotional support. Few of these women had friends or were able to establish ties with neighbors or the community. Their social isolation and estrangement from their spouses and families made it impossible for them to reach out toward others during times of stress. No one was available to help them with the usual crises of childrearing.

These mothers often turned to their children for assistance and nurturance during these times, which is the reverse of the normal parental behavior. This phenomenon is known as *role reversal* and may be expressed in different ways depending on the child's age. School-age children are often required to cook, clean house, and care for their younger siblings. Toddlers are expected to achieve premature toilet training, motor skills, and a general independence which is clearly beyond their capacity. Role reversal with an infant occurs when the mother regards its feeding and responsiveness primarily in terms of her own gratification. These women become angry when the baby refuses to suck from the breast or bottle, is unable to gain weight, or is difficult to comfort. The mother perceives these various signs of unresponsiveness as a personal rejection by the infant, and as confirmation of her maternal incompetency.

What all these examples of role reversal have in common is that the maternal demands for the child's responsiveness or performance exceed the child's developmental capacity. The unresponsive child is then unconsciously equated with the mother's own rejecting and critical parent. As a result, the mothers typically regarded the abused child as the most deviant or difficult child in the family, and the one who required the most attention of all of the siblings. The abused child, of course, is the one who cannot comply with the demands for role reversal.

Thus far, these comments might indicate that it is the mothers who are primarily responsible for child abuse, but this impression is incorrect. The fathers were the abusing parent in exactly half of these 60 cases. An interesting pattern in the abusing fathers was their tendency to abuse their wives along with the scapegoated child. The nonabusing mother of an abused child is surprisingly similar to the abusing mother with respect to background, childrearing attitudes, and psychodynamics. These mothers experience the same hostility and anger towards the children, but they allow their men to act out these impulses for them. These women often assume the role of the abuser when their spouses leave.

Having explored the child abuse syndrome from the vantage points of both the parent and the child, and their mutual interaction, we may now achieve a better understanding of this phenomenon. Child abuse is basically a *dysfunction of parenting*. The abusers never learned appropriate parenting behavior, because of their own unfavorable childhood experiences. Their parents usually provided poor models for childrearing. The learned nature of parenting has been described by Benedek as memories of and an identification with the parenting behavior experienced in earliest years. This is supported by Harlow's primate studies, which demonstrated that infant female monkeys reared without their mothers by wire or cloth surrogates failed to develop maternal behavior. These maternally deprived monkeys eventually subjected their offspring to physical attack.

CHILD ABUSE: A SYNDROME OF PATHOLOGICAL FAMILY INTERACTION

The etiology of child abuse is based on three potentiating factors: 1) the abuse-prone personality of the parent; 2) the characteristics of the child which make him or her vulnerable for scapegoating; and 3) any environmental stress which increases the burden of child care.

The abuse-prone personality traits of the parent include poor impulse control, a devalued self-concept, and excessive use of the defense mechanisms of denial, projection, and externalization. These individuals desperately need to maintain a positive facade, so they defend themselves against the awareness of inadequacy and worthlessness by projecting their negative attributes onto the child. Contrary to popular belief, only a small minority of abusing parents are psychotic. About 10% display evidence of psychotic behavior, which is usually chronic in nature.

The contributions of the child towards the abuse include any physical or behavioral deviancy which increases the burden of childrearing. Children who are premature or physically ill, as well as those with brain damage, psychosis, or congenital defects, are difficult to manage and readily evoke the defective self-concepts of their parents. Other children are scapegoated because they remind the parent of a hated person or situation. For example, a mother might beat a child who resembles a despised husband or boyfriend. Another mother will abuse a child whose conception forced her into an unhappy marriage.

The third essential factor is environmental stress, which can trigger abuse by upsetting the delicate equilibrium between the childrearing resources and the childrearing pressures in the family. The physical illness of a parent, desertion by a spouse, and loss of a babysitter or a supportive relative reduce the caretaking capacity of a family. Sickness of a child and the birth of a new baby increase the childrearing burdens. When environmental conditions increase the discrepancy between the limited parental capacity and the increased demands for child care, the better integrated parent seeks help from a parent, spouse, or friend. The more isolated, abusing parent turns to the child for support instead. Alcoholism and drug abuse further interfere with the ability of the parent to perceive the needs of the child, to care for the child, and to control destructive and aggressive impulses.

The following psychodynamic pattern then ensues. The scapegoated child is incapable of satisfying the parental needs, and the mother unconsciously equates the child with her own rejecting parent. Her resulting sense of rejection, inadequacy, and low self-esteem becomes intolerable and is displaced onto the child through mechanisms of denial and projection. A shift occurs, and the mother identifies with her own punitive parent and attacks the child, who now represents her past and current "bad" self-image. In hitting the child, the mother symbolically punishes her own bad parent, her bad self, and other despised individuals consciously or unconsciously linked to the child. If the abused child is removed from the home, the mother's rage might become internalized, resulting in severe depression, or another child might be chosen for scapegoating. The availability of a scapegoat seems to be necessary for the abusing parent's psychological equilibrium.

The relative strengths of these three variables contributing to the child abuse syndrome vary from one case to another. For example, a severely hyperactive and demanding child, who might be retarded or brain-damaged, will require lower levels of parental abuse-proneness and environmental stress to become a victim of abuse. On the other hand, if a normal and relatively undemanding child in a stable family environment was abused, one would predict that the parent had an unusually high level of abuse-proneness. Average parents might abuse an average child only in very stressful environmental situations where extreme childrearing pressures exist.

SEXUAL ABUSE

As noted earlier, sexual abuse has been reported with rapidly increasing frequency in the past decade, although there is no clear evidence that it is actually occurring more often than in the past. It may occur with children of all ages from infancy on through adolescence, and can include all varieties of sexual activity from genital fondling to masturbation, oral-genital relations, anal contact, intercourse, and rape. It may be either heterosexual or homosexual. The perpetrators may be family members of all ages and relationships. Only a small percentage of sexual abuse is done by strangers, although in the past such cases have been the ones which came most often to public attention. *Incest* is the most common form of sexual abuse, occurring most frequently between fathers or stepfathers and their daughters, or between a mother's lover and her daughter. Sexual activity related to childhood curiosity and exploration is quite common between brothers and sisters, and is usually not considered to be abusive unless it progresses to intercourse or other forced sexual activity. Sexual relationships between girls and other male

relatives occur with less frequency. Intrafamilial homosexual relationships are much commoner than thought in the past, particularly between boys and their fathers or stepfathers. Abuse of either girls or boys by female relatives is reported less often, and mother-son incest is probably the least common form of sexual abuse.

Sexual abuse has many features in common with physical abuse and neglect. Children may be physically abused early in life and sexually abused later on, or the two may occur concurrently. There are also cases in which sexual abuse has occurred without any history of previous physical abuse. Sexually abusive parents, or other caretakers, commonly give histories of significant deprivation, neglect, or abuse in their early lives. And there is frequently a history of generational incest quite analogous to the generational repetition of physical abuse. As in other forms of maltreatment, there is no overall correlation between sexual abuse and socioeconomic level, educational achievement, cultural group, or ethnic derivation. In some cases, alcohol and crowded living conditions precipitate or increase the frequency of individual acts of sexual abuse. There is often an unconscious condoning on the part of the nonabusive parent, or even a conscious awareness and disregard of the incestuous activity. Sometimes there is actually a subtle or obvious instigation of the incest by the nonabusive parent. Sexual abuse is not a sudden, new phenomenon in a family, but rather the culmination of, as well as an attempted solution for, long-lasting family tensions and conflicts. Preexisting difficulties between the parents in the areas of mutual respect, understanding, and communication, and especially in the sexual sphere, are the common predisposing factors, and the incestuous activity is the result of family problems rather than the cause of them.

As in physical abuse and neglect, the deleterious effects of sexual abuse are long-lasting, and are much more the result of psychological trauma and subsequent distortion of psychosexual development than they are the result of any physical injury or physical effects of the sexual abuse itself. The earlier in life that the abuse occurs and the more it is accompanied by aggression or violence, the more severely will the subsequent psychosexual development be disturbed. The later in the child's life that the sexual abuse occurs and the more that it is accompanied by a gentle seduction and persuasion, the less severe will the psychological damage be, although some degree of disturbance seems to be inevitable. In the direct sexual sphere, the long-term, deleterious effects are seen in the form of complete sexual avoidance or inhibition, or in the opposite direction, promiscuity and sometimes prostitution in both sexes. More general psychological sequelae include disturbances in gender identity and sexual role, very low self-esteem with a sense of being damaged and worthless, social isolation and shallow interpersonal relationships, poor marriages, fears of raising children, and serious problems of unresolved rage and guilt. Sexually abused children of school age may often show severe problems in learning or truancy, or on the other hand, may overcompensate by compulsive studying and straight "A" performance. The single most damaging element in sexual abuse is the callous exploitation of a child's obedience to parental authority and natural need to be loved for the selfish satisfaction of the adult's desires, far in excess of the child's psychological ability to understand and to cope.

THE TREATMENT OF CHILD ABUSE

Any plan for the prevention or treatment of child abuse must attempt to modify the three important variables of the pathological family interaction. It is important to involve the abusive parent in a corrective emotional experience with an accepting, uncritical adult. The helping person, who may be a psychiatrist, social worker, nurse, or parent aide, tries to develop a trusting relationship with the parent. The therapist provides the parents with some of the dependency gratifications which they were unable to obtain from their own spouses and family, thereby eliminating the need for role reversal and unrealistic demands made on the child. Another goal of treatment is to make the parent aware of the intrusion of the past into his or her distorted relationship with the child. Group psychotherapy has proven especially helpful to abusing parents in this respect. An organization known as Parents Anonymous, started in Los Angeles by a woman by the name of Jolly K., in association with other abusive mothers, works on the basis of similar principles.

The contributions of the child to the abuse may be dealt with by parental counseling and individual psychotherapy. If the child is physically or behaviorally impaired, the nature of the problem should be carefully explained to the parents so that their expectations of the child can be realistically adjusted. Outpatient play therapy with the abused child has proven to be quite successful in reversing some of the psychological damage resulting from the ongoing trauma. This form of psychotherapy allows the children to recreate and master their traumatic experiences in play and fantasy. The ego deficits and cognitive impairment of so many of the abused youngsters require an initially supportive therapeutic technique designed to strengthen ego functioning and to contain drives and impulses. Psychoeducational assistance is often required by school-age abused children because they manifest a high incidence of speech and language dysfunction and learning disability.

Environmental stress can be alleviated by providing such services as homemakers, visiting nurses, and day-care facilities for abused infants and preschool children. Emergency social services should also be provided where appropriate. It is obvious that traditional modes of outpatient psychiatric treatment must be greatly modified and expanded in order to meet some of the basic needs of families involved in child abuse.

All of these principles are also applicable in the treatment of sexual abuse. The treatment of sexually abused children must be carefully designed and individualized according to the age of the child, the duration and severity of the abuse, and the particular family dysfunctions which have led to the abuse. The family itself must receive treatment inasmuch as the sexual abuse is a symptom of severe family breakdown. Thus, it is necessary not only to care for the abused child, but also to treat the perpetrator of the sexual abuse and to help the perpetrator's spouse become a more alert and more protective caretaker. In this connection, the child, too, must be helped to regain a sense of privacy and control over his or her own body, and to feel supported in saying "No" to any further abuse. As a rule, long-term treatment, in either individual or group psychotherapy, is necessary to accomplish these goals.

Suggested Readings

Chase NF: *A Child Is Being Beaten: Violence Against Children, An American Tragedy.* New York, Holt Rinehart, 1975.
D'Ambrosio R: *No Language But a Cry.* New York, Dell, 1970.
Finkelhor D: *Sexually Victimized Children.* New York, The Free Press, 1979.
Fontana VJ: *Somewhere A Child Is Crying.* New York, Macmillan, 1973.

Green A, Gaines R, Sandgrund A: Child abuse: pathological syndrome of family interaction. *Am J Psychiatry* 131:882, 1974.

Green A: *Child Maltreatment: A Handbook for Mental Health and Child Care Professionals.* New York, Jason Aronson, 1980.

Helfer RE, Kempe CH (eds): *The Battered Child,* ed 3. Chicago, University of Chicago Press, 1980.

Herman J: *Father-Daughter Incest.* Cambridge, Harvard Univ. Press, 1981.

Justice B, Justice R: *The Broken Taboo: Sex in the Family.* New York, Human Science Press, 1979.

Kempe CH, Silverman FN, Steele BF, Droegemuller W, Silver HK: The battered-child syndrome. *JAMA* 181:17, 1962.

Martin HP (ed): *The Abused Child: A Multidisciplinary Approach to Developmental Issues and Treatment.* Cambridge MA, Ballinger, 1976.

Meiselman KC: *Incest: A Psychological Study of Causes and Effects with Treatment Recommendations.* San Francisco, Jossey-Boss, 1978.

Steele BF: Parental abuse of infants and small children. In Anthony EJ, Benedek T (eds): *Parenthood: Its Psychology and Psychopathology.* Boston, Little, Brown, and Co, 1970, p 449.

References

Benedek T: Parenthood as a developmental phase. *J Am Psychoanal Assoc* 7:389, 1959.

Caffey J: Multiple fractures in the long bones of infants suffering from chronic subdural hematoma. *Am J Roentgenol* 56:163, 1946.

Coppolillo HP: A conceptual model for study of some abusing parents. In Anthony EJ, Koupernik C, Chiland C (eds): *The Child in His Family: Vulnerable Children.* New York, John Wiley & Sons, 1978, p 231.

Emslie GJ, Rosenfeld A: Incest reported by children and adolescents hospitalized for severe psychiatric problems. *Am J Psychiatry* 140:708, 1983.

Morris MG, Gould RW: Role reversal: a concept in dealing with the neglected/battered child syndrome. In *The Neglected/Battered Child Syndrome.* New York, Child Welfare League of America, 1963, p 29.

Sandgrund A, Gaines R, Green A: Child abuse and mental retardation: a problem of cause and effect. *Am J Ment Def* 79:327, 1974.

Silverman FN: The roentgen manifestations of unrecognized, skeletal trauma in infants. *Am J Roentgenol* 69:413, 1953.

Yates A: Children eroticized by incest. *Am J Psychiatry* 139:482, 1982.

Section M/The Middle and Later Years of Life

CHAPTER **46** ## Middle Age and the Climacterium

Dorothy Strauss, Ph.D. and
George L. Mizner, M.D.

THE "MID-LIFE CRISIS"

The term, "mid-life crisis," has become so established in our common usage that it has lost specificity and become a generalized label. Today, nearly all emotional disturbances experienced by men as well as women between the ages of 40 and 65 are readily ascribed to a "mid-life crisis" by magazine articles, television programs, and popular novels. The problem with respect to medical practice is that the physician may be tempted to go along with the public's lay diagnosis or the patients' self-diagnosis of a "mid-life crisis." Since an increasing segment of the population is entering these middle years and, incidentally, consulting physicians about their problems, it is obvious that resorting to the "mid-life crisis" explanation has limited value for the management of any particular individual. Biological changes do frequently aggravate emotional disturbances during these years, but in unique and different ways for each and every patient.

THE DEVELOPMENTAL CONTINUUM

Until recently, the life cycle that was considered worthy of scientific investigation was a very shortened one. It was assumed that the turmoil and uncertainty of childhood and adolescence are replaced by the confidence, predictability, and emotional control of early adulthood, and that at this point the peak of development occurs. It was possible to hold this view for so long because it dovetailed nicely with the work ethic of Western society and because, until recently, the average life span for both men and women did not exceed by very much their years of high productivity, reproduction, and responsibility. However, as the likelihood of living into the 70's became an expectation rather than an exception, and earlier demise more a matter of serious disease or accident, there has emerged a growing discomfort with the idea that the early 40's and 50's inevitably usher in a period of mental and social deterioration, with a universal slowing down of the capacity for new learning.

Generativity vs. Stagnation

Erik Erikson (Figure 46.1) was one of the first to make us aware that development does not stop as adolescence draws to a close—that in fact, development is a lifelong process. Erikson expresses his life stages in terms of opposites: one representing a successful resolution of a phase specific developmental task and the other an unsuccessful resolution. He sees adulthood and middle age as providing an opportunity for *generativity*. By this concept he means a concern with nurturing and guiding the next generation, and later the taking on of the "mentor" role and

Figure 46.1. Erik Erikson.

the creation of spiritual and intellectual heirs. The opposite of this is *stagnation*, by which Erikson means the pervasive intellectual, psychological, and interpersonal impoverishment that results from a failure of generativity. He describes such individuals as indulging themselves "as if they were their own one and only child." He feels they lack "some faith, some belief in the species, which would make a child appear to be a welcome trust" and which would enable them to engage in the altruistic task of being truly nurturant to the next generation whether or not it includes their own biological children.

Development in Adult Life

Since Erikson, a number of authors have attempted systematic studies of the life cycle with special emphasis on development in adult life. Daniel Levinson and his group at Yale emphasize the discontinuities and transitions of adult life. The thesis of the Yale group is that there are distinct adult life cycle stages initiated by well-defined periods of change in which new life tasks need to be coped with in new ways. Like Erikson, they feel that failure to change and failure to deal with the new intrapsychic and interpersonal challenges of adulthood lead to

stagnation, impoverishment of the personality, and difficulties later on—in short, a faulty life structure. Levinson's book, *The Seasons of a Man's Life*, is based on a total of 40 men, 10 each from four different occupations, who are followed through the mid-life transition. Levinson particularly stresses the conscious choices that these men make about work, marriage and family, friends, and life goals during age-defined stages of the middle years.

George Vaillant's study, *Adaptation to Life*, follows 95 Harvard freshmen into middle age, and places more emphasis on the maturation and evolution of preexisting adaptational styles and defense mechanisms than it does on the discontinuities of personality development. For Vaillant, the boy is indeed the father of the man, and he regularly finds in his college subjects the very strengths or flaws that lead to successful or unsuccessful adaptation in later life. As a corollary, Vaillant also finds that in mid-life, physical health accompanies emotional health. Those of his subjects who were identified early as having the poorest psychological adjustment also showed the greatest incidence of serious physical disease and the highest mortality rates as they reached their 40's and 50's. Furthermore, no single childhood factor accounted for happiness or unhappiness by age 50; rather, it was the stability of the childhood environment and the sustained social supports available in the adult environment that appeared to be the most crucial factors.

Roger Gould of the University of California at Los Angeles, in his book, *Transformations*, likens middle age to adolescence in that both periods are marked by great self-questioning and the potential as well as the need for change. There is a tendency to question what one has done with one's life, accompanied by a wish to change in some important way. Frequently, this is tied to feelings of dissatisfaction with the way life has turned out and disgust with what one has become. Such deep-seated "negative self-images" are not confined to those who have utterly failed to achieve their life goals, but are found also in successful individuals who feel that the emotional price that they have paid for their success has been too great.

Finally, Calvin Colarusso and Robert Nemiroff, in their book, *Adult Development*, extend psychodynamic and psychoanalytic theory through the second half of the life cycle. They review current adult developmental research, and discuss the practical implications and the clinical importance of this research for the most effective diagnosis and treatment of adult patients.

Since the current cultural climate emphasizes self-realization more than duty and responsibility, today's middle-aged man may be more apt to break with tradition and to involve himself with new and different careers, commitments, and relationships. A drastic break with the past may take a heavy toll in the demand made for major readjustments in the self or in the dislocations brought to the lives of those who are dependent upon these men for stability and support. Not only wives and children, but others as well, may become casualties.

The studies quoted above are confined mostly to men and are based on small numbers of subjects, and therefore it is probably too early to conclude that adulthood can be divided into stages that are as clearcut, predictable, and invariable as the stages of development in infancy, childhood, and adolescence. What seems certain is that development continues during the adult years and that these years which we label middle age require a more thoughtful reappraisal. The altered circumstances of life confront middle-aged people with a new view of themselves and new opportunities on the one hand, and problems and conflicts on the other. It is undeniable that traumatizing life events tend to accelerate with the passage of time; but it is not correct to assume that all of these are experienced by the majority of older adults as crises of despair. The work of resolution and reaccommodation is the stuff of which ongoing development consists.

THE FEMALE CLIMACTERIUM

The female climacterium has been a source of much medical concern and comment for years. First of all, it is essential to flesh out the skeleton of biological facts with an awareness that both psychological and social factors have profound impacts upon how different women experience and react to the stresses of mid-life. Social norms, and the psychological resources available for accommodation to those norms, play a tremendous role in the way a particular woman is going to react as the biological changes of the climacterium begin to become apparent.

The female climacterium is best described as a process which extends over a variable time span which has its onset somewhere between the ages of 40 and 53. Physical signs and symptoms vary from mild to severe. However, it is often the psychological problems which motivate the patient to seek relief. The menopause is relatively simple to discuss because the picture is fairly clear. Physically, there is the dramatic change which signals the end of the reproductive phase of life. With the loss of ovarian function and the final discontinuation of menstruation, we say that the menopausal phase has been completed. Prior to the actual cessation of menses, however, there may be a period when physical symptoms such as excessive or irregular bleeding may develop, or signs of vasomotor imbalance may become apparent. Diminishing ovarian function need not and often does not occur in the form of a rapid change, and the symptoms of a hypothalamic-pituitary-ovarian imbalance may appear intermittently at first and then intensify as estrogen secretion decreases. The entire phase lasts, on the average, from two to five years. During this time, or for an even longer period, women commonly experience some symptoms of autonomic nervous system imbalance but in varying degrees of severity. Some are sorely distressed by hot flashes and sweats; others barely notice them. Additionally, there are metabolic and other organic changes which may produce distressing symptoms. Nevertheless, the most common complaints are still basically psychological; and while the menopause cannot be implicated as the causative factor, it is frequently an aggravating element.

It is important to remember that episodes of anxiety and depression so commonly associated with the menopause are often essentially referable to the basic premenopausal personality structure of the individual. Those women whose life histories are replete with coping difficulties may be expected to run true to form when they reach the menopause. The girl who was regularly distressed by menstruation, who had endless trouble deciding whether or not to get married or to become pregnant, whose pregnancy was an ordeal only to be exceeded by the trials of parenting, becomes the woman for whom the climacterium is a catastrophe. But this type of reaction is not the case for the vast majority of women, as Bernice Neugarten has convincingly demonstrated in a number of studies. In fact, Neugarten suggests that, for the healthy, adaptable woman, menopause and the departure of children can bring a new sense of freedom and spontaneity.

We have the impression that the women's movement, careers for women, less emphasis on childbearing and rearing as the only valid social roles for women, greater openness about sexuality, and a breaking down of myths about the loss of sexual interest after menopause have made the climacterium less of a threat and trauma for women than it used to be. In today's world, the woman in middle life whose orientation was essentially domestic seems better able to decide that she has fulfilled her obligations toward the next generation, and that now it is time for her to try her hand at something that will provide new enrichment for her for the rest of her life.

A number of other changes in our society (better health care, greater affluence, the pursuit of higher education by women, and a tendency during the last half century towards earlier childbearing) have all enabled women to look forward to many years of postmenopausal productivity and vigorous good health. Additionally, the recent emphasis on diet and exercise has enabled many women to maintain their youthful attractiveness for many more years than used to be the case. Menopause appears to be occurring somewhat later (on the average, in the late rather than in the middle 40's), and hormonal replacement can reduce or eliminate many of the physical changes that accompany the loss of ovarian function. Both of these factors help smooth the transition by increasing preparatory time and by providing a sense of some control over distressing physical symptoms.

In this connection, a word needs to be said about hormone replacement therapy for the postmenopausal woman because this is still a subject of considerable medical uncertainty and controversy. At a conference on estrogen use in postmenopausal women held by the National Institute on Aging and the National Institutes of Health in September 1979, it was recognized that estrogens are effective in overcoming the atrophy of the vaginal epithelium and the associated symptoms of vaginal dryness, burning, itching, and pain on intercourse which occur in women whose endogenous estrogen production has declined. It also seems likely that estrogens are effective in treating vasomotor instability ("hot flashes") and in retarding the bone loss which normally follows menopause and which

eventually results in osteoporosis and an increased risk of fractures. However, the conference found no convincing evidence that estrogen will retard wrinkling of the skin, greying of the hair, or other physical manifestations of aging. Nor does the evidence suggest that estrogen is useful in the treatment of primary psychological problems. However, the use of estrogens may help some women feel better physically, and that result may lead to an improvement in psychological status as well.

The hazards of estrogen therapy were also discussed at this conference. The conference found no convincing evidence that exogenous estrogens in customary doses increase the risk of thromboembolic phenomena, stroke, or heart disease in women who have undergone natural menopause. However, evidence was presented that the risk of uterine endometrial carcinoma increases with the duration of estrogen use and declines after discontinuation. The incidence of uterine cancer increases four- to eight-fold after two to four years of use. A recent study by Antunes, Stolley, and coworkers found that women who use estrogen for five years or more are 15 times more likely to develop uterine cancer. Most of this increase is accounted for by early stage, low grade endometrial lesions which are easily detected and readily treated. As a result, the *mortality rate* due to uterine cancer does not seem to have risen in response to estrogen replacement therapy, despite the increased incidence of uterine cancer associated with prolonged estrogen use. In contrast, the incidence of breast cancer has not changed parallel with estrogen use. Nevertheless, this remains an area of considerable concern because of the high incidence and relatively poorer prognosis of breast cancer, and because of the association between estrogens and breast cancer in certain experimental animal studies. Finally, there is some evidence to suggest that long-term users of estrogen have an increased rate of gallstones, incur an increased risk of hypertension, and experience abnormal changes in their blood clotting mechanisms. In November 1979, the American Council on Science and Health issued a report urging that each woman must carefully assess the severity of her true menopausal symptoms against the risks of long-term estrogen use, and should realize that estrogen therapy cannot provide all of the many youth-oriented and psychological benefits that have been claimed for it for so many years.

THE MALE CLIMACTERIUM

The male climacterium has no clearcut biological marker equivalent to menopause in the woman. Muscle strength, speed, and endurance decline but exercise can do much to preserve physical vigor. Male hormone levels decrease only slightly in mid-life, and many men remain not only sexually vigorous but also fertile into their late 60's or 70's. Physicians nonetheless often find themselves providing reassurance to men in their 50's and 60's whose anxiety over an occasional lapse in sexual efficiency results in further dysfunction as a by-product of panic. For the most part, the mid-life transition presents basically psychological rather than physiological stresses to men. To quote Howard Spierer: "For many men, mid-life brings the realization that they will not move any higher in their occupations. They will therefore need to scale down their aspirations and anticipated achievement levels. In the process their confidence in themselves, their feelings of personal control over their own destinies and their belief in their work competence are likely to suffer." What is largely unique to men, namely the scaling down of their career expectations, may in the future apply as well to women as more of them pursue careers prepared for and entered early in adulthood. At the present time, the single most traumatizing aspect of mid-life for men may well be the tarnishing of the once shining expectations of their youth.

Even those who are highly successful and achieve their life work goals are likely to wonder if their sacrifices have been worthwhile. What did they miss of their children's lives and development because of their ardent pursuit of career objectives? What of the novels not read, the rivers not fished, the vacations postponed, the friendships let lapse, and the marriages neglected because they could not refuse assignments and tasks that were to take them up the next rung of the career ladder?

The staggering financial burdens of this time of life exacerbate the emotional problems. The mid-life generation is literally *in the middle*, caught between children approaching adulthood and parents moving into the later years of life. College and graduate education have outpaced in cost most other segments of an inflationary economy. Limited employment opportunities may mean continued support for the job-seeking child. Aging parents may become financially dependent, in spite of social security benefits. The problem of how to help a parent who is physically and/or mentally incapacitated has no easy solutions and can generate a tremendous burden of guilt even when financial assistance is not an issue. A recent study by Lieberman suggests that caring for elderly parents has become a major source of stress in middle age, and may seriously undermine the quality of family life.

The workplace may also lose much of its previously positive aspects. Many men cite financial pressures as the sole reason for maintaining a pace at work which has become too strenuous or for remaining in a job which has become boring or unfulfilling. The declining employment opportunities for persons past 40 and restrictive (nonvested) pension plans are additional reasons why so many men stay in dead-end jobs. Relationships at work change too. The middle-aged man may suddenly find himself regarded with unaccustomed respect by younger colleagues, and he becomes aware that he is being looked to for advice and guidance, not just for some specific work problem, but on how to live life and plan a career. This brings him a heightened sense of responsibility for the work enterprise and for nurturing a younger generation of successors to carry on knowledge and traditions. But this is also a reminder that power and influence are soon to be relinquished. Alternately and less flatteringly, he may be passed over, shunned or pitied as already being over the hill, out of the mainstream, and no longer useful.

OPPORTUNITIES AND STRESSES OF MIDDLE AGE

Careful observation and the contributions of researchers in the field of aging suggest strongly that chronological age in and of itself is much less important than the stresses which are experienced during this phase of life and the efficiency of the coping mechanisms. To quote Bernice Neugarten: "It is not the fact that one reaches 40, 50, or 60 which is itself important, but rather 'How am I doing for my age?'"* Perhaps the most salient thing to be said for people in this age span is that, being *in the*

---

* Time, age, and the life cycle. *Am J Psychiatry* 136:888, 1979.

middle, they receive conflicting messages from the young, from their grown and semigrown children, from their younger associates, from their elderly parents, and even from each other.

Several writers, Gutmann in particular, have pointed out that culturally and socially dictated differences between the sexes tend to become less so with age. The speculation is that with the passing of parenting responsibilities, suppressed personality attributes, i.e., aggressiveness in women and desire for emotional attachment in men, are allowed more open expression. In order to be successful in childrearing, women may have to inhibit aggressive and competitive tendencies, postpone outside interests, and defer career choice until they relinquish maternal responsibilities. Men on the other hand, in making their way professionally, are taught to be as aggressive and competitive as possible, and to renounce the more feeling or "feminine" side of their personalities. Anything "feminine" tends to be perceived by the young man as a dangerous threat to his career ambitions. As a result, he cannot express or live out those aspects of himself until in mid-life he has attained sufficient security about his "manliness" and his accomplishments to permit himself to give expression to the less stereotypically "masculine" aspects of his personality.

One might expect that as the result of these changes in both men and women, couples would find more in common and draw closer in middle age. Indeed, this may be the result in some instances. Frequently, however, the husband is beginning to seek closer family life and more communication in his marriage, just as the wife may be looking to free herself from the confines of the family in an attempt to make her mark in the world outside the home and gain a new identity for herself. Since they no longer have the rearing of children as a common endeavor, they now must reexamine their commitment to each other and decide if they wish to spend the rest of their lives together. Old marital disappointments, continuing irritations and dissatisfactions, as well as new opportunities have to be evaluated and explored before a decision can be made and the marriage either terminated or redirected toward a new period of stability. For people who have never married, this too may be a difficult time as they are forced to come to terms with the fact that now it may be too late. For many, the spectre of a lonely old age, without the companionship and support of spouse

and children, becomes a very frightening prospect.

Relationships with children also change as the children mature. Parents come to view their own success in life at least partially in terms of how well the children turn out. The traditional parental role has to be relinquished if the child—now a young adult—is to emancipate fully and yet maintain the affectionate bonds so crucial to the emotional well-being of both generations. New sons-in-law and daughters-in-law must be welcomed into the family and new relationships forged with them, their parents, and their relatives. Grandparenthood (Figure 46.2) is eagerly welcomed by most people and may bring with it new satisfactions without the daily responsibilities of childrearing. However, it also serves as yet another reminder of the inexorable forward movement of the life cycle.

The aging of parents also gives people in midlife an increasing appreciation of their role as a link between successive generations. We acquire greater sympathy and understanding of old people. In looking at them, we wonder about ourselves, and we watch them with hope or fear regarding our own aging and death. When they

Figure 46.2. *Old Man and Small Boy* (1930) by Gustav Vigeland. Bronze. Placed in the Vigeland Sculpture Park, Oslo, Norway. (By permission of Vigeland Museum, Oslo, Norway.)

do die, we are forcefully reminded of the passage of time and of the inevitability of our own future death. A subtle change accompanies this growing awareness of one's own ultimate demise. Instead of thinking about how many years we have lived, we start to wonder about the number of years we may have left. By the age of 40 or 45 we become aware that we have less than half of our lives left to live, and this profoundly influences our view of the world and of ourselves.

Many people during middle age have their first brush with serious illness. Perhaps it is a nonfatal heart attack or a successful cancer operation. Such an event cannot help but confront us further with our own mortality, and such confrontation leads to a serious reevaluation of life goals, lifestyle, and life priorities. Even those who escape such an experience personally, inevitably have friends and colleagues who succumb. The result is what Neugarten refers to as "the rehearsal for the heart attack" by men, while women, who live longer and tend to marry men older than themselves, prepare themselves psychologically for widowhood. In fact, Dr. Robert Butler has noted that the number of women age 45 to 64 will "skyrocket" to 36 million between 1990 and 2010—and many of these women will be either widowed or divorced. The average age of widowhood is now in the mid to late 50's. And, of the 11 million widows currently in this country, many live below the official poverty line and two-thirds live alone.

In middle age both sexes become more preoccupied with their health and tend to undertake activities designed to ameliorate chronic illness and maintain good physical condition. For as much as we may be distressed by the encroaching shadow of our own personal death, perhaps we are even more frightened by the spectre of slipping into an aged existence without meaning or purpose, over which our capacity for control will be progressively eroded until it disappears entirely.

But middle age should not be characterized solely in terms of losses, be they physical or emotional. For an increasing number of individuals, it is really the prime of life. Although we think of ourselves as a youth-oriented society, we are not necessarily a young society. Power and responsibility are vested in the middle-aged. They govern in politics and in industry and make the crucial decisions. As a consequence, they are often envied by the young, who are confident that they could do it better and are impatient to get into the saddle, and by the elderly, who are equally convinced that, given a second chance, they would surely improve on their own past record. Many people in middle age compensate for any physical and psychological slowing down with increased experience, superior judgment, improved frustration tolerance, humor, and the acquisition of wisdom. Hopefully, the senior executive or professional has learned to cut through red tape, to guard against unwelcome distractions, and to order priorities. When asked if they would like to be young again, most people in mid-life shudder at the thought. They may wish to feel and look young again to recapture their youthful vitality, but they do not usually wish to live their lives over, and they are unwilling to relinquish the advantages that rank, power, and experience have given them.

Bernice Neugarten (Figure 46.3), whom we have quoted repeatedly and to whose research and writings we owe much of our understanding of middle age, points out that time and timing are crucial factors in self-evaluation throughout life. At every stage of our life cycle, we compare ourselves with others of similar age to determine how well we are doing and whether or not we are keeping up with our contemporaries. "Leav-

Figure 46.3. Bernice L. Neugarten.

ing the parents' home, marriage, parenthood, occupational achievement, one's own children leaving home, the climacteric, grandparenthood, retirement—these are the normal turning points, the punctuation marks along the life line. They call forth changes in self-concept and identity, but whether or not they produce crises depends on their timing."* Most of us have ample opportunity to think about these events well in advance—to rehearse them ahead of time in our minds so that when we are actually confronted by them we feel prepared. In middle age, as at other times in life, it is the unexpected that causes the most distress. The premature death of a spouse, the lingering incapacity of a parent, debilitating illness in ourselves, the expected promotion that does not materialize, the unanticipated loss of a job, or the adult child who, instead of leaving home, remains dependent and is unable to find a place in life—these are the true stresses of middle age—the "mid-life crises" that may cause emotional or physical breakdown.

But even these unexpected crises do not have to be "bad" in their ultimate effect. In the same way that growth and development occur early in life by the mastery of various anxieties and conflicts, and by the successful transitions from one stage to the next, so also can psychological maturation continue until the very end of the life cycle. The basic process by which human growth and development takes place has not changed. It has simply been extended to include those added years of life which have become the heritage of a sizable percentage of the population. Within the total framework of the life cycle, the climacterium anticipates the later years. It is the time for a reintegration of the biological, the psychological, and the social components so that a new balance can be established. It is the essential prologue to successful old age, that final segment of the life cycle which will be discussed in the chapter which follows.

Suggested Readings

Butler RN, Lewis MI: *Aging and Mental Health: Positive Psychosocial and Biomedical Approaches*, ed 3. St. Louis, C.V. Mosby Co 1982.

Colarusso CA, Nemiroff RA: *Adult Development: A New Dimension in Psychodynamic Theory and Practice*. New York, Plenum Press, 1981.

---

* Time, age, and the life cycle. *Am J Psychiatry* 136:888, 1979.

Eichorn DA, et al: *Present and Past in Middle Life*. New York, Academic Press, 1981.

Erikson EH: Generativity vs. stagnation. In *Childhood and Society*. New York, W.W. Norton, 1950, p 231.

Erikson EH: Growth and crises of the healthy personality. In *Identity and the Life Cycle*. Psychological Issues, vol 1, no 1. New York, International Universities Press, 1959, p 97.

Gould R: *Transformations*. New York, Simon & Schuster, 1978.

Levinson DJ, et al: *The Seasons of a Man's Life*. New York, Alfred A. Knopf, 1978.

Lidz T: The middle years. In *The Person*. New York, Basic Books 1976, p 486.

Mandell AJ: *Coming of Middle Age: A Journey*. New York, Summit Books, 1977.

Neugarten BL (ed): *Middle Age and Aging: A Reader in Social Psychology*. Chicago, University of Chicago Press, 1968.

Neugarten BL: Dynamics of transition of middle age to old age: adaptation and the life cycle. *J Geriatr Psychiatry* 4:71, 1970.

Neugarten BL: Time, age, and the life cycle. *Am J Psychiatry* 136:887, 1979.

Vaillant GE: *Adaptation to Life* Boston, Little, Brown, and Co, 1977.

References

Antunes CMF, et al: Endometrial cancer and estrogen use: report of a large case-control study. *N Engl J Med* 300:9, 1979.

Bart PB, Grossman M: Menopause. In Notman MT, Nadelson CC (eds): *The Woman Patient. Vol. 1*. New York, Plenum Press, 1978, p 337.

Gutmann DG: Parenthood: a key to the comparative study of the life cycle. In Datan N, Ginsberg L (eds): *Life-Span Development Psychology*. New York, Academic Press, 1975.

Hospels A, Musaph H (eds): *Psychosomatics in Peri-Menopause*. Baltimore, University Park Press, 1979.

Hull R, Reubsaat HJ: *The Male Climacteric*. New York, Hawthorne Books, 1975.

Jaques E: Death and the mid-life crisis. *Int J Psychoanal* 46:502, 1965.

Lieberman GL: Children of the elderly as natural helpers: some demographic considerations. *Am J Community Psychol* 6:489, 1978.

Masters WH, Johnson VE: Sexual inadequacy in the aging male. In *Human Sexual Inadequacy*. Boston, Little, Brown, and Co, 1970, p 316.

Masters WH, Johnson VE: Sexual inadequacy in the aging female. In *Human Sexual Inadequacy*. Boston, Little, Brown, and Co, 1970, p 335.

Notman MT: Is there a male menopause? In Rose L (ed): *The Menopause Book*. New York, Hawthorn Books, 1977, p 130.

Notman MT: Midlife concerns of women: implications of menopause. In Nadelson CC, Notman MT (eds): *The Woman Patient. Vol 2*. New York, Plenum Press, 1982, p 135.

Perlmutter JF: A gynecological approach to menopause. In Notman MT, Nadelson CC (eds): *The Woman Patient. Vol 1*. New York, Plenum Press, 1978, p 323.

Report on Postmenopausal Estrogen Therapy. New York, The American Council on Science and Health, 1979.

Report on Postmenopausal Estrogen Therapy. Bethesda MD, National Institute on Aging and National Institutes of Health, 1979.

Rose L (ed): *The Menopause Book*. New York, Hawthorne Books, 1977.

Sheehy G: *Passages*. New York, E.P. Dutton, 1976.

Spierer H: Major transitions in the human life cycle. Academy for Educational Development, June 1977, p 38.

Stearns EL, et al: Declining testicular function with age-hormonal and clinical correlates. *Am J Med* 57:761, 1974.

Wittenberg CK: Estrogen widely prescribed for emotional ills. *Psychiatric News*, February 15, 1980.

CHAPTER 47 Later Adulthood and Old Age

George L. Mizner, M.D., Dorothy Strauss, Ph.D.,
and Richard C. Simons, M.D.

THE AGING OF AMERICA

On his 80th birthday, a well-known entertainer was asked how it felt to be old. He replied: "Great!—when you consider the alternative." At the beginning of this century that alternative, namely, death at an early age, was the rule. In 1900, average life expectancy at birth was less than 40 years, and the median age of the population when the first census was taken in 1790 was 16 years. An infant born today can expect to live for more than 70 years, and the median age of the population has moved up to 30 and will be 35 by the year 2000. Medical and social advances have not only increased longevity, but also have greatly improved the health of the population at large. The average age of persons entering nursing homes is now 80, as compared with 70 just a few years ago. This is a reflection of two trends: 1) better support services to enable the aged to continue independent living; and 2) an actual improvement in health and in the quality of life during the later years. Until recently, advances in maternal health care, child health care, and public health measures accounted for most of the increase in longevity. In the past 20 years, however, much of the increase in longevity has come about in people over 65.

This is the first century in which nearly everyone has the opportunity to grow old. Two hundred years ago, only 20% of the newborn babies made it into their 60's. Now 80% reach that age. To take a more recent example: in 1920, a 10 year old boy or girl had only a 40% chance of having two grandparents alive. Today his or her chance of having two living grandparents has nearly doubled to better than 75%.

In 1984 there were 26 million Americans over the age of 65—11.5% of the population, up from 9.9% in 1970. In 40 years' time, when many of the postwar baby boom generation will have reached retirement age, there will be almost twice as many older Americans. By the year 2020, at least 20% of the population will be over 65, and a disproportionate number of those are likely to be women. As recently as 1950, the life expectancy for men was greater than that for women. Today a newborn baby girl can expect to live eight years longer than a boy born on the same day, and a married woman is destined for an average of 10 years of widowhood. This gap in life expectancy between men and women continues to widen. It will be interesting to see if the greater prevalence of career women will reverse this trend.

This increased longevity is presumably what we have always wanted. It gives the majority of our population the opportunity to survive, to taste and experience every stage of life, and to enter old age in good physical health with some sense of dignity and fulfillment. What is true for the majority is unfortunately not the case for a sizable minority. It is important to remember that at least some of our elderly live at or below the poverty line, and that most pensions and Social Security payments fail to keep up with recent inflationary trends. Forecasts concerning future deficits in the Medicare system further threaten the financial security of our older population.

In 1948, more than 50% of men over age 65 were still in the work force. Today, less than 20% of men over 65 are working and, despite the preponderance of elderly widows, the percentage for women is even lower. Newer studies have shown that most people genuinely enjoy the freedom from responsibility, increased leisure, and opportunity to pursue their own interests that accompany retirement. Retirement does not have a uniformly deleterious effect upon physical or mental health, and some studies suggest that, once an initial period of anxiety of variable duration is over, the health and outlook of the retiree may actually improve. Thus, the years from 65 to 75, when not complicated by poverty, ill health, or loneliness, have, for an increasing number, come to be among the most pleasurable and rewarding of the entire life span.

Gerontology (the study of aging) and *geriatrics* (the care of the aged) are new disciplines. Even the words are new, having been coined early in this century. Professional societies in these fields were first established in the 1940's. But it has only been recently that their membership in the United States has comprised more than a handful of people, and it is also only within very recent years that the aging of America has been brought forcefully to the attention of politicians, physicians, and the general public. Senior citizens' groups and many individuals have been involved in this effort to sensitize us to old people and to the problems of aging in a society that has been traditionally youth-oriented. One of the most active in this effort has been Dr. Robert Butler, a psychiatrist and psychoanalyst, who was named as the first Director of the National Institute on Aging (Figure 47.1). This, the youngest of our National Health Institutes, was established by Congress in 1974 and became operative in 1976. Since then, the National In-

stitute on Aging has been active in promoting research on aging, in lobbying for the needs of the aged in Congress and before the public, and in combating the prejudices, the unflattering stereotyping, and the many myths about aging that Dr. Butler has come to term *ageism*. We shall now look at a number of these myths.

THE MYTH OF AGING AS A PATHOLOGICAL PROCESS

It is beyond the scope of this chapter to address the question of how the acceleration of the physiological aging process occurs or what triggers the faster ticking of the biological clock. There has been widespread biomedical and popular interest in hypotheses which attach major importance to one or a combination of such factors as: genetic programming, efficiency of the immune system, specific enzyme action upon body "pacemakers" such as the hypothalamus, inability of the organism to cope with an unfavorable environmental situation, poor nutrition, and numerous other conditions which alter each individual's chances for reaching the maximal limit of the human life span—itself an unknown quantity.

What we will address, however, is the tendency among professionals as well as the general public to regard the "elderly" as a homogeneous group. We overlook differences in levels of functioning, in background, in class and cultural values, in the degree of lifelong inner direction, and in the balance between deficits and assets— all of which must be assessed on an individual basis. Because the degree of success or failure with which previous developmental phases have been negotiated is critical for establishing the way in which the final years of life are to be experienced, there is even less justification for stereotyping the over 65 individual than someone at a younger age level.

To begin with, any assessment of psychological functioning requires that the previous life history and present environment be considered as well as the chronological age, which is the least reliable of all indices. Undesirable traits ascribed to the aging process may really be exaggerations of traits present all along in the individual's life history. We move through life not only in terms of the calendar, but also along biological, social, and psychological tracks, a perspective often lost when we consider the aged. This is probably due to the fact that the

Figure 47.1.   Robert N. Butler.

elderly who are sick are more in the public eye than their healthy counterparts. As a result, the myth has emerged that aging itself is a pathological process which reduces the organism to a state of physical and mental helplessness and dependence.

It is true that there are physical changes which are age-related, albeit not "old age" specific. There is loss of elasticity in the tissues, manifested most commonly as wrinkling of the skin. Hearing and visual deficits tend to become prominent. Postural changes may become more pronounced along with the "shrinking" phenomenon. However, empirically, there is an abundance of evidence which refutes any correlation between these physical changes and some fixed starting point in time. By identifying all of old age as a disease, we tend to underestimate the importance of diagnosis and treatment for the separate and specific disease processes which afflict aged individuals. Furthermore, many medical procedures and treatments which formerly were reserved for younger patients are now considered safe and appropriate for use in older age groups, and may result in a reduction of morbidity and an extension of many active and meaningful lives. Since aging is, itself, progressive, the quest for a "cure" is of less importance than the maintenance of an adequate level of function. With the greater availability of modern medical safeguards, the possible benefits from active treatment procedures generally outweigh the risks.

THE MYTH OF INEVITABLE DEMENTIA

It has been a popular assumption that if an individual lives long enough, dementia becomes inevitable because it was believed that the normal physiological decline of old age extends also to the brain. While the majority of healthy, elderly persons show some measurable cognitive decline, this is not sufficiently severe to warrant the term "dementia." Diminutions in rapid recall and the capacity for new learning are often balanced by improvements in judgment, expanded vocabulary, and other advantages of the increased life experience that comes with age.

In the area of intelligence and productivity, it is essential to remember that some individuals retain mental ability and creativity well into their advanced years without appreciable loss, while others, because of disuse, lack of motiva-

tion, or disease, suffer considerable loss. Intelligence is as much a matter of individual differences among the elderly as among individuals of any other age group, and, to date, there is no adequately supported evidence that documents the universality of steady intellectual decline among the aged.

There is evidence that the general efficiency of the sensory processes declines, due largely to decreases in visual and auditory functions. However, these decrements, consisting of neural and nonneural changes, affect the various sensory modalities differently, allowing for degrees of compensation. And, since adaptive ability is highly variable among individuals, such decrements should not be interpreted as precursors of a failing brain. In the absence of disease, the capacity for new learning is related to the basic level of intelligence, to the degree of motivation, and to the continued exercise of intellectual ability.

THE MYTH OF INEVITABLE PHYSICAL INCAPACITATION

In recent years, some basic research has been conducted on the biomedical and environmental factors that retard or accelerate the process we describe as aging. These research studies have been conducted at several centers in the United States. Of particular note is a longitudinal study in progress since 1955 at the Duke University Medical Center. Beginning with 271 persons aged 60 to 90, survivors have made themselves available for examination and testing throughout the years. A monograph published in 1970, which reported and analyzed the findings, concluded that, while there is a trend toward a general decline in physical function, there are also exceptions among the subjects. Some have even demonstrated improvement in certain physical functions, such as cardiopulmonary status, skin condition, circulation, and sexual activity. The inference is that an increased rate of physical incapacitation is neither inevitable nor uniformly irreversible.

A second longitudinal study, begun at Duke University Center in 1968, included 502 subjects at the outset. One of the conclusions based upon both research studies at Duke suggests that work satisfaction, particularly among men, is a remarkably reliable predictor of longevity, and that both men and women who perceive their roles in later years as useful live longer than those who do not (Figure 47.2). The interdependence between a sense of physical well-being and emotional health is never more critical than among the aged. Several studies which have focused upon populations over age 60 report that self-rated health was of greater significance to the individuals questioned than the judgments of either their physicians or their families. This should not be so surprising, since the awareness of diminishing physical resources can sometimes best be compensated for by subjective judgments which are hopeful and reassuring.

THE MYTH OF LOSS OF SEXUALITY

It is questionable whether any activity has a greater potential for both physical and psychological reassurance than sexuality. While frequency and intensity diminish with age in both men and women, research data, beginning with Kinsey and continuing with Masters and Johnson and the Duke University Center studies,

attest to a continued interest in sexual activity in individuals in their seventies, eighties, and even nineties. It is indeed a myth that sexuality is lost with aging. Certainly, for the aged, the psychological gratifications of sex have just as great an importance as the physical pleasures of lovemaking. There is the reassurance of still being a man or a woman, of sharing an intimate companionship, of having the capacity to meet another's deep, personal needs. In short, one remains a desired, hence meaningful, person.

Unfortunately, there are often physical and social obstacles in the way of relaxed sexual pleasure for the aged. Of these, the physical may be the more easily managed. In the case of rapid fatigability, fear of exertion, some level of disability, or other age-related impediments to relaxed sexual expression, an empathic doctor can readily supply whatever information and instruction will be helpful, provided the doctor is not too uncomfortable about talking to his or her elders concerning sex.

Social barriers to sexual expression among the

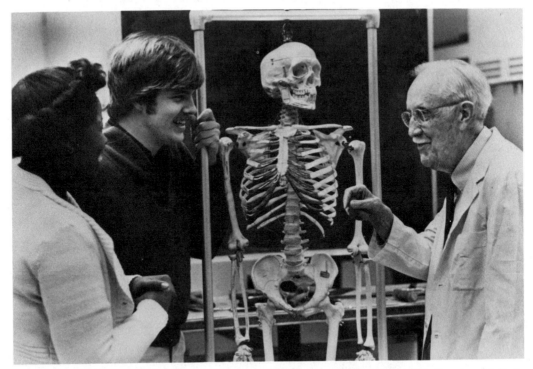

Figure 47.2.   Dr. Leslie B. Arey served as Chairman of the Department of Anatomy at Northwestern Medical School in Chicago, Illinois for 32 years, from 1924 to 1956, retiring at the age of 65. Here he is at the age of 94, working as a Laboratory Instructor in the same department, still teaching medical students—and making them laugh in the process. Even the skeleton seems to be enjoying the joke.

elderly are often more of a problem than physical ones. Loss of a partner through death creates a sexual void not easily filled. We still live in a time when sex between aged partners is regarded as somewhat grotesque, so that the elderly widow or widower may tend to suppress sexual interests for fear of appearing foolish. There are also economic problems which complicate later-life remarriages. A growing number of older men and women live together without legalizing their relationship, rather than suffer a reduction in financial benefits because of a change in marital status. Thus, we are confronted with the peculiar phenomenon of unconventional living among those who are probably least comfortable with an unconventional life style. Yet, the benefits of sharing an intimate relationship are often sufficient to override guilt feelings, family disapproval, or other negative reactions. Sexuality in the aged has been described by some as "regressive" since being cared for may be a more important goal than sexual pleasure. This attitude is highly questionable, since the component of caring and being cared for figures prominently at younger ages, too. When caring is absent, sexuality between people of any age becomes exploitative, mechanical, and impersonal. In young and old alike, to be able to feel sexual desire and to perform sexually are affirmations of being fully alive.

There are, of course, just as many neurotic reasons for seeking sexual alliances during the later years as during any other phase of life. As self-perceived deficits increase, so does vulnerability. One may then attempt to recapture one's youth by choosing a much younger partner. However, in situations where there is a marked differential between partners either in age or in health and vigor, the primary counseling responsibility is not to condemn but to insure that the mind does not make a contract that the body cannot fulfill.

The continuing need for male-female companionship has been well established by many studies. Sexual interest and activity during later life continue to be important to a vast majority of men and a smaller majority of women. This finding may be less a matter of inherent differences in sexual interest between men and women, and more the result of longevity differences which reduce the availability of male partners for older women. There is also much more cultural desexualization of the older female than of the older male. With the observed and projected growth of our older population, institutions and agencies which deal with the aged are increasingly obliged to recognize such prejudicial attitudes. It is particularly difficult for children to think of their parents as sexual beings. This difficulty often persists into adulthood, and results in middle-aged men and women being unable to accept their aging parents' continuing sexual needs. Attaching a negative connotation to sexual activity for the elderly may well impair both the physical and the mental health of these individuals.

THE MYTH OF SOCIAL WITHDRAWAL AND DISENGAGEMENT

There is an obvious inconsistency between according sexuality an important role in the maintenance of physical and psychic function in the elderly, and the concept that the older individual inevitably enters into a progressive process of social withdrawal and disengagement. This is another one of the myths of aging that needs to be reexamined.

It has been suggested by some authors that social withdrawal and disengagement from interaction with others are natural and inevitable consequences of growing older, independent of the attitude of the surrounding environment. While this may be true for some few older people, for many others, social withdrawal is clearly precipitated and accelerated by a rejecting and inhospitable environment. There are some societies and cultures which support the aged. Many do not. It would be quite incorrect to assume that victory over the environment can always be within reach of each of us as we move toward advanced age. One need only observe the general tendency toward rapid decline among the institutionalized aged to realize that more is required than willpower or determination. In our opinion, this precipitous and tragic decline may in some cases be due to the noxious conditions of institutionalization (which have been recently documented in public exposés of some geriatric facilities and nursing homes), and to the personal and cultural insult which removal from the mainstream of life imparts. These factors are beautifully depicted in the film *Peege* (Figure 47.3), in which a young man is able to establish a meaningful contact with his supposedly "senile" and "disengaged" grandmother who has been institutionalized for many years in a nursing home.

Figure 47.3. A young man talks to his grandmother in a nursing home. From the film *Peege.* (By permission of Phoenix Films Inc., 470 Park Avenue South, New York, N. Y. 10016.)

The human being is a social creature who exists within a network of interpersonal relationships. Even the narrowest reading of personality theory includes social and cultural input as necessary for the establishment of a subjective sense of identity. This is why adaptation to change within a familiar setting is often more effective and less stressful than in strange surroundings. This is especially true for the aged. Depending on the individual, either continued involvement and activity, or gradual change to a more contemplative, inward-directed mode, can both be healthy and appropriate ways of adjusting to the later years of life.

There is always the temptation to move from theory to actual examples of persons who continue to be highly involved in the affairs about them even though they have reached advanced age. We find them in the arts, the judiciary, the sciences, industry, and politics. Indeed, in government, "old soldiers" are remarkably resistant to fading away. The disadvantage of pointing to such lists is that it implies that only the most outstandingly high achievers are likely to be the ones who retain their capacity for social interaction with aging. Our experience has been that there are many elderly people who are not famous, and yet who have maintained an ability to function actively and generatively, and to assume nurturant and responsible roles. They are men and women who find it possible to develop either new interests beyond those of their earlier work and family-rearing years, or else show continued fidelity to earlier interests and activities (Figure 47.4). With the expansion of the older segment of our population, it is

Figure 47.4. Elizabeth Castellano, retired after 50 years of teaching in the New York City public school system, volunteers to help hospitalized children keep up with their school work. Photograph by Bob West. (Courtesy of Downstate Medical Center, Brooklyn.)

likely that the opportunities for satisfying social interaction among the elderly will increase, not merely because there will be more older persons to interact with each other but because our society will come to attach less social stigma and devaluation to its older members.

EGO INTEGRITY VS. DESPAIR

To go on living requires ways of adapting to losses and separations, especially since these are expected to occur more frequently in the later years of life. Bernice Neugarten has suggested that separations and losses may have constructive as well as destructive potentials, and that continued growth as well as pathology is a possibility for older individuals. This concept of continued growth and development throughout the life cycle has been particularly stressed by Erik Erikson. He calls his last stage of psychosocial development *ego integrity*, and contrasts it with the *despair* that is felt by those who fail to achieve a final integration of their lives. By ego integrity, Erikson means "the acceptance of one's one and only life cycle as something that had to be and that, by necessity, permitted of no substitutions." It means making peace with one's parents and with oneself, and taking responsibility for how one's life has turned out. Failing this, the individual is subject to despair, disgust, or a chronic, contemptuous displeasure with others which serves to mask an underlying self-contempt and fear of death.

As we have already indicated, earlier assumptions about the inevitability of serious mental impairment, ranging from pathetic forgetfulness through confusional states to a final subhuman, vegetative end, have come to be recognized as misconceptions. However, the stress of life events (particularly repeated losses), in combination with the physical changes of aging, can render an aged person particularly vulnerable to emotional breakdown. We will discuss some of the psychopathology of aging shortly, but it is worth noting now that the judicious and prompt use of psychotherapy may be extremely helpful in returning an anxious or depressed older person to a healthier level of coping, and should not be neglected for reasons having to do with age alone. Depression and despair are not inevitable consequences of aging.

PSYCHOPATHOLOGY IN THE LATER YEARS

Only 5% of people over age 65 are confined to nursing homes, but that percentage rises rapidly after age 75. Over one-half of America's elderly live with their spouses in independent households. One-quarter live alone, often in housing projects specifically designed for the elderly, and only 15% live with their children. However, approximately 80% of the elderly are in direct contact with some family member each week, and are by no means deserted or abandoned. Most stay in communities where they have roots—partly by choice, partly because they cannot afford to move. Only a minority head for Leisure World, Sun City, and other retirement communities. In the older population at large (those over 65 living both in and outside of institutions) it is estimated that about 15% suffer from some significant mental disorder, either psychogenic or organic. The split between the two is about half and half, with a shift towards organic brain disease in the over age 75 segment of the population.

Chronic Organic Mental Disorder

There is an entire chapter devoted to the organic mental disorders later in the book, but it is important for us to note here that even among physicians, there has been a great deal of confusion about the causes, symptoms, course, and even the diagnosis of these conditions. For example, we diagnose *chronic organic mental disorder* (or *dementia*) almost twice as frequently in this country as in other English-speaking countries (Great Britain, Canada) where gerontology and geriatric medicine are more advanced. This is not because there is more chronic organic mental disorder in the United States, but because we tend to overlook treatable causes of *acute organic mental disorder* (or *delirium*) and treatable functional psychiatric disorders which are misdiagnosed as being due to "senility." Because of the myths about aging which we have just discussed, there is an unwarranted attitude of hopelessness and therapeutic nihilism which encourages inaccurate diagnosis, resulting in less active treatment than is possible and desirable.

It used to be thought that most cases of the chronic organic mental disorder known as *senile dementia* were due to arteriosclerosis of the brain ("hardening of the arteries"). We now think that the clinical diagnosis of arteriosclerotic dementia is only justified when there is evidence of multiple strokes producing sudden exacerbations in the dementing process (*multi-infarct dementia*) as opposed to the relatively smooth decline found in most cases of dementia. Neuropathologists are finding that only 15% to 20% of senile dementia is due to cerebrocirculatory problems; by far, the more common cause is neuronal degeneration leading to cerebral atrophy. Useful clinical distinctions between the so-called *presenile dementias* (Alzheimer's disease, Pick's disease) and senile dementia cannot be drawn except on the arbitrary criterion of age. They are all characterized by cerebral atrophy for which there is no established etiology. The current tendency is to move away from the terms presenile and senile dementia, and to refer to all of these conditions as *Alzheimer's disease*. This is the disease which so many people dread and which is so devastating to the sufferer and to his or her family. It is estimated that over two million people in the United States suffer from Alzheimer's disease, which afflicts one out of every 20 individuals between the ages of 65 and 75, and one out of every five over the age of 80. It is the fourth most common cause of death in this country, and is responsible for over 50% of all nursing home admissions. The annual cost of caring for the victims of this disease is estimated to be in the billions of dollars.

Alzheimer's Disease

Early symptoms of Alzheimer's disease (phase I, the "forgetfulness phase") involve a tendency toward forgetfulness. The individual has difficulty remembering names, places, appointments, and may need to write things down in order to remember them. The cognitive deficit is primarily subjective, and may lead to an increase in anxiety. With progression of the disease (phase II, the "confusional phase") there is a definite and observable impairment of cognitive functioning particularly in regard to memory of recent events. The earlier anxiety may now be replaced by denial. Eventually (phase III, the "dementia phase") the individual becomes severely disoriented with impairment of remote memory for past events as well as recent memory. The capacity for abstract thinking is decreased, and thought processes become more concrete and impoverished. Routine activities are initially well carried out, but anything that requires new learning or understanding becomes very difficult. This is why travel, a change of residence, or transfer to a hospital or nursing home—all of them unfamiliar environments—often seem to cause an acute exacerbation of symptomatology. The patient may become severely confused, agitated, and sometimes paranoid. Emotionally, people suffering from Alzheimer's disease may become depressed, gloomy, and withdrawn, with feelings of inadequacy and hopelessness. Less often, we see a mild euphoria in which patients seem oblivious to their cognitive deficits. Either way, with progression of the disease, apathy becomes the predominant affect.

Personality changes in Alzheimer's disease tend to be characterized either by an exaggeration of premorbid traits (such as cautiousness, rigidity, or miserliness) or a breakthrough of previously inhibited traits (such as aggressiveness, boastfulness, or slovenliness). Neurological changes are also common, including aphasias, agnosias, apraxias, extrapyramidal signs,

and a return of primitive reflexes. On postmortem examination of the brain, we often (but not invariably) see a reduction of weight with shrunken gyri and widened sulci due to cortical atrophy. The ventricles tend to be enlarged. Microscopically, *senile plaques* (also called *neuritic plaques*) are the most typical finding. *Neurofibrillary tangles* and *granulovacuolar bodies* are also found. None of these changes are exclusive to Alzheimer's disease and may be found to a lesser degree in the normally aging brain.

Hypotheses in regard to the etiology of Alzheimer's disease include: 1) a viral etiology, particularly the slow virus diseases; 2) a toxic agent, possibly aluminum; 3) a defect in the immune system; and 4) genetic inheritance, possibly through trisomy 21, the same chromosome responsible for Down's syndrome. Much current research is focusing on the biochemical changes that accompany Alzheimer's disease. With age, we all undergo some reduction of choline acetyltransferase and acetylcholinesterase (two enzymes involved in the production of the neurotransmitter acetylcholine). However, a number of investigators have reported massive reduction of these two enzymes in the brains of patients with Alzheimer's disease. Choline and acetylcholine have been found to be necessary for normal memory, and it is possible that a disturbance in the cholinergic neurotransmitter system is responsible for the memory impairment seen in Alzheimer's disease. There are now a number of promising studies underway with various drugs that increase the formation of acetylcholine, decrease its destruction, or directly stimulate acetylcholine receptors in the brain. Some of these drugs appear to improve memory, and the so-called cerebral metabolic enhancers (such as the ergot alkaloids) may exert similar effects. Whatever the etiology of Alzheimer's disease, ultimately it may be necessary to correct multiple, interacting neurochemical dysfunctions in the brain in order to reverse the memory and other cognitive defects of this illness. Despite the greatly increased interest in and research on Alzheimer's disease, much more work needs to be done before we can hope to treat it successfully or prevent its occurrence.

Acute Organic Mental Disorder

Acute organic mental disorders are discussed in more detail in a subsequent chapter. Suffice it to say that there are traumatic, infectious, metabolic, nutritional, and iatrogenic causes of acute brain syndrome in the elderly. Infections may occur without fever or leukocytosis, and heart attacks may be accompanied by very little pain, but both of these can cause sudden cognitive impairment and an acute organic mental disorder which may mistakenly be assumed to be chronic in nature. The same is true for congestive heart failure and hypothyroidism. *Normal pressure hydrocephalus* presents with the triad of urinary incontinence, mild dementia, and a typical CT scan showing enlargement of the lateral ventricles with little cortical atrophy. Surgical shunting procedures are frequently successful in eliminating the dementia and the incontinence.

Depression

The number of psychogenic and so-called functional psychiatric disorders with which one has to be concerned in old age is really quite small. *Depression* is by all odds the most common and the most serious. Then comes *hypochondriasis*, followed by *paranoid disorders*, *anxiety disorders*, and *sleep disturbances.* Two psychiatric disorders that are frequently found in old age but that have their onset in earlier life are *alcoholism* and *schizophrenia.* In this chapter, we shall only discuss depression and sleep disturbances.

It is important to distinguish grief from depression in old people. There are many reasons for grief among the elderly, since the losses and relinquishments of old age are many and often overwhelming. Furthermore, the recuperative capacities may be so depleted in the elderly that prolonged grieving may be difficult to differentiate from depression. It is important to remember that both the grief reactions and the depressions are treatable.

Suicide, always a risk in depression, becomes an even greater danger in old age. Nearly one-third of all successful suicides occur among the elderly. This figure is higher still for men and is highest of all for single or widowed white men, living alone without adequate support systems. According to Dr. Jack Weinberg, the losses that lead to depression and suicide are not only losses of friends and relatives, prestige and position, money and material things, but also of some form of mastery in many areas. This is the reason why some elderly may refuse to wear glasses or hearing aids. To do so is to admit failing capacities and to relinquish mastery in areas where their previous functioning had been adequate. The more they lose, the more the elderly will want to hold on to physical objects and mementoes. Quite normally, they surround themselves with pictures and other reminders of people and places that once were meaningful and that now may be lost to them.

Even older people who have constant caretaking are likely to complain of always being alone. Such complaints do not necessarily indicate senile distortion but rather a perceived isolation from significant personal contacts. When such complaints are made to family members, they may represent a way of saying that the relative who is being addressed holds an irreplacable position in the psychic life and well-being of the older person, who is pleading not to be abandoned.

One of the characteristics of depression in the elderly is that it lacks the guilt-ridden, self-accusatory quality that tends to characterize depressions earlier in life. What we see instead is depression which is associated with feelings of loss, helplessness, hopelessness, inadequacy, and inferiority. Loss of interest in people and activities is common, as are somatic complaints such as weakness and fatigue. Atypically, depression may present itself as a *pseudodementia* with the psychomotor retardation being so severe that the patient gives the appearance of being demented. In the elderly, poor nutrition and self-neglect as well as sleep disturbances are frequently seen as symptoms of depression. A history of unwarranted and premature retirement as well as unwarranted changes of residence and living conditions should also serve to alert the physician to the possibility of an underlying depression.

The psychotherapy of these conditions requires the capacity to empathize accurately with what the older person has lost and what he or she is feeling, to listen attentively and without impatience even if the complaints are repetitive, and to offer oneself as a caring link into the present and the future (Figure 47.5). The very fact that the health professional cares enough to be concerned, to listen, and to want to help, indicates to the patient that he or she is not as alone, forgotten, and hopeless as had been thought. The relationship with the physician

Figure 47.5. A physician and his elderly patient. (Reproduced with permission from *The Geriatric Patient,* William Reichel, M.D. and Mal Schechter, eds., HP Publishing Co., Inc., New York, New York, 1978. Photograph by Frank B. Ritter.)

can serve as a stepping stone to other relationships which can then replace those that have been lost. Some physical contact, the laying on of hands, which many physicians have largely abandoned, may also be particularly important and helpful with the elderly. It is our impression that many old people die or develop symptoms of senility before their time because they have lost the people who were most important to them and have been unable to replace them with new relationships. Without someone to care or to care for, we are lost, and there seems to be no point to survival. We all depend for our emotional well-being on having something useful to do, something to hope for, and someone to love. If in old age we lose all three, what reason is there to go on living?

Psychotherapy and drugs usually work better in combination than either treatment modality by itself. The tricyclics are the drugs of choice in unipolar depressions accompanied by the classical signs. It is probably also worth trying them, however, when symptoms of depression are less clearcut and less typical. It is important to remember that the tricyclics are potent anticholinergics, and the aggravation of cardiac and other conditions are common side effects. It is necessary therefore to start with lower doses and to work up gradually to a therapeutically effective dose. The problems and risks of using tricyclics in the elderly are such that many psychiatrists feel that hospitalization and a thor-

ough medical work-up are prerequisites for initiating this form of treatment. The obtaining of drug blood levels may also be useful where these assays are available. Before prescribing any drugs in an elderly patient, it is important to remember that there is a greatly increased incidence of physical illness in this age group. Frequently, the patient is taking other drugs for other illnesses, and therefore the likelihood of undesirable drug interactions increases greatly.

We noted at the beginning of this chapter that the elderly comprise 11% of our population. But this 11% accounts for 25% of all prescriptions written, 50% of all health care dollars spent by the federal government, and 70% of all acute hospital beds. Yet, despite this attention to their health care needs, mismedication and overmedication are two of the most serious hazards that the elderly face. Since aging leads to slower absorption, metabolism, and secretion of drugs, a normal adult dose of any medication may be dangerously high and possibly even lethal for an elderly person. It is therefore essential that all physicians carefully monitor and individualize the medications that they prescribe to their elderly patients, and remain current in their knowledge about how the interactions and the side effects of these drugs may affect the increased mental and physical vulnerability of the aged.

Sleep Disturbances

The only other functional disturbance to be discussed in this chapter has to do with the difficulty that older people often have in sleeping. Anxiety states and depressions are frequently the cause of disturbed sleep patterns. What is not so well-known to physicians and laymen alike is that the normal sleep pattern of the elderly is drastically different from the normal sleep pattern of the younger adult. Old people have reduced stage 3 and stage 4 sleep. They awaken easily and usually can go back to sleep fairly easily as well. Several awakenings during the night occur normally in the healthy older person. Additionally, one or more brief naps during the day are normal and decrease the need for nighttime sleep. The overall sleep requirement of the elderly is as great or greater than it was in earlier life, but periods of wakefulness during the night are not uncommon, especially if there have been several naps during the day. Under these circumstances, it makes very little sense to worry about sleeplessness. Many elderly people like to get up during the night, take a small snack, and read for an hour or two before going back to bed. It is important to be aware of these normal sleep patterns in the elderly so that the physician does not become stampeded into prescribing a variety of hypnotics which rapidly lose their effectiveness, frequently keep the elderly person in a perpetual state of mild delirium, and may even push an already impaired brain over the edge into dementia.

DETERMINANTS OF LONGEVITY

We have emphasized that people are living longer than they used to, but we have said little as yet about the factors that contribute to longevity. Heredity is clearly of importance. If our parents and grandparents lived to a ripe old age, our statistical chance of being long-lived is greatly improved. Similarly, an absence of hereditable diseases in the family increases the likelihood of our longevity. A predisposition to heart attacks, strokes, hypertension, diabetes, thyroid disorders, chronic lung disease, certain cancers, and some allergic diseases is present in some families.

Diet and lifestyle are also significant. It seems important not to be grossly overweight, and it is probably wise to eat red meat, animal fat, and other sources of cholesterol in very moderate quantities. The relationship between smoking and lung cancer, chronic lung disease, and increased mortality has become more firmly established. Lung function in smokers is comparable to lung function in nonsmokers who are approximately 10 years older. The more one smokes, the more profound are the adverse effects, but with the cessation of smoking, normalization of lung function becomes possible. Interestingly enough, moderate drinkers (one to two drinks per day) live longer than those who do not drink at all. The reason for this is not clear and may have more to do with personality differences between drinkers and nondrinkers than with the inherently beneficial effects of small doses of alcohol. Heavy drinkers show vastly increased morbidity and mortality rates.

Moderate exercise seems to be beneficial and probably increases longevity. Regular vigorous exercise is possibly even better although this is as yet not certain, but sporadic, vigorous exercise in an otherwise sedentary individual is dangerous. A corollary of this is that people whose work involves physical activity (provided that the activity is not dangerous) live longer than those whose work is sedentary. Another interesting finding is that people who sleep a great deal (nine or more hours per night) have a shortened life expectancy. Once again, the reasons for this finding are not clear. It may relate to insufficient physical activity, or it may be that physical or psychological illnesses are the cause of both the prolonged sleep and the increased mortality. Sleeping six or less hours per night also appears to be related to decreased life expectancy.

Regular breast examinations and pap smears for women over 30, and proctoscopic examinations for men over 40, are related to improved life expectancy, presumably because of earlier cancer detection. There is also a positive correlation between years of schooling and longevity—probably not because education in itself enables one to live longer but because it is associated with a higher income level and thus greater access to good health care. This finding is true except at the highest levels of earned income where one sees a drop in life expectancy. The reasons for this drop are not clear. The stresses and pollution common to urban living also seem to take their toll, because city people do not live as long as their country counterparts despite the fact that the latter have less access to good health care.

Other lifestyle factors also appear significant in the mortality tables. People who are married live longer than those who are single, divorced, or widowed. The latter groups are more prone to depression and suicide than the married, and they also die from physical illnesses at a greater rate. People who have friends and strong social support systems live longer than those who do not. Work appears to be conducive to good health as we noted earlier. People who retire early do not live as long as those who remain occupationally active. Alternatively, those who are in poor health, physically or emotionally, may be the ones who retire early. Calm, relaxed Type B personalities live longer than the more intense, aggressive, and competitive Type A personalities. Finally, it seems that happiness contributes to longevity. People who are content live longer than those who are worried, tense, and guilty.

CONCLUSION

Perhaps the single most important fact to be recognized about aging is that it belongs within the normal life span of the healthy human being. Aging itself cannot be equated with disease. While some diminished functioning in various areas is characteristic, there is neither a predetermined order nor consistency to these changes. Both individual differences and environmental factors affect the rate and nature of biological, psychological, and social aging.

Every culture develops its own stereotypes of the aged. We have certainly not escaped the negative results of this process. We seem inclined to remove older individuals from the work force, often prematurely. The family networks to which they belong frequently wish to make them as invisible as possible. Sexuality among the elderly is rejected out of hand. Long before the healthy aged man or woman arrives at the

> . . . last scene of all
> That ends this strange eventful history*

he or she is at risk of being dismissed as unnecessary. Wisdom, compassion, and foresight urge a dramatic revision of these attitudes. As Robert Butler and others have pointed out: The aged are our future selves. If we continue to have discriminatory attitudes towards the aged, we ourselves are likely to become the victims of those prejudices.

Suggested Readings

Busse EW, Pfeiffer E (eds): *Behavior and Adaptation in Late Life*. Boston, Little, Brown, and Co, 1969.

Busse EW, Pfeiffer E: *Mental Illness in Later Life*. Washington, DC, American Psychiatric Association, 1973.

Butler RN: *Why Survive? Being Old In America*. New York, Harper & Row, 1975.

Butler RN, Lewis MI: *Aging and Mental Health: Positive Psychosocial and Biomedical Approaches*, ed, 3. St. Louis, C.V. Mosby Co, 1982.

Colarusso CA, Nemiroff RA: *Adult Development: A New Dimension in Psychodynamic Theory and Practice*. New York, Plenum Press, 1981.

---

* Shakespeare, *As You Like It*, Act II, Scene 7.

Erikson E: Ego integrity vs. despair. In *Childhood and Society*. New York, W.W. Norton, 1950, p 231.

Kaplan HS: The effects of age on sexuality. In *The New Sex Therapy*. New York, Brunner/Mazel, 1974, p 104.

Kimmel DC: Biological and intellectual aspects of aging. In *Adulthood and Aging: An Interdisciplinary, Developmental View*. New York, John Wiley & Sons, 1974, p 343.

Lidz T: Old age. In *The Person*. New York, Basic Books, 1976, p 511.

Mendelson MA: *Tender Loving Greed*. New York, Alfred A Knopf, 1974.

Miller E: *Abnormal Aging: The Psychology of Senile and Presenile Dementia*. New York, John Wiley & Sons, 1977.

Neugarten BL (ed): *Middle Age and Aging: A Reader in Social Psychology*. Chicago, University of Chicago Press, 1968.

Palmore E (ed): *Normal Aging: Reports From the Duke Longitudinal Study, 1955–1969*. Durham, NC, Duke University Press, 1970.

Pfeiffer E: Sexuality and the aging patient. In Green R (ed): *Human Sexuality: A Health Practitioners' Text*, ed 2. Baltimore, Williams & Wilkins, 1979, p 124.

Reichel W (ed): *The Geriatric Patient*. New York, H.P. Publishing, 1978.

Schneck MK, Reisberg B, Ferris SH: An overview of current concepts of Alzheimer's disease. *Am J Psychiatry* 139:165, 1982.

Thompson TL, Moran MG, Nies AS: Psychotropic drug use in the elderly. *N Eng J Med* 308:134 and 194, 1983.

Usdin G, Hofling CK (eds): *Aging: The Process and the People*. New York, Brunner/Mazel, 1978.

References

Berezin MA: Psychodynamic considerations of aging and the aged: an overview. *Am J Psychiatry* 128:1483, 1972.

Berkman LF, Breslow L: *Health and Ways of Living: The Alameda County Study*. New York, Oxford University Press, 1983.

Binstock RH, Shanas S (eds): *Handbook of Aging and the Social Sciences*. New York, Van Nostrand Reinhold, 1976.

Birren JE, Schaie KW (eds): *Handbook of The Psychology of Aging*. New York, Van Nostrand Reinhold, 1977.

Cumming E, et al: Disengagement—a tentative theory of aging. *Sociometry* 23:23, 1960.

Eisdorfer C, Lawton MP, *The Psychology of Adult Development and Aging*. Washington, DC, American Psychological Association, 1973.

Finch CE, Hayflick L (eds): *Handbook of The Biology of Aging*. New York, Van Nostrand Reinhold, 1977.

Grinspoon L (ed): Geriatric psychiatry. In *Psychiatry 1983: Annual Review II*. Washington, DC, American Psychiatric Press, 1983, p 169.

Howells JG (ed): *Modern Perspectives in the Psychiatry of Old Age*. New York, Brunner/Mazel, 1975.

McKinsey ME: Interdisciplinary research in the service of the aged. *Geriatrics* 30:112, 1975.

Nicholas CR, Busse EW: Some aspects of mental health and illness in the aged. *North Carolina Med J* 19:352, 1958.

Sternschein I: The experience of separation-individuation in infancy and its reverberations through the course of life: maturity, senescence and sociological implications. *J Am Psychoanal Assoc* 21:633, 1973.

Strauss D: Relationship between perception of the environment and the retrenchment syndrome. New York University, 1963. Unpublished doctoral dissertation.

Zinberg NE, Kaufman I (eds): *Normal Psychology of the Aging Process* New York, International Universities Press, 1963.

CHAPTER **48 Loss, Grief, and Mourning in Adults**

Carl T. Wolff, M.D. and
Richard C. Simons, M.D.

Parting is all we know of heaven,
And all we need of hell.

Emily Dickinson

THE UBIQUITY OF LOSS

Loss takes many forms in our lives. There are *real losses,* in which there is the actual loss of a specific person who is of significance to us. There are also *threatened losses* in which one has to deal with the impending loss of an important person. And, uniquely in human beings, there are *symbolic losses.* One can lose not simply a person, but a belief or an ideal or a way of life or a country (Figure 48.1). There are also *fan-*

Figure 48.1. A Frenchman weeps at the fall of France. Marseilles, February 1941. (By permission of Movietone News.)

tasied losses, in which individuals react to an event as if it were a loss when there is no apparent reason to believe that it represents an actual loss for the person. Drs. Simons, Rubinstein, and Franks will be talking further about these various kinds of losses later in their chapter on depression.

In the book thus far, we have talked about the development of the human being from birth through adulthood, and we have seen how each new developmental stage involves some kind of loss and separation — the infant's loss of oneness with the mother, the toddler's loss of the mother as a constant figure, the oedipal child's loss of the parents as sexual objects, the adolescent's loss of the parents as caretakers, the middle-aged and aging person's loss of youth and physical strength. Indeed, all of the life cycle can be conceptualized as variations on the theme of separation and individuation.

In addition to these sequential losses inherent in growth and development, there are losses that are less predictable. The most irrevocable such loss, of course, is the death of a significant person. But one can also experience a permanent loss through divorce, or any other kind of separation in which the individual does not return. Sometimes a person may react to a change in the status of the loved one. A wife whose husband suddenly becomes preoccupied and involved in his work may react to the loss of his affection or his emotional investment in her, and go through a kind of mourning.

Another major kind of loss for any individual involves physical illness. Certainly, such events as amputations, or any operations that result in the loss of body parts, are a very major kind of loss for all of us. One can also experience a loss if there is impaired functioning of any part of the body, or even a change in overall functioning such as sometimes occurs during the climacter-

498

ium. Any organic illness involves some loss in one's healthy functioning. This is especially true if the illness is a chronic one, where the cure may also involve a loss. For example, individuals with rheumatic heart disease may have adapted to a restricted life of semi-invalidism. Then, with the advent of cardiac surgery, and the opportunity it provides for a normal life, the individual may actually go through a process of mourning the loss of his previously restricted adaptation. Even though he is healthy again and is now able to truly enjoy life, he still has to adjust to giving up his old way of relating to people, and this may involve a very difficult transition. As Byron says in his poem, *The Prisoner of Chillon:*

> My very chains and I grew friends
> So much a long communion tends
> To make us what we are: — even I
> Regained my freedom with a sigh.

There are other kinds of more distant losses that can provoke a bereavement reaction — the loss of status; the loss of membership in a group; even the loss of a social institution or of an institutional figure. Remember the country's grief over the assassination of President John F. Kennedy. We did not know him personally, yet we felt his loss acutely (Figure 48.2). Other such losses may include the loss of a home, the loss of a job, the loss of one's possessions. We have seen a good deal of bereavement in individuals who, for example, have been subjected to urban redevelopment, and who have had to give up not only their homes in being moved to another part of the city, but sometimes their very way of life. Another potential loss to keep in mind involves pets. There are many isolated and withdrawn individuals whose major relationship in life is to an animal, and the loss of this pet may provoke an intense grief reaction.

GRIEF AND MOURNING

The response to loss has been called *mourning* or *bereavement* or *grief*. For the sake of clarity, we are going to term the entire process mourning or bereavement, and restrict the term grief to the specific affective or emotional manifestations of this mourning process.

Bereavement or mourning is a normal phenomenon — normal in the sense that it is a necessary part of the response to loss. If one looks carefully at individuals who go through this process of mourning, it becomes clear that

Figure 48.2. Young black boy holding a candle and crying at President John F. Kennedy's funeral. Photograph by Enrico Sarsini. (By permission of Time-Life Picture Agency, Copyright Time Inc.)

grief work has a function, and that its function is to free the individual from some of the ties to the lost person. The man who grieves and mourns for his wife who has died, must do so before he can be free to begin new activities and to form new relationships. This is clearly a very difficult task, one that is very painful but also one that is very necessary. In this sense, if one looks through a wider biological telescope, we can see that mourning also occurs in many higher animals. In animals that form attachments to other animals, especially primates and domesticated animals, a response very similar to bereavement in human beings can be observed, as Dr. Rosenblum has discussed earlier in his chapter on ethology.

As we discuss the usual course of mourning, it is important to keep in mind that there is a wide range of variability in the normal mourning process. There are wide oscillations in mood and in behavior, and there may be differences from one day to the next. Of course, the degree of mourning depends on the nature of the relationship, not only how intense it was and how meaningful the person was who died, but also on how much ambivalence there may have been towards the person. It depends on the circumstances of the loss as well — a sudden loss (Figure 48.3) may provoke a much more intense response than an expected one that comes after a long period of waiting (Figure 48.4).

Dr. Dubovsky has already cited George Engel's work on sudden death in response to situations involving loss, and Dr. Levy has described the more protracted "giving-up-given-up complex" as a reaction to loss and feelings of helplessness and hopelessness. As one poignant example of a fatal reaction to a sudden loss, Dr. Charles H. Best, the codiscoverer of insulin with Dr. Frederick Banting, died in 1978 at the age of 79. He was stricken with a ruptured blood vessel in his abdomen immediately after hearing that his 46 year old son had died of a heart attack.

In fact, the reaction of most parents of any age to the loss of a child is usually more intense and prolonged than that of adults who lose another adult. It has been estimated that over 75% of the marriages of those parents who have lost a child become dysfunctional for varying periods of time, and many end in divorce. There is a high rate of alcoholism, depression, suicide attempts, and sexual difficulties in surviving parents. And surviving siblings not only feel guilty over still being alive, but they also take their parents' anguish as proof that the dead brother or sister had been the best loved. Mourning also varies from culture to culture. The extent to which a culture either facilitates or inhibits the expression of the mourning process

Figure 48.3. *Killed in Action* (1921) by Käthe Kollwitz. (By permission of Philadelphia Museum of Art: The Print Club Permanent Collection.)

Figure 48.4. *Anguish — The Dead Child* by Käthe Kollwitz. (Courtesy of Lloyd and Sue Joshel, Denver, Colorado. Photograph by Judith K. Thorpe.)

will alter the response that one sees in various people.

THE PHASE OF PROTEST

Mourning can be conveniently divided into three phases. The first phase is called the *phase of protest*. It is characterized by very frantic attempts on the part of the bereaved individual either to maintain the relationship with the lost person or to recover it. What form does this protest take? The first reaction is usually one of numbed disbelief and denial. The individual may say, "No, I don't believe it. It has not happened." This kind of protest can be intense and prolonged, or it may be only momentary. This is an important clinical point.

In this first phase, one will sometimes see people who simply cannot accept or in any way tolerate the idea that the person is dead, and they will continue to behave as if nothing has happened. "It isn't so. It can't have happened. I just don't believe it." A related form that the protest sometimes takes is what people refer to

as "shock," in which there seems to be a total dulling of all senses. This is seen in the person who says, "I was stunned, shocked. I felt nothing. I saw nothing. I heard nothing. I was in a trance." Such a blocking out of the entire world during this very early phase of protest really represents a sort of massive defense against any acknowledgment of the loss.

Emily Dickinson describes this state of shock beautifully:

> There is a pain — so utter —
> It swallows substance up —
> Then covers the Abyss with Trance —
> So Memory can step
> Around — across — upon it —
> As one within a Swoon —
> Goes safely — where an open eye —
> Would drop Him — Bone by Bone.*

---

* From *The Complete Poems of Emily Dickinson,* edited by Thomas H. Johnson. Copyright © 1929 by Martha Dickinson Bianchi. Copyright © 1957 by Mary L. Hampson. (Reprinted by permission of Little, Brown, and Co.)

At the same time, one may see another kind of behavior that indicates some awareness of the loss but in a very unrealistic way. Someone has died, but there is still a strong urge to recover the lost person. At the bedside of her dead husband, his wife may shake him and say, "No, come back. Wake up. Don't leave me now." In other words, there is a very strong attempt to bring the dead person back to life in spite of the knowledge that he is dead and will not return.

Weeping may represent both a protest and an attempt to recover the lost person. If one thinks about children who are separated from their mothers, the first thing they do is to weep. One function of the weeping is to alert the world to the loss, and in most instances, the weeping brings some attention and may even bring back the mother. An adult may also weep in order to try to get the love object to return. At the same time, one very often sees, in this early phase of the bereavement reaction, considerable anger and hostility. This may be directed at various people. Very often the bereaved person will turn to the doctor and say, "You didn't save him. You didn't do what you should have done. You could have done more." This is also true for complaints against oneself. "If I had only been there. If I had only done something or other. Perhaps I could even make it different right now." And similarly, the reaction to the dead person may be an angry one. "How can you do this to me? You just shouldn't have done it. I needed you. How could you leave me at this point in my life? You should come back."

THE PHASE OF DISORGANIZATION

The phase of protest may last only minutes; it may last days; it may last weeks or months. But gradually it gives way to the second phase which has been called the *phase of disorganization,* or the phase of developing awareness of the loss. Erich Lindemann was the first to systematically describe the symptoms of this phase following his work with the survivors and the bereaved relatives of the 500 victims of the terrible Cocoanut Grove Fire in Boston in 1942.

Characteristic of this phase is the growing realization that the loved person is gone. Emotions during this phase are intensely painful. The affect is primarily one of sadness, with a deep yearning for the lost loved one. The person may also be experiencing anger and guilt, but the predominant affect seems to be one of profound sadness. At such a time, when a person experiences this kind of grief, the world seems a very poor, empty, and meaningless place. But in contrast to someone with a true clinical depression, the grieving person's self-esteem is still intact. This is very important clinically. If one talks to a person in mourning, he will say that although the world seems impoverished and meaningless, he himself still feels that he is worthwhile and of value. He does not think of himself as evil or bad or worthless, as someone who is suffering from a depressive illness is very likely to do.

Along with the grief may come various somatic symptoms such as digestive disturbances, an empty feeling in the stomach, loss of appetite, tightness in the throat, choking sensations, deep sighing respirations and, characteristically, a feeling of weakness, lack of energy, and physical exhaustion. These symptoms are often evoked by memories of the dead person, by reminders in the external world, by friends who may make comments. Most people find these symptoms so intensely painful that they try to avoid looking at any reminders of the dead person, but rarely are they successful.

Another aspect of this phase of a developing awareness of the loss is a sense of unreality, a kind of withdrawal from the world. People at this time become introverted; they do not seem to want relationships. Their other relationships may lack their usual spontaneity and warmth.

Grieving people are often irritable, and may feel a good deal of guilt and a good deal of anger towards other individuals. One will often see individuals react with hostility to friends and acquaintances and relatives who come and offer their sympathies. If a comforter says, "What a terrible thing this is. How deeply sorry I am for you," grieving individuals may react with anger and hostility because this is not what they want to hear. They want someone to come and say, "I will help you get your loved one back."

At the same time, one may see a kind of disorganized aimlessness and restlessness in the behavior of the bereaved person. Often, grieving individuals complain that they just cannot sit, that they have to pace about. They also complain that, in retrospect, when they look back on the experience of mourning, it was as if they were going through the motions — they did all their daily chores, they did everything that had to be done, but all this was done in a kind of automatic, unfeeling, uninvolved way, that took considerable effort.

The most characteristic feature of this phase is the mental activity of the individual. Following the phase of protest, the bereaved person becomes preoccupied with the lost person. The man who has lost his wife at first protests and says it has not happened and refuses to acknowledge the loss. Then he becomes more and more preoccupied with his memories of his relationship with her. Characteristically, this process first involves memories of her at the time of her death. He will think about her last days and hours and minutes. These memories often come spontaneously, without the person intentionally wanting to think about them; in fact, most people do not want to recall them because they are so painful. But over and over again, one will find such memories coming suddenly into consciousness. They are very intense and they are very painful.

What is happening? What seems to be happening is that the strong attachment to the person, suddenly broken, is transferred onto the memories of the relationship. What is so painful about this process is that with each memory, with each recollection of a fond event in the life of the relationship, one has to consciously acknowledge that it can no longer be. In a sense, this is piecemeal reality testing of the loss — moment by moment and bit by bit, one thinks over these memories, and as they come into consciousness, one is painfully reminded that the relationship is over forever. It is this repeated disappointment, as one remembers each of these events, that leads eventually to the relinquishment of the attachment and to the third phase of the mourning process. At the same time, as this process is going on, the individual will sometimes return to denial and to protest — "It isn't so."

Very often during this period, individuals will have dreams, clearly wish-fulfilling dreams, in which the dead person comes back and is alive, and things are just as they had been before. Daytime hallucinations of the deceased may even occur, and bring with them fears of going crazy. But such experiences are a normal — albeit sometimes terrifying — part of mourning.

Just as the second phase of disorganization may fluctuate with the first phase of protest and be interchanged with it in this fluid and dynamic

way, so, too, the second phase begins to give way to the third phase and may be interchanged with it. This cyclical nature of grief has been vividly described by C.S. Lewis in his book, *A Grief Observed,* written after the death of his wife, Joy. This is what Lewis says just as he thinks he is beginning to resolve his grief:

> For me at any rate the program is plain. I will turn to her as often as possible in gladness. I will even salute her with a laugh. The less I mourn her the nearer I seem to her. An admirable program. Unfortunately it can't be carried out. Tonight all the hells of young grief have opened again; the mad words, the bitter resentment, the fluttering in the stomach, the nightmare unreality, the wallowed-in tears. For in grief nothing "stays put." One keeps on emerging from a phase, but it always recurs. Round and round. Everything repeats. Am I going in circles, or dare I hope I am on a spiral. But if a spiral, am I going up or down it?*

THE PHASE OF REORGANIZATION

The third phase is one of *reorganization,* in which the individual begins to reinvest his or her energies and interests in the world. Again, the duration of this phase varies greatly. For some people it may take months to years; for others it may happen more rapidly. Characteristically, the individual in this phase begins to give up the intensity of investment in the lost person. Very often, individuals will describe how for a number of weeks or months they could not bear to do anything to the house. The pictures were still around, the beds were as they had been, the table was set as before, the clothes were in the closet, and there was the feeling, "I can't touch anything. I just can't change anything yet." A little later in this third phase, the individual will begin to alter some of his or her behavior and begin to give away or put away some of the belongings of the dead wife or husband.

In addition, the memories begin to fade. They do not become quite so intense or painful anymore. In this third phase, people finally arrive at the point where they can think back to the

---

* From *A Grief Observed* by C.S. Lewis. Copyright © 1961 by N.W. Clerk. Used by permission of The Seabury Press, Inc., New York.

relationship without intense grief and distress, but rather with pleasure and affection, and these remembrances become an important part of the life of the individual from then on. In addition, new activities are begun, and very often, the extent to which new things are started which had never been done before by the person is quite striking. Thus, new activities and new relationships begin, and old relationships are reestablished. However, for a long period of time the person may experience a good deal of guilt over enjoying life again, or of even being alive and having survived the lost one. Survivor guilt is an enormously powerful emotion as William Niederland has demonstrated in his description of the *survivor syndrome* among surviving victims of the Nazi concentration camps. This guilt may be heightened considerably by a feeling of disloyalty if a new love object enters the person's life.

But regardless of whatever changes take place, there are some aspects of the old relationship that are always maintained. First of all, the memories remain. Secondly, most people continue to maintain some fantasy of reunion. This is supported and encouraged by most religions, namely, the idea that at some point in the future we will again see the people we have lost and be reunited with them. Finally, the relationship is maintained through the process of identification. Individuals over time may become very much identified with the attitudes and values and even the activities of the departed loved one. There are examples of women whose husbands die, and who initially take over the business because they have to take it over — somebody has to do it. Then a year or two later, someone may say, "You know, she runs the business just the way her husband did," even though the woman herself may be quite unaware of the degree of her identification with her dead husband. Emily Dickinson has described this phenomenon as well:

> The distance that the dead have gone
> Does not at first appear —
> Their coming back seems possible
> For many an ardent year.
>
> And then, that we have followed them,
> We more than half suspect,
> So intimate have we become
> With their dear retrospect.*

Out of all of this comes, hopefully, a phenomenon of growth. We have talked about all of the critical phases in the life cycle that can lead to greater maturation and mastery. Mourning can work in a similar way, because if the grief is experienced and resolved, then very often new things happen to an individual — new values, new attitudes, new talents, new strengths. Individuals who have gone through mourning successfully feel that they are stronger and more independent, better able to take care of themselves, more capable of coping with whatever crisis life may bring.

PATHOLOGICAL MOURNING

What about the abnormal kinds of grief and mourning that one sees? (Table 48.1). In each of these, in one way or another, the individual has been unable to come to terms with the loss, either to acknowledge it consciously, or to give up the yearning for the person. The most striking example of an abnormal form of grief is the delayed or absent grief reaction, in which people avoid grieving altogether. They feel no pain, no sadness, they have none of the somatic symptoms, they do not become preoccupied with memories of the dead person. Often such an individual will, a year later or five years later, perhaps on the anniversary of the death, experience for the first time a grief reaction. Or, the grief may be delayed until much later in life, at the time of another loss. For example, a man's wife dies, and he may then suddenly find himself grieving not only for her, but also for the mother for whom he never grieved 30 years before.

One may also see, in some individuals, the onset of grief when they reach the same age at which somebody else had died in the past. A very famous example in recent years was the singer Elvis Presley. For many years, he had a premonition his life would end on the anniversary of his mother's death, and at the same age. During the last weeks of his life, he was haunted by a recurring dream of his mother reaching out from the grave and beckoning him to join her. On August 16, 1977, at the age of 42, Elvis Presley died. His mother had died at the age of 42 on August 14, 1958 — 19 years earlier almost to the day.

Another abnormal response is the persistence

---

* From *The Complete Poems of Emily Dickinson,* edited by Thomas H. Johnson. Copyright © 1929 by

Martha Dickinson Bianchi. Copyright © 1957 by Mary L. Hampson. (Reprinted by permission of Little, Brown, and Co.)

Table 48.1
*Normal and Pathological Mourning**

Signs of Normal Mourning	Signs of Pathological Mourning
1. Protest, disbelief, denial, shock	1. Persistence of denial with delayed or absent grieving
2. Profound sadness and survivor guilt, but self-esteem is intact	2. Depression with impaired self-esteem, suicidal thoughts and impulses with self-destructive behavior
3. Multiple somatic symptoms without actual organic disease	3. Actual organic disease and medical illness
4. Sense of unreality, withdrawal from others	4. Progressive social isolation
5. Anger and irritability	5. Persistent anger and hostility leading to paranoid reactions, especially against those involved in the medical care of the deceased, or else suppression of any expression of anger and hostility
6. Disruption of normal patterns of conduct, with restlessness, aimlessness, automatic behavior	6. Continued disruption of normal patterns of conduct, often with a persistent hyperactivity unaccompanied by a sense of loss or grieving
7. Preoccupation with memories of the deceased, dreams of deceased, hallucinations, fears of going crazy	7. Continued preoccupation with memories of the deceased to the point of searching for reunion
8. Identification with certain traits or abilities of the deceased	8. Conversion symptoms similar to the symptoms of the deceased

* Table by Richard C. Simons.

of the sense of unreality and withdrawal from others to the point of progressive social isolation. The profound sadness and guilt over having survived the lost loved one may develop into a clinical depression in which the bereaved person experiences self-hatred and worthlessness, and feels that he or she is a vicious and evil person who does not deserve to live. Often this has to do with the existence of hostile feelings towards the dead person which cannot be expressed, which are not acceptable, and which are then turned against the self. Dr. Glickman will be discussing this phenomenon in much greater depth in his chapter on suicide.

Another abnormal response to loss is medical illness. It has been well documented by Colin Murray Parkes in England and by James J. Lynch in this country that, following the loss of a spouse, there is a significant increase in both mortality and morbidity among the survivors. The death rates among widows and widowers is considerably higher during the first year of bereavement than for matched populations of the same age and sex who still have a spouse. Divorced persons also have a physical illness and

physician visit rate that is much higher than matched married controls in the first year following the divorce. And even though the remarriage rate is very high among the recently divorced, this is not true for those who lose a spouse through death. There are approximately 12 million persons in the United States today whose spouses have died, and 85% of these 12 million are women. Three out of four American women outlive their husbands, the average age of these widows is 56, and only 7% of them will remarry. This enormous segment of our population is at risk physically and emotionally if their grief is not resolved.

In addition to these kinds of physical responses, there are those in which feelings of anger and hostility may persist and develop into paranoid reactions, especially against the physicians involved in the care of the deceased. The disruption of normal patterns of conduct may also continue, often with a persistent hyperactivity unaccompanied by a sense of loss or grieving.

Another very interesting variant of the normal mourning process is the development of conversion symptoms similar to those of the deceased. One young woman, whose mother died of a brain tumor, came to the hospital one year after the mother's death, with severe headaches — an identification with the symptoms of her deceased mother.

There are other individuals who remain so preoccupied with memories of the deceased that they carry out conversations with the dead person and have fantasies that they can continue to do all the things that they used to do together. This denial may exist side by side with a conscious awareness that the person is gone. Such a person will usually say, "Well, of course I know my husband is no longer living, but I still have these conversations with him." In a sense, there is a split between one part of the person that is very much aware of the loss, and another part which functions as if the loss never happened. Such splitting can be seen in the extreme in people who wander around looking for the dead person, searching in other parts of the city or other parts of the country. Sometimes this is a conscious search, but more often it is unconscious. Such people will just say that they feel restless and they are looking for something, but they do not know what. As long as this yearning is unconscious, it cannot be confronted and is not subject to the reality testing of the mourning process. Anne Morrow Lindbergh, writing about the kidnapping-murder of her 18 month old son in 1932, poignantly describes the search: "Like Orpheus, one tries to follow the dead on the beginning of their journey. But one cannot, like Orpheus, go all the way, and after a long journey one comes back."*

THE PHYSICIAN AND THE MOURNING PROCESS

The attitudes of physicians and the rest of the medical profession can either facilitate the mourning process or impede it. Think of how the staff in any hospital usually reacts to death. One of the first things that happens is the removal of the body. This is done as quickly as possible so that no one will be "upset." Very often, a family will come and want a last look, want to see their father or their mother or their grandparent who has died, and the hospital will say, "No, you can't. The body's gone." What

does this do? Well, presumably it spares people pain. But it also delays one of the first steps in the mourning process — the acceptance of the loss. If you do not see the body, it is somewhat harder to truly believe that the person is dead than if you do see it.

This is one of the functions of the funeral. It is a cultural recognition that death has occurred. The viewing of the body in the casket has the same purpose. It is painful, to be sure, but it is also enormously important for the process of mourning. This is also a basic principle of self-help support groups and bereavement centers around the country — to help bereaved people face the reality of their loss.

What can we as physicians do to help a person during bereavement? First of all, we must be prepared to listen to people who are grieving and to talk to them. Most physicians, indeed most people, feel uncomfortable about grief, and want to avoid it. The fact that we may have been the physician of the dead person makes it even more difficult for us. To some extent we all have our grandiose fantasies that we should be able to help everybody, and this is especially true for physicians. So there are many reasons why a physician might want to avoid a person who is in mourning. But an empathic physician can do a great deal to facilitate the process of mourning — by listening, by acknowledging the pain of the loss, by accepting the bereaved person's anger and guilt and sadness, perhaps even by crying with them.

If the physician has a good relationship with the grieving individual or family, they may be helped and encouraged to immediately talk about the loss, and to review what happened. They will want to know what the disease was, what its causes were, what the autopsy findings were, everything about it. The mourning process can be facilitated greatly in this way. There are also some specific things about which many people are concerned during bereavement. They often worry about whether they are going crazy. Most people do not ordinarily experience this kind of intense feeling during their lives, and the grief response is a very painful one and a very strong one. This may frighten many people. They may feel that they are losing control, that they are going insane, that their feelings are inappropriate, that it is wrong for them to feel such hostility. The physician can reassure them that all of these grief reactions are normal and necessary.

---

* "Open To Love — Or Suffering," by Anne Morrow Lindbergh. *The New York Times,* March 1, 1973.

The physician can also serve in a very real way as a new object for the bereaved person, as someone to whom the patient can turn with some trust and confidence. In fact, it may very well be through this kind of contact with a physician that the reorganization process can begin, and the person may then have the courage to begin to establish other relationships and to return to a social life. In short, grief is necessary, painful, and inevitable. If we can fully appreciate this, then physicians and all health care professionals can be of enormous assistance during this important and universal human experience.

Suggested Readings

Lewis CS: *A Grief Observed.* New York, The Seabury Press, 1963.

Lindemann E: Symptomatology and management of acute grief. *Am J Psychiatry* 101:141, 1944.

Lindemann E: *Beyond Grief: Studies in Crisis Intervention,* New York, Jason Aronson, 1979.

Lynch JJ: *The Broken Heart: The Medical Consequences of Loneliness.* New York, Basic Books, 1977.

Nemiah JC: The phenomenology of depression and grief. In *Foundations of Psychopathology.* New York, Oxford University Press, 1961, p 145.

Nemiah JC: Pathological grief. In *Foundations of Psychopathology.* New York, Oxford University Press, 1961, p 168.

Parkes CM: *Bereavement: Studies of Grief in Adult Life.* New York, International Universities Press, 1972.

References

Bowlby J: Pathological mourning and childhood mourning. *J Am Psychoanal Assoc* 11:500, 1963.

Bowlby, J: *Attachment and Loss. Vol. I: Attachment.* New York, Basic Books, 1969.

Bowlby J: *Attachment and Loss. Vol. II: Separation: Anxiety and Anger.* New York, Basic Books, 1973.

Bowlby J: *Attachment and Loss. Vol. III: Loss: Sadness and Depression.* New York, Basic Books, 1980.

Cassem NH: Resolution of the grieving process. Paper presented at the University of Colorado Medical Center, Department of Psychiatry. January 15, 1979.

Cohen RE, Ahearn FL: *Handbook for Mental Health Care of Disaster Victims.* Baltimore, Johns Hopkins University Press, 1980.

Engel GL: Psychological responses to major environmental stress: grief and mourning; danger, disaster and deprivation. In *Psychological Development in Health and Disease.* Philadelphia, W.B. Saunders, 1962, p 272.

Fleming J, Altschul S: Activation of mourning and growth by psychoanalysis. *Int J Psychoanal* 44:419, 1963.

Freud S (1917): Mourning and melancholia. In *The Standard Edition of the Complete Psychological Works of Sigmund Freud,* vol 14. London, Hogarth Press, 1957, p 237.

Niederland WG: Psychiatric disorders among persecution victims. *J Nerv Ment Dis* 139:458, 1964.

Niederland WG: Clinical observations on the survivor syndrome. *Int J Psychoanal* 49:313, 1968.

Schiff HS: *The Bereaved Parent.* New York, Penguin Books, 1978.

Schoenberg B, et al: *Anticipatory Grief.* New York, Columbia University Press, 1974.

Stern G: *The Buffalo Creek Disaster: The Story of the Survivors' Unprecedented Lawsuit.* New York, Random House, 1976.

Zisook S, et al: Measuring symptoms of grief and bereavement. *Am J Psychiatry* 139:1590, 1982.

CHAPTER 49 The Dying Adult

A. Historical and Religious Perspectives

Sidney L. Werkman, M.D.

When faced with the fact of inevitable death, patient and physician alike must abandon the beguiling search for a cure. Both set out in a new territory unexplored by medicine until recently, that of philosophy, religion, and bioethics. It is instructive to study the many transformations that our knowledge of death has undergone, from prehistory to the present, for evidences of early views continue to affect both patient and physician in surprising ways. When we understand these transformations better, our own clinical work with dying patients will be enriched and our patients will be better served.

Throughout history there has been an intertwining of medical and religious perspectives in regard to death. The doctor and the priest have alternatively fought, cooperated, and withdrawn from each other. When I studied medicine at a fine teaching hospital during the post World War II period, my fellow students and I concentrated on scientific medicine and were given no exposure to chaplains, religious issues, bioethics, or teaching about the care of dying patients. The situation has changed radically with the introduction of value issues and ethical concerns into medical education and patient care. This chapter is an attempt to offer some historical perspective about that change and the evolution of our current views about death.

THE FACT OF DEATH IN PREHISTORY

Prehistoric man, in contrast to his animal cousins, recognized the fact of death and paid attention to it with ceremonial burial. Burial sites going back to 100,000 B.C. have been discovered. Tombs from every culture of prehistory and early antiquity attest to man's long concern with continuity of the spirit and even of the

body itself. No other living creature buries its dead. Our early ancestors conceived of death as a dynamic stage of a continuing drama, and nearly all religions have evolved elaborate explanations for the continuity of life. Even the eminent writer on death, Dr. Elisabeth Kübler-Ross, has stated: "The more I go into this after-death research, the more some scientific people want to shred me to pieces. But I already have more than enough evidence that there is an afterlife."

The combination of a bewildering environment of storms, floods, droughts, and threatening beasts, matched against man's exposed body and expanding consciousness, placed him in a paradoxical position that continues to the present. Man was master of many things but was also aware of his own vulnerabilities. The tiger was physically powerful but free of any perplexity about its place and continuity in the universe. Illness and pain shatter the sense of continuity and invulnerability that accompany good health. Like a sick person of today, the human of 100,000 B.C. must have looked for ways to explain pain, disfigurement, and death. The explanations fashioned with a primitive knowledge of physiology and anatomy centered on the invasion of evil spirits, punishment, or a departure of the healthy soul from the body. Interestingly, patients still invent similar explanations for disease today. They say: "The pain gripped me," as if pain were some invasion from the outside, or "I had a heart attack because I was living too wild a life" as if a myocardial infarction were a punishment from the outside. The ultimate pain, of course, was death, and death became conceptualized, not as a natural event, but as the ultimate punishment. And when that became too painful to consider, man began to evolve both pleasant and terrifying concepts of an afterlife.

Prehistoric man concurrently developed the use of medicinal herbs for combatting pain and disorder. The infectious diseases and trauma probably were treated by rational medical means even in the earliest times, but the chronic illnesses and death were referred for care to the wisdom of religion. Psychological rituals were used to control demons and restore a sense of coherence. Individuals who possessed a natural talent for influencing others gradually evolved into our professional ancestors—witch doctors, medicine men, shamans, and sorcerers. These early "doctors" developed fascinating techniques meant to return the healthy soul to the body, or free the body of evil spirits that had invaded it. The earliest treatments seemed to have been guided by a simple logic. A person with head pain or, perhaps, disturbing thoughts, was assumed to have had his head invaded by an evil spirit. The treatment for such possession was to trephine the skull in order to allow the spirit to escape. Trephined skulls dating from 10,000 B.C. have been discovered.

Other means of banishing evil spirits or returning a "lost soul" or sense of coherence to the body were elaborated into rituals, prayers, and magic incantations directed to restore health. Such incantations or formulas typically contained elements of confession of sin, prayer to be freed of evil influence from enemies, or the imploring help from an outside agency. We see a continuation of such practices in the ordinary experience of even the nonreligious patient in pain who cries out, "God, please help me." Ironically, the ancient concept of healing the whole person, not simply the physical body, has returned to medicine today in our recognition that illness and health are biopsychosocial issues. This complex tradition of technical therapeutic intervention combined with psychological or spiritual involvements has existed for as long as man has puzzled over his place and meaning in the universe.

THE ASCENDANCY OF RELIGION

Though simple infections or traumatic events were treated by ordinary medical means even in ancient times, the major illnesses and death have always triggered concerns about the possibility of an afterlife. Explanations for life and death, "Where we came from, why we are here, and where we are going," are fundamentally religious matters. Despite their central importance for most religions and philosophies, medical education until the last several decades has ignored these concerns as objects of serious study and instead, focused on the scientific, technical aspects of patient care.

Ancient Greek medicine was not unlike American medical education prior to the recent resurgence of concern with philosophical, religious, and bioethical traditions. Influenced by the Epicurean view that death was the end of life and that pain was without supernatural meaning but simply a natural consequence of bodily alteration, the Greeks made a clean separation between medicine and religion. As Hippocrates put it: "Every disease has its own nature and arises from external causes." He derided the concept of sacred diseases and sacred cures while noting that "Our natures are the physicians' of our diseases."

With the exception of Greek medicine, most cultures have turned to religion to find meaning and comfort for patients who face death. The basic Western religion, Judaism, is firmly committed to the sanctity of life, though it introduced conflicting views about life after death that have remained thorny problems to the present. On the one hand, the Jewish Pharisees of biblical times adhered to the doctrine of personal immortality, while another group, the Sadducees, conceptualized death as an eternal sleep. Still other sects defined death as a finality. Jewish theology spawned complex conceptualizations of a fiery hell and beatific heaven that continue to evolve today. These trends were balanced later by the teachings of such philosophers as the 12th Century Maimonides, who denounced the concepts of everlasting bodily torture or happiness that were so prevalent in medieval times.

When Christianity swept over Europe, religious orders increasingly assumed the responsibility for medical care. This was a natural development, since religious organizations combined a commitment to helping others with a high level of education. Large hospitals were founded in Rome and Constantinople by the Christian Roman Emperor Constantine in the 4th Century. Disabled, handicapped, and dying people congregated in the monasteries and hospitals of Christian orders and, as patients died, it was natural that they would be ministered to with rituals based on a religious understanding of death. Thus, dying was a matter, not only for patient and family, as it is so often today, but also became intertwined with the religious tradition that permeated the medieval world. The doctor-priest and nurse-nun were experts in the religious rituals that evolved from their tradition. Also, they became most familiar with the physical experience of dying and death. Plague victims, the poor, and the homeless, shunned by the rest of society, fell into the helping hands of the religious medical establishment where death was not an enemy, as it is so often viewed by medicine now, but as an avenue of reconciliation with God and an entrance into heaven. Thus, the inevitability of death was cushioned by a sense of meaning and promise, whether of an afterlife or another kind of immortality in the form of ceremonials and memorials. The medieval physician gave meaning to illness and death, while cure or redemption were sought through the intercession of God. Human helplessness was balanced by belief.

Despite the importance placed on an afterlife and on varying forms of consciousness in most religions and philosophies, medical education has tended until recently to ignore these concepts as objects of serious study. The continuing controversy over parapsychological research and the various attempts to validate extrasensory perception attest to our uneasy preoccupation with unusual realms of consciousness. Since these problems are still unanswered by modern medicine, it is small wonder, then, that ancient man would have difficulty with such questions. For us today it is important that we recognize that these questions are still viable ones for vast numbers of people, particularly those who are facing death.

THE BEGINNINGS OF MODERN MEDICINE

The Reformation introduced a radical change in religious sensibility and an extraordinary flowering of scientific inquiry that profoundly influenced medical care. That change might be dated from the reign of King Henry VIII of England (1510–1543), whose break from Catholicism resulted in the closing of Catholic hospitals, and in the diminished power of the church-based medical care system. The state gradually took over the responsibility for providing medical care through the institution of sec-

ular hospitals. The medical profession as we now know it was born in these hospitals, where physicians directed their efforts to understanding disease rather than ministering to the spiritual needs of patients. We can see the development of modern medicine in microcosm through this historical pattern that developed in England.

St. Bartholomew's Hospital, which was established in London in 1662, pioneered a new type of scientifically based medical school concerned with the description and cure of disease in place of the care of the patient. Henri de Mondeville, a famous doctor of the time, wrote that the physician "should refuse as far as possible all dangerous cases, and he should never accept desperately sick ones." Because of this focus on cure, hospitals and medical schools turned away from the care of chronically ill and dying patients. This trend is best exemplified by a sign placed at the door of St. Thomas' Hospital in London in 1700 stating: "No incurables are to be received."

Modern medicine and the era of acute care had begun. From that time on the tension between care of the patient and cure of disease has been a central one for medicine. Advances in surgical techniques and medical knowledge, followed by the introduction of precise pharmaceutical agents and antibiotics, characterize the long sweep of medicine from the 17th century to the present time. Doctors became soldiers in a battle against disease rather than ministers to ill and dying patients. In such a climate, death has become an enemy, while the person who harbors the disease may suffer from neglect. Post World War II American medical education and research have tremendously advanced the study of the physiology and pathology of disease patterns. Competence in diagnosis and the application of accurate, scientifically based treatment is the glory of our time. Research into disease mechanisms and treatments flourishes.

This emphasis on the understanding and cure of disease may result in neglect of the subjective, inner experiences of the patient, or as Lewis Thomas put it, medicine advanced by an emphasis on "meticulous, objective, even cool observations of sick people." Technological advances in medicine encourage the view of a patient as a series of systems and mechanisms similar to a machine. The doctor's concern terminates when the machinery no longer functions. After an autopsy, the dead patient, and the patient's family as well, may be discarded by the medical profession, just as old computers are consigned to junk heaps. Contemporary medical students who have received little instruction that would help them work with dying patients may find themselves baffled by the inevitable questions that their patients ask about pain, suffering, and impending death. With little knowledge or tradition to call upon in answer to these questions, it is no surprise that many physicians treat illness with skill yet ignore a patient's emotional, philosophic, and religious concerns. Our contemporary value systems and patterns of medical education ignore religious and historical traditions, and do not prepare the future physician to deal with the most poignant concerns of many dying patients: "Why am I in such pain? Why do I have to die? What will it be like to die?"

The sick person's puzzled questions and the dying patient's desperate ones can only be understood and addressed from a philosophic or religious point of view, so often omitted in medical education. Furthermore, contemporary attitudes toward dying and death, strongly influenced by an Anglo-Saxon, Calvinist suppression and denial of feelings, foster an ethic that excludes the experience and expression of emotion. As a dying nurse wrote to Dr. Ned Cassem, a psychiatrist-priest involved with counseling dying patients: "All I want to know is that there is someone who can hold my hand when I need it. Death may be routine to you but it is new to me." The surviving wife of a young man emphasized this point in a letter to Dr. Cassem about her husband: "The importance to him was not so much to know that he would be mourned after he died, but the reality of knowing that he was loved while he lived. Speaking freely of death allowed us to taste more fully of life."*

NEW DEVELOPMENTS IN MEDICAL CARE FOR THE DYING

The Hospice Movement, inspired by the work of Dr. Cicely Saunders of St. Christopher's Hospital in England, has demonstrated how important it is for a patient to die at home or in a supportive environment among friends and loved ones (Figure 49.1). Hospice programs are

---

* From "New Hospital Practices Reflect a Need to Help Dying Patients Prepare for Death," by Bill Kovach, *The New York Times*, January 21, 1973.

therapeutically sound and economically beneficial. Cancer self-help programs also offer great psychological support as well as practical advice about prostheses, wigs, and dietary aids. The recognition that seriously ill patients can take considerable responsibility for their illnesses has helped many people find meaning in their final days as they move toward "a good death."

These innovations have developed separately from the scientifically grounded medical tradition of the recent past. Though not in conflict with current research developments, they represent a distinct break from the tradition of emphasis on technical intervention at the expense of humane involvement between physician and patient. They represent a recognition of the wish for patients to understand their diseases thoroughly and to become active participants in their own treatment, and they have been accompanied by an extraordinary revitalization and flowering of religious and philosophic concerns about death and dying. A strongly resurgent Christian concern with dying focuses on the profound meaningfulness of each individual life and the important continuities in the cycle of life and death. A powerful Existential position, exemplified by the writing of Viktor Frankl, affirms mankind's search for understanding and meaning in life as a unique aspect of the human condition. Recent publications within the Jewish tradition have highlighted the problem of suffering and the need for benevolent, compassionate involvement with dying patients. The field of bioethics has added a powerful, new dimension to medical education through the addition of philosophers to medical school faculties. As a whole, these trends have already greatly influenced the way we function as professionals, and constitute a direction of potentially great importance for the future medical care of the dying patient. Fear has increasingly been replaced by the understanding and acceptance of death described by Sir Thomas Browne, a physician, and the author of *Religio Medici*: "We all labor against our own cure, for death is the cure of all diseases."

GUIDES FOR WORKING WITH DYING PATIENTS

In light of all that I have said above, I would like to conclude this chapter by listing a few of

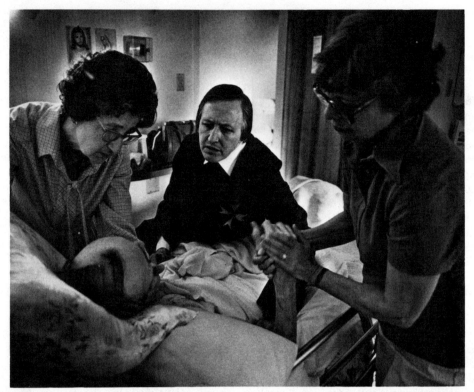

Figure 49.1. A dying man and his grieving family are comforted by Father Paul von Lobkowitz, the Czechoslovakian monk who is director of the Hospice of the Holy Spirit in Lakewood, Colorado. Copyright © 1979—John Sunderland/Denver Post.

the issues that address both the medical and the spiritual concerns of the dying patient.

1. *Competence*: The first thing a seriously ill patient wants is a competent doctor in whom he or she can place confidence and trust. Be certain that you have adequate scientific and clinical knowledge of the patient's illness and treatment. Do not hesitate to ask for consultations from colleagues whenever needed.

2. *Caring*: This is the quality most valued by a dying patient. Be sure you know your patient well as a human being, and are prepared to attend seriously to each and every question presented to you.

3. *Comfort*: Patients do not die of "cancer" but rather of infections that can be treated. They suffer less from "carcinoma" than from odors, skin rashes, weight loss, hair loss, difficulty swallowing and breathing, and pain. People worry less about their incurable illnesses than they do about treatable discomforts. Reassure the patient that you will make every effort to provide symptomatic relief for these treatable discomforts.

4. *Communication*: There is no one right thing to say. The question is not what you are supposed to tell a dying patient, but rather what you can do to allow your patient to speak openly with you. Make an effort to know something of your patient's background, hobbies, family, and personal life interests. A patient may wish to review his or her life with you in the hope that you will learn from that life, not unlike the dying Hamlet who told Horatio: "If thou didst ever hold me in thy heart, absent thee from felicity awhile and in this harsh world draw thy breath in pain, to tell my story."

5. *Cheerfulness*: A dying patient once told me, "I don't want a sour puss for a doctor. I want someone who can talk with me about the World Series, who has a sense of humor, who can make my life a little brighter."

6. *Respect*: This includes respect for the patient as a unique human being, and also as a unique psychological being with mechanisms of defense that may be absolutely essential for coping with his or her impending death. One of the most important of these defense mecha-

nisms is denial. A dying patient who says, "I know I'm getting better," is not asking for a lecture on ominous changes in blood chemistries or irreversible disruptions in immune systems or inoperable metastases.

7. *Control*: Emphasize the availability of effective pain control medications that can be administered immediately before pain becomes excruciating. Be certain that a patient who is terrified of suffocating or choking to death has ready access to a bell or buzzer to call medical personnel.

8. *Touch*: To hold a patient's hand during a painful time may offer more comfort than any medication or technical procedure.

9. *Visits*: Encourage visits from relatives and set a definite schedule for rounds by medical personnel. Clinical experience regrettably confirms that doctors and relatives decrease the frequency of their visits as death approaches, the very time that a patient needs the most support.

10. *Hope*: A dying patient lives one day at a time; goals change as an illness progresses. At a certain point a patient may value the discontinuation of uncomfortable IV medications more than cure of the disease. The anticipation of a relative's visit can help a distressed patient withstand pain with greater equanimity. Many dying patients welcome the opportunity to help the medical profession through participation in research on experimental medications or through being examined by medical students. Some wish to donate eyes, limbs, or other organs. Hope

eases pain and despair. It is best nurtured through the medium of an empathic relationship between doctor and patient. And as Hippocrates indicated long ago, one never knows when hope may actually lead to recovery: "Some patients, though conscious that their position is perilous, recover their health simply through their contentment with the goodness of the physician."

Suggested Readings

Aries P: *Western Attitudes Toward Death: From the Middle Ages to the Present.* Baltimore, Johns Hopkins University Press, 1974.

Feifel H (ed): *The Meaning of Death.* New York, McGraw-Hill, 1959.

Kastenbaum R, Aisenberg R: *The Psychology of Death.* New York, Springer, 1972.

Kushner HS: *When Bad Things Happen to Good People.* New York, Avon Books, 1981.

References

Ackerknecht EH: *A Short History of Medicine.* New York, Ronald Press, 1978.

Bodemer CW: Physicians and the dying: a historical sketch. *J Fam Prac* 9:827, 1979.

Boshes B: Death: historical evolution and implication of the concept. *Ann NY Acad Sci* 315:11, 1978.

Choron J: *Death and Western Thought.* New York, Macmillan, 1963.

Frankl VE: *Man's Search for Meaning.* Boston, Beacon Press, 1959.

Saunders C, Baines M: *Living with Dying: The Management of Terminal Disease.* New York, Oxford University Press, 1983.

Sigerist H: *The History of Medicine. Vol I: Primitive and Archaic Medicine* (1951) and *Vol II: Early Greek, Hindu, and Persian Medicine* (1961). Oxford, England. Oxford University Press.

Thompson JD, Goldin G: *The Hospital: A Social and Architectural History.* New Haven, Yale University Press, 1975.

Veatch R: *Death, Dying, and the Biological Revolution: Last Quest for Responsibility.* New Haven, Yale University Press, 1976.

B. The Clinical Perspectives

Ursula Thunberg, M.D.

"May you live all the days of your life."
— *Jonathan Swift*

THE UNIVERSALITY OF DEATH

The experience of dying and finally of death is a universal experience that we, as humans, share with all living organisms. It is the final

phase of the individual human life in both a psychological and a physical sense. This final moment of dying and death has created fascination, awe, and fear in people down through the ages and in all cultures of human history.

If we compare the religious, poetic, and anthropological material on the theme of death existing in many different cultural groups, we can see many similar emotions and reflections. The following three poems were written by Mexican Indians many centuries ago in the Nahuatl language and were translated into Spanish in the 16th century:

> just like the flowers I will go
> my fame will be nothing
> someday
> nothing of my name will be left
> to the last flower the last song
>
> we disappear
> eagles tigers
> nothing in the gold
> nothing in the emeralds
> nothing in the feathers
> nothing in the world
>
> where are we going Oh where are we going
> are we dead are we still alive
> is this where time ends is there time some-
>   where else
> people are only here on earth
> with pungent flowers and with songs
>   and out of words
> surely
> they make truths!

Although many individual statements have been made by dying people describing the experience, this information has not generally been collected, and if, as in the *Tibetan Book of the Dead*, such information is formally gathered together, the culturally strange religious concepts make it difficult for most of us to understand the material. Over the ages man has wrestled with the enigma of death, and his searchings have taken all kinds of form — religious, poetic, and scientific. The following is an example from an African setting:

The Chameleon and the Lizard

When Death first entered the world, men sent the chameleon to find out the cause. God told the chameleon to let men know that if they threw baked porridge over a corpse, it would come back to life. But the chameleon was slow in returning and Death was rampant in their midst, and so men sent a second messenger, the lizard.

The lizard reached the abode of God soon after the chameleon. God, angered by the second message, told the lizard that men should dig a hole in the ground and bury their dead in it. On the way back the lizard overtook the chameleon and delivered his message first, and when the chameleon arrived the dead were already buried.

Thus, owing to the impatience of man, he cannot be born again.

a Margi story
(Central African Republic)

These poems and stories express the same basic feelings and raise the same problematic questions that we are asking in our age at a different time and in a different culture. Scientifically and intellectually, death is defined simply as the end of life and the cessation of all physical and mental functions. However, when we encounter death in family members or in our patients, or when we have to contemplate our own death, we approach this scientific and intellectual reality on a totally different level. We have emotional reactions, and experience feelings of fear, anxiety, anger, and helplessness (Figure 49.2). All of us must work out our own answers to the questions of our life and our death. Why am I here? What is the purpose of my life? What will happen when I die?

THE STAGES OF DYING

In the following material I will focus predominantly on adult patients dying of chronic fatal

Figure 49.2. *Death Seizes a Woman* (1934) by Käthe Kollwitz. (By permission of The Library of Congress.)

diseases, because in most cases of death by accident or an acute illness such as a heart attack or a massive lung embolus, the patient has no time to face the issue of impending death emotionally or intellectually. A patient with a chronic fatal disease will initially suffer from certain symptoms that will bring him or her to a physician. In the course of the illness the patient will pass through a process that will begin with the initial diagnostic procedures, followed by various modalities of treatment, possibly leading to a remission. If the illness continues, several relapses may be followed by further remissions until finally the illness reaches a terminal stage characterized by generalized weakness, debilitation, and, finally, death.

I emphasize this process of dying because, all along its course, the patient, informed about the illness or not, will pick up clues about the state of his or her health from the surroundings. These clues may be given by family members, who suddenly appear more concerned or anxious, or more helpful to the patient than they had been in the past. Clues may also be given by health care personnel during the course of treatment, in the form of nonverbal facial expressions, or avoidance of a patient's request for some specific information, or discussions between health care professionals within hearing range of the patient. The patient is also given many clues from the state of health of his or her own body, the growing inability to do things, the failing capacity of bodily functions, culminating in an overwhelming feeling of exhaustion. Only a person who has been very ill will have a true understanding of what it feels like to be very sick. In most cases, the health care professional is younger than the patient with a fatal disease, and if the professional has always enjoyed good health, that person may be completely unable to empathize with the dying patient.

In recent years many investigators have been exploring the emotional and psychological aspects of death and dying. One of the most outstanding of these workers is Dr. Elisabeth Kübler-Ross, who has become well known for her work with dying patients. She began interviewing them, inquiring into their thoughts and feelings about their illnesses. The material from many years of this work is described in her book *On Death and Dying.* As she began to analyze this clinical material, it seemed to her that there were five separate stages that the dying patient experiences when faced with his or her impending death. Although she presents them as five sequential stages, in actuality they represent five specific issues with which at some time or other the dying patient will have to deal.

The Stage of Denial

The first stage that Kübler-Ross describes, the *stage of denial* and isolation of affect, can be seen when the person who has been told that he or she has a fatal disease says, "No, it can't be true, not me." Recently I met a young woman 23 years old who had been diagnosed as having a tumor of the pituitary gland. Since she came from a very well educated family with a medical background, she was aware of the implications of the diagnosis. She told me that when she learned the diagnosis, her first reaction was, "No, it is not possible. It can't be me. It is a bad dream."

The Stage of Anger

The next reaction after this first realization has been described as the *stage of anger:* "Why does it have to be me? What have I done?" One patient may experience a full range of intense feelings of bitterness, rage, and envy, while the anger in another patient may be much more muted. This may be especially the case in a patient with low self-esteem, with strong guilt reactions, or with masochistic, self-destructive personality characteristics, who may see the terminal illness as a punishment, and possibly even a punishment that is deserved.

The Stage of Bargaining

The third *stage of bargaining,* namely bargaining with the assumed invisible powers that control our lives, has strong magical overtones. As we know, magical thinking is the belief that our thoughts and wishes can in some way affect reality, and it is rather typical for the young child below the age of five. It is also a mode of interpreting the world used by normal adults who are in severe emotional stress. In this third stage many patients return to the religious orientations of their youth, or begin to search for the deeper meanings of their lives. Some time ago I listened to an interview with the father of a leukemic child who had died. I was struck by the strong feelings expressed by the father, who happened to be a minister, that if he had more totally committed himself to the service of God, his son's life might have been spared. I have had the repeated experience that this magical bargaining can exist side by side with normal intellectual functioning and intact reality testing. Many times the patient expresses the wish for a magical rescue and at the same time is aware of the futility of such a wish.

The Stage of Depression

The fourth stage really has two phases, *preparatory grief* and *final grief*. During the first phase, the patients gradually detach themselves from their surroundings, relinquish their wider social relationships and family responsibilities, and begin the process of mourning the anticipated cessation of all these emotional bonds. Even patients who have been separated from their families for a long period of time will begin reflecting about these past relationships, and may even try to rectify wrongs that they may have committed in the past. The second phase is characterized by an increasing preoccupation with the patient's own life coming to an end. This period is often filled with reflections about the total meaning of life and existence, and all degrees of depression may be seen.

The Stage of Acceptance

The fifth stage is described as the *stage of acceptance*. Dr. Kübler-Ross describes this stage as an emotionally neutral stage, almost devoid of feelings. This has not been my experience with the dying adult patient, especially during the last 36 to 48 hours before loss of consciousness. Generally, I have found the terminal adult patient somewhat euphoric, rarely anxious, and generally very much at peace (Figures 49.3 and 49.4). I would like to state that I am talking about patients whom I knew over a period of many weeks, patients with whom I had established a relationship through daily contact. I have found that in this final phase of dying, patients may experience a very different emotional state from any that had appeared in the earlier stages.

SOME CLINICAL EXAMPLES

I have worked as a consultant for a religious nursing home specializing in the care of the

Figure 49.3. *Woman Reaching Out Her Hand To Death* (1934) by Käthe Kollwitz. (By permission of National Gallery of Art, Washington, D.C., Rosenwald Collection.)

Figure 49.4. *Death as a Friend* (1934) by Käthe Kollwitz. (By permission of National Gallery of Art, Washington, D. C., Rosenwald Collection.)

clearly identified terminal patient. This home has a very personal, comfortable setting with individualized patient care. What immediately impressed me was the ease with which staff and patients related to one another and the apparent comfort of these very ill patients. To corroborate my own clinical observations, I asked for the staff's impressions about the final emotional status of their dying patients, who come from various socioeconomic, cultural, and religious backgrounds. The staff had the same impression that I have just described about the emotional status of many of these patients during their last hours.

Mary

Here is an actual example from some years ago. Mary was a 42 year old black woman with a professional education as a teacher, who was hospitalized in the final phase of cancer of the colon with shortness of breath and inability to eat. She was on the ward three weeks before she died. I was an intern at the time, and I began to see her daily. After one week on the ward she called me to her bed and asked me what I thought about her illness. Not knowing what to say at that time, I asked her what her thoughts were about it. She informed me that she was aware that she was dying of cancer, and that she had told her teenage children that she would not be returning home again. When asked why she thought so, she explained that though she had been hospitalized before, this time she had a very strong feeling that she would not leave the hospital alive.

Neither her physician nor her husband and family had shared any information with her about her illness during the three years that she had been ill. She had made her own conclusions following a major exploratory operation which resulted in a large abdominal scar. She said, "I know that they must have been exploring my abdomen for cancer, because in my age group there is no other reason for such a big scar on the abdomen." She reflected a great deal in the next two weeks about the worth of her life. She felt that she had had 22 good years with her husband, that she had enjoyed her profession, and that her children were intelligent and attractive. She felt that it had been a good life. During the last days she often smilingly spoke about her mother, who had died five years earlier. She expressed the knowledge that she would die soon and that she was not afraid. On the day that she slipped into a terminal coma, she talked smilingly about her children, stated that she looked forward to their daily visits, expressed no physical discomfort in spite of apparent severe shortness of breath, and in the late afternoon lost consciousness. At no time did she seem to experience distress or emotional turmoil. She

was a good example of Stewart Alsop's observation: "A dying man needs to die, as a sleepy man needs to sleep, and there comes a time when it is wrong, as well as useless, to resist."

Betty

Betty was a German immigrant whom I also saw as an intern. Her husband had recently died of cancer, and now she had breast cancer in the final stages. She had developed a lymphedema of the arm which resulted in constant drainage, and I had to change her dressings. I would always talk with my patients as I did these procedures, and so Betty and I chatted many times each day and got to know each other pretty well. One day she said to me, "You know, don't you, Dr. Thunberg, that I'm dying of cancer," I said to her, "How do you know?," and she said, "Oh, you know, I have the same thing my husband had. He died of cancer of the prostate and had lymphedema of the leg." She said that her arm looked exactly the same way. She died shortly after Christmas. I remember being on duty that Christmas Eve. Betty had ordered three bottles of champagne and she invited all of the medical staff to a champagne party at her bed so as to wish us a merry Christmas. She said, "I think it's going to be the last bottle of champagne I will drink in this life." The next day was Christmas, and when I went to visit her the room was packed with relatives. They were all standing around her, saying, "Oh Betty, you will get better," and so on and so on, and she said, "No, no, I will not get better, right Dr. Thunberg?" Well, the relatives looked at me with horrified expressions. I did not know what to say, so I looked at her and said, "Betty, you know." She looked very satisfied and pleased at that, and the relatives were speechless. Two days before she died she told me, "You know, it's going to come to an end soon," and it did. For the last 24 hours she was confused and hallucinating, and then she drifted into a coma and died. But for several days before her death, she had a clear awareness that she was about to die.

THE UNIQUENESS OF DYING

It is important to recognize that dying, like living, is a total process involving the entire human being. This means that all aspects of a human personality will experience and participate in this process. When we try to understand what happens when people are involved in the process of dying, we like to categorize, to systematize, to put the whole process into a schema that allows us to talk about it and intellectually get control of it, and thus make it less threatening for us. It is very hard for us to accept the reality that there are certain things in life that we cannot control, such as death. This is something that is especially difficult for anyone working in the health care fields, where the major professional goal has been defined as the saving of life. Any death may therefore represent a failure in our professional expectations, and a harsh confrontation with our limitations, our fallibility, and our own mortality.

It is important to recognize that death is an integral and natural part of human life experience and living. Indeed, it is the final phase of life. As a person approaches this final phase, inner psychic shifts will occur which will not be accessible to outside observers unless we can help the dying patient to talk about this inner state. One of the changes that takes place is an inner sense of time which is unique to the patient. This is something that has to be respected. Dr. Elisabeth Kübler-Ross described this phenomenon very clearly at the beginning of her work in Chicago, when she wanted to interview the first patient for her seminar. She postponed the interviewing for the benefit of the students whom she wanted to have present, and then learned that the patient was not able to talk any longer at the time the students were available. It is essential that all of us who work with dying patients respect these changed states of the patients. We have to be available when they feel the need for us. All too often our medical or theoretical or educational procedures ignore the needs of the dying patient. We want the dying patient to adjust to us, rather than the other way around.

TO TELL OR NOT TO TELL

One of the major points that always seems to emerge in any discussion of the issues related to the dying patient, is the question of whether or not one should tell the patient of his or her disease and its implications. In a 1961 study by Oken, 219 physicians at Michael Reese Hospital in Chicago were asked about their preferences on this issue with patients who had cancer. Twelve per cent said that they usually told the patients, while 88% said that they did not tell their patients. However, 60% of these same physicians stated that they themselves would like

to be told if they had cancer. In a parallel investigation of the opinions of cancer patients, about 80% of them said that they wanted to be told. So there is a major discrepancy here between what doctors as physicians prefer, what doctors as patients prefer, and what the patients of these doctors prefer.

However, by 1977, using Oken's same questionnaire, Novack and his colleagues found a complete reversal of attitudes among 264 physicians at Strong Memorial Hospital in Rochester. Ninety-eight per cent said that they generally told their patients the diagnosis, 100% said that they would prefer to be told if they themselves had cancer, and 100% indicated that they thought the patient had the right to know the diagnosis. Novack attributes improved therapy for many forms of cancer, increased public awareness of cancer, greater comfort among physicians in relating to dying patients, and more understanding among physicians about the dying process as factors in bringing about these marked changes in physicians' attitudes.

John Hinton feels that a careful exploration of the patient's already existing knowledge about the disease is the first and most important step, without prejudging what the final decision will be. Some patients will need to know everything, whereas many other patients will be too frightened to know too much too soon. Elisabeth Kübler-Ross similarly expresses the belief that the question is not so much *if* the patient should or should not be told about the illness, but rather *how* and *when* this information should be shared with the patient. She suggests that talking freely with the patient about the malignancy, without equating it with impending death, is the approach to take initially. Norman Cousins makes the same point:

> Lives can be profoundly affected or even lost because of the way information is conveyed. Admittedly, patients vary in their ability to live with the truth, and sometimes the truth can complicate and impair treatment. Truth, misplaced or poorly conveyed, can crush two vital ingredients in treatment—hope and the will to live. . . . Truth can be told in a way that can potentiate a patient or devastate him. It can lead to challenge or set the stage for shattering defeat.*

---

* *The Healing Heart, Antidotes to Panic and Helplessness* by Norman Cousins. Reprinted by permission of W. W. Norton & Company, Inc., New York. Copyright © 1983 by Norman Cousins. Page 142.

Often the more central question is not whether the patient can tolerate the anxiety of talking about death, but whether the physician can tolerate it. As Hinton rightfully observed, "It is to be remembered that while doctors are trying to judge their patient's capacity to stand unpleasant news, many patients are equally making their intuitive judgments of whether their doctor can bear sincere but difficult questions."

It is essential that those of us who are health care professionals develop a deep respect for the uniqueness and individuality of each patient's life experience. Conditioned as we are to think in categories throughout our medical training, we can so easily fall into the trap of approaching a patient with a chronic malignant disease as a statistic moving toward death in a routine manner. We forget that this human being has no equal and will never come again, that his or her life is a unique one, never to be lived again in the same manner. It is important that we approach the dying patient in the same manner as we would like to be treated if we were that patient. Based on this realization, we also should recognize the importance of the patient's being able to utilize his last years, months, or weeks of life according to what he considers to be the priorities for himself. If there is not free and open communication with the physician about the illness, to the degree that the patient can deal with it, the patient may not be able to make the best use of the time that is left. Later, when it is too late, he will feel cheated out of this last precious time.

For example, the wife of a man with a malignancy of the abdomen told the man's private physician that she did not want him to tell her husband about his illness, "Because my husband cannot take it." In the meantime, the patient was becoming increasingly anxious. After repeated hospitalizations, he had started to lose weight. He expressed his concerns to the nursing staff, who had been informed by the physician not to talk with the patient about his illness. This created great tension among the ward staff, and a social worker was called in to start working with the wife, eventually helping her to recognize the implications of her attitude for the patient, for herself, and for their relationship during the short time they still had together.

How essential this final time is for the patient and his family is something we often forget. Things might need to be said that had never been expressed before. Decisions may have to be made that can never be made later. In terms of a relationship of trust to be established between the patient and the physician, open and honest communications are essential. If the patient concludes that his physician is not honest and trustworthy, what implications does this have for their relationship, especially towards the end, when the patient needs the support of his doctor more than ever before? No matter what rationalization the physician might utilize to explain to himself a dishonest approach to the patient, will it not gradually affect his own sense of trustworthiness and integrity? A breakdown in communication between physician and patient, or between patient and family, will inevitably lead to feelings of loneliness, of isolation, and of heightened anxiety and fear, and since pain is the acceptable language of the hospital, many patients may communicate their fear and loneliness in a disguised manner by asking for pain medications. What they are really asking for is the attention and concern of the medical and nursing staff. This form of pain as an expression of emotional discomfort must be differentiated from actual organic pain in order for appropriate help to be given to the patient.

It is evident that, in order to help the dying patient, physicians, nurses, and all of the medical staff must first be able to deal with the reality of death themselves. Many times the staff avoids the dying patient because they are afraid of dealing with this eventual reality in their own lives, and are afraid of being confronted with their own helplessness in the face of this inevitable end that awaits all of us. Hopefully, the widening interest in the exploration of care for the dying patient, including the introduction of seminars on death and dying in medical school and nursing school curricula across the country, will enable health care professionals to face their own anxieties about death, so as to be better prepared to help their dying patients face this last stage of life.

A PERSONAL EXPERIENCE

Just before the second edition of this book went into print, I developed a malignancy. I will conclude this chapter by sharing with the reader the impact of that experience on my life. About two years after the death of my son's father from leukemia, I observed changes in a mole on my back, changes which I initially ignored. I think the reason for my denial was not only fear, but also the fact that I could not emotionally face the possibility that my son's other parent also might have a malignant illness, one which generally is known to have a very poor prognosis. As a result, I did nothing for two or three months until one morning when I found blood on the back of my night gown. I remember looking at the mole in the mirror and then suddenly having the extremely painful realization: "This is a malignant melanoma. There is no way I can continue ignoring this any longer." And with that thought I broke into tears. I then called an oncologist, who referred me to a well-known skin specialist. He confirmed the diagnosis of malignant melanoma. My immediate concerns were not so much about myself, but rather about my son: "What will happen to him and how do I tell him?" He was 11 years old at the time. Within the preceding two years he had lost both his father (from leukemia) and his godmother (from abdominal cancer). I was deeply worried for him.

When I told him that I had a cancerous mole and would have to go to the hospital for two operations (first, excision of the mole and a skin graft, then lymph node resection), his eyes widened. It was as though he was visualizing his father deteriorate in the course of a single year from a tall, vigorous, vivacious man in his forties to a bald, paralyzed, helpless figure who looked like a wizened old man. My son's expression froze, his voice rose in pitch, and he said with great emphasis: "I don't want to go to school tomorrow. They are going to the Museum of Natural History. But I am not going!" Without arguing, I asked what he wanted to do instead. He said he wanted to stay home and play with his toys. There was no further discussion of my illness that day, as he obviously was too overwhelmed. Two days later, he called me while taking a bath: "I want to talk to you!" Without looking at me, but swishing his body from side to side in the water, he said: "I hope these two operations are going to help you; otherwise I will be very sad." I told him that I was going to have the operations so as to be able to live, and that although his father and godmother had died of cancer, not everyone who has cancer dies. Over the next few days we had several discussions initiated by him regarding when people and animals die. It was apparent that he had many concerns about death and dying, as indeed did I. But I had to help him with his concerns first, before I could deal with my own. He also had many concerns about the technical details of the operations: What part of my body was the doctor going to cut? How was he going to do it? Would

I be asleep? Would I feel any pain? Would I wake up during the operation? As we talked about all of these matters, I remember thinking that we sounded like two old philosophers, discussing life and death, pain and fear, hope and trust.

Eventually as he became calmer, I looked to myself. First, I made a will, and discussed with friends and family the various alternatives for my son's care in the event of my death. Then I became preoccupied with more personal and existential issues. What had I accomplished in my life? Would my passing really be noticed by the crowds of people moving along the streets of New York City? Would there be any kind of existence beyond this life? Would I have any control over the outcome of my illness? While there was sadness mixed with these thoughts, there also emerged a more intense appreciation of the uniqueness of the living moment. My life had been rich in so many ways, and I decided that whatever was left of it was meant to be lived, not mourned.

I will not go into very much detail about my two operations, except to say that I experienced all of the complications that seem to be inevitable when physicians become patients—extreme pain, insomnia, septic fevers, skin rashes secondary to an allergic reaction to penicillin, transient kidney failure, and dangerously low hemoglobin levels that turned out to be in error! I did have many dreams in the hospital—nightmares about dying— but also happy dreams about living. I remember thinking as I awoke from the anesthesia that I must write some time about how reassuring the pain was, because it meant that I was alive. However, I also remember a few days later standing at the window and looking out at the snow falling. Tears were running down my face, partly out of exhaustion and self-pity, and partly because the pain was so severe that dying would feel like a relief. I felt as though there was just a thin thread of will power left, going from somewhere to somewhere in my body, with no emotions and no thought attached. My surgeon came into the room at that very moment on his daily rounds. I turned around and, embarrassed about the tears, said to him: "Shit, did you have to come in just now?" Tactful man that he was, he pretended not to see the tears and proceeded to examine the surgical dressing in a kind but businesslike manner.

After leaving the hospital, I stayed a week at home, then went back to work. I had just started to develop a new program with a new staff at the time when the melanoma was diagnosed. I was concerned about the impact my illness would have on this new program. I decided to be completely honest with the staff. From years of experience working with the families of children who had malignancies, I knew that secretiveness would only backfire in the long run. Also, in our relatively educated society, if a chief of service has two operations within a period of three months, the staff would surely begin to wonder about the nature of my illness. I gathered the staff together, told them the diagnosis and the possible prognosis, discussed the reasons for the two operations, and reviewed the estimated time for recovery postoperatively. The response of the staff was marvelous. They worked hard with me in preparation for my being away, and they were very supportive when I came back after each operation. There was no unmanageable crisis during my absence, and the staff did not discuss my illness with anyone else. Looking back now, I believe that I made the right decision. My open communications made the staff less anxious; they felt trusted by me and therefore they in turn trusted me. I shall always remember their warm human support with deep gratitude.

I am now approaching the five year anniversary of the surgery and have every reason to be hopeful that I will survive my malignancy. Has this experience changed my life? Absolutely. My priorities have truly changed. I have very little patience with superficial relationships. If I want to do something, I do it instead of postponing it until some later time. I am more aware of the transience of human life, but also of its uniqueness. I am also much more aware of the common bonds that link all of us to one another, and therefore my empathy for others has deepened and increased. I can appreciate much better now why each of us in our different ways searches for a sense of meaning to our existence. Rather than becoming more afraid of death, I have become more open to life. My son is older and more secure, and I feel more confident of his future. My illness brought us even closer than we were before. Perhaps most important of all, I have come to realize that I as an individual am unique and special, and yet at the very same time I am only a small part of that great mass of humanity that has moved from birth to death since the beginning of time. My cancer confronted me with the fragility of my existence and the inevitability of my death. But it also

helped me see more clearly the essentials of my own life and my common bond to all of the other lives that have existed on this earth before me, and all of the lives that will come to be after I have gone. Norman Cousins has said it very well:

> Death is not the enemy; living in constant fear of it is. I have no intention of swathing myself in cotton to soften a possibly fatal episode. I will continue to live and think as actively and creatively as it is physically possible for me to do, knowing that longevity by itself can be sterile but that vital feelings and thoughts give meaning and depth to life and provide a true sense of the possibilities of human existence.*

---

* *The Healing Heart, Antidotes to Panic and Helplessness* by Norman Cousins. Reprinted by permission of W. W. Norton & Company, Inc., New York. Copyright © 1983 by Norman Cousins. Page 224.

Suggested Readings

Alsop S: *Stay of Execution.* Philadelphia, Lippincott, 1973.

Cassem NH: The dying patient. In Hackett TP, Cassem NH (eds): *Massachusetts General Hospital Handbook of General Hospital Psychiatry.* St. Louis, C.V. Mosby, 1978, p 304.

Cousins N: *The Healing Heart. Antidotes to Panic and Helplessness.* New York, W. W. Norton & Co., 1983.

Freud S (1916): On transience. In *The Standard Edition of the Complete Psychological Works of Sigmund Freud,* vol 14. London, Hogarth Press, 1957, p 303.

Gonda TA: *Death and Dying.* Menlo Park, CA, Addison-Wesley, 1981.

Hinton JM: *Dying.* Baltimore, Penguin Books, 1967.

Hinton JM: Facing death. *J Psychosom Res* 10:22, 1966.

Kübler-Ross E: *On Death and Dying.* New York, Macmillan, 1969.

Lewis JM: Dying with friends: implications for the psychotherapist. *Am J Psychiatry* 139:261, 1982.

Norton J: Treatment of a dying patient. *Psychoanal Study Child* 18:541, 1963.

Saunders C: The moment of truth: care of the dying person. In Pearson L (ed): *Death and Dying.* Cleveland, Case Western Reserve University Press, 1969, p 49.

Shneidman E: *Voices of Death.* New York, Harper & Row, 1980.

Weisman AD: *On Dying and Denying: A Psychiatric Study of Terminality.* New York, Behavioral Publications, 1972.

Werkman SL: *Only a Little Time.* Boston, Little, Brown, and Co, 1972.

Zinsser H: *As I Remember Him.* Boston, Little, Brown, and Co, 1940.

References

Becker E: *The Denial of Death.* New York, The Free Press, 1973.

Beier V (ed): *The Origin of Life and Death: African Creation Myths.* London, Heinemann Educational Books, 1966.

Berg S (ed): *Nothing in the Word: Versions of Aztec Poetry.* New York, Grossman Publishers.

Evans-Wentz WY: *The Tibetan Book of the Dead.* London, Oxford University Press, 1960.

Novack DH, Plumer R, Smith RL, et al: Changes in physicians' attitudes toward telling the cancer patient. *JAMA* 241:897, 1979.

Oken D: What to tell cancer patients: a study of medical attitudes. *JAMA* 175:1120, 1961.

PART IV

Psychopathology: The Continuum Between Health and Illness

Section N/Normality and Abnormality

CHAPTER 50 **Normality Versus Abnormality, and the Concept of Mental Illness**

Herbert Pardes, M.D.

In the previous chapters we have been tracing the gradual unfolding of events that transform the human infant into the human adult. We have found that the factors affecting the specific nature of the individual are numerous. They are present even before the conception of the child. They include the genetics of his or her family, the social and economic status of the family, the status of the mother during pregnancy, and her physical and psychological health. We have gone on to trace the various environmental factors that act upon the developing child and have found that the individual has a substantial potential to develop in a wide variety of directions. The child uses this potential in an attempt to gain a homeostatic balance. By that we mean that the individual has to mediate the various forces acting upon him or her, both forces originating from inside as well as forces originating from outside. In order to do this, the child uses methods derived from its own innate abilities, from the learning that it does from models in the environment, and also from continuous modification due to learning from additional models and from new experiences. The previous experiences affect the methods used and the various reactions to stresses. Thus, the techniques of the adult for handling stress and for realizing his or her full potential are determined by countless interweaving forces.

THE CONCEPT OF ADAPTATION AND CHARACTER

Gradually, however, certain habitual interests and reaction patterns develop. For example, if you were entering one of your clinical clerkships and some attending on the ward said that he was going to conduct bedside rounds, and you happened to know that that person was a particularly demanding attending, you would likely have some idea as to which of your colleagues might immediately move to the front of the group as the rounds began, which of your colleagues might tend to shrink a bit toward the back, which of your colleagues might suddenly find that this was an opportune time to take a bathroom break, and perhaps even which of your colleagues might at that particular moment find it necessary to make a call home to his family. In other words, there is a certain predictability to the behavior of human adults. We would see the same thing in a psychiatric hospital ward if a paranoid patient were admitted. The patient may have decided that neighbors around him, friends, family — all were part of an extensive communist plot against him. Accordingly, you could pretty well predict that in short order the psychiatric staff and all of the various people on the ward would be included in that plot. So there is a certain predictability to the behavior of individuals.

Now the organized and individualized structure which encompasses the predictable patterns of behavior, the various responses to stress situations, and the techniques for realizing the organism's different potentials, is referred to collectively as the *character* or *personality* of the individual. Thus, character is the sum of the attitudes and patterns of behavior typical for the given individual in adapting to the various inner and outer forces operative in his life. And by an *adaptation* we refer to the necessity to minimize the tension from the conflicting forces playing upon him. We do *not* mean simply an adaptation to a given culture or society.

At times this adaptation may cause the individual so much trouble that either he or others become aware of it. At that point it is considered maladaptive and pathological. For example, as part of an overall adaptation, an individual may develop what is referred to as an *obsession*. This can be particularly distressful to the given individual. An obsession is a persistent thought which is ego-alien and cannot be excluded from consciousness by any conscious process. There are individuals who are plagued by continuing and recurring thoughts about possibly killing one of their family members. This would be an obsession. A second kind of pathological adaptation might include *delusions*. In this instance the individual might not experience much subjective distress, but the person's thinking would be seen by others as clearly abnormal. A delusion is a false fixed belief which is maintained despite incontrovertible evidence to the contrary and which is not usually accepted by the individual's culture or subculture. For example, we see patients who tell us that they are Jesus Christ. We see other patients who tell us that they are the victims of extensive communist plots or plots from literally any kind of organization. These types of deviations from the broad spectrum of normal adaptations constitute *psychopathology*. Our primary focus in these first several chapters will be to introduce the concept of psychopathology.

THE PREVALENCE OF PSYCHOPATHOLOGY

What is the prevalence of psychopathology? In order to get some idea we can examine two studies done in quite different kinds of settings. One was done by Alexander Leighton in Sterling County, which is a semi-agricultural lumbering and fishing area. Another was done by Thomas Rennie and his coworkers in the east side of Manhattan. They both used interviews to elicit the presence or absence of psychogenic symptoms. The results were roughly the same. They found that about 30% of people were seriously bothered by symptoms. They found another 30% who were moderately troubled by symptoms, 25% who reported relatively mild and inconsequential symptoms, and 15% who were asymptomatic. One would not propose that those figures are exact, but they do suggest that much of the population reports some kind of psychological distress. More recent studies show that up to 30% of patients going for help to general practitioners and internists suffer from some diagnosible psychiatric disorder.

There are other statistics of particular interest when one talks about the prevalence of psychopathology. Approximately 2 million people were hospitalized for psychiatric illnesses in 1983. The likelihood is that all of us will have a close friend or relative who at some point will have a severe mental illness. For example, the estimated prevalence of schizophrenia in a year is approximately 1% of the population. In other words, within a given year about two million people are likely to be diagnosed schizophrenic. A far larger number will have affective disorders within a given year. The prevalence for affective disorders has been estimated at approximately 6% of the population. These include people with a variety of different types of depressions and other affective disorders, such as mania. While many of these people may receive treatment, a large number do not. The annual number of reported suicides in the United States is about 25,000 per year, and it has been estimated that two to three times that many suicides may go unreported. In fact, suicide constitutes the fourth most frequent cause of death in the age range 25 to 44, and the second most frequent cause of death in the ages 15 to 24, being surpassed only by accidents. Recent evidence suggests that around 20% of the population needs some form of treatment for diagnosable mental illness within a given year. I will not present any additional statistics, but I assume that this will give some general idea of the widespread occurrence of psychiatric illness.

NORMALITY VS. ABNORMALITY

A question that follows is the separation of normal functioning from pathological functioning. This is often most difficult but obviously quite important.

How does one decide whom to refer for help? How does one decide who needs preventive help? The question of normality as opposed to abnormality is often a critical one. We can take a look at some of the criteria that one could use in making such a determination. First of all we can look at what typifies the majority or the average individual. What is true of most people? Is the person showing something that the majority of people would also show? But one gets into difficulty with this criterion because, for example, most people suffer from dental caries, just as the majority of people also suffer from some kind of visual defect. So this criterion, the law of the majority or of the average, in and of itself, does not distinguish normality from abnormality.

One could go on to look at the presence or absence of symptoms, assuming that those who have complaints manifest psychopathology. However, as mentioned before in the two studies in Manhattan and in Sterling County, only 15% of people were asymptomatic. So in effect, with this criterion, one would be deciding that 85% of the population had a mental illness or some kind of psychological disturbance. Obviously this criterion, in and of itself, would not adequately distinguish psychological disturbance from normality.

One could go on to use as a criterion the subjective physical and emotional well-being of an individual. Is the person relatively confident and relatively secure? Does the person have a sense of adequacy to handle most situations? However, one can go to a psychiatric state hospital and find a grossly disturbed manic patient who will tell you that he is perfectly fine. One can speak to a person who has chronic alcoholism, in the midst of an alcoholic bout, and he will tell you he has never been happier. So the criterion of the subjective physical and emotional well-being of an individual in and of itself also does not suffice.

Finally, one can talk in terms of an evaluation of the *overall functioning* of an individual which would include a large number of questions or issues to be evaluated. For example, what is the relation of the individual to reality? What kinds of relationships does that person have with other people? Can he or she tolerate some anxiety? Some frustration? The usual separations of life? The depressions that everybody experiences at one point or another? Can the person delay gratification, or must he have either the cake or the drink or the smoke, and therefore not be able to tolerate any delay in getting it? What kinds of defense mechanisms does the person use? For example, how does the person handle aggression? Does he or she do it by projecting it to other people (a relatively primitive mechanism) and say, "I'm not angry, it's really everybody around me who is yelling"? Or does the individual sublimate aggression and put it to some constructive use? Is there some organization, some synthesis to the total assets, the total interests, and the total activities of the individual? Or are his life and his goals rather fragmented? How does the person respond to normal situations when one might expect a certain degree of regression? Does the person have the capacity of a Ph.D. but, because of inadequate adaptation, is unable to secure the degree or to do any work in his field? All of these and more would be involved in a comprehensive understanding of a person's level of functioning, and the best that one can do in terms of distinguishing normality from abnormality, is to use these criteria collectively and try to examine in detail each individual situation. In recent years a greater attention to observable phenomena associated with specific illnesses has resulted in a more differentiated classification of the mental disorders. This classification, which will be discussed further in the next chapter, complements the more comprehensive assessment of function that I have just described above.

Still there are many grey areas. Often, it is particularly difficult to decide. Owing to the vast complexity of human behavior, it is hard even for people who are well trained in psychiatry or psychology to always reach agreement and to predict all behavior. In fact, often the newest people in the field are the ones who show the best diagnostic skills and this tends to decrease with age. The reader may be familiar with the story of the medical student who went to his medical clerkship for the first day both quite anxious and quite interested, and his first patient came in suffering from low back pain. The medical student went right to work. He did his five hour examination, wrote up a 10 page report, did the physical, did the lab work, and put it all in the chart. The intern came, saw the patient for about an hour, also did his history and physical, wrote his one page note in the chart, and informed the resident that a new patient had entered the hospital. The resident saw the patient for ten minutes and put a paragraph in the chart. The staff presented the patient to the attending who signed the chart.

Well, this was a very complicated case, and as a result they brought in chief residents, specialty groups, and literally every conceivable service to take a look at the patient. While they were testing and evaluating and reexamining, the patient got worse and worse and finally died. One can imagine that with all this interest, there was a tremendous turnout for the autopsy. At the autopsy it was determined that the patient had sarcoma of the spleen, and the chief of medicine was most distressed. How was it that nobody had any idea that this patient was suffering from sarcoma of the spleen? The chief of medicine decided to examine microscopically every detail of that chart to see if there were any clues. As he was going through the chart he came to the medical student's work-up, and number one under his diagnostic impressions was sarcoma of the spleen! The chief of medicine was dumbfounded. He decided he had to see this budding genius immediately. He called the medical student into his office and he said, "Dr. X, I'd like to congratulate you; you are off to a fantastic start in medicine, I've never seen anything like this before. This is wonderful. I want you to keep up the good work, but I have just one question for you. How did you know this patient had sarcoma of the spleen?" And the medical student, feeling rather pleased and self-satisfied, said, "Well, after all, what else causes low back pain?"

THE APPROACH TO A PSYCHIATRIC PATIENT

I would now like to discuss the initial approach to patients generally and then approach a patient with psychopathology in a way comparable to the one we would use to approach a patient with nonpsychiatric medical pathology. We do that by asking three general questions. First: *What?* In other words, we identify the descriptive pathology. What are the patient's complaints? What are our observations? All of these answer the question, what. Second: *How?* How does this descriptive pathology develop? In other words, what dynamic mechanisms operate

to produce the signs and symptoms? Third: *Why?* In other words, why did this come about and what were the causes that set these mechanisms in motion? So we have three different aspects of pathology, the answer to the question *what*, or the descriptive, the answer to the question *how*, or the dynamic, and the answer to the question *why*, or the developmental and genetic.

How does this work? Let us first take a patient in medicine. The patient comes into our office complaining about frequent respiratory attacks. Often at night, he coughs, wheezes, has shortness of breath, and at the end of the attack produces a great deal of sputum. The attacks are sudden, and at other times he is relatively healthy. These are his complaints. We examine him during the attack and find that he is anxious and that he is having trouble breathing. His thorax is hyperexpanded and his diaphragm is very low, his expirations are prolonged, and he has a whistling sound to his breathing. When we listen with the stethoscope, we hear wheezes and rhonchi throughout the chest, mainly in expiration. All of these findings answer the question, what. This is the descriptive part of the pathology.

Then we move on to the question, how. How did this come about? What were the forces and mechanisms that produced these wheezes and this dyspnea? To answer this question we must refer to a body of knowledge about the forces that produce this picture. They include the mechanisms of contraction of bronchial and bronchiolar muscles, the edema of mucous membranes, and the accumulation of bronchial secretions. The contraction of the muscles interferes with the movement of air in and out of the chest. There would be increased difficulty in transporting the air as a result of the edema of mucous membranes. The accumulation of secretions, and a narrowing of bronchial and bronchiolar muscles, may cause wheezes and rhonchi. Accumulation of secretions accounts for the sputum at the end of the attack. We could continue talking about defensive reactions to allergens, psychological forces in producing the attacks, and many other factors, but all of these would be the variety of dynamic forces which produced the manifest picture and which answer the question, how.

But we have one further question: why? Why did this person react this way to an allergic or psychological stimulus? Why did the particular stimulus cause the attack but not other stimuli?

We know that familial elements are important in bronchial asthma, but of what importance would that be for this particular person? If the person had an inherited predisposition, why is it expressed in this person and not in others? These are the developmental and genetic questions. In other words, they represent an inquiry into the causes of the illness, and are an attempt to answer the question, why. The patient is aware of his symptoms, but he is unaware of the forces and the causes that have brought them about.

What about psychopathology? A patient tells of his complaints, but there is much of which he is unaware. Also, there is much that the patient will be reluctant to say. This gives the psychiatrist the additional task of being able to elicit the relevant material from the patient. The psychiatrist scrutinizes the patient's attitude and behavior as he discusses his complaints. What is troubling him primarily? What may be of less consequence? The psychiatrist attends to the patient's manner of speaking in relation to the content. He also attends to what the patient does not say. A pregnant patient of mine, who was particularly distressed and anxious, spoke about everything but the one most glaring recent change in her life — her pregnancy! And it was only when I started talking to her about it, that one could see that this was indeed what was causing much of her distress. So we attend to what the patient does not say as well as to what the patient does say. The patient may be able to speak about less sensitive areas but may refrain from the most charged issues in his life.

Like the general practitioner or the internist, the psychiatrist gets a history plus a detailed description of symptoms and then conducts his own examination. This is referred to as a *mental status*. A mental status is a comprehensive survey of the psychological status of a given individual at a particular time. It includes observations of the person's general health and appearance, of his or her habits of dress, of his general moods and affects, of the patterns of his speech, of his facial expressions, as well as his motor activity. It involves a focus on the content of the person's thought and also on the logic of his thought processes. It involves an examination of his state of awareness or confusion, of his ability to absorb as well as to recall. It involves an estimate of his general intellectual capacity, of his judgment, of his insight, and many other aspects of his behavior.

AN INTERVIEW WITH A PATIENT

Let us now look at a portion of an interview conducted some years ago by Dr. John Frosch, keeping in mind what we have described above. J. R. is the patient, and we start a bit after the beginning of the interview.

J. R.: . . . leading up to the actual kidnapping of my daughter on February the 15th. I have that annotated down on the calendar. Having heard her voice, help me God first, and then Jim — help.

Dr. F.: Excuse me if I interrupt you from time to time but I have to get something clear in my mind. You mention the kidnapping of your daughter?

J. R.: Correct.

Dr. F.: Was she actually kidnapped?

J. R.: She was actually kidnapped, doctor.

Dr. F.: By whom?

J. R. Shall I say either one or possibly two chaps who lived in the neighborhood who are obviously by me only suspects at this time since I actually did not see with my own eyes.

Dr. F.: You didn't see the actual kidnapping?

J. R.: No, sir.

Dr. F.: Well, how did you know that this was a kidnapping?

J. R.: Doctor, my daughter has not shown up which is entirely a wrong thing. She would have obviously been home.

Dr. F.: How long is this now since she has not . . . ?

J. R.: The point, the simple point, no, that has nothing to do with it, doctor. The point now is this, that February the 15th was when she disappeared.

Dr. F.: And you haven't seen her since?

J. R.: And doctor, there were any number of indications and I was told repeatedly one thing after another which didn't formulate any boogie-boogie or anything like that. It was simply a basic fact that they were implying that she had been kidnapped.

Dr. F.: Who was implying?

J. R.: Now, doctor, first of all in a year, a year prior to my daughter's kidnapping several fellows, boys on the block, and one who did not belong in the block who came in with the boys on the block — I had shown them a bankbook with $999,999.99 in the bank balance. Things have disappeared and they knew where the bankbook was because I had opened the drawer in my desk.

Dr. F.: What did they do with the bankbook?

J. R.: I don't know. I don't know, but it simply disappeared, period. Now it seems to me that if they had, if they personally had been responsible for the entry in the house and the theft of the bankbook, Good Heavens, there was only $5 left in the account in the book. I mean, I mean they just simply did not see the same amount above, the small amount below that million bucks, that's simply, that's all, the figures of the 9999 etc., occluded any possibility in their thoughts and they, my God, who would ever keep a million dollars in the bank account? Let's not kid about it. I mean that would be utter foolishness but to show the mental age of these kids and their lack of experience with bank balances, why obviously . . .

Dr. F.: What happened subsequent to that?

J. R.: Pardon!

Dr. F.: What happened subsequently?

J. R.: Subsequent to that was a gradual buildup of . . . hm . . . his word wasn't too good and so on and so forth, I give you a . . .

Dr. F.: A gradual buildup?

J. R.: That is correct.

Dr. F.: What does that mean?

J. R.: Simply this. To the effect that anything that I might have to say later could be discredited very handily by anybody.

Dr. F.: Well when you say his word wasn't any too good — I don't understand. Did people talk about it or what?

J. R.: For example, oh, yes, Mrs. Jones in particular was in the forefront of the diminution of my word as to its value.

Dr. F.: Diminution of your word?

J. R.: The reduction of my word in any value. In other words, so that I was a fool. "You'll never see her again, Jim." How do you like that? It's too late, Jim.

Dr. F.: It's too late, Jim?

J. R.: Yes, or Jimmy.

Dr. F.: Did they ever try to get you . . .

J. R.: No, not here. Well, here, here is what the story is is this. That they intended by hook or crook to get the house, and they thought they were going to get a lot of money. I think they still think that there's money. Let them think it because there isn't any.

Dr. F.: Who are these people, Jim?

J. R.: Well, one, Smith whom I had known lived in the top floor back of 17 Sixth Avenue. I'd known him for quite a while. I didn't know it

at the time but he was in prison and received, his mother received . . .

Dr. F.: Excuse me, were any of these people the people you showed your bankbook to?

J. R.: Not to Smith or either to Howell.

Dr. F.: This is a different group entirely?

J. R.: That is correct. I just told you the kids. Now the point is this. That the kids talked to a slightly older person and the older person would pass the word around. Believe me . . .

Dr. F.: Pretty soon the whole neighborhood knew about all of this?

J. R.: Oh, yes, without any hesitation.

Dr. F.: I see, and then these guys got together and . . .

J. R.: Whatever they cooked up was up to them. I don't know.

Dr. F.: What was the ultimate goal?

J. R.: Well, the ultimate goal is obviously to get a hold of the property and any money they can get a hold of, period.

Dr. F.: Did they . . .

J. R.: Now, there were several things, doctor. In my marriage to Sally King . . .

Dr. F.: Before you get to that, let me ask you one more question.

J. R.: Just a little bit more, please doctor. I'm not totally unaware of time passing on and so on . . .

Dr. F.: Oh, we have plenty of time. I just want to ask you one more question. Was part of their ultimate goal also to do away with you?

J. R.: That I am not quite sure of but I understand that the order for no violence went out about a year and a half ago when things started cooking up during the summer, and the show was put on for me.

Dr. F.: The show put on for you?

J. R.: Oh, the prostitutes going past with their foul mouths and making dirty cracks when I was sitting out on the stoop.

Dr. F.: At you? About you? To you? Did they try to proposition you?

J. R.: Yes, they did everything in the world. Oh, good Lord, that was about it.

Dr. F.: What would they say, for instance?

J. R.: Well, oh, foul mouthed.

Dr. F.: Use the words.

J. R.: No, I'd rather not. I'm going to be . . . I'm sorry I have to get a little prissy about this situation because fundamentally the four letter Anglo-Saxon words . . .

Dr. F.: Did they say, for instance, "Hey, Jim, do you want to fuck," or something like that?

J. R.: That's exactly just about it and why the hell don't you. Do you want to work it by yourself or . . .

Dr. F.: Give me the exact words, Jim.

J. R.: They were . . . you used them. One morning I was sitting out on the stoop. This was pretty early, about seven o'clock and I say pretty early. It's fairly early for the neighborhood. I was sitting out on the stoop and a cab drove up across the street and a gal stepped out of the cab and says, "About the birds, the beasts, and the flowers, how about it?"

Dr. F.: The birds and the beasts?

J. R.: The birds, the beasts, and the flowers.

Dr. F.: Beasts? What did she mean by the beasts?

J. R.: That's the way she put it.

Dr. F.: What did she mean by that?

J. R.: Well, she meant the birds and bees obviously, you know that was pretty much pat.

Dr. F.: Why would she say beasts?

J. R.: I don't know but that's just exactly the way she said it.

Dr. F.: Can you surmise what she meant by that?

J. R.: I don't . . . I . . . what her connections are I don't know but I got a laugh out of it.

Dr. F.: Tell me, are any of these remarks irritating?

J. R.: She said, as I say, about the birds and the beasts and the flowers.

Dr. F.: Yes.

J. R.: Then no answer from the guy that had driven her up in the car. "So you want to do it yourself, huh?" That isn't . . . what the hell did she say? That isn't . . . I think it was . . . I doubt if it was wise. It was some other word that had a similar connotation to "that isn't wise" to it and I got a kick out of the situation. I kid you not because it was so darned obviously for me. She spoke so darn loud that it came across the street.

Dr. F.: Obviously, it was intended for your ears?

J. R.: Obviously it was intended for my benefit.

Dr. F.: Did they also make any cracks about you . . . that because you didn't respond, you might be a fairy or queer.

J. R.: Absodamnlutely! Remember when they were having the big raid on the stores on Main Street?

Dr. F.: What about it?

J. R.: A couple of gals and two guys came and ran in the car and they parked in front of the house and they were taking stuff out of the rumble seat of the car to take over into 16 Sixth Avenue and the gals went up in the stoop in 16 and one called across the street. This was the first one that I mentioned to you.

Dr. F.: Yes.

J. R.: It was simply this. "You're a faggot," or something like that. Or, "Do you want to do it by yourself?" Now one of the gals was coming along with a guy looking right at me and I was looking past her. Believe me, I couldn't tell what her face looked like because I was actually not looking at her face, but she was looking right straight at me and she got just about as far from here to well, just to the edge of that sofa over there at the gate. It came out as, well, she'd rather fuck than eat. How do you like that!

Dr. F.: What did that mean to you?

J. R.: That was the implication and then when they had gone past . . .

Dr. F.: She'd rather fuck than eat? What did the eating refer to?

J. R.: Obviously her food. This is far as I can see. So, anyway, the point was that they had gone past the house and past the tree and toward the fire hydrant. Now you don't know the location of these things.

Dr. F.: It's all right. Go ahead.

J. R.: I'm simply setting a stage for you on the street, on the sidewalk, in front of my house, I'm 17 Sixth Avenue. The fire hydrant is between 17 and 19. The tree is directly in front of 17 and it's a little tree but anyway he turned around and was looking at me . . .

Dr. F.: The fellow with her?

J. R.: Yes, and she said "Good God, he didn't even look at me." He said . . . "Don't worry. He saw you," and now, I never saw her before in my life and I wouldn't be able to . . .

Dr. F.: What did he mean "Don't worry. He saw you?"

J. R.: They were pulling the trick. That's all.

Dr. F.: What trick?

J. R.: It was part of the bit. They were playing this thing up to the hilt.

DISCUSSION OF THE INTERVIEW

I do not intend to demonstrate a complete mental status at this point, but let us focus on some of the prominent features of this interview.

First, the patient speaks frequently in a strange, rather incomprehensible way. At times he is very vague. He also demonstrates an intriguing use of language. There were such comments as, "which is entirely a wrong thing" or "in the forefront of the diminution of my word," or "didn't formulate any boogie boogie" or "abso-damnlutely." He tells of people talking about him, calling him names, making false accusations and insinuations, persecuting him. Enough is known about his actual life situation to say that this is not in fact happening.

What do we see then? First, we see what are referred to as *illusions*. Illusions are misinterpretations or misperceptions of actual external stimuli. For example, Jim may hear people clear their throat or say something to the cab driver; he perceives that as a verbalized threat. Somebody else might smell the odor of cooking and tell you what they have smelled is the odor of a dead body. The first would be an auditory illusion, the second would be an olfactory illusion, and there can be illusions of every sensory modality. Second, although not as clearly in this part of the interview, we see *auditory hallucinations*. Hallucinations are sensory perceptions in the absence of an external stimulus. Again, this can affect any sensory modality. In another part of the interview, for example, he speaks about being able to hear people talking several blocks away in a cellar. As far as we could tell, there was no external stimulus to trigger that perception.

Third, we see *delusions of persecution*. As I mentioned earlier, a delusion is a false, fixed belief maintained despite incontrovertible evidence to the contrary and not usually accepted by the person's culture or subculture. Again there can be various sorts of delusion. There can be *somatic delusions*: patients will tell us that they have no organs in their body. There can be *delusions of grandeur*: somebody says that he is Christ or he is God. And as demonstrated in the interview there can be delusions of persecution. Here people are trying to hurt, provoke, harm Jim. They want to get his house, steal his bankbook, kidnap his daughter. Also we see *ideas of reference*. By that we mean that a person interprets things going on in the environment as having a special and personal reference to him, as Jim does with the various talk and activities of the neighborhood. He describes a show being put on for him alone. All of this is descriptive

and answers the question, What? And one could go further, because there is a good deal of material that emerges even in this brief portion of the interview.

But what about the second question: How? How did this come about? What are the forces and mechanisms that produce this kind of descriptive picture? As with the asthmatic patient we would look to knowledge acquired over time about what produces these kinds of pathological pictures. Jim has certain internal conflicts. He has conflicts around impulses which are felt as unacceptable, and we can speculate about what some of these conflicts and concerns may be. He says that someone is trying to get his property and his money. This may refer to his own wish or fantasy. He is the one who originates the idea of a million dollars in a bankbook. He refers to some men kidnapping his daughter. We might wonder if he had inclinations toward his daughter that aroused guilt in him. Or does his daughter's absence become disturbing to him and humiliating, such that it is much better to rationalize it by saying she has been kidnapped, rather than to admit that she left him? He spoke about prostitutes putting on a show for him. They demeaned him as a result of the fact that he made no response and showed no interest. They referred to him as a faggot. We might speculate that perhaps he has impulses associated with homosexuality which are repugnant to him. What he does is to paint the picture of an extensive plot throughout the entire neighborhood. The particular nature of the plot is determined by issues of importance to him. Just like a projective test, he uses his own fantasies, his own concerns, his own preoccupations, and sees them in what is really a relatively neutral situation. He may use particular aspects of the situation to construct the story, but more as a tool rather than as a critical determining force. The force comes from him.

So if he is troubled by avaricious, by homosexual, by incestuous, or by other impulses, he defends against them by pushing them away from himself, by trying to repress them, by trying to forget them. But the forces reassert themselves. A person's internal psychology is always active, always dynamic. So he goes to a more drastic defense. He pushes them out of himself. He denies them in himself, and he attributes them to other people. Now he can feel somewhat more comfortable. He is more comfortable because the impulses are seen as outside of him. In that way he is better able to fight them. This is the essence of the mechanism of *projection*; he has projected many of his own unacceptable impulses to the people around him. But there are other aspects as well. The *principle of multiple function* sets forth the idea that many different psychological forces express themselves concomitantly in a person's behavior. Jim's delusions also serve to gratify certain grandiose needs. According to his delusions he is the central figure for a host of activities in the neighborhood, and the prime figure of interest to all of the people there. This actually denies the relatively inconspicuous position he has in life. Now in order to understand more of the dynamics, one would have to work further with Jim. But these are some attempts to answer the question: How?

We have a third question, however, the question: Why? Here we would have to look for earlier experiences which led to an interference in Jim's psychological development. Under stress Jim regresses to patterns more consistent with earlier stages of development. Thus, he is using techniques from a point in psychic development when things on the inside and things on the outside are not clearly differentiated. He ascribes to people on the outside things that really originate within himself. He may have been more prone to use these techniques, or to suffer from his earlier experiences, as a result of constitutional elements, and we will discuss the constitutional, genetic determinants of mental illness in a subsequent chapter. At this point we do not know anything about the genetic factors in Jim's case. We would have to learn more by being able to talk further to him or his family. The main point, however, is that we are trying to explain the why of his psychopathology, and to do so we would have to explore more about his early development, about his family life, and about his hereditary background, and this takes a good deal of time. Also, the process is hampered by the problems of any retrospective examination.

But we have some additional problems. We are dealing here with ideas, with feelings and emotions, all of which are often very difficult to demonstrate, especially in an initial interview. In more extensive treatment with an individual, such phenomena often come more clearly into focus, and the relationship between the dynamic and the descriptive aspects of behavior are much more blatantly demonstrated. One patient, for example, whom I had been seeing in treatment for a while, once had the following experience. After he had been smoking some pot, he developed an impression that he could see his father in his grave, with a twisted face, and the patient felt that the father had a kind of murderous look on his face directed toward the patient. This was related to many aggressive impulses and feelings the patient had expressed earlier in the treatment toward the father. Also, one can see these dynamic issues much more clearly in a patient in the borderland of psychosis, in which the person fluctuates between seeing the impulses as his own, versus seeing them as coming from the outside. Some patients may be so severely disturbed that they have in their conscious awareness ideas of which normal people are usually unaware. One such patient came to a psychiatric emergency room openly talking about wanting to murder his mother, and on the other hand wanting to lie on her breast. This is content of which most people would not be aware. Generally, however, the dynamic factors are difficult to demonstrate immediately in psychiatry, and it may take an even longer period of time before the developmental and genetic factors become clear. That is because there exists outside the awareness of both patient and observer a part of the mind called the unconscious, which I will discuss further in a later chapter.

Suggested Readings

Leighton AH: *My Name is Legion.* New York, Basic Books, 1959.

MacKinnon RA, Michels R: *The Psychiatric Interview in Clinical Practice.* Philadelphia, W.B. Saunders, 1971.

Offer D, Sabshin M: Normality. In Kaplan HI, Freedman AM, Sadock BJ (eds): *Comprehensive Textbook of Psychiatry,* ed 3, vol. 1. Baltimore, Williams & Wilkins, 1980, p 608.

Srole L, Langner TS, Michael ST, Opler MK, Rennie TAC: *Mental Health in the Metropolis: The Midtown Manhattan Study,* vol 1. New York, McGraw-Hill, 1962.

Richard C. Simons, M.D. and
Herbert Pardes, M.D.

We would like to begin by reviewing the general classification of the mental disorders and then proceed to an overview of the multiple factors involved in the etiology of mental illness.

THE DIAGNOSIS OF MENTAL ILLNESS

Diagnosis of mental illness has undergone many changes in the past decade as a result of research advances in phenomenology, epidemiology, and the neurosciences. A new diagnostic system was introduced in 1980 in the *Diagnostic and Statistical Manual of Mental Disorders—Third Edition* (DSM-III). This system emphasizes observable phenomena and decreases the reliance on inference in diagnosis. It also attempts to remain free of any particular theories regarding the etiology of mental illness. Finally, it fosters the development of homogeneous groups of disorders and increases the reliability of diagnostic categories. We are not assuming a detailed mastery of this diagnostic nomenclature for the purposes of this book, but we will review some of the broad categories, some of the basic concepts, and some of the outstanding features of the mental disorders. One of the major innovations of DSM-III is the *multiaxial system* that utilizes five separate axes for evaluating diagnosis, planning treatment, and predicting outcome. *Axis I (Clinical Syndromes)* and *Axis II (Personality Disorders)* together constitute the entire classification of the mental disorders. We will begin by discussing the major clinical syndromes of Axis I.

The first major category among the *Clinical Syndromes of Axis I* involves *disorders usually first evident in infancy, childhood, or adolescence.* Among these, the syndrome of *mental retarda-* tion is of major importance. Mental retardation refers to subnormal general intellectual functioning, starting in the developmental period and associated with impairment in adaptive behavior. There are a host of causes that may be responsible for mental retardation. Many are of known organic etiology. The majority of cases, however, seem to have as their cause sociocultural factors. Mental retardation will be discussed in more detail in a later chapter. Other syndromes within this first major category include *pervasive developmental disorders* (previously called the psychoses of childhood), *attention deficit disorder* and *specific developmental disorders** (the learning disabilities), *conduct disorder* (including delinquency), *eating disorders* (obesity, anorexia nervosa, and bulimia), and the so-called *symptom disorders of childhood.* These latter include *anxiety disorders* (such as phobias), *stereotyped movement disorders* (such as various tics), and *other disorders with physical manifestations* (stuttering, enuresis, encopresis, sleepwalking disorder, and sleep terror disorder). Each of these disorders will also be discussed in more detail in later chapters.

The second major category in Axis I consists of the *organic mental disorders.* In DSM-III a distinction is made between *organic brain syndrome*, which designates a constellation of signs and symptoms without reference to etiology (for example, delirium, dementia, intoxication, withdrawal); and *organic mental disorder*, which designates a particular organic brain syndrome in which the etiology is known (for example, alco-

---

* Specific developmental disorders are listed in Axis II in DSM-III.

hol withdrawal delirium, multi-infarct dementia). Some key signs and symptoms in the organic mental disorders include impairments of consciousness, orientation, memory, and other cognitive deficits.

The third major category in Axis I consists of the *substance use disorders*. This diagnostic class involves maladaptive and undesirable behavioral changes (inability to control drug use, impaired social or occupational functioning, development of withdrawal symptoms) associated with more or less regular use of substances that affect the central nervous system. These conditions are to be distinguished from nonpathological substance use for recreational or medical purposes. They are also to be distinguished from the drug-induced organic mental disorders which involve the direct acute or chronic effects of these substances on the central nervous system. One of the major agents in this group is alcohol, which is associated with a wide array of mental and physical syndromes and an enormous social cost. Alcohol is estimated to be involved in 30% of all suicides, 40% of all assaults, 50% of all fatal automobile accidents, and 65% of homicides. It is estimated that over 10 million Americans are dependent on or abuse alcohol and other drugs.

A fourth major category in Axis I that has already been discussed earlier in this book involves the *psychosexual disorders* (the psychosexual dysfunctions, the paraphilias, and the gender identity disorder of transsexualism). Two other categories that have also been discussed in the book are the relatively common *somatoform disorders* (conversion disorder, hypochondriasis, idiopathic pain disorder, and somatization disorder or Briquet's syndrome), and the relatively rare *factitious disorders*.

A seventh major category in Axis I is *adjustment disorder*. This involves a maladaptive reaction to an identifiable psychosocial stressor, defined as occurring within three months after the onset of the stressor. It is not merely a single instance of a pattern of overreaction to a stressor or an exacerbation of one of the mental disorders previously described. The stressor may seem to vary in intensity, and the severity of the reaction may not be completely predictable from the severity of the stressor as perceived by others. The stressors may be single (e.g., death of a loved one) or multiple (e.g., ongoing marital difficulties); they may occur only once or be recurrent; they may affect an entire group or

community (a natural disaster) or only an individual (the developmental stress of going to school or getting married).

We will spend much of the remainder of this chapter on the two other major categories in Axis I, the *neurotic disorders* and the so-called *"functional" psychotic disorders*, as well as the *personality disorders* that constitute Axis II of DSM-III. However, before doing that we would like to briefly describe the other three axes of DSM-III. *Axis III* is called *Physical Disorders or Conditions*. This axis allows the clinician to indicate any current physical condition or disorder from which the patient may be suffering. It also allows the clinician to list any psychological factors that may have contributed either to the onset or the exacerbation of a physical condition. Axis III includes all of the *psychophysiological disorders* that were described by Dr. Levy in his overview of the basic concepts of psychosomatic medicine (Chapter 12). *Psychosomatic medicine* is defined by Sheehan and Hackett as the study of the reciprocal relationships among biological, psychological, and sociological factors in maintaining health and influencing the onset and cause of diseases. In Chapter 13 Dr. Dubovsky demonstrated this broadened definition of psychosomatic medicine in his discussion of the psychophysiology of health, illness, and stress. Axis III represents the recognition of this broadened definition in our diagnostic nomenclature.

Axis IV provides for a coding and rating of the *Severity of Psychosocial Stressors* that may have contributed to the onset or the exacerbation of the current mental disorder. Such stressors should be listed as clearly and specifically as possible. Treatment outcome may become more predictable through the use of Axis IV, since the prognosis may be better when a mental disorder develops as the result of a severe psychosocial stressor rather than when it develops as the result of a mild stressor, or in the absence of any stressor.

Axis V provides for an estimate by the clinician of the *Highest Level of Adaptive Functioning During the Past Year* as reflected in social relationships, occupational functioning, and use of leisure time. Treatment outcome may become more predictable through the use of Axis V since this axis allows for an assessment of the patient's strengths, assets, and motivation for treatment. Furthermore, many patients return to their previous level of adaptive functioning once they have recovered from their mental disorder.

We will now discuss the three broad categories of the mental disorders: the *neurotic disorders* (Axis I), the *functional psychotic disorders* (Axis I), and the *personality disorders* (Axis II). The neurotic disorders and the functional psychotic disorders are broad, overriding diagnostic categories that are composed of a number of different sub-categories in Axis I. The personality disorders are listed on a separate Axis II because very often a patient may be manifesting the signs and symptoms of both a personality disorder and a clinical syndrome. However, because of the more acute and dramatic presentation of the clinical syndrome, the more chronic and less dramatic presentation of the personality disorder was often overlooked in the past. (The same is also true for the specific developmental disorders.) The presence of a separate Axis II for the personality disorders (and the specific developmental disorders) encourages clinicians to diagnose these conditions in addition to the clinical syndromes whenever it is appropriate to do so. We will now attempt to differentiate clinically between these three broad categories of the mental disorders (Table 51.1).

DIFFERENTIATION OF THE MENTAL DISORDERS

Attitude of Patient Toward Illness

In the previous chapter the concept of adaptation was discussed—namely, the typical behavior patterns and defense mechanisms and personality traits that an individual develops in response to stress. These patterns are used repetitively, they are part of what makes an individual unique. For example, one person, if particularly anxious, might become very talkative and very active, while a second person in the same situation might tend to withdraw and become quiet. The sum total of these various defense mechanisms and behavior patterns and personality traits constitute the character or personality of the individual. Now some individuals choose patterns that may solve certain problems for them, but do so relatively inefficiently and in fact may even cause additional problems. Such behavior patterns may affect their lives continually, yet often in a very subtle way. In order to see this clearly it often becomes necessary to look at the entire life of the individual and observe the way in which it has been stamped by certain *maladaptive behavior patterns*, certain rigid and inflexible attitudes and personality traits that have caused repetitive problems for the person. One has to look closely because often the behavior is only slightly different from the behavior of other people. In fact, if one spoke to the people around the person, they might say that the person is simply "idiosyncratic." When the character or personality of an individual utilizes maladaptive behavior patterns and inflexible attitudes to such a degree that effective social or occupational functioning is repetitively impaired, we say that a personality disorder exists.

One of the distinguishing features of a personality disorder is that such a person generally seems less distressed, less troubled than an individual with a neurotic disorder. In a neurotic disorder a person usually identifies certain of their thinking or behavior as *symptoms*. These are seen as foreign, as not consistent with the person's general psychology, as alien, and therefore we refer to such symptoms as *ego-alien* or *ego-dystonic*. In contrast, for the individual suffering from a personality disorder, his or her behavior is *ego-syntonic*. It is considered part of the person, not alien, and is consistent with the person's ongoing interests, feelings, and general psychology. It is not seen by the person as a sign of illness.

For example, if a person is characterized as rigidly scheduling everything, as being particularly orderly and thrifty, as being perhaps excessively clean, a person who is involved in an excessive amount of thinking about relatively inconsequential things, a person who doubts himself repeatedly or who may have to procrastinate before coming to any decision, such a person would be considered as having an *obsessive compulsive personality disorder*. He might organize a rather elaborate schedule and arrange all kinds of pencils and paper for several hours, and then work for about 10 or 15 minutes. If you asked him about this, he would say, "In order to be efficient, I have to have things organized. I have to have things scheduled. I just can't work in a mess." If you talked to him about his attitude regarding money, he would say, "Well, of course it's important not to waste money." If you asked him why it takes him so long to come to a decision, he might reply, "I have to take everything into account before I can make a

Table 51.1
*Differentiation between the Neurotic Disorders, the Functional Psychotic Disorders, and the Personality Disorders**

	Neurotic disorders	Functional psychotic disorders	Personality disorders
Ego functions	Mild to moderate impairment but reality testing is intact	Severe impairment with reality testing always impaired	Mild to moderate impairment but reality testing is intact
Developmental stage	Conflicts generally related to later developmental stages and danger situations	Regression to very early fears of annihilation, fragmentation, and disintegration	Conflicts generally related to later developmental stages and danger situations
Onset	Acute	Acute	Chronic
Attitude of patient toward illness	Symptoms are viewed as ego-alien, ego-dystonic	Variable	Maladaptive behavior patterns are viewed as ego-syntonic
Attitudes of others toward patient	Moderate concern	Great concern, fear	Annoyance, anger
Genetic and other biological factors	Undetermined, possibly present in some subcategories	Present in some sub-categories	Undetermined, possibly present in some subcategories

*Table by Richard C. Simons and Herbert Pardes.

critical decision." In other words, all of this behavior would be ego-syntonic for that individual. On the other hand, if you had a person with an *obsessive compulsive neurotic disorder* who was having thoughts that he might kill somebody in his family, or who, in order to prevent anxiety, must kiss his or her spouse on each side of the cheek before they separate for the day, you would find that this person would tend to disavow these obsessional thoughts and compulsive actions. He or she would see such symptoms as a sign of illness, as foreign, in other words as ego-alien. The neurotic individual is regularly aware of certain ego-alien aspects of his or her life, whereas the individual with the personality disorder is not.

For the individual suffering from a psychotic disorder, this criterion (the attitude of the patient toward the illness) is quite variable. Some psychotic patients may be terrified by their hallucinations or other symptoms, and view them as ego-alien. Other psychotic patients may only be able to explain their inner chaos through a fixed delusion, and therefore that delusion becomes ego-syntonic.

Onset

Manifestations of personality disorders are generally seen by the time of adolescence or even earlier. They are usually chronic and per-

sist throughout adult life, in contrast to the more acute onset of the neurotic and psychotic disorders. In order to make the diagnosis of a personality disorder, it should be clear that the identified characteristics are typical of the person's functioning on a long-term basis and are not limited to discrete episodes of illness. One of the key problems with someone suffering from a personality disorder is that, by virtue of the "ego-syntonic" nature of the person's behavior, there is often minimum motivation for change. This makes the possibility of ensuring a cooperative interaction with any person offering therapeutic help particularly difficult.

Attitudes of Others Toward Patient

This inability of individuals with a personality disorder to recognize the maladaptiveness of their behavior patterns, defense mechanisms, and personality traits may cause others in their environment to become annoyed or angry at them, or to view them as "a little different" or "idiosyncratic." In contrast, the individual with a neurotic disorder may elicit moderate concern from others because of the mental pain and suffering that is conveyed. The individual with a psychotic disorder may elicit even greater concern from others because of the serious disorganization that is evident in the individual's functioning. At times one may even experience fear in the presence of someone suffering from a psychotic disorder because of the strangeness and possibly also the dangerousness of the person's behavior. Such fear should be a clue that can be used in making the diagnosis.

Ego Functions

In order to differentiate a psychotic disorder from a neurotic disorder or a personality disorder, one would have to carefully evaluate the ego functioning of an individual through a *mental status examination* (Table 51.2). There are five main functions that should be assessed. First, the so-called *autonomous functions* that may develop independent of conflict include perception, memory, orientation, thinking, affects (emotions, moods), motor behavior, speech, and language. Second, the *adaptive functions* mentioned in the discussion of Axis V of DSM-III include social relationships, occupational functioning, and use of leisure time, as well as any special talents or creative capacities. Third, the *defensive functions* include the defense mechanisms, behavior patterns, and personality traits that are used in dealing with anxiety and conflict. Fourth, the *synthetic functions* are reflected in the ability to organize and integrate the various demands of the inner and outer worlds. Judgment and insight could be considered manifestations of these functions. Fifth, there is the function of *reality testing*.

One of the ego functions that is particularly useful in evaluating the presence of a psychotic disorder is reality testing. By reality testing we mean the capacity to distinguish inside from outside, to have a definite idea of one's ego boundaries so that the individual does not see things which originate within himself as existing or originating outside of himself. A marked impairment of any of the various ego functions may indicate the presence of a psychotic process, but certainly reality testing is one of the main criteria for differentiating a psychotic disorder from both a neurotic disorder and a personality disorder. However much the functioning of patients with neurotic disorders and personality disorders may be impaired in various ways, there is no substantial impairment of their reality testing, whereas the reality testing of the psychotic patient is invariably impaired.

Developmental Stage

The main conditions that constitute the neurotic disorders are the *anxiety disorders*, the *dissociative disorders*, certain of the *affective disorders*, and in some instances certain of the *somatoform disorders* and *psychosexual disorders* as well. One of the central features of the anxiety disorders is that the individual is either experiencing substantial anxiety or is trying to use a variety of defense mechanisms in dealing with that anxiety. In some, the anxiety is directly experienced, and these are known as the *anxiety states*. The individual may experience the anxiety in a variety of situations, and either continually in a generalized persistent way (*generalized anxiety disorder*), or more suddenly and unpredictably (*panic disorder*). In other anxiety disorders the individual develops defense mechanisms for dealing with the anxiety, but often these mechanisms develop into symptoms that cause such distress that the individual com-

Table 51.2
Mental Status Exam*

1. Autonomous functions
   a. Perception
   b. Memory
   c. Orientation
   d. Thinking
   e. Affects (emotions, moods)
   f. Motor behavior (including appearance)
   g. Speech and language
2. Adaptive functions
   a. Social relationships
   b. Occupational functioning
   c. Use of leisure time (hobbies, interests, recreation)
   d. Special talents and creative capacities
3. Defensive functions
   a. Defense mechanisms
   b. Behavior patterns
   c. Personality traits
4. Synthetic functions
   a. Organizing, integrative capacities
   b. Judgment
   c. Insight
5. Reality testing

* Table by Richard C. Simons and Herbert Pardes.

plains about these ego-alien or ego-syntonic symptoms rather than the anxiety that is causing the symptoms. For example, as mentioned earlier, a person with an *obsessive compulsive disorder* develops obsessional thoughts and compulsive rituals in order to contain the anxiety. They will then come to their family physician or to a psychiatrist complaining that they are tortured by their symptomatic thoughts or impaired by their symptomatic compulsions. The *phobic disorders* represent another group of anxiety disorders in which the inner anxiety is displaced onto an external object, activity, or situation which can then be avoided through the phobic symptom. As we have already discussed, the individual with a personality disorder deals with anxiety through the development of rigid, persistent maladaptive behavior patterns that are ego-syntonic rather than through the development of ego-alien symptoms. Yet, in both the anxiety disorders (and the other neurotic disorders) and the personality disorders, the individual feels intact, however impaired he or she may be in various ego functions.

The situation is very different for the psychotic patient. That individual is generally struggling with problems related to very early stages of development, with marked regression to primitive fears of annihilation, fragmentation, and disintegration. Such fears stand in sharp contrast to the separation anxieties, mutilation and castration anxieties, and guilt that play such an important role in the development of the neurotic disorders and the personality disorders (see "Primary Danger Situations," Table 18.1, Chapter 18). For example, a psychotic patient might be concerned about such issues as being able to survive, as being able to hold onto reality, as being able to maintain physical and psychological integrity. He or she may talk about disintegrating, merging, or fragmenting. The neurotic patient, on the other hand, might focus on a failure to fulfill certain standards, or on certain wishes that violate his or her own sense of ethics and morality, while a patient with a personality disorder might never be able to deal effectively with any situation that involves separation from or competition with other people.

Genetic and Other Biological Factors

The term "functional" psychotic disorders refers to psychotic conditions in which a clear-cut organic cause has not as yet been established, in contrast to the organic mental disorders in which the organic etiology is established. The main conditions under this category are the *schizophrenic disorders*, the *paranoid disorders*, and certain of the *affective disorders*. As will be described in Chapter 52, there is increasingly powerful evidence for the presence of genetic, neurochemical, and other biological factors in the etiology of many of these "functional" psychotic disorders. The overall evidence for genetic, neurochemical, and other biological factors in the etiology of the neurotic disorders and the personality disorders is much less convincing at this point, but is suggestive in the case of some sub-categories of these disorders.

THE MULTIPLE ETIOLOGIES OF MENTAL ILLNESS

With this general overview of the major syndromes of psychopathology as a frame of reference, we would now like to move on to the question of the etiology of these mental illnesses. What are the various factors that have to do with the development of psychopathology? One way to approach this question would be through the *biopsychosocial* model discussed earlier in the book. Using this model, one would be curious about the biological factors (Chapter 52), the psychological factors (Chapters 53 and 55), and the sociocultural factors (Chapter 54) that may be contributing to any given mental disorder. Another way to approach this question would be to take a *chronological model*, and in this model one would be interested in the ongoing interaction between both nature and nurture. First, there are the *constitutional factors*, referring to everything with which the individual enters the world. These include all of the *genetic factors* having an effect on the potential for health or illness. Second, there are the *experiential factors* which interact with the constitutional potential for good functioning or for psychiatric difficulties. These experiential factors can be divided into the *early developmental factors* and the *current psychosocial stressors*. We recognize that the current stresses include some which may be part of the innate developmental process, e.g., the various stages of the life cycle and especially those that involve profound biological changes such as puberty and the climacterium. These will involve inevitable stresses with which the individual will have to deal. But there are also accidental and adverse events which may impinge upon the particular individual. All of these current stresses can be considered *precipitating factors*. So, in evaluating the origin of any mental disorder, one would look at three factors. First, there would be the constitutional, that with which the individual entered life; second, the early developmental, which would interact with the genetic and other constitutional factors to gradually produce a certain type of personality; and finally the current psychosocial stressors and the precipitating factors, which would interact with that personality to set a given psychopathological process into motion. Table 51.3 depicts the integration of the *biopsychosocial model* with: 1) the *descriptive model* of DSM-III which attempts to describe *what* strengths and liabilities are present in any given psychiatric patient using five different axes of investigation; 2) the *dynamic model* which attempts to explain *how* a given syndrome of psychopathology has come about through the interaction of multiple etiological factors; and 3) the *developmental-genetic model* which attempts to explain *why* a given syndrome of psychopathology has come about through the ongoing chronological interaction of nature (genetic and other constitutional factors) and nurture (developmental factors and experiences).

At times it would be clear that one set of factors is clearly predominant. For example, with phenylketonuria the main factor is constitutional; this illness involves an autosomal recessive gene which, if undetected, leads to marked mental retardation. On the other hand, in the neurotic disorders and the personality disorders, the factors most significantly involved seem to be early developmental ones and certain later precipitating ones. In regard to the functional psychotic disorders, the delineation of the role of genetic, neurochemical, and other biological and constitutional factors in the etiology of these disorders constitutes one of the most exciting areas of current psychiatric research. The best current view of the role of various factors in these major psychiatric disorders such as the schizophrenic disorders and the affective disorders is that there is a likely interplay of biological, psychological, and sociocultural factors which can lead to the precipitation of a given episode of illness in any given individual at any given time.

As one proceeds to explore other constitutional factors in both personality development and mental illness, one finds there have been various workers who have tried to relate certain types of body morphology and temperament to psychopathology. For example, Kretschmer, a German psychiatrist, divided people into four

Table 51.3
Evaluation of the Psychiatric Patient*

Models	Descriptive	Dynamic	Developmental-genetic
Biological	*Physical exam* Current physical strengths Current physical disorders or conditions (DSM-III Axis III)	Biological factors in mental illness	History of genetic and other constitutional factors History of physical illness, injuries, operations, medications
Psychological	*Mental status exam* Current psychological strengths and adaptive functioning (DSM-III Axis V) Presence of one or more mental disorders (DSM-III Axis I and Axis II)	Psychodynamic factors in mental illness Learning factors in mental illness	Developmental factors and experiences in infancy, childhood, adolescence, and adulthood
Sociocultural	*Life setting* Current psychosocial supports (DSM-III Axis V) Current psychosocial stressors (DSM-III Axis IV)	Sociocultural factors in mental illness	Family history Racial, religious, cultural, and socioeconomic background

* Table by Richard C. Simons

body types and found that certain body types were characteristic for certain diseases. There have been others who have attempted to develop the same thesis. However, morphological type is not currently seen as a critical factor in the etiology of mental illness. Attempts to correlate mental illness with such constitutional factors as race or ethnic background have been rather unconvincing to date, although the cultural definition of what constitutes mental illness and "deviant" behavior is an important factor in the statistical reporting of mental illness in various cultures, countries, and ethnic groups, as Dr. Mumford will indicate in her chapter on sociocultural factors in mental illness.

With regard to sex, there tends to be an increased incidence of the anxiety disorders (especially phobias) and the affective disorders in women, while men tend to show a higher incidence of the organic mental disorders, alcoholism, and the personality disorders (especially antisocial personality).

With regard to marital status, it has been found that there is a somewhat increased incidence of mental illness in single people, possibly as a result of the reduced social support systems available to them, or possibly because of preexisting emotional problems that may have prevented them from establishing a stable marital relationship.

Other factors existing prior to birth, which would be relevant in the development of psychopathology, would include the state of the mother during pregnancy. We are aware of the fact that German measles and syphilis may have marked effects on the developing fetus. There is also increasing evidence which indicates that alcohol and other drugs ingested by the pregnant mother may cause gross birth defects and perhaps other subtle defects which we cannot as yet detect.

One other element present in the inherent constitutional structure of the individual is the drives. These would manifest themselves as intense urges, needs, and desires demanding gratification in a most compelling way. It is felt by many neonatal researchers that individuals show considerable variation in the strength of their drives, even at birth. There have been many efforts to relate such behaviors as the frequency and the intensity of crying, of sucking, and of various other activity patterns to different strengths of drives in the neonate. Furthermore, the individual may enter the world with a given strength to these drives, and then have them modified by a variety of experiential factors throughout life.

Thus, there are a large number of more or less fixed factors, the irreducible minimum with which a person enters the world. These are the constitutional factors, and while substantial work is necessary in order to delineate all of them, they are clearly related to personality development and, in some instances, to the development of mental illness. And while our understanding of the role of genetic, neurochemical, and other biological factors in the etiology of mental illness obviously is not complete, it is steadily increasing and remains a fascinating area for further research and exploration, as we shall see in the next chapter.

Suggested Readings

Diagnostic and Statistical Manual of Mental Disorders, ed 3. Washington, DC, American Psychiatric Association, 1980.

Goodwin DW, Guze SB: *Psychiatric Diagnosis*, ed 3. New York, Oxford University Press, 1984.

Leigh H, Reiser MF: *The Patient: Biological, Psychological, and Social Dimensions of Medical Practice.* New York, Plenum, 1980.

Spitzer RL, Williams JBW, Skodol AE: DSM-III: the major achievements and an overview. *Am J Psychiatry* 137:151, 1980.

Section O/The Multiple Etiologies of Mental Illness

CHAPTER **52** **Biological Factors in Mental Illness**

A. Genetic Factors in Mental Illness

Martin Reite, M.D.

During the past several decades we have witnessed a marked increase in both interest in and research on the relationship between genetics and psychiatry. Substantial evidence now exists suggesting that genetic factors are of significant importance in the major mental illnesses, and basic data relating to genetic influences in other areas of both normal and abnormal behavior are emerging at a rapid rate. This renewed interest in genetic influences on human behavior reflects both a fundamental increase in substantive empirical data and improved measuring techniques, as well as a change in attitude on the part of serious students of human behavior. The relationships being described today have been there waiting to be observed, but our research strategies were not sufficiently refined, and furthermore perhaps the intellectual climate was not optimal prior to this time. There were several reasons for the latter. First, much of the early work on genetic influences on human behavior was performed by German investigators and published in the German literature, and thus was not available to all. Subsequently, the entire area fell into disrepute with the rise of the Third Reich and its distortion of the science of genetics. Second, the intellectual climate during the early part of the 20th century was heavily influenced by both the behaviorism of Watson and the American translation of Freud's psychoanalysis, both of which tended to stress environ-

mental influences and downplay the importance of genetic or constitutional factors in human behavior. It was also thought at the time that to say something was "genetic" (or "constitutional") was to imply it was immutable, forever fixed, and not accessible to modification or change.

Fundamental changes in these areas have led to the current state of willingness to consider, and actively search for, genetic contributions to human behavior, both normal and abnormal. Largely as an outgrowth of the spectacular advances in molecular biology, our knowledge of the subtle and complex manner in which genetic influences may be affected, especially in development, has required a fundamental revision of older concepts of immutability and determinism. Indeed, the evidence in support of genetic contributions to certain major mental illnesses has become so compelling that it can no longer be ignored.

Our coverage of genetics and psychiatry in this chapter will be selective. There are many, by now well defined, genetically based metabolic disorders that have associated behavioral disturbances as a major component, including such entities as phenylketonuria, the lipochondrodystrophies, and other inborn errors of amino acid, sugar, and lipid metabolism. Similarly, chromosomal anomalies such as Down's syndrome, Klinefelter's syndrome, and Turner's syndrome have important psychiatric implications. These areas are well covered in other textbooks, and have been briefly discussed in this book in the chapters on mental retardation and transsexualism. I will limit my discussion to those psychiatric disturbances for which evidence of important genetic influences is beginning to appear. Further, I will assume that the reader possesses a basic knowledge of the science of genetics.

RESEARCH STRATEGIES IN PSYCHIATRIC GENETICS AND THE SCHIZOPHRENIC DISORDERS

The Problem of Diagnosis

Research in psychiatric genetics is complicated by the fact that the disorders in which we are interested are difficult to diagnose with precision since reliable biological markers do not yet exist. The areas where the most progress has been made in clinical human genetics are areas where definitive diagnoses are possible. For example, in PKU, serum phenylalanine levels are elevated, and phenylpyruvic acid is found in the urine. The other inborn errors of metabolism also have characteristic biochemical findings associated with them, and therefore accurate diagnoses can be made. This greatly facilitates genetic research. In most medical conditions we have reliable, objective, empirically derived biological markers. When a patient consults us complaining of symptoms suggestive of pneumonia, we can obtain objective indicators that substantiate our diagnosis, e.g., a chest film with lobar consolidation or a sputum culture positive for diplococcus. If a patient describes symptoms suggestive of temporal lobe epilepsy, we might benefit from observing a seizure, but an accurate diagnosis depends upon specific EEG abnormalities. In the case of most psychiatric disorders, the primary data we have upon which to base our diagnosis is that provided by the patient's history, subjective complaints, and behavior during a psychiatric interview. We have as yet no objective biological markers, no reliable laboratory tests, to assist in making an accurate diagnosis. Thus, we have the definite possibility that a single clinical syndrome may include several different disorders with several different etiologies. This is a problem that enormously complicates genetic research in psychiatric illness.

Definitions

Several definitions are of importance in our discussion of research strategies in psychiatric genetics. These are: 1) *lifetime risk*, 2) *prevalence*, and 3) *period of risk*.

Using the common cold as an example, its prevalence would be represented by how many people in a given place such as a school classroom have a cold at a given time. During the winter months, this figure could perhaps be as high as 10% to 20%. The lifetime risk of the common cold, by comparison, is a figure representing how many individuals will, at some time during their lives, contract a cold; the lifetime risk of the common cold would therefore be approximately 100%. In the case of schizophrenia, the lifetime risk of the population at large is approximately 1%. This means that, from a statistical standpoint, approximately one out of 100 individuals can be expected to develop schizophrenia at some time during their lives. The concept of period of risk is important when we think of psychiatric genetics. This term refers to that portion of a person's life during which they are most likely to develop or exhibit the illness in question. Again, in the case of the common cold, people are at risk over their entire life span, for be they infants, children, adults, or elderly, they can still contract a cold. With certain of the psychiatric disorders, however, the period of risk is limited. For example, most new cases of schizophrenia are diagnosed in individuals beginning in their teens and extending up through perhaps 45 years of age. Relatively few cases are found before adolescence, and it is rare for a new case of schizophrenia to be diagnosed in an individual over 45. The period between adolescence and about age 45 therefore constitutes the period of risk for schizophrenia. In the case of the major affective disorders, the period of risk generally is thought to be roughly between the ages of about 25 and 55 or 60 (although some cases of bipolar disorder appear in younger individuals) and, thus, while overlapping a portion of the period of risk for schizophrenia, it is significantly different from it. The important issue here is that if you are studying the lifetime risk or prevalence of a disorder, you must be certain your population is in the period of risk age-wise. It would make little sense to try to study genetic influences on bipolar disorder in young children, or genetic influences on acute paranoid schizophrenia in the elderly, for neither of these populations would be at significant risk for the disorder in question. The word risk is often used in another manner in the general area of psychiatric genetics. It is often said, e.g., that an individual's "risk" of developing schizophrenia is about 1%; in this case, risk is used to mean lifetime risk. Also, persons from families that have a schizophrenic family member are more likely to develop the disorder than otherwise (their "risk" is about 10%, and they are often referred to as being "at risk"). Thus, the term risk may be used in several different ways, although the meaning is generally similar.

In our discussion of research strategies, we will use the example of research on the schizophrenic disorders for illustrative purposes. Most psychiatric genetic research has focused on this disorder, and numerous studies utilizing all the various research strategies have been published in the scientific literature.

Pedigree Analysis

Pedigree analysis is perhaps the easiest way to examine possible genetic contributions to a disorder, and is represented by the well-known family tree in which members of a family who are affected with an illness are represented by solid or filled squares or circles and unaffected members by open squares or circles. The family relationship between all individuals is apparent, and it is easy to trace the illness in question from one generation to another. This technique is useful when studying relatively uncommon disorders that are constant in their penetrance and in their clinical expression. However, family histories are published only if there is a concentration of affected individuals, and they do not provide us with much data as to how the illness is represented in the population at large. Furthermore, with pedigree analysis, there is no control for social, familial, or environmental influences. This is crucial in psychiatry, for we are dealing with behavioral disturbances, and we know that environmental influences can precipitate, modify, and cause disorders of behavior. Thus, we have to be able to separate out social and environmental factors. It is not so crucial when we are talking about a disorder of amino acid metabolism, where we assume that environmental influences are not going to have a great deal to do with whether one has an enzyme deficiency or not. Accordingly, pedigree analysis is of generally limited usefulness in learning about the genetics of psychiatric disorders.

Family Risk Studies

The second major research strategy in psychiatric genetics is the *family risk study* (also sometimes called *consanguinity studies*). What one does in this case is to compare the occurrence of a given disorder, for instance schizophrenia, among the relatives of patients who have the illness, compared to the prevalence in a normal or control population. Those individuals who are diagnosed as having the disorder in question are usually called *index cases* or *probands*. If one finds, among the family or biological relatives of an index case, a greater number of cases than one would expect from a similar sample size of the population at large, then there is presumptive evidence of a genetic contribution to (or influence on) the disorder.

A large number of family risk studies have fairly well established that the lifetime risk of schizophrenia is much higher in those individuals who have a close biological relative with the disorder. In a family with normal parents, if one child is schizophrenic the chance of another child (a sibling) also developing the disease is about 8.5%, which is over eight times higher than in the normal population. In a family with a single schizophrenic parent, the lifetime risk of a child also developing the disease is about 14%. If both parents are schizophrenic, the chance of a child developing the disease is 25%. Thus, the lifetime risk of schizophrenia in children with two schizophrenic parents is 25%; they are considered at high "risk" for the disease.

Family risk or consanguinity studies demonstrate that an individual's risk of developing schizophrenia increases dramatically if the individual has close family members with the disease. But such studies cannot separate environmental from genetic influences. It is certainly stressful to be raised by a schizophrenic parent or parents, and it has been proposed that perhaps it is the stress of living with a schizophrenic family member that accounts for the higher incidence in other family members. The family risk or consanguinity studies are not powerful enough strategies to separate out such influences. In 13th century France, leprosy was thought to run in families as a sort of hereditary disorder, for cases of leprosy were found to cluster in affected families. We now know that this was due to close and crowded living conditions over a long time span that permitted spread of what is normally not a particularly contagious disease from one family member to another. In the absence of such knowledge, however, a family risk study of leprosy would have led to the conclusion that genetic influences may be important.

Twin Studies

The third major research strategy involves *studies of twins*, technically called *gemellology*. First developed by Francis Galton in the 19th century, this strategy depends on the fact that monozygotic, or identical, twins have the same genotype, whereas dizygotic, or fraternal, twins have different genotypes. Therefore, if a disorder is genetic, and if one twin of a monozygotic pair has it, the likelihood should be much higher that the other member of the twin pair will also have it, since they share the same genotype. The risk in dizygotic twins, on the other hand, should be no greater than in nontwin siblings. By way of definition, if in twin studies both twins have the disease in question, they are called *concordant*. If only one has it and the other does not, they are called *discordant*. So one would expect, in a genetically determined illness, to see a higher frequency of concordance than discordance in monozygotic twins.

The work of Franz Kallmann during the first half of this century was instrumental in reawakening interest in the genetics of mental illness; in an extensive series of twin studies, Kallmann found a far higher incidence of concordance for schizophrenia in identical twins as compared to fraternal twins. A number of subsequent studies by other investigators have confirmed that the concordance for schizophrenia in identical twins is high, approximately 40% to 50%, whereas in fraternal twins the concordance rate is only about 10%, which is approximately the same as for nontwin siblings. Thus, twin studies are also supportive of a genetic contribution to schizophrenia.

There are, however, problems with twin studies as well. Twins are often very special people. Identical twins especially are often raised in

quite atypical environments where they are dressed and treated the same, and they may almost lose their individual identities at times. One might wonder, therefore, whether one twin could in a sense "learn" to be schizophrenic by observing and/or interacting with the other twin (it is important to note, however, that being a twin per se does not increase the risk of schizophrenia); and, again, with twin studies, where the twins are raised by their natural parents, we cannot separate out environmental influences. Even with monozygotic twins, the fact that they have the same genotype does not in any sense mean they are going to have the same environment. For instance, in the case of monozygotic twins especially, the two twins are usually subjected to rather marked differences in the intrauterine environment. There is usually one smaller twin, and it usually has a very different blood supply than the larger twin, so such environmental influences start very early. There is also a higher risk of birth trauma with twins.

The very fact that the concordance rate for schizophrenia in identical twins is less than 100% (which is the rate you would expect if a disorder was completely determined by the genotype) documents the fact that environmental influences must have some influence in the appearance of the disorder, at least insofar as *preventing* its development in an individual genetically predisposed to it or in *precipitating* its development in the same individual. What the critical environmental influences may be, however, is as yet unclear. Such influences can, of course, be myriad, including intrauterine differences, birth traumas, forceps injuries, cord compression, nutritional deficiencies, and the whole gamut of social, familial, and environmental difficulties that can be encountered as one is growing up. Evidence for incomplete expression of genotypes is also found in studies of discordant identical twins, since the "normal" twins of discordant pairs apparently transmit schizophrenia to children at the same increased rate as the schizophrenic twins do.

Adoption Studies

It was largely because of the problems associated with separating environmental from genetic influences that the *adoption* research strategies were developed. The central issue in such studies is that an infant shares a certain percentage of the genotype of his biological parents.

If that infant is adopted away shortly after birth and is raised by another set of parents, with whom it shares no common genes, then genetic influences (provided by the biological parents) can be separated from environmental influences (provided by the adoptive parents).

There are several ways to do research involving adoption. For example, one can study the children of schizophrenic parents who were adopted away at birth, compared to the children of nonschizophrenic parents adopted away at birth. If a genetic influence is present, and assuming the adoptive parents of both groups are similar, the children of the biological parents who are schizophrenic should have a higher incidence of schizophrenia compared with the children of biological, nonschizophrenic parents. Or conversely, one might identify a population of adults who have schizophrenia and who were adopted away from their biological parents as infants, and one can find another group also adopted away as infants who do not have schizophrenia as the control group. Then one can go back through family records and study the biological and the adoptive relatives of both of these groups, and then determine whether or not the biological relatives of those adults who have schizophrenia showed a greater percentage of schizophrenia than one would expect on the basis of what is known about the incidence of the disease in the population at large or among the biological relatives of the control group. Most of this type of work has been done in the Scandinavian countries where very accurate records are kept of family histories, births, deaths, records of hospitalization, diagnoses, and the like.

A number of adoption studies of schizophrenia have been performed, most notably by Seymour Kety and David Rosenthal and their collaborators. In one such major study, these investigators identified all adoptions that took place in the city of Copenhagen between 1924 and 1947 inclusive, where the adoptive parents were not related biologically to the child. There were a total of 5,483 such adoptions. Of this group, 33 individuals had developed schizophrenia at the time of the study. Most subjects were between 20 and 40 years of age, so they had gone through the period of risk for the most part. These 33 were called the index cases. For each one of these 33 index cases who had been adopted many years back, a control subject was found, matched for age and sex, who had been adopted but who

had not developed schizophrenia. Thus, there were 33 index and 33 control cases.

These investigators then identified all possible close biological relatives and the comparable group of adoptive relatives for both groups. A total of 463 relatives were identified for their 66 subjects. They then examined the medical records of all relatives for evidence of what they described as "schizophrenic spectrum disorders." It was postulated that if there was indeed a significant genetic contribution to schizophrenia, then the biological relatives of the index cases should have a much greater incidence of schizophrenic spectrum disorders than the biological relatives of the control cases. In the case of adoptive relatives, both groups should have a similar and low incidence of schizophrenic spectrum disorders.

Of the total of 150 biological relatives of the index cases, 13 were found to have schizophrenic spectrum disorders, whereas of the total of 156 biological relatives of the control cases, only three were found to have schizophrenic spectrum disorders. This difference was highly statistically significant. Among the 74 adoptive relatives of the 33 index cases, two had schizophrenic spectrum disorders, and among the 83 adoptive relatives of the control cases, three had schizophrenic spectrum disorders. These differences were not statistically significant.

This study provided strong evidence for a genetic influence in the development of schizophrenia, a view supported by a number of subsequent studies using adoption research strategies. There has been considerable recent argument in the scientific literature as to just how these findings should be interpreted (for example, see Lidz and Blatt, 1983; Kety, 1983; and Grove, 1983), but the overwhelming weight of the evidence strongly supports a major role for genetic influences in this disorder. In this regard, Crow (1983) has proposed the interesting hypothesis that schizophrenia may be a viral disease (many of the genetic studies would be compatible with such an explanation), and that the genetic influence may in fact represent a genetically determined susceptibility to such infection. The need for further studies in this area is clear.

The major difficulty in this research is the high probability that schizophrenia is a symptom complex representing a group of disorders with similar appearance but very different etiologies, of which genetics is but one. In the absence of reliable biological markers which allow us to define with more clarity those various disorders that eventually are clinically diagnosed as schizophrenia, we can expect little further resolution of the question of genetic contribution. A recent study suggests it may be useful to divide schizophrenia on the basis of whether it is familial (those patients with a schizophrenic first degree relative) or sporadic (patients with a negative family history for schizophrenia). One would expect to find a significant genetic contribution only to the first type, and evidence of some type of environmental causation (toxic, traumatic, infectious, psychosocial) more prominent in the latter.

In our discussion of research strategies in psychiatric genetics, it is apparent that as one moves from pedigree analysis through family risk to adoption studies, the ability to separate environmental from genetic influences increases markedly; so, however, does the difficulty, cost, and complexity of the research. It is relatively easy to construct family pedigrees; it is time consuming, difficult, and expensive to conduct an adoption study. The natural history of genetic research on specific psychiatric syndromes tends to move from simpler strategies to more complex and costly ones. Initially, perceptive clinicians observe that certain illnesses seem to run in families. They may construct several family pedigrees to document this impression, and this may be then followed by a family risk study. As a rule, only if this is positive will more complex and powerful research strategies be brought into play. We have seen this progression in studies of schizophrenia, and now we will observe it once again in genetic research on affective disorders and alcoholism.

AFFECTIVE DISORDERS

Nomenclature

The affective disorders constitute the largest category of severe, often incapacitating, mental illnesses. This group of disorders has undergone extensive changes in its nomenclature over the past few years, and this complicates the comparison of older studies (which used an earlier nomenclature) with newer studies. Currently DSM-III uses the term bipolar disorder (mixed, manic, or depressed) for what used to be called manic-depressive psychosis, and major depres-

sion (single episode or recurrent) for what used to in the main be called psychotic depression or involutional melancholia. (The term unipolar disorder is also still in use for major depression without evidence of mania.) The relationship between bipolar disorder and major depression or unipolar disorder is not yet clear, although as many as 10% of initially depressed patients eventually develop bipolar disorders.

Evidence for Genetic Causation

It is perhaps in the area of the affective disorders that we have seen some of the most impressive recent advances in psychiatric genetics, including recent work that has focused on the mode of genetic transmission of certain of these disorders. Additionally, the important concept of *genetic vulnerability* has been highlighted by research on genetic contributions to the affective disorders. This concept implies that persons, who for genetic reasons are vulnerable to the development of a disorder, carry evidence of their biological vulnerability even when clinically well and exhibiting no symptoms. It then becomes enormously important to examine such individuals when they are well so as to study their biological vulnerability without the extra contaminants produced by the presence of the illness per se (e.g. the intrinsic stress that results from having a major illness, illness-induced physiological changes, or the effects of drugs and other therapies).

Most studies have placed the lifetime risk of bipolar disorder at about 1%, roughly similar to that of schizophrenia, although this figure varies somewhat from study to study and from country to country. The incidence of both unipolar and bipolar disorders as well as other forms of significant depression may be in excess of 5%, which is clearly a major public health problem and a source of considerable suffering for the many affected individuals. Family risk studies of bipolar disorder have generally shown the risk in siblings or parents of affected patients to be in the general vicinity of 10%, with a lesser figure (ranging from 1–4%) for major depression only. Different studies provide somewhat different figures, probably due to variation in the sample base. The risk for second degree relatives (uncles, aunts, grandparents, grandchildren) is generally about half that of first degree relatives. A number of twin studies (reviewed in Gershon,

1976) have consistently demonstrated a significantly higher concordance rate for affective disorder in identical as compared to fraternal twins. Such studies have provided strong support for a major genetic contribution to at least some of the affective disorders.

As pointed out earlier, however, adoption studies are critical in providing hard evidence in support of a genetic contribution to an illness. While they do not completely differentiate genetic from possible prenatal and perinatal influences, the importance of adoption studies is nonetheless significant. In a 1977 adoption study of bipolar adoptees, Mendlewicz and Rainer found evidence of affective disorder in 31% of the biological parents of their probands compared to 12% in the adoptive parents. The morbid risk in these biological parents was comparable to the risk found in parents of nonadopted bipolar patients (26%), and was significantly higher than it was in the biological or adoptive parents of normal adoptees (2% and 9%, respectively).

Mode of Genetic Transmission

The affective disorders have proven to be fertile ground for studies of possible modes of genetic transmission, and in these studies pedigree analyses have proven quite useful. Specific genetic hypotheses can be tested in such cases by examining chromosomal linkage markers or evidence of specific physiological vulnerabilities in the members of a pedigree, and then determining to what extent they travel with the affective disorder. In a recent review of the mode of genetic transmission, Gershon (1983) proposed two major classes of models, called *unitary* and *heterogeneous*. In unitary models, all patients with a given diagnosis (e.g., affective disorder) are considered to be part of a single type of genetic liability. Heterogeneous models on the other hand state that within a given clinical syndrome (again affective disorders), some cases are caused by one type of genetic disorder, and some by another. For example, it has been generally well established that some cases of bipolar disorder seem linked to the X-chromosome (high rates of apparent mother-son transmission, and virtually absent father-son transmission), whereas others do not. This would conform to a heterogeneous model. Turner and King hypothesized that a subgroup of bipolar illnesses

(called BPD$_1$) may be involved with X-linked inheritance, while the second subgroup (BDP$_2$) may have an autosomal dominant genetic inheritance pattern linked with the HLA (human leukocyte antigen) gene on chromosome 6, distal to the short arm. In a 1981 paper Weitkamp and Stancer reported that depressive illness segregates along with HLA in certain families. Since HLA is known to be associated with the body's immune system, this linkage may help to explain the reported disturbances of certain immune functions in some patients with major affective disorders, or in other patients following a major loss. It should be noted however that the above findings have been criticized on methodological grounds and have not been replicated by other investigators. Thus their significance is far from clear at the present time.

Genetic Markers in Affective Disorders

A major goal in psychiatric genetics is to eventually be able to identify distinct entities that are genetically transmitted, and that travel with the clinical syndromes of interest, and are present and measurable even though the affected individual may not be exhibiting clinical symptoms at the time in question. Such *genetic markers* would therefore be able to successfully predict which members of a pedigree are at risk and which members are not. Gershon (1983) outlines the following as the qualifications necessary (but not sufficient) for such a genetic marker: 1) The characteristic must be associated with an increased likelihood of the psychiatric illness. (On the other hand, the proposition that persons who have the illness should generally show the characteristic need not be true since there may be biological heterogeneity in the illness.) 2) The characteristic must be heritable and must not be a secondary effect of the illness. 3) The characteristic must be observable (or evokable) in the well state, so that its presence can be determined independently of the illness.

To date, several potential genetic markers of affective illness have been identified, including certain measures of monoamine metabolism (e.g., several measures of monoamine oxidase, catechol-O-methyltransferase, and dopamine-βhydroxylase), various measures of cell membrane permeability and transport (e.g., lithium transport), and the presence of atypical brain proteins (e.g., Duarte protein). None of these measures have proven satisfactory as yet, but they provide an indication of some of the exciting directions in which genetic research on affective disorders appears to be moving.

SCHIZOAFFECTIVE DISORDER

The diagnosis of schizoaffective disorder is a difficult one from a nosological standpoint, since this syndrome is even less well-defined than the schizophrenic and affective disorders, containing as it does aspects of both. As biological markers are developed for both schizophrenia and the various subgroups of the affective disorders, these nosological difficulties should be clarified.

Most genetic studies indicate that schizophrenia and manic-depressive psychosis are distinct and separate genetic disorders; i.e., the lifetime risk of schizophrenia is no greater in the relatives of manic-depressive patients than it is in the population at large. In addition, no twin study has yet to report a pair of monozygotic twins where one of the pair was schizophrenic and the other manic-depressive, although Kendler and Tsuang have described a single, probably monozygotic, twin pair who apparently progressed together from an affective disorder, unipolar in one and bipolar in the other at age 31, to a more typical schizophrenic syndrome several years later. Also, in a 1954 study, Kallmann demonstrated that the incidence of schizophrenia was from three to four times higher in the relatives of patients with "involutional melancholia" (an affective disorder that today would most likely be called either unipolar depression or psychotic depression) than in the general population. If there was genetic overlap between schizophrenia and manic-depressive illness, we would expect the children of schizophrenic and manic-depressive patients to demonstrate a higher incidence of schizoaffective illness. This has not been observed, and affected children will generally develop either a schizophrenic or a manic-depressive illness.

There have been some recent studies, however, suggesting a possible genetic link between schizoaffective disorder and the broad category of affective disorders. In a large study of 260 twin pairs where at least one member of each pair had either manic-depressive psychosis, schizophrenia, or a schizoaffective psychotic disorder, Cohen and his colleagues found the mon-ozygotic concordance rate for schizoaffective illness to be more than twice that of schizophrenia, and similar to that of manic-depressive illness. These findings support a possible relationship between schizoaffective and affective disorders. Other family risk studies have suggested that not only is there a genetic link between schizoaffective disorder and affective disorders generally, but that X-chromosome transmission may also be involved in schizoaffective disorder. Most data are also consistent with a polygenic mode of inheritance, although nothing more precise can be said at this time.

INFANTILE AUTISM

Infantile autism is a rare (incidence about 4 per 10,000 children or 0.04%), but serious psychotic disorder of infancy characterized by severely impaired communication, a fascination with objects and an associated disinterest in people, an obsessive concern with keeping the environment unchanging, and marked social withdrawal with lack of response to holding, cuddling, and contact. While there is a similarity to childhood schizophrenia, some authors tend to differentiate the two by noting that childhood schizophrenia has a much later onset and may be preceded by a period of fairly normal development, whereas infantile autism has a very early onset with no evidence of preceding normal development.

In a study of 21 same-sex twin pairs, at least one of whom had infantile autism, Folstein and Rutter found that 4 of 11 monozygotic twin pairs were concordant for autism, but none of the 10 dizygotic pairs were concordant. It is noteworthy that 9 of the 11 monozygotic twin pairs were concordant for some form of cognitive disorder (including autism). These findings suggest that there likely is a genetic component to the disorder, and that this genetic component is related to an as of yet unspecified cognitive disturbance. There is some evidence of cognitive disabilities in the siblings of autistic probands as well, also suggesting a relationship to genetically determined cognitive functions.

The syndrome of infantile autism, or one very similar, has also been noted to follow congenital rubella and perinatal brain injury, and some autistic children have been found to have the so-called *fragile X syndrome*, an abnormality on the long arm of the X-chromosome. It has also been reported that parents of autistic children may share significantly more HLA antigens than otherwise would be expected. Thus it is quite likely that once again we may have a clinical syndrome in infantile autism that includes several different specific disorders with different etiologies, at least one type of which has a genetic component. This likelihood is strengthened by the fact that a subgroup of autistic children appear to have ventricular enlargement on CT scan.

ALCOHOLISM

It is a common truism that alcoholism seems to run in families, and family risk studies have documented the truth of this. In a 1979 review of the familial incidence of alcoholism, Cotton found that in studies over the last four decades, nearly one-third of any sample of alcoholics will have at least one parent who was alcoholic. It has also been common, however, to hold that this increased family risk of alcoholism was in significant part the result of learning—children of alcoholic parents, by growing up in such an environment, would simply learn the behavior from their parents, or they would be led to alcoholism by the poor environmental conditions that are often part of the alcoholic parent's condition. While environmental influences may certainly play a role in the development of alcoholism, during the past decade an extensive body of research, to which Dr. Donald Goodwin has been a major contributor, has demonstrated that genetic influences may be very important in the development of alcoholism. In a 1973 study, Goodwin and his collaborators studied a group of 55 men (the probands) who had been separated from their biological parents, at least one of whom was an alcoholic, before six weeks of age, and raised by nonalcoholic adoptive parents. Compared to a matched control group, significantly more of the proband group had a history of drinking problems (and the incidence of divorce was three times as high in this group). They interpreted their findings as supporting the idea that genetic factors play a role in the development of alcoholism. In a similar study, these investigators studied the sons of alcoholic parents, adopted in infancy and raised by nonalcoholic adoptive parents, in comparison to their brothers who had been raised by the alcoholic biological parents. Both groups had high

rates of alcoholism, and the results suggested that, at least in this sample, environmental factors contributed little if anything to the development of alcoholism.

Two more recent studies performed by investigators at Washington University School of Medicine in collaboration with investigators at Umea University School of Medicine in Sweden examined the inheritance of alcoholism in men and women independently. In a study of 862 Swedish men who were adopted by nonrelatives at an early age, 151 were found to have some record of alcohol abuse, and 51 had severe abuse. Examining the patterns of alcohol consumption overall, two patterns or types of abuse were found that appeared to have different genetic and environmental causes. Type 1 (called milieu limited) alcohol abuse was more common (seen in 13% of adopted men). It was of usually isolated or mild severity (although occasionally severe), and both biological parents tended to show a pattern of mild alcohol abuse with minimal criminality. Importantly, the postnatal environment tended to determine both frequency and severity of abuse in the congenitally predisposed sons. The relative risk for developing alcoholism in congenitally predisposed sons was 2 if alcohol abuse was present in the postnatal environment, and 1 (no increase in risk) if there was no abuse in the postnatal environment. Type 2 (male-limited) alcoholism was less common (4% prevalence, compared to 13% for Type 1), it was usually recurrent and of moderate severity (although occasionally severe), and while biological mothers tended to be normal, biological fathers showed a history of both severe alcohol abuse and severe criminality. The postnatal environment had no effect on frequency, although it did appear to affect severity of abuse. In these cases, the relative risk of developing the syndrome was 9 in congenitally predisposed sons regardless of the postnatal milieu. This study was important in demonstrating that there clearly appears to be more than one type of alcoholism, and genetic/environmental contributions vary according to the type of the disorder.

In a similar study by the same investigators of 913 Swedish women adopted by nonrelatives at an early age, there was a threefold increase of alcohol abusers among the adopted daughters of alcoholic biological mothers compared with daughters of nonalcoholic mothers. And, while there was an excess of alcohol abuse among the daughters of alcoholic biological fathers who were not criminals, biological fathers who were both severe alcoholics and criminals had no excess of alcoholic daughters, in marked contrast to the previously described situation in male children. This study demonstrated further the heterogenity of the syndrome and the importance of sex differences.

The question naturally arises, if alcoholism has a genetic component, exactly what, on a biochemical basis, is different in those who are genetically at risk? Research in both fraternal and identical twins has suggested that the rate at which ethanol is metabolized is under genetic control, and it has been found that, in family members of alcoholics, blood acetaldehyde concentrations were elevated to a significantly greater degree after a single dose of alcohol compared to a normal control group. It is well-known that individuals of Mongoloid origin may be more sensitive to the effects of alcohol; recent research has suggested that genetically determined differences in the enzyme aldehyde dehydrogenase may account for these apparent racial differences. Thus, there are several indicators that the way alcohol is metabolized is both genetically influenced, and may differ in alcoholics and nonalcoholics. Similarly, there is some evidence that patients with Wernicke-Korsakoff syndrome, an occasional outcome of alcoholism, have a specific enzyme deficiency that impairs their utilization of thiamine. It has also recently been found that the young sons of alcoholic fathers, who are at high risk for the development of alcoholism, may have in common with their fathers an apparently genetically determined low voltage fast EEG pattern. It has been suggested that this EEG pattern, which is heritable, relates in some way to the risk of developing alcoholism, and that it may serve as a biological marker.

CRIMINALITY

The consideration of criminal behavior in a textbook of psychiatry must be qualified: If we consider psychiatry as a medical specialty whose proper focus involves all aspects of human behavior, including that considered "deviant" by varying cultural and societal norms, it is proper to consider criminality. But by so doing, we should not imply that criminal behavior per se is a sign of psychopathology or mental illness,

for this is a hotly and justifiably debated topic better left to more philosophical treatises.

The investigation of genetic contributions to criminal behavior is complicated by the broadness of the definition of what exactly constitutes criminal behavior in a given culture or social system, and by the fact that environmental influences (such as poverty, adolescent peer pressure, and the like) are known to be important in influencing certain behaviors of this type. Nonetheless, there exists a notion that in the case of certain individuals, who can be found in many cultures and from many different family and environmental backgrounds, there exists a "criminal personality" that cannot be explained by customary psychological or sociological theories. Data supporting this view is developed in the recent work of Yochelson and Samenow who posit a specific disturbance in patterns of thinking that lead to repetitive criminal behavior in this group of individuals.

Research attempting to demonstrate a genetic contribution to criminal behavior has followed the conventional path, beginning with family risk, then twin, and finally adoption studies. In a 1977 report Christiansen found a much higher concordance for criminal behavior in male-male identical twins than in male-male fraternal twins. A study reported in 1982 by Bohman, Cloninger, and colleagues of 862 Swedish men adopted by nonrelatives at an early age found that while most of the violent criminal behavior was related to alcohol abuse, there was evidence of a significant genetic contribution to nonviolent criminal behavior. More recently Mednick et al. reported a study based upon court convictions of 14,427 children adopted by nonrelatives in Denmark between 1924 and 1927 after being separated from the natural parents at birth or a young age. They found a statistically significant correlation between adoptees and their biological, but not adoptive, parents for property crimes. No such correlation was found for violent crimes. These investigators stated: "The findings imply that biological predispositions are involved in the etiology of at least some criminal behavior." What such biological predispositions are or might be remain unclear, and, of course, the role of environment is certainly highly significant. Thus, while an improved understanding of how genetic and environmental factors interact to result in criminal behavior would be of very great importance, it is not yet within our grasp.

OTHER PSYCHIATRIC DISORDERS

The study of possible genetic influences on the neurotic disorders and the personality disorders has not progressed as far as is the case with the psychotic disorders or alcoholism. Nonetheless, recently emerging evidence suggests that there may well be genetic contributions to these disturbances as well.

Many writers over the years have commented upon the apparently familial nature of panic disorder. A family risk study reported by Cohen et al. in 1951 found a very high prevalence (67%) of neurocirculatory asthenia or anxiety neuroses (which today would be primarily included in the diagnosis of panic disorder) in family members of patients with neurocirculatory asthenia. These authors interpreted their findings as strongly supporting a genetic etiology. A subsequent family history study by Noyes et al. of 112 patients with anxiety neurosis and 110 control patients demonstrated that anxiety neurosis was present in 114 of 919 first degree relatives of the patients with anxiety neurosis but in only 19 of 904 relatives of the controls. These differences were highly statistically significant. Two more recent studies, a family study by Crowe et al. and a twin study by Torgersen, both support the idea that there may be a significant genetic component in the etiology of panic disorder. While the nature of this genetic component is far from clear, one group of investigators has suggested that patients with panic attacks may have a biologically based (and possible genetically determined) disorder in the metabolism of certain inhibitory neurotransmitters.

The issue of genetic contributions to the personality disorders is less convincing, although several investigators believe such influences to exist. A number of studies have addressed the issue of possible genetic contributions to antisocial personality disorder, and there is evidence strongly suggestive of a genetic mode of transmission, or at least a genetic contribution to this disorder. Studies of antisocial personality are closely related to studies of criminality, however, for one frequently leads to the other, and they may be hard to separate. Various investigators have published reports suggesting possible genetic contributions to borderline personality disorder, schizotypal personality disorder, paranoid personality disorder, and obsessive compulsive personality disorder, as reviewed in a 1983 paper by Siever et al. In none of these conditions have the studies been as rigorous or convincing as is the case for schizophrenia, affective disorders, or alcoholism. In time, when more data become available, the picture will hopefully become clearer.

IMPLICATIONS OF GENETIC RESEARCH

In this brief review of genetic factors in mental illness, I have not covered one area that may prove to be of considerable interest and importance in the near future—this is the area of genetic influences on normal character structure and personality type. Some evidence is beginning to emerge, primarily from studies of identical twins separated early in life and raised apart, suggesting that basic aspects of character structure, physiological patterns and reactivity, behavioral mannerisms, and the like may all be significantly influenced by genetic factors. This area of research is still too new to permit any definite conclusions to be made, but it is one of considerable potential importance, from which interesting new data will likely be emerging during the next few years.

In closing, one occasionally hears the complaint that assigning a genetic etiology to a mental disorder will lead to therapeutic nihilism. Nothing could be farther from the truth. There are three very good reasons for the vigorous pursuit of possible genetic and other specific etiological contributions to major mental illness. First, only by clearly defining the etiology of an illness can a correct diagnosis and rational treatment be undertaken. The major mental illnesses have tended to baffle the best clinicians. They still cannot be diagnosed with certain precision, and their treatment, while far more successful than a decade or two ago, is still in part trial and error, with outcome difficult to predict. A genetic etiology may ultimately lead to the uncovering of a specific biochemical abnormality, at which time rational treatments can be designed to correct the error. Second, a great deal of harm has been done by well-meaning but misinformed authors who in the past routinely tended to lay the blame for illnesses such as infantile autism and schizophrenia on the parents, or on a "schizophrenogenic mother." Such blame can cause great suffering for the unjustly accused, and do little good for the affected patients. To the extent that specific etiologies are found for such disorders, knowledge will replace prejudice in imputing causation, to the ultimate benefit of all involved. Finally, if a genetic predisposition to an illness such as schizophrenia is identified, then it may be possible to identify those individuals known to be at high risk for the development of the disorder before it becomes clinically manifest, and provide preventive assistance in such a manner as to diminish the likelihood of the disorder developing. Alternatively, by providing immediate intervention and treatment at the first signs of the disorder, it may be possible to decrease the length or severity of the illness.

Suggested Readings

Andreasen NC: *The Broken Brain. The Biological Revolution in Psychiatry.* New York, Harper & Row, 1984

Crow TJ: Is schizophrenia an infectious disease? *Lancet* 1:173, 1983.

Deitrich RA, McClearn GE: Neurobiological and genetic aspects of the etiology of alcoholism. *Fed Proc* 40:2051, 1981.

Gershon ES: The genetics of affective disorder. In Grinspoon L (ed): *Psychiatry 1983: Annual Review II.* Washington, DC, American Psychiatric Press, 1983, p 434.

Goodwin DW: Genetic component of alcoholism. *Ann Rev Med* 32:93, 1981.

Gottesman II, Shields J: *Schizophrenia. The Epigenetic Puzzle,* Cambridge, Mass., Cambridge University Press, 1982.

Rosenthal D, Kety SS (eds.): *The Transmission of Schizophrenia.* New York, Pergamon Press, 1968.

References

Agarwal DP, Harada S, Goedde HW: Racial differences in biological sensitivity to ethanol: the role of alcohol dehydrogenase and aldehyde dehydrogenase isozymes. *Alcoholism: Clin and Experimental Res* 1:12, 1981.

Bohman M: Some genetic aspects of alcoholism and criminality. *Arch Gen Psychiatry* 35:269, 1978.

Bohman M, Sigvardsson S, Cloninger CR: Maternal inheritance of alcohol abuse: cross-fostering analysis of adopted women. *Arch Gen Psychiatry* 38:965, 1981.

Bohman M, Cloninger CR, Sigvardsson S, von Knorring A: Predisposition to petty criminality in Swedish adoptees. I. Genetic and environmental heterogeneity. *Arch Gen Psychiatry* 39:1233, 1982.

Brown WT, et al: Autism is associated with the Fragile-X syndrome. *J Autism Dev Disord* 12:303, 1982.

Cambell M, et al: Computerized axial tomography in young autistic children. *Am J Psychiatry* 139:510, 1982.

Christiansen KO: A review of studies of criminality among twins. In Mednick SA, Christiansen KO (eds): *Biosocial Bases of Criminal Behavior.* New York, Gardner Press, 1977, p 88.

Cloninger CR, Bohman M, Sigvardsson S: Inheritance of alcohol abuse: cross-fostering analysis of adopted men. *Arch Gen Psychiatry* 38:861, 1981.

Cloninger CR, Sigvardsson S, Bohman M, von Knorring A: Predisposition to petty criminality in Swedish adoptees. II. Cross-fostering analysis of gene-environment interaction. *Arch Gen Psychiatry* 39:1242, 1982.

Cohen ME, et al: The high familial prevalence of neurocirculatory asthenia (anxiety neurosis, effort syndrome). *Am J Hum Genet* 3:126, 1951.

Cohen SM, Allen MG, Pollin W, Hrubec Z: Relationship of shizoaffective psychosis to manic-depressive psychosis and schizophrenia. *Arch Gen Psychiatry* 26:539, 1972.

Coryell W, Gaffney G, Burkhardt PE: The dexamethasone suppression test and familial subtypes of depression—a naturalistic replication. *Biol Psychiatry* 17:33, 1982.

Cotton NS: The familial incidence of alcoholism: a review. *J Stud Alcohol* 40:89, 1979.

Crowe RR, Noyes R, Pauls DL, Slymen DJ: A family study of panic disorder. *Arch Gen Psychiatry* 40:1065, 1983.

Fieve RR, Rosenthal D, Brill H (eds): *Genetic Research in Psychiatry.* Baltimore, Johns Hopkins University Press, 1975.

Folstein S, Rutter M: Infantile autism: a genetic study of 21 twin pairs. *J Child Psychol Psychiatry* 18:297, 1977.

Gabrielli WF, Mednick SA, et al: Electroencephalograms in children of alcoholic fathers. *Psychophysiol* 19:404, 1982.

Gershon ES, et al: The inheritance of affective disorders: a review of data and of hypotheses. *Behav Genet* 6:227, 1976.

Grove WM: Comment on Lidz and associates' critique of the Danish-American studies of the offspring of schizophrenic parents. *Am J Psychiatry* 140:998, 1983.

Kallmann FJ: Genetic principles in manic-depressive psychoses. In Hoch P, Zubin J (eds): *Depression.* New York, Grune & Stratton, 1954.

Kallmann FJ: *Heredity in Health and Mental Disorder.* New York, W.W. Norton & Co, 1953.

Kendler KS: Overview: a current perspective on twin studies of schizophrenia. *Am J Psychiatry* 140:1413, 1983.

Kendler KS, Hays P: Familial and sporadic schizophrenia: a symptomatic, prognostic, and EEG comparison. *Am J Psychiatry* 139:1557, 1982.

Kendler KS, Tsuang MT: Identical twins concordant for the progression of affective illness to schizophrenia. *Br J Psychiatry* 141:563, 1982.

Kety SS: Mental illness in the biological and adoptive relatives of schizophrenic adoptees: findings relevant to genetic and environmental factors in etiology. *Am J Psychiatry* 140:720, 1983.

Kinney DK, Matthysse S: Genetic transmission of schizophrenia. *Ann Rev Med* 29:459, 1978.

Kruszewski SP: The familial subtyping of depression: a reexamination of the endocrine, clinical and hereditary subgroups data in affective disorders. *Res Comm Psychol Psychiat Beh* 8:207, 1983.

Levitas A, et al: Autism and the fragile X syndrome. *Dev Behav Pediat* 4:151, 1983.

Lidz T, Blatt S: Critique of the Danish-American studies of the biological and adoptive relatives of adoptees who become schizophrenic. *Am J Psychiatry* 140:426, 1983.

Mednick SA, Gabrielli WF, Hutchings B: Genetic influences in criminal convictions: evidence from an adoption cohort. *Science* 224:891, 1984.

Mendlewicz J: Genetic studies in schizoaffective illness. In Gershon ES, Belmaker RH, Kety SS, Rosenbaum M (eds): *The Impact of Biology on Modern Psychiatry.* New York, Plenum Press, 1977, p 229.

Mendlewicz J, Linkowske P, Wilmotte J: Linkage between glucose-6-phosphate dehydrogenase deficiency and manic-depressive illness. *Br J Psychiatry* 137:337, 1980.

Mendlewicz J, Rainer JD: Adoption study supporting genetic transmission in manic-depressive illness. *Nature* 268:327, 1977.

Noyes R, Clancy J, Crowe RR, Hoenk PR, Slymen DJ: The familial prevalence of anxiety neurosis. *Arch Gen Psychiatry* 35:1057, 1978.

Sheehan DV, Ballenger J, Jacobsen G: Treatment of endogenous anxiety with phobic, hysterical, and hypochondriacal symptoms. *Arch Gen Psychiatry* 37:51, 1980.

Siever LJ, Insel TR, Uhde TW: Biogenetic factors in personalities. In Frosh JP (ed): *Current Perspectives on Personality Disorders.* Washington, DC, American Psychiatric Press, 1983.

Sigvardsson S, Cloninger CR, Bohman M, von Knorring A: Predisposition to petty criminality in Swedish adoptees. III. Sex differences and validation of the male typology. *Arch Gen Psychiatry* 39:1248, 1982.

Stubbs G: Shared parental HLA antigens and autism. *Lancet* 2:534, 1981.

Torgersen S: Genetic factors in anxiety disorders. *Arch Gen Psychiatry* 40:1085, 1983.

Turner WJ, King S: BPD₂: an autosomal dominant form of bipolar affective disorder. *Biol Psychiatry* 18:63, 1983.

Weitkamp LR, Stancer HC, et al: A gene on chromosome 6

than can affect behavior. *N Engl J Med* 305:1301, 1981.

Winokur G, et al: Is a familial definition of depression both feasible and valid? *J Nerv Ment Dis* 166:764, 1978.

Yochelson S, Samenow SE: *The Criminal Personality, Vol. I: A Profile for Change*, 1976. *Vol. II: The Change Process*, 1977. New York, Jason Aronson.

B. Neurochemical, Neuroendocrine, and Psychopharmacological Factors in Mental Illness

Robert Freedman, M.D.

The psychopharmacological treatment of schizophrenia, depression, mania, and other mental disorders has developed extensively over the past 30 years with the introduction of several classes of psychoactive drugs. This chapter describes each of the major classes of these psychotherapeutic drugs: antipsychotics, antidepressants, lithium carbonate, antianxiety agents, and stimulants. For each class of drugs, a brief history of its discovery, its current clinical usage, and the implications for a biological understanding of the respective mental illness will be outlined. A final section in the chapter will describe new findings in neurobiology which may someday contribute further to the understanding and treatment of mental illness.

ANTIPSYCHOTIC DRUGS IN THE TREATMENT OF SCHIZOPHRENIA

No group of drugs in psychiatry has had quite as dramatic an impact on the treatment of mental illness as the *antipsychotic drugs*. These drugs have changed the attitude of both professionals and society as a whole towards schizophrenia from one of hopelessness and disinterest to one of optimism and a regard for the patient as a human being. The prototypic drug, *chlorpromazine*, a *phenothiazine*, was discovered accidentally. Chlorpromazine was known to be an antihistamine, and it was also known to have effects on temperature regulation which might be of benefit to patients undergoing surgery. As was common at the time, the drug was tested on a ward of chronic schizophrenic patients. These

individuals were thought to be incurable, and because of their deteriorated condition, good subjects for human experimentation. Fortunately, the psychiatrists assigned to this ward were capable observers and noted that the patients were much improved by the drug. The patients were not sedated, but rather they appeared more relaxed. Delusions and hallucinations were diminished in both frequency and severity. Patients who had been hyperactive became less so, and patients who had been withdrawn became more active. Thus, unlike the barbiturates which improved schizophrenic patients to some extent by depressing all mental functioning, chlorpromazine seemed to alleviate symptoms of schizophrenia more specifically. Chlorpromazine and its analogues and derivatives have therefore been termed antipsychotic drugs.

These drugs have had a major impact on the treatment of schizophrenia. The number of patients hospitalized on a virtually permanent basis in large state mental hospitals had been steadily increasing for a number of years. After the introduction of chlorpromazine in 1956, this population began to fall dramatically (Figure 52.1). Mental health treatment could then concentrate on the return of schizophrenic patients into the community as functioning citizens, rather than upon the "warehousing" of incurables.

Rigorous tests of the efficacy of these drugs have been performed. Because many illnesses improve transiently as a function of the patient's and doctor's expectations and hopes, a new

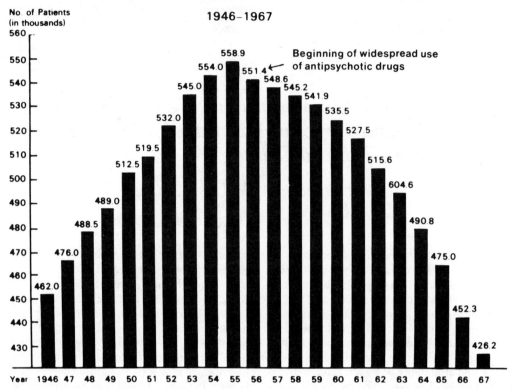

NUMBER OF RESIDENT PATIENTS IN STATE AND LOCAL GOVERNMENT MENTAL HOSPITALS IN THE UNITED STATES

1946–1967

Figure 52.1. Relationship of number of patients in U.S. mental hospitals to the introduction of chlorpromazine and other antipsychotic drugs. (Modified from Davis and Cole, 1975.)

methodology, the *double blind* study, was developed. The patient and his family are offered the opportunity to participate in a study of a new drug which may be of benefit to the patient's mental condition. The patient is told that at some time in the study, a *placebo* may be substituted for the drug. The patient and all nurses and doctors with whom he comes in contact do not know the contents of the capsules he takes. Both patient and staff are thus "blind." Only one or two persons know the actual medication being administered. All ratings of change in illness are done by the "blind" medical staff. Using this methodology, about three quarters of schizophrenic patients are significantly improved on antipsychotic drugs. The other one quarter improve only a minimal degree or not at all. On placebo, only one-quarter improve. Thus, the drugs are significantly more effective than placebo in the treatment of psychosis. Similar studies show that they are also effective in the prevention of relapse after successful treatment.

Other treatments of schizophrenia, besides antipsychotic drugs, have been proposed. Good results have been reported by advocates of megavitamin therapy, for example. In the case of megavitamins, however, double blind studies have shown an actual worsening of schizophrenia.

A number of side effects have been seen after the administration of antipsychotic drugs. These effects are related to two areas of the brain, the basal ganglia and the hypothalamus. Administration of antipsychotic drugs causes movement disorders similar to those of Parkinson's disease, including rigidity, dystonias, akinesia, Parkinsonian-like tremors, and akathisia, a form of motor restlessness. These effects are mediated by the action of the drugs in the basal ganglia, and are often controlled by the use of anticholinergic agents, which are also useful in the control of Parkinson's disease. Patients on antipsychotic drugs may also experience an increase in appetite leading to weight gain, and an inability to control their body temperature, which can lead to hypo- or hyperthermia. These effects are mediated by the action of the drugs in the hypothalamus.

The close resemblance of these side effects to Parkinson's disease suggested to neurobiologists a possible mechanism of action for the antipsychotic drugs. Since Parkinson's disease is known to be caused by a decrease in the innervation of the basal ganglia from the dopamine-containing substantia nigra in the midbrain, it was hypothesized that antipsychotic drugs block the actions of the *neurotransmitter, dopamine* (DA), in the basal ganglia. (A neurotransmitter is a neurochemical that transmits impulses across the connections or synapses between neurons.) This hypothesis has been confirmed in numerous studies in laboratory animals. It was then further hypothesized that an excess of dopamine may be the cause of schizophrenia. This idea has been called the *dopamine hypothesis*. The principal evidence for it is the finding that antipsychotic drugs block the action of dopamine in the basal ganglia. A second piece of evidence is the finding that amphetamine, a drug which causes the release of dopamine, can cause a paranoid psychosis in human beings which resembles paranoid schizophrenia. Unfortunately for the theory, schizophrenic patients excrete normal amounts of dopamine, so that there is as yet no direct and conclusive evidence of dopamine excess in the brain cells of schizophrenic patients.

The finding of an antidopamine action with chlorpromazine has been used to develop other antipsychotic drugs by screening for their ability to develop signs of basal ganglia dysfunction in animals. Over 50 different drugs have been thus developed, none of which are more effective in treating psychosis than chlorpromazine. However, some of them, such as *haloperidol*, a *butyrophenone* derivative, are 100 times more potent. The more potent drugs tend to be less sedating, but they also produce more dysfunction in motor behavior. A clinician selects between these various drugs based on the particular side effects which his patient can best tolerate.

One additional side effect has been of increasing concern. After many years of antipsychotic drug treatment, some patients were noted to develop a choreoathetotic movement disorder, principally involving grotesque protrusion of the tongue and mouth, but also often jerking of the arms and legs as well, now termed *tardive dys-*

kinesia. "Tardive" means that the disorder appears late in treatment, in contrast to the other movement disorders which all appear in the first several months. Tardive dyskinesia does not abate when the drug is withdrawn, but rather it appears to get worse. Anticholinergics also worsen it. It generally improves slowly over several weeks to months, but it may not completely resolve. The incidence in a group of chronically drug-treated patients is about 20%, so that a significant number of patients are affected. The current hypothesis holds that the chronic blockade of dopaminergic neurotransmission in the basal ganglia produces a supersensitivity to dopamine. This supersensitivity is a general phenomenon in the nervous system, which occurs as a response of a nerve or muscle cell to denervation. The cell becomes supersensitive to the neurotransmitter which has been removed by the denervation. In this case, the denervation is functionally caused by a drug which blocks neurotransmission. As the blockade continues, the neuron becomes more and more sensitive until the small amounts of dopamine which are not blocked by the drug become effective, and the movement disorder results. Removing the drug makes the situation temporarily worse by allowing more dopamine to contact the sensitive cell. Eventually, however, in most cases, the sensitivity abates. Although this explanation is attractive, data to support it are scanty. The clinician and the patient who has tardive dyskinesia thus face a dilemma. They must decide whether to treat the psychosis with drugs and thereby worsen the tardive dyskinesia, or to withhold drugs and see the psychosis exacerbate. A careful discussion with the patient and his family of the risks and benefits is therefore necessary.

A number of questions concerning the neurochemical etiology of schizophrenia are currently being investigated. One of the principal lines of inquiry continues to be an attempt to find which neuronal systems are involved in antipsychotic drug action. My own work has centered on a second neuronal system, the norepinephrine-containing neurons of the pontine brain stem nucleus locus coeruleus. *Norepinephrine* (NE) and dopamine are the two principal catecholamine neurotransmitters in the central nervous system. We have found that norepinephrine and dopamine mediated neurotransmission are blocked by antipsychotic drugs, and increased by several drugs, such as amphetamine or phencyclidine ("angel dust"), which can also cause psychoses. Pursuing this inquiry further, we have asked how changes in noradrenergic or dopaminergic physiology might produce or alleviate psychotic symptoms. In most areas of the brain, these neurotransmitters account for less than 1% of all synapses. Instead of carrying specific bits of information, these systems appear to have a modulatory role. Increase in catecholaminergic neurotransmission makes neurons which receive catecholamine-containing synapses hyperresponsive to activity arriving over other neuronal pathways. This hyperresponsiveness can be diminished by antipsychotic drugs, which block the actions of catecholamines. Many psychotic patients have been characterized as hypervigilant, and because of their hypervigilance, they are unable to attend selectively to important messages and to filter out distracting messages. One of the principal therapeutic effects of antipsychotic drugs seems to be to restore this perceptual disability to a more normal state. Perhaps the neuronal mechanisms which I have just described underlie this therapeutic effect.

An increased biological understanding of how antipsychotic drugs act may help answer a number of important clinical questions. How can those patients who will respond to the drugs be identified? Why are the drugs effective for some manifestations of schizophrenia, but not for others? Can alternative antipsychotic drugs be designed which are not dopamine antagonists? If schizophrenia is not due to a dopamine excess, what other mechanism can be postulated?

Researchers have shown that several abnormalities in brain structure and function exist in schizophrenic patients. For the most part, these abnormalities are not reversed by antipsychotic drugs. The relative size of the cerebral ventricles is enlarged in a subset of schizophrenic patients, particularly those with more chronic psychotic pictures. There are also abnormalities in several parameters of sensory evoked potentials and in some forms of eye movements.

The efficacy of the antipsychotic drugs in the treatment of schizophrenia should not be used to exclude the importance of other forms of treatment. Certainly, some characteristics of schizophrenia, such as social isolation, require psychological intervention in addition to drug treatment. Even if a drug were found which completely reversed all of the biological abnormalities in schizophrenia, the patient would still have experienced the tragedy of the regression

and the fragmentation of functioning to be described later in this book. Careful psychological treatment would still be necessary to allow even a partial completion of personal development and integration of functioning.

ANTIDEPRESSANT DRUGS IN THE TREATMENT OF DEPRESSION

A number of related observations in both patients and in animals over the past 25 years have also greatly enhanced our capacity to understand and to treat depression. Depression for these purposes is defined as an illness in which a disturbance of mood ("dysphoria") is a prominent feature, but other symptoms may also be present. The dysphoria may include emotions of sadness, irritability, agitation, helplessness, hopelessness, worthlessness, and guilt. The other symptoms may include loss of appetite and decrease in weight, decreased energy and ability to work, decreased sexual drive, sleep disturbance with early morning awakenings, other physical complaints, and suicidal tendencies. Several or all of these may be present. To avoid confusion between this illness and the more common reactions everyone experiences to defeats or losses, including mourning over the loss of a loved one, modern psychiatric terminology calls this illness an *affective disorder*, and this illness will be discussed in more detail later in the book. For now, it will suffice to say that there are two forms of affective psychosis (as distinct from a schizophrenic psychosis). The first is the *unipolar* form of depressive illness, that is a depressive reaction that does not alternate with episodes of mania. The *bipolar* form of depressive illness consists of alternating attacks of mania and depression, the so-called manic-depressive psychosis.

In the 1950's, *reserpine*, a *rauwolfia* alkaloid, was introduced as an antihypertensive agent. It was observed that about 10% of patients receiving this drug became severely depressed; many of them even attempted suicide. Simultaneously, neurobiologists noted that reserpine depleted three monoamine neurotransmitters in the brains of laboratory animals: dopamine, norepinephrine, and *5-hydroxytryptamine* (5-HT), also known as *serotonin*. Thus, a drug which caused depression had a definable neurochemical action. Also in the 1950's, *iproniazid*, a drug used to treat tuberculosis, was noted to make the tubercular patients euphoric. It was also effective as an antidepressant for depressed patients.

This drug was subsequently shown to be a *monoamine oxidase* (MAO) *inhibitor*. Monoamine oxidase is an enzyme which degrades these monoamine neurotransmitters. Its inhibition therefore raises the level of monoamine neurotransmitters in the brain. Thus, a drug which alleviates depression acts to raise the level of the same substances which reserpine, a drug which causes depression, depletes. A second class of drugs was also noted to have antidepressant action. These drugs, called *tricyclics* because of their three-ringed chemical structures, also affected the monoamines. Monoamines are normally taken back into the nerve terminals which initially released them. This "reuptake" process thus terminates the action of monoamine neurotransmitters. Tricyclics block the reuptake process, which thus prolongs the presence of the neurotransmitters in the synaptic cleft, and thereby effectively potentiates the action of the neurotransmitters. Thus, two different classes of *antidepressant drugs*, the monoamine oxidase inhibitors and the tricyclics, both act to increase monoaminergic neurotransmission (Figure 52.2). Since tricyclics do not block dopamine reuptake very effectively, attention has centered primarily on norepinephrine and serotonin.

Unlike the dopamine hypothesis of schizophrenia, which has not led to the finding of a specific biochemical disorder, the *norepinephrine and serotonin hypotheses* of affective disorder have led to the actual demonstration of biochemical deficiencies in depressed patients. Norepinephrine is one of the neurotransmitters released by nerve cells in the brain when a person takes amphetamine and gets "high," and appears to be related in its functioning to arousal, alertness, euphoria, and possibly mania. Serotonin, on the other hand, may have some relationship to states of drowsiness and falling asleep. The first to be explored was norepinephrine. Although norepinephrine is present in the peripheral sympathetic and the central nervous system as well as the adrenal medulla, it is metabolized by different pathways in each system. The central nervous system primarily produces 3-methoxy-4-hydroxyphenylglycol (MHPG), an end product which is excreted into the cerebrospinal fluid and ultimately into the urine. The level of this product in the spinal fluid is found to be lower in some, but not all, depressed patients. Cerebrospinal fluid levels of serotonin metabolites are also low in some depressed patients. All of these findings lend support to the hypothesis that "depression" is a

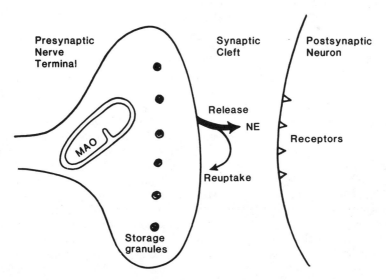

Figure 52.2. Sites of drug action at a noradrenergic synapse. Reserpine depletes norepinephrine in *storage granules*, and thus decreases the amount of norepinephrine which can be released during neurotransmission. Monoamine oxidase inhibitors inhibit the activity of the mitochondrial enzyme, monoamine oxidase (*MAO*), which normally metabolizes norepinephrine; the amount of norepinephrine which can be released is thus increased. Amphetamine facilitates *release* of norepinephrine. Tricyclic antidepressants prevent its *reuptake*, thereby prolonging its presence in the synaptic cleft and facilitating neurotransmission. (Antipsychotic drugs block *receptors* on postsynaptic neurons, thus blocking neurotransmission.)

group of physiologically heterogeneous illnesses that may essentially be differentiated by specific biochemical criteria. For example, MHPG spinal fluid levels tend to be lower in manic-depressive patients when they are in the depressed phase, and higher during the manic phase. Patients suffering from unipolar depression tend to fall into two categories: 1) those with low MHPG levels when depressed, and 2) those with normal or high MHPG levels when depressed. An intriguing recent finding is that some patients supposedly suffering from unipolar depression who have very low MHPG urine levels and who are treated with tricyclics then develop manic symptoms. This suggests that these patients may have been suffering from an underlying bipolar depression that had not yet manifested itself clinically.

Modern treatment of the affective disorders generally begins with the tricyclics. During the first week of treatment, the patient is noted to have his sleep pattern regularized, and appetite and energy are increased. The improvement is not impressive to the patient himself, who continues to complain of depression, but it will be obvious to the treating staff and to the patient's family. Only by the third week does the patient himself feel better. The reason for the delay is unknown. Approximately 70% of depressed patients respond to a tricyclic antidepressant. Generally, all symptoms of the depressions are alleviated. By contrast, the treatment of schizophrenia results in a patient who is markedly improved, but not fully normal. If the depressed patient fails to respond, it is worthwhile to measure the plasma level of drug. For some tricyclics, there is a "therapeutic window." Levels which are too low or too high result in a poor response. If a patient fails to respond to an adequate trial of one drug, it is warranted to try another. In particular, if the first drug was a predominantly norepinephrine reuptake blocker, then the second choice might be a predominantly serotonin reuptake blocker.

There are several problems associated with using the tricyclics. They are cardiac depressants and they can cause arrhythmia and postural hypotension. Careful cardiovascular monitoring is essential. The toxic to therapeutic ratio is low, approximately 10:1. Since many patients are suicidal, intentional overdosage is not uncommon. Doses as low as 1.5 grams, a week's supply, can be fatal. Obviously, close

monitoring of suicidal intent, arrangement of family support, and hospitalization where appropriate, are all important parts of the management of depression. Some of the symptoms of tricyclic intoxication are caused by the potent anticholinergic effects of these drugs. A syndrome of hot flushed skin, dilated pupils, tachycardia, and confusion or coma is noted. These symptoms may be temporarily reversed by using physostigmine to block central nervous system acetylcholinesterase, the enzyme which degrades another neurotransmitter, *acetylcholine* (Ach).

The monoamine oxidase inhibitors are generally used in cases of atypical depression in which anxiety, phobic, and hypochondriacal complaints are prominent. Dietary control is important, because an important function of the enzyme monoamine oxidase is to protect the body from monoamines in the diet. The worst offender is tyramine, found in foods such as cheeses, red wines, and beer. Tryamine not destroyed by monoamine oxidase releases norepinephrine from the peripheral sympathetic nervous system, and causes a hypertensive crisis which may be fatal. Other indirectly acting sympathomimetics, such as nasal decongestants, should also be avoided.

Depressed patients who do not respond to pharmacotherapy will generally respond to treatments with electric shock, termed *electroconvulsive therapy* (ECT). Depressed patients had been noted before the drug era to improve after spontaneous epileptic seizures. The mechanism of action of ECT is unknown, but a seizure, not just the passage of current, is crucial. The patient is given a short acting barbiturate for general anesthesia, and then briefly paralyzed with succinyl choline to prevent muscle contractions during the seizure. Bone fracture is thus minimized. Electrical current is applied across the head, or, in some cases, only to the nondominant side of the brain. Six to twelve treatments are given, one every other day. The chief side effect is confusion and memory loss, which are generally transient. Older reports of severe brain damage following ECT were the result of excessive current, excessive number of treatments, and poor anesthesia technique, leading to anoxia. ECT is by far the fastest and most effective treatment for severe depression. Limitations on its abuse by poorly trained doctors who give it indiscriminately are certainly warranted, but unfortunately, in some states, its use for depressed and suicidal patients has been curtailed excessively by restrictive legislation.

Increasing interest is being paid to *neuroendocrine* functions of the brain in depression. Abnormalities in brain regulation of the adrenal cortex and the thyroid have been noted in depressed patients. Since hormonal regulation can be measured by sampling hormones such as cortisol or thyroid-stimulating hormone in the peripheral circulation, neuroendocrine techniques provide yet another means to assay brain function non-invasively. In the *dexamethasone suppression test* (DST), for example, a low dose of dexamethasone (an artifical steroid) normally suppresses plasma cortisol levels for 24 hours through its effects on the temporal lobe, an important sight of regulation of the neuroendocrine axis responsible for ACTH production. However, a substantial subgroup of patients with major depressive symptomatology (about 40%) are nonsuppressors, in that they show an "escape from suppression" within 24 hours. In the *thyrotropin-releasing hormone* (TRH) *stimulation test*, levels of thyroid-stimulating hormone (TSH) are monitored before and after an infusion of TRH. The effect of TRH on TSH release from pituitary cells is diminished or blunted in about 30% of patients with major depressive symptomatology. This diminished release may correlate with diminished serotonergic neurotransmission, and provides another sample of how neuroendocrine techniques can be used to assess brain function in patients with psychiatric illness.

LITHIUM CARBONATE IN THE TREATMENT OF MANIA

Many depressed patients are also troubled by periodic episodes of euphoria, hyperactivity, irritability, and a flight of ideas that may take on paranoid, grandiose, delusional properties. This phase is called mania, or the manic phase of manic-depressive illness. Mania may be thought of as the opposite of depression. Many of the biochemical studies performed on patients with depressive illness described in the previous section have also been performed on patients with mania. Some manic patients switch from depression to mania in one day; preceding the switch, they have been found to have a marked increase in the level of norepinephrine excre-

tion. Figure 52.3 shows how one of these patients switches from depression to mania. Plotted above the clinical ratings are the mean values for norepinephrine excretion from a group of such patients. Note that the increase in norepinephrine excretion precedes the transition into the manic state. Most of the norepinephrine excreted in the urine comes from the peripheral sympathetic nervous system, not the central nervous system. However, the precise role of brain norepinephrine in mania still remains uncertain.

Although antipsychotic drugs may be helpful in mania, they are not sufficient treatment. The treatment of mania has been profoundly influenced by the accidental discovery of the effectiveness of lithium carbonate. An Australian physician, Jon F. K. Cade, was experimenting with the urine of manic patients. He injected the urine into guinea pigs, and they died. He then decided to isolate the toxic component and tried sodium urate. As a control, he used lithium urate. The lithium ion, he decided, had

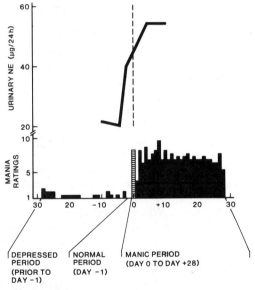

Figure 52.3. Relationship of urinary norepinephrine levels to the onset of a manic episode. *Bar graph* shows onset of mania with daily ratings of manic symptoms for a rapidly cycling manic-depressive patient. *Line graph*, on the same time scale, shows average change in urinary norepinephrine levels for a group of such patients. Note that the increase in norepinephrine excretion precedes the transition into mania. (Modified from Bunney et al., 1972.)

a calming effect for the guinea pigs, so he gave it to the manic patients, who were also calmed. The treatment was initially thought by physicians in this country to be too dangerous. Early experience with lithium salts as substitutes for sodium in cardiac patients' diets had been disastrous. Intake of large amounts of lithium salts caused all types of nervous dysfunction, including coma and death. Control of dosage by blood level monitoring was developed, however, and is now used routinely.

Lithium carbonate is used today as a safe and effective treatment for manic-depressive illness. It is effective in reversing mania and also in preventing its recurrence. Depressive episodes are also decreased in severity and frequency. The drug is remarkably well tolerated. Side effects include some minor, but measurable, decrease in mental ability, nontoxic goiter, nephrogenic diabetes insipidus, and leukocytosis. Some reports have suggested the possibility of permanant kidney damage after long-term usage, but a 1982 review by Ramsey and Cox concluded that the loss of kidney function does not appear to be significant in the great majority of patients on long-term lithium therapy.

The mechanism of action of lithium is unknown. It interferes with sodium exchange in red blood cells, but its specific action in the treatment of manic-depressive illness has still not been determined. It has been demonstrated to block the actions of norepinephrine, but it also interferes with many other neural processes. One of the most interesting results of lithium treatment is its effect on psychiatric diagnosis. American psychiatrists had generally diagnosed any paranoid, grandiose, or delusional patient as schizophrenic. British psychiatrists called such patients manic if they fit other criteria for mania. When custodial care was the only treatment modality, the debate was academic. The development of lithium as a specific treatment modality, however, made accurate diagnosis extremely important. Most psychiatrists today use the British criteria, and this has resulted in the more frequent diagnosis and successful treatment of mania.

ANTIANXIETY DRUGS IN THE TREATMENT OF ANXIETY

Unlike the psychiatric diseases previously described, anxiety is a symptom, not a disease. Its treatment by pharmacological means must be placed in the context of a diagnosis and an overall treatment plan. For example, anxiety may be a symptom of panhypopituitarism, or chronic obstructive pulmonary disease, or hyperthyroidism, or delirium tremens. All these conditions require specific medical treatment. Premature treatment with an *antianxiety agent* might mask important signs and symptoms. For a large number of people, however, anxiety occurs in a setting in which it is not a symptom of an organic illness. Typical causes include job related stress, marital discord, and other life crises. About 10% of the population each year will receive treatment with an antianxiety agent for such a problem. The most commonly used agents are the *benzodiazepines*, such as *chlordiazepoxide, diazepam*, and *alprazolam.*

Double blind studies have been difficult to perform with antianxiety agents, because anxiety is a highly subjective feeling and responses to placebo are much more pronounced than placebo responses in other illnesses. Nonetheless, significant drug effects have been demonstrated. Most of the studies have been short-term; effects are observable for three weeks. Safety has also been an important question. These drugs replaced the barbiturates, with which fatal overdoses and fatal withdrawal seizures were common. The benzodiazepines are less problematic. Fatal overdose is much rarer, although it can occur in combination with alcohol. Tolerance and dependence occur, but they are much less frequent than with the barbiturates. Nonetheless, withdrawal can lead to seizures and delirium. The benzodiazepines are best limited to short-term use around an identifiable crisis. They do not seem to be effective in long-term use, and such use can lead to both psychological and physical dependence.

STIMULANT DRUGS IN THE TREATMENT OF THE ATTENTION DEFICIT DISORDER IN CHILDHOOD

Minimal brain dysfunction (MBD), unlike depression or schizophrenia, is not yet a well-defined clinical entity. As Dr. Christ will describe later in the book, it may be one of the causes of the attention deficit disorder in children who demonstrate hyperactivity, distractibility, impulsivity, and specific learning disabilities. *Stimulant drugs*, such as *amphetamine* or *methylphenidate*, are an effective treatment for those cases of the attention deficit disorder which are due to MBD. It is less certain whether they are effective in those cases of learning disability which are due to developmental lags or psychogenic conflicts. The child becomes more attentive, better able to learn, and less hyperactive. Amphetamine and methylphenidate both release the brain catecholamines, norepinephrine and dopamine. Perhaps the modulatory role of these neurotransmitters described earlier is responsible for the clinical effects observed. Children who have the severest perceptual difficulties have been shown to have the best response to stimulants in some studies. It is true that these drugs have been overused with many children in different settings. Nonetheless, for those children suffering from the attention deficit disorder due to MBD, these drugs can be extremely valuable and often achieve results which cannot be achieved by special education or psychotherapy alone. The principal side effect of the drugs seems to be growth retardation due to interference with the hypothalamic regulation of the release of growth hormone. This side effect is minimized by careful attention to the growth pattern of the child, and periodic "holidays" off the drug.

POSSIBLE FUTURE CONTRIBUTIONS OF BRAIN RESEARCH TO PSYCHIATRY

The drugs discussed so far were all discovered accidentally. Rather than being the product of research, the discovery of these drugs stimulated research to try to explain how they worked. The success of the drugs, on the other hand, has made future "accidental" discoveries less likely. Seriously ill psychiatric patients are no longer regarded as hopeless cases to be experimented upon at will. Thus, future progress will involve further working out of how presently available drugs act. Many of the current explanations involve norepinephrine and dopamine. More precise explanations may involve more detailed descriptions of how these monoamines function in various diseases. Other, as yet undiscovered, neuronal systems may be important also. Several new findings hold promise for increasing the understanding of brain function, and may provide the basis for new psychiatric treatments. These include the discovery of new receptor sites, endogenous opiates, metabolic brain imaging, and brain transplantation.

The endogenous opioid peptides called *endor-*

phins and *enkephalins* were discovered within the past decade. The striking effects of opiates such as morphine or heroin on human and animal behavior suggested that these substances must have a specific interaction with specific receptors within a particular brain system, perhaps imitating a neurotransmitter normally found in the brain. In 1973, specific opiate receptors were identified. Then, in 1975 and subsequently, brain substances were discovered which seem to function like natural, internal opiates. In the hypothalamus, there are macromolecules called endorphins, which have opiate-like activity and can circulate in the blood. They are closely related to other hypothalamic hormones, such as ACTH. In other areas of the brain, smaller polypeptides which have opiate-like activity are present. These molecules are called enkephalins. The functions of endorphins and enkephalins are not clear. They are sometimes found within neurons which contain other neurotransmitters. Many neurons are sensitive to them; in some areas of the brain, they are excitatory, but in other areas, inhibitory. They do profoundly depress the activity of the norepinephrine-containing neurons of the important nucleus locus coeruleus.

In many areas of the brain, their activity is blocked by *naloxone*, a drug developed to block the actions of morphine. This finding suggested that naloxone could be used to identify the effects of endorphins and enkephalins in normal people. In one experiment, patients were given placebo as a pain reliever after dental surgery. About one-third of the patients experienced relief of physical pain. This subset of patients was then given either placebo or naloxone after repeat dental surgery. The group who received placebo again experienced relief, but the naloxone-treated group did not. This finding suggested that the placebo effect was mediated by endorphins or enkephalins. Whether they also play some role in mediating psychological pain and stress is still to be determined. Attempts have been made to see if schizophrenia or depression is caused by endorphin or enkephalin dysfunction. Results have been initially promising, but have not yet been confirmed in double blind evaluation.

The discovery of opiate receptors, and subsequently of the endorphins and enkephalins, led to the more recent discovery of receptor sites for the benzodiazepines, and is prompting the search for a natural, internal antianxiety agent that normally occupies these receptor sites. Such a substance has been described as the "brain's own tranquilizer," and if it is isolated, could provide the basis for even more effective antianxiety drugs which do not have the side effects of the benzodiazepines.

One of the goals of neuroscientists has been to devise means for visualizing the activity of the brain in patients. Electroencephalography has been helpful, as has the measurement of excreted chemicals such as MHPG, the metabolite of norepinephrine. A recently developed technique known as *metabolic brain imaging* is also promising. When brain cells are active, they metabolize glucose. 2-deoxyglucose, like glucose, is taken up into nerve cells, particularly when they are active. The neurons normally use glucose for energy, but 2-deoxyglucose is not metabolized. Its accumulation in the neuron thus may reflect its activity. If the 2-deoxyglucose is radioactive, it can be detected on histological preparations of an animal brain (Figure 52.4), or by positron emission tomography, also known as the PET scan (Figure 52.5). This technique may allow detection of brain metabolic abnormality in psychiatric illness. Many neurotransmitters, like dopamine, cause a neuron to use increased amounts of glucose, so that such metabolic abnormalities may reflect excesses or deficiencies in neurotransmitter activity.

The brain has long been thought to be generally incapable of growth or change after maturity. Neurons were believed to be stereotyped, with little potential for development outside of their normal role, so that if a particular neuronal system were lost or damaged, other neurons could not replace it. Recent work on *brain transplantation* has suggested other possibilities. Initial work showed that parts of the brain, such as the cerebellum or the hippocampus, could be transplanted to the eye of an adult rat from a fetus. There, they attach to the iris and develop the typical structure and physiological activity of the part of brain from which they came. If two structures which normally innervate each other are transplanted together, such as substantia nigra and caudate nucleus, one of the basal ganglia, the innervation forms in the eye (Figure 52.6). This technique allows rigorous study of drug action on one part of the brain isolated from other parts. The technique has been carried further to allow grafting within the brain itself. Rats which lose the substantia nigra

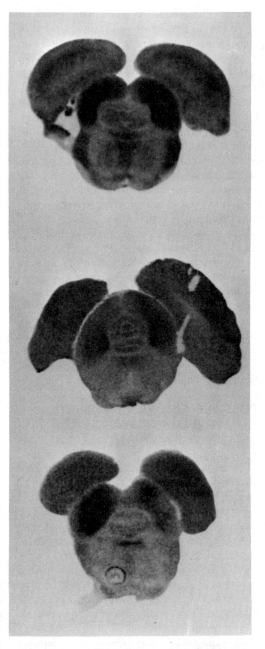

Figure 52.4. [¹⁴C]DG autoradiographic visualization of the effects of altered auditory input on the local glucose utilization of some central auditory structures in the conscious albino rat. *Upper figure*: normal conscious rat. *Middle figure*: both external auditory canals were obstructed with wax and the animal was placed in a sound-proof room. *Lower figure*: only one auditory canal (contralateral to the side of the brain with reduced optical density in auditory structures) was obstructed. Note the inferior colliculi, lemnisci, and superior olives. (From Sokoloff, 1976).

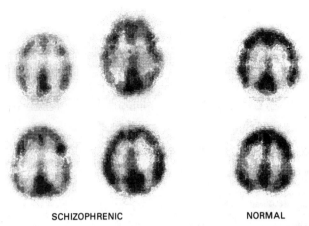

SCHIZOPHRENIC   NORMAL

Figure 52.5. Positron emission tomograms (PET) from four schizophrenic and two normal subjects. Each shows the relative accumulation of radioactive deoxyglucose in a tomographic slice of brain above the ventricles. In normal subjects the frontal lobes (*top*) show more accumulation than the occipital lobes (*bottom*). In schizophrenic subjects, however, there is diminished accumulation in the frontal lobes (Illustration from Buchsbaum et al., 1982).

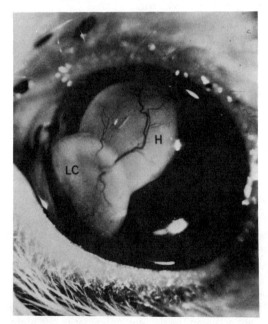

Figure 52.6. Eye of an adult rat containing two grafts of fetal brain tissue. The two portions, the hippocampus (*H*) and the locus coeruleus (*LC*), form functional synaptic connections with each other. (From Olsen et al., 1980.)

on one side of their brain rotate within cages after stimulation of the dopaminergic-containing circuitry. The rotation is caused because only the caudate nucleus on one side of the brain now receives dopamine synapses. The rotation can be blocked by grafting a fetal substantia nigra to the caudate which has lost its own substantia nigra, thus restoring the innervation. This technique is simplified by the fact that the brain does not mount an immunological reaction to transplanted tissue. The technique may be useful in diseases like Parkinson's disease in which this same dopaminergic-innervation is lost in the disease process. The problem of obtaining donor material may be solved by the preliminary finding that the animal's own peripheral sympathetic neurons or even adrenal medulla cells may be used in place of substantia nigra neurons. This approach to the therapy of severe Parkinson's disease has been attempted in several human subjects to date.

All of this work on the discovery of new receptor sites and of the endogenous opiates, the search for endogenous antianxiety agents, the development of metabolic brain imaging, and the exploration of brain transplantation, offers far reaching possibilities for the future contribution of basic brain research to problems in clinical psychiatry.

Suggested Readings

Baldessarini RJ: *Biomedical Aspects of Depression and Its Treatment.* Washington, DC, American Psychiatric Press, 1983.

Barchas JD, Berger PA, Ciaranello RD, Elliott GR (eds): *Psychopharmacology from Theory to Practice.* New York, Oxford University Press, 1977.

References

Andreasen NC, et al: Ventricular enlargement in schizophrenia: relationship to positive and negative symptoms. *Am J Psychiatry* 139:297, 1982.

Andreasen NC: *The Broken Brain. The Biological Revolution in Psychiatry.* New York, Harper & Row, 1984.

Buchsbaum MS, et al: Cerebral glucography with positron tomography. *Arch Gen Pscyhiatry* 39:251, 1982.

Bunney WE, et al: The "switch process" in manic-depressive illness. *Arch Gen Psychiatry* 27:295, 1972.

Davis JM, Cole JO: Antipsychotic drugs. In Freedman AM, Kaplan HI, Sadock BJ (eds): *Comprehensive Textbook of Psychiatry*, ed 2, vol 2. Baltimore, Williams & Wilkins, 1975, p 1921.

Freedman R: Interactions of antipsychotic drugs with norepinephrine and cerebellar neuronal circuitry: implications for the psychobiology of psychosis. *Biol Psychiatry* 12:181, 1977.

Freedman R, Adler LE, Waldo MC, Pachtman E, Franks RD: Neurophysiological evidence for a deficit in inhibitory pathways in schizophrenia: comparison of medicated and drug-free patients. *Biol Psychiatry* 18:537, 1983.

Greenblatt DJ, Shader RI: *Benzodiazepines in Clinical Practice.* New York, Raven Press, 1974.

Holzman PS, et al: Pursuit eye movements in schizophrenia. *Arch Gen Psychiatry* 41:136, 1984.

Hughes J: Isolation of an endogenous compound from the brain with pharmacological properties similar to morphine. *Brain Res* 88:295, 1975.

Klawans HL, Jr: The pharmacology of tardive dyskinesias. *Am J Psychiatry* 130:82, 1973.

Maas JW: Biogenic amines and depression: biochemical and pharmacological separation of two types of depression. *Arch Gen Psychiatry* 32:17, 1975.

Olsen L, et al: Conditions for adrenergic hyperinnervation in hippocampus. I. Histochemical evidence from intraocular double brain grafts. *Exp Brain Res* 39:277, 1980.

Perlow M, et al: Brain grafts reduce motor abnormalities produced by CNS damage. *Science* 204:643, 1979.

Ramsey TA, Cox M: Lithium and the kidney: a review. *Am J Psychiatry* 139:443, 1982.

Schildkraut JJ: Biogenic amines and affective disorders. *Ann Rev Med* 25:333, 1974.

Snyder SH: A model of opiate receptor function with implications for a theory of addiction. In Snyder SH, Matthysee S (eds): *Opiate Receptor Mechanisms.* Cambridge, MIT Press, 1975, p 137.

Snyder SH, et al: Drugs, neurotransmitters, and schizophrenia. *Science* 184:1243, 1974.

Snyder SH: *Biological Aspects of Mental Disorder.* New York, Oxford University Press, 1980.

Sokoloff L: Auditory stimulation. In Plum F, Gjedde A, Samson FE (eds): *Neuroanatomical Functional Mapping by the Radioactive 2-Deoxy-D-Glucose Method. Neurosci Res Program Bull* 14:1976.

Targum SD, Sullivan AC, Byrnes SM: Neuroendocrine interrelationships in major depressive disorder. *Am J Psychiatry* 139:282, 1982.

Wender P: *Minimal Brain Dysfunction in Children.* New York, Wiley-Interscience, 1971.

C. Biological Rhythms

Thomas J. Crowley, M.D.

To understand important behavioral and medical information about patients, modern physicians need to understand the biological periodicity which characterizes man and other organisms. Physicians also should know that subtle biological rhythms may modify everyday "normal" behavior profoundly and may contribute to pathological behavior.

BIOLOGICAL PERIODICITY

Periodic changes are inherent in nearly all biological functions. Although the eminent physiologist, Claude Bernard, emphasized the importance of homeostasis, modern research shows that neither constancy nor random variation is the rule of life; most biological and behavioral functions show regular, rhythmic, periodic changes.

It has been suggested that such rhythmic variation reflects a direct astronomical influence. For example, it could be argued that the regular daytime increase and nighttime decrease in human motility, which is seen as part of the sleep-wake cycle, is due to a direct action of the sun and other light sources. However, we will see evidence that this rhythm in motility persists in the absence of any solar influence; the rhythm appears to be an inherent property of the organism. On the other hand, it is clear that the light-dark cycle does synchronize this rhythm among different individuals, so that most people are active in the day and quiescent in the night. We shall see that, without the synchronizing effect of the sun, slightly different rest-activity cycles emerge among different people.

In the past it also was suggested that *all* biological rhythms were a *response* to a basic rhythm of sleep and wakefulness. But we now know that rhythms with a period of approximately 24 hours persist in organs isolated from the rest of the body. Moreover, many biological functions begin to change before the usual time of awakening. For instance, the late-night rise in adrenal steroid production may be viewed as a preparation for the period of expected wakeful activity, rather than as a response to that activity.

It unfortunately is necessary to divorce any discussion of rhythms in biology from "Biorhythms." No satisfactory scientific evidence supports the claim that from the moment of birth we are continually under the influence of three rhythms of fixed frequency, but a considerable profit from the sale of Biorhythm calendars and calculators probably assures that this nuisance will be with us for some time.

DEFINITIONS

Wave-like biological functions are defined in terms of their period, frequency, phase, level, and amplitude.

The *period* of a biological rhythm is the time interval from a point on one wave to the corresponding point on the next wave. For example, the human body temperature rhythmically rises and falls once each 24 hours; the time interval from peak to peak is thus 24 hours, and therefore the period of the rhythm is 24 hours.

The *frequency* of a biological rhythm is the number of waves per unit time. In the temperature example, just given, the frequency is one cycle per 24 hours. There is an inverse relationship between frequency and period ($f = 1/p$).

The *phase* of a biological rhythm is the time relationship between the peak of that rhythm and some other regularly recurring event, usually at the same frequency. For example, the daily peak in the rhythm of human motility closely coincides with the daily peak in the rhythm of temperature, and the two are said to be approximately "in phase" with one another. But the daily peak in adrenocorticosteroid secretion occurs about eight hours before the daily temperature peak, and the two rhythms are said to be "out of phase" with one another by that many hours.

The *level* (or "mesor") of a biological rhythm is the mean height of the wave. If the peak of a man's temperature rhythm is 38°C, and the trough is 37°C, the level would be approximately 37.5°C.

The *amplitude* of a biological rhythm is a measure of the height of the wave; amplitude is half of the peak-to-trough height.

Two other terms also need definition. A *synchronizer* is an environmental event which influences the phase or frequency of a biological rhythm. For example, the timing or phase of the human sleep-wake cycle is synchronized by social stimuli and by the light-dark cycle; people around us and the regular recurrence of night and day influence our times of arising and retiring.

A *biological rhythm* is a periodic biological event which is amenable to frequency synchronization by an environmental event, but which persists in the absence of such synchronizers. For example, the human sleep-wake cycle is synchronized to a 24 hour period by the solar light cycle, but the sleep-wake cycle persists (usually with a period slightly different from 24 hours) among people isolated in caves and unable to see the sun.

Drs. J. Aschoff and R. A. Wever in Germany have studied many volunteers who lived alone in soundproof underground chambers with no clocks, TV, newspapers, or other time cues. Such subjects usually show a fairly regular cycle of rest and activity, but with a period averaging around 25 hours rather than 24. They arise and retire a little later each day (in relation to solar time) until eventually they are completely out of phase with the rest of society. Thus, the sleep-wake cycle persists but is said to *free-run* with a period slightly different from 24 hours in the absence of a synchronizing solar light cycle.

SPECTRUM OF BIOLOGICAL RHYTHMS

Our rhythms do not all beat in unison. An earlier example comparing the adrenocorticosteroid and temperature rhythms showed that two biological rhythms with 24 hour periods could be *out of phase* with one another. Many other biological rhythms do not have a *period* of 24 hours. Indeed, there is a whole spectrum of different frequencies. Electroencephalographers may observe rhythms of up to 32 cycles per second in normal brain waves. The heart beats rhythmically at about one cycle per second, and respirations typically occur at about 20 cycles per minute. During sleep, REM episodes of rapid eye movements and dreaming recur about once every 90 minutes. Temperature, motility, the sleep-wake alternation, and adrenocortical secretion all cycle about once per 24 hours. The menstrual rhythm has a period of about 28 days. Some physiological functions and mating behavior in many animals cycle annually, and there are some suggestions of annual physiological rhythms in human beings.

Recognizing this spectrum in the frequency of biological rhythms, and recognizing that frequencies vary slightly in free running conditions, Professor Franz Halberg at the University of Minnesota provided the field with three more definitions. A *circadian (circa + dies,* about a day) rhythm is one with a period of 20 to 28 hours. An *ultradian* rhythm has a period less than 20 hours and therefore has a frequency considerably greater than one cycle per 24 hours. An *infradian* rhythm has a period greater than 28 hours and therefore a frequency considerably less than one cycle per 24 hours.

NEURAL CONTROL OF CIRCADIAN CYCLING

Circadian rhythms are found in plants, single-celled animals, and even in isolated organs. But in complex animals the brain has assumed the role of synchronizing the different circadian functions, of "conducting the circadian orchestra." A retinohypothalamic pathway runs through the optic nerve, terminating near the chiasm in the suprachiasmatic nuclei of the hypothalamus. Bilateral destruction of this pathway, or destruction of the nuclei, severely disrupts circadian timing, indicating that the nuclei utilize information about light cycles received over the retinohypothalamic pathway to synchronize sleep-wake cycles and various biochemical cycles. However, an animal functionally blinded by severance of the optic tracts behind the chiasm maintains circadian cycling in synchrony with light-dark cycles because the retinohypothalamic path and suprachiasmatic nuclei are anterior to this lesion and remain intact. In man, tumors of the hypothalamus sometimes first disrupt circadian sleep-timing, resulting in complaints of insomnia or daytime drowsiness. Presumably, such complaints reflect dysfunction in the suprachiasmatic area.

DISRUPTION OF NORMAL BIOLOGICAL RHYTHMS

Isolation experiments help us to understand how human circadian rhythms respond to various stressing conditions. Circadian rhythms persist in volunteers isolated from clocks, social cues, and the solar day-night cycle. But in isolation the intrinsic circadian rhythms usually "free-run" with periods different from 24 hours. Moreover, different subjects may display different periods, with about 25 hours being most common. Even within the same subject, different physiological and behavior functions may show different intrinsic periods. In such a subject, for example, the circadian rhythms for urinary excretion gradually may drift out of phase with the circadian sleep-wake cycle because the two rhythms develop somewhat different periods; this is called *internal desynchrony.* Other important individual differences also may appear. Some individuals have free running circadian periods shorter than 24 hours, while others have periods considerably longer than 24 hours. In some individuals deprived of social and light-dark cues, normal circadian periodicity is disrupted and fragmented. Apparently, in isolation experiments which eliminate the usual social and light-dark synchronizers, synchronizing mechanisms less efficiently "conduct the circadian orchestra," permitting some rhythms to be disrupted and some subjects to undergo internal desynchrony. But it must be emphasized that, in general, rhythms persist during isolation.

Blind people are deprived of the normal synchronizing effects of the light-dark cycle. But circadian rhythms appear to be normal in most of these people. Apparently, they use social synchronizers to organize regular, rhythmic cycling. But some blind people do show abnormalities of circadian timing. A blind person's impairment of circadian synchronization may have important behavioral effects. At least one case has been reported of a blind person whose life was seriously disrupted by intermittent daytime drowsiness. When he was allowed to set his own time for arising and retiring, he showed a typical pattern of free running, going to bed and getting up a little later on each successive day, and showing no daytime drowsiness. When he was forced to follow a more regular schedule, episodes of drowsiness and sleep occurred at about the times when he would have retired if he were allowed to set his own schedule and free-run.

Rotating shift workers now include 27% of the American male, and 16% of the American female, work force. All of these people, and also the nonrotating permanent night workers, live on mixed schedules; much of their personal business must be done in the day. Such workers continually must oppose effects of usual social and light-dark circadian synchronizers. Accordingly, the circadian rhythms of such people are disturbed. For example, the amplitude of the circadian temperature curve is notably flattened in night workers. Shift work brings about increased physical, psychological, and social complaints in workers, and the longer the workers continue with shift work, the more complaints they have. Commencing night work produces a physical stress reaction with greater secretion of adrenaline and increased serum levels of cholesterol and uric acid. Although permanent night work results in better adaptation than alternating night and day shifts, adaptation remains incomplete.

Schedules for shift workers may further complicate their problems. It apparently is more difficult for human beings to change shifts by advancing their rhythms counterclockwise (night shift to evening shift to day shift) than to delay those rhythms clockwise (night to day to evening). Also, such adjustments are made slowly, and rapid rotation through shifts prevents accommodation to any circadian cycle. Accordingly, after arranging clockwise shift changes which occurred only once every three weeks, Dr. Charles Czeisler and his colleagues demonstrated improved satisfaction, fewer health complaints, reduced personnel turnover, and increased productivity among workers in an industrial plant. Human circadian rhythms are not infinitely flexible, and workers' productivity, satisfaction, and safety all can be enhanced by industrial medicine's careful attention to the limits which those rhythms impose.

In another example, nuclear submariners of the U.S. Navy work six hours and rest 12. Human beings cannot adapt to this 18-hour cycle, so these sailors experience continuing circadian desynchrony. Civilization's future may rest, but may rest fitfully, with these desynchronized men.

Jet lag is a more posaic, but also more common example of disruption of circadian synchrony. After rapidly moving across several time zones the traveler arrives with circadian rhythms out of phase with the social and light-dark cues at his destination. Nocturnal insomnia, daytime drowsiness, irritability, headaches, and some impairment of concentration are common complaints until the traveler resynchronizes to the new time. Jet lag has practical behavioral implications. Statesmen and businessmen often delay important transactions until some resynchronization has occurred.

THE MENSTRUAL RHYTHM

Moving from the circadian domain, it is interesting to consider the potential behavioral concomitants of the infradian *menstrual rhythm*. The possibility that there may be rhythmic changes in human emotions and behavior related to the menstrual rhythm has in the past been used as an argument to deny responsible positions to women. There certainly is no scientific evidence at this time indicating that the menstrual rhythm is accompanied by large-scale behavioral changes which would warrant such exclusions. But to reject out of hand the possibility that some behavioral change may parallel the menstrual rhythm would seem extreme, given the profound hormonal changes associated with that rhythm. Women regularly report physical discomfort and symptoms of water retention in the premenstrual days of the cycle. There also appears to be some consensus in research reports suggesting a small to moderate average increase in spontaneous motor activity and mental arousal around mid-cycle. Probably, however, the task for clinicians and researchers in this area increasingly will be to focus upon repetitive, periodic changes in individual women, as opposed to previous efforts to find average changes characterizing most or all women. For example, a small subpopulation of women have significant and disabling premenstrual emotional changes (irritability, depression, tension, restlessness, and mood swings) and physical changes (swelling with water retention, painful or tender breasts, weight gain, aches and pains). This has come to be known as the *premenstrual syndrome* or *PMS*. Whether these changes are physiologically or psychologically determined (or both) remains an important research question, but for these particular women, the important clinical fact is that they experience profound, rhythmic waxing and waning of physical and emotional distress in connection with their menstrual cycle.

BIOLOGICAL RHYTHMS AND BEHAVIORAL PATHOLOGY

Psychiatrists increasingly have become interested in the possibility that impaired regulation of biological rhythms may contribute to behavioral pathology.

For example, *drugs* are known to affect circadian rhythms. The choice among certain drugs may be guided in part by the side-effects of those drugs on circadian rhythms. For example, the night-time sedative, flurazepam, has such a prolonged effect that spontaneous motility is depressed on the day following a bedtime dose; the drug exerts an unwelcome disruption of the rest-activity cycle. In another example, 1-α acetyl-methadol is a long-acting opioid drug which has been proposed as a replacement for methadone in the treatment of heroin addicts. It seems convenient because it is given only once every two days, but the drug severely disrupts circadian cycles of rest and spontaneous motility; it stimulates excessive motility on the day of its administration and suppresses motility on the day between doses. This disruption of circadian motility rhythms is so great that the drug seems a poor choice as a potential replacement for methadone.

Other research indicates that estrogens, thyroid medications, and tricyclic drugs all may increase the frequency of circadian rhythms in certain experimental circumstances, while lithium and ethanol may reduce the frequency of those rhythms. Thus, there is considerable evidence that commonly used medications may have subtle but potentially important effects upon circadian behavioral rhythms.

The syndrome of *delayed sleep-phase onset* is another example of behavioral pathology associated with abnormal regulation of biological rhythms. These patients typically feel energetic and active in the evening and early night, and are unable to fall asleep before 3:00 A.M. They describe themselves as "evening persons" on standardized questionnaires, and they show no consistent pathology in electroencephalographic sleep records, nor in standardized psychological tests such as the Minnesota Multi-Phasic Personality Inventory. When these patients are encouraged to go to bed successively later each night, they soon are retiring in the morning, then in midday, then in the afternoon, and eventually at usual bedtime. Thereafter, these patients reportedly are able to fall asleep after retiring at normal bedtime.

Recurring affective disorders also may be caused in part by desynchrony of biological rhythms. Years ago, Professor Halberg speculated that "internal desynchrony" could lead to intermittent mood disorders. If, for example, each of two biological functions normally had rhythmic variations with a frequency of one cycle every 24 hours, and one then began to free run with a frequency of one cycle per 25 hours, the two functions gradually would drift out of phase with one another. If their peak times coincided initially, after about 12 days the peak time of one would coincide with the trough time of the other, and about 12 days later the peaks again would coincide. If the physiological functions in question had an additive effect on behavior, then that behavior gradually would wax and wane in an intermittent fashion every few weeks. And if the difference in periods was small (e.g., 24 vs. 24.1 hours), the waxing and waning would be much slower.

In manic-depressive patients some physiological and behavioral functions apparently do free run with a circadian period slightly different from 24 hours, while other functions maintain the usual 24 hour circadian period. Thus, it seems likely that internal desynchrony does occur in at least some manic-depressive patients. Working on the hypothesis that circadian regulation might be important in patients with affective disorders, Dr. Thomas Wehr at the National Institute of Mental Health abruptly shifted the light-dark cycle in a small number of depressed patients. Dr. Wehr observed that the patients temporarily became less depressed when he moved the daily cycle of sleep and activity to earlier in the day, through changes in lights-on and lights-off times. These various studies increasingly suggest that disruption of the synchrony of biological rhythms may contribute to the development of certain affective disorders.

SUMMARY

Numerous subtle biological changes undoubtedly contribute to the puzzling fluctuations and vagaries of human behavior seen both in everyday life and in psychiatric disturbance. This chapter has reviewed some of the manifold behavioral expressions of one of those biological factors, rhythmic biological variation. It is already clear that biological rhythms are associated with subtle but profound changes, both normal and pathological, in human behavior.

Suggested Readings

Moore-Ede MC, Sulzman FM, Fuller CA: *The Clocks that Time Us.* Cambridge, Harvard University Press, 1982.

Wever RA: *The Circadian System of Man: Results of Experiments under Temporal Isolation.* New York, Springer-Verlag, 1979.

References

Abramowitz ES, Baker AH, Fleischer SF: Onset of depressive psychiatric crises and the menstrual cycle. *Am J Psychiatry* 139:475, 1982.

Akerstedt T, et al: *Shift Work and Well-being.* Report 63b, Laboratory for Clinical Stress Research, Karolinska Institute, Stockholm, 1977.

Aschoff J: Circadian systems in man and their implications. *Hosp Pract* 11:51, 1976.

Crowley TJ, Hydinger-Macdonald M: Bedtime flurazepam and the human circadian rhythm of spontaneous motility. *Psychopharmacology* 62:157, 1979.

Crowley TJ, et al: Every-other-day acetylmethadol disturbs circadian cycles of human motility. *Psychopharmacology* 62:151, 1979.

Czeisler CA, et al: Rotating shift work schedules that disrupt sleep are improved by applying circadian principles. *Science* 217:460, 1982.

Czeisler CA, et al: Successful non-drug treatment of delayed sleep phase syndrome with chrono-therapy: resetting a biological clock in man. *Sleep Res* 8:179, 1979.

Halberg F: Implications of biological rhythms for clinical practice. *Hosp Pract* 12:139, 1977.

Haskett RF, et al: Severe premenstrual tension: delineation of the syndrome. *Biol Psychiatry* 15:121, 1980.

Kokkoris CP, et al: Long-term ambulatory temperature monitoring in a subject with a hypernychthermeral sleep-wake cycle disturbance. *Sleep* 1:177, 1978.

Kripke DF, et al: Circadian rhythm disorders in manic-depressives. *Biol Psychiatry* 15:335, 1978.

Miles LEM, Raynal DM, Wilson MA: Blind man living in normal society has circadian rhythms of 24.9 hours. *Science* 198:421, 1977

Moore-Ede MC, et al: Circadian timekeeping in health and disease. Part 1. Basic properties of circadian pacemakers. *N Engl J Med* 309:469, 1983. Part 2. Clinical implications of circadian rhythmicity. *N Engl J Med* 309:530, 1983.

Rubinow DR, Roy-Byrne P: Premenstrual syndromes: overview from a methodologic perspective. *Am J Psychiatry* 141:163, 1984.

Weber AL, et al: Human non-24-hour sleep-wake cycles in an everyday environment. *Sleep* 2:347, 1980.

Wehr TA, et al: Phase advance of the circadian sleepwake cycle as an antidepressant. *Science* 206:710, 1979.

Weitzman ED, et al: Delayed sleep-phase syndrome: a biological rhythm sleep disorder. *Sleep Res* 8:221, 1979.

D. Sleep and Sleep Disorders

Martin Reite, M.D.

HISTORICAL BACKGROUND

In 1892, George Trumball Ladd, Professor of Mental and Moral Philosophy at Yale, hypothesized the existence of eye movements during sleep and accompanying dreaming. Professor Ladd, however, apparently did not actually watch people while they were sleeping to see if in fact their eyes were moving. It remained for Aserinsky and Kleitman to empirically document the existence of such eye movements during the early 1950's. Studying sleeping adults, they described periods of rapid, jerky, and binocularly symmetrical eye movements occurring during the night, and noted that when the subjects were awakened during these eye movement periods they would often report that they had just been dreaming. Dement and Kleitman, studying these phenomena more thoroughly, found human sleep to be of a cyclic nature and to be composed of various "stages," with different electrical and physiological concomitants. These observations, made in the 1950's, incorporated the use of electroencephalography (a technique developed by a German psychiatrist Hans Berger) to record brain waves (a technology not available to Professor Ladd), and were the foundations of Sleep Disorders Medicine as we know it today. This development is a good example of how new measuring techniques and technology combined with keen observation can bring about major advancements in medical science.

THE STAGES OF SLEEP

Electroencephalography of Sleep

In general, it is convenient to describe and categorize the stages of sleep on the basis of brain electrophysiology as depicted by the electroencephalogram (EEG), as well as by the presence or absence of rapid eye movements as measured by the electrooculogram (EOG). There are two entirely different kinds of sleep: *rapid eye movement* (REM) *sleep* and *nonrapid eye movement* (NREM) sleep or *slow wave sleep* (SWS).

Shortly after the development of electroencephalography it was observed that when human beings went to sleep, brain waves in general became slower and of higher amplitude. This so-called slow wave sleep (SWS) is now divided into four stages, Stages 1, 2, 3 and 4, as a function of EEG morphology. Stage 1, seen as normal individuals move from wakefulness into slow wave sleep, is characterized by disappearance of normal waking alpha activity and the appearance of generalized low voltage, somewhat slower theta activity. Subjects are in fact asleep during Stage 1 sleep, but are easily aroused. They may rarely experience transient hypnogogic hallucinations, which are vivid dream-like images, and occasional hypnic jerks, often consisting of a subjective sensation of taking a step, missing it, and waking up with a body jerk. Stage 1 is normally followed by Stage 2, characterized by somewhat higher voltage slower activity, and the presence of sleep spindles and K-complex activity. Spindle activity consists of rhythmical EEG bursts that wax and wane in amplitude (therefore the term spindle), predominantly seen over midline fronto-central regions. K-complexes are high voltage occasionally somewhat sharp transients, often accompanied by spindle bursts, and usually seen over central or parietal regions. They are thought to represent cerebral responses to external or internal stimuli of various sorts. Stage 3 sleep is characterized by 20% to 50% high voltage slow delta activity with occasional spindle and K-complex activity intermixed. Stage 4 sleep is characterized by generalized high voltage delta activity comprising more than 50% of the record. Stage 3 and 4 sleep are often lumped together and called "Delta" sleep because of their high content of slow EEG (delta) activity. The four stages of SWS are also frequently grouped together and called NREM sleep.

Sleep onset usually consists of an orderly transition from wakefulness through Stages 1 to 4 sleep. Normally, about 90 minutes after sleep onset, the EEG pattern suddenly changes, becomes lower voltage and faster, with occasional sawtooth waves, similar to but not identical with a waking type brain wave pattern, and the observer will notice rapid eye movements beneath the closed eyelids. This is REM sleep, and if the subject is awakened, he or she will often report having been dreaming. EEG patterns associated with SWS (or NREM) and REM sleep are illustrated in Figure 52.7. REM periods last anywhere from a few to 20–30 minutes (even longer in the early morning hours), and occur periodically throughout the night at approximately 90 minute intervals. A normal adult spends between 20% and 25% of sleep time in the REM state. Most of the Stage 3 and 4 slow wave sleep occurs early in the night. REM periods tend to get somewhat longer later in the night or in the early morning hours. If a person sleeps later than usual in the morning, as for example, on a weekend, they may, shortly before waking up, be spending nearly 50% of their time in REM sleep, which is the reason why dreams are often more frequently remembered when waking up at those times.

Physiological Correlates of Sleep Stages

Slow wave (NREM) sleep is normally accompanied by slight decreases in heart rate and respiration rate, with regularization of both, a slight diminution in resting muscle tone compared to the waking state, and a slight decrease in blood pressure. Autonomic physiology is generally stable. REM sleep, by comparison, is accompanied by marked deviations in physiological patterns. Heart and respiratory rate often accelerate, frequently become irregular, and, in addition to the presence of rapid eye movements, there is a striking diminution in skeletal muscle tone. In fact, the electromyogram (EMG) records its lowest levels during REM sleep. REM sleep is normally accompanied by penile erections, and the presence of such erections during REM sleep is a good way to physiologically evaluate erectile dysfunction. If the erectile dysfunction has a physiological origin, there will be an impairment of REM erections, whereas if it is psychologically determined, REM erections will likely be normal.

Characteristic changes in certain circulating

Awake low voltage—random, fast

50 μV

1 sec

Drowsy 8 to 12 cps—alpha waves

Stage 1 3 to 7 cps—theta waves

theta waves

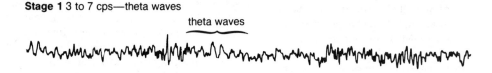

Stage 2 12 to 14 cps—sleep spindles and K complexes

sleep spindle

K complex—

Delta Sleep ½ to 2 cps—delta waves >75 μV

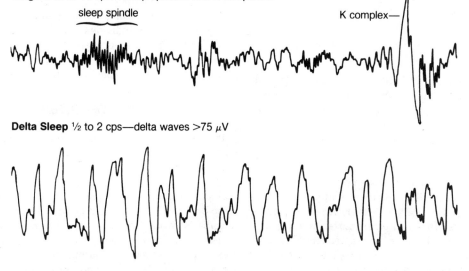

REM Sleep low voltage—random, fast with sawtooth waves

sawtooth waves   sawtooth waves

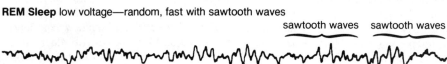

Figure 52.7. Human sleep stages. (Reprinted by permission from P. Hauri, *The Sleep Disorders*. Scope Publications, The Upjohn Company, Kalamazoo, MI, 1982.)

hormones are also noted during sleep. For example, in normal adults growth hormone is preferentially secreted during the first episode of slow wave sleep early in the night. If the subject stays up all night and then goes to sleep, growth hormone will not be secreted during the night but will once again be secreted when slow wave sleep occurs. Growth hormone, therefore, is considered to be entrained to the sleep rhythm. Prolactin secretion in adults usually peaks during NREM sleep, with minimal values during REM periods. If the sleep cycle shifts, prolactin shifts with it, and thus it too is entrained to the sleep cycle. By comparison, steroid hormones are usually maximally secreted during the early morning hours, i.e., during the last half of the sleep cycle. If an individual stays up all night, and then goes to sleep the next day, he or she will still have the peak steroid secretion during the early morning hours even though still awake, and the latter part of the next sleep period will not be accompanied by an increase in secretion of steroid hormones. Thus, these hormones are not sleep entrained, and possess an intrinsic circadian rhythm of their own. It may take up to ten days following a major change in time zones or sleep schedule for steroid hormone secretion to once again come into synchronization with sleep patterns. The same type of relationship holds between a number of other physiological variables and sleep patterns. Some are sleep entrained, others are independent of sleep (e.g., body temperature).

Neurophysiology and Neurochemistry of Sleep

Slow wave or NREM sleep appears to depend upon the balance between an arousal system, including the reticular activating system, and a rather widespread forebrain sleep-inducing system. Thus the onset of slow wave sleep involves both decreased activity in arousal systems and increased activity in slow wave sleep-inducing systems. Serotonergic systems have been implicated in controlling the onset and maintenence of slow wave sleep. However, recent evidence implicates other neurotransmitter systems, including acetylcholine and catecholamines, as being important in modulating interactions between sleeping and arousal systems. REM sleep appears to involve the activity of several deep midline structures located in the mesencephalic, medullary, and pontine reticular systems, as well as other midline nuclei including the locus coeruleus. Active work is continuing on efforts to elucidate the specifics of the neurophysiological and neurochemical basis of REM sleep. Both cholinergic and aminergic systems appear involved in the onset and maintenance of REM sleep. There is also evidence from several laboratories of the presence of a circulating sleep-inducing substance or factor, possibly peptide in nature. Recently, a glycopeptide called "factor S" has been isolated from human urine that appears to produce a slow wave sleep when infused into the brain of experimental animals.

Changes in Sleep Patterns Over the Life Span

Major changes in the distribution of sleep stages are noted from birth through adult life to old age. Premature infants may spend as much as 80% of their time, or more, in REM sleep, while newborn infants spend about 50% of their sleep time in REM sleep. The percent of time spent in REM sleep decreases to adult values (20–25%) by the time a child is several years of age. Stage 3 and 4 slow wave sleep increases in amount in latency age children and young adolescents, and it is difficult to arouse them from a Stage 3 and 4 sleep. Thus, it is possible to pick up a child who has recently gone to sleep, and who is in Stage 3 and 4 sleep, and carry him or her about without their being awakened. With increasing age, beginning normally in late middle-aged and older individuals, sleep tends to become more fragmented; Stage 3–4 sleep tends to decrease, more time is spent awake, and complaints of sleep disturbances tend to increase.

FUNCTIONS OF SLEEP

In spite of intensive research efforts over the past several decades, we still have little knowledge of exactly what purpose sleep serves. It is generally known that sleep is necessary for normal body restorative functions, and rats that are sleep-deprived for prolonged periods become ill and die, showing lesions in several organ systems. At one time it was thought that REM sleep was necessary for normal psychological functioning, but this idea is now disputed. It has also been suggested that REM sleep may be a period of time during which new experiences are processed and integrated with older memories, but this hypothesis has yet to be substantiated. All we can say for sure at this time is that we cannot function normally (or feel rested) without optimal sleep, and we cannot function at all without some sleep.

On the average, normal healthy young adults sleep approximately seven and three-quarters hours per night. There is marked individual variation, however, with some people requiring up to 10 hours sleep to feel rested during the day, and others getting along without any obvious ill effects with no more than three to four hours of sleep per night throughout their lives. Sleep can be experimentally shortened to about six hours per night, and once that stage is reached, individuals tend to remain at the shorter sleep times without evidence of impairment in functioning, although they do tend to complain of being somewhat more tired during the day. The proper amount of sleep for a given individual can perhaps best be described as that amount necessary to feel rested and "not sleepy" the following day.

There have been descriptions of personality characteristics of both long and short sleepers, with long sleepers tending to be somewhat more introspective, moody, and obsessional, and short sleepers tending to be more action-oriented, less introspective, and less moody. Which comes first, the personality type or the sleep pattern, remains to be determined, however.

SLEEP DISORDERS

Prevalence of Sleep Disorders

It has been estimated that up to 20 million people in this country suffer from sleep disorders, that about 10 million see a physician for their sleep difficulty, and that about five million receive a prescription for sleeping medication. Of this latter group, more than two million take sleeping pills each night over several months, despite many serious questions about the safety and effectiveness of long-term, nightly sedative use. Nearly 40% of these sedative prescriptions are written for persons over age 60, yet this is the very age group that is more vulnerable to both psychological and physiological side effects from these drugs, as will be discussed later in the chapter.

Classification of Sleep Disorders

Clearly, sleep disorders rank among one of the most common complaints physcans hear from their patients. These complaints generally fall into three different areas and can be succinctly summarized as: 1) "Doctor, I can't go to sleep" or "Doctor, I can't stay asleep,"; 2) "Doctor, I sleep too much"; or 3) "Doctor, strange things happen when I sleep." The first is what we generally call *insomnia*, and is now more technically known as *Disorders of Initiating and Maintaining Sleep* (DIMS). Until the recent past, this general complaint of inability to sleep was almost universally dealt with by the prescription of a sedative hypnotic drug. We now know that there are a variety of separate disorders which may result in the common symptom of insomnia. In many such disorders, hypnotic medication is not the treatment of choice. The second major group of disorders, that of *excessive daytime sleepiness* or *hypersomnia*, is included under the general diagnostic categorization of *Disorders of Excessive Sleepiness* (DOES). Formerly thought to consist primarily of psychological disturbances and narcolepsy, it is now known that there are a number of separate disease entities that contribute to this same general symptom of excessive daytime sleepiness (EDS). The third group of disorders consist of such phenomena as sleepwalking, (somnambulism), sleeptalking, enuresis (bed wetting), night terrors (pavor nocturnus), and bruxism (tooth grinding). For the most part these *parasomnias* are now thought to represent disorders of arousal that occur early in the night at the time of most deep Stage 3–4 sleep. They are often thought of as phenomena that would be normal if carried out in a waking state, but are not normal when the patient is asleep. In a single chapter I cannot hope to cover in detail all of the present known sleep disorders. I will only discuss those that are most common, and those which will probably be seen with considerable frequency by most primary care physicians. But first, I will make a few comments about the diagnosis of sleep disorders.

Diagnosis of Sleep Disorders

Proper diagnosis of sleep disorders is multifaceted. It begins with a complete sleep history, medical history, and physical examination. A bed partner interview is very important, as the bed partner may report events suggesting the possibility of a sleep disorder of which the patient is unaware. A psychiatric examination, including perhaps several psychological tests, is important to establish whether or not the patient is clinically anxious or depressed, or has other significant psychopathology. Laboratory examinations, if indicated, may include several studies. One of these is *polysomnography*, which is the all-night recording of EEG sleep stages and a number of physiological variables. These variables may include EKG, oxygen tension by ear oximetry, several measures of breathing (including nasal and oral thermistors), intercostal EMG, measures of chest and diaphragmatic expansion, and the recording of anterior tibialis EMG. A *multiple sleep latency test* (MSLT) is often indicated in patients complaining of excessive daytime sleepiness. The MSLT consists of a polysomnogram recording at five two-hour intervals during the day, e.g., 1000, 1200, 1400, 1600, 1800 hours, at which times the patient is requested to lie down and attempt to go to sleep. In normal subjects, the mean sleep onset time for these five two-hour naps is usually 12 to 15 minutes or more, showing some variation as a function of time of day. Patients with excessive daytime sleepiness show a significant reduction in mean sleep onset time, which permits quantification of the severity of their disorder, as well as a way to monitor improvement with treatment. Other tests, such as nocturnal penile tumescence (NPT), are used when indicated in the sleep laboratory evaluation.

DISORDERS OF INITIATING AND MAINTAINING SLEEP

Disorders of initiating and maintaining sleep are most frequently subsumed under the global term "insomnia." Insomnia is generally classified by how long it has persisted: transient (less than three weeks) or chronic (more than three weeks). Transient insomnias usually have a clear-cut precipitant such as physical illness, acute life stress, irregular rest-activity schedules, or jet lag. They occur in otherwise normal persons who usually have a normal sleep history. They often resolve in the case of jet lag. Short term use of appropriate hypnotics may be beneficial. Chronic insomnias are more long lasting, persisting well beyond the initial stressful event (if one was present), and present more complex diagnostic and therapeutic decisions. In sections following, the major causes of chronic insomnia will be discussed.

Psychiatric-Related Insomnias

Psychiatric disturbances are the most frequent causes of insomnia. Most often these are the *anxiety disorders* and the *depressive disorders*, both of which frequently include disturbances in sleep as a major symptom. The diagnosis must be made by a careful psychiatric evaluation and appropriate sleep evaluation, such that the other causes of insomnia can be systematically excluded. It is possible to have more than one cause of insomnia. There is, for example, nothing to prevent an individual with a depression-related insomnia from also having symptomatic nocturnal myoclonus, or sleep apnea. It is quite common for sleep problems to be intimately intertwined with other symptoms in patients with complex and chronic psychopathologies. Such individuals may focus on their sleep problems to the exclusion of or as a way of avoiding having to deal with their other problems. Insomnia secondary to a psychiatric disorder is best managed by the appropriate treatment of the underlying psychiatric problems with perhaps judicious short-term use of hypnotics if appropriate.

The early hope that certain of the major psychiatric disorders, such as schizophrenia, would have unique sleep disturbances accompanying them has not been fulfilled. Sleep may certainly be disturbed in such patients; in the acute phase of a schizophrenic illness the patients may remain awake until they are exhausted, then sleep only poorly and awaken unrefreshed. Some schizophrenic patients deprived of REM sleep fail to show a REM rebound during recovery sleep as normal persons do. However, there appears to be nothing unique about polysomnographically recorded sleep in schizophrenic patients that would aid in diagnosing (or understanding) their illness.

With the affective disorders, the situation is somewhat different. There is mounting evidence that some depressed adults may show an unusually short nighttime REM latency (i.e., early onset of REM sleep), a finding that has been used diagnostically. Current thinking suggests that an adult with nocturnal REM latency of 50 to 60 minutes or less (age may also be an important variable in this regard) should be suspected of having an affective disorder, and examined appropriately. It has also been recently shown that in certain depressed patients, their sleep patterns may change the night following a test dose of 50 mg of the tricyclic antidepressant amitriptyline. Increased REM latency and reduced difficulty in sleep onset after amitriptyline appear to be predictors of a subsequent positive therapeutic response to tricyclic antidepressant therapy.

These nocturnal sleep patterns in depressive patients would be more typical of sleep in normals that was delayed until early morning hours, where the tendency to have REM sleep is greater, and REM latencies are shorter. This and other physiological data suggest that REM sleep (and body temperature) circadian rhythms may be phase advanced in certain depressed patients relative to their sleep-wake schedules, as discussed by Dr. Crowley in the preceding part of this chapter. Experimentally advancing the sleep-wake schedule has been shown to result in short-term improvement in depressive symptoms in some depressed patients, perhaps by temporarily compensating for their own internal disturbances in rhythms. Such data, as well as evidence that both sleep deprivation and REM deprivation may result in short-term improvement in depressive symptoms, lends credence to the hypothesis that certain affective disorders may be closely linked to disturbances in the regulation of internal phase relationships of several biological rhythms.

Although not usually considered a psychiatric disorder per se, mention should be made of sleep disturbances, usually insomnia, accompanying the grief that follows a major separation or loss. The response to separation and loss includes a set of physiological symptoms in which sleep complaints figure prominently. While exhibiting considerable variability and usually improving significantly over a period of several weeks, in some individuals the grief response is difficult and protracted, extending over a period of months. This may be representative of underlying individual differences in the physiological disorganization precipitated by loss. While the mechanisms underlying such atypical and prolonged grief responses are not well understood, they might best be considered, in turns of management, to represent an affective disorder.

Psychophysiological Insomnia

Psychophysiological insomnia ranks with the psychiatric insomnias as one of the most frequent causes of insomnia. Psychophysiological insomnia consists essentially of conditioned arousal in a sleep setting. In contrast to patients with anxiety or depression, the daytime work

adaptation in these patients, as well as their interpersonal relationships, are good except for feeling chronically tired. They usually have little evidence of significant psychopathology. They do complain of muscular tension and a sense of being "wired" as they try to go to sleep, which may be associated with anxiety about the process of going to sleep per se. They often sleep better away from home and not infrequently when recorded in a sleep laboratory they exhibit normal sleep. They often can fall asleep easily when not trying to, such as while watching TV. Such individuals appear to have been conditioned to remain awake in the normal sleep environment of their bedroom.

The differential diagnosis of psychophysiological insomnia includes all of the many causes of insomnia, especially psychiatric insomnia. Once the diagnosis is established, the treatment consists of improvement of sleep hygiene, which includes such items as regularization of the sleep-wake cycle, not going to bed to do anything except sleep, not staying in bed while worrying or obsessing about various concerns, institution of a program of regular daily exercise, avoidance of excessive caffeine, avoidance of alcohol before sleep onset, and limited use of hypnotics. Selected patients may benefit from appropriate use of biofeedback, which may include theta or sensorimotor-rhythm (SMR) biofeedback. Biofeedback therapy should be instituted only by well-qualified professionals.

There may be types of insomnia that are essentially "primary," with onset early in life, and characterized by intrinsic excessive reticular activating system activity and/or deficiencies in slow wave sleep-inducing CNS systems. Such individuals, for whom treatment is difficult, would likely appear in the "psychophysiological" or "childhood-onset" insomnia diagnostic category.

Drug- and Alcohol-Related Insomnia

Insomnia related to drug and alcohol abuse is thought to be the third most common cause of insomnia, following the psychiatric disorders and psychophysiological insomnia. Chronic heavy use of alcohol and sedative medication may result in decreases of both Stage 3–4 sleep and REM sleep, disorganization and mixing of sleep EEG patterns, impaired sleep efficiency, and disturbance in normal sleep cycling. Until

the recent past, sleeping pills, most often barbiturates, were dispensed quite freely for sleep-
related complaints, resulting in excessive use
(and abuse) and usually worsening of the sleep
complaints. Withdrawal of these compounds is
compromised by the REM rebound phenomena
that will be described later in the chapter. Heavy
use of alcohol, often for the alleged purpose of
preventing insomnia, inevitably worsens the underlying sleep disorder, and further aggravates
rebound phenomena upon alcohol withdrawal.
A high incidence of suspicion as to the existence
of drug- or alcohol-related insomnia can be obtained by a very careful history. Again, an interview with a close relative or bed partner may
also be helpful, since such patients are frequently prone to understate their drug or alcohol
use.

Treatment consists of a slow withdrawal, perhaps accompanied by temporary replacement
with more suitable hypnotics. Counseling or psychotherapy is usually a necessary adjunct. Other
forms of treatment that provide patients with a
sense of having some control over their ability
to relax and sleep (formerly provided by the
drug), such as progressive relaxation or biofeedback techniques, may be helpful when used ju-
diciously as part of the total treatment program.
Such patients are difficult at best, however, and
there often remains an underlying psychiatric
or characterological disturbance that facilitated
adoption of the original drug abuse habit. They
require considerable firmness and patience on
the part of their physicians. Particular mention
should be made here of insomnia related to
excessive caffeine consumption. Although the
general public has an awareness of this problem,
the physician will not infrequently be presented
with a complaint of insomnia that can be traced
to caffeine, and which will respond to withdrawal of caffeine-containing beverages.

Nocturnal Myoclonus

Nocturnal myoclonus is a syndrome recognized with increasing frequency of late. It is
characterized by periodic contractures of the
leg musculature, beginning with the anterior
tibialis muscles, occurring approximately every
20 to 40 seconds. These contractures arouse the
patient and result in subjective insomnia,
although the patient is usually not aware of the
leg jerking. While polysomnography is required
for a definitive diagnosis, the bed partner

interview can provide a high level of suspicion.
The etiology is unknown, and the incidence of
the disorder increases with increasing age. The
term *periodic movements in sleep* (PMS) is often
used instead of nocturnal myoclonus, because a
variety of other disorders have in the past been
subsumed under the term nocturnal myoclonus.
Nocturnal myoclonus has been effectively
treated with 0.5 mg of clonazepam (Clonapin)
at bedtime, but the drug has a variable effect. It
has also been suggested that tricyclic
antidepressants aggravate the condition. This is
another example of the importance of making
an accurate diagnosis of the cause of insomnia
before instituting treatment.

A related disorder, *restless legs syndrome*, may
occur either independently of or associated with
PMS. This is characterized by uncomfortable
"creeping" sensations in the legs that appear
only at rest (but while awake) and require that
the patient get up and move about to terminate
the uncomfortable sensations. While not
painful, they are sufficiently disturbing to
produce insomnia in some individuals. Restless
legs syndrome has been reported to respond to
oxycodone (Percodan) or codeine, which
suggests that it may have opiate-related etiology.
It has also been reported to respond to
carbamazepine (Tegretol) as well as vitamin E,
caffeine withdrawal, and dopamine agonists. At
the present time its etiology and optimal
treatment are not well understood.

Sleep Apnea Insomnia

Some cases of insomnia are related to *sleep
apnea*, most often of the central type. It frequently occurs that the patient has an apnea,
awakens, and remembers the awakening but is
unaware of the apnea. Again the bed partner
interview may be helpful in raising the suspicion
of this disorder. Polysomnography is indicated
for a definitive diagnosis. Treatment is somewhat problematic, as will be discussed shortly.
Sleep apnea insomnia must not, of course, be
treated with hypnotics, as they may further aggravate the apnea. This again emphasizes the
importance of accurate diagnosis prior to instituting treatment for any insomnia.

Circadian Rhythm Disorders

Several disorders of the sleep-wake cycle have
recently been described, some of which result in

insomnia. The by now generally well established discipline of *chronobiology* has made us aware that many biological functions have 24-hour circadian rhythms. The sleep-wake cycle is one of these.

Most normal individuals, when placed in an environment free of time cues, such as in a deep cave, will move to a 25-hour sleep-wake rhythm, which appears to be the frequency of our free-running circadian clock. By virtue of the fact that we live in an environment with a 24-hour light-dark cycle, we must phase advance our internal biological clock by one hour each day to stay in synchronization with our externally imposed 24-hour rhythms. Long distance travellers who move through a number of time zones rapidly are forced to re-entrain their circadian rhythms to new 24-hour cycles. There is evidence that some individuals are more adept at such re-entrainment than others. The phenomena of *jet lag*, in which the various circadian biological rhythms are out of synchronization with each other, and which results in fatigue and impaired performance, is by now well known to most travelers. Eastbound travel usually results in more difficulties, as travelers are required to phase advance their sleep-wake rhythms. Westbound travel is not as disruptive, as our bodies find it easier to re-entrain rhythms that are phase-delayed than those that are phase-advanced. A study by Seidel et al. suggests that the use of the short acting benzodiazepine triazolam to induce sleep in normal individuals who have experienced a sudden 12-hour shift in their sleep cycle (akin to flying half way around the world) resulted in both improved sleep and improved daytime performance compared to either placebo or the long-acting benzodiazepine flurazepam.

The late Elliot Weitzman and his colleagues developed a classification of disorders of the sleep-wake cycle, some of which result in subjective insomnia, and such individuals may present to the doctor initially complaining of insomnia. Perhaps the most common of these disorders is the *delayed sleep-phase onset syndrome* described by Dr. Crowley in the preceding part of this chapter. These patients report a chronic inability to fall asleep at the desired clock time to meet our conventional school-work cycle, but are able to fall asleep easily in the early morning hours, at which point their sleep is polysomnographically normal. They characteristically have a great deal of trouble awakening in the morn-

ing, since they have not had enough sleep, and they feel fatigued and sleepy during the day. They may sleep very late on weekends. They often are described as "night people" or "evening persons" and have in the past been thought to have a type of sleep onset insomnia. Many such patients can be successfully treated by "chronotherapy," which involves delaying their time of going to sleep by three hours each day (i.e., a temporary 27-hour sleep-wake cycle), until they have moved their sleep onset time around the clock and are going to sleep at the desired time (e.g., 10:00 or 11:00 p.m.). Once they have reached this goal, they can often maintain the new rhythm so long as they do not artifically interfere with their sleep-wake cycle by staying up unusually late. Attempting to modify their sleep onset time in the other direction, i.e., by shortening their sleep-wake cycle, is generally not successful.

Shift workers are also subject to sleep difficulties due to their frequent rhythms. It has recently been shown that if shift workers arrange their shift changes to result in phase delays, the change in work schedules are more easily adapted to than if they work schedules that result in phase advances.

Coexisting Medical Disorders

A number of unrelated disease entities can result in impaired sleep. Hyperthyroidism may result in shortened and fragmented sleep that contains an increased amount of delta sleep. Hypothyroidism may result in excessive sleepiness and a lack of delta sleep. Sleep disorders due to thyroid dysfunction may last a number of months (up to a year) after the thyroid disorder is treated medically. Chronic renal insufficiency may also result in shortened, fragmented, and disorganized sleep. Sleep disorders due to uremia usually improve temporarily after dialysis. Any disorder that has chronic pain as a component can also worsen sleep and result in insomnia. Chronic fibrositis has been associated with a peculiar sleep pattern called alpha/delta sleep, in which alpha activity intrudes into slow wave sleep and results in what is called *nonrestorative sleep*. With nonrestorative sleep, although the patient may sleep for a normal time period, he or she does not feel rested when they awaken. Such medical disorders, and other diagnosable illness that may interfere with sleep, should be sought as part of the sleep workup, which includes a medical history and appropriate laboratory studies. Coexisting medical conditions are of course most common in elderly patients, where special emphasis should be placed on their detection.

Sleep Problems in the Elderly

The highest percentage of sleep complaints can be found in the elderly. There are several reasons for this. First, sleep patterns are known to change with age, with elderly individuals exhibiting significantly less deep slow wave (Stage 3 and 4) sleep, more frequent arousals during the night, and frequently less total sleep time. These changes may be perceived as insomnia and the patients may so complain. Secondly, elderly individuals are frequently afflicted with other medical disorders that impair their health, and which may be associated with chronic pain or other disturbances which significantly interfere with sleep. Thus, disturbances in sleep frequently accompany other chronic illnesses. Finally, recent research has demonstrated that there is a higher incidence of sleep apnea and nocturnal myoclonus in normal elderly individuals. The reason for this remains to be determined, nor is there yet any clearly effective therapy (if any is indicated), but these conditions could certainly contribute to the perception of disturbed sleep in the elderly. Additionally, the elderly, because of physical or other limitations, are frequently forced into significant changes in living habits, the most profound of which are those encountered with chronic hospitalization or nursing home environments. In these situations, the normal day-to-day activity and sleep-wake cycles may be significantly altered. There may be frequent daytime napping, and thus the maintenance of normal circadian activity patterns may be disturbed, with the resulting circadian rhythm disturbances appearing as insomnia. Opportunity for physical activity and exercise may be decreased. All of these factors, along with the recognized observation that elderly individuals metabolize medication significantly differently (usually more slowly) than younger persons, make the evaluation and management of sleep disturbances in the elderly an area of special concern.

The evaluation of a sleep complaint in the elderly must be comprehensive and multifaceted. What is the day-to-day work and activity cycle? Does the patient have sufficient physical activity, and is a normal sleep-waking schedule in effect? Are there any underlying unrecognized, improperly diagnosed, or inadequately treated medical illnesses present? Has the patient's mental status been adequately evaluated? As noted in Chapter 47, unrecognized and inadequately treated depressive disorders (with accompanying insomnia) are frequently seen in elderly people where they are misdiagnosed as symptoms of dementia. Finally, assuming a thorough evaluation and proper treatment of other environmental, social, and medical conditions, the choice and use of hypnotics must be weighed against the possibility of aggravating a possible underlying central sleep apnea, and of interacting in a toxic way with other concomitantly administered medications. This by no means suggests that hypnotics should not be used in the elderly, but only that they must not be used indiscriminately. They must be intelligently chosen with respect to type, purpose of administration, dose, metabolic fate, and interaction with other agents. As our elderly population increases, these issues will increase in importance.

The Use and Abuse of Hypnotics

Let us now consider some of the basic issues relative to the effects of drugs on sleep, since hypnotics are still one of the major treatment modalities available for the treatment of certain of the insomnias. Two important facts to keep in mind are: 1) any drug that effects sleep also changes sleep, and 2) many sedative hypnotics have a fairly short duration of effective action. For illustrative purposes, I will begin by discussing the effects of barbiturates, which until recently were the most commonly prescribed hypnotic for insomnia.

Barbiturates, as do many other older sedative hypnotics, strongly suppress REM sleep when administration is first begun. If, however, a therapeutic dose, normally about 100 mg, is administered nightly on a continual basis, after a period of a few days to a week, REM sleep returns to normal levels in terms of percent of total sleep. If then, after a several week period, the drug is suddenly discontinued, a phenomena known as *REM rebound* occurs. This consists of a marked increase in the present time spent in

REM sleep during the first several nights following drug discontinuation, and this REM sleep is often associated with unusually vivid and frequently frightening nightmares.

An example of REM suppression and rebound is illustrated in Figure 52.8, where the vertical axis is REM sleep in percent, and the horizontal axis is time. Initial placebo administration is accompanied by normal amounts of REM sleep, about 20% of total sleep. When a REM suppressant drug is started, such as a barbiturate, REM % decreases, and then slowly returns to normal, only to show a marked rebound when the drug is stopped and the placebo reinstituted. The neurochemistry underlying this rebound phenomena is not well understood, but its clinical implications are considerable, because the initial tendency is for the patient to immediately reinstitute the medication to help correct what is perceived as an increasingly severe problem with sleep.

A second major consideration in the use of barbiturate-like compounds is the fact that their effectiveness diminishes rapidly after the first few days of administration. While they may be effective in decreasing sleep latency (the period

of time measured from "lights out" to the onset of sleep) and in decreasing the number of awakenings for the first several nights, by the end of a week or so, this effect has in large part worn off, and even though the drug is continued, sleep patterns in insomniac patients remain as disturbed as prior to the onset of drug administration. There is then a frequent problem with the patient increasing the dose, so as to obtain once again a short-term improvement in sleep patterns. As a result, such individuals can rather easily become habituated to higher and higher doses of these medications.

Many of the older sedative hypnotic agents also modify or enhance the activity of certain hepatic enzyme systems in such a way as to alter the metabolic rate of other simultaneously administered medications. As an example, the barbiturates stimulate hepatic enzyme activity so as to increase the metabolism of anticoagulants, steroid compounds, other sedatives such as alcohol, and tricyclic antidepressants. If barbiturates or similar drugs are prescribed for an individual who is, for example, stabilized on an anticoagulant, some difficulty in maintaining the anticoagulant status can be anticipated. The

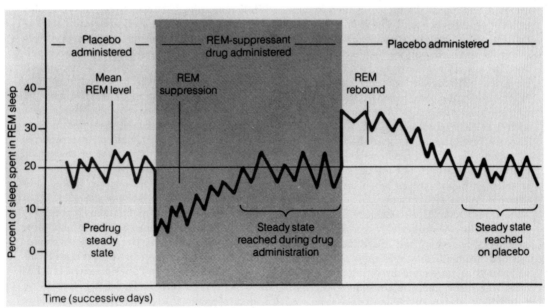

Figure 52.8. REM deprivation and rebound. (Reprinted by permission from P. Hauri, *The Sleep Disorders.* Scope Publications, The Upjohn Company, Kalamazoo, MI, 1982.)

benzodiazepine compounds, on the other hand, are thought not to alter hepatic enzyme activity, although they may potentiate the action of alcohol and other sedatives.

The use of barbiturates and other older sedative hypnotics has now diminished considerably in the treatment of insomnia, and instead some of the more newly developed benzodiazepine compounds are proving to be both safer and more effective. These compounds enjoy the advantage of less toxicity, with a much greater latitude between the therapeutic range and the potentially lethal dose range. They also have been shown to be effective in improving sleep for much longer periods of time, up to at least a month in some studies. They are associated with less of a disturbance in sleep patterns than are barbiturates and other agents. The benzodiazepines also tend to decrease Stage 3–4 slow wave sleep, which can be used to advantage in treating certain of the parasomnias, where reduction in slow wave sleep may be associated with clinical improvement.

They do, however, have some problems of their own. Several benzodiazepine hypnotics, such as flurazepam (Dalmane), have active metabolites with a very long half-life, on the order of 70 to 100 hours or more. Thus, it takes a number of days for a single dose to be totally excreted, and repeated daily doses tend to build up blood levels over a period of days. These long half-life agents may be associated with considerable daytime sedation in some patients. This may be advantageous in an anxious patient, where some daytime sedation may be desirable. It is not advantageous, however, in individuals who must be maximally alert during the day, such as truck or bus drivers, pilots, or policemen. The discontinuation of benzodiazepine compounds may result in a syndrome called *rebound insomnia*. With short half-life benzodiazepines, rebound insomnia occurs when an individual who has taken a therapeutic dose nightly for some time suddenly discontinues the medication, and sleep is subjectively worse for one or two nights. With long half-life benzodiazepines, rebound insomnia may not appear for five to seven days or more after discontinuation of the drug. Very short half-life benzodiazepine hypnotics have also been reported to produce an early morning insomnia in some patients, consisting of an increase in time awake during the

early morning hours of drug nights. This usually occurs after several weeks of nightly administration, when tolerance has begun to develop. This syndrome, like rebound insomnia, may be due to a lag in production of endogenous benzodiazepine compounds as the serum level of the drug diminishes.

The metabolic fate of different benzodiazepines varies considerably. Several of the longer acting compounds (e.g., flurazepam and diazepam) undergo hepatic oxidation, a metabolic pathway more likely to be impaired by liver disease or impaired liver function. Others (e.g., temazepam and oxazepam) undergo hepatic conjugation and renal excretion; this metabolic pathway is less likely to be interfered with by impairment in hepatic function. Furthermore, evidence of withdrawal symptoms, including insomnia, has been described in patients who have been on long half-life benzodiazepines (e.g., flurazepam) for prolonged periods, and who are then switched to short half-life benzodiazepines. Such symptoms may persist for several weeks, and should be distinguished from reemergence of the underlying anxiety held in check by the long-acting compounds.

Because of these many complications with the benzodiazepines, considerable efforts have been made over the years to find a "natural" hypnotic. While something like the peptide "factor S" may ultimately prove to be such, the amino acid L-tryptophan, a precursor of serotonin, has been shown to be effective in inducing sleep in otherwise normal subjects, at a dose of about four grams. As of yet, however, it has not lived up to expectations in the treatment of insomnia.

Several basic questions should be kept in mind whenever one is prescribing a hypnotic compound. These include: 1) What is its duration of hypnotic action (how many days or weeks will it continue to be effective if administered nightly)? 2) How safe is it (that is, how close is the therapeutic dose to the toxic dose)? 3) What is its serum half-life and metabolic pathway (especially important for the elderly and those with liver disease)? 4) Does it affect hepatic enzyme activity? 5) To what extent does it distort sleep patterns? 6) To what extent is REM rebound a problem? 7) To what extent is rebound insomnia a problem?

It is advisable for a physician to know the answers to all of these questions before prescribing any hypnotic compound for the treatment of insomnia.

DISORDERS OF EXCESSIVE SLEEP

Disorders of excessive sleep are a group of disorders formerly characterized as the hypersomnias. These are the most serious of the sleep disorders from a medical standpoint, and such complaints must be taken very seriously by the physician. As noted earlier, a nocturnal polysomnogram, perhaps followed by a multiple sleep latency test the day following the polysomnogram, is necessary for an accurate diagnosis of these disorders.

Narcolepsy

Narcolepsy is a disorder characterized by frequent, sudden, and overwhelming urges to sleep that occur periodically throughout the day. These *daytime sleep attacks* result in patients uncontrollably going to sleep in difficult, embarrassing, and dangerous circumstances such as on the job, during conversations, and while driving. In addition to the attacks of daytime sleepiness, narcoleptic patients frequently complain of *cataplexy* (sudden bouts of muscular weakness, usually brought about by strong emotions), *hypnogogic hallucinations* (vivid, visual hallucinary episodes occurring at sleep onset), and *sleep paralysis* (waking up from sleep being paralyzed and unable to move voluntary musculature with the exception of the eyes). These four sets of symptoms taken together, i.e., daytime sleep attacks, cataplexy, hypnogogic hallucinations, and sleep paralysis, have been sometimes termed the "narcoleptic tetrad." The onset of narcolepsy is usually in adolescence or early adulthood, and the daytime sleep attacks usually precede the development of the other symptoms.

Narcolepsy appears to be a disorder of REM sleep. The cataplectic attacks and sleep paralysis appear to represent a breakthrough into the waking state of the descending muscular inhibition normally associated with REM sleep. Severe cataplectic attacks may terminate within several minutes in a full-blown REM sleep episode. There is evidence of a significant genetic contribution to the narcoleptic syndrome, and a very similar syndrome has been found in several species of dogs that has a clear genetic component. Hopefully, animal model studies will ultimately result in our improved understanding of the fundamental pathophysiology of narcolepsy in man.

The diagnosis of narcolepsy requires a careful history, and both polysomnography and the MSLT. While an all night polysomnogram may not show marked deviations in narcoleptic individuals, not infrequently a *sleep onset REM period* is noted which is helpful in diagnosis. A sleep onset REM period is a REM period that occurs within ten minutes of sleep onset (a rare finding in the normal population). A polysomnogram will also help differentiate other causes of excessive daytime sleepiness, such as sleep apnea or nocturnal myoclonus (both of which, incidentally, are seen more frequently in patients with narcolepsy). The MSLT is often diagnostic in narcolepsy. As a group, narcoleptics will have very short mean sleep latencies, on the order of three to four minutes for the five testing periods. If two or more sleep onset REM periods are noted during the MSLT, this is further strong evidence of narcolepsy, especially when the symptoms of cataplexy, sleep paralysis, and hypnogogic hallucinations are present. Abusers of stimulant drugs not infrequently become quite proficient in reciting the appropriate sleep history in order to obtain the diagnosis of narcolepsy and a prescription for stimulants. Thus, it is advisable to obtain empirical documentation of the diagnosis by means of sleep laboratory studies before instituting treatment.

The treatment of narcolepsy remains symptomatic. Stimulants such as dextro-amphetamine sulfate or methylphenidate are useful in controlling the daytime sleep episodes. The tricyclic antidepressants such as imipramine or protriptyline have been shown to be efficacious in helping to control severe symptomatic cataplexy, although they appear to have little effect on the daytime sleep attacks. An important part of the treatment regimen of any narcoleptic patient is regularization of the sleep-wake cycle so as to protect nocturnal sleep, provision of several naps during the day, and helping the patient design a lifestyle compatible with the disorder. Patients have to be made aware of the dangers of sleep attacks or cataplectic episodes in intrinsically dangerous situations such as swimming, mountain climbing, driving and related activities. The American Narcolepsy Association (an association of individuals afflicted with the disorder) has proved helpful in providing both the latest information on treatment and etiology as well as support for afflicted individuals.

The Sleep Apnea Syndromes

The other major cause of excessive daytime sleepiness are the sleep apneas, or cessation of breathing during sleep. There are two main types: (1) *central apneas*, i.e., decrease of the central respiratory drive during sleep, and (2) *obstructive apneas*, i.e., collapse of the nasopharyngeal upper airway so as to preclude air exchange. Most sleep apnea syndromes include aspects of both central and obstructive forms, and are called *mixed apneas*. Often, for example, an initial central apnea will be followed by collapse of the airway with a resultant secondary obstructive episode. Recently, episodes of diminished breathing, called *hypopneas*, have also been observed during sleep, and have been in large part attributed to a decrease in central respiratory drive. The apneas, especially the obstructive apneas, represent serious medical disorders that justify vigorous diagnosis and treatment. Chronic severe obstructive apnea can result in severe hypoxemia, with resultant pulmonary hypertension ultimately leading to cor pulmonale and right heart failure. Systemic hypertension is also a frequent complication. In infants and young children, obstructive apnea syndromes can lead to chronic hypoxemia resulting in CNS damage. While the majority of sleep apnea patients present as mildly hypertensive, overweight, middle-aged males with a history of snoring, this is not universally true, and a sleep apnea syndrome should be suspected in any case of excessive daytime sleepiness, at any age. Symptoms of sleep apnea may include, in addition to excessive daytime sleepiness, impaired work performance and psychological changes including depression. In fact the psychological disturbances are not infrequently the presenting complaint. Additionally, some apnea syndromes may present with a chief complaint of insomnia. The sleep laboratory workup includes polysomnography for quantification of the type of severity of apnea and the degree of associated oxygen desaturation, evaluation of any accompanying cardiac arrhythmias, and an

MSLT evaluation for quantification of the severity of the excessive daytime sleepiness, to be used both as a guide to severity of the disorder and as a way to measure improvement with treatment. Other laboratory procedures that may be necessary include radiographic studies and/or computerized tomography of the upper airway, and visualization of the nasal and oropharynx with fiberoptic endoscopes.

Snoring as a symptom of possible sleep apnea should be taken seriously. Snoring is quite common in the general population; it is estimated that 45% of adults snore occasionally, and up to 25% may be habitual snorers. Snoring is three times more common in the obese, and more frequent in men than women. Some individuals snore only when the nasal airway is obstructed, such as when they have a cold, or during the allergy season. In others it may be a symptom of more chronic airway obstructions, such as maxillary polyps, or enlarged adenoids or tonsils (in children, for example). Snoring can be a source of considerable interpersonal and marital discord, which should be taken into account as part of its evaluation.

Sleep apnea syndromes are found in infants and children as well as adults. School age youngsters who are noted to fall asleep frequently in class, and who display impaired school performance (some of whom were formally thought to be "lazy") may in fact have an obstructive sleep apnea disorder. Often these youngsters may be slightly overweight, with mild hypertension, and may complain of morning headaches. Infants and young children ranging from newborn to approximately age three may also develop obstructive sleep apnea syndromes. Such children may have a history of labored breathing while asleep but look perfectly normal when awake. The diagnosis is often long delayed. Even though they may have been brought to the physician by worried parents, since their daytime exam looks normal, no diagnosis is made. It is not infrequent that an accurate diagnosis is not made until major symptoms occur, which may include failure to thrive, cor pulmonale, or neurological dysfunction secondary to apnea-induced cerebral hypoxia. Once again, the importance of obtaining an adequate history about sleep from the parents is important, and concerns voiced about peculiar breathing behavior while sleeping should be taken seriously by the pediatrician or family physician.

The treatment of sleep apnea is complex and multifaceted. It is, of course, imperative that an accurate diagnosis be made first, for the treatment of central and obstructive apneas can be quite different. The treatment of central apneas has proven to be difficult. Evening alcohol consumption and nighttime hypnotics can aggravate the condition. Some recent work suggests that acetazolamine may prove to be quite beneficial, both symptomatically and in terms of reducing the number and severity of central apneas, although this effect is more common for patients living at high altitude (e.g., > 5000 ft) than for those living at sea level. In severe cases, diaphragmatic pacing may be necessary. In regard to the obstructive apneas, hypnotics and alcohol may again severely aggravate the problem. Weight loss has been beneficial to some patients with obstructive apnea syndromes, perhaps by reducing fatty infiltrates in pharyngeal tissue. Some patients have responded to tongue retaining devices. Several medications have been helpful in managing obstructive apnea, including protriptyline, medroxyprogesterone acetate, and theophylline. Until the recent past, tracheostomy was a surgical treatment of last resort for severe cases of obstructive apnea. While curative of obstructive apnea, the procedure has a high incidence of side effects. New surgical procedures such as the uvulopalatopharyngoplasty (UPPP) procedure are being developed. These involve reconstructive surgery of the pharyngeal area with removal of excessive tissue. They offer the promise of being effective in some cases, especially where heavy snoring is involved. It should be noted that severe snoring is frequently improved by pharyngeal reconstructive surgery such as the UPPP, independent of the effect of the surgery on the apnea. The treatment of obstructive apnea in children is frequently surgical in nature and involves the removal of excessive lymphoid tissues, such as tonsils and adenoids. The results in such cases are often very good.

PARASOMNIAS

Sleepwalking Disorder

Somnambulism, or *sleepwalking disorder*, is relatively common in children between ages five and 10, and has been estimated to occur in from 5% to 15% of normal children, more commonly in males. It can usually be diagnosed by history from the parents. While sleepwalking the child has a blank, staring face and can be wakened only with great difficulty. The next morning there is amnesia for the route travelled and for other events that occurred during the sleepwalking episode. The differential diagnosis should include temporal lobe epilepsy. Major therapeutic considerations are to protect the child, as somnambulists have been known to walk into furniture, fall down flights of stairs, or rarely (fortunately), fall out of windows. The benzodiazepines, which suppress Stage 3–4 sleep, have been used successfully to treat somnambulism in adults. Small ultrasonic burglar alarms can also be helpful, at least by turning on a light or ringing a bell so as to alert someone else in the house that the somnambulist is out of bed. Somnambulism has been occasionally described as a complication of thioridazine (Mellaril) treatment due to its tendency to enhance NREM sleep.

Sleep Terror Disorder

Night terrors, also called *pavor nocturnus*, classically present with a child sitting up in bed, screaming loudly, breathing rapidly and perspiring, looking wild-eyed and frightened, with tachycardia and dilated pupils, and being very difficult to arouse or console. The child will normally fall back to sleep, and have little or no memory for the episode the following day. Most children grow out of night terrors without treatment. It occurs in one to four percent of normal children, more commonly in males. Management primarily involves reassurance and education of the parents. Severe cases (several episodes per week) may be treated with benzodiazepines to reduce Stage 3–4 sleep. The onset of night terrors has frequently been observed to follow febrile illnesses by several months. Differential diagnosis includes temporal lobe epilepsy and nightmares. *Nightmares* are frightening dreams (which are usually clearly remembered) occurring during REM sleep, with few of the signs of autonomic arousal typical of night terrors. Nightmares are fairly common in children, especially between the ages of four and seven, and may result from frightening events (or stories) during the day. They often need no treatment. In severe cases they may be representative of individual or family psychopathology and may require counseling or psychotherapy.

Night terrors are seen in adults as well (where they are called "incubus"), and may include marked autonomic arousal and a variety of relatively uncoordinated movements, such as sitting up in bed, thrashing about, and the like. Adults, like children, rarely remember these episodes in the morning and are also very difficult to arouse. The initial complaints often come from their bed partners, who are concerned about the well-being of themselves as well as the patient during these episodes. While psychiatric evaluation is warranted, many cases occur in the absence of major evidence of psychological disturbances, and there may be a genetic component to the etiology. In adults, treatment may include reducing Stage 3–4 sleep with benzodiazepine drugs; in some cases tricyclic antidepressants (e.g., imipramine) have proven helpful in reducing the frequency and severity of symptoms.

Sleep-Related Enuresis

Sleep-related enuresis is also considered to be another of the parasomnias, and will be discussed in Chapter 61 as one of the symptom disorders of childhood.

SUMMARY

Sleep Disorders Medicine is a new specialty area in which knowledge is growing rapidly. What we think is true today may be shown to be untrue tomorrow. It is wise, therefore, to consult the latest literature, or a Sleep Disorders Center, before embarking on any treatment of complicated sleep disorders. What I hope to have accomplished is to demonstrate that sleep disorders are real, diagnosable, and treatable, but also very complex. They must be taken seriously if we, as physicians, are to maximize the help we can provide to our patients.

Suggested Readings

Guilleminault C (ed): *Sleep and Waking Disorders: Indications and Techniques.* Menlo Park, CA, Addison-Wesley Publishing Co., 1982.
Hauri P: *The Sleep Disorders.* Kalamazoo, MI, The Upjohn Company, 1982.
Kales A, Kales JD: *Evaluation and Treatment of Insomnia.* New York, Oxford University Press, 1984.
Orr WC, Altschuler KZ, Stahl ML: *Managing Sleep Complaints.* Chicago, Year Book Medical Publishers, 1982.

References

Allen RM: Attenuation of drug-induced anxiety dreams and pavor nocturnus by benzodiazepines. *J Clin Psychiatry* 44:106, 1983.
Aserinsky E, Kleitmam N: Regularly occurring periods of eye motility, and concomitant phenomena during sleep. *Science* 118:273, 1953
Broughton RJ: Sleep disorders: disorders of arousal? *Science* 159:1070, 1968.
Brouillette RT, Fernbach SK, Hunt CE: Obstructive sleep apnea in infants and children. *J Pediatr* 100:31, 1982.
Brownell LG, et al: Protriptyline in obstructive sleep apnea. A double-blind trial. *N Engl J Med* 307:1037, 1982.
Carskadon MA, Dement WC: Respiration during sleep in the aged human. *J Gerontol* 36:420, 1981.
Cartwright RD, Samelson CF: The effects of a nonsurgical treatment for obstructive sleep apnea. *JAMA* 248:705, 1982.
Coleman RM, Roffwarg HP, Kennedy SJ: Sleep-wake disorders based on a polysomnographic diagnosis. *JAMA* 247:997, 1982.
Conell LJ, Berlin RM: Withdrawal after substitution of a short-acting for a long acting benzodiazepine. *JAMA* 250:2838, 1983.
Cotton RT: Uvulopalatopharyngoplasty: commentary. *Arch Otolaryngol* 109:502, 1983.
Czeisler CA, Moore-Ede MC, Coleman RM: Rotating shift work schedules that disrupt sleep are improved by applying circadian principles. *Science* 217:460, 1982.
Dement W, Kleitman N: Cyclic variations in EEG during sleep and their relation to eye movements, body motility, and dreaming. *EEG & Clin Neurophysiol* 9:673, 1957.
Fujita S, et al: Surgical correction of anatomic abnormalities in obstructive sleep apnea syndrome: uvulopalatopharyngoplasty. *Otolaryngol Head Neck Surg* 89:923, 1981.
Greenblatt DJ, et al: Benzodiazepine hypnotics: kinetic and therapeutic options. *Sleep* 5:518, 1982.
Haponik EF, et al: Computerized tomography in obstructive sleep apnea. *Am Rev Respir Dis* 127:221, 1983.
Hartmann E, Chung R, Ching-Piao C: L-Tryptophan and sleep. *Psychopharmacologia (Berl)* 19:114, 1971.
Hauri PJ, et al: The treatment of psychophysiologic insomnia with biofeedback: a replication study. *Biofeedback Self Regul* 7:223, 1982.
Hernandez SF: Palatopharyngoplasty for the obstructive sleep apnea syndrome: technique and preliminary report of results in ten patients. *Am J Otolaryngol* 3:229, 1982.
Hobson JA: Sleep mechanisms and pathophysiology: some clinical implications of the reciprocal interaction hypothesis of sleep cycle control. *Psychosom Med* 45: 123, 1983.
Jouvet M: Biogenic amines and the states of sleep. *Science* 163:32, 1969.
Kales A, et al: Hereditary factors in sleepwalking and night terrors. *Br J Psychiatry* 137:111, 1980.
Kales A, et al: Early morning insomnia with rapidly eliminated benzodiazepines. *Science* 220:95, 1983.
Kripke DF, Ancoli-Israel S, Okudaira N: Sleep apnea and nocturnal myoclonus in the elderly. *Neurobiol Aging* 3:329, 1982.
Krueger JM, Pappenheimer JR, Karnovsky ML: The composition of sleep-promoting factor isolated from human urine. *J Biol Chem* 257:1664, 1982.
Kupfer DJ, et al: Sleep and treatment prediction in endogenous depression. *Am J Psychiatry* 138:429, 1981.
Ladd GT: Contribution to the psychology of visual dreams. *Mind*, Series 2, Vol 1. pp 299–304, 1892.
Maugh TH: Sleep promoting factor isolated. *Science* 216:1400, 1982.
Mullen PE: Sleep and its interaction with endocrine rhythms. *Br J Psychiatry* 142:215, 1983.
Rechtschaffen A, et al: Physiological correlates of prolonged sleep deprivation in rats. *Science* 221:180, 1983.

Reynolds CF, et al: Electroencephalographic sleep, aging, and psychopathology: new data and state of the art. *Biol Psychiatry* 18:139, 1983.

Scrima L, et al: Increased severity of obstructive sleep apnea after bedtime alcohol ingestion: diagnostic potential and proposed mechanism of action. *Sleep* 5:318, 1982.

Seidel WF, et al: Treatment of a 12-hour shift of sleep schedule with benzodiazepines. *Science* 224:1262, 1984.

Simmons FB, Guilleminault C, Silvestri R: Snoring, and some obstructive sleep apnea, can be cured by oropharyngeal surgery. *Palatopharyngoplasty Arch Otolaryngol* 109:503, 1983.

Smith PL, et al: The effects of protriptyline in sleep-disordered breathing. *Am Rev Respir Dis* 127:8, 1983.

Spinweber CL, et al: L-tryptophan: effects on daytime sleep latency and the waking EEG. *Electroencephalography Clin Neurophysiol* 55:652, 1983.

Tan T-L, et al: Biopsychobehavioral correlates of insomnia: diagnosis based on DSM-III. *Am J Psychiatry* 141:357, 1984.

Wehr TA, et al: Phase advance of the circadian sleep-wake cycle as an antidepressant. *Science* 206:710, 1979.

Weitzman ED: Sleep and its disorders. *Annu Rev Neurosci* 4:381, 1981.

Weitzman ED, Czeisler CA, et al: Delayed sleep phase syndrome. *Arch Gen Psychiatry* 38:737, 1981.

White DP, et al: Central sleep apnea. Improvement with acetazolamide therapy. *Arch Intern Med* 142:1816, 1982.

CHAPTER 53 Psychodynamic Factors in Mental Illness, and the Concepts of Fixation, Regression, and the Unconscious

Herbert Pardes, M.D.

THE UNCONSCIOUS

The Topographic Model

Many of the psychodynamic factors in mental illness exist in a sphere of the mind referred to as the *unconscious*. The idea of a part of the mind exerting a powerful influence on the individual's behavior without his awareness was developed by Freud into an operational concept for understanding behavior. According to Freud and his coworkers, the unconscious was divided into two parts, the preconscious and the true or dynamic unconscious. Preconscious material is material that, although not conscious at the time, can be made conscious with some effort, while the area of the true unconscious is firmly blocked from consciousness and requires special techniques in order to become conscious. Thus, Freud spoke in terms of three spheres of the mind. The first is the *conscious* sphere. For example, I am consciously concentrating on what I am writing right now. The second is the *preconscious* sphere. I am not thinking about what I had for breakfast this morning, but if I wanted to I could get it back into my mind with a simple conscious effort. The third is the *unconscious* sphere, where wishes and memories of events related to an earlier time of life exist, and which I could not retrieve by any conscious effort. These three spheres of the mind constitute Freud's *topographic* model of mental functioning.

The Structural Model

Later, when Freud discovered that the unconscious comprises not only our repressed childhood wishes, but also many other current aspects of our personality including much of our conscience, he substituted for the topographic model the *structural* model of mental functioning. According to this model, the unconscious is a reservoir of the basic instinctual drives, wishes, and needs, referred to as the *id*. It also contains certain hidden facets of the personality, referred to as the *unconscious part of the ego*. These are automatic devices which the individual employs to protect himself and defend himself against tension or conflicts resulting from the interplay of the various inner and outer forces acting on him. These are used automatically without the person's awareness, and are referred to as the mechanisms of defense. The unconscious also contains features of the psyche which exert an influence on the morals and taboos of the individual. These are the source of what is seen externally as a sense of conscience, of right and wrong, in other words, the *superego*. All of these lie in an area out of the awareness of the individual, yet they exert a most powerful influence on the individual's behavior.

The Unconscious in Everyday Life

As I have emphasized before, this is a dynamic unconscious. It is constantly operating. One does not simply "turn off" one's impulses, wishes, feelings, defenses, or conscience. Freud found that elements of the unconscious manifest themselves in various ways that we can all recognize in our everyday lives. First of all they emerge in *dreams*. All of us at one time or another dream of things which cause us surprise, embarrassment, shame, or guilt. These may include a hostile attack on someone with whom we are close. They may include romantic or sexual intimacies with people ostensibly forbidden to us. They may include situations in which we usurp the role of others. Such dreams represent the coming to the surface of wishes that are typically unconscious. Second, elements of the unconscious may be seen in certain *behaviors*. For example, one may see a child smile at the sight of his or her sibling getting physically hurt. The child may be experiencing the gratification of an unconscious hostile wish towards the sibling, while at the same time he or she may verbally express sympathy and concern. Third, unconscious elements emerge in what are referred to as *parapraxes*. These include slips of the tongue, mislaid objects, and lapses of memory. These are widespread and of enormous variety. At times we may sense our own reluctance to recall a dentist appointment or a dinner date with someone about whom we have some ambivalence. We may even try maneuvers to force ourselves to remember only to find that we often still forget. The fact that we may have to work so hard to remember these particular things in contrast to others may signal that we have some unconscious negative inclinations against which we are struggling.

These expressions of our unconscious are constantly with us. For example, one patient who had very ambivalent feelings about a colleague of his, was supposed to pick up the colleague to go to a social event, but forgot to pick him up. The colleague arrived, was angry, and told off my patient. After settling that, they agreed to get some refreshments, with my patient offering to get the drinks while the colleague got the food. My patient went to get the drinks and lo and behold came back with one drink. One can also see evidence of elements of the unconscious in psychoses where what is usually hidden from a person's awareness breaks through.

Freud found that one could facilitate the recovery of unconscious material through hypnosis, through the use of certain drugs, and through the use of the psychoanalytic method of free association which he developed. He also found that what is unconscious, is unconscious for good reasons. Thus, if we try to have the person face some unconscious wish or impulse, the same reasons which made it unconscious will make it very hard for the person to accept or to comprehend. If a person is told that some aspect of his behavior demonstrates a hostile impulse on his part toward somebody whom he feels he loves, he will try to rationalize the behavior, deny it, get rid of it, do anything to keep from acknowledging it.

The Unconscious in Psychopathology

The unconscious can be demonstrated to a greater or lesser extent in all of the syndromes of psychopathology. As Dr. Console and Dr. Simons will discuss in a later chapter, *unconscious fantasies* are often powerful etiological factors in the development of the anxiety disorders and the dissociative disorders. But unconscious fantasies may also play an important etiological role in the development of many of the psychotic disorders as well, along with biological and sociocultural factors. The following clinical material is from a patient suffering from a psychotic disorder.

TRANSCRIPT FROM TWO INTERVIEWS

I am now going to present a portion of two interviews with a patient which I think shows unconscious elements breaking through rather dramatically. These were video tape interviews made by Dr. John Frosch with a woman who was hospitalized and severely distressed psychologically. She was suffering from a manic-depressive psychosis. After being treated in the hospital she returned for a second video tape interview with Dr. Frosch while being continued in treatment as an outpatient. During this second interview she was shown the earlier video tape which was made when she was actively disorganized. The transcript will first focus on her inpatient interview with Dr. Frosch when she was acutely disturbed, then switch to the time when she was in much better health and was being seen as an outpatient. What I particularly want to emphasize is the breakdown of her defenses in the first interview, and the spilling into consciousness of material which is ordinarily repressed in the unconscious.

Description

The patient appears on a split screen (Figure 53.1). On one-half of the screen she appears in a hospital gown, and is quite agitated, showing marked mood swings between euphoria and depressed crying. Periodically during the interview, she lifts up her hospital gown to well above

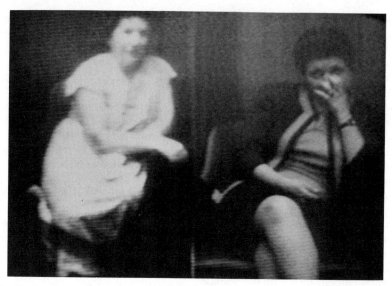

Figure 53.1. Patient hospitalized (on left). Patient recovered (on right) watching herself as an inpatient.

the knees, particularly when she is talking about her sexual experiences. On the other half of the screen the patient appears much different. She is calm, well groomed, appropriate in her emotional responses, and dressed attractively, as she views the first interview made when she was in the hospital.

Inpatient Interview

Ruth: . . . I married a goy, and I thought God was punishing me because I was a religious girl and here I went against his wishes by marrying a Gentile even though he did convert. I'm so Jewish conscious, I had even worked for the Hebrew school when I was 17. In fact, I was brought up practically on the floor of the shul. As a baby, when growing up, we would always have to go to shul. My mother was very orthodox . . . Was? She still is! My mother is alive! My mother and father are alive! You know that? I thought they were both dead!

Dr. F.: Really?

Ruth: Really.

Dr. F.: How did you have that idea?

Ruth: Honestly. I thought that my mother died when she was 58. She had high blood pressure. I hated her. That had something to do with why she died. But it was my mother-in-law I hated, not her. But in my fantasy I wouldn't give in to that. I wouldn't say that it was I who was right. I thought I was a . . . I hated my mother! I hated her and I could have killed

her! (Quite agitated) She was mean but I guess . . . look, we all have our reasons. She acted the way she did because she had a hard life, too. I never had a doll! I never had a party! I had to always be perfectly clean! I couldn't go dirty! I had to be perfect! I went to school! I went to Hebrew school and I took piano lessons and I was told to clean the house too and how much could one person do! (Crying)

Dr. F.: So what happened?

Ruth: I wish she were dead.

Outpatient Interview (Figure 53.2)

(Patient has been reacting with intense interest and surprise while viewing the above portion of her interview in the hospital.)

Ruth: My parents are dead. They were dead at that time. My mother was not mean. It isn't true that I hated her because she wanted me to be clean and perfect.

Dr. F.: These other things that you said, were they true?

Ruth: Yes. I don't recall having a doll. I may be wrong about it but I don't recall having a doll. I don't recall having birthday parties, though I questioned my brother about that, and he claimed that there was an acknowledgement of some kind on my birthdays. When I said party, I meant inviting friends and things like that. He said that he did recall that they made a little fuss when my birthday did come around.

Dr. F.: But you come out here with such hatred for your mother.

Ruth: My mother, yes.

Dr. F.: Did you feel it?

Ruth: I don't think I ever felt it. I never showed it.

Dr. F.: Do you feel it now?

Ruth: No.

Dr. F.: Well, did you feel it at all at any time in your adult life, this hatred for your mother? Are you aware at any time of consciously hating your mother?

Ruth: I resented my mother dying on me when she did.

Dr. F.: What do you mean?

Ruth: She picked the wrong time to die.

Dr. F.: Why?

Ruth: I felt, if she were alive, I would still have my son with me. I, that, . . . my husband wouldn't have acted the way he did.

Dr. F.: You mean when he took the child away?

Ruth: Yes.

Dr. F.: To the best of your knowledge, you never consciously expressed this hatred towards your mother that you do here? You never felt it even?

Ruth: My mother was always ill. First of all, she practically died when she had me. This was impressed on me. She always suffered from high blood pressure. She was a sickly woman, and everyone was supposed to be gentle and kind to her and . . . I mean, she placed all her hopes and desires in me. I was the only girl she had and the youngest.

Dr. F.: Yes, but I do want to get this one point clear. Now you . . .

Ruth: I never expressed hatred toward her that I recall.

Dr. F.: You never felt it openly, even to yourself?

Ruth: I may have . . . I don't know . . . oh, there were times that I did when I was a child.

Dr. F.: Like this?

Ruth: No, never like that, no.

Dr. F.: Where do you think this comes from? This hatred, this expression of hatred? Is it really towards your mother?

Ruth: I don't know.

Dr. F.: Well, think about it and talk about it further in your treatment with Dr. James. Shall we look some more?

Ruth: O.K. Boy, I was really emotional in that interview.

Dr. F.: Which part of it evoked the most emotion in you as you watched it just now?

Ruth: Letting out the hatred.

Dr. F.: Letting out the hatred? Sometimes that helps.

Ruth: I would never let out things.

Figure 53.2.   Patient (on right) talking to Dr. John Frosch (on left) about the inpatient interview she had just witnessed.

Dr. F.: Do you remember telling me that part at all?

Ruth: No. Not at all.

Inpatient Interview

Ruth: Well, I don't want to get anybody into trouble because actually what happened, I think, is these people were trying to really help me. I don't think . . .

Dr. F.: You had relations with him though?

Ruth: Not exactly. What do you call relations? Like now I have these . . . When I would get these burning sensations in my feet and that was due to nerves and tensions and he would rub them.

Dr. F.: Massage them?

Ruth: Massage them, you know, like this. (She pulls up her hospital gown) And even now my feet feel good when I . . .

Dr. F.: What has this got to do with your vagina? Your foot is not your vagina.

Ruth: It seems as if, as he was rubbing he was going higher and higher and higher until he was . . . then he just used his finger.

Dr. F.: Did you enjoy it?

Ruth: Oh, I loved it. I just loved it, but I felt guilty.

Dr. F.: Why?

Ruth: Because he wasn't my husband.

Dr. F.: I see. Well, but you told me that one of them . . .

Ruth: But then one time I did let him insert his penis.

Dr. F.: Insert his penis?

Ruth: Yes, and I had a baby. I like to think of sex. It makes me feel very good.

Dr. F.: You get sexually excited when you think of it?

Ruth: Yes, I can have an orgasm just thinking of it.

Dr. F.: Did you have an orgasm just now as we were talking of it?

Ruth: No, not then, but I'm talking to you now and I'm trying to concentate on that rather than . . .

Dr. F.: When you think about it, you could have an orgasm?

Ruth: Bet if I think about it, I could. Yes. If I lie down, I can even go through the actual movements. I think I've done it previously while I've been in the hospital. That's what pulled me out of it many times.

Dr. F.: Do you masturbate when you do it? Do you rub yourself?

Ruth: Well, I'm not sure because . . . I'm not really sure. I just do sort of a movement. I don't think I actually masturbate. Masturbate is touching yourself, right?

Dr. F.: Sure, it's one way. But do you move your legs and that sort of thing? Do you move your legs against each other?

Ruth: Yes.

Dr. F.: In that way you get excited?

Ruth: Yes.

Dr. F.: Have you had orgasms in that way since being here in the hospital?

Ruth: Yes.

Outpatient Interview

Dr. F.: You haven't spoken in as much detail to Dr. James as you did here to me in this first interview?

Ruth: No. Not the detail that was mentioned here.

Dr. F.: What about this-out-of-wedlock baby?

Ruth: That's true, it's not me but . . .

Dr. F.: You didn't have it?

Ruth: I didn't have it but I mentioned . . .

Dr. F.: It's getting sort of confusing . . .

Ruth: Someone I knew had the baby, not me.

Dr. F.: Now look, Ruth, we're not going to look at any more . . .

Ruth: Yes, I know.

Dr. F.: What do you think of this entire experience right now? Could you tell me? How do you feel about it?

Ruth: Well, I feel very good that I saw this. I think it's given me some insight into some of my feelings.

Dr. F.: Some of the things that really exist within you?

Ruth: Right. In fact I'm so sorry that Dr. James didn't see it.

Dr. F.: Would you like him to see it?

Ruth: I would very much like him to see it.

Dr. F.: Why?

Ruth: Because though I will discuss it with him, I don't think I could possibly show him in the same way. My whole reaction. The getting up, the pains, my lapse of memory, my going from one thought into the other, my confusion. I mean I touch so much.

Dr. F.: It would make it easier for you to talk to him about it if he saw this first? Is that it?

Ruth: Yes.

Dr. F.: You'd be a little embarrassed to tell him directly?

Ruth: I don't know if it's a question of embarrassment, but in discussing it with him, it's possible that I may omit certain things which this would show, and then he would know better what things to touch on in the process of the therapy.

Dr. F.: I see.

Ruth: Whereas I have a way of getting off on a tangent into something else.

Dr. F.: Seeing this interview, do you think it relieved anything within you?

Ruth: Oh, I feel a tremendous relief.

Dr. F.: In what way?

Ruth: The feelings about my mother. That was a big point. My feelings about sex. Another big point. And my feelings about my boyfriend which basically I know I'll always have. I still have guilt. Down deep, I still have guilt feelings over our relationship, even though I've continued it a long time. I don't think I'll ever erase that actually.

DISCUSSION OF THE TWO INTERVIEWS

What kinds of things do these two interviews emphasize particularly? First of all, I think it is clear that in the first interview this woman had a great deal of difficulty with regard to reality. She said that her mother was alive. Her mother in fact was dead at the time. She may be expressing a wish that she have her mother back, and being this sick, her reality testing was so disturbed that she in fact thought the mother was back with her. She also referred to an out-of-wedlock baby as being hers. In fact she had no out-of-wedlock baby. The baby was born to a friend of hers. So her reality testing was substantially impaired.

In addition, one can see the eruption of her enormous anger and resentment toward her mother in the first interview. She said, "I hated my mother! I hated her and I could have killed her! She was mean." She was no longer aware of this hatred when she was not as disturbed, when she came back as an outpatient for the second interview. She did mention something which is of great interest to us, and that is that the mother almost died giving birth to her. The mother apparently told this to her repeatedly as

a child, thus causing her to feel very guilty. As a result, she felt she had to comply with literally whatever the mother wanted, and she then detailed the various things she was obliged to do. She accepted very little for herself.

She *repressed* the thoughts linked to her anger toward her mother, and as a result she was not aware of them consciously, either before her breakdown or after her recovery. As a matter of fact, she repressed many parts of the first interview. Also her disturbed state allowed facts about her sexual experiences and her feelings regarding her boyfriend to emerge. Further, her behavior generally was quite erotic during the first interview. She had not discussed these matters with her outpatient therapist, because she was unaware of both the content and the intensity of many of the ideas and feelings that emerged during her breakdown. This is essentially what is meant by the power of unconscious forces.

So in studying the etiology of mental illness, insofar as psychodynamic factors are concerned, we will repeatedly be dealing with elements that originate in the unconscious sphere of a person's mental life. We will also be dealing with many early developmental forces, and I will now briefly consider two of those, namely fixation and regression.

PSYCHOSIS AND EARLY DEVELOPMENTAL FORCES

The neonate enters the world with certain constitutional endowments and, at this point, a critical change occurs. Whereas before, all of the basic needs of the infant had been satisfied in utero, the infant now must begin to function in a different environment, one in which he or she must take an active part. The infant must develop mechanisms for negotiating with the outside environment as well as for attending to the various drives acting from within.

There is an essential difference in the early life of the human child as opposed to all other animals, and this is extremely important in the total future development of the individual. That difference refers to the fact that, unlike other animals, the human infant needs support from its environment in order to develop the necessary physiological and psychological mechanisms for continued existence. Because of this long contact and dependence on the supporting environment, we can see that the early setting with its various experiences is a critical factor in the development of later psychopathology. Thus, it is especially important for psychiatry to study the nature of the early environment and to try to comprehend how the emerging infant experiences it. Since we cannot directly ask the infant, we use two general approaches. One is to attempt to reconstruct childhood experiences from patients in intensive psychotherapy or in psychoanalysis. The second is to use direct observations of infants so as to supplement this data from reconstructions. Taking the two approaches collectively, we then develop hypotheses about the nature of these earlier stages of development.

Looking at these earlier stages, we can assume that the child's relationship to the environment is at first vague and confused. The differentiation of the infant as a discrete self is unclear. The infant's body image, in other words, that mental representation of what its body looks like, of where its body ends and where the world begins, probably forms only gradually and is completed much later. At first the demarcation is rather indefinite. The infant may include as part of himself certain features of the environment, for example, some of his clothes, his mother's breast, or other proximal objects. So, at this point in development the organism's representation of himself consists of an almost total fusion with his surroundings, rather than one of separateness. As was described earlier in the book, this is referred to as the autistic stage of psychic development.

If we try to understand psychopathology developmentally, we can see that derivatives of these very early stages of psychic development are reflected in the psychoses and to some extent in the most severe forms of personality disorders, whereas derivatives of later stages of psychic development are reflected in the neurotic disorders and the less severe forms of personality disorders. For example, a schizophrenic patient described what he called a "total communication," one so total that he became the whole universe. His body boundaries were gone, there were no limits, and he became what he experienced. He described this experience of fusion while taking LSD, but he also described it during intercourse when he was not on LSD. In this particular interview he went on to report that he also was having the same experience with the interviewer. Since he experienced this

state of fusion at times when he did not want it, he was not in control of it, and it was not something that he could turn on or off. This *state of fusion* is remarkably similar to the early developmental state described above in the newborn.

Another feature of this early stage, in addition to the lack of differentiation, is *fragmentation*. Early in development we assume that the various components forming the total and comprehensive percept of the self or of other objects are not yet integrated. This applies to thoughts and to language as well. We assume that these do not start as unified phenomena, but first consists of fragments. In language the fragments might include a variety of factors, for example the sounds of consonants, vowels, syllables, and the various letter combinations that eventually compose the word. This word in turn would be linked to an image of the object which itself originates from different fragments. This earliest phase then is characterized by fragmentation as well as nondifferentiation. With growth we expect the child to advance from this stage. We expect fragments to unite with an emerging sense of unity. We expect the development of a sense of identity, with an increased capacity to discriminate the infant's self from what is nonself. We expect an increasing synthesis of the elements of language, as well as the elements composing the percepts of different objects. But when there is an interference with the appropriate integration of these fragments into a unified whole, we have the beginnings and the prototypes of psychotic symptoms which may later appear as derivatives of this earliest stage of development.

FIXATION AND REGRESSION

Two psychic operations are particularly relevant here. One is *fixation*. Fixation occurs if, as a result of significant pathological experiences at a given stage in psychic development, there is an overinvestment in this particular stage and consequently an interference with subsequent development. The interference may be with the acquisition of advanced patterns of behavior, for example a child who is having difficulty in working out one particular phase may not be prepared adequately to cope with new stresses or challenges in subsequent phases. Fixation may also continue to exert a pull, so that even though the individual does progress through subsequent phases, these earlier patterns and conflicts may at times be reactivated. This second psychic operation is *regression*. By this we refer to the tendency of an individual to revert to earlier patterns of behavior. This might happen particularly in the face of a current threat, or if the individual had great difficulty in mastering a new developmental task. However, it is important to remember that regression is not always pathological. In fact, it may serve many protective and adaptive needs for the individual. This is true, for example, when a person develops a physical illness. When adults become sick, they very frequently behave like children, and seek attention and succor as a child would do from a parent. Preoperative patients often regress to such a point that their reverence and trust for their physicians become reminiscent of the young child's awe for the "superhuman" parents. The advantages for the patient in such a transient regression include a reduction in anxiety.

In psychopathology, however, an individual with a fixation at one point in development may regress permanently to that point. Consequently, we see derivatives of the earlier period in the symptoms that emerge. This does not mean that the person totally regresses. In fact, we usually see mixtures in any given individual of areas of regression coexisting with areas of normal functioning. There are many people suffering from schizophrenia or psychotic depressions, for example, who function quite adequately in certain areas of their lives while showing marked regression in other areas. One patient who illustrated this was hospitalized on a psychiatric ward with a psychotic depression. She was a very bright, articulate college graduate, who nihilistically believed that she was still within her mother's womb, and as a result she was literally vegetating. In many ways she was nonfunctional, and yet she could engage in a perfectly sensible and reasonable conversation, and she impressed everyone with her brightness and with her logical thinking. So regression is an uneven process, and when we evaluate any psychologically disturbed individual, we are interested in both the areas of pathology, as well as all residual ego strengths. A knowledge of these is integral to the determination of how well the person can function in society despite his or her illness. This determination is of great significance, given the value of patients being able to function outside of hospital settings and in the community whenever possible.

THE ORAL STAGE OF DEVELOPMENT

The infant then goes on to other developmental stages, and these too can be examined specifically in terms of their relationships to later psychopathology. For example, the symbiotic stage and the beginnings of the separation-individuation stage follow the autistic stage in the first year of life, and all three stages constitute what was first conceptualized by Freud in psychosexual terms as the oral stage of development.

In the oral stage the relationship to objects is of critical importance, and one figure in particular becomes dominant in the infant's environment. That is the mothering figure. At this time of life the most pressing needs for the infant center around nutrition, which becomes the infant's main contact with the environment. Thus, the mouth is an especially important organ for the infant; he or she explores literally everything with the mouth. Give an infant a new toy and he invariably puts it into his mouth. But the oral stage involves more than just activities of the mouth. It also involves the evolving relationships with the important people around the baby. During this first year of life the task of getting accustomed to repeated contacts and separations with the critical objects and particularly with the mothering object is paramount. Fondling the child, holding the child, touching the child, playing with the child, all are of great importance in this stage, and all of these pleasant experiences of being gratified and loved are connected with feeding. In fact, a relationship eventually develops between tension reduction and the ingestion or introduction of warm food.

One may see certain difficulties begin at this time. For example, one may find babies who start to have difficulty eating, babies who begin vomiting, and babies with weaning reactions. But of greater interest to us in this discussion is the fact that subsequent development may be affected. We see in this stage prototypes of patterns manifested later during stressful situations. If, during this stage, the infant was overindulged, deprived, or subjected to markedly inconsistent and erratic caretaking, its subsequent development may be impaired. As a result one may see a regression to oral behavior in any stressful situation, or more marked oral fixation reflected in such conditions as obesity or repeated depressions or chronic alcoholism or drug abuse.

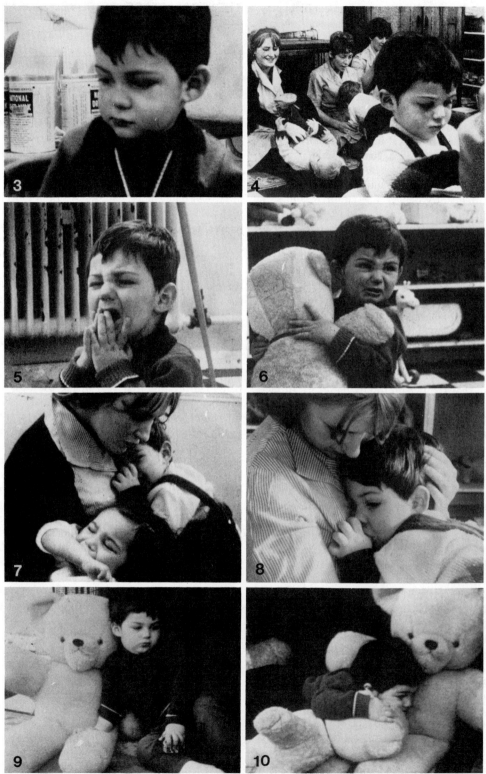

Figures 53.3–53.10. From the 1969 film *John—17 Months—Nine Days in a Residential Nursery.* (By permission of James and Joyce Robertson, Robertson Centre, 51 Corringham Road, London, England. Distributed by New York University Film Library, New York, N.Y., in black and white sound. Also distributed by Canadian Film Library.)

An example of a sudden and dramatic regression has been poignantly depicted by James and Joyce Robertson in their film, *John—17 Months—Nine Days in a Residential Nursery.* John (Figure 53.3) is a 17-month old boy who is brought to a residential nursery by his father when his mother enters the hospital to have a second baby. At first he seems to be adjusting satisfactorily (Figure 53.4). However, by the fourth day he is starting to cry (Figure 53.5), and is clinging to his teddy bear (Figure 53.6). By the fifth day he is inconsolable—crying continually and sucking his thumb (Figure 53.7). By the sixth day he is refusing to eat, even though hungry. By the seventh day he is no longer protesting the separation from his parents. His cry is weak and pitiful, and he is passively withdrawn, sucking his thumb, and no longer responsive to his favorite nurse's attention (Figure 53.8). By the eighth day he is depressed and apathetic (Figure 53.9), and lies on his teddy bear in a withdrawn state for long periods of time (Figure 53.10). When his mother comes to take him home on the ninth day, he cries when he sees her and throws himself about uncontrollably. Only after a long struggle does he allow her to cuddle him, and even then he is screaming, sucking his thumb, and staring at her with a look of profound resentment and bitterness.

One kind of personality disturbance that appears to be related to the oral period is referred to as the *impulsive personality disorder.* For such individuals tension is intolerable. They must have immediate gratification. They are action oriented, and there is little thinking before the action. Often such individuals need people in a desperate way. They have great difficulty in dealing with separations and in attempting to individuate. One such patient whom I treated could not tolerate any regular work situation. She could not study. When she was at her job, she needed total freedom. On impulse she would often abruptly leave home. She drank a great deal and, whenever she was alone, she would become depressed. She could not work unless she had people around her. With these people she would relate in a most demanding way. She always was seeking their immediate love and affection. However, her feelings would change very rapidly, and as a result she had a number of relationships over a very short period of time. In a treatment situation she could not tolerate the slightest frustration or inattention from the therapist. She functioned in many ways like an infant who required the continuing presence of a mothering object offering a constant stream of love. While not as bizarre in their behavior as many psychotic patients, people with these types of personality disorders still display pervasive and profound disturbances in their behavior.

We could examine fixations in later developmental stages, and attempt to relate other personality disorders as well as the neurotic disorders to these fixations. But the main point is to note the relationship of specific developmental phases to specific psychological illnesses. Generally, the earlier the developmental disturbance, the more primitive and profound the later illness. The impact of early stages on later adult behavior and psychopathology is what accounts for the importance that mental health professionals place on the study of and attention to early development.

Thus, early childhood is of central concern to us, and we have spent much time with it in this book. We have seen that early childhood makes a critical contribution to the psychology of individuals throughout the rest of life. We have seen character traits and behavior patterns laid down at this time. We have seen fixations develop that become the ground work for future illnesses. But development does not end here. The child is now exposed more and more to society, a society not buffered for the child by his or her parents. This means increased stresses and coping techniques which may have to be even more complex; but still we see indications of earlier techniques. Each stage of psychic development is incorporated into the psychic structure and then influences all subsequent stages of psychic development. Thus, there is a continuity to psychic development, and as a result, events separated by a considerable number of years are still related. At any point in time, a given stress and what the person brings to that stress may lead either to further maturation and development, or to the precipitation of mental illness.

Suggested Readings

Arlow JA, Brenner C: *Psychoanalytic Concepts and the Structural Theory.* New York, International Universities Press, 1964.

Freud A: The concept of developmental lines. In Harrison SI, McDermott JF (eds): *Childhood Psychopathology.* New York, International Universities Press, 1972, p 133.

Freud S (1901): The Psychopathology of Everyday Life. In *The Standard Edition of the Complete Psychological Works of Sigmund Freud,* vol 6. London, The Hogarth Press, 1960.

Nemiah JC: Psychological conflict. In *Foundations of Psychopathology*. New York, Oxford University Press, 1961, p 35.

Nemiah JC: The unconscious and repression. In *Foundations of Psychopathology*. New York, Oxford University Press, 1961, p 56.

Nemiah JC: Past in present: the childhood roots of emotional disorders. In *Foundations of Psychopathology*. New York, Oxford University Press, 1961, p 74.

54 Sociocultural Factors in Mental Illness, and the Epidemiology of the Mental Disorders

Emily Mumford, Ph.D.

CORRELATION DOES NOT MEAN CAUSATION

Long before the term "correlation" came into use as a designation that one property is statistically associated with another, people tried to locate the cause of specific diseases by observing what factors seemed to "go with" them.

The history of informed opinions about pellagra recapitulates some of the problems involved in the epidemiology of mental illness. The disease appeared concentrated in poor populations, where many people had to subsist on rotting maize by the time spring came. Had survey methods and statistics been available then, there would no doubt have been statistical correlations to the 0.05 level of significance between the group attribute "high consumption of spoiled maize" and the other group attribute, "many cases of pellagra." Moreover, at a time in history when it was known that bad food could make one sick, the causal association was logical.

At the same time, plague epidemics appeared to spread from foul smelling sections of towns where narrow streets were often awash with offal. The impact of noxious odors in places where the disease appeared concentrated led to the likely conclusion that the smells caused the disease. Doctors' costumes during epidemics assumed masks with beaks to hold aromatic spices to sweeten the air they breathed (Figure 54.1). The only problem in both pellagra and plague was that the conclusion was wrong—as it often is when two mistaken assumptions are made. The first mistaken assumption is that correlation between two attributes of a *group* necessarily means that the same association would hold when *individuals* are considered. The second mistaken assumption is that a correlation is a statement of causation.

Then came the breakthroughs of Semmelweis and Lister, and others who followed in rapid succession, to demonstrate that germs could cause disease. At about the same time, in America two widely held notions were consistent with the idea that filth and squalor bred germs, which in turn caused pellagra. The first idea was that "cleanliness was next to godliness." In the 1890's, the *Woman's Home Companion* was filled with articles extolling charity, thrift, and cleanliness as well as work; they also have detailed advice about boiling every dish taken from any sick room. Nicety and chastity were sanctified. Victoria ruled England, and Victorian morality appeared to rule American women.

The second notion consistent with using the squalor-pellagra correlations as a statement of causation was that of Social Darwinism. The idea of social survival of the fittest was an intellectually reassuring basis for exploiting or at least for ignoring the situation of poor people simply by defining them as "inferior," or "willing to live with filth" and thus basically unredeemable. Communities with many cases of pellagra did tend to be the ones with many squalid homes. Again, the "conclusions" about the causation of an illness were based on a correlation between the two group properties (squalor and high rates of pellagra), and again the conclusions were compatible with popular beliefs as well as with the medical thinking of the time (the germ theory of disease).

It was not until Joseph Goldberger looked at individuals within populations that he came to his insight about dietary deficiency and pellagra. Asylums and prisons housed many victims of pellagra, but within asylums and within prisons it was the inmates and not the custodians who were stricken. Still, the germ theory was so entrenched that Goldberger felt compelled to go to great lengths to prove his theory—including

Figure 54.1. *Plague Mask* (1656) by Paulus Furst. Physicians of the 17th and early 18th centuries wore costumes and masks for quarantined areas of the plague. The beak of the mask was filled with spices to "purify" the air breathed. The wand was supposed to allow the doctor to "feel the pulse" of the victim. (By permission of The Bettmann Archive, New York.)

injecting himself and his family members with excrement of pellagra victims!

THE CONCEPT OF MULTIPLE CAUSATION

Rapid advances in statistics, sampling theory, survey methods, and computers have facilitated the development of epidemiology so that this science now includes a history of the health of populations, an assessment of health within a given community, a determination of probabilities for risk, and an identification of syndromes. Probably most important—and most dependent on newer research techniques—epidemiological studies have turned attention to multiple causation in illness. Again, this coincides in time with medicine becoming aware of the limitations

of the "single cause" concept, and the larger society becoming concerned about life style, pollution, stress, and nutrition as important influences on health. Disease, in the new frame of reference, occurs within the interaction of three factors: 1) stimuli from the environment; 2) responses from a host that are influenced by both heredity ("nature") and development ("nurture"); and 3) the conglomeration of thoughts and traits and practices which we call culture. The inclusion of "culture" as a factor is a recognition that disease is not only an objective physical state but it is also a social fact. Nowhere is this more obvious than in attempts to enumerate and compare rates of specific chronic diseases across cultures.

The pellagra example is instructive today because we still tend to make the two errors epitomized in the history of beliefs about pellagra. The first is the mistake of taking a correlation as a statement of causation. Whether a correlation is arrived at through homely observation, as in the "maize disease," or the plague, or whether the correlation appears in a study using sophisticated methods, the fact of covariance by itself does not prove that one thing is causing another.

The second error exemplified by the history of beliefs about pellagra is that the association or correlation of one group property with another property of a group says nothing about whether there is the same association when each individual is considered. It was not until Goldberger observed that prison and asylum life in itself did not affect inmates and custodians in the same way, that he was able to move effectively away from the popular germ theories of his time. If this seems elementary, then no one will ever again be heard to suggest that the high rates of hospitalization for mental illness in parts of cities where there is crowding is "because" crowding causes mental illness.

This brings us immediately to the complexities of the epidemiology of mental illness. I shall first outline briefly the history of the field, then spend more time on problems of methodology, and finally discuss some of the findings to date and where they seem to lead us.

MENTAL ILLNESS: A NEW SUBJECT FOR EPIDEMIOLOGY

When the Milbank Memorial Fund held a 1949 conference on the epidemiology of mental illness, the joining of these two terms was relatively new, though as early as the 17th century there had been census-like recordings of admissions to and discharges from "mental institutions" in Europe. Great Britain's Committee on the Epidemiology of Mental Disorder was formed in 1959. Several large prevalence studies, a few very interesting small ones, and a host of review articles reflected concern about the burden of mental illness in modern societies. The problem was not new, but it had gained the attention of people actively searching for new and improved means toward health. Private foundations and the government turned to the search for the prevention of mental illness, for early case finding, and for the development of treatment facilities. Often based on the number of hospitalized patients, including the senile who were beginning to be sent out of the family into newly opened facilities, these early studies gave rise to a flurry of articles about "tremendous increases in mental illness." Also, the studies were consistent with impressions of physicians who observed more cases in their practices as people began to be more willing to ask for help for emotional difficulties. In this case, epidemiology did not serve one of its major functions, i.e., to counteract impressions based on the selectivity of clinical practice. An increase in presentation of a symptom or a disease in a practice may reflect a change in referrals to the particular physician, or a change in what people believe should be presented to medicine, or even the physician's selective attention to a particular medical problem.

Physicians, as well as social commentators, were asked to explain the cause of the "alarming increase." The answers were various and generally included the expert's own particular bias about society. Changes in family structure or the "breakdown of the family," urban sprawl, air pollution, threat of nuclear war, and changing morality, were each cited as the cause for these startling facts, which were not real, but only apparent. The situation recalls Tristam Shandy's observation, "How finely we argue on mistaken facts."

THE PROBLEM OF INDICATORS: MEDICAL DIAGNOSIS

At first glance, it should be easy to determine who is well and who is sick. It seems logical to take the clearly objective fact of a doctor's di-

agnosis as the indicator of illness. Or, to assess the rate of severe illness, hospitalization should be a neat indicator. One is either hospitalized or not, and indeed hospitalization is the ultimate source of legitimacy or the final "say" at any point in time about whether or not one is really ill. More importantly, the figures on hospitalization are reasonably available and reliable.

In the spirit of the 1930's Lee Deets reported his finding that there was practially no mental illness among the Hutterites—members of a religious sect, who lived together in stable, rural, seemingly idyllic communities. Deets had used hospitalization as his indicator for mental illness, and not a few articles in the professional as well as the lay press used his data to support the contention that "modern city life," "crowding," "noise," "fast pace of life," and "family breakdown," "caused" mental illness. However, Joseph Eaton and Robert Weil later replicated the study, but this time with a door-to-door survey of Hutterite communities, and they found—contrary to Deets' report—that these stable, rural groups had rates of severe psychological impairment comparable to those found in urban centers. The Hutterites, however, tended to contain mentally ill members in their homes rather than send them to hospitals.

People have very different ideas about what should be brought to the attention of physicians, so that the frequency of any illness that physicians see coming from different populations can vary widely even though the rates of illness within the same populations may be identical. Moreover, availability of hospital beds can also influence hospitalization figures, and insurance regulations have still further impact on hospitalization rates as well as length of stay.

In 1949, Herbert Goldhammer and Andrew Marshall, in their book, *Psychosis and Civilization*, challenged the popular assumption that mental illness had spiraled upward since the "good old days." As they demonstrated, the essential difference over a hundred years' time was in the locus of where the mentally ill were kept, and in age differences in the population, not in the differences of rates of illness. After Dorothea Dix and the crusades of other reformers, giant mental hospitals had been built to serve a large, previously "invisible population" which had been managed at home or in jail, pesthouse or almshouse, or else died young. This in turn greatly influenced the numbers of people hospitalized for mental illness.

Since 1958, August Hollingshead and Frederick Redlich, among others, have presented formidable evidence that serious mental illness is not primarily "a disease" of the cities, nor of the striving and the ambitious. Rather, some types of mental illness are more likely to receive medical treatment at earlier stages among the rich compared with the poor, and in cities compared with rural areas. Since that time many cross-cultural studies have reported somewhat comparable rates of severe mental illness in a wide variety of cultures—from the Yoruba in Africa, to Nova Scotia, to Midtown Manhattan, and including the Hutterites.

In 1962, *Mental Health in the Metropolis* reported a major survey of the 1950's, the Midtown Manhattan Study, and demonstrated the feasibility and fruitfulness of gathering a wide range of data for locating untreated, as well as treated cases in a carefully drawn sample. This was an advance in method which was more free from cultural bias than hospitalization rates. At least its figures on the prevalence of mental illness, by class, were not influenced by differences in a family's disposition to seek or obtain help or to allow for hospitalization.

The diversity in definitions about which persons are mentally ill—even at one point in time—has been demonstrated by Bruce and Barbara Dohrenwend, who presented 87 Manhattan community leaders with a series of six briefly described psychiatric cases and compared the leaders' responses to those gathered in other settings. Each of the six cases had been diagnosed by a panel of 34 psychiatrists as requiring hospitalization. The identical cases were also presented to a sample of 178 respondents in a small Canadian town and a larger sample of nearly 2000 respondents in Baltimore. The closest agreement came with the one case diagnosed as "paranoid schizophrenic." Each of the community leaders, as had the psychiatrists, indicated that the person needed hospitalization. Also 91% of the respondents in Baltimore agreed that the case required hospitalization. But only 69% of the respondents in the small Canadian town thought the person should go to a hospital.

A second case presented to the same four panels of respondents was diagnosed as "simple schizophrenia" by the psychiatrists. This is the case as it was presented to each respondent.

Now here's a young woman in her twenties, let's call her Betty Smith ... she has never had a job, and she doesn't seem to want to go out and look for one. She is a very quiet girl, she doesn't talk much to anyone—even her own family, and she acts like she is afraid of people, especially young men her own age. She won't go out with anyone, and whenever someone comes to visit her family, she stays by herself and daydreams all the time, and shows no interest in anything or anybody.

In contrast with the recommendation of each of the panel of psychiatrists at that time, only 72% of the community leaders, 78% of the Baltimore sample, and 36% of the small town respondents felt that Betty Smith required hospitalization. The other cases presented to these four samples—including one of severe compulsive-phobic behavior, one alcoholic, and one anxiety neurotic—showed even wider disparity in people's disposition to consider hospitalization. Compounding the problem is the fact that there are changes in medicine even over brief time spans around whether hospitalization is the preferred treatment for a specific illness.

By now, 80 different studies have attempted to count untreated as well as treated or hospitalized cases—in cities and villages in North and South America, Europe, Asia, and Africa. Consistently the finding has been that only a small portion of the "cases" was ever hospitalized. A study in New York State found that for every patient in a psychiatric facility, there were four outside who were judged by the psychiatrist-investigators to be sick enough to require certification for admission to a mental hospital or other psychiatric inpatient facility. This ratio of hospitalized to nonhospitalized at any one time is a function not only of a person's disposition to seek help, and the facilities available; it also varies depending on current social policies as well as psychiatric thinking about the most propitious and/or economical location for the treatment of various forms of mental illness. In chronic illness, in mild or nonthreatening conditions, and in social settings where, though ill, the person may still continue to function at least in a marginal way, hospitalization figures are particularly unreliable as a measure of true prevalence. Fortunately, the move away from reliance on hospital statistics opens a path toward increasingly meaningful studies.

THE PROBLEM OF OTHER INDICATORS: SYMPTOM CHECK LISTS

Developed by teams of psychiatrists, social psychologists, and sociologists, symptom check lists have been employed in several impressive surveys. These lists, painstakingly developed and tested and modified by clinicians to identify degrees of impairment, have several advantages.

First, they allow for careful sample selection and training of field interviewers who can probe appropriately. This use of lists, of course, can only eliminate bias from the sample when the sample is carefully drawn by experts, and when the canvas is monitored with determined efforts and call-back to assure that the hard-to-reach are adequately represented. (It is a common fallacy that one can ignore refusals, or casually substitute for them—a fallacy which leads to overrepresentation of the easily accessible whose social and emotional status may differ considerably from the inaccessible.)

The survey that uses symptom check lists also avoids the problem of guessing backwards from group properties, and it casts a net over rich as well as poor, and those who incline to seek medical attention at the first hiccup as well as those who steadfastly refuse to seek medical help though nearly prostrated. The check list also reduces the problem of different dispositions to admit to illness. It does not ask the respondent whether he is ill, but asks whether he has experienced each of a series of feelings, thoughts, and behaviors. Then the psychiatrists determine the degree of impairment.

Such lists seem a major step forward. They allow the giant computer to probe for relationships among a wide range of variables about the respondent's past and present life and a wide range of specific symptoms. They also provide the researcher with an efficient way to look at clusters of symptoms, and the possibility of additive effects of various attributes of individuals and their life situations. Surveys employing such lists do not underenumerate the doctor-shy people; they deal with objective data, but still have the benefit of psychiatric insight. It all sounds very good, but there are some problems.

First, when we begin to count illness through symptoms, we run the risk of stimulating the pulse we take. Careful probes into any indication of symptoms or fears, frustrations, aches, and uncertainties present in a population which otherwise would seem healthy can produce statistics that will be viewed with alarm. In England, in the course of a study of respiratory disease, it was discovered that a two hour interview with a long schedule of symptoms, and interviewers who probed sympathetically, re-

sulted in a very high rate of respiratory disease per 1000 respondents. But a brief interview conducted at the same time, and with a matched sample of respondents, not surprisingly found a markedly lower rate of disease in the same population. If the two studies had been done in two different countries, or at two different times, headlines might have pronounced the "alarming" differences in rates.

A second problem of symptom check lists is that, in looking for symptoms, there may be a tendency to miss how well the individual is actually functioning day to day.

There is a third problem in large surveys of treated as well as untreated cases of mental illness, and this is the issue of diagnosis. So far we have spoken of mental illness as though it were a single category. Unfortunately, many epidemiological studies have tended to concentrate on symptoms which might be incapacitating socially. A consequence is that organic psychoses, addictive disorders, severe depression, schizophrenia, and even mental retardation, might all be lumped together in such rates. As we move to the reality of the wide range of symptoms and etiologies included under the umbrella "mental illness," we necessarily open another box of problems. In psychiatry, as in other specialities, there are differences between clinicians in their disposition to diagnose specific illness. It is said that liver disease (maladie de foie) is more likely to be picked up at earlier stages by French than by American physicians. One cross-cultural study of psychiatric diagnosis more than 10 years ago found that Dutch psychiatrists tended to designate fewer patients as schizophrenic than did American psychiatrists, when the two panels were presented identical cases. However, the cross-cultural difference did disappear when only the most severely ill cases were compared. In diagnosis, as with the tendency to bring a patient to a psychiatrist for help, there is apparently more cultural impact on figures that refer to the middle or mild ranges of symptom impairment than there is on figures reflecting severe forms of illness. More recently, interrater reliability has improved, i.e., two or more psychiatrists presented the same list of symptoms or behaviors will independently each offer the same diagnosis. Mental retardation, organic brain syndrome, and alcoholism are the categories showing highest agreement. Leo Srole and his colleagues from the Midtown Manhattan Study have processed responses to their symptom lists by computer and found that the computer-derived mental health ratings yield extremely high correlation (0.83) with psychiatrists' ratings. In fact, the computer ratings were closer to the combined ratings of the psychiatrists than the psychiatrists' individual ratings were to each other.

A fourth problem is that ethnic groups vary in their willingness to admit to having certain symptoms, as well as in their willingness to admit to certain diseases. The respondent in a culture where it is not considered bizarre to see and talk with a grandmother dead these two years, is more likely to agree readily to a question about whether she ever hears voices. One study of widows in England, on the other hand, found that only after long interviews did a sizable portion confess to hallucinatory experiences that followed shortly after the death of their husbands. These women in a straight interview with a simple check list would not have admitted to the experience. Ethnic groups also vary in their tendency to "yea-say" or "nay-say." Bruce and Barbara Dohrenwend found that Irish respondents tended to be "nay-sayers," denying almost every symptom. Even when quite benign questions were interjected, the Irish respondents said, "No." In contrast, the Puerto Rican respondents in the same study seemed more disposed to respond with, "Yes," throughout their interviews. In this connection, many clinicians report the apparent agreeableness of Puerto Rican females. We called a Puerto Rican mother of a male adolescent psychiatric patient to ask whether we could make a home visit. She quickly said, "Yes." When we arrived, she said that she had worried all day about what she had agreed to! Whether these reports reflect differences in cultural tendencies to deny illness compared with tendencies to couch problems in somatic terms, or whether the differences relate to general response to strangers or to authority figures, the effect in surveys is the same—cultural bias in results.

A fifth and last artifact in surveys of health status needs consideration. This is the matter of transient response to situational factors. The lady who answers "yes" to questions about sleeplessness, loss of appetite, and inability to concentrate might score high on a symptom list. However, if it were known that her husband had died the previous week, her responses might be differently interpreted. The Dohrenwends interviewed a panel of respondents to determine life situations and also symptom status. Then they repeated the interview of the same respondents two years later. Nearly 78% of the respondents who had experienced unfavorable life events during the two year period had more symptoms at the end of the two year period than they had at the beginning. There was no comparable increase in symptoms among respondents who had not experienced unfavorable events. Thus, caught up in surveys of the prevalence of mental illness that use symptom lists is a small portion of the population who may have negligible underlying pathology, but who are struggling through some real crisis and showing signs of that.

QUESTIONS TO ASK OF EPIDEMIOLOGICAL FINDINGS

The point is that in epidemiology, just as in experimental science, findings are influenced by the methods used to obtain them. In neither experimental nor survey research does it make sense to accept findings for what they seem without weighing the impact of the method on the findings. It is, of course, equally specious to disregard findings from clinical, or experimental, or from survey research in an offhand way because there might be some artifact of method reflected in them. The first step toward advance in the science of epidemiology, as elsewhere, is recognition of the provisional nature of all findings. Careful enumeration is important, but it is not everything.

Three questions should be addressed to epidemiologic findings in mental illness. The first can be summarized by the broad question, "How much of the illness counted is an outbreak of the disease and how much is simply an outbreak of reporting of the disease?" The second can be summarized, "Is the relationship a property of a group compared with rates of disease in the group, or is it a direct relationship between an individual's attribute and the presence or absence of the disease in the same individual?" Third, "Are the findings reported accurate reflections of incidence, or of prevalence, of the disease in the population?"

Incidence is the rate of known *new* cases in a given population. *Prevalence* is the rate of *all* known cases in a given population. Incidence is obviously the measure of choice in a search for causation. With prevalence, some consequences of the disease can easily be mistaken for cause. For example, if a chronic illness causes individuals to lose jobs, then prevalence figures may show a high correlation between unemployment and the disease, but that does not mean that unemployment causes the disease.

Unfortunately, incidence is hard to determine in the chronic diseases. With some acute infectious diseases or other conditions of sudden onset, it may be relatively easy to establish a new case with reasonable assurance. But in mental illness, for example, first hospitalization may simply be the middle or late event in a long illness. Hospitalization may be precipitated by some change in the patient's life that makes the old behavior a new problem, or at least newly visible to someone in a position to get the problem to medical attention. Thus, an association between first hospitalization and a changed work situation may suggest that change in work caused such stress that it precipitated illness— or that the change precipitated someone to define previously acceptable behavior as needing hospitalization. Or the association could mean that the illness caused a change in jobs and a subsequent search for help.

What we usually see reported in the epidemiology of mental illness is prevalence rates, i.e., *the total number of cases*, new, middle, and of long duration, per thousand population, or how the illness prevails in the population. This means that prevalence rates over time can be markedly influenced by treatment methods that are effective in keeping the patient alive for a long time. As medicine is more successful, diabetics live longer, resulting in an accumulation of old cases and, therefore, increased prevalence rates. On the other hand, as medicine is more successful in case-finding at early stages of any illness, incidence rates may increase, even in the absence of real change in the proportion of actual first occurrence of the illness in the population.

THE FINDINGS

When we have sifted out the artifacts of method, what do the many epidemiological studies of mental illness tell us? First, beginning with Goldhammer and Marshall we see there is *no* conclusive evidence that there has been a major increase in the amount of severe symptom impairment over the past 100 years.

Second, from a wide range of cross-cultural studies we find *no* conclusive evidence of major differences between societies—from here to Nigeria to India to China—in the prevalence of severe impairment. Comparisons between urban and rural areas leave room for doubt about any romantic claims for a relative absence of psychiatric problems in lovely little towns. Bruce Dohrenwend summarized findings from the surveys that have compared rural and urban populations. Total rates for all functional psychoses combined were found to be more prevalent in rural than urban settings in five out of the seven studies. However, rates for neuroses and personality disorder were found to be higher in urban than in rural settings in some studies, but not in others.

Third, there are differences across cultures. There is variation in the style of presenting symptoms, and in the content or topics in delusions and hallucinations (as I discussed in the chapter on culture). Related to this there appear to be cross-cultural differences in prevalence of the various diagnostic categories within the functional psychoses, even though there are no cross-cultural differences in total prevalence of all forms of severe mental illness.

Fourth, the disposition to seek medical help and the tolerance of groups to accommodate to bizarre behavior vary considerably, and beyond that, the response of kin and community to the fact of hospitalization varies dramatically. Some groups appear to be able to live with a wide range of behavior and to include under the rubric of "normal" many behaviors that in another group are regarded as pathological. However, where people are reluctant to designate behavioral deviation as mental illness, once the person is finally called "insane" or "loco" or "mentally ill," he tends to be regarded as irreparably damaged, or even dangerous, and he is thus excluded and essentially abandoned. Reflecting this fact, there are differences in the frequency with which family members from different groups visit the patient in a psychiatric hospital. Lower socioeconomic status families tend to be more despairing once the diagnosis is made that the patient is sick enough to be hospitalized for mental illness. Related to such family attitudes as well as to other factors, length of hospital stay tends to be longer for poorer patients.

Fifth, physical health status is closely correlated with psychological health. Unfortunately, this is not something that has been included in many studies, but the findings suggest that it should be.

Sixth, according to preliminary results (reported in 1984) from an extensive epidemiological survey sponsored by the National Institute of Mental Health, nearly 20% of American adults over the age of 18 suffer from a diagnosable mental disorder, but only one in five of those afflicted seek help for their condition. This survey reported that anxiety disorders (especially phobias) are the most common mental disorder in this country (8.3%), followed by alcoholism and other drug abuse (6.4%), affective disorders (6%), schizophrenic disorders (1%), and antisocial personality disorder (0.9%).

Seventh, this same survey found that the overall rates of mental disorder among men and women are comparable. However, men had higher rates for substance abuse, organic mental disorder, and antisocial personality disorders, whereas women had higher rates for anxiety disorders and depressive disorders. People under the age of 45 were twice as likely to have a mental disorder than those over 45. There was virtually no difference between blacks and whites in the rates of mental illness or the type of mental disorders in these two groups.

Eighth, there is persistent evidence of a correlation between low socioeconomic status and severe symptom impairment, particularly schizophrenia. More than 33 surveys have included socioeconomic status and have used highly sophisticated methodology and door-to-door surveys rather than hospitalization statistics, and in 28 of these surveys the highest overall rates have been found in the lowest socioeconomic stratum (Class V in the Hollingshead-Redlich scale). This relationship shows up most clearly in urban settings. However, neurotic symptoms of anxiety and depression in lower socioeconomic groups are very often presented as somatic symptoms in emergency rooms and clinics. These patients may not be very psychologically minded. It is often mistakenly assumed by physicians that these patients in the lower socioeconomic groups do not suffer from job stress, and also that it is "wrong" for them to bring their social and emotional problems to a medical setting. Therefore, poor patients are rarely diagnosed as neurotic, and a self-fulfilling prophecy then confirms the belief that patients with symptoms of anxiety and depression are concentrated in the upper socioeconomic classes.

SOCIOECONOMIC STATUS AND PSYCHOSIS

The meaning of the persistent association between low socioeconomic status or social class and severe symptom impairment is unclear. In the first place there is the possibilty of *downward drift*. That is, the mentally ill person may be less competent to hold a job or to fend for himself, and may drift downward occupationally and also socially. Since most of the studies deal with prevalence, there is the possibility that some segments of the poor or lower class patients who are mentally ill may have moved into that class consequent to the illness. On the other hand, Leo Srole, who compared the symptom-impairment score of the respondent with the socioeconomic status of the respondent's father, found that only 9.5% of sons whose fathers were in the lowest stratum were relatively symptom free—but 24.4% of the respondents whose fathers were in the highest stratum were free of symptoms of mental illness. The statistical relationships between the father's socioeconomic status and the patient's impairment score suggest that some part of the correlation is not accounted for by downward drift. In other words, "drift" accounts for a small portion of the association, but it does not seem to be enough to explain fully the relationship.

In the second place, there is evidence that there may be higher incidence of severe life stress at the bottom of the social ladder. Loss of home, being the victim of crime, poor physical health, marital separation, abandonment, and tenuous job situations that offer little in the way of personal initiative or rewards—all common among the poor—are among these stressful events, and the association between symptom impairment and low socioeconomic status may, therefore, also reflect transient responses to these life situations as well as impairment from long-term stress of life at the bottom of a social pyramid.

However, the conditions of social deprivation and pressure experienced by children and adults in the lowest socioeconomic status are not enough in themselves to explain self-perpetuation of psychological disorder in otherwise normal human beings. Situational factors may only contribute to the correlations. But fatalism or a sense of hopelessness may make poorer people more vulnerable to the damaging effects of unfortunate events. *Secondary gain* among the most deprived may also contribute. In view of the very poor person's position at the bottom of the community, the role of patient may be for some a relatively acceptable alternative in a hopeless world, which in turn could contribute to tendencies to admit to symptoms readily, and to see oneself as "damaged."

Additional factors that have received some attention in the epidemiology of mental illness include child rearing practices that may be class related as well as related to ethnic groups. Also, gross nutritional deficits in pregnancy and the neonatal period, as well as later, may contribute to the correlation between low socioeconomic status and symptom impairment. Finally, genetic factors may play a role in the schizophrenic and affective disorders, a possibility already discussed by Dr. Reite.

MIDTOWN FOLLOW-UP STUDY

A 20-year follow-up and reinterviews with the large sample of people who were originally interviewed in the major Midtown Manhattan Study provided the basis for testing some common assumptions about mental illness. Leo Srole and his associates were able to locate and reinterview 695 of the original 1660 respondents who in the first survey were within the ages of 20 through 59 (299 of the original sample were known deceased). Because the research team of this survey did not have to guess about whether impairment came after or before major life crises, or change in social status, some of the blurring due to multiple causation may finally begin to be clarified.

An early report from this follow-up study casts new light on the impact of aging on mental health. We tend to assume a necessary decline in emotional status as well as intellectual and physical ability with age. The Midtown Manhattan investigators in 1954 had found evidence of this assumption when they compared their younger with their older respondents. But when they went back in 1974, they were surprised to find that the whole issue of the impact of aging on mental health was far more complex. When they looked at the *same* people 20 years later, 40.9% were the same, 32.5% had gotten better, and 26.6% had gotten worse. We know that death rates are particularly high among the severely impaired, and particularly hospitalized, psychiatric patients. Even so, among the survivors in this severely impaired category, there were still some who had gotten better over the course of 20 years. One of the reasons for this surprising finding appears to be related to changes in our society over the past 20 year period. The sociocultural environment in 1974 appears to be more conducive of emotional well being for older people (particularly women) than in 1954. It would seem that a decline in mental health is by no means inevitable with aging.

Another way of looking at the same data is to compare age groups or generations rather than comparing the same individual, over time. When the Midtown investigators took people in their 50's in 1954 and compared that group with another group of people who were in their 50's in 1974, they found further evidence of improvement. When they compared males and females in their 50's at these two points in time (1954 and 1974), they found a particularly dramatic change for the better in women in their 50's. Whether improved physical health of older women, or certain social advantages related to the women's liberation movement, or other possibilities explain these differences between women in their 50's in 1954 compared with women in their 50's in 1974, is yet to be determined.

CONCLUSION

With each step through the tangles of correlations, advance will come only if the epidemiologist keeps in close touch with medical scientists and clinicians. Knowledge of other methods and different perspectives is essential if we are to achieve more than approximate successive stabs at causation.

Suggested Readings

Dohrenwend B: Sociocultural and social-psychological factors in the genesis of mental disorders. *J Health Soc Behav* 16:365, 1975.

Srole L: Measurement and classification in sociopsychiatric epidemiology: Midtown Manhattan Study (1954) and Midtown Manhattan Restudy (1974). *J Health Soc Behav* 16:347, 1975.

References

Deets L: *The Hutterites.* Gettysburg, PA, Times Publishing Company, 1939.

Dohrenwend BP, Dohrenwend BS: *Social Status and Psychological Disorder.* New York, John Wiley & Sons, 1969.

Dohrenwend BP, Egri G, Mendelsohn FS: Psychiatric disorder in general populations: a study of the problem of clinical judgment. *Am J Psychiatry* 127:1304, 1971.

Dohrenwend BP, Dohrenwend BS: Psychiatric epidemiology: an analysis of "true prevalence" studies. In Golann SE, Eisdorfer C (eds): *Handbook of Community Mental Health.* New York, Appleton-Century-Crofts, 1972, p 283.

Dunham H: *Community and Schizophrenia.* Detroit, Wayne State University Press, 1965.

Eaton J, Weil RJ: *Culture and Mental Disorders: A Comparative Study of the Hutterites and Other Populations.* Glencoe, Ill, Free Press, 1955.

Goldhammer H, Marshall AW: *Psychosis and Civilization.* Glencoe, Ill, Free Press, 1953.

Gove WR: Societal reaction as an explanation of mental illness: an evaluation. *Am Sociol Rev* 35:873, 1970.

Hollingshead AB, Redlich FC: *Social Class and Mental Illness.* New York, John Wiley & Sons, 1958.

Kessler RC, McRae JA: Trends in the relationship between sex and attempted suicide. *J Health Soc Behavior* 24:98, 1983.

Lapouse R: Problems in studying the prevalence of psychiatric disorder. *Am J Public Health* 57:947, 1967.

Leighton AH: *My Name is Legion.* New York, Basic Books. 1959.

Lemkau P, Crocetti G: Vital statistics of schizophrenia. In Bellak L (ed): *Schizophrenia: A Review of the Syndrome.* New York, Grune & Stratton, 1958, p. 64.

Mechanic D: Methodological perspectives in the study of disease processes. In *Medical Sociology.* New York, Free Press, 1968, p 195.

Mishler E, Scotch N: Sociocultural factors in the epidemiology of schizophrenia. *Int J Psychiatry* 1:258, 1965.

Murphy JM: Psychiatric labeling in cross-cultural perspective. *Science* 191:1019, 1976.

Myers J, Bean L: A *Decade Later: A Follow-up of Social Class and Mental Illness.* New York, John Wiley & Sons, 1968.

Pasamanick B: What is mental illness and how can we measure it? In Sells SB (ed): *The Definition and Measurement of Mental Health.* U.S. Public Health Service Publication. 1968, p 30.

Robins E, Myers J, Shapiro S: Preliminary results of the NIMH epidemiological survey. *Psychiatric News,* November 18, 1983.

Srole L, et al: *Mental Health in the Metropolis: The Midtown Manhattan Study,* vol 1. New York, McGraw-Hill, 1962.

CHAPTER 55

Learning Principles, Biofeedback, and Behavioral Medicine

Johann Stoyva, Ph.D.

"HUMAN NATURE"

"You can't change human nature." This sentiment is one which has often been voiced over the course of the centuries by thinkers as diverse as cooks and philosophers, prophets and saloon keepers, archbishops and streetwalkers. Opinions on the issue have differed dramatically. Proponents of reform have believed that the character of man can be altered. But a long line of thinkers, mainly conservative, have believed that human nature is not open to fundamental change.

In the judgment of St. Augustine, man is born inherently corrupt. And even to argue that man, through his own efforts, can be improved is not only wrong but heretical. The English philosopher and political intriguer, Thomas Hobbes, expressed similar views: we are self-seeking and prone to violence. Society is a war of all against all and should be organized accordingly. Dostoyevsky was likewise pessimistic, even though he lived during a period of brilliant scientific progress. In his estimation, even though humans come to understand the scientific laws that govern them, this will not allow them to manage their lives more effectively. The demonic and the irrational will still overwhelm us.

Against those gloomy prognoses may be placed an array of more cheerful pronouncements. Philosophers and writers of the enlightenment period, as for example, Locke, Diderot, Condorcet, and Jefferson, spoke not just of improving man, but of human perfectibility; and a long line of 19th century reformers and visionaries (Godwin, Fourier, Saint-Simon, and Robert Owen, as well as the anarchist, Prince Kropotkin) were similarly enthusiastic about the prospects of fundamental change.

One suspects that a great deal hinges upon how we interpret the phrase "human nature." If we mean the individual's "central emotional disposition," then perhaps not much change is possible (although religious conversion experiences might be an exception). Despite various life experiences, the individual still retains the same basic outlook on life, feels like the same person he has always been, and maintains the same basic emotional disposition.

But, if we shift our emphasis to the individual's behavior, then great change is demonstrably possible. A few historical examples will underscore the point. Well into the 19th century, the practice of dueling was fairly common both in Europe and America. Many considered it to be an ineradicable part of human nature (particularly in the male). Yet, the practice has changed. And, as Bertrand Russell has remarked, few of us feel thwarted because we are not allowed to fight duels! Or consider the habit of spitting on sidewalks, a practice which seems to have been common in the 19th century. This behavior, too, has shown a commendable decrease, partly as a result of anti-tuberculosis campaigns. Or, take the staging and witnessing of public executions, a form of diversion for which there was a long-unquenchable popular enthusiasm. This, also, is another practice which has fallen into disuse.

With the recognition that behavior can indeed be changed, the learning principles governing the modification of behavior, and the larger question of how the organism adapts to its environment, have become central issues in 20th century psychology. There are three main types of learning, and I shall now discuss each of them: 1) *classical conditioning*, 2) *operant (or instrumental) conditioning*, and 3) *modeling (observational learning)*.

CLASSICAL CONDITIONING

Ivan Pavlov was the great Russian physiologist who formulated the principles of classical (or Pavlovian) conditioning. Pavlov first did important work in the physiology of the digestive system. Remarkably gifted in surgery, he succeeded in developing techniques to measure the glandular secretions of dogs by means of a fistula. The results of this work earned him a Nobel Prize. In his later years, Pavlov became something of a monument in Soviet society since it was thought that his research might provide a scientific basis for Leninist-Marxist theories pertaining to the development of the new Soviet man. A gentleman of forthright views, Pavlov enjoys the rare distinction of having disagreed with Stalin and yet dying a natural death.

Early in his investigations, Pavlov observed that a dog would sometimes begin to salivate even though a food stimulus was not physically present in its mouth. In this type of learning, a previously neutral stimulus had become capable of producing a particular reaction. It is known, for example, that meat powder in a dog's mouth will automatically produce salivation. Therefore, it is called an *unconditioned stimulus* (UCS). The response of salivating to meat powder is called an *unconditioned response* (UCR), since it does not have to be learned.

Pavlov was intrigued to note that after a time his dogs would begin salivating even before they got the meat powder; e.g., the mere sight of the keeper or the sound of his footstep had become sufficient to trigger salivation. In other words, a previously neutral stimulus (the keeper)—because he had been regularly associated with feeding—had now become a *conditioned stimulus* (CS) for salivation. More typically, a bell or a light is used as the conditioned stimulus. For example, with a trained dog, we sound a bell (the CS) and salivation occurs, which is now termed the *conditioned response* (CR).

Classical conditioning occurs in three phases. In the *acquisition phase*, the organism learns the response. In the *extinction phase*, the conditioned response diminishes when the keeper (the CS) appears many times and is *not followed* by meat powder (the UCS). The *spontaneous recovery phase* occurs after extinction has taken place. Here, the conditioned response spontaneously comes back, then again diminishes. For example, the dog will again (for a brief time) begin to salivate at the sight of the keeper.

Stimulus generalization occurs when a stimulus reasonably *similar* to the original conditioned stimulus also produces the conditioned response. For example, the dog begins to salivate when he sees someone else who looks like the keeper—perhaps because this person also wears a white lab coat. Classical conditioning can also occur to a painful or unpleasant stimulus. For example, a laboratory dog learns that a buzzer is the signal for electric shock to his paw. After *avoidance conditioning* has occurred, the sound of the buzzer alone will cause foot withdrawal as a means of avoiding the painful shock. A common clinical example: after a visit to the dentist, a child learns that a white coat will be followed by a needle in the gum. Classical avoidance conditioning also shows the three phases of acquisition, extinction, and spontaneous recovery.

OPERANT CONDITIONING

The American psychologist, B. F. Skinner (Figure 55.1), has been centrally concerned with the production of change in behavior and in determining the lawful regularities in such change. Beginning with intensive work on animals, he has subsequently proposed that the same body of learning principles applies to both humans and animals. Although a gentle-mannered individual, he has been the subject of much controversy, and has been vigorously attacked, especially by literary intellectuals. Why? One reason may be his thorough-going *environmental determinism*. Just as Freud believed that human behavior is determined by an individual's inner psychological forces as governed by predictable scientific laws (*psychic determinism*), Skinner believes that human behavior is determined by an individual's environment, also as governed by predictable scientific laws. Skinner has no place for what he calls the "autonomous man" of political and literary thinkers.

Unlike the work of most great learning theorists, Skinner's ideas have already demonstrated considerable practical utility: in the teaching of animals, in the ward management of chronic psychotic patients, and in teaching of the mentally retarded through token economies; in the

Figure 55.1. B. F. Skinner (By permission of Wide World Photos.)

development of programmed learning; and in the management of addictive disorders such as obesity and smoking. Skinner stresses that it is of utmost importance that we address ourselves to the problems of behavior. The greatest and most overriding issues facing the human species involve the behavior of its members: war, crime, population growth, racial prejudice, pollution, and addictive disease. It is unlikely, says Skinner, that these are issues which will increasingly yield to sophisticated physiochemical research. We must instead focus on the principles governing behavior and behavioral change.

Reinforcement

Skinner's fundamental thesis is enshrined in the concept of *reinforcement* and in the idea that behavior is governed by its *consequences* for the individual. In this thesis he has maintained a remarkable, almost unnerving, consistency in the course of his career. The beginnings of his reinforcement concept were formulated in papers written during the early 1930's.

A *reinforcer* may be defined as something which *follows* a particular item of behavior and which alters the probability that this behavior will occur again in the future. For example, if a pigeon is given a grain of wheat after it pecks at a blue dot, the behavior of pecking at the blue dot is likely to increase. In this example, the grain of wheat is the reinforcer, and pecking at the blue dot is the behavior-to-be-reinforced. The wheat grain is termed as *positive reinforcer* since it acts to increase the probability that the behavior preceding it will occur again. In contrast, *punishment* is something which acts to decrease the probability that the behavior preceding it will occur again. A *negative reinforcer*— actually a somewhat confusing term—refers to the elimination of something unpleasant. Suppose we complain about a loud noise coming from a neighbor's stereo, and the loud noise stops. Cessation of the noise is an example of a negative reinforcer. The behavior of complaining has been reinforced by elimination of an unpleasant stimulus.

A central feature of operant conditioning is that reinforcement for the correct response should come quickly—preferably right after the correct response has occurred. (This feature of prompt knowledge of results is also incorporated into the biofeedback techniques, to be described later). If reinforcement for the correct response is delayed—even by minutes—then the rate of learning is greatly slowed. Skinner, incidentally, maintains that much of our academic learning is very inefficient because reinforcement is subject to long delays and may even be of a capricious nature. When students write essays, for example, their grades (the reinforcer in this case) are often slow in coming and thereby uncertain in their effects on subsequent behavior.

Distinction between Operant and Classical Conditioning

In operant conditioning, it is not the presentation of a preceding stimulus that evokes or controls the response. Often, no preceding stimulus can be identified. On the contrary, it is the *consequences* of the behavior which determine whether it will occur again. Another critical difference between operant and classical conditioning is that in operant conditioning the organism *must first do something before reinforcement occurs*; e.g., a rat must press a bar before he receives a food pellet. Put another way, the animal must first *operate on the environment* before reinforcement takes place.

A significant advantage of operant conditioning over classical conditioning is its much greater flexibility as a training procedure. A particular reinforcer can be used to reinforce any response of which the organism is capable. A food pellet, for instance, could be a reinforcer for scratching, pecking, jumping, sniffing, tapping, and so forth. First the behavior occurs, then it is quickly reinforced.

Contingencies of Reinforcement

A central integrating theme in Skinner's work is the concept of *contingencies of reinforcement,* the patterning or scheduling of reinforcement. Several important different schedules of reinforcement have been described. One of the most important consists of *partial (intermittent) reinforcement.* Thus, a pigeon might be reinforced for only every fifth peck instead of each peck. A striking characteristic of intermittent reinforcement is that it leads to behavior which is highly resistant to extinction. By gradually "stretching" the reinforcement ratio, Skinner has taught pigeons to peck as many as 10,000 times before earning their reinforcer.

Many instances of the powerful effects of intermittent reinforcement can be seen in human behavior. *Gambling* is a good example. The dedicated gambler will persist through many disappointments. In Las Vegas, one sees vast rows of gleaming slot machines, and the customers show remarkable persistence, even though they know the pay-offs are not very frequent. Persistence of behavior in the face of scarce reinforcers is apparent in many areas of human endeavor: in sports such as fly-fishing or hunting, in playing the stock market, in scientific research, and in clinical work. Many practitioners take special pride and satisfaction in dealing with the difficult patient, despite their awareness of the gloomy prognosis.

Shaping

Very important in the Skinnerian scheme of things is the idea of the *shaping* of behavior. What shaping involves is the *reinforcement of successive approximations to the finally desired behavior.* Suppose we want to teach a dog to jump through a hoop three feet above the ground. How can the dog be taught to do this? This is an act he is quite unlikely to perform spontaneously. Therefore, we shape his behavior

to the desired goal. We begin with the initial *random variability* of the dog's behavior. He will poke around corners of the room, scratch himself, come to be petted, lie down to take a nap, and so forth. At first, we reinforce any behavior which is in the desired direction; e.g., if the dog moves from a corner toward the hoop, we offer reinforcement. Later, he must move closer to the hoop in order to be reinforced. In subsequent steps, he must put his nose in the hoop to be reinforced. Later, the hoop would be gradually elevated. Finally, he would have to jump through a hoop to be reinforced. The shaping principle is very important and can be seen in many areas of human behavior. In school, for example, we begin with fundamentals in the elementary years and, then, through the various grades, go on to more complex matters. In sports, especially in the acquisition of motor skills, shaping techniques are widely applied. Skiers, for example, are now taught alpine skiing by means of the Graduated Length Method (GLM). One begins with a very short ski which is easy to maneuver. Then, as expertise increases, one moves on to progressively longer and more formidable skis. The same principle is involved in teaching young children to play tennis.

MODELING

Along with classical conditioning and operant conditioning, modeling is one of the three major types of learning. Very important in child development, it is basically an *observational type of learning.* For example, a child will observe how his parents hold a knife and fork, then attempt to do the same. Or, the child will adopt the speech, mannerisms, and behavior of someone whom he admires and respects. Modeling is often seen in sports—the beginner in tennis will try to swing his racket the way the pro does. In Albert Bandura's work, it was found that when an adult behaved aggressively towards a Bobo doll, a child who had been watching would follow suit.

Modeling has been employed in *fear reduction.* In one study, children who suffered from dog phobias watched films of other children handling and playing with dogs. The children who had watched the films showed a marked diminution in their fear of dogs which was not displayed by the children in the control group.

BEHAVIOR THERAPY: THE CLINICAL APPLICATION OF LEARNING PRINCIPLES

In order to illustrate the clinical application of learning principles in the treatment of mental illness, three examples of *behavior therapy* will be described.

Token Economy

This is a technique based on the principles of operant conditioning. It has been employed in the management of chronic schizophrenic patients in mental hospital wards and in the care of the mentally retarded. The basic idea is that when the patient engages in acceptable behavior, then "goodies" come his way, i.e., the desirable behavior is reinforced. For example, if a patient makes his own bed, he is allowed to see a movie that evening.

The procedure requires careful observation of behavior by the ward staff, and both patients and staff should be clear on the ground rules—which behavior will be reinforced and which will not. Ideally, the reinforcer should come quickly after the desired behavior. Since this is often not practical, the patient initially receives *token reinforcers* such as wooden coins after the desired task has been performed (hence the term, *token economy*). These tokens (or points) are totaled, then later translated into more tangible reinforcers (such as cigarettes, desserts, entertainment). A token economy not only can make a ward a good deal easier to manage, but can assist in the patient's learning behavior which will help him to reestablish himself in the community.

The token economy method has also been widely used in the institutional management of the mentally retarded. Often, dramatic gains are made in the ability of these individuals to clothe and feed themselves and to make proper use of toilet facilities through the use of token reinforcers.

Systematic Desensitization

This is a widely used technique in the treatment of phobias and specific anxiety disorders. Developed by the psychiatrist, Joseph Wolpe, formerly from South Africa, it provided a major impetus to the growth of behavior therapy in the sixties and seventies. The technique grew out of Wolpe's earlier experiments on the production of conditioned fear responses in animals. Wolpe found that if he introduced a response incompatible with fear, such as eating, then the fear response was diminished (inhibited). He then reasoned that this observation might prove useful in the treatment of anxiety in humans. If he could introduce a response incompatible with anxiety, then the anxiety would be inhibited or diminished. For practical reasons, the response he chose for this task was muscular relaxation.

Systematic desensitization is based on the idea that profound muscle relaxation leads to parasympathetic dominance in the autonomic nervous system. This can be used as a *competing response* which is *incompatible with anxiety*, since the latter is based upon sympathetic dominance in the autonomic nervous system. Thus, the patient who is extremely relaxed is unlikely to be anxious. In systematic desensitization, the anxious patient is first taught muscular relaxation. With the help of the therapist, the patient then forms a graded hierarchy of six to 12 anxiety scenes focused around the anxious situation. Suppose the patient suffers from severe public speaking anxiety. The hierarchy items range from scenes that cause only mild anxiety (for example, accepting an invitation to talk one month from now) to a scene of severe anxiety (the moment before beginning a talk to a large and critical audience). The patient first visualizes the mild anxiety scene while maintaining relaxation (and absence of anxiety). As he progressively masters the anxiety scenes (by maintaining relaxation), he goes on to more difficult ones and, finally, all the way through the anxiety hierarchy. He has been desensitized to the anxiety situation and now is able to think about it, yet remain tranquil. This procedure generally takes six to 14 sessions. An important additional phase of the procedure is that as the patient progressively masters the anxiety scenes, he gradually begins to face (and master) these same situations in his everyday life.

Sex Therapy

Behavior therapy, often in combination with other approaches, has been used to treat a variety of sexual dysfunctions as discussed in Chapter 36.

BIOFEEDBACK: THE LEARNED MODIFICATION OF PHYSIOLOGICAL ACTIVITY

Fundamental Principles

A type of learning which has stirred up much popular excitement, as well as scholarly interest, is known as *biofeedback* (a contraction of "bioelectric information feedback"). Biofeedback, which can be regarded as an extension of operant conditioning, involves the learning of voluntary control over various sorts of physiological activity. The essence of this training is to provide the individual with a flow of precise information about a particular sort of physiological activity. For example, electromyographic (EMG) activity of the frontalis muscle of the forehead can be signalled by means of a tone of varying pitch. When the muscle is tense, the tone is high in pitch; as the individual relaxes the muscle, the pitch of the tone which he hears through his headphones simultaneously decreases. In other words, the tone serves to track what the muscle is doing, and the subject receives virtually immediate feedback as to what his level of muscular tension is. The same information feedback technique can in principle be applied to any physiological activity which is measurable (especially if the activity is under neural control).

Three fundamental principles are involved in biofeedback training. First, it must be possible to *detect* and measure accurately the particular physiological activity of interest. Normally, the signal-to-be-detected is a bioelectric one, e.g., EMG activity, or a brain rhythm such as alpha or theta EEG, or heart rate (EKG). Other (non-bioelectric) types of signals can also be monitored such as blood pressure (Korotkoff sounds) and peripheral temperature (a function of blood flow at the probe site). Second, there must be a flow of continous or near-continuous *information feedback* for the subject. Finally, since biofeedback is very much a matter of voluntary control, the subject must be *motivated* to learn. There is nothing automatic about this type of learning; usually much practice is required.

Note the fundamental similarity between biofeedback and operant conditioning. *Before* the individual hears the low-pitched tone that tells him his muscle tension is low, he must *first relax the muscle.* He first executes the response of muscle relaxation; then he very quickly receives reinforcement (in the sense of the feedback tone telling him he is performing the correct response—or at least going in the right direction).

With respect to clinical applications of biofeedback in psychology and psychiatry, two main streams of endeavor have emerged. One involves training in the voluntary control of autonomic activity; the other consists of training in relaxation of the striate musculature.

Biofeedback for Voluntary Control of Autonomic Activity

That autonomic activity can be brought under some degree of learned or voluntary control is a very recent development within psychology. Even the name "autonomic" nervous system (ANS) implies something which governs itself. Its discoverer, Bichat, called it the "vegetative" nervous system, a term still commonly used in Europe. Again, it implies something which runs itself as well as being of fairly lowly status!

Within experimental psychology it had long been held that "involuntary" autonomic activity was not amenable to voluntary control through operant (instrumental) conditioning. What could be controlled by both classical and operant conditioning was the activity of the voluntary striate muscle system. Admittedly, there were some fascinating exceptions to the foregoing view of the autonomic nervous system, such as the case of the celebrated magician, Houdini, who was able to extricate himself from all sorts of awkward situations. Subsequent to his death it was learned that Houdini had trained himself to a high degree of voluntary control over the esophageal swallowing response. After practicing for many hours with a piece of potato tied to a string, he had been able to overcome the normal gag reflex. Prior to a performance, he would swallow a skeleton key which he would hold in his upper esophagus, and which would remain undetected. Later, he would regurgitate the key and use it to slip out of chains, handcuffs, and padlocks. Also, from the 19th century onwards, there had been reports filtering out of India about the mysterious powers of the yogis, who were reported to show remarkable control over a great many autonomic visceral responses such as heart rate, blood pressure, intestinal activity, and the like. Generally, though, these reports were not taken seriously by the Western scientific community.

With the advent of biofeedback techniques,

however, it has been demonstrated that a degree of voluntary control over autonomic responses is possible. These observations are of particular interest to psychosomatic medicine since, in the psychophysiological disorders, it is frequently some autonomic activity which has gone awry—as for example, in essential hypertension, peptic ulcer, asthma. Consequently, there has been much interest in whether biofeedback training of autonomic activity might be useful in the treatment of psychosomatic diseases, afflictions which are so prevalent in modern society.

Peripheral temperature regulation is the autonomic response which has thus far received the most clinical use (Figure 55.2). The experiments of Taub have shown that normal subjects can acquire some control over hand temperature. Over four training sessions, each of which lasted about a half hour, volunteers learned to increase hand temperature by about 2°F. Others learned to decrease temperature by about the same amount. Selected individuals showed very large changes—increases of 6° or 7°F and decreases of about the same order. Moreover, subjects were able to retain this control quite well after an interval of several months during which feedback training had been absent.

A particular application of temperature feedback has been in cases of *migraine headache*, a vascular disorder. A key etiological feature of this headache is an initial phase of vasoconstriction in the cerebral arteries followed by a subsequent rebound phase during which marked vasodilatation of the extracerebral arteries occurs. Although the precise mechanism of the pain, especially the biochemical aspects of it, remains somewhat obscure, there is good agreement that the headache pain is closely associ-

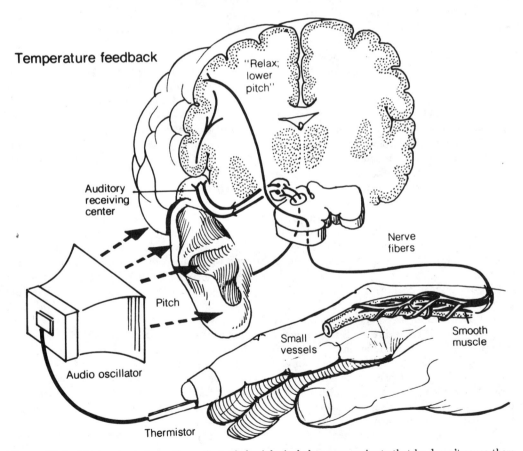

Figure 55.2. Electronics informs the patient of physiological changes so minute that he doesn't sense them normally. In temperature feedback, a patient who hears peripheral vascular dilation as warmth "felt" by the thermistor can consciously alter the oscillator's pitch by willful vascular changes. (Courtesy of Patient Care Publications, Inc.)

ated with the rebound vasodilatation occurring in the extracranial arteries.

It was accidentally noted by Green, Sargent, and their associates that certain volunteers who suffered from migraine headache were much improved after they were successful in increasing hand temperature. By now, many practitioners, mostly clinical psychologists and psychiatrists, have employed the hand warming technique with migrainous patients, and numerous successful outcomes have been reported. It should be emphasized that considerable uncertainty still surrounds the use of hand warming techniques in the treatment of migraine headache. To begin with, the causal mechanisms are unknown. How does hand warming have an effect upon the superficial cranial arteries that are the focus of the pain? Some have suggested that hand warming acts to increase the defective vasomotor tone of the migrainous patient. Others maintain that what is essentially involved is a relaxation response.

Another problem is the scarcity of controlled outcome studies, even though by now the number of cases treated by this method over the past 10 years must run well into the thousands. On the favorable side of the balance, however, must be weighed the observation of many practitioners that certain patients will respond well to this treatment even though they have been resistant to other treatment approaches for some years. It seems, especially for the classic type of migraine patient in whom a premonitory aura is present, that the hand warming approach is useful. Another favorable aspect of the approach should be emphasized: when it is successful, drug dependence of the patient is eliminated or greatly diminished, quite an important consideration.

By now, a great deal of work on the learned control of autonomic functions has been conducted. Heart rate, electrodermal activity, and salivation are all amenable to a degree of voluntary modification. A major characteristic of such autonomic learning is the presence of very great individual differences; some subjects can produce large changes, others, hardly any. A particularly valuable series of experiments has been conducted by Bernard Engel and his associates in which patients with *cardiac arrhythmias*, such as premature ventricular contractions and Wolff-Parkinson-White syndrome, learned to diminish the frequency of their arrhythmias. A pioneering figure in this area for many years, Neal E. Miller, continues to explore the voluntary learning of various autonomic responses and the possible far reaching therapeutic effects of biofeedback in the treatment of many different illnesses, especially those of a psychosomatic nature. Similar efforts have also been made to train patients with *epilepsy* to increase their levels of the sensorimotor rhythm (SMR), an EEG wave emanating from the area of the Rolandic fissure. Enhancement of this rhythm appears to have an inhibiting effect on epileptic seizures.

Regarding the clinical application of biofeedback, it should be emphasized that there is nothing automatic about it. Many sessions of training are usually required, and the cooperation of the patient is vital. He or she is not the passive recipient of the therapist's ministrations, but must become an active partner in the therapeutic endeavor.

Biofeedback for Relaxation

Another major applied use of biofeedback has been in the induction of relaxation, a procedure having a surprising number of uses. Indeed, the Western world has only recently come to recognize the value of relaxation for man's physical and emotional well being, although that value has for centuries been part of Eastern culture in the form of yoga, Zen, and transcendental meditation. Clinical applications have been developed both for disorders involving localized muscular tension and in disorders characterized by excessively high arousal which is of psychogenic origin, as in many cases of anxiety.

In recent years, relaxation procedures have been widely used in *tension headache*, which is also known as muscle-contraction headache. The classic symptom of this disorder is a pain that is fairly steady, bilateral, gradual in onset, not associated with throbbing or nausea, and which is likely to occur at times of stress or emotional turmoil. In biofeedback treatment of this problem, patients typically receive two sessions of frontalis muscle EMG feedback per week. In addition, they are told to practice relaxation on their own twice a day for about 15 minutes each time. To test the efficacy of this procedure, we designed a study which involved an experimental group and two control groups (Budzynski, Stoyva, Adler, and Mullaney, 1973). The experimental group received genuine EMG feedback as a means of assisting relaxation; one control group was a no-treatment condition; the other was a "placebo-suggestion" group who *believed* it was receiving relaxation training. The outcome was clearly in favor of the EMG feedback group who showed statistically significant reductions in both frontal EMG levels and on ratings of head pain. Additionally, they showed large reductions in medication usage. Since this experiment was completed, a number of other investigators have similarly reported that relaxation training is useful in the treatment of tension headache. There is some debate, however, as to whether EMG feedback is required for the requisite degree of relaxation. Some investigators maintain that an adequate degree of relaxation can be reached by means other than biofeedback, for instance, by means of verbal instructions to relax. At any rate, it can be concluded that relaxation training is a clinically useful approach in tension headache and is now receiving wide use. What is the most effective and economical form of relaxation training will no doubt be determined in future comparative studies.

EMG feedback has also been utilized in several other disorders involving localized muscle tension: in *temporomandibular joint pain* (where there is cramping and pain in the jaw muscles), in *bruxism* (toothgrinding), in localized *muscle cramps*, and in *dysphagia* (difficulty in swallowing owing to spasticity of the esophagus).

Another major type of application of EMG feedback has been in the induction of a general (whole-body) relaxation response. My colleague and I (Stoyva and Budzynski, 1974) have hypothesized that a general relaxation response has physiological effects opposite in nature to those produced by psychological stress. Basically, psychological stress leads to a high arousal condition (as reflected in the activity of various physiological systems). A generalized relaxation condition, on the other hand, is a state of low arousal. It will be recalled that muscle relaxation is utilized in the systematic desensitization of phobias and circumscribed anxieties as a condition incompatible with anxiety (see earlier section describing the work of Wolpe).

Relaxation training appears useful in at least two conditions which are often stress related, or at least exacerbated by psychological stress. One is *sleep-onset insomnia*. The other is *chronic* or *free-floating anxiety*, an affliction thought to be present in at least 5% of the population. This disorder is also referred to as *generalized anxiety*

disorder. It fails to respond very well to systematic desensitization as it is ordinarily conducted. Yet, two careful studies that have included appropriate control groups indicated favorable results when EMG feedback was used as a means of relaxation training. In the 1975 study of Townsend and Addario (1975), EMG feedback patients showed significant decrements in anxiety which were not seen in the matched control group treated with group psychotherapy. Similarly, in the 1977 study by LaVallee and colleagues, patients receiving EMG feedback assisted relaxation training showed larger and more lasting decrements in anxiety than those receiving Valium. It should be emphasized, however, that patients with chronic, pervasive anxiety are complex and difficult; no one procedure solves the whole problem. A many faceted and persistent approach is required. Relaxation training, however, if it is thoroughly done, is a useful beginning.

BEHAVIORAL MEDICINE

Over the past several decades, there has been a growing recognition that the individual's behavior, especially his habitual behavior, can have important consequences for health and disease. As one example, the work of the British physician and biochemist, Thomas McKeown, strongly emphasizes the importance of behavioral and environmental factors in health and disease. According to McKeown, the popular view is that one-to-one personal medical care has been the source from which all improvements in health have flowed. Yet, McKeown's researches on the history of improvements in health in 19th century England and Wales show that the practice of medicine was only one of several factors contributing to better health in the population. In terms of rank, the major factors were the following: 1) limitation of family size (behavioral change), 2) an increase in food supplies (which allowed better nutrition), 3) a healthier physical environment, and 4) specific preventive and therapeutic measures in medical care.

A recent document published by the Canadian government echoes McKeown's sentiments. Principally authored by the Canadian Minister of Health, Marc LaLonde, this 1974 report stresses the etiological significance of behavioral and environmental influences in disease. A point underscored in this document, titled *New Per-*

spectives on the Health of Canadians, is that traditional one-to-one medical practice may have reached a point of diminishing returns. In the United States, for example, between the years 1950 and 1975, health expenditures increased from 4.6% of the Gross National Product to 8.3%; yet, mean longevity showed virtually no change. A major conclusion of the LaLonde report is that, if we are serious about fostering health and increasing longevity, then we must place far greater weight on the environmental and behavioral determinants of health than we have up to the present.

The idea that one's habitual behavior has consequences for health dates back to ancient times. It was, for example, a concept enshrined in the Hippocratic teachings. Why, then, was more not done to pursue the implications of the idea? Probably a major reason was the lack of any body of well defined procedures for changing behavior. It is in this respect that the principles of learning and behavior change may prove increasingly useful. An emerging area dealing with the application of learning principles to health and disease has been termed *behavioral medicine*. I shall conclude this chapter by discussing the application of learning principles to two of the health problems most frequently encountered in our society today, obesity and cardiovascular disease.

Obesity

Obesity is a major public health problem in the United States and in the entire Western world. Clearly, there is some truth to the old saying that "we dig our graves with a knife and fork." From the perspective of learning principles, obesity may be viewed as the consequence of the maladaptive behavior of overeating. The question then becomes: can we change this maladaptive behavior? Over the past 15 years, much valuable work has been conducted on this question. The four major steps in the behavioral treatment of obesity are clearly described in a 1979 article by Stunkard. They are as follows:

Description of the behavior to be modified. This is the baseline phase and is very important in all behavior interventions. Before we know whether a particular type of behavior has changed or not, it is necessary to know what its level has been prior to treatment. In the case of obese patients, individuals are asked to keep careful records of the food they eat: where?

when? how much? with whom? how did they feel? These records often prove to be surprisingly revealing. People may be surprised at how much they eat and under what circumstances they eat. In what is known as *behavioral analysis*—the diagnostic phase of a behavioral treatment program—there are two main points of focus. First, what are the *antecedent stimuli* which elicit (trigger) the behavior? For example, it may be noted that food advertisements are likely to bring on eating. Second, what are the *consequences* of the behavior? For some individuals, eating may act to reduce anxiety. Information regarding antecedent stimuli leads directly to the second phase of treatment.

Control of stimuli leading to eating. A variety of measures may be directed to this task. The patient is encouraged to limit the amount of high calorie food kept in the house, to stop subscribing to Gourmet Magazine, or to take a route home from work which which does not lead past the delicatessen window. Activities associated with eating are also modified. For example, much eating may have been occurring along with television watching or during reading. The patient is instructed to do all his eating in one place. This reduces the number and potency of stimuli leading to eating.

Changing the behavior of eating. Various techniques are used to make patients aware of the components of eating and to gain control over these components. Patients are encouraged to decrease their speed of eating. Delays in eating are introduced. Patients learn to put down their utensils after every third mouthful until that mouthful has been finished. Then progressively longer delays are introduced. The meal is arranged so that second helpings are difficult to obtain, e.g., a trip from the dining room to the kitchen is required. Additionally, family members are encouraged to compliment the patient on his improved ways of eating.

Modification of the consequences of eating. In the program described by Stunkard, separate reward schedules were established for changes in eating behavior and for weight loss. It appears that rewards for changing behavior were the most potent of the two. An important principle in behavior change is that a reward (reinforcement) should follow quickly after desirable behavior has occurred. This is accomplished through the use of intermediate or *secondary reinforcers*. These are things which are not reinforcing in themselves but, through previous association with primary reinforcers such as food or social approval, have come to be regarded as desirable. A good everyday example would be money. In the case of the obese patients, points are awarded when they engage in adaptive behavior such as: recordkeeping, pausing during the meal, counting chews and swallows, eating in a particular place, and so forth. At a later time, these points, which act to provide immediate reinforcement for desirable behavior, are converted into more tangible rewards such as trips to the movies, relief from household chores, and so forth. Note the parallels with token economies described earlier.

What are the outcome data on this approach? A large number of controlled studies have been carried out which generally testify to the usefulness of the technique and also serve to throw light on the components involved. Patients do indeed shed weight in these programs, and more than with traditional approaches. Yet, at the end of a year, weight loss averages only a few pounds. Stunkard suggests that it may be valuable to combine behavioral approaches with methods employed by self-help groups such as TOPS (Take Off Pounds Sensibly). Behavioral components could be added to the traditional programs made up of inspirational lectures, nutrition counseling, and social pressure. Some promising steps in this direction have already been taken.

Cardiovascular Disease

In the area of cardiovascular disease, several types of behavior have been identified as important risk factors: smoking—as indicated in the Framingham Study and other investigations; obesity and hyperlipidemia—associated with the behavior of overeating; and lack of exercise. Additional nonbehavioral risk factors include presence of diabetes, hypertension, and a family history of heart disease.

In recent years, an additional psychological component has been identified as a risk factor of great significance in coronary artery disease. Known as *Type A* behavior, this factor was brought to light through the investigations of the San Francisco cardiologists Meyer Friedman and Ray Rosenman. They maintain that the individual who is at risk for coronary artery disease exhibits a cluster of related behavioral characteristics. They typify a "high pressure" individual who, oddly enough, corresponds

rather well to the European stereotype of the American businessman. Major characteristics of the Type A individual are an overriding sense of time urgency, an obsession with deadlines, great emphasis on competitive relationships with others which is often accompanied by an element of hostility, an emphasis on quantifiable achievement (e.g., money, votes, publications, depending upon the profession), an emphasis on the quantity of things rather than their quality, and a strong need to feel in control of the situation in which he finds himself. It is the belief of Friedman and Rosenman that Type A individuals can change their behavior and thereby prolong their lives.

An interesting recent example of a large scale program designed to alter behavior related to risk of heart disease was the Stanford Three-Community Study by Farquhar and colleagues. As Stunkard has noted, even though much of the program was not explicitly behavioral, it did in fact mainly grow out of research on behaviorally oriented interventions and was aimed at producing behavior change. Three towns of approximately 14,000 each were involved. Two of the towns were exposed to an intensive media educational campaign about coronary artery disease which involved television and radio spot advertisements, newspaper columns, and posters and billboard advertising, as well as direct mailings over a two year period. In one of the two towns, the media campaign was supplemented by a face-to-face counseling program which was directed at high risk individuals and which was designed to change behavior involving coronary risk factors. One town served as a control and received no campaign.

The results were quite striking, especially among the high risk participants. By the end of the second year, risk of coronary disease had decreased by 17%, as measured by the Cornfield risk index, in the two communities exposed to the media campaign. In the control community, there had actually been an increase of 6%. Even more striking was the change in higher risk individuals who had received face-to-face instruction for whom a decrease of 30% in the risk index occurred. As Stunkard emphasizes, such a decrease in coronary risk is comparable to an increase in life expectancy of five years for someone aged 45. This represents "... a greater increase in life expectancy for middle-aged men than that achieved by all the medical advances which have occurred during the present century." Considering the wide prevalence of cardiovascular disease in Western societies, it would seem that such endeavors in behavioral medicine warrant extensive support.

Suggested Readings

Agras WS: Behavioral medicine. In Freedman AM, Sack RL, Berger PA (eds): *Psychiatry for the Primary Care Physician.* Baltimore, Williams & Wilkins, 1979, p 273.

Basmajian JV: *Biofeedback: Principles and Practice for Clinicians.* Baltimore, Williams & Wilkins, 1979.

Goldstein A, Foa E (eds): *Handbook of Behavioral Interventions: A Clinical Guide.* New York, John Wiley & Sons, 1980.

Green E, Green A: *Beyond Biofeedback.* New York, Delacorte Press, 1977.

Hamburg DA, Elliott GR, Parron DL: *Health and Behavior: Frontiers of Research in the Biobehavioral Sciences.* Washington, DC, Institute of Medicine and National Academy Press, 1982.

Miller NE: Applications of learning and biofeedback to psychiatry and medicine. In Kaplan HI, Freedman AM, Sadock BJ (eds): *Comprehensive Textbook of Psychiatry,* ed 3, vol 1. Baltimore, Williams & Wilkins, 1980, p 468.

Skinner BF: *Beyond Freedom and Dignity.* New York, Alfred A. Knopf, 1971.

Stuart RB (ed): *Adherence, Compliance and Generalization in Behavioral Medicine.* New York, Brunner/Mazel, 1982.

Wolpe J: *The Practice of Behavior Therapy.* New York, Pergamon Press, 1973.

References

Bandura A: *Principles of Behavior Modification.* New York, Rinehart & Winston, 1969.

Budzynski TH, et al: EMG biofeedback and tension headache: a controlled outcome study. *Psychosom Med* 35:484, 1973.

Budzynski TH, Stoyva JM, Peffer KE: Biofeedback techniques in psychosomatic disorders. In Goldstein A, Foa E (eds): *Handbook of Behavioral Interventions: A Clinical Guide.* New York, John Wiley & Sons, 1980, p 186.

Dubos R: *Man Adapting.* New Haven, Yale University Press, 1965.

Farquhar JN, et al: Community education for cardiovascular health. *Lancet* 1:1192, 1977.

Friedman M, Rosenman RH: *Type A Behavior and Your Heart.* New York, Alfred A. Knopf, 1974.

Lalonde M: *A New Perspective on the Health of Canadians.* Ottawa, Canada, Ministry of Health and Welfare, 1974.

LaVallée YJ, et al: Effects of EMG feedback, diazepam and their combination on chronic anxiety. *Psychosom Res* 21:65, 1977.

McKeown T: *The Modern Rise of Population.* New York, Academic Press, 1977.

Passmore J: *The Perfectibility of Man.* New York, Scribner's, 1970.

Russell B: An outline of intellectual rubbish. In Engner RE, Denonn LE (eds) *The Basic Writings of Bertrand Russell.* New York, Simon & Schuster, 1967, p 73.

Sargent JD, Walters ED, Green EE: Psychosomatic self-regulation of migraine headaches. In Birk L (ed) *Biofeedback: Behavioral Medicine.* New York, Grune & Stratton, 1973, p 55.

Stoyva JM: Musculoskeletal and stress-related disorders. In Pomerleau OF, Brady JP (eds): *Behavioral Medicine: Theory and Practice.* Baltimore, Williams & Wilkins, 1979, p 155.

Stoyva JM, Budzynski TH: Cultivated low arousal—an anti-stress response? In DiCara LV (ed): *Recent Advances in Limbic and Autonomic Nervous Systems Research.* New York, Plenum Press, 1974, p 369.

Stunkard AJ: Behavioral medicine and beyond: the example of obesity. In Pomerleau OF, Brady JP (eds): *Behavioral Medicine: Theory and Practice.* Baltimore, Williams & Wilkins, 1979, p 279.

Taub E, Emurian C: Feedback-aided self-regulation of skin temperature with a single feedback locus. I. Acquisition and reversal training. *Biofeedback Self Regul* 1:147, 1976.

Townsend RE, House JF, Addario D: A comparison of biofeedback-mediated relaxation and group therapy in the treatment of chronic anxiety. *Am J Psychiatry* 132:598, 1975.

Weiss T, Engel BT: Operant conditioning of heart rate in patients with premature ventricular contractions. In Birk L (ed): *Biofeedback: Behavioral Medicine.* New York, Grune & Stratton, 1973, p 79.

Section P/The Major Mental Disorders of Childhood and Adolescence

CHAPTER 56 **The Syndrome of Mental Retardation**

Herbert Pardes, M.D.

THE TRAGEDY OF RETARDATION

In this chapter, I would like to focus on a specific group of illnesses, illnesses that for many people and many families can represent a potentially most devastating crisis. This is the syndrome of mental retardation. Perhaps I can illustrate this with a case history. A few years ago I began seeing a young man who had come to treatment for a variety of problems. The primary ones included an absolute inability to have any social contact with women, and a preoccupation with repetitive thoughts which frequently interfered with his ability to work and to study. Over a period of time the man made substantial changes, and eventually he married. He had shown considerable improvement in his professional work, and he was generally advancing rather nicely when the couple had their first child. At this point, tragedy struck. Actually this was not a tragedy that arose suddenly, but one that came on in stages.

Their child did not show the customary developmental landmarks that would be expected. They found that the child could not hold his head up, and was not responding as their friends' children were. Then the child began to develop seizures, and the parents resorted to all sorts of explanations and rationalizations. But these symptoms continued until finally they took the child to a specialist, who had to tell them that the child was mentally retarded and furthermore, that it was a case of rather profound mental retardation. Now what does this mean? Well, it means that the wife was staying home with a small child who could not respond or control himself, who wanted constant attention, but who offered nothing in the way of any response to the parents. The child could not show any progressive development, could not give the usual pleasure to the parents of seeing him master certain tasks. The child just lay there as a very substantial burden on this mother. As a result the mother became increasingly upset and irritable with the husband. The husband, who had begun to develop a rather substantial sense of confidence, who was doing rather well in his work, and who felt rather positive and optimistic about his developing family life, began to reexperience his old devalued self-image.

The inevitable solution was suggested that they should send the child to an institution. By this time, however, the child was about a year and half to two years old, and regardless of the lack of response, the mother did not want to give up the child. It was very difficult for her to conceive of sending this little baby whom she had nurtured day by day for almost two years to some cold, impersonal institution. But as long as the child remained at home, the husband and the wife thought of everything from divorce to suicide to infanticide. This then is the problem

619

of mental retardation, and as one can see, it is not merely a problem which affects the mentally retarded individual, but really involves the entire family. For example, the retardation of this child had effects not only on the parents, but also on the rest of the family, on the grandparents, and the uncles and the aunts. Incidentally, the article by Leo Kanner listed under the suggested readings is particularly interesting in terms of the various kinds of parental responses and reactions to the birth of a retarded child.

DEFINITION OF MENTAL RETARDATION

What is mental retardation? Mental retardation is a syndrome, in other words, a constellation of symptoms. The most commonly used clinical definition includes the following requirements: first, that there is significant impairment in intellectual functioning; second, that there is a similar impairment in adaptive behavior; third, that these be concurrent (in other words both the intellectual impairment and the impairment in general adaptation should exist at the same time); and fourth, that the onset of these clinical manifestations takes place before the age of 18. This syndrome is not an etiological entity. As we will see, many different causative factors have been identified. Most clinicians agree that mental retardation should not be diagnosed unless the I.Q. is at least two standard deviations below the mean; in other words, below approximately 70.

THE MEASUREMENT OF INTELLIGENCE

I want to say a few words about intelligence generally. If one talks in terms of an individual, in contrast to a cultural or racial group, then genetic influence can have a substantial effect on the level of intelligence for a given individual. For example, monozygotic twins will tend to show a much higher degree of concordance for their general level of intelligence than will dizygotic twins. But many, many environmental factors are also important when one looks at the level of intelligence for any individual. For example, there was one study done with children who were adopted, and although the children's intelligence levels tended to correlate very highly with those of their natural parents, there

was still a substantial modification of their intelligence level, depending upon the nature of the adoptive family's home. If the environment tended to be particularly stimulating, then the individual's intelligence level would tend to be somewhat on the high side in comparison with his or her natural parents, and vice versa if the environment to which the child had been adopted was rather unstimulating and did not encourage intellectual growth.

Other factors can affect intelligence and certainly the measurement of intelligence. The particular emotional state of an individual will have a substantial impact on the level of intelligence. If an individual develops a mental illness, this will very definitely have a negative impact on the level of intelligence. The nature of the person's formal education will have an impact on intelligence. Also, with regard to the specific testing of intelligence, the motivations of the child or adult at any particular point will have substantial impact on the tested intelligence. In addition, most I.Q. tests are not free of the impact of cultural background, and they are often biased in favor of the middle class white population. As a result there is a search for culture-free tests, and more recently for culture-specific tests.

It might be interesting to take a moment and look at one of these culture-specific tests, the Dove Counterbalance Intelligence Test, developed by Adrian Dove. Take this test yourself right now, and see how many of the questions you can answer. The answers are listed at the conclusion of the test. I dare say that most people raised in a conventional white middle class background would do just as poorly on this test as someone from a ghetto might do on some of the middle class-biased I.Q. tests (Table 56.1).

THE CLASSIFICATION OF MENTAL RETARDATION

The classification of retardation has traditionally been on the basis of the general level of intelligence, with descriptors dividing the levels of retardation as borderline, mild, moderate, severe, and profound. The American Psychiatric Association uses these terms as follows: *borderline* (I.Q. 71 to 84); *mild* (I.Q. 50 to 70); *moderate* (I.Q. 35 to 49); *severe* (I.Q. 20 to 34); and *profound* (I.Q. below 20). The same terms and criteria are used by the World Health Organization (see Table 56.2).

Table 56.1
The Dove Counterbalance Intelligence Test*

1. "T-Bone Walker" got famous for playing what?
   (a) Trombone   (b) Piano   (c) "T-Flute"   (d) Guitar   (e) "Hambone"
2. Whom did "Stagger Lee" kill (in the famous blues legend)?
   (a) His mother   (b) Frankie   (c) Johnny   (d) His girl friend   (e) Billy
3. A "Gas Head" is a person who has a
   (a) Fast moving car   (b) Stable of "lace"   (c) Process   (d) Habit of stealing cars   (e) Long jail record for arson
4. If a man is called a "Blood," then he is a
   (a) Fighter   (b) Mexican-American   (c) Negro   (d) Hungry Hemophile   (e) Redman or Indian
5. If they throw the dice and "7" is showing on the top, what is facing down?
   (a) "Seven"   (b) "Snake eyes"   (c) "Boxcars"   (d) "Little Joes"   (e) "Eleven"
6. Jazz pianist Ahmad Jamal took an Arabic name after becoming really famous. Previously he had some fame with what he called his "slave name." What was his previous name?
   (a) Willie Lee Jackson   (b) LeRoi Jones   (c) Wilbur McDougal   (d) Fritz Jones   (e) Andy Johnson
7. In "C.C. Rider," what does "C.C." stand for?
   (a) Civil Service   (b) Church Council   (c) County Circuit, Preacher of an old-time rambler   (d) Country Club   (e) "Cheating Charley" (the "Boxcar Gunsel")
8. Cheap "chitlings" (not the kind you purchase at the frozen-food counter) will taste rubbery unless they are cooked long enough. How soon can you quit cooking them to eat and enjoy them?
   (a) 15 minutes   (b) 2 hours   (c) 24 hours   (d) 1 week (on a low flame)   (e) 1 hour
9. "Down Home" (the South) today, for the average "Soul Brother" who is picking cotton (in season from sunup until sundown), what is the average earning (take home) for one full day?
   (a) $0.75   (b) $1.65   (c) $3.50   (d) $5.00   (e) $12.00
10. If a judge finds you guilty of "holding weed" (in California), what's the most he can give you?
    (a) Indeterminate (life)   (b) A nickel   (c) A dime to call your lawyer   (d) A year in county   (e) $100.00
11. "Bird" or "Yardbird" was the "jacket" that jazz lovers from coast to coast hung on
    (a) Lester Young   (b) Peggy Lee   (c) Benny Goodman   (d) Charlie Parker   (e) "Birdman of Alcatraz"
12. A "Hype" is a person who
    (a) Always says he feels sickly   (b) Has water on the brain   (c) Uses heroin   (d) Is always ripping and running   (e) Is always sick
13. Mattie Mae Johnson is on the county. She has four children and her husband is now in jail for non-support, as he was unemployed and was not able to give her any money. Her welfare check is now $286.00 per month. Last night she went out with the biggest player in town. If she got pregnant, then nine months from now how much more will her welfare check be?
    (a) $80.00   (b) $50.00   (c) $35.00   (d) $150.00   (e) $100.00
14. "Hully Gully" came from
    (a) "East Oakland"   (b) Fillmore   (c) Watts   (d) Harlem   (e) Motor City
15. What is Willie Mays' last name?
    (a) Schwartz   (b) Matauda   (c) Gomez   (d) Turner   (e) O'Flaherty
16. The opposite of square is
    (a) Round   (b) Up   (c) Down   (d) Hip   (e) Lame
17. Do "The Beatles" have soul?
    (a) Yes   (b) No   (c) Gee Whiz, or maybe
18. A "Hankerchief Head" is
    (a) A cool cat   (b) A porter   (c) An "Uncle Tom"   (d) A hoddi   (e) A "preacher"
19. What are the "Dixie Hummingbirds"?
    (a) A part of the KKK   (b) A swamp disease   (c) a modern Gospel group   (d) A Mississippi Negro, para-military strike force
20. "Jet" is
    (a) An "East Oakland" motorcycle club   (b) One of the gangs in *West Side Story*   (c) A news and gossip magazine   (d) A way of life for the very rich

For 21–24, fill in the missing word or words that sound best.
21. "Tell it like it
    (a) Thinks I am"   (b) Baby"   (c) Try"   (d) is"   (e) Y'all"
22. "You've got to get up early in the morning if you want to
    (a) Catch the worms"   (b) Be healthy, wealthy, and wise"   (c) Try to fool me"   (d) Fare Well"   (e) Be the first one on the street"

Table 56.1 (continued)
The Dove Counterbalance Intelligence Test

23. "Walk together, children,
    (a) Don't you get weary—there's a great camp meeting"   (b) For we shall overcome"   (c) For the family that walks together talks together"   (d) By your patience you will win your souls" (Luke 21:19)   (e) Find the things that are above, not the things that are on Earth" (Cor. 3:3)
24. "Money don't get everything, it's true
    (a) But I don't have none and I'm so blue"   (b) But what it don't get I can't use"   (c) So make with what you've got"   (d) But I don't know that and neither do you"
25. "Bo-Didley" is a
    (a) Camp for children   (b) Cheap wine   (c) Singer   (d) New dance   (e) Mojo call
26. Which word is most out of place here?
    (a) Splib   (b) Blood   (c) Gray   (d) Spook   (e) Black
27. How much does a "short-dog" cost?
    (a) $0.15   (b) $2.00   (c) $0.35   (d) $0.05   (e) $0.86 + tax
28. True or False: A "Pimp" is also a young man who lies around all day.
    (a) True   (b) False
29. If a Pimp is up-tight with a woman who gets California State aid, what does he mean when he talks about "Mother's Day"?
    (a) Second Sunday in May   (b) Third Sunday in June   (c) First of every month   (d) None of these   (e) First and Fifteenth of every month
30. Many people say that "Juneteenth" (June 19) should be made a legal holiday because this was the day when
    (a) The slaves were freed in Jamaica   (b) The slaves were freed in California   (c) Martin Luther King was born   (d) Booker T. Washington died   (e) The slaves were freed in Texas

Answers:

1. d	7. c	13. c	19. c	25. c
2. e	8. c	14. c	20. c	26. c
3. c	9. d	15. b	21. d	27. c
4. c	10. c	16. d	22. c	28. a
5. a	11. d	17. b	23. a	29. c
6. d	12. c	18. c	24. b	30. b

* By Adrian Dove. From *The Psychology of Black Language* by J. Haskins and H.F. Butts, M.D. Copyright 1973 by J. Haskins and H.F. Butts, M.D. (By permission of Harper & Row. Barnes & Noble.)

About 8% of the overtly diagnosed mentally retarded are so severely impaired as to require constant care for survival, because they cannot distinguish between safety and danger. A larger proportion, approximately 12%, is capable of making such distinctions but fail when daily tasks require symbolic communication, in other words reading, writing, and arithmetic. In educational terms this group is usually described as the *trainable group*. The larger segment of the retarded population, about 80%, can acquire certain basic skills in symbolic communication. This group would encounter major difficulties only when called upon to think abstractly or to make rather complex judgments, and in educational terms this group has been referred to as the *educable group*.

Since the second requirement of the definition of mental retardation concerns impairment in general adapation, and there are not any specific tests which can measure this criterion very accurately, a critical clinical task involves the assessment of general adaptation. This becomes important because very frequently it is poor adaptation that raises the question of possible retardation rather than the results of any intelligence test. The third requirement of the definition deals with the problem posed by the fact that there are many individuals who show poor adaptation despite high intelligence, and others who do very well socially despite relatively low intellectual endowment. Thus, the admonition is made not to diagnose members of either of these groups as being retarded. The impairment in intelligence and adaptation should be concurrent. Finally, mental retardation is a developmental aberration, and hence the onset should be during the developmental years. This is what leads to the fourth criterion, i.e., that this syndrome should develop before age 18.

Table 56.2

Developmental Characteristics of the Mentally Retarded*

This table integrates chronological age, degree of retardation, and level of intellectual, vocational, and social functioning.

Degree of Mental Retardation	Preschool Age 0–5 Maturation and Development	School Age 6–20 Training and Education	Adult 21 and over Social and Vocational Adequacy
Profound	Gross retardation; minimal capacity for functioning in sensorimotor areas; needs nursing care	Some motor development present; may respond to minimal or limited training in self-help	Some motor and speech development; may achieve very limited self-care; needs nursing care
Severe	Poor motor development; speech minimal; generally unable to profit from training in self-help; little or no communication skills	Can talk or learn to communicate; can be trained in elemental health habits; profits from systematic habit training	May contribute partially to self-maintenance under complete supervision; can develop self-protection skills to a minimal useful level in controlled environment
Moderate	Can talk or learn to communicate; poor social awareness; fair motor development; profits from training in self-help; can be managed with moderate supervision	Can profit from training in social and occupational skills; unlikely to progress beyond 2nd grade level in academic subjects; may learn to travel alone in familiar places	May achieve self-maintenance in unskilled or semiskilled work under sheltered conditions; needs supervision and guidance when under mild social or economic stress
Mild	Can develop social and communication skills, minimal retardation in sensorimotor areas; often not distinguished from normal until later age	Can learn academic skills up to approximately 6th grade level by late teens; can be guided toward social conformity	Can usually achieve social and vocational skills; adequate to minimum self-support but may need guidance and assistance when under unusual social or economic stress

* Reprinted from *Comprehensive Textbook of Psychiatry*, ed. 2. A.M. Freedman, H.I. Kaplan, and B.J. Sadock, editors. Williams & Wilkins, Baltimore, 1975. Published by permission.

Since there are many social role requirements before school entrance and during adult life that can be performed with a degree of intelligence considerably lower than the average, many preschool children and even adults with I.Q.'s between 50 and 70 are often not suspected of being mentally retarded. The correlation between intelligence and adapation is highest during the school years because if it does anything, the I.Q. does tend to predict academic performance, and adequate learning is our society's most important expectation of school age individuals. About 3% of the United States' population, in other words between six to seven million people, score below 70% on the customary I.Q. tests. However, about two-thirds of these people are not considered clinically retarded because their adaptation is adequate. There is also a clear trend regarding sex distribution in retardation. Males predominate in ratio of something like 65 to 35. Aside from the basic problems of the retardation, the mentally retarded are highly vulnerable to a variety of superimposed handicaps both physical and psychological in nature.

THE CLINICAL AND SOCIOCULTURAL GROUPS

The mentally retarded can be separated into two distinct groups when one talks in terms of causation. The first constitutes the so-called *clinical types* and the second, the *socioculturally retarded*. This last group, the socioculturally retarded, is referred to as mental retardation associated with psychosocial disadvantage.

In the clinical types the impairment is generally either moderate or profound. This type of retardation is not social class related, and usually somatic or laboratory findings will indicate some degree of organic involvement. On the other hand, sociocultural retardation is highly social class dependent. A rough estimate is that in the United States about 25% of the retarded group are in the clinical category, while some 75% are in the sociocultural group. Sociocultural retardation is usually not diagnosed until school entrance. Retardation tends to be mild in this group, with I.Q.'s ranging between 50 and 70, and there are usually no readily demonstrable physical signs or pathognomonic laboratory tests. Recent observations have called attention to the fact that many children and adolescents who function at the retarded level in the classroom perform quite adequately in their customary social milieu. The families of the socioculturally retarded often do not detect major differences in the performance of these children, and it is only when the school system encounters the children that psychometric tests are arranged which then tend to confirm the diagnosis.

ETIOLOGICAL FACTORS

Focusing more carefully on some of the etiological factors, one finds that they are legion. But most distressing is that fact that it is only in the 25% of cases that constitute the clinical group that one can find a definitive, biomedical, etiological factor. Most of the mentally retarded are in the mildly retarded sociocultural group, and among these, socioeconomic, nutritional, and environmental factors appear to play a major etiological role. Unfortunately, such factors are often very difficult to define.

Clinical Group

With regard to the specific factors, I am not going to try to cover them all, but I will try to focus on some of the key ones. First of all, there are the *prenatal infections*, and the major ones are rubella (German measles) and syphilis. There has been a rubella vaccine available for several years, and this is being administered to children under the age of 10 so that in time all girls will be immunized before they reach childbearing age. Unfortunately, syphilis, which had been under relatively good control, is again reaching epidemic proportions, and the number of cases of congenital syphilis with secondary mental retardation has been increasing. Furthermore, many newly trained doctors do not think of syphilis nor do they know how to diagnose it clinically.

There are a variety of other factors such as *postnatal cerebral infections, trauma,* and *intox-*

ication. For example, heavy maternal alcoholic consumption during pregnancy can cause *fetal alcohol syndrome* (FAS) which includes a variety of anomalies of the skull, face, and limbs along with mental retardation and retarded growth. The precise mechanism is unknown, but it is likely the result of the direct effect of alcohol on the fetus. It is not known what minimum level of alcohol ingestion is necessary to produce the syndrome. Six drinks per day significantly increases the risk to the fetus, and one study showed that two ounces of alcohol (four to five drinks) resulted in a 12% incidence of FAS. Indeed, some authorities do not consider any alcohol consumption during pregnancy to be safe. While not yet fully understood, FAS is suspected by some investigators to be a relatively frequent cause of mental retardation. I would also like to focus briefly on *galactosemia*, which is one of the *metabolic* causes of retardation. This is carried by an autosomal recessive gene, and in this disease entity, the newborn is unable to tolerate milk because he cannot metabolize the galactose that is a breakdown product of the lactose in milk. The galactose is then deposited in the eyes, in the liver, and in the central nervous system, producing cataracts, cirrhosis of the liver, and mental retardation. If a galactose-free diet is instituted early, it allows for normal physical and mental development.

Another metabolic cause of retardation of some note is one of the amino acid disorders, *phenylketonuria* (PKU). Phenylketonuria is also transmitted as an autosomal recessive gene, and involves a deficiency in the liver phenylalanine hydroxylating system. Kaufman has elegantly described a variety of molecular sites which can produce such a deficiency. The findings of various sites account for the fact that there have been different clinical responses of the patients afflicted with this disease when therapeutic attempts have been made. Compulsory screening of all newborn babies is now required in over 40 states, and this has resulted in the early identification of a number of such affected children. However, tests done before discharge from the hospital, in other words prior to about three days of age, fail to identify some of the infants who have a late rise in the phenylalanine. Untreated children are frequently, but not always, retarded. They may also exhibit hyperkinetic features, autistic behavior, seizures, and other relatively characteristic findings. These include a tendency to be light skinned and light haired, the presence of eczema, and the emission of a relatively characteristic odor. The low phenylalanine diet necessary to control this disorder is usually continued until about five years of age, but there is some question as to whether the diet should be continued after that age. Although elevated phenylalanines may not have a particular effect on the adult, their effect on the developing fetal brain in a pregnant woman and on other developing organs can be devastating. Children of PKU mothers who are untreated during their pregnancies are retarded in 100% of the cases, and therefore this has been used as an argument for the continuation of the diet in such affected women. Also, it has been suggested that routine tests be done for any woman who has had more than one retarded child or more than one child with a learning problem. The children of an affected individual will be PKU carriers, and the risk that they will actually have PKU is about 1 in 100.

I would like to move on to one of the prominent *chromosomal* causes of mental retardation, and that is *Down's syndrome*. This is the single most common clinical, etiological entity in mental retardation. Down's syndrome is equated with what has been called *mongolism*. At one point this entity accounted for about 15% to 20% of the institutionally mentally retarded. Although there is no single clinical finding that is pathognomonic, there are many associated abnormalities including poor muscle tone (hypotonia), epicanthal folds, slanting of the eyes, small or low set ears, a short neck, a single palm crease with fingers that are short and curved inward, and a protruding tongue (Figure 56.1). Mental retardation is present in every case, and usually the intellectual or I.Q. level is about 30 to 50; in other words, moderate to severe intellectual impairment. Approximately 40% of these children will have congenital cardiac defects, and GI tract anomalies are also not uncommon.

Pathologically there is accumulating evidence that patients with Down's syndrome suffer a decline in brain activity with age. Many autopsied brains of older Down's syndrome patients show the degeneration of nerve cells and reduced enzyme activity that characterize Alzheimer's disease. Research using positron emission tomography (PET Scan) shows 30–40% increased use of brain glucose in young adult Down's syndrome patients compared to normals. This suggests the disorder may be associated with an alteration of brain metabolism. As the patient

Figure 56.1. Child with Down's syndrome (mongolism), with characteristic facial features, thickened tongue, and curved fingers. From the film *Somebody Waiting*. (By permission of University of California Extension Media Center, Berkeley, California, 94720.)

with Down's syndrome gets older, recent findings suggest that brain glucose use declines.

Much is known about the genetics of Down's syndrome. The most frequent genetic defect in Down's syndrome is *trisomy 21*, which means that there are three 21 chromosomes rather than the usual two. This defect occurs in about 1 in 700 births, but what is of particular importance is that the likelihood is markedly increased in women over age 35. By monitoring all pregnancies occurring in women over 35, it would be possible to identify approximately 1700 Down's syndrome fetuses prenatally every year. (The total number of Down's babies is about five or six thousand per year in this country.) At the very least, diagnosis should be made as soon after birth as possible. A chromosome analysis is recommended whenever Down's syndrome is suspected, both to confirm the diagnosis and to identify those babies who have the other genetic defect which frequently can cause Down's syndrome, that of *translocation*. Once having had a baby with trisomy 21, the risk for the mother having a second such baby is about 1%, and for this reason it is suggested that *amniocentesis* (evaluation of the amniotic fluid) be done in future pregnancies.

The second genetic defect I referred to, translocation, does not involve an additional chromosome, but rather there is a fusion between two chromosomes, especially chromosomes 21 and 15. Physically and mentally these children are identical to those with trisomy 21, but approximately one-third of these translocations is inherited, and the remaining two-thirds have arisen de novo in the child with Down's syndrome. Therefore, in contrast to trisomy 21, it is essential to arrange for a chromosome analysis on both parents whenever translocation is suspected. The translocation carrier is physically and mentally normal, but is at risk for having further children with Down's syndrome. If the mother carries translocation, her risk for another child with Down's is 10% to 15%. If the father is the carrier, the risk for another Down's syndrome baby is 4%, and approximately half of his children will be carriers for the translocation although they are not affected. Thus, compared to trisomy 21, the risks are very much higher and the indications for amniocentesis greater.

A recently discovered genetic defect called the *fragile X syndrome* (due to a fragile site at the end of the long arm of the X-chromosome) has also been found to cause mental retardation, particularly in males. Women who carry the fragile X have a 50% risk of bearing a retarded son, and some workers in the field have estimated the incidence of the fragile X syndrome at about one in 1000, a close second to Down's syndrome among the chromosomal causes of mental retardation. Further studies are necessary to determine the exact incidence. The clinical features include large testicles, large ears, elongated face, poor eye contact, speech and language dysfunction, and behavioral problems. Levitas and coworkers have reported a high incidence of autistic behavior among retarded patients with the fragile X syndrome. If this finding is verified by other studies, a subgroup of autistic children may be identified in which there is a specific neurophysiological dysfunction associated with the specific chromosomal anomaly of the fragile X.

Another group of etiological factors related to retardation has to do with *gestational disorders*. These include prematurity, low birth weight, and also at times postmaturity. The one thing I would particularly emphasize here is that an increased incidence of low birth weight infants occurs among lower socioeconomic groups because of greater problems involving poor maternal nutrition, inadequate prenatal care, anemia, and a variety of prenatal illnesses. There are also instances of retardation which arise in conjunction with childhood psychiatric illnesses, particularly some of the early childhood psychoses that will be discussed in the following chapter.

Sociocultural Group

Finally, we have the group referred to as the group of retarded children with psychosocial disadvantage. Three sets of etiological factors have been invoked, but the specific etiology is still an enigma, and this is a subject of considerable discussion and controversy. The first factor that has been suggested involves some genetic factor that has thus far remained unidentified. This is related to the very controversial question of the relationship between genetics and intelligence. At this point, one can only say that while polygenic inheritance may play a role in the general distribution of intelligence and in the production of certain brilliant individuals, its contribution to the phenomenon of sociocultural retardation is not demonstrable. Hypotheses of this nature have led to assumptions of a decreased intellectual endowment or cognitive capacity in different economic, social, or racial groups, but there is no substantive evidence to support these assumptions.

The second set of proposed factors involves noninheritable, environmental, somatic factors. The mothers of socioculturally retarded children usually have high levels of prematurity (in fact, probably about twice the national average), relatively poor prenatal care, poor nutrition, and poor general health care. As a result, these children are often exposed to a variety of noxious agents such as infections, traumata, and intoxications. It is reasonable to assume that the cumulative effects of organic insults to the nervous system result in minute but important consequences which, though not ascertainable by physical examination, do become manifest as an impairment of intellectual performance and general adaptation. Thus, this group of factors may play some role in the development of such retardation.

Finally, the third set of factors involves early childhood rearing experiences. These children are frequently unwanted, unplanned, and conceived accidentally. They are often raised in broken homes with absent fathers and with emotionally and physically unavailable mothers. They spend much of their infancy and early childhood unattended. Most people in the field assign the greatest etiological role to these early experiential factors and a somewhat lesser role to the noninheritable, environmental, somatic factors.

There is one last point to be made about diagnosis. Generally speaking, the younger the age at which the diagnosis of retardation is made, the more severe the degree of retardation and the more likely it is that a specific etiological factor can be isolated.

GENETIC COUNSELING

I would like to say a few words about genetic counseling. As a result both of the control of infections and the greater recognition of genetic disorders, an increasing proportion of childhood mortality is now attributed to genetic disorders. For example, chromosome abnormalities are present in about 1% to 2% of all newborns. (Estimates suggest that actually 4% of all conceptions are chromosomally abnormal, but many of these are spontaneously aborted.) A technique of particular importance in genetic counseling is amniocentesis. This involves an examination of the amniotic fluid, especially in the early part of the second trimester. In this process there is an examination of amniotic cells to explore the possibility of genetic abnormalities or the presence of a hereditary disease. It is especially useful for mothers of all ages who have had a previous child with Down's syndrome and, as I mentioned earlier, for older mothers who have increased chances of having a Down's baby. Usually one cannot get the cells until about the 16th week and in fact, in order to do the process, it at times requires a repeat examination at the 20th week. Rapid expansion of facilities for amniocentesis could lead to quick returns in the prevention of Down's syndrome. If made available for all pregnant women of 35 years or more who desire it, probably more than 1000 cases of Down's syndrome could be prevented each year. And a new research technique, chorion biopsy, may soon enable even earlier examination of the condition of the fetus. Certainly more active genetic counseling can play a large role in reducing the incidence of mental retardation. Currently, only about 5% of families of the retarded ever receive genetic counseling.

Genetic counseling, of course, is preventive.

Many things, however, can be done for a retarded child of a therapeutic and rehabilitative nature. Of great help in the improvement of care for the mentally retarded has been the establishment of special education classes in the public schools for both educable and trainable children. Whereas, in the past it was not unusual for a mentally retarded youngster to be institutionalized purely for educational reasons, this indication for admission has tended to disappear. Recently there have been specific services designed to improve the intellectual capacity of the mentally retarded, as well as attempts to place the mentally retarded in larger groups whenever possible to augment the possibility of socialization and normalization for them. Also of critical import is the therapeutic work done with the family, since retardation in one child has enormous impact on the other members of the family.

Let me emphasize in closing that mentally retarded children are not simply to be thought of in a homogeneous way. They are individuals with a specific illness and a specific difficulty, just like any other patient, and if we think of them in that way and if we focus on working very intensively with them, they can often make substantial progress in treatment.

Suggested Readings

Cytryn L, Lourie RS: Mental retardation. In Kaplan HI, Freedman AM, Sadock BJ (eds): *Comprehensive Textbook of Psychiatry*, ed 3, vol 3. Baltimore, Williams & Wilkins Co, 1980, p 2484.

Davis JC: Decisions about reproduction: genetic counseling. In Notman MT, Nadelson CC (eds): *The Women Patient. Volume 1: Sexual and Reproductive Aspects of Women's Health Care*. New York, Plenum Press, 1978, p 33.

Hall JE: Sexuality and the mentally retarded person. In Green R (ed): *Human Sexuality: A Health Practitioner's Text*, ed 2. Baltimore, Williams & Wilkins, 1979, p 164.

Kanner L: Parents' feelings about retarded children. In Harrison SI, McDermott JF (eds): *Childhood Psychopathology*. New York, International Universities Press, 1972, p 761.

Reissman F: The hidden I.Q. In Harrison SI, McDermott JF (eds): *Childhood Psychopathology*. New York, International Universities Press, 1972, p 744.

Thomas A, Sillen S: The genetic fallacy. In *Racism and Psychiatry*. New York, Brunner/Mazel, 1972, p 23.

References

Hagerman RJ, McBogg PM (eds): *The Fragile X Syndrome*. Dillon, CO, Spectra Publishing Co, 1983.

Kaufman S, et al: Hyperphenylaianinemia due to a deficiency of biopterin *N Engl J Med* 299: 673, 1978.

Levitas A, et al: Autism and the fragile X syndrome. *Develop Behavioral Pediatrics* 4:151, 1983.

Streissguth AP, et al: Teratogenic effects of alcohol in humans and laboratory animals. *Science* 209:353, 1980.

CHAPTER 57

The Pervasive Developmental Disorders of Childhood

Adolph E. Christ, M.D. and
Gordon K. Farley, M.D.

At the turn of this century, severely deviant children were diagnosed as either retarded or brain damaged and often consigned to a life in an institution. In 1906 Professor Sante de Sanctis first referred to *childhood psychosis*. He identified a number of children who seemed to have normal development up until the sudden onset of the disorder, which was characterized by intellectual deterioration, sudden and unexplained panic attacks, constricted or inappropriate affect, uncontrollable and unprovoked outbursts of rage, resistance to change in the environment, fixed postures and peculiar hand movements, abnormalities of speech such as echolalia (repetition of the words of others), and self-mutilation. In an amazingly modern sounding paper, he struggled with the differentiation between mental retardation and central nervous system disease, stating that some cases of severe childhood psychopathology were neither one but rather were more like dementia praecox (which was later renamed schizophrenia). In 1919, Lightener Witmer, who established the first child guidance clinic in the United States in Philadelphia in 1896, described the successful treatment of a two and a half year old child suffering from what we would now call infantile autism. As late as 1937, Lutz reviewed the world literature on childhood schizophrenia, and concluded that only 14 of the by then 60 reported cases of childhood schizophrenia, with onset before age 10, were unequivocal examples of this disease. Thus, the symptoms of these children have defied easy recognition and classification, perhaps in part because it is so difficult for all of us to accept the profound and pervasive disruption of functioning that occurs in these children.

THE PARADOXICAL SYMPTOMS OF PSYCHOTIC CHILDREN

The symptoms of psychotic children are strange, often frightening, and full of paradoxes.

The following are examples of actual cases, all patients of one of the authors (A. E. Christ). A child may be unresponsive to the approach of a child or an adult. Suddenly, this same child may viciously attack the shunned person. Occasionally, a microscopic look at the antecedents of the behavior may show the reason. It may have been precipitated by the adult sharing a moment of tenderness with another child. A child who usually appears very dull may at moments exhibit amazing intelligence and even cunning. For example, one young boy was fearful of stepping from the linoleum to the wooden part of the floor, yet he would stack chairs on a table and fearlessly walk on the edge of the top chair. Another boy sustained first and second degree burns when he bumped into a steam pipe, yet did not give evidence of being in pain. Several days later, however, he cried in pain when his forearm was lightly scratched. Joy and pleasure are not usually seen in these children, and yet, gleeful sadomasochistic laughter may suddenly erupt. The sadomasochistic outbursts can result in violent self-injury, as in the case of Robert, who, after knocking out several of his teeth quite purposefully on a table and repeatedly hitting his head on a wall, was finally fitted with a specially designed football helmet. More frequently, these children will slap their faces, even to the point of causing permanent injury. One young girl was idiot-like in her total lack of intellectual competence, yet was able to multiply two three-digit numbers in her head in 10 seconds, never erring. One boy kept many toys in boxes, never playing with them, but he became panicky if these boxes were opened or moved. He had a small red truck, which he always carried in his hand. He misplaced it on one occasion and screamed in a rage for hours while the entire family looked for the lost truck. Another boy masturbated almost incessantly, anally and genitally, yet looked tense and frantic, never pleased or relaxed. Many of these children spend hours staring vacantly while moving their fingers in front of their eyes. Wilbur was more integrated than many such children, and came to the outpatient clinic twice a week for treatment. He knew every bus schedule in San Francisco. His favorite project was taking a large sheet of paper and making a few tiny, connected lines in an apparently random way on various parts of the sheet. After many hours of such meticulous work, other lines would be added and connected, and eventually an amazingly precise map of San Francisco would emerge.

Stanislaus Szurek, as a result of his extensive work at the Langley Porter Neuropsychiatric Institute in San Francisco with these children and their parents, felt that the psychoses of childhood are part of a continuum with the neuroses, and that these psychotic children simply suffer from earlier, more severe, and more pervasive emotional difficulties than neurotic children. In contrast, Lauretta Bender at Bellevue Hospital in New York City was particularly impressed with the existence of organic factors in the development of childhood psychosis. She concluded that an hereditary predisposition is essential, along with some neurophysiological developmental unevenness, for the development of these severe disorders.

Let us now look at some of the specific subgroups of these disorders, beginning with infantile autism.

INFANTILE AUTISM

In 1943, Leo Kanner described a specific subgroup of these psychotic children who appeared abnormal almost from birth. He highlighted the following features: 1) autism, namely a marked aloneness, a nonresponsiveness to and active avoidance of parents and other adults; 2) severe difficulties in communication; 3) an obsessive insistence on sameness; and 4) a fascination with objects, and not with people. He designated this syndrome *infantile autism*. The following are some examples of children with infantile autism, again all patients of Dr. Christ.

Jim was a seven year old boy who was brought to my office by his mother. A small, slender, attractive boy, he was held by the wrist, his hand dangling limply below his mother's grasp. He walked on his toes, leaning forward as if his center of gravity was six inches in front of him. He never looked directly at me, but rather appeared to be focusing on an area several miles away. Despite this, he seemed bright—not at all vacuous as a retarded child might appear. Once the door was closed, his mother collapsed into a comfortable chair. As though looking with eyes out of the side of his head, he had spotted a light switch to which he ran, and turned it on and off, on and off.

His mother explained that he had a number of these rituals. He would spend hours turning light switches on and off, and in fact he had worn out several at home. He would take magazines, hold them close to his face and fan the edges, perhaps listening to the sound, smelling the newsprint, and feeling the light breeze against his eyes. His mother described another symptom, which I was to experience directly later when I did a home visit. Jim had learned to run the family hi-fi. He had excellent fine motor coordination, and never broke anything. Somehow, he would always pick out one record, whether in its jacket or out, would place it on the turntable, and put the needle on exactly one spot. It was Ferde Grofé's *Grand Canyon Suite*—the spot where the donkey is walking. As soon as that phrase finished, he would put the needle back on the same spot, over and over again, for several hours! Saturday was an especially difficult day. Mother vacuumed the living room, which meant that she had to move Jim's armchair. Jim would have a screaming fit until the chair was replaced, in exactly the same place, with this particular record jacket on it. Another youngster, who was four years old, opened and closed doors, particularly those with magnetic catches. He would lie on the floor, thumb in mouth, head close to the door, and literally spend hours opening and closing the doors, again as if interested in the sound, smelling the door as a whiff came past his nose, or feeling the breeze of the door against his face.

Interest in waterplay is shared by nearly every infantile autistic child. Jim found the washbasin as soon as I stopped his lightswitch play. It had a movable spigot as is found in many hospitals. Jim moved it to one side, turned the water on, and looked at the turning, swirling water. There was a near hypnotic quality to his looking at it, similar to his staring at the turning phonograph records at home. This type of repetitive looking at swirling, turning, spinning records or water would last for 15 or 30 minutes at a time, with these youngsters remaining in what seemed to be a trancelike state.

So far we have looked at some of the repetitive acts, and the interaction of these children with inanimate objects. Both of these are emphasized by Kanner in his 1943 description of these children. What about their relation to animate objects, to people? His parents took Jim and his younger brother to a beach. Jim was very intrigued by the color yellow, anything yellow. While the parents were spreading out the blanket and taking out the picnic lunch, Jim saw a yellow ball fly through the air and land 100 feet away. The shortest distance between two points is a straight line, and this is the one that Jim took. He stepped on people, on lunches, on faces on his way to the desired spot—as if all the people were simply tufts of grass. In the playroom he spotted a yellow box on a shelf behind my chair. He climbed on the chair to get it, quite oblivious of the fact that I was sitting in the chair. His mother apologized, saying that he dealt with people as if they were inanimate things. In fact, if Jim wanted something, he would often take his mother's arm and use it as if it were an extension pole for his personal use.

Jim's mother described how almost from the day he was born, he would fuss whenever he was picked up or cuddled by her, refusing the bottle unless it were propped up without the mother present. She described his body as "curving away" from her each time that she picked him up. There was a profound difference between Jim and his younger brother. The younger brother smiled at three or four months when the mother appeared. He cuddled back when she picked him up, and at six months he clearly was pleased when she or her husband came into his room. By 14 months he would jump with joy when he saw his father drive up in the car after work. These were all new experiences for the parents, because Jim had never done any of these things. As the mother said, "I guess he needed me to get things for him, but I never got the feeling that he needed me as a person, or even that he would be bothered if I suddenly ceased to exist."

This uninvolvement with people can have rather startling effects. During a home visit, Jim's parents took me out to the back yard, which actually resembled a prison. The high wooden fence was topped with another wire fence, and on top of that was another inclined piece of fence. Jim not only had excellent fine motor coordination, but he was also extremely agile. From the time that he could walk, he would wander away from home giving no warning, no evidence of fear of separation from his parents, no apprehension when he was picked up blocks away from home by strangers or the police. As he grew older, the fence in the back yard became higher and higher as the parents tried to contain him, and in this way stop him from his unwelcome wanderings throughout the countryside.

So far we have described the stereotyped and ritualistic behavior, and the relationships to inanimate objects and to people, all of which are abnormal (Figures 57.1 and 57.2). The language of these autistic children is also strange, prompting some to think that there may be a central nervous system defect that affects the speech

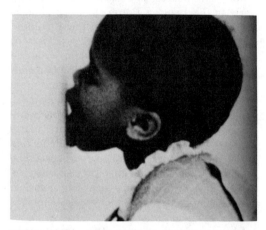

Figure 57.1. A two year old autistic girl engaged in ritualistic behavior. From the film *Looking For Me* by Janet Adler. (By permission of University of California Extension Media Center, Berkeley, California, 94720.)

Figure 57.2. A five year old autistic girl showing stereotyped mannerisms. From the film *Looking For Me* by Janet Adler. (By permission of University of California Extension Media Center, Berkeley, California.)

center predominantly. For example, Jim had no speech. He said two or three words once or twice when he was two years old, but none after that. The prognosis for such children who have no usable speech is very grave indeed, as we will see a little later. Another four year old did have speech, but he never said, "I." His speech was echolalic (he would usually speak by saying that which he had heard being said). If he wanted a cookie, he would say, "Henry want a cookie?" never changing the interrogative to the more appropriate declarative form. The repetition of television commercials is amazingly common with these children. The same television commercial may be repeated while playing alone with objects, with a more anxious tone of voice when a ritual is being interrupted, or with a panicky tone of voice when a physician is about to give a penicillin shot. It is as if the words themselves have no meaning, and the tone of voice may be the only indicator that the child is upset.

We could spend much more time describing the strange and fascinating behavior of autistic children. Let us mention just a few more symptoms that are usually found in youngsters with a diagnosis of infantile autism. One thing that is very puzzling about these children is that, although they may test as retarded, they look very bright, and they often have some unusual capabilities. A seven year old nonverbal child was an inpatient in a hospital. He was never without a string, and with the help of expertly placed saliva, he made the most fantastic "live" sculptures by twirling the string with his thumb and forefinger. No cowboy with a rope ever came close to this boy's whirling dexterity. Another three year old taught himself to read. At five he could read the *New York Times* with few errors. However, he seemed not to understand a single word of what he read.

The amazing memory of some of these children can be maddening. An eight year old was driven to the clinic by his father three times a week. The father took the identical route for a number of weeks. Once, when he took a different turn, the boy screamed and cried inconsolably until the father retraced his steps and continued on the usual route. This kind of memory, combined with an unusual need for the maintenance of sameness, is further exemplified by another example from Jim, the boy I described before. He had always had extraordinary skill in assembling puzzles, but he would turn the puzzles

upside down, so that he did not see the pictures. As part of the routine in the day care unit, Jim met with the occupational therapist every day. Every time a new activity was learned, it had to be added to the end of the list of his previous activities, a list which could not be altered. For example, he would do the two-, then the three-, then the four-, the five-, the eight-, the 12- and the 15-piece puzzle, one after the other in that sequence. Next he would string four different bead patterns, and so on and so on. Every time that the occupational therapist tried to alter the sequence, Jim screamed, cried, and appeared quite inconsolable.

Finally, let us look at the families of these children. Originally, Leo Kanner was impressed with the unusual intellectual competence of the parents of these children. Of the original 11 children that he described in 1943, the number of M.D.'s, Ph.D.'s, and unusually gifted mothers and fathers was far beyond the normal distribution. Several subsequent studies have found discrepancies with Kanner's original findings, particularly in regard to the unusual abilities of the mothers, so that this original sample may have been a biased one. In addition, Kanner was impressed with a somewhat detached, cold, "refrigerator" quality of many of these parents, a finding that was also not substantiated in later studies. The unanswered question of course is how much of this "detached" quality was inherent in the parents and pathogenic, and how much was a reaction to years of stressful living with such a difficult child. In fact, the parents of autistic children have not been found to be different in any specific demonstrable way from the parents of normal children, except for their understandable anxiety and concern for their disturbed child.

As other mental health workers became familiar with these criteria, many of the above symptoms were also seen in children who were severely retarded, brain damaged, deaf, blind, or aphasic. Thus, what started out as possibly a highly specific disease expanded into a group of possibly unrelated disorders. Rimland developed a symptom check list in which a youngster must earn 20 points to be considered as suffering from infantile autism. Over 2,000 of these forms were sent to him by parents who had filled them out, and whose children had been diagnosed as having infantile autism. Rimland found that only about 10% of these children actually fit the diagnosis on the basis of his check list. He quotes

Kanner, who also found that only about 10% of the children sent to him by other physicians with the diagnosis of infantile autism actually fit this syndrome. A particularly interesting study was done by Prior and his coworkers, who asked a computer to come up with the "best classification." The answer was that it may be better to do away with the designation of infantile autism altogether, and simply talk about psychosis in children with early onset before the age of three, where aloneness and withdrawal present as the primary symptoms.

Do you remember the rubella (German measles) epidemic of 1964? It is estimated that 20,000 to 30,000 children were born with congenital malformations secondary to the mothers' having had German measles while pregnant. Stella Chess studied 243 of these children in New York City, and found that about 7% of them had a complete or partial syndrome of autism! This is particularly impressive when you consider that a British study by Totter found the incidence of autism or partial autism to be 4.5 per 10,000 children of the same age, and a Japanese survey by Suwa reported an incidence of 0.52 per 10,000 total population. The congenital German measles group therefore represents at least a 100-fold increase in incidence over the expected! In addition, a rather large number (about 25%) of autistic children develop epilepsy in adolescence, thus again suggesting that central nervous system damage may play an important role in infantile autism.

What happens to these children as they grow up? An interesting study in New South Wales by Harper and Williams separated 131 autistic children into a natal and an acquired group. Twenty-eight per cent had symptoms from birth, 72% before age three. The natal group developed less speech, had more neurological symptoms, had a lower I.Q., and in general showed much more progressive deterioration than the other group.

How about those that do improve and get better? Leo Kanner obtained information on 96 children he himself had diagnosed as having infantile autism. Of these now 23 to 35 year olds, 11 were "mingling, working, and maintaining themselves in society." The rest, about 90%, were not self-sufficient. All of those who improved went through an adolescent period of increasing self-assessment with considerable efforts to fit themselves into the community, regardless of how difficult it might have been for

them to do so. They tried to belong, even after rebuffs because of their strangeness. All had jobs, and many of them had their own cars. Several of them had entered military service, even though most of them had to be discharged medically, usually by the end of one year. Despite these efforts at socialization, none of them had any close personal friendships, nor any interest in sexual involvement with others, nor any thoughts about marriage. Kanner further pointed out that all of these 11 had developed speech before the age of five, and all were raised outside of institutions, but he questioned the specificity of this finding, since many of the other youngsters who were not self-sufficient had also not been institutionalized.

In summary, then, infantile autism is a syndrome originally described by Leo Kanner in 1943, in which the affected children have a severe uninvolvement with people, a peculiar overinvolvement with inanimate objects, an obsessive need for sameness, and an abnormal language development. The onset of symptoms is before the third year of life, with DSM-III specifying onset before 30 months of age. A large number have symptoms from birth. The prognosis is extremely poor, but worse if the symptoms exist at birth, if there are neurological symptoms, if the I.Q. is below 50, if usable speech does not develop by age five, and if there is no effort to change in relation to societal expectations during adolescence. One further point is that there are usually three to four boys to every one girl who develop this syndrome.

CHILDHOOD ONSET PERVASIVE DEVELOPMENTAL DISORDER

Although symbiotic psychosis is not identified as a separate diagnostic entity in DSM-III, children with symbiotic psychosis represent another interesting example of severe developmental deviation and arrest. In 1949 Margaret Mahler described children who, unlike the infantile autistic group, develop fairly normally at first. However, as a result of some event such as the birth of a sibling, or a move to a new house, or some other unsettling occurrence, these children react quite markedly. They become irritable and whiny, and cling excessively to the mother. They panic at even a mild separation, and they begin a frightening and relentlessly deteriorating course, losing speech, developing mannerisms, withdrawing, in short, looking more and more like Kanner's infantile autistic children. Some come out of this early panic state, and continue to develop normally. Others remain in this clinging, easily panicked state, which Mahler referred to as *symbiotic psychosis*. Although quite clearly psychotic, they are not as pathological as the typical infantile autistic children. Mahler became fascinated by this turn of events, and made a major contribution to our understanding of the normal development of children by meticulously studying the transition from the symbiotic to the separation-individuation stages of development. This group of children seems unable to separate from their mothers, and they do not develop a comfortable sense of their own separate identities. The exaggerated panic resulting from any separation is a cardinal feature in these children. The mothers play an equally important part in the illness, and fear separation as much as the children do.

Barbara was such a child, first seen in treatment at age seven. She made very rapid progress, speaking well, developing an active imagination as she played out scenes of separation with the dolls, becoming interested in many new things, and developing a warm relationship with the therapist. Although the mother was seen in treatment herself, and could stay in the playroom or watch through a one-way mirror to minimize her fear of separation from her daughter, her daughter's developing independence was too much for her. The mother became paranoid, convinced that her daughter's therapist was going to kidnap her daughter. When she threatened suicide, her husband insisted that treatment for the child be stopped. "I feel I am choosing between my wife's and my daughter's sanity. For now, I must choose my wife's."

Infantile autism and symbiotic psychosis represent a small but relatively homogeneous group of the totality of children with "childhood schizophrenia" or what is now called *pervasive developmental disorder* in DMS-III. At one time, nearly all of the psychoses of childhood were lumped together under the single classification of "childhood schizophrenia," but gradually various distinct entities have been identified, i.e. infantile autism with onset before 30 months of age, and *childhood onset pervasive developmental disorder* (including symbiotic psychosis) with onset after 30 months of age. Most workers in this area feel that infantile autism and childhood onset pervasive developmental disorder are two different and distinct disease processes with dif-

ferences in age of onset, symptom picture, and prognosis. Although there are many similarities, in childhood onset pervasive developmental disorder the onset is after the age of 30 months, whereas in infantile autism the onset is before 30 months. In childhood onset pervasive developmental disorder one observes islands of relatedness, especially with mothering and fathering figures, but there is a general pattern of withdrawal from others. In infantile autism, especially early in the illness, extreme emotional withdrawal from all humans is seen. Children with childhood onset pervasive developmental disorder usually have some speech which may be bizarre and abnormal but is still used for communication. Autistic children have little speech that is used for communication. Finally, the prognosis in infantile autism is generally poorer than those cases where the onset of the pervasive developmental disorder occurs at a later age.

MENTAL RETARDATION

If psychotic symptoms are a seriously maladaptive reaction to stress, it stands to reason that mentally retarded individuals, who have fewer resources available to deal with stress, will indeed be more vulnerable to all types of emotional disorders, including psychosis. The term *propfschizophrenia* was used to designate retarded individuals who develop a secondary psychosis. The prognosis of these children is much better than for the nonretarded psychotic child. A close working alliance with the parents, along with special schools for the retarded, can help to mobilize support systems to which the child can quickly respond.

John was a 16 year old retarded boy with an I.Q. of 52. He had adjusted well to a special school class for the retarded, and to the vocational rehabilitation classes which he attended. A tall, strong, good-looking boy, he enjoyed walking to the neighborhood supermarket and bagging groceries at the checkout stand. He was proud of the occasional tips that he received. The death of his father altered the whole family balance. John's behavior became quite bizarre. He refused to go to school, literally clinging to his mother and sister when they tried to go to work. He stood in front of the apartment door, barring it so that they could leave only with great difficulty. He telephoned his mother at work every five minutes, crying and screaming.

A few weeks of individual and family therapy, during which the family was able to begin the process of mourning, resulted in a rapid amelioration of John's symptoms, and he returned to his school and to his work in the supermarket.

SCHIZOPHRENIA WITH ONSET IN LATER CHILDHOOD

The "adult" disease of schizophrenia, with Bleuler's primary symptoms of autism, associational difficulties, abnormality of affect, and ambivalence, and the accompanying secondary symptoms of delusions and hallucinations, seems to be a disease different from these pervasive developmental disorders of early childhood. In the adult disease, there is a much higher incidence in the lower socioeconomic classes, with a higher genetic loading, especially on single egg and double egg twin studies. Schizophrenia most often has its onset in adolescence or young adulthood, but there is a growing acceptance that a form of childhood schizophrenia that is similar to the adult form may have an onset at around age 10 to 12. Indeed, the symptoms of the older child may include symptoms of delusions and hallucinations, symptoms which are never found in the younger autistic or severely psychotic child. Thus, the lower social class, the higher genetic loading, the later age of onset, the equal incidence of males and females with later childhood schizophrenia, and the presence of the secondary symptoms of adult schizophrenia in these children are quite different from what is seen in the pervasive developmental disorders of early childhood. The physician is often called upon to make a differentiation between these various entities. Table 57.1 lists some of the major differentiating characteristics between infantile autism, childhood onset pervasive devel-

Table 57.1

Differentiation of the Pervasive Developmental Disorders, Severe Mental Retardation, and Schizophrenia with Onset in Later Childhood *

	Infantile Autism	Childhood Onset Pervasive Developmental Disorder	Severe Mental Retardation	Schizophrenia with Onset in Later Childhood
Age of onset	Before 30 months	After 30 months	From birth	Around age 10 to 12
Sex ratio	Males–females 4 to 1	Males–females 1 to 1	Males–females 2 to 1	Males–females 1 to 1
Motor-muscular landmarks	Normal	Normal	Markedly delayed	Normal or slightly delayed
Relationships with people	Avoidant	Variable	Immature	Variable
Relationships with inanimate objects	Prefers inanimate objects to people	Variable	Normal	Variable
Differentiation of self from environment	Unable to differentiate	Variable	Variable	Variable
Language development	Abnormal	Variable	Markedly delayed	Variable
Delusions and hallucinations	Absent	Absent	Absent	Present in some cases
Clinical course	Usually stable	Variable	Stable	Exacerbations and remissions
Prognosis	Poor	Variable	Poor	Variable
Genetic loading	Suggestive in some cases	Variable	Present in some cases	Present in some cases
Parental factors	Not present	Present in some cases	Not present	Present in some cases
Socioeconomic class	No difference	No difference	No difference	↑ incidence in lower socioeconomic class

* Table by Gordon K. Farley and Richard C. Simons.

opmental disorder, severe mental retardation, and schizophrenia with onset in later childhood.

DISINTEGRATIVE PSYCHOSIS

There are a very few youngsters who have the onset of their severe symptoms between the ages of three and five. Initially, there are symptoms of vague illness, followed by restlessness, irritability, hyperactivity, and anxiety for several weeks. There is then a gradual loss of functions, including loss of speech, loss of ability to comprehend language, a decrease in intellectual functions, loss of social skills, impairment of interpersonal behavior, and a loss of interest in objects. The stereotyped behavior and peculiar mannerisms include many of the symptoms that we have described in autistic children. The prognosis is usually very bad in *disintegrative psychosis*, with very few responding to treatment. There is considerable agreement that this group may actually be responding to some sort of central nervous system degenerative disease. Indeed, Heller's description of *dementia infantilis* in 1930 fits this syndrome. On autopsy, all of the patients that Heller had described were found to have some degree of central nervous system damage. Although ICD-9 (International Classification of Diseases—Ninth Revision) retains this diagnosis, DSM-III lists it as Organic Brain Syndrome with Dementia.

ETIOLOGY OF THE PERVASIVE DEVELOPMENTAL DISORDERS

Central Nervous System Dysfunction Factors

Controversy reigns in the literature about which psychotic children to include in the "organic" group. All workers agree that children with such hard findings on neurological examination as pathological reflexes, motor impairments, and sensory deficits are suffering from a localized brain defect. However, Bender, Goldfarb, and Birch each independently called attention to less localizing findings that could best be summarized as "soft neurological signs." These include autonomic nervous system incoordination, multiple modality incoordination (e.g., hearing, vision, touch), major discrepancies between different intellectual functions (e.g., ver-

bal vs. motor intelligence), incoordination in body movements, speech difficulties, confused laterality, and spatial disorientation. The reason this becomes important is that as excellent a researcher as Goldfarb finds "neurological dysfunction" present in 70% of his series of 40 schizophrenic children, whereas equally careful studies by Szurek of 264 psychotic children found only 17% who were primarily retarded or who had evidence of central nervous system pathology. It is quite probable that these two groups of children were not selected differently, but rather that the 17% vs. 70% neurological dysfunction represents a significantly different interpretation of "soft neurological findings."

Since the advent of computerized axial tomography and a number of other brain imaging techniques, additional knowledge regarding "organic" causes for the pervasive developmental disorders has accumulated. A number of *different* kinds of abnormalities have been found, but no single abnormality has been found in even a majority of children with these disorders. In autistic children, some of the CT scan findings have been: 1) reversed posterior cerebral asymmetry; 2) ventricular dilation asymmetries; 3) unilateral densities; 4) other scan abnormalities. Newer brain imaging techniques such as positron emission tomography (PET scan) and nuclear magnetic resonance (NMR) are just now beginning to be used diagnostically with children with these severe disturbances. Other researchers such as the Wings, Ornitz and Ritvo, the DeMeyers, and Birch and Walker have found a variety of sensory-motor and perceptual disorders in children with pervasive developmental disorder. Boullin, Coleman, and O'Brien found an abnormality of serotonin efflux from blood platelets. Although all these findings are suggestive of an abnormally functioning central nervous system in these children, such causation cannot at this point be considered as proven.

Genetic Factors

Adult schizophrenia is known to occur in families and as Dr. Reite has discussed in Chapter 52, the closer the genetic relationship between the individuals, the higher the concordance for schizophrenia. This genetic factor has been less convincingly demonstrated for the pervasive developmental disorders of childhood. However, in a series of 14 identical twins collected by Rimland, where one twin had infantile autism, 11 of the other 14 twins were also afflicted. The study by Folstein and Rutter has already been described by Dr. Reite in Chapter 52. One fairly recent exciting lead is the demonstration of the fragile X syndrome. In this syndrome a certain behavioral pattern (autistic behavior, mental retardation, hyperactivity) with identifiable physical features (large testicles, unusual facial characteristics, hyperextensible joints) is associated with a typical fragile site on the long arm of the X-chromosome. If a subgroup of autistic children can be identified in which there is a specific neurophysiological dysfunction associated with the specific chromosomal anomaly of the fragile X, this would have great implications for both prevention as well as treatment.

Psychogenic Factors

The issue of parental pathology is probably the most controversial issue in the etiology of the pervasive developmental disorders. Berlin states that most psychopathology in children results from conflictual relations between the parents and the child. Szurek carefully avoids blaming the parents, with attendant guilt and shame, and works instead in psychotherapy with the parents toward an increased self-awareness that hopefully results in an alteration of the pathological family interaction. He underlines the relief the parents experience as they clarify the unconscious origins of these interactions in unresolved conflicts from their own childhoods. In contrast, Rimland feels that " . . . psychogenesis is a . . . pernicious hypothesis . . . " which damages and torments parents.

It does seem that those who have worked most intensively with the parents of psychotic children usually have found rather profound psychopathology in these parents. For example, Jane, during her eight years of hospitalization, exhibited multiple sexual symptoms, including vaginal and rectal masturbation, exhibitionism, and a voyeuristic pulling up of the dresses of the nurses. Her sister exhibited herself in school at age eight. The maternal grandfather had been arrested for molesting minors. Yet the mother, in an extended course of psychotherapy, only twice spontaneously made fleeting references to sexuality! But it must again be stressed that anyone living or working closely with these very disturbed children experiences great stress. In addition, it has not been demonstrated that the parents of these children are different in any

specific way from the parents of normal children. Regardless of the initial reasons for their psychoses, these children bring out severely conflictual feelings in nursing staff, psychiatric residents, and child fellows, as well as all other adults who must work closely with them, and the stress on the parents of these children is enormous.

THE FAMILY PHYSICIAN

Why does a family physician, a pediatrician, a nurse, or a mental health specialist need to know about this group of relatively rare syndromes? Is it not enough to refer any questionable child to a child psychiatrist? As more careful assessment methods of premature, of neonatal, and of young babies are being developed by pediatricians like Dr. Brazelton, and by a growing group of child psychiatrists and psychologists, very early manifestations of abnormal responses are being identified, responses that can take on added significance when compared to the similar symptoms of the severe disturbances described in this chapter. The aim of all work is ultimately toward primary prevention, prevention that may only be possible with very early intervention. The key to this whole approach is that there will be a group of family physicians, of pediatricians, and of mental health workers who can recognize deviations in the very young baby, deviations that will prompt referral for treatment rather than the more usual response of: "He will grow out of it." Without early intervention and treatment, he may not "grow out of it."

Suggested Readings

Bender L: Childhood schizophrenia. In Harrison SI, McDermott JF (eds): *Childhood Psychopathology.* New York, International Universities Press, 1972, p 628.

Ekstein R, Wright DG: The space child. In Harrison SI, McDermott JF (eds): *Childhood Psychopathology.* New York, International Universities Press, 1972, p 710.

Goldfarb W: An investigation of childhood schizophrenia: a retrospective view. In Harrison SI, McDermott JF (eds): *Childhood Psychopathology.* New York, International Universities Press, 1972, p. 688.

Kanner L, Lesser LI: Early infantile autism. In Harrison SI, McDermott JF (eds): *Childhood Psychopathology.* New York, International Universities Press, 1972, p 647.

Mahler MS: On child psychosis and schizophrenia: autistic and symbiotic infantile psychoses. In Harrison SI, McDermott JF (eds): *Childhood Psychopathology.* New York, International Universities Press, 1972, p 670.

Ornitz EM, Ritvo ER: The syndrome of autism: a critical review. *Am J Psychiatry* 133:609, 1976.

References

Bender L: Childhood schizophrenia. *Psychiat Q* 27:663, 1953.

Berlin IN, Christ AE: The unique role of the child psychiatry trainee on an inpatient or daycare unit. In Szurek SA, Berlin IN (eds): *Clinical Studies in Childhood Psychoses*. New York, Brunner/Mazel, 1973, p 163.

Berlin IN, Szurek SA: Parental blame: an obstacle in psychotherapeutic work with schizophrenic children and their families. In Szurek SA, Berlin IN (eds): *Clinical Studies in Childhood Psychoses*. New York, Brunner/Mazel, 1973, p 115.

Bettelheim B: *The Empty Fortress: Infantile Autism and the Birth of the Self*. New York, The Free Press, 1967.

Birch H: The problem of brain damage in children. In Birch H (ed): *Brain Damage in Children: The Biological and Social Aspects*. Baltimore, Williams & Wilkins, 1964, p 3.

Birch H, Walker H: Perceptual and perceptual motor dissociation: studies in schizophrenia and brain-damaged children. *Arch Gen Psychiatry* 14:113, 1966.

Bleuler E: *Dementia Praecox*. New York, International Universities Press, 1950.

Bomberg D, Szurek SA, Etemad JG: A statistical study of a group of psychotic children. In Szurek SA, Berlin IN (eds) *Clinical Studies in Childhood Psychoses*. New York, Brunner/Mazel, 1973, p 303.

Boullin D, Coleman M, O'Brien R: Abnormalities in platelet 5-hydroxytryptamine efflux in patients with infantile autism. *Nature* 226:371, 1970.

Chess S: Autism in children with congenital rubella. *J Autism Child Schizo* 1:33, 1971.

Christ AE: Sexual countertransference problems with the psychotic child. In Szurek SA, Berlin IN (eds): *Clinical Studies in Childhood Psychoses*. New York, Brunner/Mazel, 1973, p 481.

Christ AE, et al: The role of the nurse in child psychiatry. *Nurs Outlook* 13:1, 1965.

Christ AE, Griffiths R: Parent nurse therapeutic contact on a child psychiatry unit. *Am J Orthopsychiatry* 35:589, 1965.

Christ AE, Wagner N: Prevention of iatrogenic factors in child residential treatment. In Masserman J (ed): *Current Psychiatric Therapies*, vol 1. New York, Grune & Stratton, 1966, p 46.

De Myer M, et al: Imitation in autistic, early schizophrenic, and non-psychotic subnormal children. *J Autism Child Schizo.* 2:264, 1972.

de Sanctis S: Sopra alcune varieta della demenza precoce. Rivista Sperimentale di Freniatria 32:141, 1906. Translation by Mary Jeffress, M.S.W. In Szurek SA, Berlin IN (eds): *Clinical Studies in Childhood Psychoses*. New York, Brunner/Mazel, 1973, p 31.

Goldfarb W: *Childhood Schizophrenia*. Cambridge, Harvard University Press, 1961.

Harper J, Williams AS: Age and type of onset as critical variables in early infantile autism. *J Autism Child Schizo* 5:1, 1975.

Heller T: About dementia infantilis. *Z Kinderforsch* 37:661, 1930. Reprinted under Hulse WC: Dementia infantilis. *J Nerv Ment Dis* 119:471, 1954.

Howells JG, Guirguis WR: Childhood schizophrenia 20 years later. *Arch Gen Psychiatry* 41:123, 1984.

Kanner L: Autistic disturbances of affective contact. *Nerv Child* 2:217, 1943.

Kanner L: Follow-up study of eleven autistic children originally reported in 1943. *J Autism Child Schizo* 1:119, 1971.

Kanner I, Rodriguez A, Ashenden B: How far can autistic children go in matters of social adaptation? *J Autism Child Schizo* 2:9, 1972.

Levitas A, McBogg PM, Hagerman RJ: Behavioral dysfunction in the fragile X syndrome. In Hagerman RJ, McBogg PM (eds): *The Fragile X Syndrome*. Dillon, CO, Spectra Publishing Co, 1983.

Lutz J: Über die Schizophrenie im Kindesalter. Schweiz. *Arch Neurol Psychiatry* 39:335, 1937; 40:141, 1937.

Mahler MS, Ross JR, Fries de Z: Clinical studies in benign and malignant cases of childhood psychosis. *Am J Orthopsychiatry* 19:295, 1949.

Mahler MS: *On Human Symbiosis and the Vicissitudes of Individuation*. New York, International Universities Press, 1968.

Mahler MS, Pine F, Bergman A: *The Psychological Birth of the Human Infant*. New York, Basic Books, 1975.

Prior M, Perry D, Gadzago C: Kanner's syndrome or early onset psychosis: a taxonomic analysis of 142 cases. *J Autism Child Schizo* 5:71, 1975.

Rank B: Adaptation of the psychoanalytic technique for the treatment of young children with atypical development. *Am J Orthopsychiatry* 19:130, 1949.

Rapoport JR, Ismond DR: Biological research in child psychiatry. *J Am Acad Child Psychiatry* 21:543, 1982.

Rimland B: *Infantile Autism*. New York, Appleton-Century-Crofts, Division of Meredith Publishing Company, 1964.

Rutter M: Psychotic disorders in early childhood. *Brit J Psychiatry* 113:133, 1967.

Rutter M: Childhood schizophrenia reconsidered. *J Autism Child Schizo* 2:315, 1972.

Rutter M, Lockyer L: A five to fifteen year follow-up study of infantile psychosis. *Br J Psychiatry* 113:1169, 1967.

Rutter M, Schopler E (eds): *Autism: A Reappraisal of Concepts and Treatment*. New York, Plenum Pess, 1978.

Suwa N, et al: Survey of autistic children on Hokkaido Island. *Psychiatr Neurol Jpn* 72:6, 1970.

Szurek SA: Childhood schizophrenia: a psychogenic hypothesis. In Szurek SA, Berlin IN, Boatman MJ (eds): *Inpatient Care for the Psychotic Child*. Palo Alto, CA, Science and Behavior Books 1971, p 92.

Wing L, Wing J: Multiple impairments in early childhood autism. *J Autism Child Schizo* 1:311, 1971.

Witmer L: What I did with Don. Historical introduction by Gianascol AJ. In Szurek SA, Berlin IN (ed): *Clinical Studies in Childhood Psychoses*. New York, Brunner/Mazel, 1973, p. 48.

CHAPTER 58 **The Learning Disabilities of Childhood: Attention Deficit Disorder and Specific Developmental Disorders**

Adolph E. Christ, M.D.

MULTIPLE DIAGNOSES

The titles that have been used to define the *learning disabilities of childhood* are legion. As you read the brief history behind this syndrome, which I will describe shortly, I hope it will become clearer why there have been so many labels for a disability that affects such an enormous number of children. Some of the terms that you will come across for this disorder in the pediatric, neurological, and psychiatric literature are: minimal cerebral dysfunction, minimal brain damage or dysfunction (MBD), organic behavior disorder, hyperkinetic syndrome, perceptual disorder, Strauss syndrome, and hyperactive child syndrome to list only a few. In DSM-III the term given to this condition is *attention deficit disorder* (ADD) since difficulties with attention are virtually always present in these children. DSM-III describes two subtypes of the disorder, one with hyperactivity and the other without hyperactivity.

What are these children like? Their symptoms may include motor awkwardness, perceptual disturbances, hyperactivity, distractibility, impulsivity, excitability, antisocial behavior, emotional lability, and other various problems. One unusual parent described this as " . . . not a nice handicap." Such technical terms as "catastrophic behavior" are translated by the outside world as "spoiled, bratty, bad-mannered, ill-behaved, badly brought up, undisciplined, obnoxious," and by other children as "queer." To all this we must add one more adjective, "interesting." Of these children, 50% exhibit what has been termed a "paradoxical reaction" in that they become wide awake and even more excitable when given a hypnotic drug such as Phenobarbital, but will relax and attend better on stimulant drugs such as Dexedrine, Ritalin, and Cylert.

By now the reader may be asking, "Why the term learning disability?" Remember the symptoms just described in the above paragraph? These attributes make these children particularly problematic for educators. Indeed, there is a large and sophisticated literature that is emerging from teachers and educational psychologists who are looking closely at these children from this perspective of learning. As you review the educational literature, therefore, you will find the diagnostic label, *learning disability*, used a great deal. Although children with learning disabilities have specific learning difficulties in reading, arithmetic, language, and articulation, reading problems have been the most intensively studied and are the most common. DSM-III places all of these *specific developmental disorders* in Axis II, and describes five subtypes: 1) *developmental reading disorder*; 2) *developmental arithmetic disorder*; 3) *developmental language disorder, expressive type*; 4) *developmental language disorder, receptive type*; and 5) *developmental articulation disorder*. In contrast to the pervasive developmental disorders where *multiple* functions are affected due to a *distortion* in development, in each specific developmental disorder only a *single* function is affected due to a *delay* in development.

Specifically, a child is defined as having a learning disability if he or she is significantly behind in achievement in the particular area (for example, reading) that one might predict on the basis of the child's actual I.Q. Thus, a youngster with an I.Q. of 90 would be expected to have a reading score consistent with this I.Q. test score. If, however, his reading ability is two or more years behind the expected norm corrected for I.Q., such a youngster would be considered to have a developmental reading disorder.

There is still considerable disagreement about the actual causes of the learning disabilities. The most popular opinion about the etiology has shifted in the past 20 years from "psychogenic" to "minimal brain damage" to "developmental dysmaturation." Thus, the causes of the learning disabilities are probably multiple and complex (Figure 58.1). Most of us would agree that there is a group of youngsters, perhaps 20%, whose learning disability is primarily the result of underlying psychogenic disorders, either neurotic or psychotic, that may also involve social and cultural factors. There is another group, perhaps again about 20%, whose learning disability seems to be related to identifiable organic central nervous system (CNS) damage and other biological factors. The area of the brain that is damaged is quite important. For example, the

spastic group of cerebral palsied children has a much higher incidence of learning problems than the choreoathetoid group of cerebral palsied children. Finally, the largest group, perhaps 60%, has symptoms (hyperactivity, distractibility, impulsivity, and excitability) of the *attention deficit disorder* in which there may be multiple (developmental, neurological, and psychogenic) etiological contributions to the disturbance (Table 58.1).

The number of children having such disorders is not inconsequential. Several recent studies suggest that up to 20% of the school population in this country may suffer from some form of learning disability. Boys are affected four to seven times more often than girls. We do know that 15% of American adults have serious reading problems, and the same number lack the literacy necessary to function adequately in society. In some pediatric and child psychiatric

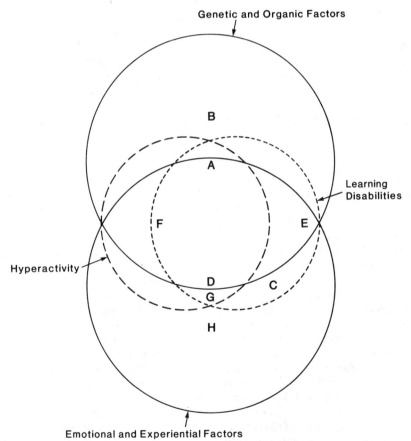

Figure 58.1. The interaction of psychogenic and sociocultural factors with organic and other biological factors in the hyperactive and learning disabled populations. (Figure by Adolph E. Christ.)

Table 58.1
*Differential Diagnosis of the Hyperactive Child**

	Incidence	Past Neurological Injury	Neurological Review of Systems	Neurological Exam	Mental Retardation	Family History	Age of Onset	Severe Emotional Problems
	%							
1. Developmental hyperactivity	42	−	−	−	−	Often	Birth	−
2. Neurological hyperactivity	15							
A. "Minimal brain dysfunction"		+	±	+ ("Soft signs")	−	−	Variable	±
B. Organic brain damage		+	+	+ ("Hard signs")	−	−	Time of injury	±
3. Mental retardation	6	±	−	±	+	−	Variable	−
4. Psychogenic hyperactivity	37							
A. Mild (e.g., situational depression or anxiety, or parental overreaction)		−	−	−	−	−	After age 2	−
B. Severe (e.g., maternal deprivation, childhood psychosis, severe neurosis)		−	−	−	−	−	After age 2	+

* *Differential Diagnosis of the Hyperactive Child.* After table prepared by Barton D. Schmitt, Harold P. Martin, Gerhard Nellhaus, Jere Cravens, Bonnie W. Camp, and Kent Jordan.

outpatient clinics serving lower socioeconomic groups, as many as 40% of the children seen each year receive the diagnosis of learning disability. Pediatric clinics that serve predominantly middle class children find that the proportion of learning-disabled children is quite a bit less.

HISTORICAL OVERVIEW

I have found that our current thinking about this group of children is best understood if we first look at some historical facts. Dr. Kurt Goldstein worked in a hospital whose population included men who had sustained central nervous system injuries during World War I. Over the years he observed that these brain-damaged men seemed compelled to keep their lockers immaculate, and their soap dishes and toothbrushes were always in the same place day after day. In addition to being very concrete and meticulous, they would perseverate (be unable to leave a task easily and go on to the next one), and they had stereotyped responses to stimuli. When these various defensive behaviors broke down, the patients would often become violent, and even suffer a total personality disorganization. Goldstein referred to this breakdown as a *catastrophic reaction*, and viewed the perseveration, concreteness, and meticulousness of the patients as defensive attempts to prevent this catastrophic reaction from occurring.

One sees catastrophic reactions most clearly in elderly geriatric patients with organic mental disorders if they are pushed to answer questions that they are no longer able to solve, such as: "How much change would you get if you bought a 30 cent candy bar and a 43 cent can of soup, and you gave the clerk a one dollar bill?" A woman who had been a bookkeeper or a man who had owned a store remember themselves as they were, i.e., as always able to solve simple problems such as these. Being unable to solve such simple problems is devastating for them. If pushed to give an answer, they will show a "catastrophic reaction," i.e., they will become furious and possibly even begin to hallucinate, or else become totally inarticulate and retreat to bed, picking at the bedcovers. Characteristic of the catastrophic reaction is the rapid improvement, often within minutes, when the cognitive stress is removed. These same patients would happily talk for hours about some philosophical or religious topic that does not reveal their cognitive deficits. Similarly devastating reactions are sometimes seen in children who have learning disabilities. Most commonly, it is the psychological test part of the total evaluation that brings out this response. As with the geriatric patients, being forced to recognize cognitive deficits is enormously upsetting.

About the same time that Goldstein described these findings, the severe influenza epidemic of 1918 left residual problems. Some adults developed Parkinson's syndrome, while some children developed hyperactivity, impulsivity, and distractibility. Alert pediatricians and psychiatrists such as Lauretta Bender read about this syndrome, and found that in their practices there were a number of children who had identical symptoms even though they had no history of, nor any other signs of, CNS damage. Since most of the postinfluenza children showed no gross neurological signs, such as cranial nerve defects, or motor, sensory, or reflex changes, the possibility was raised that minimal brain damage existed in these "hyperactive" children.

In 1933, Werner and Strauss, largely influenced by Goldstein's finding with adults, started to study the consequences of true brain damage in mildly retarded children. They separated retarded children into two categories: "endogenous" (i.e., familial, genetic) and "exogenous" (i.e., secondary to possible central nervous system damage). Following Goldstein's lead, they studied the perceptual and perceptual-motor performance of these children. The "exogenous" (brain-damaged) children copied a form board totally capriciously, with no apparent organization. In addition, they seemed unable to separate a picture from its background, a figure from its ground, the relevant from the irrelevant. These children (see A in Figure 58.1) were more hyperactive, distractible, impulsive, excitable, uncoordinated, and socially unacceptable than the endogenous retardates (see B in Figure 58.1). Hence, the term *Strauss syndrome* began to be another diagnostic label applied to this group of children.

Then Benjamin Pasamanick and Hilda Knobloch, starting in the 1940's, conducted a number of prospective and retrospective studies on children from the Baltimore area. They found that in the lowest socioeconomic population, there is a higher incidence of prematurity, of fetal death, and of perinatal mortality. Most of these deaths are secondary to central nervous system damage. From these investigations Pasamanick developed his concept of a *continuum of reproductive casualty*. He argued that where central nervous system damage results in deaths, there must be many more children where there is central nervous system damage that is somewhat less and which does not result in fatalities. He then did a study that indeed showed that the mothers of youngsters with reading disabilities had a significantly greater history of prematurity, toxemia, bleeding during pregnancy, maternal malnutrition, and infection, and that the youngsters had had other prenatal and perinatal difficulties,

including head injuries and anoxia during or shortly after birth.

The theory that learning disabilities might be due to subtle brain damage found further support in the research of William Windle in the 1960's. He reduced the oxygen supply to a group of experimental monkeys for a few minutes immediately after birth, and then compared these monkeys with a control group over the next several years. The experimental monkeys had motor and sensory difficulties similar to those shown by children with certain learning disabilities.

At the same time, other studies were also being done that pointed more to social deprivation than to central nervous system damage as a possible etiological factor. A number of investigators began to find that sensory and emotional deprivation of the infant has major consequences. Spitz described the severe intellectual deterioration of infants who were raised in emotionally sterile environments, or who were separated from their mothers at an early age. Harold Skeels showed that the I.Q. can go up or down significantly, depending on the stimulation of the children and the presence of maternal contacts. He followed a group of 12 orphans, with a mean I.Q. of 87, who lived in a deprived orphanage setting, and who showed a drop in I.Q. to 61 over a two year period. An experimental group of 13 orphans were cared for in the same orphanage by institutionalized retarded women for a number of months and then placed in adoptive homes that provided love and affection and normal life experiences. These 13 received much more stimulation and nurturance. The lower original mean I.Q. of 64 in this group of 13 subjects increased to a mean I.Q. of 92 over the same two year period! A 21 year follow-up study was even more dramatic. In the original control group of 12, one had died in adolescence following continued residence in a state institution for mentally retarded. Four were still wards of institutions, the others were only marginally employed, only two had married, and median educational level was less than the third grade. In sharp contrast, all 13 of the children in the experimental group were self-supporting, none was a ward of any institution, 11 of the 13 had married, and the median educational level was the twelfth grade. In fact, four of the 13 had taken one or more years of college work, and one had even graduated from college!

Such deprivation is not found only in orphanages. Pavenstedt, Deutsch, Wortis, and many others have reported that very low socioeconomic families are often highly unstable. They may exist on a day-to-day, crisis-to-chaos basis. Infants are at times neglected, isolated in cribs without toys, or in dark rooms with no stimulation except the unusable and intensive stimulation of loud radios and television, and any exploratory interests are disliked and discouraged by the adults. All of these findings have prompted Sameroff and Chandler to state that even if a "continuum of reproductive casualty" does exist, it is also necessary to postulate a *"continuum of caretaking casualty"* in order to explain the range of different behavioral outcomes of children with the same "organic" background.

Although it is dangerous to infer from animal studies to human situations, some experimental work just cannot be done with humans, and so we must borrow from animal experiments to see if we can learn more about the effects of sensory deprivation. Valverde raised mice in the dark, and found a 20% reduction in the number of dendritic spines in the nerve cells of the visual cortex. Bell and others found that mice raised in very crowded conditions had slowed neuronal development, reduced brain protein and nucleic acids, and decreased intracellular RNA. Finally, Rosenzweig and coworkers Bennett and Diamond raised one group of rats in a stimulus-rich environment which included ladders, wheels, and boxes, and another group in individual cages out of sight of other rats. The occipital cortex of the stimulus-rich group was 4% to 12% thicker than the other group. Thus, we can see that deprivation can affect the central nervous system in animals.

But are the symptoms of hyperactivity, distractibility, and impulsivity always correlated with central nervous system damage? Those of us who have worked closely with neurologists and neurosurgeons have seen children with gross neurological damage who did not have these symptoms. I vividly remember a pretty, friendly, three year old girl (see *B* in Figure 58.1) who had been a terror before her hospitalization. She had Sturge-Weber syndrome (hemangioma of the brain and face), and her right cerebral hemisphere had to be surgically removed. Postoperatively she had none of the symptoms of the attention deficit disorder, even though she unquestionably had a large part of her central nervous system removed.

Let us summarize. Goldstein's work on brain-

damaged adults inspired Werner and Strauss to look for similar difficulties in children. The exogenous retardates they studied had symptoms much like the postencephalitic children described by Lauretta Bender. The studies of Pasamanick showed a higher incidence of prenatal and perinatal problems, problems secondary to central nervous system damage in children with learning and reading disabilities. However, other factors such as severe emotional and sensory deprivation can also cause major changes in I.Q. Further, animal studies show rather clearly that such factors as sensory deprivation can alter the central nervous system. Finally, some children with clear evidence of brain injury do not show the cardinal symptoms of the attention deficit disorders. At this time, therefore, it may be wiser to consider that hyperactive and learning disabled children can be depicted as in Figure 58.1, and that the etiology of each child's disorder may have a larger or smaller contribution from genetic and organic factors on the one hand, and emotional and experiential factors on the other.

We shall now look at five clinical examples of children with learning disability problems, each emphasizing a different etiology for the learning disability.

CASE HISTORIES

Learning Disability of Neurotic Etiology

A 13 year old girl (see *C* in Figure 58.1) was referred for psychiatric evaluation. She was the middle of three children from an upper middle class family. The girl was very popular in the private school which she attended, and she was able to adapt and maneuver well in the difficult cultural life of this most elite school. However, her reading ability was in the third percentile (97% of youngsters her age read better than she did), while her arithmetic and writing were from the 40th to the 60th percentile. Yet her I.Q., if corrected for the reading difficulty, was at the level of the average college graduate student.

She felt herself to be a total mismatch in her family. Her parents were brilliant professionals for whom intellectual competence was most important. Both siblings were straight "A" students. Her social competence, her aspirations to be a model, and her artistic interests never received the recognition from her parents that her siblings' bookishness received. In general, it is hard to be a middle child; the oldest is special for being first, the youngest for being the baby. This girl had an additional burden; all her interests and talents were of little interest to her parents, while her reading disability was the only thing that would rouse real interest and concern in them. She was only dimly aware of the extent of her underlying rage at her parents, but her dreams and nightmares of horrendous violence and mutilation alerted me to her unconscious rage. If she needed to express anger, it would be hard to think of a symptom that would be more vengeful in this particular family. Indeed, it would be like the vengeance of an anorexic patient whose parents are renowned gourmet cooks!

Phyllis Blanchard presents three case examples of psychoneurosis where reading disability is one of the symptoms. She points out that "... there is no single situation or personality adjustment which can be isolated to explain the development of reading disability ... " A careful evaluation is needed to diagnose the neurosis, and to get a complete picture that helps explain the choice of a particular symptom such as reading disability. As in all neurotic situations, there are always many motivations for the choice of any symptom. In addition to the "vengeance" motive, this girl had always had a hard time growing up. In most ways she was almost too grown up, but there was a part, hidden from her awareness, that was afraid of being grown up. Being a very poor reader had been one way of remaining a little girl.

Learning Disability of Psychotic Etiology

Reading difficulties can be present in more severely disturbed children as well. A nine year old boy (see *D* in Figure 58.1), who was diagnosed as suffering from childhood schizophrenia, could not bear to look at a printed page. The letter "C" looked like a mouth with big teeth that would bite and swallow him. He was quite hyperactive, as are many of these psychotic children. Another very disturbed child described getting confused every time he saw the letter "F." It reminded him of "Fuck," and would trigger disturbing images that persisted.

Learning Disability with Possible "MBD"

A 10 year old boy (see *E* in Figure 58.1) came into my office and announced, "I have been informed I must see you. My parents insist, so I must comply." His polysyllabic speech contin-

ued in like vein for much of the interview. Unlike most learning-disabled children, he was an avid reader. A few weeks later, he tentatively began to show his disability. He could count, add, and subtract, but he could not coordinate counting to 12 with the checkers that he took out of the box for our game. Similarly, in an "eeny meeny miney mo" to determine who would have the first checkers move, he could not coordinate the "words" with himself or me. He boasted that he was ambidextrous, when actually he could not tell left from right on his body or on mine! His spelling was atrocious, his handwriting illegible. Printing was a bit better, but he used p and q, b and d, interchangeably. His disorganization was revealed for all to see on paper, where he would produce excessive material on one corner, and very little on the rest of the page. At other times he would print a letter using one space, followed by many spaces between other letters. His teacher stated that his desk was like a "rodent's nest"—papers and books all helter-skelter. To help him, his parents bought him a ring binder with separate sections for each subject. Somehow, arithmetic, social studies, and writing all ended up on the same page, and his parents would spend much time each evening helping him to organize his homework. They had warned me of his total lack of spatial orientation, but I was not prepared for his losing his way from my office to the bathroom two doors away after he had been seeing me for six months.

Rather than being distractible and hyperactive with a short attention span, his attention problem was the opposite. Once he started reading, shouts by his teacher could not stop him. Indeed, she put him at the front desk so that she could touch him to get his attention. He was a lonely and unhappy boy. His fear of being stupid and "a retard" mobilized massive defenses. He antagonized all his classmates by being a bossy know-it-all, always showing off his talents. Only after a great deal of treatment did he become aware that he was trying to prove to others (and to himself!) that he was not "a retarded creep." But unfortunately what the other children saw was the defense—an opinionated, bossy "creep!"

Physical and neurological examinations were normal. His electroencephalogram was also quite normal. It was not possible to localize a neurological lesion in any part of his brain. So here was a severe learning difficulty with spatial disorientation, massive left-right confusion, and an inability to coordinate counting in a boy whose reading and verbal ability was superior. This case is a good example of why many of us suspect that such children have "a minimal brain damage," either an alteration in the normal development of the central nervous system after birth, or most probably, I believe, some as yet unidentified maturational interference with the smooth coordination of higher cortical centers and functions.

Learning Disability in a Hyperactive Child

The next case illustrates the most frequent situation seen in child psychiatric facilities. A nine year old boy (see *F* in Figure 58.1) was referred to the psychiatric clinic as a severe management problem in the school. He did not do his homework, he would daydream, he was always in the middle of any class disturbance. His current teacher had been warned by his second grade teacher that he never sat still, would fidget, could not concentrate on anything more than five minutes, and was very distractible. His current teacher had seen all these things within a few days of the youngster's being in her classroom. His last teacher had moved him to the rear seat in the classroom, because he would continually jump and run to the window to look for the source of any street noise, and consistently turn around and look at anyone moving or making a noise behind him. At least by being in that rear seat, he did not distract as many children as he had when she had him sitting in the front row.

In my office he came in sullenly, only gradually describing that he knew that he was bad and stupid. He tried to sit still, but quickly started fidgeting, fingering whatever was within reach. He ran to the window when a truck drove by. After 10 minutes he seemed ready to explode with inner tension, so I continued the interview while we walked outside. He seemed more comfortable, but the distractions were still too much. He could not really focus on a topic for more than a few sentences.

The parents described him as much harder to manage than the two older siblings. He was a breech presentation at birth, and was kept in the hospital a couple of extra days after the mother went home. The obstetrician was described as being a bit worried—the boy had been somewhat listless at first, but seemed to pick up well after seven days, so he was discharged. The parents described the first year as a nightmare. "It's like he never slept. He kept us up most of the night, needing feedings every two to three hours for the first six months." Once he started to crawl and walk, he would never sit still, and always seemed to get into trouble, breaking things, or falling and hurting himself. He seemed clumsier than the other children had been. As he got older, he did not busy himself like the other children, but always wanted company. Outside he was not careful like his two older brothers. Without looking he might dash out into the street, so that the mother constantly worried that he might be run over by a car.

School had been a disaster from the start, culminating in the referral to the clinic. The boy responded well to dextroamphetamine sulfate. He lost most of his hyperactivity, distractibility, and impulsivity. As a matter of fact, 48 hours after he was started on his medication, his teacher called excitedly to describe his marked improvement. He was now sufficiently attentive so that the psychologist could reevaluate him, and found a rather typical reading disability. His intelligence was normal, but his reading was at the first grade level. He could read a few words that he had learned before, but had no idea how to sound out letters to figure out a new word. He was transferred to a school that had a special remedial reading class.

By now the reader will recognize in this boy the attention deficit disorder with symptoms of hyperactivity, distractibility, and impulsivity. Unfortunately, these symptoms are as difficult on the parents and teachers as they are on the child. This boy probably best fits into the category of developmental hyperactivity (Table 58.1). Whether he had some central nervous system damage at birth always remained questionable. The neurological examination and the electroencephalogram were never conclusive. Emotionally, he was a troubled youngster, but it had more to do with his long experiences of failure in school. The boy was not involved in an entangled neurotic interaction with his parents, nor they with him. As a matter of fact, once his major symptoms subsided, his parents quickly shifted their concerns to other matters. There are other children, however, who in addition to the rather typical picture presented above, also have major emotional problems. It is most important not to miss a severe family problem or an emotional problem that may be masked by the reading disability or the attention deficit disorder.

Learning Disability with Truancy

Finally, there is another group of youngsters who may also have very low achievement scores in school. A 15 year old boy (see *G* in Figure 58.1) was referred to the child psychiatric clinic by the Family Court. He and several friends had stolen a car. The Family Court felt that a special psychiatric day care program for court-referred adolescents might be better than a short jail sentence. The boy's hyperactive history was in some ways similar to our previous case, except that he was so impulsive that he began truanting from school in the third grade, and by the sixth grade he was spending more days out of than in school. He lived at home with four siblings, fathered by two different men. The mother was on welfare and had never married.

A frequent reading score of adolescents who end up in a correctional facility for criminal behavior is between the second and third grade. Like many of these children, this 15 year old boy had never had either his attention deficit disorder or his reading disability diagnosed. The horrendous family problems, the truancy, and the increasing problems with the law, culminating in the last arrest, seemed much more pressing when he came to the attention of the authorities at all previous times.

There are many other adolescents like this boy who have severe problems with the law, and who have low achievement scores in all areas. Adding together the total number of days that they have actually been in school can be very suprising! For example, one adolescent (see *H* in Figure 58.1) who had reading, writing, and arithmetic scores at the third grade level, actually had spent a total of no more than 430 days in school up until the time he was seen in the clinic. In short, his low achievement scores had probably more to do with other emotional problems leading to truancy than they had to do with any particular learning disability or attention deficit disorder. It is important to separate in one's own thinking youngsters who may have been truant from school, and in addition who may have had extremely poor school experiences, from youngsters who have specific learning disabilities as described in our other cases.

SUMMARY

Some youngsters with learning disabilities are quite clearly suffering from a neurotic disturbance, with the reading disability only one of the symptoms of an underlying neurosis. The 13 year old girl in the first case presented is an example of this group. Other children may be psychotic, as in our second case. Other youngsters with learning disabilities are quite clearly organically impaired, as was probably true of the 10 year old boy in the third case history. The converse, however, is not true. Not all organically impaired youngsters have either the attention deficit disorder or a learning disability. Finally, the large group of youngsters with the attention deficit disorder or hyperkinetic syndrome who comprise the great majority of these cases may have developmental, neurological, and psychological factors involved in the etiology of their learning disturbance. The organic subgroup was studied by Werner and Strauss in their "exogenous" (mildly) mentally retarded children, and by Pasamanick. The environmental contributions were highlighted by Spitz and Skeels, who showed the remarkable changes in I.Q.'s brought about in infants by sensory and/or maternal deprivation. All of these deprivational factors are factors that Pavenstedt, Wortis, and others have pointed out are also unfortunately often present in higher proportions among the lowest socioeconomic groups. The psychological factors may be primary, but if not, they are at least always a secondary contributor. Being "dumb" and disliked by teachers and students alike are the painful sequelae of a learning disability, and these children feel like failures from their earliest school contacts.

This large group of children, who have attention deficit disorder symptoms as well as learning difficulties, remains an etiological enigma. The first label (attention deficit disorder) is preferred by the medical profession, the latter label (learning disability) by the teaching profession. However, it is important to remember that these labels are more on a par with terms like fever, which can be the result of a pneumonia, of a renal infection, or of a meningoencephalitis. We cling to these labels because these children have so much in common, and because we are not yet sufficiently clear about the specific etiological factors in many of these children to develop a more etiologically based nomenclature.

THE TREATMENT OF THESE CONDITIONS

As with the psychoses of childhood, early detection and treatment of potential learning problems are extremely important, and can help to prevent the vicious cycle of the child and others coming to the premature conclusion that he or she is an educational failure. A combination of treatment approaches is always required in the treatment of any learning disability. A careful family and developmental history needs to be taken, including an exploration of the meaning of academic success and failure for the parents. A thorough neurological work-up is also important. Whatever the cause of the learning disability, both the parents and the child will need support and counseling, possibly even psychotherapy and/or behavior therapy. In addition, the teachers and the school must be an integral part of the treatment program, and the educational tutoring that may be required needs to be individualized for each child.

There have been many special methods developed for working with these children with learning disabilities. For example, Gittman stresses the importance of developing perceptual-motor skills with such exercises as practice in general coordination on the balance walking beam, practice in eye-hand coordination, practice in eye movements and form recognition. In short, he recommends efforts to try to train these children in those functions in which they may be "neurologically" impaired. His feeling is that training in these basic functions is absolutely essential for proper learning of such skills as reading.

Finally, pharmacological therapy can be of great help in indicated cases, but stimulant medication should not be used as the sole treatment. Optimum treatment requires a combination of remediation, school consultation, medication, family counseling, psychological support of the child, and, according to some, perceptual-motor training. To date, it has not been proven that any substances in our food (e.g., food additives, food preservatives, artificial colors and flavors, and naturally occurring salicylates) cause either the attention deficit disorder or any of the specific developmental disorders. Therefore, the so-called *defined-diets* that are supposedly free of these substances are not recommended in the treatment of these conditions at the present time.

As health care specialists, whether physicians, nurses, or others, we are often asked our opinions about these perceptual-motor, special exercise, and remedial teaching methods by teachers and parents. An excellent summary of many of these methods can be found in the Hallahan and Cruickshank book listed in the suggested readings at the end of the chapter. These various approaches that have been used by the learning disability specialists are based on our growing recognition and knowledge of central nervous system function. As we gain a better understanding of the interrelationship between the neurophysiological and the psychological functions of the brain, hopefully we will be able to be even more effective in our treatment of these children.

Suggested Readings

Birch H (ed): *Brain Damage in Children: The Biological and Social Aspects.* Baltimore, Williams & Wilkins, 1964.

Blanchard P: Psychoanalytic contributions to the problems of reading disabilities. In Harrison SI, McDermott JF (eds): *Childhood Psychopathology.* New York, International Universities Press, 1972, p 487.

Cantwell DP: The hyperkinetic syndrome. In Rutter M, Hersov L (eds): *Child Psychiatry: Modern Approaches.* London, Blackwell Scientific, 1977.

Eisenberg L: Hyperkinetic reactions. In Noshpitz JD (ed): *Basic Handbook of Child Psychiatry,* vol II. New York, Basic Books, 1979, p 439.

English OS, Pearson GHJ: Difficulties in learning. In Harrison SI, McDermott JF (eds): *Childhood Psychopathology.* New York, International Universities Press, 1972, p 445.

Farley GK, Eckhardt LO, Hebert FB: Hyperkinetic syndrome. In *Handbook of Child and Adolescent Psychiatric Emergencies.* New York, Medical Examination Publishing, 1979, p 78.

Hallahan DP, Cruickshank WM: *Psychoeducational Foundations of Learning Disabilities.* New Jersey, Prentice-Hall, 1973.

McDevitt JB: Learning disturbances. In Wiedeman GH (ed): *Personality Development and Deviation.* New York, International Universities Press, 1975, p 148.

Rutter M: Syndromes attributed to "minimal brain dysfunction" in childhood. *Am J Psychiatry* 139:21, 1982.

Schmitt BD, et al: The hyperactive child. In Wolman IJ (ed): *Clinical Pediatrics,* vol. 12. Philadelphia, J. B. Lippincott Co, March 1973, p 154.

Silver L: The minimal brain dysfunction syndrome. In Noshpitz JD (ed): *Basic Handbook of Child Psychiatry,* vol II. New York, Basic Books, 1979, p 416.

Wender P: *Minimal Brain Dysfunction in Children.* New York, Wiley-Interscience, 1971.

References

Bell RW, et al: Effects of population density and living space upon neuroanatomy, neurochemistry, and behavior in the C57B l/10 mouse. *J Comp Physiol Psychol* 75:258, 1971.

Bender L: Post-encephalitic behavior disorders in childhood. In Neal JB (ed): *Encephalitis: A Clinical Study.* New York, Grune & Stratton, 1942, p 361.

Birch HG, Gussow JD: *Disadvantaged Children.* New York, Grune & Stratton, 1970.

Christ AE: Attitudes toward death among a group of acute geriatric psychiatric patients. *J Gerontology* 16:56, 1961.

Deutsch M: Facilitating development in the pre-school child: social and psychological perspectives. *Merrill-Palmer Q* 10:249, 1964.

Frostig M, Horne D: *The Frostig Program for the Development of Visual Perception: Teacher's Guide.* Chicago, Follett, 1964.

Kawi AA, Pasamanick B: Prenatal and paranatal factors in the development of childhood reading disorders. *Monographs of the Society for Research in Child Development,* vol 24, 1959.

Kephart NE: *The Slow Learner in the Classroom*, ed 2. Columbus, OH, Charles E. Merrill, 1971.

Pasamanick B, Knobloch H: Brain injury and reproductive casualty. *Am J Orthopsychiatry* 30: 298, 1960.

Pasamanick B, Knobloch H: Epidemiologic studies on the complication of pregnancy and the birth process. In Harrison SI, McDermott JF (eds): *Childhood Psychopathology*. New York, International Universities Press, 1972, p 825.

Pavenstedt EA: Comparison of the child-rearing environment of upper-lower and very low-lower class families. *Am J Orthopsychiatry* 35:89, 1965.

Rosenzweig MR: Environmental complexity, cerebral change, and behavior. *Am Psychologist* 21:321, 1966.

Rosenzweig MR, Bennett EL, Diamond MC: Chemical and anatomical plasticity of brain: replications and extensions. In Gaito J (ed): *Macromolecules and Behavior*, ed 2. New York, Appleton-Century-Croft, 1970, p 205.

Rutter M, Yule W: The concept of specific reading retardation. *J Child Psychol Psychiatry* 16:181, 1975.

Sameroff AF, Chandler MJ: *Frontiers of Psychiatry*, June 1, 1975.

Skeels HM, Dye HB: A study of the effects of differential stimulation on mentally retarded children. *Proceedings of The American Association on Mental Deficiency* 44:144, 1939.

Skeels HM: Adult status of children with contrasting early life experiences: a follow-up study. *Monographs of the Society for Research in Child Development*, vol 31, 1966.

Spitz RA: Hospitalism: an inquiry into the genesis of psychiatric conditions in early childhood. *Psychoanal Study Child* 1:53, 1945.

Spitz RA: Anaclitic depression. *Psychoanal Study Child* 2:313, 1946.

Strauss AA, Kephart NC: Behavior differences in mentally retarded children measured by a new behavior rating scale. *Am J Psychiatry* 19:1117, 1940.

Valverde F: Apical dendritic spines of the visual cortex and light deprivation in the mouse. *Exp Brain Res* 3:337, 1967.

Wortis H, et al: Child-rearing practices in a low socioeconomic group. *Pediatrics* 32:298, 1963.

CHAPTER **59** Conduct Disorder, and the Problem of Juvenile Delinquency

Adolph E. Christ, M.D.

DSM-III defines *conduct disorder* as a repetitive pattern of conduct in which either the basic rights of others or major social norms are violated. DSM-III then describes four subtypes: 1) the *undersocialized*, characterized by a failure to establish affectionate relationships with others; 2) the *socialized*, characterized by affectionate relationships with some people but callous or manipulative behavior toward "outsiders"; 3) the *aggressive*, characterized by aggressive conduct in which the rights of others are violated (physical violence, theft); and 4) the *nonaggressive*, characterized by absence of physical violence against a victim, but rather persistent conflicts such as truancy, substance abuse, running away from home, lying, vandalism, firesetting, and theft that does not involve direct confrontation with a victim. All of the above mentioned conduct is more serious and persistent than the occasional pranks and misbehavior of most children and adolescents.

The term, *juvenile delinquency*, will not be found in any of the official diagnostic manuals. Still, the term "juvenile delinquency" persists. It persists for a reason. Judges, attorneys, police, mental health workers, sociologists, and many other professionals with diverse backgrounds are interested in studying, treating, and preventing this phenomenon, and yet a common frame of reference, a common vocabulary, has not yet been established by these disciplines. Furthermore, acts of delinquency have one thing in common. They are acts against society. The impersonal aspect of many of these acts frightens all of us. High rents are paid in large cities for "safe neighborhoods," and large sums of money are paid for protection by police, courts, and jails. Even as rational a society as ancient Greece executed Socrates because he was supposedly "corrupting" youth!

MISINFORMATION ABOUT DELINQUENCY

The seeds of some of our current misinformation about delinquency were planted long ago. In the 18th century, man was seen as a free moral agent. His behavior was considered to be totally a matter of choice and free will. By the latter half of the 19th century, largely as a result of Mendel's and Darwin's findings, species selection and heredity were much talked about, and the hereditary aspect of criminality was stressed. Hence, one was not truly morally free, but limited by heredity. The delinquent was seen as an atavistic throwback to man's beginnings. Lombroso, writing his original work in 1876, spent many years "documenting" the physical correlates of this hereditary degeneracy. To this day the lay public often describes such physical attributes as closely spaced eyes, deformed ears, and "a lean hungry look" as typical of the criminal. About 40 years later, Goring showed that such supposedly recognizable "stigmata" of degeneracy are distributed equally in both the criminal and noncriminal populations.

Around this time, physicians were clinically impressed with the higher incidence of mental retardation in the criminal population. Goddard translated Binet's intelligence test from French into English in 1910, then two years later tested incarcerated offenders, and found that 50% were feeble minded! His conclusion that mental deficiency was the primary cause of delinquency is therefore understandable.

As psychological tests of intelligence became more sophisticated, the intelligence quotients (I.Q.) of large groups of incarcerated delinquents were found to average around 92. Maller in New York City, and Lichtenstein and Brown in Chicago, compared the I.Q. of juvenile delinquents with the I.Q. of children from similar socioeconomic backgrounds, and found little difference in intelligence. Hence, the idea that delinquency is caused by low intelligence is no longer tenable. This is indeed an apt moment to quote Galileo: the goal of science is not to prove infinite wisdom, but to set limits on infinite error!

THE EPIDEMIOLOGY OF DELINQUENCY

Before we look at specific case histories of delinquents, let us review a few of the major epidemiological findings on juvenile delinquency:

1. Delinquency is a serious problem. As was noted in Chapter 43, the rate of armed robbery, rape, and murder among adolescents has tripled over the past 20 years. There have been concomitant increases in drug and alcohol abuse in schools, vandalism of school property, and assaults on teachers. If these trends continue, it is estimated that one out of every nine youngsters will appear in juvenile court for offenses other than speeding before the age of 18!

2. Delinquency rates vary with age. In many studies, it has been found that age 16 carries the highest rate of delinquency, falling to one-half that rate by age 21, with a lower rate under age 15 (FBI data).

3. Delinquency rates vary with sex. Boys clearly outnumber girls in a ratio of five to one. The most frequent delinquency found in girls is running away and sexual offenses. As a group, the runaways are a bit brighter than the sexual offenders. On the other hand, sexual offenses are extremely rare in adolescent boys, whereas car theft is almost never seen in girls.

4. Delinquency appears to be related in certain ways to socioeconomic class. Lower socioeconomic class male delinquents tend to be more involved with gangs. Higher socioeconomic class male delinquents, and delinquent girls at all socioeconomic levels, tend to commit more individual crimes, and more often come from troubled families. Shaw and McKay began ecological studies in the early 1940's which were followed by many others. They reported a higher incidence of juvenile delinquency in the dilapidated slum areas of large cities, with a gradual decrease in incidence proportional to the distance from the city center. Hence, much lower rates were found in suburbs; the lowest rates, in rural areas.

What is fascinating is that the same slum area continues to have high crime rates, even when the population of this particular slum area changes. For example, in the mid 19th century, Irish, Scandinavian, and German immigrants occupied the slums. In the late 19th century they were replaced by Italians, Poles, and Jews. In the 1940's to the present, they in turn were replaced by Blacks, Puerto Ricans, and Chicanos. As the slum dwellers moved out of the slums, the incidence of juvenile delinquency decreased in this particular population. However, the new slum dwellers, those who replaced the ones who were leaving, maintained the high rate of delinquency! The logical conclusion would seem to be: tear down the slums, relocate people to adequate housing in adequate neighborhoods, and delinquency will decrease.

However, housing and the neighborhood are not the whole story by far. Most youngsters raised in the slums do not become criminals, especially those from three immigrant groups. These are the Jews, and the Japanese, and the Chinese. The Italian and Jewish immigrants bear interesting comparisons in this regard. Both groups moved into the United States at approximately the same time, and both stress a very close family involvement. However, the Jews, very much like the Chinese and Japanese, stress education, especally for the boys. The schools facilitated the transition of immigrant Jews to the new culture, and provided access to increased social class status on the basis of good academic performance. This was not true to the same degree among the Italian immigrants.

5. Delinquency seems to be related to broken homes. Divorce and desertion are often seen in the backgrounds of delinquent youngsters. However, factors leading up to the divorce or the separation are often more important than the presence of single parent homes. For example, the death of a father is not correlated with higher delinquency rates. A working mother also does not seem to affect delinquency rates. The death of a mother, on the other hand, does increase the rate of delinquency, particularly in younger girls.

6. Delinquency also appears to be related to a lack of consistent discipline. In general, parents, even in the worst slums, can raise nondelinquent children, if they are interested in their children and care about them, and provide consistent and concerned discipline. The worst combination seems to be a criminal father who

is cruel and neglecting, and a lax, uninvolved mother, or vice versa.

These facts all have to do with the ecology of juvenile delinquency—incidence, age, sex, socioeconomic class, and family background. Perhaps the best way to gain a better understanding of the inner experiences of individual delinquents is to study some case histories.

CASE HISTORIES OF DELINQUENT ADOLESCENTS

John

John is 23, a bright, competent, graduate student at a good university. He feels settled into a way of life that he hopes will include an engineering degree, possibly a graduate degree in business administration, then a position in his father's firm. Life was not always like that. I knew him as a troubled teenager. At age 16 psychotherapy was a condition of probation on a charge of drug dealing at his local high school.

His parents described him as a colicky baby, relieved finally when he was put on a soybean milk diet. He had allergic rhinitis, so the family could never have cats. He was a robust, active toddler, but had more than his share of bumps. His mother said, "I often wondered if he were accident prone. I don't have a single picture of him before he was 10 without a scab or a bump on his face." He had problems in school in the first few grades, especially with reading. His mother tutored him. He was on the periphery of the other children, even up to the sixth grade. He was never ostracized, but he also was never really accepted. John felt lonely, collected rocks, coins, and stamps, and occasionally made transient friends with other collectors.

Junior high school was a change. The school was much larger. John made friends with a few boys who were experimenting with drugs and were also somewhat on the fringe of the overall group. John felt more accepted by this group, and as he gained knowledge and experience with various drugs, he gained further status. By the ninth grade, John was much more involved in drugs. One of his friends from the sixth grade had access to a high school boy who was dealing heavily in drugs, and he in turn was John's main supplier. By now, most of the youngsters were also experimenting with drugs, and John was often asked for pills. Almost imperceptibly, John began dealing himself. At first he never charged

more than he paid for the pills, but gradually he took a commission.

The extra money meant easier dates, and a few expensive items that in turn increased his status with the others. "At times I felt guilty, but I really couldn't get out of it." Too many kids relied on John for drugs, and the extra $20 a week was too hard to give up. By now, older boys, possibly 19 or 20, would buy from and sell to John, and he began to feel twinges of fear as he heard about police raids or about others who had been picked up for selling drugs. John stayed with ups, downs, cocaine, and marijuana, refusing to become involved with heroin. In that middle class school, the youngsters made a clear distinction between those who experienced occasional "highs" at parties, and those who became addicted or drifted into heroin.

Finally, at 16, John was caught. One of the older boys turned out to be a narcotics agent. "I was getting careless. I guess I didn't care." John was arraigned and appeared before a judge, who requested psychiatric evaluation before sentencing. John's parents had vaguely sensed that something was wrong. Perhaps he seemed to have a bit too much money at times, but they tended to disregard this because he seemed to be doing so well in school. By now he had many friends, his telephone was always ringing, he had a girlfriend, and he was doing well in his studies. John's being caught was like an awakening shock to the family, just as it was to John. John readily agreed to weekly psychotherapy and probation for six months. In talking with the parents, I learned that there had been some marital problems, more marked when John was first starting in school. John was very special to his mother. He reminded her of her favorite brother. "I often confided in John. He was very sensitive." Even when he did poorly in school, the mother was convinced that he was unusually bright, and she felt a good deal of pride when he began doing better in school. In fact, she felt that she had saved him by her tutoring. But when John started junior high school, the mother became angry at him. She said, "He changed. I couldn't confide in him. He was always going out." As the mother began to talk further and understand herself better in the course of treatment, she said, "Although I didn't recognize it at the time, I guess I was angry at him for growing up."

John never returned to drugs. After a year of treatment, he stopped. He saw me again for a couple of times after he had been in college for two years. As he thought back on the whole episode, he felt the police experience gave him the courage to stop. None of his friends could really blame him for not jeopardizing himself by getting back into drugs after he had been caught. In college he made other friends. He did not have to experiment with drugs as many of the others did. "That was old hat to me. I went to a couple of parties and felt very bored. The other kids were going through things I went through at 15. That was just not my scene."

By definition, John was a juvenile delinquent. Had he been 18 or 19, he might have been sentenced, perhaps even jailed. The boundary between normalty and delinquency indeed becomes a bit hazy at times. Peter Blos has commented, "Such typical acting out behavior is usually transient, benign, and in the service of progressive development."

In a broad sense, John's history follows the adolescent process as outlined by Blos. As he entered junior high school, he became much less involved with his family, particularly his mother. The drugs facilitated a great increase in his self-absorption and self-involvement. John described the hours he spent thinking about his different reactions to the various drugs, especially his two experiences with LSD, which he shared in a narcissistic way with others. Finally, at 16 he started to date one girl, and became very involved with her. As that happened his interest in drugs, and in that type of self-absorption, decreased. Blos' shorthand description of this stage is: progressive uninvolvement with mother, followed by excessive self-involvement, finally leading to heterosexual involvement. However, there were other features in John's background which made his drug taking not a transient, benign acting out in the service of progressive development as is the case with the normal adolescent.

John's earliest difficulties, manifested in the symptoms of colic, allergies, school difficulties, and social isolation, played a crucial role in his going too far in the acting out of his underlying problems. The marital conflict of the parents and the excessive preoccupation of the mother with John also presented special problems for him.

Various authors have called attention to a number of psychological features in the *neurotic delinquent*, all seen in John. First, there is an excessive impulsiveness, a proclivity for action. Second, there are rather intense narcissistic needs and an intolerance of tension. Third, there

are early psychological traumata. The relationship to people tends to be shallow. John, for example, became transiently involved with collectors, but one collector was as good as another. In his early junior high school contacts, his male friends were never really friends, and were easily exchanged one for the other. There are other important factors at work in the neurotic delinquent, such as the concept of the superego lacunae which will be described in the fourth example. The following case examples bring out some of the more complex factors seen in delinquents raised in difficult social settings such as the ghetto.

Bill

Bill was 15. He stole $20 to $30 per week, picking pockets if alone, or demanding money from strangers when participating with a gang. When the victim refused to give money, he got beaten up by the gang. Bill used to carry a .22 caliber pistol, which he once fired at a boy, but missed. Bill stabbed a boy in the leg during one of these holdups, was picked up by the police, and referred to a child psychiatry clinic.

Bill seemed generally eager to participate in a special, court-related, adolescent program. Many other adolescents accept this type of program as a better alternative than going to jail, but in no way express or show their eagerness. Bill was different. The psychiatrist, social worker, and psychologist each saw him alone during the first days, and all described him as cooperative, shy, anxious. He was quite embarrassed about his stuttering, asking if he could get help for this problem. His verbal intelligence was quite a bit lower (I.Q. of 74) than his performance (I.Q. of 96), in part because he gave up much more quickly on any difficult verbal questions. He had truanted from school for many years, since he had never really been able to master the routine demands of school. (One large study found that 83% of delinquent children had a reading disability.) Bill did not see himself as being able to be assertive, or to do anything about his difficulties. When asked his plans for the future, he said, "I can't be anything. I can't read or talk."

A slum has many different sections, and Bill's house was in the worst part. There were no stores or shopping areas for blocks around. On one side of the street all of the houses were deserted. Most of the windows and doors were boarded up. Even during the day there was an eerie quiet, which the staff doing the home visit found quite frightening. The apartment was clean, the furniture very simple. There were no expensive items at all, not even a radio or a television.

Bill was a sad, lonely boy, spending a great deal of time in what he called his "apartment"— a room he had furnished with a few chairs and a mattress in a neighboring block of deserted houses. He went there to get some privacy, because home included his asthmatic mother and five siblings. The oldest son of the seven children was in the service. The mother never married, and there were five different fathers for these seven children. The fathers all disappeared, providing no financial support for any of the children. Bill's mother felt totally overwhelmed. When the children started to bicker or fight, she would leave the house; otherwise she would develop an attack of asthma. Bill's stuttering abruptly started when he was eight years old during one of these fights when his older brother broke his arm. At that time his fantasies of killing began, fantasies that specifically involved killing his brother. Later on these fantasies were not limited to his brother, but included anyone who angered him. At times he would climb to the top of the building, thinking about all the people he could shoot. His younger siblings would tease him about his stuttering, and he would imagine stabbing and clubbing them to death.

The contrast between this inner violence which broke out at times when he was with his gang, and his usual quiet, shy, anxious appearance was quite marked, as it is with so many of these *gang-oriented delinquents*. The hopelessness he felt was accentuated by the mother's retreat to asthma in any tense situation. The gang provided excitement, a new set of values with high prestige on toughness and smartness, and a vehicle through which Bill could act out his sadistic impulses, now directed at the unknown stranger who is being mugged rather than at his family.

Manuel and Robert

In marked contrast to these children is the more overtly *psychotic delinquent*. Manuel and Robert were hospitalized on the psychiatric ward. These eight year old boys had murdered Robert's mother, but were incarcerated before they could kill Manuel's mother. The boys were small for their age, and had been close compan-

ions for one year. Robert's father was alcoholic, and his mother believed that she was a voodoo witch. She was convinced of her superhuman powers, as were many in her neighborhood. She punished Robert by dressing in her voodoo garb, and then threatening him with spirits who would kill him or maim him if he misbehaved or continued to wet to bed. Robert and Manuel spent hours together talking about their terror, exaggerating the feelings rather than relieving them through this talk. Robert's symptoms included hearing voices, and seeing death, mutilation, and destruction in what to other people might be rather neutral stimuli. For example, when he was asked to tell a story about a picture, as in the *Thematic Apperception Test*, or to describe what he saw in ill-defined ink blots, as in the *Rorschach Test*, Robert's murderous and mutilating fantasies clearly emerged.

There is a phenomenon described in the psychiatric literature where two individuals, who are very close, influence each other to the point of developing the same delusional system. This has been called *folie-à-deux*, madness shared by two (*shared paranoid disorder*). In the case of Manuel and Robert, these two small boys, terrified quite literally out of their minds by the reality of Robert's situation, were involved in a feedback system in which the individual terror of each was increased by their mutual interaction. Both, for different reasons, were isolated and ostracized by other children. They had no one else with whom to interact, no one else who could correct their progressively psychotic solution to their problems. Robert's father was alcoholic, angry when sober, brutal under the influence of alcohol. Manuel's parents were excessively rigid—"Children should be seen but not heard" to the extreme. Neither boy had ever experienced a sympathetic, let alone a warm or kind relationship with anyone else that would allow them to express their innermost fears. And so they had to find their own solution to their fears—the murder of their mothers.

Juanita

The ghetto is not uniform. It includes many different life styles. Juanita was a very pretty, attractive 15 year old girl. She came to the attention of the Family Court as a result of a PINS (person in need of supervision) petition filed by her parents. Her parents felt totally unable to control Juanita. She began truanting from school in the fifth grade. As she got older, her truancy problem rapidly escalated, until it began to include some petty larceny. The parents were very worried about what she did when she was not in school. The truant officer pressured them. The mother's depression, which she felt was caused by her sense of being a total failure as a mother, culminated in a suicide attempt by drinking two-thirds of a bottle of cleaning fluid. Juanita was not the only source of worry for the mother. The oldest son had a nonfunctioning kidney, surviving only because of regular renal dialysis. The parents helped to take care of this son's six year old daughter. Juanita developed epilepsy at the age of nine. The youngest brother, age 13, had rather severe asthma. He too had been expelled from school many times for truancy. The oldest sister, who was married and living away from home, was heavily involved in drug abuse, adding to the mother's worry about Juanita's behavior when truanting from school.

The parents were born and raised in a small isolated fishing village in Puerto Rico. Life was very different there than in the New York City ghetto. All the villagers knew each other, and the parents lived a few blocks from each other while they were growing up. Children just naturally did what they were told. The father was highly respected in this village. He graduated from high school, and was trained as a machinist. After he married, he moved to New York City to better his financial situation. In marked contrast to his adjustment in the fishing village, the father was suddenly overwhelmed in the large city. He never was able to reestablish that feeling of well-being and self-esteem that he had had as a developing youngster and as a young man in Puerto Rico. He began to drink, and by the time that I began to see Juanita, he was well on his way to becoming a chronic alcoholic.

The parents could not understand this new culture, the culture quickly embraced by their children as they grew up. The parents moved to a better section of the ghetto, one with many more senior citizens, and also more upwardly mobile Black and Puerto Rican residents who had more easily integrated into the American culture. However, the mother, though having lived in the United States for 20 years, was still clinging to her familiar culture. She had not even learned English beyond that required for simple shopping. The added stresses of the children's physical problems and their troubles with the law were too much for her. The father withdrew, drinking more and more. The mother worried—helplessly, painfully, and in great isolation. Once Juanita and her younger brother were referred to a specialized adolescent treatment program, the initial evaluation included a number of sessions with the entire family. There was quite a bit of fondness and warmth among the family members that emerged rather rapidly, and these affectionate ties proved to be a great asset in the subsequent treatment of Juanita and her brother.

Two important additional factors became apparent, *generation blending* and *superego lacunae*. The parents, Juanita, and her brother were seen together as a family for family therapy. The arguing, bickering, teasing, and playfulness appeared to be that of four siblings, rather than two parents and two children. There was no clear authority exercised by the parents. Although both parents tried to be firm in their authority with the children, it rapidly became clear that their wish to be friends with their children was more important to them than being parents. This was a particularly important insight because Juanita and her brother, in their interaction with the treatment staff, provoked and tested limits until it became clear that the staff fully intended to be firm and consistent in its exercise of authority. Once this was clear, both Juanita and her brother relaxed and did very well in the program, including their school work.

Some years ago Adelaide Johnson and Stanislaus Szurek described an interaction often seen in more middle class families with delinquent children, which they named "superego lacunae" or "holes in the conscience." They were struck by the subtle ways that the parents, without being aware of it, encouraged the delinquent behavior of the children. For example, during one of the family sessions, the younger brother described how he had fooled the teacher. He went to school and sat in the classroom for three days after he was expelled without the teacher noticing it. Juanita and her parents laughed with the brother at his ability to fool the teacher. One drop does not make an ocean. It is the pervasiveness and persistence of the subtle encouragement day in and day out that convey the message to the child that this type of antisocial behavior is not only permissible, but perhaps even unconsciously desired by the parents.

Barbara

Barbara was 15. She lived in an exclusive suburb with her parents. She was a beautiful girl, and her appearance would not be a handicap in her plans to become a model. Her parents arranged for a psychiatric evaluation because Barbara announced that she intended to drop out of high school. In the course of the evaluation it became clear that Barbara came home at three A.M. on some week days, and five or six A.M. on weekends. Barbara was much too tired to get up at eight A.M. to go to school. But it was not until Barbara said that she planned to quit school that the parents felt that something had to be done about the hours that Barbara was keeping.

When I asked what they thought their daughter was doing until three or five or six A.M., both said, "having fun." The mother described how she had been raised by a rigid, autocratic father and a very weak, uninvolved mother. She escaped her father's autocracy by marrying at 18. "I promised myself that my child would be able to have fun, and not live like I did. I had to be in right after school. I was never allowed to go to any school functions, or even to date until I graduated from high school at 17." Barbara's father denied ever worrying about his daughter. "She is very sensible. She can take care of herself." He became annoyed when I questioned whether she might be getting sexually involved, or might be getting in over her head in antisocial activities. He was quite indignant about such suggestions. The fact of the matter was that Barbara already had a reputation among her classmates as the "school whore."

The encouragement of such antisocial activity can be explicit, as in the example of Juanita and her brother, or implicit as in this situation with Barbara. There are certain behaviors that cry out for questioning by the parents. Not questioning is tantamount to permission, and the adolescent knows it and resents it. Another example is even more dramatic. An 18 year old boy told me he had "come out" as a homosexual two years before. One year later he had gotten false eyelashes. Before he went out evenings, he would put them on, using other makeup as well. He wore silver elevator shoes, and a silk ruffled shirt. His dress and gestures had all the exaggerated effeminate features associated with some male homosexuals. I asked what his parents' reaction was to all of this. He said, "I don't

know. I don't hide my makeup. They have never said anything. I am not sure they even are aware." In talking with the parents, I was able to confirm the boy's sense of his parents' non-recognition or nonacknowledgment of his homosexuality. They had been unconsciously sanctioning their son's homosexuality as a vicarious way of expressing some of their own sexual difficulties.

THE PSYCHOLOGY OF DELINQUENCY

In the early part of this chapter, I reviewed a few of the sociological and cultural findings on delinquency. I also looked at some of the early false explanations, including those involving genetics and low intelligence. Hopefully, our case examples began to demonstrate some of the diversity and complexity of the psychology of delinquency.

In the early years of this century, William Healy began pioneering psychiatric work with delinquents under the auspices of the newly formed juvenile court in Chicago. The entire child guidance movement, which resulted in the opening of dozens of child guidance clinics in the 1930's, was actually developed primarily to study, treat, and prevent juvenile delinquency. Healy began a revolution in our thinking about delinquency. He insisted that each boy or girl must be understood as a unique and individual person. The delinquency can only start to make sense if one knows about the child's or adolescent's inner life, his intellect, his family, his school, and his cultural environment. Healy particularly emphasized that an unconscious conflict underlies every specific delinquent act.

Meanwhile, August Aichhorn, a teacher in Austria, became the director of an institution for delinquent boys. He studied psychoanalysis, and began to report his growing understanding of the psychodynamics of such children and why they became delinquent. His book, *Wayward Youth*, is a classic. Aichhorn felt that there was a latent period in delinquent children before they became overtly delinquent during which they were particularly receptive to treatment and education. Aichhorn emphasized the development of the superego or conscience in every child, feeling that all children have wishes that must be curtailed by proper upbringing by the parents. If the parents are unable to fulfill this task, then the conscience or superego of the child does not develop normally, and hence adequate self-control is not achieved.

Franz Alexander also wrote about the superegos of delinquents, and described a particular type of *neurotic character* in which an unconscious need for punishment is a major motivating force for antisocial behavior.

We should add a few more names to this brief overview of the psychological factors that may operate in delinquency. John Bowlby studied 44 habitual thieves, and found that almost all of them had lost emotional contact with their mothers or foster mothers in early childhood, and had developed *affectionless characters*. And as noted earlier, Adelaide Johnson and Stanislaus Szurek called attention to the important concept of superego lacunae as exemplified in the cases of Juanita and Barbara. They pointed out that the child acts out the unconscious forbidden wishes of the parents, which are conveyed to the child by the parents' sanctioning, condoning, and encouraging the antisocial behavior of the child.

THE TREATMENT AND PREVENTION OF JUVENILE DELINQUENCY

The treatment of the criminal adolescent or adult is notoriously prone to failure. As a society, we seem helpless, continuing to jail criminals, even though jail only seems to serve as a finish-

ing school for more criminals (Figure. 59.1). David Reiser and Charles Malone described three to five year old children who were referred for treatment because of extreme amounts of disruption of home and neighborhood, running away, killing animals, frequent biting, scratching, stealing, fire setting, and vandalism. Reiser's patients were from the middle and upper classes, Malone's from lower class families. A follow-up four to 14 years later by Reiser showed that nine of the 26 children had become delinquents, but 17 had not. In his discussion of Reiser's paper, Theodore Lidz made the point that young children with such severe "antisocial" behavior often grow up to be schizophrenic, whereas adult criminals almost never have such bizarre histories as young children.

Working the other way around, the Gluecks studied 500 seriously delinquent boys, ages 11 to 17, and compared them with 500 nondelinquent boys of the same age, living in the same neighborhoods, of matched ethnoracial origin, and of matched intelligence. They studied the sociocultural, somatic, intellectual, and emotional-temperamental aspects in each of these 1,000 families. They developed a delinquency prediction scale that was supposed to predict future delinquency at the age of six. To date, no such scale, including this one, has proven reliable or truly predictive of eventual delinquency. Quite obviously, the wish is to find a way to

Figure 59.1. An adolescent boy in jail for delinquent behavior. From the film *Adolescence: The Winds of Change* by John Janeway Conger, in consultation with Jerome Kagan. (By permission of Harper & Row, New York, N.Y.)

predict delinquency in young children, so that efforts can be made toward prevention.

As we can see, juvenile delinquency, if defined as those acts which, if committed by an adult, would be considered a crime, includes many very different kinds of children and adolescents. The schizophrenic adolescent who sets a fire because a voice tells him to do so is very different from the retarded adolescent who is a peripheral member of a gang, and this retarded adolescent who gets caught because he does not have the sense to run away is very different from the rest of the gang. There are children who are quite clearly unloved and unwanted, whose hatred is expressed in all directions, and there are those who are unwisely and excessively loved, without restriction of discipline or limits. There are children and adolescents whose consciences are defective in those very areas where their own parents have defective consciences, and there are those who have such massive guilt that only punishment can relieve it. The parents of delinquents are just as varied. There are tragic parents who seek a new life in the United States, who hope to improve the lot of their children, only to find that their children have become strangers as they acculturate faster than the parents. There are other parents whose own despair and loneliness leave them with too little strength to withstand the added burdens of the poverty and the lawlessness of the ghetto.

Delinquency and criminality are frightening. The impersonality of some of this behavior is too unpredictable, leaving the victim helpless to prevent a recurrence. And yet, as we get to know the perpetrator of the crime, he, too, appears a victim, his rage and helplessness almost too understandable. More than any of the other psychopathological entities, juvenile delinquency can really only be understood if we look very closely at those sociocultural factors that contribute to the behavior of the delinquent child. Quite clearly, psychological factors do play a role and a very important role in each of these youngsters. The possibility of organic brain damage with a very high incidence of severe reading disability in this population cannot be ignored. However, particularly as one approaches the ghetto, the pull of poverty, the pull of the excitement of the gang, the pull of the acculturation forces outside of the home, are often too much for the counterpull of the closeness of the family, the parental discipline, and

the other factors that might mitigate against the development of delinquency in many of these children and adolescents.

Suggested Readings

Aichhorn A: *Wayward Youth.* New York, Viking Press, 1935.

Cloward RA, Ohlin LE: Some current theories of delinquent subcultures. In Harrison SI, McDermott JF (eds): *Childhood Psychopathology.* New York, International Universities Press, 1972, p. 540.

Eissler KR (ed): *Searchlights on Delinquency.* New York. International Universities Press, 1949.

Johnson AM: Sanctions for superego lacunae of adolescents. In Harrison SI, McDermott JF (eds): *Childhood Psychopathology.* New York, International Universities Press, 1972, p. 522.

Keniston K: *The Uncommitted: Alienated Youth in American Society.* New York, Dell, 1967.

Lindner R: *Rebel Without a Cause.* New York, Grune & Stratton, 1944.

Menninger K: *The Crime of Punishment.* New York, Viking Press, 1968

Offer D, Marohn RC, Ostrov E: *The Psychological World of the Juvenile Delinquent.* New York, Basic Books, 1979.

Quay HC (ed): *Juvenile Deliquency* New York, Van Nostrand Reinhold Co, 1965.

Redl F, Wineman D: *Children Who Hate.* New York, Free Press of Glencoe, 1951.

Redl F, Wineman D: *Controls From Within.* New York, Free Press of Glencoe, 1952.

Redl F, Wineman D: *The Aggressive Child.* New York, Free Press of Glencoe, 1957.

References

Alexander F: The neurotic character. *Int J Psychoanal* 11:292, 1930.

Blos P: The concept of acting out in relation to the adolescent process. In Rexford EN (ed): *A Developmental Approach to Problems of Acting Out.* New York, International Universities Press, 1966, p 118.

Bowlby J: *Fourty-Four Juvenile Thieves.* London, Bailiere, 1946.

Eichorn JR: Delinquency and the educational system. In Quay HC (ed): *Juvenile Delinquency.* New York, Van Nostrand Reinhold Co, 1965, p. 298.

Glueck S, Glueck ET: *Unravelling Juvenile Delinquency.* Cambridge, Harvard University Press, 1959.

Goddard HH: *Juvenile Delinquency.* New York, Dodd, Mead, 1923.

Goring CS: *The English Convict.* His Majesty's Stationary Office, London 1913. Reprinted by Patterson Smith, Montclair, NJ, 1972.

Healy W, Bronner AF: *New Light on Delinquency and Its Treatment.* New Haven, Yale University Press, 1936.

Johnson AM, Szurek SA: The genesis of antisocial acting out in children and adults. *Psychoanal Q* 21:323, 1952.

Lewis DO, et al: Homicidally aggressive young children: neuropsychiatric and experiential correlates. *Am J Psychiatry* 140:148, 1983.

Lichtenstein M, Brown AW: Intelligence and achievement of children in a delinquency area. *J Juvenile Res* 22:1, 1938.

Lombroso C: *Crime: Its Causes and Remedies.* New York, Little Brown, 1911.

Maller JB: Juvenile delinquency in New York City. *J Psychology* 3:1, 1937.

Malone CA: Some observations on children of disorganized families and problems of acting out. In Rexford EN (ed) *A*

Developmental Approach to Problems of Acting Out. New York, International Universities Press, 1966, p 22.

McCord W, McCord J, Zola I: *Origins of Crime.* New York, Columbia University Press, 1959.

Miller WB: Lower class culture as a generating milieu of gang delinquency. *J Soc Issues* 14:5, 1958.

Reiser DE: Observations of delinquent behavior in very young children. In Rexford EN (ed): *A Developmental Approach to Problems of Acting Out.* New York, International Universities Press, 1966, p 50.

Shaw RC, McKay HD: *Juvenile Delinquency and Urban Areas.* Chicago, University of Chicago Press, 1942.

CHAPTER 60 # The Eating Disorders, and the Psychophysiological Disorders of Childhood and Adolescence

Adolph E. Christ, M.D.

I will begin this chapter by discussing the clinical manifestations of the eating disorders and two of the most common psychophysiological disorders of childhood and adolescence, namely asthma and ulcerative colitis. I will then conclude the chapter by describing general systems theory, and attempt to show how this theoretical perspective can add greatly to our understanding of the mental disorders in general, and of the psychophysiological disorders in specific.

EATING DISORDERS

Jules Hirsch and Herbert Weiner have recently summarized our current knowledge about the interaction of biological and psychological factors in the eating disorders. In this brief introduction I will focus primarily on the interaction of sociocultural and psychological factors in these disorders. There is a cartoon which shows a gangster staggering into his mother's kitchen, bullet holes gushing blood. She is standing with a plate of soup in her left hand, a spoon going towards his mouth in her right, as she says, "Eat, eat, my son." This dying man could easily have come from any one of a number of different ethnic groups.

Certainly the prevailing cultural attitudes about health and beauty have a great deal to do with eating patterns. It is hard to overestimate their importance, even though they can markedly change in a relatively short period of time. For example, until the 1920's slenderness was feared because tuberculosis was felt to result from frailty. Actually, weight loss is the result of tuberculosis and not the cause, but many thin children were force fed to prevent this illness. A

little earlier, the long dress and bustle hid the obesity that was necessary to insure the mark of beauty in the woman—a well formed cleavage exposed by a plunging neckline. Obesity as a sign of beauty and wealth persists to this day in countries where moderate to severe poverty exists. In contrast, today's American fashion model is extremely slender. It may surprise readers, as it did me, to learn that fainting, secondary to near starvation, is a frequent occupational hazard of today's models.

Not only do prevailing cultural attitudes about health and beauty influence the way a family interacts around eating, but unconscious psychological attitudes and conflicts can very readily find expression through the continuing ritual of eating. Eating is such a basic and repetitive function that if it does become a focus for parent-child interactional pathology, the results can be quite unfortunate. A school teacher father brought a verbatim account of one such meal to Leo Kanner. In order to get even with his wife, this father went into an adjoining room, and took notes of the breakfast dialogue between five year old Martin and his mother.

Breakfast Scene

(Wheaties are served at 8:15 A.M.)
Mother: (Much coercing, yelling, threatening.)
Martin: (Crying, almost vomiting, refusing to eat, threatened to be put to bed.)
Mother: Did you get me out of bed for this? Tomorrow you can holler for your breakfast all day, but you won't get it. You are going to eat this whether you want it or not. (Pause.) Hurry up! You

are going to sit here all day until you eat.

Martin: (Cries.) My stomach hurts. I don't want it. I won't eat it.

Father: (From adjoining room, to mother.) Don't start any feeding methods! The doctor said to wait until he gets well. Don't force food! Take it away. (Diverts the child's attention until he stops crying. To Martin): Your stomach has plenty of room. I'll feed it and, as you eat the wheaties, I'll ask the stomach if it has room. Stomach says: Come on, wheaties! ... Thank God! (It is now 9:35. Soft boiled egg. Father leaves the dining room to listen from the adjoining room.)

Mother: (Pleasantly conversing with Martin.) Go on! Hurry up! Keep it up until you are finished! Don't look around until you are finished! You won't make me mad again. Don't talk to me!

Martin: Too much salt.

Mother: (Disgustedly.) Aw, you!

Martin: See this?

Mother: Watch what you are doing! Is it any wonder that you get everything all over yourself? Can't pick them, can you?

Martin: I'll get 'em.

Mother: Come on! Hurry up! You move so slow no wonder you give it a chance to get off your spoon.

Martin: I get it in my tummy.

Mother: We gave him the works. (Egg finished at 9:47. 9:49: Chocolate milk.)

Mother: Go ahead! Drink it!

Martin: Stomach hurts.

Mother: Keep drinking! Go ahead!

Martin: My stomach.

Mother: (Puts her hand on Martin's abdomen.)

Martin: (Drinks a little. Puts glass down.)

Mother: Never mind massaging the stomach! You never see people rubbing stomachs in a restaurant. I'll take you back to the hospital. I'll take a blanket, wrap it around you, take a cab, and they'll straighten your stomach out.

Martin: My stomach is upset.

Mother: Pick the glass up! Pick the glass up! Pick it up! ... Without that sour puss. Well, do you want to go outside? You have been sitting here two hours.

You want to sit here another hour?

Martin: My stomach.

Mother: I don't think it's your stomach. I think you ought to have your head examined.

Martin: Stop hollering at me!

Mother: Drink it down.

Martin: I can't.

Mother: Yes, you can. You want me to put it down your throat?

Martin: (Crying and whimpering.) I don't want.

Mother: Go on! You want me to give it to you?

Martin: Please! Please!

Mother: Don't set it down so much! Pick it up! Pick it up! I said: Pick it up! (Martin cries.) That means nothing to me. I am used to seeing that mug.

Martin: (Tries to belch.) I can't drink it.

Mother: (Sarcastic.) I am so sorry. Do you want me to cry with you?

Martin: (Yelling.) I don't want any more.

Mother: Shut up! You are going to drink it. You don't want to stay here. You want to go to the hospital.

Martin: No! No! I don't want to go.

Mother: Holler a little louder so everybody can hear you!

Martin: (Half crying and half yelling.) I don't want any more.

Mother: You are going to drink. I have plenty of time. I like to see how you get all full of spasms.

Martin: (Hits, kicks, and pinches his mother.)

Mother: That's fine. I can take it. All nice boys do that. Good boys pinch, kick, and hit their mothers and daddies. (Two minutes of silence.)

Mother: Do you think Shirley Temple pinches and hits her mother? Do you think she would like it?

Martin: Yes.

Mother: I'll write her a letter and see what she says. I'll bet she'll want her picture back.

Martin: Don't write to her!

Mother: Well, why do you do that?

Martin: Because I want to. (Follow five minutes of silence. Martin sitting and milk not finished.)

Martin: Go and do something and I'll drink it. You go and do your work!

Mother: I am going to sit right here until you drink it. You don't do what I tell you anyhow. Pick that glass up! Are you going to start all over again? Pick it up!

Martin: (Drinks some.) I want to take a rest.

Mother: How much more have you got?

Martin: (Wants to kiss his mother, then finishes milk. Finished at 10:15.)

Martin: (Proudly.) Didn't I drink it up?

Mother: I won't forget that you hit your mother. Only bad little boys do that.*

Obesity

Obesity is defined as weighing 20% or more above the ideal body weight for the person's height and skeletal frame. Obesity is a very common problem in America, and the percentage of people in each decade of life who are obese steadily increases until the age of 50, following which there is a sharp decline. The major reason for the decline is that obese people die at a much greater rate after age 50. Obesity is a major risk factor for several of the most common fatal illnesses of middle age, including coronary artery disease, hypertensive cardiovascular disease, and diabetes. Some obese people may live to be quite old, but statistically the odds for longevity favor people who are thin or close to their ideal body weight.

Obesity is more common in members of the lower socioeconomic class in this country than in the middle or upper classes. The number of adipose tissue cells a person has for life may be partially influenced by nutrition during infancy, and so overfed babies may actually develop more adipose cells. Vigorous physical activity not only burns off calories but may also decrease appetite and food intake in some individuals. Very rarely brain damage in the ventromedial or lateral hypothalamus (hunger and satiety centers) may influence appetite. And as Hirsch has pointed out in his review article, we are still only at the beginning in our understanding of the subtle biological and psychobiological factors in the etiology of obesity. On the basis of our current knowledge, it is still probably safe to say that many, if not most individuals overeat for emotional reasons. The anxious or depressed person

---

* From Kanner, Leo. *Child Psychiatry*, ed 3. Charles C Thomas, publisher. Springfield, IL, 1966. Published by permission.

may find a large meal sedating and tranquilizing. Insomniacs may find food a helpful soporific. Those with body image disturbances who feel their body is unattractive or grotesque may eat to enlarge their self-image. Any stress may prompt the obese person to overeat. Indeed, obese persons are more likely to manifest emotional conflicts than are a matched population of nonobese persons, but the diversity of dynamic factors among these individuals argues against the existence of any single constellation of personality characteristics specific to obesity.

Hilda Bruch's name is synonymous with the study of obesity and anorexia nervosa. She states that "the experience of hunger is not innate, but contains important elements of learning." She has found that people suffering from obesity or anorexia have a poor recognition of hunger and satiation, as well as more general bodily sensations. With Coddington she introduced measured amounts of food into the stomachs of different subjects, and found that obese and anorexic patients were significantly less able than normal subjects to recognize whether food had been put into their stomachs or how much had been introduced. Similarly, Schachter found that obese subjects are much more affected by external stimuli, such as the sight of food or the passage of time, whereas normal subjects eat when they are hungry.

Genetic factors may play some role in the etiology of obesity. In 1927 Danforth first described a genetic form of obesity in a specific strain of mice. This was particularly exciting at the time, opening up many research possibilities. However, Bruch subsequently followed many obese adolescents into adulthood, and found that those adolescents who had been in psychiatric treatment and had resolved some of their basic problems around obesity raised no obese children, even if they themselves remained obese. Angel did a very extensive study to determine the genetic aspects of obesity, and concluded that, "Whatever the genetic determinants ... they are complicated by the effects of environmental factors, faulty eating habits, psychic influences, and traumatic events." Obesity in children is very rarely the result of hypothyroidism or hypopituitarism. It is indeed unfortunate that so many physicians, either because of their own feelings of hopelessness or because of the parents' coercion, will prescribe thyroid or other types of hormones to these children in the hope that, even though all hormonal evaluations are normal, such drugs might do something.

As I indicated earlier, the overfeeding and the inability to take cues from the child about food are inevitably seen in families who produce severely obese children. These interactional patterns can be subtle, as is often the case in anorexia nervosa, or they can be markedly overt, as is often the case in obesity. What is clear, however, is that they are persistent. I consulted in a pediatric obesity clinic for several years, and the parent-child interaction of the obese children and their mothers in the waiting room was fascinating. The mothers usually took off the coats and rubbers of these six to 12 year old children and hung them up. The children sat in the chairs, and if there were not enough chairs, the mothers would stand. The automatic passivity and compliance of these obese children, and the overprotectiveness of the mothers, were quite marked. As these children's weight increased to 70 or 100% above normal, less and less of their bodies moved, until there was almost no hand or finger motion.

In general, most of these children had been obese all of their lives, even as small babies. At times one wonders whether there are critical points beyond which, if obesity has existed, it is there for life. Bruch describes a rarely encountered situation that helps to answer this question. A two year old boy was 100% overweight. The parents had lost their jobs during the depression years, and had taken a position together in a wealthy household. The child was fed every time he whimpered in order to keep him quiet. The father was so disgusted with his son's appearance that he could neither pay attention to him nor play with him. Up until this point, the situation was a typical one for obese children. But then it changed. The couple moved. The mother no longer felt the constraints of keeping her child quiet, so that she now permitted him a free choice of food. The father, encouraged by some of the changes in his son, started playing and enjoying sports with him. Without any diets or any coercion, by age five he was a chubby, but active, friendly, and outgoing child. At the age of 10 he was a good athlete. By the age of 18 he was described as tall and slender. Thus, in order for obesity to develop, a persistent interactional pattern between parents and child had to be present. This case demonstrated that even severe obesity up to the toddler age does not necessarily result in permanent obesity unless the pathological parental interaction continues. Bruch found that, of all the parental factors studied, the parents' encouragement of excessive dependence and discouragement of any independence in their children seemed the most important variables.

What happens, however, if the obesity persists? It appears that where there is a good accepting relationship between the obese child and his or her family, much of life can be fairly normal. In fact, many obese people maintain a comfortable steady weight, be it 50% or even 100% above average weight. For many obese people, efforts to reduce below this weight mean a life of constant preoccupation with food and weight. However, where there is not this type of an accepting relationship by the family, the obese child is invariably a very unhappy child who develops into a very unhappy obese adolescent and adult.

With regard to adolescent obesity, it is important to remember that normal adolescence is a period of dramatic body change, which may not be at all smooth and even. One slender boy was six feet three inches tall at the age of 17. He had a marked growth spurt from age 13 to 15, but all of it was in his legs! His long legs and tiny thorax earned him the temporary nickname of "Stork." Girls not unusually go through periods of 10% to 20% weight deviation from the normal, either too much or too little, but this gradually evens out. Many girls welcome the appearance of feminine curves, while others resent not being able to fit into the male jeans that they had been wearing until then, and they may temporarily go on crash diets to correct this "obesity." When adolescents have a good sense of identity, a sense of themselves as separate and well differentiated individuals, the final physical outcome, be it to become slender or obese adults, does not have to hamper their subsequent development.

The disturbed adolescent, on the other hand, may eat when he or she is anxious, angry, sad, or depressed. Indeed, I have had patients describe this kind of eating as a "hunger in the mouth," a need to chew, to swallow, to fill a terribly empty feeling inside. Not only do such patients have difficulty recognizing true hunger, but anxiety, anger, sadness, and depression are also often vague and unrecognized feelings. To the question "How did that make you feel?", a puzzled look is not an unusual response. Much of the normal adolescent's conflict revolves around the question of choice and duty, or as Bruch points out, between self-initiated and superimposed activities. This is really not so different from Peter Blos' concept of adolescence as a second separation-individuation stage. However, in the case of a disturbed adolescent, the severity of the underlying psychopathology markedly distorts this normal conflict. In adolescence the battle between dependence and independence is only partly waged between the parents and the adolescent. It is also partly waged within the adolescent. The precarious balance of the emotionally disturbed, obese adolescent can sometimes be tipped by such stresses as going away to college or sudden reducing. A neurosis, a period of acting out, or at times even a profound difficulty such as a schizophrenic disorder or a major depression, may emerge under the impact of these stresses. When this follows a period of dieting, one begins to see that the obesity itself may have served as a defense and protection from too much contact with people, and may have helped to ward off some of the more disturbed underlying feelings. Indeed, this type of obesity can generally best be understood as a symptom of a more pervasive underlying emotional disturbance.

Anorexia Nervosa

Jane was 14 when she was admitted to the hospital. She was 5 feet 5 inches tall, and at 72 pounds she was markedly emaciated. There was hardly any bone in her body that was not clearly outlined. Since around 10% of patients with *anorexia nervosa* eventually die of the self-imposed starvation, treatment in a hospital setting is often essential. This is one of the few emotional diseases of adolescence where the incidence is greater in girls than boys, with a ratio of 10:1. An early description of this illness in 1868 by William Gull is still timely. This is not a disease of poverty. Nearly all reported cases come from well-to-do families where food is plentiful.

There is a marked similarity in the histories of most of these cases. Before the onset of the disease, the youngsters have been excellent students, thoughtful, obedient to a fault at home and in school. The overt pathological family interactions of the obese child are rare. Indeed, the initial contact with the parents often gives one the impression of a loving, highly concerned involvement with the patient. The slight body

shift that occurs in early adolescence, with the hip and breast enlargement, may precipitate severe worries in the girl about getting fat. An initial diet may be welcomed by all, especially if the girl was a bit overweight. But the "diet" that is so innocently begun in adolescence soon takes an ominous turn.

Weight continues to drop, more and more foods are stricken from the diet, exercises are done "to burn off the fat." Menstruation ceases. The body contours flatten out, and many of the secondary sexual characteristics are lost. By now, the family is alarmed, and strange interactions around eating become manifest. In Jane's family the mother ceased to talk about food because it provoked totally uncharacteristic, defiant refusals in her previously compliant daughter. The father went to Jane's room every hour, suggesting food that she might want to eat, and offering to cook it for her any time of the day or night. However, Jane remained intensely afraid of becoming obese, even as her weight loss progressed.

Jane continued to go to her ballet lessons, as well as to the swimming pool. By now she weighed 80 pounds, and was truly a skeleton (Figure 60.1). She was oblivious to her peculiar appearance, and seemed unable to comprehend why the ballet teacher wanted her to discontinue her lessons, or why her friends began to shun her at the pool. This apparent inability to realistically perceive their body image is quite characteristic of youngsters with anorexia nervosa. They continue to see themselves as "fat" regardless of how much weight they lose.

Jane was eventually hospitalized in the psychiatric ward at a weight of 72 pounds. She denied that she felt hunger, and quickly insisted on a specific diet: a cup of black coffee for breakfast, lettuce without any dressing for lunch, and a glass of skimmed milk for supper. When she was forced to eat, she only pretended to eat, lied about the amount that she ate, and then threw it into the garbage can until she was caught. She next tried to vomit surreptitiously by putting her finger down her throat after meals. The denial of hunger is felt by Bruch to be part of the more global denial and unawareness of general bodily sensations described in the previous section on obesity. It is a highly characteristic symptom in youngsters with anorexia nervosa. Another nearly universal characteristic is the excessive amount of physical activity in which these patients engage. After

Figure 60.1. Giacometti, Alberto. *Man Pointing* (1947). Bronze, 70 1/2″ high, at base 12 × 13 1/4″. Collection, The Museum of Modern Art, New York. Gift of Mrs. John D. Rockefeller III.

her third day on the ward, the occupational therapist reported, "I wonder if we should let her use the exercise equipment. The way she uses that equipment is unbelievable!" Despite her emaciation she walked and paced for hours, oblivious of what must have been extreme fatigue due to this hyperactivity. Others will attempt to lose more weight by abusing laxatives, enemas, and diuretics.

In a classic paper on this syndrome, Waller, Kaufman, and Deutsch felt that the central conflict in some of these young women is a fear of femininity, and they presented case material that demonstrated the self-induced vomiting and progressive weight loss to be defenses against oral impregnation fantasies. For example, many anorexics gorge themselves (bulimia), then become terrified of the "bulge in the stomach" and quickly induce vomiting to "get everything out." Associated with the fear of femininity is a pervasive fear of the responsibilities of adulthood and the inevitable separation from the parents. The emaciation certainly maintains the patient in a dependent state, forces continued attention from the frantic parents, and delays separation and adulthood.

In her series of 70 patients, Bruch was particularly impressed with the paralyzing sense of ineffectiveness of these patients. In her book, *The Golden Cage*, Bruch has described many of these patients as not feeling adequate to meet the expectations placed upon them by their families. They feel like "a sparrow in a golden cage." The refusal to eat is seen by them as perhaps the only way in which they can exercise control and self-direction. Treatment therefore only becomes effective when this feeling of helplessness, of total absence of any kind of constructive self-direction, is gradually resolved. I can only repeat what was said earlier about the obese adolescent. Many of the conflicts of the anorexic patient revolve around the question of self-initiated versus superimposed activity. Thus, severe obesity is one side of the coin; severe emaciation, resulting at times even in death, is the other.

Bulimia

Bulimia, or the *binge-purge syndrome*, is a disorder that has recently been differentiated from anorexia nervosa. The essential features are episodic binge eating (rapid consumption of a large amount of food in a short period of time), termination of such eating episodes with self-induced vomiting or laxatives, awareness that the eating pattern is abnormal, fear of not being able to stop eating voluntarily, and depressed mood with self-critical thoughts following the eating binges. As with anorexia nervosa the disorder occurs predominantly in middle or upper class females, but unlike anorexia nervosa the weight loss is never so extreme as to be life-threatening. While many cases of anorexia nervosa may begin at puberty, the binge-purge syndrome is more likely to begin in college and then persist for many years among these well-educated, high-achieving women. Finally, bulimia appears to be a much more common disorder than anorexia nervosa. In one study by Pope and coworkers, 304 females over 12 years of age, randomly selected in a shopping center, were asked to complete a one page confidential questionnaire dealing with eating habits. Of the 300 who responded, 10.3% met the DSM-III criteria for a lifetime history and diagnosis of bulimia, whereas only 0.7% met the DSM-III criteria for a lifetime history and diagnosis of anorexia nervosa.

ASTHMA

An asthmatic attack is always frightening, not only to the child, but also to the parents and siblings. The child has the feeling that he is choking to death. His face is pale. He breathes rapidly, inhaling quickly, but then wheezing as he tries to push out the air. He feels the need to breathe in even as he is exhaling, so as to take in enough air to keep alive.

Everyone in the home is affected by an attack. Inhalants, syringes, adrenalin, aminophyllin suppositories are all carefully arranged and readily available. A rapid trip to the emergency room may become necessary, not infrequently with a period of hospitalization that disastrously affects the family budget. Every feature of the house is altered. Pets, especially cuddly dogs and cats, even birds and hamsters, are banned. Furniture becomes stark and vinyl covered. Curtains and rugs begin to disappear. A dust-free home requires meticulous, time consuming housekeeping.

In the more serious forms of this disease, corticosteroids may be given, and they may cause a number of reactions or side effects, such as a bloated appearance. John, age 12, expressed his reaction to these drugs as follows: "My stomach is big, my cheeks are like a hamster's, my shoulders are like a buffalo's hump. I don't mind all that. That will go away when I stop taking the medicine. But what I care about is that my growth may be stunted." This bloated appearance is not attractive, and it adds to the child's and the family's distress.

As a disease asthma is not benign. In a followup 20 years after the onset of symptoms, Rackemann and Edwards found the following: 70% had no more symptoms of asthma if the patient avoided offending allergens, even if some (21%) had other allergic diseases. Twenty-six per cent had some asthmatic symptoms, and

about half of those (13%) had a serious health problem with asthma. One per cent had died of asthma.

Even when the asthma is outgrown, there may be major characterological consequences. Kiell attempts a fascinating reconstruction of President Theodore Roosevelt's life from the perspective of the effects of his being asthmatic until adulthood. Extremely close to his mother, whom he addressed as "Darling, beloved motherling," he had a similar infantilized relationship with his sister. At age 11 he wrote in his diary, "I read until Mama came in, and then she lay down and I stroked her head and she felt my hands and nearly cried because they were fevered." He was coddled until age 18, and had only private tutors. We can only speculate how much of his later life was a reaction formation to this infantilization, but he climbed the Matterhorn, was a hero in the Spanish-American war, roughed it on the badlands of the Dakotas, hunted lions in Africa, and played polo when other men his age were playing croquet. He was overjoyed when his four sons enlisted in the military service, taught them to swim by throwing them into deep water as children, and took them on hikes that were far beyond their abilities. Thus, asthma not only kills, but it can also have serious psychological effects on the developing child and on the parents. At times, the sum of the individual's ways of dealing with the asthmatic experiences may be largely constructive. Often, however, the outcome can hamper effective functioning. For example, one individual considered himself so weak and vulnerable even after outgrowing the asthma, that he unnecessarily restricted all of his physical activities in adulthood.

What is asthma? The current medical term for asthma is reactive airway dysfunction. The person's tracheobronchial tree is hyperreactive and various physical, allergic, or emotional stresses may elicit the bronchoconstrictor response. It is the leading cause of chronic illness in children, affecting boys to girls in a ratio of two to one until adolescence, when the incidence becomes equal. Although it is more common in males, females tend to have more severe asthma. It is also important to realize that adults may develop the illness at any age without having had any prior symptoms.

What causes asthma? Although we are learning more and more as a result of research, much remains unknown. *Atopy* is a term referring to a constellation of findings in some allergic individuals, including a high incidence of asthma, hay fever, and eczema in close relatives (hereditary factor), a predilection to selective formation of a particular antibody (reagin) on exposure to allergenic substances, a hyperreactivity of the respiratory airways to many physical environmental factors, and a probable abnormality in the metabolism of cyclic adenosine $3':5'$-monophosphate (cyclic AMP), manifested by abnormal responses to histamine and adrenalin.

In regard to immunological factors, *extrinsic (allergic) asthmatic* attacks can follow exposure to environmental pollutants such as house dust and pollens. *Intrinsic asthmatics* seem not to be allergic to such substances, even on skin tests. The onset of asthma in this intrinsic group is earlier (around age two), and follows no seasonal pattern. The role of infection is also fascinating. Respiratory infections often precipitate asthmatic attacks, especially in the intrinsic (nonallergic) type of asthma. Recent work suggests this is so only with certain viral infections, such as parainfluenza virus. Bacterial infections and other viral respiratory infections, such as the adenovirus and the Hong Kong influenza viruses, do not precipitate asthmatic attacks. In regard to endocrine factors, little is known about their specific effect. That endocrine factors play a role is suggested by the fact that women have more asthmatic attacks during the premenstrual part of their menstrual cycle. There is also a much greater incidence of asthma in individuals with Addison's disease. Furthermore, asthmatics who also have thyrotoxicosis cannot have the asthma controlled until the underlying endocrine disease is treated.

Psychological factors must always be considered in any discussion of asthma. The question has been whether they are primary in the etiology of this disease, or arise secondarily as reactions to the disease. Certainly anxiety from any cause may lead to bronchospasm in asthmatics. Asthmatics participating in an experiment were given a drug which induced bronchospasm and were later told they were being given the drug again but were given a placebo. The anxiety of anticipating an asthmatic attack caused bronchospasm to occur even when only a placebo was given.

In another study on the experimental induction of anxiety in asthmatic and nonasthmatic individuals, Peter Knapp has reported: "Both groups were roughly the same with one excep-

tion—anger. Nonasthmatics got angry at the nasty experiment, but the asthmatics suppressed the emotion and did not report anger." Knapp went on to quote Hippocrates: "Asthmatics must guard against anger."

Some authors have stressed that the mother of the asthmatic child is often quite rejecting of the child. However, more recent evidence contradicts this with the finding that actually there is an excessive closeness between the mother and her asthmatic child. In the treatment of asthmatic children and their parents, it becomes very difficult to determine all of the reasons for this extreme closeness. One mother poignantly described her difficulty in balancing the dependent and the independent needs of her child. Too much running, any sudden exposure to cold weather, viral infections, all of these could precipitate an asthmatic attack. When she let him run out and play in the winter and he then had an asthmatic attack, her guilt was not alleviated by the pediatrician's insisting that she watch him more carefully.

Thus, frequent asthmatic attacks may change a parent's natural response to a child. In one family, the two older siblings were quite independent, outgoing, active children. On the other hand, the youngest child, who was asthmatic, was spoiled and pampered by all. This is in marked contrast to a situation where the parents tend to cling to all of their children. For example, one mother was orphaned at the age of 13. She missed the intimacy of family life during her adolescence, and wanted to provide this closeness to her children. Her overprotection of her asthmatic child was indeed excessive, but she tended to be that way with all of her children. A younger child, who was not asthmatic, persistently but gently pushed the mother away and developed more independently.

A more difficult situation is one where the psychopathology of the parent is more profound. One woman suffered from a severe psychosomatic disorder herself, and had a series of excessively close but sadomasochistic relationships with her own parents and her husband. Her son's asthma often infuriated her because of the excessive demands that his illness made on her. Her own infantile character made it difficult for her to evaluate her son's dependent and independent needs. At times she quite clearly rejected and provoked him. He then cried and screamed, precipitating an asthmatic attack. The father was also quite infantile and ineffectual in interacting with his wife. Although very bright, he did not allow himself to comprehend what was transpiring between his wife and son during these episodes.

By now it should be clear that there are many different kinds of parents of asthmatic children who will interact with their child in important but very different ways. The children themselves are also very different. The total separation of the child from the family, labeled "parentectomy" by Peshkin, is practiced in such institutions as the National Asthma Center and National Jewish Hospital and Research Center in Denver, Colorado. Such radical treatment is obviously limited to intractably asthmatic children. Bernstein and Purcell described different patterns in youngsters hospitalized at this center. One group rapidly remits, and remains symptom-free without medication for the full year of hospitalization. These children in general have more neurotic symptoms, and the mothers have more autocratic and hostile rejecting attitudes towards their children. In contrast, the steroid-dependent children remain symptomatic. Attempts to withdraw this group from medication produce rapid relapses. Arnoldsson found that placebo medication could not replace the steroids. These children had many fewer neurotic symptoms, and the parental attitudes were also quite different. In still another group, separation, or even the threat of separation from the mother, can precipitate an asthmatic attack. This is obviously in marked contrast to the rapid improvement seen in the asthmatic youngsters who are totally separated from their parents by hospitalization.

How can we make sense out of all of this? Marvin Stein has recently summarized our current understanding of the multiple biological, psychological, and sociocultural factors involved in asthma. It appears to be an allergic disease with probable hereditary, biochemical alterations resulting in altered reactions to a variety of stimuli. The symptoms are terrifying, producing psychological reactions in both child and parents, and the normal interaction of parent and child is skewed by such a serious illness. There are idiosyncratic backgrounds in some of these parents, which further affect their coping mechanisms. Although there is little evidence that asthma initially starts solely as a reaction to emotional stresses or conflicts, there is overwhelming evidence that emotional factors play an important role in the prolongation of the disease in many cases, in the precipitation of attacks in some cases, and in the alteration of the relationship between the asthmatic child and his or her parents in nearly all cases.

ULCERATIVE COLITIS

This is a chronic disease punctuated by variable periods of remissions, during which any hope that the abdominal pain and bloody diarrhea are finally over can be dashed by a sudden recurrence of the colitis, even after a five year remission. One adult patient described the following: "When I take a taxi, my main worry is whether, if I suddenly have to go to the bathroom, the cab can stop in time so that I can find a bathroom before I have an accident." Shopping in a department store means determining where the bathrooms are on each floor in case of sudden diarrhea. Repeated urges to defecate at night, with severe abdominal cramps just before a bowel movement, are not unusual. As the disease progresses, weight loss, nausea and vomiting, anemia, even emaciation and growth retardation may occur. A thorough evaluation may be necessary to confirm the diagnosis and observe the progression of the illness. Sigmoidoscopy to visualize the bleeding mucosa, ragged ulcers, and pseudopolyps, rectal biopsy for micropathological confirmation, and barium enema X-ray studies to see the hyperactive colon, ulcers, or later the shortened rigid colon, may all be required procedures.

These various procedures are not only uncomfortable; they are also very intrusive. A prim and proper 14 year old girl described the indignity and horror of these procedures. She was very modest and shy, and indeed it was only after we had developed a trusting relationship after six months of psychotherapy that she was able to begin to talk about her fear and her rage at having her privacy so blatantly invaded. Fortunately, she had a very sensitive pediatrician who had known her since infancy. He had carefully explained all of the procedures to her, had allowed her maximum privacy, and had the nurse drape her with heavy sheets so as to increase her feeling of being covered and protected. After the tests were completed, he explained all of the findings to her. Nevertheless, she still felt that she had been exposed and victimized.

Ulcerative colitis can start in infancy, although this is uncommon. It is primarily a disease of adolescents and young adults. This is not a benign disease. The overall mortality rate has been estimated at about 5%. Forty per cent to 50% of childhood cases continue with symptoms into adulthood, the rest have prolonged remissions. One complication can be neoplastic degeneration, which becomes an increasing risk when the colitis has persisted for more than 10 years. Thus, colectomy may be required not only for refractory bleeding or perforation of the colon, but also prophylactically because of the risk of cancer after the first decade of this illness. However, the decision to remove the colon surgically, leaving an ileostomy for life, is not an easy one. A close working alliance of child psychiatrist, pediatrician, and pediatric surgeon is imperative in the care of such a complicated disease.

The causes of this disease remain unclear. A genetically determined organ vulnerability is probably present since it may run along family lines. Regional enteritis (Crohn's disease) appears to be a similar disorder, except the vulnerable organ is the small, rather than large, intestine. Theories on infectious, immunologic, and psychogenic causes have been proposed, but the etiology is still uncertain. Certainly the severe emotional problems present in the child, and in the parent-child interactions, are most persuasive, if not as etiological, then at least as major contributory factors in the repeated exacerbations of ulcerative colitis.

What are these children like? The first descriptive studies on these patients were done 30 or more years ago when the very sizable group of children with milder ulcerative colitis was not yet appreciated. Therefore, the youngsters who were reported in some of these early studies may represent a very select group with severe colitis and emotional problems who were referred for psychiatric evaluation. For example, Dane Prugh found a group of children with ulcerative colitis to be relatively passive, rigid, overly dependent on parental (especially maternal) figures, socially inhibited, emotionally immature, and needing to an exaggerated degree to conform to social norms. These children seemed unable to express strong feelings of anger or resentment to authority figures. In a study of 17 cases of ulcerative colitis, Stuart Finch also found these children to have great difficulty in expressing anger. In addition, he found them to be depressed and borderline in their thinking, but not psychotic, whereas in Aaron Karush's follow-up

study of 30 adult chronic ulcerative colitis patients who had had psychotherapy, about one-half (14) had been psychotic.

An important consideration here is the stressful effect that the disease process itself may have on the patient and his or her personality. It is not surprising that a child with painful abdominal cramps, bloody diarrhea, and chronic weakness would be relatively dependent, inhibited, passive, and depressed. Many other aspects of the disease are also psychologically stressful, including perianal disease, arthritis, amenorrhea (in women), and the embarrassment of frequent and urgent diarrhea. The associated treatment may also induce emotional problems in the patients as well. Since oral sulfasalazine is efficacious in lessening the chance for relapse, daily medication is needed even when the patient is completely asymptomatic. This may present a financial burden and arouse feelings about the ongoing dependence on drug therapy. In association with corticosteroid therapy, one must consider the fear of major adverse side effects, including mood disturbances and unflattering cosmetic changes. Seriously ill children may experience growth retardation, and major weight loss may cause body image problems in patients regardless of age. In addition, there is the ongoing requirement for occasional intrusive, uncomfortable procedures, such as sigmoidoscopies and barium enemas, as well as the possibility of colectomy mentioned earlier.

Perhaps a case report will help to make the diagnosis of this illness more vivid.

Janet was 15 when she was referred to me by her pediatrician. She had recently recovered from a severe bout of ulcerative colitis. She was certain she would never have another attack. She had the "active" characteristics seen in Karush's study as correlated with better prognosis. She fought her dependency needs and actively tried to change her environment. Indeed, in the last year of treatment, she won a hard fought battle with her mother, getting help from her mother's therapist and from me to go to college away from home. The father was seldom mentioned. He was an ineffectual man who combined a civil service job with some petty thievery. The thievery often involved stealing clothes for Janet. She gradually became aware of her anger and resentment at this behavior, and ultimately refused to accept any more clothes from him unless she could see the bill of sale. An older brother was a college student, living at home, clearly very dependent on the mother. Janet was fond of him, but also contemptuous of his passivity.

A major focus of the three years of treatment was her dependency on her mother, and her fight for independence. At first it was a question of becoming aware of how she felt about her inadequate allowance, her compliance with an inappropriately early curfew, her not being allowed to go out of the home after dark. As she clarified each of these areas and became aware that she indeed was angry, she then began to disagree with her parents, particularly her mother, until she was able to effect some changes.

But independence is not only a battle with others. Every few months she lost the house keys, making her parents furious. They would take away all her privileges, and treat her like an incompetent little child. At first she complained bitterly about this. Gradually she became aware that she unconsciously lost the keys in order to get this attention, and to have the pleasure of being taken care of and treated like a little girl. Now she really fought the hard battle. "It's unfair. Growing up has too many responsibilities." Anger changed to sadness as she became aware that growing up, being competent, getting straight A's in school, having privileges, and being independent produced no response from her parents. Only when she was sick, "bad," or dependent, did her mother pay any attention to her. Her choice of friends and boyfriends changed, and she became more involved with boys who were competent and competitive, rather than passive and ineffectual like her brother and father.

Any chronically ill child can often use psychiatric treatment. Similarly, such treatment becomes much more helpful when the significant parent or parents are also in psychiatric treatment. Whether it is to help the parents deal with the excessive and unresolved needs of a chronically ill child, or to understand and alter ways in which they may unknowingly worsen the child's illness, psychotherapy for both the child and the parents should always be considered in the management of such a chronic life-threatening disorder as ulcerative colitis.

PSYCHOPHYSIOLOGICAL DISEASE AND GENERAL SYSTEMS THEORY

The more traditional way of thinking about disease processes has been named the *linear*

model, to contrast it with the *multiple feedback model*. The linear model in essence is a cause-effect model: the tubercle bacillus causes tuberculosis, and certain psychological dynamics lead to certain psychological diseases. In the multiple feedback model, certain family dynamics cause parents to deal with their children in ways which lead to conflicts in the children, which in turn are partially resolved or expressed through the formation of psychiatric symptoms, which are then reacted to in different ways by the parents.

Ludvig von Bertalanffy developed a theoretical point of view which can most easily be defined as follows: A whole which functions as a whole by virtue of the interdependence of its parts is called a *system*, and the method which aims at discovering how this is brought about in the widest variety of systems is *general systems theory*. This approach becomes necessary in the study of human behavior because biological processes, unlike the physical sciences, are too complex for the linear method. The linear method is adequate for *closed systems*. However, biological systems are not closed systems, but rather are *open systems*. The earlier goal of closed systems, to transform energy from one state to another, and to produce work as a consequence, marked the beginning of the Industrial Revolution and man's replacement by a machine. World War II shifted the emphasis to the processing of information, first to guide antiaircraft guns, then to automate industry, finally to take information and computerize it. This "purposefulness," this ability to make ongoing corrections, is basic to *cybernetics*, the science of communication and control. As a result, a biological system, such as a human being, can now be conceptualized not only as an engine, but also as a decision-making system.

The importance of informational feedback that allows for correction was originally emphasized by von Bertalanffy. Such terms as "positive feedback loops" (encouraging change) and "negative feedback loops" (discouraging change, setting limits) allowed a more precise description of the types of communication used at different moments in a family. A particularly impressive report of success in the treatment of severely ill children using family therapy has been reported by Salvador Minuchin. The three diseases were juvenile diabetes, intractable asthma, and anorexia nervosa. Remember the difficulty in the treatment of intractable asthma in steroid-dependent children in a hospital setting? Minuchin reported that with six to 22 months of family therapy, eight steroid-dependent children were taken off steroids, and on one to three year follow-up they had continued to do well, using bronchodilators only occasionally, and missing just a few days of school per year. Minuchin emphasizes the open systems model. He looks beyond the psychosomatically ill child to that individual child's social context and to the feedback processes between the child and his or her family. Minuchin feels that "certain types of family organization are closely related to the development and maintenance of psychosomatic symptoms in children, and children's psychosomatic problems (in turn) play a major role in maintaining family homeostasis."

What is necessary for the development of a psychophysiological disorder? The child is physiologically vulnerable, and has a physical symptom. Minuchin feels that the emotional exacerbation that accompanies the physical symptom sets the stage for a truly chronic physical disease. What causes this emotional exacerbation? Minuchin outlines four transactional characteristics present in the "psychosomatogenic" family organization. The first is *enmeshment*, defined as the excessive involvement and responsiveness of all family members. He describes the "handkerchief flutter," where everyone pulls out a handkerchief and offers it when one sneezes. The second is *overprotectiveness*, where all are excessively protective over each other's welfare. This retards the child's development of autonomy and competence. The third is *rigidity*, the need to retain the status quo. This means that the usual changes, such as those that occur as the child moves into various developmental stages, are not allowed. The fourth characteristic is *lack of conflict resolution*. As family tensions increase, requiring some new resolution, the child gets sick, so that attention is diverted from the cause of the tension to the sick child. There is thus great relief in the family, and this serves as a positive reinforcement for the child to remain ill.

How is the child involved? There are three ways in which the sick child may be "used" at times of stress or conflict. One pattern, termed *triangulation*, involves putting the child in the position of siding with one or the other parent at different times. A second pattern is *parent-child coalition*, where there is a stable siding of the child with one parent against the other parent. A third pattern is *conflict detouring*. Here the parents are united, and any conflict that arises between the parents is detoured to the scapegoated child. The parents then agree that all would be well if it were not for the fact that the child is sick. The treatment of the psychophysiological disorder becomes a matter of changing these fixed pathological interactions. Therapeutic efforts are directed towards the child, the parents, and the feedback processes within the family so as to bring about more adaptive ways of dealing with stress and conflict.

Let us again look at a case history to illuminate some of these principles. Julie was a 13 year old girl who was referred to me because she had severe, acute, spasmodic abdominal pains. She had been operated on five months before for a possible acute appendix. The appendix had been removed, but had been found to be only minimally inflamed. She had again been referred to a pediatric surgeon for a possible second surgery. By then she had been out of school for six weeks. The surgeon and a pediatric neurologist suspected a psychiatric problem. Her groans of pain could be heard even before she came to my office, accompanied by her apprehensive parents.

The younger of two daughters, she described herself as "the peacemaker" in the family. Her 19 year old sister had returned home after one year of college, and was involved in a silent war with the father. When I suggested that the sister join us for the fourth family session, both parents were apprehensive that speaking openly about the disagreement between the father and daughter would create an irreparable rupture, and the girl would move out forever. The mother, whose parents had immigrated from Italy, could not tolerate the fact that her unmarried daughters would move out of the home before marriage. The father came from a very strict Irish Catholic background. He had hypertension, and occasional chest pains. He felt particularly close to Julie, and explained, "I had morning sickness for three months when my wife was pregnant with Julie." He also did not want his children to move out of the home.

Julie's symptoms had disappeared by the third session, and in the fourth session her parents described her as radically changed. She was expressing her anger openly. The family was also changed. The father and other sister still disagreed, but not violently. The father also described a major change in himself: "I speak up now. I feel much better about it." Both sisters described how they did not allow him to clam up, as he used to do, but pursued him until he said what was on his mind. Julie described another change in herself in the seventh and last interview: "I used to be like a leaf, bending each way. It felt like I had all of them inside me, and I needed to take each of their sides so as to make peace." She stopped doing this, raised some hell of her own, and let the rest of the family make their own peace.

Was this family permanently altered? Certainly the transactional patterns had been changed for the better. More adaptive communicational feedback processes had been established. The family's interactional characteristics had indeed been altered. Julie was asymptomatic for six weeks, returned to school after the third interview, and expressed the feeling that she now felt free to go ahead in her development as a woman. On subsequent follow-up the family was functioning at this improved level.

Our more recent understanding of the power of family transactions and of faulty communications, and the search for open systems models that enlarge the horizons of our understanding of families, groups, and communities are exciting developments. A more complete understanding of the psychophysiological disorders of children, and indeed of mental illness in general, will come as we integrate our advancing knowledge of the biological, psychological, and sociocultural components of development, and general systems theory offers an important conceptual framework for this integration.

Suggested Readings

Bruch H: *Eating Disorders: Obesity and Anorexia Nervosa and the Person Within*. New York, Basic Books, 1973.

Bruch H: *The Golden Cage: The Enigma of Anorexia Nervosa*. Cambridge, MA, Harvard University Press, 1978.

Bruch H: Anorexia nervosa: therapy and theory. *Am J Psychiatry* 139:1531, 1982.

Fleck S: A general systems approach to severe family pathology. *Am J Psychiatry* 133:669, 1976.

Herzog DB: Bulimia: the secretive syndrome. *Psychosomatics* 23:481, 1982.

Hirsch J: The psychobiology of obesity. In West LJ, Stein M (eds): *Critical Issues in Behavioral Medicine*. Philadelphia, J. B. Lippincott, 1982, p 183.

Knapp PH: The asthmatic child and the psychosomatic problem of asthma: toward a general theory. In Harrison SI, McDermott JF (eds): *Childhood Psychopathology*. New York, International Universities Press, 1972, p 591.

Miller JG: *Living Systems*. New York, McGraw-Hill, 1978.

Minuchin S: *Families and Family Therapy*. Cambridge, MA, Harvard University Press, 1974.

Minuchin S: *Psychosomatic Families*. Cambridge, MA, Harvard University Press, 1978.

Pope HG, Hudson JI: *New Hope of Binge Eaters: Advances in the Understanding and Treatment of Bulimia*. New York, Harper and Row, 1984.

Prugh DG: Psychophysiological disorders. In *The Psychosocial Aspects of Pediatrics*. Philadelphia, Lea & Febiger, 1983, p 336.

Stein M: Biopsychosocial factors in asthma. In West LJ, Stein M (eds): *Critical Issues in Behavioral Medicine*. Philadelphia, J. B. Lippincott, 1982, p 159.

Stunkard AJ: *The Pain of Obesity*. Palo Alto, CA, Bull Publishing Co, 1976.

Weiner H: Psychobiological and psychosomatic aspects of anorexia nervosa and other eating disorders. In West LJ, Stein M (eds): *Critical Issues in Behavioral Medicine*. Philadelphia, J. B. Lippincott, 1982, p 193.

References

Angel JL: Constitution in female obesity. *Am J Phys Anthrop* 7:433, 1949.

Arnoldsson H: Long term ACTH and corticosteroid therapy in bronchial asthma: a clinical evaluation. *Acta Allergol (Kbh)* 12:1, 1958.

Bernstein L, Purcell K: Institutional treatment of asthmatic children. In Schneer HI (ed): *The Asthmatic Child*. New York, Harper & Row, 1963, p 224.

Blos P: *On Adolescence*. New York, The Free Press of Glencoe, 1962.

Coddington RD, Bruch H: Gastric perceptivity in normal, obese, and schizophrenic subjects. *Psychosomatics* 11:571, 1970.

Enzer NB, Hijmans JC: Ulcerative colitis beginning in infancy: a report of five cases. *J Pediatrics* 63:437, 1963.

Finch SM, Hess JH: Ulcerative colitis in children. *Am J Psychiatry* 118:819, 1962.

French TM, Alexander F: *Psychogenic Factors in Bronchial Asthma. Psychosom Med*. Monograph, National Research Council, Washington, DC, 1941.

Gull WW: Anorexia nervosa. In Harrison SI, McDermott JF (eds): *Childhood Psychopathology*. New York, International Universities Press, 1972, p 567.

Kanner L: *Child Psychiatry*, ed 3. Springfield, IL, Charles C Thomas, 1966.

Karush A, et al: The response to psychotherapy in chronic ulcerative colitis. *Psychosom Med* Part I: 30:225, 1968. Part II: 31:201, 1969.

Kendell RE, et al: The epidemiology of anorexia nervosa. *Psychol Med* 3:200, 1973.

Kiell N: Effects of asthma on the character of Theodore Roosevelt. In Schneer HI (ed): *The Asthmatic Child*. New York, Harper & Row, 1963, p 84.

Lamont JH: Which children outgrow asthma and which do not? In Schneer HI (ed): *The Asthmatic Child*. New York, Harper & Row, 1963, p 16.

Luparello T, et al: Influences of suggestion on airway reactivity in asthmatic subjects. *Psychosom Med* 30:819, 1968.

Peshkin MM: Diagnosis of asthma in children past and present. In Schneer HI (ed): *The Asthmatic Child*. New York, Harper & Row, 1963, p 1.

Pope HG, Hudson JI, Yurgelun-Todd D: Anorexia nervosa and bulimia among 300 suburban women shoppers. *Am J Psychiatry* 141:292, 1984.

Prugh DG: The influence of emotional factors on the clinical course of ulcerative colitis in children. *Gastroenterology* 18:339, 1951

Rackemann FM, Edwards MC: Asthma in children: a follow-up study of 688 patients after an interval of 20 years. *N Engl J Med* 246:815, 858, 1952.

Schachter S: Obesity and eating. *Science* 161:751, 1968.

Sperling M: A psychoanalytic study of bronchial asthma in children. In Schneer HI (ed): *The Asthmatic Child*. New York, Harper & Row, 1963, p 138.

Spiro HM: *Clinical Gastroenterology*. Toronto, Macmillan, 1970, p 534.

von Bertalanffy L: *Organismic Psychology and Systems Theory*. Worcester, MA, Clark University Press, 1968.

Waller JV, Kaufman MR, Deutsch F: Anorexia nervosa: a psychosomatic entity. *Psychosom Med* 2:3, 1940.

Wiener N: *Cybernetics*. Cambridge, MA, Technology Press, 1948.

61 **The Symptom Disorders of Childhood**

Gordon K. Farley, M.D.,
Louis L. Fine, M.D.,
William V. Good, M.D., and
Richard C. Simons, M.D.

INTRODUCTION

The so-called symptom disorders of childhood are a group of relatively common mental disorders of children. These disorders are loosely bound together by the fact that it is the symptom presented by the child or seen in the child that is the disturbing element. The underlying causes are quite diverse, and they can be biological, psychological, sociocultural, or a combination of all of these. Symptom disorders in children are among the most frequent clinical conditions encountered by pediatricians and family practitioners. Studies performed both in the United States and in Europe show that around 80% of children have had some kind of emotional or behavioral symptom before the age of 16. Such symptoms usually disappear with time and are not related to any other type of maladjustment. Nonetheless, these symptoms are troublesome to the parents and to the child, and these children are frequently brought to family physicians and pediatricians because of parental concern over these symptoms. It should be noted that all the above symptom disorders are more frequent in children who have been separated for some reason from their parents. However, separations from parents do not inevitably lead to harmful consequences. The effect of separation depends on the age of the child, the circumstances of the separation, the child's previous relationships with the parents, the care provided during the separation, the length of the separation, the financial condition of the family, the circumstances of the reunion, and the mental health of the child and the parents. It should also be noted that brief, pleasant separations can be helpful in preparing the child for later developmentally necessary separations.

In this chapter we shall look at three main categories that together constitute the symptom disorders of childhood: 1) the anxiety disorders; 2) the stereotyped movement disorders; and 3) other disorders with physical manifestations.

THE ANXIETY DISORDERS

Normal Childhood Fears

Most children show fears of something or someone at some time during their lives. There is a developmental sequence to these childhood fears. The newborn is afraid of intense, sudden, sensory stimulation and loss of support from someone who is holding him or her. The six to eight month old child is afraid of strangers and unfamiliar objects. The toddler is afraid of separation from the mother or other caretaking persons, and may be afraid of specific objects such as animals, moths, insects. The toddler may be also afraid of loss of the mother's, father's, or other caretaker's love. The preschooler may be afraid of the dark, and the schoolage child may be afraid of kidnappers, burglars, pain, physical harm, or embarrassment. In a study of children's fears, Jersild found that only about 5% of five to 12 year old children stated that they had no fears. Such fears are very common among children and often evanescent in nature, disappearing nearly as rapidly as they appear. These normal childhood fears do not indicate significant emotional conflict in the child. It is only when such fears persist and affect the functioning of the child that the physician should become concerned.

Separation Anxiety Disorder

In this disorder the child experiences excessive anxiety on separation from those to whom the child is attached. Such children often become preoccupied with fears that something bad will happen to them or to their parents during a separation, and they may refuse to sleep overnight at friends' homes or attend summer camp or even go to school. They may be unable to sleep in a room by themselves in their own home, or they may need someone to stay with them until they fall asleep. Nightmares that express the fears of separation are common. During the day they may "shadow" the parents around the house. Physical symptoms (headaches, stomachaches, nausea, vomiting) often appear when the separation is anticipated or occurs, as well as temper tantrums, crying, and pleading with the parents not to leave.

Avoidant Disorder

In this disorder the child experiences excessive anxiety when confronted with the need for contact with strangers. The persistent avoidance of contact with strangers may become so severe as to interfere with social functioning in peer relationships and with educational functioning in teacher relationships.

Overanxious Disorder

In this disorder the child experiences excessive anxiety manifested by excessive worrying and fearful behavior that is not focused on a specific situation (such as separation) or persons (such as strangers).

School Phobia

A *school phobia* may result from either a separation anxiety disorder or an avoidant disorder. School phobia usually has a fairly abrupt onset, most commonly between the ages of five to 10. The child expresses a very strong fear of attending school and an equally strong wish to remain at home. This fear is often precipitated by an actual or threatened loss to the child. This loss could be in the form of a death of a parent,

sickness of a parent, a change in a parent's work schedule, or a move to a new neighborhood. The relationship between the child and mother is often characterized by a hostile, dependent quality. The child expresses the fear that something frightening will happen during a separation from the mother. Ambivalence on the part of the mother regarding separation also exerts a prominent influence on the clinical picture. The mother often states that she fears something bad will happen to the child if the child goes to school, communicating this fear to the child in many subtle ways. School phobia is often seen in the context of previous separation problems, sometimes dating back to preschool or kindergarten. The clinical picture that presents to the physician is: 1) a marked fear of attending school; 2) a fear of being separated from a parent, usually the mother, under any conditions; and 3) a fear of specific people at school or on the way to school. The child will often select a school teacher, a bully, or a janitor. The child may also complain of somatic symptoms without physical findings. These symptoms include: headaches, fatigue, stomachaches, nausea, vomiting, fever, chills, muscular aches and pains, diarrhea, and constipation.

School phobia should be differentiated from truancy. In school phobia, a child is afraid to leave home and to go to school; in truancy, a child can leave home but does not go to school. One also can differentiate these two conditions by noting where the child goes after leaving school. The truant child usually does not go home. A truant child may be involved with delinquency, does not have a particularly dependent relationship with the mother, is apt to be underachieving at school, is not particularly anxious, and does not have marked physical complaints. It should be noted that severe school phobia in teenagers may be reflective of more significant psychopathology, and may possibly indicate the onset of a severe psychiatric illness such as adolescent schizophrenia.

The treatment for school phobia is usually very successful. Treatment should be directed toward the immediate return of the child to the school and strict enforcement of the child's presence at school. A meeting of school attendance authorities, teachers, school nurse, parents, the child, and the physician to formulate an attendance plan for the child may be necessary. Family treatment should focus on the relationships of the child to other important family members, especially the parents. Individual psychotherapy may be recommended for the child. In this type of therapy, the focus is on the child's underlying conflicts of loss, anger, and dependency, so that more adaptive coping resolutions and solutions can be achieved. Behavior modification treatments intended to desensitize the child to the feared situation at the school or the feared situation of separation may be effective, along with rewarding the child for attending school. Minor tranquilizers may also be needed temporarily to decrease the child's anxiety while in the phobic situation.

THE STEREOTYPED MOVEMENT DISORDERS

One of the most disfiguring problems of childhood is that of *tics*. Mostly occurring about the eyes, face, and neck, these motor movements are recurrent, repetitive, involuntary, rapid, and purposeless. They can be either transient (*transient tic disorder*, with duration of at least one month but not more than one year) or chronic (duration of at least one year). In *chronic motor tic disorder* no more than three muscle groups are involved at any one time for a duration of at least one year, whereas in *Tourette's disorder* multiple muscle groups are affected for a duration of at least one year. In Tourette's disorder multiple vocal tics are also present (clicks, grunts, barks, coughs), and 60% of the cases have the symptom of *coprolalia*, an irresistible urge to utter obscenities. In all three of these disorders the movements can be voluntarily suppressed for minutes to hours. The incidence of tics in childhood is probably 3% to 5% with an increased predilection for boys. The average age of onset of tics is around seven years.

The etiology of some tics is clearly psychogenic in origin. Tics can represent symbolic expressions of unconscious psychological conflict, and therefore actually be a conversion disorder. They also can be a simple motoric outlet for increased psychological tension and anxiety. The treatment for such tics can take several forms, including psychotherapy and behavior modification. However, there is also a growing body of evidence that suggests that some tics can be caused by central nervous system dysfunction. For example, tics seem to occur more commonly in children with a relative who suffered tics. Tourette's disorder is often indistinguishable in its early phases from psychogenic tics and yet is probably a disorder of brain dopamine overactivity.

In regard to the differential diagnosis, there are a number of other disorders that present with abnormal motor movements. For example, diseases of the extrapyramidal system may present with *choreiform movements* (dancing, random, irregular, nonrepetitive movements) and *athetoid movements* (slow, irregular, writhing movements, usually in the fingers and toes). Generally, such movements cannot be voluntarily suppressed as can tics and they are usually random and irregular rather than recurrent and repetitive. Adolescent schizophrenia sometimes presents with *dyskinesias*, irrespective of whether the patient has been treated with neuroleptics. Dyskinesias are silent, oral-buccal-lingual, masticatory movements in the face and choreoathetoid movements in the limbs. The tic disorders of childhood are probably not associated with an increased risk of schizophrenia (or intellectual deterioration). However, a child who develops tics should be screened for schizophrenia, particularly if he or she is in early adolescence.

OTHER DISORDERS WITH PHYSICAL MANIFESTATIONS

This category of the symptom disorders includes those disorders in which the disturbance is in a physical function: speech (stuttering), urination (functional enuresis), defecation (functional encopresis), and sleep (sleepwalking disorder and sleep terror disorder).

Stuttering

Stuttering is defined in DSM-III as frequent repetitions or prolongations of sounds, syllables, or words; or frequent, unusual hesitations and pauses that disrupt the rhythmic flow of speech. Approximately 1% of all children have a persistent problem with stuttering that extends into adolescence, with boys affected more commonly than girls. Shame and embarrassment may become intense, especially with teasing from peers. If recovery does not take place, there may be a lifelong limitation in social relationships and occupational functioning.

Functional Enuresis

The treatments suggested for enuresis range from the ridiculous to the sadistic. In 1950, in the Merck Manual, cantharides (Spanish Fly) was suggested as a treatment for enuresis. As recently as 1960, the Merck Manual recommended methyltestosterone for enuresis as well as silver nitrate infusion into the bladder and passage of urethral sounds to increase bladder irritability. Previous attempts to treat enuresis have included penile clamps, ligatures, and corks; collodium on the tip of the penis at the urethral opening; various and assorted drugs; as well as other very punitive methods. The variety of treatment modalities attest to the efforts made to control the symptom. However, it has only been with understanding of the symptom that rational treatments have evolved.

Functional enuresis is defined in DSM-III as repeated, involuntary voiding of urine during the day or at night, not due to any physical disorder, and after an age at which bladder control is expected. *Nocturnal enuresis* occurs at night during sleep. *Diurnal enuresis* occurs during waking hours. Enuresis is defined as *primary* if it is present in a child who has never achieved consistent bladder control, and as *secondary* if it has been preceded by a period of urinary continence for at least one year. As Dr. Reite has already indicated, most cases of nocturnal enuresis occur during arousal from Stage 3–4 nonREM sleep and are classified as one of the parasomnias. Wide cultural variations exist regarding the age by which a child is expected to achieve bladder control. As children get older, an increasing number of them achieve bladder control and also achieve it without relapse. Longitudinal studies by Oppel and colleagues have shown that by the age of five, 81% of children have achieved bladder control (64% with no relapse), and by the age of six 87% of children have achieved bladder control (70% with no relapse). Furthermore, at any given age more males are enuretic than are females.

What are the causes of enuresis? The etiologies of enuresis can be divided into three general categories. The first includes the organic causes, the second category is developmental delay, and the third includes the psychogenic causes. The percentage of children with an organic cause is around 5%. These may include congenital anomalies in the urinary tract, obstruction to the distal outflow of urine, and genital-urinary tract infections. A very unusual cause of enuresis is problems in the central nervous or peripheral nervous system, including defects in bladder innervation and spina bifida occulta. Other rare

organic causes may be diabetes mellitus, diabetes insipidus, sickle cell anemia, and food allergies. The second fairly common cause of enuresis is what can be termed developmental delay in maturation of the genital-urinary system. There are a number of characteristics of enuretics that are now well known and that reflect such a developmental delay: 1) most enuretics void more frequently but not more copiously during the day than do nonenuretics; 2) most enuretics have a smaller functional bladder capacity, and enuresis is known to be very uncommon in children with bladder capacities of over 300 to 360 cu cm; 3) enuresis usually occurs during NREM and not during REM sleep; 4) a 68% concordance rate exists between monozygotic twins for enuresis, and a 43.5% rate between dizygotic twins.

A third common cause consists of psychogenic and environmental factors. A fairly frequent family pattern exists among enuretic children in that the enuresis often follows an episode of separation, family illness, or the birth of a sibling. A number of similar personality patterns are also noted in many of these children. They are often anxious, depressed, unable to take responsibility for their actions, and unable to express anger and resentment directly. Frequently these children have a history of coercive toilet training at the hands of the parents, and the enuresis at times is an indirect expression of anger against the parents.

What does one need to do in the evaluation of a child with enuresis? First, a careful family history should be taken which inquires about the following: the onset of the enuresis; concurrent family events at the time of onset; what makes the enuresis worse; what makes it better; the frequency of episodes and the amount voided; is there a seasonal or weekly variation; what time of day or night does it occur; is there a family history of enuresis; what is the impact of the symptom on the family life; what is the parents' method of dealing with enuresis; what are the sleep patterns; and what are the family sleeping locations? The physical workup for a child with enuresis can be brief yet comprehensive. One should watch the child urinate, observing any deviation of the stream, the caliber of the stream, the strength of the stream, and whether the child is able to stop the stream of urine suddenly. One should also note the bladder capacity as compared with normal children of the same age and one should perform a urinalysis and a urine culture. If all of the above are normal, no further diagnostic tests such as an intravenous pyelogram or cystoscopy need be done.

The treatment of enuresis is rewarding and productive. We must remember that development and maturation are on our side and even if untreated, most cases of enuresis cure themselves. One part of treatment should always be counseling and supportive guidance for both the child and the parents, so as to help the parents take the pressure off the child. One should also try to evaluate in what ways the parents may unconsciously reinforce or reward the symptom. Asking the parents to keep a diary, noting the nights that the child is enuretic without criticism, and offering the child praise when he or she is not enuretic, can help a great deal. Bladder training, that is exercises to increase the bladder capacity of a child with a small bladder, may also help. There are a number of methods for doing this but one method is to ask the child to retain urine during the day for as long as possible and then measure the amount voided. As the child works harder on this, the bladder capacity increases and the enuresis becomes less frequent. Fluid restriction in the evening and conditioning using the "bell and pad" may also help the child overcome the enuresis. The use of drugs (imipramine is commonly prescribed at present) should only be a last resort, since the risks may far outweigh any advantages, and drugs should only be used in conjunction with all of the above approaches.

Functional Encopresis

Functional encopresis is defined as repeated voluntary or involuntary passage of feces of normal or near-normal consistency in inappropriate settings. It is not due to any physical disorder. In our children's psychiatric day hospital we have seen stools in such diverse locations as in the shower, on the floor, in the swimming pool, in the bed while the child was awake, on a rooftop, and on one occasion in a lunch box. Functional encopresis is defined as *primary* (or continuous) if it occurs after the child has reached the age of four without being preceded by a period of fecal continence for at least one year, and as *secondary* (or discontinuous) if it has been preceded by a period of fecal continence for at least one year. As shown in Table 61.1 there are distinctive differences be-

Table 61.1

Differentiation Between Primary (Continuous) Encopresis and Secondary (Discontinuous) Encopresis*

Primary encopresis
1. Usually associated with enuresis
2. Low-pressure toilet training by impulsive parents
3. Low levels of aspiration and achievement for mother
4. Social and emotional regression marked
5. Obsessional traits usually absent
6. Antisocial behavior present
7. "Leakage symptoms" generally prominent
8. Reaction formations usually absent
9. Reaction to encopresis—little shame, guilt, or anxiety
10. Child usually rejected and neglected by the parents
11. Child usually doing poorly in school

Secondary encopresis
1. Usually dissociated from enuresis
2. High-pressure toilet training by obsessional parents
3. High levels of aspiration and achievement for mother
4. Social and emotional regression much less marked
5. Obsessional traits usually present
6. Antisocial behavior absent
7. "Leakage symptoms" seldom present
8. Reaction formations usually a striking feature
9. Reaction to encopresis—shame, guilt, and anxiety
10. Child usually overprotected by the parents
11. Child usually doing well in school

* Modified from earlier table by E. James Anthony, 1957.

tween these two types of functional encopresis. However, in both types the children are often small, pale and sickly looking, without friends, poor in athletics, and poor in their school work. Yet beneath this passive facade, there may be an angry, sullen, and defiant child. Many of these children express marked fears of defecation. One child was heard to say that a blue frog lived in the toilet and would bite him if he wasn't careful. Another child said that he thought he might fall into the toilet and disappear. Another said that a shark was swimming in the toilet water and would bite his "weiner" off if he sat on the toilet.

The prevalence of encopresis varies somewhat with the population being studied. In the Children's Hospital Medical Center in Boston, Levine found an incidence of 3% in a normal population of children coming into the clinic for other problems. In our children's psychiatric day hospital we find an incidence of about 8%. It should be recognized that there are wide cultural variations in the age when bowel control is expected. In the United States it is about two years of age; in Sweden, four to five years of age; and in many nonindustrial countries, bowel control is not expected until age seven or eight. The male/female ratio for encopresis is about six boys to one girl.

In evaluating a child with encopresis the same principles of history taking apply that were delineated for enuresis. A rectal examination should be done in order to evaluate rectal sphincter tone, determine whether there are feces in the rectum, and inspect the anal area and perineum for fissures and fistulae. A barium enema, proctoscopic examination, and rectal mucosal biopsy are indicated only if there are positive physical findings and/or a history suggestive of Hirschsprung's disease (congenital aganglionic megacolon). In Hirschsprung's disease the defective neurological control of the colon leads to constipation without fecal incontinence soon after birth, with a subsequent history of frequent episodes of intestinal obstruction and an empty rectum on physical examination. In contrast the child with functional encopresis presents with fecal incontinence during the second year or later, with no episodes of intestinal obstruction, and with the rectum filled with feces on physical examination.

As in the treatment of enuresis, the treatment of encopresis consists of ongoing counseling and guidance for the parents and the child. One purpose is to further evaluate the psychological contributors to the encopresis, such as fears of defecation, insensitivity to bodily cues, coercion around toilet training, parental anger towards the child as reflected in both rejection and intrusiveness, and the child's anger towards the parents. Another purpose of treatment is to take the pressure off both the child and the parents, and to suggest more appropriate and less punitive ways of handling the soiling. Keeping a diary of what is going on in the family when encopresis occurs can be very useful. Having the child draw what he thinks is causing the encopresis can also be useful. The use of the gastro-ileo reflex (the feeling of fullness in the rectum after eating a meal) can aid in toilet training and in developing greater sensitivity to bodily cues. One should also insure that the stools

remain soft, and this can be done by encouraging the child to eat foods such as prunes, bran cereal, and high-bulk vegetables (spinach, lettuce, cabbage, corn), and by drinking extra water.

Symptom Disorders of Sleep

Sleepwalking disorder (somnambulism), sleep terror disorder (night terrors or pavor nocturnus), and nightmares have already been discussed by Dr. Reite in Chapter 52D. These sleep disorders are common in children, partly because of delays in neurophysiological development, and partly because going to sleep for children often involves conflicts over giving up control, separating from the daytime world, and being compliant with parental suggestions or demands. Physicians can be helpful by explaining to the parents and the child that all of these conditions are usually developmental in that they start and stop during a particular period, yet may be exacerbated or precipitated by environmental events. They usually decrease in frequency with advancing age, and unless there is clear evidence of excessive conflict in the child, no specific treatment is needed.

Suggested Readings

Anders TF, Weinstein P: Sleep and its disorders in infants and children: a review. *Pediatrics* 50:312, 1972.

Anthony EJ: An experimental approach to the psychopathology of childhood: encopresis. *Br J Med Psych* 30:146, 1957.

Bruun RD, et al: A follow-up of 78 patients with Gilles de la Tourette's syndrome. *Arch Gen Psychiatry* 133:944, 1976.

Coolidge JC, Brodie RD: Observations of mothers of 49 school phobic children: evaluated in a 10-year follow-study. *J Am Acad Child Psychiatry* 13:275, 1974.

Farley GK, Eckhardt LO, Hebert FB: *Handbook of Child and Adolescent Psychiatric Emergencies.* Garden City, NY, Medical Examination Publishing Co, 1979.

Fisher C: A psychophysiological study of nightmares and night terrors. III Mental content of stage 4 night terrors. *J Nerv Ment Dis* 157:75, 1973.

Kahn JH, Nursten JP: School refusal: a comprehensive view of school phobia and other failures of school attendance. *Am J Orthopsychiatry* 32:707, 1962.

Starfield B: Enuresis: its pathogenesis and management. *Clin Pediat* 11:343, 1972.

Waldfogel S, et al: The development, meaning and management of school phobia. *Am J Orthopsychiatry* 27:754, 1957.

References

Azrin NH, Besalel VA: A parent's guide to bedwetting control. New York, Pocket Books, 1979.

Azrin NH, Foxx RM: Toilet training in less than a day. New York, Pocket Books, 1974.

Bemporad JR, et al: Characteristics of encopretic patients and their families. *J Am Acad Child Psychiatry* 10:272, 1971.

Coolidge JC, et al: A ten-year follow-up study of sixty-six school phobic children. *Am J Orthopsychiatry* 34:675, 1964.

Dittman KS, Blinn J: Sleep levels in enuresis. *Am J Psychiatry* 111:913, 1955.

Fisher C, et al: A psychophysiological study of nightmares and night terrors. The suppression of stage 4 night terrors with diazepam. *Arch Gen Psychiatry* 28:252, 1973.

Golden GS: Tourette syndrome—the pediatric perspective. *Am J Dis Child* 131:531, 1977.

Jersild AT: *Child Psychology*, ed 3. New York, Prentice-Hall, 1947.

Keith PR: Night terrors—a review of the psychology, neurophysiology, and therapy. *J Am Acad Child Psychiatry* 14:477, 1975.

Levine MD: Children with encopresis: a descriptive analysis. *Pediatrics* 56:412, 1975.

Levine MD, Bakow H: Children with encopresis: a study of treatment outcome. *Pediatrics* 58:845, 1976.

Miller LC, et al: Comparison of reciprocal inhibition, psychotherapy, and waiting list control for phobic children. *J Abnorm Psych* 79:269, 1972.

Oppel WC, et al: The age of attaining bladder control. *Pediatrics* 42:614, 1968.

Schmitt BD: School phobia—the great imitator: a pediatrician's viewpoint. *Pediatrics* 45:422, 1971.

Shapiro AK, et al: Treatment of Tourette's syndrome with haloperidol, review of 34 cases. *Arch Gen Psychiatry* 28:92, 1973.

Section Q/The Major Mental Disorders of Adulthood

CHAPTER **62** ## The Schizophrenic Disorders

Mark Rubinstein, M.D.,
Ronald D. Franks, M.D., and
Richard C. Simons, M.D.

DEFINITION

Schizophrenia may be defined as a group of disorders characterized by profound disturbances in thinking, feeling, and behavior. While we will describe the many abnormal signs and symptoms of this syndrome, there is no universally accepted definition of this serious mental illness, and its causes are probably the least understood of all the psychopathological disorders. It is best to think of schizophrenia as representing a group of heterogeneous disorders with multiple etiologies rather than a single disease entity.

To give you a more vivid picture of these disorders, we will begin this chapter by describing the onset of a paranoid schizophrenic disorder in a young man whom we shall call Bobby.

THE CASE OF BOBBY—PRESENTING SYMPTOMS

Bobby, a 23 year old college graduate, was admitted to the psychiatric hospital in an acutely psychotic state. He was belligerent, suspicious of everyone around him, and convinced that a group of men were hunting him down, wanting to assassinate him. He was plagued by voices (auditory hallucinations) that would not cease their badgering criticisms of him. He could not go to the police because he was sure that they were also pursuing him. His wife, Diana, reported that when he returned home from a poker party, Bobby was in a state of panic. There was an incomprehensible and bizarre quality to his words and actions. His wife knew instinctively that something was dreadfully wrong. Bobby's speech was broken and fragmented, and made little sense. He was agitated, pacing the room, sweating, and gesturing with his hands in a very peculiar way. Diana was sure that only Bobby and no one else knew the meaning of these strange gestures. He refused to talk and sat motionless while staring at a wall. Finally, he began to giggle as though responding to some inner joke that he could not share with her. Diana then called a family physician who advised her to bring Bobby to the nearest hospital emergency room.

On the way to the general hospital Bobby pushed Diana out of the car and drove off. He sped back to the house, scrawled a message to her on a piece of scrap paper, took some money, and drove the car toward the freeway. Bobby thought that the people in the other cars were staring at him, so he drove faster. Thinking a police car was following him, he sped off the highway and took the service road, returning to the main road only when he was certain all was clear.

After three hours of high-speed driving he stopped at a roadside diner. As he entered the restaurant, he felt as though things seemed unreal, as if he were living in a dream. He could not eat. He was sure that others in the diner were staring at him, and that they all knew that the police were following him. He glanced at a group of truck drivers sitting in a corner, and it seemed as though one of the men was winking and smiling at him. Bobby was furious. He shrieked, "What are you doing?!", and then began cursing and threatening the men, even accusing them of being after him. They sat and did nothing, recognizing that he was severely disturbed. Bobby ran from the restaurant, his fears mounting, convinced now that the truck drivers would also follow him. He then began to hallucinate, hearing voices calling him "faggot," "gay," and "queer." These voices became increasingly mocking and derogatory, torturing him with their accusations of his homosexuality. Not daring to stop again, too restless and disturbed to sleep, he drove through the night.

At three A.M. the next morning he arrived exhausted at his mother's house and entered through the basement door. Later that morning his mother discovered him asleep on the living room couch, only partly clothed, disheveled and unshaven. She wondered what was wrong. When he awoke, Bobby told her about his fears of being pursued and about the voices. He was trapped and desperate, and begged his mother to hide him. She realized that Bobby was mentally ill, and persuaded him to be seen by a trusted general practitioner, who recognized the seriousness of what was happening and arranged for Bobby to be hospitalized. Thus, while it is unusual for nonpsychiatric physicians or health care professionals to become involved in the total treatment of someone suffering from an acute schizophrenic breakdown, it is quite likely that they may very well be the first to diagnose this most serious of all mental disorders, and then to intervene immediately to prevent further regression and disorganization.

At the time of admission to the psychiatric hospital, Bobby's conversations were very difficult to follow. It was as if Bobby had constructed special meanings for his words, with his own individual but incoherent language. His behavior was increasingly ritualistic and peculiar. He appeared very suspicious and guarded, occasionally alluding to a special power allowing him to control people's thoughts and behavior. His pattern of speech was striking in that, although he was clearly very frightened, he talked in a flat monotone with a flattened emotional expression.

HISTORICAL REVIEW OF SCHIZOPHRENIA

Who is to say how many of the ecstatic religious and philosophical experiences that have been chronicled and described over many thousands of years were essentially manifestations of a disorder that would today be termed schizophrenia? The earliest religious writings contain references to visions and voices, to premonitions and ineffable experiences that foretold the future and bode well or ill for men. Early writings from all civilizations describe disturbed states that were considered to be brought on by devils and demons, and that were characterized by hallucinations, delusional thinking, and bizarre behavior. At varying times throughout man's history the schizophrenic person has alternatingly been regarded as a saint and a healer, entitled to priestly privileges, or as an afflicted and cursed individual whose fate was that of persecution or extrusion from the company of other men. Some remnants of these superstitions and fears still prevail today. Most people feel uncomfortable when confronted with a person who is mentally ill, and many still consider it desirable to extrude such patients from society.

The term *dementia praecox* (démence précoce) was first used by Morel, a Belgian psychiatrist, in 1856. He described a boy of 14 who had previously been functioning very well, and who rapidly deteriorated to a withdrawn state and appeared to have become prematurely "demented." Morel interpreted this disorganization of personality as an arrest of development, and considered it a form of mental deficiency and "moral degeneracy" resulting from hereditary factors.

In 1896 Emil Kraepelin distinguished between dementia praecox and manic-depressive psychosis, and began to bring order to what had been a chaotic system of classification of mental diseases. Before Kraepelin, numerous psychiatric syndromes had been described, but there was little unity to the methods of classification or description. Kraepelin was able to take a number of apparently separate diseases and unify them by recognizing the elements common to them all. He described an apparent lack of external causes in dementia praecox, its occurrence in young and previously healthy-appearing people, and the inevitability of ultimate deterioration.

In 1911 Eugen Bleuler introduced the term schizophrenia, which translated literally means "split-mindedness." He described four primary disturbances, which have subsequently been characterized as the "four A's": 1) an *autistic* withdrawal from reality into fantasy; 2) a loosening of *associations*; 3) an inappropriateness of *affect*; and 4) *ambivalence* of motility and volition. Bleuler considered hallucinations and delusions to be secondarily derived from these four primary disturbances. In contrast to Kraepelin, Bleuler did not consider ultimate deterioration to be an essential or inevitable part of schizophrenia. Implicit in his conceptualization was the idea that the disorder was a psychopathological reaction involving underlying disturbances in certain psychological processes, and was not a form of dementia, mental deficiency, or moral degeneracy.

In the 1950's Kurt Schneider described "first rank" hallucinatory and delusional symptoms which he considered to be pathognomonic of schizophrenia. These included the following: 1) audible thoughts (hallucinatory voices that echo or speak the patient's thoughts aloud); 2) voices debating or disagreeing (hallucinatory voices engaged in debate or disagreement about the patient); 3) voices commenting (hallucinatory voices that comment on the patient's actions); 4) thought broadcasting (the delusion that one's thoughts are broadcast from one's mind to the external world so that others can hear them); 5) thought insertion (the delusion that thoughts are inserted into one's mind); 6) thought withdrawal (the delusion that thoughts are withdrawn from one's mind); and 7) "made" feelings, impulses, and acts (the delusion that one's feelings, impulses, and actions are not one's own, but are imposed and controlled by some external force).

As we can see, much of the history of schizophrenia has involved the classification of its varied and confusing signs and symptoms. It is difficult for us today to appreciate the monumental achievement that was required to bring unity to the clinical description of this wide variety of strange and incomprehensible behaviors that had for centuries been regarded as the work of devils or angels, and whose very nature was the furthest imaginable from that of scientific inquiry and understanding.

DSM-III DIAGNOSTIC CRITERIA

DSM-III describes a characteristic onset, course, and symptom picture for the schizophrenic disorders, and then delineates several different types within this group of disorders.

Onset

Onset is usually during adolescence or early adulthood, but by definition in DSM-III it must occur before age 45.

Course

For the diagnosis of schizophrenia to be made, DSM-III specifies that continuous signs of the illness must be present for at least six months. There is often a *prodromal phase* during which a clear deterioration from a previous level of functioning takes place. In the *active phase* characteristic symptoms involving multiple psychological functions are prominent. During the *residual phase* some of the psychotic symptoms may persist, but with less intensity. A complete return to premorbid functioning is possible but unusual.

Symptoms

The characteristic symptoms of schizophrenia involve multiple psychological functions that have been described earlier in the book in Chapter 19 and then listed in more detail in Table 51.2 in Chapter 51 (Mental Status Exam). While there are many different ways of conceptualizing the symptoms of schizophrenia as we have seen in our historical review, we shall attempt in this chapter to describe them according to the particular psychological function that is impaired. In that way we shall also be able to illustrate how a mental status exam might be conducted on a patient suffering from a schizophrenic disorder.

Types

DSM-III delineates five different types within the schizophrenic disorders: disorganized, catatonic, paranoid, undifferentiated, and residual. We shall comment in particular on the catatonic and paranoid types in our discussion of the characteristic symptoms of schizophrenia.

Differential Diagnosis

The differentiation between schizophrenia and *mania* will be discussed in the next chapter on the affective disorders. The various *paranoid disorders* present with persistent persecutory delusions or delusional jealousy, but without prominent hallucinations, and without the severe disturbances in form of thought (loosening of associations, incoherence) or content of thought (bizarre delusions) characteristic of the schizophrenic disorders. In *schizophreniform disorder* the clinical symptoms are identical to schizophrenia with the exception that the duration (including prodromal, active, and residual phases) is less than six months but more than two weeks. In a *brief reactive psychosis* there is a sudden onset of psychotic symptoms following a recognizable psychosocial stressor that would evoke significant symptoms of distress in almost anyone. In contrast to schizophrenia there is no prodromal phase of increasing psychopathology immediately preceding the psychosocial stressor, the psychotic symptoms do not last for more than two weeks, and there is an eventual return to the premorbid level of functioning. Finally, *schizoaffective disorder* is a controversial diagnosis that should be used only in those instances where it is not possible to differentiate between a schizophrenic disorder and an affective disorder.

ETIOLOGY

One of the most challenging and important areas of inquiry for clinicians and researchers in years to come will be the elucidation of the different etiologies of the schizophrenic disorders. While much has been learned and understood in recent years, a fundamental and unitary understanding of schizophrenia has not yet been achieved. While earlier clinicians such as Kraepelin regarded it as a neuropathological disease with an inevitably fixed outcome, a great deal has been learned subsequently to suggest that the onset of schizophrenia is most probably due to a highly complex and multifaceted interaction of many factors.

Dr. Reite has discussed the evidence for the presence of *genetic* factors in Chapter 52A, and Dr. Freedman has presented the evidence for the dopamine hypothesis and other possible *neurochemical* factors in Chapter 52B. A *psychodynamic* model for the onset of schizophrenia that emphasizes the concepts of early fixation and regression has been presented by Dr. Pardes in Chapter 53, and Dr. Mumford has discussed some of the possible *sociocultural* factors in Chapter 54. There has also been increasing interest in recent years in possible *neurophysiological* factors in the etiology of schizophrenia, based on evidence of enlarged cerebral ventricles, abnormalities in several parameters of sensory evoked potentials, various cognitive impairments, and impaired eye movements and visual tracking in certain groups of schizophrenic patients.

Finally, it has been hypothesized that disturbances in *family interactions* may lead to a schizophrenic disorder in one or more of the family members. In Chapter 60 Dr. Christ discussed some of the family interactions that may play a role in the development of psychosomatic disease in children. In regard to schizophrenia, Lidz and coworkers described various patterns of chronic parental disharmony among the parents of schizophrenic patients, whereas Bateson and Jackson were impressed with the frequent contradictory ("double bind") communication patterns in such families. Wynne and Singer developed a different concept, that of "pseudomutuality," to explain the family interactions in schizophrenia. In these families, any conflict or difference is viewed as a threat to the family's existence and is therefore suppressed. A variety of mechanisms are used to pressure family members into preserving an illusion of complementarity, and any member who fails to cooperate becomes a "scapegoat." Perhaps the most compelling scientific work on the importance of family interactions in schizophrenia is that by Vaughn and Leff who discovered that extended exposure to criticism by family members can have an adverse effect on prognosis and/or recurrence of the illness.

As further research continues, it is hoped that various subgroups within the schizophrenic disorders can be more specifically identified on the basis of specific etiological factors. Even if a particular etiological factor only applies to a very small percentage of the total population of individuals suffering from schizophrenia, it can serve as a model for future research and treatment in the same manner that the discovery of phenylketonuria served as a model for subsequent research and treatment in the area of mental retardation.

THE CHARACTERISTIC SYMPTOMS OF SCHIZOPHRENIA

Autonomous Functions

Thinking is a function that is necessary if one is going to deal with the realities of the world. The person whose psychological functioning undergoes the kind of massive regression that is characteristic of schizophrenia gives up the capacity to think as an adult. He relinquishes his ability to think in Aristotelian and universally accepted logical terms. His thinking assumes a concrete, illogical, bizarre quality in both the *form of thought* and the *content of thought*. In regard to the *form* of thought, normally when we speak, our words follow our ideas, and irrelevant and extraneous thoughts are scanned and selectively suppressed from our stream of conversation. Hence, we usually speak in a reasonably ordered, goal-directed, and understandable fashion, in which each idea is meaningfully and coherently linked to the one preceding it and the one following it. The schizophrenic person's ability to screen his thoughts and eliminate irrelevant words and tangential links is compromised. His speech may suffer from such an intrusion of associated ideas and trends that he may speak in an incomprehensible manner. This has been termed *loosening of associations*, and it may be so pronounced as to render the patient completely incoherent. His speech becomes fragmented, and his language is no longer used as a means of communication with others but rather becomes entirely a means of self-expression. This disturbance in the form of thought has also been referred to as *formal thought disorder*.

For example, a schizophrenic patient, while on a psychiatric ward, wrote the following disjointed note to his physician in an attempt to explain his illness: "It should be extrusively notated (and annotated) that my imago has been ensnared in the viscosity of time. That is why my transcendent self has been importuned (but not without resisting) despite the hydraulic pressure I have succinctly initiated in an attempt to

limitate and delineate those theotons (the ultimately microscopic, particulate hydrole) whose essential god-like characteristics have been laminated into an irreducibly miniscultate, atomized, and indeed lionized cannister. Such is the enraptured entrapment of my condition."

In another example a schizophrenic patient was noted to be piling one mattress on top of another and when asked why she was doing so, replied, "Because I want to be closer to God when I sleep." A schizophrenic man was seen wrapping sterile gauze and bandages around his head and gave as his reason, "I want to keep all unclean thoughts out of my head." Another disturbed patient, when brought to the hospital emergency room, asked why he had been brought to a police station and wanted to know the nature of the crime he was accused of having committed. When asked why he thought he was in a police station, he noted the presence of two policemen in the hallway and hence, the hospital was, for him, a police station. While his observation of the police was correct, he failed to recognize the many nurses and doctors hurriedly going about their business, and he came to the conclusion that he was in a police station upon a minor and incomplete bit of evidence that was only partly relevant to the circumstances at the time. This patient did what many schizophrenic people do. He assumed a sweeping similarity in two events or objects that share only one small property in common. Such reasoning is *paralogical*, childlike, magical, and concrete, suffering from many flaws in structure and misguided concepts of causality. It results in a greatly compromised ability to understand and deal with the world.

Another characteristic of schizophrenic thinking is an abrupt *blocking* of the stream of thought. This usually occurs at a moment when the person is about to experience an emotionally unpleasant sensation and defends against this by blocking out the thought. When the thoughts return, the patient may feel that someone had stolen them from his mind.

This brings us to the disturbance in *content* of thought known as a *delusion*. A delusion is a false, fixed belief, not shared by others in the culture, and one to which the person adheres despite ample evidence to the contrary. The delusional person has regressed in his thinking to the earliest stages of logic characteristic of childhood. He believes what he wants and needs to believe despite all opposing evidence. In addition, he can accept two mutually exclusive events occurring simultaneously and not be bothered by the logical contradiction involved. For example, a schizophrenic patient on the hospital ward maintained steadfastly that he was the all-powerful son of God. He found no inconsistency in the fact that he had been committed to a hospital and was not free to leave whenever he wanted, and that prior to his hospitalization he had been unable to obtain enough money to feed and clothe himself.

As was mentioned in the historical review, delusions of thought broadcasting, thought insertion, thought withdrawal, and of being controlled by external forces are more common in the schizophrenic disorders than in the other psychotic disorders. Delusions of reference (events are given unusual significance, usually of a negative nature) are also common. Somatic and nihilistic delusions may also be seen, although these are more common in the affective psychoses. Persecutory delusions, grandiose delusions, and delusional jealousy are especially characteristic of *paranoid schizophrenia*.

Affect or emotion is another function that may be markedly impaired in schizophrenia. There is often a reduced emotional response, an apathetic *flattening* and shallowness, and a barren emotional landscape to the schizophrenic person's inner experiences. His emotional shallowness may be such that he loses his ability to empathize with others and thus he seems dull, disinterested in, and uninvolved with others and with the world around him. Due to this flatness, the observer often has the feeling that there is an emotional chasm separating the schizophrenic person from himself—a gulf that is unbridgeable. This has been described as the *praecox aura*—a feeling of impenetrable and inaccessible aloofness that is conveyed by the schizophrenic person to others (Figure 62.1).

The affective disturbance also includes an emotional response to given life circumstances that is often quite *inappropriate*. Normally our inner feeling state is reflected by our physical appearance and facial expressions. Our emotions cause us to give many signs and clues as to how we feel, and thereby we convey to others our inner experiences. For example, a sad face, a drooped head, a softer timbre of the voice, and a tearing of the eyes are only some of the many external clues that an observer might note in a person who has become depressed. In other words, the affect that we display to others is generally appropriate to our prevailing inner thoughts. This is often not the case with a person who is schizophrenic. A schizophrenic person may break out laughing when there is no apparent reason for such a reaction. He may describe the death of someone in his family and

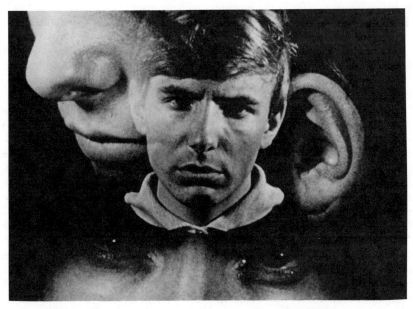

Figure 62.1. A schizophrenic young man. From the film *World of the Schizophrenic*. (By permission of Sandoz Pharmaceuticals, East Hanover, NJ. Distributed by Association-Sterling Films, New York, NY.)

in talking about the loss he may smile or even laugh, a reaction that seems incomprehensible and frightening to the normal observer. Or he may describe the most terrifying experience in a bland and indifferent manner, as though he is describing a neutral event which is of no consequence to him.

This startling inappropriateness of affect is partly responsible for Bleuler's having termed the disorder schizophrenia, or "splitting of the mind." There is a disturbance in the person's ability to think and feel synchronously, and it is these functions of thinking and feeling that are fragmented and disassociated from each other. The ability to integrate the thinking component and the feeling (affective) component of one's inner psychological world is thereby lost.

This disruption in the integration of thinking and feeling constitutes the essence of schizophrenia. Here, too, the defensive nature of the symptom becomes evident. The person retreats from all feelings into a barren emotional life and thereby attempts to protect himself or herself from the depressed or anxious feelings that may befall others.

Perception, a function which is crucial to our negotiating the demands of life, is often affected in a schizophrenia process. Sensory experiences without corresponding external stimuli are common experiences in schizophrenia. Such experiences are termed *hallucinations*. Most common are auditory hallucinations—usually the hearing of voices. The voices may be those of God or the devil. They may be soothing or threatening. They may even command the patient's movements and activities. The schizophrenic patient may hear a voice that torments him and eventually orders him to leap in front of a train or out of a window, or to kill someone else. Suicide and homicide may then become tragic complications of a schizophrenic illness (Figure 62.2). Visual hallucinations occur infrequently in schizophrenia, but *illusions* in the visual sphere are fairly common. The patient frequently reports "strange" experiences. Objects and people change their shapes and sizes, and the patient frequently misinterprets visual and auditory stimuli in his environment. An ordinary, innocent conversation between two people in the street becomes for the schizophrenic patient a whispered and clandestine plot to destroy him.

Other perceptual disturbances may occur in regard to the sense of self. Patients frequently tell of dream-like and surrealistic impressions

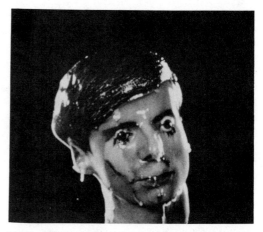

Figure 62.2. Image of a wax head melting away under water, to portray a schizophrenic young man in a catatonic state responding to terrifying voices that order him to drown himself. From the film *World of the Schizophrenic.* (By permission of Sandoz Pharmaceuticals, East Hanover, NJ. Distributed by Association-Sterling Films, New York, NY.)

that the world seems to be changing, or possibly even coming to an end. Streets and landmarks that were ordinarily familiar now seem strange and foreign, as though they are being seen for the first time. The patient may also feel that his body is changing in some inexplicable way (Figure 62.3), and he may even seek medical consultation for this symptom. Hallucinations may occur in any of the sensory modalities and, when present, may cause the patient to become completely preoccupied. He may sit for hours listening to the "voices" and may be rendered oblivious to the people and environment around him. This is often part of the overall picture of schizophrenic withdrawal.

Motor behavior, or the freedom to use the body in a goal-directed manner, is another vital function. Often the schizophrenic patient feels that he has lost his freedom of will (*volition*) and can no longer move as he would like. The patient is often plagued by feelings of *ambivalence*, so that he cannot decide if he wants to sit down or stand up, or if he wishes to walk into a room or stay outside, and so he may remain at the doorway for hours. In the more extreme cases as seen in *catatonic schizophrenia*, the patient may fail to react to the environment (catatonic stupor), resist all attempts to be moved (catatonic negativism), maintain a rigid posture (catatonic rigidity), assume inappropriate or bizarre postures (catatonic posturing), or engage in stereotyped, excited motor movements that are not influenced by external stimuli (catatonic excitement).

Speech and *language* may also be severely disturbed in schizophrenia. The person's ability to communicate meaningfully with others may become impaired even further as he develops his own private language. Words may lose their communicative value and cease to be symbols for abstract ideas or objects. The words themselves become objects—a phenomenon called *desymbolization of language.* A schizophrenic person may use a word only because it rhymes with one before it and not because it communicates an idea to another person. Occasionally he may create a completely new word or expression in order to describe or express an idea for which no ordinary word exists. Such words are called *neologisms* (new words). For example, a young woman was describing her difficulty in getting along with other people, and her psychiatrist asked her to elaborate on these troubles. She began talking and then suddenly said angrily, "I wish you'd stop making such *cellunoid* comments to me." The doctor asked her the meaning of the word *cellunoid,* and she replied that a *cellunoid* comment is one that is too penetrating. "It's a comment that gets inside my *cells* and *annoys* me. It's an annoying question."

Another woman, while speaking to the psychiatrist on the ward where she was hospitalized, mentioned her fear that another patient would commit '*r-monkey.*" The doctor inquired as to the meaning of this expression, and she informed him that the word meant "*rape*": "*r-ape.*" She was concerned about being raped. It is evident that the retreat from the use of adult language and from the consensually accepted symbolic use of words, into a private and idiosyncratic usage, serves to keep from consciousness frightening thoughts and feelings. The schizophrenic person's regression in the use of language is a retreat to a more primitive mode of communication which is similar to the condensation, displacement, and symbolism of *primary process thinking* found in dreams. There are many other specific and fascinating disorders involving the usage of language that characterize the various forms of schizophrenia, and the interested reader may wish to consult some of the references and suggested readings for these examples.

Memory and *orientation* are other psychological functions that belong to the group of "autonomous functions." They are so called because they are part of the natural endowment of an individual and may remain relatively unaffected by conflict. The illnesses in which the functions

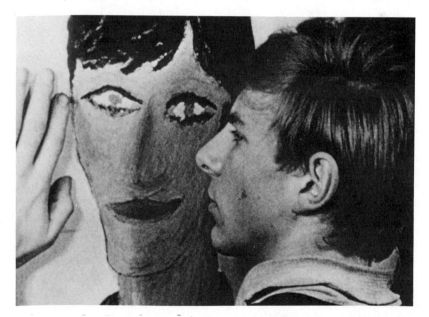

Figure 62.3. A schizophrenic young man looking in a mirror and seeing a distorted self-image in the reflection. From the film *World of the Schizophrenic.* (By permission of Sandoz Pharmaceuticals, East Hanover, NJ. Distributed by Association-Sterling Films, New York, NY.)

of memory and orientation are most affected are the organic brain syndromes, which will be discussed by Dr. Glickman in a later chapter. In general, the schizophrenic person's memory and orientation remain intact despite the massive impairment of other functions.

Adaptive Functions

It is because of his failure to *adapt to reality* that the schizophrenic person most often is brought to the attention of mental health workers. Now the concept of adaptation to reality is not synonymous with conformity. Conformity is not necessarily a virtue, and it is usually the efforts of extraordinary individuals who have refused to conform to prevailing standards at any given time in history that have accounted for most of the progress in the world. Indeed, these are many prevailing mores and values in all areas of human life that deserve to be actively resisted and to which "adaptation" is only a measure of passivity and cowardice. Conformity is *not* to be equated with mental health, and disagreement or dissent is *not* synonymous with mental illness.

By adaptation to reality we mean the person's ability to arrive at some balance between his impulses and his conscience, and then to use good judgment in assessing his options in reality and in meeting the realistic demands of life. If he is able to "adapt" in this sense to the demands that reality imposes on him, then the chances are that he will function effectively in the world. The schizophrenic person's ability to function in such a way is sorely compromised. It is not rare for severely disturbed patients to wander the streets in winter, ignoring the weather and without proper clothing. Or, a person may be walking idly into the middle of a busy intersection, oblivious to the onrushing cars. Such maladaptive behavior is obviously dangerous and indicates a profound disturbance in a person's ability to function in an independent manner in the real world.

A very reliable indicator of the state of a person's adaptive functioning is the quality of his or her *social relationships (object relations)*. The schizophrenic person's object relations often suffer massively. There is almost always a social withdrawal and a distancing from others to the extent that Bleuler considered one of the cardinal signs of the disorder to be *autism*. Autism is a profound preoccupation with one's inner mental life to the exclusion of the outer world and the people who inhabit it. It is quite characteristic of schizophrenic patients. It is not rare for such people to remain in their rooms for days at a time, not venturing out into the company of others. Families of such people frequently visit psychiatric emergency rooms asking that something be done to draw them out of their rooms. Often these people have locked themselves inside for days or even weeks, sitting silently and meditating. They may be preoccupied with philosophical profundities or even with auditory hallucinations, and during these weeks alone they may neglect to take care of basic needs such as eating or bathing.

It is frequently observed that such patients, even before becoming acutely ill, began a slow and insidious social withdrawal and often suffered from the feelings of shyness, inadequacy, and social ineptness that are characteristic of the *schizoid* and *schizotypal personality*. They were often loners and "dreamers" who could not relate to people on a meaningful level. Here, too, the defensive nature of the symptom is evident. Anxiety which might be generated by contact with other people is avoided by withdrawal. The paucity and barrenness of their social relationships are a price that schizophrenic people have to pay for at least some relief from the panic that might otherwise completely and terrifyingly overwhelm them (Figure 62.4).

Figure 62.4. *The Scream* (1893) by Edvard Munch. (By permission of National Gallery, Oslo, Norway.)

Defensive Functions

Defenses are an integral part of every personality structure. Unfortunately, many students develop the idea that defenses are "pathological," and that the tactics of treatment include taking them away from the patient. Nothing could be further from the truth. Defenses are necessary for all of us so that we can deal with the conflicts of life and not be overwhelmed by anxiety. Defenses are necessary, and in fact their strength and intactness are important indications of healthy functioning. When defenses are fragile, the result can be an anxiety of panic proportions and a disruption of the person's ability to function.

In a schizophrenic reaction, the patient attempts to defend himself from anxiety that threatens to become intolerable. But his defenses begin to falter and may not be sufficient to stem the tide of anxiety that has been produced by innumerable conflicts. Hence, at the beginning of a schizophrenic disorder, we may see a patient whose defensive structure is crumbling and whose thoughts reflect a breakthrough of the most frightening impulses. The patient may be consciously aware of thoughts and feelings that most of us only dare to dream about—and even when we dream of them they are represented in distorted and disguised fashion. These often have to do with incestuous, homosexual, murderous, or other forbidden sexual and aggressive wishes. Ordinarily such impulses are banished from consciousness because they are so unacceptable that even to think of them arouses more anxiety and guilt than most people can tolerate. In the face of these impulses, and with failing defenses to ward off the anxiety which they generate, the schizophrenic person must find other defenses. He thus regresses to the use of more primitive and less adaptive defenses.

He begins to use denial and projection almost exclusively—defenses that were developed and used most often at an earlier time in life. In so doing, he does not have to tolerate the unacceptable ideas and impulses as originating from within himself, but can experience them as coming from others. Hence, it is not *he* who wants to kill others; *they* want to kill him. It is not *he* who has sexual feelings about other men. Rather, *other men* whisper about him and impugn his manliness. The patient has struck a bad bargain, but a bargain nonetheless. He pays a terrible price for the disavowal of such primitive and frightening thoughts, but the price is less than the fragmenting anxiety that such thoughts and feelings would arouse if he acknowledged them as his own. The reader may also have noticed that in regressing to the exclusive use of such primitive defenses, the patient has failed to distinguish events occurring inside himself from those outside. His inner experiences are projected outside himself onto others. There is a consequent breakdown of the boundaries between himself and others, and by virtue of such a breakdown, he has lost the ability to test reality correctly.

Reality Testing

Reality testing is the function responsible for the correct perception of the reality of the external world. This important function is a major determinant in the assessment of whether or not a patient is psychotic. This ability to distinguish self from nonself, and inner fantasy from external reality, is profoundly compromised in the schizophrenic disorders. A person who experiences his inner feelings and fantasies as being a part of the world outside himself is a person who can no longer differentiate self from nonself. Hence, a person who is experiencing auditory hallucinations and believes that they are the voices of others commanding him to do certain things, is a person whose ability to test reality has been lost.

In a more general sense, a loss of the ability to test reality involves a loss or a compromise of the integrity of one's "ego boundaries," a sense of where one person ends and another begins. Many schizophrenic patients report feelings of fusion with others, or feelings that they can read the minds of others, or that others can read their minds. Some patients will talk of being controlled by others—by "influencing machines" from outer space, or by hostile and unseen forces that follow and torment them. The loss of the ability to distinguish what is externally real from what is not, what is self from that which is not part of the self, reflects the massive regression back to the earliest stages of development, when the infant, with its poorly developed and immature mental functions, could not make these distinctions.

Synthetic Functions

The reader may be struck by the apparent lack of success in the schizophrenic patient's attempts to cope with his fragmenting and disintegrating world. However, it is crucial to understand that these very symptoms that we have been describing in schizophrenia are defensive and adaptive attempts by the patient to make sense and order out of an overwhelming and incomprehensible world. The disturbances that we see—the hallucinations, the shallowness of emotional response, the delusions, the autistic withdrawal, and the disordered thinking and language of the schizophrenic patient—are all defensive attempts at reordering and at restructuring his world so as to achieve some synthetic balance. They are attempts by the patient to deal with a crumbling personality structure brought about by overpowering anxiety. These efforts to avoid panic and the threat of fragmentation and annihilation (Figure 62.5) are partly successful to the extent that the person is not destroyed and some areas of psychological functioning may even remain relatively intact.

An analogy that may be useful is that of a retreating army that has suffered a massive defeat at the battlefront. Its troops are in frantic disarray, and in their flight from the pursuing enemy they erect whatever feeble defenses they can so as to ward off a final assault and destruction that would be inevitable if they did nothing.

THE CASE OF BOBBY—PAST AND PRESENT HISTORY

With this presentation of both the etiology and the characteristic symptoms of schizophrenia in mind, let us now return to the case of Bobby.

Bobby had recently married. He and his wife, Diana, moved away from his home despite the protestations of his mother with whom he had been living, and to whom he felt very attached. Bobby found the adjustment difficult. His marriage was not the romantic and fulfilling experience he had hoped it would be. He and Diana argued frequently. There were few jobs available. Bobby was working as a bank teller, a job for which he felt ill-suited and overeducated. Diana could not find work, and after a few months she was talking disparagingly about their financial situation and their marriage.

Figure 62.5. Image of a doll broken into pieces, to reflect the fragmentation of body image and fear of annihilation present in the schizophrenic process. From the film *World of the Schizophrenic*. (By permission of Sandoz Pharmaceuticals, East Hanover, N.J. Distributed by Association-Sterling Films, New York, N.Y.)

The night before he was hospitalized, Bobby was playing cards with some friends, all men. He was enjoying the companionship and the joking, until at one point he felt that he was becoming sexually aroused. He did not understand these feelings since there were no women present. What had at first been a pleasant evening had now become an uncomfortable experience of excessive closeness with a group of men. Bobby's anxiety increased. He was feeling more and more sexually stimulated, obsessed with the thought of embracing one of the men. He began to experience palpatations and sweating. He could no longer concentrate on the conversation or the jokes, having become preoccupied with his thoughts which seemed to be echoing loudly. One of the men had jokingly undressed. He displayed himself to the others who were laughing uproariously, with the exception of Bobby, who felt an intense wave of anxiety, nausea, and revulsion. He began to furiously pace about the room; then he bolted from the house into the night and raced home. Diana's reaction to Bobby on his arrival has already been described.

Later in his hospitalization, as he began to recover, Bobby told his psychiatrist about himself. He was an only child, whose mother had given him all of her attention. He had even labeled her "smother mother," a name reflecting his mixed feelings about her. Her attentions were constantly bestowed on Bobby because she and her husband had never related well. She became dependent on her son for the comfort and love that she had never received from her husband, and Bobby in turn became very dependent on her. Bobby's father, a heavy drinker, was frequently away from home. He had little time for either his wife or his son. Bobby had never found it easy to make friends, preferring instead to stay home and read, often feeling awkward and shy at social gatherings. Thus there were both schizoid and dependent features to his personality. Diana was the first woman with whom he had ever had a relationship of consequence. She was very protective and domineering, in many ways reminding Bobby of his mother. They married after only a few dates.

Diana quickly recognized the powerful hold that Bobby's mother exercised over him, and Diana insisted that they move out of the mother's house and to a different state. Thus, the maternal role was transferred to Diana, who at first enjoyed it, but later began resenting her husband's withdrawn and dependent attitudes.

These feelings about Bobby became stronger, and the relationship became more burdensome to her when the couple began to have financial troubles. At that point Diana became contemptuous of her husband's difficulties, criticizing him for not being more "aggressive" and "masculine," and for failing to support her adequately.

Thus, while Bobby's psychosis began abruptly on the night of the card game, the difficulties preceding it began many years earlier. There was a family history of "eccentric" behavior among several maternal relatives, and a family history of alcoholism and possibly abusive behavior by the paternal grandfather. Bobby's parents had a very conflicted marriage, and their attitudes toward Bobby ranged from the extremes of aloof rejection on the part of father, to suffocating closeness on the part of the mother. For reasons having to do with her own psychological past, Bobby's mother never allowed him to separate from her and become a person in his own right. As a result, he suffered all the doubts and anxieties of someone who has never developed a true sense of individuality and capability. Because of the disordered relationships in the home it was difficult for Bobby to attain an independent, masculine self-image, and to feel reasonably certain that he could handle life's demands. He impulsively married a woman who, he hoped, could affirm his heterosexuality, and whose needs might complement his own. During the first few months of the marriage a balance was struck. But when difficulties arose, the precarious balance became endangered by Diana's repeated attacks on Bobby's already diminished sense of self-sufficiency and masculinity. The stage was then set for the tragedy to come.

The evening of the card game was the onset of Bobby's overt psychosis. Bobby experienced a surge of frightening and forbidden homosexual feelings that precipitated his panic and disorganization. His attempt at resolution of the panic involved a regression to a predominant use of the defense mechanisms of denial and projection. He first denied and disavowed his sexual feelings toward these other men, and turned his sexual feelings into revulsion and hatred. He then projected this hatred onto the external world and developed the paranoid delusion that he was the object of vengeful and murderous rage on the part of the other men. His delusional conviction that he was being pursued by the other men, while frightening to him, was not nearly as frightening as the forbidden homosexual impulses which he had earlier experienced. In his paranoid state, Bobby reordered and restructured reality to fit in with his conflicts, and in a maladaptive way he made sense and order out of what had been a crumbling world. However, in the process he lost the ability to distinguish that which was occurring inside of him from the reality of the world outside. The most frightening of his inner experiences were no longer his homosexual thoughts and wishes, but rather the voices that were yelling at him—"faggot," "gay," "queer." Bobby's frantic journey home to his mother was a retreat, both realistically and psychologically, to the past. It was a regression to earlier chronological and developmental times when his world was a different and more secure place. Bobby's new world was not the world of reality. It was the world of the schizophrenic.

TREATMENT AND PROGNOSIS

Antipsychotic Drugs

As described by Dr. Freedman in Chapter 52B, one of the most important discoveries in psychiatry during the past 30 years has been the usefulness of the phenothiazines and other antipsychotic drugs in the treatment of schizophrenia. With few exceptions, these agents greatly improve the patient's course and outcome, and add greatly to the success of other treatment modalities. However, medication alone is not sufficient for most patients. Approximately one-third of schizophrenic patients treated only with drugs will relapse within a year. If the remaining two-thirds are taken off drugs, half of them will show a relapse within the ensuing year. Thus other treatment modalities are usually necessary.

Psychotherapy

Psychotherapy with schizophrenic patients is effective, especially if it is supportive and reality oriented in its focus and is combined with antipsychotic medications. In fact, individual psychotherapy combined with medication has been shown to be more effective than either modality by itself, particularly if the psychotherapy helps the patient adapt to everyday problems in living.

Such problems may be those within the family, as elegantly documented by Vaughn and Leff. They have demonstrated that when families are supportive and noncritical of the schizophrenic patient, the relapse rate is quite low (12–15%), regardless of whether the patient takes medication or not. With a very critical family, however, the relapse rate is much higher (50%). Within such critical families, medication is crucial, reducing the relapse rate to one comparable with supportive families. Without medication, the relapse rate jumps three-fold, increasing to over 90% for patients spending more than 35 hours a week in such a critical family environment.

Hospitalization

Most schizophrenic patients require hospitalization at some point during their lives, usually during an acute psychotic episode. The psychiatric hospital can be used to initiate medication, while helping the patient to also begin to regain his or her former level of functioning. Most studies indicate that lengthy hospitalization (three months or longer) provides little more benefit than a short-term hospitalization, provided the patient is carefully reintegrated into the community once the acute psychosis is resolved. Looking at all groups of schizophrenic patients in various forms of treatment, approximately 70% are relatively asymptomatic within three months of their first psychotic episode. After five years, 60% are socially recovered, although evidence of the illness may still be present. Thirty percent will demonstrate a significant social handicap, requiring considerable financial and/or emotional support, while the remaining 10% will require some form of long-term institutional care, usually hospitalization.

Other Prognostic Variables

A number of additional factors influence the outcome of schizophrenia. A worse prognosis is associated with patients who become ill at an early age, especially if there is an insidious onset. Premorbid characteristics of aloofness, shallowness, inappropriate affect, and evidence of brain damage (including enlarged ventricles on CT scan) are also associated with a poor prognosis. By contrast, patients with a good premorbid history (people who are well educated, who are married, who can sustain a good work relationship), or who develop an acute illness at a later age have a far better prognosis. The presence of affective illness within the family improves the prognosis as does the presence of symptoms of depression or mania combined with the schizophrenic symptoms.

Nancy Andreasen has suggested a classification of schizophrenia based upon prognosis. In her category of *positive schizophrenia*, the onset is often acute, the premorbid history is good, and the prognosis is favorable. In this form of schizophrenia the patient presents with at least one of the following intense psychotic symptoms: 1) positive formal thought disorder (characterized by loosening of associations, incoherence, illogicality, and pressure of speech); 2) delusions; 3) hallucinations; or 4) bizarre behavior. In her category of *negative schizophrenia*, the onset is often insidious, the premorbid history is poor, and the prognosis is unfavorable. In this form of schizophrenia the patient presents with at least two of the following "five A's": 1) alogia (poverty of speech); 2) affective flattening; 3) anhedonia (inability to experience pleasure) and asociality (few social contacts); 4) avolition-apathy (lack of energy and persistence); and 5) attentional impairment (difficulty in attending to environmental stimuli). Andreasen believes that there are focal neurochemical processes involved in positive schizophrenia that are reversible with treatment, whereas diffuse neurophysiological and other structural processes are involved in negative schizophrenia (as reflected in high ventricular-brain ratios) that are not reversible with treatment. Further research will be necessary to document the validity of Andreasen's classification, but at this point it appears to have both clinical and research promise.

Suggested Readings

Andreasen NC: *The Broken Brain. The Biological Revolution in Psychiatry*. New York, Harper & Row, 1984.

Cancro R (Preceptor): The Schizophrenic Disorders. In Grinspoon L (ed): *Psychiatry 1982*. Washington, DC, American Psychiatric Press, 1982, pp 79–255.

Frosch J: *The Psychotic Process*. New York, International Universities Press, 1983.

Green H: *I Never Promised You a Rose Garden*. New York, Holt, Rinehart, and Winston, 1964.

Niederland WG: *The Schreber Case*. New York, Quadrangle/ The New York Times Book Co, 1974.

Peters F: *The World Next Door*. New York, Farrar Straus and Co, 1949.

Sechehaye M: *The Autobiography of a Schizophrenic Girl*. New York, Grune & Stratton, 1951.

References

Andreasen NC, et al: Ventricular enlargement in schizophrenia: definition and prevalence. *Am J Psychiatry* 139:292, 1982.

Andreasen NC, et al: Ventricular enlargement in schizophrenia: relationship to positive and negative symptoms. *Am J Psychiatry* 139:297, 1982.

Arieti S: *Interpretation of Schizophrenia*, ed 2. New York, Basic Books, 1974.

Bellak L (ed): *Disorders of the Schizophrenic Syndrome*. New York, Basic Books, 1979.

Berger MM (ed): *Beyond the Double Bind*. New York, Brunner/Mazel, 1978.

Bleuler E: *Dementia Praecox or the Group of Schizophrenias*, translated by J. Zinkin. New York, International Universities Press, 1950.

Freedman R, et al: Neurophysiological evidence for a deficit in inhibitory pathways in schizophrenia: comparison of medicated and drug-free patients. *Biol Psychiatry* 18:537, 1983.

Holzman PS, et al: Pursuit eye movements in schizophrenia. *Arch Gen Psychiatry* 41:136, 1984.

Howells JG, Guirguis W: *The Family and Schizophrenia*. New York, International Universities Press, 1982.

Schneider K: *Clinical Psychopathology* (translated by M.W. Hamilton). New York, Grune and Stratton, 1959.

Sederer LI: Schizophrenic disorders. In Sederer LI (ed): *Inpatient Psychiatry: Diagnosis and Treatment*. Baltimore, Williams & Wilkins, 1983, p 42.

Taylor MA, Abrams R: Cognitive impairment in schizophrenia. *Am J Psychiatry* 141:196, 1984.

Vaughn CE, Leff JP: The conflict of family and social factors on the course of psychiatric illness. *Br J Psych* 129:125, 1976.

CHAPTER **63** **The Affective Disorders**

A. Mania and Bipolar Disorder

Mark W. Rhine, M.D.,
Ronald D. Franks, M.D., and
Richard C. Simons, M.D.

In contrast to the schizophrenic disorders, where the essential feature is a disturbance in thinking, in the affective disorders the essential feature is a disturbance of mood (affect, emotion). The mood may be either elevated and euphoric (mania) or depressed and dysphoric (the depressive disorders). We shall first discuss mania.

DEFINITION

The nosology of mania has been clarified in recent years. Mania can be distinguished as either *primary* or *secondary*. *Primary mania* is the mania of a primary affective disorder, whereas Krauthammer and Klerman view *secondary mania* as the mania that occurs secondary to a variety of organic disorders, including drug ingestion (especially steroids and stimulants such as amphetamine, ritalin, and cocaine), infections (encephalitis, influenza, tertiary syphilis), CNS neoplasms, epilepsy, and various metabolic disturbances (including postoperative states and hemodialysis). One should be particularly alert to such possible etiologies if a first episode of mania occurs in an individual over 55, especially if there is no family history of affective disorder. In such cases, a thorough medical and neurological workup is indicated.

According to DSM-III, primary mania may be seen in one of three conditions: 1) *bipolar disorder, manic,* (where only a manic episode is present); 2) *bipolar disorder, depressed* (where there is a history of manic episodes, but currently only a major depressive episode is present); and 3) *bipolar disorder, mixed* (where the current episode involves the full symptomatic picture of both manic and major depressive ep-

isodes, intermixed or rapidly alternating every few days).

THE CHARACTERISTIC SYMPTOMS OF MANIA

My conquering imagination soon tricked me into believing that I could lift myself by my bootstraps ... and having no boots to stand in, I used my bed as boots. I reasoned that for my scientific purpose a man in bed was as favorably situated as a man in boots. Therefore, attaching a sufficient number of my felt straps to the head and foot of the bed (which happened not to be screwed to the floor), and, in turn, attaching the free ends to the transom and the window guard, I found the problem very simple. For I next joined these cloth cables in such manner that by pulling downward I effected a readjustment of stress and strain, and my bed, *with me in it*, was soon dangling in space. My sensations at this momentous instant must have been much like those which thrilled Newton when he solved one of the riddles of the universe. Indeed, they must have been more intense, for Newton, knowing, had his doubts; I, not knowing, had no doubts at all. So epoch-making did this discovery appear to me that I noted the exact position of the bed so that a wondering posterity might ever afterward view and revere the exact spot on the earth's surface whence one of man's greatest thoughts had winged its way to immortality ... Meanwhile I felt sure that another sublime moment of inspiration would intervene and clear the atmosphere, thus rendering flight of the body as easy as flight of the imagination.

This remarkable description of mania is taken from Clifford Beers' account of his own mental illness, entitled *A Mind That Found Itself*, written in 1907. This book is fascinating reading not only because Beers describes from his own perspective what it is like to have a manic-depressive illness, but also because he documents the inhumane treatment of psychotic patients that often prevailed at that time. Beers later crusaded for better conditions for the mentally ill, culminating in his founding of what is now the National Mental Health Association.

In many ways a manic episode is the mirror image of a major depressive episode. In mania the *mood is elevated*, and the patient is expansive, euphoric, and full of infectious good humor. This expansive mood is labile, however, and when the manic patient is criticized or frustrated, he or she can become suddenly irritable, argumentative, and threatening. At other times, especially when a mixed bipolar disorder is present, sadness, tearfulness, suicidal thoughts, and other depressive symptoms may suddenly break through.

The speech of the manic patient is in stark contrast to the slow, laborious discourse of the depressed patient. The manic talks loudly and incessantly, in voluminous and rapid detail, in what is known as *pressure of speech*. The content of the manic's speech is consistent with his euphoric mood, and though he jumps rapidly from topic to topic (a phenomenon known as *flight of ideas*), the listener usually has no difficulty in following his meaning. At times his speech may include rhyming, punning, bad jokes, and so-called *clang associations* in which the sound of a word may stimulate an association to a word with a similar sound.

In contrast to the depressed individual (who has no energy, no interest in his usual activities, for whom everything is an exhausting chore, and who prefers to withdraw from people and activity), the manic person is tireless, always on the go, constantly preoccupied with *grandiose* plans, changing from one activity to another, requiring little sleep, until he finally collapses with exhaustion. Because of this *hyperactivity* and *distractibility*, the manic patient often becomes overinvolved socially and sexually, and shows *poor judgment* in interpersonal and business affairs. He or she may form indiscrete sexual liaisons, impulsively marry, enter into ill-considered business ventures, spend money lavishly and unwisely, and eventually have to be protected from personal embarrassment and financial ruin during the manic phase. Such individuals are obviously very difficult to live with, and the divorce rates of manics are high.

When delusions or hallucinations are present, their content is usually consistent with the predominant mood (mood-congruent). For example, the manic patient may develop a grandiose delusion involving a special relationship to God or some world-famous person, or the possession of God-like powers (Figure 63.1). Or God's voice may be heard in an hallucination that announces to the person the existence of special powers or a special mission. Clifford Beers provides a vivid description of his own delusions of grandeur:

> Gravity being conquered, it was inevitable that I should devote some of my time to the invention of a flying machine. This was soon perfected—in my mind.... As usual I was unable to explain how I should produce the result which I so confidently foretold. But I believed and proclaimed that I should, ere long, fly to St. Louis and claim and receive the one hundred thousand dollar reward offered by the Commission of the Louisiana Purchase Exposition for the most efficient airship to be exhibited. The moment the thought

Figure 63.1. *Realization* by Philip Moore. (By permission of Philip Moore.)

winged its way through my mind, I had not only a flying machine, but a fortune in the bank. Being where I could not dissipate my riches (he was in the hospital), I became a lavish verbal spender. I was in a mood to buy anything, and I whiled away many an hour planning what I would do with my fortune.

MANIA AND SCHIZOPHRENIA

These descriptions by Clifford Beers give us a glimpse of what mania is like. They also demonstrate how easily someone might mistake mania for schizophrenia, given the unusual thinking in both. Despite the strong similarities, however, mania has been recognized as a separate disease for almost 2,000 years. Aretaeus in the second century described both mania and melancholia, noticing a relationship between the two. He saw mania occurring more in the young and melancholia more in the old. He also observed that mania nearly always converted to melancholia but not the reverse. Kraepelin, at the turn of the 20th century, helped with this distinction by developing descriptive criteria for both schizophrenia and mania, emphasizing that the social and mental decline which he felt was inevitable in schizophrenia (dementia praecox) did not occur in mania. Despite these efforts, however, little attention was seriously paid to mania as a separate disease entity until the early 1950's when Cade discovered that lithium carbonate was a specific and effective treatment for mania. This discovery has led to increasing efforts toward diagnosing mania whenever possible, given its better prognosis than schizophrenia. Table 63.1 outlines some of the main differentiating features between mania and schizophrenia.

Because of the relatively brief length of manic episodes, studies of prevalence and incidence are much more difficult to obtain with mania than with schizophrenia. The best estimate of the lifetime risk of mania or bipolar disorder is approximately 1%, roughly similar to that of schizophrenia. In some studies women may be slightly more likely to develop this disease than men, but in other studies bipolar disorder appears to be equally common in both sexes. The age of onset (in the 20's) is somewhat later than for schizophrenia. Also unlike schizophrenia, mania does not seem to be as strongly linked with any particular socioeconomic class, al-though some studies suggest that it may be more prevalent in the upper classes. Finally, again in contrast to schizophrenia, mania has a more variable prevalence among different cultures, being proportionately higher among Jews, Irish, and the Hutterites, while lower in Asian societies, especially those where Hinduism or Buddhism is the predominant religion.

ETIOLOGY

As with schizophrenia, primary mania is probably best viewed as a syndrome that is the result of multiple etiological factors. Dr. Reite has presented the evidence for genetic factors in the etiology of mania (Chapter 52A), and Dr. Freedman has discussed some of the possible neurochemical causes (Chapter 52B). There is also evidence that a disturbance in biological rhythms may play a role in the etiology of mania, as discussed by Dr. Crowley in Chapter 52C. Neurophysiological abnormalities in sensory evoked potentials during the manic state suggest that mania may also be related to a disruption in normal sensory processing. Sociocultural factors and family interactions do not at this point appear to play a significant role in the etiology of mania, although further research in these areas is needed. Finally, Lewin and others have suggested that mania can be understood psychodynamically as a defense against and a denial of depression, since manic episodes sometimes occur following a significant loss instead of the depression that might be expected. Furthermore, although recovered manic patients appear to adapt successfully in their social and work relationships, Cohen and coworkers observed that these individuals are often dependent and insecure, and in need of the continuing approval and reassurance of others. However, MacVane and coworkers did not find these dependent personality features in bipolar patients who were well stabilized on lithium, and Cassano, Maggini, and Akiskal suggest that such traits as dependency and low self-confidence are more likely to be chronic sequelae and postpsychotic complications of manic (and major depressive) episodes rather than prepsychotic etiologic factors.

TREATMENT

Most cases of mania will be treated by the psychiatrist. However, the nonpsychiatric phy-

Table 63.1
*Differentiation of Mania and Schizophrenia**

	Mania	Schizophrenia
Mood or affect	Elated, euphoric, consistent with content of speech (underlying sadness and anger).	Flat, bland, inappropriate to content of speech (underlying panic and suspiciousness).
Thinking	Pressured speech. Flight of ideas, with content more logical and easier to follow. Delusions and hallucinations less common. Delusions when present tend to be grandiose and mood-congruent.	Fragmented speech. Concrete, illogical, bizarre, difficult to understand. Delusions and hallucinations more common. Delusions tend to be persecutory in nature or bizarre and mood-incongruent.
Behavior	Hyperactivity. Behavior appears to be more influenced by external factors and relationships. Poor judgment. Socially over-involved and intrusive. May be assaultive but rarely homicidal.	Agitation. Behavior appears to be more influenced by internal factors. Socially withdrawn. May be assaultive and homicidal.
Object relations	Better social skills and relations with people. Fear of loss of object. Better work history.	Isolated. Poor social skills and relations with people. Fear of annihilation. Often a deteriorating work history.
Reaction of interviewer	Patient is likeable, makes us laugh, occasionally makes us feel overwhelmed or angry.	Patient seems distant, strange, and often threatening. Makes us feel puzzled and frightened.
Typical age of onset	25–55.	Adolescence to 45.
Socioeconomic	All socioeconomic groups.	Tend toward lower socioeconomic status.
History	History of previous episodes of mania and/or depression. History of mood swings. Family history of affective disorder common.	History of acute episodes followed by reconstitution or chronic deterioration. Family history of schizophrenia common.
Prognosis	Generally better.	Generally poorer.

* Table by Ronald D. Franks, Mark W. Rhine, and Richard C. Simons

sician has an important role to play in diagnosing the illness in its early stages, when the lay person is apt to regard it merely as excessive good spirits. At that point the physician can provide invaluable help by urging the patient or the family to get immediate psychiatric help. The physician must also be alert to the fact that his or her manic patients are apt to discontinue their medical regimens for their various physical illnesses as they enter a manic or major depressive episode.

Hospitalization is frequently required during the height of a manic episode in order to interrupt the patient's self-destructive course. Poor judgment is a hallmark of mania and may result in aggressive outbursts, impulsive sexual encounters, and the reckless spending of a lifetime's savings unless the patient is placed briefly in a protective setting. But whether in the hospital or not, these patients should be given a trial of lithium carbonate. Approximately 70% of manic patients will notice a sharp reduction in the acute symptoms as well as a reduction in the frequency and intensity of manic and major depressive episodes. Other antipsychotic medications (phenothiazines, butyrophenones) may also be useful in controlling mania, especially in the beginning stages of treatment, since lithium usually requires one to three weeks before its effect is noticed. Carbamazepine appears to be quite promising as an alternative to lithium for those manic patients sensitive to some of lithium's side effects. But the dramatic impact of one drug—lithium—in offering hope in place of despair for these patients cannot be overstated. One manic patient used poetry to express his gratitude:

To Lithium
Moon in my hand, I thank you
for your discipline through my blood,
your salty ways,
how much do I owe you
beyond obedience
and freedom from forgetfulness?
How clearly I see your strength
in keeping my feet on the ground
and putting my head someplace near the
    Earth,
removed from other planets
someplace on my shoulders,
not burning with imaginations
condemned to suffer wanderings,
a life spent unable to match
a plug to a socket
But honed to life and true,
focused and sized aright
delivered to me by you.

Freddy Bosco

Individual psychotherapy with the manic patient is very difficult. Most manic patients do not want to relinquish the elation and grandiosity of mania despite the disruption that their unrealistically inflated self-esteem is causing for them. Thus, a supportive rather than an insight-oriented approach is most effective, but usually only in combination with medication. As with schizophrenia, involving the patient's family, friends, employer, and other environmental resources can be critical to the success of treatment.

PROGNOSIS

The natural course of bipolar disorder prior to the introduction of lithium resulted in manic periods of usually two to four months with depressive periods lasting four to six months. Of those patients experiencing their first attack, only 25% would not have another episode. Most (75%) would experience a second, with 65% having a third and 45% a fourth or more. Now, with effective treatment these statistics are greatly improved. The most striking feature about bipolar disorder, however, is that in between episodes of mania and depression, less than 10% of patients will show any evidence of mental illness. This characteristic is probably the most important difference between mania and schizophrenia, since nearly 70% of schizophrenic patients show evidence of some chronic, persistent symptoms of their illness.

Suggested Readings

Akiskal HS: The bipolar spectrum: new concepts in classification and diagnosis. In Grinspoon L (ed): *Psychiatry Update Vol II.* Washington, DC, American Psychiatric Press, 1983, p 271.
Andreasen NC: *The Broken Brain. The Biological Revolution in Psychiatry.* New York, Harper & Row, 1984.
Beers CW: *A Mind That Found Itself.* New York, Doubleday, 1907.
Clayton PJ (Preceptor): Bipolar Illness. In Grinspoon L (ed): *Psychiatry Update Vol. II.* Washington, DC, American Psychiatric Press, 1983, pp 267–345.
Sederer LI: Mania. In Sederer LI (ed): *Inpatient Psychiatry: Diagnosis and Treatment.* Baltimore, Williams & Wilkins, 1983, p 28.

References

Cassano GB, Maggini C, Akiskal HS: Short-term, subchronic, and chronic sequelae of affective disorders. *Psychiatr Clin North Am* 6:55, 1983.
Cohen MB, et al: An intensive study of 12 cases of manic-depressive psychosis. *Psychiatry* 17:103, 1954.
Krauthammer C, Klerman GL: Secondary mania. *Arch Gen Psychiatry* 35:1333, 1978.
Lewin B: *The Psychoanalysis of Elation.* New York, W. W. Norton & Co, 1950.
MacVane JR, et al: Psychological functioning of bipolar manic-depressives in remission. *Arch Gen Psychiatry* 35:1351, 1978.

B. Depression and the Depressive Disorders

Richard C. Simons, M.D.,
Mark Rubinstein, M.D., and
Ronald D. Franks, M.D.

INTRODUCTION

This chapter on depression and the depressive disorders involves one of the most complex areas in psychiatry. The complexity stems in part from the fact that depression can present in at least three forms: 1) as a normal affect or emotion such as sadness; 2) as a sign or symptom of a situational reaction; and 3) as an illness or clinical syndrome in the form of an affective disorder. Furthermore, all three of these forms of depression may exist on a continuum. For example, someone may feel sad in response to a loss. This emotion of sadness may then develop into the situational reaction of grief or bereavement, with depression as one of the signs or symptoms. The depression may then progress to the full clinical syndrome of an affective disorder in which occupational, social, and bodily functions are disrupted. Further complexity arises from the fact that depression as a primary affective disorder can present with either psychological symptoms or physical symptoms or both, and also that some physical illnesses can present with depression as their main or possibly their only symptom (secondary depression). In this chapter we will present a classification of depression that attempts to address these various complexities.

THE THREE MEANINGS OF DEPRESSION

Depression as a Normal Emotion

The distinction between depression as a clinical syndrome and depression as a mildly altered mood state such as sadness or unhappiness is one that can be confusing. Sadness and unhappiness are not clinical conditions but are, rather, normal and universal phenomena that constitute part of the human condition. At times, we

are all unhappy with ourselves, with the people in our lives, or with our situations, and there is sometimes little that we can do to alter such feelings. Sadness and unhappiness over the inevitable disappointments of life are universal experiences. Depression as a clinical syndrome, on the other hand, is something quite different. The distinction is illustrated by the following vignette. A group of medical students was asked if anyone could distinguish between unhappiness and clinical depression. There was silence for a moment, and then a young man made the following reply: "Clinical depression is when you apply to 10 medical schools, and you end up being rejected by every one of them. Unhappiness is when you're *in* medical school." That is as good a distinction as can be made!

Depression as a Situational Reaction

Situational depression is continuous with the transient states of sadness and unhappiness described above, but tends to last somewhat longer. Perhaps the most familiar example of situational depression is that of grief and mourning, listed in DSM-III as *uncomplicated bereavement.*

Mourning or bereavement is also a normal phenomenon. It is usual to see this reaction following a meaningful loss, especially after the death of someone very close and very loved. Mourning is purposive and serves an important function in preparing the mourner to adaptively face the future. It enables the bereaved person to eventually relinquish the emotional ties to a loved one who has died, so that new attachments and emotional investments may begin. It is a slow and very painful process, and has been described by Dr. Wolff and Dr. Simons in a previous chapter. The predominant affects involved are intense sadness, and a profound yearning or longing for the lost person. The bereaved person's perception of the world may be as the grieving Hamlet's, ("How weary, stale, flat and unprofitable seem to me all the uses of this world"), and his feelings may be colored by a pervasive emptiness, but his self-esteem is still intact. This is a crucial distinction between mourning and clinical depression. While the world may seem empty and lacking in meaning to the mourning person, he still feels that he is basically worthwhile. He does not suffer the profound feelings of self-loathing and unrelenting guilt that characterize the depressed person's state of mind. This important distinction is basic in understanding clinical depression as a *disorder*, while bereavement, although a *deviation* from the usual state of functioning, is a normal response to a loss (Figure 63.2).

The other familiar example of situational depression that we all experience during the course of our lives is the *sadness associated with each new stage of development*. Even as we are enjoying the pleasure and happiness that come with new accomplishments, and with further individuation and independence, we are also feeling a bittersweet sadness at relinquishing all that must be left behind. In a sense, the whole of life

can be viewed as a series of developmental milestones, each one characterized by elements of loss and separation, as well as by elements of gain and individuation. These paradoxes are perhaps seen most poignantly as one becomes older (Figure 63.3). In a youth-oriented culture where a high premium is placed on the ephemeral virtues of youth and beauty, aging can become a relentless insult and, depending upon the emotional investment one has made in appearance, strength, and youth, the process of aging can be extremely stressful.

Joseph Heller described many of these feelings very beautifully in his novel, *Something Happened*. The central figure of the novel is Bob Slocum, a middle-aged advertising executive. As he watches his son grow older and become disinterested in him, Slocum begins to contemplate his own future as an old man:

> I don't want him to go. My memory's failing, my bladder is weak, my arches are falling, my tonsils and adenoids are gone, and my jawbone is rotting, and now my little boy wants to cast me away and leave me behind for reasons he won't give me.

Figure 63.2. *The Survivors* (1923) by Käthe Kollwitz. (By permission of National Gallery of Art, Washington, DC., Rosenwald Collection.)

Figure 63.3. *Self-Portrait in Profile to the Right* (1938) by Käthe Kollwitz. (By permission of National Gallery of Art, Washington, DC, Rosenwald Collection.)

What else will I have? My job? When I am fifty-five, I will have nothing more to look forward to than Arthur Baron's job and reaching sixty-five. When I am sixty-five, I will have nothing more to look forward to than reaching seventy-five, or dying before then. And when I am seventy-five, I will have nothing more to look forward to than dying before eighty-five, or geriatric care in a nursing home. I will have to take enemas. (Will I have to be dressed in double-layer, waterproof undershorts designed especially for incontinent gentlemen?) I will be incontinent. I don't want to live longer than eighty-five, and I don't want to die sooner than a hundred and eighty-six.

Oh, my father—why have you done this to me? I want him back.*

———
* From *Something Happened*, by Joseph Heller. Copyright © 1966 and 1974 by Scapegoat Productions, Inc. (Reprinted by permission of Ballantine Books, a division of Random House, New York.)

Bob Slocum poignantly epitomizes an ironic contradiction of human existence, one that was expressed by Jonathan Swift's aphorism: "Every man desires to live long, but no man would be old." For while old age brings with it a potential for ripened pleasures, it also demands major adjustments and adaptations which are difficult for many people to make.

First of all, the inevitable losses of later life are many. Loved ones and friends may move away or die. As Bob Slocum is aware, retirement may bring with it feelings of uselessness, lassitude, and loss of status. But the infirmities of aging with their consequent reminders of our own mortality may be the most distressing of all. Loss of one's health and the integrity of one's own body often accompanies old age, and may have devastating effects on a person (Figure 63.4). People may become depressed because of the limitations that a physical illness imposes upon them. They may become depressed after the loss of function of an organ or after the loss of the organ itself, and they may become depressed by the threat that the physical illness poses to life itself.

Figure 63.4. *Trauernder Mann* ("Grieving Man") (1890) by Vincent van Gogh. (By permission of Rijksmuseum Kröller-Müller, Otterlo, Holland.)

Depression as an Affective Disorder

Depression as normal sadness, and depression as a situational reaction, are rarely so severe as to cause a major disruption in work, social interaction, or bodily function. Depression as an affective disorder, however, does cause such severe disruptions. The depressed mood is deeper and more protracted. Work or school performance is significantly disturbed. The patient's interest in maintaining close relationships sharply declines. Bodily functions deteriorate; the patient loses interest in eating (anorexia) and in sexual activity. Sleep is harder to obtain and is not restful. The patient becomes noticeably slowed down (psychomotor retardation) or else very restless (psychomotor agitation). Feelings of helplessness, hopelessness, and worthlessness are nearly constant, often progressing to suicidal proportions. This is not just the affect of depression as seen in normal sadness or in various situational reactions. This is the full clinical syndrome of an affective disorder.

As with primary mania and secondary mania, it is helpful to separate depression as an affective disorder into *primary depression* and *secondary depression* (Figure 63.5).

In contrast to normal sadness and situational reactions, primary depression as an affective disorder appears to be grossly out of proportion to any life events or life stresses that may have preceded it, and the intensity and duration of the mood disturbance reaches the point of morbid despair. In his book *The Varieties of Religious Experience* William James conveys this difference eloquently:

> There is a pitch of unhappiness so great that the goods of nature may be entirely forgotten, and all sentiment of their existence vanish from the mental field. For this extremity of pessimism to be reached, something more is needed than observation of life and reflection upon death. The individual must in his own person become the prey of a pathological melancholy.... Such sensitiveness and susceptibility to mental pain... one seldom finds in a healthy subject even where he is the victim of the most atrocious cruelties of outward fortune... it is positive and active anguish, a sort of psychical neuralgia, wholly unknown to healthy life.*

So also does Joseph Heller's Bob Slocum:

> I do indeed know what morbid compulsion feels like. Fungus, erosion, disease. The taste of flannel in your mouth. The smell of asbestos in your brain. A rock. A sinking heart, silence, taut limbs, a festering invasion from within, seeping subversion, and a full pressure on the brow, and in the back regions of the skull. It starts like a fleeting whim, an airy, frivolous notion, but it doesn't go; it stays; it sticks; it enlarges in space and force like a somber, inhuman form from whatever lightless pit inside you it abides in; it fills you up, spreading steadily throughout you like lava or a persistent miasmic cloud, an obscure, untouchable, implacable, domineering, vile presence disguising itself treacherously in your own identity, a double agent— it is debilitating and sickening. It foreshadows no joy—and takes charge, and you might as well hang your head and drop your eyes and give right in.†

In contrast to primary depression, secondary depression (like secondary mania) appears in connection with some other serious medical or psychiatric disorder. Woodruff and colleagues, and then Robins and Guze proposed the category of secondary depression to designate those states of demoralization, hopelessness, and helplessness that are often found as reactions to serious nonaffective mental disorders, especially schizophrenia and alcoholism. Subsequently Klerman and Barrett proposed extending the concept of secondary depression to those depressions associated with various medical and neurological illnesses (see Table 14.1 in Chapter 14C), and also to those depressions that appear as adverse reactions to various drugs (see Table 14.2 in Chapter 14C). The following is a case example of a clinical depression secondary to a serious medical illness.

Mrs. B was 39 and a successful lawyer at the time she was seen in psychiatric consultation. Her first marriage at age 30 lasted only three years. At the time of her divorce, one of the major problems was the patient's wish for a family, a wish her first husband did not share. At age 36, the patient became involved with a new man whom she married approximately one

---

*From *The Varieties of Religious Experience* by William James, 1902. Dolphin Books, Doubleday & Co, Garden City, NY, pp 136, 138.

---

†From *Something Happened*, by Joseph Heller. Copyright © 1966 and 1974 by Scapegoat Productions, Inc. (Reprinted by permission of Ballantine Books, a division of Random House, New York).

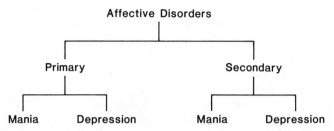

Figure 63.5. Classification of the affective disorders, following Robins and Guze (1972), Klerman and Barrett (1973), and Krauthammer and Klerman (1978).

and one-half years later. As she approached her late 30's, she became increasingly concerned over whether she would ever have children. In response to this concern, she put great pressure on her husband to begin a family. Her husband resisted, feeling that the marriage needed strengthening before either partner could successfully function as a parent. The patient began to feel depressed. She had symptoms of fatigue, loss of appetite, weight loss (20 pounds over six months), insomnia, and abdominal pain, similar in nature to that experienced several years earlier with a duodenal ulcer. The patient also developed mild to moderate hypertension, diagnosed by her physician to be secondary to the degree of psychological stress that she was experiencing. Her routine blood and urine tests showed no abnormalities. Over a six-month period, the patient received marital therapy from her minister, noticing a temporary improvement that lasted for one or two days after each session. Unfortunately the depression would quickly return. Because of the lack of resolution, a psychiatric consultation was obtained by the patient's internist, who was concerned about the continued weight loss and the persistent physical complaints. At the patient's insistence, he also admitted her to a general hospital for a more complete diagnostic workup. On abdominal CT scan, the patient was found to have a large tumor, later diagnosed as carcinoma of the body and tail of the pancreas, which had invaded her left kidney. The patient's secondary depression was the first clue to a serious physical illness. At the onset of her depression, however, the patient's symptoms and history were more consistent with a primary rather than a secondary depression, and this confusing picture delayed prompt diagnosis. The psychological issues troubling the patient were certainly important. Unfortunately, the patient's abdominal pain and hypertension had also been seen as psychological in origin. It is important to remember that carcinoma of the pancreas is only one of a number of medical and neurological illnesses which may initially present with the clinical syndrome of depression. It is also important to remember that this patient, like all psychiatric patients, actually presents a greater risk of developing an associated physical illness than does someone without psychiatric problems, as Dr. Mumford has pointed out in Chapter 6.

HISTORICAL REVIEW OF THE CLASSIFICATION OF DEPRESSION

The ubiquity of depression has been noted and described throughout the ages. Hippocrates called it "melancholia," which literally means "black bile." He believed depression to be caused by an accumulation of black bile within the body. Depression has been described in literature and poetry, from the times of the prophets, Homer, and Shakespeare up to the present day. Some of the most prominent people in history have been afflicted with this disease, and of all mental disorders, it is the one most frequently described in the various arts. We are often able to see the importance of depression in its relation to the arts, but we can only speculate as to the influence of this mood disorder upon the course of history itself.

Scientific investigations of depression are only about 100 years old. In the late 19th century Kraepelin was the first to distinguish recurrent depressive episodes with melancholia from the elated mood swings of mania. He brought all of these conditions together under his concept of *manic-depressive psychosis*, which he separated from *dementia praecox* or *schizophrenia*. Subsequently, there have been many different attempts to classify the various subtypes of depression. Earlier classifications tended to focus on severity (*mild* vs. *severe*) or on the presence or absence of certain symptoms (*neurotic* vs. *psychotic, agitated* vs. *retarded*), whereas later classifications have tended more to focus on course (*chronic* vs. *episodic, single episode* vs. *recurrent*) and chronology (*primary* vs. *secondary*). Earlier classifications also tended to focus on the presence or absence of an external precipitating event (*reactive* or *exogenous* vs. *endogenous*) or on the assumed etiology (*characterological* vs. *biological*). In 1957 Leonhard originally proposed separating depressed patients with a history of manic episodes (*bipolar*) from those depressed patients with a history of recurrent depressive episodes without mania (*unipolar*). It is this classification of *bipolar* vs. *unipolar* that is used by most clinicians, and that formed the basis for the DSM-III classification of affective disorders, even though the term "unipolar" is not used in DSM-III. Finally, in 1978 Winokur and his colleagues presented a classification of primary, unipolar depression based upon specific familial constellations. In this classification the categories are *familial* (pure depressive disease or PDD, depression in an individual who has a first degree relative with depression, but not one with mania, antisocial personality disorder, or alcoholism) vs. *sporadic* (sporadic depressive disease or SDD, depression in an individual who has no first degree relative with psychiatric illness) vs. *spectrum* (depression spectrum disease or DSD, depression in an individual who has a first degree relative with antisocial personality and/or alcoholism).

As outlined in Figure 63.6, DSM-III groups all of the primary affective disorders together on a purely descriptive basis, independent of any presumed etiologies, whether biological, psychological, or sociocultural. As noted in the previous section on mania, bipolar disorder is divided into manic, depressed, and mixed types. Major depression may present in three forms— without melancholia, with melancholia, and with psychosis. Other specific affective disorders include cyclothymic disorder and dysthymic disorder. And, for the purposes of this chapter, we will discuss a fourth category—adjustment disorders with depressed mood associated with an identifiable psychosocial stressor.

THE CHARACTERISTIC SYMPTOMS OF DEPRESSION

The characteristic symptoms of schizophrenia were presented in the context of a mental status examination of various psychological functions, and the characteristic symptoms of mania were presented through the autobiographical accounts of Clifford Beers. To present the characteristic symptoms of depression, we will choose a patient who can serve as a prototype for us.

Mr. K is a 42 year old business executive who is beginning to feel "down." The onset may have been related to a decline in his business, although it is not clear whether the decline occurred before or after the depression began. There is a history of a similar episode of depression six years ago, but no history of manic episodes. There is a family history of depression

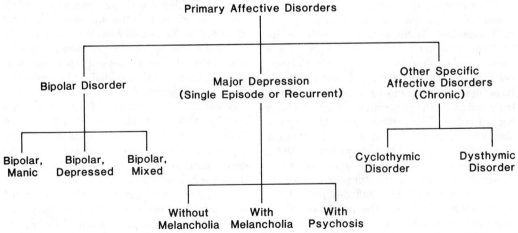

Figure 63.6. Classification of the primary affective disorders according to DSM-III, modified from Andreasen (1983) and Klerman (1983).

among several close relatives. Mr. K's physical health is good, and physical examination by his family physician is normal. He denies the abuse of drugs or alcohol, and he is not currently on any medications. When not ill the patient is described as very hard working (10 to 14 hours per day), quite perfectionistic, but somehow not as successful as one might imagine given the investment in his work. He has even been called a "workaholic" by his business associates who speak of the patient as "always busy." Let us now follow the course of his depression.

First, there is a *disturbance of mood.* Our patient is somewhat preoccupied. He may complain of feeling "blue" and "down in the dumps." He no longer wakes up in the morning with the same vigor and zest that he usually feels, and there is a hollow and lackluster quality to the day's agenda. Events have lost their flavor and do not seem as enjoyable as they were before. The day begins to feel as though it is dragging on. Ideas and thoughts do not come to him as quickly as they formerly had, and he finds that he has some *difficulty in concentrating.* He is distracted and indecisive, and his work begins to suffer.

There is an accompanying feeling of nervousness and *restlessness.* At work he has to get up and walk around a good deal. He begins to experience a sense of dread and loneliness and emptiness. He soon begins to ruminate about the events that led to his present state of mind. He begins to wonder, "Is it worth it? Where am I going? Do I really care about this job? Do I care about my wife and kids?"

Accompanying the sadness and the rumination is a waning of interest in the world around him—a slow *withdrawal of interest in pleasurable activities* such as food and sex. His thoughts turn repeatedly to the idea that perhaps he is not the person he should be. He begins to have derogatory and *depreciative thoughts* about himself, with *feelings of worthlessness and helplessness.* As a result he feels increasingly dependent on sympathy, reassurance, and support from others.

He approaches the people closest to him—his family. At first his wife is very supportive. She tells him, "Don't worry. You're all right. The business isn't so important." In other words, she tries to fill the void that the depression is creating. She may succeed to some extent, but it is not enough. His *self-esteem has plunged,* and it will take more than a few supportive words from

his wife to bring it back to its former level. He continues to withdraw and to seek reassurance until his wife's patience is taxed. She may eventually explode and angrily criticize the patient, rather than continue with her encouragement. When this occurs, everything that the patient had been feeling about himself is confirmed. This is the ironic predicament in which the depressed person finds himself. It is the self-fulfilling prophecy of depression. The person feels badly and lacks self-esteem, and in his repeatedly seeking and even demanding external support he eventually manages to antagonize those closest to him, thus confirming his own self-derogatory feelings. The world is then ready to accommodate the depressed person's self-punitive needs.

The patient withdraws further. The withdrawal is reminiscent of that observed in primates after their mothers have been removed from the environment, and in the anaclitically depressed infants following separation from their mothers. Our patient is now depressed enough to entertain *suicidal thoughts.* In addition, he has developed some of the *somatic* (or so-called "vegetative") *signs of depression.* He looks sad, haggard, and drawn (*psychomotor retardation*). He is not sleeping well—awakening early each morning and then feeling *fatigued* during the day. In addition to the *insomnia*, he has *lost his appetite* for food almost completely, and has begun to *lose weight.*

At this point the patient is suffering from a *major depression.* Yet despite the severity of his symptoms he may not have presented himself to a physician. He may have been able to continue functioning at his work, although his abilities have been greatly compromised and a pervasive sense of pessimism colors his outlook. The patient's *mood disturbance now becomes more profound.* An engulfing sense of *guilt*, shame, and emptiness begins to prevail. His thinking and ability to concentrate become so impaired that he feels as though his mind is disorganized and that he is mentally paralyzed. His loss of interest in the world around him and his *withdrawal from all pleasurable activities* and former interests become so profound that even the most casual observer is aware that something is terribly wrong with the patient (Figure 63.7).

He no longer craves sympathy or support. He no longer wonders if he is worthy of love and affection. He knows that he is worthless. His

Figure 63.7. *Despair* (1892) by Edvard Munch. (By permission of the Theil Gallery, Stockholm, Sweden.)

suicidal ruminations become more intense and occupy most of his waking time. He can no longer work or function as he did in the earlier phase of the depression. He now *eats nothing*, and his *weight loss becomes noticeable.* He can hardly sleep. If he falls off to sleep, it is fitful and for only a few hours at a time. He *awakens very early in the morning*, and feels *most depressed* and fatigued at that time. Even the simplest activities seem to be too complicated and overwhelming. Everything seems to require too great an effort, and he has to summon all his reserve and will to accomplish the most minor task. He suffers vague feelings of fullness in the head and chest. His feet feel heavy and leaden, and nothing offers him solace or help. His sense of helplessness and hopelessness is difficult for anyone else to fathom. The patient's major depression has now progressed to *melancholia*.

The despair and hopelessness may progress even further. The patient may fall into a *depressive stupor*. He may remain seated for hours on end with fixed facies, eyes staring blankly downward, head bowed, mouth agape, and with his hands hanging limply between his knees. Or he may become agitated and pace back and forth,

wringing his hands in despair. He may sit and rock in a chair, moaning and whispering to himself. It is now obvious to any observer that the patient is in the midst of a *psychotic depression*.

He may begin to *hallucinate* and become totally absorbed in the voices that he hears. They are condemning voices that call him names and tell him that he is rotten and no good. They accuse him of wrongdoing and confirm for him the worst feelings he ever had about himself. They call him useless and stupid, and even though they are merely auditorizations of his own self-loathing thoughts, he experiences them as emanating from outside himself.

Most dramatic may be the development of a full-blown delusional system. Delusions, when they occur, tend to take one of three mood-congruent forms. First, there may be *delusions of worthlessness and sinfulness*. They are so striking to the observer because they are remarkable distortions, and the listener is immediately struck by the marked contradictions that these self-derogating ruminations convey. A man who has always been a fine and upstanding member of the community, a loving husband and father, a man who has always tried to earn an honest living, may state with complete conviction that he is a wretched criminal and that he is worth nothing, that he is debased and deserves nothing. He may state that he is the world's greatest failure, or that he is the most evil person ever to walk the face of the earth, and that all mankind would benefit by his death. The reader may note the striking grandiosity inherent in these self-depreciatory claims, and the extent to which the psychotic process has taken over.

Then there may be *delusions of nihilism*. The patient feels that all is hopeless and without meaning. He may become thoroughly convinced that he is nothing and that he has even ceased to exist, and he may also state despairingly that the world is useless and that it too has ceased to exist. All is emptiness and nothingness. In this delusional perception of the world, the patient conveys the psychotic extent to which he has regressed in his psychological functioning. He has completely lost touch with reality. He interprets the world and all that it contains in conformity with his own inner percepts and needs, and since he believes he no longer exists, neither does the world.

Finally, a system of delusions may develop

involving the patient's body—*somatic delusions*. Such beliefs may evolve from the somatic concerns which the patient developed in the earlier phase of the depression. Usually the patient's self-preoccupation is accompanied by an increase in bodily concerns, as the rest of the world is being excluded. In the earlier phase of the depression he may seek medical help because of these somatic symptoms. When he is psychotic he may become convinced, despite realistic evidence to the contrary, that his body is cancerous and rotting. He may believe that his intestines are plugged up and are being eroded by disease, or he may be convinced that he is suffering from a heart condition, or that his brain is on fire. Any bodily organ may become the focus of such a somatic delusion and, when present, such a belief may fully occupy every waking moment of the patient's day.

Our patient has progressed from a major depression, to melancholia (with a loss of pleasure in all activities and a lack of reactivity to usually pleasurable stimuli, along with a worsening of other depressive symptoms), and finally to a psychotic depression (with depressive stupor, hallucinations, delusions, and impaired reality testing). The patient's inner mood—his own psychic reality—has taken the place of the outer reality of the real world. His ability to determine what is real and what is not real has been totally compromised. The patient is psychotic because of the profound and global regression that his functioning has undergone. Like the infant, he cannot distinguish events occurring inside himself from those occurring outside, and this is the essence of psychosis. It is the profound disturbance of *mood* that distinguishes the *affective psychosis* just described from a *schizophrenic psychosis* where there is a more global fragmentation of all mental functions and where it is rare for depression to be the initial and major symptom before the onset of psychotic features. However, it may be more difficult to differentiate bipolar depression from unipolar depression, and therefore some of the distinguishing features between these two disorders are listed in Table 63.2

OTHER SPECIFIC AFFECTIVE DISORDERS

The essential features of these disorders are: 1) a chronic course of at least two years' duration, often beginning in early adult life without a clear onset; 2) a mood disturbance that is not of sufficient severity to meet the criteria for either a manic episode or a major depressive episode (full affective syndrome); and 3) absence of psychotic symptoms. In DSM-III there are two disorders in this category: *cyclothymic disorder* and *dysthymic disorder*.

Cyclothymic Disorder

In *cyclothymic disorder* there are numerous periods of depression and hypomania that may be separated by periods of normal mood, or may be intermixed, or may alternate. The depressive and hypomanic periods often involve *paired sets of symptoms*, as indicated in Table 63.3. Akiskal and his coworkers (1977) have presented a number of validating criteria for considering cyclothymic disorder to be a mild or attenuated form of bipolar disorder. These include: the similarity of symptoms in the two disorders; the increased frequency of affective disorders in the biological relatives of patients with cyclothymic disorder, and the increased frequency of cyclothymic disorder in the biological relatives of patients with bipolar disorder; the significant proportion of cyclothymic disorders that evolve into bipolar disorder; and the similar tendency of patients with cyclothymic disorder and bipolar disorder to respond favorably to lithium therapy and to develop hypomanic responses to tricyclic therapy. However, there are other patients with cyclothymic disorder who do not demonstrate this close affinity with bipolar disorder, and who might more accurately be considered to be suffering from a *cyclothymic personality disorder* rather than an affective disorder. Further research will be necessary to clarify this issue.

Dysthymic Disorder

A similar issue exists in regard to dysthymic disorder, where the depressive symptoms listed in Table 63.3 appear but are not of sufficient severity to meet the criteria for a major depressive episode. Akiskal (1983) has demonstrated that one group of dysthymic patients (whom he designates as "subaffective dysthymic disorders") has short REM latencies similar to patients with major depression and responds favorably to antidepressants. However, there is another group of chronically depressed patients (whom Akiskal calls "character-spectrum disorders") with normal REM latencies who are not responsive to antidepressants. Klerman

Table 63.2
*Differentiation of Bipolar Depression and Unipolar Depression**

	Bipolar Depression	Unipolar Depression
History of mania	Present	Absent
Prevalence	10% of affective disorders	90% of affective disorders
Sex ratio	Equal	Females:males 2:1
Premorbid personality	Often cyclothymic	May appear in a wide range of personality types—depressive, masochistic, obsessional, dependent, narcissistic, histrionic, borderline
Age of onset	Before 30 usually	After 30 usually
Type of onset	Often abrupt	Often gradual
Duration of episode	Usually shorter	Usually longer
End of episode	Often abrupt	Often gradual
Number of episodes	May be numerous	Usually fewer
Impairment	May be considerable with psychotic features	May be considerable with psychotic features
Complications	Substance abuse and consequences of impulsive actions	Suicide
Lithium	Usually effective	Usually ineffective
Antidepressants	May precipitate mania	Usually effective

* Modified from earlier table by Hagop Souren Akiskal (1981).

Table 63.3
*Paired Symptoms of Cyclothymic Disorder**

During **depressive** periods there is depressed mood or loss of interest or pleasure in all, or almost all, usual activities and pastimes, and at least three of the following:

1. Insomnia or hypersomnia
2. Low energy or chronic fatigue
3. Feelings of inadequacy
4. Decreased effectiveness or productivity at school, work, or home
5. Decreased attention, concentration, or ability to think clearly
6. Social withdrawal

7. Loss of interest in or enjoyment of sex

8. Restriction of involvement in pleasurable activities; guilt over past activities

9. Feeling slowed down
10. Less talkative than usual
11. Pessimistic attitude toward the future, or brooding about past events
12. Tearfulness or crying

During **hypomanic** periods there is an elevated, expansive, or irritable mood and at least three of the following:

1. Decreased need for sleep
2. More energy than usual
3. Inflated self-esteem
4. Increased productivity, often associated with unusual and self-imposed working hours
5. Sharpened and unusually creative thinking
6. Uninhibited people-seeking (extreme gregariousness)
7. Hypersexuality without recognition of possibility of painful consequences
8. Excessive involvement in pleasurable activities with lack of concern for the high potential for painful consequences, e.g., buying sprees, foolish business investments, reckless driving
9. Physical restlessness
10. More talkative than usual
11. Overoptimism or exaggeration of past achievements
12. Inappropriate laughing, joking, punning

* *Diagnostic and Statistical Manual of Mental Disorders*, ed 3 (DSM-III). American Psychiatric Association, Washington, DC, 1980, p 220.

(1983) has pointed out another subgroup of dysthymic patients with *masked depression* or *depressive equivalents*, especially patients suffering from hypochondriasis and chronic idiopathic pain, and in some instances conversion disorder. Thus dysthymic disorder appears to be a rather heterogeneous category that may consist of at least four subgroups: 1) patients with a *true affective disorder* in a mild or attenuated form; 2) patients with a *somatoform disorder* that is a depressive equivalent presenting with somatic symptoms rather than a mood disturbance; 3) patients with a *depressive personality disorder* or a *masochistic personality disorder* presenting with an impaired sense of self-esteem and various maladaptive personality traits rather than a mood disturbance; and 4) patients with an *adjustment disorder with depressed mood* where the psychosocial stressor may not be clearly identifiable or may not have been accurately diagnosed. We shall now look at three common examples of the latter.

ADJUSTMENT DISORDERS WITH DEPRESSED MOOD

Pathological Mourning

The signs and symptoms of *pathological mourning* (or complicated bereavement) have been described in Chapter 48 and listed in Table 48.1. Not uncommonly patients will present to physicians with various medical illnesses and conversion symptoms that are actually due to a pathological grief reaction, and yet they may be completely unaware of the relationship of their physical symptoms to a previous loss. In other instances patients will develop a clinical depression following a loss, and will also be unaware that their depression is a pathological grief reaction. *Physicians should routinely ask about recent losses in their work-ups of every patient.*

The Anniversary Reaction

Physicians should also routinely ask about *past losses* as well, since the *anniversary reaction*, often depressive in nature, is much more common than is generally recognized. There are many people who become depressed at a particular time every year. This may occur year after year on or about the same date. The date upon which the anniversary reaction occurs is associated with a meaningful loss from the past, and is often the birth date or date of death of a loved

one. The reaction need not be a depression. It can take the form of an anxiety attack or a conversion symptom or a psychophysiological disorder. But even if these are the presenting symptoms, they are further examples of the depressive equivalents just described. In other words, they are physical symptoms that serve to mask the underlying sadness and depression. The symptoms and their exact meanings vary from person to person, but they usually represent some conflict concerning the loss of a loved one in the past.

Dr. George Engel (1975) has documented his own anniversary reactions to the deaths of his father and his identical twin brother in a courageous and profoundly insightful paper, in which he reveals his ongoing self-analysis, and his unresolved grief and mourning over a 10 year period. This paper vividly demonstrates the power and the timelessness of unconscious conflicts, as well as the diversity of conversion, psychophysiological, and depressive symptoms that may occur in relation to the anniversaries of the loss of loved ones. This intensely human document should be read by anyone who wishes to appreciate more deeply the meaning and the power of the past, and particularly the way in which grief and mourning may be expressed in anniversary reactions.

Paradoxical Depression

Paradoxical depression, also known as the "promotion depression" or the "success neurosis," is illustrated by the case of the politician who, after winning an election, falls into a state of deep depression, or the business executive who, after being promoted, similarly becomes depressed. The "paradox," of course, is that these people, after achieving a long-sought goal that is viewed by others as a crowning success and would seem to be a cause for happiness or even elation, experience instead a depression. They are truly people who are "wrecked by success." How can we make sense out of this? We have talked about loss, diminished self-esteem, and guilt, and these factors are not immediately apparent in this situation.

However, when we get to know these people in depth and learn about their past histories and family backgrounds, some important connections emerge. For them, the idea of success is associated with an aggressive, possibly even a murderous, triumph over some important person from their past, usually a parent or a sibling.

Hence, success for these people is a tragedy. It is not success in the usual terms, but rather it is a sin, one for which the person must atone. It is a Pyrrhic victory. There is also a loss involved in any success or promotion—a loss of the security of the less responsible position. For some people, the added responsibility of the new position may be experienced as a burden and a threat, and lead to depression instead of pleasure and happiness.

A CASE HISTORY

We used a prototype of a patient to illustrate the continuum between major depression, melancholia, and psychotic depression. Let us now look at an actual case history which illustrates many of the concepts we have just discussed.

Mr. L, a 75 year old man, was hospitalized for a medical evaluation of his persistent vomiting. He had suffered from this symptom for one month, and had lost about 12 pounds as a result. All diagnostic tests were normal. Mr. L had experienced his first bout of nausea and vomiting the day after the unveiling of the tombstone at his wife's grave. The day of the unveiling was two days prior to the first anniversary of his wife's death and only one day before what would have been the couple's fifty-third wedding anniversary. Mr. L's wife had died after a prolonged and debilitating course of cancer of the gastrointestinal tract. During the last four months of her life Mr. L had nursed her at home rather than send her to a hospital. She spent the last few days of her life at the hospital where Mr. L was now a patient.

A conversation with his daughters revealed that he had told them just before his wife died that he thought his wife would be better off dead. "It was terrible for her to have to suffer any longer." She had been in a great deal of pain and had been *unable to eat* toward the end of her life. At her funeral, both daughters noticed that Mr. L did not cry and seemed to react to the events in a somewhat indifferent fashion. One daughter mentioned that he had always been an "unemotional man"—rarely showing his feelings. The family had jokingly nicknamed him, "Mr. Indifferent," because of his ability to remain calm and unruffled in the face of any crisis. Indeed, he had always prided himself on being a strong man and had always taken care of things himself. While in the hospital he sud-

denly remembered that his wife, prior to her death, had been vomiting and had lost a great deal of weight. He then had the thought that perhaps he too had developed cancer. It was at that point that Mr. L felt suicidal. He did not want to suffer as his wife had. He felt that he had been in pain long enough.

The reader may have noted some striking aspects about the case of Mr. L. He became transiently suicidal when it suddenly dawned upon him that he might have cancer of the gastrointestinal tract, the very disease from which his wife had died one year earlier. His symptoms of nausea and vomiting began immediately after a ceremony commemorating his wife's death. The ceremony took place on the anniversary of her death but also on the anniversary of their marriage 53 years earlier. Mr. L had nursed his wife during the last months of her life. He had watched her suffer, and he had wished for an end to his wife's torments. When she did finally die, Mr. L did not mourn as most people would. Instead, as had always been his tendency, he isolated his feelings and kept them in check. He did not go through the various phases of normal mourning. He had not worked out the guilt that we all feel when a loved one dies, especially if for whatever reason we may have wished that person dead.

A year later, on a double anniversary, he developed the same symptoms that his wife had prior to her death. He did not think of this consciously. Rather he developed persistent vomiting and sought medical treatment. This was an anniversary reaction that took the form of a conversion disorder. In this anniversary reaction, he identified with his wife and became as she had been. He developed the same symptoms. He even hospitalized himself in the same hospital in which she had died, and developed the idea that he had precisely the same disease that she had had. He then became suicidal. His suicidal thoughts represented both a wish to be reunited with his wife in death and also an attempt to expiate the guilt he felt for having wished her dead. Mr. L developed many of the symptoms of unresolved grief and pathological mourning described in Chapter 48.

Many depressed patients will first present themselves for treatment as Mr L did, namely with somatic symptoms, and his case illustrates the complexities of dealing with a depressed patient. Many internists and family physicians have estimated that a very large percentage of their practices is comprised of depressed patients who first present with physical symptoms, in other words depressive equivalents that mask the mood disturbance. An exhaustive diagnostic search by the physician for an organic explanation of the symptoms, combined with a failure to explore the patient's emotional state and current life situation, may actually lead to a worsening of the depression and increase the risk of suicide.

ETIOLOGY

As with schizophrenia, one of the most challenging and important areas of inquiry for clinicians and researchers in the years to come will be the further elucidation of the multiple etiologies of the depressive disorders, and the identification of various subgroups within the depressive disorders on the basis of specific etiological factors. It is beyond the scope of this chapter to review in detail all of the various biological, psychological, and sociocultural theories regarding the etiology of depression. The

most prominent and widely accepted theories are listed in Table 63.4 according to the model, the proposed mechanism, and the major proponents of the theory. For any single patient with depression, it is probable that several of these etiological factors may be interacting with each other, and certainly a combination of these factors in any given individual may sharply increase the risk of developing a depressive disorder.

TREATMENT

Antidepressant Drugs

As Dr. Freedman indicated in Chapter 52B, the use of the tricyclic antidepressant drugs has brought about significant improvement in the treatment of the depressive disorders. Approximately 70% of patients with a major depression will respond to one of the tricyclic antidepressants. Their effectiveness is reduced sharply, however, in those depressions that are psychotic in nature. Such patients usually require the addition of an antipsychotic medication (e.g., phe-

Table 63.4
*The Multiple Etiologies of Depression**

Model	Mechanism	Reference
1. Psychological		
a. Psychoanalytic	Aggression turned inward	Freud, Abraham
	Object loss and separation	Spitz, Bowlby
	Loss of self-esteem	Bibring
	Predisposing personality traits	Chodoff
b. Cognitive	Negative cognitive view of the self, of one's experiences, and of the future	Beck
c. Behavioral	Learned helplessness	Seligman
	Loss of positive reinforcements	Lewinsohn
d. Existential	Loss of meaning of existence	Becker
2. Sociocultural	Loss of social or cultural role status	Bart, Weissman & Klerman
3. Biological		
a. Genetic	Genetic transmission through several possible mechanisms	Kallman, Gershon, Winokur
b. Neurochemical	Impaired norepinephrine and serotonin neurotransmission	Schildkraut
c. Neuroendocrine	Impaired hypothalamic-pituitary-adrenal secretion	Carroll, Loosen & Prange
d. Neurophysiological	Impaired limbic-diencephalic function leading to disturbances in the normal neurophysiology of sleep, sensory evoked potentials, and biological rhythms	Kupfer, Buchsbaum, Wehr
e. Neuroanatomical	Impaired neuroanatomical structures	Andreasen

* Modified from earlier table by Akiskal and McKinney (1975).

nothiazines) to the antidepressant. Recently new classes of antidepressants have emerged, including benzodiazepine derivatives. This new generation of antidepressants with a lower toxic to therapeutic ratio may result in fewer side effects and risk, especially when taken in large doses, since intentional overdose is always a danger with depressed patients who are suicidal. As also noted by Dr. Freedman, the monoamine oxidase inhibitors are generally used in cases of atypical depression in which anxiety, phobic, and hypochondriacal symptoms are mixed with the depressive symptoms, and the usual somatic or vegetative signs of depression (psychomotor retardation, anorexia, weight loss, early morning awakening, fatigue) are absent. Here again the physician needs to be alert to possible side effects, especially hypertensive crises following the ingestion of foods with a high tyramine content (cheddar cheeses, beer, red wines, herring, yogurt; liver). Excessive amounts of caffeine and chocolate can also cause hypertensive crises with these drugs.

When clinicians try to decide whether to use antidepressants, they look for any factors which are associated with a good response, such as a good previous response in either the patient or a biologically related member of the patient's family who was depressed. The presence of any of the somatic or vegetative symptoms just described have also been associated with a good response to antidepressants, especially the tricyclics. A higher socioeconomic status and the presence of compulsive personality traits may also improve the chances of a good response. Negative predictors of response include multiple previous episodes of depression, psychosis, and the presence of a severe personality disorder.

Lithium

As described in the previous section on mania, lithium has been used primarily in patients who have bipolar disorder. It is effective with 70% of these patients in reducing symptoms acutely, and in reducing the severity and frequency of recurrence. Lithium may also be useful for patients who have recurrent unipolar depressions, although these studies are less convincing. Recent work also suggests that lithium may be a useful adjunct to tricyclic antidepressants with certain treatment-resistant depressions.

Other Drugs

Antipsychotic drugs such as the phenothiazines, as described earlier, are sometimes helpful in the treatment of patients with psychotic depression. They almost always must be combined with an antidepressant medication in order to be effective. The use of stimulants, such as amphetamines, has limited usefulness in the treatment of depression, and only in rare cases are they justified. For example, the depressed elderly patient who cannot tolerate the anticholinergic, sedative, and cardiovascular side effects of the tricyclics may benefit from low doses of amphetamine.

Electroconvulsive Therapy (ECT)

Few procedures in psychiatry have caused more social controversy than the use of ECT. This in large part stems from its excessive use for a wide variety of mental disorders when first discovered and to serious side effects due to poor anesthesia technique. Currently, however, ECT is used primarily for severe depressions, especially if the patient is unresponsive to antidepressant medications and psychotherapy. Only rarely is it now used for acute schizophrenia or severe mania. ECT is effective to some degree in 85–95% of depressed patients, especially the more severely depressed, and it will significantly benefit approximately half of those people who have shown no response to various combinations of antidepressant medications, yet are suffering from a major depression. The procedure has been described by Dr. Freedman in Chapter 52B. ECT is usually performed three times a week for three to four weeks and results in a dramatic and sharp reduction of the depressed symptoms, often as early as the third treatment. This is in contrast to the use of tricyclic antidepressants which usually require ten days to three weeks before the gradual onset of improvement. Side effects with ECT are transient, with most of the patients experiencing some difficulty with short-term memory. Chronic memory problems are now exceedingly rare, as are any serious complications to the brief general anesthesia.

Psychotherapy

The use of psychotherapy in the treatment of depression is currently receiving considerable research attention. Recent data suggest that psychotherapy is approximately equal in effectiveness to antidepressant medications, and that either medication or psychotherapy alone is inferior to the two combined. The type of psychotherapy indicated depends in large part on the interest of the patient and the particular theoretical perspective of the clinician. Given the right patient, insight-oriented therapy, supportive therapy, cognitive therapy, and behavior therapy all may be helpful. It would appear, in fact, that for many patients, combining techniques from all of these therapeutic approaches may lead to the greatest success.

Hospitalization

Depression does not lead to hospitalization as frequently as does mania or schizophrenia. It is estimated that hospitalization is required for only 6% of depressed females and 3% of depressed males. Those patients who do require hospitalization usually suffer from marked suicidal preoccupations and suicidal behavior, or a severe reduction in the ability to manage life outside of a highly structured environment. Hospitalization is best kept relatively short-term with the goal of reintegrating the patient as soon as possible into his or her usual environment once safety and everyday functioning permit.

PROGNOSIS

The usual course of depressed patients who do not receive psychotherapy or medication is six to nine months between the onset of the illness and return to usual functioning. With medications and/or psychotherapy, the patient's return to normal is significantly shorter (weeks to a few months). Despite treatment, however, 10% to 15% of all depressed patients suffer from a chronic form of the illness with considerable residual social and occupational impairment. This is more likely when there are frequent recurrent episodes. Indeed recurrence rates for unipolar depression are as high as 50%, and these individuals with recurrent major depressions are also at greater risk for developing a bipolar disorder than are those individuals with only a single episode of major depression. Furthermore, the overall suicide rate among patients who have been hospitalized for depression is around 15%. Thus the clinician must be alert

to any patient who gives a history of depression, whether as a symptom of a situational reaction or as part of the full clinical syndrome of an affective disorder. Furthermore, the clinician must always remember that a depressive disorder may present in a masked form with somatic symptoms as the only presenting complaint.

Suggested Readings

Akiskal HS: A biobehavioral approach to depression. In Depue R (ed): *The Psychobiology of the Depressive Disorders.* New York, Academic Press, 1979, p 409.

Andreasen NC: The diagnosis and classification of affective disorders. In Davis JM, Maas JW (eds): *The Affective Disorders.* Washington, DC, American Psychiatric Press, 1983, p 135.

Andreasen NC: *The Broken Brain. The Biological Revolution in Psychiatry.* New York, Harper & Row, 1984.

Anthony EJ, Benedek T (eds): *Depression and Human Existence.* Boston, Little, Brown, and Co, 1975.

Davis JM, Maas JW (eds): *The Affective Disorders.* Washington, DC, American Psychiatric Press, 1983.

Engel GL: The death of a twin: mourning and anniversary reactions. Fragments of 10 years of self-analysis. *Int J Psychoanal.* 56:23, 1975.

Klerman GL (Preceptor): Depressive Disorders. In Grinspoon L (ed): *Psychiatry Update,* Vol 2. Washington, DC, American Psychiatric Press, 1983, pp 351–548.

Klerman GL: The nosology and diagnosis of depressive disorders. In Grinspoon L (ed): *Psychiatry Update,* Vol 2. Washington, DC, American Psychiatric Press, 1983, p 356.

Paykel ES (ed): *Handbook of Affective Disorders.* New York, Guilford Press, 1982.

References

Akiskal HS, McKinney WT: Overview of recent research in depression: integration of ten conceptual models into a comprehensive clinical frame. *Arch Gen Psychiatry* 32:285, 1975.

Akiskal HS, et al: Cyclothymic disorder: validating criteria for inclusion in the bipolar affective group. *Am J Psychiatry* 134:1227, 1977.

Akiskal HS: Clinical overview of depressive disorders and their pharmacological management. In Palmer G (ed): *Neuropharmacology of Central Nervous System and Behavioral Disorders.* New York, Academic Press, 1981, p 38.

Akiskal HS: Dysthymic disorder: psychopathology of proposed chronic depressive subtypes. *Am J Psychiatry* 140:11, 1983.

Andreasen NC, Winokur G: Secondary depression: familial, clinical, and research perspectives. *Am J Psychiatry* 136:62, 1979.

Freud S (1916): Some character types met with in psychoanalytic work: those wrecked by success. In *The Standard Edition of the Complete Psychological Works of Sigmund Freud,* vol 14. London, Hogarth Press, 1957, p 316.

Hirschfeld RMA, Klerman GL: Personality attributes and affective disorders. *Am J Psychiatry* 136:67, 1979.

Klerman GL, Barrett J: Clinical and epidemiologic aspects of affective disorders. In Gershon ES, Shopsin B (eds): *Lithium: Its Role in Psychiatric Research and Treatment.* New York, Plenum Press, 1973.

Krauthammer C, Klerman GL: Secondary mania. *Arch Gen Psychiatry* 35:1333, 1978.

Leonhard K: *Aufteilung der Endogenen Psychosen.* Berlin, Akademie Verlag, 1957.

Pollock GH: Anniversary reactions, trauma and mourning. *Psychoanal Q* 39:347, 1970.

Robins E, Guze SB: Classification of affective disorders. In Williams TA, Katz MM, Shield JA (eds): *Recent Advances in the Psychobiology of the Depressive Illnesses.* Washington, DC, U S Govt Printing Office, 1972, p 283.

Woodruff RA, Murphy GE, Herjanic M: The natural history of affective disorders. *J Psychiatry Res* 5:255, 1967

References for Table 63.4

Abraham K (1911): Notes on the psychoanalytic investigation and treatment of manic-depressive insanity and allied conditions. In *Selected Papers on Psychoanalysis.* London, Hogarth Press, 1927, p 137.

Andreasen NC: The diagnosis and classification of affective disorders. In Davis JM, Maas JW (eds): *The Affective Disorders.* Washington, DC, American Psychiatric Press, 1983, p 135.

Bart P: The sociology of depression. In Roman P, Trice H (eds): *Explorations in Psychiatric Sociology.* Philadelphia, F.A. Davis Co, 1974, p 139.

Beck AT: The development of depression: a cognitive model. In Friedman RJ, Katz MM (eds): *The Psychology of Depression: Contemporary Theory and Research.* New York, John Wiley & Sons, 1974, p 3.

Becker E: *The Revolution in Psychiatry.* Glencoe NY, Free Press of Glencoe, London, Collier-Macmillan Ltd, 1964, p 108.

Bibring E: The mechanism of depression. In Greenacre P (ed): *Affective Disorders.* New York, International Universities Press, 1953, p 13.

Bowlby J: Grief and mourning in infancy and early childhood. *Psychoanal Study Child* 15:9, 1960.

Buchsbaum MS: The average evoked response technique in the differentiation of bipolar, unipolar and schizophrenic disorders. In Akiskal HS, Webb WL (eds): *Psychiatric Diagnosis: Exploration of Biological Predictors.* New York, Spectrum, 1978, p 411.

Carroll BJ: Clinical applications of the dexamethasone suppression test for endogenous depression. *Pharmacopsychiatry* 15:19, 1982.

Chodoff P: The depressive personality. *Arch Gen Psychiatry* 27:666, 1972.

Freud S (1917): Mourning and melancholia. In *The Standard Edition of the Complete Psychological Works of Sigmund Freud,* vol 14. London, Hogarth Press, 1957, p 243.

Gershon ES: The genetics of affective disorders. In Grinspoon L (ed): *Psychiatry Update,* Vol 2. Washington, DC, American Psychiatric Press, 1983, p 434.

Kallmann FJ: Genetic principles in manic-depressive psychosis. In Hoch PH, Zubin J (eds): *Depression.* New York, Grune & Stratton, 1954, p 1.

Kupfer DJ: Application of the sleep EEG in affective disorders. In Davis JM, Maas JW (eds): *The Affective Disorders.* Washington, DC, American Psychiatric Press, 1983, p 107.

Lewinsohn P: A behavioral approach to depression. In Friedman RJ, Katz MM (eds): *The Psychology of Depression: Contemporary Theory and Research.* New York, John Wiley & Sons, 1974, p 157.

Loosen PT, Prange AJ: Serum thyrotropin response to thyrotropin-releasing hormone in psychiatric patients: a review *Am J Psychiatry* 139:405, 1982.

Schildkraut JJ: The catecholamine hypothesis of affective disorders. *Am J Psychiatry* 122:509, 1965.

Schildkraut JJ, et al: Biological discrimination of subtypes of depressions. In Davis JM, Maas JW (eds): *The Affective Disorders.* Washington, DC, American Psychiatric Press, 1983, p 31.

Seligman M: Depression and learned helplessness. In Friedman RJ, Katz MM (eds): *The Psychology of Depression: Contemporary Theory and Research.* New York, John Wiley & Sons, 1974, p 88.

Spitz RA, Wolf KM: Anaclitic depression: an inquiry into the genesis of psychiatric conditions in early childhood. *Psychoanal Study Child* 2:213, 1946.

Wehr TA, Wirz-Justice A, Goodwin FK: Circadian rhythm disturbances in affective illness and their modification by antidepressant drugs. In Davis JM, Maas JW (eds): *The Affective Disorders.* Washington, DC, American Psychiatric Press, 1983, p 333.

Weissman MM, Klerman GL: Depression in women: epidemiology, explanations, and impact on the family. In Notman MT, Nadelson CC (eds): *The Woman Patient,* Vol 3. New York, Plenum Press, 1982, p 189.

Winokur G, et al: Is a familial definition of depression both feasible and valid? *J Nerv Mental Dis* 166:764, 1978.

Lewis Glickman, M.D.

THE LOGIC OF SUICIDE

Suicide is a Latin translation of the English word "self-killer." Latin translations of English words describing sexual and excretory functions and death were introduced about 200 years ago when English words began to be considered too blunt and too upsetting. Graveyards became cemeteries, undertakers became morticians, and self-killers became suicides. Suicide is upsetting because it raises perplexing and frightening questions about human nature and hence about ourselves. Actions speak louder than words, and the suicide's action tells in the strongest possible terms that he does not accept those beliefs about life that seem so self-evident to the rest of us. Self-preservation may be Nature's first law, but it is not his. He believes, "Where there's death, there's hope." He cares as little for his inalienable right to life as he does for the liberty or the pursuit of happiness endowed to him by his Creator and promulgated in the Declaration of Independence.

While the suicide has reasons for what he does, the logic he is obeying is not that of common sense and everyday reality. Except in relatively uncommon situations in which his motive is to escape the pain of an incurable illness or death by torture, the suicide marches to a different drummer, and we cannot understand his reasons by using our common sense. Our common sense reaction to the person who kills himself is like that of Omar Khayyam to the wine merchant. He wondered what the vintner bought that was worth half as much as what he sold. We wonder what the suicide gains that is worth half as much as what he has lost. I believe we must make the assumption that the suicide believes he is gaining something more precious than what he is losing. We should therefore expect that the logic of suicide will seem fantastic, even bizarre. To understand him, to follow the course of his reasoning and bring to light his motivations, we must follow the trail marked out for us by those who have suicided, by those who knew them, and by storytellers—poets, novelists, dramatists—who have been able to translate their own suicidal inclinations into poems and stories. But even here, their motives may be hidden from themselves, concealed in their own unconscious. As Anne Sexton, a distinguished poet who died a suicide, wrote:

> But suicides have a special language.
> Like carpenters they want to know *which tools.*
> They never ask *why build.**

Sylvia Plath, another great poet who committed suicide, wrote:

> Dying
> Is an art, like everything else.
> I do it exceptionally well.
> I do it so it feels like hell.
> I do it so it feels real.
> I guess you could say I've a call.†

THE INCIDENCE OF SUICIDE

Understanding the suicide's motives is no mere academic exercise. It has a practical value, as it is likely to put us in a better position to prevent this tragedy in the patients we see. Suicide is the 10th most frequent cause of death in this country, the second most common cause of death on the college campuses, the leading cause of death among medical students, and the third leading cause of death in the 15 to 19 age group. There are over 25,000 suicides in the

---

* From the poem *Wanting to Die* from the book *Live or Die* by Anne Sexton. (Reprinted by permission of Houghton Mifflin Co, Boston.)

† From the poem *Lady Lazarus* from the book *Ariel* by Sylvia Plath. (Reprinted by permission of Harper & Row, New York.)

United States each year, and approximately 10 times that many unsuccessful attempts. The true incidence of suicide is likely to be much higher than the reported statistics, probably over 50,000 or more each year. There are realistic reasons why the suicide or his family might wish to conceal the fact that suicide was the cause of death. Most life insurance policies carry a clause limiting liability if suicide occurs within two years of the purchase of the policy. Relatives may also be concerned with the reputation of the family and the effect on the children, since suicide carries a social stigma and evokes guilt in the survivors. These factors certainly influence the decisions and certifications of coroners, medical examiners, and judges.

Suicide may also be underreported because of our inability to be certain in many cases whether death is due to suicide or an accident. For example, we usually cannot be reasonably certain whether fatal single car collisions are suicides or accidents unless a so-called psychological autopsy is performed. In the psychological autopsy, the associates and relatives of the deceased are interviewed as to his behavior and statements in the days prior to his death. Few medical examiner's offices conduct such investigations. Fatal single car collisions which cannot be proven to be suicides are therefore reported as accidents. Instances in which there may not have been a conscious intent, but in which the individual acted in such a way as to bring about his death, for example driving while drunk, are also reported as accidents rather than suicides. Another possible reason for the underreporting may have to do with the guilt of the attending physician, since suicide is likely to occur relatively soon after contact with a physician. In one study of 60 suicides, over 80% had seen a physician within the preceding six months, and over 50% within the preceding month or less of the suicide. Unfortunately, the physician, rather than preventing the suicide, sometimes helps the potential suicide achieve his goal. Twenty percent of suicides die by ingesting the very sedatives prescribed by a physician, and in one study over 50% had obtained the means to kill themselves in a *single* prescription from their doctors. Thus, the physician often "puts the gun" in the patient's hands in spite of the fact that he is aware that the patient is depressed. I will discuss a possible cause for this phenomenon later in the chapter.

THE EPIDEMIOLOGY OF SUICIDE

Before we study the lives and thoughts of some individuals who have suicided, we might attempt an overview of the types of people who kill themsleves. What kind of a person is most likely to do this? Suicide appears to be associated with maleness, aging, loneliness (the unmarried, divorced, or separated), isolated living arrangements, unemployment, overt physical and emotional illness, loss of a parent before the age of 15 by death, divorce, or separation (twice the expected rate), previous psychiatric hospitalization (12 times the expected rate), and a previous suicide attempt (20 times the expected rate). It is also associated with being a male physician (15% higher than the expected rate), being a female physician (three to four times the expected rate), residence in Nevada (two times the expected rate paralleling the high divorce rate in Nevada), economic depression (the rate in 1932 was the highest ever reported in the United States, 17.5/100,000), Christmas holidays (5% to 10% increase), being an American Indian (twice the expected rate), and being a male veteran with a history of both psychiatric hospitalization and a previous suicide attempt (90 times the expected rate). However, suicide rates fall sharply during wars, mass strikes, and popular uprisings.

Seventy percent of suicides are men. Three-quarters of all suicides occur after age 40. Suicide is much more common among whites than blacks. However, the rates among adolescents, women, and blacks are increasing rapidly. Women attempt suicide more often than men, but men are more often successful. Men are the victims of three out of four successful suicides. Why do men often succeed, while women do not? It is probably because men tend to keep their problems to themselves without seeking help, and then choose more violent and aggressive and hence more certain methods, such as jumping, shooting, and stabbing (Figure 64.1), whereas women are more likely to choose the less certain method of sedative overdose. The incidence in men reaches a peak between ages 20 to 30, falls back somewhat until age 60, then surpasses the earlier peak, reaching a maximum at ages 75 to 79 when the rate is nearly 50/100,000 per year. The incidence in American Indians and black males reaches its peak between the ages of 25 and 35 and then declines.

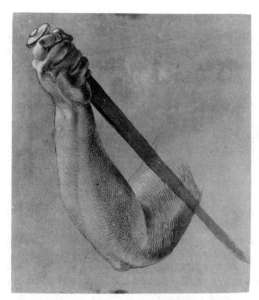

Figure 64.1. *Arm with Dagger* by Albrecht Dürer. (By permission of Albertina Museum, Vienna, Austria.)

In women the incidence rises until age 55 and then declines. Unmarried, single, or divorced men have twice the rate of married men. And, almost all suicides are emotionally ill. Most suicides are either depressed, or else are suffering from alcoholism, drug addiction, or a schizophrenic psychosis.

Patterson and colleagues have suggested an acronym of SAD PERSONS that summarizes 10 major risk factors for suicide. The letters in the acronym stand for: sex (male), age (over 40), depression, previous attempt, ethanol abuse, rational thinking loss, social supports lacking, organized plan, no spouse, and sickness (physical illness). I believe the acronym helpful, except that I would substitute recent loss of object relationships and of self-esteem, since I consider that to be a far greater risk factor than rational thinking loss.

Suicide statistics from other countries are difficult to interpret or compare with our own. Hungary, Sweden, Austria, and Denmark have the highest reported rates. What does this mean? It may simply mean that these countries keep better statistics and/or that their citizens are more frank. Catholic countries such as Spain and Ireland tend to report low rates. Does this mean that the greater social and religious stigma leads to a lower rate or to greater con-

cealment? Norway has a much lower rate than Sweden. Does this relate to child rearing practices? Or do Norwegians habitually report drownings as accidents rather than suicide, and is drowning the suicide method preferred by Norwegians?

THE DYNAMICS OF SUICIDE

The risk factors in suicide strongly suggest that suicide is statistically associated with the triad described by Karl Menninger (Figure 64.2) many years ago—*the wish to kill, the wish to be killed,* and *the wish to die.* The last is often the result of a wish for reunion with a lost parent.

The greater incidence of suicide in men than in women suggests that the greater aggressivity in the male which causes men to commit 85% of all murders may also lead more men to commit suicide as well. Changes in cultural expectations for female behavior may also be contrib-

Figure 64.2. Karl A. Menninger.

uting to the increasing incidence of both murder and suicide among women in recent years.

The increasing incidence of suicide with age strongly suggests that object loss and loss of self-esteem are important predisposing or precipitating factors. Growing old in our culture is likely to involve a series of object losses and of blows to self-esteem, the first by deaths and separations, the second by loss of work and physical attractiveness (Figure 64.3). The peak incidence of suicide in women at age 55 may be

Figure 64.3. *Old Man with a Rope* (1925) by Käthe Kollwitz. (By permission of National Gallery of Art. Washington, DC, Rosenwald Collection.)

correlated with the cessation of menses and their consequent self-perception as no longer sexually desirable or fertile. The increasing incidence with age in men, especially in times of economic depression, may reflect the diminished desirability of the older man in the work market and hence a self-perception as worthless and unmanly. The higher rates in young black males and American Indians may be related to a self-perception as being worthless and unmanly in a culture which does not value their contributions, and to alienation from a culture whose goals and beliefs they may not share. The object loss may not be a person but rather a deeply valued goal or purpose in life. Loss can occur because of an inability to find purpose and values, or because of an inability to live up to the ideals one has. Aggression may be turned against the self when the individual does not attain the standards he has set for himself. In addition, social and geographic mobility is often achieved at a cost of isolation from extended family and close friends. Adoption of new value systems is often achieved at the cost of conflict with the older values with which one has been raised, and the choice of many different value systems in an open society can lead to confusion and depression. These factors may well be responsible for the increasing suicide rate among 10 to 24 year olds. Suicide, while far away from the home and family and values, was described in Rudyard Kipling's short story *Thrown Away*. *Thrown Away* is the story of a young man's suicide because of his inability to adjust to his sudden freedom in India after being brought up in England by overprotective parents.

A CASE HISTORY

Let us now look at some of these dynamics at work in an actual patient. The patient I will discuss was someone I never met. I heard about her from her coworkers after she had killed herself, and I had the opportunity to observe the effect of her suicide on her associates. The woman who killed herself was a professional in her early sixties. She had six of William Shakespeare's seven motives for suicide. She felt she bore "the whips and scorns of time, the oppressor's wrong, the proud man's contumely, the pangs of dispriz'd love, ..., the insolence of office, and the spurns that patient merit of the unworthy takes." She lacked only "the law's delay." The one thing that seems to have changed since Shakespeare's time is the method. Medical science now allows us to make our "quietus" not with a "bare bodkin" but with sleeping pills prescribed by a physician.

The facts which led up to the suicide as known to her coworkers were as follows: She worked in a fairly large office for many years, but had only one friend at work, her secretary. The woman in question was extremely conscientious and hardworking but so aggressive and domineering that she managed to antagonize nearly everyone who worked with her. For example, she would frequently need her colleagues' immediate help when she knew they were at lunch. She never married, but lived with her father until he died six months before her suicide. She seems to have functioned well at her work, if not in her relationships with her colleagues, until additional personnel were added to her organization, and these people had to be accommodated in the same quantity of office space. A space committee consisting of the senior staff was appointed to allocate offices, and this woman, by virtue of her seniority and status, was appointed to the committee.

She then did a curious thing. Instead of taking the position offered to her and attending the meetings, she sent her one friend, her secretary, as her proxy. The committee met, and the senior staff who were members all arranged for private offices for themselves on the prestigious ground floor. The secretary, however, was not able to obtain this for her friend, who was shunted to an upper floor with the more junior staff and given a segment of a large room in which she was separated by a divider from her coworkers. She bitterly complained to the director of the organization, and asked that he ignore the recommendations of the space committee and obtain a larger office for her. He pointed out that many others were also unhappy with their new, smaller offices, and that if he did as she requested others would also ask to be changed. He could not accede to her request without acceding to theirs as well. She became very angry and handed in her resignation. The director, recognizing that she was emotionally distraught, refused to accept it and told her to think about it for a while. She did so for two weeks, but then resubmitted her resignation. At this point the director accepted it and set about to hire a successor.

She had a comfortable pension and would be well provided for. A few weeks later a successor was hired. Soon thereafter the woman asked for her job back. The director felt that he could not now fire the person who had taken her place and explained he could not rehire her. She returned home and was found dead of an overdose a week later. When her coworkers heard of her suicide there was a great deal of guilt and recrimination. Those who were not on the space committee felt the committee members were responsible. Those on the committee felt the director was responsible. The secretary felt she was responsible. I do not know what the director felt.

Based on these events what can we say about this woman's motivations? She seemed to have suffered an overwhelming loss to her self-esteem. Perhaps the death of her father, for whom she had cared all her adult life and for whom she had given up marriage and children, had contributed to her depression. Perhaps she had distributed her investments of love into too few baskets—her father, her secretary, the director, her office, and her job. When she lost all of these in such a short period of time, she lost everything in life that was important to her. We can speculate that these losses caused her to feel angry, but her conscience would not allow her wish for revenge direct expression against those whom she perceived as the authors of her plight. She then turned her wish to kill against herself and achieved her revenge indirectly. She punished her enemies by causing them to feel guilty, and at the same time she punished herself for her hatred.

The suicide punishes those he holds responsible for his plight. This is clearly seen in Kipling's story, *Thrown Away*. The author-narrator holds the parents responsible for the young man's suicide because of their overprotection of him. The author points out that their son's suicide note would have destroyed the parents if delivered to them. They would blame themselves for his suicide, feeling they had failed as parents in not preparing him for the stresses he would find in India. The story details the successful attempt of the narrator and another man to conceal the fact that the son killed himself, so as to protect the parents from their son's unconscious wish for revenge.

THE WISH TO KILL

That the suicide aims at the destruction of others as well as himself is recognized in many primitive tribes, where suicide is a socially approved method of obtaining revenge by the weaker person who feels himself injured by someone stronger. If a man has an enemy he wishes to kill but is too weak to do so, he can kill himself after accusing his enemy of being responsible. His relatives are then obliged to kill the enemy. In Western Europe the awareness that suicides wanted revenge led to the custom in earlier centuries of burying them at a cross roads with a stake through their hearts. The theory was that unless these precautions were taken, the suicide would return as a vampire who would suck the blood from the living. If the stake through the heart did not kill the vampire, the pressure of continued walking over the grave would keep him confined. These precautions were based on psychological reality. The suicide does want revenge.

In his book on suicide, *The Savage God*, A. Alvarez wrote that every suicide is fundamentally an attempt at exorcism. By that he meant that the suicide not only wishes to kill those closest to him, he also wants to kill someone he has made part of himself. Unlike Dr. Frankenstein, who created a monster outside of himself who kills others, the suicide has created a monster within himself whom he kills. Often this "monster" is the parent who has died or who left the child, and to whom the child has attributed his own angry feelings. Wishes to kill exist in all of us and can be readily activated by any frustration of our wishes. Freud pointed out that this truth is more acceptable from poets than from scientists. He quoted Heinrich Heine, who said that all he wanted out of life was a small cottage in the country. There would be flowers before his window, fresh milk and butter, and a few fine trees. And for his happiness to be complete, he would like to see six or seven of his enemies hanging from those trees. He would forgive them, of course—after they were dead! This is funny because it is so true for all of us. But we do not like to admit it. It is far more comfortable to attribute such wishes to others. Few of us have Pogo's insight when he says: "We have met the enemy and he is us!"

THE WISH TO BE KILLED

Both the child and the adult want to attribute their own unacceptable wishes to others. However, as adults we generally have learned the difference between thoughts and actions, and we know that thoughts by themselves do not harm. The child has difficulty making this distinction

and tends to feel as guilty for his thoughts as for his actions. He is likely to feel so guilty for his wishes to harm his parents, that he attributes his own anger to them. "I don't hate you. You hate me. I don't want to kill you. You want to kill me." Now if the child experiences rejection and abandonment by the parents in reality, then he will feel even more rage. However, his rage causes him great anxiety and guilt, because he also needs his parents to survive. In a complicated process that we cannot describe in detail here, the child identifies with the parents (*identification with the aggressor*), and then turns his rage against the parent or parents *whom he has made a hidden part of himself.* Thus, in suicide, the patient destroys the parent who has become part of himself, and at the same time punishes himself for his murderous rage—the wish to kill and the wish to be killed.

In all suicides, the parent is viewed unconsciously to a greater or lesser degree as more murderous than he or she actually is. The parent who really wishes to kill the child does so by assault or neglect, and the child will not survive to suicide. If the child, who has internalized a loved and hated parent, then grows up and loses someone whom he has put in place of the parent—a spouse, lover, employer—the same process is now reactivated. "I don't want to kill you—You want to kill me," and then another step: "You're in me. I will kill you before you kill me."

Perhaps the best way to appreciate that we all have such wishes to kill and to be killed is to recall our nightmares in which we are either being killed or killing someone else. All the characters in our dreams, ourselves and others, killers and victims, represent aspects of our own personality. The terror we experience during such nightmares is due to the emergence of these murderous impulses. The potential suicide is further terrified by the loss of the person whom he both hates and loves.

TALES OF HORROR

The terror evoked by such losses can best be appreciated if we recall our own reactions as a child or adolescent to the first horror movie we saw. Indeed, the themes of the most popular horror novels and movies are the hidden themes of suicide—monsters who return from the dead and demonic possession. These novels and movies are popular because they evoke a childhood reality and a childhood terror which the reader or viewer can reexperience and master. Roller coasters also allow a childhood experience of terror and helplessness to be safely reexperienced and mastered. "I am not as helpless as I was before. This time I made it happen, and I came through all right."

Two of the most popular horror stories of all time—*Frankenstein* and *Dracula*—deal with the theme of the return of the dead and their revenge upon the living. And two of the most popular movies in recent years—*Psycho* and *The Exorcist*—deal with the same theme, each in a different way. In *Psycho*, the young man's mother did not want him to have a relationship with any other woman. In an effort to free himself from her domination, he kills her. However, instead of becoming free from her, her murder binds him to her more closely, because he then becomes his mother. He wears a mask of her face and a wig of her hair, dresses up in her clothes, talks and walks the way she did. While dressed as his mother, he kills a young woman who has come to stay at his motel. He thus makes his mother the murderer that he is in fact, and maintains a union with her even after her death. In the same manner, the suicide maintains the union with the person he has lost by becoming reunited with that person in death.

In *The Exorcist*, the Devil, rather than a murdered parent, possesses the soul. The Devil is the figure we endow with the qualities we have which we wish to disavow. The Devil is the bad part of ourselves. The movie concludes that the only way to exorcise the bad part of ourselves is by suicide. It describes the attempt by two priests to remove the Devil from a young girl. They are sitting with her in her room attempting to exorcise the Devil. One of them leaves for a few minutes. When he returns, he finds his colleague dead. He becomes very upset and beats on the girl's chest, saying to the Devil inside, "Take me! Take me!" The Devil then leaves the girl's body and enters the priest's body. The priest then jumps out of the window and kills himself in an attempt to kill the Devil who is now within him.

THE WISH TO DIE—THE WISH FOR REUNION

Suicide as a reunion with a loved and hated parent lost in childhood is perhaps best illustrated in the writings of Sylvia Plath, a poet who died a suicide. She made three suicide attempts. The first is described in her autobiographical novel, *The Bell Jar*. Her father died when she was 10. When she was 20, she visited his grave, returned home, went into a hole in the wall of the cellar, and took 50 sleeping pills. She was found by chance and saved. After some months of treatment in a psychiatric hospital she returned to her poetry, married, and had two childen. Ten years later she had some difficulties with her husband and separated from him. She then almost killed herself in an auto crash while driving alone. Six months later, at the age of 31, she successfully suicided by turning on the gas and placing her head in the oven. A great deal of her poetry deals with her relationship with her father, in which intense love and a wish for reunion are mixed with intense hate and wish to kill.

As she wrote in her poem *Daddy*:

> I was ten when they buried you.
> At twenty I tried to die
> and get back, back, back to you.
> I thought even the bones would do.*

At the same time she accused him of being the suicide she later became. As I mentioned previously, vampires were once thought to be suicides who had returned from the grave.

> If I've killed one man, I've killed two
> The vampire who said he was you
> And drank my blood for a year,
> Seven years, if you want to know.
> Daddy, you can lie back now.
> There's a stake in your fat black heart
> And the villagers never liked you.
> They are dancing and stamping on you.
> They always *knew* it was you.
> Daddy, daddy, you bastard, I'm through.†

THE WISH TO BE RESCUED

It is important for physicians to realize that in addition to the triad of wishes that Karl Menninger has described, the suicidal patient

---

* From the poem *Daddy* from the book *Ariel* by Sylvia Plath. (Reprinted by permission of Harper & Row, New York.)

† From the poem *Daddy* from the book *Ariel* by Sylvia Plath. (Reprinted by permission of Harper & Row, New York.)

has a fourth wish, and that is *the wish to be rescued*. A careful history of the period preceding the suicide attempt will in nearly every instance demonstrate the existence of this wish. It can certainly be seen in what we know of Sylvia Plath's suicide. Alvarez was a close friend of Sylvia Plath's, and she asked him to come by and see her on Christmas Eve, 1962. She was clearly agitated and depressed, and she read to him her last poems. As he has recalled in *The Savage God*, there was no mistaking the meaning of these poems. In all of her earlier poems about death, there was something that survived and triumphed and lived on. But in these poems, death was not to be denied. She presented herself as a corpse:

> I do not stir.
> The frost makes a flower,
> The dew makes a star,
> The dead bell,
> The dead bell.
>
> Somebody's done for‡

Alvarez recognized the depth of her depression, but was unable to respond. As he says in *The Savage God*, he knew that he had let her down in some final and unforgivable way, but he could not help himself. He never again saw her alive. She committed suicide on February 11, 1963. It is only in the epilogue of *The Savage God* that we fully realize why Alvarez was unable to help—a few years earlier, *on Christmas Eve*, Alvarez himself had made a suicide attempt by swallowing 45 sleeping pills and almost died.

After failing to be rescued by Alvarez, Sylvia Plath still was hoping to be saved. She wrote a psychotherapist for an appointment but somehow the letter went astray, and the therapist's reply arrived a day or so after she died. She had arranged for a new cleaning girl to come for an interview at nine o'clock on the morning she turned on the gas. The cleaning girl arrived promptly at nine and knocked loudly on the door, but there was no answer. The downstairs neighbor would normally have been up by then to open the door, but he had overslept. The cleaning girl left to check the address with the employment agency, and returned again. It was now 11 o'clock. This time the smell of gas was

‡ From the poem *Death and Company* from the book *Ariel* by Sylvia Plath. (Reprinted by permission of Harper & Row, New York.)

very strong, and some builders nearby broke down the door. Sylvia Plath's body was still warm. She had left a note asking that her family physician be called, leaving his name and telephone number. But it was too late. She was already dead.

Many suicides are arranged in this fashion. A wife is depressed because her husband drinks too much or is involved with another woman. She takes an overdose of pills at a time when she can still be revived if her husband comes directly home from work. On the other hand, if he stops off to drink or to see his girl friend, then she will be dead when he arrives. She thus forces him to live with the guilt for her death. Several years ago, Robert Morse, the United States Attorney for the New York District, was profoundly depressed and impulsively handed in his resignation to the judge who was his superior. Mr. Morse then sat mute and immobile for half an hour in the judge's office. The judge sensed that something was terribly wrong but did not know what to do. Mr. Morse then returned to his apartment and immediately killed himself by jumping out of the window. Civil libertarians and others who are concerned with a person's right to commit suicide miss the essential point: that every suicide at least to some degree wants to be rescued, and wants to feel that someone desires him to live and feels that he deserves to live. He sets his attempt up in such way that there is at least the possibility of rescue if someone cares enough.

If we say to the person perched on a roof threatening to jump, "It's O.K. with us," this increases the person's belief that he is bad and deserves to die. Rescuing the suicidal patient from his own impulses and enforcing a period of hospitalization usually is sufficient to bring about a remission in the intensity of the suicidal drive. Sylvia Plath was placed in a mental hospital for a number of months following her first suicide attempt. She was then released and had 10 years in which she was able to marry, have two children, and establish herself as a poet of the very first rank before she succeeded in killing herself. It is possible that if she had been rescued again in February, 1963, she might have gone on for another 10 years or possibly even for the rest of her life without making another attempt. The drive to suicide is intermittent, not continuous. This brings us to the concluding section of this chapter—the myths surrounding suicide, the prevention of suicide, and the treatment of the suicidal patient.

SOME MYTHS ABOUT SUICIDE

"People who talk about suicide will not try it." "Suicides occur without warning." "Suicidal individuals are fully intent on dying and do not want to be rescued." "Asking about suicide may put a dangerous idea into the patient's head." "Suicidal people are suicidal forever." "People who try suicide and fail are not serious about it, and will not try again." "Only the poor commit suicide." "Only the rich commit suicide." "Only psychotic individuals commit suicide." From all that I have discussed thus far, I hope that we can see these statements for what they are—dangerous myths that may cause the suicidal person to feel even more worthless and alienated, and ultimately more suicidal.

THE PREVENTION OF SUICIDE

Because the suicidal impulse is often transient, simply making the means of suicide less available has been shown to decrease its incidence. For example, removing carbon monoxide from domestic gas in England between 1963 and 1970 reduced the suicide rate during those years. Total suicides decreased from approximately 5,700 in 1963 to 4,000 in 1970 while the number of attempts continued to increase. Similarly, limiting to 25 the number of sedatives which could be prescribed at one time in Australia in 1967 caused a decline in the suicide rate for the five subsequent years although the rate had been rising until 1967. In the United States the increase in the suicide rate during the last 30 years is accounted for primarily by the increasing number of deaths by firearms. According to Boyd, suicide by firearms increased from 4.9/100,000 in 1953 to 7.1/100,000 in 1978, while the age-adjusted rate for all other means remained essentially the same (5.9 in 1953 and 5.4 in 1978). Since 83% of all suicides by firearms are by handguns, it is likely that the suicide rate would fall if handgun sales were restricted in this country, just as it fell when carbon monoxide was removed from domestic gas in England and when the number of sedatives in a single prescription was limited in Australia. Additional evidence for this hypothesis is that states which have strict gun-control laws have lower suicide rates than those which do not.

THE TREATMENT OF THE SUICIDAL PATIENT

The specifics involved in the various somatic treatments for severe depression, such as pharmacotherapy and electroconvulsive therapy, are beyond the scope of this chapter. What I will discuss will be the basic principles of psychotherapy with the suicidal patient. I want to emphasize that any psychotherapy of the suicidal patient must be based on an understanding of the logic of the suicide and not on the logic of common sense. Psychotherapeutic approaches based on common sense not only do not work, but actually increase the suicidal drive by increasing guilt and decreasing self-esteem. Examples of such common sense approaches are, "Pull yourself together." (He's already tried that.) "Think about what you are doing to your family." (One of the reasons he feels so guilty is precisely because of what he is doing and what he wants to do to his family.) "There are other people worse off than you are." (This is like telling the patient in pain that there are other people in the world who have pain which is worse.)

Jane Austen, writing at the beginning of the 19th century, was aware of the harmfulness of common sense in treating the suicidally depressed. In her novel *Sense and Sensibility*, common sense approaches were used initially in treating Marianne, the heroine, and succeeded only in causing her to become more depressed and eventually attempt suicide. Marianne became depressed when her lover Willoughby deserted her. Her sister Elinor (the "sense" of the title; Marianne is the "sensibility") says to her, "Exert yourself, dear Marianne, if you would not kill yourself and all who love you. Think of your mother; think of her misery while you suffer; for her sake you must exert yourself." Marianne replies, "I cannot. Leave me if I distress you; leave me, hate me, forget me!" Marianne's mother is, in fact, in part responsible for Marianne's unhappiness, since she had encouraged Marianne to behave imprudently in her relationship with Willoughby.

Elinor later tells Marianne, hoping to "settle her mind," that her lover Willoughby has impregnated and abandoned another young girl. Elinor believes that when Marianne "considers the wretched and hopeless situation of this poor girl, . . . with an affection for him as strong, still as strong as her own, and with a mind tormented by self-reproach which must attend her through life, surely this comparison must have its use with her. She will feel her own sufferings to be nothing. They proceed from no misconduct, and can bring no disgrace." When Marianne heard this, "her mind did become settled, but it became settled in gloomy dejection." Thus, common sense did not work. This may be why efforts by volunteers to simply befriend patients who call suicide prevention centers may not significantly reduce the suicide rate.

The psychotherapeutic approach to the suicidal patient is based on decreasing the intensity of the wishes to kill, to be killed, and to die. After the initial rescue, the therapist hopes to allow some outlet for the wishes to kill and to decrease the wishes to be killed and die. The first can be done by providing an external outlet for the patient's rage; the second by decreasing the patient's guilt and increasing his self-esteem; the last by providing in the relationship with the therapist a partial substitute for the relationship the patient has lost.

Sometimes even one of these is sufficient to help a particular patient. For example, establishing a relationship of trust with the patient may be enough by itself, and a caring and dependable nonpsychiatric physician may very often be able to sustain a depressed patient without referring the patient to a psychiatrist. This can happen even if the physician is not necessarily aware that he is treating depression and that the patient might well suicide if it were not for the relationship.

This can be illustrated by a study done at Kings County Hospital Center between Jan. 1, 1961 and Dec. 31, 1978. During this period of time, there were 30 suicides by inpatients being treated on the medical and surgical wards. Seven of these were from the chronic pulmonary disease wards. These patients all had poor medical prognoses, with either far advanced tuberculosis or emphysema, or both, and all were severe alcoholics. All seven of the suicides from these wards occurred between 1961 and 1968. In 1968, the medical service on the chronic pulmonary wards underwent a reorganization. Because the medical house staff had been unhappy with their rotation on the chronic service, they were no longer assigned to it. Full-time attendings were assigned to these wards instead. These attendings, unlike the house staff who were unhappy with their rotation on the chronic service, were interested in the treatment of patients with chronic pulmonary problems. They did not ro-

tate every month or two, and unlike some of the house staff, did not become discouraged or angry if the patients did not get well quickly, did not follow their dietary or medical regimens, or went on drinking binges. They simply cared for the patients and their illnesses in a continuing, dedicated, nonjudgmental manner. The patients benefited by having a single doctor to whom they could relate, and whom they could come to trust. They did not have to adjust continually to new physicians. There have been no suicides since 1968 on the chronic pulmonary disease service, whereas there were 10 suicides from 1968 through 1978 in the rest of the general hospital.

Similar good results in preventing suicide by providing a caring relationship have been reported from an American Indian Reservation. American Indians have the highest rate of suicide of any ethnic group in the country, and these rates peak at ages 15 to 24. The suicide is most frequently preceded by recurrent episodes of public drunkenness and disorderly conduct. Formerly these youths were arrested, sentenced to a few days or weeks in jail, and then released without supervision, only to repeat their behavior until they killed themselves in single car auto accidents, or by freezing to death while drunk, or by gunshot wounds. In an effort to reduce the suicide rate, all youths convicted of public drunkenness or disorderly conduct were returned to their reservations instead of being jailed. In their communities, they received supportive care from a physician, a social worker, and Indian volunteers. In the two years after the program went into operation, there were no suicides in the under 30 age group, although two or three would have been expected. We can best understand this result by thinking of the caretakers as substitute parents for these youngsters. The youth's response may then well be, "If they want me alive, maybe I'm not as bad as I think I am."

The doctor-patient relationship is both more crucial in the treatment of the suicidal patient than in the treatment of most other patients and also more likely to be disrupted. It is more crucial because the penalty the patient may pay for loss of the relationship is his life. The nonsuicidal patient who loses his relationship with his doctor is likely to simply find another doctor. The suicidal patient is likely to kill himself. At the same time that the suicidal patient desperately needs his relationship with his doctor, he is also likely to try to provoke his physician to break off the relationship—to say to him as Marianne did to her sister, Elinor, who was trying to act as her therapist, "Leave me, hate me, forget me."

The suicidal patient tries to provoke the therapist both to test the therapist ("If you know what I'm really like, can you still accept me?") and to repeat the trauma of loss he has suffered in an attempt to master it ("Being deserted isn't so bad. I can make it happen."). He will therefore try to anger the therapist so that the therapist rejects him as a patient. The patient often attacks the therapist in the very areas in which the therapist's own self-esteem is vulnerable in order to achieve his goal of arousing counter hostility and abandonment.

He may attack the therapist on the basis of his age, race, sex, religion, training, competency, income, or any other area in which the therapist feels insecure. The therapist must allow the patient to express these feelings without retaliation so as to reduce the amount of hatred he has left to turn against himself. Sidney Tarachow tells the story of the depressed, suicidally preoccupied woman whom he saw once a week for psychotherapy, who told him at the end of each session, "I don't know if I'll be back next week." Each week he would worry that she had killed herself until he saw her again. After a time he realized that the outlet for her sadism which he provided for her by worrying all week was what kept her from suicide.

Treating the suicidal patient is very difficult because the patient in time begins to show the therapist the Frankenstein he has created, made part of himself, and wishes to kill. If the therapist flinches at the sight and turns away, the patient may be lost. The therapist, faced with the patient's deepest hatreds and murderous wishes, may find the treatment sessions increasingly painful and may become increasingly angry with the patient. If he does not understand what is happening, he may start to withdraw from the patient. The therapist has many opportunities to rationalize his retreat from the suicidal patient. In a beautiful paper entitled *The Anatomy of a Suicide*, Leston Havens describes the case of an older woman who had become depressed over the impending marriage of her daughter. She was hospitalized and slowly established trusting relationships with a resident therapist, a head nurse, and a female medical student. Then the resident was promoted to chief resident and had to reduce the number of therapy patients in order to take on his addi-

tional administrative duties. In this situation it is the suicidal patient, who can tolerate transfer the least, who is often the first to be transferred. Such was the case here. The patient had little trust in the new therapist. Then, within a period of days, her daughter married, the head nurse fell ill, and the female medical student completed her rotation on the service. The patient went home on a weekend pass and leaped off a high cliff into the ocean below.

Jane Austen was aware that successful psychotherapy of the suicidal patient requires a continuing relationship, an external outlet for rage, and reduction of guilt. In *Sense and Sensibility*, after demonstrating the ineffectiveness of common sense, she demonstrates successful psychotherapy based on a dynamic understanding of the suicidal patient's needs. Marianne knowingly has exposed herself to a life-threatening fever. Willoughby, who had cruelly rejected her after leading her to believe he wished to marry her, is told that Marianne is dying of a fever because of his cruel treatment of her. He realizes that this accusation is true, and he rides to Marianne's bedside to save her. He arrives after the crisis is passed, but he insists on giving a message to her sister Elinor to deliver to Marianne. The message ends, "Tell her of my misery and of my penitence . . . tell her that my heart was never inconstant to her, and if you will, that at this moment she is dearer to me than ever."

Willoughby provides an outlet for Marianne's rage ("Tell her of my misery and of my penitence."). He is unhappily married. She can take joy in the fact that he is suffering as much or more than she is. She does not have to turn her rage against herself. He reduces her guilt and increases her self-esteem when he says, "Tell her that my heart was never inconstant to her." Marianne's self-esteem is in large part based on her belief that she is extremely perceptive. She is more upset by the thought that she had been mistaken in her belief that Willoughby loved her, than by the fact that he left her. Willoughby tells her that she was not a fool, that indeed he did love her. He also tells her he still maintains a relationship with her from afar, that he will always love her, that . . . "she is dearer to me than ever." Thus, she has not really lost him even though he is married to another woman.

Willoughby's message is conveyed by her sister Elinor to Marianne a few weeks later, after Marianne has recovered from her fever but is still depressed. Elinor tells her of Willoughby's suffering and of his repentence. Marianne's re-action is dramatic. The next day Marianne tells her mother: "It is a great relief to me what Elinor told me . . . I have now heard exactly what I wish to hear . . . I am now perfectly satisfied. I wish for no change." Willoughby loved her, will always love her, and is unhappily married. Her depression is cured, and two years later she marries the very man whom Willoughby has told Elinor he can least accept as Marianne's husband!

The therapy of the suicidal patient, like the therapy of any patient, was summed up by Francis Peabody in 1927: "The secret of the care of the patient is in caring for the patient." Caring for the suicidal patient is often very difficult because he believes he is not worth such caring, and he will summon all of his ingenuity and perseverance to convince his doctor that his own evaluation of himself is correct. If he succeeds, he suicides. The doctor must be willing to engage himself in the treatment and face the depths of the patient's rage and self-disgust. As Havens says at the conclusion of his paper: "Here is the great challenge of suicide: to stay with the battle and feel, not running from what must be borne." Many centuries ago, the Roman philosopher Seneca commented on this same challenge, but this time from the viewpoint of the loneliness of the suicidal patient:

> For who listens to us in all the world, whether
> He be friend or teacher, brother or servant?
> Does he listen, our advocate, or our husbands or wives,
> Those who are dearest to us?
>
> Do the stars listen, when we turn despairingly away
> From men, or great winds, or the sea or
> The mountains? To whom can any man say—Here I am!
> Behold me in my nakedness, my wounds, my secret
> Grief, my despair, my betrayal, my pain,
> My tongue which cannot express my sorrow, my
> Terror, my abandonment.
> Listen to me for a day—an hour—a moment!
> Lest I expire in my terrible wilderness, my
> Lonely silence. O God, is there no one to listen?

Suggested Readings

Alvarez A: *The Savage God: A Study of Suicide*. New York, Random House, 1972.

Havens LL: The anatomy of a suicide. *N Engl J Med* 272:401, 1965.

Menninger KA: *Man Against Himself*. New York, Harcourt, Brace, 1938.

References

Barraclough B, et al: A hundred cases of suicide: clinical aspects. *Br J Psychiatry* 125:355, 1974.

Boyd JH: The increasing rate of suicide by firearms. *N Engl J Med* 308:872, 1983.

Brown JH: Suicide in Britain: more attempts, fewer deaths, lessons for public policy. *Arch Gen Psychiatry* 36:1119, 1979.

Dizmang LH, et al: Adolescent suicide at an Indian Reservation. *Am J Orthopsychiatry* 44:43, 1974

Eyer J, Sterling P: Stress-related mortality and social organization. The Review of Radical Political Economics, 1977, cited in the *Wall Street Journal*, October 2, 1979.

Farberow NL (ed): *The Many Faces of Suicide: Indirect Self-Destructive Behavior*. New York, McGraw-Hill, 1980.

Farberow NL, Shneidman ES (eds): *The Cry for Help*. New York, McGraw-Hill, 1961.

Finkle BS, McCloskey KL, Goodman LS: Diazepam and drug associated deaths. *JAMA* 242:429, 1979.

Frederick CJ: Current trends in suicidal behavior in the United States. *Am J Psychotherapy* 32:172, 1978.

Freud S (1917): Mourning and melancholia. In *The Standard Edition of the Complete Psychological Works of Sigmund Freud*, vol 14, London, Hogarth Press, 1957, p 237.

Glickman L: Suicide among medical and surgical inpatients at Kings County Hospital from 1961 to 1973. Paper presented at Medical Staff Day, Kings County Hospital Center, Brooklyn, NY, May 1973.

Glickman L: Suicidal patients. In *Psychiatric Consultation in the General Hospital*. New York, Marcel Dekker, 1980.

Goldney RD, Katsikitis M: Cohort analysis of suicide rates in Australia. *Arch Gen Psychiatry* 40:71, 1983.

Holinger PC: Adolescent suicide. *Am J Psychiatry* 135:754, 1978.

Jensen VW, Petty TA: The fantasy of being rescued in suicide. *Psychoanal Q* 27:327, 1958.

Lester D, Murrell ME: The influence of gun control laws on suicidal behavior. *Am J Psychiatry* 137:121, 1980.

Maltsberger JT, Bruce DH: Countertransference hate in the treatment of suicide patients. *Arch Gen Psychiatry* 30:625, 1974.

Murphy GE: The physician's responsibility for suicide. *Ann Int Med* 82:301, 1975.

O'Brien JP: Increase in suicide attempts in drug ingestion. *Arch Gen Psychiatry* 34:1165, 1977.

Orgel S: Sylvia Plath: fusion with the victim and suicide. *Psychoanal Q* 43:262, 1974.

Patterson WM, et al: Evaluation of suicidal patients: the SAD PERSONS scale. *Psychosomatics* 24:343, 1983.

Peabody FW: The care of the patient. *JAMA* 88:877, 1927.

Resnik HL (ed): *Suicidal Behaviors: Diagnosis and Management*. Boston, Little, Brown, and Co, 1968.

Shneidman ES, Farberow NL (eds): *Clues to Suicide*. New York, McGraw-Hill, 1957.

Shneidman ES (ed): *Essays in Self-Destruction*. New York, Science House, 1967.

Stengel E: *Suicide and Attempted Suicide*. Baltimore, Penguin Books, 1964.

Tarachow S: *An Introduction to Psychotherapy*. New York, International Universities Press, 1963.

Tefft BM, Pederson AM, Babigian HM: Patterns of death among suicide attempters, a psychiatric population, and a general population. *Arch Gen Psychiatry* 34:1155, 1977.

65 Violence and the Physician

John M. Macdonald, M.D.

Many persons are so fascinated by violence that they spend endless hours watching mediocre television programs of armed robbery, kidnapping, and murder. Of course, medical students would not fritter away their time in this manner, but what would you prefer, a book on *The Lives of the Saints* or *The Memoirs of Jesse James*? Crime fascinates us, but it also repels us. We do not like to think of crime in our homes, our neighborhoods, or our hospitals. We like to think that crime will not affect us and that we will not have criminals as patients. But not all criminals are behind bars in penitentiaries. They are on the streets, many of them have jobs, and when ill, they come to our private offices, to our emergency rooms, and to our hospitals. They bring their children to the pediatrician and their elderly parents to the clinic.

The public belief that criminals have shifty eyes, distinctive ear lobes, or a generally sinister appearance is fostered on television as well as in literature. Movie directors select clean-cut heroes and repulsive villains who create a sense of brooding evil. But criminals have no mark of Cain which betrays their violent nature. They do not come to us with their FBI rap sheet in hand. Victims of violence may also pass unrecognized. We do not see what we do not want to see, and physicians are perhaps even quicker than others to turn a blind eye or a deaf ear to evidence of personal violence. Such denial may make the world seem more pleasant than it is, but denial by physicians may not always be in the best interests of their patients. Serious physical injuries are too readily accepted as being due to accidents because we cannot think the unthinkable, and consider the possibility of deliberate violence. The patient who states he was walking down the street when a car pulled alongside him and the driver shot him in the leg, may in fact have been shot by the owner of a liquor store during an attempt to rob the store at gunpoint. A youth walking down a country road,

who "kicked a tin can which exploded," may have been injured in the premature explosion of a bomb which he himself had made.

VIOLENCE IN THE HOME

Injuries due to violence within the home are often attributed to "accidents" by both victim and assailant. The injured patient conceals the true origin of his or her wounds, and the family joins in the conspiracy of silence. A child with a fractured skull "fell out of bed"—he was really beaten by his father. A wife with broken bones "fell down the basement stairs"—she was thrown down the stairs by her husband. A husband with a gunshot wound was "cleaning his pistol when it discharged"—he was shot by his wife. An elderly grandmother "tripped on a rug" and fractured her hip—she was shoved by her daughter.

Yet, despite all the publicity in recent years about battered children and battered wives, it is easy to overlook assaults within the family when the victim makes no mention of violence, provides a reasonable explanation for the injuries, and is accompanied by an apparently concerned relative. The victim's peculiar silence may proceed from the assailant's threats of death or serious injury in the event of exposure of the truth. It may also stem from embarrassment over who the assailant is. Teenage children have been known to assault their parents, sometimes a case of "the biter bit." There are also battered husbands, but many of them are too ashamed to reveal beatings by their wives. However, most studies show a much higher incidence of wife beating than of husband beating, and furthermore, the greatest physical harm in spouse abuse is to women because of the greater incidence of serious assaultive behavior by men. Women also tend to endure abuse and physical harm much longer, usually because they feel trapped in the marriage or the relationship for a variety of psychological, sociological, and economic reasons.

"Granny bashing" should also not escape notice. Elderly people can be just as tiresome and just as infuriating as small children. When grandmother is a little slow coming to the dining table, her daughter yanks on her arm and dislocates her shoulder. In the emergency room, no reference is made to her daughter's impatient act because the old lady is fearful that the daughter may send her to an old people's home. Sensitive inquiry by a physician or nurse may reveal the true source of the injury and save the grandmother from a return visit to the hospital six months later with a fractured hip.

Attempted suicide and homicide may also be dismissed as "attacks" or "accidents." A young woman reported that "a burglar broke in her home and shot her when she resisted his attempt to rape her"—she had actually shot herself in the chest in an attempt to take her own life. A youth was admitted to the hospital with deep cuts in both hands from "accidentally putting his hands through a window." While still in the hospital he was arrested on charges of stabbing his parents to death, the cuts in his hands being due to the knife slipping during the alleged homicides.

A significant number of patients admitted to hospitals with burns have deliberately burned themselves to obtain attention, in an attempt at suicide, or for some other reason. Some of these patients attribute their burns to "accidents." There may indeed have been an accident. A housewife with severe burns said she was "using paint thinner when it was ignited by ashes from her cigarette." In fact, she had deliberately set a fire in her living room with the intention of making a claim on her insurance company for fire damage due to an electrical short circuit. The fire flared up faster than she anticipated and she became a victim. (There is a saying among arsonists that you must know what you are doing or you will be the first to burn.)

Even though the patient tells the doctor about violence or threats of violence within the home, this important message may be disregarded by the doctor. A man states that he is so angry at his wife that he is going to burn the house down while she is asleep. The doctor replies, "Oh no, you wouldn't do that . . . do you still have those ulcer pains?" The doctor may squelch meaningful inquiry into the risk of serious injury, or even homicide, by responding to a patient's statement, "I've just had a fight with my wife" with the comment "Tell me how the argument started." The patient takes the hint and there is an intellectual discussion on marital disharmony rather than a frightening account of the use of brute force. The doctor should have responded, "Did you strike her? Did you give her a black eye? Did you break any bones? Did you break her nose? Did you choke her? You did. Was this to the point of unconsciousness? Does this happen very often?" Patients are very quick to pick up a doctor's reluctance to talk about violence or his disapproval of such behavior either in words or looks.

The patient may not complain of either injuries or violence, yet the symptoms may provide a clue, for example, a vaginal discharge or pregnancy in a 14 year old girl. She may blame the pregnancy on her boyfriend, when in fact she is the victim of incest and her father has threatened to kill her if she reveals this information. Battered wives often appear with complaints such as headaches, choking sensations, asthma, chest pain, gastrointestinal symptoms, pelvic pain, and allergies. These symptoms may be connected to previous episodes of battering but there may be no direct connection between these symptoms and the current battering. Patients may return again and again with "uncontrolled" diabetes or "uncontrolled" epilepsy. They do not take their insulin or their anticonvulsant medication as prescribed because they know that the only way they can escape their husbands is through admission to the hospital. As in all interviews, we must listen with a third ear. Remember that incest and violence are more common than any of us care to think.

VIOLENCE ON THE HIGHWAY

Motor vehicle wrecks due to attempted suicide or attempted homicide are often attributed to careless driving, drunkenness, loss of control at high speed, or falling asleep at the wheel. This is not surprising, since the person at fault, if he survives, has good reasons for concealing his motives from the police. If the person does die in the wreck, it is usually not possible to determine suicidal or homicidal intent in the absence of a written note or verbal statement of such intent prior to the wreck. A 32 year old schizophrenic woman was out driving with her husband and five children when the voices told her that she would have to be born again. In order to be born again one has to die first, so she deliberately crashed her car into the rear of another car at 80 mph. Both cars overturned, but fortunately no one was seriously injured, and she was fined $10 for careless driving. Her husband neglected to tell the court or police about his wife's mental disorder. Three days later he was forced to take her for treatment to a psychiatric hospital.

When any patient is brought to an emergency room with injuries following an automobile wreck, the possibility of nonaccidental intent should be considered. Otherwise, the patient, upon recovery from his injuries, may later succeed in taking his own life and possibly the lives of others as well. Injured passengers, aware of the reason for a close call with death, may also be unwilling to talk to the police. A young man, angry at his wife, attempted to kill her and himself by aiming his car at a tree. The wife was naturally tearful and upset, but the police assumed that this was due to her shock over the accident and the pain from her head striking the windshield. The officer told her husband, "I know what must have happened. Your front tire blew out and you lost control of your car and hit the tree." Neither the husband nor his wife told the policeman that the tire blew out because it hit the edge of the sidewalk at high speed when the husband tried to kill his wife and himself.

VIOLENCE IN HOSPITALS

Each month there are three or four assaults of hospital staff in the busy emergency room of a large city hospital, usually by patients under the influence of alcohol or of an hallucinogenic drug such as phencyclidine ("angel dust"). On the wards, a delirious patient suffering from an acute organic brain syndrome may become assaultive in response to paranoid delusions or hallucinations of a frightening nature. Psychotic patients suffering from a schizophrenic illness, especially those with long standing paranoid delusions, may also become violent. Antisocial or sociopathic personalities, with their low tolerance for frustration, also make their contribution to physical attacks within a hospital. The psychotically depressed person, feeling that life is miserable and that there is no hope for the future, may come to believe that death is the only solution for the whole family.

The physician who wishes to avoid the risk of assault must treat all his patients with respect and be polite, courteous, and considerate, rather than impatient, irritable, and critical. Patients are very sensitive to negative feelings whether communicated in words or in facial expressions. Above all, we must not make any comments that reflect on a patient's masculinity, and we must beware of the patient under the influence of alcohol or drugs, and of the angry, belligerent, or paranoid patient. Tattoos indicating membership in a gang or an outlaw motorcycle club, as well as tattoos such as "Born to kick ass" and "Born to lose," scars from bullet or knife wounds, needle tracks, and nicknames such as "Paranoid Al," "Crazy Joe," "Mad Dog," or "Snap-Cap" convey the suggestion of a lifestyle very different from that of the doctor.

The patient may volunteer information which suggests that violence is on his mind. Fantasies of rape and murder should not be lightly disregarded. A 15 year old high school student wrote a theme on a proposed book for his teacher: "This book does not have a title, but it is the story of a boy who was fed up with living. His name doesn't matter. It's what he will do that will shock you. One night when his parents went to bed, he got up from his bed, took his shotgun, loaded it, and went quietly into their bedroom. His mother and father were sleeping, he took aim, and shot his father first. His mother screamed and he shot her." That night the student went to his parents' room and wounded both of them with two shots.

This is a dramatic and unusual case, but fantasies, threats, and symbolic acts of violence suggest the need for very careful evaluation. The homicidal threat, the hand drawn across the throat, and the knife thrust in the pillow may be messages of doom. Prior acts of violence are the best predictors of future violence. Even though patients may boast of such behavior, their bragging may cover shame. In talking with these patients, it is better to avoid words such as rape, mugging, and murder. Euphemisms such as cutting rather than stabbing make it easier for these patients to reveal themselves.

ORIGINS OF VIOLENT BEHAVIOR

Sociologists draw attention to subcultures of violence in our larger cities. Wolfgang notes that when a blow of the fist is casually accepted as a normal response to certain stimuli, when knives are commonly carried for personal defense, and a homicide is as frequent as Saturday night, then social control against violence is weak. The following notice on the wall of a local tavern in downtown Denver hints at a high level of violence in that neighborhood:

> PLEASE BROTHERS NO WEAPONS!
>
> If you don't bring a weapon, then my brother won't have to carry his weapon. Then our sisters & mothers may feel free to come in for a beer, cocktail or food,
>
> > WITHOUT FEAR OF BEING CUT
> > OR SHOT BY MISTAKE
> > THANKS FOR BEING
> > A BROTHER & SISTER
> >
> > LOVE AND PEACE "BIG AL"

As Dr. Christ noted in his chapter on juvenile delinquency, there are many factors in childhood which may contribute to violence. Parental indulgence, rejection, seduction, or brutality all may generate aggression in the child and provide a negative model for future behavior, but this is not predictable. Freud noted that so long as we trace development backwards, the chain of events appears continuous and we feel that we understand the patient's behavior. But Freud added the warning that if we proceed the reverse way, if we start from the beginning, from the time of the patient's birth, then we no longer get the impression of an inevitable sequence of events.

Thus, a child who has been savagely and repeatedly beaten by his father may indeed later kill someone or commit other crimes of violence. He may savagely beat his own children as his father did to him, or he may become a social worker in a program to help battered children, or an author who writes empathic novels around the theme of child abuse, or a loving father. Any of these events could be attributed in part to the childhood beatings. The final outcome is dependent on the influence of many other experiences in life.

Other parental attitudes and behaviors may contribute to a child growing up with unusual needs for attention, for companionship, and for reassurance of masculinity or femininity. Some of these needs can be obtained through acts of violence. The man unsure of his masculinity, whether because of physical weakness, below average height, or parental behavior that encourages effeminacy, may attempt to prove his masculinity through assaultive behavior. The weak and timid gain instant power with a .38

caliber revolver—the power of life and death over others. And in regard to needs for attention, it is better to be wanted by the police than not to be wanted at all.

Other motives for an act of violence may involve such obvious conscious emotions as anger, resentment, revenge, jealousy, and sexual desire. Often, indeed, there is clear evidence of such factors, but even when they are present, they seldom provide an adequate explanation for the violence. The assailant himself may attempt to explain his conduct in this manner. Yet the mainsprings of human conduct are so complex as to cast doubt on such simple explanations. There may also be motivations beyond the conscious awareness of the assailant. In rape, for example, a deep-seated hatred and contempt of women, perhaps derived from an embittered relationship with the mother in childhood, is usually far more important than any kind of sexual desire as a motive. In addition, exploration of a violent act should always include review of the role of the victim.

VICTIMS OF VIOLENCE

Some persons become *victims by chance* alone, simply because they are in the wrong place at the wrong time. The patient who walks into an emergency room cannot anticipate that he will be attacked by a brain injured, disoriented, delirious patient who misidentifies his victim as a dangerous aggressor. *Vulnerable victims* of violence include children, the elderly and physically handicapped, hitchhikers and drivers who pick up hitchhikers, alcoholics, drug pushers and users, persons in high-crime areas, employees working alone at night in convenience stores, prostitutes, and clients of prostitutes. These persons are either less able to defend themselves or they place themselves in situations of danger.

There are also *victims who provoke violence*. In almost one-third of 578 consecutive criminal homicides in Baltimore, the victim was the first to show and use a deadly weapon or to strike a blow in an altercation—in short, the first to resort to violence. Words and looks can wound as well as blows and bullets. Harsh criticism, belittling sarcasm, or a contemptuous glance in a moment of crisis may provoke an assailant into an act of homicide. Women threatened with firearms by their husbands have responded with provocative comments such as, "What are you going to do, big man, kill me?" and "You haven't got the guts to kill me." Husbands in turn have provoked their wives into killing them through repeated brutal beatings over many years. Some victims take inadequate steps to protect themselves. A very vain young woman did not say, "Don't shoot me," but rather "Don't shoot me in the face." Her boyfriend altered his aim and shot her in the chest. How different the response of a child when his severely depressed mother said she was going to kill him; "Oh no, momma, I know you wouldn't do that." In other words, some victims are not always blameless.

PREJUDICE

I would like to conclude this chapter with a very brief mention of a phenomenon which underlies much of the violence in the world today. *Prejudice* may be defined as an irrational hatred of a person, group, race, religion, or nation. The prejudiced person may, or may not, act out his prejudices, and as Allport notes, discrimination as a consequence of prejudice has more immediate and serious social consequences than prejudice alone. The origins of prejudice include *scapegoating*, whereby attention is diverted from one's own shortcomings to those of others. Forbidden aggressive and sexual impulses are projected onto others who are then regarded as hostile, dangerous, dirty, and immoral. Blaming the victim has long been popular. Disadvantaged groups are regarded as deserving their inferior state. The poor are poor because they are ignorant, lazy, squander their money, and do not keep their homes in good condition. Resistance to change is also involved. Minority groups with different values and ideals threaten the establishment and arouse resentment. Hostile sentiment between groups is likely in times of economic recession and is fostered in wartime. Thus, during the Vietnam war, the Viet Cong were dehumanized and were referred to as "gooks." Some authorities have attempted to explain prejudice in terms of the *authoritarian personality*, but this concept alone does not explain the widespread extent of prejudice nor the hatred and violence that have been turned against so many people during the course of civilization as a result of prejudice.

Suggested Readings

Macdonald JM: *The Murderer and His Victim*. Springfield, IL, Charles C Thomas, 1961.

Macdonald JM: *Rape: Offenders and Their Victims*. Springfield, IL, Charles C Thomas, 1971.

Macdonald JM: *Bombers and Firesetters*. Springfield, IL, Charles C Thomas, 1977.

References

Allport GW: *The Nature of Prejudice*. Cambridge, MA, Addison-Wesley, 1954.

Carmen E (Hilberman), Rieker PP, Mills T: Victims of violence and psychiatric illness. *Am J Psychiatry* 141:378, 1984.

Criminal Justice Commission. Criminal homicides in Baltimore, Maryland 1960–1964. Baltimore, 1967 (processed).

Dobash RE, Dobash RP: *Violence Against Wives*. New York, The Free Press, 1979.

Freud S (1920): The psychogenesis of a case of homosexuality in a woman. In *The Standard Edition of the Complete Psychological Works of Sigmund Freud*, vol 18. London, Hogarth Press, 1955, p 145.

Gelles RJ: *The Violent Home: A Study of Physical Aggression Between Husbands and Wives*. Beverly Hills, CA, Sage, 1974.

Goodstein RK, Page AW: Battered wife syndrome: overview of dynamics and treatment. *Am J Psychiatry* 138:1036, 1981.

Hilberman E: Overview: the "wife-beater's wife" reconsidered. *Am J Psychiatry* 137:1336, 1980.

Langley R, Levy RC: *Wife Beating: The Silent Crisis*. New York, E.P. Dutton, 1978.

Roy M (ed): *Battered Women: Psychological Study of Domestic Violence*. New York, Van Nostrand Reinhold, 1977.

Steinmetz SK: *The Cycle of Violence: Assertive, Aggressive and Abusive Family Interaction*. New York, Praeger, 1977.

Steinmetz SK, Straus MA (eds): *Violence in the Family*. New York, Harper & Row, 1974.

Straus MA, Gelles RJ, Steinmetz SK: *Behind Closed Doors: Violence in the American Family*. New York, Anchor Books, 1981.

CHAPTER 66 The Substance Use Disorders

Thomas J. Crowley, M.D. and
Mark W. Rhine, M.D.

DEFINITIONS

A *drug* is any chemical agent that affects living processes. Only food and water are usually excluded from this very broad definition, so the term *drug abuse* (or *substance abuse*) also is broad, encompassing abuse of the drugs alcohol and nicotine, as well as such compounds as heroin, LSD, or methamphetamine.

We define *substance abuse* as the *repeated nontherapeutic use of any drug in doses or schedules which produce a significant risk of adverse effects to the user or others*. The term *nontherapeutic use* excludes circumstances in which an admittedly toxic drug, such as a cancer chemotherapeutic agent, is given with the expectation that its therapeutic benefits outweigh its potential risks. The phrase *any drug* specifically includes the abuse of alcohol or tobacco.

The ingestion of a drug at certain *doses* might not produce adverse effects, while ingestion at other doses clearly would. For example, there is no evidence that low dose (1 or 2 shots per week) use of alcohol has adverse effects, while a pint per day of distilled liquor is a very risky level of consumption. But the *schedule of administration* also must be considered. If a person drinks a quart of distilled liquor in a year, that might seem safe; but if he drinks the entire quart on his birthday each year, he could die.

Adverse effects are at the heart of our definition. Drug use may cause medical, financial, legal, social, psychological, or family problems. If the drug use produces problems, or a significant risk of problems, for the user or others, that is substance abuse and deserves treatment. In regard to medical problems, the abuse of alcohol, tobacco, and other drugs contributes to death from a long list of causes, including cancer, cardiovascular disease, trauma, infection,

and overdose. In fact, the National Institute on Drug Abuse estimates tht 25% of all deaths in this country are premature deaths in which substance abuse is a contributing cause. Thus substance abuse may well be the greatest medical problem of our time.

Legal problems also deserve special comment. Societies often partially determine the adverse effects of substance abuse. For example, it is said that early Persian rulers discouraged the use of tobacco by pouring molten lead down the throats of smokers. The United States outlaws heroin even for therapeutic use, although it is used commonly in medical treatment abroad. Moslem laws, which forbid the use of alcohol, apparently are more lenient toward cannabis derivatives, while the reverse is true in the United States. Physicians often recognize that such laws are pharmacologically and medically irrational, and they may work to modify those laws. But being jailed is an adverse effect of drug use; when a patient's use of drugs puts him at serious legal risk, the same physicians who work to change drug laws have the obligation to counsel their patients to live within those laws.

DSM-III distinguishes two categories within the *substance use disorders: substance abuse and substance dependence*. Substance abuse requires a pattern of pathological use that leads to an impairment in social or occupational functioning and that is present for a duration of at least one month. Substance dependence requires physiological dependence, evident by either tolerance or withdrawal. *Tolerance* means that increased amounts of the substance are needed to achieve the desired effect or there is diminished effect with regular use of the same dose. *Withdrawal* means that a substance-specific syndrome follows abstinence from a substance that previously was used on a regular basis.

PHYSICIANS' ATTITUDES TO ALCOHOLISM AND OTHER SUBSTANCE ABUSE

Although alcoholism has been referred to as the most neglected health problem and the most treatable untreated illness in the United States today, physicians have always been pessimistic about the treatment of alcoholics as well as other drug abusers. Doctors tend to stereotype "the alcoholic" as a skid row derelict, a panhandler who drinks cheap Muscatel and sleeps in doorways. Similarly, they stereotype "the drug abuser" as a person from the inner city ghetto who indulges in a life of crime to support his heroin habit. Since less than 3% of alcoholics live on skid row, doctors with this stereotype will miss the diagnosis of alcoholism in the vast majority of their patients, overlooking those who still have such resources as a job, family, and home, and are thus most likely to benefit from treatment. It is no wonder then that such physicians would be discouraged if they persistently attempted to diagnose and treat only those alcoholics least likely to profit from treatment. Imagine how discouraged cancer surgeons would be if they operated only on patients with widespread metastases and refused those with *carcinoma in situ!*

This bias in physicians probably comes from several sources. The skid row alcoholic and the ghetto drug user are common stereotypes in our society which the student is likely to bring along when he or she enters medical school. As a clerk and house officer on the wards and in the emergency room, the young physician is repeatedly confronted with cirrhosis, esophageal varices, peripheral neuritis, Korsakoff's psychosis, delirium tremens, and other frustrating medical complications of late-stage alcoholism. Until recently, students were unlikely to be taught anything else in medical school about alcoholism other than these physical complications, and so their picture of the alcoholic becomes very warped indeed. They are not taught that alcoholism affects a wide spectrum of the population, male and female, young and old, from all socioeconomic groups. It therefore may not occur to physicians that when a 40 year old executive becomes suddenly unmanageable three days postcholecystectomy, the patient might be going through alcohol withdrawal, nor that the attractive housewife with "heartburn" might be

suffering from alcoholic gastritis, nor that the teenager in the car crash may have been intoxicated. Similarly, because physicians tend to identify "drug abusers" with the individual who has hepatitis or bacterial endocarditis as a complication of intravenous use of drugs, they do not consider in the same category the housewife to whom they give repeated prescriptions of opioids for her headaches or amphetamines for her weight control.

It is important to recognize that there is no such person as "the" alcoholic or "the" drug abuser. People from a wide variety of backgrounds use and abuse alcohol and other drugs for a wide variety of reasons. Our definition of substance abuse given at the beginning of this chapter includes not only those with the medical complications of drug abuse or late-stage alcoholism, but also those who are just beginning to have problems at work or with their spouse or family, and for whom much may be done if the problem is recognized and addressed in its early stages.

SCREENING AND EVALUATING SUBSTANCE ABUSERS IN MEDICAL PRACTICE

Given the prevalence of substance abuse in our society, every patient in every medical practice should be evaluated for this problem. Physical findings and laboratory tests may contribute to the screening process, but an effective screening procedure is simply to ask, "Was there ever a time in your life when you were using more alcohol or other drugs than you think was good for you?" This question focuses on *problems* from drug use, and *problems* are at the heart of our definition of substance abuse. The question also permits the patient initially to respond in the past tense, avoiding the embarrassment which sometimes leads to denial of current problems.

If the initial screening suggests the possibility of drug abuse, the physician can then obtain a more detailed drug history. Questions to be asked include the following: *What have you used?* The physician asks about the use of each of the major drug classes (tobacco, alcohol, other general depressants, opioids, stimulants, and hallucinogens), now and in the past. *How much do you use?* Drug by drug, the physician asks about weekly intake: How many packs of cigarettes? How many shots or ounces of hard liquor, cans of beer, and glasses of wine (1.5 ounces of hard liquor, a 12 ounce can of beer, and a six ounce glass of wine contain about equal quantities of absolute alcohol). How many "hits" of LSD or other hallucinogenic drugs? How many pills or capsules of benzodiazepines, barbiturates, or amphetamines, and what size of each? How many ounces or grams of cocaine? How many dollars worth of heroin? *When have you used the drugs?* At what periods in his or her life did the patient use the drugs? At what times of day? For women, was there any relationship between drug use and time in the menstrual cycle? How does current use compare with past use? Has the patient been abstinent at intervals, and for how long? When was the last day the patient went without any drugs? *What was the source of your drugs?* Were the drugs obtained from street suppliers, thievery, multiple prescriptions obtained through "doctor shopping," forged prescriptions, friends, or relatives? *How did you use the drugs?* What was the route of administration (oral, intravenous, pulmonary inhalation, or intranasal insufflation)? What preparation and procedures were used to administer the drug? *With whom did you use the drugs?* Did the patient take the drug alone, at parties, in sexual settings, or with selected friends? *Under what circumstances did you use drugs?* Does a seasonally employed patient mainly use drugs during periods of unemployment? Does the patient use drugs after events of social rejection? Does use typically follow fights with the spouse? Does use occur when living with the parents, but not when living independently? Or does the patient seem to use drugs continually, regardless of current conditions? *What problems or cost resulted from the drug use?* Financial problems may include debts incurred because of drug purchases or drug-related unemployment. Patients may commit burglary or prostitution to get funds for drugs. Legal problems often involve arrests for public drunkenness, for fighting, for driving while intoxicated, or for drug possession or sale. Medical problems may include withdrawal symptoms, cirrhosis, subacute bacterial endocarditis following intravenous drug use, hepatitis, and a host of other toxic phenomena. Patients may develop mental problems such as acute or chronic organic mental disorders. The loss of friends is a major social problem. Vocational and school problems include days missed because of intoxications or hangovers, confron-

tations with supervisors or teachers, loss of productivity or declining grades, drug related loss of professional licenses or certificates, and job or school dismissals. Family problems may appear as arguments with spouses, rebelliousness or impaired school performance in children of the user, anxiety and depression in other family members, and divorce. *What are the payoffs or rewards in the drug use?* The physician asks about how the drug makes the patient feel, and what favorable or beneficial effects the patient believes the drug may have upon his or her behavior. The physician also determines how the response of others to the patient's drug use may reinforce continued use; does the spouse cover up for the drinking, or do the parents excuse aggressiveness because "It is just the bottle talking"? *Who else in your family has had drug problems?* The physician inquires whether familial influences (either genetic or learned) may have contributed to the patient's drug problem.

The patient's answers to these questions indicate which of many etiological factors may contribute to the substance abuse behavior. The answers also usually suggest which treatment interventions may help this individual patient.

THE MULTIPLE ETIOLOGIES OF SUBSTANCE ABUSE

Consider trying to predict which children, of all those in the world, are at greatest risk to become substance abusers. What pharmacologic, social, and personal factors increase the danger that any particular person will become harmfully involved with drugs? In Figure 66.1 such etiologic factors appear schematically on a

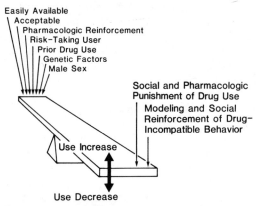

Figure 66.1. The multiple etiologies of substance abuse. (Figure by Thomas J. Crowley.)

seesaw; some increase, and some decrease, the risk that a given person will abuse a particular drug.

Availability

People are much more likely to abuse drugs which are easily available to them. For example, in wine-producing France alcohol is cheap and widely available, but only a few hundred miles away in Norway alcohol is heavily taxed, more expensive, and more difficult to obtain. These differences appear to affect the prevalence of alcoholism in the two countries. Deaths from liver cirrhosis (a common public health measure of alcoholism) claim about 45 of each 100,000 Frenchmen and only about 5 of each 100,000 Norwegians. Similarly, during Prohibition in the United States and in several Canadian provinces the prevalence of cirrhosis declined dramatically. Although it often is said that Prohibition "didn't work," it seems clear that there was less alcoholism when alcohol was less available. Other data show that when increased sales taxes make alcohol less easily available, there is less excessive drinking.

Still another example may arise in the ready availability of drugs to physicians; although there are no convincing prevalence figures, more physicians than, for example, lawyers, appear to abuse those prescription drugs which are so readily available to doctors. This observation suggests a simple rule to reduce drug availability and drug abuse among physicians: *they should not prescribe potentially abusable medications to themselves.* Placing the responsibility for such prescribing in the hands of another doctor makes abusable drugs no more available to physician-patients than to other patients.

Persons attempting to achieve abstinence should try to make drugs less available to themselves. They should be counselled to vigorously terminate contacts with dealers and to avoid friends who might casually supply some drugs. In addition, such patients should avoid places of high availability, which may include certain neighborhoods, or particular bars or nightclubs, or parties with known drug abusers. Decreased availability does decrease the risk of drug use.

Acceptability

Availability of a drug is not enough to promote its use; that drug also must be accepted and used by at least some of one's associates. For example, although marijuana grows wild in the American Midwest, it rarely was harvested for smoking until the 1960's. But then illicit harvesting became common; marijuana was not more available in the fields, but there had been a major change in society's acceptance of marijuana smoking.

Acceptance of the use of a drug may get new users started in two ways. First, the neophyte learns how to use the drug by simple observation of friends or family. This teaching and learning by simple observation is called *modeling,* and thus the beginner learns in this way to smoke tobacco rather than to eat it, or to drink alcohol rather than to burn and smoke it. Second, a new user's ingestion of a drug probably will be applauded by associates who use it. Users of a drug may enjoy drug-centered social contacts with other users, while excluding nonusers from their company. A particularly clear example of such *social reinforcement* for drug use arose in 1966 when a balladeer, Donovan, sang "Electrical banana is gonna' be a sudden craze," and youngsters began to search for a "banana high." Soon, underground newspapers published recipes for preparing banana skins to smoke, and groups of young people in banana costumes were attending "banana rallys"; they sang banana music as they smoked "banana grass." Of course, it was a hoax; banana skins contained no hallucinogens. But many young people used this "mellow yellow" despite its lack of pharmacologic effect. The fun of a rebellious but harmless activity, and the pleasure of joining in a carnival-like pastime apparently were social reinforcers for the self-administration of banana smoke.

The expectation of social reinforcement appears to be very important in initiating drug use. For instance, youths often report that they began smoking tobacco so that their friends would view them as more adult. Similarly, invitations to secret "beer blasts" are among the rewards for adolescent drinking. Treatment is complicated when most of a patient's social contacts and social rewards come from such drug-centered activities. Adolescent drug users may never have experienced age-appropriate social excitement and fun without drugs, and even adults who had such experiences before their drug involvement may have given them up completely. Such patients may need specific counseling and support from their doctors to begin, or resume, socially rewarding drug-free activities.

Pharmacologic Reinforcement

Introduction. Mellow yellow was a passing fad; it "hooked" no one. But many of those who similarly experiment with drugs such as heroin or cocaine are "hooked" into compulsive, repetitious self-administration. These drugs differ pharmacologically from the mellow yellow placebo, and one pharmacologic difference is that these drugs compellingly drive continued use. How do they do so? In the past this tendency to "get hooked" was ascribed mainly to physical dependence; a heroin addict gets sick when he abstains, and it was suggested that drug use persisted so that the user could avoid this withdrawal syndrome. But stimulants such as cocaine produce very little abstinence illness. Moreover, a high percentage of heroin users relapse back to drug use many months or years after their acute withdrawal syndrome abates. So, "getting hooked" apparently is not simply the result of avoidance of an abstinence illness.

Some suggest that drugs make people feel much better psychologically, either producing a wonderful euphoria or suppressing unpleasant dysphoric feelings, so that the user is driven to maintain that pleasant state. Certainly, some users of many abused drugs do experience very pleasant feelings after a dose. However, many frequent, high-dose users report that their drug eventually produced very weak positive effects and very profound negative effects on their feelings, but they also report that they still could not desist from further use! When chronic alcoholics are given free access to alcohol in research wards, their mood does not improve during drinking binges; in fact, they become so depressed that some of these studies have been stopped because of fears that the subjects might commit suicide. In another example, many tobacco smokers continue using their drug, and there is a very high relapse rate even among those who fear smoking's health consequences and attempt to stop; but few tobacco smokers claim that the drug produces any nirvana-like psychological states. Considering all of these facts, it seems improbable that most drug abuse occurs because drugs make people feel good psychologically.

Reinforcement in Animals. Indeed, with appropriate access to drugs, even animals that presumably lack man's complex feeling states and symbolic capacity will self-administer drugs repeatedly and compulsively to the point of death, in ways highly analogous to those of human substance abusers. In such studies researchers implant one end of a flexible cannula in a vein of a rat or monkey and attach the other end to an automatic pump. A lever in the animal's cage operates as a switch, so that a press on the lever briefly activates the pump, driving a small amount of drug-containing fluid into the vein. Out of curiosity, or even by accident, the animal will bump the lever a few times. After those first injections the animal then will press the lever with increasing frequency if the fluid contains alcohol, barbiturates, nonbarbiturate sedative-hypnotics, benzodiazepines, cocaine, amphetamines, nicotine, or such opioids as heroin, morphine, methadone, codeine, or acetylmethadol. But if the pump contains only saline, or one of many drugs not abused by human beings, the animal soon stops pressing the lever.

If an event systematically follows some behavior, and if the behavior then occurs with increasing frequency, that event is defined as a *reinforcer.* If commonly abused drugs are given to animals when the animals emit some behavior, that behavior will occur with increasing frequency; by definition then, these drugs reinforce that behavior. For the monkeys in these experiments, and for human drug abusers, the behavior which just precedes the arrival of the drug into the body is the act of self-administering the drug, and the drug itself pharmacologically reinforces (drives the repetition of) that self-administration behavior. *Reinforcement of repetitious self-administration behavior is one of the pharmacological properties of these drugs,* apparently mediated in the brain at least in part by the catecholamine-containing medial forebrain bundle and its connections in the ventral tegmental area and nucleus accumbens. Through this mechanism of reinforcement, the drug drives the user to repeat compulsively the self-administration of the drug, and this neuropharmacologic driving of behavior can occur even when the drug no longer produces euphoric feelings.

Another animal study supports the view that passive exposure to a drug does not promote drug-seeking, whereas systematic presentation of the drug after some self-initiated behavior will do so. Self-administration behavior was studied by Drs. J. R. Weeks and R. J. Collins in a one-week test period in which rats could press a lever to obtain morphine injections. For three weeks before the test, one group of rats had the opportunity to use the apparatus to inject themselves with morphine. In those three pretest weeks, another group of rats received automatically timed injections of morphine in comparable doses, without any opportunity for lever pressing. An additional group of rats had no prior experience with the drug until the test period. In the test week animals with prior exposure to the lever and the drug quickly resumed self-administration, and animals with no prior drug experience gradually learned to press the lever to obtain morphine injections. But those rats which passively had received automatic injections for three weeks avoided the lever during the test, pressing *less* frequently than those with no prior drug exposure. Thus, passive exposure did not enhance drug-seeking. Abused drugs drive organisms to repeat behaviors which previously had preceded the arrival of the drug into the brain; that process is *pharmacologic reinforcement*.

Reinforcement in Humans. We are now in a better position to understand why "drug craving" or "drug hunger" apparently does not result from repeated passive exposures to the drug. The pain of some terminally ill patients requires enough morphine to produce physical dependence upon the drug, which often is injected on a regular schedule by a hospital nurse. But these patients do not appear to be obsessed with thoughts of the drug, nor to "crave" or actively seek it. But outpatients with prescriptions to *self-administer* injectible morphine more frequently appear to develop pernicious drug-seeking behavior. This develops when a *personal* act of self-administration is quickly followed by the arrival of the drug at certain brain sites. The drug then reinforces the *self-administration* behavior, meaning that it activates brain mechanisms which increase the likelihood that the behavior will recur.

Physicians have only three methods for reducing the effect of pharmacologic reinforcement among patients attempting to give up drug abuse. First, narcotic antagonists such as naltrexone competitively block opioid receptors, so that a heroin injection no longer exerts its pharmacologic effects, including the reinforcing effect. The second method employs methadone, an opioid agonist with many morphine-like effects. Methadone maintenance treatment, described more fully later in this chapter, raises patients' tolerance to opioids so that the usual street-doses of heroin are too small to exert much reinforcing effect; heroin use then tends to taper off. Third, nicotine-containing chewing gum is analogous to methadone. Nicotine-dependent persons can obtain nicotine by chewing

the gum, thereby avoiding exposure to the toxic tars of tobacco smoke. Nicotine cigarettes are less reinforcing for patients who are already dosed with nicotine from the gum.

In a very mechanistic way, it appears that certain drugs neuropharmacologically "program" patients' brains, so that patients repeat the acts which previously had put those drugs into the body. This process of behavioral reinforcement, and our limited tools for reducing it, probably help to account for the high relapse rates which plague these patients.

Reinforcement by "Neutral" Stimuli. Neutral stimuli which have been associated regularly with drug reinforcement in the user's prior experience may themselves become reinforcers for drug-using behaviors. For example, Dr. Travis Thompson trained a monkey to press a lever to obtain morphine injections. A light also flashed during the injections. Thus, the monkey associated the reinforcing effects of morphine entering the body with the flashing light. Eventually, morphine injections were discontinued, but the light still flashed whenever the animal pressed the lever. The experiment continued for two more months, and the monkey pressed frequently every day, obtaining only the flashing light and no drug. Apparently, after the prolonged association of the light with the sensations of the injections, the light itself became sufficiently reinforcing to maintain lever pressing. A similar process may underlie the strange "needle freak" behavior of some drug abusers. For example, a scientist who was very knowledgeable about chemistry used amphetamines intravenously. He maintained a stock solution, which he carefully diluted for each injection. After finally exhausting the stock solution, he washed saline into the bottle to obtain the lingering traces of amphetamine, and he injected the saline wash. He repeated these washings and injections several times a day for several weeks, despite his knowledge that essentially no amphetamine remained in the bottle. The visual and tactile stimuli of drawing up the wash solution, putting on a tourniquet, placing a needle in the vein, and depressing the plunger had been associated for so long with amphetamine reinforcement that these stimuli themselves apparently reinforced the scientist's continuing injections even in the absence of the drug. As with the monkey looking at the flashing light, stimuli long associated with drug reinforcement maintained the scientist's self-administration behavior although the drug no longer was available.

Negative Reinforcement. Laymen equate "negative reinforcement" with punishment, but behavioral scientists apply the term to situations in which a behavior is reinforced by the organism's escape from, or avoidance of a noxious, aversive condition. Although many people abuse drugs without experiencing euphoria and relief from unhappiness, some people do appear to use drugs to avoid aversive, destructive, or empty life circumstances. For example, some patients report that they use alcohol or other sedative drugs to become "blotto," in an attempt to blot out their awareness of degrading or humiliating or depressing life situations. Perceiving their lives as repetitive, boring, and dull, other people welcome any novel, drug-induced changes in feelings, perceptions, or thoughts. The effect may be comparable to a short vacation; the user temporarily experiences a "change in the scenery." Indeed, this seeking of altered experiences may be the principle reason for the use of hallucinogenic drugs, which in animal studies do not pharmacologically reinforce self-administration behavior. Users' descriptions of the hallucinogenic drug experience as "a trip" may support the view that hallucinogens, like vacations, are taken mostly to provide some variety and novelty in a boring or depressing life situation.

Nevertheless, the importance of aversive environments may have been overemphasized in earlier theories of substance abuse, which hypothesized that improvements in unhappy life circumstances would lead users to abandon drugs. In fact for many, substance abuse is not a *solution* to unhappiness; it is instead the principle *source* of unhappiness. Moreover, it seems unlikely that the third of adult Americans who smoke tobacco have lives markedly unhappier than those of nonsmokers. Aversive life circumstances probably do contribute to substance abuse behavior and should be considered in treatment plans for substance abusers, but physicians now rarely attempt to induce abstinence by first trying to improve patients' mood states or their aversive environments. The first step usually is to bring about abstinence by the other approaches described here. The patients' mood and environmental relationships almost always improve, and any continuing conflicts or problems can then be addressed with counseling and psychotherapy.

The aversiveness of the *withdrawal* or *abstinence syndrome* requires special comment. Different drugs produce different withdrawal states (these will be discussed later in this chapter and also in the next chapter on organic mental disorders). Resumed use of the missing drug reduces the uncomfortable abstinence symptoms, rapidly in the case of opioids and more slowly with general depressants. When a user becomes physically dependent, and discovers that taking the drug now stops the abstinence syndrome, the onset of any withdrawal symptoms may promote further drug use. The drug's termination of that aversive withdrawal state then obviously adds to the total reinforcing effect of the drug. But, as already noted, people and animals without physical dependence will repeatedly and harmfully self-administer drugs, and therefore physical dependence in and of itself can no longer be invoked as the sole cause of compulsive drug use. The major cause appears to be pharmacologic reinforcement.

The Risk-Taking User

Even where pharmacologically reinforcing drugs are acceptable and easily available, not everyone abuses those drugs. For example, surveys indicate that in a recent year only about two-thirds of adult Americans had used any alcohol, and only about 10% reported experiencing alcohol-related life problems. What distinguishes those who become substance abusers from those who do not? Is it personal psychopathology that leads some people to abuse drugs? Despite references in the early psychiatric and psychoanalytic literature to the psychopathology of "the addictive personality," it is now evident that no one psychopathological syndrome is common to all drug abusers. Indeed, many abusers of drugs show little psychopathology beyond their destructive drug use. Although many other abusers do show major psychopathology, especially personality disorders and depressive disorders, such disorders may be the product, rather than the cause, of a lifetime of addiction. As Dr. George Vaillant concludes from his 40 year follow-up study of male college students: "I would not deny the importance of psychopathology in the genesis of alcoholism, but would instead emphasize the importance of alcohol abuse in the genesis of psychopathology . . . The average alcoholic does not drink as an adult because his childhood was unhappy and he was unusually anxious. Rather, he is unhappy and anxious in adulthood as a result of his past alcohol abuse."

But in other studies of people before and after the development of drug abuse problems, one characteristic does emerge: Risk-takers seem more likely than others to become substance abusers, or stated differently, those who cautiously refrain from chancy, risky activities are unlikely to abuse drugs. In one such study alcoholics who averaged 34 years of age had routinely taken psychological tests in college an average of 13 years earlier (before they developed serious alcohol problems). Those tests were compared with randomly-selected tests from other students of the same era. The scores showed no true maladjustment or psychopathology that distinguished the prealcoholic students from the others, but the prealcoholics were much *more* likely to agree with such statements as: "In school I was sometimes sent to the principal for cutting up ... Most people will use somewhat unfair means to gain profit or an advantage rather than to lose it ... Most people are honest chiefly through fear of being caught ... If I could get into a movie without paying and be sure I was not seen I would probably do it ... I can remember 'playing sick' to get out of something ... My parents have often objected to the kind of people I went around with ... In a group of people I would not be embarrassed to be called upon to start a discussion or give an opinion about something I know well." The prealcoholics were much *less* likely than their classmates to say: "I go to church almost every week." The prealcoholics emerge as being more impulsive, less conforming, and more gregarious than their classmates, but these characteristics were not strong enough to constitute true psychopathology.

One obviously must risk breaking society's rules to experiment with widely comdemned, illegal drugs, such as heroin. Even among those who experiment, some will respond to early signs of developing problems, or to the disapproval of friends and family, and desist from further use. But those most willing to continue a dangerous, chancy, risky activity may persist in using the drug until they are "hooked" fully by its reinforcing properties. So rule-breaking risk-takers appear more likely to become addicted to available but widely condemned drugs. Even with that least-disapproved and legal drug, tobacco, risk-takers apparently are more likely to use it,

and to use it heavily. Hans Eysenk developed a test to measure extraversion—a propensity toward taking chances, craving excitement, sticking one's neck out, acting impulsively on the spur of the moment, and being tempermental and aggressive. The converse, introversion, is a tendency to "look before you leap," to control feelings, and to distrust impulse. In studies of large numbers of people, despite considerable overlapping among groups, Eysenk found small but quite significant progressive increases in average extraversion scores from groups of nonsmokers to groups of light, and then to medium, and then to heavy smokers. Apparently, even with a drug which is not strongly condemned in a society, risk-takers are more likely than others to experiment with that drug and to become heavily involved with it. In keeping with the view that cigarette smokers may tend to be risk-takers is the observation that deaths of smokers by accident, violence, or suicide are about 20% above expected rates. But a risk-taking tendency is not per se a psychopathologic syndrome. It may even be an advantage, for example, to a professional soldier or a stock market investor.

People become risk-takers in many ways. For example, manic-depressive patients often show poor judgment, embark on risky enterprises, and drink alcohol excessively in their manic periods. Patients with antisocial personalities characteristically engage in dangerous or illegal activities, and such patients comprise about 15% of heroin addicts in recent studies of methadone-maintenance programs. Families and peer groups may also contribute to a risk-taking lack of restraint which facilitates drug involvement. For example, compared to nondrinking youths, teens who drink alcohol heavily sense less parental disapproval of drinking, more approval by peers for drinking, and a lack of parental affection and involvement. A propensity to take risks is revealed in the adolescent drinkers' other problems: precocious sexual activity, delinquency, use of marijuana and other drugs, truancy, and classroom misbehavior. Similarly, in neighborhoods where heroin was widely available, Dr. Isidor Chein compared youthful users and nonusers of the drug. The fathers of the users more frequently were absent from the family, or else hostile and nonsupportive. Users' families were less cohesive, and users more often had to assume adult responsibility prematurely. Thus, with the same neighborhood exposure to drugs, youths with more stable and supportive families were significantly less likely to risk heroin experimentation. It appears that in supportive, affectionate homes where appropriate limits are set, children learn attitudes of enlightened restraint and attention to self-care which are incompatible with extensive drug experimentation.

So for an available but widely condemned drug, people with the greatest and most deviant risk-taking propensity appear most likely to experiment with the drug, to persist in its use despite warnings and early signs of problems, and eventually to become "hooked" by the reinforcing properties of the drug. And even with a drug which is more condoned in a society, those who tend (for whatever reason) to take risks are more likely to use, and to abuse, that drug.

Accordingly, therapists of drug abusers often promote restraint, attention to self-care, and a reduction in risk-taking with such varied questions as, "Do you really think that action would be safe and good for you?"; "When did you last have a physical examination?"; or "Don't you think you're worth enough to look out for yourself and take care of yourself?"

Prior Drug Use

By definition, for a drug to be considered reinforcing, previous abusers of that drug must have a high likelihood of resuming that abuse. And indeed, many abstinent alcoholics and abusers of other drugs experience one or more relapses. A history of prior drug abuse definitely is associated with an increased risk of future drug abuse. Accordingly, physicians who seek "cures" among substance abusers may become frustrated or angry. A more reasoned and modest approach will be to assume that substance abuse is a chronic condition characterized by remissions and relapses, and therefore the physician should aim to prolong remissions and to limit the duration and harmful consequences of relapses.

Genetic Factors

As Dr. Reite has already indicated in Chapter 52A, genetic or other constitutional factors appear to make an important contribution to substance abuse behavior. Adoption studies show that, despite being raised apart from their biological families, the children of alcoholics are significantly more likely to develop alcoholism in adulthood then are the children of nonalcoholics. Thus, the well-known tendency for alcoholism to run in families is not due to learning alone, but probably involves genetic or other constitutional influences as well.

Unfortunately, at the present time we have little information on *what* is inherited by these potentially vulnerable children. It could be, for example, a greater risk-taking propensity, a nervous system more responsive to the reinforcing properties of alcohol, a reduced tendency to limit drinking as adverse physiological or psychological consequences develop, or some difference in how alcohol is metabolized. Some studies have favored a metabolic explanation, suggesting that tetrahydroisoquinolines formed during alcohol metabolism actually promote further drinking. But problems in replicating those findings have left the issue clouded in controversy. So while genetic (or other inborn constitutional) factors contribute to the risk that a given person will become alcoholic, the mechanism by which that occurs remains unidentified.

Genetics also may influence tobacco smoking. Significantly more twins both smoke, or both abstain, among monozygotic (identical) twin pairs, than among dizygotic (fraternal) twin pairs. The greater concordance, or similarity, in smoking behavior among identical twins suggests a genetic contribution to the probability that a person will become a smoker. The long-term hope in such genetic research would be to find "markers" which identify children at high risk, so that they could receive appropriate preventive education and counseling.

Sex

Males outnumber females among substance abusers. Recent surveys show, for example, that about 57% of cigarette smokers and about two-thirds of heavy drinkers of alcohol are males. Similar ratios hold for most abused drugs in the United States, although females may achieve or pass parity in the abuse of medically prescribed sedatives and analgesics. Although we know that boys are more likely than girls to become substance abusers, we do not know whether this difference results from greater societal strictures against drug use by women, or because women generally engage less often in risky activities, or because of other unknown influences.

Social and Pharmacologic Punishment of Drug Use

The adverse consequences of drug abuse often develop too late, or with insufficient certainty, to deter further use effectively; the remote threat of late-life lung cancer, for example, may not keep an adolescent from smoking tobacco. To be effective in reducing drug abuse, punishment should be immediate and certain. But punishment in the criminal justice system is neither immediate nor certain. Before purchasing cocaine a modern user can reassure himself that the odds of being caught are not great, and that even if one is caught, appeals, plea bargains, and other maneuvers may delay or eliminate any punishment. Unable to respond with immediate and certain punishment, governments sometimes rely instead on drastic punishments for drug abuse; in the past tobacco smokers in Japan were threatened with death, and in Russia with terrible beatings. Nevertheless, the use of tobacco spread in those two countries, as elsewhere. But more immediate and predictable punishment, which need not be drastic, *is* a deterrent. For instance, drug-abusing physicians take drugs dramatically less often when they know that they will have to produce frequent urine samples, and that they will lose their medical licenses immediately if any sample contains drugs.

Patients sometimes voluntarily arrange for such rapid and certain *social punishment* (punishment from others) to be applied in treatment, in order to deter themselves from further drug use. In a treatment called *contingency contracting*, patients may hire therapists to monitor urine samples and to apply an agreed-upon punishment (such as forfeiture of a large sum of money) if the patient produces any drug-containing urine. Such arrangements appear effective for inducing a period of abstinence, during which other treatments may be initiated. To motivate drug-using patients to enter treatment and become abstinent, doctors sometimes arrange dramatic confrontations between the patient and others. In such meetings a spouse may tell an alcoholic patient that, unless treatment begins and drinking stops, the spouse will leave. At the same time the alcoholic's employer may state that the patient will be fired unless those same changes occur. Drug abusers commonly fear the long-term marital and job consequences

of their drug use; making these long-term consequences much more immediate through confrontational meetings is not without risk. But, such interventions have motivated many drug abusers to begin treatment, providing another example of the judicious use of social punishment in treating drug abusers.

Disulfiram (Antabuse) provides a somewhat comparable *pharmacologic punishment*. A disulfiram-treated alcoholic patient becomes very ill immediately upon drinking alcohol. The illness punishes concurrent use of alcohol and disulfiram, and patients usually stop taking one or the other of the drugs. Unfortunately, it is not uncommon that they stop using disulfiram first, so that they can resume using alcohol.

Modeling and Social Reinforcement of Drug-Incompatible Behavior

If the coach of a high-school sports team says, "Students who drink alcohol cannot play on this team," and if the coach has reasonably effective means for discovering who drinks, then the alcohol-drinking student has to choose between the social rewards of that sport, versus the social and pharmacologic rewards of alcohol. Under these circumstances a student cannot have both; the two are incompatible. The coach and other team members teach the student how to play the sport—they model the behavior. The cheers of the crowd and the camaraderie of the team socially reinforce the activity and make it attractive. The student must then decide between alcohol and the sport. Employee assistance programs apply this principle of choice widely in the workplace. Such programs of companies and unions identify substance abusers through deficient work performance and then require improved performance. Unless improvement occurs (which generally means that the worker has entered treatment and become abstinent), the worker will be fired. The attractive, rewarding job is made incompatible with continued abuse of alcohol or other drugs, requiring a choice by the worker.

SPECIFIC DRUG SYNDROMES

Polydrug Abuse

Although most of this section describes the effects of individual classes of drugs, physicians now recognize that many substance abusers use multiple drugs. Marijuana and alcohol are commonly combined, and many alcoholics also are heavy smokers of tobacco. Alcoholics appear to be especially prone to develop problems with other general depressant drugs. Heroin abusers often also have serious alcohol problems, and when heroin is in short supply, these people may shift to nonopioid drugs. A user of stimulants may take depressants to "come down." Thus, physicians caring for drug-abusing patients should carefully assess the patients' full pattern of drug use.

Tobacco

Tobacco is the most widely abused drug in the United States. About a third of adult Americans use tobacco, and all doses appear to increase health problems. The Surgeon General of the United States reports that one pack of cigarettes per day reduces the life expectancy of a young man by approximately four years; two packs per day reduce it by approximately eight years. Lung cancer, very rare among nonsmokers, is much more frequent among smokers. Other health problems associated with tobacco smoking include cardiovascular disease, peptic ulcer, reduced birthweight in the children of smoking mothers, bronchitis, emphysema, and oral and laryngeal cancers.

Tobacco smoking has been accepted widely in our society, and until recently there have been few social controls on the use of this drug. Indeed, a powerful industry advertises and lobbies to expand this form of drug abuse. Paradoxically, while the United States government pays other countries to destroy fields of marijuana or opium poppies, exportable but lethal American tobacco receives Federal crop supports.

Tobacco smoke apparently has few behavioral effects aside from reinforcing its own self-administration; that is, the drug's main behavioral effect is to increase the probability of further smoking. Thus, there is no immediate intoxication syndrome, and the adverse health consequences develop very slowly. The relative absence of immediate adverse consequences no doubt has contributed to the view that tobacco smoking was not drug abuse. But tobacco's profoundly adverse effects, now clear, erase any doubt that the use of this drug in any dose must be considered drug abuse.

Alcohol

According to the National Council on Alcoholism, there are more than 100 million persons over the age of 15 in this country who are consumers of alcohol. Of these, an estimated 10 million suffer from alcoholism. Alcoholism is clearly the most serious of all drug problems in terms of loss of productivity (approximately 25 billion dollars annually), the total human tragedy, the extent of physical damage to the body, and the number of fatalities from withdrawal symptoms as a result of the development of tolerance and physical dependence. The statistics are awesome: 50% of all fatal automobile accidents in this country involve alcohol, 65% of murders, 35% of rapes, 30% of suicides, 40% of all assaults, and 60% of cases of child abuse. When alcoholism is treated, associated violent behavior decreases. The suicide rate of alcoholics is nearly 60 times that of nonalcoholics, and the overall death rate of alcoholics is two and one half times higher than the rest of the population. The number of known women alcoholics has doubled since World War II, and an estimated 3.3 million teenagers are showing signs of early alcoholism.

We have already discussed the various questions that may be helpful in eliciting a history of alcohol or other drug abuse. For patients who may be reluctant to admit openly that they have a problem, it may be useful to give a questionnaire, such as the Michigan Alcohol Screening Test (MAST) for the patients to answer in the privacy of their own homes; they can score the test themselves and decide whether or not they have an alcohol problem. One example was an attorney, about to be fired by his firm unless he controlled his drinking, who steadfastly denied any drinking problem; he had the notion that an alcoholic must be someone who drank more than he did. After taking home the MAST to score himself, he returned, ready to accept the fact that he did indeed have a problem, and entered into treatment.

Many people are unable to admit that they have an alcohol problem when they are first confronted, but may come back later if they recognize that the physician is willing to discuss the problem with them in a nonjudgmental manner. Usually it takes some crisis to make a person believe that he or she is an alcoholic, such as a spouse deciding to end the marriage, the threat of being fired from a job, an arrest for drunken driving, or the diagnosis of liver impairment. What does the physician do when the patient is ready to acknowledge that he or she has a drinking problem? We begin by obtaining the detailed history which we described earlier. Note that one question which we do *not* ask is "Why do you drink?" Some alcoholics may indefinitely postpone dealing with the fact that they *are* drinking excessively while they engage in a search for elusive "causes." For these particular individuals, psychotherapy to understand the "whys" of their behavior may be useful, but usually only *after* they achieve sobriety through other treatment modalities.

The next step is to recognize that alcoholic patients can be motivated for treatment. Doctors who have labored on a medical ward with a patient hemorrhaging from esophageal varices secondary to alcoholic cirrhosis, transfusing unit after unit of blood to save his life, only to see him return to drink within hours after his discharge, will understandably see the alcoholic as "unmotivated." There is no question that alcoholic patients make great use of the psychological defense mechanism of denial, that it takes time for them to acknowledge that they have a problem and even longer for them to want to do something about the problem, and that some alcoholics seem unwilling ever to give up drinking. But numerous studies have shown that it is simply not true that alcoholics in general are "unmotivated" for treatment. As a group, alcoholics tend to be ashamed of their drinking and very sensitive to rejection and they are not, therefore, likely to become involved in a program where they do not feel welcome. Dr. Morris Chafetz has shown how the simple measure of assigning an individual to act as "ombudsman" for the alcoholic during his stay in the emergency room, explaining to him what was happening and assuring him that he had a place to go when he left, increased from 1% to 65% the number of alcoholic patients following through on a referral to the alcoholic clinic. Other studies have shown that similar measures such as follow-up letters or phone calls or the elimination of waiting lists have resulted in marked increases in the number of alcoholic patients utilizing treatment facilities.

Ample evidence is now accumulating that not only can the alcoholic be motivated for treatment, but also that he or she can profit from that treatment. About one-third of alcoholics in treatment stop drinking entirely, another one-third show marked improvement in their drinking, and one-third show no improvement. Improvement in drinking leads to improvement in other areas of life, such as work and family. Those individuals who drop out of a treatment program, even if they feel they are doing well and have the problem mastered, are more apt to relapse than those who maintain contact with the program, whether it be in a medical or psychiatric setting or a self-help program such as Alcoholics Anonymous. Many alcoholics will have to make repeated attempts to stop drinking before they ultimately do so. Dr. Richard Fox has described a skid row detoxification program with an open-door policy permitting the alcoholic to return to dry out as often as necessary. Although the only goal of the program was to provide medical detoxification, and although no pressure was put on the patient to change his or her drinking behavior, nevertheless a third of this group was able to attain a sustained period of sobriety. When one realizes that these patients represented perhaps the most difficult portion of the alcoholic population to treat because they were hard-core, skid row alcoholics with virtually nothing going in their favor, the results are all the more impressive.

It is also important to recognize the necessity of individualizing the treatment program for every alcoholic patient. Some may be able to utilize outpatient facilities, but others will need to be hospitalized and enter into various inpatient rehabilitation programs. In the long-term treatment of alcoholism, it is also useful to appreciate the fact that alcoholism is a chronic disease, marked by periods of remission and exacerbation, such as one would see in a patient with chronic heart disease, diabetes, or multiple sclerosis. The physician needs to understand that at times of stress the patient may return to drinking. The danger at the time of relapse is that the physician may get angry at the patient, or may feel guilty for not having been a better doctor. It is crucial that the physician set realistic goals in the treatment of the alcoholic. If we can keep in mind that the patient may not have had even one day of sobriety in the past year, then even a week of sobriety may be a considerable accomplishment early in treatment.

The patient may regard a return to drinking

as a setback, a failure, or a sign of moral weakness and lack of willpower. The doctor should avoid such moral judgments and handle the relapse as would be done with any chronic illness. It may even be a useful opportunity to review with the patient what may have precipitated the drinking, with an eye to learning different ways to cope with such stresses in the future. The patient's shame at returning to alcohol is common, and it is often necessary to reach out to get patients back into treatment at such times. Physicians who have patience and are available and nonjudgmental at times of crisis will serve their patients well. It is important for physicians to realize that not all of their patients will recover, but neither should they be discouraged from working with alcoholics because of a false pessimism about the prognosis.

Finally, the physician should not attempt to work in isolation in treating alcoholic patients. Alcohol treatment programs are available through most mental health centers, and Alcoholics Anonymous chapters exist everywhere, as do Al-Anon chapters for the spouses of alcoholics and Al-A-Teen chapters for the children of alcoholics. These self-help groups provide tremendous support for the patients and their families during a difficult period in their lives.

Other General Depressant Drugs

The barbiturates, the nonbarbiturate sedative-hypnotics such as methaqualone (Quaalude), ethchlorvynol (Placidyl), or meprobamate (Miltown), and the benzodiazepines such as chlordiazepoxide (Librium) or diazepam (Valium) are, like alcohol, general depressant drugs, and continued use leads to the development of tolerance and physical dependence.

General depressant drugs usually are taken orally but may be injected intravenously. Street users may purchase the drugs illegally on the black market, but occasionally they are obtained in "doctor-shopping" visits to multiple doctors, or from an unethical "script doc" who literally sells prescriptions. The general depressant *intoxication syndrome* resembles that of alcohol, with confusion (impaired cognition), lethargy (decreased level of activity and consciousness), and ataxia (motor incoordination). Higher doses produce coma, respiratory depression, and death. The alcohol and general depressant *abstinence syndrome* may be life threatening, and Dr. Glickman will describe this syndrome further in the next chapter.

Opioid Drugs

Opioid drugs such as morphine, heroin, methadone, codeine, meperidine (Demerol), and hydromorphone (Dilaudid) all activate opioid receptors in the central nervous system. These drugs are taken orally, intravenously, by intranasal insufflation, and sometimes by smoking. Of the opioid drugs, heroin probably is most widely abused; it is estimated that there are several hundred thousand American heroin users. Since heroin is not used medically in the United States, the entire supply is smuggled into this country. Heroin abusers are usually of lower socioeconomic status and commonly are found in economically depressed, inner city areas. Opioid-abusing physicians, nurses, pharmacists, and other health professionals with access to legal opioids more commonly abuse morphine, meperidine, hydromorphone, or one of the other opioids used in therapy.

Injection of an opioid drug produces a pleasant, dreamy mental state, alternating motor stimulation or motor suppression, miosis, constipation, and some loss of interest in events. High doses cause confusion, lethargy, and ataxia, and eventually induce coma, respiratory depression, and death, as do the general depressant drugs. Continued opioid use leads to physical dependence, and drug withdrawal produces nausea and vomiting, diarrhea, "goose flesh," mydriasis, chills, and muscle aches. However, the opioid withdrawal syndrome is never fatal unless there are other complications. It is not a medical emergency, and it compares in severity to "the flu." Physically dependent heroin users must "shoot up" every four to eight hours to avoid withdrawal symptoms. During those few hours they must spend some time "nodding" or "coasting," get the money for the next injection (this may cost $100 to $200 per day), find a dealer and purchase more of the drug, and prepare for the next injection. This schedule usually renders heroin use incompatible with most traditional jobs and family life.

In recent years, government-sponsored clinics have provided methadone to opioid users. Unlike heroin, methadone retains much of its activity after oral administration, and it has a much longer serum half-life. Therefore, one daily oral dose of methadone prevents abstinence, and the drug's relatively slow absorption from the gastrointestinal tract avoids the peak blood levels which produce nodding. But patients in methadone maintenance treatment remain physically dependent upon opioid drugs, and they still feel some opioid "high." Therefore, the treatment often is criticized for "merely substituting one drug for another." But methadone is subject to rigorous quality control, is taken orally instead of by nonsterile injection, permits patients to resume more normal social relations and work because they no longer rapidly alternate from "coasting" to abstinence, and is dispensed by health professionals rather than criminals, at a cost which does not require such illegal activities as burglary or prostitution. These advantages also make patients available for rehabilitation, and some 80,000 Americans are now in methadone maintenance treatment.

There also is wide interest in opioid antagonists for reducing opioid abuse. The antagonists tie up opioid receptors without activating them, thereby blocking heroin's access to the receptors. Naltrexone, an opioid antagonist which can be taken orally every two to three days, has almost no physiological or behavioral effect of its own. But because naltrexone blocks opioid receptors for several days, it also blocks the effects of street heroin during that time. An estimated 10% of heroin abusers, who are well motivated but who intermittently are exposed to the persuasion of heroin-using friends, find naltrexone useful in staying free of opioids; when tempted, they know that the reinforcing effects of heroin are unavailable to them.

Stimulant Drugs

Recent years have seen an explosion of cocaine use. About 20% of young Americans (ages 18–25) used the drug in 1982 alone, and it is suggested that sales by America's cocaine smugglers would rank their industry in size between the Ford Motor and Gulf Oil corporations. The drug is insufflated ("snorted") into the nose, injected intravenously, or smoked in a chemically derived "free-base" preparation which survives high, volatilizing temperatures better than does the more common hydrochloride salt.

As with other stimulant drugs (and in contrast to alcohol, the other general depressants, and the opioid drugs) cocaine intoxication results in euphoria and hyperalertness, restlessness, hyperactivity, and, in higher doses, seizures, respiratory depression, or paranoid thinking which may resemble acute paranoid schizophrenia. Irritability, unpredictability, and moodiness com-

plicate the social interactions of these patients. Anorexia (loss of appetite) commonly occurs, and high-dose users may undergo severe weight loss. Intravenous use may lead either to chemical or infectious hepatitis, and some users have lost limbs by accidentally injecting stimulants into an artery rather than a vein. Social, financial, and vocational disruptions are very common among cocaine abusers, some of whom spend as much as $150,000 per year on the drug. A periarteritis-like vascular disease and cerebrovascular strokes sometimes follow prolonged or high-dose cocaine or amphetamine use. If the stimulant abruptly is withdrawn after high-dose and continued use, the abstinence syndrome is uncomfortable but not life threatening. It is characterized by fatigue, prolonged sleep (especially excessive REM sleep), overeating with weight gain, and emotional depression. The depression (sometimes a cause for the initial use of these euphoriant drugs) may lead to resumed use, and the vicious cycle continues.

Because these abstinence signs are relatively mild, cocaine abusers may reassure one another that the drug is not "addicting." On the other hand, cocaine is highly reinforcing in animal studies. Monkeys will self-administer cocaine until they die in status epilepticus during free-access experiments. People also report a very compelling reinforcement by the drug, often saying that they cannot stop using it even when tolerance has eliminated most of the positive effects. Therapists find users of cocaine and other stimulants difficult to treat, probably because these drugs are so reinforcing of self-administration behavior; users frequently relapse and drop out of treatment. Cocaine's adverse effects are limited by its availability and cost, but it is extremely disruptive for those with regular access to it.

The amphetamines, dextroamphetamine (Dexedrine), methamphetamine (Methedrine), and several other drugs with amphetamine-like actions produce effects quite similar to those of cocaine, although their duration of action is more prolonged. They are commonly used by the oral route, although intravenous "speed" use still occurs among some "street people."

The caffeine in coffee, tea, and cola drinks is a mild stimulant. It reinforces animal self-administration behavior. But caffeine use does not usually meet our definition of drug abuse, because usually it does not produce problems. However, some individuals, drinking 20 cups or more of coffee per day, may suffer caffeine-induced anxiety, tremors, and restlessness. Caffeine also stimulates gastric acid secretion, which is dangerous for people with peptic ulcer disease. Thus, in selected persons, caffeine use does constitute drug abuse, and withdrawal may even be accompanied by "caffeine-withdrawal" headaches.

Hallucinogenic Drugs

These numerous drugs have diverse behavioral and physiological effects with widely differing mechanisms of action. Perhaps their only shared effect is the production of an "altered state of consciousness." This term implies altered perceptions with changed physical sensations, thinking, or affect.

Probably the most widely used hallucinogen now is delta-9-tetrahydrocannabinol (THC), the psychoactive agent in marijuana and other cannabis derivatives. In the United States, THC usually is taken by smoking parts of the marijuana plant, but more concentrated oils and resins from the plant sometimes are available, especially abroad. Illusions or hallucinations are rather uncommon with the less concentrated preparations. These produce giddiness with some impairment of short term memory, learning, problem-solving ability, and motor coordination in, for example, automobile driving. There is still some question as to whether THC lowers testosterone levels and sperm counts in males to the point of affecting growth and fertility. Recent studies suggest that THC may have some potential therapeutic effects in glaucoma, nausea resulting from cancer-chemotherapy drugs, and bronchial asthma. But the latter is more than outweighed by evidence of chronic pulmonary disease among chronic marijuana users. Marijuana smoke is even more irritating to the lungs than tobacco smoke, and a recent report from the National Institute on Drug Abuse indicated that smoking less than one "joint" per day decreases the vital capacity of the lungs as much as smoking 16 tobacco cigarettes per day. There is no apparent withdrawal syndrome from THC as it is used in the United States. The drug does not reinforce self-administration behavior in animals, and users generally seem able to discontinue marijuana if they find that it is causing problems for them. We suspect that social reinforcement, and the association of the drug with good times and pleasant friends, may play more of a role than phar-macological reinforcement in marijuana's current wide use in the United States.

"PCP" (*PeaCe Pill*) is a street term for phencyclidine, an experimental anesthetic agent which was not marketed for human use because it produced frequent psychoses. The drug seemed free of adverse effects in some animals, however, and it was used extensively in veterinary medicine. The drug, also called Angel Dust, is synthesized rather easily by amateur chemists, and the same mental changes which led to its medical disuse make it attractive to street people, who take it orally, smoked on tobacco or marijuana, or by injection. The effects of low doses in human beings are subject to some speculation at this time, but high-dose intoxication produces delirium with confusion and disorientation, hallucinations, delusions, strange posturing and possibly extrapyramidal motor abnormalities, perseveration of speech, unpredictable and at times dangerous aggressive behavior, hypertension, seizures, and coma. Prolonged psychoses resembling schizophrenia or psychotic depression may occur. PCP reinforces self-administration behavior in animals. There is no clear evidence at the present time for an abstinence syndrome following the use of this drug.

LSD (*d*-lysergic acid), or "acid," is an unusually potent drug, effective in doses as low as 200 micrograms. It induces perceptual changes and illusions, interpreted by different people either as mind-expanding or terrifying. The LSD intoxication syndrome will be described in more detail by Dr. Glickman in the next chapter. The drug usually is taken orally, and its effects last several hours. It does not reinforce self-administration behavior in animals, and most human users take it only infrequently. A few people, however, take the drug daily; they become tolerant to its effects, and no abstinence syndrome occurs upon withdrawal. Regular daily use is uncommon, and the failure of animals to self-administer the drug suggests that this is due to the drug's lack of pharmacologically reinforcing properties.

Atropine-like belladonna alkaloids and other psychoactive compounds occur in a number of plants which sometimes are ingested for their hallucinogenic effects. These include, among others, nutmeg, Morning Glory seeds, fly-agaric mushrooms, Angel's Trumpet flowers, Jimson (or Jamestown) weeds, and peyote cacti (Mescaline). In addition to altered perceptions, illusions, and hallucinations, these plant drugs also may produce nausea, vomiting, cardiac irregularities, convulsions, and coma. But American Indians carefully have ritualized controlled doses of peyote into the ceremonies of their Native American Church.

Nonnarcotic Analgesic Drugs

Aspirin, phenacetin, and acetaminophen are abused with surprising frequency in a manner that may be of considerable medical importance. In a study in our psychiatric hospital, patients without chronic inflammatory diseases ingested at home an average of 6.3 grams per month, and those with neurotic diagnoses averaged nearly 11 grams per month, of these drugs. Continued use of these nonnarcotic analgesics may damage the kidneys. These analgesic drugs do not reinforce self-administration behavior in animals, and only rarely do patients say that they feel much better after using the drugs, whereas such reports are common with those drugs which vigorously reinforce self-administration behavior in animals. These users have appeared to us to be rather dependent persons who express considerable concern for their physical health and seem to be relieved by medical interventions, including pill taking, aimed at relieving physical discomforts. Analgesic withdrawal does not appear to produce an abstinence syndrome.

CONCLUSION

Substance abuse is probably the most common behavioral problem in medical practice. Numerous factors contribute to the probability that a given person will or will not abuse a particular drug. Physicians who are knowledgeable about the many etiological factors in substance abuse, and who can understand the similarities and differences in the abuse of various drugs, will be in a position to identify substance abuse problems among their patients, and to either treat or refer for treatment those among their patients with drug problems.

Suggested Readings

Bean MH, Zinberg NE (eds): *Dynamic Approaches to The Understanding and Treatment of Alcoholism.* New York, Free Press, 1981.

Cohen S: *The Substance Abuse Problems.* New York, The Haworth Press, 1981.

Senay EC: *Substances Abuse Disorders in Clinical Practice.* Boston, John Wright-PSG, Inc, 1983.

Vaillant GE: *The Natural History of Alcoholism: Causes, Patterns, and Paths to Recovery.* Cambridge, MA, Harvard University Press, 1983.

References

Angrist BM, et al: Banana smoking. *NY State J Med* 67:2983, 1967.

Bean M: Alcoholics Anonymous. *Psychiatric Ann* 5:45 and 83, 1975.

Bozarth MA: Opiate reward mechanisms mapped by intracranial self-administration. In Smith JE, Lane JD (eds): *Neurobiology of Opiate Reward Processes.* Amsterdam, Elsevier/North-Holland Biomedical Press, 1983, p 331.

Braucht GN: Problem drinking among adolescents: a review and analysis of psychosocial research. In National Institute on Alcohol Abuse and Alcoholism, *Special Population Issues: Alcohol and Health Monograph No. 4,* Rockville, MD, 1981.

Chafetz ME, Blane HT, Hill MJ: *Frontiers of Alcoholism,* New York, Science House, 1970.

Chein I, et al: *The Road to H.* New York, Basic Books, 1964.

Cohen M, et al: Alcoholism: controlled drinking and incentives for abstinence. *Psychol Rep* 28:575, 1971.

Deneau G, Yanagita T, Seevers MH: Self-administration of psychoactive substances by the monkey. *Psychopharmacologia* 16:30, 1969.

Department of Health, Education, and Welfare Publication No. (PHS) 79-50066. *Smoking and Health.* Washington, DC, Government Printing Office, 1979.

Department of Health, Education, and Welfare Publication No. (ADM) 80-945. *Marihuana and Health Effects: 8th Annual Report to the United States Congress.* Washington, DC, US Government Printing Office, 1980.

Emrick CD: A review of psychologically oriented treatment of alcoholism. *Quart J Studies Alc I.* 35:532, 1974. II. 36:88, 1975.

Eysenck HJ: Personality and cigarette smoking. *Life Sci* 3:777, 1963.

Fox RP, Graham MD, Gill MJ: A therapeutic revolving door. *Arch Gen Psychiatry* 26:179, 1972.

Friberg L, et al: Smoking habits of monozygotic and dizygotic twins. *Br Med J* 1:1090, 1959.

Goodwin DW: Alcoholism and heredity. *Arch Gen Psychiatry* 36:57, 1979.

Goodwin DW, et al: Alcohol problems in adoptees raised apart from alcoholic biological parents. *Arch Gen Psychiatry* 28:238, 1973.

Iglauer C, Woods JH: Concurrent performances: reinforcement by different doses of intravenous cocaine in rhesus monkeys. *J Exp Anal Behav* 22:179, 1974.

Kammeier ML, Hoffmann H, Loper RG: Personality characteristics of alcoholics as college freshmen and at time of treatment. *Quart J Stud Alc* 34:390, 1973.

Kissin B, Begleiter H (eds): *The Biology of Alcoholism, Vol. I: Biochemistry* (1971). *Vol. II: Physiology of Behavior* (1972). *Vol. III: Clinical Pathology* (1973). *Vol. IV: Social Biology* (1976). *Vol. V: Treatment and Rehabilitation of the Chronic Alcoholic* (1977). New York, Plenum Press.

Kornetsky C, et al: Intracranial self-stimulation thresholds: a model for the hedonic effects of drugs of abuse. In *Problems of Drug Dependence 1978.* Committee on Problems of Drug Dependence, Inc, 1979, p 462.

Krasnegor NA (ed): *Cigarette Smoking as a Dependence Process.* NIDA Research Monograph 23, DHEW Publication No. (ADM) 79-800. Washington, DC, US Government Printing Office, 1979.

Levine DG: "Needle freaks": compulsive self-injection by drug users. *Am J Psychiatry* 131:297, 1974.

Loper RG, Kammeier ML, Hoffman H: MMPI characteristics of college freshman males who later became alcoholics. *J Abnormal Psych* 82:159, 1973.

MacAndrew C, Edgerton RB: *Drunken Comportment: A Social Explanation.* Chicago, Aldine, 1969.

Murray RM, Timbury GC, Linton AL: Analgesic abuse in psychiatric patients. *Lancet* 1:1303, 1970.

Myers RD, Melchior CL: Alcohol drinking: abnormal intake

caused by tetrahydropapaveroline in brain. *Science* 196:554, 1977.

Petersen RC, Stillman RC (eds): *PCP Phencyclidine Abuse*: *An Appraisal*. NIDA Research Monograph 21, DHEW Publication No. (ADM) 79-728. Washington, DC, US Government Printing Office, 1979.

Raaschow-Nielsen E: Smoking habits in twins. *Dan Med Bull* 7:82, 1960.

Selzer ML: The Michigan alcoholism screening test. *Am J Psychiatry* 127:1653, 1971.

Solm H: Alcoholism in Europe. In Seixas FA, Eggleston S (eds): *Works in Progress on Alcoholism. Ann NY Acad Sci* 273:24, 1976.

Stein L: Chemistry of reward and punishment. In Efron DH (ed): *Psychopharmacology: A Review of Progress 1957–1967*. Public Health Service Publication No. 1836. Washington, DC, US Government Printing Office, 1968, p 105.

Thompson T, Bigelow G, Pickens R: Environmental variables influencing drug self-administration. In Thompson T, Pickens R (eds): *Stimulus Properties of Drugs*. New York, Appleton-Century-Crofts, 1971, p 193.

Thompson T, Pickens R: An experimental analysis of behavioral factors in drug dependence. *Fed Proc* 34:1759, 1975.

Tinklenberg JR, et al: Drug involvement in criminal assaults by adolescents. *Arch Gen Psychiatry* 30:685, 1974.

Todd GF, Mason JI: Concordance of smoking habits in monozygotic and dizygotic twins. *Heredity* 13:417, 1959.

Vaillant GE: Natural history of male psychological health: VIII. Antecedents of alcoholism and "orality." *Am J Psychiatry* 137:181, 1980.

Weeks JR, Collins RJ: Factors affecting voluntary morphine intake in self-maintained addicted rats. *Psychopharmacologia* 6:267, 1964.

Winokur G, et al: Alcoholism: III. Diagnosis and familial psychiatric illness in 259 alcoholic probands. *Arch Gen Psychiatry* 23:104, 1970.

Winokur G, Rimmer J, Reich T: Alcoholism: IV. Is there more than one type of alcoholism? *Br J Psychiatry* 118:525, 1971.

Woods JH, Ikomi F, Winger G: The reinforcing property of ethanol. In Roach MK, McIsaac WM, Creaven PJ (eds): *Biological Aspects of Alcohol*. Austin, University of Texas Press, p 371.

Woods JH, Winger GD: Alcoholism and animals. *Prev Med* 3:49, 1974.

Woody GE, et al: Psychotherapy for opiate addicts-does it help? *Arch Gen Psychiatry* 40:639, 1983.

CHAPTER **67** # The Organic Brain Syndromes and the Organic Mental Disorders

Lewis Glickman, M.D.

DEFINITIONS

In DSM-III a distinction is made between *organic brain syndromes* and *organic mental disorders.* The term "organic brain syndrome" (OBS) refers to a constellation of objective signs and subjective symptoms without reference to etiology—for example, delirium, dementia, intoxication, withdrawal. The term "organic mental disorder" refers to a particular organic brain syndrome in which the etiology is known—for example, alcohol withdrawal delirium, multi-infarct dementia, substance-induced intoxication. The essential feature of all of these disorders is either a transient or a permanent dysfunction of the brain.

Brain neurons can be damaged or destroyed by either a primary disease of the brain or by a systemic illness that secondarily affects the brain. Thus, a long list of possible causes must always be considered: toxic substances, electrolyte imbalances, metabolic disorders, nutritional deficiencies, cardiovascular and cerebrovascular disorders, infectious diseases, cranial and extracranial neoplasms, and trauma. Regardless of the cause, when neurons are damaged but not destroyed, the resulting mental dysfunction is potentially reversible if the damaged neurons can be returned to normal function. When the neurons are destroyed, the resulting mental dysfunction is irreversible because dead neurons can neither be revived nor replaced. In the past, a reversible organic brain syndrome was called an *acute brain syndrome* (or *delirium*), and an irreversible organic brain syndrome was called a *chronic brain syndrome* (or *dementia*). However, equating acuteness with reversibility and chronicity with irreversibility has not always proven to be clinically warranted, and therefore this linkage has been abandoned in DSM-III. Acute and chronic are best used in their usual medical meaning, namely to refer to mode of onset and duration, and not to prognosis.

For example, potentially reversible brain syndromes may have a slow, insidious onset and a prolonged, chronic course. Examples can be seen in patients with slowly developing and persistent metabolic problems such as liver, kidney, or endocrine diseases. These patients are occasionally found in mental hospitals after they have been confined for months or years mistakenly diagnosed as suffering from schizophrenia or depression. Conversely, irreversible brain syndromes can be of sudden and acute onset, for example, brain damage due to lack of oxygen secondary to cardiac arrest. Every organic brain syndrome should, however, regardless of type of onset or duration, be considered to be potentially reversible until proven otherwise. It has been said that the potentially reversible causes of progressive intellectual deterioration probably represent the most commonly overlooked treatable medical conditions in America today.

SIGNS OF OBS AND DIFFERENTIAL DIAGNOSIS

What are the signs of organic brain syndrome, and how do these differ from the signs of the functional mental disorders? The distinction is extremely important since the treatment for each is quite different. In the treatment of functional mental disorders, although psychopharmacological medications may be used, we are not certain of the precise neurochemical or neuroendocrine disturbance which may be causing the disorder and therefore we do not know precisely how the medications correct the disturbance. In the treatment of the organic mental disorders, we try to restore a known biochemical or hormonal or anatomical imbalance, or treat a known toxic or infectious disease process.

In all organic brain syndromes, there is a *loss* of higher brain function. In addition, there may be *release* of lower functions, impulses, or emotions from control by higher centers. Signs or symptoms produced by loss of higher functions are called *negative* or *deficit* signs or symptoms. Signs or symptoms produced by release of lower functions, impulses, or emotions are called *positive* signs or symptoms because something appears which was not present before. This concept of positive and negative signs and symptoms was developed by Hughlings Jackson, a 19th century neurologist.

Functions are lost in the opposite sequence from which they were acquired in the life history both of the species and of the individual. The latest acquisition, both in the development of our species and in our individual development, is our *intellectual* or *cognitive function*. This is the first to be lost in organic brain syndrome. Just as left heart failure, regardless of etiology, causes a decreased ability to function physically, brain failure, regardless of etiology, causes a decreased ability to function intellectually. The presence of intellectual or cognitive deficit is generally both a necessary and a sufficient condition for the diagnosis of OBS to be made. Intellectual function is preserved in OBS only in diseases which involve areas of the brain which are not concerned with cognition; or in certain drug intoxications, endocrine disorders, and other extracranial diseases. For example, frontal lobe lesions produce changes solely in mood, judgment, and behavior. Steroids, reserpine, and pancreatic cancer can produce a clinical picture identical with a severe depression, whereas pheochromocytoma, hyperthyroidism, and excessive caffeine can produce symptoms of severe anxiety. Chronic and excessive use of amphetamines can produce a clinical picture identical to paranoid schizophrenia. These and other medical conditions that present with psychiatric symptoms have been discussed in Chapter 14C.

In spite of the above exceptions most patients with an OBS suffer from a cognitive impairment, and the presence of a cognitive impairment almost always indicates the presence of an OBS. Some depressed patients may appear to have a cognitive impairment, but in fact because of their depression they are too apathetic or uninterested to cooperate in tests of intellectual function. This has been called "depressive pseudodementia." After the depression is successfully treated, intellectual function can be seen to be intact. Some schizophrenic patients may also appear to have a cognitive impairment, but again this is rarely the case. The following story illustrates this point. A man gets a flat tire in front of a mental hospital. A patient watches him from behind the fence as the man takes off the tire and puts the lugs in the hubcap. Some boys come by and run away with the hubcap with the lugs in it. The man does not know how he can put his wheel back on. As he scratches his head in perplexity, not knowing what to do next, the patient, who was watching all this from behind the fence, says to him, "I have a suggestion. Why don't you take one lug off each of the other wheels and put it on the wheel with the flat and drive to the nearest gas station and get some more lugs there." The man says, "Why you're right. That's brilliant. You know I would have asked your advice but I thought you were a patient there at the hospital." The patient replies, "I am a patient. I may be crazy but I'm not stupid."

OBS is differentiated from mental retardation on the basis of the fact that in OBS there has been a *decrease* from a previously normal or superior level of intellectual function, while in mental retardation intellectual function was never normal.

Often *motor function* and *level of consciousness* are also impaired in OBS. Motor function tends to be lost after intellectual function, and level of consciousness or wakefulness after motor function. Decrease in motor function may manifest itself first as inability to perform fine movements accurately with the fingers and later may progress to inability to walk, stand, or sit up. Decrease in level of consciousness may progress from apathy to lethargy, somnolence, stupor, coma, and finally, death. This sequence may be seen in the person drinking alcohol. First there is mental confusion, recent memory loss, and poor social judgment, then difficulty with balance and slurred speech, and then stupor, coma, and death. This sequence may also be punctuated by episodes of sexual and aggressive behavior due to the breakdown of the patient's defenses against wishes and impulses on a psychological level and to the release of cortical inhibition of the limbic system on a physiological level.

The sequence of loss of cognition, then motor function, then level of consciousness, and finally death is based on the phylogenetic sequence of the brain structures which are depressed. Cognition is lost with the neocortex, the most recent addition to our brain. Motor function and coordination are lost with the motor cortex and cerebellum. Level of consciousness is based in the midbrain and is depressed when midbrain function is depressed. Finally, when the function of the oldest part of all, the medulla, is depressed, the respiratory center fails. If respiration is supported and the insult to brain function continues to progress, then the vasomotor center fails and the patient goes into hypotensive shock and dies, since our circulatory center is older than our respiratory center. For example, the blood level of barbiturates necessary to paralyze the circulatory center is double the level necessary to paralyze the respiratory center.

Cognitive defects, motor deficits, and decreased level of consciousness are negative signs. The presence of any of them indicates strongly that there is an organic etiology to the mental disorder regardless of whatever other signs may be present as well. If an organic brain syndrome is present, it may be a potentially correctable one that must be diagnosed relatively rapidly in order to prevent neuronal death. This would occur, for example, if anoxia or hypoglycemia were the cause of the neuronal damage. The physician, therefore, must always consider the possibility that mental dysfunction may be due to an organic condition.

Differential diagnosis between various organic brain syndromes, as well as between organic and functional mental disorders, may be confusing for several reasons. First of all, organic brain syndromes due to the same etiology may present with different signs and symptoms, whereas organic brain syndromes due to different etiologies may present with the same signs and symptoms. Second, many organic brain syndromes present with positive signs as well as negative signs. With organic insult to the brain, the patient's reality testing and defenses against impulses may begin to deteriorate, so that in addition to impairment in cognition, motor function, and consciousness, there may also be perceptual, affective, and behavioral abnormalities. These latter positive signs may or may not be present. Not every patient with organic brain syndrome will hallucinate or become delusional, assaultive, anxious, or depressed. These symptoms are more likely to occur in individuals whose reality testing or impulse control was somewhat unstable prior to the organic insult. When they do occur,

they are likely to lead to diagnostic difficulty, since positive signs involving breakthroughs of affects and impulses *may be identical* in both organic and functional disorders. Since they are more dramatic than the negative signs, they often mislead the physician into believing the patient has a functional psychiatric disorder. The physician's attitude toward the patient may also lead him into error if he loses his objectivity when confronted with positive signs which provoke fear or anger.

Affects and behavior which are unacceptable to the individual or to society tend to break out at the point where defenses are weakest. This was known to the Romans as "In Vino Veritas." This translates literally as, "There is truth in wine," meaning our true nature manifests itself when we are drunk. This is also true when we are uremic, hypoglycemic, hyper- or hypothyroid, suffering from a brain tumor, or senile. The same thought was expressed by Henry Fielding in his novel, *Tom Jones:*

> To say truth, nothing is more erroneous than the common observation, that men who are ill-natured and quarrelsome when they are drunk, are very worthy persons whey they are sober: for drink, in reality, doth not reverse nature, or create passions in men which did not exist in them before. It takes away the guard of reason, and consequently forces us to produce those symptoms, which many, when sober, have art enough to conceal. It heightens and inflames our passions (generally, indeed, that passion which is uppermost in our minds), so that the angry temper, the amourous, the generous, the good-humoured, the avaricious, and all other dispositions of men, are in their cups heightened and exposed.

Expressed in psychodynamic terms, organic factors damage defenses against impulses at the point where they previously have been weakest. What Fielding called "that passion which is uppermost in our minds," we now call our mental *set.* The patient's life situation at the time of the onset of the organic brain syndrome and the circumstances in which it develops is called the *setting.* Both set and setting are important determinants of the type, extent, and content of the positive signs.

Anything that increases fear and apprehension will increase the likelihood that positive symptoms will occur. The patient's ability to employ more mature defenses such as repression, already undermined by organic factors, will often be insufficient to cope with the anxiety aroused by his perception of a sudden decrease in his cognitive ability. The individual who sets a high value on intellectual function and/or who must function in an intellectually demanding job is likely to become more upset by intellectual loss than a person with different values and vocation. Anxiety is also generally greatest in rapidly progressing lesions where there is insufficient time to mobilize defenses. Positive signs are also more likely to occur in those organic brain syndromes which do not decrease the level of consciousness, as these patients remain able both to perceive their defects and to respond with anxiety. Organic brain syndromes which do not cause a decrease in the level of consciousness are those which are the result of an overstimulation rather than to a depression of neural function. These include sedative or alcohol withdrawal (for example, delirium tremens); hallucinogen and stimulant intoxication (for example, LSD or amphetamines); and sensory deprivation, sensory overstimulation, and sleep deprivation (for example, ICU delirium). These rather unusual organic mental disorders will be discussed in the last part of this chapter.

CLASSIFICATION OF THE ORGANIC BRAIN SYNDROMES

The patient's most prominent symptoms, whether positive or negative, are used as the basis for the classification of the organic brain syndromes in DSM-III. If the most prominent symptom is a loss of intellectual abilities (memory, abstract thinking, judgment, and other higher cortical functions), of sufficient severity to interfere with social or occupational functioning, *dementia* is present. If the most prominent symptom is a clouding of consciousness with reduced awareness of and attention to the environment, *delirium* is present. In the *organic amnestic syndrome* the predominant symptom is memory impairment, both short-term (inability to learn new information) and long-term (inability to remember information that was known in the past). However, there is no loss of other intellectual abilities as in dementia, and no clouding of consciousness as in delirium. In *organic delusional syndrome* delusions are the predominant clinical feature; in *organic hallucinosis* persistent or recurrent hallucinations are

the predominant clinical feature; in *organic affective syndrome* the most prominent symptom is a disturbance of mood; and in *organic personality syndrome* the most prominent symptom is a marked change in behavior or personality. *Intoxication* is defined in DSM-III as the development of a substance-specific syndrome that follows the recent ingestion of that substance. *Withdrawal* is defined as the development of a substance-specific syndrome that follows the cessation of or reduction in intake of a substance that was previously used on a regular basis.

MENTAL STATUS EXAMINATION

The mental state of the patient with OBS is produced by a combination of positive and negative signs and symptoms, and islands of intact function. These in turn are a result of the patient's premorbid personality, the extent of the organic insult, the circumstances under which it occurs, and the speed with which it develops. The patient's mental status is assessed by the mental status examination just as his physical status is assessed by means of the physical examination. Those aspects of the mental status examination which assess memory, orientation, motor function, and level of consciousness are especially useful in determining whether the patient is suffering from an organic or functional mental disorder. In addition, certain types of hallucinatory symptoms occur much more frequently in OBS than in functional psychiatric illnesses. These five areas should be assessed in every complete physical and neurological examination as well as in the mental status examination, since organic brain syndrome is common in many neurological and medical diseases and is sometimes the first sign of these illnesses. For example, intellectual impairment may herald the onset of diseases as diverse as hyperparathyroidism, systemic lupus erythematosis, meningioma, encephalitis, porphyria, hypertension, congestive heart failure, and pernicious anemia.

Memory and Orientation

When we test cognitive function, we do not test for the highest type of intellectual function, the ability to abstract, as this is too closely related to general intelligence. Ability to abstract is also the one area of intellectual functioning which is lost in schizophrenia. As tests of abstraction do not help us in differentiating between organic brain syndrome, schizophrenia, and mild intellectual retardation, we use tests which are not particularly related to intelligence, at least above a certain minimum—and which anybody who has completed the sixth grade should be able to answer correctly. These are tests involving memory and orientation.

Memory is well developed in childhood, unlike the ability to abstract which does not develop fully until adolescence. It is therefore not lost until after the ability to abstract. It is possible that some early cases of OBS in which only abstraction is lost may be missed if we use memory loss as the sole criterion for the diagnosis. Even so, signs of memory loss are likely to appear earlier on mental status exam than physical signs of OBS on laboratory tests such as the EEG and CT scan (computerized tomography).

We test *memory* by asking the patient, "When did you come to the hospital? How long have you been here? How old are you? When were you born? How long have you been married? What was the date of your marriage?" *Remote memory* is generally preserved longer than *recent memory*. For example, the patient is much more likely to know the date of his birth than to know his age, and to know the date of his marriage than to know how long he has been married. The most recent memory of all is something that we teach the patient while conducting the mental status. We call this *retention* and *recall* of short-term memory. We give the patient a task, for example, to repeat three objects, to remember them, and to repeat them back to the examiner five minutes later. We test *concentration span* which also is related to memory by asking the patient to subtract seven from 100 and keep subtracting seven from his answer all the way down. The patient has to keep the task in mind until he completes it. The three objects and the 100-minus-seven tests are probably the tasks most frequently given to patients to test their memories.

Orientation for time, place, and *person* simply means, "Does the patient know where he is in time, where he is in his physical and social environment, and who the people around him are?" We ask him, "What day is today? What month is it? What year is it? Where are you now? What kind of place is this? Who are you? Who am I?" Orientation for time is generally lost before orientation for place, and orientation

for place before orientation for person. Orientation for time is lost first because there are no sensory cues available to help the patient determine the day, month, or year as there are to help him determine where he is or who the people around him are. Orientation for day or date is lost before orientation for month, and orientation for month before orientation for year. This occurs because we know the day or date for less than 24 hours while we may know the month for 30 days and the year for 365 days. The longer we know something the more likely we are to remember it. Not only is the last ability we acquire the first we lose, but the last information we acquire is the first we lose in the presence of an organic insult. The patient will always know who he is except in certain types of dissociative disorders such as psychogenic amnesia and psychogenic fugue. We learn our names very early and remember them even after severe brain damage. Patients with functional psychotic disorders may lose orientation for place and/or person as part of their loss of reality testing. However, these patients place themselves in environments which are bizarre and consistent with their delusional thinking, while patients with organic brain syndromes tend to place themselves in familiar places with familiar people. For example, a psychotically depressed patient with the delusion that he has committed an unforgivable sin may believe he is in hell and the doctor is the devil, whereas a hospitalized patient with OBS may believe that he is at home and that the doctor is a friend or relative.

Some physicians do not examine patients as to orientation and memory because they are afraid of insulting them by asking obvious questions. However, if you explain to the patient that you would like to test his memory as part of your examination, he will generally cooperate without difficulty. The patient who does become insulted after an explanation of this kind is likely to be covering over an intellectual deficit of which he does not want to be made aware, as it is too upsetting to him. This is why many patients with organic brain syndrome become depressed. The depressive symptoms may cause them to seek psychiatric help, and they may not complain of the intellectual impairment that caused the depression in the first place.

Motor Function

In organic brain syndrome we often find loss of motor function. There may be some degree of impaired coordination (ataxia), involuntary to-and-fro movements of the eyeballs (nystagmus), slurred speech, incontinence, and involuntary up and down movements of the hand when it is held hyperextended at the wrist (asterixis). Asterixis looks as if the patient is waving goodbye.

Level of Consciousness

We ascertain the level of consciousness by observing the patient and listening to his voice as he speaks to us. If the patient looks disinterested, apathetic, or sleepy, as if he has been sedated, or if his speech is soft or slurred, the patient has a decreased level of consciousness. These signs are so obvious that they may strike one as not worth mentioning. However, their significance may be missed by otherwise thorough physicians. Patients with organic brain syndrome may fall between the interests of different specialists. Medical specialists in organic disease who have increasingly sophisticated laboratory procedures at their disposal may look at X-rays and laboratory tests, rather than at how awake the patient is or how soft or slurred his speech is. The psychiatrist may study the intrapsychic conflicts or interpersonal stress rather than consider a physical cause for the patient's symptoms.

If the patient looks sleepy or if his speech is slurred, this is of great diagnostic significance. These signs are extremely rare in patients with functional mental disorders, who are instead usually agitated, upset, and hyperalert. Only a few types of organic brain syndromes are associated with sustained hyperalertness and sustained hyperexcitability. In most types of OBS, if hyperalertness occurs, it is secondary to anxiety and is episodic, alternating with periods of decreased wakefulness, apathy, or somnolence. The worsening of the patient's condition at night ("sundowning") may also be an important sign of organic disturbance.

Hallucinations

Two types of breakthrough symptoms in organic brain syndromes are different from those commonly found in functional psychotic disorders. When hallucinations occur, for some reason they tend to be *visual*. It is as if in OBS,

dreaming slips over into the waking state and the patient sees things. Visual hallucinations are unusual in functional psychoses. When they do occur, as, for example, in schizophrenia, the patients see things which are closely related to their delusions. If a schizophrenic patient is preoccupied with religious delusions, he may see the Virgin Mary or a saint or some figure of religious significance. In contrast, the organic patient may see little men or little animals which often appear to be unrelated to his delusions or preoccupations. Auditory hallucinations may be present in OBS as well as in functional psychoses. However, when auditory hallucinations occur in organic brain syndromes, they usually occur within the so-called psychic horizon. That is, *they have their origin in a place from which the patient could ordinarily hear* (for example, from outside the door, or under the bed, or the street outside). The patient with schizophrenia will hear voices but will seldom locate their source. It is not enough, therefore, to know that the patient is hallucinating. The examiner must inquire as to the type and the content of the hallucination, and if auditory, the source.

After the physician decides on the basis of his mental status examination that the patient is likely to be suffering from an organic brain syndrome, the next question is whether it is reversible or irreversible. This question cannot be answered by mental status examination. The mental status of the patient with reversible brain syndrome is identical to that of the patient with irreversible brain syndrome. They can be differentiated only by history, physical examination, and in most instances by laboratory tests. A common error is to assume that all brain syndromes in older patients are due to *primary degenerative dementia* (Alzheimer's disease) and hence are irreversible rather than treatable. Correctable causes of brain syndrome occur in the elderly as well as in younger patients. Medical and surgical knowledge has advanced greatly since Shakespeare wrote, "A good old man sir, he will be talking, as they say, 'when the age is in, the wit is out.'" An old person's wit may be out as a result of a subdural hematoma, brain tumor, uremia, hyper- or hypothyroidism, or a host of other medical and surgical illnesses. The various physical and laboratory findings in these and other diseases which may cause organic brain syndromes are outside the scope of this chapter.

TREATMENT

Treatment of brain syndromes is of two types: etiological and symptomatic. In reversible brain syndromes, both are necessary. In irreversible brain syndromes, only symptomatic treatment is possible.

Etiological treatment is aimed at the correction of the condition which has caused the neuronal damage or dysfunction. For example, treatment of the underlying liver, cardiac, renal, or endocrine disease, withdrawal of the medication which is causing the toxic state, removal of the brain tumor or hematoma. If successful, treatment will result in a return of the neurons to normal and the disappearance of both the negative and the positive symptoms.

Symptomatic treatment is aimed at correction of the positive symptoms, rather than at the underlying neuronal damage or dysfunction. It is divided into two types: psychological and pharmacological. Psychological treatment is of most value in early stages or in less severe brain damage where the patient retains sufficient cognitive function and consciousness to perceive and retain environmental stimuli. In the treatment of patients with irreversible brain syndrome, as in the treatment of any patient whose condition is not amenable to specific therapy, the major emphasis must be on a doctor-patient relationship that aims at making the patient as comfortable as possible within the limitations imposed by his disease. Psychological treatment consists of simple measures directed toward helping the patient retain his hold on reality and providing him with interested, active, reassuring caretakers. In hospitalized patients, it may consist of repeated explanations as to what is happening, reassurance that the patient will get well, and continued orientation to reality by verbal means, by keeping the bedside lights on at night, and by providing clocks and calendars. In essence, this is the approach used in "talking down" LSD users who are experiencing a "bad trip." The "talker" uses his own reality testing and cognitive functions as a substitute for those functions which are defective in the LSD user, just as the ground controller "talks down" an airplane when the pilot is blinded by fog or defective instruments. Using a therapist's cognitive and reality testing functions as substitutes for the patient's is often necessary for patients who are hospitalized for medical and surgical

illnesses and who develop delirium. This therapy can be performed by a nurse or a relative. One or the other should be allowed to be with the patient at all times. Psychological methods often must be combined with pharmacological ones, especially if a nurse or relative cannot be continually present with the patient.

Positive symptoms such as anxiety, agitation, hyperactivity, belligerence, or assaultiveness may require treatment with major tranquilizers in doses sufficient to diminish excessive affects and psychomotor activity. The major tranquilizers are generally used since these, unlike the minor tranquilizers or sedatives, can calm extremely agitated patients without decreasing their level of consciousness (except as a transient side effect). With the proper use of major tranquilizers, the physician can almost always avoid institutionalization and custodial care for those with irreversible brain syndromes. The patient can be kept calm and manageable by his family at home even though negative signs such as defective memory and disorientation are not improved. In the withdrawal deliria, minor tranquilizers and sedatives are both etiological and symptomatic therapies, in that they substitute for the drug from which the patient has been too rapidly withdrawn and thereby diminish the severity of the biochemical derangement while simultaneously calming the patient.

SOME ATYPICAL ORGANIC MENTAL DISORDERS

Many of the organic mental disorders produced by specific substances have already been described by Dr. Crowley and Dr. Rhine in the preceding chapter on substance use disorders. I will conclude this chapter by discussing four which are atypical in that they produce an intoxication or a delirium characterized by a *sustained increase in wakefulness and alertness* due to overstimulation rather than depression of neuronal function. Positive symptoms are almost always present, because of the rapid onset, the hyperalert state, and the frequency with which these conditions are associated either with preexisting emotional instability or with current life stress or both. They are also of special interest to physicians because they occur very frequently in hospitalized patients.

LSD Intoxication

Lysergic acid diethylamide (LSD), like other hallucinogens and stimulants, in sufficient doses will cause a delirium characterized by both positive and negative symptoms as well as hyperalertness. Although positive symptoms may be of any variety, the LSD intoxications that physicians see clinically are characterized by hallucinations, delusions, or affects which are painful to the user—the so-called "bad trips." Physicians are seldom if ever asked to see patients who find the subjective experiences of intoxication pleasant or neutral. The type of positive symptoms present with LSD, as with the other drugs mentioned, depends in large measure on the premorbid personality and the current life stress (set and setting), just as the signs of alcohol intoxication (amorousness, conviviality, bellicosity) vary with the personality of the drinker and the circumstances in which he or she drinks. LSD differs from other hallucinogens in that it is active in much smaller doses.

Certain symptoms have been described as characteristic of LSD intoxication, for example, synesthesias (hallucinations in which there is a merger of two sensory modalities, i.e., seeing colors when a loud sound occurs). There is some question as to whether these signs are related to the pharmacological properties of LSD or to the expectations of the users. Many LSD users were conditioned by reading or hearing the accounts of the LSD experiences of Aldous Huxley and Timothy Leary. For a period in the sixties, LSD was advocated by Timothy Leary as the sacrament of a new religion and as an aid to realizing a secular vision of "Heaven on earth" and "Better living through chemistry." "Turn on, tune in, drop out" was the slogan. The writings of Huxley and Leary exerted a strong proselytizing effect in recruiting new users by advocating the ingestion of LSD as a means of gaining strength and self-knowledge. Some youths hoped that LSD would help them cope with their personal conflicts and developmental problems. Initially, many reported that after taking LSD they did indeed feel new strength and found new and better directions in their lives. Judging by the apparent decrease in use in subsequent years, the initial promise of this drug has not been fulfilled. The entire LSD phase, with its early enthusiasm, exaggerated claims, and quick abandonment, is reminiscent of exaggerated claims in years past surrounding the introduction of many pharmacologically ineffective drugs into medical therapy. These episodes illustrate the truth of the adage, "Use new drugs early before they lose their efficacy."

Amphetamine Intoxication

The clinical picture of an amphetamine intoxication may resemble that of paranoid schizophrenia rather than that of an OBS. There may be no visual hallucinations or disorientation, and the most prominent or only signs may be paranoid delusions and an affect appropriate to this type of ideation, either fear or anger. These patients may be diagnosed incorrectly as paranoid schizophrenics on admission to mental hospitals. Their symptoms generally remit, however, in days rather than weeks or months as in true paranoid schizophrenia.

Amphetamine intoxication is almost always caused by continuous ingestion of increasing doses of the drug rather than by a single dose as in the case of LSD intoxication. Amphetamine users tend to gradually increase the dose they take as tolerance develops to the mood-elevating effects of the drug. As tolerance to the effects of LSD lasts only a few days, the user has no incentive to increase his dose. The amphetamine user, like the user of sedatives or opiates, takes the drug to relieve depressive affects, feelings of inadequacy, and low self-esteem. However, unlike most sedative or opiate users, the amphetamine user is usually interested in increasing his drive and initiative. Whatever their goals, users of all these drugs find they must take more and more to achieve the results they want. As the dose is increased, side effects appear. In high doses, opiates and sedatives produce confusion (impaired cognition), lethargy (decreased level of consciousness), and ataxia (impaired motor function). In high doses, amphetamines cause an increase in the level of consciousness and elation, grandiosity, loquacity, restlessness, sweating, tremors, hyperactivity, hyperalertness, sleeplessness, and finally psychosis with visual hallucinations and/or paranoid delusions. The cause of the characteristic clinical picture of amphetamine intoxication is unknown. It probably is related to both the pharmacological effects of amphetamines as well as the personality characteristics of those who become psychologically dependent on this drug. Physical dependence and an abstinence syndrome occur with amphetamines, but it is mild and neither dangerous nor uncomfortable. The abstinence or withdrawal syndrome is characterized by prolonged sleep, fatigue, overeating, and depression. It is associated with EEG changes and an increase in the percentage of REM sleep time. This can be understood as a rebound phenomenon—amphetamines tend to depress sleep and dreaming to less than normal levels, and these increase to greater than normal levels when amphetamines are withdrawn.

Alcohol Withdrawal Delirium (Delirium Tremens)

The clinical picture of delirium tremens is similar to that of the LSD and amphetamine intoxications in that the patient is hyperalert and hypervigilant. The patient with delirium tremens is also likely to have paranoid delusions. Like the patient with amphetamine intoxication, he often sweats profusely. The clinical picture of delirium tremens, however, may differ from amphetamine intoxication in that the patient with delirium tremens does not have a clear sensorium (i.e., he is disoriented for time, place, and person). He also is often febrile. While LSD and amphetamine intoxications are due to the toxic effect of these drugs, delirium tremens is due to the effect of *withdrawal* of alcohol, which has been transformed after continuous ingestion over a period of weeks and months from a toxic agent to a component of metabolic processes necessary for brain function and sometimes for life as well. The transformation from toxic agent to essential metabolite which occurs with continued use of alcohol as well as other general depressant drugs and opioids is called *physiological dependence*. The *abstinence* or *withdrawal syndrome* is the clinical condition following withdrawal of the drug in a physically dependent individual.

Tolerance means that larger and larger doses are necessary to achieve the same effect. There is a cross-tolerance between alcohol, sedatives, and minor tranquilizers, and also a cross-tolerance between the various narcotics (i.e., any one can be used to prevent the development of a withdrawal syndrome in a patient physically dependent on any other). For example, the mi-

nor tranquilizers, Valium and Librium, or paraldehyde, a sedative, may be used to prevent as well as to treat delirium tremens; methadone, a nonopiate analgesic, may be used to prevent or treat the heroin withdrawal syndrome.

The alcohol withdrawal or abstinence syndrome consists of a sequence of tremors, anxiety, sweating, easy startle (hyperactivity to environmental stimuli), restlessness, nausea and vomiting, *nocturnal hallucinations, grand mal seizures*, and then delirium during the day as well as at night. This sequence develops over a period of about 72 hours. The delirium lasts for 48 to 72 hours except in patients with a complicating medical or surgical illness where the delirium can last for as long as several weeks. Thirty years ago the mortality rate of the fully developed alcohol withdrawal syndrome (delirium tremens) was reported to be 9% in uncomplicated cases and 24% in cases with complicating organic disease. In recent years the mortality rate has declined to zero in several published series. The reason for the decline in mortality is probably due to an enhanced appreciation on the part of the medical profession that delirium tremens is a life-threatening emergency. Consequently, greater attention is now paid to nutrition, hydration, electrolyte balance, and sedation in these patients.

The same signs (tremors, hallucinations, seizures, and delirium) develop in the same sequence when sedatives and minor tranquilizers are withdrawn suddenly from those who are physically dependent on them. The more slowly the drug is metabolized, the more the symptoms are delayed and the more they are muted. Patients who have become physically dependent on sedatives which are rapidly metabolized such as alcohol, chloral hydrate, paraldehyde, and short-acting barbiturates such as secobarbital, develop withdrawal symptoms within a few days of abstinence. *These withdrawals are dangerous to life.* Patients who are dependent on long-acting barbiturates such as phenobarbital or minor tranquilizers such as Valium or Librium, which are slowly metabolized, develop withdrawal symptoms as late as a week after abstinence, and the symptoms are much less dangerous. Patients dependent on these latter drugs may develop anxiety, restlessness, and grand mal seizures but are unlikely to become delirious. The alcohol and sedative withdrawal syndrome resembles a rebound phenomenon from the effects of these drugs, just as the opiate withdrawal syndrome resembles a rebound phenomenon from the effects of opiates. However, brain function does not become dependent on opiates, and therefore delirium does not occur when they are withdrawn. *Sudden withdrawal of opiates such as heroin never causes death.*

It is important for the physician to try to obtain an accurate history of drinking and sedative ingestion from all hospitalized patients because of the frequency of withdrawal deliria in the medically and surgically ill and the associated mortality. In one study, delirium tremens developed after admission in 1% of male patients on a general surgical service. Alcoholics and drug addicts are more prone to trauma as well as to other conditions which often lead to hospitalization, such as tuberculosis, cirrhosis, pancreatitis, peptic ulcer, and ruptured esophageal varices. Patients who are admitted to any hospital with a history of steady drinking, previous episodes of delirium tremens, and/or early signs of alcohol withdrawal should be evaluated for physical dependence with a test dose of 200 mgm of secobarbital. If the patient shows no signs of intoxication after one hour (nystagmus, lethargy, ataxia, or slurred speech), he or she should be reintoxicated with a sedative or minor tranquilizer. Once delirium tremens has developed, large doses repeated until the patient is asleep and then continued at regular intervals for several days until the delirium clears are generally necessary. These patients must be kept well sedated, because they have been known to suicide or assault other patients while in a delirious state.

ICU Delirium

For intact CNS function, we need adequate amounts of sensory input from our environment, and we need sleep. When we receive either too much or too little sensory input or too little sleep over too long a period, a delirium characterized by increased wakefulness, disorientation, and visual hallucinations is produced. The delirium is indistinguishable on mental status examination from a toxic or withdrawal delirium.

The effects of sensory deprivation can perhaps most readily be appreciated if we remember our childhood fear of the dark, or recall the difference between walking alone at night down a dark street and hearing footsteps behind and having the same experience during the day. Darkness tends to undermine our ability to distinguish reality from fantasy. Simply turning on a light restores reality testing. With the cutting off of each additional sensory modality, psychosis or delirium becomes more likely to occur. When normal subjects are cut off from all sensory input by being suspended in a tank of water so as to simulate weightlessness with their eyes and ears covered, they will become delirious in a few hours. It is as if the mind "abhors a vacuum." When denied sensory input from the external environment, it creates an internal environment from which stimuli flow. Florid visual and auditory hallucinations take the place of the external emptiness.

Sleep deprivation and sensory overstimulation also can produce delirium, especially when combined with sensory deprivation. The police of some nations produce delirium by the use of all these modalities in an attempt to obtain confessions. This is well illustrated in the movie *The Day of The Jackal.* The French police have captured an OAS colonel and wish to obtain as much information as possible about a plot to assassinate De Gaulle. The colonel resolves to tell them nothing of what he knows. The police keep bright lights on him, beat him, and keep him awake by interrogating him in relays. One policeman says to the prisoner, who is groggy, sweating, covered with bruises, and half blinded by the light shining in his eyes, "You know, Colonel, everyone cracks with this treatment. You've administered it often enough yourself. Why are you wasting our time?" Although French, he does not respond appropriately to this irrefutable logic. He becomes delirious and eventually dies of beatings and exhaustion. The French police tape what he has said in his delirium, and this gives them the leads they need to begin their efforts to find the assassin.

Sensory deprivation, sensory overstimulation, and sleep deprivation deliria are of importance to all physicians because of the increasing frequency with which they are produced by modern methods of hospital treatment. As older methods of treatment which produced sensory deprivation have been abandoned, newer methods have been introduced and applied to increasing numbers of patients. Up until about 30 years ago both eyes of patients with bilateral cataracts were operated on at the same time, causing the patient to be blind for a week. This reduced the anesthetic risk, as a single anesthesia was sufficient for both procedures, but greatly increased the risk of sensory deprivation delirium. Many of these patients were elderly and had hearing difficulties as well, and many became psychotic. This was called "black patch delirium." This does not occur with the current procedures in which cataracts are extracted one at a time, with sufficient interval between so that the bandage is removed from the first eye before the second is operated on. Also up until about 30 years ago, patients with poliomyelitis that affected their respiratory muscles were confined in tank respirators—the so called "iron lung." They were immobilized, had a limited visual field, and were subjected to the continuous monotonous noise ("white sound") of the respirator motor. Some of these patients became delirious. This reaction disappeared with the introduction of respirators which did not require complete immobilization.

As these procedures and devices were abandoned or modified, the ICU (Intensive Care Unit) was introduced to provide better care for patients by concentrating the sickest patients, the most sophisticated diagnostic and therapeutic devices, and the best trained personnel in one area. As with all improvements in medical care, a price was paid. Just as steroids can cause side effects, ICU's can cause delirium. ICU patients are confined to bed, often immobilized by traction or cardiac monitoring devices or respiratory assisting devices, and exposed to a white sound background of whirring motors or regular blips or beeps. Lights are kept on all the time, sometimes in a room with no windows, clocks, or calendars to measure the passage of time, and sometimes with no opportunity for conversation with relatives except for five minutes every hour. The doctors and nurses caring for the patients are distracted by their responsibilities of monitoring the complex life-support systems. The patients are afflicted by frequent injections and have tubes in most of their body orifices. The atmosphere is one of monotony interrupted at irregular intervals by terror. Without warning, alarm bells sound and staff rush to care for patients with cardiac or respiratory arrests. Patients hear and see deaths of other patients, and fear for their own fate.

The rapidity with which the ICU syndrome develops depends on the arrangements of the particular ICU—the amount of visiting allowed, the number of windows in the room, and the degree of immobilization of the patient. In one surgical ICU where there were no windows and where visitors were limited to five minutes every hour, patients in neck traction became delirious by the sixth day. Those who were not in neck traction became delirious by the 18th day. ICU delirium starts with the patients becoming confused as to whether they are asleep and dreaming or awake. For the first day they can be reassured that they are indeed awake and can be brought back into contact with reality by the staff. They then become increasingly agitated and frightened by paranoid fears and visual hallucinations over the next 24 hours.

ICU delirium can best be understood as being essentially similar to the "combat fatigue" or the "three day schizophrenia" of World War II or the "shell shock" of World War I, as well as to the delirium produced by police interrogators in order to obtain information from suspects. In combat there is the same combination of sensory monotony alternating with periods of sensory overstimulation, sleep deprivation, and fear of death as in the ICU. In World War II it was well-known that *all* of the troops exposed to combat, regardless of their preexisting mental stability, would eventually develop "combat fatigue." Depending on the intensity of the fighting, the period of exposure would vary from several weeks to several months. As the period approached its end point, the percentage of psychiatric casualties increased. At that point the troops had to be withdrawn to the rear to rest (Table 67.1).

The treatment for all types of sensory deprivation, sensory overstimulation, and sleep deprivation deliria is restoration of the normal amounts of stimuli and sleep. Treatment of "combat fatigue" or "three day schizophrenia" is withdrawal of the soldier to a point behind the lines, but close enough to combat to hear the sound of the guns. Soldiers who are withdrawn so far to the rear that they can no longer hear the sound of guns will recover but will relapse immediately upon return to combat. These soldiers react to the sound of guns by intense anxiety. Soldiers cared for in a supportive environment while still hearing gunfire are not conditioned to the same extent to react with anxiety to the sound. The hospitalized patient with an ICU delirium can be cured simply by

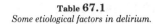

Table 67.1
Some etiological factors in delirium.

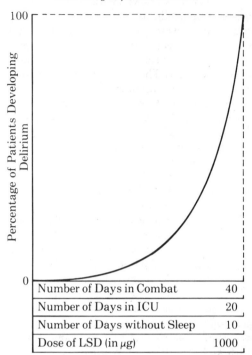

Number of Days in Combat	40
Number of Days in ICU	20
Number of Days without Sleep	10
Dose of LSD (in μg)	1000

transferring him out of the ICU to the regular hospital environment. If he is too ill to be transferred, tranquilization sufficient to produce a state of apathy or somnolence is necessary. The syndrome can be prevented or delayed if ICU patients are allowed more varied sensory input. Calendars, clocks, radios, and TV's should be supplied. ICU's should be built so that patients can look out of windows, and relatives should be allowed to stay with patients. Staff members should be encouraged to engage patients in conversation, and to keep them oriented to reality by explanations and reassurance. This may be difficult to carry out in practice because an ICU staff is often shorthanded and preoccupied with physical procedures, and some relatives become quite upset by the atmosphere of an ICU. Also, some doctors and nurses find it difficult to work while they are constantly under the eye of relatives. Hopefully, in the future there will be greater success in diminishing the psychological hazards associated with ICU treatment.

Suggested Readings

Andreasen NC: *The Broken Brain: The Biological Revolution in Psychiatry.* New York, Harper & Row, 1984.

Engel GL, Romano J: Delirium: a syndrome of cerebral insufficiency. *J Chronic Dis* 9:260, 1959.

Glickman L: *Psychiatric Consultation in the General Hospital.* New York, Marcel Dekker, 1980, pp 55–114.

Kornfeld DS: The hospital environment: its impact on the patient. In Lipowski ZJ (ed): *Advances in Psychosomatic Medicine, Vol. 8: Psychosocial Aspects of Physical Illness.* Basel and New York, Karger, 1972, p 252.

Lipowski ZJ: *Delirium: Acute Brain Failure in Man.* Springfield, IL, Charles C Thomas, 1980.

Lipowski ZJ: A new look at organic brain syndromes. *Am J Psychiatry* 137:674, 1980.

Lipowski ZJ: Transient cognitive disorders (delirium, acute confusional states) in the elderly. *Am J Psychiatry* 140:1426, 1983.

Plum F, Posner J: *The Diagnosis of Stupor and Coma*, ed 2. Philadelphia, F.Y. Davis, 1972.

References

Blumenfield M, Glickman L: Ten months experience with LSD users admitted to a county psychiatric receiving hospital. *NY State J Med* 67:1849, 1967.

Connell PH: *Amphetamine Psychosis.* Maudsley Monographs No 5. London, Chapman & Hall, 1958.

Glickman L, Blumenfield M: Psychological determinants of "LSD reactions." *J Nerv Ment Dis* 145:79, 1967.

Glickman L, Herbsman H: Delirium tremens in surgical patients. *Surgery* 64:882, 1968.

Jackson JH: *Selected Writings.* New York, Basic Books, 1958.

Kramp P, Raphaelson OJ: Delirium tremens: a double-blind comparison of diazepam and barbital treatment. *Acta Psychiat Scand* 58:174, 1978.

Linn L, et al: Patterns of behavior disturbance following cataract extraction. *Am J Psychiatry* 110:281, 1953.

Mendelson J, Solomon P, Lindemann E: Hallucinations of poliomyelitis patients during treatment in a respirator. *J Nerv Ment Dis* 126:421, 1958.

CHAPTER **68** **Psychiatric Emergencies in Medical Practice**

Michael P. Weissberg, M.D.

THE PROBLEM

"I tell my residents never to get involved in how the patient got injured or hurt. I tell them 'What you don't know can't hurt you.'"
A Medical School Professor

Unfortunately, psychiatric emergencies occur in medical practice with a great degree of regularity. Often, however, if the physician is not alert to them they may go undetected until too late. The medical practitioner very often has the opportunity for early detection, emergency treatment, and referral of psychiatric emergencies. This offers an excellent chance for the prevention of morbidity and mortality, since the medical practitioner may be able to intervene early in the course of an impending emergency before a dangerous situation becomes inevitable. For instance, as Dr. Glickman indicated earlier, one study of 60 successful suicides showed that over 80% of these individuals had seen their doctors within six months before they killed themselves, and over 50% of this same group of patients had seen their doctors within one month or less of their deaths. Over two-thirds of these patients had histories of previous suicides or threats, yet these histories were known to only two-fifths of the physicians responsible for their care. There was substantial evidence of depressive illness in three-quarters of these patients, yet the diagnosis was rarely made and therefore the depression was not treated.

Child abusers visit their physicians preceding or during the abusive crisis, while perpetrators and victims of spouse abuse frequently suffer from a host of somatic complaints for which they seek medical care in addition to presenting with the physical manifestations of violence. Victims of incest come to the attention of med-

ical personnel with a variety of complaints only some of which are related to the genitourinary system. Even murderers experience somatic ills during the build-up phase before the killing. However, the majority of these cases are missed—many even by psychiatrists.

Medical practitioners may also inadvertently "promote" dangerous behavior in their patients. In another study of 32 patients who had committed suicide with an overdose of medication, 29 (91%) had seen a physician within six months of their deaths. Of these 29, 16 (55%) had obtained the means to kill themselves in a *single* prescription from their physicians within a week or less before their suicides. Patients may go from emergency rooms to clinics collecting medicines as a means of suicide. A 35 year old, divorced woman came to a medical emergency room complaining of insomnia of three weeks' duration. She was given 60 capsules of Dalmane 30 mg. and a follow-up appointment to the medical clinic. When her chart was reviewed, she was called back the next day. She admitted to collecting medicines for a suicide attempt and was grateful to be offered psychiatric consultation. She was relieved to been "found out."

Even though all patients are not as open to intervention as this woman, medical practitioners must be alert to the possibility of a psychiatric emergency in their patients. Psychiatric emergencies may be defined as *any* alteration of feeling, thinking, or behavior that, if left unattended, may lead to harm either to the patient or to someone in the patient's environment. The emergency may be identified by the patient, his family or friends, or only by the physician. In all cases, psychiatric emergencies occur when there is a failure of the patient's normal coping mechanisms in response to stress. The stress may be external (loss of job, health, a loved one),

759

internal (a psychological conflict), or a pathophysiological process (intoxication). Often a number of factors are present. For example, a divorce may reactivate unresolved grief about the earlier death of a parent, which may lead to suicidal behavior in a patient whose coping mechanisms have already been weakened by excessive use of alcohol. Patients may present their difficulties either directly or indirectly, but it is the physician's responsibility to suspect the presence of an emergency in *any* patient who appears to be under stress.

THE STRESS RESPONSE

It is useful to think of the manifestations of psychiatric emergencies as resulting from maladaptive responses to stress and as representing attempts to re-establish psychological homeostasis. Many violent behaviors represent distorted attempts to regain control over situations gone awry. Patients are trying to solve problems, albeit in destructive ways.

We normally respond to stress in phasic ways. For instance the loss of one's car keys may be denied at first. This initial stage of *denial* may be followed by a period of *disorganization and symptom formation* characterized by anger or anxiety. *Maladaptive responses*, such as kicking the car, may be tried before a locksmith is called, and psychological *re-equilibration* is regained. Patients rarely see their physicians during the stage of *denial*. Patients more typically seek medical attention during the stage of *symptom formation and disorganization* or because of problems associated with the stage of *maladaptive responses*. *Re-equilibration* then follows, but not necessarily to the patient's previous level of functioning. For example, a dangerous situation occurred when a marginally adjusted mother felt stressed because her electronic baby-sitter, her TV, broke. As the household became disorganized, she sought help for her worsening tension headaches. In the midst of this crisis, she physically abused her youngest child before returning to an emergency room where the true scope of her difficulties was finally understood.

A stress contains within it a threat to security and self-esteem, and precipitates fears of loss or failure. It may be only privately perceived or it may be an overwhelming event which affects everyone such as the development of a physical illness. Normal life events can precipitate psy-

chiatric emergencies in those so prone. For example, the risk for both spouse abuse and incest is high during pregnancies. Seventeen percent of father-daughter incest occurs when the mother is pregnant. Intercurrent factors can also decrease stress resistance and increase the danger. For instance, the perimenstrum is associated with a higher risk of child abuse and suicide. Sleep deprivation, or the presence of an organic brain syndrome, can make destructive behavior more likely.

SOME HIDDEN PRESENTATIONS OF PSYCHIATRIC EMERGENCIES

The following are some of the covert ways that psychiatric emergencies present to the physician:

1. With vague *somatic complaints*, with symptoms and signs of *anxiety* or *depression*, or with complaints that are *out of proportion* to the physical findings.

2. With *multiple visits* that involve complaints about medical care. One patient visited a single emergency room 23 times before a psychiatric consultant diagnosed the presence of spouse and child abuse.

Patients in these first two groups routinely evoke antipathy in physicians. They are labelled as crocks, turkeys, GOMERS (Get Out of My Emergency Room) or WADAO'S (Weak And Dizzy All Over). Pejorative labels such as hypochondriac, hysteric, or somatizer also express hostility and the urge to get rid of these people.

3. With *accidents* or other *manifestations of trauma*. Violent death (accidents, suicide, and homicide) is the third leading cause of death in the United States and the first cause for people under the age of 39. Accidents can be the result of intentional suicide and homicidal behavior, or be due to "accident proneness." Patients may use the explanation of accidental injury to "explain" dangerous behavior, especially in spouse abuse and child abuse. *The presence of a psychiatric emergency should be considered in any patient who presents with trauma no matter what the reported explanation.*

4. With *dissociative states* such as fugues, amnesias, or episodes of depersonalization. One patient came to the emergency room complaining of night terrors and feelings of unreality. Another said that the world seemed hazy and not real. They both revealed a history of sexual

abuse. The use of such primitive defenses when under stress is not an uncommon finding among those who were physically or sexually abused as children.

5. With symptoms and signs of *family disruption*. In one such family the initial history was as follows: the father had a "slight" alcohol problem; the marriage was "falling apart"; and the daughter had run away from home twice and was having "problems" in school. Upon further psychiatric evaluation the following was discovered: the father was actively suicidal; the marital discord had reached the point of physical abuse; and the father had been sexually molesting his daughter.

6. With the *obvious presence of one dangerous behavior* hiding the existence of another. Dangerous behaviors often overlap. Spouse abuse and child abuse are often found in the same family. Sexual abuse and physical abuse of children often co-exist. Problems with alcohol and suicide occur in all of these syndromes as well. When one problem is found, the others must be looked for.

THE DANGER SCREEN

The physician must maintain a high index of suspicion for psychiatric emergencies since the diagnosis depends more on the history than on specific physical findings. A number of screening questions may be used. Patients will answer honestly, especially if the physician appears to be nonjudgmental. Since these patients feel extremely sensitive, questioning should be done with tact and *in private*. The following questions may be used after a relationship with the patient has been established: 1. "Are there things going on at home which you find upsetting?"; 2. "Are there things of a personal nature which you haven't told me?"; 3. "Have you been feeling hopeless, sad, ashamed, or frightened about anything?"

The actual form of the question is less important than the questioner's willingness to listen to the answer.

COMMON ERRORS IN EVALUATING DANGEROUSNESS

Why is the potential for dangerous behavior so often overlooked in patients? There are many

reasons for this. Sometimes it can be due to a lack of knowledge or training. For instance, if a physician does not know what to look for, ask about or do, then important clues to dangerousness may be overlooked. Also, the issues of suicide, homicide, child abuse, spouse abuse, and incest usually are anxiety provoking for the physician, and therefore their presence may be denied, as has been indicated in earlier chapters on these subjects.

Some physicians will not ask about dangerous behavior because they feel they are putting ideas into their patient's heads by asking about these matters. No doubt the approach has to be a tactful one, but most patients are relieved to find someone interested enough to ask about personal difficulties. Physicians cannot suggest suicide or homicide to someone who is not contemplating it already. In fact, it has been my experience that the real embarrassment in a full, frank discussion with a patient mostly comes from the doctor and not the patient. Patients will only be as comfortable and open as their doctor allows them to be. People will not talk about personal matters unless the doctor signals a willingness for them to do so. Similarly, physicians sometimes feel that asking questions about violence may be demeaning or insulting to the patient. This again is a rationalization and a way to avoid subjects that physicians find anxiety provoking.

Potential emergencies may also not be inquired about (or taken seriously) because of feelings that psychiatric problems are "made up" by the patient, and therefore they are not "real." For example, a 24 year old man was brought to the emergency room following an eight pill overdose of sleeping pills. The situation was not thought serious because of the number of pills taken and therefore the patient was viewed as "manipulating." The patient was sent home with his father only to be brought back the next day with a fatal self-inflicted gunshot wound through the heart. The patient may have been "manipulating" but also was seriously suicidal.

Often the physician is not specific enough while obtaining the history of violence. This, too, is a way of avoiding a difficult subject. For example, as Dr. Macdonald indicated in his chapter on violence, when asking about homicidal impulses one must find out if the patient has ever hurt anyone, how, with what, and whether the victim was hospitalized. The same is true for suicidal impulses. Physicians should inquire *directly* about suicide in any patient who appears to be depressed or under stress. The patient should be asked, for example, "Have things ever seemed so bad that you thought of taking your life?" If the answer is yes, the details about past attempts and current plans must be obtained. Getting the specifics will help the clinician reach a much more complete and realistic evaluation of how lethal the present situation really is.

It is important for the physician to be aware of his or her own prejudices which could interfere with the fullest evaluation. of a patient's crisis. For example, most people are horrified by child abuse or incest but it must be inquired about if the situation warrants it. Awareness of, and attempting to control, one's own feelings and prejudices will help to widen the scope of inquiry and not limit what the patient is allowed to talk about.

Some people have the attitude that personal violence, particularly suicide and spouse abuse, should not concern the physician, that these behaviors are private matters. Although philosophical questions should concern every physician, these attitudes usually indicate that the doctor is very uncomfortable with the question of personal violence. In many cases where "Doesn't the patient have a right to die?" is heard, the patient is either disliked, or it is the doctor who feels hopeless and helpless.

THE WORK-UP

When faced with a possible emergency, two questions must be answered initially: 1. Is the patient suffering from a *physical* illness?; 2. How *dangerous* is the present situation? During a psychiatric emergency, everyone is anxious—the patient, the family, and the doctor. It is in just these situations that important details may be overlooked. It therefore is critical that the work-up be organized in such a way that nothing is forgotten.

I would recommend six basic steps in organizing the work-up: 1. Observe the outward behavior of the patient, including his mood and appearance. This can be deceiving. A calm patient may be highly dangerous, while an agitated patient may not be suicidal or homicidal at all. Some patients appear to relax after deciding to die or kill someone else. 2. Take a history from the patient. Why is the patient here now? Par-

ticular inquiry should be made about the precipitating event, previous level of functioning, and past coping mechanisms in other stressful situations. 3. Obtain a history from friends or relatives, especially if the patient seems confused, withholding, or if the story just does not seem to hang together. Are the friends and relatives part of the problem? Or will they be reliable allies and help with the treatment? 4. Do a mental status examination. This will help in establishing whether the patient is suffering from a functional psychosis or is suffering from a pathophysiological process which is causing psychological symptoms (organic brain syndrome). 5. Do a physical examination. Special note should be made of signs of frequent fights, or signs attributable to past suicide attempts. Do not forget that psychiatric emergencies can occur within the context of physical disease. 6. Finally, evaluate your own emotional reaction to the patient. The physician's response to the patient can be an extremely important diagnostic tool. For example, in social situations it is normal to avoid disquieting people; in medicine this is cause for further psychological investigation. If the examiner feels sad while talking to a patient, a depression should be looked for. If the examiner feels frightened, he should ask himself what is frightening about this patient and explore the situation further.

COMMON ERRORS IN TREATING DANGEROUS BEHAVIOR

Some doctors may take a moralistic or condemning attitude toward violent behavior once it is discovered. This will only serve to alienate the patient and increase the potential danger. Others may do just the opposite, and offer reassurances that "everything will be all right." Even though the doctor should always transmit hope to the patient, empty reassurances will make the patient feel even less understood and will create further problems.

Sometimes doctors react to a dangerous person by trying to "out macho" the patient, by trying to be overly "cool," challenging, or even humiliating. Patients who resort to violence are extremely sensitive to any slight. This approach is never helpful, and may be a very dangerous course of action because it may force the patient toward further action to assauge his already injured pride.

At times, in the excitement of the encounter, the doctor may forget to take necessary precautions. For instance, he may see an obviously excited or angry patient alone, in a small room where there is not enough distance between them, with no immediate help available, with the door closed. The clinician may threaten force with no backup to enforce the threat, or the patient may be carrying a weapon and has not been disarmed. These courses of action are obviously dangerous. Therefore, planning ahead is a must. Under no circumstances should the physician be a hero or be hesitant to ask for help, including from the police. If, unfortunately, the choice becomes either letting the patient escape or placing the doctor in danger, the patient must be let go.

Many physicians also are unclear about their legal and ethical responsibilities when faced with potential violence. All states have laws in the area of child abuse; most allow *all* physicians to hospitalize patients against their will if it seems that they are likely to be a danger to themselves or others. Although holding someone against their will can be very unpleasant, most suicidal and homicidal patients are seeking external controls and are usually relieved to have been "found out" and stopped in time.

EMERGENCY TREATMENT

The two primary principles of treatment in psychiatric emergencies are: 1. Maintain the patient's self-esteem by warm, empathic, and interested listening; and 2. Maintain the patient's life by proper diagnosis, evaluation, and treatment. This includes the use of physical or chemical restraints when necessary.

The therapeutic benefits of a thorough psychological evaluation should not be underestimated. Patients in crisis are often confused as to what really is wrong and can benefit from the objectivity of another person. During a successful psychological evaluation, a chaotic story may become intelligible to both the patient and the physician. The delineation of the precipitant and the conflict may in and of itself be highly beneficial. People in crisis suffer from markedly lowered self-esteem; they are ashamed, bewil-

dered, and may feel guilty. A hopeful and kind listener can help many patients regain lost confidence in themselves and in their environment.

I have delineated six steps in the work-up of psychiatric emergencies. I will conclude this chapter by suggesting six areas which the physician should keep in mind as he or she is preparing the immediate treatment plan for a patient in crisis.

1. Do I really understand why the patient presented now and the circumstances of the present decompensation, or am I missing some important information? 2. Do I understand the seriousness of this patient's condition, or am I going along with the patient's or the family's denial of how bad things are? 3. Has the crisis passed, or is the patient still overwhelmed by what initially caused the emergency? 4. Do I dare let the patient go home, or am I sending him back into a pathogenic environment where nothing has really been changed or resolved? 5. Do I need an immediate consultation with a psychiatrist? 6. If I am going to send the patient home, what kind of follow-up have I arranged? Will the patient follow the treatment plan? Or is it too dangerous for the patient to be alone?

Ultimately, the physician has to follow his or her own educated opinions and intuitive feelings about what would be useful in psychiatric emergencies. If the use of force and involuntary hospitalization is considered, it should be done without undue fear of legal retribution. It is my experience that successful malpractice suits will more likely result from neglecting a potentially lethal situation than from making an honest clinical mistake.

Suggested Readings

Dubovsky SL, Weissberg MP: Psychiatric emergencies. In *Clinical Psychiatry in Primary Care*, ed 2. Baltimore, Williams & Wilkins, 1982, p 254.

Farley GK, Eckhardt LO, Hebert FB: *Handbook of Child and Adolescent Psychiatric Emergencies*. New York, Medical Examination Publishing, 1979.

Weissberg MP: *Dangerous Secrets: Maladaptive Responses to Stress*. New York, W. W. Norton & Co., 1983.

References

Murphy GE: The physician's responsibility for suicide. *Ann Int Med* 82:301, 1975.

Weissberg MP: Emergency room medical clearance: an educational problem. *Am J Psychiatry* 136:787, 1979.

69 The Anxiety Disorders and the Dissociative Disorders

William A. Console, M.D. and
Richard C. Simons, M.D.

In this chapter we will be discussing the various anxiety disorders and dissociative disorders. What we hope to convey is the fundamental proposition that in our work with these disorders, we are dealing with disturbances of thoughts and feelings and behavior, at the center of which is *anxiety* over some *unconscious fantasy*. Whatever the ultimate (and probably multiple) etiologic factors may be in these disorders, the common dynamic element in all of them is the presence of unacceptable unconscious wishes and impulses and fantasies which must be defended against in various ways.

THE ANXIETY DISORDERS

In this group of disorders, anxiety is either the predominant symptom (as in the *anxiety states* of *panic disorder* and *generalized anxiety disorder*), or anxiety is experienced if the individuals attempt to confront the feared situation (as in *phobic disorder*) or attempt to resist their obsessions and compulsions (as in *obsessive compulsive disorder*). Let us begin by discussing phobic disorders since the process of neurotic symptom formation is especially clear in these disorders.

Phobic Disorders

A *phobia* is a persistent, irrational fear of an object or situation (the *phobic stimulus*). A phobia is obviously not related to reality. If a wild tiger walked into the room, and we developed a fear about that, this would be a normal reaction in the face of a real situation. This is not a phobia; it is a fear of real danger. But in the phobia the danger is within the person. The danger is a matter of the pushing towards consciousness of an unacceptable wish or impulse or fantasy, and the mechanisms of defense are first *repression*, and then *displacement*. The wish which is internal is now transferred to some external object or situation. This gives the individual the potential of *avoiding* that object or that situation, and thereby effecting some kind of reduction in his or her anxiety. DSM-III has divided the phobic disorders into three types: 1) *agoraphobia*, in which the individual experiences either a marked fear of being alone, or else a marked fear of being in open spaces or public places from which escape might be difficult, such as crowds, tunnels, bridges, elevators, or public transportation; 2) *social phobia*, in which the individual experiences a marked fear of being exposed to scrutiny by others that will lead to humiliation or embarrassment; and 3) *simple phobias*, such as *acrophobia* (the fear of heights), *claustrophobia* (the fear of closed spaces), and fears of various animals (dogs, cats, snakes, insects, and mice). Dynamically what is important to remember is the sequence of repression, displacement, and then avoidance that constitutes the essence of all of these phobic disorders.

These dynamics are illustrated by a woman who came to treatment with her mother and said that in the course of the past six months she had become increasingly afraid to go out of the house to do any shopping. She was able to describe the exact onset of her difficulty. She was in the butcher shop, and she was waiting her turn when she was suddenly seized with an overwhelming anxiety which she could not explain, but which upset her so much that she had to leave the store before making her purchase. The next day she attempted to use a *counterphobic mechanism* by going back to the store. But it did not work. She got to the store, and she again went into a panic and had to leave.

She was then unable to do any further shopping in the butcher shop. As the days and weeks went by, in a manner similar to throwing a pebble in a pond, the phobia spread. It became the grocery, the laundry, the drug store, the cleaners, until ultimately she could not go out of the house at all unless accompanied by her mother. This person is referred to as the *phobic partner*, and the phobic partner affords protection. In this particular case the woman had been having some difficulty with her husband. She was not sexually responsive, and often made excuses so as to avoid having intercourse. On that day in the butcher store, another woman who was being served had asked for a pound of salami, and the butcher had winked at this woman and said, "You want it in one piece?" It was at that point that the patient became anxious. The fantasies and the wishes behind her defensive indifference to her husband had been reactivated, and she felt a sexual attraction to the butcher which frightened her. Freud has described a similar case, a woman who was afraid of going out on the street. He was able to establish that she was afraid to walk the street because she was afraid of being a "streetwalker." Her prostitution fantasies were operative and were being displaced from within herself externally onto the street. "It is not what is within me that is so threatening; it is something out there."

Here is the case of another woman who experienced her first overwhelming anxiety at the hairdressers. She was having her hair done, and suddenly she told the hairdresser that she had a splitting headache. She said she would come back some other time, but she did not go back again. Again the phobia spread, so that she too became virtually a prisoner in her own apartment. In this situation careful history revealed the following. She too was not having the best relationship with her husband, partly because she had always thought of her father as the most wonderful man in the world. Her father was number one, and her husband was only number two. On the night before the incident just described, she had been visited by the father who lived in another city. In the course of the visit the father was seated in a chair. She was sitting on the floor at his feet, and he was playfully touching her head and stroking her hair. At the time she was not aware of any unacceptable idea or feeling. As a matter of fact, it was a nice conversation, with her husband seated right

there, and her father caressing her hair. But on the following day when the hairdresser was touching her hair, there was a reactivation of some of her earliest wishes and desires, desires which involved wanting to have her father leave the mother and go off with the patient. We can now see more clearly the role of the phobic partner. The unconscious wish is to get rid of the mother and go off with the father. This results in the need for the person to always have the mother in sight, to make certain that no harm is coming to the mother. In men the phobia commonly has to do with aggressive impulses towards the father, expressed as a fear and hatred of animals. The hatred and fear of father are displaced onto an external object which can then be avoided, and in that way a moderately reasonable relationship with the father can be maintained.

The Process of Neurotic Symptom Formation

Thus the phobic system affords the individual a *compromise solution* to his or her conflict, but a price is paid for the peace and comfort that come from this temporary resolution of the conflict. This is the case for all of the neurotic disorders of which the anxiety disorders are only one example. Conversion disorders would be another example. As Dr. Levy has already discussed in Chapter 10, in conversion a forbidden wish or impulse or fantasy is repressed and then symbolically converted into a somatic symptom. This somatic symptom serves multiple purposes. It expresses the forbidden wish in a symbolic way; it defends against the wish; it provides punishment for the wish; and it allows some adaptive gain—all at the same time. The gain may be a *primary gain* (i.e., keeping the conflict out of conscious awareness through the unconscious mechanism of forgetting known as repression) or a *secondary gain* (i.e., allowing the individual to avoid some frightening activity). Perhaps we can illustrate more clearly these essential aspects of neurotic symptom formation by discussing a rather dramatic case of conversion disorder.

A 24 year old married woman is admitted to the ward of a general hospital around noon on a Monday with a chief complaint of an inability to walk because of paralysis of both legs. The history obtained upon her admission was that she had gone to bed Sunday night feeling perfectly well and had no reason to get up or do anything in the course of the night, but upon awakening found that she could not move her legs. She was then brought to the hospital. With such a history of a seemingly sudden onset of paralysis in a previously healthy woman, what is the first thing that one would think of as a possible cause? We would first think of some kind of vascular accident.

So we examine her and we find that both legs are warm. Her ankles are as warm as her knees, and her knees are as warm as her elbows. Her calves are as warm as her thighs and her forearms. There is no change in temperature. We feel a good pulse in both extremities. The color of the skin is perfectly normal. It is pink, with no blanching. So we say, no vascular accident here. What is the next thing we think? Spinal cord lesion. We think of a possible neurological lesion, but she has knee jerks. She has ankle jerks. She has no Babinski reflexes. Muscle tone is good. Everything is just fine. There is absolutely no indication of interference with the nervous system. Every test that we do is negative, perfectly normal.

In the course of our neurological examination, we remember that she says that she cannot feel her legs. So we take a wisp of cotton, and we rub it on her calf, and we say to her, "Tell me when you feel something." She is quiet as we go up and up and up, but as we pass the knee, she says, "Yes, something is tickling me." We take a pin, and we stick the pin in her foot. She does not budge. We stick the pin in her calf. No reaction. We stick the pin in her thigh, and she says, "Ouch." We continue to do this very carefully, and we establish that she has an anesthesia from the tip of her toe to just above the knee on both legs; and if we go all around, we find that there is a fairly clear demarcation between the anesthesia and the sensitivity. It circles her legs just above the knees. However, the books say that the cutaneous nerves do not clearly demarcate in this way. They do not stop in this fashion just above the knee. This woman has what the books describe as a *stocking anesthesia*. She has an anesthesia of that portion of the lower extremities covered by a stocking. At that point we begin to think that possibly we are dealing, not with some organic change, but rather with some functional change. We are dealing with

some psychological phenomenon, translated into a somatic symptom, but a very real somatic disability because in truth she cannot move her legs.

Is she malingering? Is there a difference between malingering and what we are about to call *conversion disorder*? As Dr. Levy indicated in an earlier chapter, there is a very fundamental difference, because in malingering the person is consciously aware of what is happening. The person knows what he or she is doing. This woman does not know. What has taken place has taken place in her unconscious mind. She did not deliberate and decide, for whatever reason, that she was going to develop a paralysis of the legs.

We are now very interested in how this came about, and as we obtain our history, we ascertain the following. She is 24 years old. She is married. Her husband is in the army, stationed overseas. She is living with her in-laws. The family includes a brother, her brother-in-law. The brother-in-law is a nice-looking man who from time to time has made little suggestions to her that go beyond brotherly interest. The previous day, a Sunday, the family had all been at home. There had been Sunday dinner, and while sitting around watching television and talking, the brother-in-law had again expressed his interest in our patient, and had made the suggestion that he might visit her in her bedroom that night. Later that night, as she was lying in bed and thinking about what he had said, she thought she heard someone at the door. She even thought she saw the door knob turn. She said, "My God, he wasn't fooling. Maybe he is coming in." She lay there, and she struggled with this conflict. She thought, "Should I get up and let him in? Or bolt the door? Or lie quietly and make believe that I don't hear him?" In her conflict one side of her said, "No. This is wrong. This is immoral. This is a brother-in-law. It's like a brother. It's incest." And the other side said, "But, it's been a long time. And he is nice. And I do need love and affection." Then the other side responded, "But it's my husband's brother. How could I betray my husband?" And in the course of this uncertainty she fell asleep, and awoke the next morning with the solution to her dilemma. Because if indeed it had been the brother-in-law at the door and she could not walk, then she could not run away or move to defend herself, and whatever might take place would not be her fault. Whatever might happen, she was not responsible and could not be blamed. This is the essence of neurotic symptom formation as illustrated in a conversion disorder.

Obsessive Compulsive Disorder

Let us tell you another story. A 10 year old boy is going to school. He gets up in the morning. Has his breakfast. Leaves his house. Walks half a block, turns left, walks two long blocks, and there on the corner is his grade school in Brooklyn. And as he is walking, he steps over every crack. He takes a long step, then a short step, misses every crack, and this is his routine. How many readers have had a similar experience? Probably a great many of you. But when you were doing this, you had not yet read this textbook, so you did not get that idea from us. So where did this almost universal idea originate? Why is it that virtually all of us have had this same experience? Some readers may even remember that with this particular activity, certain lines went through our heads, and what were they? "Step on a crack and break your mother's back." Now what kind of crazy business is this? "Step on a crack and break your mother's back?"

In 1924, A. A. Milne wrote this poem, *Lines and Squares*:

> Whenever I walk in a London Street,
> I am ever so careful to watch my feet;
>   And I keep in the squares,
>   And the masses of bears,
> Who wait at the corners all ready to eat,
> The sillies who tread on the lines of the
>   street,
>   Go back to their lairs,
>   And I say to them, "Bears,
>   Just look how I'm walking in all of the
>   squares!"*

That was London. We were talking about Brooklyn. So this experience has a universality which goes beyond the confines of Flatbush Avenue and the Brooklyn Bridge. Again we ask, from whence does this come? Why should it be that all of us had these kinds of thoughts when

we were children? The reason is because we are human beings who had fathers and mothers, and because, at certain stages of our development, we got into various kinds of conflicts with our fathers and mothers, and we developed *ambivalence*. We developed feelings of hatred as well as of love. It is this fundamental dilemma of the human condition—the polarity of hate and love for the same people—that accounts for this behavior that all of us have experienced. And it is this polarity of love and hate that is the essence of the *obsessive compulsive disorder*.

The hallmark of the obsessive compulsive disorder is the presence of a recurrent, persistent, unacceptable thought (the *obsession*) which is experienced as senseless and possibly even repugnant. The individual attempts to ignore or suppress the thought, usually without success. The person may then call upon some kind of action or ritual (the *compulsion*) that attempts to ward off the thought and protect against it, usually through the defense mechanism of *undoing* ("If I walk around the block three times, I will undo having stepped on the crack"). Another way to deal with the thought is to change it into its opposite through the defense mechanism of *reaction formation* ("I am not angry at my mother. I love her. In fact, I love her all the time"). Still another way to deal with the thought is through the defense mechanism of *isolation*, in which the thought is separated from any emotions ("If I step on a crack, it will break my mother's back. But I have no feelings about that"). The difference between the childhood situation which we have described and the clinical syndrome of an obsessive compulsive disorder in an adult has to do with the role of anxiety. It is very likely that if, as children, we inadvertently stepped on something forbidden, we might then go back and kind of redo it or undo it by missing it. On the other hand, if we were late for school and were in a great hurry, we might not go back. We might have some uneasiness about it all, but it would not destroy our day. But with the obsessive compulsive disorder, interference with the compulsion gives rise to overwhelming anxiety.

The most common *obsessions* involve thoughts of violence, contamination, and doubt. What are some of the typical *compulsions*? There are hundreds of them. Let us take some historical ones. Let us take Shakespeare. Lady Macbeth washes her hands and says, "Out, out

---

* From *When We Were Very Young*, by A. A. Milne. Copyright © 1924, by E. P. Dutton & Co, Inc; renewal, 1952, by A. A. Milne. Reprinted by permission of the publishers, E. P. Dutton & Co, Inc.

damned spot." She cannot wash it away. She cannot wash away the guilt of her murderous behavior. It may very well be that in your practice you will see someone who comes to you with both arms excoriated to the elbows, red, cracked, oozing with fluid, because the person has the compulsive need to wash his or her hands and arms 30, 40, 50 times a day. And then the red, oozing fluid itself becomes even more contamination that has to be washed off frantically. It is in *Macbeth* also that Macbeth himself says, "What's done, cannot be undone." The obsessive compulsive patient has it figured just the opposite. What is done *can* be undone. Here is the defense mechanism of undoing, of going back and missing the crack that undoes the touching. We see this undoing when people report to us that they go to bed at night, and just as they get into bed, they have the thought, "I didn't turn the gas off." They have to go downstairs and check the stove. Turn it on. Turn it off. Go back upstairs. Having gotten upstairs, again, "I'm not sure. I turned it on. Then I turned it off. But did I really turn it off? I have to go back and check." Another form of this undoing can be seen in the ritual of checking the front door. "Did I leave it open? Somebody's going to come in and murder us. Better go down and check. Fiddle with it."

What we are dealing with here are very thinly veiled aggressive, hostile impulses. The impulse is really to leave the gas on, to asphyxiate everyone in the house, or to leave the door open and thus invite some assault, usually against the spouse or the children. Here we come across another fundamental principle in psychiatric thinking, and that is the concept of *the return of the repressed*. In these situations, the repressed, hostile urges actually break through all of the compulsive efforts to keep them repressed. For by turning the gas on and off repeatedly, the person increases the likelihood that on one of those occasions, he or she will in fact leave it *on*.

A young man in treatment was describing how fastidious he was, and in this instance the polarity mentioned earlier of love versus hate is reflected in the derivative polarity of clean versus dirty. This is very, very common among obsessive compulsive patients. The idea of contamination is very disturbing to them, and the reaction formation against it is to become scrupulously and fastidiously clean about everything. This man was describing his fastidious cleanliness, and when he got to the matter of personal hygiene he said that he was so clean that whenever he had a bowel movement, he would meticulously wipe himself again and again. And then he said, "Well, God damn it. Don't you know what happens? Practically every time that I'm wiping myself my finger breaks through the toilet paper!" You can predict what he would then do. He would smell his finger to find out whether any feces had gotten on it! This man is showing very clearly how the repressed urge to be dirty, to play with dirt, even to smell it and get it close to the mouth, "breaks through" in the most literal sense imaginable. His fastidious and meticulous cleansing ritual allows his finger to "break through" the toilet paper and touch his anus.

Not infrequently, the concern with cleanliness in the obsessive compulsive disorder is reflected in considerable anxiety over touching smooth porcelainized objects, especially in bathrooms. If such people touch the bathtub or the wash basin, they have to wash their hands immediately. So they scrupulously avoid touching these objects. Thus, people suffering with this disability who have to avoid touching all kinds of things, or who have to go through some series of seemingly senseless acts to undo the horror they think they have done, become enormously restricted, and incapable of functioning in any meaningful way. Another young man suffered from a central fear that combined both a social phobia and an obsessive compulsive disorder. He had to do everything within his power to avoid urinating in the presence of another person. Therefore he could not use any public toilet because there was always the danger that someone else might enter. He structured his entire life around this central fear. He would plan ahead that at such-and-such a time in the day he would probably have to empty his bladder, and he would have to arrange to be near a private toilet at that time so as to eliminate any danger that another person might appear.

We cite this case to give you some feeling for what these people have to go through in their efforts to deal with an impulse that is so horribly threatening to them. The fear of germs, which goes along with the fear of dirt, is another very common obsessional concern. A veterinarian with a germ phobia is a good example. He was crippled in his work, absolutely crippled. Whenever he touched a cat or a dog, he would immediately have to wash his hands, and thus he could not really get any work done. We hope we have conveyed how very real these psychological conditions are, how these illnesses in which there is no organic factor are just as crippling and just as incapacitating as having two broken legs or pneumonia or any other physical illness. Furthermore, the treatment of obsessive compulsive patients is very difficult. One of the reasons for this has to do with the degree of emotional isolation that is present. Despite the fact that their symptoms cause them great distress, they tend to isolate many of their emotions from their obsessional thoughts, and in turn they may be little affected by the interaction with the therapist. They tend to talk about all kinds of external circumstances utilizing another defense mechanism of *intellectualization*, rather than talking about their inner lives and their feelings.

Anxiety States

The *anxiety states* were previously known as the *anxiety neuroses* (Figure 69.1). DSM-III has divided the anxiety states into two categories: *panic disorder* and *generalized anxiety disorder*. The essential difference between the two is that in panic disorder, the anxiety attacks occur suddenly and unpredictably, whereas in generalized anxiety disorder, the anxiety attacks are more generalized and persistent. In both conditions the anxiety attacks are accompanied by somatic symptoms of excessive autonomic arousal—dyspnea, palpitations, chest pain, choking and suffocating sensations of a "lump in the throat," dizziness and light headedness with fainting sensations, paresthesias that cause tingling in the hands and feet, hot and cold flashes throughout the body, flushing of the face and body, sweating, clammy hands, dry mouth, indigestion, abdominal pains and discomfort, frequent urination, and diarrhea—literally "every symptom in the book." In addition, because of the generalized and persistent nature of the anxiety attacks in generalized anxiety disorder, we also see in these individuals: 1) signs of motor tension—shakiness, restlessness, trembling, muscle aches including tension headaches, inability to relax, fatigability, eyelid twitches, strained facial expression, and exaggerated startle response; 2) signs of apprehensive expectation that something bad will happen to themselves or to others;

and 3) signs of excessive vigilance—hyperalertness eventually resulting in distractibility and difficulty concentrating, insomnia, irritability, impatience, always feeling "on edge." Frank Netter's drawing of a tense and anxious woman sitting on the edge of her chair (Figure 69.1) beautifully captures many of these features of the generalized anxiety disorder.

We refer to the anxiety that is present in the anxiety states as *free-floating anxiety*, because it is not connected to anything specific in the patient's conscious mind. In contrast, the phobic patient tells us that he cannot go out into the street—the anxiety is connected to the street. The obsessive compulsive patient tells us that he has no difficulty at all going out into the street, but if, while walking down the street, he does not touch every third lamppost, he becomes terribly distressed, and he has to go back to make sure that he has magically protected him-

GENERALIZED ANXIETY DISORDER
"Doctor, I'm worried, but I don't know why. I'm just worried, I have no reason to be, but I am."

Figure 69.1.   Copyright © 1957 CIBA Pharmaceutical Company, Division of CIBA-GEIGY Corporation. Reproduced, with permission, from *Clinical Symposia*, illustrated by Frank H. Netter, M.D. All rights reserved.

self. The patient in an anxiety state simply tells us about his anxiety, but he has no idea from where it comes. Our task is to ascertain with what it is connected, because it is really free-floating only in appearance. It is attached to some idea that is beyond the patient's conscious awareness. Sometimes the patient in an anxiety attack may breathe so rapidly as to cause a drop in CO_2 that leads to respiratory alkalosis and cerebral hypoxia (*the hyperventilation syndrome*). The resulting neurological symptoms (lightheadedness, dizziness, paresthesias in the fingers and mouth, headache, tetany-like contractions of the distal extremities), gastrointestinal symptoms (difficulty swallowing, abdominal pains), and cardiac symptoms (palpitations, chest pains) all reinforce the excessive autonomic arousal, and lead to a vicious cycle of increasing panic and increasing hyperventilation. Slowing of the EEG and nonspecific changes in the EKG may confuse the diagnosis and aggravate further the patient's panic. Recent research suggests possible genetic and familial factors in the etiology of panic disorder (as discussed by Dr. Reite in Chapter 52A), and certain antianxiety agents may bring rapid symptomatic relief for some of these patients (as discussed by Dr. Freedman in Chapter 52B).

Post-traumatic Stress Disorder

In Chapter 35 Dr. Dickes and Dr. Fleming discussed one example of a *post-traumatic stress disorder*, namely the rape trauma syndrome. In addition to rape, other stressors generally outside the range of usual human experience that might produce this disorder include physical assault, military combat, natural disasters (floods, earthquakes), accidental man-made disasters (car accidents, plane crashes, fires), or deliberate man-made disasters (torture, concentration camps, warfare against civilians). The essential feature of the disorder involves a reexperiencing of the traumatic event through recurrent (usually painful and intrusive) recollections of the event, recurrent dreams or nightmares of the event, and possibly even dissociative states in which aspects of the event are relived. Diminished responsiveness to the external world often occurs ("psychic numbing" or "emotional anesthesia"), with detachment or estrangement from other people, diminished interest in previously enjoyed activities (especially

sexuality), and diminished ability to feel emotions of any kind (especially those associated with intimacy). This disorder is listed among the anxiety disorders because these individuals often develop many of the symptoms of excessive autonomic arousal found in the anxiety states, as well as symptoms of excessive vigilance such as hyperalertness, insomnia, and exaggerated startle response. Many of these patients experience intense survival guilt, and their symptoms are intensified when they are exposed to situations that resemble or symbolize the traumatic event.

The post-traumatic stress disorder is a striking example of a common tendency in human beings—the need to gain active mastery over a terrifying trauma that once was experienced in a passive and helpless state. Certainly the repetitive dreams and nightmares in which the traumatic event is relived over and over again reflect this continuing effort at resolution and mastery. The Greek dramatist Aeschylus described this same process many centuries ago in these words:

> In our sleep pain that cannot forget
> falls drop by drop upon the heart.
> And in our despair, against our will,
> comes wisdom—through the awful
> grace of God.

The Role of Anxiety in Neurotic Symptom Formation

Anxiety, like guilt, constitutes a normal and universal aspect of the human condition. Anxiety serves as a *signal* that alerts us to the repetition in adult life of the primary danger situations of early childhood (Table 18.1 in Chapter 18), and to the possible dangers to ourselves and others of our inner wishes, impulses, and fantasies. However, when the anxiety threatens to become overwhelming or *traumatic*, then the process of neurotic symptom formation is set in motion. It is this pathological form of anxiety that is experienced directly in the anxiety states, indirectly through neurotic symptoms in the phobic disorders and obsessive compulsive disorder, and both directly and through symptoms in the post-traumatic stress disorder. The existential philosopher, Soren Kierkegaard (who died the year before Freud was born) understood well the relentless and incapacitating nature of this form of anxiety:

> No Grand Inquisitor has in readiness such terrible tortures as has anxiety, and no spy knows how to attack more artfully the man he suspects, choosing the instant when he is weakest, nor knows how to lay traps where he will be caught and ensnared, and no sharp-witted judge knows how to interrogate, to examine the accused, as anxiety does, which never lets him escape, neither by diversion nor by noise, neither at work nor at play, neither by day nor by night.

THE DISSOCIATIVE DISORDERS

The *dissociative disorders* are rare but fascinating conditions in which there is an alteration in the person's state of consciousness. The disturbance may be limited to the function of memory (*psychogenic amnesia*), in which the repression is so extensive that the individual is unable to recall important personal information about his or her life. Or the disturbance may be limited to the perception of one's own identity or reality (*depersonalization disorder*), in which the person experiences a sense of self-estrangement or unreality. *Psychogenic fugue* combines features of both of the above. In this disorder the individual suddenly travels away from home, is unable to recall memories of his or her past identity, and assumes a new identity. The most extreme alteration in consciousness occurs in *multiple personality*, where two or more distinct personalities exist within the individual. Each personality is dominant at different times. Each personality is a complex, integrated unit with its own memories, behavior patterns, and social relationships. And each personality may be completely unaware of the existence of the other personalities. In multiple personality we see perhaps the most powerful and persuasive evidence for the existence of unconscious fantasy. One set of unconscious fantasies coalesce to form a distinct personality that is separate (and often opposite) from the unconscious fantasies in each of the other distinct personalities. *The Three Faces of Eve* and *Sybil* are vivid case histories of patients with multiple personalities.

UNCONSCIOUS FANTASIES AND NORMAL FUNCTIONING

In this chapter we have stressed the role that unconscious fantasies play in both the anxiety disorders and the dissociative disorders. We would like to conclude by stressing the role that unconscious fantasy plays in normal functioning as well. Our unconscious fantasies become the wellspring for our creativity, our capacity for love and empathy, and our uniqueness as individuals. So we should not be too concerned about the fact that we have within us so many unconscious fantasies. It does not mean that we are "sick." It only means that we are human.

Suggested Readings

Nemiah JC: *Foundations of Psychopathology.* New York, Oxford University Press, 1961, pp 85–144.
Pasnau RO (ed): *Diagnosis and Treatment of Anxiety Disorders.* Washington, DC, American Psychiatric Press, 1984.
Schreiber FR: *Sybil.* New York, Warner Books, 1973.
Thigpen CH, Cleckley HM: *The Three Faces of Eve.* New York, McGraw Hill, 1957.

References

Arlow JA: Unconscious fantasy and disturbances of conscious experience. *Psa Quart* 38:1, 1969.
Brenner C: *The Mind in Conflict.* New York, International Universities Press, 1982.
Freud S (1926): Inhibitions, symptoms, and anxiety. In *The Standard Edition of the Complete Psychological Works of Sigmund Freud,* vol 20. London, Hogarth Press, 1959.

CHAPTER 70 The Personality Disorders

Richard C. Simons, M.D. and
John M. Macdonald, M.D.

"Character is destiny." *Heraclitus*

CHARACTER AND PERSONALITY

The term *character*, derived from a Greek word for "scratch" or "distinctive mark," refers to those mental qualities of an individual that distinguish him as a *personality*. A person does not invariably react in exactly the same way to any given situation, but he or she does tend to respond in a relatively typical or characteristic manner. An individual's *character* or *personality* is revealed in typical behavior patterns and in characteristic responses to life events and to stress situations. These behavior patterns and responses reflect a complex interaction between the pressures of the person's needs and wishes, the demands of the person's conscience, and the effectiveness of that individual's various ego functions (autonomous, adaptive, defensive, synthetic, and reality testing).

PERSONALITY TRAITS AND PERSONALITY DISORDERS

Personality traits is a term used to describe the above typical behavior patterns and characteristic responses that constitute an individual's character or personality. Personality traits are enduring but *flexible* patterns of perceiving and relating to both the external world and oneself. It is only when these personality traits become so rigid and *inflexible* and maladaptive, and thereby cause *significant impairment in social and occupational functioning*, that they then constitute a *personality disorder*. The essential difference is that personality traits are adaptive by virtue of their flexibility, whereas a personality disorder is maladaptive by virtue of its inflexibility. Personality traits allow for a widened range of responses to life situations, whereas a personality disorder limits and re-

stricts a person's range of responses to life situations.

PERSONALITY DISORDERS AND THE PHYSICIAN

The physician who is familiar with the various personality disorders is in the advantageous position of being able to recognize the presence of a personality disorder, to anticipate difficulties likely to arise in the physician-patient relationship as a result of the personality disorder, and to take preventive measures. The brief descriptions of the diagnostic features of the personality disorders provided in this chapter cannot do justice to the rich and often mixed clinical pictures encountered in medical practice, nor to the unconscious dynamics involved in each personality disorder. Examples from literature provide for the interested student illustrative case histories, unburdened by psychiatric terminology and closer to the true complexity of human nature.

CLASSIFICATION OF THE PERSONALITY DISORDERS

DSM-III groups the personality disorders into three clusters: 1) those individuals who appear "odd" or eccentric (for example, paranoid and schizoid personality disorders); 2) those individuals who appear dramatic, emotional, or erratic (for example, histrionic and borderline personality disorders); and 3) those individuals who appear anxious or fearful (for example, avoidant, dependent, and obsessive compulsive personality disorders). We would suggest a somewhat different classification that we believe is more clinically useful, one that is based on the broad classification of the mental disorders that is outlined in Table 51.1 of Chapter 51. We have found it helpful to divide the personality disorders into the following three clusters: 1) those that are often associated with the neurotic disorders; 2) those that are often associated with the functional psychotic disorders; and 3) those that are not usually associated with either. It is this latter classification that we will be presenting in this chapter.

PERSONALITY DISORDERS OFTEN ASSOCIATED WITH NEUROTIC DISORDERS

Obsessive Compulsive Personality Disorder

These persons, who love order and discipline, are conscientious, dependable, punctual, and precise, but they do not adapt easily to sudden changes, and they appear to others as unduly fussy, perfectionistic, overly strict, rigid, and inflexible. They are much concerned with orderliness, cleanliness, neatness, and the need to observe strictly even petty rules and regulations. They live by routines, and like to have everything in its place and a place for everything. A picture which is hanging at a slight angle is returned to the correct position, and their desk is kept immaculate. They may be thrifty to the point of miserliness, and stubborn to the point of obstinacy.

They are more concerned with facts and figures than with feelings, so that they may be rather cold and distant in their relationship with others. For example, the father of a girl admitted to a psychiatric ward wrote to her physician: "It would be greatly appreciated if further correspondence could be sent by airmail. Thank you for your letter dated August 19, postmarked August 23rd and received August 26th. She (referring to his daughter) has been inconsistent in seeking advice from her parents and following such advice when given." At the end of the letter he wrote: "This report was prepared by Nancy's father with the testimony and assistance of her mother and sister." It should be obvious how difficult it would be for a young child to relate to the author of such a letter.

The obsessive compulsive patient sets high standards not only for himself or herself but also for others, making quite unreasonable demands on the family and on subordinates at work. His sense of obligation to his employer makes it difficult for him to relax and to reduce his workload, even while recovering from a heart attack.

The obsessive compulsive research worker, despite his diligence, may be so handicapped by indecision, doubt, and need for perfection that he is never able to see "the big picture" and his research is never complete. All of these perfectionistic tendencies enter into the doctor-patient relationship. The obsessive compulsive patient arrives at his doctor's office well in advance of the time of his appointment. The stubborn quality of his character shows itself in his insistence upon telling the history of his illness at great length, despite all efforts by the physician to move ahead more quickly. His doubt and uncertainty are revealed in his return to the doctor's office five minutes after his departure to make sure that he mentioned some minor detail. That night there is a telephone call to correct some statement made earlier in the day to the doctor. Invariably such a patient will expect the physician to explain precisely all aspects of the diagnosis and prognosis, and to predict accurately the entire course of the treatment—in other words, to be perfect. (Figure 70.1)

Reaction formation, isolation of affect, intellectualization, and undoing are the major mechanisms of defense. Obsessive compulsive disorder is more likely to develop in the obsessive compulsive personality, who is also particularly prone to depression because of his failure to meet his own perfectionistic standards of behavior and to achieve the high goals he sets for himself.

Examples from literature of the obsessive compulsive personality disorder would be Soames Forsyte in *The Forsyte Saga* by John Galsworthy and Arthur Dimmesdale in *The Scarlet Letter* by Nathaniel Hawthorne.

Histrionic (Hysterical) Personality Disorder

In contrast to the obsessive compulsive personality, who tends to be conservative in outlook and restrained in the expression of feelings, the histrionic or hysterical personality is quick to embrace new ideas and uninhibited in the public display of exaggerated emotional reactions. He or she is usually a relatively dependent person who is constantly seeking love and attention. The sympathy or good favor of others is sought through subtle praise, open admiration, or frank adoration. If this friendly and ingratiating approach fails, there may be a less kindly reaction such as an angry outburst or a temper tantrum.

OBSESSIVE COMPULSIVE PERSONALITY DISORDER
Preoccupied with the smallest detail, these patients often bring notes along and go over and over the same theme. However, they are quite reticent about their obsessional ideas, fearing them to be signs of severe mental disturbance.

Figure 70.1. Copyright © 1957 CIBA Pharmaceutical Company, Division of CIBA-GEIGY Corporation. Reproduced, with permission, from *Clinical Symposia*, illustrated by Frank H. Netter, M.D. All rights reserved.

Dramatic and histrionic behavior attracts attention, and the observer may not at first recognize the exhibitionistic quality of the behavior. Tears and sobbing engender sympathy, but the physician may note that the feelings seem shallow and lack genuine depth. The volatile moods change like April showers. One moment the person appears to be grief-stricken, the next moment there is light-hearted laughter as if there were not a care in the world. The mood of a severely depressed person does not change so quickly, and does not respond so readily to a telephone call, or encouragement and support from the physician. The patient with an histrionic personality disorder tends to exaggerate his physical complaints, describing them in superlatives. His headaches are terrible, his nerves are shattered, there is no hope for the future, and he is going to take his life. However, he does have confidence that his doctor will help him. Indeed, his doctor is the first person who has

ever really understood him. Our first reaction, of course, is one of delight at having such an intelligent and perceptive patient, but then one soon realizes that it is still only the first interview, the patient has done all the talking, and there is very little basis in reality for this rapid assessment of our talents.

Some doctors may be drawn into intensive relations with these patients, who often seek out older persons of the opposite sex as a substitute for some important figure from the past, such as a parent. They can be quite seductive in their words, gestures, appearance, and other behavior. For example, an appointment is requested in the evening when other staff are not present in the clinic or office. This flirtatious and seductive behavior may eventuate in the expression of direct sexual feelings for the physician, but, as Dr. Franks pointed out in an earlier chapter, these patients are rarely looking for a lasting and meaningful sexual relationship. Rather, they are trying to deal with other painful feelings, such as loneliness, anxiety, and guilt, as well as a basically impaired sense of self, through the medium of sexuality.

These patients may make great demands on those around them, and when their needs for love and reassurance are not fulfilled, they may threaten suicide. Such suicidal gestures are made to gain attention, to arouse sympathy, or to frighten others into submission. The suicidal intent is rarely serious. However, fatal accidents can occur: the patient may lean too far out of a window, overdose with drugs believed to be harmless, or misjudge the time of a spouse's arrival home to turn off the gas jets on the stove. Here death becomes a tragic accident in a dramatic setting.

Repression is the major defense mechanism. The histrionic or hysterical personality may give a past history of conversion symptoms or dissociative disorders such as amnesic episodes or fugue states.

Examples from literature of the histrionic or hysterical personality disorder include Emma Bovary in *Madame Bovary* by Gustave Flaubert, Sue Bridehead in *Jude the Obscure* by Thomas Hardy, and Julien Sorel in *The Red and the Black* by Stendahl.

Masochistic Personality Disorder

The masochistic personality seems driven to seek out suffering whether through failure at work, financial loss, humiliation, or physical pain. Whenever the physician encounters a patient who has suffered an unusual series of misfortunes in life, he should ask himself whether the patient has created his own private hell on earth. The life history may include victimization in many ways: repeated rapes or other forms of sexual abuse, beatings or other inflictions of humiliation and suffering by brutal marital partners, exploitation by employers, swindling by dishonest businessmen, and unnecessary surgery by physicians who have not recognized the patient's unremitting but unconscious need for pain and punishment.

As described earlier in the book, in the syndrome of polysurgery these patients may attempt to satisfy their need for punishment by encouraging surgeons to remove any part of the human anatomy not essential to life: tonsils, appendix, gallbladder, portions of the stomach and bowels, uterus and ovaries, to mention only a few. Surgical removal of the organ may be followed by temporary relief of pain, but soon the pain reappears in another site, and the presenting symptoms suggest yet another "diseased" organ. Nearly all of these patients are attempting to deal with unconscious guilt, a chronic underlying depression, and a defective sense of the self through their masochistic behavior. They are at risk for developing overt depressive disorders.

Examples from literature of the masochistic personality disorder include Anna Karenina in *Anna Karenina* by Leo Tolstoy, Terry Dunn in *Looking for Mr. Goodbar* by Judith Rossner, Ethan Frome in *Ethan Frome* by Edith Wharton, and Tess in *Tess of the D'Urbervilles* by Thomas Hardy.

Depressive Personality Disorder

In contrast to the masochistic personality disorder, the depressive personality does not provoke punishment from others in the external environment. Rather, the conflict has become internalized, and the patient becomes his or her own torturer. As a result, such individuals are often gloomy, pessimistic, brooding, extremely self-critical and self-derogatory, and so preoccupied with their inadequacies and failures that they are unable to enjoy the pleasures of their successes. In fact, such individuals may become "wrecked by success" and develop the so-called "success neurosis," because the unconscious meanings for them of success lead to anxiety and guilt instead of pleasure and happiness.

While these individuals do not provoke their physicians into unnecessary medical and surgical interventions as does the masochistic personality, physicians need to be alert for this disorder all the same. Such patients may not be able to tolerate success in their physical health any better than they can tolerate success in their love or work relationships, and they may need to unconsciously sabotage the physician's good medical or surgical care. They are also at risk for developing overt depressive disorders, and in contrast to the histrionic personality, their suicidal attempts are usually quite serious and unfortunately often successful DSM-III classifies depressive personality disorder among the affective disorders as a dysthymic disorder rather than classifying it among the personality disorders. However, because of the stability and chronicity of this behavior pattern, we believe there is clinical validity for classifying depressive personality as a personality disorder as well as an affective disorder. Further research will determine which of these classifications is most appropriate.

Two examples from literature of the depressive personality disorder would be Hamlet from Shakespeare's *Hamlet* and Clemence from *The Fall* by Albert Camus.

Avoidant (Phobic) Personality Disorder

Avoidant or phobic personalities are extremely sensitive to any potential rejection, humiliation, or shame, and become devastated by the slightest suggestion of criticism or disapproval. Their self-esteem is severely impaired, and despite their desire for affection and acceptance they tend to withdraw from social contacts and close interpersonal relationships.

Individuals with this personality disorder may develop overt phobic symptoms, and such symptoms would then lead to an even greater restriction of their social relationships. An example of an avoidant or phobic personality disorder in literature is Laura Wingfield in *The Glass Menagerie* by Tennessee Williams.

PERSONALITY DISORDERS OFTEN ASSOCIATED WITH FUNCTIONAL PSYCHOTIC DISORDERS

Paranoid Personality Disorder

Individuals with a paranoid personality disorder show a pervasive, unwarranted suspiciousness of people. Their lives are spent mistrusting others. They are extremely sensitive to any slight, real or imagined, and are quick to take offense and counterattack. They tend to blame others for any and all misfortunes in their lives, especially physicians. Such people are constantly on guard, expect others to take advantage of them, and are always ready to go to court to protect their rights. Pathological jealousy is often prominent. Projection and denial are the major mechanisms of defense for these individuals, and their paranoid personality disorder may eventually develop into an overt paranoid psychotic disorder. A good example from literature of a paranoid personality disorder would be Captain Ahab in Herman Melville's *Moby Dick*.

Schizoid and Schizotypal Personality Disorders

The shy, aloof, distant, and reserved person who often lives alone, avoids social relationships, and lives in a world of daydreams and fantasies is described as a schizoid personality. Such individuals seem to be indifferent to either praise or criticism, and seem to be unable to feel warm, tender emotions toward others. In addition to these characteristics, the schizotypal personality disorder also manifests eccentricities of thought (e.g., magical thinking), perception (e.g., recurrent illusions), speech (e.g., circumstantiality), and behavior (e.g., complete social isolation). Both the schizoid personality and the schizotypal personality may be at risk for developing an overt schizophrenic psychotic disorder. An example from literature of a schizoid personality disorder would be Bartleby in *Bartleby, The Scrivener* by Herman Melville.

Cyclothymic Personality Disorder

As with depressive personality, DSM-III classifies cyclothymic disorder among the affective disorders rather than among the personality disorders. Again, because of the stability and the chronicity of this behavior pattern we believe there is clinical validity for classifying cyclothymic disorder as a personality disorder as well as an affective disorder. Further research will determine which of these classifications is most appropriate. Individuals with a cyclothymic personality disorder manifest a tendency toward mood swings, with hypomanic periods (periods of elation and increased activity) alternating or

intermingling with depressive periods (periods of depression and decreased activity). Such individuals may in the course of their lives develop a manic episode or a major depressive episode or a bipolar (manic-depressive) episode. Moses Herzog in Saul Bellow's *Herzog* shows the repeated mood swings of the cyclothymic personality disorder.

Borderline Personality Disorder

The very term "borderline" suggests that this personality disorder is "on the border" between a neurotic disorder and a psychotic disorder. Indeed the diagnosis has been criticized because so many of its signs and symptoms are shared with other disorders. The essential feature of the borderline personality disorder is *instability* in a variety of areas. Instability in interpersonal relationships is seen in the tendency of these patients to quickly shift between idealization and devaluation of other people. Instability of mood is seen in rapid fluctuations from a normal mood to intense depression, anger, anxiety, and other affects. Instability of behavior is seen in impulsive and unpredictable actions that are often self-destructive (sexual and financial indiscretions, substance abuse, overeating) and possibly even physically self-damaging (recurrent accidents, physical fights, self-mutilation, suicide attempts). Instability of identity is reflected in the person's uncertainty about self-image, self-esteem, gender identity, and long-term personal and professional goals. Instability of autonomy is manifested in an intolerance of being alone, and chronic feelings of emptiness and boredom.

Such a patient may speak admiringly of the physician one day, only to turn on the physician with anger and abuse the next, accompanied by complaints to the local medical society or threats of legal action for medical malpractice. Their self-destructive behavior includes a tendency to antagonize and provoke others, especially physicians, yet they cannot tolerate rejection and may become suicidal if they succeed in driving the physician away. Their impulsivity and unpredictability threaten the continuity of any long-term treatment regimen. For example, they may refuse to take the medications prescribed, or they may overdose with those very same medications in a suicide attempt. They may call the physician at all hours of the day or night, and then later lash out at the physician for not being sufficiently caring and attentive. Furthermore, the stress of physical illness may cause even further regression in these patients, sometimes to the point of brief but stormy psychotic episodes.

It is important for the physicians of such patients to set realistic goals for the treatment, to show sensitivity for the stresses likely to upset the patient, and to establish firm but nonpunitive limits on immature, hostile, and self-destructive behavior. The reasons for these limits should be explained to the patient, and the limits should be enforced promptly by everyone involved in the treatment of the patient. It is also important to avoid unnecessary referrals to other physicians, and to avoid the use of excessive or addicting medications. Perhaps most important of all—and most difficult of all—is for the physician to remember that the patient's abuse and criticism are manifestations of a serious mental disorder. These patients who abuse so readily are the very ones most desperately in need of a stable relationship with a physician to protect them from the destructive instability that pervades every aspect of their lives.

The fascinating character of Dmitri Karamazov in *The Brothers Karamazov* by Fyodor Dostoyevsky shows many of the features of a borderline personality disorder.

PERSONALITY DISORDERS NOT USUALLY ASSOCIATED WITH EITHER NEUROTIC OR PSYCHOTIC DISORDERS

Dependent Personality Disorder

These persons show a childlike dependency on others, passively allowing others to assume responsibility for their lives because of their inability to function independently. They lack confidence in themselves, and tend to cling to others, especially when they are under stress. When ill, they make unusual demands upon their doctors and will often beseige them for advice and reassurance, not only regarding their illnesses but also in other matters. They need to be given to constantly, and the early oral conflicts of these individuals may eventuate in the dependent form of hypochondriasis, alcoholism, drug dependence, and other impulse and addictive disorders as discussed earlier in Chapter 53. Patients with dependent personality disorder

who are seriously ill or who are recovering from a major operation require and receive much medical attention, and during these times they may regress to an even more childlike, dependent state. Upon resolution of the medical or surgical crisis, a sudden reduction in the physician's time spent with the patient may lead to the appearance of new physical symptoms or some more overt psychological crisis. Physicians need to spend more time with these patients than might appear necessary during their recovery, so as to be able to respond to their heightened dependent needs as appropriately as possible.

An example of the dependent personality disorder from literature is Skipper in *Second Skin* by John Hawkes.

Passive-Aggressive Personality Disorder

The passive-aggressive personality has difficulty in expressing openly his feelings of anger, resentment, and hostility. He will often deny to himself as well as to others the presence of such feelings, which find expression in passive and indirect forms of aggression or rebellion as described earlier by Dr. Franks in his discussion of the angry patient, and also in the hostile type of hypochondriacal patient as described by Dr. Rhine and Dr. Thompson. The patient's anger may be cloaked by a friendly attitude. His or her resentment may be hidden behind words of agreement and respect. Indeed, the manifestation of hostility may be so subtle that it becomes almost impossible for the recipient of these feelings (namely, the physician) to prove that he is being attacked. Attempts at confrontation meet with a slightly condescending attitude of hurt dismay at such an unjust accusation. This adds to the frustration and exasperation of those who have to live or work with passive-aggressive personalities. The frustration may lead to an outburst of anger which strengthens the claim of the passive-aggressive personality that it is not he who is the angry person but rather the other person. Although they will not openly rebel against persons in authority, they may quietly but effectively encourage others to do so. Thus, they may raise an issue at a ward meeting knowing full well that there is a major and potentially disruptive disagreement among the staff on the particular issue.

Passive procrastination, stubbornness, and obstructionism are seen in many relationships with physicians. The passive-aggressive patient expresses great confidence in the physician but "forgets" appointments and fails to take any medications despite repeated promises to do so. There is always some excuse which satisfies the patient, if no one else. "I mislaid the prescription and didn't want to bother you for another one." "I thought I was only supposed to take the pills if my pain came back after leaving the hospital." "I felt better and I thought you wouldn't want me to continue taking them." "It just slipped my mind." "I wasn't sure whether the drugstore gave me the right brand," and so on. The patient is deeply hurt by questions about his cooperation but conceals his resentment, at least while talking to the doctor. All of the personality disorders pose potential problems for the doctor-patient relationship, but passive-aggressive patients, along with masochistic, paranoid, borderline, narcissistic, and antisocial personalities, are among the most difficult to treat for many physicians.

An example from literature of the passive-aggressive personality disorder is Roger Chillingsworth in *The Scarlet Letter* by Nathaniel Hawthorne.

Narcissistic Personality Disorder

Narcissistic personalities have a grandiose sense of their self-importance and uniqueness. They see themselves as very important, talented, powerful figures and, in their relationship with others, they tend to be haughty, arrogant, and condescending. In conversation they are preoccupied with their own achievements and do not welcome attempts to interrupt their soliloquies. Their grandiosity and exhibitionism conceal inner doubts, and they have a great need for constant attention and admiration. Their sense of entitlement leads them to expect special favors from others without assuming reciprocal responsibilities, and they can become enraged when these expectations are not met. This sense of entitlement also leads them to exploit others for their own purposes, without regard for the needs and rights of others.

When they become ill, they demand the services of leading specialists. Only the best internists or surgeons can take care of someone so important. When admitted to a hospital, such patients respond to medical residents and interns with lordly disdain and indifference, and they are reluctant to provide their medical his-

tory, preferring to deal only with the Chief of Service. Narcissistic personalities are more likely to cooperate in medical or surgical treatment when physicians respond to their special needs for attention and praise.

Examples from literature include Peter Petrovich Luzhin, the wealthy suitor of Raskolnikov's sister, in *Crime and Punishment* by Fyodor Dostoyevsky. Peter Luzhin wanted a poor girl for a wife, who would not be a threat to his power, domination, and control. Mrs. Ramsay in *To the Lighthouse* by Virginia Woolf is another example of a narcissistic personality disorder.

Antisocial (Sociopathic) Personality Disorder

Antisocial or sociopathic personalities are social misfits who from an early age prove a prob-

ANTISOCIAL PERSONALITY DISORDER
"I like to gamble, I've lost a lot of money, mine and the company's, but that never worried me. As a matter of fact, I've written bad checks for as much as $1800."

Figure 70.2. Copyright © 1957 CIBA Pharmaceutical Company, Division of CIBA-GEIGY Corporation. Reproduced, with permission, from *Clinical Symposia*, illustrated by Frank H. Netter, M.D. All rights reserved.

lem to themselves as well as to society. They are unstable, reckless, irresponsible persons who have difficulty tolerating frustration. Lacking persistence, they go from one job to another in quick succession. Although many do not come in conflict with the law, their intolerance of the social and legal restrictions of everyday life contributes to impulsive and antisocial behavior that may include crimes of great violence. There is often a striking absence of conscious remorse or guilt for such behavior. Such individuals seem to lack the capacity to feel with and for others, yet on first meeting they may be very charming and impressive (Figure 70.2). Thus they may be able to form quick social and sexual relationships, but are unable to maintain them because of their callous and self-centered disregard for the needs of others and for the truth. Their irritability, aggressiveness, and impulsivity may lead them into repeated fights and physical assaultiveness, including spouse abuse and child abuse. The abuse may take the form of actual beatings of the spouse and children, or it may take the form of neglecting the physical and emotional needs of the spouse and children. Many individuals with an antisocial personality disorder seem unable to benefit from experience, treatment, or punishment, but others begin to mature in their late thirties or forties. It should be mentioned that the unreliability and irresponsibility do not show themselves in every situation. Not all personal and financial obligations are neglected and not all promises remain unfulfilled. Impulsivity does not preclude self-restraint in some areas, and disregard for the truth is not seen in every statement.

The physician should be aware of the problems likely to be encountered in diagnosis and treatment. The antisocial patient with an obscure fever may report a history of malaria in Vietnam (although he has never been abroad), may sell medicines prescribed for him, and may pay the bill for professional services with a check written on the "East Bank of the Mississippi."

Examples from literature of the antisocial or sociopathic personality disorder include Felix Krull in *The Confessions of Felix Krull* by Thomas Mann, Michael Corleone in *The Godfather* by Mario Puzo, and Mr. Hyde in *Dr. Jekyll and Mr. Hyde* by Robert Louis Stevenson.

Suggested Readings

Barchilon J: *The Roots of Horror, The Roots of Beauty: The Novel as an Expression of the Unconscious.* In press.

Frosch JP (ed): *Current Perspectives on Personality Disorders.* Washington, DC, American Psychiatric Press, 1983.

Kernberg OF (Preceptor): Borderline and narcissistic personality disorders. In Grinspoon L (ed): *Psychiatry 1982.* Washington, DC, American Psychiatric Press, 1982, pp 411–532.

Millon T: *Disorders of Personality. DSM-III: Axis II.* New York, John Wiley & Sons, 1981.

Nemiah JC: *Foundations of Psychopathology.* New York, Oxford University Press, 1961.

References

Akiskal HS, Hirschfeld RMA, Yerevanian BI: The relationship of personality to affective disorders: a critical review. *Arch Gen Psychiatry* 40:801, 1983.

Kahana RJ, Bibring GL: Personality types in medical management. In Zinberg NE (ed): *Psychiatry and Medical Practice in a General Hospital.* New York, International Universities Press, 1964, p 108.

Stoudemire A, Thompson TL: The borderline personality in the medical setting. *Ann Int Med* 96:76, 1982.

CHAPTER 71 An Overview of the Psychiatric Therapies

Joanne H. Ritvo, M.D.,
Eugene V. Friedrich, M.D.,
Jonathan I. Ritvo, M.D., and
Kenneth L. Weiner, M.D.

"The mind of man is capable of anything because everything is in it, all the past as well as all the future."

Joseph Conrad
Heart of Darkness

INTRODUCTION

What does a clinician do when a man's mind, with all of its capability and potential, becomes disturbed and causes great distress and suffering? To treat the mind of man, the physician must understand that mind, in all of its many facets. From one perspective, this entire book has tried to describe, and where possible, to explain, the multiple factors and influences that must be considered if one is to attempt to understand human behavior in both health and illness. As the conclusion to this part of the book that has dealt with psychopathology, this chapter will provide an overview of the range of psychiatric therapies currently available to help individuals who are suffering from mental disorders.

DIAGNOSIS AND TREATMENT IN PSYCHIATRY

The Diagnostic Process in Psychiatry

In order to prescribe treatment rationally, the physician must first make a diagnosis and then formulate a plan for determining the etiology of the illness. In psychiatry this task is made more complex by several factors: 1) the need to make a diagnosis along the five different axes of DSM-III, as described in Chapter 51; 2) the multiple etiological factors that may be involved in many,

if indeed not all of the mental disorders, as outlined in Table 51.3 in Chapter 51; 3) the frequent lack of correlation between specific mental symptoms and specific etiological factors; and 4) the difficulty that many psychiatric patients may have in describing their thoughts, feelings, and behavior in a reliable way.

The nonpsychiatric physician will, in the absence of pathognomonic signs and symptoms, gather more data to increase the probability of an accurate diagnosis. This additional data may come from further history and more extensive physical examination, but usually includes selected laboratory tests and other diagnostic procedures. An integration of all of this data should point to the most likely etiology and diagnosis, and thus provide a guide for treatment. In psychiatry the organic mental disorders probably come the closest to this biomedical model, but even here, the identification of a specific organic etiology, such as a brain tumor or drug intoxication, does not begin to explain the specific content of a patient's paranoid delusion. Earlier in the book, in Chapter 13, the advantages of Dr. George Engel's biopsychosocial model over the traditional biomedical model were presented, not only for psychiatry but for all of medicine. We will not repeat those arguments here, except to say that not only is our diagnostic reliability enhanced through the use of the biopsychosocial model (see Table 51.3 in Chapter 51 again), but our therapeutic effectiveness as well. Within psychiatry there are many diverse treatment interventions which can be very efficacious for a range of mental disorders if appropriately prescribed according to a specific diagnosis *and* if skillfully administered. The various treatment interventions can be classified according to Dr. Engel's "biopsychosocial model," that is, biological, psychological, and social therapies. They are overlapping and interrelated but will be considered separately for the sake of clarity.

Biological (Somatic) Therapies

Biologic or somatic therapies are based on the assumption that there is a pathophysiologic process affecting the central nervous system which is producing the disturbed behavior. These treatments are aimed at reversing the pathophysiologic mechanisms by altering the balances of certain neurotransmitters and synaptic receptor sites. The two most important of these somatic therapies have already been described in Chapter 52B: the *psychopharmaco-therapies* (antipsychotic drugs, antidepressant drugs, lithium carbonate, antianxiety drugs, and stimulant drugs) and *electroconvulsive therapy* (ECT). Other much less widely used somatic therapies include various *nutritional therapies* and *psychosurgery*. The removal of the toxic effects of drugs and the treatment of medical illnesses which cause organic mental disorders and other psychiatric symptoms could also be included here. Severely disturbed and possibly dangerous behavior, such as psychotic agitation, homicidal assaultiveness, suicidal depression, or overwhelming panic frequently require somatic treatments. In such situations specific target symptoms can be readily identified and the treatment response is often dramatic.

Psychological Therapies

Psychological therapies are based on the assumption that unconscious conflicts and maladaptive learning can affect an individual's psychological functioning and interaction with the environment. The two most prominent psychological therapies are *psychotherapy* (based on a psychodynamic model of the mind as described in Chapter 53) and *behavior therapy* (based on a learning theory model of the mind as described in Chapter 55). Two less widely used psychological therapies are *hypnosis* (based on a psychodynamic model) and *biofeedback* (based on a learning theory model). Let us first briefly discuss the various psychotherapies.

Psychotherapies may differ in their contexts—*individual, group, family,* and *psycho-* *drama*. They may differ in their lengths—*crisis, short-term,* and *long-term*. And they may differ in their goals—*supportive* or *insight-oriented*. *Psychoanalysis* would thus be considered one of the individual psychotherapies in which the frequent visits over a long period of time are designed to achieve meaningful insight into and resolution of chronic intrapsychic and interpersonal conflicts that cannot be effectively addressed by more short-term approaches. *Crisis intervention,* on the other hand, provides immediate relief for someone in acute distress who does not need or does not wish further help once the crisis is resolved. Whatever the context or the length or the goal of the particular psychotherapy, the quality of the therapist-patient relationship is crucial. It is within this relationship that the patient finds the immediate support and security necessary to observe himself, his vulnerabilities, his patterns of responding to other people, and his ways of handling stressful situations. Such knowledge may allow the patient to perceive himself and his environment more accurately, and to behave more adaptively. In a more long-term psychotherapy or psychoanalysis, the patient may then be able to uncover the unconscious meanings of his maladaptive behaviors, reconstruct their origins and determinants from his past experiences, and use these insights to significantly change many aspects of his life.

In contrast to the various psychotherapies, behavior therapy is much more *symptom-oriented*. The primary effort in behavior therapy is directed toward identifying the antecedent stimuli, the maladaptive symptom or response triggered by the stimuli, the consequences of that response, and the various reinforcers that maintain the response. The patient is then helped to unlearn or extinguish the maladaptive response and to learn more adaptive behavior regardless of the origin and meaning of the symptoms. Some of the examples and applications of behavior therapy that have been described in Chapter 55 include *token economy, systematic desensitization,* and *sex therapy,* as well as biofeedback and the emerging area of behavioral medicine.

Social (Environmental) Therapies

Social or environmental therapies are based on several general assumptions. First, environmental stress may produce symptomatic behavior. The stress may be a personal loss or a natural disaster or some other traumatic event over which the patient has no control. Or the stress may be one of a long series of crises provoked by the patient's chronic, maladaptive behavior. Second, environmental forces may reinforce maladaptive behavior and limit or undermine adaptive behavior. For example, a wife who continually covers up for her husband's gambling or alcoholism, or a husband who only responds to his wife when she is complaining of pain, each may provide the secondary gain that maintains the symptoms regardless of whatever somatic or psychological therapies are attempted. Third, environmental pressures may increase at times of major developmental change, such as leaving home for college, marriage, or retirement.

Social therapies which attempt to alter the patient's environment in a positive way include *hospitalization* with *milieu therapy, day treatment programs* that may involve *occupational therapy* and *creative arts therapies, residential placement, sheltered workshops,* and *family therapy.*

An environment which becomes more supportive and realistic in its expectations and demands on the individual will be less stressful and more growth promoting. Although family therapy is traditionally considered a form of psychotherapy for promoting new learning and insight, it also offers the opportunity for facilitating change in a crucial part of the patient's environment. Various *self-help groups* may also provide a different and more supportive environment for troubled individuals.

A Multidimensional Treatment Approach

Each of the psychiatric therapies has benefits but also risks, and therefore indications as well as contraindications. A specific review of the indications and the contraindications of each of the psychiatric therapies is beyond the scope of this chapter. However, the importance of a multidimensional approach is worth emphasizing. Although some clinicians may become overcommitted to a particular theoretical view of human behavior, the most efficacious and competent approach is invariably a *multidimensional* one which is based on a comprehensive and integrated understanding of the patient and his or her life situation. The result may be the prescription of only one type of intervention, or

several different interventions simultaneously, or several different interventions at different times. In short, the treatment should be tailored to fit the patient's needs, rather than fitting the patient to the theoretical bias of the therapist. The following case history will illustrate the use of a multidimensional treatment approach for a patient suffering from anorexia nervosa.

THE CASE OF MARY

In Chapter 60 Dr. Christ discussed the eating disorders, and the interaction of biological, psychological, and social factors that have led to a significant increase in recent years in the incidence of anorexia nervosa and bulimia. As Dr. Christ indicated, the treatment of anorexia nervosa must aim at restoring normal body weight and normal biological functions. But it must also aim at strengthening the fragile sense of identity and psychological control held by these patients, and at helping the family deal with a life-threatening illness.

The case of Mary, like Dr. Christ's patient Jane, illustrates the combination of psychiatric therapies often utilized in the treatment of anorexia nervosa. As is typical of many patients with this illness, separations, losses, and developmental milestones were major stresses for Mary. Her father had died when she was three and her sister five. Mother was a rather inflexible woman, depressed, proper and tidy. Although still young when her husband died, she never remarried but devoted herself totally to her children and her teaching profession. She regarded Mary as the "perfect daughter," totally compliant. Thus, when Mary began to lose weight in high school, mother could not believe that it might be an emotional problem. Mary was finally seen by her family physician who immediately recognized the seriousness of the problem and hospitalized her. She was 16 years old, 5'5" tall, and her weight had fallen to about 55 pounds.

Mary's hospital treatment combined individual psychotherapy, behavior therapy, family therapy, and pharmacotherapy. Initially, she refused to cooperate with either the psychotherapy or the behavioral program. She struggled with her psychiatrist and the nurses just as she had struggled with her mother over eating. Prior to being weighed, she often stuffed rocks in her robe pockets and drank large amounts of water. She did exhausting calisthenics for hours. She continued to sabotage her treatment until she realized that her discharge was contingent upon weight gain. At that point a behavioral approach of positive reinforcement for weight gain which Mary was allowed to control at her own pace was a turning point in the treatment. Antidepressant medication helped to alleviate some of the chronic depression and self-destructive tendencies that were being expressed through the anorexia, and then she became more amenable to the individual supportive psychotherapy. Here the focus was on helping her find more adaptive ways of asserting herself and establishing her identity as someone other than simply her mother's "perfect daughter." Family therapy then became an integral part of the treatment. Both mother and daughter learned to tolerate each other's anger and depression better, and began to respect each other as separate individuals. Mary began to learn to say "No" to her mother verbally rather than by refusing to eat, and the mother in turn began to see that Mary's "No" did not represent a personal attack or a lack of love.

Once out of the hospital Mary returned to high school. Although chronically preoccupied with food, she appeared significantly improved and maintained her weight at a normal level until it became time for her to leave home for college. The separation from home and from mother precipitated a severe relapse. She had been in college only a few weeks when she began to "diet" again. She was away from home for the first time. The social scene was threatening and competitive. A first sexual relationship was deteriorating. She decided she would feel better about herself if she were thinner. However, after several months of 400 to 700 calories per day, she could no longer concentrate on her studies. Her weight loss was noticeable to everyone around her, she was amenorrheic, and her treasured long blond hair was falling out. She consulted a psychiatrist, requesting outpatient psychotherapy.

After assessing her physical and nutritional state, the doctor agreed to treat her as an outpatient but only for as long as that made good medical and psychiatric sense. Outpatient psychotherapy was designed first to restore her physical health to the point where she could actively participate in treatment (it is well recognized that people in a starvation state have cognitive difficulties). The psychiatrist then began to work with her to help her identify alternative, healthier coping mechanisms to deal

with her conflicts. Only at this point was Mary able to begin to look at her sexual fears, her fears of becoming a woman and especially a mother, and her fears of adult responsibilities and pleasures. As therapy progressed and became more insight-oriented, she was also able to modify her rigid perfectionism so that she became more tolerant of herself for not being a "perfect daughter" or a "perfect straight A student." After working on these conflicts for some period of time in individual psychotherapy, Mary was then able to benefit from a group psychotherapy experience with other anorexic patients. In this group Mary's tendency to deny the seriousness of her illness and to deny the lifelong possibility of relapses and exacerbations could no longer be maintained. Mary eventually graduated from college, and although she has remained chronically preoccupied with food and with thinness, she nevertheless has been able to establish a professional career and several meaningful personal relationships.

CONCLUSION

It is our belief that the multiple psychiatric therapies that were made available to Mary at each step along the way, as determined by her needs alone, allowed her to overcome a serious mental illness and begin to achieve a full and satisfying life. Her case provides a good example of the importance of a multidimensional approach to both the etiology and the treatment of any mental disorder. While it is unlikely that any clinician would be able to master all of the various psychiatric therapies discussed in this chapter (especially as these therapies become increasingly complex, specific, and effective), a multidimensional approach allows the focus to be on the patient's needs rather than on the clinician's talents and interests. The concerned and committed clinician can then refer the patient for the appropriate therapy or therapies that are required. If this approach is taken, then we believe that the range of psychiatric therapies currently available compare very favorably in both specificity and effectiveness with the therapies available in all other areas of medicine.

Suggested Readings

American Psychiatric Association Commission on Psychiatric Therapies, TB Karasu, Chairman: *The Psychiatric Therapies*. Washington, DC, American Psychiatric Press, 1984.
Halleck SL: *The Treatment of Emotional Disorders*. New York, Jason Aronson, 1978.

PART V
Conclusion

(**Left**) *The Doctor and the Doll* (1929) by Norman Rockwell. (Reprinted with permission from *The Saturday Evening Post*, Copyright © 1929. The Curtis Publishing Company.) (**Right**) Cover from January 1, 1976 issue of *Modern Medicine* by John Berkey. (By permission of Modern Medicine Publications and the New York Times Media Company, Inc)

Section R/Why Teach Human Behavior?

CHAPTER 72 **Human Behavior and the Physician of the Future**

Richard C. Simons, M.D.

Miss Polly had a dolly who was sick-sick-sick.
So she called up the doctor to come quick-quick-quick.
The doctor came with a satchel on his back
And he knocked on the door with a tap-tap-tap.
He looked at the dolly and he shook his head
He told Miss Polly, "Put her right to bed."
He wrote on his paper for a pill-pill-pill.
"I'll be back in the morning with a bill-bill-bill!"

A few years ago a five year old girl brought this poem home from her kindergarten class, where she and her schoolmates had learned it. It is hard to imagine any child learning that poem at the turn of the century, or even in 1929 when Norman Rockwell painted his famous *The Doctor and the Doll*. But times have changed, as can be seen in the January 1976 cover of *Modern Medicine*—an updated version of Rockwell's kindly family doctor, now listening with his stethoscope to a computer instead of to a little girl's doll.

As we come to the conclusion of this book, what can we foresee for the physician of the future? There can be little doubt that the explosion of medical knowledge and the increasing need for specialization of the past decades will continue. But does this necessarily mean a concomitant preoccupation with financial rewards

(as Miss Polly's poem suggests) or a further dehumanization of the practice of medicine and the relationship between physician and patient (as depicted by the *Modern Medicine* cover)? Let us hope not. If there has been one unifying theme throughout all of the chapters of this book, it is that the physician of the future can master the increasing knowledge of medical science without losing sight of the human beings who are to be the beneficiaries of that knowledge. None of us would want to return to the days before antibiotics and steroids and immunization, when half of one's children never lived to adulthood. Nevertheless, our increasing technological advances require that we constantly keep in mind what a doctor ought to be. Norman Cousins has expressed his opinion:

> I pray that medical students will never allow their knowledge to get in the way of their relationship with their patients. I pray that all the technological marvels at their command will not prevent them from practicing medicine out of a little black bag if they have to. I pray that when they go into a patient's room they will recognize that the main distance is not from the door to the bed but from the patient's eyes to their own, and that the shortest distance between those two points is a horizontal straight line—the kind of straight line that means most when the physician bends low to the patient's loneliness, fear, pain, and the overwhelming sense of mortality that comes flooding up out of the

unknown, and when the physician's hand on the patient's shoulder or arm is a shelter against darkness. Even as medical students attach the highest value to their science, they should never forget that it works best when combined with their art, and that their art is what is most enduring in their profession. Ultimately, it is the physician's respect for the human soul that determines the worth of his science.*

This integration of science and art, of knowledge and humanity, is not easy. Those increasing numbers of medical students who are choosing to become general practitioners and family practitioners will have the task of accepting the limitations of their knowledge and expertise, and of acting accordingly in the best interests of their patients. Specialists, on the other hand, have the equally difficult task of maintaining their expertise in one area of medicine, while often feeling woefully inadequate in nearly all other areas. And both general practitioners and specialists have a further task that requires not only effort and humility, but courage as well. Life is indeed joyful. But it is also ultimately sad. For we all inevitably must lose those who are dearest to us, either through their deaths or through our own. Across the centuries the greatest of artists have recognized this bitter truth of human existence. But physicians must forge this insight from the crucible of their everyday experience, and then be able to face the ultimate end of life with each and every patient.

The drawings, etchings, and lithographs of the great German artist, Käthe Kollwitz, have been one of the continuing visual themes of this book. She could portray great joy, as in her drawings of mothers and children, but she knew great sorrow as well, and she expressed this in her art as few others have been able to do. Her many self-portraits all convey her grief and sadness (Figure 72.1). Her younger son, Peter, was killed in World War I in 1914. When Hitler came to power in 1933, her work was systematically outlawed by the Nazis. She was forced to resign from the Prussian Academy of Arts (the first woman ever to be elected to the Academy), and her art was removed from all German mu-

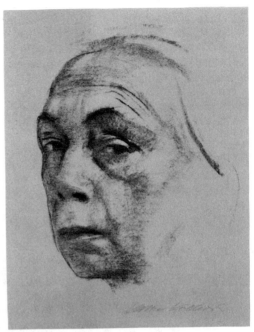

Figure 72.1. *Self-Portrait* (1924) by Käthe Kollwitz. (By permission of National Gallery of Art, Washington, D.C., Rosenwald Collection.)

seums. Despite this persecution she continued to work. In 1936, she and her husband, Dr. Karl Kollwitz (a physician who dedicated his life to caring for the poor) were interrogated by the Gestapo and threatened with imprisonment in a concentration camp. Following the outbreak of World War II, her husband died (1940), her grandson Peter was killed in action on the Russian front (1942), and her home in Berlin was destroyed in an air raid (1943). Her involvement in life, and her kindness and concern for others never ceased despite these many tragic losses. Yet she was also ready for "the call of death" which she drew in 1935 and which finally came in 1945 at the age of 78 (Figure 72.2).

How difficult it is for most of us to attain that degree of commitment, compassion, and acceptance. Yet, the ultimate mourning that we all have to face is the mourning for our own deaths. It is the unique responsibility of physicians to anticipate and experience that mourning themselves so that they can in turn help their patients to face it. As have so many artists before him, Gerard Manley Hopkins tried to prepare us for this inevitable grief of life in his poem to a young child entitled *Spring and Fall*. The girl is sad over the falling leaves of autumn, and Hopkins attempts to comfort her:

---

* *The Healing Heart, Antidotes to Panic and Helplessness* by Norman Cousins. Reprinted by permission of W. W. Norton & Company, Inc. Copyright © 1983 by Norman Cousins, p 137.

Figure 72.2. *The Call of Death* (1935) by Käthe Kollwitz. (By permission of Philadelphia Museum of Art: The Print Club Permanent Collection.)

Margaret, are you grieving
Over Goldengrove unleaving?
Leaves, like the things of man, you
With your fresh thoughts care for, can you?
Ah! as the heart grows older
It will come to such sights colder
By and by, nor spare a sigh
Though worlds of wanwood leafmeal lie;
And yet you will weep and know why.
Now no matter, child, the name:

Sorrow's springs are the same.
Nor mouth had, no nor mind, expressed
What heart heard of, ghost guessed:
It is the blight man was born for,
It is Margaret you mourn for*

---

* From *The Poems of Gerard Manley Hopkins*, 4th ed, Oxford University Press, 1967. Copyright © 1967, The Society of Jesus. (Reprinted by permission of The English Province of The Society of Jesus.)

Name Index

Abraham, K., 709, 712
Abram, H.S., 120
Abramov, L.A., 357
Abramowitz, E.S., 569
Abrams, R., 691
Abt, L., 292
Ackerknecht, E.H., 513
Adams, J.B., 238
Addario, D.A., 615, 618
Adelson, J.B., 269
Ader, R., 100
Adler, C.S., 614
Adler, J., 630
Adler, L.E., 564
Adoptee's Liberty Movement
  Association, 288
Aeschylus, 770
Agarwal, D.P., 552
Agras, W.S., 618
Ahearn, F.L., 507
Aichhorn, A., 654, 656
Akerstedt, T., 569
Akiskal, H.S., 694, 696, 705, 706, 709,
  711, 779
Alan Guttmacher Institute, 130
Al-Anon, 742
Al-A-Teen, 742
Alcoholics Anonymous, 741, 742
Aldrete, J.A., 59
Alexander, F., 79, 80, 81, 82, 84, 88,
  655, 656, 670
Allen, M.G., 552
Allen, R.M., 584
Allport, G.W., 292, 729
Alsop, S., 517, 521
Altschul, S., 507
Altschuler, K.Z., 584
Alvarez, A., 718, 720, 724
Amdur, M.A., 35, 37
American Council on Science and
  Health, 481
American Medical Association, 348,
  350
American Narcolepsy Association,
  582
American Psychiatric Association,
  323, 376, 397, 620
American Society for Prevention of
  Cruelty to Animals, 470
Ammon, 320
Ancoli-Israel, S., 584
Anders, T.F., 676
Anderson, J.C., 35, 37
Andreasen, N.C., 552, 564, 691, 696,
  702, 709, 711, 712, 758
Angel, J.L., 660, 670
Angrist, B.M., 745
Anisman, H., 100
Anna, O., 24–26
Anthony, E.J., 149, 270, 298, 451, 675,
  676, 711
Anthony, S., 303, 314
Antunes, C.M.F., 481, 485

Arensberg, C.M., 233, 239
Aretaeus, 694
Arey, L.B., 489
Aries, P., 239, 513
Arieti, S., 413, 691
Aristotle, 197
Arlow, J.A., 595, 771
Arms, S., 149
Arnoldsson, H., 666, 670
Arthur, R.J., 418, 422
Aschoff, J., 565, 569
Aserinsky, E., 569, 584
Ashenden, B., 637
Asher, S.J., 469
Association of American Medical
  Colleges, 423, 432
Austen, J., 721, 723
Azrin, N.H., 676

Babigian, H.M., 35, 37, 724
Bach, J.S., 404
Badgley, R., 440
Bagley, R.W., 239
Bahnson, C.B., 96, 100
Bahnson, M.B., 96, 100
Baines, M., 513
Bak, R.C., 389
Baker, A.H., 569
Baker, E.L., 375
Bakow, H., 677
Bakst, H., 100, 113
Bakwin, H., 298
Baldessarini, R.J., 563
Balint, M., 26
Ballenger, J., 552
Bandura, A., 610, 618
Banting, F., 500
Baran, A., 288, 292
Barchas, J.D., 563
Barchilon, John, 112
Barchilon, Jose, 88, 779
Barefoot, J.C., 94, 100
Barglow, P., 136
Barnes, A.B., 112
Barraclough, B., 724
Barrett, J.E., 421, 700, 701, 711
Barsky, A.J., 78
Bart, P., 709, 712
Bart, P.B., 485
Bartollas, C., 400
Basch, S.H., 59
Basedow, H., 19, 20, 26
Basmajian, J.V., 618
Bateson, G., 681
Beach, F.A., 400
Bean, L., 606
Bean, M.H., 745
Beck, A.T., 709, 712
Becker, E., 521, 709, 712
Becker, H.S., 432
Becker, M., 47
Beecher, H.K., 62, 67
Beers, C.W., 693, 694, 696, 702

Beethoven, L., 404, 467
Begleiter, H., 745
Beier, V., 521
Bell, A.P., 394, 395, 397, 398, 400
Bell, R.Q., 149
Bell, R.W., 642, 646
Bellak, L., 691
Bellini, G., 70
Belliveau, F., 375
Bellow, S., 776
Belt, B.G., 113
Bemporad, J.R., 298, 676
Bender, L., 629, 635, 636, 637, 641,
  642, 646
Benedek, T., 136, 149, 451, 474, 477,
  711
Benfield, D.G., 154, 157
Benjamin, H., 389
Bennett, E.L., 642, 647
Benson, E.B., 440
Berezin, M.A., 497
Berezin, N., 157
Berg, B., 157
Berg, S., 521
Berger, H., 569
Berger, M.M., 691
Berger, P.A., 563
Bergman, A., 181, 196, 637
Bergmann, K., 36, 37
Berkey, J., 785
Berkman, L.F., 96, 100, 497
Berlin, I.N., 636, 637
Berlin, R.M., 584
Berman, E., 456, 457, 463
Bernard, C., 564
Bernard, J., 459, 463
Bernstein, L., 666, 670
Besalel, V.A., 676
Best, C.H., 500
Bettelheim, B., 637
Bibring, E., 709, 712
Bibring, G.L., 26, 54, 59, 123, 136,
  226, 248, 269, 779
Bichat, 612
Bieber, I., 396, 400
Bigelow, G., 746
Binet, A., 158, 648
Binstock, R.H., 497
Birch, H.G., 144, 150, 159, 164, 635,
  637, 646
Bird, B., 52, 58
Birns, B., 149
Birren, J.E., 497
Bissell, L., 440
Blachy, P.H., 113
Blake, W., 403
Blanchard, P., 643, 646
Blane, H.T., 745
Blatt, S., 545, 552
Bleuler, E., 634, 637, 680, 684, 691
Blinn, J., 676
Bloch, D.A., 239
Block, J.L., 140, 150

Blom, G.E., 286
Bloom, B.L., 469
Blos, P., 257, 269, 651, 656, 662, 670
Blum, H.P., 226
Blumberg, E.M., 96, 100
Blumenfield, M., 59, 758
Blumer, D., 67
Bodemer, C.W., 513
Bohannan, P., 465, 469
Bohman, M., 136, 550, 552
Bomberg, D., 637
Borg, B., 153, 154, 157
Bosco, F., 696
Boshes, B., 513
Boston Women's Health Book
  Collective, 136
Boullin, D., 635, 637
Bowden, C.L., 26
Bowes, W.A., 149
Bowlby, J., 100, 286, 298, 507, 655,
  656, 709, 712
Boyd, J.H., 721, 724
Boyle, B.P., 431, 432
Bozarth, M.A., 745
Bradley, R.A., 149
Braucht, G.N., 745
Brazelton, T.B., 143, 149, 180, 196
Brearley, M., 254
Bree, G., 2
Brenner, C., 595, 771
Brenner, M.H., 416, 422
Breslow, L., 100, 497
Breuer, J., 24, 25, 26, 69, 72
Brighton, J.R., 440
Brill, H., 552
Brodie, R.D., 676
Brody, D., 47
Brody, S., 149
Bronfenbrenner, U., 462, 463
Bronner, A.F., 656
Broughton, R.J., 584
Brouillette, R.T., 584
Brown, A.W., 648, 656
Brown, C.A., 469
Brown, E., 136
Brown, J.H., 724
Brown, W.T., 552
Browne, T., 511
Brownell, L.G., 584
Brownmiller, S., 357
Bruce, D.H., 724
Bruch, H., 660, 661, 662, 663, 670
Bruegel, P., 241
Brustein, R., 453, 463
Bruun, R.D., 676
Buchsbaum, M., 563, 564, 709, 712
Budzynski, T.H., 614, 615, 618
Buffum, J., 357
Bunney, W.E., 559, 564
Bureau of Labor Statistics, 443
Burgess, A.W., 106, 354, 357
Burgess, E.W., 456, 463
Burkhardt, P.E., 552
Burlingham, D.T., 181
Burnap, D.W., 349, 357
Burstein, A.G., 26
Burt, C., 249
Busse, E.W., 497
Butler, J., 136
Butler, R.N., 484, 485, 487, 497
Butterfield, P.M., 149
Butts, H.F., 622
Byrnes, S.M., 564
Byron, Lord, 499

Byyny, R.L., 67

Cade, J.F.K., 559, 694
Caesar, 319, 320
Caffey, J., 477
California Medical Association, 431
Call, J.D., 149, 180, 196
Calvin, J., 321
Cambell, M., 552
Camerino, M., 100
Camp, B.W., 640
Campos, J.J., 150
Camus, A., 2, 775
Cancro, R., 691
Cannon, W.B., 19, 26, 88, 100
Cantwell, D.P., 646
Carlson, G.A., 440
Carlyle, T., 403
Caron, H., 41, 47
Carrier, J.M., 400
Carroll, B. J., 709, 712
Carroll, V., 422
Carskadon, M.A., 584
Cartwright, A., 44, 47, 431, 432
Cartwright, R.D., 584
Caruso, E., 406
Cassano, G.B., 694, 696
Cassell, E.J., 58
Cassem, N.H., 59, 93, 100, 507, 511,
  521
Castellano, E., 491
Castelnuovo-Tedesco, P., 113, 136
Cath, S.H., 149, 180
Catullus, 319
Ceriani, E.G., 434
Chafetz, M.E., 741, 745
Chandler, M.J., 642, 647
Chagall, M., 406
Chase, N.F., 476
Chein, I., 737, 745
Chertok, L., 136, 149
Chess, S., 144, 145, 150, 632, 637
Chez, R.A., 157
Ching-Piao, C., 584
Chodoff, P., 709, 712
Chopin, F., 407
Choron, J., 513
Christ, 403, 525
Christ, A.E., 637, 639, 646
Christiansen, K.O., 550, 552
Chung, R., 584
Churchill, W., 400
Ciaranello, R.D., 563
Cicero, 320
Cirillo, D.P., 59
Clancy, J., 552
Clayton, P.J., 696
Cleckley, H.M., 771
Cloninger, C.R., 550, 552
Cloward, R.A., 656
Cobb, S., 298
Coddington, R.D., 660, 670
Cohen, K.A., 157
Cohen, M., 745
Cohen, M.E., 551, 552
Cohen, M.B., 694, 696
Cohen, R.E., 507
Cohen, S., 745
Cohen, S.M., 548, 552
Colarusso, C.A., 451, 479, 485, 497
Cole, J.O., 554, 564
Cole, T.M., 357
Coleman, A.D., 136

Coleman, E.M., 400
Coleman, J.R., 416
Coleman, L., 136
Coleman, M., 635, 637
Coleman, R.M., 584
Coleman, R.W., 149
Coleridge, S.T., 79
Collins, J.A., 136
Collins, R.J., 734, 746
Comarr, A.E., 357
Comer, J.P., 292
Committee on Adolescence, American
  Academy of Pediatrics, 132, 136
Condorcet, M., 607
Conell, L.J., 584
Conger, J.J., 180, 196, 226, 248, 253,
  264, 270, 655
Connell, P.H., 758
Connelly, J.C., 440
Connolly, P.B., 358, 375
Conrad, J., 780
Console, W.A., 13, 113
Constantine, 509
Coolidge, J.C., 676
Coombs, R.H., 428, 431, 432, 440, 456,
  463
Copans, S., 91
Coppolillo, H.P., 477
Corbalan, R., 100
Cornwell, D., 107
Coryell, W., 552
Cotton, N.S., 549, 552
Cotton, R.T., 584
Council of Macon, 320
Council of Trent, 320
Council of Troyes, 412
Cousins, N., vii, 14, 16, 17, 18, 91, 93,
  99, 100, 518, 521, 786, 787
Cox, M., 463, 464, 469, 560, 564
Cox, R., 463, 464, 469
Cravens, J., 640
Crawford, J.T., 107
Crocetti, G., 606
Crow, T.J., 545, 552
Crowley, T.J., 569, 732
Crowe, R.R., 551, 552
Cruickshank, W.M., 646
Cullberg, J., 153, 157
Culpan, R., 35, 37
Cumming, E., 497
Cumming, E., 272, 280
Cumming, J., 272, 280
Currey, H.L.F., 357
Cytryn, L., 627
Czeisler, C.A., 567, 569, 584, 585

Dahlstrom, W.G., 94, 100
Dalton, K., 149
D'Ambrosio, R., 476
Danforth, 660
Dante, 412
Danzger, B., 144, 150
D'Arcy, C., 35, 37
Darwin, C., 197, 648
Davenport, W., 400
Davies, B., 35, 37
Davis, J.C., 627
Davis, J.M., 554, 564, 711
Davis, M., 40, 41, 47
Deets, L., 599, 605
deFries, Z., 400, 637
Deitrich, R.A., 552
deLaTour, G., 147
Dement, W.C., 569, 584

DeMeyer, M., 635, 637
Deneau, G.A., 745
deMondeville, H., 510
deSanctis, S., 628, 637
deTocqueville, A., 273, 278
Deutsch, F., 79, 88, 663, 670
Deutsch, H., 113, 342
Deutsch, M., 642, 646
Devine, R., 60, 67
deVries, J.V., 55
DeWalt, R., 446
Diamond, M., 354, 357
Diamond, M.C., 642, 647
Dickes, R., 112, 357, 389, 390
Dickinson, E., 498, 501, 504
Dickinson, R.L., 326, 327
Dick-Read, G., 138, 149
Diderot, D., 607
Dinitz, S., 400
Dittman, K.S., 676
Dix, D., 599
Dizmang, L.H., 724
Dlin, B.M., 113
Dobash, R.E., 729
Dobash, R.P., 729
Dodson, F., 149
Dodsworth, R.O., 212
Doering, S.G., 149
Dohrenwend, B.P., 419, 421, 600, 602, 603, 605
Dohrenwend, B.S., 419, 421, 600, 602, 605
Dolger, H., 46, 47
Donovan, 733
Dörner, G., 384, 389
Dostoyevsky, F., 73, 607, 777, 778
Dove, A., 620, 621, 622
Doyle, B.B., 440
Drachman, R., 47
Droegemuller, W., 477
Dubey, D., 100
Dubos, R., 618
Dubovsky, S.L., 59, 67, 78, 98, 118, 120, 763
Dulit, E.P., 270
Dunbar, F., 79, 80, 88
Dunham, H., 605
Durer, A., 715
Duszynski, K.R., 100
Dye, H.B., 647

Eastham, E.J., 36, 37
Eastwood, M.R., 37
Eaton, J., 599, 605
Eckhardt, L.O., 248, 286, 314, 646, 676, 763
Edel, L., 413
Edgerton, R.B., 745
Edwards, M.C., 664, 670
Egri, G., 605
Ehrhardt, A.A., 226, 385, 389
Eichorn, D.A., 485
Eichorn, J.R., 656
Eisdorfer, C., 497
Eisele, S.G., 390
Eisenberg, L., 646
Eisendrath, R., 59
Eisenstein, V.W., 463
Eissler, K.R., 656
Ekstein, R., 636
Eliot, R.S., 94, 99
Elkind, D., 252
Ellenberg, M., 351, 357
Elling, R., 47

Elliott, G.R., 563, 618
Ellis, F.W., 100
Emde, R.N., 149, 150, 165, 170, 181
Emrick, C.D., 745
Emslie, G.J., 477
Emurian, C., 618
Engel, B.T., 614, 618
Engel, G.L., 9, 13, 64, 66, 85, 86, 88, 90, 91, 95, 96, 99, 100, 112, 113, 500, 507, 707, 711, 758, 780, 781
English, O.S., 226, 646
Entwisle, D.R., 149
Enzer, N.B., 670
Erikson, E.H., 160, 163, 164, 172, 180, 184, 196, 225, 226, 245, 248, 259, 270, 288, 292, 443, 448, 451, 456, 478, 479, 485, 492, 497
Escalona, S.K., 181
Esman, A.H., 270
Etemad, J.G., 637
Etzel, B.C., 150
Evans, A.E., 314
Evans, R.B., 400
Evans-Wentz, W.Y., 521
Eyer, J., 724
Eysenk, H., 737, 745

Falstein, E.I., 248
Farberow, N.L., 724
Farley, G.K., 248, 286, 314, 634, 646, 676, 763
Farquhar, J.N., 617, 618
Fasanella, 404
Feifel, H., 513
Feinstein, S.C., 270
Feldberg, R., 469
Feldman, S.S., 150
Felice, M., 357
Ferenczi, S., 79, 88
Fernbach, S.K., 584
Ferris, S.H., 497
Fielding, H., 749
Fieve, R.R., 552
Fildes, L., 1, 40
Finch, C.E., 497
Finch, S., 270, 667, 670
Fine, L.L., 270
Finkelhor, D., 476
Finkle, B.S., 724
Fisher, C., 676, 677
Flaubert, G., 774
Flavell, J.H., 254
Fleck, S., 670
Fleischer, S.F., 569
Fleming, J., 314, 507
Flexner, A., 423
Foa, E., 618
Follman, J.F., 35, 37
Folstein, S., 548, 552, 636
Fontana, V.J., 476
Ford, C.S., 400
Ford, C.V., 78, 133, 136
Forssman, H., 134, 136
Fox, R.P., 741, 745
Foxx, R.M., 676
Foy, J.L., 136
Fraiberg, S.H., 140, 141, 150, 180, 196, 226
Francke, L.B., 463
Frankl, V.E., 511, 513
Franks, R.D., 106, 564, 695
Frederick, C.J., 724
Freedman, A.M., 623
Freedman, N., 47

Freedman, R., 564, 691
French, T.M., 88, 670
Freud, A., 165, 181, 262, 263, 270, 292, 298, 595
Freud, S., 26, 50, 69, 72, 86, 158, 159, 160, 180, 188, 197, 213, 215, 216, 217, 218, 221, 240, 259, 287, 292, 322, 323, 341, 342, 377, 402, 414, 422, 441, 442, 450, 451, 460, 463, 507, 521, 541, 586, 587, 593, 595, 608, 709, 711, 712, 718, 724, 728, 729, 765, 770, 771
Friberg, L., 745
Friedman, M., 100, 417, 422, 617, 618
Friedman, R., 157
Friedman, R.M., 292
Frosch, J., 528–530, 587–591, 691
Frosch, J.P., 779
Frost, R., 405, 408, 409
Frostig, H., 646
Fry, J., 34, 37
Fujita, S., 584
Fuller, C.A., 569
Fuller, M., 106
Funkenstein, D.H., 432
Furman, E., 314
Furman, R.A., 314
Furst, P., 598

Gabbard, G., 131, 136
Gabrielli, W.F., 552
Gadpaille, W.J., 389, 391, 400
Gadzago, C., 637
Gaensbauer, T.J., 149, 181
Gaffney, S., 552
Gagnon, J.H., 400
Gaines, R., 477
Galbraith, J.K., 274
Galenson, E., 149, 180, 196
Galileo, 403, 411
Galsworthy, J., 773
Galton, F., 544
Gardner, G.G., 302
Gaskill, E.B., 113
Gebhard, P.H., 451
Gedo, J.E., 413
Geer, B., 432
Geiger, K., 239
Gelles, R.J., 729
Gerall, A., 383
Gerard, M.W., 248
Gershon, E.S., 546, 547, 552, 709, 712
Gersick, K.E., 465, 469
Gesell, A., 159
Getto, C.J., 67
Gewirtz, J.L., 150
Giacometti, A., 405, 663
Gill, M.J., 745
Ginsburg, H., 254
Giotto, 404
Gitlin, M.J., 113
Gittman, 646
Glaser, B.G., 239
Glass, G.V., 36, 37
Glass, R.M., 115, 120
Glenn, J., 348
Glicken, A.D., 157
Glickman, L., 59, 724, 758
Glueck, E.T., 655, 656
Glueck, S., 655, 656
Goddard, H.H., 648, 656
Goddard, K.E., 150
Goedde, H.W., 552
Goldberger, J., 597, 598

Golden, G.S., 677
Golden, J.S., 349, 357
Goldfarb, W., 159, 164, 635, 636, 637
Goldhammer, H., 599, 603, 605
Goldin, G., 513
Goldney, R.D., 724
Goldstein, A., 618
Goldstein, J., 292
Goldstein, J.H., 59
Goldstein, K., 640, 642
Goldstein, S., 463
Goldstein, S.G., 357
Goldwyn, R.M., 113
Gonda, T.A., 521
Gonne, M., 444
Goode, W.J., 239, 463
Goodenough, D., 47
Goodman, L.S., 724
Goodstein, R.K., 729
Goodwin, D.W., 540, 549, 552, 745
Goodwin, F.K., 712
Gordon, K.K., 143, 150
Gordon, R.E., 143, 150
Goring, C.S., 648, 656
Gottesman, I.I., 552
Gould, Robert, 298
Gould, Roger, 456, 463, 479, 485
Gould, R.W., 477
Gove, W.R., 605
Goy, R.W., 383, 390
Gradstein, B., 157
Graham, M.D., 745
Graham, S., 279
Grant, R.L., 120
Green, A., 618
Green, Arthur, 473, 477
Green, A.W., 357
Green, E., 614, 618
Green, H., 691
Green, M., 47, 314
Green, R., 357, 360, 375, 389, 390,
  400, 444, 451
Greenacre, P., 342, 390
Greenblatt, D.J., 564, 584
Greene, W.A., 96, 100
Greenglass, E.R., 136
Greenson, R.R., 390, 451
Griffiths, R., 637
Grinspoon, L., 497
Groban, S.E., 67
Grofé, F., 629
Grollman, E., 462
Grossman, B., 47
Grossman, M., 485
Grossman, S., 59, 67, 120
Groth, M., 453
Group for the Advancement of
  Psychiatry, 357
Grove, W.M., 545, 552
Groves, J.E., 106
Grundlach, R.H., 400
Guerra, F., 59
Guilleminault, C., 584, 585
Guirguis, W.R., 637, 691
Gull, W., 662, 670
Gunderson, E.K.E., 418
Gurwitt, A.R., 149, 180
Gussow, J.D., 646
Gutmann, D.G., 483, 485
Guze, S.B., 540, 700, 701, 711

Habenstein, R.W., 239
Hackett, T.P., 57, 59, 66, 93, 100, 113,
  534

Hader, E., 39
Hadrian, 320
Hagberg, K., 47
Hagerman, R.J., 627, 637
Haggerty, R.J., 33, 37
Halberg, F., 566, 568, 569
Hale, M.L., 120
Hall, E., 279, 280
Hall, J.E., 627
Hall, R.C.W., 115, 117, 120
Hallahan, D.P., 646
Halleck, S.L., 783
Hamburg, D.A., 618
Hammersmith, S.K., 400
Hammurabi, 470
Hampson, J.G., 390
Hampson, J.L., 389, 390
Hampson, R.B., 292
Haponik, E.F., 584
Harada, S., 552
Hardy, M., 41, 47
Hardy, T., 774, 775
Hare, S., 89
Harlow, H.F., 165, 170, 181, 201, 202,
  203, 204, 212, 474
Harlow, M.K., 212
Harmon, R.J., 154, 155, 157, 181
Harper, J., 632, 637
Harper, L.V., 149
Harris, H.I., 35, 37
Hartmann, E.L., 584
Hartmann, H., 463
Haskett, R.F., 569
Haskins, J., 622
Hauri, P., 571, 579, 584
Havens, L.L., 723, 724
Hawkes, J., 777
Hawthorne, N., 773, 778
Haylick, L., 497
Haynes, R.B., 47
Hays, P., 552
Hazell, L.D., 150
Healy, W., 654, 656
Hebert, F.B., 248, 286, 314, 646, 676,
  763
Heilbronn, M., 67
Heine, H., 718
Heinzelmann, F., 239
Helfer, R.E., 477
Heller, J., 698, 699, 700
Heller, T., 635, 637
Hendin, H., 270, 398, 400
Heraclitus, 772
Herbsman, H., 758
Herjanic, B., 270
Herjanic, M., 712
Herman, J., 477
Hernandez, S.F., 584
Herschkowitz, S., 390
Herzog, D.B., 670
Hesiod, 415
Hess, J.H., 670
Hetherington, E.M., 463, 464, 469
Hickler, H., 270
Hijmans, J.C., 670
Hilberman, E., 357, 729
Hill, M.J., 745
Hinde, R., 198
Hinton, J.M., 518, 519, 521
Hippocrates, 16, 19, 79, 509, 513, 616,
  665, 701
Hirsch, J., 658, 660, 670
Hirschfeld, R.M.A., 711, 779
Hitchfield, E., 254

Hite, S., 442, 451
Hittelman, J., 150
Hitzig, W., 14
Hobbes, T., 607
Hobson, J.A., 584
Hoenk, P.R., 552
Hoffmann, H., 745
Hofling, C.K., 497
Holinger, P.C., 724
Holistic Medicine Movement, 17
Hollander, M.A., 113
Hollender, M.H., 20, 26, 46, 47
Hollingshead, A.B., 600, 604, 606
Holmes, T.H., 9, 13, 87, 88, 417, 418,
  419, 421, 422, 428
Holmstrom, L., 354, 357
Holzman, P. S., 564, 691
Homer, 701
Hooker, E., 400
Hoon, E.F., 400
Hoon, P.W., 400
Höpker, T., 188
Hopkins, G.M., 787, 788
Horne, D., 646
Horne, R.L., 96, 100
Hospels, A., 485
Houdini, H., 612
House, J.F., 618
Howells, J.G., 136, 497, 637, 691
Hrubec, Z., 552
Hudson, J.I., 670
Huffman, J.W., 113
Hughes, J., 564
Hull, R., 485
Humanistic Medicine Movement, 17
Hunt, C.E., 584
Hunt, D.D., 389, 390
Hunt, M.M., 323, 442, 451
Huston, A.C., 180, 196, 226, 248, 270
Hutchings, B., 552
Huxley, A., 754
Hydinger-Macdonald, M., 569

Ibsen, H., 452, 453
Iglauer, C., 745
Iker, H., 96, 100
Ikomi, F., 746
Ilgenfritz, M.P., 464, 469
Imperato-McGinley, J., 383, 390
Inhelder, B., 254
Insel, T.R., 552
Ipsen, J., 150
Ismond, D.R., 637

Jacklin, C.N., 226
Jackson, D.D., 681
Jackson, H., 748, 758
Jackson, R.W., 357
Jacobsen, G., 552
Jacobson, E., 226
James, W., 700
Jaques, E., 485
Jefferson, T., 607
Jensen, V.W., 724
Jersild, A.T., 671, 677
Jessner, L., 136, 286
Johnson, A.M., 248, 298, 653, 655, 656
Johnson, R.P., 440
Johnson, V.E., 126, 129, 136, 142, 150,
  322, 324–337, 338, 341, 342, 343,
  348, 359–375, 392, 394, 400, 485,
  489
Johnson, W.E., 357
Jolly, K., 476

Jones, R.W., 440
Jordan, K., 640
Josselyn, I.M., 270
Jost, A., 383, 390, 444
Jouvet, M., 584
Justice, B., 477
Justice, R., 477

Kagan, J., 180, 196, 226, 248, 264, 270, 655
Kahan, E.B., 113
Kahana, R.J., 26, 54, 59, 226, 248, 269, 779
Kahn, J.H., 676
Kaij, L., 150
Kales, A., 584
Kales, J.D., 584
Kallmann, F., 544, 548, 552, 709, 712
Kammeier, M.L., 745
Kanner, L., 620, 627, 629, 631, 632, 633, 636, 637, 658, 660, 670
Kantner, J.F., 136
Kaplan, E.H., 348
Kaplan, H.I., 623
Kaplan, H.S., 357, 359, 360, 364, 368, 370, 371, 373, 375, 457, 463, 497
Kapostins, E., 143, 150
Karacan, I., 357
Karasek, R., 417, 422
Karasu, T.B., 100, 783
Kardener, S.H., 106
Karlen, A., 350, 357, 391, 400
Karmel, M., 149
Karnovsky, M.L., 584
Karp, S., 47
Karush, A., 667, 670
Kashani, J.H., 298
Kastenbaum, R., 314, 513
Katsikitis, M., 724
Katz, M.M., 712
Kaufman, A., 357
Kaufman, I., 497
Kaufman, I.C., 212
Kaufman, M.R., 663, 670
Kaufman, S., 624, 627
Kawi, A., 646
Kaye, H.E., 396, 400
Keith, P.R., 677
Kellerman, J., 302
Kelly, J.B., 461, 463, 469
Kempe, C.H., 59, 470, 477
Kendall, R.E., 670
Kendler, K.S., 548, 552
Keniston, K., 270, 432, 656
Kennedy, J.A., 100, 113
Kennedy, J.F., 499
Kennedy, S.J., 584
Kennell, J.H., 141, 149, 150, 157
Kephart, N.E., 647
Kernberg, O., 779
Kessler, R.C., 606
Kety, S.S., 545, 552
Khayyam, O., 713
Kiell, N., 664, 670
Kierkegaard, S., 770
Kilmann, P.R., 375
Kimball, C.P., 59, 113, 120
Kimmel, D.C., 451, 497
King Henry VIII, 510
King, S., 271, 279, 280
King, S., 547, 553
Kinney, D.K., 552
Kinsey, A.C., 371, 375, 393, 400, 442, 451, 489

Kipling, R., 716, 717
Kirk, P., 157
Kirkendall, L.A., 456, 463
Kirscht, J., 47
Kissin, B., 745
Kitzinger, S., 139, 149, 150
Klaus, M.H., 141, 149, 150, 157
Klawans, H.L., 564
Kleitman, N., 569, 584
Klerman, G.L., 78, 421, 692, 696, 700, 701, 702, 705, 709, 711, 712
Kliman, G.W., 149
Knapp, P.H., 665, 670
Knapp, R.J., 154, 157
Knights Templars, 412
Knobloch, H., 164, 641, 647
Knudson, A.G., 314
Kohen, J.A., 464, 469
Kohut, H., 298
Kokkoris, C.P., 569
Kollwitz, Karl, 787
Kollwitz, Käthe, 4, 10, 148, 297, 304, 315, 500, 501, 514, 516, 698, 699, 716, 787, 788
Kolodny, R., 368, 374, 375
Koos, E., 280
Koranyi, E.K., 115, 120
Korner, A., 181
Kornetsky, C., 745
Kornfeld, D.S., 120, 758
Korsch, B., 44, 47
Kovach, B., 511
Kraepelin, E., 268, 679, 681, 694, 701
Kramp, P., 758
Krasnegor, N.A., 745
Krauthammer, C., 692, 696, 701, 711
Krementz, J., 292
Kretschmer, E., 539
Kripke, D.F., 569, 584
Kris, E., 149
Kriz, V., 53
Kron, R.E., 150
Kropotkin, 607
Krueger, J.M., 584
Kruszewski, S.P., 552
Kübler-Ross, E., 157, 237, 302, 508, 515, 516, 518, 521
Kupfer, D.J., 584, 709, 712
Kushner, H.S., 513
Kuzma, K., 292

Ladd, G.T., 569, 584
LaLonde, M., 615, 618
Lamaze, F., 62, 130, 138
Lamb, C., 48
Lamb, E., 136
Lamont, J.H., 670
Langley, R., 729
Langner, T.S., 532
Lapouse, R., 606
Lasker, J., 153, 154, 157
Lassen, C.L., 375
LaVallée, Y.J., 615, 618
Lawton, M.P., 497
Lazare, A., 72
Lear, M.W., 356, 357
Leary, T., 754
Leboyer, F., 150
Leff, J.P., 681, 690, 691
Leibs, S.A., 157
Leigh, H., 13, 26, 59, 540
Leighton, A.H., 525, 532, 606
Lemkau, P., 606
Leonhard, K., 702, 711

LeShan, L., 96, 100
Lesser, L.I., 636
Lester, D., 724
Leurgans, S., 136
Levi, L., 417, 419, 422
Levine, D.G., 745
Levine, D.M., 432
Levine, M.D., 675, 677
Levinger, G., 463, 464, 465, 469
Levinson, D.J., 456, 463, 479, 485
Levitan, S.J., 120
Levitas, A., 552, 626, 627, 637
Levy, N., 113
Levy, N.B., 57, 59, 88, 89
Levy, R.C., 729
Lewin, B., 694, 696
Lewinsohn, P., 709, 712
Lewis, C.E., 432
Lewis, C.S., 503, 507
Lewis, D.O., 656
Lewis, J.M., 521
Lewis, M., 181
Lewis, M.I., 485, 497
Leynes, C., 134, 136
Licht, H., 323
Lichtenstein, M., 648, 656
Lichtenstein, R., 53
Lidz, T., 180, 196, 226, 239, 248, 270, 451, 485, 497, 545, 552, 681
Lieberman, G.L., 482, 485
Lief, H.I., 348, 350, 357, 456, 457, 463
Lilley, M.C., 235
Lindbergh, A.M., 506
Lindemann, E., 155, 157, 298, 502, 507, 758
Lindner, R., 656
Linkowske, P., 552
Linn, L., 758
Linton, A.L., 745
Lipowski, Z.J., 113, 120, 758
Lipsitt, D.R., 78
Lipton, R.C., 150
Lister, J., 597
Lobitz, W.C., 375
Locke, J., 607
Lockyer, L., 637
Lombroso, C., 648, 656
Long, K.D., 136
Longfellow, C., 469
Loosen, P.T., 709, 712
Loper, R.G., 745
Lorenz, K., 172, 173, 198
Lothstein, L.M., 390
Lourie, R.S., 627
Lown, B., 93, 100
Luce, J.M., 67
Luparello, T.J., 78, 670
Luria, A.R., 159, 164
Lusk, L., 421
Luther, M., 321
Lutz, J., 628, 637
Lynch, J.J., 505, 507
Lyon, J.M., 75, 78

Maas, J.W., 564, 711
MacAndrew, C., 745
Maccoby, E.E., 150, 226
Macdonald, J.M., 729
Macdonald, M., 44, 47
Macfarlane, J.A., 147, 150
Mack, J.E., 270
MacKinnon, R.A., 532
MacVane, J.R., 694, 696

Maggini, C., 694, 696
Mahan, J.L., 418
Mahler, M.S., 159, 160, 170, 172, 174, 181, 182, 196, 632, 633, 636, 637
Mai, F.M., 136
Maimonides, 509
Malinowski, B., 280
Maller, J.B., 648, 656
Malone, C.A., 655, 656
Maltsberger, J.T., 724
Mandell, A.J., 485
Mann, E.C., 125, 136
Mann, T., 86, 89, 779
Margolis, R., 421
Marks, R.M., 63, 67
Marmor, J., 390, 400
Marohn, R.C., 656
Marshall, A.W., 599, 603, 605
Martin, C.E., 375, 400, 451
Martin, H.P., 477, 640
Martin, L.M., 357
Martin, M.J., 117, 120
Mary Ellen, 470
Mascagni, P., 406
Mason, J.I., 746
Mason, W.A., 212
Masters, W.H., 126, 129, 136, 142, 150, 322, 324–337, 338, 341, 342, 343, 348, 359–375, 392, 394, 400, 401, 485, 489
Masuda, M., 35, 37
Matthysse, S., 552
Maugh, T.H., 584
Mazor, M.D., 136
McArthur, C., 13, 440
McBogg, P.M., 627, 637
McCarthy, J., 136
McCary, J.L., 348
McClearn, G.E., 552
McCloskey, K.L., 724
McCord, J., 657
McCord, W., 657
McCue, J.D., 440
McDermott, J.F., 463
McDevitt, J.B., 196, 646
McDougall, W., 198
McDowell, E., 107
McGinley, P., 450
McKay, H.D., 649, 657
McKegney, P.F., 120₁
McKeown, T., 615, 618
McKinney, W.T., 709, 711
McKinsey, M.E., 497
McRae, J.A., 606
Mechanic, D., 419, 422, 606
Mednick, S.A., 550, 552
Megadux Notarus, 322
Meiselman, K.C., 477
Melchior, C.L., 745
Melville, H., 776
Melzack, R., 61, 67
Mendel, G., 648
Mendelson, J., 758
Mendelson, M.A., 497
Mendlewicz, J., 547, 552
Menken, J., 136
Menning, B.E., 134, 135, 136
Menninger, K.A., 109, 113, 425, 432, 440, 451, 656, 715, 719, 724
Mensh, I.N., 106
Merskey, H., 61, 67
Meyer, B.C., 56, 59, 67
Meyer, J.K., 375, 389, 390
Michael, S.T., 532
Michelangelo, 404, 407

Michels, R., 532
Miles, L.E.M., 569
Miller, D.C., 440
Miller, E., 497
Miller, G., 100
Miller, J.G., 164, 670
Miller, L.C., 677
Miller, N.E., 614, 618
Miller, P.R., 447
Miller, Sara, 18
Miller, Stuart, 18
Miller, S.J., 400
Miller, W.B., 657
Millon, T., 779
Mills, K.H., 375
Mills, T., 729
Milne, A.A., 238, 767
Minuchin, S., 668, 669, 670
Mirsky, I.A., 80, 81, 88
Mishler, E., 606
Mitchell, W.D., 120
Mitford, J., 239
Moles, O.C., 463, 464, 465, 469
Money, J., 195, 226, 382, 385, 389, 390
Monica, 95
Moore, H., 450
Moore, P., 693
Moore-Ede, M.C., 569, 584
Moos, R.H., 48, 59, 89
Moran, M.G., 120, 497
Morel, B., 679
Moroney, R.M., 239
Morris, M.G., 477
Morse, R., 720
Mozart, W.A., 404
Mullaney, D.J., 614
Mullen, P.E., 584
Mumford, E., 36, 37, 279, 280, 421, 432
Munch, E., 310, 445, 447, 448, 449, 523, 686, 704
Murphy, G.E., 100, 712, 724, 763
Murphy, J.M., 606
Murray, R.M., 745
Murrell, M.E., 724
Musaph, H., 485
Muslin, H., 113
Mussen, P.H., 180, 196, 226, 248, 270
Myers, J., 606
Myers, R.D., 745

Nadelson, C.C., 133, 136, 292, 428, 432, 451, 463
Nagy, M., 303, 314
Nanninga, J.B., 113
National Council on Alcoholism, 740
National Institute of Mental Health, 3, 568
National Institute on Aging, 481
National Institute on Drug Abuse, 730, 744
National Institutes of Health, 481
National Mental Health Association, 693
Native American Church, 745
Natterson, J.M., 314
Negrete, V., 44, 47
Nellhaus, G., 640
Nelson, J.B., 226
Nemiah, J.C., 26, 59, 507, 596, 771, 779
Nemiroff, R.A., 451, 479, 485, 497
Netter, F.H., 769, 774, 778
Neugarten, B.L., 480, 482, 484, 485, 491, 497
Newman, L.E., 390

Nicholas, C.R., 497
Nichter, M., 280
Niederland, W.G., 413, 504, 507, 691
Nies, A.S., 120, 497
Nietzsche, 279
Niggemeyer, E., 127
Nilsson, A., 150
Nixon, R.M., 418
Norton, J., 521
Notman, M.T., 112, 113, 136, 292, 428, 432, 451, 463, 485
Novack, D.H., 518, 521
Noyes, R., 551, 552
Nursten, J.P., 676

O'Brien, J.P., 724
O'Brien, R., 635, 637
O'Connor, V.J., 113
Odoroff, C.L., 35, 37
Offer, D., 268, 270, 532, 656
Offer, J.B., 268, 270
Ohlin, L.E., 656
Oken, D., 518, 521
Okudaira, N., 584
Olsen, L., 563, 564
Opler, M.K., 278, 280, 532
Oppel, W.C., 674, 677
Opper, S., 254
Orgel, S., 724
Ornitz, E.M., 635, 636
Orr, W.C., 584
Osler, W., 423, 431
Osofsky, H.J., 149
Osofsky, J.D., 144, 149, 150
Ostrov, E., 656
Ovesey, L., 390, 400

Page, A.W., 729
Palenski, C.O., 157
Palmore, E., 497
Pannor, R., 288, 292
Pachtman, E., 564
Pappenheimer, J.R., 584
Pardes, H., 421, 536, 537
Parents Anonymous, 476
Parkes, C.M., 87, 89, 100, 237, 239, 505, 507
Parron, D.L., 618
Parsons, T., 238, 239
Pasamanick, B., 163, 164, 606, 641, 642, 645, 646, 647
Pasnau, R.O., 113, 771
Passmore, J., 618
Patterson, W.M., 724
Pauls, D.L., 552
Pauly, I.B., 357, 389, 390
Pavenstedt, E.A., 642, 645, 647
Pavlov, I.P., 608
Paykel, E.S., 150, 421, 422, 711
Peabody, F.W., 13, 26, 724
Pearson, G.H.J., 226, 646
Pearson, M.M., 440
Pederson, A.M., 724
Peffer, K.E., 618
Pellegrino, E., 271, 280
Peppers, L.G., 154, 157
Perlman, A., 113
Perlmutter, J.F., 485
Perlow, M., 564
Perry, D., 637
Perry, S., 67
Persky, H., 463
Person, E., 390
Peshkin, M.M., 666, 670

Peters, F., 691
Petersen, A.C., 270
Petersen, R.C., 746
Peterson, O., 432
Petrich, J., 422
Petty, T.A., 724
Pfeffer, C.R., 298
Pfeiffer, E., 497
Phillips, J.L., 254
Phipps-Yonas, S., 136
Phoenix, C.H., 390
Piaget, J., 159, 160, 180, 191, 193, 241,
    249–254, 263
Picard, R.S., 96, 100
Picasso, 402
Pickens, R., 746
Pierce, C.M., 248
Pierson, G., 280
Pine, F., 181, 196, 637
Pizer, H., 157
Planned Parenthood, 130
Plath, S., 713, 719, 720
Plato, 18, 228, 299, 403
Platt, B.B., 149
Plimpton, T., 421
Plum, F., 758
Plumer, R., 521
Pollin, W., 552
Pollock, G.H., 26, 88, 89, 113, 314, 711
Pomeroy, W.B., 375, 400, 451
Pope, H.G., 664, 670
Posner, J.B., 758
Poznanski, E.O., 298
Prange, A.J., 709, 712
Pratt, L., 43, 47
Presley, E., 504
Price, G., 77
Prior, M., 632, 637
Prizant, G., 35, 37
Proust, M., 405
Provence, S., 149, 150
Prugh, D.G., 181, 196, 226, 248, 270,
    286, 314, 667, 670
Prusoff, B.A., 422
Purcell, K., 666, 670
Puzo, M., 779

Quasimodo, 404
Quay, H.C., 656
Queen, S.A., 239
Quinlan, K., 236

Raaschow-Nielsen, E., 746
Rackemann, F.M., 664, 670
Rada, R.T., 358
Rahe, R.H., 9, 13, 87, 88, 89, 417, 418,
    419, 421, 422, 428
Rainer, J.D., 547, 552
Ramsey, T.A., 560, 564
Rangell, L., 72
Rank, B., 637
Raphael, 404
Raphaelson, O.J., 758
Rapoport, J.R., 637
Raskin, M., 432
Rasmussen, K.L.R., 212
Raynal, D.M., 569
Reader, G., 47
Rechtschaffen, A., 584
Redl, F., 656
Redlich, F.C., 600, 604, 606
Reich, P., 100, 358
Reich, T., 746
Reichel, W., 497

Reichsman, F., 57, 59, 88, 89, 95, 100
Reisberg, B., 497
Reiser, D.E., 18, 26, 59, 432, 655, 657
Reiser, M.F., 13, 26, 59, 81, 88, 540
Reiss, A.J., 400
Reiss, D., 239
Reissman, F., 627
Reite, M., 212
Reiterman, C., 136
Rennie, T.A.C., 525, 532
Resnik, H.L., 724
Resolve, 135
Reter, D.J., 389, 390
Reubsaat, H.J,. 485
Reynolds, C.F., 585
Rhine, M.W., 695
Rhoads, J.M., 440
Richards, D.H., 113
Richter, C.P., 95, 100
Richter, L., 375
Richter, M., 75
Rieker, P.P., 729
Rimland, B., 631, 635, 636, 637
Rimmer, J., 746
Ringrose, C.A.D., 136
Ritter, F.B., 495
Ritvo, E.R., 635, 636
Robertson, James, 281, 282, 286, 594,
    595
Robertson, Joyce, 594, 595
Robins, E., 400, 606, 700, 701, 711
Robinson, J., 168, 181
Rochlin, G., 303, 314
Rockwell, N., 3, 785, 786
Rodgers, D.A., 113
Rodin, A., 445
Rodriguez, A., 637
Roeske, N.C.A., 113
Roffwarg, H.P., 584
Rogers, M.P., 100
Roghmann, K.J., 33, 37
Romano, J., 113, 758
Roosevelt, T., 664
Rose, K.D., 440
Rose, L., 485
Rose, R.M., 421
Rosen, D.H., 18, 26
Rosen, J.S., 113
Rosenblum, L.A., 181, 212
Rosenbluth, D., 286
Rosenfeld, A., 149, 477
Rosenman, R.H., 100, 417, 422, 617,
    618
Rosenthal, D., 545, 552
Rosenzweig, M.R., 642, 647
Rosow, I., 440
Ross, J.M., 149, 180, 226
Ross, J.R., 637
Rossner, J., 775
Roth, C., 41, 47
Rowe, J., 153, 157
Roy, M., 729
Roy-Byrne, P., 569
Rubinow, D.R., 569
Rubinstein, A., 402
Rubinstein, M., 13, 59, 113
Russell, B., 607, 618
Rutter, M., 150, 548, 552, 636, 637, 646,
    647

Sabshin, M., 532
Sachar, E.J., 63, 67
Sacks, S., 456, 463

Sadock, B.J., 623
Sadock, V.A., 329, 337
Saez, J.M., 390
Sagarin, E., 393, 400
Sager, C.J., 457, 463
Saghir, M.T., 400
Saint Augustine, 321, 607
Saint Jerome, 321
Saint Paul, 320
Samelson, C.F., 584
Samenow, S.E., 550, 553
Sameroff, A.F., 144, 150, 642, 647
Sanchez, C., 310
Sanchez, S., 310
Sander, F.M., 463
Sander, L.W., 147, 150
Sandgrund, A., 447
Sargent, J.D., 614, 618
Sarnoff, C.A., 248
Sarsini, E., 499
Satterfield, S., 389, 390
Saunders, C., 237, 511, 513, 521
Schachter, S., 660, 670
Schafer, R., 226
Schäfer, S., 395, 400
Schaffer, J.W., 100
Schaie, K.W., 497
Schechter, M.D., 288, 292
Scheiber, S.C., 440
Schelkun, R., 298
Schiavi, R.C., 100, 358
Schiff, H.S., 157, 507
Schildkraut, J.J., 564, 709, 712
Schleifer, S.J., 100
Schlesinger, B., 464, 469
Schlesinger, H.J., 36, 37
Schmale, A.H., 9, 85, 86, 88, 96, 100
Schmitt, B.D., 640, 646, 677
Schneck, M.K., 497
Schneider, K., 680, 691
Schoenberg, B., 507
Schopler, E., 637
Schreiber, F.R., 771
Schroder, A.K., 18, 432
Schur, M., 80, 89
Schwab, J.J., 120
Schwartz, M.F., 401
Schweitzer, A., 18
Schwiebert, P., 157
Scotch, N., 606
Scrima, L., 585
Sechehaye, M., 691
Sederer, L.I., 691, 696
Seeman, B., 47
Seevers, M.H., 745
Segal, H.L., 88
Segraves, R.T., 358
Seidel, H.M., 432
Seidel, W.F., 577, 585
Seiden, A.M., 150
Seligman, M.E., 100, 709, 712
Seligmann, A., 47
Selye, H., 417, 422
Selzer, M.L., 746
Semans, J.H., 359, 371, 375
Semmelweis, I.P., 597
Senay, E.C., 133, 136, 745
Seneca, 415, 724
Sexton, A., 713
Shader, R.I., 564
Shakespeare, W., 231, 295, 345, 352,
    404, 415, 444, 445, 497, 701, 716, 752,
    767, 775
Shanas, S., 497

Shapiro, A.K., 677
Shapiro, A.P., 100
Shapiro, S., 606
Shaw, C., 298
Shaw, G.B., 403
Shaw, N.S., 150
Shaw, R.C., 649, 657
Sheehan, D.V., 534, 552
Sheehy, G., 485
Sherfey, M.J., 328, 342, 348
Shield, J.A., 712
Shields, J., 552
Shneidman, E., 521, 724
Shopper, M., 7–8, 9
Shore, E.G., 136
Siegal-Gorelick, B., 292
Siegel, R.E., 157
Siever, L.J., 551, 552
Sigerist, H., 513
Sigvardsson, S., 136, 552
Sillen, S., 627
Silver, H.K., 477
Silver, L., 646
Silverman, F.N., 477
Silverstein, S., 214, 224, 247
Silvestri, R., 585
Simmons, F.B., 585
Simon, W., 400
Simons, R.C., 13, 51–52, 78, 113, 160, 382, 505, 536, 537, 539, 634, 695
Singer, E., 37
Singer, M., 681
Singer, T., 91
Sivarajan, E.S., 358
Skeels, H.M., 641, 645, 647
Skinner, B.F., 608, 609, 610, 618
Sklar, L.S., 100
Skodol, A.E., 540
Slymen, D.J., 552
Smith, C.K., 35, 37
Smith, P.L., 585
Smith, R.L., 521
Smith, W.E., 434
Snortum, J.R., 401
Snyder, S.H., 564
Sobowale, N.C., 13, 440
Socrates, 648
Sokoloff, L., 562, 564
Solberg, D., 136
Solm, H., 746
Solnit, A.J., 140, 150, 292, 314, 463
Soloff, L.A., 358
Solomon, G.F., 89
Solomon, P., 758
Sophocles, 218
Sorenson, R.C., 270
Sorosky, A.D., 288, 292
Sosa, R., 138, 150
Spark, R.F., 351, 358, 360, 375
Spas, R., 272
Sperling, M., 670
Spierer, H., 482, 485
Spinweber, C.L., 585
Spiro, H.M., 670
Spiro, H.R., 67
Spitz, R.A., 95, 100, 146, 150, 161, 165, 170, 178, 181, 184, 196, 200, 365, 641, 645, 647, 709, 712
Spitzer, R.L., 540
Spock, B., 181, 238
Srole, L., 532, 604, 605, 606
Stafford-Clark, D., 37
Stahl, M.L., 584
Stalin, J., 608

Stancer, H.C., 547, 553
Starfield, B., 676
Stark, M.H., 140, 150
Starr, A., 113
Stearns, E.L., 485
Steele, B.F., 473, 477
Stein, L., 746
Stein, L.I., 432
Stein, M., 99, 100, 666, 670
Steinberg, S., 314, 447, 451
Steinmetz, S.K., 729
Stendahl, 774
Stengel, E., 724
Sterling, P., 724
Stern, D.N., 149, 150
Stern, G., 507
Sternschein, I., 497
Stevenson, R.L., 779
Stewart, M., 157
Stinson, P., 302
Stinson, R., 302
Stoller, R.J., 195, 226, 368, 375, 377, 386, 387, 388, 389, 390
Stolley, P.D., 481
Stoudemire, A., 99, 100, 120, 440, 779
Stoyva, J., 614, 615, 618
Strain, J.J., 50, 59, 67, 120
Straus, M.A., 729
Strauss, A.A., 638, 641, 642, 645, 647
Strauss, A.L., 239
Strauss, D., 497
Streissguth, A.P., 627
Strindberg, A., 453, 454
Stuart, R.B., 618
Stubbs, G., 553
Stuart, I., 292
Stunkard, A.J., 47, 616, 617, 618, 670
Sullivan, A.C., 564
Sullivan, H.S., 228
Sultan Mehmet, 322
Sulzman, F.M., 569
Surman, O.S., 112
Suwa, N., 632, 637
Suzuki, B., 149
Svejda, M.J., 150
Svendsen, M., 248
Swanson-Kauffman, K., 154, 157
Swedberg, J., 149
Swift, J., 513, 699
Syme, S.L., 96, 100
Szasz, T.S., 20, 26
Szurek, S.A., 248, 629, 635, 637, 653, 655, 656

Talbott, G.D., 440
Tan, T.-L., 585
Tanzer, D., 140, 150
Tarachow, S., 723, 724
Targum, S.D., 564
Taub, E., 618
Tavormina, J.B., 292
Taylor, M.A., 691
Tchaikovsky, P.I., 402, 405
Tefft, B.M., 724
Terkel, S., 414, 422
Thaler, M., 81, 88
Theorell, T.T., 417, 419, 422
Thigpen, C.H., 771
Thomas, A., 144, 145, 150, 627
Thomas, C.B., 96, 100
Thomas, L., 510
Thompson, J.D., 513
Thompson, T., 735, 746
Thompson, T.L., 59, 67, 115, 117, 118,

120, 497, 779
Thompson, W.L., 117, 120
Thorpe, J.K., 4, 297, 446, 501
Thorpe, W.H., 198
Thurber, J., 357
Thuwe, I., 134, 136
Tietze, C., 136
Timbury, G.C., 745
Tinbergen, N., 198
Tinkham, C.B., 112
Tinklenberg, J.R., 746
Titchener, J.L., 113
Todd, G.F., 746
Tolstoy, L., 450, 775
Toolan, J.M., 298
Torgersen, G., 553
Totter, 632
Townsend, R.E., 615, 618
Trause, M., 157
Trethowan, W.H., 136
Troyat, H., 451
Tsuang, M.T., 548, 552
Turner, W.J., 547, 553
Tyson, R.L., 149, 180, 196

Udry, J.R., 459, 463
Uhde, T.W., 552
Usdin, G., 497

Vaillant, C.O., 422
Vaillant, G.E., 13, 99, 100, 414, 422, 430, 432, 437, 438, 440, 479, 485, 736, 745, 746
Valverde, F., 642, 647
Vanggaard, T., 323
vanGogh, V., 404, 699
Vaughn, C.E., 681, 690, 691
Veatch, R.M., 302, 513
Verdi, G., 404
Verrier, R., 100
Viederman, M., 59
Vietze, P.M., 150
Vigeland, G., 121, 140, 145, 184, 245, 446, 483
Vincent, C.E., 239
Virgin Mary, 412
Vollman, J.H., 157
Voltaire, 45
vonBertalanffy, L., 668, 670
vonKnorring, A., 552
vonLobkowitz, P., 512
vonMunchausen, B., 65

Wabrek, A.J., 113
Wabrek, C.J., 113
Wagner, G., 329, 330, 331, 332, 333, 334, 335, 336, 360, 375
Wagner, N., 136, 637
Wagner, N.W., 358
Waldfogel, S., 286, 676
Waldo, M.C., 564
Walker, H., 635, 637
Wall, P.D., 61, 67
Waller, J.V., 663, 670
Wallerstein, J.S., 461, 463, 469
Wallin, P., 463
Walters, E.D., 618
Ward, I., 383, 390
Waring, E.M., 13, 440
Warner, R., 302
Watson, E., 298
Watson, J., 198, 541
Weber, A.L., 569
Weeks, J.R., 734, 746

Wehr, T.A., 568, 569, 585, 709, 712
Weigert, E., 136
Weil, R.J., 599, 605
Weinberg, J., 494
Weinberg, M.S., 394, 395, 397, 398, 400, 401
Weinberg, T.S., 401
Weiner, H., 81, 82, 88, 658, 670
Weinstein, E., 278, 280
Weinstein, P., 676
Weir, D.R., 136
Weir, W.C., 136
Weisman, A.D., 59, 81, 89, 113, 521
Weisman, C.S., 432
Weiss, J., 314, 447, 451
Weiss, R.S., 463, 465, 469
Weiss, T., 618
Weissberg, M.P., 59, 78, 118, 120, 763
Weissman, M.M., 709, 712
Weitkamp, L.R., 547, 553
Weitzman, E.D., 569, 577, 585
Weller, E.B., 270
Weller, R.A., 270
Wellisch, D.K., 96, 100
Wender, P., 564, 646
Werkman, S.L., 521
Werner, H., 641, 642, 645
West, L.J., 89
West, P.M., 100
Wever, R.A., 565, 569
Wharton, E., 775
White, D.P., 585
White, K.L., 280

White, R.A., 358, 375
White, S.W., 469
Whitfield, J.M., 157
Whittemore, R., 47
Wieder, H., 288, 292
Wiener, N., 670
Williams, A.S., 632, 637
Williams, C.J., 398, 401
Williams, J.B.W., 540
Williams, R.B., 94, 100
Williams, T., 775
Williams, T.A., 712
Wilmotte, J., 552
Wilson, M.A., 569
Windle, W., 641
Wineman, D., 656
Wing, J., 635, 637
Wing, L., 635, 637
Winger, G., 746
Winnie, A.P., 59
Winokur, G., 553, 702, 709, 711, 712, 746
Wirz-Justice, A., 712
Wiseman, F., 420, 429, 431
Witkin, H., 41, 47
Witmer, L., 628, 637
Wittenberg, C.K., 485
Wolf, J.E., 390
Wolf, K.M., 150, 181, 712
Wolf, S.G., 89, 100
Wolfe, S., 440
Wolff, H.G., 80, 89
Wolff, J., 131, 136

Wolff, P.H., 181
Wolpe, J., 611, 615, 618
Woodruff, R.A., 700, 712
Woods, J.H., 745, 746
Woody, G.E., 746
Woolf, V., 778
World Health Organization, 303, 620
Worthington, R.E., 96, 100
Wortis, H., 642, 645, 647
Wright, D.G., 636
Wright, F.L., 230
Wyeth, A., 407
Wynne, L., 681

Yager, J., 96, 100
Yanagita, T., 745
Yates, A., 477
Yeats, W.B., 444, 445
Yerevanian, B.I., 779
Yochelson, S., 550, 553
Young, W.C., 383, 390
Yule, W., 647
Yurgelun-Todd, D., 670

Zborowski, M., 278, 280
Zelnik, M., 136
Ziegler, F.J., 113
Zinberg, N.E., 497, 745
Zinsser, H., 521
Zisook, S., 507
Zohar, J., 113
Zola, I., 277, 280, 419, 422, 657

Subject Index

Abandonment, 459, 462, 649, 718
Abortion
  habitual, 125
  spontaneous, 80, 125, 152, 154
  therapeutic (induced), 133–134
Abstinence, *see* Celibacy
Abstinence syndrome, *see* Withdrawal syndrome
Acceptance, 516, 787
Accident-proneness, 64, 461, 471, 525, 760
Acetaldehyde, 550
Acetaminophen, 745
Acetylcholine (Ach), 493, 558, 572
Acetylcholinesterase, 493, 558
Acetylmethadol, 568
Achieved status, 232, 415–416
Acid, *see* LSD
Acquired immune deficiency syndrome (AIDS), 399
Acquisition phase, 608
Acromegaly, 351
Acrophobia, 764
Action specific energy, 198
"Active," 385
Active phase of schizophrenia, 680
Acupuncture, 61
Adaptation, 295, 392, 398, 459, 479, 491, 499, 524–525, 620, 622, 686, 760
Adaptation syndrome, 417
Adaptation to Life, 479
Adapting to Parenthood, 141
Adaptive functioning (Axis V), 534
Adaptive functions, 537, 686, 772
Addiction, *see* Substance use disorder
Addictive personality, 736
Addison's disease, 116, 351
Adherence behavior, *see* Responses to medical advice
Adjustment disorder, 143, 534
Adjustment disorder with depressed mood, 702, 707–709
Adolescence, 159, 160, 162, 254, 255–270, 282, 289, 292, 311–314, 366, 381, 438, 441, 450, 455, 460, 461, 469, 498, 648–657, 661–670
Adolescence: The Winds of Change, 264, 655
Adoption, 134, 135, 287–292
Adoption studies, 544–545, 547, 549, 550, 738
Adrenal-cortical activation, *see* Pituitary-adrenal-cortical activation
Adrenogenital syndrome, 382, 384
Adulthood, 369, 315–521
  early, 441–451
  later, 486–497
  middle, 478–485
  provisional, 456

Affect, 180, 229–231, 232, 532, 537, 556, 586, 634, 680, 683, 684, 749, 750, 754, *see also* Specific affects
Affectionless characters, 655
Affective disorders, 90, 99, 525, 537, 538, 540, 546–548, 556, 568, 574–575, 578, 593, 604, 692–712
  see also Bipolar disorder
  see also Depression and the depressive disorders
  see also Mania
Afrodex, 373
Agapetae, 320
Ageism, 487–491
Aggression, 64, 185–187, 201–204, 240–247, 257, 260–262, 287–289, 322–323, 377, 473–476, 483, 493, 496, 528–532, 687, 709, 713–724, 725–729, 744, 765, 767–769, 776–779
Aggressive conduct disorder, 648
Agitation, 117, 556, 704, 753, 781
Agnosia, 493
Agoraphobia, 117, 764
Akathisia, 554
Akinesia, 554
Alarm reaction, 466
Alcohol withdrawal delirium, *see* Delirium tremens
Alcoholism, 3, 58, 109, 352, 354, 428, 429, 437, 443, 458, 462, 474, 475, 494, 496, 500, 534, 540, 549–550, 593, 601, 604, 652, 653, 700, 715, 722, 727, 728, 730–742, 748, 755–756, 760, 761, 777, 782
Aldehyde dehydrogenase, 550
Alertness, 159, 557
Alienation, 462
Allergens, 664
Alpha waves, 570, 571
Alprazolam (Xanax), 560
Altruism, 438, 440
Aluminum, 493
Alzheimer's disease, 116, 492–493, 752
Ambisexuality, 394
Ambivalence, 70, 219–225, 308, 398, 461, 466, 500, 587, 634, 672, 680, 684, 719, 767–769
Amitryptyline (Elavil), 557
Amnesia
  see Organic amnestic syndrome
  see Psychogenic amnesia
Amniocentesis, 137, 151, 625, 627
Amphetamines, 246, 352, 555, 557, 560, 581, 692, 710, 732, 735, 743, 748, 754–755
  amphetamine intoxication, 555, 743, 754–755
Amplitude, 565
Amputations, 56, 61, 283, 307–308, 385, 498
Anaclitic depression, 161, 178, 200
Anal intercourse, 393, 399, 475
Anal stage, *see* Psychosexual development

Analgesic drugs, 745

Anatomical sex, 382–383, 384–389, 444

Anatomy of a Suicide, The, 723, 724

Anatomy of an Illness, 14, 16, 18, 91

Androgens, 383, 384, 388, 391, 444

Anesthesia
during delivery, 137, 142, 166
reactions to, 55–56, 106–107, 558

Anesthesias, 69, 78, 766
glovelike, 69
stocking, 69, 766

Angel dust, *see* Phencyclidine

Angel's Trumpet flowers, 744

Anger, 22–23, 52, 56, 57, 63, 66, 73–74, 80, 94, 98, 101–
103, 107, 110, 117, 119, 132, 133, 134, 135, 156,
193, 260–262, 263, 283, 288, 295, 297, 306, 310,
312, 313, 354, 362, 363, 369–374, 379, 386, 387,
393, 398, 437, 445, 455–463, 464–469, 472–476,
502, 505, 514, 515, 559, 567, 586, 591, 595, 643,
652, 661–670, 673, 674, 675, 676, 693, 717–724,
725–729, 743, 754, 760–763, 767–769, 776, 777–
779

Angry Boy, 184

Anguish, 501

Animism, 180, 251

Anna Karenina, 775

Anniversary reaction, 64, 96, 114, 134, 156–157, 504,
707–708, 720

Anorexia, 700, 703–704, 743

Anorexia nervosa, 125, 269, 285, 443, 533, 662–663,
668, 782–783

Antecedent stimuli, 616, 781

Antianginal drugs, 117

Antianxiety drugs, 35, 62, 93, 560, 673, 781

Antiasthmatic drugs, 117

Anticancer drugs, 353, 730, 744

Anticholinergic drugs, 554

Anticoagulants, 579

Anticonvulsants, 117

Antidepressant drugs, 35, 556–559, 705, 709–710, 781,
783

Antihistamine drugs, 553

Antihypertensive drugs, 117, 353

Antiinflammatory drugs, 117

AntiParkinsonian drugs, 117

Antipsychotic drugs, 35, 553–556, 690, 695, 709–710,
753, 781

Antisocial behavior, 163, 269, 638, 645, 648–656, 725–
729

Antisocial personality disorder, 269, 540, 604, 727, 737,
778–779

Anxiety, 4, 28, 33, 48, 49, 50–52, 57, 58, 62, 63, 66, 69,
71, 73, 78, 79, 80, 94, 98, 107, 108, 110–112, 114–
118, 120, 123–130, 133, 142, 144, 148, 152, 153,
162, 166, 191, 220, 284, 299–314, 361, 369–374,
378–381, 435, 436, 437, 439, 457, 460, 464, 465,
472, 473, 480, 482, 485, 486, 492, 493, 495, 514,
519, 537, 538, 560, 580, 593, 615, 651, 660–666,
673, 674, 678–679, 687–690, 707, 718, 736, 744,
748, 749–750, 753, 754, 755, 760–763, 764–771,
774, 775, 776
and danger situations, 50, 52, 159, 160, 189, 214–
218, 225, 378–381, 538, 770
fear of annihilation, 50, 536, 538, 688
fear of bodily injury, 50, 52, 56, 108, 110–112, 160,
214–218, 378–381, 436–437
fear of castration, *see* Castration anxiety
fear of conscience, 160, 225, *see also* Guilt; Superego
fear of failure (in sexual performance), 360–361, 363,
371–374, *see also* Performance anxiety
fear of loss of control, 52, 55, 107, 363, 366, 370
fear of loss of love of the object, 50, 160, 189, 378–
381, *see also* Separation anxiety
fear of loss of the object, 50, 160, 189, 378–381, *see
also* Separation anxiety
fear of penetration, *see* Mutilation anxiety
fear of strangers, 50, *see also* Stranger anxiety
in flight-fight, 92–94
signal, 770
traumatic, 770

Anxiety disorders of adulthood, 494, 537, 540, 551,
574, 587, 604, 611, 615, 764–771

Anxiety disorders of childhood, 533, 671–673

Anxiety states, 537, 764, 769–770

Apathy, 56, 116, 117, 297, 493, 595, 748

Aphasia, 493

Aphrodisiacs, 352, 353

Apraxia, 493

Ariel, 713, 719, 720

Arm with Dagger, 715

Arson, *see* Fire setting

Artificialism, 251

As You Like It, 497

Asceticism, 263, 321

Ascribed status, 231

Aspirin, 33, 745

Assaultiveness, 109, 443, 462, 534, 649, 725–729, 740,
749, 753, 756, 781

Associations
clang, 693
loosening of, 634, 680, 682

Asterixis, 752

Asthma, 30–31, 79, 80, 85, 283, 284, 652, 664–666, 668,
744

Ataxia, 742, 752, 754

Atherosclerosis of penile vessels, 351

Athetoid movements, 673

Atlas of Human Sex Anatomy, 326, 327

Atopy, 664–665

Atropine, 744

Attachment, 134, 141–142, 151–157, 172–174, 503

Attention, 78, 162, 473

Attention deficit disorder (ADD), 162, 246, 533, 560–
561, 638–647

Attraction, 447

Auletrides, 319

Authoritarian personality, 729

Autism, *see* Autistic behavior

Autistic behavior, 140–141, 170, 201–204, 624, 626, 629–632, 634, 636, 680, 686
Autistic stage, 159, 160, 170, 172, 376, 592–593
Automobile accidents, 534, 714, 722, 726–727, 740, 760, 770
Autonomic nervous system, 79–80, 369, 480, 612, 770
Autonomous functions, 180, 537, 682–686, 772
Autonomy, 160, 183–184, 191, 776
Auxiliary ego, 184
Average expectable environment, 168
Aversive stimulus, 736
Avoidance, 225, 538, 764
Avoidance conditioning, 608
Avoidant disorder of childhood, 672
Avoidant personality disorder, 225, 775
Axis I of DSM-III, 533–540
Axis II of DSM-III, 533–540
Axis III of DSM-III, 534, 539
Axis IV of DSM-III, 534, 539
Axis V of DSM-III, 534, 539

Babinski reflex, 167
Backache, 60, 349
"Bad trip," *see* LSD
Barbiturates, 117, 246, 352, 553, 560, 576, 578–580, 638, 742, 749, 755
Bargaining, 515
Bartleby, The Scrivener, 776
Basal ganglia, 554, 562
Basic trust, 160, 172, 174
Battered child syndrome, 470, 725
Battered husband syndrome, 725
Battered wife syndrome, 725, 726
Behavior disorders of childhood and adolescence, *see* Conduct disorder
Behavior patterns, 524–525, 535, 537, 595, 772
Behavior therapy, 61, 62, 400, 611, 646, 673–676, 711, 781, 782–783
Behavioral analysis, 616
Behavioral medicine, 615–618, 781
Behaviorism, 198, 541
Bell Jar, The, 719
Belladonna alkaloids, 744
Benzodiazepine receptor sites, 561–562
Benzodiazepines, 117, 560, 580, 583, 584, 710, 742
Bereavement, *see* Mourning
Binge-purge syndrome, 663–664
Biofeedback, 61, 94, 609, 612–615, 781
Biological rhythms, 147, 564–569, 575, 709
Biological therapies, 781
Biomedical model, 90–91, 112, 780
Biopsychosocial model, 90–91, 112, 114–120, 538–539, 780
Biorhythms, 565
Bipolar disorder, 546, 556, 587–591, 692–696, 702, 706, 737, 776
  depressed, 692, 702
  manic, 692, 702
  mixed, 692, 702

Birth, 137–150, 166, 237–238
  home births, 137–138
  hospital births, 137–138
  premature, 137, 141, 147, 153, 163, 626, 641
  prepared childbirth, 138–139
  postmature, 626
  stages of labor, 138–139
  theories of, 166
Birth control, *see* Contraception
Birthing centers, 138
Birthing rooms, 138
Bisexuality, 317–320, 394
Black patch delirium, 757
Blindness, 69, 140, 566
Blocking, 682
Body image, 56, 57, 104, 108, 171, 179, 250, 283, 311, 436, 473, 592, 660, 688
Body language, 68–72
Body morphology, 539–540
Bombing, 725
Bone-pointing, 19–20, 271
Borderline personality disorder, 551, 776–777
Boy Seated in a Tree, 245
Breast envy, 217
Breasts, 111, 325, 329, 330
Brief reactive psychosis, 681
Briquet's syndrome, *see* Somatization disorder
Brothers Karamozov, The, 777
Bruxism, *see* Tooth grinding
Buddenbrooks, 86
Bulimia, 533, 663–664, 782
Burns, 286
Butyrophenones, 555, 695

Caesarian sections, 123, 137, 138, 153
Caffeine, 576, 743–744, 748
Call of Death, The, 315, 788
Cancer, 54, 58, 61, 66, 96, 98, 99, 110–112, 116, 299–314, 438, 481, 484, 496, 517, 667, 708, 740
Cancer-prone personality, 96
Cancer self-help programs, 511
Cantharides (Spanish fly), 353, 673
Carbamazepine (Tegretol), 576, 695
Cardiac arrhythmia, 48, 93, 558, 614, 745
Cardiovascular disease, 617–618, 660, 740, 741, 747, 750
  see also Cardiac arrhythmia
  see also Cerebrovascular strokes
  see also Hypertension
  see also Myocardial infarction
  see also Sudden (cardiac) death
Caretaking casualty, 642
Cartoon Classics From Medical Economics, 66, 75, 102, 457
Case of Anna O., 24–26
Case of Monica, 95
Castration anxiety, 50, 160, 215–216, 222–225, 242, 282, 380–381, 444, 538
Cataplexy, 581

Catastrophic reaction, 640
Catatonic schizophrenia, 680–681, 684–685
  catatonic excitement, 685
  catatonic negativism, 684
  catatonic posturing, 684
  catatonic rigidity, 684
  catatonic stupor, 684
Catecholamines, 48, 92, 93, 555–561
Catholicism, 510
Caudate nucleus, 562
Causation, 597, 598
Cavalleria Rusticana, 406
Celibacy, 320–321
Central nervous system infections, 624, 692, 747, 750
Central nervous system neoplasms, 116, 692, 747
Central nervous system toxins, 747
Central nervous system trauma, 624, 747
Central nervous system tumors, 116, 750, 752
Cerebellum, 749
Cerebral arteriosclerosis, *see* Multi-infarct dementia
Cerebral atrophy, 492–493
Cerebral palsy, 639
Cerebral ventricles, 556, 681, 691
Cerebrovascular strokes, 492, 743
Cervical incompetence, 125, 135
Character, *see* Personality
Character disorders, *see* Personality disorders
Character traits, *see* Personality traits
Chief cells of the stomach, 81
Child abuse, 134, 141, 203, 230, 291, 462, 470–477, 718, 725, 728, 740, 759–763, 779
Child neglect, *see* Child abuse
Child Psychiatry, 660
Child support, 464
Childhood and adolescence, 121–314
Childhood and Society, 163
Childhood fetish, 380
Childhood onset pervasive developmental disorder, 633–636
Childhood psychoses, *see* Psychoses of childhood
Childhood schizophrenia, 628, 634–635, 643
Children and Their Mothers, 127, 188
Chloral hydrate, 755
Chlordiazepoxide (Librium), 35, 560, 742, 755
Chlorpromazine (Thorazine), 553–556
Choice of Weapons, A, 450
Cholesterol, 496, 567, 617
Choline, 493
Choline acetyltransferase, 493
Choreiform movements, 673
Chorion biopsy, 627
Christianity, 320–321, 392, 509, 511
Christina's World, 407
Chronobiology, 577
Cimetidine, 117, 353
Circadian rhythm, 566, 576
Circumcision, 345–347
Circumstantiality, 776
Cirrhosis, 731, 756

Civil Rights Movement, 443
Civilization and its Discontents, 414
Clang associations, *see* Associations
Classical conditioning, 608, 609–610
Claustrophobia, 764
Climacterium, 478–485, 538
  female, 480–481
  male, 482
Clinical syndromes (Axis I), 533–540
Clitoris, 330–332, 338
Cloaca, 195, 340, 436
Clonidine, 117
Closed systems, 668
"Coasting," 742
Cocaine, 352, 692, 743
Codeine, 742
Cognitive development, 159, 160, 164, 249–254
  concrete operational stage, 160, 161, 241, 253
  formal operational stage, 160, 253–254, 263
  preoperational stage, 160, 191, 215, 218, 250–253, 282
  sensory motor stage, 160, 180, 249–250
Cognitive function, *see* Intellectual function
Colectomy, 667
Collected Poems of William Butler Yeats, 444
Colostomy, 56, 104, 356
Coma, 742, 744, 745, 748
Combat fatigue, 757
Communication, 360–363, 369–374, 392, 455, 458, 464, 475, 483, 512, 519, 629, 681
Comparative behavioral research, 197–199
Compensation, 51
Competitiveness (in medical school), 426–427
Complete Poems of Emily Dickinson, The, 501, 504
Compliance, *see* Responses to medical advice
Comprehensive Textbook of Psychiatry, 623
Compromise solution, 765
Compulsion, 536, 767–769
Compulsive personality disorder, *see* Obsessive compulsive personality disorder
Computerized tomography (CT scan), 118, 494, 549, 635, 690, 701, 751
Concentration, 703, 769
Concentration span, 751
Concordance, 544
Concrete operational stage, *see* Cognitive development
Condensation, 685
Conditioned response (CR), 608
Conditioned stimulus (CS), 608
Conditioning, 166, 171, 187
Conduct disorder of childhood and adolescence, 246, 443, 533, 648–657
Confessions of Felix Krull, The, 779
Conflict, 29, 68–72, 159, 224–226, 361–362, 396, 397, 455, 531, 669, 760, 764–771, 781, 783
  see also Anxiety
  see also Guilt
Conformity, 459, 686
Confusion, 116, 117, 493, 742, 744, 748, 754

Congenital defects, *see* Handicapped children
Consanguinity studies, 543
Conscience, *see* Superego
Conscious, 20–21, 377, 396, 398, 403, 457, 525, 586, 748–752, 771
Consciousness, *see* Conscious
Consequences of behavior, 609–610, 616, 781
Conservation, 252–253
Conservation-withdrawal reaction, 94–99
Consonance, 145
Constitution, 97–99, 538–539
Consultation-liaison psychiatry, 17, 20, 28–31, 97, 108, 113–120
Contingency contracting, 739
Continuous growth adolescents, 268
Contraception, 131, 134, 254, 353, 354, 442, 460
Contributions to the Psychology of Love, 460
Control by knowing, 50
Control of drives, 179
Conversion disorder, 24–26, 51, 65, 68–72, 78, 79, 97, 98, 505, 506, 534, 673, 707, 708, 765–767, 774
Cooperative response to medical advice, 47
Coping ability, 283, 480, 487, 595, 759–760, 783
Coprolalia, 673
Coprophilia, 376
Core gender identity, 186, 386
Coronary Care Unit (CCU), 93
Correlation, 597, 598
Corticosteroids, *see* Steroids
Counseling, *see* Psychotherapy
Counterphobic mechanism, 764
Countertransference, 23–26, 101–106, 285–286, 438, 721–724
Couvade syndrome, 128
Creative arts therapy, 782
Creativity, 402–413, 450, 771
Crime and Punishment, 778
Criminality, 443, 550, 648–656, 725, 779
Culture, 41–45, 271–280, 500, 506, 540, 602, 603, 658, 674
Cunnilingus, 317, 318
Curandero, 20, 271, 272
Curiosity, 357, 361, 366, 475
Cushing's disease, 116, 351
Customs inspection, 174
Cybernetics, 668
Cyclic AMP, 665
Cyclothymic disorder, 702, 705, 706
Cyclothymic personality disorder, 705, 776

Daddy, 719
Danger screen, 761
Danger situations, *see* Anxiety
Data of psychiatry, 165
Dawn of Abdominal Surgery, The, 107
Day care, 292, 462, 476
Day Grandpa Died, The, 296
Day of the Jackal, The, 756
Day treatment programs, 782

Daytime sleep attacks, 581
Dead Mother, The, 310
Deafness, 69
Death and Company, 720
Death and dying
  child's awareness of, 299–304
  ethical perspectives, 299–302, 518–519
  fears of, 9, 55, 108, 179, 354, 483, 492
  historical and religious perspectives, 234–237, 508–513
  in adolescents, 311–314, 438
  in adults, 9, 10, 58, 434, 483–485, 492, 508–521, 787–788
  in children, 284, 285, 299–311, 500
  in surgical patients, 10, 55, 436
  new developments in care, 511–513
  perinatal, 151–157
  stages of, 514–516
Death and the Maiden, 447, 449
Death as a Friend, 516
Death Seizes a Woman, 514
Death Swoops Into a Group of Children, 304
Defense mechanisms, 49, 51–52, 71, 98, 99, 180, 262–263, 283, 479, 531, 535–538, 586, 687, 748, 750, 764–771, 772–779
Defensive functions, 537, 687, 772
Delayed sleep-phase onset syndrome, *see* Sleep-onset insomnia
Delinquency, *see* Juvenile delinquency
Delirium, 108, 109, 492, 496, 533, 727, 744, 747, 750, 755–758
Delirium tremens, 560, 731, 747, 755–756
Delta waves, 570, 571
Delusion, 56, 66, 108, 109, 115, 116, 389, 525, 531, 536, 553, 559, 603, 634, 678–679, 680, 682, 683, 688–690, 693, 704–705, 727, 744, 749, 750, 754, 755
  mood-congruent, 693
  of grandeur, 531, 683, 693
  of jealousy, 683
  of nihilism, 683, 704
  of persecution, 531, 678–679, 683, 688–690
  of reference, 683
  of worthlessness, 704
  somatic, 78, 531, 683, 704–705
  thought broadcasting, 680, 683
  thought insertion, 680, 683
  thought withdrawal, 680, 683
Dementia, 117, 488, 490, 492, 496, 533, 578, 747, 750
Dementia infantilis, 635
Dementia praecox, *see* Schizophrenic disorders
Denial, 4, 8, 45, 48, 49, 51, 52, 57, 58, 61, 65, 71, 73, 78, 90, 93, 94, 96, 98, 108, 284, 295, 312, 355, 378, 381, 389, 439, 461, 472, 474, 493, 501, 503, 505, 506, 515, 531, 662, 687, 689, 694, 725, 741, 776, 777, 783
Denial of pregnancy, 125
Denial phase of stress response, 760
Dependency
  in anorexia nervosa, 662–663

Dependency—*continued*
  in asthma, 664–666
  in child abuse, 476
  in duodenal ulcer, 80–84
  in hospitalized patients, 10, 283
  in hypochondriasis, 74–78
  in mania, 694
  in pain patients, 62, 63, 66
  in psychophysiological disorders, 80–85
  in school phobia, 672–673
  in ulcerative colitis, 667–668
  with anesthesia, 55
  with hemodialysis, 57
  with surgery, 108
  with transplantation, 57
  see also Dependent personality disorder
Dependent personality disorder, 54, 78, 283, 745, 777
Depersonalization disorder, 760, 771
Depressant drugs, *see* General depressant drugs
Depression and the depressive disorders, 3, 4, 12, 48,
    52, 57, 58, 63, 76, 78, 79, 87, 90, 95, 96, 98, 103,
    108, 109–110, 110–112, 114–118, 120, 131, 133,
    135, 140, 142, 143, 153, 154, 162, 174, 178, 237,
    268, 283, 299–314, 363–364, 387, 388, 397, 404,
    405, 408, 411, 437, 461, 464, 473, 475, 480, 492,
    493–496, 498, 500, 502, 505, 516, 556–559, 567,
    574–575, 593, 595, 653, 660, 661, 667, 674, 693,
    694, 697–712, 713–724, 727, 729, 736, 743, 748,
    749, 751, 754, 759–763, 773, 775, 776, 781, 782,
    783
  adjustment disorder with depressed mood, 702
  agitated, 702
  as a normal emotion, 697
  as a situational reaction, 697–699
  as an affective disorder, 700–701, 702–711
  atypical, 558, 710
  biological, 702
  bipolar, *see* Bipolar disorder
  characterological, 702
  chronic, 702
  cyclothymic, *see* Cyclothymic disorder
  dysthymic, *see* Dysthymic disorder
  endogenous, 702
  episodic, 702
  exogenous, 702
  familial (PDD), 702
  in adolescents, 268
  in children, 298
  in divorce, 460, 461, 464
  in infant monkeys, 208–212
  in the aged, 494–495
  major depression, 143, 546, 662, 702, 703–705, 776
  melancholia, 701, 702, 704
  mild, 701
  neurotic, 702
  paradoxical, 53, 64, 96, 707–708, 775
  postoperative, 109–110
  postpartum, 142–143
  preoperative, 108

  primary, 700, 701, 702, 702–712
  psychotic, 702, 704–705
  reactive, 702
  recurrent, 702
  retarded, 702
  secondary, 700, 701, 702
  severe, 701
  single episode, 702
  spectrum (DSD), 702
  sporadic (SDD), 702
  unipolar, 546, 556, 702, 703–705, 706
  see also Affective disorders
Depressive equivalents, 707, 709, 711
Depressive personality disorder, 78, 707, 775
Depressive pseudodementia, 494, 748
Depressive stupor, 704
Descriptive model, 527–532, 539
Desertion, *see* Abandonment
Desipramine (Pertofrane), 557
Despair, 480, 491–492, 704
Despair, 704
Desymbolization of language, 685
Detouring, 669
Developmental arithmetic disorder, 638
Developmental articulation disorder, 638
Developmental casualty, 163
Developmental-genetic model, 527, 538–539
Developmental language disorder (expressive type),
    638
Developmental language disorder (receptive type), 638
Developmental reading disorder, 638, 642–645, 651,
    656
Dexamethasone suppression test (DST), 559
Dextroamphetamine (Dexedrine), 638, 743
Diabetes insipidus, 560, 674
Diabetes mellitus, 43, 46, 56, 87, 90, 166, 283, 284, 313,
    351, 360, 617, 660, 668, 674, 726, 741
*Diagnostic and Statistical Manual of Mental Disor-
    ders—3rd Edition (DSM-III)*, 69, 323, 376, 533–
    540, 546, 632, 633, 638, 648, 664, 673, 674, 680,
    692, 697, 702, 705, 706, 730, 747, 750, 764, 769,
    772, 775, 776, 780
Dialogues of Plato, 18
Diazepam (Valium), 35, 560, 580, 615, 742, 755
"Difficult" patient, 101–120
  "Difficult" medical patient, 113–120
  "Difficult" surgical patient, 106–113
Digitalis, 117
Digoxin, 353
Disability neurosis, 65
Discipline, 184–185, 187–189, 260–262, 464, 466–467,
    649, 651–656
Discordance, 544
Discrimination, *see* Prejudice
Disengagement, 490
Disidentification, 392, 444
Disintegrative psychosis, 635
Disorders of excessive sleepiness (DOES), *see* Hyper-
    somnias

Disorders of initiating and maintaining sleep (DIMS), *see* Insomnias
Disorganization phase of grief, 502–503
Disorganization phase of stress response, 760
Disorganized schizophrenia, 680
Disorientation, *see* Orientation
Displacement, 51, 52, 73, 76, 101–106, 180, 225, 262, 283, 538, 685, 764
Dissociation, 51
Dissociative disorders, 537, 587, 760, 770, 771, 774
Dissonance, 145
Distractibility, 162, 560, 638–646, 693, 769
Disulfiram (Antabuse), 739
Divine Comedy, 412
Divorce, 131, 154, 230–231, 459–463, 464–469, 484, 496, 498, 500, 505, 619, 649, 693, 700, 714, 760
Divorce and Separation, 464
Doctor and the Doll, The, 785, 786
Doctor-patient relationship, 14–47, 432–440
    and responses to medical advice, 38–47
    and the angry patient, 101–103
    and the "difficult" medical patient, 113–120
    and the "difficult" surgical patient, 106–113
    and the expectant couple, 129–130
    and the infertile couple, 134–136
    and the nuclear family, 234–239
    and the pain patient, 66
    and the seductive patient, 103–106
    and the suicidal patient, 714, 721–724
    dissatisfaction in, 33–37, 38–47, 430–431
    during birth and postpartum, 137–149
    in adolescent pregnancy, 132
    in hypochondriasis, 75–77
    in perinatal loss, 154–157
    in psychotherapy, 781
    in unwanted pregnancy, 133–134
    model of activity-passivity, 20–21
    model of guidance-cooperation, 21
    model of mutual participation, 21
    models of, 19–26
    mutual collaboration in, 17–18
    participants in, 14–18, 58
    sexual involvement in, 106
    the patient, 14–15, 33–37
    the physician, 15, 27–30
"Doctor shopping," 35, 75, 77, 78
Doll's House, A, 452
"Doorknob comment," 66
Dopamine (DA), 555–561, 673
Dopamine hypothesis, 555
Double bind, 681
Double blind study, 554, 560, 561
Double standard, 443, 459
Doubt, 160, 183–184, 191, 767–769, 773
Dove Counterbalance Intelligence Test, 620–622
Down's syndrome, 164, 541, 625–626, 627
Downward drift, 604
Dr. Jekyll and Mr. Hyde, 779
Dracula, 719

Dreaming, 117, 393, 410, 503, 586, 685, *see* Nightmares
Drives, 179, 377–378, 442, 540, 586, 686, 687
Drug abuse, *see* Substance use disorders
Drug and alcohol related insomnia, 575–576
Drug history, 731–732
Drugs in the elderly, 495
Duarte protein, 547
Duodenal ulcer, *see* Ulcer
Dynamic model, 527–532, 539
Dyskinesias, 673
Dyspareunia, 352
Dysphagia, 615
Dysphoria, 556
Dyssomnias, *see* Parasomnias
Dysthymic disorder, 702, 705, 707
    character spectrum dysthymic disorder, 705
    subaffective dysthymic disorder, 705
Dystonia, 554

Eating disorders, 435, 533, 658–664
Eclampsia, 124, 132, 641
Education, 496
Educational tutoring, 646
Effeminate behavior, 196, 320, 386, 395, 399, 443, 654
Egalitarianism, 459
Ego
    definition of, 179
    development, 159, 160
    functions, 179, 180, 537, 772
    ideal, 221, 225, 266, 268
    psychology, 179
    unconscious part, 179
Ego-alien, 525, 535–538
Ego and the Mechanisms of Defense, The, 263
Ego boundaries, 687
Ego-dystonic, *see* Ego-alien
Ego-syntonic, 535–538
Egocentrism, 250–251, 254
Ejaculatory inevitability, 347
Elation of mood, *see* Euphoria
Electrocardiogram (EKG), 612, 770
Electroconvulsive therapy (ECT), 558, 710, 781
Electroencephalogram (EEG), 542, 570–572, 612, 614, 643, 751, 755, 770
Electromyogram (EMG), 570–572, 612, 614–615
Electrooculogram (EOG), 570–572
Embryo transfer, 135
Emergency room history, 760–763
Emergency rooms, 420–421, 759–763
Emotional anesthesia, 770
Emotional fit, 285
Emotions, *see* Affects
Empathy, 9, 102, 104, 105, 156, 285–286, 298, 313, 435, 436, 437, 439, 489, 506, 771
Emphysema, 351, 722, 740
Encopresis, 248, 533, 675–676
    continuous, 675
    discontinuous, 675
    functional, 675–676

Encopresis—*continued*
    primary, 675
    secondary, 675
Endometriosis, 135, 352
Endorphins, 61, 561
Enemy of the People, An, 452
Enkephalins, 61, 561
Enmeshment, 669
Enuresis, 12, 31, 247–248, 443, 533, 573, 584, 673–675
    diurnal, 674
    functional, 673–675
    nocturnal, 674
    primary, 674
    secondary, 674
Environmental determinism, 608
Environmental setting, 162–163, 404, 474, 490
Environmental therapies, *see* Social therapies
Enzymes
    5-alpha-reductase, 382
    5-hydroxytryptamine, 556
    17-beta-hydroxysteroid-dehydrogenase, 382
Ephedrine, 117
Epidemiology of mental disorders, 597–606
Epilepsy, 69, 284, 285, 542, 583, 614, 692, 726
Epinephrine, 92
Erectile dysfunction, 12, 31, 56, 110–111, 351–353, 366, 368, 373, 428, 570
Ergot alkaloids, 493
Esophageal varices, 731, 756
Estrangement, 462, 770
Estrogens, 117, 383, 385, 480–481
Ethan Frome, 775
Ethchlorvynol (Placidyl), 742
Ethics
    in death and dying, 299–302, 511
    in homosexuality, 399–400
    in psychiatric emergencies, 763
    in sex therapy, 368
Ethology, 197–212
Euphoria, 116, 117, 493, 516, 556, 558, 559, 693, 696, 743, 754, 776
Evaluation of Sexual Disorders, The, 359
Evening Shadow, The, 405
Evocative memory, 175, 193
Evoked potential, 556, 681, 694, 709
Excessive daytime sleepiness (EDS), *see* Hypersomnias
Excitability, 638–646, 752, 753–758
Excitement phase, *see* Sexual response cycle
Exhibitionism, 216, 377
Exhibitionistic behavior, 215–216, 386, 774
Existentialism, 511, 709
Exorcist, The, 719
Expectant couple, 122–136
Experiential factors, 538–539
Experiment in the Teaching Methodology of Sensate Focus, An, 365
Extended family, 122, 146, 168, 229–231, 234–239, 434, 462, 716

Externalization, 474
Extinction phase, 608
Extramarital affairs, 129, 142, 456
Extrapyramidal signs, 493
Extrasensory perception, 510
Extraversion, 737
Extrinsic asthmatics, 665
Eye movements in schizophrenia, 556, 681

Factitious disorder, 65, 534
Factor S, 572, 580
Failure to thrive, 161, 178, 471
Fall, The, 775
Family disorganization, 462
Family Group, 450
Family interactions in schizophrenia, 681, 690
Family risk studies, 543–544, 546, 551
Family romance, 287–289
Family setting, 161
Family structure and functions, *see* Sociology
Family systems
    affectionate, 228
    bilineal, 227
    companionate, 228
    matriarchal, 227
    matrilineal, 227
    matrilocal, 227
    monogamous, 227
    neolocal, 227
    patriarchal, 227
    patrilineal, 227
    patrilocal, 227
    patronymic, 233
    polyandrous, 232
    polygamous, 232
    polygynous, 232
Family therapy, 476, 653, 668–670, 672–676, 781, 782, 783
Fantasies
    about bodily functions, 435, 436–437
    about death, 299–300, 303–304
    about sexual organs, 338–348
    about transplanted organs, 57–58
    development of, 192–193
    homicidal, 652, 727
    in pregnancy, 124–125, 151–157
    in the oedipal stage, 213–226
    masturbatory, 265–266, 366, 393, 399
    of adopted children, 287–289
    of children regarding divorce, 461, 466
    of divorced partners, 466
    of fetishists, 378–381, 386
    of oral impregnation, 663
    of reunion, 13, 295, 461, 466, 502, 504, 505, 708
    of transvestites, 381–382, 386
    prostitution, 765
    suicidal, 713–729
    unconscious, 587, 764–771
Father, The, 453–454

Father and Child, 140
Fatigue, 117, 349, 494, 703, 743, 755, 769
Fear, *see* Anxiety
Feces, 187–189, 378–381
Feeding
 and culture, 278–279
 difficulties, 174
 model of, 169–170
Feelings, *see* Affects
Fellatio, 316, 317, 393
Femininity, 111–112, 125–129, 131, 135, 185–187, 193–
 196, 216–218, 219–222, 242–243, 383–389, 391–
 400, 443–444, 483, 663, 728
Feminism, 394, 459
Feminizing syndrome, 382
Fetal alcohol syndrome (FAS), 624
Fetal monitoring, 137, 166
Fetishism, 376, 378–381, 386, 388
Fetishistic cross dressing, 382
Fibrositis, 577
Field dependence, 41
Fire setting, 648, 655, 726
Fixation, 591–596
Flatness of affect, 634, 683
Flexner report, 423–424
Flight-fight reaction, 52, 80, 92–99
Flight of ideas, 559, 693
Flurazepam (Dalmane), 568, 577, 580, 759
Fly-agaric mushrooms, 744
Folie-à-deux, 652
Formal operational stage, *see* Cognitive development
Formal thought disorder, *see* Thinking
Forsyte Saga, The, 773
Foster care, 290–292, 462
Fragile X syndrome, 548, 626, 636
Fragmentation, 536, 538, 592, 684, 688
Frankenstein, 719
Free association, 322, 587
Free-floating anxiety, 615, 769
Free running, 565
Frequency, 565
"Frigidity," *see* General sexual dysfunction
Frotteurism, 377
Fugue state, *see* Psychogenic fugue
Functional psychoses
 see Affective disorders
 see Schizophrenic disorders
Furosemide, 117
Fusion, 592, 687

Galactosemia, 624
Gambling, 443, 610, 782
Gang-oriented delinquent, 652
Gangs, 245, 248, 649–656
Gastric fistula, 95
Gastrocolic reflex, 187
Gemellology, 544
Gender identity, 191, 193–196, 224, 382–389, 392, 443–
 444, 476, 776

Gender identity disorder, *see* Transsexualism
General depressant drugs, 742
General sexual dysfunction, 368, 369–370
General systems theory, *see* Systems theory
Generalized anxiety disorder, 537, 615, 764, 769–770
Generation blending, 653
Generativity, 448, 478–479, 491
Genetic counseling, 152, 437, 627
Genetic epistemology, 249
Genetic factors
 in affective disorders, 538–540, 546–548, 605, 709
 in alcoholism, 549–550, 738
 in Alzheimer's disease, 493
 in childhood schizophrenia, 634
 in creativity, 404
 in criminality, 550, 648
 in Down's syndrome, 625–626
 in duodenal ulcer, 83
 in galactosemia, 624
 in homosexuality, 396
 in infantile autism, 548–549, 635–636
 in longevity, 487, 496
 in mental illness, 538–540, 541–553
 in narcolepsy, 581
 in normal development, 159, 164, 166, 170, 185, 195,
 551
 in obesity, 660
 in panic disorder, 551
 in personality disorders, 551
 in phenylketonuria, 624–625
 in schizoaffective disorder, 548
 in schizophrenic disorders, 542–546, 605
 in sexual identity, 382
 in smoking, 738
 in transsexualism, 386
Genetic markers, 547–548, 738
Genetic transmission, 547
Genetic vulnerability, 546
Genital stage, *see* Psychosexual development
Genitality, 266
Geographic mobility, 230, 462, 716
Geriatrics, 487, 492
German measles, *see* Rubella
Gerontology, 487, 492
Gestational disorders, 626
Ghetto, 163, 651–653
Ghosts, 452
Girl at the Mirror, 3
Giving-up-given-up complex, 9, 48, 72, 80, 85–88, 96,
 500
Glass Menagerie, The, 775
Glucose, 562
Godfather, The, 779
Golden Cage, The, 663
Gonadal factors in sexual identity, 382
Goodness of fit, 145
Grade school child, 160, 240–248, 443–444, 461
Graduate, The, 262
Grand Canyon Suite, 629

Grand mal seizures, 755, *see also* Epilepsy
Grandiosity, 54, 506, 532, 559, 693, 696, 704, 754, 778
Grandparenthood, 2, 292, 293–294, 441, 483, 485, 486, 490
"Granny bashing," 726
Granulovacuolar bodies, 493
Greece, 317–319, 509
Green Light, The, 406
Grief, 2, 56, 61, 78, 85–88, 96, 101, 103, 134, 135, 136, 140, 151–157, 237, 293–298, 299–314, 419, 452, 461, 465, 494–495, 498–507, 575, 697–699, 707–709, 713–721, 760, 787
Grief Observed, A, 503
Grief work, 499
Group therapy, 373–374, 476, 615, 781, 783
Growth retardation, 561, 667
Guided imagery, 61
Guilt, 24, 30–31, 49, 51, 52, 54, 57, 58, 64, 78, 98, 107, 109, 112, 124, 126, 133, 134, 135, 142, 152, 160, 213, 225, 251, 265, 285, 295, 321, 354, 362, 369–374, 378, 386, 403, 439, 452, 453, 461, 466, 468, 476, 490, 494, 497, 502, 505, 531, 538, 556, 586, 591, 636, 656, 687, 698, 703–705, 707–709, 717–724, 741, 763, 770, 774, 775, 779

Habituation, 171
Hallucinations, 109, 115, 117, 143, 172, 295, 503, 531, 536, 553, 602, 603, 634, 640, 678, 680, 684, 693, 704, 727, 744, 749, 750, 752, 754, 755, 756, 757
  auditory, 531, 678, 680, 684, 704, 756
  mood-congruent, 693
  nocturnal, 755
  visual, 684, 752, 754, 756, 757
Hallucinogenic drugs, 592, 727, 744–745
Haloperidol (Haldol), 353, 555
Hamlet, 775
Hand-eye-mouth coordination, 175
Handicapped children, 140–141, 407, 474
Head Start, 244
Headache, 60, 68, 72, 117, 349, 354, 582, 672, 726, 731, 769, 770
  caffeine-withdrawal, 744
  migraine, 80, 117, 613–614
  tension, 73, 614–615, 769
Healing Heart, The, vii, 17, 518, 521, 787
Health care professionals
  see Doctor-patient relationship
  see Physicians
Heart of Darkness, 780
Heart Sounds, 356
Hedda Gabler, 452, 453
Helplessness, 9, 85–88, 95–96, 102, 430, 494, 500, 514, 519, 556, 663, 700, 703, 704
Hemodialysis, 57, 88, 118, 312, 692
Hermaphrodism
  pseudo, 382
  true, 382
Herniorrhaphy, 56, 361
Heroics (among physicians), 430–431

Heroin, 352, 561, 737–738, 742, 756
Herzog, 776
Hetaerae, 319
Hippocampus, 563
Hirschsprung's disease, 676
Histrionic personality disorder, 54, 68, 78, 104, 773–774
HLA (human leucocyte antigen), 547, 549
Hodgkins disease, 105, 351
Homeostasis, 524, 564
Homicide, 117, 443, 462, 534, 649, 652, 684, 687, 715, 725–729, 740, 759–763, 781
Homosexuality, 224, 292, 317–320, 322, 323, 376–377, 381–386, 391–401, 405, 443, 475, 531, 654, 687
  asexual, 395, 397
  close-coupled, 395, 397
  coupled, 395, 397
  developmental, 393
  dysfunctional, 395, 397
  enforced, 393
  exploitative, 393
  functional, 395, 397
  ideological (political), 394
  open-coupled, 395
  preferential (exclusive, obligatory), 376–377, 381–386, 391, 393, 394–400
  pseudo, 393
  situational, 393
  variational, 394
Hope, 513
Hopeless, 53
Hopelessness, 9, 85–88, 95–96, 98, 99, 430, 493, 494, 500, 556, 700, 704
Hormonal factors in sexual identity, 382–384
Hospice Movement, 511, 512
Hospital, 420, 429, 431
Hospitalism, 146, 161, 178, 200
Hospitalization
  and diagnosis, 599–603
  and hospital culture, 276–277
  as treatment, 690, 695, 711, 782
  reactions of adults to, 10–11
  reactions of children to, 281–286
Hostility, *see* Anger
Human sexuality
  differences between the sexes, 442–443
  uniqueness of, 442
Human Sexuality: A Health Practitioners' Text, 354
Human Sexuality: Heterosexual Intercourse, 447
Hydromorphone (Dilaudid), 742
Hyperactivity, 162, 246, 475, 505, 553, 559, 560, 638–646, 663, 693, 743, 753, 754, 755
  developmental, 639, 640, 644
  neurological, 639, 640, 643–644
  psychogenic, 639, 640, 642, 643
Hyperalertness, 743, 752, 753–758, 769, 770
Hyperemesis gravidarum, 124–125
Hyperhidrosis, 73
Hyperkinetic syndrome, *see* Attention deficit disorder

Hyperlipidemia, 617
Hyperparathyroidism, 116, 750
Hyperprolactinemia, 351
Hypersomnias, 573, 581–583
Hypertension, 28, 41, 46, 79, 80, 85, 94, 481, 558, 582, 613, 617, 660, 701, 710, 744, 750
Hyperthyroidism, 79, 80, 85, 116, 560, 577, 665, 748, 752
Hyperventilation syndrome, 73, 98, 99, 770
Hypnogogic hallucinations, 581
Hypnosis, 25, 61, 62, 93, 94, 587, 781
Hypnotics, 496, 578, 578–581, 742
Hypochondria, 73
Hypochondriasis, 34, 65, 71, 72, 73–78, 90, 97, 98, 115, 494, 534, 707
    dependent type, 74–75, 777
    hostile type, 73–74, 777
Hypoglycemia, 116
Hypogonadism, 351
Hypomania, 705, 706, 776
Hypoparathyroidism, 116
Hypopituitarism, 351, 560, 660
Hypopnea, 582
Hypothalamic-pituitary-adrenal axis, 559, 709
Hypothalamic-pituitary-gonadal axis, 135, 351, 360, 480
Hypothalamus, 384, 391, 487, 554, 561, 566, 660
Hypothyroidism, 116, 577, 660, 752
Hysterectomy, 55, 56, 111–112, 354, 388
Hysterical childbirth, 25
Hysterical personality disorder, *see* Histrionic personality disorder

Id, 586
Idealism (in medical school), 425–426
Idealization, 22, 51, 257, 262, 264, 266, 288, 296, 445, 456, 776
Ideas of references, 531
Identification, 24, 51, 57, 64, 69, 70, 184, 185, 191, 217, 218–224, 241, 262, 266, 296, 298, 386, 396, 398, 435, 439, 443–444, 465, 467, 472, 474, 504, 505, 708, 718
Identification with the aggressor, 474, 718
Identity, 160, 259, 266–267, 269, 288–290, 416, 445, 448, 450, 467–468, 491, 592, 633, 661, 771, 776, 782, 783
Identity disorder, 267
Ileostomy, 56, 356, 667
Illusion, 295, 531, 684, 744, 776
Imipramine (Tofranil), 557, 584, 675
Imitation, 184, 185, 241, 298
Immune systems, 98, 99, 487, 493, 547
"Impotence," *see* Erectile dysfunction
Imprinting, 172, 173, 198
Improvising response to medical advice, 46
Impulses, *see* Drives
Impulsive personality disorder, 595
Impulsivity, 473–474, 560, 638–646, 737, 749, 776, 777, 779

In vitro fertilization, 135
Inadequacy, *see* Self-esteem
Inappropriateness of affect, 634, 680, 683–684
Incest, 475, 531, 687, 726, 759–763, 766, *see also* Child abuse
Incest taboo, 229, 444
Incidence, 602
Inclusion-exclusion, 457–459
Incontinence, 29–30, 52
Incubus, 584
Independence, 257, 260–262, 425, 460
Index case, 543
Individualism, 459
Industry, 160, 245–246
Infant, 160, 165–181, 498
Infant observation, 165, 592
Infanticide, 143, 470, 619
Infantile autism, 170, 178, 548–549, 628, 629–636
Inferiority, 160, 245–246, 494, *see also* Self-esteem
Infertility, 134–136, 152, 287
Inflation, 462, 482, 486
Influencing machines, 687
Infradian rhythm, 566
Inhibited sexual desire, 366, 368, 374
Inhibition, 96
Initiative, 160, 225
Insight, 537
Insomnias, 78, 117, 118, 573–581, 660, 703–704, 769, 770
Instability, 776–777
Instinct theory, 198
Insulation (in medical school), 425
Insulin, 117
Integrity, 425, 491–492
Intellectual development, 158
Intellectual function, 488, 534, 620, 748–751
Intellectualization, 51, 263, 286, 425, 769, 773
Intelligence quotient (IQ) 158, 620–623, 638–639, 642, 648, 649, 651
Intelligence tests, 620–623
Intensive care unit (ICU) delirium, 10, 57, 756–758
Internal desynchrony, 566, 568
Internalization, 185, 186, 213, 219–224, 243–245
Interracial adoption, 290
Intimacy, 269, 398, 443–447, 455–458, 770
Intoxication syndromes, 533, 742–745, 747, 750, 754–755, 760
Intrapsychic conflict, *see* Conflict
Intrinsic asthmatics, 665
Introjection, 51
Introversion, 737
Invention of the Adolescent, 228, 258, 259
Involutional melancholia, 76, 548
Iproniazid, 556
Iron lung delirium, 757
Irritability, *see* Anger
Irritable colon syndrome, 73
Isolation (as defense mechanism), 51, 71, 190, 767, 769, 773

Isolation (as failure of intimacy), 443–447, 456
Isolation experiments, 566
Isoniazid, 117

Jet lag, 567, 577
Jimson (Jamestown) weeds, 744
John, 594, 595
Joy, 139, 296, 298
Judaism, 509, 511
Jude the Obscure, 774
Judeo-Christian tradition, 459
Judgment, 537, 693, 748, 751
Juvenile delinquency, 248, 269, 285, 443, 462, 533, 648–657, 672, 728, 737

K complex, 570, 571
Kibbutz, 146
Killed in Action, 500
Kinderspiele, 241
Kiss, The, (Munch), 447, 448
Kiss, The, (Rodin), 445
Klinefelter's syndrome, 382, 541
Korsakoff's psychosis, *see* Wernicke-Korsakoff syndrome

La belle indifference, 71, 78
Labia majora, 332
Labia minora, 332
Laboratory tests, 16–17, 31, 71, 77, 109, 114, 118, 780
Lady Lazarus, 713
Language, *see* Speech
Latency stage, *see* Psychosexual development
Laxatives, 663
Learned helplessness, 709
Learning, *see* Learning theory
Learning disabilities, 161, 162, 163, 246, 443, 473, 476, 533, 560, 638–647
Learning theory, 144, 182, 184, 198, 392, 397, 442, 478, 524, 607–618, 733–736, 739, 781
Leisure time, 534, 537
Leprosy, 544
Lethargy, 742, 748, 754
Leukemia, 96, 283, 284, 285, 299–314, 471, 515
Level, 565
Level of consciousness, 748–752
Levodopa, 117
Liaison psychiatry, *see* Consultation-liaison psychiatry
Libido, 198
Lidocaine, 117
Life cycle, 1–5, 12–13, 122, 146, 257, 296, 298, 315, 437, 441, 448, 478, 485, 498, 504, 538, 787–788
Life setting, 9, 85–88
Lifetime risk, 542
Light-dark cycle, 564–569
Limbic system, 709, 748
Linear model, 668
Lines and Squares, 767
Lipochondrodystrophies, 541

Lithium carbonate, 559–560, 694, 695, 696, 710, 781
Live or Die, 713
Locomotion, *see* Motor function
Long Time to Grow, A, 192
Longevity, 486, 496–497
Looking for Me, 630
Looking for Mr. Goodbar, 775
Loosening of associations, *see* Associations
Loss
    fantasied, 498
    fetal, 151–157
    in adults, 498–507
    in children, 293–298
    in depression, 697–699, 709
    in menopause, 12
    in middle age, 482–485
    in old age, 491, 494–495
    in postoperative depression, 109
    in school phobia, 672–673
    in sudden death, 96
    in suicide, 716–724
    in the angry patient, 101–103
    in the giving-up-given-up complex, 85–88
    in the pain-prone patient, 64
    in the seductive patient, 103–106
    neonatal, 151–157
    of a child, 500
    of a grandparent, 293–294
    of a parent, 309–310, 447, 464, 714
    of a peer, 310–311
    of a pet, 499
    of a sibling, 308–309, 447
    of body part, 52, 61, 109, 297, 307–308, 498
    of feces, 187–189
    of job, 7–8, 9, 12, 90, 414–422, 485, 714
    of physical attractiveness, 12
    of spouse, 87, 96, 97, 99, 485, 708, *see* Divorce
    of the infant-in-utero, 148
    of the perfect baby, 140–141
    perinatal, 151–157
    real, 498
    symbolic, 498
    threatened, 498
    see also Depression
    see also Grief
    see also Mourning
Love, 263–266, 402, 442–450, 455–456, 458, 771
Lupus erythematosis, 117, 750
Lysergic acid diethylamide (LSD), 352, 592, 651, 744, 753, 754
    LSD intoxication, 744, 754

Macbeth, 767–768
Madame Bovary, 774
Major depression, *see* Depression
Malignant melanoma, 519–521
Malingering, 71, 72, 77, 246, 766
Malpractice, 56, 106, 109, 114, 431, 437, 763, 776
Man and Woman, 446

Man and Woman, Boy and Girl, 385
Man Pointing, 663
Mania, 557, 559–560, 681, 692–696, 700, 701, 776
    primary, 692, 700, 701
    secondary, 692, 700, 701
Manic-depressive psychosis, *see* Bipolar disorder
Marijuana, 352–353, 737, 744
Marital bond, 465
Marital dysfunction, 154, 428, 429, 437, 452–463, 500, 761
Marital separation, 154, 231, 459–463, 464–469
Marital therapy, 363, 457–459
Marriage, 441, 447–450, 452–463, 483, 485, 496, 540
    adolescent, 130–131, 460
    contract, 457
    group, 463
    homosexual, 463
    one-profession, 456
    open, 463
    sadomasochistic, 458
    two-profession, 456
Masculinity, 110–111, 135, 185–187, 193–196, 215–216, 222–224, 242, 383–389, 391–400, 443–444, 483, 727, 728
Masked depression, *see* Depressive equivalents
Masochistic personality disorder, 54, 58, 64, 66, 377, 458, 515, 707, 774–775
Masochistic perversion, *see* Sexual masochism
Mastectomy, 56, 61, 111, 388
Master Builder, The, 452–453
Mastery, 11, 249, 464, 485, 494, 504, 770
Masturbation, 214, 215–216, 256, 260, 265–266, 322, 338–339, 347–348, 350, 356, 364–367, 382, 388, 393, 399, 475, 628
"Maternity blues," 143
Medical history, 15, 27–32, 71, 75, 114–118, 349
Medical illness presenting as a psychiatric disorder, 115–118, 700
Medical school training, 36–37, 423–427
Medicare, 486
Medicine
    as a profession, 416, 423–440
    origins of modern medicine, 510–511
Medicine man, 19–20, 509
Meditation, 61, 62, 94, 614
Medulla, 749
Megavitamin therapy, 554
Melancholia, *see* Depression and the depressive disorders
Memory, 2, 78, 116, 159, 169–170, 175, 180, 295, 396, 466, 493, 503, 533, 537, 587, 631, 685, 710, 744, 748, 750–751, 771
Memory trace, 169, 179
Men, Women and Dogs, 357
Menarche, 255–256
Menopause, 12, 480–481, 716
Menstruation, 216, 384, 480, 567–568, 662
Mental disorders
    classification of, 323, 376, 397, 533–540

    of adulthood, 678–779
    of childhood and adolescence, 619–677
Mental Health in the Metropolis, 600
Mental illness
    and creativity, 409–411
    biological factors, 541–585
    concept of, 524–532
    diagnosis of, 533–540, 599–603
    learning factors, 607–618, 781
    multiple etiologies of, 538–540, 541–618
    psychodynamic factors, 586–596, 781
    sociocultural factors, 597–606
    statistics of, 2–4, 113–114, 525
Mental representation, 175, 179, 250, 442, 592
Mental retardation, 161, 162, 163, 284, 443, 475, 533, 539, 542, 601, 611, 619–627, 633, 634, 656, 748
    classification of, 620, 622, 623
    clinical group, 623–626
    educable group, 622
    etiology of, 624–627
    sociocultural group, 623–624, 626–627
    trainable group, 622
Mental status examination, 78, 118, 527–532, 537, 680, 682–688, 750–752, 762
Meperidine (Demerol), 742
Meprobamate (Miltown), 742
Mescaline, *see* Peyote cacti
Mesor, 565
Metabolic brain imaging, 562, 635
Methadone, 742, 755
Methamphetamine (Methedrine), 743
Methaqualone (Quaalude), 352, 742
Methyldopa, 117
Methylphenidate (Ritalin), 560, 581, 638, 692
Methylxanthines, 117
MHPG, 557, 558, 562
Michigan Alcohol Screening Test (MAST), 740
Midbrain, 749
Middle age, 441, 478–485, 498
Mid-life crisis, *see* Middle age
Midtown Manhattan Study, 36, 525, 600, 601, 605
Milieu therapy, 782
Mind-body relationship, 48–120, 122–125
Mind That Found Itself, A, 693, 694
Minimal brain dysfunction (MBD), 161, 246, 560–561, 638–643
Minnesota Multi-Phasic Personality Inventory (MMPI), 94, 568
Miscarriage, *see* Abortion (spontaneous)
Miserliness, 493, 773
"Missionary" position, 352
Mistrust, 160, 172
Mitral valve prolapse, 117
Moby Dick, 776
Modeling, 610, 733, 739
Modern Medicine, 785, 786
Mona Lisa, 402
Mongolism, *see* Down's syndrome
Monkeys, 95, 199–212

Monkeys—*continued*
  Bonnet macaque, 199–212
  Pigtail macaque, 199–212
  Rhesus macaque, 199–212
Monoamine oxidase, 547
Monoamine oxidase (MAO) inhibitors, 353, 557–558, 710
Mood, *see* Affects
Moral degeneracy, 679, 680
Morbidity rates in psychiatric patients, 35–36, 99, 115
Morning Glory seeds, 744
Moro reflex, *see* Startle reflex
Morphine, 352, 561, 742
Mortality rates in psychiatric patients, 35–36, 99, 115
Mother and Child, 121, 145
Mother With Child in Arms, 148
Motherhood and Mourning, 157
Mothering figure, *see* Parenting
Motherless-mother monkeys, 203–204
Motility, *see* Motor behavior and function
Motivation, 398–400, 612, 741
Motor behavior and function, 176, 180, 183, 186, 191–192, 537, 680, 684, 748–752
Motor cortex, 749
Mourning
  and depression, 697–699, 707, 708–709
  pathological mourning in adults, 504–507, 707–709
  pathological mourning in children, 296–298
  stages of in adults, 501–504, 505
  stages of in children, 294–296
  see also Grief
Multiaxial system of DSM-III, 533–535, 539
Multi-infarct dementia, 492, 533, 747
Multiple causality, 254, 598
Multiple feedback model, 668
Multiple personality, 771
Multiple sclerosis, 116, 351, 741
Multiple sleep latency test (MSLT), 574, 581
Munchausen's syndrome, *see* Factitious disorder
Murder, *see* Homicide
Muscle cramps, 615
Mutilation anxiety, 50, 160, 215, 216–218, 363, 538
Myasthenia gravis, 116
Myelinization, 187–189
Myocardial infarction, 7–12, 28–29, 46, 48, 49, 53, 57, 65, 66, 68, 69, 71, 77, 93–99, 102, 108, 114, 237, 351, 356, 484, 500, 515
Myths
  about aging, 487–491
  about divorce, 459–462
  about food, 278–279, 435
  about heterosexuality, 338–348, 350–353, 361, 366
  about homosexuality, 391–400
  about marriage, 455–459
  about newborns, 168
  about parenting, 143–147
  about suicide, 721

Naloxone, 561
Naltrexone, 743

Narcissism, 263, 264, 398, 403, 436, 455, 651
Narcissistic personality disorder, 54, 778
Narcolepsy, 581–582
Narcotics, 56
Natural childbirth, 123, 138
Nature and Evolution of Female Sexuality, The, 328
Nature and nurture, 165, 397, 538–539
Nausea of pregnancy, 124
Necrophilia, 376
"Needle freak," 735
Needs, 5, 167, 179, 402–404, 489, 540, 586, 772
Negation, 51
Negative feedback loops, 668
Negative schizophrenia, 691
Negative symptoms (in OBS), 748
Negativistic behavior, 185
Neocortex, 749
Neologism, 685
Neonatal Behavioral Assessment Scale, 143
Neonate, 143–147, 166–172
Neuritic plaques, *see* Senile plaques
Neurochemistry, 538–540, 553–564, 572
Neurodermatitis, 79, 85
Neuroendocrinology, 559
Neurofibrillary tangles, 493
Neurological development, 159, 473, 635, 639–642, 643–644
Neurological illness presenting as a psychiatric disorder, 115–118, 700
Neurophysiology, 556, 572, 681, 694, 709
Neuropsychology, 159, 164
Neurotic character, 655
Neurotic delinquent, 651
Neurotic disorders, 90, 98, 162, 190, 224–226, 322, 458, 490, 534–540, 592–595, 603, 643, 662, 764–771
Neurotransmitters, 555–564, 572, 781
New Perspectives on the Health of Canadians, 615–616
New Sex Therapy, The, 359
Newborn, *see* Neonate
Newborn, The, 147
Nicotine, *see* Tobacco
Night terrors, *see* Sleep terror disorder
Night workers, *see* Shift workers
Nightmares, 117, 224–225, 285, 354, 579, 583–584, 643, 676, 718, 770
"No," concept of, 184–185, 187–189, 190
No More Tears, 53
Nocturnal myoclonus, 576, 578
Nocturnal penile tumescence (NPT), 574
"Nodding," 742
Nonaggressive conduct disorder, 648
Nonrapid eye movement (NREM) sleep, *see* Sleep
Norepinephrine (NE), 92, 555–561, 709
Norepinephrine hypothesis, 557
Normal pressure hydrocephalus, 116, 494
Normality and abnormality, 524–532
Nortriptyline (Aventyl), 557
Not Me Alone, 130, 139
Notes From Underground, 73–74
Now We Are Six, 240

Nuclear family, 126, 228–231, 234–239, 434
Nuclear magnetic resonance (NMR), 635
Nucleus locus coeruleus, 561, 563, 572
Nurses
  see Doctor-patient relationship
  see Physicians
Nursing homes, 486, 490, 491, 492, 493, 516–517, 578
Nutmeg, 744
Nutritional therapies, 781
Nystagmus, 752

Obesity, 58, 496, 533, 593, 616–617, 660–662
Object choice, 376–377, 378–381, 385, 442–443
Object constancy, 193, 250
Object permanence, 250
Object relationships, 159, 160, 179, 263–266, 376–377, 473, 534, 537, 686
Object representation, 193, 250
Obsession, 525, 536, 767–769
Obsessive compulsive (neurotic) disorder, 190, 243, 536, 538, 764, 767–769, 773
Obsessive compulsive personality disorder, 54, 243, 360, 535, 551, 773, 774
Obstetrics as a specialty, 437
Occupation, *see* Work
Occupational therapy, 782
Oedipal stage, *see* Psychosexual development
Oedipus complex, 218–226, 262, 265, 287–289, 396, 406, 410, 444, 452, 454, 468, 498, 765
Oedipus Rex, 218
Old age, 483, 486–497, 498, 605, 698–699
Old Man and Small Boy, 483
Old Man with a Rope, 716
Omnipotence, 430, 431
On Adolescence, 257
On Death and Dying, 515
Oophorectomy, 112
Open systems, 668
Operant conditioning, 608–610
Opiate receptor sites, 561
Opioid drugs, 561, 731, 742–743
Oral genital contact, 110–111, 317–318, 475
Oral personality, *see* Passive-dependent personality
Oral stage, *see* Psychosexual development
Orality
  in monkey isolates, 201–202
  in monkeys separated from mother, 208, 210
  in oral stage, 593–595
  in together-together monkeys, 204
Orchiectomy, 56, 110
"Organ recital," 75, 78
Organ vulnerability, 80–85, 91, 98, 99
Organic affective syndrome, 750
Organic amnestic syndrome, 750
Organic brain syndrome (OBS), 108, 109, 116, 117, 533–534, 601, 656, 686, 727, 747–758, 760, 762, *see also* Organic mental disorder
  acute, 747
  chronic, 747
Organic delusional syndrome, 750

Organic hallucinosis, 750
Organic mental disorder, 78, 492–494, 533–534, 540, 604, 640, 747–758, 780, 781, *see also* Organic brain syndrome
Organic personality syndrome, 750
Organizers of the psyche, 170
Organizing capacities, 537
Orgasm
  female, 328, 331–334, 341–342, 442–443
  male, 329, 347
  multiple, 342
  simultaneous, 342–343, 361
Orgasmic dysfunction, 366, 368, 370–371, 442–443
Orgasmic phase, *see* Sexual response cycle
Orgasmic platform, 333
Orientation, 78, 493, 533, 537, 643, 685, 744, 750, 751
Osteoporosis, 481
Our Bodies, Ourselves, 143
Ovaries, 112, 135
Overanxious disorder of childhood, 672
Overprotectiveness, 669
Overwork (among physicians), 430
Oxazepam (Serax), 580
Oxycodone (Percodan), 576

Pagliacci, 406
Pain, 55, 56, 60–67, 78, 97, 108, 512, 519, 561
  acute, 62, 69
  and punishment, 63–64
  chronic, 62–63, 69, 577, 578, 707
  clinics, 63
  congenital absence of, 61
  gate control theory of, 61
  idiopathic pain disorder, 62, 69, 534, 707
  in the terminally ill, 63
  phantom, 61, 308
  postoperative, 63, 69
  psychogenic, 65, 69
  sociocultural factors in, 277–278, 602
  types of, 60–61
Pain-prone patient, 64, 97
Palmar grasp reflex, 167
Pancreatic carcinoma, 116, 700–701, 748
Pancreatitis, 756
Panic, 116, 117, 378, 393, 465, 482, 633, 678–679, 686, 688–690, 764, 781
Panic disorder, 537, 551, 764, 769–770
Paradoxical depression, 53, 64, 96, 707–708, 775
Paraldehyde, 755
Paralyses, 69, 78, 765–767
Paranoid behavior, 453, 493, 505, 524, 528–532, 555, 559, 743, 748, 754, 755, 757, 775–776
Paranoid disorders, 494, 538, 681, 776
Paranoid personality disorder, 54, 58, 108–109, 551, 775–776
Paranoid schizophrenia, 528–532, 555, 600, 678–679, 681, 683, 688–690, 727, 743, 748, 754
Paraphilias, 376–382, 443, 534
Paraplegia, 352, 458
Parapraxes, 587

Parapsychology, 510
Parasomnias, 573, 583–584, 674, 676
Parasympathetic nervous system, 79, 80–85, 92–99, 368
Parental dysfunction, 470–477
Parent-child coalition, 669
Parent-infant interaction, 140–142, 143–149
Parentectomy, 666
Parenthood
  see Parent-infant interaction
  see Parenting
Parenting
  and step-parenting, 292, 460
  and the obstetrician, 437
  and the pediatrician, 435–436
  and the single parent, 287, 292, 461, 462, 464–469
  and violence, 728
  in child abuse, 470–477
  in creativity, 404
  in homosexuality, 396–397
  in schizophrenia, 681
  in the childhood psychoses, 631–636
  in transsexualism, 387–388
  motives for, 441, 447–450
  of the adolescent, 260–262
  of the adopted child, 287–290
  of the asthmatic child, 665–666
  of the child, 161–163, 183–189
  of the neonate, 168, 172–174
  of the obese child, 661
  of the physically ill and dying child, 284–285, 299–314
  of the ulcerative colitis child, 667–668
  other arrangements for, 292
Paresthesias, 769, 770
Parkinson's disease, 351, 554, 563, 640
Partial sexual drives, 377
"Passive," 385
Passive-aggressive personality disorder, 283, 777–778
Patient interviews, 7–8, 528–530, 587–591
Pavor nocturnus, *see* Sleep terror disorder
Pederasty, 318–320
Pediatrics as a specialty, 435–436
Pedigree analysis, 543
Pedophilia, 376
Peege, 490, 491
Peer group, 243–245, 257, 311, 366, 550
Pellagra, 597, 598
Pelvic inflammatory disease (PID), 135, 352
Pemoline (Cylert), 638
Penis, 334–335, 343–347
Penis envy, 217
Pepsinogen, 81–84, 95, 99
Peptic ulcer, *see* Ulcer
Perception, 180, 537, 638, 684, 744
Perceptual-motor training, 646
Perfectionism, 438–440, 662–663, 767–769, 773, 782–783
Performance anxiety, 360–361, 363, 371–374

Period, 565
Period of risk, 542
Periodic movements in sleep (PMS), 576
Periodicity, 564–569
Peripheral neuritis, 731
Pernicious anemia, 117, 750
Perseveration, 640, 744
Personality, 524–525, 535, 750, 772
Personality disorders (Axis II), 54, 90, 190, 534–540, 551, 592–595, 603, 736, 772–779
Personality profile, 79
Personality traits, 80, 190, 525, 535, 537, 595, 772,
Pervasive developmental disorders, 533, 628–637
Perversion: The Erotic Form of Hatred, 377
Pets, 499
Peyote cacti, 744
Peyronnie's disease, 352
Phallic stage, *see* Psychosexual development
Phantom limb, 308
Phantom pain, 61, 308
Phase, 565
Phenacetin, 745
Phencyclidine (PCP), 555, 727, 744
Phenobarbital, 755
Phenothiazines, 553–556, 695, 709–710
Phenylalanine, 625
Phenylketonuria (PKU), 539, 541, 542, 624–625, 682
Pheochromocytoma, 116, 748
Phobic disorder, 153, 224–225, 354, 533, 538, 540, 604, 610, 611, 764–765, 775
Phobic partner, 765
Phobic personality disorder, *see* Avoidant personality disorder
Phobic stimulus, 764
Physical dependence, *see* Substance dependence
Physical development, 159
Physical disabilities, 281–286
Physical disorders or conditions (Axis III), 533, 539
Physical examination, 15–16, 31, 71, 103, 114–118, 780
Physical illness
  and loss, 496, 498, 505
  as punishment, 4, 12–13, 29–30, 52, 53, 54, 109, 112, 251, 283, 508, 515, 775
  ethnic differences in, 277–278, 602
  fantasies about, 54–55
  in divorce, 461
  in grief, 505
  in psychiatric patients, 35–36
  previous experiences with, 53–54
  reactions of adults to, 4, 6–13, 21, 36, 48–59
  reactions of children to, 281–286
  reactions of family to, 284–285
  reactions of hospital staff to, 285–286
  social meanings of, 271–280
Physicians
  alcoholism in, 429, 437, 733
  and child abuse, 472
  and dying adolescents, 311–314
  and dying adults, 234–237, 511–521

and dying children, 299–311
and homosexuality, 391–393, 398–400
and human behavior, 1–5, 786–788
and marital/parental difficulties, 447–450
and organic brain syndromes, 749, 751, 753, 756–758
and psychiatric emergencies, 759–763
and rape victims, 355
and sexual myths, 338–348
and sexual response cycle, 324–337
and sexuality, 316–317, 349–358
and the childhood psychoses, 636
and the latency age child, 246–248
and the learning disabilities, 645–646
and the mourning process, 506–507
and the nuclear family, 234–239
and the personality disorders, 772–779
and the suicidal patient, 714, 721–724
and violence, 725–729
angry feelings in, 102–103, 119
attitudes toward alcoholism and other substance abuse, 731, 740–742, 745
characteristics of, 23, 438–440
cultural expectations of, 271–280
drug abuse in, 8, 429, 437, 733, 739, 742
emotional illness in, 437–438, 440
emotional reactions in, 34, 58
families of, 428, 435
life experiences of, 17
marriages of, 428, 429, 437, 456, 457
sexual feelings in, 105–106, 349
suicide in, 8, 429, 438, 714
Physiological dependence, *see* Substance dependence
Physiological Responses of the Sexually Stimulated Female in the Laboratory, 329–334
Physiological Responses of the Sexually Stimulated Male in the Laboratory, 334–336
Physostigmine, 558
Pick's disease, 492
Pituitary-adrenal-cortical activation, 92, 98, 166, 382–385, 565
Placebo, 31–32, 91, 360, 554, 561, 557, 577, 615
Plague, 597, 598
Plague Mask, 598
Plateau phase, *see* Sexual response cycle
Play
in children, 192–193
in infants of monkey isolates, 203
in monkey isolates, 201–203
in together-together monkeys, 204
joint play, 192
parallel play, 192
Poems of Gerard Manley Hopkins, The, 788
Poetry of Robert Frost, The, 408, 409
Pollution, 496, 609
Polydrug abuse, 739–740
Polysomnography, 574–584
Polysurgery, 12–13, 58, 109, 775
Population growth, 609

Pornae, 319
Porphyria, 116, 750
Positive feedback loops, 668
Positive schizophrenia, 691
Positive symptoms (in OBS), 748
Positron emission tomography (PET scan), 562–563, 635
Postnatal cerebral infections, 624
Postpartum, 142–143, 147–149
    depression, 143
    disorders, 143
    psychosis, 143
Post-traumatic stress disorder, 354, 770
Poverty, 487, 550, 649, 651–654, 656, 729, 737
Power, 457–459
Practicing period, 182
Praecox aura, 683
Preadolescence, 255–257
Precipitating factors, 539
Preconscious, 403, 586
Predator-prey relations, 198
Preeclampsia, 124, 132
Pregnancy, 12, 78–79, 104, 122–136, 355, 410, 437, 443, 480
    adolescent, 130–133
    out-of-wedlock, 130–134
    stages of, 125–129
    unwanted, 133–134
Prehistory, 508–509
Prejudice, 290, 324, 398, 400, 443, 487–491, 609, 729, 762
Premarital sex, 263–266, 441, 456
Premature ejaculation, 366, 368, 371–373
Prematurity, *see* Birth (premature)
Premenstrual syndrome (PMS), 567–568
Prenatal hormones, 383–384
Prenatal infections, 624
Prenatal period, 166, 383
Preoedipal stages, 159
Preoperational stage, *see* Cognitive development
Preparatory grief, 516
Pre-school child, 160, 213–226, 461
Presenile dementia, 492
Pressure of speech, 693
Prevalence, 542, 602
Priapism, 353
Primary danger situations, *see* Anxiety
Primary degenerative dementia, *see* Alzheimer's disease
Primary gain, 765
Primary process, 180, 685
Primate research, *see* Ethology
Primitive Erotic Art, 346, 347
Principle of multiple function, 532
Prisoner of Chillon, The, 499
Proband, 543
Prodromal phase of schizophrenia, 680
Professional role, 276
Projection, 51, 108, 193, 455, 474, 532, 687, 689, 776

Prolactin, 571–572
Promiscuity, 395, 398, 476, 649, 654, 693
Promotion depression, *see* Paradoxical depression
Propfschizophrenia, 633
Propranolol, 117, 353
Prostate, 110, 135
Prostatectomy, 56, 110
Prostitution, 319, 324, 476, 531, 728
Protection, 231
Protest phase of grief, 501–502, 505
Protracted adolescence, 267–268, 441
Protriptyline (Vivactil), 583
Pseudocyesis, 125
Pseudoindependence, 80–84
Pseudomutuality, 681
Psychiatric emergencies, 759–763
Psychiatric-related insomnias, 574–575
Psychiatric therapies, 780–783
Psychic determinism, 608
Psychic horizon, 752
Psychic numbing, 770
Psycho, 119
Psychoanalysis, 165, 226, 360, 395, 400, 541, 587, 592,
     654, 781
Psychogenic amnesia, 760, 771, 774
Psychogenic fugue, 760, 771, 774
Psychological autopsy, 714
Psychological reactions to physical illness, *see* Physi-
     cal illness
Psychological therapies, 781
Psychology of Black Language, The, 622
Psychomotor agitation, 700
Psychomotor retardation, 494, 700, 703
Psychoneuroimmunology, 99
Psychopathology, 492–497, 523–783
Psychopharmacology, 495, 553–564, 781, 782, 783
Psychopharmacotherapy, *see* Psychopharmacology
Psychophysiological disorders, 65, 71, 72, 79–89, 534,
     613, 664–670, 707
Psychophysiological insomnia, 575
Psychophysiology of stress, 90–100
Psychoprophylactic, 138
Psychoses of childhood, 159, 443, 533, 628–637, *see
     also* Pervasive developmental disorders of child-
     hood
Psychosexual development, 158–159, 160, 164, 254,
     392, 398, 475
  anal stage, 160, 188, 193
  genital stage, 160, 259
  latency stage, 159, 160, 161–162, 240–248
  oedipal stage, 159, 160, 218–226
  oral stage, 160, 179, 193, 593–595
  phallic stage, 160, 213–218
Psychosexual disorders, 534, 537
Psychosexual dysfunctions, *see* Sexual dysfunctions
Psychosis, 52, 58, 66, 98, 99, 104, 108, 115, 116, 117,
     118, 153, 310, 386, 474, 591–595, 643, 652, 744,
     754
  functional psychotic disorders, 90, 91, 114, 534–540,

     587, 762
  postoperative, 55–56, 109
  postpartum, 143
  situational, 98, 99
  toxic, 116, 117
Psychosis and Civilization, 599
Psychosocial development, 160, 161–163, 254
Psychosocial stressor (Axis IV), *see* Stressor
Psychosomatic disorders, *see* Psychophysiological dis-
     orders
Psychosomatic entity, 97
Psychosomatic medicine, 90, 97, 534
Psychosurgery, 781
Psychotherapy, 31, 118, 132–136, 165, 226, 310, 355,
     360, 363, 364–375, 388, 395, 399, 400, 409, 476,
     492, 494, 561, 576, 584, 592, 636, 646, 650, 667–
     668, 669, 672–676, 690, 696, 710–711, 721–724,
     740–742, 763, 781, 782–783
  crisis, 763, 781
  family, 476, 653, 668–670, 672–676, 781, 782, 783
  group, 373–374, 476, 615, 781, 783
  individual, 781, 782–783
  insight-oriented, 781, 782–783
  long-term, 781, 782–783
  psychodrama, 781
  short-term, 781, 782–783
  supportive, 781, 782–783
Psychotic delinquent, 652
Puberty, 255–257, 380, 441, 442, 538
Punishment, 609, 739
  pharmacologic, 739
  social, 739

Racial prejudice, *see* Prejudice
Rape, 83, 248, 319, 353–355, 377, 393, 462, 475, 649,
     727, 728, 740, 775
Rape crisis teams, 355
Rape trauma syndrome, 354–355, 700
Rapid eye movement (REM) sleep, *see* Sleep
Rapprochement, 182
Rationalization, 51, 282, 283, 519
Rauwolfia, 556
Reaching Orgasm, 367
Reaction formation, 51, 190, 664, 767, 773
Reading disability, *see* Developmental reading disor-
     der
Reagin, 665
Reality testing, 171–172, 180, 366, 503, 505, 516, 536,
     537, 591, 687, 705, 749, 753, 756, 772
Realization, 693
Rebound insomnia, 580
Recall, 751
Recent memory, 493, 751
Receptors on postsynaptic neuron, 557
Recognition memory, 175
Red and the Black, The, 774
Re-equilibration phase of stress response, 760
Reflexes in newborn, 167
Reformation, 321, 510

Refueling, 182
Regional enteritis, 667
Regression, 21, 49, 50, 51, 63, 122, 211, 283, 461, 490, 536, 538, 591–595, 687, 705, 777
Reinforcement, 609–610, 667, 675
  contingencies of, 610
  negative, 184, 609, 736
  partial (intermittent), 610
  pharmacologic, 734–736
  positive, 61, 182, 185–186, 198, 609, 709
  social, 733, 739
Reinforcer, 609, 734, 781, 782
Relaxation methods, 61, 94, 611, 614–615
Religio Medici, 511
Religion, 411–413, 509–510, 511, 516, 715
Relinquishment of baby, *see* Adoption
REM latency, 574–575, 705
REM rebound, 574, 576, 578–580
Remembrance of Things Past, 405
Remote memory, 493, 751
Reorganization phase of grief, 157, 503
Repression, 51, 68, 78, 96, 226, 322, 396, 531, 591, 750, 764, 765, 768, 771, 774
Reproduction, 442, 443, 478, 480
Reproductive casualty, 641
Reserpine, 117, 556
Residency training, 427–430, 786, 787
Residential placement, 782
Residual phase of schizophrenia, 680
Residual schizophrenia, 681
Resolution phase, *see* Sexual response cycle
Resomatization, 80
Respiratory depression, 742, 743, 749
Responses to medical advice, 11, 17–18, 34–37, 38–47, 119, 297, 421
Restless legs syndrome, 576
Restlessness, 117, 502, 567, 703, 743, 744, 754, 755, 769
Retarded ejaculation, 368
Retention, 493, 751
Reticular activating system, 92, 572
Retirement, 7–8, 12, 415, 417, 419, 486, 496
Retreatist response to medical advice, 45
Return of the repressed, 768
Reversal of affect, 262
Reversibility, 253
Rheumatic heart disease, 499
Rheumatoid arthritis, 79, 85, 87–88, 352
Rigidity, 619
Risk-taking, 736–738
Rites of passage, 257
Ritualistic behavior, 629, 630, 767–769
Ritualistic response to medical advice, 45–46
Road Not Taken, The, 408
Role diffusion, 160, 259, 267
Role reversal, 473, 476
Romantic love, 455–456
Rome, 319–320
Romeo and Juliet, 232, 295

Rooting reflex, 167, 169
Rorschach Test, 652
Rosmersholm, 452
Rubella, 166, 540, 624, 632
Running away, 648, 649

SAD PERSONS acronym, 715
Sadistic perversion, *see* Sexual sadism
Sadness, 78, 152, 295, 296, 297, 308, 461, 466, 502, 505, 661, 693, 697, 698, 787
  see also Depression
  see also Grief
Savage God, The, 718, 720
Savage Sword of Conan, The, 92
Sawtooth waves, 570, 571
Scapegoating, 474, 669, 681, 729
Scarlet Letter, The, 773, 778
Schizoaffective disorder, 548, 681
Schizoid personality disorder, 54, 686, 776
Schizophrenic disorders, 78, 90, 99, 116, 117, 162, 268–269, 283, 494, 525, 528–532, 538, 542–546, 553–556, 563, 574, 592, 593, 600–605, 611, 655, 656, 662, 672, 678–691, 694, 695, 700, 705, 715, 726–727, 748, 752, 776
Schizophreniform disorder, 681
Schizophrenogenic mother, 551
Schizotypal personality disorder, 551, 686, 776
School phobia, 161, 162, 246–247, 672–673
School setting, 161–162, 244–245, 443–444
Scientific Revolution, 322
Scream, The, 523, 686
Scrotum, 335
Seasons of a Man's Life, The, 479
Secobarbital (Seconal), 755
Second Skin, 777
Secondary gain, 64, 77, 604, 765, 782
Secondary mania, 629
Secondary reinforcers, 616–617
Secularism, 459
Sedatives, *see* Hypnotics
Seductiveness, 54, 68, 103–106, 774
Selective emotional reactions, 285
Self-esteem, 76, 96, 103, 104, 108, 110–112, 135, 190, 283, 355, 356, 367, 436, 437, 464, 468, 474, 476, 479, 502, 505, 515, 653, 694, 696, 698, 700, 703–709, 716–724, 754, 760, 763, 775, 776
Self-fulfilling prophecy, 271
Self-help groups, 782
Self-image, 87, 102, 109, 685, 776
Self-mutilation, 201, 473, 776
Self-Portrait, 3, 787
Self-Portrait in Profile to the Right, 699
Self-representation, 193, 250, 376
Seminal emissions, 255–256
Senile dementia, 492
Senile plaques, 493
Senility, *see* Dementia
Sensate focus exercises, 364, 369
Sense and Sensibility, 721–724

Sense of self, 684, 709, 771, 775
Sense of unreality, 502, 505, 684, 760, 771
Sensory deprivation, 57, 642, 756–758
Sensory motor stage, *see* Cognitive development
Sensory overstimulation, 57, 756–758
Separation anxiety, 12, 50, 160, 175–179, 189, 281, 282, 378–381, 538, 633, 663, 672, 709
Separation anxiety disorder of childhood, 672
Separation-individuation, 146, 159, 160, 162, 175–178, 182–191, 257–258, 260, 311, 376, 387, 498, 593, 633, 662, 698
Serial monogamy, 227, 463
Serotonin (5-HT), 556–558, 572, 635, 709
Serotonin hypothesis, 557
Set, 749
Setting, 749
Sex and Gender, 386–387
Sex flush, 330
Sex skin, 332
Sex therapy, 364–375, 458, 611, 782
Sexual abuse, *see* Child abuse
Sexual aversion, 368, 374
Sexual desire disorders, 368, 374
Sexual deviations, *see* Paraphilias
Sexual dysfunctions, 90, 135, 224, 350–356, 359–375, 400, 428, 458, 476, 500, 534, 611
Sexual history, 11, 350, 392, 399
Sexual identity, 58, 186, 382–385, 393, 394
Sexual masochism, 377
Sexual murder, 377
Sexual orientation, 376–378, 382, 385, 391–400
Sexual perversions, *see* Paraphilias
Sexual response cycle, 322, 324–337, 368
  excitement phase, 325, 328, 329
  genital vasocongestion phase, 368
  in females, 325–334
  in males, 329, 334–336
  in older men, 337
  in older women, 336
  orgasmic phase, 325, 328, 329
  plateau phase, 325, 328, 329
  reflex clonic contractions phase, 368
  resolution phase, 325, 328, 329
  stages of, 325, 328, 329
Sexual role behavior, 382, 385
Sexuality
  and adolescent pregnancy, 130–133
  and drugs, 352–353
  and physical illness, 11, 52–53, 350–352
  and sexual myths, 338–348, 351, 361
  and sexual response cycle, 324–337
  and surgery, 110–112
  and the sexual dysfunctions, 359–375
  and the single parent, 468–469
  during middle age, 480–482
  during pregnancy, 123, 126–129
  during postpartum, 142–143
  historical and cultural perspectives, 316–323
  in adolescence, 255–257, 259, 262–266, 441
  in adulthood, 316–401
  in childhood, 26, 185–187, 193–196, 213–226, 240–247, 289
  in general medical practice, 349–358
  in monkey isolates, 201–203
  in old age, 336–337, 348, 489–490
  in the hospital, 355–357
  repression of in women, 443
Sexual sadism, 377
Shaman, 509
Shame, 52, 57, 58, 107, 135, 160, 183–184, 191, 354, 378, 461, 464, 586, 636, 673, 742
Shaping, 144, 610
Shared paranoid disorder, *see* Folie à deux
Shell shock, 757
Sheltered workshops, 782
Shift workers, 567
Shock, 501, 505
Siblings, 64, 308–309, 311–313, 447, 455, 473, 475, 500, 543–544
Sick role, 65, 238, 276
Sick Room, The, 235
Sickle cell anemia, 23, 351, 674
Simple phobias, 764
Simple schizophrenia, 600
Single parent, *see* Parenting
Six Million Dollar Man, The, 307
Sleep, 159, 168, 569–585
  and longevity, 496
  deprivation, 57, 430, 578–580, 756–758, 760
  disorders, 573–585
  functions of, 572–573
  in anxiety disorders, 574
  in depressive disorders, 574–575
  in schizophrenia, 574
  neurochemistry of, 572
  nonrestorative, 577
  NREM sleep, 495–496, 570–572, 574–584, 674
  physiology of, 570–572
  problems in children, 174–175
  problems in the aged, 494–496, 578
  REM sleep, 570–572, 574–584, 743, 755
  SWS sleep, 570–572, 574–584
  sleep-wake cycle, 564–569
  stages, 570–572
Sleep apnea
  central, 582
  insomnia, 576, 578
  mixed, 582
  obstructive, 582
Sleep disorders medicine, 584
Sleep-onset insomnia, 568, 577, 615
Sleep onset REM period, 581
Sleep paralysis, 581
Sleep spindle, 570, 571
Sleep terror disorder, 533, 573, 583–584, 676
Sleeping Beauty myth, 242, 366
Sleeptalking, 573
Sleepwalking disorder, 533, 573, 583, 676

Slips, *see* Parapraxes
Slow virus, 493
Slow wave sleep (SWS), *see* Sleep
Smiling response, 170–171
Smoking, *see* Tobacco
Snoring, 582–583
Social control, 231
Social Darwinism, 597
Social deprivation and isolation, 473, 476, 494, 505, 519, 566, 641–642
Social isolation rearing in monkeys, 199–203
Social maladjustment, 248
Social phobia, 764, 768
Social Readjustment Rating Scale, 419
Social relationships, *see* Object relationships
Social smile, *see* Smiling response
Social supports, 96, 468, 494, 496, 540
Social therapies, 781–782
Social withdrawal, 297, 456, 490–491, 493, 499, 502, 505, 535, 548, 553, 629–632, 686, 702–705, 770, 775, 776
Socialization, 192–193, 231, 243–245
Socialized conduct disorder, 648
Socioeconomic status, 604–605, 649
Sociology, 227–239
Sociopathic personality disorder, *see* Antisocial personality disorder
Sodomy, 320
Soft neurological signs, 635
Somatic Consequences of Emotional Starvation in Infants, 178
Somatic entity, 97
Somatic symptoms, *see* Somatization
Somatic therapies, *see* Biological therapies
Somatization, 52, 98, 99, 502, 707–711, 760, 769–770
Somatization disorder, 534
Somatoform disorders, 534, 537, 707
Somatopsychic-psychosomatic process, 80–85
Somebody Waiting, 625
Something Happened, 698, 699, 700
Somnambulism, *see* Sleepwalking
Somnolence, 748, 752
Sonnet 129 (Shakespeare), 445
Spanish fly, *see* Cantharides
Specialization, *see* Residency training
Specific developmental disorders, 533, 638
Specificity hypothesis, 80–85, 91
Spectatoring, 360, 366, 369
Speech, 180, 182–183, 191–192, 537, 592, 630, 631, 685, 693
Speed, 743
Splitting, 264–265, 360, 444, 505
Spontaneous recovery phase, 608
Spouse abuse, 725, 726, 759–763, 775, 779
Spring and Fall, 787, 788
Squeeze Technique, 372
Squeeze technique, 371–373
St. Francis in Ecstasy, 69, 70
Stagnation, 478–479

Startle reflex, 167
Startle response, 769, 770
Starvation, 297
Status epilepticus, 285
Status orgasmus, 342
Status placement, 231
Stealing, 163, 245, 248, 309, 462, 648, 651, 655, 725
Stereotyped movement disorders, 533, 673
Stereotypes
    of the aged, 487–491, 497
    sex-role, 185–187, 193–196, 459
Sterility, 110–112, 744
Sterling County Study, 525
Steroids, 58, 117, 166, 572, 579, 664–669, 692, 748, 786
Stigmata, 69, 71
Stillbirth, 153
Stimulant drugs, 560–561, 646, 692, 710, 743–744, 781
Stimulus generalization, 608
Stop-start technique, 366, 370, 371
Storage granules, 557
Stranger anxiety or distress, 50, 174–175, 281
Strauss syndrome, 638, 641
Stress
    and sexual behavior, 383–384
    of life events, 9, 33–34, 85–88, 283–284, 414–422, 464, 492, 604, 759–760, 782
    psychophysiology of, 90–100
    response, 417, 760
Stressor, 417, 534, 538–539, 681, 702, 707
Structural model, 586
Studies in Erotic Art, 317, 318, 341, 344
Stupor, 748
Sturge-Weber syndrome, 642
Stuttering, 533, 651, 673
Subdural hematoma, 116, 752
Sublimation, 52, 255, 406, 436
Substance abuse (definition of), 730, 739–745
Substance dependence, 560, 730, 739–745, 755–756
Substance use disorders, 3, 90, 109, 166, 268, 355, 428, 429, 437, 443, 462, 474, 534, 593, 604, 609, 648, 649, 650–651, 715, 730–746, 776, 777
Substantia nigra, 555, 562, 563
Success neurosis, *see* Paradoxical depression
Sucking reflex, 167, 169
Sudden death, 96–97
Suicide and suicide attempts, 3, 58, 90, 96, 108, 118, 143, 283, 316, 355, 389, 397, 404, 428, 429, 438, 443, 452, 462, 465, 473, 494, 496, 500, 505, 525, 534, 556, 619, 653, 684, 693, 700, 703, 704, 708, 709, 711, 713–724, 726, 740, 756, 759–763, 774, 775, 776, 781
    dynamics of, 715–721
    epidemiology of, 714–715
    in adolescence, 268, 714, 716
    in American Indians, 714, 716, 722
    in Blacks, 714, 716
    in children, 298, 716
    in physicians, 8, 429, 438, 714
    in the aged, 494, 714, 716

Suicide and suicide attempts—*continued*
  in the lonely, 714
  in wives of physicians, 428
  prevention of, 721
  treatment of the suicidal patient, 721–724
Sundowning, 752
Superego, 185, 191, 193, 219–226, 240–241, 242, 243,
    265, 266, 268, 269, 380, 586, 651, 653–656, 686,
    717–724, 772
Superego lacunae, 651, 653–656
Support groups, 156
Surgent growth adolescents, 268
Surgery
  and postoperative delirium, 108, 109
  and postoperative depression, 109–110
  and postoperative psychosis, 56
  and the depressed patient, 95–96, 108
  and the paranoid patient, 108–109
  as a specialty, 58, 436–437
  cardiovascular, 56
  in transsexualism, 388–389
  multiple surgery, *see* Polysurgery
  neurosurgery, 56, 111
  on the ears, 56
  on the eyes, 52, 56
  on the reproductive organs, 55, 56, 110–112
  patients who refuse, 108
  plastic, 56, 108, 109, 356
  reactions of adults to, 10, 12, 29–30, 52, 55–56, 106–
    112
  reactions of children to, 281–286
  the "difficult" surgical patient, 106–113
Surrogate mothers, 135
Survivor guilt, 54, 109, 504, 770
Survivor syndrome, 504
Survivors, The, 698
"Swapping," 463
"Swinging," 463
Sybil, 771
Symbiosis, 387
Symbiotic psychosis, 178, 632–633
Symbiotic stage, 159, 160, 172–174, 178, 376, 593
Symbolic function, 68, 69, 78, 159, 250, 384, 409, 685
Symbolization, 52
Sympathetic nervous system, 79, 80, 92–99, 368
Symptom check lists, 600–602
Symptom disorders of childhood, 224–225, 533, 671–
    676
Symptom formation in the neuroses, 765–767, 770–
    771
Symptoms, 535–538, 760, 781
Synchronizer, 565
Synesthesias, 754
Synthetic functions, 537, 688, 772
Syphilis, *see* Venereal disease
Systematic desensitization, 611, 615, 781
Systems theory, 158, 163–164, 458–459, 668–670
  biological perspective, 159–161
  psychological perspective, 158–159

  sociocultural perspective, 161–163

Tardive dyskinesia, 555
Teahouse of the August Moon, The, 272
Temazepam (Restoril), 580
Temperament in adults, 539
Temperament in newborns, 144–146, 167
Temperomandibular joint pain, 615
Tension states in newborns, 167, 169, 179
Tenting effect, 333
Terbutaline, 117
Tess of the D'Urbervilles, 775
Test tube baby, 135
Testes, 110, 135, 335–336
Testosterone, 373, 382, 383, 482, 744
Tetrahydrocannabinol (THC), *see* Marijuana
Tetrahydroisoquinoline (THQ), 738
Theatre of Revolt, The, 453
Thematic Apperception Test, 652
Theophylline, 583
Theta waves, 570, 571
Thinking, 180, 213, 537, 682–683
  abstract, 159, 184, 191–192, 493, 750, 751
  animistic, 180, 251
  bizarre, 682–683
  causal, 250
  concrete, 215, 493, 682
  content of thought, 682–683
  contrary to fact, 254
  deductive, 254
  disorder, 116, 117, 682
  form of thought, 682–683
  magical, 24, 213, 218, 241, 243, 282, 515, 682, 776
  paralogical, 682
  propositional, 254
  scientific, 254
Thioridazine (Mellaril), 353, 583
Three day schizophrenia, 757
Three Faces of Eve, The, 771
Thrown Away, 716, 717
Thyroid-stimulating hormone (TSH), 559
Thyrotoxicosis, *see* Hyperthyroidism
Thyrotropin-releasing hormone (TRH) stimulation
    test, 559
Thyroxine, 177
Tibetan Book of the Dead, 514
Tics, 533, 673
To Earthward, 409
To the Lighthouse, 778
Tobacco smoking, 58, 496, 617, 730, 736, 738, 739, 740,
    744
Toddler, 160, 182–196, 498
Together-together monkeys, 204
Toilet training, 187–189, 189–191, 195, 473, 673–676
Token economy, 608, 611, 781
Tolerance, 560, 730, 754, 755
Tom Jones, 749
Tomboy behavior, 196, 242, 384, 387, 395, 399, 443
Tooth grinding, 573, 615

Topographic model, 586
Tourette's disorder, 673
Toxemia of pregnancy, *see* Eclampsia
Tranquilizers, *see* Antianxiety drugs and Antipsychotic drugs
Transactional systems, 456–458
Transference, 21–26, 101–106, 721–724
  "negative," 22–23
  "positive," 22
Transformations, 479
Transitional objects, 176–178, 378–381
Translocation, 625
Transplantation
  brain, 562–563
  kidney, 57–58, 311, 356
Transsexualism, 196, 376, 384, 385–389, 443, 534, 542
Transvestism, 216, 376, 380, 381–382, 386–389
Trauernder Mann, 699
Tremors, 744, 754, 755
Triangular relationship, 218
Triangulation, 669
Triazolam (Halcion), 577
Tricyclics, 353, 495, 557–558, 579, 581, 584, 709
Trisomy 21, 493, 625
Truancy, 163, 245, 246, 462, 476, 645, 648, 651, 653, 672, 737
Tryptophan, 580
Tubal ligation, 353, 354
Tuberculosis, 40, 41, 87, 447, 557, 722, 756
Tumultuous growth adolescents, 268
Turner's syndrome, 382, 541–542
Twin studies, 544, 546, 548, 551, 738
Twins, 12–13, 109, 385
Two Year Old Goes to the Hospital, A, 281, 282
Two-point touch, 171
Type A personality, 94, 496, 617
Type B personality, 94, 496
Type O blood, 83
Tyramine, 558, 710

Ulcer, 79, 80–85, 98, 99, 613, 740, 744, 756
Ulcerative colitis, 79, 80, 85, 283, 666–668
Ultradian rhythm, 566
Ultrasound, 137, 151, 153, 166
Uncomplicated bereavement, 697
Unconditioned response (UCR), 608
Unconditioned stimulus (UCS), 608
Unconscious, 21–26, 49, 73, 74, 76, 101–106, 109, 158, 226, 322, 340, 349, 377, 378–381, 387, 394, 396, 398, 403, 406, 409–412, 438, 450, 473–475, 505, 532, 586–591, 636, 653–656, 673–676, 718, 764–771, 775, 781
Undersocialized conduct disorder, 648
Undifferentiated schizophrenia, 681
Undifferentiated state, *see* Autistic stage
Undoing, 52, 190, 767, 768, 773
Unemployment, 416, 417, 419, 714
Unemployment, 10
"Unworried sick," 36

Urbanization, 462
Uremia, 351, 577, 752
Ureterostomy, 356
Urinary system, 110
Urophilia, 376
Uterus, 111, 135, 333–334
Uvulopalatopharyngoplasty (UPPP), 583

Vagina, 332–333, 339–340, 343, 388
Vaginismus, 340, 352
Vandalism, 649
Varieties of Religious Experience, The, 700
Vas deferens, 110, 135
Vasectomy, 110, 135, 353, 354
Vasomotor instability, 480–481
Vegetative signs, 703
Venereal disease, 55, 134, 135, 355, 398–399, 452, 540, 624, 693
Ventricular-brain ratio (VBR), *see* Cerebral vertricles
Victorian Period, 321–322
Violence, 393, 453, 462, 475, 651–653, 713–724, 725–729, 740, 759–763, 779
Visual tracking in schizophrenia, 556, 681
Volition, 680, 684
Vomiting, 124–125, 663–664, 672, 708, 745, 755
Voodoo, 19–20, 95, 652
Voyeurism, 216, 377
Vulva, 332

Wakefulness, 159, 168, 171, 753–758
Wanting to Die, 713
Wayward Youth, 654
Weary Country Doctor, 434
Wernicke-Korsakoff syndrome, 550, 731
When a Child Enters the Hospital, 282
When We Were Very Young, 767
When You Are Old, 444
Where The Sidewalk Ends, 214, 224, 247
Who's the Patient Here? Portraits of the Young Psychotherapist, 91
Widowers, 505
Widows, 484, 486, 496, 505, 602
Wilson's disease, 117
Wish for reunion, 715, 719
Wish to be killed, 715, 718
Wish to be rescued, 719–721
Wish to die, 715, 719
Wish to kill, 715, 717–718
Wishes
  see Dreams
  see Fantasy
  see Needs
Witch doctor, 18, 509
Withdrawal (social), *see* Social withdrawal
Withdrawal syndromes, 109, 533–534, 560, 730, 736, 740, 742–745, 747, 750, 755–756
Wolff-Parkinson-White syndrome, 614
Woman Reaching Out Her Hand to Death, 516
Womb envy, 217

Women's Liberation Movement, 443, 459, 481
Work, 265, 266, 362, 402–440, 442, 450, 462, 482, 486, 488, 534, 537, 703, 716
Working, 414
World of the Schizophrenic, 683, 684, 685, 688
"Worried well," 36, 73

Worthlessness, *see* Self-esteem

X-chromosome, 547, 548, 626, 636

Zoophilia, 376